OXFORD MEDICAL PUBLICATIONS

Oxford textbook of psychiatry

own below.

Oxford textbook of psychiatry

MICHAEL GELDER
Professor of Psychiatry, University of Oxford

DENNIS GATH
Clinical Reader in Psychiatry, University of Oxford

RICHARD MAYOU
Clinical Reader in Psychiatry, University of Oxford

OXFORD   NEW YORK   TORONTO
OXFORD UNIVERSITY PRESS

Oxford University Press, Walton Street, Oxford OX2 6DP

Oxford New York Toronto
Delhi Bombay Calcutta Madras Karachi
Kuala Lumpur Singapore Hong Kong Tokyo
Nairobi Dar es Salaam Cape Town
Melbourne Auckland

and associated companies in
Beirut Berlin Ibadan Mexico City Nicosia

Oxford is a trade mark of Oxford University Press

British Library Cataloguing in Publication Data
Oxford textbook of psychiatry. — (Oxford medical
publications)
1. Psychiatry
I. Gelder, M. G.   II. Gath, D.
III. Mayou, R.
616.89   RC454
ISBN 0-19-261428-2
ISBN 0-19-261294-8 pbk

Library of Congress Cataloguing in Publication Data
Gelder, Michael Graham.
Oxford textbook of psychiatry.
(Oxford medical publications)
Bibliography: p.
Includes index.
1. Psychiatry. I. Gath, Dennis. II. Mayou, R.
III. Title. IV. Series. [DNLM: 1. Psychiatry.
2. Mental disorders WM 100 G3150]
RC454.G42 1983   616.89   83-4035
ISBN 0-19-261428-2 (U.S.)
ISBN 0-19-261294-8 (U.S.: pbk.)

Printed in Great Britain by
M & A Thomson Litho Ltd.
East Kilbride, Scotland

Preface

This book is written primarily as an introductory textbook for trainee psychiatrists, and also as an advanced textbook for clinical medical students. We hope that the book will also be useful, for purposes of revision and reference, to psychiatrists who have completed their training and to general practitioners and other clinicians.

The subject matter of this book is the practice of clinical psychiatry. Recent years have seen the increasing development of sub-specialties such as child and adolescent psychiatry, forensic psychiatry, and the psychiatry of mental retardation. This book is mainly concerned with general psychiatry, but it also contains chapters on the sub-specialties. Throughout the whole book, our purpose has been to provide an introduction to each subject, rather than a fully documented account. It is assumed that the trainee psychiatrist will go on to consult more comprehensive works such as the *Handbook of psychiatry* (Shepherd 1983), the *Comprehensive textbook of psychiatry* (Kaplan *et al.* 1980), and specialized textbooks dealing with the sub-specialties. In some chapters references are made to basic sciences such as psychology, genetics, biochemistry, and pharmacology. Discussion of these subjects is based on the assumption that the reader already has a working knowledge of them from previous study.

The chapters dealing with psychiatric treatment fall into two groups. First, there are three chapters wholly devoted to treatment and concerned only with general issues. In this group, Chapter 17 deals mainly with drug treatment and electroconvulsive therapy; Chapter 18 deals with psychological treatments; and Chapter 19 discusses the organization of services for the rehabilitation and care of patients with chronic psychiatric disorders. Second, there are the various chapters on individual syndromes, which include sections on the treatments specific to those syndromes. In these chapters, treatment is usually discussed in two parts. The first part examines the evidence that a particular treatment is effective for a particular syndrome; the second part discusses (under the heading of management) practical issues in treatment, such as ways of using various treatments singly or in combination at different stages of a patient's illness. The separation of chapters on general issues from those on specific issues means that the reader has to consult more than one chapter for complete information on the treatment of any disorder. None the less this arrangement is preferred because a single treatment may be used for several syndromes. For example, antipsychotic drugs are used to treat mania and schizophrenia, and supportive psychotherapy is part of the treatment of many disorders.

In this book there is no separate chapter on the history of psychiatry. Instead certain chapters on specific topics include brief accounts of their history. For example the chapter on psychiatric services contains a short historical review of the care of the mentally ill; and the chapter on abnormal personality includes some information about the development of ideas about that subject. This arrangement reflects the authors' view that, at least in an introductory text, historical points are more useful when related to an account of modern ideas. The historical references in this book can be supplemented by reading a history of psychiatry such as that by Ackerknecht (1968) or Bynum (1983).

The use of references in this book also needs to be explained. As this is an introductory postgraduate text, we have not provided references for every statement that could be supported by evidence. Instead we have generally followed two principles: to give references for statements that may be controversial; and to give more references for issues judged to be of topical interest. In an introductory text it also seemed appropriate to give references mostly to the Anglo–American literature. For all these reasons the coverage of the literature may seem uneven; but – as explained above – the book is written in the expectation that the trainee psychiatrist will progress to other works for more detailed literature surveys. Suggestions for further reading are given at the end of each chapter.

Oxford
May 1983

M.G.
D.G.
R.M.

Acknowledgements

In writing this book we have been greatly helped by advice and comments generously given by colleagues. We wish to thank:

Dr S. Abel, Dr J. Bancroft, Mr J. Beatson, Miss V. L. Bellairs, Dr S. Bloch, Dr L. Braddock, Dr S. Crown, Professor J. E. Cooper, Dr J. Corbett, Dr P. Cowan, Dr N. Eastman, Professor Griffith Edwards, Dr G. Forrest, Dr K. W. M. Fulford, Professor D. P. B. Goldberg, Dr G. Goodwin, Professor D. G. Grahame Smith, Professor J. C. Gunn, Dr J. Hamilton, Dr K. E. Hawton, Dr A. Hope, Dr T. Horder, Professor R. E. Kendell, Professor I. Kolvin, Professor M. H. Lader, Dr J. P. Leff, Dr R. Levy, Dr P. F. Liddle, Professor W. A. Lishman, Professor H. G. Morgan, Dr J. McWhinnie, Dr D. J. Nutt, Dr W. Ll. Parry-Jones, Professor E. S. Paykel, Dr J. S. Pippard, Miss S. Rowland-Jones, Dr G. Stores, Dr C. A. Storr, Dr T. G. Tennent, Dr C. P. Warlow, Dr G. K. Wilcock, and Dr H. H. O. Wolff.

We are also grateful to many other colleagues who have given advice and to our secretaries. We are particularly indebted to Mrs Susan Offen who has given invaluable help at all stages of the preparation of the typescript and the checking of references.

While every effort has been made to check drug dosages in this book, it is still possible that errors have been missed. Furthermore, dosage schedules are being continually revised and new side-effects recognized. For these reasons the reader is strongly urged to consult the drug companies' printed instructions before administering any of the drugs recommended in this book.

Contents

1. Signs and symptoms of mental disorder

Psychiatry can only be practised if the psychiatrist develops two distinct capacities. One is the capacity to collect clinical data objectively and accurately by history taking and examination of mental state, and to organize the data in a systematic and balanced way. The other is the capacity for intuitive understanding of each patient as an individual. When the psychiatrist exercises the first capacity, he draws on his clinical skills and knowledge of clinical phenomena; when he exercises the second capacity, he draws on his general understanding of human nature to gain insights into the feelings and behaviour of each individual patient.

Both capacities can be developed by accumulating experience of talking to patients, and by learning from the guidance and example of more experienced psychiatrists. From a textbook, however, it is inevitable that the reader can learn more about clinical skills than about intuitive understanding. In this book the first four chapters are concerned with various aspects of clinical skills. This greater coverage of clinical skills in no way implies that intuitive understanding is regarded as unimportant but simply that it cannot be learnt from reading a textbook.

The psychiatrist can only acquire skill in examining patients if he has a sound knowledge of how each symptom and sign is defined. Without such knowledge, he is liable to misclassify phenomena and make inaccurate diagnoses. For this reason, questions of definition are considered in this first chapter, before the examination of patients is described in the next.

Once the psychiatrist has elicited a patient's symptoms and signs, he needs to decide how far these phenomena resemble or differ from those of other psychiatric patients. In other words, he must determine whether the clinical features form a syndrome, which is a group of symptoms and signs that identifies patients with common features. The purpose of identifying a syndrome is to be able to plan treatment and predict the likely outcome by reference to accumulated knowledge about the causes, treatment, and outcome of the same syndrome in other patients. The principles involved are discussed in Chapter 4, which is concerned with classification, and also in the chapters dealing with the different syndromes.

Since the present chapter consists mainly of definitions and descriptions of symptoms and signs, it may be less easy to read than those which follow. It is suggested that the reader should approach the chapter in two stages. The first reading can be applied to the introductory sections and to a general understanding of the more frequent abnormal phenomena. The second can focus on details of definition and the less common symptoms and signs.

Before individual phenomena are described, it is important to consider some general issues concerning the methods of studying symptoms and signs and the terms used to describe them.

Psychopathology

The study of abnormal states of mind is known as **psychopathology,** a term which denotes two distinct approaches.

The first approach, **phenomenological psychopathology** (or **phenomenology**), is concerned with the objective description of abnormal states of mind in a way that avoids, as far as possible, preconceived theories. It aims to elucidate the basic data of psychiatry by defining the essential qualities of morbid mental experiences and by understanding what the patient is experiencing. It is entirely concerned with conscious experiences and observable behaviour. According to Jaspers (1963), phenomenology is 'the preliminary work of representing, defining and classifying psychic phenomena as an independent activity'.

The second approach, **psychodynamic psychopathology,** originates in psychoanalytical investigations. Like phenomenological psychopathology, it starts with the patient's description of his mental experiences and the doctor's observations of his behaviour. However, unlike phenomenological psychopathology it goes beyond description and seeks to explain the causes of abnormal mental events, particularly by postulating unconscious mental processes. These differences can be illustrated by the two approaches to persecutory delusions. Phenomenology describes them in detail and examines how they differ from normal beliefs and from other forms of abnormal thinking such as obsessions. On the other hand, the psychodynamic approach seeks to explain the occurrence of persecutory delusions, in terms of unconscious mechanisms such as repression and projection. In other words, it views them as evidence in the conscious mind of more important disorders in the unconscious.

This chapter is concerned mainly with phenomenological psychopathology, although reference will also be made to relevant ideas from dynamic psychopathology.

The most important exponent of phenomenological psychopathology was the German psychiatrist philosopher, Karl Jaspers. His classical work, *Allgemeine Psychopathologie [General psychopathology],* first appeared in 1913, and was a landmark in the development of clinical psychiatry. It provides the most complete account of the subject and contains much of interest, particularly in its early chapters. The seventh (1959) edition is available in an English translation by Hoenig and Hamilton (Jaspers 1963). Alternatively, useful outlines of the principles of phenomenology have been given by Jaspers (1963) and by Scharfetter (1980).

The significance of individual symptoms

Individual psychological symptoms are not necessarily evidence of pathology. Even hallucinations, which are often regarded as hallmarks of mental illness, are sometimes experienced by healthy people, for example when falling asleep. Symptoms are often recognized as abnormal because of their intensity and persistence. None the less, even when intense and persistent, a single symptom does not necessarily indicate illness. It is the characteristic grouping of symptoms into a syndrome that is important.

Primary and secondary symptoms

The terms primary and secondary are used in describing symptoms, but with more than one meaning. The first is temporal; primary meaning antecedent and secondary meaning subsequent. The second is causal; primary meaning directly related to the pathological process and secondary meaning a reaction to the primary symptom. The two meanings are often related – the symptoms appearing first in time are those most directly related to the pathological process.

It is preferable to use the terms primary and secondary in the temporal sense, since this is factual rather than arbitrary. However, when first seen, many patients cannot give a clear account of the chronological development of their symptoms. If this happens, it is only possible to conjecture whether one symptom could be a reaction to another; for example, whether the fixed idea of being followed by persecutors could be a reaction to hearing voices.

The form and content of symptoms

When psychiatric symptoms are described, it is usual to distinguish between form and content, a distinction that can be best explained with an example. If a patient says that, when he is entirely alone, he hears voices calling him a homosexual, then the form of his experience is an auditory hallucination (i.e. a sensory perception in the absence of an external stimulus) while the content is the statement that he is homosexual. A second person might hear voices saying he is about to be killed: the form is still an auditory hallucination but the content is different. A third might experience repeated intrusive thoughts that he is homosexual but realize that these are untrue. He has an experience with the same content as the first (concerning homosexuality) but the form is different – in this case an obsessional thought.

DESCRIPTION OF SYMPTOMS AND SIGNS

Introduction

In the following sections, symptoms and signs are described in a different order from the one adopted when the mental state is examined. This is because it is useful to begin with the most distinctive phenomena – hallucinations and delusions. This should be borne in mind when reading Chapter 2 in which the description of the mental state examination begins with behaviour and talk rather than hallucinations and delusions.

The definitions in this section generally conform with those in the Present State Examination (PSE) a widely used standardized rating system described by Wing *et al.* (1974) and adopted by the World Health Organization for an international study of major mental disorders. The PSE definitions were developed in several stages. The original items were chosen to represent the clinical practice of a group of psychiatrists working in western Europe. The first definitions were modified progressively through several editions. The seventh edition was used in a large Anglo-American diagnostic project; the eighth included modifications arising from a study of schizophrenia carried out in countries in Europe, Asia, and the Americas; while the ninth, published in 1974, incorporates further refinements suggested by analysis of the previous studies. The PSE therefore provides useful common ground between psychiatrists working in different countries and contains definitions that can be applied reliably.

Before we consider individual symptoms it is appropriate to remind the reader that it is important not only to study individual mental phenomena but also to consider the whole person. The doctor must try to understand how the patient fulfils social roles such as worker, spouse, parent, friend, or sibling. He should consider what effect the disorders of function have had upon the remaining healthy parts of the person. Above all he should try to understand what it is like for this person to be ill, e.g. to care for small children while profoundly depressed or to attempt to live as a schizophrenic. The doctor will gain such understanding only if he is prepared to spend time listening to patients and their families and to interest himself in every aspect of their lives.

DISORDERS OF PERCEPTION

Perception and imagery

Perception is the process of becoming aware of what is presented through the sense organs. **Imagery** is an experience within the mind, usually without the feeling of reality that is part of perception. **Eidetic imagery** is a visual image which is so intense and detailed that it has a 'photographic' quality. Unlike perception, imagery can be called up and terminated by voluntary effort. It is usually obliterated by seeing or hearing. Occasionally, imagery is so vivid that it persists when the person looks at a poorly structured background such as plain wallpaper. This is called **pareidolia,** a state in which real and unreal percepts exist side by side, the latter being recognized as unreal. Pareidolia can occur in the delirium of fever and a few people can induce it deliberately.

Alterations in perception

Perceptions can alter in intensity and quality. They can seem more intense than usual, e.g. when two people experience the same auditory stimulus, such as the noise of a door shutting, the more anxious person may perceive it as louder. In mania, also, perceptions often seem very intense. Conversely, colours may seem less intense to someone who is depressed. Changes in quality occur in schizophrenia, sensations sometimes appearing distorted or unpleasant. For example, a patient may complain that food tastes bitter or that a flower smells like burning flesh.

Illusions

Illusions are misperceptions of external stimuli. They are most likely to occur when the general level of sensory stimulation is reduced. Thus at dusk a common illusion is to misperceive the outline of a bush as that of a man. Illusions are also more likely to occur when the level of consciousness is reduced, as for example in an acute brain syndrome. Thus a delirious patient may mistake inanimate objects for people when the level of illumination is normal, though he is more likely to do so if the room is badly lit. Illusions occur more often when attention is not focused on the sensory modality, or when there is a strong affective state ('affect illusions'), e.g. a person who is afraid in a dark lane is more likely to misperceive the outline of a bush as that of an attacker. (The so-called **illusion of doubles** or **Capgras syndrome** is not an illusion but a form of delusional misinterpretation. It is considered under paranoid syndromes in Chapter 11).

Hallucinations

A hallucination is a percept experienced in the absence of an external stimulus to the sense organs, and with a similar quality to a true percept. A hallucination is experienced as originating in the outside world (or within one's own body) like a percept, and not within the mind like imagery. Hallucinations may appear more or less real, varying from an experience that seems to have all the reality of a sensory experience to one that is little more real than mental imagery.

Hallucinations are not restricted to the mentally ill. A few normal people experience them, especially when tired. Hallucinations also occur in healthy people during the transition between sleep and waking; they are called

hypnagogic if experienced while falling asleep and **hypnopompic** if experienced during awakening.

Pseudohallucinations

This term has been applied to abnormal phenomena that do not meet the above criteria for hallucinations and are of less certain diagnostic significance. Unfortunately the word has two meanings which are often confused. The first, originating in the work of Kadinsky, was adopted by Jaspers (1913) in his book *General psychopathology*. In this sense, pseudohallucinations are especially vivid mental images; that is, they lack the quality of representing external reality and seem to be within the mind rather than in external space. However, unlike ordinary imagery, they cannot be changed substantially by an effort of will. The term is still used with this meaning (see, for example Scharfetter 1980). The second meaning of pseudohallucination is a hallucination that the subject recognizes as having no correlate in the external world. This is the sense in which the term is used by Hare (1973) and Taylor (1979).

Both definitions are difficult to apply because they depend on the patient's ability to give precise answers to difficult questions about the nature of his experience. Judgements based on the patient's recognition of the reality of his experience are, not surprisingly, difficult to make reliably because the patient is often uncertain himself. Although the percepts must be either in the external world or within the mind, patients often find this distinction difficult to make.

Taylor (1981) has suggested that two groups of pseudohallucinations should be recognized: 'imaged' pseudohallucinations that are experienced within the mind and 'perceived' pseudohallucinations that are experienced as located in external space but recognized as unreal. In everyday clinical work it seems better to abandon the term pseudohallucinations altogether, and simply to maintain the term hallucination as defined at the beginning of this section. If the clinical phenomena do not meet this definition, they should be described in detail rather than labelled with a technical term that provides no additional information useful for diagnosis. Readers requiring a more detailed account of these problems of definition are referred to Hare (1973), Taylor (1981), and Jaspers (1963, pp. 68–74). Further information about the phenomena themselves will be found in Sedman (1966).

Types of hallucinations

Hallucinations can be described in terms of their complexity and their sensory modality (see Table 1.1). The term **elementary hallucination** is used for experiences such as bangs, whistles, and flashes of light; **complex hallucination** is used for experiences such as hearing voices or music, or seeing faces and scenes.

Hallucinations may be auditory, visual, tactile, gustatory, olfactory, or of deep sensation. **Auditory hallucinations** may be experienced as noises, music, or voices. Hallucinatory 'voices' are sometimes called **phonemes,** but this usage

Table 1.1. *Description of hallucinations*

1. According to complexity
   elementary
   complex

2. According to sensory modality
   auditory
   visual
   olfactory and gustatory
   somatic (tactile and deep)

3. According to special features
   (a) auditory: second person
                   third person
                   Gedankenlautwerden
                   Écho de la pensée
   (b) visual: extracampine

4. Autoscopic hallucinations

of the term is at variance with its dictionary definition of a specific sound in a specific language. Voices may be heard clearly or indistinctly; they may appear to speak words, phrases, or sentences; and they may address the patient or sound as if talking to one another, referring to the patient as 'he' or 'she' (**third person hallucinations**). Sometimes voices seem to anticipate what the patient thinks a few moments later, or speak his own thoughts as he thinks them, or repeat them immediately after he has thought them. In the absence of concise English technical terms, the last two experiences are sometimes called *Gedankenlautwerden* and *écho de la pensée* respectively.

Visual hallucinations may also be elementary or complex. They may appear normal or abnormal in size; if the latter, they are more often smaller than the corresponding real percept. Visual hallucinations of dwarf figures are sometimes called lilliputian. **Extracampine visual hallucinations** are experienced as located outside the field of vision, that is, behind the head. **Olfactory and gustatory hallucinations** are frequently experienced together, often as unpleasant smells or tastes.

Tactile hallucinations, sometimes called **haptic hallucinations,** may be experienced as sensations of being touched, pricked, or strangled. They may also be felt as movements just below the skin which the patient may attribute to insects, worms, or other small creatures burrowing through the tissues. **Hallucinations of deep sensation** may occur as feelings of the viscera being pulled upon or distended, or of sexual stimulation or electric shocks.

An **autoscopic hallucination** is the experience of seeing one's own body projected into external space, usually in front of oneself, for short periods at a time. This experience may convince the person that he has a double (*doppelganger),* a theme occurring in several novels, including Dostoevsky's *The double.* In clinical practice this is a rare phenomenon, mainly encountered in a small minority of patients with temporal lobe epilepsy or other organic brain disorders (see Lukianowicz 1958 and Lhermitte 1951 for detailed accounts).

Occasionally, a stimulus in one sensory modality results in a hallucination in another, e.g. the sound of music may provoke visual hallucinations. This experience, sometimes called **reflex hallucinations,** may occur after taking drugs such as LSD, or rarely in schizophrenia.

As already mentioned, **hypnagogic** and **hypnopompic hallucinations** occur at the point of falling asleep and of waking respectively. When they occur in normal people, they are brief and elementary – as for example of hearing a bell ring or a name called. Usually the subject wakes suddenly and recognizes the nature of the experience. Hallucinations of this kind are common in narcolepsy; here the experience is different, as the patient may spend a long time between sleeping and waking and may have elaborate hallucinations.

Diagnostic associations

Hallucinations may occur in all kinds of psychosis, in hysterical neuroses and, at times, among healthy people. Therefore the finding of hallucinations does not itself help in diagnosis. However, certain kinds of hallucinations do have important implications for diagnosis.

Both the form and content of **auditory hallucinations** can help in diagnosis. Of the various types – noises, music, and voices the only ones of diagnostic significance are voices heard as speaking clearly to or about the patient. As explained already, voices which appear to be talking to each other, referring to the patient in the third person (e.g. 'he is a homosexual') are called **third person hallucinations.** They are associated particularly with schizophrenia. Such voices may be experienced as commenting on the patient's intentions (e.g. 'he wants to make love to her') or actions (e.g. 'she is washing her face'). Of all types of hallucination, commentary voices are most suggestive of schizophrenia.

Second person hallucinations appear to address the patient (e.g. 'you are going to die') or give commands (e.g. 'hit him'). In themselves they do not point to a particular diagnosis, but their content and especially the patient's reaction may do so. For example, voices with derogatory content suggest depressive psychosis, especially when the patient accepts them as justified (e.g. 'you are wicked'). In schizophrenia the patient more often resents such comments.

Voices which anticipate, echo, or repeat the patient's thoughts also suggest schizophrenia.

Visual hallucinations may occur in hysteria, affective disorders, and schizophrenia, but they should always raise the possibility of an organic disorder. The content of visual hallucinations is of little significance in diagnosis.

Hallucinations of taste and smell are infrequent. When they do occur they often have an unusual quality which patients have difficulty in describing. They may occur in schizophrenia or severe depressive disorders, but they should also suggest temporal lobe epilepsy or irritation of the olfactory bulb or pathways by a tumour.

Tactile and somatic hallucinations are not generally of diagnostic significance although a few special kinds are weakly associated with particular disorders. Thus, hallucinatory sensations of sexual intercourse suggest schizophrenia, especially if interpreted in an unusual way (e.g. as resulting from intercourse with a series of persecutors). The sensation of insects moving under the skin occurs in people who abuse cocaine and occasionally among schizophrenics.

DISORDERS OF THINKING

Disorder of thinking is usually recognized from the patient's speech or writings. It can also be inferred from actions; for example, a previously efficient librarian, who developed schizophrenia, became unable to classify books because each one seemed to belong to many different categories. Some psychological tests of thought disorder require the person to sort objects into categories.

The term disorder of thinking can be used in a wide sense to denote four separate groups of phenomena (Table 1.2). The first group comprises particular kinds of abnormal thinking – delusions and obsessional thoughts. The second

Table 1.2. *Disorders of thinking*

1. Particular kinds of abnormal thoughts
   Delusions
   Obsessions

2. Disorders of the stream of thought (speed and pressure)

3. Formal thought disorder (linking of thoughts together)

4. Abnormal beliefs about the possession of thoughts

group, disorder of the stream of thought, is concerned with abnormalities of the amount and the speed of the thoughts experienced. The third group, known as disorders of the form of thought, is concerned with abnormalities of the ways in which thoughts are linked together. The fourth group, abnormal beliefs about the possession of thoughts, comprises unusual disturbances of the normal awareness that one's thoughts are one's own.

The second and third groups are considered here, whilst the first and fourth will be discussed below.

Disorders of the stream of thought

In disorders of the stream of thought both the amount and the speed of thoughts are changed. At one extreme there is **pressure of thought,** when ideas arise in unusual variety and abundance and pass through the mind rapidly. At the other extreme there is poverty of thought, when the patient has only a few thoughts, which lack variety and richness, and seem to move through the mind slowly. The experience of pressure occurs in mania; that of poverty in depressive disorders. Either may be experienced in schizophrenia.

The stream of thought can also be interrupted suddenly, a phenomenon which the patient experiences as his mind going blank, and which an observer notices as a sudden interruption in the flow of conversation. Minor degrees of this experience are common, particularly in people who are tired or anxious. However, thought blocking, a particularly abrupt and complete interruption, strongly suggests schizophrenia. Because thought blocking has this importance in diagnosis, it is essential that it should be identified only when there is no doubt about its presence. Inexperienced interviewers often wrongly identify a sudden interruption of conversation as thought blocking. There are several other reasons why the flow of speech may stop abruptly: the patient may be distracted by another thought or an extraneous sound, or he may be experiencing one of the momentary gaps in the stream of thought that are normal in people who are anxious or tired. Thought blocking should only be identified when interruptions in speech are sudden, striking, and repeated, and when the patient describes the experience as an abrupt and complete emptying of his mind. The diagnostic association with schizophrenia is strengthened if the patient also interprets the experience in an unusual way, e.g. as having had his thoughts taken away by a machine operated by one of his persecutors.

Disorders of the form of thought

Disorders of the form of thought can be divided into three subgroups, flight of ideas, perseveration, and loosening of associations. Each is related to a particular form of mental disorder, so that it is important to distinguish them, but in none of the three is the relationship strong enough to be regarded as diagnostic.

In **flight of ideas** the patient's thoughts and conversation move quickly from one topic to another so that one train of thought is not completed before another appears. The links between these rapidly changing topics are understandable because they occur in normal thinking, a point that differentiates them from loosening of associations (see below). In practice, the distinction is often difficult to make, especially when the patient is speaking rapidly. For this reason it may be helpful to tape record a sample of speech and listen to it several times. The characteristics of flight of ideas are: preservation of the ordinary logical sequence of ideas, using two words with a similar sound (clang associations) or the same word with a second meaning (punning), rhyming, and responding to distracting cues in the immediate surroundings. Flight of ideas is characteristic of mania.

Perseveration is the persistent and inappropriate repetition of the same thoughts, as judged by the patient's words or actions. In response to a series of questions, the patient gives the correct answer to the first, but continues to answer subsequent different questions with answers to the first. It is associated with dementia but not confined to them.

Loosening of associations denotes a loss of the normal structure of thinking. To the interviewer this appears as muddled and illogical conversation that cannot be clarified by further enquiry. Several features of this muddled thinking have been described (see below), but in the end it is usually the general lack of clarity in the patient's conversation that makes the most striking impression. This differs from the difficulties of understanding people who are muddled through anxiety or low intelligence. Anxious people give a more coherent account when they have been put at ease, while those with subnormal intelligence can express ideas more clearly if the interviewer simplifies his questions. When there is loosening of associations, the interviewer has the experience that the more he tries to clarify the patient's thoughts the less he understands them. Loosening of associations occurs in schizophrenia.

Loosening of associations can take several forms. **Knight's move** or **derailment** refers to a transition from one topic to another, either between sentences or in mid-sentence, with no logical relationship between the two topics and no evidence of the forms of association described under flight of ideas. When this abnormality is extreme it disrupts not only the connections between sentences and phrases but also the finer grammatical structure of speech. It is then called **word salad** or **verbigeration.**

One effect of loosened associations on the patient's conversation is sometimes called **talking past the point** (also known by the German term *Vorbeireden*). In this, the patient seems always about to get near to the matter in hand but never quite reaches it.

Several attempts have been made to devise psychological tests for loosening of associations, but the results have not been particularly useful to the clinician. Attempts to use the tests to diagnose schizophrenia have failed.

In addition to these disorders of links between ideas, thought may become illogical through widening of concepts, i.e. the grouping together of things that are not normally regarded as closely connected with one another.

Neologisms

Although not a disorder of the form of thought, neologism is conveniently described here. In this abnormality of speech the patient uses words or phrases invented by himself. Neologisms must be distinguished from incorrect pronunciation, the wrong use of words by people with limited education, dialect words, obscure technical terms, and the 'private words' which some families invent to amuse themselves. The interviewer should always record examples of these words and ask the patient what they mean.

Theories of thought disorder

Many theories have been proposed but none is convincing (see Payne 1973 for a review). Each theory attempts to explain a particular aspect of the thought disorder found in schizophrenia. Thus Goldstein (1944) built his theory round the apparent difficulty in forming abstract concepts ('concreteness'), while

Cameron (1938) developed Bleuler's original observation that there is a 'loosening of associations', i.e. that the boundaries between concepts are less clear than in normal people. Payne and Friedlander (1962) developed the theory that concepts are too wide (over-inclusive) and devised ways of testing this with problems requiring the sorting and classification of objects. Bannister (1962) used Kelly's personal construct theory as the basis of a similar scheme, in which schizophrenics were supposed to have constructs that are not as consistent as those of other people and not as well structured. Bannister and Fransella (1966) devised an ingenious test for these aspects of personal constructs, asking subjects to rate photographs of unknown people for a number of attributes such as kindness, honesty, and selfishness. Although the test provides a method of measuring one aspect of thought disorder, the theory has not succeeded in explaining how the abnormality arises.

Delusions

A delusion is a belief that is firmly held despite evidence to the contrary and is not a conventional belief that the person might be expected to hold given his educational and cultural background. This definition is intended to separate delusions, which are indicators of mental disorder, from other strongly held beliefs found among healthy people. A delusion is usually a false belief, but not invariably so (see below).

Delusions are beliefs that are held with great conviction and cannot be altered by presenting evidence that contradicts them. For example, a patient who holds the delusion that there are persecutors in the adjoining house will not be convinced by evidence that the house is empty; instead he will retain his belief by suggesting, for example, that the persecutors left the house before it was searched. However, some of the non-delusional ideas of normal people are equally impervious to reasoned argument. Thus delusions have to be distinguished from the shared beliefs of people with a common religious or ethnic background. For example a person who has been brought up to believe in spiritualism is unlikely to change his convictions when presented with contrary evidence that convinces a non-believer.

Delusions must also be distinguished from **overvalued ideas,** i.e. deeply held personal convictions that are understandable when the patient's background is known; for example, a person whose mother and sister contracted cancer one after the other, may develop the strong conviction that cancer is contagious. Although the distinction between delusions and overvalued ideas is not always easy to make, this seldom leads to practical difficulties since diagnosis of mental illness depends on more than the presence or absence of a single symptom.

The definition of delusion emphasizes that the belief must be firmly held. Although this is true at the stage when the delusion is fully formed, it may not always be so at times before and afterwards. Thus, although some delusions arrive in the patient's mind fully formed and with a sense of total conviction, others develop more gradually; and during recovery the patient may pass through a stage of increasing doubt before finally rejecting the ideas as false. The term **partial delusion** is sometimes used (as in the Present State Examination see p. 4) to describe these phenomena. It is safest to use this term only when it is known that a full delusion was previously present or, with hindsight, that the partial delusion later developed into a full delusion. Partial delusions are sometimes found during the early stages of schizophrenia. When they are encountered, a careful search should be made for other phenomena of mental illness, and the patient re-examined later, but the finding cannot be given much weight by itself.

Finally, although a patient may be wholly convinced that a delusion is true, this conviction does not necessarily influence all his feelings and actions. This **double orientation** occurs most often in chronic schizophrenics; such a patient may, for example, believe that he is a member of a Royal Family whilst living contentedly in a hostel for discharged psychiatric patients.

Although delusions are as a rule false beliefs, in exceptional circumstances they can be true or subsequently become true. Thus a man may develop a jealous delusion about his wife, in the absence of any reasonable evidence of infidelity. Even if the wife is being unfaithful at the time, the belief is still delusional if there is no rational grounds for holding it. Exceptions of this kind remind us that it is not the falsity of the belief that determines whether it is delusional but the nature of the mental processes that led up to it. Conversely, it is a well-known pitfall of clinical practice to assume that an idea is false because it is odd, instead of checking the facts or finding out how the idea was arrived at. For example, improbable stories of persecution by neighbours or of attempts at poisoning by a spouse may turn out to be correct and arrived at through normal processes of logical thinking.

Delusions are of many kinds. These will now be described; the reader may find it helpful to refer to Table 1.3 as he reads the section which follows.

Primary, secondary, and shared delusions

A **primary** or **autochthonous** delusion is one that appears suddenly and with full conviction but without any mental events leading up to it. For example, a schizophrenic patient may be suddenly and completely convinced that he is changing sex, without ever having thought of it before and without any preceding ideas or events which could have led in any understandable way to this conclusion. The belief arrives in the mind suddenly, fully formed, and in a totally convincing form. Presumably it is a direct expression of the pathological process causing the psychosis – a primary symptom. Not all primary delusional experiences start with an idea; a **delusional mood** (sometimes known by the German word *Wahnstimmung*) or a **delusional perception** can also arrive suddenly and without any antecedents to account for them. Of course, patients do not find it easy to remember the exact sequence of such unusual and often distressing mental events and for this reason it is difficult to be certain what is

Table 1.3. *Descriptions of delusions*

1. According to fixity
     complete
     partial

2. According to onset
     primary
     secondary

3. Other delusional experiences
     delusional mood
     delusional perception
     delusional memory

4. According to theme
     persecutory (paranoid)
     delusions of reference
     grandiose (expansive)
     delusions of guilt and worthlessness
     nihilistic
     hypochondriacal
     religious
     jealous
     sexual or amorous
     delusions of control
     delusions concerning possession of thought
     delusions of thought broadcasting

5. According to other features
     shared delusions

primary. Inexperienced interviewers usually diagnose primary delusional experiences too readily because they do not probe carefully enough into their antecedents. Primary delusions are given considerable weight in the diagnosis of schizophrenia, and it is important not to record them unless they are present for certain.

Secondary delusions can be understood as derived from some preceding morbid experience. The latter may be of several kinds, such as: a hallucination, e.g. someone who hears voices may come to believe that he is being followed; a mood, e.g. a person who is profoundly depressed may believe that people think he is worthless; or an existing delusion, e.g. a person with the delusion that he has lost all his money may come to believe he will be put in prison for failing to pay debts. Some secondary delusions seem to have an integrative function, making the original experiences more comprehensible to the patient, as in the first example above. Others seem to do the opposite, increasing the sense of persecution or failure, as in the third example.

The accumulation of secondary delusions may result in a complicated **delusional system** in which each belief can be understood as following from the one before. When a complicated set of interrelated beliefs of this kind has developed the delusions are sometimes said to be **systematized.**

Shared delusions: as a rule, other people recognize delusions as false and argue with the patient in an attempt to correct them. Occasionally, a person who lives with a deluded patient comes to share his delusional beliefs. This condition is known as shared delusions or **folie à deux.** Although the second person's delusional conviction is as strong as the partner's whilst the couple remain together, it often recedes quickly when they are separated. The condition is uncommon. When it does occur, it usually involves two people who have a close relationship with one another and little contact with anyone else, e.g. elderly sisters living together in a remote place (see also Chapter 10).

Delusional ideas, moods, perceptions, and memories

As a rule, when a patient first experiences a delusion he also has an emotional response and interprets his environment in a new way. For example, a person who believes that a group of people intend to kill him is likely to feel afraid. At the same time he may interpret the sight of a car in his driving mirror as evidence that he is being followed. In most cases, the delusion comes first and the other components follow.

Occasionally, however, the order is reversed. The first experience may be a change of mood, often a feeling of foreboding that some sinister event is about to take place. In German this is called *Wahnstimmung,* a term which is usually translated as **delusional mood.** The latter is an unsatisfactory term because there is really a mood from which a delusion arises. At other times, the first change may be attaching a new significance to a familiar percept without any reason. For example, a new arrangement of objects on a colleague's desk may be interpreted as a sign that the patient has been chosen to do God's work. This is called **delusional perception:** this term is also unsatisfactory since it is not the patient's perceptions that are abnormal, but the false meaning that has been attached to a normal percept. Although both terms are less than satisfactory, there is no generally agreed alternative and they have to be used if the experience is to be labelled. However, it is usually better simply to describe what the patient has experienced and to find out the order in which changes have occurred in beliefs, affect, and the interpretation of sense data.

A related disorder occurs when a patient sees a familiar person and believes him to have been replaced by an impostor who is an exact double of the original. This symptom, usually called by the French term *illusion de sosies* (illusion of doubles) may be so persistent that a syndrome, **Capgras syndrome,** has been described in which it is the central feature (see Chapter 10). The opposite false interpretation of experience occurs when the patient recognizes a number of people as having different appearances, but believes they are all a single persecutor in disguise. This symptom is called **Fregoli's illusion** after a talented actor who had an exceptional ability to alter his appearance. Both experiences are, of course, not illusions but delusions.

Finally, some delusions concern past rather than present events, and are known as **delusional memories.** For example, if a patient believes that there is a plot to poison him he may attribute new significance to the memory of an occasion when he vomited after eating a meal, long before his delusional system began. This experience has to be distinguished from the accurate recall of a delusional idea formed at the time. This term is unsatisfactory because it is not the memory that is delusional, but the interpretation that has been applied to it.

Types of delusion

For the purposes of clinical work, delusions are grouped according to their main themes. This is useful because there is some correspondence between these themes and the major forms of mental illness. However it is important to remember that there are many exceptions to the broad associations mentioned below.

Persecutory delusions are often called **paranoid,** a term which strictly speaking has a wider meaning. The term paranoid was used in ancient Greek writings in the modern sense of 'out of his mind', and Hippocrates used it to describe febrile delirium. Many later writers applied the term to grandiose, erotic, jealous, and religious, as well as persecutory, delusions. For this reason, it is preferable not to use the term paranoid to describe a persecutory delusion. However, the term paranoid applied in its wide sense to symptoms, syndromes and personality types retains its usefulness (see Chapter 10).

Persecutory delusions are most commonly concerned with persons or organizations that are thought to be trying to inflict harm on the patient, damage his reputation, make him insane, or poison him. Such delusions are common but of little help in diagnosis, for they can occur in organic states, schizophrenia, and affective psychosis. However, the patient's attitude to the delusion may point to the diagnosis: in a severe depressive disorder he characteristically accepts the supposed activities of the persecutors as justified by his own guilt and wickedness, but in schizophrenia he resents them often angrily. In assessing such ideas, it is essential to remember that apparently improbable accounts of persecution are sometimes true and that it is normal in certain cultures to believe in witchcraft and to ascribe misfortune to the malign activities of other people.

Delusions of reference are concerned with the idea that objects, events, or people have a personal significance for the patient: for example, an article read in a newspaper or a remark heard on television is believed to be directed specifically to himself. Alternatively a radio play about homosexuals is thought to have been broadcast in order to tell the patient that everyone knows he is a homosexual. Delusions of reference may also relate to actions or gestures made by other people which are thought to convey something about the patient; for example, people touching their hair may be thought to signify that he is turning into a woman. Although most delusions of reference have persecutory associations thay may also relate to grandiose or reassuring themes.

Grandiose or expansive delusions are beliefs of exaggerated self-importance. The patient may think himself wealthy, endowed with unusual abilities, or a special person. Such ideas occur in mania and in schizophrenia.

Delusions of guilt and worthlessness are found most often in depressive illness, and are therefore sometimes called depressive delusions. Typical themes are that a minor infringement of the law in the past will be discovered and bring shame upon the patient, or that his sinfulness will lead to divine retribution on his family.

Nihilistic delusions are strictly speaking beliefs about the non-existence of some person or thing, but they are extended to include pessimistic ideas that the patient's career is finished, that he is about to die, that he has no money, or that the world is doomed. They are associated with extreme degrees of depressive mood change. Comparable ideas concerning failures of bodily function (e.g. that the bowels are blocked with putrefying matter) often accompany these nihilistic delusions. The resulting clinical picture is called **Cotard's syndrome** after the French psychiatrist who described it (Cotard 1882). The condition is considered further in Chapter 10.

Hypochondriacal delusions are concerned with illness. The patient may believe wrongly, and in the face of all medical evidence to the contrary, that he is ill. Such delusions are more common in the elderly, reflecting the increasing concern with health among mentally normal people at this time of life. Other delusions may be concerned with cancer or venereal disease, or with the appearance of parts of the body, especially the nose. Patients with delusions of the last kind sometimes request plastic surgery (see p. 359).

Religious delusions: delusions with a religious content were much more frequent in the nineteenth century than they are today (Klaf and Hamilton 1961), presumably reflecting the greater part that religion played in the life of ordinary people in the past. When unusual and firmly held religious beliefs are encountered among members of minority religions, it is advisable to speak to another member of the group before deciding whether the ideas (e.g. apparently extreme ideas about divine punishment for minor sins) are abnormal or not.

Delusions of jealousy: these are more common among men. Not all jealous ideas are delusions; less intense jealous preoccupations are common, and some obsessional thoughts are concerned with doubts about the spouse's fidelity. However, when the beliefs are delusional they have particular importance because they may lead to dangerously aggressive behaviour towards the person thought to be unfaithful. Special care is needed if the patient follows the spouse to spy on her, examines her clothes for marks of semen, or searches her handbag for letters. A person with delusional jealousy will not be satisfied if he fails to find evidence supporting his beliefs; his search will continue. These important problems are discussed further in Chapter 10.

Sexual or amorous delusions: both sexual and amorous delusions are rare but when they occur, they are more frequent among women. Delusions concerning sexual intercourse are often secondary to somatic hallucinations felt in the genitalia. A woman with amorous delusions believes that she is loved by a man who is usually inaccessible, often of higher social status, and someone to whom she has never even spoken. Erotic delusions are the most prominent feature of **de Clérambault's syndrome** which is discussed in Chapter 10.

Delusions of control: the patient who has a delusion of control believes that his actions, impulses, or thoughts are controlled by an outside agency. Because the symptom strongly suggests schizophrenia, it is important not to record it unless definitely present. A common error is to diagnose it when not present. Sometimes it is confused with the experience of hearing hallucinatory voices giving commands that the patient obeys voluntarily. At other times it is mis-diagnosed because the patient has mistaken the question for one about religious beliefs concerning the divine control of human actions. The patient with a delusion of control firmly believes that individual movements or actions have been brought about by an outside agency; for example that his arms are moved into the position of crucifixion not because he willed them to do so, but because an outside force brought it about.

Delusions concerning the possession of thoughts: Healthy people take for granted the experience that their thoughts are their own. They also assume that thoughts are private experiences which other people can only know if they are spoken aloud, or if facial expression, gesture, or action gives them away. Patients with delusions about the possession of thoughts may lose these convictions in several ways. Those who have delusions about **thought insertion** believe that some of their thoughts are not their own but have been implanted by an outside agency. This differs from the experience of the obsessional patient who may be distressed by unpleasant thoughts but never doubts that they originate within his own mind. As Lewis (1957) said, obsessional thoughts are 'home made but disowned'. The patient with a delusion of thought insertion will not accept that the thoughts have originated in his own mind. Patients who have **delusions of thought withdrawal** believe that thoughts have been taken out of the mind. This delusion usually accompanies thought blocking, so that the patient experiences a break in the flow of thoughts through his mind and believes that the 'missing' thoughts have been taken away by some outside agency, often his supposed persecutors.

In **delusions of thought broadcasting** the patient believes that his unspoken thoughts are known to other people, through radio, telepathy, or in some other way. Some patients also believe that other people can hear their thoughts (a belief which also accompanies the experience of hearing one's own thoughts spoken, *Gedankenlautwerden*).

All three of these symptoms occur much more commonly in schizophrenia than in any other disorder.

The causes of delusions

So little is known about the processes by which normal beliefs are formed and tested against evidence, that it is not surprising that we are ignorant about the cause of delusions. This has not, however, prevented the development of several theories, mainly concerned with persecutory delusions.

One of the best known was developed by Freud. The central ideas were expressed in a paper originally published in 1913 (Freud 1958): 'the study of a number of cases of delusions of persecution has led me as well as other investigators to the view that the relation between the patient and his persecutor can be reduced to a simple formula. It appears that the person to whom the delusion ascribes so much power and influence is either identical with someone who played an equally important part in the patient's emotional life before illness, or an easily recognizable substitute for him. The intensity of the emotion is projected in the shape of external power, while its quality is changed into the opposite. The person who is now hated and feared for being a persecutor was at one time loved and honoured. The main purpose of the persecution asserted by the patient's delusion is to justify the change in his emotional attitude'. Freud further summarized his view as follows: delusions of persecution are the result of the sequence "I do not *love* him – I *hate* him, because he persecutes me"; erotomania of the sequence "I do not love *him* – I love *her*, because *she loves me*"; and delusions of jealousy of the sequence "It is not *I* who love the man – *she* loves him" (Freud 1958, pp. 63–4, emphases in the original). This hypothesis suggests therefore that patients who experience persecutory delusions have repressed homosexual impulses. So far, attempts to test this idea have not produced convincing evidence in its favour (see Arthur 1964). Nevertheless, the general idea that persecutory delusions involve the defence mechanism of projection has been accepted by some writers.

Several existential analyses of delusions have been made. These describe in detail the experience of the deluded patient and make the important point that it affects the whole being – it is not just an isolated symptom.

Conrad (1958), using the approach of Gestalt psychology, described the delusional experience as having four stages starting from a delusional mood which he called trema (fear and trembling), leading via the delusional idea which he called apophenia (the appearance of the phenomenon), to the person's efforts to make sense of the experience by revising his whole view of the world. These efforts break down in the last stage (apocalypse) when thought disorder and behavioural symptoms appear. While a sequence of this kind can be observed in a few patients it is certainly not invariable.

Learning theorists have tried to explain delusions as a form of avoidance of highly unpleasant emotions. Thus Dollard and Miller (1950) suggested that a delusion is a learned explanation for events which avoids feelings of guilt or shame. However, this is as unsupported by evidence as all the other theories of delusion formation. Readers who wish to find out more about the subject should consult Arthur (1964).

Obsessional and compulsive symptoms

These symptoms are more common than delusions but generally of less serious significance. The two groups of symptoms are best described separately although they often occur together.

Obsessions are recurrent, persistent thoughts, impulses, or images that enter the mind despite the person's efforts to exclude them. The characteristic feature is the subjective sense of a struggle – the patient resisting the obsession which nevertheless intrudes into his awareness. Obsessions are recognized by the person as his own and not implanted from elsewhere. He often regards the ideas as untrue or senseless – an important point of distinction from delusions. They are generally about matters which he finds distressing or otherwise unpleasant.

The presence of resistance is important because, together with the lack of conviction about the truth of the idea, it is the feature that distinguishes obsessions from delusions. However, when obsessions have been present for a long time, the amount of resistance often becomes less. This seldom causes diagnostic difficulties because by the time it happens, the nature of the symptom has usually been established.

Obsessions can occur in several forms (Table 1.4). Obsessional **thoughts** are repeated and intrusive words or phrases, which are usually upsetting to the

Table 1.4. *Obsessional and compulsive symptoms*

1. Obsessions: thoughts
                  ruminations
                  doubts
                  impulses
                  obsessional phobias

2. Compulsions (rituals)

3. Obsessional slowness

patient; e.g. repeated obscenities or blasphemous phrases coming into the awareness of a religious person. Obsessional **ruminations** are repeated worrying themes of a more complex kind; e.g. about the ending of the world. Obsessional **doubts** are repeated themes expressing uncertainty about previous actions, e.g. whether or not the person turned off an electrical appliance that might cause a fire. Whatever the nature of the doubt, the person realizes that the action has, in fact, been completed safely. Obsessional **impulses** are repeated urges to carry out actions, usually actions that are aggressive, dangerous, or socially embarrassing. For example, the urge to pick up a knife and stab another person; to jump in front of a train; to shout obscenities in church. Whatever the urge, the person has no wish to carry it out, resists it strongly, and does not act on it.

Obsessional phobias are obsessional thoughts with a fearful content; e.g. 'I may have cancer'; or obsessional impulses that lead to anxiety and avoidance; e.g. the impulse to strike another person with a knife and the consequent avoidance of knives. The term is confusing (see below under phobias).

Although the themes of obsessions are various, most can be grouped into six categories: dirt and contamination, aggression, orderliness, illness, sex, and religion. Thoughts about **dirt** and **contamination** are usually associated with the idea of harming others through the spread of disease. **Aggressive** thoughts may be about striking another person or shouting angry or obscene remarks in public. Thoughts about **orderliness** may be about the way objects are to be arranged or work is to be organized. Thoughts about **illness** are usually of a fearful kind; e.g. a dread of cancer or venereal disease. This has resulted in the name **illness phobia**, but this term should be avoided because the phenomena are not examples of anxiety arising in specific situations (which is the hallmark of a phobia, see below). Obsessional ideas about **sex** usually concern practices which the patient would find shameful, such as anal intercourse. Obsessions about **religion** often take the form of doubts about the fundamentals of belief (e.g. 'does God exist?') or repeated doubts whether sins have been adequately confessed (**scruples**).

Compulsions are repetitive and seemingly purposeful behaviours, performed in a stereotyped way (hence the alternative name of **compulsive rituals**). They are accompanied by a subjective sense that they must be carried out and by an urge to resist. Like obsessions, compulsions are recognized as senseless. A compulsion is usually associated with an obsession as if it has the function of reducing the distress caused by the latter. For example a handwashing compulsion often follows obsessional thoughts that the hands are contaminated with faecal matter. Occasionally, however, the only associated obsession is an urge to carry out the compulsive act.

Compulsive acts are of many kinds, but three are particularly common. **Checking** rituals are often concerned with safety; e.g. checking over and over again that a gas tap has been turned off. **Cleaning** rituals often take the form of repeated handwashing but may also involve household cleaning. **Counting** rituals may be spoken aloud or rehearsed silently. They often involve counting in a special way, e.g. in threes, and are frequently associated with doubting thoughts such that the count must be repeated to make sure it was carried out adequately in the first place. In **dressing** rituals the person has to lay out his clothes in a particular way, or put them on in a special order. Again, they are often accompanied by doubting thoughts that lead to seemingly endless repetition. In severe cases a patient may take several hours to put on his clothes in the morning.

Obsessional slowness is usually the result of compulsive rituals or repeated doubts but it can occur occasionally without them (primary obsessional slowness).

The differential diagnosis of obsessional thoughts is from the ordinary preoccupations of healthy people, from the repeated concerns of anxious and depressed patients, from the recurring ideas and urges encountered in sexual deviations or drug dependent patients, and from delusions. Ordinary preoccupations do not have the same insistent quality and can be resisted by an effort of will. Many anxious or depressed patients experience intrusive thoughts (for example the anxious person may think that he is about to faint, or the depressed person that he has nothing to live for), but these ideas do not seem unreasonable to them and they do not resist them. Similarly, sexual deviants and drug dependent people often experience insistent ideas and images concerned with their sexual practices or habits of drug taking, but these ideas are usually welcomed rather than resisted. Delusions are likewise not resisted, and are also firmly held to be true.

Theories about the **aetiology** of obsessions are discussed in Chapter 7, where obsessional neuroses are considered.

DISORDERS OF EMOTION

In everyday usage, the words mood and affect are used interchangeably to denote emotional states. The glossary to DSM III recommends that affect should be used for short-term states and mood for sustained ones. However, in practice, the words are often used as loosely in psychiatry as in everyday speech. In mental disorder, affect may be abnormal in three ways: its nature may be altered; it may fluctuate more or less than usual; and it may be inconsistent either with the patient's thoughts and actions or with events that are going on at the time.

Changes in the nature of emotion can be towards anxiety, depression, elation, or anger. Changes towards anxiety or depression may be associated with an obvious cause in the person's life, or arise without reason. Emotional disorders usually include several components other than the mood change itself. Thus feelings of anxiety are usually accompanied by autonomic overactivity and increased muscle tension, and feelings of depression by gloomy preoccupations and psychomotor slowness. These other features are part of the syndromes of anxiety and depressive states and as such are described in later chapters.

Abnormality in the fluctuation of mood may take the extreme form of total loss of emotion and inability to feel pleasure. The latter is sometimes called **apathy** (i.e. without feeling), a sense of the word that contrasts with the everyday usage of indolence of initiative. When the normal variation of emotion is reduced rather than lost, affect is described as **blunted** or **flattened**. When emotions change in a rapid, abrupt, and excessive way, affect is said to be **labile**. When the changes are very marked, the term **emotional incontinence** is sometimes used.

Normally, emotional expression seems appropriate to a person's circumstances (e.g. sadness after a loss) and congruent with his thoughts and actions (when a person looks sad he is likely to be thinking gloomy thoughts). In psychiatric disorders, there may be **incongruity** of affect. For example a patient may laugh when describing the death of his mother. Such incongruity must be distinguished from laughter that indicates that someone is ill at ease when talking about a distressing topic. It should be noted that failure to show emotion in distressing circumstances, although equally incongruous in the everyday sense, is called flattening of affect, not incongruity.

Changes in emotion are found in all kinds of psychiatric disorder. They are the central feature of the affective disorders (depression and elation) and of anxiety states. They are also common in other neuroses, organic psychoses, and schizophrenia.

Phobias

A phobia is a persistent irrational fear of and wish to avoid a specific object, activity, or situation. The fear is irrational in the sense that it is out of proportion to the real danger and also that the person himself recognizes that it is exaggerated. The person finds it difficult to control his fear and often tries to avoid the feared objects and situations if he possibly can. The objects that provoke the fear may be a living creature such as a dog, snake, or spider, or a natural phenomenon such as darkness or thunder. Fear-provoking situations include high places, crowds, and open spaces. Phobic patients feel anxious not only in the presence of the objects or situations but also when thinking about them (**anticipatory anxiety**).

Isolated phobic symptoms are common among normal people and have been described since the earliest medical writings (see Lewis 1976 or Errera 1962 for a historical account). The variety of objects and situations that are feared is great. In the past, Greek names were given to each one (Pitres and Regis 1902 labelled some seventy in this way), but there is nothing to be gained by this practice.

As pointed out earlier, obsessional thoughts leading to anxiety and avoidance are often called **obsessional phobias;** e.g. a recurrent thought about doing harm with knives is sometimes called a phobia of knives because the person avoids these objects. Similarly, obsessional thoughts about illness are sometimes called illness phobias (e.g. 'I may have cancer'). Strictly speaking neither of these symptoms is a phobia. Nor is dysmorphophobia, which is a disorder of bodily awareness (see p. 358).

Depersonalization and derealization

Depersonalization is a change in self-awareness such that the person feels unreal. Those who have this condition find it difficult to describe, often speaking of being detached from their own experience and unable to feel emotion. A similar change in relation to the environment is called derealization. In this, objects appear unreal and people appear as lifeless, two-dimensional 'cardboard' figures. Despite the complaint of inability to feel emotion, both depersonalization and derealization are described as highly unpleasant experiences.

These central features are often accompanied by other morbid experiences and there is some disagreement whether these are a part of depersonalization and derealization or separate symptoms. These accompanying features include changes in the experience of time; changes in the body image such as feeling that a limb has altered in size or shape; and occasionally a feeling of being outside one's own body, observing one's own actions, often from above. These features do not occur in every case (Ackner 1954*a*).

Depersonalization and derealization are experienced quite commonly as transient phenomena by healthy adults and children, especially when tired. The experience usually begins abruptly and in normal people seldom lasts more than a few minutes (Sedman 1970). The symptoms have been reported after sleep deprivation (Bliss *et al.* 1959), after sensory deprivation (Reed and Sedman 1964), and as an effect of hallucinogenic drugs (Guttman and Maclay 1936). The symptoms also occur in many psychiatric disorders, when they may be persistent, sometimes lasting for years. They are particularly associated with anxiety states, depression, and schizophrenia. Roth (1959) has drawn attention to the frequency with which these symptoms occur in phobic disorders. Depersonalization has also been described in epilepsy, especially the kind arising in the temporal lobe. Some psychiatrists, notably Shorvon *et al.* (1946), have described a separate depersonalization syndrome which is discussed in Chapter 7.

Because patients find it difficult to describe the feelings of depersonalization and derealization, they often resort to metaphor. Unless careful enquiry is made, this can lead to confusion between descriptions of depersonalization and of delusional ideas. For example, a patient's description of depersonalization may be 'as if part of my brain had stopped working', or of derealization 'as if the people I meet are lifeless creatures' – statements which must be explored carefully to distinguish them from delusional beliefs that the brain is no longer working or that people have really changed. At times, this distinction may be very difficult to make.

There are several **aetiological theories** about depersonalization. Mayer-Gross (1935) proposed that it is a 'preformed functional response of the brain' in the sense that an epileptic fit is a preformed response. Others have suggested that depersonalization is a response to alterations in consciousness (which is consistent with its appearance during fatigue and sleep deprivation in normal people) or to excessive levels of anxiety. Thus Lader and Wing (1966) described one anxious patient who developed depersonalization during an experiment in which skin conductance and heart rate were being measured. When this happened, these psychological indices of anxiety fell, suggesting that depersonalization may have been an expression of some mechanism which reduced anxiety. However, depersonalization can occur when consciousness is normal and in the absence of anxiety so that, at best, these ideas can only explain a proportion of cases. Moreover, in states with undoubted changes in consciousness (acute organic psychosyndromes) depersonalization is found in only a minority of patients and the same argument can be applied to anxiety states. Other writers have suggested that depersonalization is the expression of a disorder of perceptual mechanisms, and some psychoanalytic authors regard it as a defence against emotion. These various theories, none of which is satisfactory, have been reviewed by Sedman (1970).

MOTOR SYMPTOMS

Abnormalities of social behaviour, facial expression, and posture occur frequently in mental illness of all kinds. They are discussed in the Chapter 3 where the examination of the patient is considered. There are also a number of specific motor symptoms. With the exception of tics these are mainly observed among schizophrenic patients. They are described briefly here for reference, and their clinical associations are discussed in Chapter 9.

Tics are irregular repeated movements involving a group of muscles, e.g. sideways movement of the head or the raising of one shoulder. **Mannerisms** are repeated movements that appear to have some functional significance, for example saluting. **Stereotypies** are repeated movements that are regular (unlike tics) and without obvious significance (unlike mannerisms): for example rocking to and fro. **Posturing** is the adoption of unusual bodily postures continuously for a substantial period of time. The posture may have a meaning, e.g. standing with both arms outstretched as if being crucified; or may have no apparent significance, e.g. standing on one leg. Patients are said to show **negativism** when they do the opposite of what is asked and actively resist efforts to persuade them to comply. **Echopraxia** is the imitation of the interviewer's movements automatically even when asked not to do so. Patients are said to exhibit **ambitendence** when they alternate between opposite movements, for example putting out the arm to shake hands, then withdrawing it, extending it again, and so on. **Waxy flexibility** is detected when a patient's limbs can be placed in a position in which they then remain for long periods whilst at the same time muscle tone is uniformly increased.

DISORDERS OF THE BODY IMAGE

The body image or body schema is a person's subjective representation against which the integrity of his body is judged and the movement and positioning of its parts assessed. To the earlier neurologists the body schema was a postural model (see Head 1920). Schilder (1935), in his book *The image and appearance of the human body*, argued that this postural model is only the lowest level of organization of the body schema, and that there are also higher psychological levels founded on emotion, personality, and social interaction.

It is certainly true that, in clinical practice, abnormalities of body image are encountered that affect far more than the appreciation of posture and movement. These abnormalities arise in neurological as well as psychiatric disorders, and in many cases organic and psychological factors appear to be acting together. Unfortunately, in neither neurological nor psychiatric disorders are the causes of body image disturbances understood completely. In the account that follows, we follow broadly the scheme proposed by Lishman (1978*a*) and we recommend the relevant sections (pp. 81–94) of his book and the review by Lukianowicz (1967) to the reader who requires more detailed information about these disorders.

Phantom limb is a continuing awareness of a part of the body that has been lost. As such it is perhaps the most convincing evidence for the concept of a body schema. It occurs usually after limb amputation but has been reported after removal of breasts, genitalia, or eyes (Lishman 1978, p. 91). Phantom limbs may be experienced as painful. The phantom is usually present immediately after amputation and usually fades gradually, although a minority persist for years (see textbooks of neurology or the review by Frederiks 1969, for further information).

Unilateral unawareness and neglect is the most frequent neurologically determined disorder of body image. It usually affects the left limbs, and arises most often from lesions of the supramarginal and angular gyri of the right parietal lobe, often following a stroke. When the disorder is marked, the patient may neglect to wash one side of his body or to shave one side of his face, or may put on only one shoe. In its mildest form, it can be detected only by special testing using double stimulation (e.g. if both wrists are touched with cotton wool but the patient reports a touch from only one side, even though the sensation on the other side is present when tested on its own). Further information is given by Critchley (1953) whose book gives detailed information about syndromes arising from lesions in the parietal lobes.

Hemisomatognosis: this disorder, which is also known as hemidepersonalization, is much less frequent than unilateral unawareness. The patient reports the feeling that one of his limbs is missing, usually on the left. The disorder can occur on its own, or together with hemiparesis. There is often a coincident unilateral spatial agnosia. The nature of the patient's awareness is variable; some patients know that the limb is present though it feels to be absent, whilst others believe wholly or partly that the limb is really absent.

Anosognosia is a lack of awareness of disease, and it too is more often manifest on the left side of the body. Most often it occurs briefly in the early days after acute hemiplegia but occasionally it persists. The patient does not complain of the disability on the paralysed side and denies it when pointed out to him. There may also be denial of dysphasia, blindness (Anton's syndrome), or amnesia (most marked in Korsakov's syndrome). Pain asymbolia is a disorder in which the patient perceives a normally painful stimulus but does not recognize it as painful. Although these disorders are clearly associated with cerebral lesions, it has been suggested that there is a psychogenic element whereby the awareness of unpleasant things is repressed (see, for example Weinstein and Kahn 1955). Although it is hardly possible that structural damage could act in the absence of psychological reactions, it seems unlikely that the latter can be the sole cause of a condition that is so much more frequent on the left side of the body.

Autotopagnosia is the inability to recognize, name, or point on command to parts of the body. The disorder may also apply to parts of the body of another person, but not to inanimate objects. It is a rare condition which arises from diffuse lesions, usually affecting both sides of the brain. Nearly all the cases can be explained by accompanying apraxia, agnosia, dysphasia, or disorder of spatial perception (see Lishman 1978, p. 87).

Distorted awareness of size and shape includes feelings that a limb is enlarging, becoming smaller, or otherwise being distorted. Unlike the phenomena described so far, these experiences are not related closely to lesions of specific areas of the brain. They may occur in healthy people especially when falling asleep, or in the waking state, when very tired. They are sometimes reported in the course of migraine, in acute brain syndromes, as part of the aura of epilepsy, or after taking LSD. Changes of shape and size of body parts are also described by some schizophrenic patients. The person is nearly always aware that the experience is unreal, except in some cases of schizophrenia.

Reduplication phenomenon is the experience that part or all of the body has doubled. Thus the person may feel that he has two left arms, or two heads, or that the whole body has been duplicated. These phenomena have been reported rarely in the course of migraine and temporal lobe epilepsy as well as in schizophrenia. In an extreme form the person has the experience of being aware of a copy of his whole body, a phenomenon already described under the heading of autoscopic hallucinations.

Coenestopathic states are localized distortions of body awareness, often described as part of the body such as the nose feeling as if made of cotton wool.

DISORDERS OF MEMORY

Failure of memory is called amnesia. For clinical purposes, it is useful to think in simple terms of four memory processes: registration, retention, recall, and recognition. **Registration** is the ability to add new material to the existing store of memories; **retention** is the ability to retain the memory; **recall** is the ability to bring it back into awareness; and **recognition** is a feeling of familiarity indicating, correctly, that a particular person, object, or event has been encountered before. For clinical purposes, it is also valuable to think of three kinds of memory store, even though recent research on the psychology of memory indicates a considerably more complex arrangement (see Baddeley 1976 for a review of this and other aspects of the experimental study of memory). The first is a **short-term** store in which events are registered but quickly lost unless re-entered repeatedly, for example looking up a previously unknown telephone number, and retaining it until dialling has been completed. Unless such a number is repeated frequently it is quickly forgotten. The second is a **medium-term store** in which memories are held while some kind of sorting and organization takes place, as a result of which a proportion are laid down in the third, or **long-term store**.

The various disorders of memory encountered in clinical practice can be regarded as failures of one or more of these hypothetical processes. Thus anxious patients may complain of poor memory because they fail to register new material through lack of concentration. In Korsakov's syndrome (see Chapter 11) retention is impaired so that patients are unable to remember what has happened earlier on the same day. However, experimental studies of this condition indicate that patients can still accurately recognize some of the material that cannot be recalled (Warrington and Weiskranz 1970); hence part of the problem may be in retrieval. In dementia retention is also impaired, and more recent events are forgotten before those held in long-term storage from years before.

Other aspects of memory are impaired in certain psychiatric and neurological disorders. Some patients describe recognition of a situation or event as having been encountered before, when it is in fact novel (**déja vu**). Others have the reverse experience of failing to recognize a situation or event that has been encountered before (**jamais vu**). In Korsakov's syndrome, patients with extreme difficulty in remembering recent and past events sometimes report that they remember past events which have not taken place at the time in question (e.g. a patient who has been in the ward for a week may give a circumstantial account of going to the seaside on the previous day). This is known as **confabulation**.

Amnesia inevitably occurs after a period of unconsciousness. However, after a head injury, the period of amnesia is longer than the period of unconsciousness. **Retrograde** amnesia affects memory of events before unconsciousness, and is related to the severity of the injury, varying from minutes in mild cases to weeks in severe ones. Presumably it reflects a failure to lay down memory traces of events already experienced before the injury. **Anterograde** amnesia affects memory for events occurring after the interval of complete unconsciousness, but during the period in which recovery of consciousness was not complete.

DISORDERS OF CONSCIOUSNESS

Consciousness is awareness of the self and the environment. The level of consciousness can vary between the extremes of alertness and coma. The quality of consciousness can also vary: sleep differs from unconsciousness and stupor differs from both (see below).

Many terms have been used for states of impaired consciousness. **Coma** is the most extreme form. The patient shows no external evidence of mental activity and little motor activity other than breathing. He does not respond even to strong stimuli. Coma can be graded by the extent of the remaining reflex responses, and by the type of EEG activity. **Sopor** is an infrequently used term for a state in which the person can be aroused only by strong stimulation. **Clouding of consciousness** refers to a state in which the patient is drowsy and reacts incompletely to stimuli. Attention, concentration, and memory are impaired and orientation is disturbed. Thinking seems slow and muddled, and events may be interpreted inaccurately.

Stupor refers to a condition in which the patient is immobile, mute, and unresponsive but appears to be fully conscious, usually because the eyes are open and follow external objects. If the eyes are closed, the patient resists attempts to open them. Reflexes are normal and resting posture is maintained, though it may be awkward. (Note that in neurology the term implies impaired consciousness.)

Confusion means inability to think clearly. It occurs characteristically in organic states, but in some functional disorders as well. In acute organic disorder confusion occurs together with partial impairment of consciousness, illusions, hallucinations, delusions, and a mood change of anxiety or apprehension. The resulting syndrome has been called a confusional state or delirium, but these terms are not well defined and it is preferable to avoid them (see p. 295). Three variations of this syndrome may be mentioned. The first is an **oneiroid** (dream-like) state in which the patient, although not asleep, describes experiences of vivid imagery akin to that of a dream. When such a state is prolonged it is sometimes called a **twilight state** (see p. 295). **Torpor** is a state in which the patient appears drowsy, readily falls asleep, and shows evidence of slow thinking and narrowed range of perception.

INSIGHT

Insight may be defined as awareness of one's own mental condition. It is difficult to achieve, since it involves some knowledge of what constitutes a healthy mind, and yet doctors cannot agree among themselves about the meaning of terms such as mental health and mental illness. Moreover insight is not simply present or absent, but rather a matter of degree. For this reason it is better to ask four separate questions. First, is the patient aware of phenomena that other people have observed (e.g. that he appears to be unusually active and elated)? Second, if so, does he recognize that these phenomena are abnormal (or does he, for example, maintain that his unusual activity and cheerfulness are merely normal high spirits)? Third, if he recognizes the phenomena as abnormal, does he consider that they are caused by mental illness, as opposed to, for example, a physical illness or the results of poison administered to him by his enemies? Fourth, if he accepts that he is ill, does he think he needs treatment?

The answers to these questions are much more informative – and much more likely to be reliable – than those of the single question: is insight present or not? Newcomers to psychiatry often ask this question because they have read that loss of insight distinguishes psychoses from neuroses. While it is generally true that neurotic patients retain insight and psychotic patients lose it, this is not invariable; nor is this in practice a reliable way of distinguishing between the two. On the other hand, the four questions listed above can help the clinician to decide whether the patient is likely to co-operate with treatment.

THE MECHANISMS OF DEFENCE

So far, we have been concerned with aspects of descriptive psychopathology; or in other words with abnormal mental experiences which the patient can describe and with changes in behaviour which other people can observe. We now turn to an aspect of dynamic psychopathology that deserves special attention at this stage. It is concerned neither with mental events that the patient can describe, nor with his behaviour. Instead it is a set of processes that may help to *explain* certain kinds of experience or behaviour. These processes are called mechanisms of defence. They originate in the work of Sigmund Freud and have been elaborated by his daughter Anna Freud (1936). In the account that follows, the more important defence mechanisms are defined and brief examples given of the kinds of mental events and behaviour that they may explain. It is important to understand, at the start, that defence mechanisms are automatic and unconscious: they imply that the patient is not acting deliberately nor is he aware of his real motives at the time, though he may become aware of such motives later either through introspection or because they have been pointed out to him by another person.

Defence mechanisms have been used to account for what Freud called the psychopathology of everyday life and to explain the aetiology of mental disorders. The illustrations of mechanisms of defence that appear in the following paragraphs are all concerned with everyday thoughts and actions. This is because these kinds of explanation are useful in understanding many aspects of the day-to-day behaviour of patients whether they have psychiatric or medical conditions. In subsequent chapters consideration is given to theories that have attempted to explain neurotic symptoms and personality disorders in terms of the same mechanisms.

Repression is the exclusion from awareness of impulses, emotions, and memories that would cause distress if allowed to enter consciousness. For example, a memory of an event in which a person was humiliated may be kept out of his awareness. **Denial**, a closely related concept, is inferred when a person behaves as though unaware of something which he may reasonably be expected to know. For example, a patient who has been told that he has cancer, may subsequently speak and act as though not aware of this.

Projection refers to the unconscious attribution to another person of thoughts or feelings that are one's own, thereby rendering the original feelings more acceptable. For example, someone who dislikes a colleague may impute feelings of anger and dislike to him. In this way, his own feelings of dislike may appear justified and become less distressing.

Regression refers to the unconscious adoption of a pattern of behaviour appropriate to an earlier stage of development. It is commonly seen among physically ill people who adopt a child-like dependency on nurses and doctors. During the acute stage of illness this is often an adaptive response enabling the patient to accept the requirements of intensive medical and nursing care; however, if it persists, it can impede rehabilitation.

Reaction formation refers to the unconscious adoption of behaviour opposite to that which would reflect true feelings and intentions. For example, excessively prudish attitudes to the mention of sexual intercourse in conversation, books, or the media may occur in someone who has strong sexual drives that he cannot consciously accept.

Displacement refers to the unconscious process of transferring emotion from a situation or object with which it is properly associated, to another which will give rise to less distress. Thus a man may blame the family doctor for failing to give adequate treatment to his recently deceased wife, instead of blaming himself for putting his own work before her needs in the last months of her life.

Rationalization refers to the unconscious provision of a false but acceptable explanation for behaviour which has other, less acceptable origins. For example, a husband who neglects his wife and goes to entertainments without her may tell himself that she is shy and would not enjoy them, although this is not so.

Sublimation is a related concept which refers to the unconscious diversion of unacceptable impulses into acceptable outlets; for example, turning angry feelings into vigorous sporting activities, or turning the wish to dominate other people into organizing charitable activities.

Identification refers to the unconscious process of taking on some of the activities or characteristics of another person, often to reduce the pain of separation or loss. For example a widow may take on the same work in local government that her husband used to undertake, or she may try to think about things in the way that he would have done.

FURTHER READING

Jaspers, K. (1963). *General psychopathology*, trans. J. Hoenig and M. W. Hamilton, Chapter I; Phenomenology. Manchester University Press.

Scharfetter, C. (1980). *General psychopathology: an introduction* Trans. from the German by H. Marshall. Cambridge University Press.

Schneider, K. (1949). The concept of delusion. Reprinted and translated in Hirsch, S.R. and Shepherd, M. (ed.) (1974). *Themes and variations in European psychiatry*. John Wright, Bristol.

Shepherd, M. and Zangwill, O.L. (eds.) (1983). *Handbook of psychiatry*, Vol. 1. Cambridge University Press. (See especially: Introduction; The sciences and general psychopathology by M. Shepherd; and The historical background pp. 9–56).

Wing, J.K., Cooper, J.E., and Sartorius, N. (1974). *The measurement and classification of psychiatric symptoms* (see Glossary of definitions, pp. 141–88). Cambridge University Press.

2. Interviewing, clinical examination, and record keeping

In psychiatry, as in medicine generally, correct diagnosis depends on careful history taking and thorough clinical examination. However, psychiatry differs from the rest of medicine in that the interview is used not only to obtain the history but also as a way of eliciting clinical signs. This chapter begins, therefore, with an account of the technique of interviewing. Whilst this account draws attention to important points of technique, it should be remembered that interviewing is a practical skill that the trainee can acquire only through carrying out interviews under supervision and watching experienced interviewers at work.

THE DIAGNOSTIC INTERVIEW

Before the interview begins there are certain preliminary requirements. The interview should be carried out in a room that is reasonably soundproof and free from interruptions. The patient should not be seated directly opposite the interviewer, nor should his chair be so much lower that he has to look upwards. In this way he will feel at ease rather than under constant scrutiny. For a diagnostic interview the interviewer should sit at a writing table in order to take notes (a psychotherapeutic interview may require less formal arrangements with patient and therapist both in arm chairs). He should not attempt to memorize the interview and write notes afterwards, as this is time-consuming and likely to be inaccurate. The least obtrusive way of taking notes is to place the patient at the side of the desk, on the left side of a right-handed interviewer. This creates a suitably informal atmosphere and allows the interviewer to attend to the patient whilst writing.

The first encounter with the patient is important. The interviewer should welcome him by name, and give his own name. If the patient is accompanied by a companion it is good practice for the interviewer to welcome this person as well and to explain how long he may expect to wait before being interviewed himself. If the patient is seen at the request of a general practitioner, the interviewer should indicate that the latter has written to him, but should not reveal the contents of the letter in detail.

The interviewer should explain how he proposes to proceed: e.g. 'First, I should like to hear about your present problems. Only when I am sure that I have understood these shall I ask you how they began'. The interviewer then asks an open question such as 'Tell me about the problems' or 'Tell me what you have noticed wrong', and the patient is encouraged to talk freely for several minutes. During this time the interviewer makes two separate kinds of observations – how the patient is talking and what he has to say. The first helps the doctor decide *how* to interview the patient, whilst the second tells him *what* to ask about.

Whilst deciding how to interview the patient, the interviewer observes whether he seems co-operative, reasonably at ease, and able to express his ideas coherently. The most frequent difficulty is that the patient is overanxious. The interviewer should consider whether such anxiety is part of the presenting disorder or merely fear on coming to a psychiatrist. If the latter, the interviewer should take time to discuss the patient's apprehension before proceeding with the interview. Usually reassurance and a calm, unhurried approach will put the patient more at ease.

Sometimes the patient seems unco-operative and resentful when he begins to talk. This may be because the interview is taking place against his wishes: for example, his spouse may have persuaded him to attend, or the psychiatrist may be interviewing him after admission to a general hospital for treatment of drug overdosage. When this happens, the interviewer should talk over the circumstances of the referral and try to persuade the patient that the interview is in his own interests. Patients may appear resentful for other reasons. Some patients act in a hostile way when anxious, and some depressed or schizophrenic patients seem unco-operative because they do not regard themselves as ill. At times it becomes apparent that a patient cannot respond adequately to the interview because of impaired consciousness. When this seems likely, orientation, concentration, and memory should be tested, and if impaired consciousness is confirmed, an informant should be seen before returning to the patient.

Provided there are no immediate problems of this kind, the interviewer should consider whether there are likely to be difficulties in guiding the interview effectively. Some patients, such as successful business men, attempt to dominate the interview, especially if the interviewer is younger than themselves. Others adopt an unduly friendly attitude that threatens to convert the interview into a social conversation. In either case, the interviewer should explain why he needs to guide the patient to relevant issues.

As mentioned above, the interviewer, whilst listening to the patient's opening remarks, also begins to think what questions he should ask. These should begin with further enquiries about the *nature* of the patient's presenting symptoms. It is a common mistake to start asking about the timing of such symptoms before their nature is clearly established. For example patients sometimes say they are depressed, but further enquiry shows that they are experiencing anxiety rather than low spirits. If there is any doubt, the patient should be asked to give examples of his experiences. The interviewer should clearly understand the nature of the symptoms before asking about their timing and the factors that make them better or worse.

When all the presenting complaints have been explored in this way, direct questions are used to ask about other relevant symptoms. For example, a person who complains of feeling depressed should be asked about ideas concerning the future, sleep pattern, appetite, etc. The subsidiary questions required for each presenting symptom will be apparent from reading the chapters on the major clinical syndromes.

Next, the mode of onset of the complaint is asked about and its course noted, including any exacerbations or periods of partial remission. Considerable persistence may be needed to date the onset accurately, and if necessary it should be related to events the patient can remember accurately (e.g. was it before or after your birthday; had it already started before Christmas?).

Controlling the interview

As the interview continues, the doctor's task is to keep the patient to relevant topics by bringing him back to the point if he strays from it. In doing this the interviewer should use a minimum of leading or closed questions (a leading question suggests the answer; a closed question allows only the answers yes or no, thus preventing the person from volunteering information). Thus instead of the closed question 'are you happily married?' the interviewer might ask 'how do you and your wife get on with one another?'. When there is no alternative to a closed question, the answer should be followed by a request for an example. In this way the interviewer can confirm that the answer is valid.

Taciturn patients can often be encouraged to speak more freely if the interviewer shows non-verbal expressions of concern (e.g. leaning forward a little in the chair with an expression of interest). It is less easy to curb the flow of an over-talkative patient. Sometimes this can only be done by waiting for a natural break in the flow of speech to explain that, because time is limited, the interviewer proposes to interrupt the patient when appropriate to help him focus on the issues that are important for planning treatment. Provided this advice is given tactfully, most garrulous patients are relieved to be given it.

Although it is essential to ask direct questions about specific items of information, it is equally important to give the patient an opportunity to talk spontaneously, as unexpected material may be revealed in this way. Spontaneous talk can be encouraged by prompting rather than by asking questions, e.g. by repeating in an enquiring tone the patient's reply to previous questions or by using non-verbal prompts. Also, before ending the interview, it is useful to ask a general question such as 'Is there anything else you wish to tell me?'.

HISTORY TAKING

Whenever possible, the history from the patient should be supplemented by information from a close relative or another person who knows him well. This is much more important in psychiatry than in the rest of medicine, because psychiatric patients are not always aware of the extent of their symptoms. For example a manic patient may not realize how much embarrassment he has caused by his extravagant social behaviour, or a demented patient may not fully understand the extent to which his work is impaired. Alternatively patients may know what their problems are, but not wish to reveal them; for example, alcoholics often conceal the extent of their drinking. Also, when personality is being assessed, patients and relatives often give quite different accounts of characteristics such as irritability, obsessional traits, and jealousy.

The history should always be recorded systematically and in the same order to ensure that important themes are not forgotten by the interviewer, and to make it easier for colleagues to refer to the notes. However, it is not always possible to gather information in the same order with every patient. Some flexibility must be allowed if the patient is not to feel unduly restricted by the interviewer.

In this section, a standard scheme of history taking is given in the form of a list of topics to be covered. This will serve as a check list for the beginner, and a reminder for the more experienced interviewer, of the topics that make up a complete history. However, it is neither necessary nor possible to ask every question of every patient. Common sense must be used in judging how far each topic needs to be explored with a particular patient. The trainee must learn by experience how to adjust his questionning to problems that emerge as the interview proceeds. This is done by keeping in mind the decisions about diagnosis and treatment that will have to be made at the end of the interview.

The scheme given below is followed by notes explaining how to record the different items, and why they are important. After this the assessment of personality is discussed in more detail.

The scheme of history taking

Informant: name, relation to patient, intimacy, and length of acquaintance. Interviewer's impression of informant's reliability.

Source of referral and reasons for referral

Present illness

Symptoms with duration and mode of onset of each. Description of the time relations between symptoms and social psychological and physical disorders. Effects on work, social functioning, and relationships. Associated disturbance in sleep, appetite, and sexual drive. Any treatment given by other doctors.

Family history

Father: age or age at death. (If dead give cause of death.) Health, occupation, personality, quality of relationship with patient. **Mother:** the same items. **Siblings** Names, ages, marital status, occupation, personality, mental and psychiatric illness, and quality of relationship with patient. **Social position of family** – atmosphere in the home.

Family history of mental illness – psychiatric disorder, personality disorder, epilepsy, alcoholism. Other neurological or medical disorders (e.g. Huntington's chorea).

Personal history

Early development: abnormalities during pregnancy and birth. Difficulties in habit training and delay in achieving milestones (walking, talking, sphincter control, etc). Separation from parents and reaction to it. **Health during childhood:** serious illness, especially any affecting the central nervous system, including febrile seizures. **'Nervous problems' in childhood:** fears, temper tantrums, shyness, stammering, blushing, food-fads, sleep-walking, prolonged bed wetting, frequent nightmares (though the significance of these behaviours is doubtful, see p. 144). **School:** age of starting and finishing each school. Types of school. Academic record and sporting and other achievements. Relationships with teachers and pupils. **Higher education:** comparable enquiries. **Occupations:** chronological list of jobs, with reasons for changes. Present financial circumstances, satisfaction in work. **Service or war experience** promotion and awards. Disciplinary problems. Service overseas.

Menstrual history: age of menarche, attitude to periods, regularity and amount, dysmenorrhoea, premenstrual tension, age of menopause and any symptoms at the time, date of last menstrual period. **Marital history:** Age of patient at marriage. How long spouse known before marriage and length of engagement. Previous relationships and engagements. Present age, occupation, health, and personality of spouse. Quality of the marital relationship.
Sexual history: attitude to sex. Heterosexual and homosexual experience. Current sexual practices, contraception.
Children: Names, sex, and age of children. Date of any abortions or stillbirths. Temperament, emotional development, mental and physical health of children.

Present social situation

Housing, composition of household, financial problems.

Previous medical history

Illnesses, operations, and accidents.

Previous psychiatric illness

Nature and duration of illness. Date, duration, and nature of any treatment. Name of hospital and of doctors Outcome.

Personality before present illness

Relationships: friends, few or many; superficial or close; own or opposite sex. Relations with workmates and superiors. **Use of leisure:** hobbies and interests; membership of societies and clubs. **Predominant mood:** anxious, worrying, cheerful, despondent, optimistic, pessimistic, self-depreciating, over-confident. Stable or fluctuating. Controlled or demonstrative. **Character:** sensitive, suspicious, jealous, resentful, quarrelsome, irritable, impulsive, selfish, self-centred; timid, reserved, shy, self-conscious, lacking in confidence; dependent; strict, fussy, rigid: meticulous, punctual, excessively tidy. **Attitudes and standards:** moral and religious. Attitude towards health and the body. **Habits:** food, alcohol, tobacco, drugs, sleep.

Notes on history taking

The scheme just outlined lists the items to be considered when a full history is taken, but gives no indication why these items are important, or what sort of difficulties may arise in eliciting them. These issues are discussed in the present section, which is written in the form of notes referring to the headings used above.

The reason for referral

State in everyday language why the patient has been referred, e.g. 'severe depression, failing to respond to drug treatment'.

The present illness

In an outpatient clinic, it is usually better to consider this item first because the patient probably wants to talk about it straight away. However, with inpatients the doctor may already have substantial information about the present illness, either from doctors dealing with the case before admission, or from relatives. In these circumstances the interviewer may find it better to begin with the family and personal history.

Always record which complaints have been volunteered by the patient, and which revealed by questioning. Record the severity and duration of each symptom, how it began and what course it has taken (increasing gradually; diminishing stepwise; staying the same; intermittent). Indicate which symptoms co-vary and which take an independent course (e.g. obsessional thoughts and rituals may have fluctuated together, whilst depressed mood may have been a recent addition). Any recent treatment should be noted, together with its apparent effects. When a drug has not been effective, note whether the patient took it in the required dosage.

Family history

Mental illness among parents or siblings suggests that the cause of illness may in part be hereditary. Because the family is the environment in which the patient grew up, the personality and attitudes of the parents are important. So are separations from the parents for any reason. Ask about the parents' relationship with one another, e.g. whether there were frequent quarrels. Enquire about separations, divorce, and remarriage. Rivalry between siblings may be important, as may favouritism of one child by the parents. The occupation and social standing of the parents reflect the material circumstances of the patient's childhood.

Recent events in the family may have been stressful to the patient. Serious illness of either parent, or divorce of a sibling, are likely to be relevant problems in other family members. Finally, the family history may throw light on the patient's concerns about himself. For example, the death of an older brother from brain tumour may partly explain a patient's extreme concern about headaches.

Personal history

Pregnancy and birth: events in pregnancy are occasionally relevant, especially when the patient is mentally handicapped. An unwanted pregnancy may be followed by a poor relationship between mother and child. Similarly serious problems during delivery sometimes account for intellectual impairment, while separation in a premature baby unit may interfere with bonding between mother and child.

Early development: few patients know whether they have passed through developmental stages normally. However, this information is more important if the patient is a child or adolescent, in which case the parents are likely to be interviewed routinely. This information may also be important in cases of mental handicap, when the parents or other relative should be questionned and previous medical records should be obtained. (A summary of the main developmental milestones will be found in Chapter 20.)

Notes should also be made of any prolonged periods of separation from the mother, for example through illness. The effects of such separations vary considerably (see Chapter 20) and it is important to ask an appropriate informant whether the patient was emotionally upset at the time and, if so, for how long.

Health in childhood: there is little point in recording minor childhood ailments such as uncomplicated chicken pox; but it is appropriate to enquire about encephalitis or convulsions, any illness leading to prolonged admission to hospital, or prolonged disability.

Early neurotic traits: it is conventional to enquire about such symptoms as fears, sleep walking, shyness, stammering, and food fads. However, there is no evidence that these behaviours in childhood are precursors of neurosis in adult life.

Schooling: the school record not only gives an indication of intelligence and scholastic achievements, but also reflects social development. The type of school and examination results should be noted. The interviewer should also ask whether the patient had friends and was popular; whether he played games, and with what success; and how he got on with teachers. Similar questions are asked about **higher education**.

Occupational history: information about the present job helps the interviewer to understand the circumstances of the patient's life and judge whether he is under stress at work. A list of previous jobs is mainly relevant to the assessment of personality. If the patient has had many jobs, it is important to ask why he left each one. Repeated dismissals may reflect an awkward, aggressive, or otherwise abnormal personality (though there are, of course, many other reasons for repeated sackings). When each job is inferior to the last, it is necessary to consider declining efficiency caused by chronic mental illness or by alcohol abuse. Information about relationships with colleagues, senior and junior, helps to assess personality.

When the patient has served in the Armed Forces, or worked abroad, details should be obtained, and an enquiry made about tropical diseases later in the history.

Menstrual history: it is usual to enquire about the age of menarche and how the patient first learnt about menstruation. These questions were more important in earlier times when ignorance about sexual matters was widespread and the unexpected onset of periods in an unprepared girl could give rise to lasting anxieties. In Britain today, this rarely happens except among some immigrant groups. When interviewing immigrants to this country, or when working in other countries, the answers may be more informative. Questions about current menstrual function should be asked in all relevant cases. Dysmenorrhoea, menorrhagia, and premenstrual tension should be identified in younger women, and the menopause noted among those in middle life. The date of the last period should also be noted.

Marital history: the interviewer should enquire about previous lasting relationships with the opposite sex as well as the present marital relationship. Sexual relationships are considered in the next section: in this part of the history it is the personal aspects that are considered. Frequent broken relationships before marriage may reflect abnormalities of personality. A previous relationship may determine the patient's attitude to the present marriage, for example, when a first marriage has ended in divorce because of the husband's infidelity, a woman may overreact to minor difficulties in her second marriage.

The spouse's occupation, personality, and state of health gives information of obvious relevance to the patient's circumstances. Present difficulties can often be understood better by enquiring about each partner's original expectations of the marriage. It is also useful to ask about the sharing of decisions and responsibilities in the marriage. The dates of birth of the children, or of any miscarriages, may indicate whether marriage was forced by pregnancy.

Sexual history: it is traditional to begin the sexual history by asking how the patient acquired information about sexual matters. Such a question was more likely to give useful information in times when ignorance was more widespread than today.

In taking the sexual history, the interviewer should use common sense in deciding how much to ask the individual patient. For example, a detailed account of masturbation and sexual techniques may be essential when the patient is seeking help for sexual impotence, but the interviewer is often more concerned to find generally whether the patient's sexual life is satisfying or not. Only if there are problems need he enquire into all the details under this heading. Judgement must also be used about the optimal timing and amount of detail of questions about homosexuality.

Finally the interviewer should ask about methods of contraception and, when relevant, a woman's wishes about bearing children.

Children: pregnancy, childbirth, miscarriages, and induced abortions are important events sometimes associated with adverse psychological reactions in the mother. Information about the patient's children is relevant to present worries and the pattern of family life. Children may be affected by the patient's illness; it is important to know whether a seriously depressed woman has the care of a baby, or whether a violent alcoholic man has children in the home. If admission to hospital is being considered for a woman patient, it is important to find out about dependent children and if necessary arrange for their care. This is obvious but sometimes overlooked.

Previous illness: previous medical or surgical treatment should always be asked about, and particularly careful inquiries made about previous mental illness. Patients or relatives may be able to recall the presenting symptoms of illness, and the main points about treatment. However, details of diagnosis and treatment can usually be obtained only from the doctors who treated the patient at the time. In psychiatry the nature of previous illness is an important guide to the present disorder, and it is nearly always appropriate to request information from other hospitals.

Present circumstances: questions about housing, finances, and the composition of the household help the interviewer to understand the patient's circumstances and to judge more clearly what aspects of his life are likely to be stressful and how illness may affect him. There can be no general rule about the amount of detail to elicit, and this must be left to common sense.

Assessment of personality

Aspects of personality, such as reliability or self-confidence, are judged by asking the patient what he thinks of himself, and other people what they think of him, and by considering how he has behaved in circumstances that test these qualities. Thus, if a patient says he is self confident, we can enquire how he behaves in particular situations when he has to convince other people, or speak to a committee. In this way, the interviewer can build up a preliminary view of personality when enquiring about work and social activities.

Personality can be judged particularly well by asking about occasions when social roles are changing, such as leaving school, starting work, marrying, or becoming a parent. If this is not done, mistakes can arise from paying too much attention to the patient's own assessment of his personality. Some people give an unduly favourable account of themselves; for example antisocial people may conceal the extent of their aggressive behaviour or dishonesty. Conversely, depressed patients often judge themselves too severely, as being for example ineffectual, selfish, or unreliable, an impression that is not confirmed by other people.

It is tempting to judge personality from the patient's behaviour at interview, but it is essential to allow for the possible effects of illness. Thus, if he is depressed, a normally self-possessed and sociable person may appear shy and lacking in self-confidence.

Enquiries about personality are most fruitful when they are systematic. The following scheme is widely used and covers areas of enquiry that are most important in clinical work. In using it, it is important not to focus entirely on the abnormal, but to identify strong points in the personality as well.

The assessment begins with enquiries about **relationships** with friends and people at work. Is the person shy or does he make friends easily? Are his friendships close and are they lasting? **Leisure activities** can throw light on personality, not only be reflecting a person's interests but also by indicating his preference for company or solitude, and his levels of energy and resourcefulness.

Mood is considered next. The interviewer tries to find out whether the patient is generally cheerful or gloomy; whether he has marked changes of mood, if so, how quickly they appear, how long they last, and if they follow life-events. He should also find out whether the patient shows emotions or hides them.

Character: the interviewer will already have gathered some impression of this while taking the personal history. Further information about the patient's character should be sought; for example, by asking whether he is: reserved, timid, shy, sensitive or self-conscious; suspicious, resentful or jealous; irritable, impulsive, or quarrelsome; selfish or self-centred; lacking in confidence; strict, fussy, rigid, meticulous, punctual, or excessively tidy.

These are chiefly negative attributes of character, but it is also important to ask about positive ones. It is not appropriate to go through a complete list with every patient; commonsense will indicate what to enquire about as the picture of the patient gradually builds up. It is good practice, however, with every patient to determine how resilient he is in the face of adversity.

Answers should not always be taken at face value; for example, when readiness to anger is asked about, the interviewer should not simply accept the answer that the patient never feels angry. Instead he should persist in questioning, for example by remarking that everyone feels angry at times and asking what makes the patient angry. The interviewer should also find out whether the patient expresses anger or bottles it up; and if the former, whether through angry words or violent acts. If the patient contains anger, he should be asked how he feels at the time.

Attitudes and standards: in this part of the interview it is usual to ask about attitudes to the body, health, and illness, as well as religious and moral standards. The personal history will usually have provided general indications about these matters so that extensive questioning is seldom necessary.

Habits: this final section deals with habits of taking tobacco, alcohol, or drugs.

MENTAL STATE EXAMINATION

In the course of history taking, the interviewer will have noted the patient's symptoms up to the time of the consultation. The mental state is concerned with the symptoms and behaviour at the time of the interview. Hence there is a degree of overlap between the history and the mental state, mainly in observations about mood, delusions, and hallucinations. If the patient is already in hospital, there will also be some overlap between mental state and the observations made by nurses and occupational therapists of his behaviour outside the interview room. The psychiatrist should pay considerable attention to these accounts from other staff, which are at times more revealing than the small sample of behaviour observed at mental state examination. For example, a patient may deny hallucinations at interview, but the nurses may notice him repeatedly talking alone as if replying to voices. On the other hand, mental state examination may reveal information not disclosed at other times, for example suicidal intentions in a depressed patient.

The following paragraphs describe the examination of mental state. However, carrying out this examination is a practical skill that can be learnt only by watching experienced interviewers and by practising repeatedly under supervision. As his skills increase, the trainee psychiatrist will benefit from reading the more detailed account by Leff and Isaacs (1978), and from studying the Present State Examination, a standardized scheme described by Wing *et al.* (1974).

The mental state examination follows the headings in Table 2.1.

Table 2.1. *Summary of the mental state examination*

Behaviour
Speech
Mood
Depersonalization, derealization
Obsessional phenomena
Delusions
Hallucinations and illusions
Orientation
Attention and concentration
Memory
Insight

Appearance and behaviour

Although the mental state examination is largely concerned with what the patient says, much can also be learnt from observing his appearance and behaviour.

The interviewer should first note the patient's body build. An appearance suggesting recent weight loss should alert the observer to the possibility of physical illness, or of anorexia nervosa, depressive disorder, or chronic anxiety neurosis.

The patient's general appearance and clothing repay careful observation. Self-neglect, as shown by a dirty unkempt look and crumpled clothing, suggests several possibilities including alcoholism, drug addiction, depression, dementia, or schizophrenia. Manic patients may wear bright colours, adopt incongruous styles of dress, or appear poorly groomed. Occasionally an oddity of dress may provide the clue to diagnosis: for example, a rain-hood worn on a dry day may be the first evidence of a patient's belief that rays are being shone on her head by persecutors.

Facial appearance provides information about mood. In depression the most characteristic features are turning down of the corners of the mouth, vertical furrows on the brow, and a slight raising of the medial aspect of each brow. Anxious patients generally have horizontal creases on the forehead, raised eyebrows, widened palpebral fissures, and dilated pupils. Although depression and anxiety are especially important, the observer should look for evidence of the whole range of emotions, including elation, irritability, and anger; together with the unchanging 'wooden' expression of patients taking drugs with Parkinsonian side-effects.

The facial appearance may also suggest physical conditions such as thyrotoxicosis and myxoedema.

Posture and movement also reflect mood. A depressed patient characteristically sits leaning forwards, with shoulders hunched, the head inclined downwards and gaze directed to the floor. An anxious patient usually sits upright with head erect, often on the edge of the chair and with hands gripping its sides. Anxious people and patients with agitated depression are often tremulous and restless, touching their jewellery, adjusting clothing, or picking at the finger nails. Manic patients are overactive and restless.

Social behaviour is important. Manic patients often break social conventions and are unduly familiar to people they have just met. Demented patients sometimes respond inappropriately to the conventions of a medical interview, or continue with their private preoccupations as if the interview were not taking place. Schizophrenic patients may behave oddly when interviewed; some are overactive and socially disinhibited, some withdrawn and preoccupied, and others aggressive. Patients with antisocial personality disorders may also appear abnormally aggressive. In recording abnormal social behaviour, the psychiatrist should give a clear description of what the patient actually does. He should avoid general terms such as 'bizarre', which are uninformative. Instead he should describe what is unusual.

Finally the interviewer should watch for certain uncommon disorders of motor behaviour encountered mainly in schizophrenia (see p. 232). These include stereotypies, posturing, negativism, echopraxia, ambitendence, and waxy flexibility. He should also look for tardive dyskinesia, a motor disorder seen chiefly in elderly patients, especially women, who have taken antipsychotic drugs for long periods (see p. 380). It is characterized by chewing and sucking movements, grimacing, and choreoathetoid movements affecting the face, limbs, and respiratory muscles.

Speech

How the patient speaks is recorded under this heading, whilst what he says is recorded later. The rate and quantity of speech is assessed first. It may be unusually fast as in mania, or slow as in depressive disorders. Depressed or demented patients may pause a long time before replying to questions and then give short answers, and may produce little spontaneous speech. The same may be observed among shy people or those of low intelligence. The amount of speech is increased in manic patients and in some anxious patients.

Next the interviewer should consider the patient's utterances, keeping in mind some unusual disorders found mainly in schizophrenia. He should note whether any of the words are neologisms, that is private words invented by the patient, often to describe morbid experiences. Before assuming that a word is a neologism it is essential to make sure that it is not merely mispronounced or a word from another language.

Disorders of the flow of speech are recorded next. Sudden interruptions may indicate thought blocking but are more often merely the effects of distraction. It is a common mistake to diagnose thought blocking when it is not present. Rapid shifts from one topic to another suggest flight of ideas, while a general diffuseness and lack of logical thread may indicate the kind of thought disorder characteristic of schizophrenia (see p. 230). It can be difficult to be certain about these abnormalities at interview, and it is often helpful to record a sample of conversation for more detailed analysis.

Mood

The assessment of mood begins with the observations of behaviour described already, and continues with direct questions such as, 'What is your mood like?' or 'How are you in your spirits?'.

If depression is detected, further questions should be asked about: a feeling of being about to cry (actual tearfulness is often denied), pessimistic thoughts about the present, hopelessness about the future, and guilt about the past. Suitable questions are 'What do you think will happen to you in the future?' 'Have you been blaming yourself for anything?'.

Trainees are often wary of asking about suicide in case they should suggest it to the patient, but there is no evidence to warrant this. Nevertheless, it is sensible to enquire about suicide in stages, starting with the question 'Have you thought life is not worth living?' and if appropriate going on to ask: 'Have you wished you could die?' or 'Have you considered any way in which you might end your life?'.

Anxiety is assessed further by asking about physical symptoms and thoughts that accompany the affect. These are discussed in detail in Chapter 12; here we need only note the main questions. The interviewer should start with a general question such as 'Have you noticed any changes in your body when you feel anxious?', and then go on to specific enquiries about palpitations, dry mouth, sweating, trembling, and the various other symptoms of autonomic activity and muscle tension. To detect anxious thoughts, one can ask 'What goes through your mind when you are feeling anxious?'. Possible replies include thoughts of fainting, losing control, and going mad. Inevitably many of these questions overlap with inquiries about the history of the disorder.

Questions about **elation** correspond to those about depression; for example. 'how are you in your spirits?', followed if necessary by direct questions such as 'Do you feel unusually cheerful?'. Elated mood is confirmed by ideas reflecting excessive self-confidence, inflated assessment of one's own abilities, and extravagant plans.

As well as assessing the prevailing mood, the interviewer should find out how it varies and whether it is appropriate. When mood varies excessively, it is said to be labile; for example, the patient appears dejected at one point in the interview but quickly changes to a normal or unduly cheerful mood. Any persisting lack of affect, usually called **blunting** or **flattening,** should also be noted.

In a normal person, mood varies in parallel with the main themes discussed; he appears sad while talking of unhappy events, angry while describing things that have annoyed him, and so on. When the mood is not suited to the context, it is recorded as incongruent; for example, if a patient giggles when describing the death of his mother. This symptom is often diagnosed without sufficient reason, so it is important to record specific examples. Further knowledge of the patient may later provide another explanation for the behaviour; for example, giggling when speaking of sad events may result from embarrassment.

Depersonalization and derealization

Patients who have experienced depersonalization and derealization usually find them difficult to describe; patients who have not experienced them frequently misunderstand the questions and give misleading answers. Therefore, it is particularly important to obtain specific examples of the patient's experiences. It is useful to begin by asking: 'Do you ever feel that things around you are unreal?' and 'Do you ever feel unreal or have the experience that part of your body is unreal?'. Patients with derealization often describe things in the environment as seeming artificial and lifeless; whilst those with depersonalization may describe themselves as feeling detached from their surroundings, unable to feel emotion, or as if acting a part. If a patient has described these experiences he should be asked to explain them. Most cannot suggest a reason, but a few give a delusional explanation, for example that the feelings are caused by a persecutor (this should be recorded later under the heading of delusions).

Obsessional phenomena

Obsessional thoughts are considered first. An appropriate question is 'Do any thoughts keep coming into your mind, even though you try hard not to have them?'. If the patient says 'yes' he should be asked for an example. Patients are often ashamed of obsessional thoughts, especially those about violence or sexual themes, and persistent but sympathetic questioning may therefore be required. Before recording thoughts as obsessional, the interviewer should be certain that the patient accepts them as his own (and not implanted by someone or something else).

Some compulsive rituals can be observed, but others are private events (such as counting silently) which are detected only because they interrupt the patient's conversation. Appropriate questions are 'Do you have to keep checking activities that you know you have really completed?', 'Do you have to do things over and over again when most people would have done them only once?', and 'Do you have to repeat actions many times in exactly the same way?' If the patient answers 'yes' to any of these questions, the interviewer should ask for specific examples.

Delusions

A delusion is the one symptom that cannot be asked about directly, because the patient does not recognize it as differing from other beliefs. The interviewer may be alerted to delusions by information from other people or by events in the history. In searching for delusional ideas it is useful to begin by asking for an explanation of other symptoms or unpleasant experiences that the patient has described. For example, if a patient says that life is no longer worth living, he may also believe that he is thoroughly evil and that his career is ruined, though there is no objective evidence. Many patients hide delusions skilfully, and the interviewer needs to be alert to evasions, changes of topic or other hints of information being witheld. However, once the topic of the delusion has been uncovered, patients often elaborate on it without much prompting.

When ideas are revealed that may or may not be delusional, the interviewer must find out how strongly they are held. To do this without antagonizing the patient requires patience and tact. The patient should feel he is having a fair hearing. If the interviewer expresses contrary opinions to test the strength of the patient's beliefs, his manner should be enquiring rather than argumentative. On the other hand the interviewer should not agree with the patient's delusions.

The next step is to decide whether the beliefs are culturally determined convictions rather than delusions. This judgement may be difficult if the patient comes from another culture or is a member of an unusual religious group. In such cases any doubt can usually be resolved by finding a healthy informant from the same country or religion, and by asking him whether the patient's ideas would be shared by other people from that background.

Some special forms of delusion present particular problems. Delusions of thought broadcasting must be distinguished from the belief that other people can infer a person's thoughts from his expression or behaviour. An appropriate question is 'Do you believe that other people know what you are thinking, even though you have not spoken your thoughts aloud?'. A corresponding question about delusions of thought insertion is: 'Have you ever felt that some of the thoughts in your mind were not your own but were put there from outside?'. A suitable question about delusions of thought withdrawal is 'Do you ever feel that ideas are being taken out of your head?'. In each case, if the patient answers 'yes', detailed examples should be sought.

Delusions of control present similar difficulties to the interviewer. It is appropriate to ask 'Do you ever feel that some outside force is trying to take control of you?' or 'Do you ever feel that your actions are controlled by some person or thing outside you?'. Since these experiences are far removed from the normal, some patients misunderstand the questions and answer 'yes' when they mean a religious or philosophical conviction that man is controlled by God or the devil. Others think the questions refer to the experience of being 'out of control' during extreme anxiety; some schizophrenic patients say 'yes' when they have heard commanding voices. Positive answers must therefore be followed by further questions to eliminate these possibilities.

Finally, the reader is reminded of the various categories of delusion described in Chapter 1 namely: persecutory, grandiose, nihilistic, hypochondriacal, religious, and amorous delusions together with delusions of reference, guilt, unworthiness, and jealousy. The interviewer should also distinguish between primary and secondary delusions, and should look out for the experiences of delusional perception and delusional mood that may precede or accompany the onset of delusions.

Illusions and hallucinations

When asked about hallucinations, some patients take offence because they think the interviewer regards them as mad. Enquiries should therefore be made tactfully, and commonsense judgement used to decide when it is safe to omit them altogether. Questions can be introduced by saying: 'Some people find that, when their nerves are upset, they have unusual experiences'. This can be followed by enquiries about hearing sounds or voices when no one else is within earshot. Whenever the history makes it relevant, corresponding questions should be asked about visual hallucinations, or those of taste, smell, touch, and deep bodily sensations.

If the patient describes hallucinations, certain further questions are required depending in the type of experience. The interviewer should find out whether the patient has heard a single voice, or several; if the latter, whether the voices appear to talk to each other about the patient in the third person. This experience must be distinguished from that of the patient who hears actual people talking in the distance and believes they are discussing him (delusion of reference). If the patient says the voices are speaking to him (second person hallucinations) the interviewer should find out what they say and, if the words are experienced as commands, whether the patient feels they must be obeyed. It is important to record examples of the words spoken by hallucinatory voices.

Visual hallucinations should be distinguished carefully from visual illusions. Unless the hallucination is experienced at the time of the interview, this distinction may be difficult because it depends on the presence of a visual stimulus which has been misinterpreted.

The interviewer must also distinguish dissociative hallucinations from true hallucinations. The former are described by the patient as the feeling of being in the presence of another person or a spirit with whom he can converse. Such experiences are reported by people with hysterical personality, though not confined to them; they are encouraged by some religious groups, and have little importance in diagnosis.

Orientation

This is assessed by asking about the patient's awareness of time, place, and person. If the question of orientation is kept in mind throughout the interview, it may not be necessary to ask specific questions at this stage in the examination because the interviewer will already know the answers.

Specific questions begin with the day, month, year, and season. In assessing the replies, it is important to remember that many healthy people do not know the exact date, and that understandably patients in hospital may be uncertain about the day of the week, particularly if the ward has the same routine every day. When enquiring about orientation in place, the interviewer asks what sort of place the patient is in (such as a hospital ward or an old people's home). Questions are then asked about other people such as the spouse or the ward staff; for example, who they are and what their relationship to the patient is. If the patient cannot answer these questions correctly, he should be asked about his own identity.

Attention and concentration

Attention is the ability to focus on the matter in hand. **Concentration** is the ability to sustain that focus. Whilst taking the history, the interviewer should look out for evidence of attention and concentration. In this way he will have already formed a judgement about these abilities before reaching the mental state examination. Formal tests add to this information and provide a semi-quantitative indication of changes as illness progresses. It is usual to begin with the **serial sevens test.** The patient is asked to subtract 7 from 100 and then take

7 from the remainder repeatedly until this is less than seven. The time taken is recorded, together with the number of errors. If poor performance seems to be due to lack of skill in arithmetic, the patient should be asked to do a simpler subtraction, or to say the months of the year in reverse order. If mistakes are made with these, he can be asked to give the days of the week in reverse order.

Memory

Whilst taking the history, questions will have been asked about everyday difficulties in remembering. During the examination of mental state tests are given of immediate, recent, and remote memory. None is wholly satisfactory and the results must be assessed alongside other information about the patient's ability to remember.

Registration and **immediate memory** are assessed by asking the patient to repeat sequences of digits that have been spoken slowly enough for him reasonably to be expected to register them. An easy short sequence is given first to make sure that the patient understands the task. Then five different digits are presented. If the patient can repeat them correctly, six are given, and then seven; if he cannot, the test is repeated with a different sequence of five. A normal response from a person of average intelligence is to repeat seven digits correctly. The test involves an element of concentration, so it cannot be used to assess memory if tests of concentration are definitely abnormal.

Next, the interviewer assesses the patient's ability to learn **new information** and reproduce it straight away. It is usual to employ one of the sentences introduced by Babcock (1930): for example, 'One thing a nation must have to become rich and great is a large secure supply of wood'. Three repetitions are usually enough for correct immediate reproduction by a healthy person of average intelligence. The next test concerns the patient's ability to retain newly learned material. It is usual to give a name and address which the patient is asked to repeat (to make sure that it has been registered correctly). The interview continues on other topics for five minutes before recall is tested. A healthy person of average intelligence should make only minor errors.

Memory for **recent events** is assessed by asking about news items from the last day or two, or about events in the patient's life that are known to the interviewer (such as the ward menus on the previous day). Questions about news items should be adapted to the patient's interests, and should have been widely reported in the media.

Remote memory can be assessed by asking the patient to recall personal events or well-known public items from some years before, such as the birth dates of the patient's children or grandchildren (provided of course that the latter are known to the interviewer), or the names of earlier political leaders. Awareness of the **sequence of events** is as important as the recall of individual items.

Standardized tests of memory and learning provide a quantitative assessment that may help in diagnosis and allow changes to be followed (see Levy and Post 1982).

Assessment of memory from ward behaviour

When a patient is in hospital, important information about memory is available from observations made by nurses and occupational therapists. These include how fast the patient learns the daily routine and the names of staff and other patients; and whether he forgets where he has put things, or where to find his bed, the sitting room, and so on.

Rating scales for memory: in elderly patients, the standard questions about memory in the clinical interview discriminate poorly between those who have cerebral pathology and those who do not. For these patients there are stand-ardized ratings of memory for recent personal events, past personal events, and general events (Post 1965), which allow a better assessment of severity.

Insight

When insight is assessed, it is important to keep in mind the complexity of the concept (see Chapter 1). By the end of the mental state examination, the interviewer should have a provisional estimate of how far the patient is aware of the morbid nature of his experiences. Direct questions are now asked to assess this further. These are concerned with the patient's opinions about the nature of individual symptoms; for example, whether he believes that extreme feelings of guilt are justified or not. The interviewer should also find out whether the patient believes that he is ill (rather than, say, persecuted by his enemies); if so, whether he thinks that the illness is physical or mental; and whether he thinks he needs treatment. The answers to these questions are important because they determine, in part, how far the patient is likely to collaborate with treatment. A note that merely records 'insight present' or 'no insight' is of little value.

Some difficulties in mental state examination

Apart from the obvious problem of examining patients who speak little or no English – which requires the help of an interpreter – several difficulties arise commonly.

The unresponsive patient

The doctor will encounter occasional patients who are mute, or stuporose (conscious but not speaking or responding in any way). He can then only make observations of behaviour; but this can be useful if done properly.

It is important to remember that some stuporose patients change rapidly from inactivity to overactivity and violence. It is therefore wise to have help at hand when seeing such a patient. Before deciding that the patient is mute, the interviewer should allow adequate time for reply and should try a variety of topics. He should also find out whether the patient will communicate in writing. Apart from the observations of behaviour described earlier in this chapter, the examiner should note whether the patient's eyes are open or closed; if open, whether they follow objects, move apparently without purpose, or are fixed; if closed, whether the patient opens them on request, and, if not, whether he resists attempts at opening them.

A physical examination including neurological assessment is essential in all such cases. Also certain signs found in catatonic schizophrenia should be sought, namely waxy flexibility of muscles and negativism (see Chapter 9).

In such cases it is essential to interview an informant who can give a history of the onset and course of the condition.

Overactive patients

Some patients are so active and restless that systematic interviewing is difficult. The interviewer may have to limit his questions to a few that seem particularly important, and base his conclusions mainly on observations of the patient's behaviour and spontaneous utterances. However, if the patient is being seen for the first time during an emergency consultation, some of his overactivity may be a reaction to other people's attempts to restrain him. In such cases a quiet but confident approach by the interviewer often calms the patient enough to allow more adequate examination.

The patient who appears confused

When the patient gives a history in a muddled way, or if he appears perplexed or frightened, the interviewer should test cognitive functions early in the interview. If there is evidence of impaired consciousness, the interviewer should try to orientate the patient and to reassure him, before starting the interview again in a simplified form. In such cases every effort should be made to interview another informant.

SPECIAL INVESTIGATIONS

These vary according to the nature of the patient's symptoms and the differential diagnosis. No single set of routine investigations is essential for every case, but for patients in hospital it is reasonable to do routine tests of the urine and to arrange estimations of haemoglobin, erythrocyte sedimentation rate, white blood cells, electroytes, and urea. In the past the Wasserman reaction for syphilis was carried out routinely, but this practice has declined. The recent increase in cases of primary and secondary neurosyphilis is a reason for performing appropriate tests whenever there is the slightest reason to suspect tertiary infection. Other investigations are reviewed in the chapters on individual syndromes, particularly the section on organic psychiatry.

PHYSICAL EXAMINATION

A thorough physical examination should be completed on all patients who are admitted to hospital or attend as day patients, since the psychiatrist is then responsible for the patients's physical health as well as his mental condition. When an outpatient is seen, he is usually referred by a general practitioner or another specialist, who has often carried out the appropriate physical examination. Moreover the care of the patient is usually shared between the psychiatrist and the other doctor. However, the psychiatrist should always determine what physical examination is relevant; he should then carry it out himself, or ensure that it has been done adequately by the referring doctor, or in certain cases arrange for another doctor to complete it. The latter course may be appropriate, for example, when the referral is made by a consultant physician who knows the patient well.

How extensive the physical examination should be must be judged in every case on the basis of diagnostic possibilities. However, the psychiatrist is most likely to be concerned with examination of the central nervous (including its vascular supply) and the endocrine systems. This does not, of course, imply that physical examination should be limited to these systems and, as indicated above, any patient admitted to hospital should certainly have a full routine examination.

Additional neurological examination when an organic syndrome is suspected

When an organic syndrome is suspected a routine neurological examination should be performed. In this section it is assumed that the reader has some knowledge of clinical neurology. Those who have not should refer to a standard textbook of neurology, such as *Brain's Diseases of the nervous system* (Walton 1977). Further information about tests of parietal lobe function will be found in the monograph by Critchley (1953). These tests do not help in the localization of disorders of the frontal or temporal lobes, which are diagnosed mainly from the history (see Chapter 11).

Language abilities

Partial failure of language function is called **dysphasia.** Language may be affected in its expression or reception, or both, and in either its spoken or written form. Gross disorders of language function will have been noted when taking the history and mental state. Special tests will reveal less severe degrees of dysfunction. Before conducting them, **dysarthria** should be tested by giving difficult phrases such as 'West Register Street' or a tongue twister.

Receptive aspects of language ability are tested in several ways. The patient can be asked to read a passage of appropriate difficulty, or failing this, individual words or letters. If he can read the passage, he is asked to explain it. Comprehension of spoken language is tested by asking a patient to listen to speech. For example, he can be asked to explain what has been heard or to respond to simple commands, for example, by pointing to named objects.

Expressive aspects of language are tested by asking the patient to speak and write. He can be asked to talk about his work or hobbies, and then to name objects (for example, pen, keys, watch, and component parts of these objects) and parts of the body. Next he can be asked to write a brief passage to dictation, and then a spontaneous passage (for example about the members of his family). If he cannot do this he should be asked to copy a short passage.

Language disorders point to the left hemisphere in right-handed people. In left-handed patients localization is less certain but in many it is still the left hemisphere. The type of aphasia gives some further guide to localization: expressive dysphasia suggests an anterior lesion, and receptive dysphasia a posterior lesion; mainly auditory aphasias suggest a lesion towards the temporal region, whilst mainly visual aphasias suggest a more posterior lesion.

Construction abilities

Apraxia is inability to perform a volitional act even though the motor system and sensorium are sufficiently intact for the person to do so. Apraxia can be tested in several ways. **Constructional** apraxia is tested by asking the patient to make simple figures with matchsticks (a square, triangle, cross) or to draw them. He can also be asked to draw a bicycle, house, or clock face. **Dressing** apraxia is tested by asking the person to put on his clothes. **Ideomotor** apraxia is tested by asking him to perform increasingly complicated tasks to command, ending for example with touching the right ear with the left middle finger, while placing the right thumb on the left elbow.

Constructional apraxia, especially if the patient fails to complete the left side of figures, suggests a right-sided lesion in the posterior parietal region. It may be associated with other disorders related to this region, namely sensory inattention and anosognosia.

Agnosias

This is the inability to understand the significance of sensory stimuli even though the sensory pathways and sensorium are sufficiently intact for the patient to be able to do so. It cannot be diagnosed until it is shown that the sensory pathways are intact and that consciousness is not impaired. Several kinds of agnosia are tested. **Astereognosia** is failure to identify three-dimensional form; it is tested by asking the patient to identify objects placed in his hand while his eyes are closed. Suitable items are keys, coins of different sizes, and paper clips. **Topognosia** is failure to know the position of an object on the skin. In **finger agnosia** the patient cannot identify which of his fingers has been touched when he has his eyes shut. Right–left confusion is tested by touching one hand or ear and asking the patient which side of the body has been touched. **Agraphognosia** is failure to identify letters or numbers 'written' on the skin. It is tested by tracing numbers on the palms with a closed fountain pen or similar object. **Anosognosia** is a failure to identify functional deficits caused by disease. It is seen most often when, after a right parietal lesion, the patient is unaware of left-sided weakness and sensory inattention.

Agnosias point to lesions of the association areas around the primary sensory receptive areas. Lesions of *either* parietal lobe can cause contralateral astereognosia, agraphognosia, and atopognosia. Sensory inattention and anosognosia are more common with right parietal lesions. Finger agnosia and right left disorientation are said to be more common with lesions of the dominant parietal region.

Psychological tests

In the past, clinical psychologists were largely concerned with the assessment of patients by standardized tests. Nowadays they are more concerned with treatment, and with assessments in the form of quantified observations of the patient's behaviour.

Many standardized tests are available. For the clinician the most useful are tests of intelligence and of higher neurological functions. Other tests are still in use but have less general value, such as those of personality, 'brain damage', and thought disorder. In this section a knowledge of the principles of psychological testing is assumed; no detailed account will be attempted here. When psychological testing is an important part of assessment it will be mentioned in the chapters on clinical syndromes. At this stage a few general comments are appropriate.

In general adult psychiatry it is not necessary to have an accurate assessment of every patient's intelligence. If a patient seems to be of borderline subnormal intelligence, or if his psychological symptoms appear to be a reaction to work beyond his intellectual capacity, **intelligence tests** are essential. Such tests together with standard **tests of reading** ability are also essential in child and adolescent psychiatry (see Chapter 20) and in the assessment of mentally retarded patients (see Chapter 21).

In the past, much use was made of **'tests of brain damage'** in the diagnosis of possible organic syndromes. The recent advent of computerized axial tomography has reduced the need for such indirect ways of assessing diffuse cerebral pathology, although **specific neuropsychological tests** are still of some value as pointers to specific lesions of the frontal or parietal cortex. Such tests are also valuable in measuring the progression of deficits caused by disease. Further discussion of these issues will be found in Chapter 11.

Personality tests have some value in clinical research, but contribute little to everyday clinical practice because usually more can be learnt from the clinical assessment described earlier in this chapter. Projective tests such as the Rorschach test should not be used in assessment because their validity has not been established.

Tests of thought disorder were developed to improve the accuracy of diagnosis of schizophrenia, but proved unsuccessful. However, they are occasionally helpful in charting the progression of thought disorder.

Standardized **rating scales of behaviour** are increasingly recognized as useful applications of psychometric principles in everyday clinical practice. When no ready-made rating scale is available, a clinical psychologist can often devise *ad hoc* ratings that are sufficiently reliable to chart the effects of treatment in the individual patient. For example, in measuring the progress of a depressed in-patient, a scale could be devised for the nurses to rate to show how much of the time he was active and occupied. This could be a five-point scale, in which the criteria for each rating referred to behaviours (such as playing cards or talking to other people) appropriate to the individual patient.

SPECIAL KINDS OF INTERVIEW

Interviewing relatives

In psychiatry interviews with one or more close relatives of the patient are highly important. Generally such interviews are used to obtain additional information about the patient's condition; sometimes they are used to involve the relative in the treatment plan, and sometimes to enlist his help in persuading the patient to comply with treatment.

A history from a relative or close friend is essential when the patient is suffering from a mental illness or personality disorder severe enough to impair his ability to give an unbiased and accurate account. In less severe disorders, a relative can still help by giving another view of the patient's illness and personality. For example, a relative is sometimes more able than the patient to date the onset of illness accurately, especially if it began gradually. A relative can also give a useful indication of how disabling the illness is and how it affects other people. Finally, when it is important to know about the patient's child-hood, an interview with a parent or older sibling is important.

With few exceptions, the patient's permission should be obtained before interviewing a relative. Exceptions occur when the patient is a child (the referral usually being initiated by the parents), and when certain adult patients present as emergencies and cannot give a history because mute, stuporose, confused, violent, or extremely retarded. In other cases, the doctor should explain to the patient that he wishes to interview a relative to obtain additional information needed for diagnosis and treatment. He should emphasize that confidential information given by the patient will not be passed to the relative. If any information needs to be given to a relative, for example about treatment, the patient's permission should be obtained. It is important to remember that relatives may misunderstand the purpose of the interview. Some assume that demands will be made on them; for example the married daughter of an elderly demented woman may think that she will be asked to take her mother into her own small home. Other relatives expect to be blamed for the patient's illness; for example, the parents of a young schizophrenic may expect the doctor to imply that they have failed as parents. It is important for the interviewer to be sensitive to such ideas, and, when appropriate, to discuss them in a reassuring way. He should always begin the interview by explaining the purpose.

Adequate time should be allowed for the interview; relatives are likely to be anxious, and time is needed to put them at ease, gather facts, and impart any necessary information.

The interview will enable the doctor to discover whether the relatives are having any problems as a result of the patient's illness. If they need help, the doctor can contact their general practitioner. However, he should not become involved in the relative's problems to an extent that conflicts with his primary duty to his patient.

After the interview the psychiatrist should not let the patient know what the relative has said unless the latter has given permission. It is important to seek permission if the relative has revealed something that should be discussed with the patient, for example, an account of excessive drinking previously denied by the patient. However, if the relative is unwilling that information should be passed on, this must be respected by the doctor; for example a wife may fear violent retaliation from her husband. When this happens, the psychiatrist should try to find ways of enabling the patient to reveal the behaviour himself in a further interview.

Problems sometimes arise when someone other than the nearest relative telephones the psychiatrist about the case. Information should not be given over the telephone, even if the doctor is certain of the caller's identity. Instead the patient should be consulted and, if he agrees, an interview arranged. The psychiatrist must never allow a conspiratorial atmosphere to develop in which he conceals conversations with family members or takes sides in their disputes.

Family interviews at home

It is sometimes appropriate to add to information about the patient's social circumstances by visiting the home, or arranging for a psychiatric nurse or a social worker to do so. Such a visit often throws new light on the patient's home life. It can sometimes lead to a more realistic evaluation of the relationship between family members than can be obtained from interviews in hospital. Before arranging a visit the psychiatrist should if possible talk to the general practitioner, who often has first-hand knowledge of the family and their circumstances from home visits over the years. If another member of the staff is going to make the visit, the psychiatrist should discuss the purpose of the visit with him or her.

Emergency consultations

When time is limited and an immediate decision is required about diagnosis and management, it may be possible to obtain an outline history. However short the time it is essential to obtain a clear account of the presenting symptoms, including their onset, course, and severity. A knowledge of the major clinical syndromes will then guide the interviewer to enquiries about other relevant symptoms, including those which arise in organic brain syndromes. Recent stressful events should always be asked about, together with any previous physical or mental illness. An account of previous personality is important, though it may be difficult to obtain unless there are relatives or close friends present. Habits regarding alcohol and drugs are especially important.

The family and personal history will often have to be covered quickly by asking a few salient questions. Throughout the interview the psychiatrist should be thinking which questions need to be asked immediately and which deferred until later.

A brief but relevant physical examination should be carried out unless already performed by another doctor.

If the above points are borne in mind when conducting an emergency consultation, common sense coupled with a sound knowledge of the major clinical syndromes should prove a satisfactory guide.

Interviewing in primary care

Much of a general practitioner's work is concerned with the identification of minor psychiatric disorders among patients presenting with a combination of physical and mild psychological symptoms. A useful brief method of identifying psychiatric disorders has been described by Goldberg and Huxley (1980). It focuses on the emotional symptoms encountered most commonly in general practice, and takes account of faults in interviewing that were found by watching general practitioners at work.

In these brief interviews the first few minutes are extremely important. However short the time, it is essential to give the patient an adequate opportunity to express his problem. Family doctors sometimes omit this because they assume the patient has come back for further advice about a previous problem. Sometimes they start questioning too early, before the patient has settled in his chair; opening questions may then be answered as if they were social pleasantries (for example 'How are you feeling now?' – 'Fine thanks'). On the other hand the doctor should not sit in silence reading his previous notes, as the patient may then begin to feel ill at ease and become unable to reveal his real concerns. The interview can begin with an open question such as 'What have you noticed wrong?', and then proceed mainly by prompts and clarifying questions. As in a longer interview, the doctor should be as alert to non-verbal behaviour as he is to the spoken word.

The next task is to understand clearly the nature of the symptoms. In general practice, the presenting complaint is often physical even when the disorder is psychiatric. The patient should always be allowed adequate time to describe the complaint in his own words before questions are asked. Thus a complaint of headache should not be followed immediately by questions about the side of the head on which it is felt. Instead the patient should be encouraged to describe the symptom in more detail. It may then become apparent that he has a tight feeling over the brows rather than a painful headache. Although this may seem obvious, it was found to be a common cause of error in Goldberg and Huxley's study of interviews in general practice.

For any complaint that may have psychological causes, a simple scheme of assessment has four components: the patient's general psychological adjustment, the presence of anxiety and worries, symptoms of depression, and the psychological context. General psychological adjustment is assessed by asking about fatigue, irritability, poor concentration, and the feeling of being under stress. To enquire into anxiety and worries the interviewer asks about physical symptoms as well as tension, phobias, and persistent worrying thoughts. Symptoms of depression are covered next, including persistent depressive mood, tearfulness, crying, hopelessness, self-blame, thoughts that life is unbearable, ideas about suicide, early morning waking, diurnal variation of mood, weight loss, and loss of libido. Of these Goldberg and Huxley found that general practitioners were most likely to overlook questions concerned with depressive thoughts.

Often the family doctor already knows his patient's social circumstances, and can therefore omit some of the questions required in an interview with a new patient. However, he should think systematically about the patient's work, leisure, marriage, and other relationships, and should ask any questions needed to bring his knowledge up to date.

An interview of this kind can be conducted within the short time available for first consultations in general practice. Usually a conclusion can be reached by the end of the interview. If not, a preliminary plan can be made, and a later interview arranged for completion of a full psychiatric history and mental state examination.

CASE NOTES

The importance of case notes

Good case records are important in every branch of medicine. In psychiatry they are even more vital because there is a large amount of information collected from a variety of sources. Unless material is recorded clearly, separating facts from opinions, it is difficult to think clearly about clinical problems and to make appropriate decisions about treatment. Equally it is important to summarize the information in a way that allows essential points to be grasped readily by someone new to the case. Case-notes are not just an *aide mémoire* for a doctor's own use, but an essential source of information for others who may see the patient in the future. So they must be legible, and well thought out.

It is important to remember the medicolegal importance of good case records. On the rare occasions when a psychiatrist is called upon to justify his actions in the coroner's court, at a trial, or after a complaint lodged by a patient, he will be greatly assisted by good case notes. The psychiatrist should remember that in certain circumstances case notes can be called upon by lawyers acting for patients.

The admission note

When a patient is admitted to hospital urgently, the doctor may have limited time for the interview. It is then particularly important to select the right topics. The admission note should contain at least (i) a clear account of the reasons for admission; (ii) any information required for a decision about immediate treatment; and (iii) any relevant information that will not be available later, including details of the mental state on admission and information from any informant whose presence at a later date cannot be relied upon. The account of the mental state should include well-chosen verbatim extracts to illustrate phenomena such as delusions or flight of ideas. If there is time, a systematic history should be added. However, it is a common mistake among trainees to spend too much time on details that are not essential to immediate decisions and can be taken next day; while failing to record details of mental state that may be transitory and yet of great importance to final diagnosis.

The admission note should end with a brief statement of a provisional plan of management. This plan should be agreed with the senior nurses caring for the patient at the time.

Progress notes

Progress notes should not be written in such general terms as to be of little value when the case is reviewed later. Instead of recording merely that the patient feels better or is behaving more normally, the note should state in what ways he feels better (for example, less despondent or less preoccupied with thoughts of suicide) or is less disturbed in behaviour (for example, no longer so restless as to be unable to sit at table throughout a meal).

Progress notes should also refer to treatment. Details of drug treatment often go unrecorded in the progress notes, presumably because they appear on the prescription sheet. However, when patients' progress is reviewed, it is much more convenient to have the timing and dosage of medication recorded alongside the mental state and behaviour. Psychological treatment should also be noted. A verbatim account of a psychotherapy session is difficult to write and seldom of value in management. Instead notes should be made of the main themes of therapeutic interviews, together with any relevant observations of the patient's response. At intervals, an additional note can be made summarizing progress made in the course of several sessions.

A careful note should also be made of any information or advice given by the doctor to the patient or his relatives. This should enable anyone giving advice later to know whether or not it differs from what was said before, so that an appropriate explanation can be given.

Observations of progress are made not only by doctors, but also by nurses, occupational therapists, clinical psychologists, and social workers. As a rule, these other members of staff keep separate notes for their own use, but it is desirable that important items of information are also written in the medical record.

A careful note should be kept of decisions reached at ward rounds and case conferences, and on any other occasions when the management of the patient is discussed with the consultant or his deputy. It is particularly important to set out clearly the plans made for the patient's further care on discharge from hospital.

The case summary

This section can best be understood by referring to the specimen case summary on pages 60–1.

The case summary is usually written in two parts. The first is completed within a week of the patient's admission. It has two main purposes. First, after extensive history taking has been completed, it is a useful exercise to select the salient features of the case. Second, the Part I summary is valuable to any doctor called to see the patient when the usual psychiatrist is not available. The items included in the first summary are all those from 'Reason for referral' to 'On examination' in the specimen summary.

The Part II summary is usually prepared within a day or two of the patient's discharge; it complements the Part I summary by adding special investigations and all subsequent items in the specimen summary. The whole summary is important if the patient becomes ill again, especially if he is under the care of another psychiatrist.

Summaries should be brief but comprehensive. They should be written in telegraphic style and laid out in a standard form that makes it easy for other people to find particular items. It is sometimes appropriate to omit particularly confidential details, noting instead that relevant information will be found in the case history. The Part I summary seldom occupies more than one and a half sides of a typed page, while the Part II summary is about half a page in length. A longer summary often means that the case has not been understood clearly.

Some of the items in the summary call for comment. The reason for referral should be a brief statement avoiding technical terms; for example it might read: 'having been found wandering at night in an agitated state, shouting about God and the devil'; rather than 'for treatment of schizophrenia'. The description of personality is often the most difficult section to complete briefly but informatively. However, with practice it is usually possible to list well chosen words and phrases which bring the person to life. This part of the summary is important and repays considerable thought.

If no abnormality is found on physical examination there is no need to make a separate entry for each system; it is sufficient to enter a single statement that routine examination showed no abnormality. However, when the mental state is recorded, a comment should be made under each heading whether or not any abnormality has been found.

When possible, the entry under diagnosis should use the categories of the 9th edition of the *International classification of diseases* (or equivalent system in countries not using this). It may, however, be necessary to add some additional comment to convey the complexities of an unusual case. If the diagnosis is uncertain, alternatives should be given, with an indication of the likelihood of each.

The summary of treatment should indicate the main treatments used, including the dosage and duration of any medication. The prognosis should be stated briefly but as definitely as possible. Statements such as 'prognosis guarded' are of little help to anyone. Unless the doctor commits himself more firmly he will be unable to learn from comparing his predictions with the actual outcome. At the same time, it is appropriate to note how certain the writer is about the prognosis and why any uncertainties have arisen; for example: 'The depressive symptoms are not likely to recur in the next year provided the patient continues taking drugs. The subsequent course is uncertain because it depends on the course of her son's leukaemia'.

The plan for further treatment should specify not only what is to be done but also who is to do it. The roles of the hospital staff and of the family doctor should be made clear.

Example of a case summary

Consultant: Dr A	Admitted 27.6.81.
Registrar: Dr B	Discharged 4.8.81.

Mrs C.D. date of birth: 7.2.50.

Reasons for referral Increasingly depressed and inactive despite outpatient treatment.

Family history *Father:* 66, retired gardener, good physical health, mood swings; poor relationship with patient. *Mother:* 57, housewife, healthy, convinced spiritualist; distant relationship. *Sibling* Joan, 35, divorced, healthy. *Home* materially adequate, little affection. *Mental illness* father's brother in hospital 4 times: 'Manic depression'

Personal history *Birth and early development* normal. *Childhood health:* good. *School* 6–16 uneventful; made friends. *Occupations* 16–22 shop assistant. *Marital* several boyfriends; married at 22, husband 2 years older, lorry driver. Unhappy in last year following husband's infidelity. *Children* Jane, 7, well; Paul, 4, epileptic. *Sexual* satisfactory until last year. *Menses* no abnormality. *Circumstances* council house; financial problems.

Previous illness aged 20, appendicectomy. Aged 24 (postnatal) depressive illness lasting 3 weeks.

Previous personality Few friends; interests within the family; variable mood; worries easily, lacks self-confidence; jealous; no obsessional traits; no conventional religious beliefs but shares mother's interest in the supernatural. Drinks occasionally; non-smoker. Denies drugs.

History of present illness For 6 weeks since learning of husband's infidelity, increasingly depressed and tearful, waking early, inactive, neglecting children. Eating little. Low libido. Believes herself to be in contact with dead grandmother through telepathy. Progressive worsening despite amitriptyline 125 mg per day for three weeks.

On examination *Physical* n.a.d. *Mental* dishevelled and distraught. *Talk* slow, halting, normal form. Preoccupied with her unhappy state and its effect on her children. *Mood* depressed, with self-blame, hopelessness but no ideas of suicide. *Delusions* none. *Hallucinations* none. *Compulsive phenomena* none. *Orientation* normal. *Attention and concentration* poor. *Memory* not impaired. *Insight* thinks she is ill but believes she cannot recover.

Special investigations haemoglobin and electroytes n.a.d.

Treatment and progress Amitriptyline increased to 175 mg/day; graded activities; joint interviews with husband to improve marital relationship. Advice from social worker to husband about management of financial problems. Progressive improvement in hospital with three weekends at home before final discharge. Amitriptyline reduced to 100 mg per day at time of discharge.

Condition on discharge Not depressed but still uncertain about future of marriage.

Diagnosis Depressive illness.

Prognosis Depends on further progress with marital problems. If these improve, the short-term prognosis is good. However, vulnerable to further depressive illness in the long term.

Further management 1. Continue amitriptyline 100 mg for 6 months (prescriptions from hospital). 2. Outpatient attendance to continue marital interviews (first appointment 14.8.81) 3. Review progress and return to GP's care in 3 months.

Formulation

A formulation is a concise assessment of the case. Unlike a summary, it is a discussion of alternative ideas about diagnosis, aetiology, treatment, and prognosis, and of the arguments for and against each alternative. A good formulation is based on the facts of the case and not on speculation, but it may contain verifiable hypotheses about matters that are uncertain at the time of writing.

The formulation begins with a concise statement of the essential features of the case. This should seldom be more than two or three sentences; for example: 'Mrs Jones is a 60-year-old divorced woman with symptoms of depression which started after an operation for cancer of the bowel and which have not responded to outpatient treatment'.

The differential diagnosis is considered next. This should be a list of reasonable possibilities in the order of their probability. The writer should avoid listing every conceivable diagnosis however remote. A note is made of the evidence for and against each diagnosis, with an assessment of the balance. At the end the writer's conclusion about the most probable diagnosis should be stated clearly.

Aetiology comes next. The first step is to identify predisposing, precipitating, and maintaining causes. The reasons for any predisposition are then considered, usually in chronological order to show how each factor has built on those that went before. For example, a family history of manic-depressive psychosis suggests a genetic predisposition to similar illness; in a particular case this might have been added to by the death of the patient's mother when he was a child, and increased further by adverse influences in a children's home.

After aetiology the conclusions about diagnosis and aetiology should be summarized with a list of outstanding problems and any further investigations needed. Next a concise plan of treatment is outlined. This should mention social measures as well as psychological treatment and medication, together with the role of nurses and occupational therapists.

Finally a statement is made about prognosis. This is often the most difficult part of the formulation. As with the summary, it is wrong to avoid commitment by writing down a vague statement. It is better to make a firm prediction; for example, 'These depressive symptoms should recover quickly in hospital but are likely to recur if her husband begins to drink heavily again'. If his prediction is proved wrong the doctor can learn by comparing it with the actual outcome, but nothing can be learnt from a non-committal statement.

Example of a formulation

(*Note:* this formulation refers to the same hypothetical case that was presented above in an example of a summary. By comparing the two, the reader can appreciate the differences between the material selected for each.)

Mrs C.D. is a 31-year-old married woman who for 6 weeks has been feeling increasingly depressed and unable to cope at home, despite outpatient treatment with antidepressant drugs.

Diagnosis

Depressive illness As well as feeling depressed, Mrs C.D. has woken unusually early, felt worse in the morning and lost her appetite. She has little energy or initiative. She blames herself for being a bad mother and believes that she cannot recover. The only feature apparently against this diagnosis – her belief that she is in contact with her dead grandmother – is discussed below.

Schizophrenia Although Mrs C.D. believes that she is in contact with her dead grandmother, this idea preceded her illness. It relates clearly to her own and her mother's interest in spiritualism. It is an overvalued idea not a delusion. She has no first-rank symptoms of schizophrenia.

Personality disorder Although Mrs C.D. has mood variations from mild depression to an energetic cheerful state, these are not sufficiently intense to constitute a cyclothymic personality disorder.

Conclusions Depressive illness.

Aetiology The symptoms appear to have been *precipitated* by news of her husband's infidelity. She was *predisposed* to react in an extreme way to this news by the insecure and jealous traits in her personality. She also appears to be predisposed to develop a depressive illness in that (a) she became depressed after the birth of her first child (b) she is subject to mood variations (c) her father suffers similar, but more extreme, mood variations and his brother has been four times admitted to hospital for treatment of a manic depressive illness.

The depressive disorder may have been *maintained* in part by continuing quarrels with the husband and by worry about debts he had incurred. Her knowledge of her sister's divorce and subsequent unhappiness has added to her concerns about the future of her own marriage.

Treatment The pattern of symptoms of the depressive illness point to a response to amitriptyline given in adequate dosage. The few side-effects experienced with 125 mg per day may indicate a lower than average blood concentration. The dose should be increased to 175 mg per day. Joint interviews with the patient and her husband are needed to attempt to resolve the marital problems. (It appears that her genuine wish is for a reconciliation.) The husband should be advised by the social worker about the steps he can take to deal with his debts.

Prognosis If the marital problems improve the immediate prognosis is good. However, the several predisposing factors noted above indicate that she may develop further depressive illness particularly at times when she encounters further stressful events.

Problem lists

A problem list is a useful addition to the formulation, in cases with complicated social problems. Such a list makes it easier to identify clearly what can be done to help the patient, and to monitor progress in achieving agreed objectives of treatment.

The use of a problem list can be shown with two examples. The first is a list that might be compiled for a young married woman who had taken a small overdose impulsively and had no psychiatric illness or definite personality disorder.

As progress is made in dealing with the problems in this list, new ones may be added or existing ones modified. For example, after a few joint interviews it might appear that the patient's sexual difficulties are a cause of the marital problem rather than a result, and that counselling about sexual matters should be carried out. Item 4 would then be amended appropriately. Likewise if the

Problem	Action	Agent	Review
1. Frequent quarrels with husband	Joint interviews	Dr A	3 weeks
2. 3-year-old son retarded in speech	Assessment	General practitioner	1 week
3. Housing said to be damp and unsatisfactory	Visit housing department of local authority	Patient	2 weeks
4. Sexual dysfunction (?secondary to 1 above)	Defer		

assessment of the child by the general practitioner were to confirm speech delay, an appointment for a specialist opinion might follow.

It is often appropriate to draw up the list with the patient so that he understands which problems can be changed and what he must do himself to bring this about.

Similar lists can be a valuable aid to the review of cases during ward rounds. For this purpose, an important component of therapy is likely to be the treatment of mental illness, often by drugs. Although such treatment can be shown on the same sheet as other problems, it should be separated clearly from them, as in the following list drawn up for a 45-year-old depressed woman.

Problem	Action	Agent	Review
1. Depressive illness	Amitriptyline 150 mg/day	Dr A	3 weeks
2. Loneliness (children now grown up)	Seek paid or voluntary work	Patient and social worker	5 weeks
3. Shy and awkward in company	Social skills training group	Psychologist and nurse	4 weeks
4. Heavy irregular periods	Gynaecological opinion	Dr A	1 week

The life chart

A life chart is a way of showing the time relations between episodes of physical and mental illness and potentially stressful events in the patient's life. It is often useful when the history is long and complicated. The chart has three columns, one for life events, and one each for physical and mental illness. Its rows represent the years in the patient's life.

Completion of a life chart requires detailed enquiry into time relations, and this may clarify the relationships between stressors and the onset of illness, and also between physical and mental disorders. For example in the case of a recurrent illness previously thought to be provoked by stressful events, the chart may show it has run a regular course and that comparable events have occurred at other times without consequent illness. In another case, the chart may provide convincing evidence of a relationship between stressful events and illness.

LETTERS TO GENERAL PRACTITIONERS

When a letter is written to a general practitioner, whether after an outpatient assessment or on discharging a patient from hospital, the first step is to think what the general practitioner already knows about the patient, and what questions he asked on referral. If the family doctor's referral letter outlined the salient features of the case, there is no need to repeat them in reply. When the patient is less well known to the general practitioner, more detailed information should be given; it is then often appropriate to use sub-headings (family history, personal history, etc.) so that information can be found readily if needed later.

Similarly if the diagnosis given in the referral letter is correct, it is only necessary to confirm it; otherwise the reasons for the diagnosis should be outlined.

Treatment and prognosis are dealt with next. When discussing treatment, the dosage of drugs should always be stated. The psychiatrist should indicate whether he has issued a prescription, how long a period it covers, and whether he or the general practitioner are to issue any subsequent prescriptions. If psychotherapy, behaviour therapy, or social work are planned, the letter should name the therapist or agent concerned and indicate what profession he belongs to (for example, supportive psychotherapy from Mr Smith, hospital social worker). The date of the patient's next visit to hospital should be stated, so that the general practitioner knows whether to see the patient himself in the meanwhile.

At the time of discharge from inpatient or day patient treatment, if is often appropriate to telephone the general practitioner to discuss subsequent management before the discharge letter is written. This ensures that the division of responsibilities is acceptable to the family doctor. If this is not done, the plans formulated may be well-intentioned but inappropriate.

FURTHER READING

Engel, G.L. and Morgan, W.K. (1973). *Interviewing the patient,* pp. 26–79. W.B. Saunders, London.

Hollander, M. and Wells, C.E. (1980). Medical assessment in psychiatric practice. In *Comprehensive textbook of psychiatry* 3rd edn (eds. H.I. Kaplan, A.M. Freedman, and B.J. Sadock) Vol. 1, pp. 981–9.

Institute of Psychiatry (1973). *Notes on eliciting and recording clinical information* Oxford University Press.

Leff, J.P. and Isaacs, A.D. (1978). *Psychiatric examination in clinical practice.* Blackwell, Oxford.

3. Classification in psychiatry

In psychiatry classification attempts to bring some order into the great diversity of phenomena encountered in clinical practice. Its purpose is to identify groups of patients who share similar clinical features, so that suitable treatment can be planned and the likely outcome predicted. Most systems of classification are based on diagnostic categories, such as schizophrenia or affective disorder. Diagnosis is the process of allocating a disorder to a diagnostic category. The great majority of psychiatrists agree that diagnostic classification is essential in psychiatry, but some dissent from this view.

In general medicine, classification is fairly straightforward. Most conditions can be classified on the basis of aetiology (for example pneumococcal or viral pneumonia) and of structural pathology (lobar or bronchopneumonia). Some general medical conditions are not yet classifiable in this way (such as migraine or trigeminal neuralgia); they are therefore classified solely on symptoms. Psychiatric disorders are mainly analogous to the second group. Some psychiatric disorders have an indisputable physical aetiology (such as phenylketonuria, mongolism, or general paralysis of the insane); but most can be classified only on symptoms.

This chapter begins with a brief discussion of the concept of mental illness. Then an outline is given of the basic principles that underlie most systems of classification, and the system used in this book is summarized. Certain contentious issues are reviewed; first, objections to psychiatric classification in itself, and second the question of categorical versus non-categorical classification. Next, an account is given of methods for achieving greater diagnostic agreement between psychiatrists. This leads to a description of individual systems of classification, including the main international systems. Finally, guidelines are given on classification in everyday clinical practice.

THE CONCEPT OF MENTAL ILLNESS

In everyday speech the word 'illness' is used loosely. In psychiatric practice the term 'mental illness' is also used with little precision. To produce a good definition of mental illness is surprisingly difficult. In everyday clinical practice, this difficulty does not matter much, except in relation to certain legal issues such as compulsory admission to hospital. In forensic psychiatry, the definition of mental illness is important in relation to fitness to plead, criminal responsibility, and similar issues.

It is easy to understand why the concept of mental illness does not loom large in ordinary practice. The psychiatrist is not directly concerned with a concept of such generality. He is more interested in making sense of the wide-ranging phenomena encountered in psychiatry, so that he can plan treatment rationally and predict outcome. It turns out that the best way of doing so is to start with the basic data (symptoms and signs) and to group them into syndromes, that is constellations of symptoms that occur together frequently, and have implications for treatment and prognosis. The psychiatrist habitually works from the particular to the general, and not vice versa.

None the less, the concept of mental illness is intellectually interesting, and it does have legal implications. For these reasons an outline of the main arguments will be given here.

Many attempts have been made to define mental illness (see Wootton 1959), but little progress has been made. A common approach is to examine the concept of illness in general medicine, and to look for any analogies with mental illness. In general medicine, an important distinction is made between disease and illness. Disease refers to objective physical pathology; illness refers to subjective awareness of distress or limitation of function. A person can have a disease without being ill, as in well-controlled diabetes; or he can be ill without having a disease, as in loss of a limb by trauma. However, this distinction has little bearing on psychiatric disorders, since most of them have no demonstrable physical pathology. Most psychiatric disorders are best regarded as illnesses.

Continuing the analogy with general medicine, mental illness could be defined in three different ways: absence of health; presence of suffering; and pathological process, whether physical or psychological.

Illness of any kind can be defined as the absence of health. This changes the emphasis of the problem, but does not solve it, because health is even more difficult to define. For example, the World Health Organization defined health as, 'a state of complete physical, mental and social well-being, and not merely the absence of disease or infirmity'. As Lewis (1953) rightly commented, 'a definition could hardly be more comprehensive than that, or more meaningless'. Many other definitions of health have been proposed, all equally unsatisfactory (see Wootton 1959).

The second approach is to define illness by the presence of suffering. This ancient idea has some practical value, since it defines a group of people likely to consult doctors. Its disadvantage is that it cannot be applied to everyone who would usually be regarded as ill in everyday terms. For example, patients with mania may feel unusually well and not experience suffering, though most people would regard them as mentally ill.

Thirdly, mental illness can be defined by reference to pathological process. Some extremists such as Szasz (1960) take the view that illness can only be defined in terms of physical pathology. Since most mental disorders have no demonstrable physical pathology, on this view they are not illnesses. Szasz takes the further step of asserting that most mental disorders are therefore not the province of doctors. This kind of argument can only be sustained by taking an extremely narrow view of pathology, and it is incompatible with the available evidence. Thus, there are genetic and biochemical grounds for supposing that schizophrenia and depressive disorders may have a physical basis, though not in the form of gross structural pathology (see pp. 202 and 246).

Mental illness can also be defined in terms of psychopathology. Such a view was taken by Lewis (1955), who suggested that illness could be characterized by 'evident disturbance of part functions as well as general efficiency'. In psychiatry part functions refer to perception, memory, learning, emotion, and other such psychological functions. A disturbance of the part function of perception would be an illusion or hallucination.

Several writers (Lewis 1955; Wootton 1959) have warned strongly against defining mental illness in terms of socially deviant behaviour alone. The argument is often made that someone must have been mentally ill to commit a particularly cruel murder or abnormal sexual act (the word 'sick' is often used in this context). Although such antisocial behaviour may be highly unusual, there is no justification for equating it with mental illness. Moreover, if mental illness is inferred from socially deviant behaviour alone, political abuse may result. For example, opponents of a political system may be confined to psychiatric hospitals simply because they do not agree with the authorities.

From the above examples, it can be seen that mental illness is difficult to define. As already mentioned, the concept of mental illness need not be defined for most purposes, but the law requires psychiatrists to diagnose the presence or absence of 'mental illness' in relation to compulsory admission to hospital and certain court procedures. Faced with this task, most psychiatrists begin by separating mental handicap and personality disorder from mental illness, as explained in the next section. Whether implicitly or explicitly, they usually invoke Lewis' concept of part-functions to define mental illness; they diagnose mental illness if there are delusions, hallucinations, severe alterations of mood, or other major disturbances of psychological functions. In practice, most psychiatrists allocate psychiatric disorders to diagnostic categories, such as schizophrenia, affective disorders, organic mental states, and others; by convention, they agree to group these diagnostic categories together under the rubric mental illness. Problems may arise with certain abnormalities of behaviour such as sexual deviations or drug abuse. For the reasons given above, these deviant behaviours are not usually regarded as mental illnesses, though they are deemed suitable for treatment by doctors.

The concept of mental illness is exceedingly complicated, and in a brief space only a few of the issues can be outlined. Readers seeking more information are referred to papers by Lewis (1955), Wootton (1959), and Farrell (1979).

THE BASIC PRINCIPLES OF CLASSIFICATION IN PSYCHIATRY

Several systems of classification are used in psychiatry. Whilst these systems differ from one another in important ways, nearly all of them share similar underlying principles.

In most systems the first step is to separate mental retardation and personality disorder from mental illness. The basis of this distinction is that mental retardation is present continuously from early life, and personality disorder continuously from the end of adolescence; whereas mental illness has a recognizable onset after a period of normal functioning in adult life.

The mental illnesses are usually subdivided into two major groupings, the psychoses and neuroses, as shown in Table 3.1.

Table 3.1. *The basic classification*

Personality disorder
Mental retardation
Organic psychoses
Functional psychoses (schizophrenia; affective psychoses)
Neuroses
Adjustment disorder
Other disorders
Disorders specific to childhood

Psychoses are major mental illnesses. They are exceedingly hard to define (see below), although they are usually said to be characterized by severe symptoms, such as delusions and hallucinations, and by lack of insight. The psychoses are themselves divided into organic and functional psychoses. In the organic psychoses there is a demonstrable physical abnormality in the brain; examples are general paralysis of the insane and delirium tremens. In functional psychoses, no underlying physical disease has yet been demonstrated (though some physical basis may eventually be found). The functional psychoses include schizophrenia and the affective psychoses.

The neuroses have symptoms much closer to normal experience, such as anxiety or obsessional thoughts. They are sometimes subdivided into anxiety neuroses, obsessive–compulsive neuroses, hysteria, and so-called neurotic depression.

Since the psychoses and neuroses do not cover all mental disorders, most schemes have additional broad groupings (see Table 3.1). Some schemes include a category of **adjustment disorders,** which are mild disorders occurring as exaggerated reactions to stressful events or circumstances. A second category is for **disorders of childhood** that are not encountered in adult life. A third category is **miscellaneous disorders of behaviour** which psychiatrists treat; this group includes alcohol and drug dependence, sexual dysfunction, and sexual deviation.

The categories of mental illness are often used in a hierarchical way. Thus the category organic psychosis takes precedence over the others; for example, if a patient has a brain tumour and symptoms of a functional psychosis, the single diagnosis of organic psychosis is made. Similarly if there is a functional psychosis with additional symptoms of a neurosis, only the functional psychosis is diagnosed; for example if a patient has schizophrenia and symptoms of anxiety, only schizophrenia is diagnosed. Neurosis in turn takes precedence over adjustment disorder.

However, if either of the non-illness categories (mental handicap or personality disorder) is associated with a mental illness category, both diagnoses are made. With other disorders the practice is less consistent, but often they are recorded separately; for example, affective disorder and alcohol dependence.

As mentioned earlier, the scheme just outlined forms the basis of most systems of classification, however elaborate. This basic scheme has the advantage of simplicity, and it can be used as a rule of thumb in everyday clinical practice. However, it has certain disadvantages.

The main disadvantage is that the term psychosis is unsatisfactory, since there is no single characteristic by which it can be defined. Numerous criteria for defining psychosis have been proposed: greater severity of illness; lack of insight; inability to distinguish between subjective experience and reality; the presence of delusions and hallucinations; and marked personality change that is not psychologically understandable. Exceptions are readily found to all these criteria. Moreover, the term psychosis embraces a wide range of disparate conditions (organic; schizophrenic; affective), and there is little to be gained in bringing them together. For these reasons, the diagnostic category of psychosis is of little value in clinical practice. For decisions about treatment and prognosis, other narrower categories are more useful (see below).

Whilst the term psychosis has little value as a diagnostic category in a scheme of classification, nevertheless it is a convenient collective term in everyday clinical use, as illustrated by the names post-operative psychosis and puerperal psychosis. In short, the word psychosis is useful for communication, but not for classification. In addition, the adjective 'psychotic' is useful, as for example in the term antipsychotic drug, meaning a drug that controls delusions, hallucinations, and excitement.

Another disadvantage of the basic scheme of classification is that it splits depressive disorders between the functional psychoses (depressive psychoses) and the neuroses (so-called neurotic depression). Such a distinction is not convenient in practice.

The classification used in this book

The scheme of classification used in this book (Table 3.2) is based partly on the basic scheme outlined above and partly on the International Classification of Diseases. Mental retardation and personality disorder are used as

Table 3.2. *Classification of mental disorders*

Organic disorders
  Acute organic syndrome
  Dementia (chronic organic syndrome)
  Amnesic syndrome

Schizophrenia

Schizoaffective disorders and related syndromes

Paranoid states

Affective disorders
  Depressive disorder
  Mania

The neuroses
  Non-specific
  Anxiety neurosis
  Phobic neurosis
  Obsessional neurosis
  Hysteria
  Depersonalization syndrome

Personality disorders

Adjustment disorder

Other disorders
  Sexual dysfunction and sexual deviations
  Alcohol and drug dependence
  Miscellaneous syndromes
  Psychological factors associated with medical conditions

Mental retardation

Disorders specific to childhood

Note   Many of the conditions in this list are classified further in the chapters that follow.

separate categories. The category psychosis is not used, for the reasons given in the immediately preceding paragraphs. Instead organic disorders, schizophrenia, and depressive disorders are used as separate categories. The organic disorders are divided into acute syndromes, chronic syndromes, and those that affect memory selectively (amnesic syndrome). There are also categories for schizoaffective disorders and related intermediate syndromes, and for paranoid states.

The neuroses are kept as a separate category because they embrace disorders that have much in common, particularly the milder forms. The scheme also includes the additional categories of adjustment disorder, other disorders, and disorders specific to childhood.

The subcategories listed in Table 3.2 are explained in the chapters dealing with the main syndromes.

Objections to classification

The use of schemes of classification in psychiatry has been criticized by psychiatrists and others.

Among psychiatrists, the main critics have been psychotherapists (for example Menninger 1948), whose work is concerned more with the neuroses and personality disorders than with the whole range of psychiatric disorder. Psychotherapists tend to make two main criticisms. The first is that allocating a patient to a category detracts from the understanding of his unique personal difficulties. The second is that individual patients do not fit neatly into the available categories. Although these criticisms are important, they are only arguments against the improper use of classification. Used appropriately, classification helps to predict the course of a disorder, and to select appropriate methods of treatment. It can certainly be combined with consideration of a patient's unique qualities that affect the aetiology and treatment of individual problems. Indeed such a combination is used in preparing a formulation, see page 61.

Certain sociologists have put forward a **labelling theory**, which holds that to allocate a person to a diagnostic category is simply to apply a label to deviant behaviour (Scheff 1963; Lemert 1951). It is argued that such labelling only serves to increase the person's difficulties. There can be no doubt that terms such as epilepsy or schizophrenia attract social stigma, but this does not lessen the reality of disorders that cause suffering and require treatment. These disorders cannot be made to disappear simply by ceasing to give names to them.

Some psychologists object to diagnostic categories mainly in relation to the neuroses. Their argument is that the neuroses are quantitative variations from the normal, and it is not justifiable to make an arbitrary dividing line between the normal. Although such an argument may carry some scientific weight, an arbitrary cut-off can be of practical value in predicting the natural course and the response to treatment. An obvious example in general medicine is hypertension. As described in Chapter 6, there are practical advantages in dividing the more severe neuroses into syndromes, and in allocating individual patients to them.

In conclusion, the standpoint of this book is that the supposed disadvantages of using diagnostic categories in psychiatry are outweighed by the substantial advantages.

CATEGORICAL AND NON-CATEGORICAL CLASSIFICATION

Categorical classification

Traditionally psychiatric disorders have been classified by dividing them into **categories**, which are supposed to represent discrete entities. The categories have been defined in terms of the symptom-patterns and the course and outcome of the different disorders. Such categories have proved useful in both clinical work and research. However, certain objections are often raised against them. First, there is uncertainty about the validity of categories as representing distinct entities. Second, most systems of classification do not provide adequate definitions and rules of application, so categories cannot be used reliably. Third, many psychiatric disorders do not fall neatly within the boundaries of a category, but are intermediate between two categories; for example schizo-affective disorder, which is intermediate between schizophrenia and affective disorder. Recently multivariate statistical techniques have been used in attempts to define categories more clearly. The results have been interesting, but so far not conclusive (see Paykel 1981).

Categorical systems often include an implicit **hierarchy** of categories. If two or more diagnoses are made, it is often conventional (though not always made explicit) that one takes precedence. For example, organic mental states take precedence over functional psychoses, which in turn take precedence over neuroses. Foulds (1963) suggested that this hierarchical approach should be made an explicit basis of psychiatric classification. Foulds proposed a hierarchy of 'personal illness', of which the classes (in order of increasing priority) are: dysthymic states; neurotic symptoms; 'integrated delusions'; and 'delusions of disintegration'. According to Foulds, a high-priority condition could be accompanied by the symptoms of a condition of lower priority, but only the higher priority condition need be diagnosed. Although ingenious, this system has not been widely adopted.

Non-categorical classification

This includes the dimensional and multiaxial approaches.

The dimensional approach

The dimensional approach rejects the use of separate categories. In the past it was advocated by Kretschmer and other psychiatrists. Recently it has been strongly promoted by the psychologist Eysenck, who argues that there is no evidence to support the traditional grouping into discrete entities. Instead Eysenck (1970) has proposed a system of three dimensions: psychoticism, neuroticism, and introversion–extraversion. Patients are given scores which locate them on each of these three axes. For example, in the case of someone who would be assigned to hysteria in a categorical system, Eysenck's theory predicts that he would have high scores on the axes of neuroticism and extraversion, and a low score on the psychoticism axis. Subsequent research has not confirmed specific predictions of this kind, but the example brings out the principles.

The three dimensions were established by various procedures of multivariate analysis. They are attractive in theory, but it should be remembered that they depend considerably on the initial assumptions and the choice of methods. The dimension of 'psychoticism' bears little relation to the concept of psychosis as generally used. For example, those who score particularly highly on this dimension are artists and prisoners. The dimensions of neuroticism and introversion–extraversion have been useful in research, but in clinical practice they are difficult to apply to the individual patient.

The multiaxial approach

In one sense, the term multiaxial can be applied to the three dimensions just described. However, the term is usually applied to schemes of classification in which two or more separate sets of information (such as symptoms and aetiology) are coded. In 1947 Essen-Möller proposed that clinical syndrome and aetiology should be coded separately. It would then be possible to identify cases with a similar clinical picture on the one hand, and those with a similar aetiology on the other (Essen-Möller 1971). Such a scheme should avoid the unreliability of schemes in which clinical picture and aetiology are often combined in the definition of a single category, such as reactive depression.

Several multiaxial models have been proposed, such as the American system, DSM III, which is described later. In child psychiatry, wide use is now made of a modification of a five-axis system proposed by a WHO working party (Rutter, Shaffer, and Shepherd 1975) (see Chapter 20). Multiaxial systems are attractive, but there is an obvious danger that they will be so comprehensive and complicated as to be difficult for everyday use.

The reliability of diagnosis

Diagnosis is the process of identifying a disease and allocating it to a category on the basis of symptoms and signs. Systems of classification are obviously of little value unless psychiatrists can agree with one another when they attempt to make a diagnosis. In the past thirty years there has been increasing interest in the extent and causes of diagnostic disagreement between psychiatrists (see Kendell 1975; Leff 1977). Early studies consistently showed poor diagnostic reliability. In Philadelphia, Ward *et al.* (1962) concluded that overall disagreement was made up of the following elements: inconsistency in the patient, 5 per cent; inadequate interview technique, 33 per cent; inadequate use of diagnostic criteria, 62 per cent. The last two factors will be discussed in turn.

Interviewing technique

Psychiatrists vary widely not only in the amount of information they elicit at interview, but also in their interpretation of the information. Thus, a psychiatrist may or may not elicit a phenomenon, and he may or may not regard it as a significant symptom or sign. Variations have been found between groups of psychiatrists trained in different countries, and between individual psychiatrists in the same country. When shown filmed interviews, American psychiatrists reported many more symptoms than did British psychiatrists (Sandifer *et al.* 1968). Presumably this reflected differences in training between the two countries.

Differences in eliciting symptoms can be reduced if psychiatrists are trained to use standardized interview schedules, such as the Present State Examination (PSE) (Wing *et al.* 1974); the Schedule of Affective Disorder and Schizophrenia (SADS), which covers both the present illness and past history (Endicott and Spitzer 1978); and the National Institute of Mental Health Diagnostic Interview Schedule (DIS). Non-specialists can also be trained to use these schedules. The point of such schedules is that first they specify sets of symptoms that must be enquired about; and secondly, they define the symptoms and give instructions on rating their severity.

Criteria for diagnosis

International studies have compared the diagnostic criteria used by different psychiatrists. For example in the US–UK Diagnostic Project, American and British psychiatrists were shown the same video-taped clinical interviews, and asked to make diagnoses (Cooper *et al.* 1972). Compared with those in London, psychiatrists in New York diagnosed schizophrenia twice as often, and mania and depression correspondingly less often. Further investigation suggested that New York was not typical of North America, and that diagnostic practice in some other places in the United States and in Canada was closer to British practice.

A second study, the International Pilot Study of Schizophrenia, was carried out in nine countries (World Health Organization 1973): Columbia (Cali); Czechoslovakia (Prague); Denmark (Aarhus); England (London); India (Agra); Nigeria (Ibadan); Taiwan (Taipei); USA (Washington); and USSR (Moscow). Psychiatrists in all these countries carried out lengthy patient inter-views which included the Present State Examination. The psychiatrists made their own diagnoses, which were compared with those of the PSE computer program, CATEGO. There was substantial agreement between seven of the centres, but Washington and Moscow differed from the rest. In Washington, the findings confirmed the findings of the US–UK project described above. The Moscow psychiatrists also appeared to have an unusually broad concept of schizophrenia; this apparently reflected a particular local emphasis on the course of disorder as a diagnostic criterion.

In a third, less elaborate study, diagnostic practices were compared in France, Germany, and Great Britain (Kendell *et al.* 1974). Agreement was closest between German and British psychiatrists. French psychiatrists were notably different in diagnosing manic-depressive disorder much less frequently.

Diagnostic unreliability can be greatly reduced by providing rules for applying each category in a diagnostic scheme. The International Classification of Diseases (see p. 78) gives descriptions of categories, but they are too brief to prevent variation in interpretation. The first detailed set of rules was drawn up by Feighner *et al.* (1972) in the United States, who provided specific inclusion and exclusion criteria (see page 241 for an example of the related criteria used in DSM III). A similar approach was adopted in the Research Diagnostic Criteria

(Spitzer *et al.* 1978), and in the American system DSM III which is described later in this chapter. When criteria of this kind are used, a substantial number of patients may not fit into any of the designated categories, and may have to be allocated to an 'atypical' category. In some kinds of research, this atypical group may not matter, but it can be a problem in everyday clinical practice.

Diagnosis by computer

Computer diagnosis ensures that the same rules will be applied to every case. Computer programs to generate diagnoses have been based either on a logical decision-tree or on statistical models (see Kendell 1975). A decision-tree program evaluates a sequence of yes/no answers, and so successively narrows the diagnosis. It thus resembles differential diagnosis in clinical practice. Spitzer and Endicott (1968) first used this procedure to develop the program DIAGNO. Later Wing and colleagues (1974) developed the program CATEGO, for use with the Present State Examination. CATEGO has proved valuable in epidemiological studies of major and minor psychiatric illness, and comparison data are now available from a variety of patient groups and normal populations.

In the alternative statistical approach, data are collected from a sample of patients whose diagnoses are known. A scheme of classification is then devised from this data-base by statistical methods. Whereas the decision-tree method follows a sequence of arbitrary rules that underlie ordinary clinical practice, this second method estimates the probability that a given patient's symptoms match the symptoms of previously diagnosed patients.

The validity of schemes of classification

Whilst the unreliability of diagnosis can be reduced by the measures just described, a scheme of classification must also be valid. Even if different interviewers can be trained to reach high levels of agreement in making diagnoses, little has been achieved unless the diagnostic categories have some useful relationship to the disorders met in clinical practice. To be valid, a scheme of classification should have categories that fit well with clinical experience (face validity). The categories should also be able to predict the outcome of psychiatric disorders (predictive validity); ideally they should also point to associations between psychiatric disorders and independent variables, such as biochemical measures (construct validity).

So far little progress has been made towards establishing the validity of existing schemes of classification.

INDIVIDUAL SYSTEMS OF CLASSIFICATION

In the history of psychiatric classification, an outstanding contribution was made by the German psychiatrist Emil Kraepelin whose work was based on detailed clinical observations and follow-up studies. In successive editions of his famous textbook, he refined the distinction between organic and functional psychoses, and further divided the latter into dementia praecox (later called schizophrenia) and manic depressive illness.

In European countries systems of classification still remain largely within Kraepelin's framework. The two main exceptions are Scandinavia and France. In Scandinavia much emphasis is placed on the concept of **psychogenic** or **reactive psychoses**, which are said to have paranoid, depressive, or confusional symptoms, or sometimes a mixture of all three.

In French psychiatry, classification is based on a combination of psychopathology and elements of existential philosophy (see Pichot 1982). Certain diagnostic categories in France differ from those in Europe and North America. They include two special categories: *Bouffée délirante* – the sudden onset of a delusional state with trance-like feelings of short duration and good prognosis. Although this condition may develop into schizophrenia, it is clearly separated from acute schizophrenia and acute manic depressive illness (see Chapter 9). *Délires chroniques* – conditions which, in the ICD system, would be classified as Paranoid States and are separated from schizophrenia, a diagnosis which, in France, is used only when there is definite evidence of deterioration of personality. The *délires chroniques* are subdivided into the 'non-focused' in which several areas of mental activity are affected, and the 'focused' with a single delusional theme. The latter include several conditions such as erotomania, described in Chapter 10 Paranoid States.

In the 1920s and 1930s American views on psychiatric classification diverged widely from those in Europe. Psychoanalysis and particularly the teaching of Adolf Meyer directed American psychiatry towards a predominant concern with the uniqueness of individuals rather than with their common features. At the same time, diagnostic concepts were increasingly based on presumed psychodynamic mechanisms.

Recently in the United States attitudes towards psychiatric classification have changed considerably. An important first step was the introduction of strict criteria for classification in research, as described above (Feighner *et al.* 1972). This step was followed by the thorough work that led to the new American scheme, DSM III.

The International Classification of Diseases (ICD)

Mental disorders were not included in the International Classification of Disease until its sixth edition. The first scheme for mental disorders was widely criticized. As a preliminary to a major revision of the scheme, a survey of principles of classification in different countries was carried out (Stengel 1959), and wide variations were found. Stengel recommended a new approach based on operational definitions and supported by a glossary, but not linked to any theories of aetiology.

The eighth edition of the International Classification (ICD 8) was published in 1965. It made some progress towards solving the earlier problems but was still unsatisfactory in several ways. It contained too many categories, and allowed alternative codings for some syndromes. This probably reflected an endeavour to make the scheme widely acceptable. The glossary to ICD 8 was not published until 1972. Meanwhile glossaries had been published in America and Great Britain (General Register Office 1968). Neither of these glossaries was detailed enough; they both contained internal inconsistencies, and they disagreed with one another.

Before preparation of the latest edition, ICD 9, several WHO working parties examined the principles and practice of classification (see Kendell 1975). A new descriptive glossary (based on the British glossary to ICD 8) was drawn up. Improvements were made in the classificatory scheme, particularly in the sections on organic disorders, childhood disorders, and psychiatric disorders associated with physical illness. However, ICD 9 still remains a compromise, no doubt because it aims to be widely acceptable. It still lacks detailed rules of application. As Kendell (1975) has pointed out, depressive disorders can be classified in several alternative ways which are mutually incompatible. Despite these shortcomings, ICD is used widely and works reasonably well. It has had some success in encouraging greater uniformity of classification in different countries. It is to be expected that further versions of ICD will lead to further improvements (World Health Organization 1981).

The Diagnostic and Statistical Manual (DSM)

In 1952 the American Psychiatric Association published the first edition of the Diagnostic and Statistical Manual (DSM I) as an alternative to ICD 6 (which, as mentioned above, had been widely criticized). DSM I was influenced by the views of Adolf Meyer and Karl Menninger, and its simple glossary reflected the prevailing acceptance of psychoanalytic ideas in the United States. In 1965 work began on DSM II, in which both psychoanalytic and Kraepelinian ideas were represented.

The present third edition, DSM III, was published in 1980. It had been prepared with great care. Advisory committees had prepared detailed drafts, obtained opinions from 550 clinicians, and subjected the results to field tests. DSM III is intended to provide a comprehensive classification with clear criteria for each diagnostic category. Coding is based on American modifications of ICD 9. Definitions are mostly descriptive; theoretical statements are avoided, and aetiology is included only when clearly demonstrable, as in the organic disorders and adjustment reactions. The scheme has five axes. The two main axes are: (i) psychiatric syndrome; (ii) personality disorders. The others are: (iii) physical disorders; (iv) severity of psychological stressors; (v) highest level of adaptive functioning. An extra digit can be used in a variety of ways; for example for type of symptoms, and whether active or in remission.

During the drafting of DSM III, several diagnostic categories were particularly contentious (Spitzer and Williams 1980): neurosis; personality disorder; psychosomatic disorders; borderline personality; homosexuality; and schizo-affective disorder (the only category for which no rules could be provided). Most of these contentious issues were resolved, and the acceptance of DSM III by the different groups in American psychiatry is a measure of its success.

Despite these achievements some problems remain. It is yet to be shown that the third, fourth, and fifth axes will be used successfully in everyday clinical practice. Since the diagnostic categores are not entirely congruous with those in ICD 9, there are likely to be continuing difficulties in making international comparisons. Moreover, some categories in DSM III are not obviously better than their counterparts in ICD 9; for example, in DSM III childhood disorders of conduct are subdivided into complicated subgroups which are not wholly supported by research evidence.

Classification in everyday practice

This subject was considered briefly in the section on formulation (p. 61). It is discussed in more detail here.

A classification is made after the history and examination of mental state have been completed. The first step is to review the pattern of the symptoms occurring in the past month (as reported by the patient and any other informants) and of the symptoms and signs elicited by mental state examination. Then an attempt is made to match this pattern to one or more of the diagnostic categories in the system of classification used. Reference is made if necessary to the definitions and rules of application provided by the scheme. In practice, only a small number of categories need be considered, the rest being obviously inapplicable. An important distinction needs to be made between character-istic symptoms and discriminating symptoms. Characteristic symptoms are frequent and typical of a syndrome, but they occur in other syndromes as well. For example, suicidal thoughts occur in depressive disorder but they also occur commonly in other disorders. Such symptoms are important in planning treatment, but not in diagnosis. On the other hand discriminating symptoms are largely specific to a syndrome. They are therefore important in diagnosis, though they may cause the patient little distress or may be unimportant in treatment. An example is the delusion that thoughts are being inserted into the mind, a symptom that seldom occurs except in schizophrenia.

In attempting to match a patient's pattern of symptoms and signs to a diagnostic category, problems may arise when most symptoms fit well but one or two are incongruous. For example a patient may have depressed mood, morbid self-blame, early morning waking, and diurnal mood variation – all symptoms typical of a depressive disorder. In addition the patient may have the delusion that people talk about him on television – a typical symptom of schizo-phrenia. When this kind of incongruity occurs, the clinician should review the case thoroughly and search for other evidence of the alternative syndrome. If only a single incongruous symptoms is found among many that are congruous, generally the diagnostic category remains unchanged.

This kind of problem can sometimes be resolved by looking at the diagnostic category longitudinally as well as cross-sectionally. The process described so far is cross-sectional; that is, allocation to a category is based on present mental state and the history of symptoms in the past few weeks. The longitudinal approach deals with the nature and course of a disorder since it first began. For example, the present symptoms can be compared with those of any previous episodes of disorder. If it is found that the patient described above has had two previous episodes of clear-cut affective disorder, and no episodes of schizophrenia, then the clinician will more readily discount the current atypical symptom (the delusion of being talked about on television). If there have been two episodes of definite schizophrenia, the opposite conclusion will be justified. The time-course of previous illness is also informative; a history of intermittent episodes with complete recovery between them occurs more often with affective disorder than with schizophrenia. These principles can of course be applied to other differential diagnoses.

When discussing diagnostic classification at a ward round or in a written formulation, the best practice is to list the possible categories, and then briefly review the evidence for and against each. The list might be, for example: depressive disorder; schizophrenia; organic disorder. Evidence 'for' consists of discriminating symptoms and a typical time-course of the illness; evidence 'against' includes absence of essential symptoms, presence of incongruous symptoms, and an atypical time-course. The reader may find it helpful to refer to the example of a formulation on page 62.

FURTHER READING

American Psychiatric Association (1980). *Diagnostic and statistical manual of mental disorders.* 3rd edn. American Psychiatric Association, Washington.

Kendell, R.E. (1975). *The role of diagnosis in psychiatry.* Blackwell Scientific Publication, Oxford.

Lewis, A.J. (1953). Health as a social concept. *British Journal of Sociology* **4,** 109–24. (Reprinted in Lewis, A.J. (1967). *The state of psychiatry,* pp. 179–94. Routledge and Kegan Paul, London.)

Spitzer, R.L. and Williams, J.B.W. (1980). Classification of mental disorders and DSM III. In *Comprehensive textbook of psychiatry*, Vol. 1, 3rd edn (ed. H.I. Kaplan, A.M. Freedman, and B.J. Sadock). Williams and Wilkins, Baltimore.

World Health Organization (1978). *Mental disorders: glossary and guide to their classification in accordance with the ninth revision of the International Classification of Diseases.* World Health Organization, Geneva.

—— (1981). *Current state of diagnosis and classification in the mental health field.* World Health Organization, Geneva.

Wootton, B. (1959). *Social science and social pathology,* Chapter 7, pp. 203–26. George Allen and Unwin, London.

4. Aetiology

Psychiatrists are concerned with aetiology in two ways. First, in everyday clinical work, they try to discover the causes of the mental disorders presented by individual patients. Second, in seeking a wider understanding of psychiatry, they are interested in evidence about aetiology obtained from clinical studies, community surveys, or laboratory investigations. Correspondingly, the first part of this chapter deals with some general issues about aetiology in the assessment of the individual patient. The second part deals with the various scientific disciplines that have been applied to the study of aetiology.

When the clinician assesses an individual patient, he draws on a common fund of knowledge about aetiology built up from the study of groups of similar patients, but he cannot understand the patient in these terms alone. He must also use everyday insights into human nature. For example, in assessing a depressed patient, the psychiatrist should certainly know what has been discovered about the psychological and neurochemical changes accompanying depression, and what evidence there is about the aetiological role of stressful events and genetic predisposition. At the same time he will need intuitive understanding to recognize that this particular patient feels depressed because he has been told that his wife has cancer.

Commonsense ideas of this kind are nearly always an important part of aetiological formulation in psychiatry, but they must be used carefully if superficial explanation is to be avoided. Aetiological formulation can only be done properly if certain conceptual problems are clearly understood. These problems can be illustrated by a case-history.

For four weeks a 38-year-old married man became increasingly depressed. His symptoms started soon after his wife left him to live with another man.

In the past the patient's mother had received psychiatric treatment on two occasions, once for a severe depressive disorder, and once for mania; on neither occasion was there any apparent environmental cause for the illness. When the patient was 14 years old, his mother went away to live with another man, leaving her children with their father. For several years afterwards the patient felt rejected and unhappy but eventually settled down. He married and had two children, aged thirteen and ten at the time of his illness.

Two weeks after leaving home, the patient's wife returned, saying that she had made a mistake and really loved her husband. Despite her return the patient's symptoms persisted and worsened. He began to wake early, gave up his usual activities, and spoke at times of suicide.

In thinking about the causes of this man's symptoms, the clinician would first draw on knowledge of aetiology derived from scientific enquiries. Genetic investigations have shown that, if a parent suffers from mania as well as depression, a predisposition to depressive illness is particularly likely to be transmitted to the children. It is therefore possible that this patient received the predisposition from his mother. Clinical investigation has also provided some information about the effects of separating children from their mothers. In the present case the information is not helpful because it refers to people who were separated from their mothers at a younger age than the patient. On scientific grounds there is no particular reason to focus on the departure of the patient's mother; but intuitively it seems likely that this was an important event. From everyday experience it is understandable that a man should feel sad if his wife leaves him; and he is likely to feel even more distressed if this event recapitulates a similar distressing experience in his own childhood. Therefore, despite the lack of scientific evidence, the clinician would recognize intuitively that the patient's depression is likely to be a reaction to the wife's departure.

The same sort of intuitions might suggest that the patient would recover when his wife came back. In the event he did not recover. Although his symptoms seemed understandable when his wife was away, they no longer seem so after her return.

This simple case-history illustrates the following aetiological issues: the complexity of causes in psychiatry: the classification of causes; the concept of stress; the concept of psychological reaction; and the roles that intuition and scientific knowledge should play in aetiology. These problems will be considered in turn.

The complexity of causes in psychiatry

In psychiatry, the study of causation is complicated by two problems. Both of these problems are met in other branches of medicine, but to a less degree.

The first problem is that causes are often remote in time from the effects they produce. For example it is widely believed that childhood experiences partly determine the occurrence of neuroses in adult life. It is difficult to test this idea because the necessary information can only be gathered either by studying children and tracing them many years later, which is difficult; or by asking adults about their childhood experiences, which is unreliable.

The second problem is that a single cause may lead to several effects. For example, deprivation of parental affection in childhood has been reported to predispose to antisocial behaviour, suicide, depressive illness, and several other disorders. Conversely, a single effect may arise from several different causes. The latter can be illustrated either by different causes in different individuals, or by multiple causes in a single individual. For example, mental handicap (single effect) may occur in several children, but the cause may be a different genetic abnormality in each child. On the other hand depressive illness (single effect) may occur in one individual through a combination of causes such as genetic factors, adverse childhood experiences, and stressful events in adult life.

The classification of causes

A single psychiatric disorder, as just explained, may result from several causes. For this reason, a scheme for classifying causes is required. A useful approach is to divide causes chronologically into predisposing, precipitating, and perpetuating.

Predisposing factors

These are factors, many of them operating from early life, that determine a person's vulnerability to causes acting close to the time of the illness. They include genetic endowment and the environment *in utero*, as well as physical, psychological, and social factors in infancy and early childhood. The term **constitution** is often used to describe the mental and physical make-up of a person at any point in his life. This make-up changes as life goes on, under the influence of further physical, psychological, and social influences. Some writers restrict the term constitution to the make-up at the beginning of life, whilst others also include characteristics acquired later (this second usage is adopted in this book). The concept of constitution includes the idea that a person may have a predisposition to develop a disorder (such as schizophrenia) even though the latter never manifests itself. From the standpoint of psychiatric aetiology, one of the important parts of the constitution is the personality.

When the aetiology of an individual case is formulated, the **personality** is always an essential element. For this reason the clinician should be prepared to spend considerable time in talking to the patient and to people who know him, in order to build up a clear picture of his personality. This assessment usually helps to explain why the patient responded to certain stressful events, and why he reacted in a particular way. The obvious importance of personality in the individual patient contrasts with the small amount of relevant scientific information so far available. In the evaluation of personality, therefore, it is particularly important to acquire sound clinical skills through supervised practice.

Precipitating factors

These are events that occur shortly before the onset of a disorder and appear to have induced it. They may be physical, psychological, or social. Whether they produce a disorder at all, and what kind of disorder, depends partly on constitutional factors in the patient (as mentioned above). Physical precipitating factors include, for example, cerebral tumours or drugs. Psychological and social precipitants include personal misfortunes such as the loss of a job, and changes in the routine of life such as moving home. Sometimes the same factor can act in more than one way; for example a head injury can induce psychological disorder either through physical changes in the brain or through its stressful implications to the patient.

Perpetuating factors

These factors prolong the course of a disorder after it has been provoked. When planning treatment, it is particularly important to give attention to these factors. The original precipitating factors may have ceased to act by the time the patient is seen, and the predisposing factors may well be treatable. For example, in their early stages many psychiatric disorders lead to secondary demoralization and withdrawal from social activities, which in turn help to prolong the original disorder. It is often appropriate to treat these secondary factors, whether or not any specific measures are carried out.

The concept of stress

Discussions about stress are often confusing because the term is used in two ways. First, it is applied to events or situations that may have an adverse effect on someone; for example, working for an examination. Second, it is applied to the adverse effects that are induced, which may be psychological or physiological change. In considering aetiology it is advisable to separate these components.

The first set of factors can usefully be called **stressors**. They include a large number of physical, psychological, and social factors in the environment that have the potential to produce adverse effects. The term is sometimes extended to include events that are not experienced as adverse at the time, though they may still have adverse long-term effects. For example intense competition may produce an immediate feeling of pleasant tension, though it might in some cases lead to unfavourable long-term effects.

The effect on the organism can usefully be called the **stress reaction** to distinguish it from the provoking events. This reaction includes autonomic responses (such as a rise in blood pressure), endocrine changes (such as the secretion of adrenaline and noradrenaline), and psychological responses (such as a feeling of being keyed up).

The concept of a psychological reaction

As already mentioned, it is widely recognized that psychological distress can arise as a reaction to unpleasant events. Sometimes the association between event and distress is evident; for example, when a man becomes depressed after the death of his wife. In other cases, it is far from clear whether the psychological disorder is really a reaction to an event or whether the two have coincided fortuitously; for example, when a man becomes depressed after the death of a distant relative. Jaspers (1963, p. 392) suggested three criteria for deciding whether a psychological state is a reaction to events. First, there must be precipitating factors that seem adequate in severity and are closely related in time to the onset of the psychological state. Secondly, there must be a clear connection between the nature of the precipitating factors and the content of the psychological disorder (in the example just given, the man should be preoccupied with ideas concerning his distant relative). Thirdly, the psychological state should disappear when the precipitating factors are removed (unless, of course, it can be shown that perpetuating factors are acting to maintain it). These three criteria are quite useful in clinical practice, though they can be difficult to apply in many cases (particularly the second criterion).

Understanding and explanation

As already mentioned, aetiological statements about individual patients must combine knowledge derived from research on groups of patients, and intuitions derived from everyday experience. These two ways of making sense of psychiatric disorders have been called, respectively, *Erklären* and *Verstehen* by Jaspers (1963, p. 302). The first of these German terms is usually translated as 'explanation', and the second as 'understanding' (although 'making intelligible' may convey the meaning better than the latter). Explanation refers to the sort of causative statement that is sought in the natural sciences. It is exemplified by the statement that a patient's aggressive behaviour has occurred because he has a brain tumour. Understanding refers to an intuitive grasp of a natural connection between events in a person's life and his psychological state. It is exemplified by the statement that a patient became aggressive because his wife was insulted by a neighbour.

These distinctions are reasonably clear when we consider an individual patient. Confusion sometimes arises when attempts are made to generalize from insights obtained in a single case to widely applicable principles. Understanding may then be mistaken for exaplanation. Jaspers suggested that some psychoanalytic ideas are special kinds of intuitive understanding that are derived from the detailed study of individuals, and then applied generally. They are not explanations that can be tested scientifically. They are more akin to insights into human nature that can be gained from reading great works of literature. Such insights are of great value in conducting human affairs. It would be wrong to neglect them in psychiatry, but equally wrong to confuse them with statements of a scientific kind.

The aetiology of a single case

A discussion of how to make an aetiological formulation was given in Chapter 2 (p. 61). An example was given of a woman in her thirties who had become increasingly depressed. The formulation showed how aetiological factors can be grouped under the headings of predisposing, precipitating, and perpetuating factors. It also showed how information from scientific investigations (in this case genetics) can be combined with an intuitive understanding of personality and the likely effects of family problems on the patient. The reader may find it helpful to re-read the formulation on p. 62 before continuing with this chapter.

APPROACHES TO AETIOLOGY

Before considering the contribution that different scientific disciplines can make to psychiatric aetiology, attention needs to be given to the kinds of aetiological theory that have been employed in psychiatry.

The 'medical model'

A model is a device for ordering information. Like a theory, it seeks to explain certain phenomena, but does so in a broad and comprehensive way that cannot readily be proved false. Several models are used in psychiatric aetiology, but the so-called medical model is the most prominent. It represents a general strategy of research that has proved useful in medicine, particularly in studying infectious diseases. A disease entity is identified in terms of a consistent pattern of symptoms, a characteristic clinical course and specific post-mortem findings. When an entity has been identified in this way, a set of necessary and sufficient causes is sought. In the case of tuberculosis, for example, the necessary cause is the tubercle bacillus, but it is not by itself sufficient. The tubercle bacillus in conjunction with either poor nutrition or low resistance is sufficient cause.

This medical model has also been useful in psychiatry, though not for all conditions. It is most relevant to organic syndromes, the best example being general paralysis of the insane, which is caused by syphilitic infection of the brain. It is least appropriate to the neuroses, which seem more like an exaggeration of normal psychological reactions to events. Nowadays the medical model might be better named the organic model, particularly because general medicine now adopts a broader aetiological framework including the idea that some disorders are quantitative variations from the normal.

Reductionist and non-reductionist models

Two broad categories of explanatory model can be recognized. Reductionist models seek to understand causation by tracing back to simpler and simpler earlier stages. Examples are the medical model just described, and the psycho-analytic model. This type of model can be exemplified by the statement that the cause of schizophrenia lies in a disordered neurotransmission in a specific area of the brain.

Non-reductionist models try to relate problems to wider rather than narrower issues. The explanatory models used in sociology are generally of this kind. In psychiatry, this type of model can be exemplified by the statement that the cause of schizophrenia lies in the family to which the patient belongs: he is only the most conspicuous element in a disordered group of people.

It is unlikely that psychiatric aetiology can be approached by using either of these models exclusively. Different types of disorder are likely to require different kinds of explanation.

THE CONTRIBUTION OF SCIENTIFIC DISCIPLINES TO PSYCHIATRIC AETIOLOGY

Among the disciplines that have contributed to knowledge of psychiatric aetiology the main groups are: clinical studies and epidemiology; genetics, biochemistry, pharmacology, physiology, and neuropathology; experimental psychology, ethology, and psychoanalysis. In this section each group is discussed in turn, and the following questions are asked: What sort of problem in psychiatric aetiology can be answered by each discipline? How, in general, does each discipline attempt to answer the questions? Are there any particular difficulties in applying its methods to psychiatric disorders?

Clinical descriptive investigations

Before reviewing more elaborate scientific approaches to aetiology, attention is drawn to the continuing value of simple clinical investigations. Psychiatry was built on such studies. For example the view that schizophrenia and the affective disorders are likely to have separate causes depends ultimately on the careful descriptive studies and follow-up enquiries carried out by earlier generations of psychiatrists.

Only two examples can be given here of the many clinical investigations that have contributed in important ways to knowledge. Both are from the British literature but similar examples could have been chosen from the literature of continental Europe or America.

Anyone who doubts the value of clinical descriptive studies should read the paper by Aubrey Lewis on 'melancholia' (Lewis 1934). The paper describes a detailed investigation of the symptoms and signs of 61 cases of severe depressive disorder. It provided the most complete account in the English language, and it remains unsurpassed. It is an invaluable source of information about the clinical features of depressive disorders untreated by modern methods. Lewis' careful observations pointed to unsolved problems including the nature of retardation, the relation of depersonalization to affective changes, the presence of manic symptoms, and the validity of the classification of depressive disorders into reactive and endogenous groups. None of these problems has yet been solved completely, but the analysis by Lewis was important in focusing attention on them.

The second example is the clinical follow-up study by Roth (1955). Elderly psychiatric patients were classified on the basis of their symptoms into five diagnostic groups: affective disorder, late paraphrenia, acute or subacute delirious states, senile dementia, and arterioslcerotic dementia. These groups were found to differ in their course. Two years later, about two-thirds of the patients with affective psychoses had recovered, about four-fifths of those with senile dementia and almost as many with arteriosclerotic dementia had died; over a half of the patients with paraphrenia were alive but still in hospital; and of those with acute confusional states, half had recovered and half had died. These findings confirmed the value of the original diagnoses, and refuted the earlier belief that affective and paranoid disorders in old age were part of a single degenerative disorder that could also present as dementia. This investigation clearly illustrates how careful clinical follow-up can clarify issues about aetiology.

Although many opportunities for this kind of research have been taken already, it does not follow that clinical investigation is no longer worthwhile. For example, a recent clinical study describing the syndrome of bulimia nervosa has aetiological implications (Russell 1979). Well-conducted clinical enquiries are likely to retain an important place in psychiatric research for many years to come.

Epidemiology

Psychiatric epidemiology is mainly used in two ways – to measure the prevalence of psychiatric disorders in different groups of people and to define psychiatric syndromes. To a less extent it can also be used to investigate aetiology. It does so by examining the associations between psychiatric disorders and factors in the environment or between psychiatric disorders and other psychiatric or physical disorders. So far the main contribution of epidemiology has been to identify questions for further research. Numerous surveys have examined the associations between psychiatric disorder and age, sex, marital status, social class, economic status, and dwelling place. Although such factors sometimes contribute to causation, generally it is only justifiable to regard them as correlates of disorder, pointing to further enquiries. In the United States Hollingshead and Redlich (1958) showed that schizophrenia was eleven times more frequent in social class V than in social class I. In itself this finding throws no direct light on aetiology. It does suggest studies of other factors associated with social class (for example housing of poor quality). It also raises questions about the interpretation of associations; for example, do schizophrenics drift into the lower classes because they are disabled, or were they in the lower classes before the disorder began? Thus this study illustrates two important aspects of epidemiological research: first, the importance of specifying what variables such as social class mean in terms of living conditions; and second, the difficulty in interpreting the direction of apparent causal relationships.

Other problems of method are met in psychiatric epidemiology. One is the problem of making reliable and valid diagnoses among people interviewed in community surveys. A second problem concerns case finding. Two methods are used: the first is to enumerate all cases known to medical or other agencies (declared cases); the second is to search for both declared and undeclared cases by questioning people in the community. For most purposes hospital admission rates are unreliable, because they are affected by many extraneous variables such as the geographical accessibility of hospitals, attitudes of doctors, admission policies, and the law relating to compulsory admissions.

A third problem is that some aetiological factors in mental disorder are presumed to act many years before the illness began. Hence there is a need for longitudinal studies, in which groups of people are studied for many years. Such studies are difficult to carry out because many people move and may be difficult to find again.

Several epidemiological studies have focused on place of residence. Generally high rates of schizophrenia have been found amongst people living in districts with poor housing and a large proportion of single-person households; whilst high rates of manic-depressive psychosis and neurosis have been found amongst those living in more prosperous districts (see, for example Hare 1956). Results such as these are difficult to interpret, since it is not clear whether they are directly due to the neighbourhood environment, or whether they are mediated through social factors such as methods of child rearing or patterns of marriage. Moreover, the findings do not confirm that there is an effect at all; they could equally well reflect the movement of ill people into disadvantaged areas.

As already mentioned, epidemiological studies also examine associations between disorders. For example, it has been found that suicide is more frequent among epileptics than in the general population (see Chapter 13). Information of this kind points to further enquiries to determine the cause. Thus the association between suicide and epilepsy might be explained by an excess of depressive disorder among epileptics.

Life events research

This research uses epidemiological methods to examine the associations between illness and certain kinds of event in a person's life. The subject is currently of considerable interest, and will therefore be discussed at greater length than would otherwise by appropriate.

Wolff studied the morbidity experience of several hundred people over long periods of time. He found that episodes of psychiatric and physical illness occurred in clusters that appeared to be related to periods of environmental change (see Wolff 1962). Although this study used highly subjective measures of life-difficulties, it drew attention to the clustering of illnesses in the life span. Rahe and his colleagues (Rahe *et al.* 1967; Holmes and Rahe 1967) attempted to introduce quantification into the study of life-changes. They compiled a list of

41 life-changes concerned with occupation, residence, finance, recreations, religion, and family relationships. The items were chosen regardless of whether the change was considered to be desirable or undesirable, and whether or not it was under the person's direct control. Each item was given a weighting, according to the estimated extent of the change and of the adjustment required in the individual. Thus the death of a spouse was given a score of 100 life-change units, whilst a spell of leave was given 13 life-change units. An intensive study in the United States Navy (Rahe *et al.* 1970) showed that men with the highest scores for life-changes developed more illnesses of all kinds. In other words it appeared that the risk of developing mental and physical illnesses was greater after a period of psychological or social change than after an uneventful period.

Since this early work, the study of life-changes has been developed, and the term **life-events** has come into common use. Various modifications of method have been introduced:

1. In order to reduce memory distortion, there is restriction of the period over which events are to be recalled.

2. Efforts are made to date the onset of psychiatric illness as accurately as possible.

3. Attempts are made to exclude events that are not clearly independent of the illness, and might have been brought about as a result of the developing illness, for example, losing a job because of poor performance.

4. Additional methods of rating events have been developed; for example, scores are assigned by assessing the meaning of events to the individual patient.

5. Events are characterized in terms not only of their severity but also of their nature (such as losses or threats).

An example is provided by an investigation of depressive illness. Paykel *et al.* (1969) studied 185 depressed patients, who were compared with controls matched on social and demographic variables. A check-list was used to record life-events occurring in the six months immediately before the onset of depression. Events involving a departure of a person from the immediate social field of the respondent ('exit events') were reported by 25 per cent of the depressives but only 5 per cent of the controls. The differences, which were significant at the 1 per cent level, appear impressive in magnitude.

Paykel (1978) has pointed out that this finding is less impressive if one considers the general population as well as the case-control study. Accurate figures are not available for the incidence of depression of clinical intensity in the general population. Using an estimate of 2 per cent for new cases over the six-month period, Paykel calculated what would follow amongst 10 000 subjects in the general population. There would of course be 200 new depressives and 9800 non-depressives. The latter can be called 'normals', although they would include some old cases of depression. From the survey results, an exit would have occurred in 5 per cent of normals, that is 490 people, and in 25 per cent of the depressives, or 50 people. The total number of subjects to experience exits would be 490 plus 50, or 540. Only 50 of these (9 per cent) would become depressed. In other words, rather less than one-tenth of subjects who experience exits become depressed; most do not. The greater part of the variance in determining depression must therefore be attributed to something else.

This example has been quoted at length because it illustrates the methodological difficulties of life-events research. Paykel argues that some more appropriate means of quantifying causation is required. He suggests that an epidemiological measure known as relative risk can be approximately adapted for retrospective controlled studies. Brown *et al.* (1973*a, b*) have suggested another measure (the brought forward time) which is a mathematical formula for deriving the average amount of time by which an otherwise spontaneous onset may be considered to have been advanced by life-events.

Studies of the kind just described focus largely on acute events such as loss of job or the departure of a cherished person. However, cumulative or chronic environmental factors may also be important determinants of psychiatric breakdown. Thus, in some patients, depressive illness appears to follow a period of cumulative stressful factors, including financial worries, marital disharmony, or problems with children. An event may then act as a 'last straw' that precipitates an illness. A slightly different idea has been proposed by Brown and Harris (1978). They suggest that some circumstances of life can either protect a person against stressful life events or make him more vulnerable to them, but cannot themselves act as stressors. Amongst women, for example, having a confidant to share problems with is protective; having the care of several small children is thought to make women more vulnerable, though it does not itself induce depression. These ideas are discussed further on page 206.

Genetics

Genetic investigations are concerned with three issues – the relative contributions of genetic and environmental factors to aetiology; the mode of inheritance of disorders that have a hereditary basis; and the mechanisms of inheritance. In psychiatry, important advances have been made with the first two issues, but so far little progress has been made with the third.

The contribution of genetic factors

This is assessed by risk studies carried out in three ways – within families, between twins, or among people who have been adopted. In **family-risk studies** the investigator determines the risk of a psychiatric condition among the relatives of affected persons, and compares it with expectancy in the general population. (The affected persons are usually referred to as index cases or **probands.**) Such studies require a sample selected in a strictly defined way. Moreover, it is not sufficient to ascertain the current prevalence of a psychiatric condition among the relatives, because some may go on to develop the condition later in life. For this reason, investigators use corrected figures known as **expectancy rates.**

Family-risk studies have been used extensively. Examples will be found in the chapters on affective disorders (see p. 203) and schizophrenia (see p. 246). Since these studies cannot distinguish between inheritance and effects of the family environment, they are the least satisfactory way of determining the genetic contribution. They are useful chiefly in pointing to the need for other kinds of investigation.

In **twin studies** the investigator seeks to separate genetic and environmental influences by comparing concordance rates in uniovular (monozygous – MZ) and binovular (dizygous – DZ) twins. Such studies depend crucially on the accurate determination of zygosity. If concordance for a psychiatric disorder is substantially higher in MZ twins than in DZ twins a major genetic component is presumed. More precise estimates of the relative importance of heredity and environment can be made by comparisons between MZ twins reared together and MZ twins reared apart. A high concordance between MZ twins reared apart is strong evidence for a genetic aetiology. An example of such studies will be found in the chapter on schizophrenia (see p. 247).

Adoption studies provide another useful method of separating biological and environmental influences. These studies are concerned with children who, since early infancy, have been reared by non-related adoptive parents. Two main comparisons can be made. First, the frequency of the disorder can be compared between adopted children whose biological parents had the illness, and adopted children whose biological parents did not have the illness. If there is a genetic cause, the rate will be greater in the former. Secondly, the frequency of the disorder can be compared between the biological parents of adopted children who have an illness, and parents who reared the children. If there is a genetic cause, the rate will be greater in the former. Such studies may be affected by a number of biases, such as the reasons why the child was adopted, non-random assignment of the children on socioeconomic status, and the effects on adoptive parents of raising a difficult child. An example is provided by the studies on schizophrenia reviewed on page 248.

The mode of inheritance

This is assessed by applying special statistical models to pedigree or family-risk data. One model (segregation analysis) allows comparisons between the observed proportion of affected relatives and the proportion expected on a given model. Another (the threshold model) postulates a graded attribute of 'liability', shared by all the persons in a given population. Liability is assumed to be distributed normally in the general population and, with a higher mean value, among the relatives of affected persons. A threshold is defined, above which the disorder is manifest, the position of the threshold being a function of the prevalence of the disorder in each group. Sophisticated refinements of this method make it possible to suggest the mode of inheritance; for example, whether by single-gene transmission or polygenic transmission. Attempts to study the inheritance of psychiatric disorders in these ways have led to equivocal results.

Linkage studies

The gene for colour blindness was the first to be assigned to a specific chromosome; since then more than 200 genes have been localized on human chromosomes. These genes can serve as markers for other genes whose position is still uncertain. If the disease in question is regularly associated with one whose gene locus is known, it can be inferred that there is some linkage. By studying family pedigrees, and by using special mathematical models, it is possible to estimate the likelihood and closeness of such linkage.

Cytogenetic studies

These are concerned with identifying structural abnormalities in chromosomes and associating them with disease. In psychiatry the most important example is Down's syndrome (mongolism). In this condition two kinds of abnormality have been detected: in the first there is an additional chromosome (trisomy); in the second the chromosome number is normal, but one chromosome is unusually large because a segment of another chromosome is attached to it (translocation) (see p. 701).

Biochemical studies

These studies can be directed either to the causes of disease, or to the mechanisms by which disease produces its effects. The **methods of biochemical investigation** are too numerous to consider here, and it is assumed that the medical reader has some knowledge of them. The main aim here is to consider some of the problems of using biochemical methods to investigate psychiatric disorders.

The first problem is that the living human brain is not accessible to detailed biochemical study by ethically acceptable methods. Moreover, because most psychiatric disorders do not lead to death (other than suicide), post-mortem material is not widely available except among the elderly. Even indirect studies are difficult. Concentrations of substances in lumbar cerebrospinal fluid have an uncertain relationship to their concentrations in the brain. Concentrations in blood are even more indirectly related to those in the brain, and concentrations in the urine are more remote still.

The second problem is that in animals there is no obvious parallel to mental disorder in man. Attempts have been made to find models for behaviour seen in mental illness, for example by subjecting animals to extreme stress, but none is convincing. As pointed out in the next section, the most useful biochemical studies in animals are those linked with pharmacological investigations.

The third problem is that even when biochemical changes have been found in mental illness, it is difficult to know whether they are causal. They could be the result of alterations in diet or activity secondary to the illness, to the effects of the drugs used in treatment, or to stress responses to the experimental procedure. Moreover, even if the biochemical changes are connected with the illness itself, they may still be effects rather than a cause.

Some of the findings of biochemical research are given in subsequent chapters, especially those on affective disorders and schizophrenia. At this point a few examples will be given of the different kinds of investigation. **Post-mortem studies of the brain** provide the most direct evidence of chemical changes within it. Unfortunately, interpretation of the findings is difficult because it must be established that any changes in the concentrations of neuro-transmitters or enzymes did not occur after death. Moreover, because psychiatric disorders do not lead to death directly, the ultimate cause of death is another condition (often bronchopneumonia, or the effects of a drug overdose) that could have caused the observed changes in the brain. Even if this possibility can be ruled out, it is still possible that the chemical findings are the results of treatment rather than of disease. For example, in schizophrenic patients the density of dopamine receptors has been found to be increased in the nucleus accumbens and caudate nucleus (Owen *et al.* 1978). This finding might be interpreted as supporting the hypothesis that schizophrenia is caused by changes in dopamine function in these areas of the brain. The finding could equally be the result of long-term treatment with antipsychotic drugs, which block dopamine receptors and might lead to a compensatory increase of receptors. Owen *et al.* provided some evidence against this alternative when they demonstrated similar changes in two patients who had apparently never received antipsychotic drugs; but the point is still unsettled. In any case, even if it is eventually possible to rule out the effects of treatment, it must still be shown that the observed changes in receptors are not merely a compensatory mechanism to balance a primary disorder in another neurotransmitter system.

Even more serious problems arise when attempts are made to infer changes in the brain from **studies of cerebrospinal fluid, blood, and urine**. There are scientific doubts whether changes in the composition of lumbar c.s.f. represent changes in the brain. There are also ethical limitations on the circumstances when c.s.f should be obtained from psychiatric patients. Ingenious attempts have been made to infer biochemical events in the brain from measurements of substances in the blood. For example it is known that the rate of synthesis of brain 5-hydroxytryptamine (5HT) depends on the concentration of tryptophan in the brain; and that the latter is in turn largely determined by the concentration of unbound tryptophan in plasma. Findings of lowered free plasma tryptophan among depressed patients have therefore been interpreted as supporting the hypothesis that depressive illness is characterized by – and may be the result of – low concentrations of 5HT at crucial sites in the brain. Subsequent work has not confirmed these original findings consistently (see Green and Costain

1979). Even if the findings were to be confirmed, it would be hazardous to draw conclusions about events in the brain from such indirect evidence. The real advances that have followed investigations of blood and urine have been in the study not of mental illness but of mental subnormality. A number of rare metabolic disorders have been identified which are associated with serious forms of mental retardation. Phenylketonuria is the best known example. In these disorders, metabolites in blood and urine do give an accurate reflection of biochemical processes in the brain (see Chapter 21).

Pharmacology

The study of effective treatment of disease can often throw light on aetiology. In psychiatry because of the great problems of studying the brain directly, research workers have studied the actions of effective psychotropic drugs in the hope that the latter might indicate the biochemical abnormalities in disease. Such an approach must, of course, be used cautiously. If an effective drug blocks a particular transmitter system, it cannot be concluded that the disease is caused by an excess of that transmitter. The example of Parkinsonism makes this clear; anticholinergic drugs modify the symptoms but the disease is due to a deficiency in dopaminergic transmission, not an excess of cholinergic transmission.

It is assumed here that the general methods of neuropharmacology are familiar to the reader, and attention is focused on the particular difficulties of using them in psychiatry. There are two main problems. First, most psychotropic drugs have more than one action, and it is often difficult to decide which is relevant to the therapeutic effects. For example, although lithium carbonate has a large number of known pharmacological effects, it has so far been impossible to find one that explains its remarkable effect of stabilizing the mood of manic depressive patients.

The second difficulty arises because the therapeutic effects of many psychotropic drugs are slow to develop, while most pharmacological effects identified in the laboratory are quick to appear. For example, it has been suggested that the beneficial effect of antidepressant drugs depends on alterations in the re-uptake of transmitter at presynaptic neurones. However changes in re-uptake occur quickly, while the therapeutic effects are usually delayed for about two weeks.

The assumption is usually made that, provided a drug can pass the blood–brain barrier, its effects will be much the same in the brain as in the rest of the body. This allows inferences about activity in the brain to be drawn from experiments on peripheral tissues. Recently, interest has focused on the effects of drugs on blood platelets. Platelets are of interest because they have some receptor sites that behave similarly to those on nerve cells in the brain.

Endocrinology

Endocrine studies can be employed directly to relate concentrations of circulating hormones to disease states. For example, plasma levels of free and total cortisol are high in depressed patients because cortisol is produced at an increased rate (see Sachar 1982). This cortisol production might be secondary to the stressful experience of being ill, or it might be part of the causation of the depression. Tests of endocrine regulation have been used in an attempt to distinguish these possibilities. For example, some patients with a depressive disorder show an abnormal response to dexamethasone. This glucocorticoid normally suppresses the output of cortisol and its effect is greatest if given about midnight, when the 'programme' for the next day's output of cortisol is determined. In normal subjects, this suppression lasts throughout the following day, but in some depressed patients it is less sustained. This difference can be interpreted as showing that some depressed patients have an abnormality in the control mechanisms for cortisol production, rather than a simple increase in the circulating concentration of the hormone (see Beumont 1979 for a review).

Endocrine measurements can also be used indirectly to investigate brain function in psychiatric disorders. The connection between the two depends on the fact that the mechanisms controlling the output of hormone releasing factors involve neuronal systems that utilize transmitters such as dopamine and 5HT. From changes in the concentration of circulating hormones, it can be inferred that there are changes in the output of the corresponding releasing or inhibiting factors, and from the latter it can be inferred that there are changes in the transmitter systems that control them. Prolactin provides an example. It is controlled by an inhibiting factor that depends in part on dopaminergic neurones. For this reason prolactin levels increase when dopaminergic systems are blocked by neuroleptics (blocking an inhibitory mechanism will lead to greater release of the hormone). Conversely, it can be predicted that if dopaminergic systems are overactive in schizophrenia, there might be decreased concentrations of circulating prolactin in untreated patients. Such decreased concentrations have not been found (Johnstone *et al.* 1977). This does not, of course, disprove the hypothesis; it merely shows that, if there is a disorder of dopaminergic transmission, it is localized and does not affect the neuronal systems involved in prolactin release.

Physiology

Physiological methods can be used to investigate the cerebral and peripheral disorders associated with disease states. Several methods have been used: studies of cerebral blood flow, particularly in chronic organic syndromes; electroencephalographic (EEG) studies; and a variety of psychophysiological methods, including measurements of pulse rate, blood pressure, blood flow, skin conductance, and muscle activity. These psychophysiological measures can be interpreted in at least two ways. The first interpretation is straightforward. The data are used as information about the activity of peripheral organs in disease; for example, to determine whether electromyographic (EMG) activity is increased in the scalp muscles of patients who complain of tension headaches. The second interpretation depends on the assumption that peripheral measurements can be used to infer changes in the state of arousal of the central nervous system. Thus increase in skin conductance, pulse rate, and blood pressure are taken to indicate greater 'arousal'.

An example of this indirect use of physiological methods is provided by the work of Lader and Wing (1966), who showed that autonomic and EMG activity is high in anxious patients. They also demonstrated that the response of these systems to repeated auditory stimulation habituates more slowly in anxious patients than in normal subjects. From this they inferred that central nervous system arousal also habituates more slowly. This suggests a way in which anxiety states could be self-maintaining. If the increment of arousal caused by a stressful event fades away abnormally slowly in anxious patients, arousal might not return to normal by the time the next stimulus is encountered. In this way, a persistent state of high arousal might develop.

Neuropathology

Neuropathological studies attempt to answer the question whether a structural change in the brain (localized or diffuse) accompanies a particular kind of mental disorder. In the past, many post-mortem investigations were carried out on the brains of patients who had suffered from schizophrenia or affective disorders. No changes were found. It was therefore assumed that these were disorders of function rather than of structure (hence the name functional psychosis is sometimes used as a collective name for these conditions). Recent neurochemical studies (mentioned above) can be regarded as a logical extension of this kind of enquiry, but at a different level of organization.

Neuropathological investigations have an obvious application to the aetiology of dementia. Another important finding has been the post-mortem identification of lesions of the mamillary bodies in the brains of patients who had the amnesic syndrome. In this syndrome there is no general dementia, but profound disorder of memory (see p. 299).

Experimental and clinical psychology

A characteristic feature of the psychological approach to psychiatric aetiology is the idea that there is continuity between the normal and the abnormal. This idea leads to investigations that attempt to explain psychiatric abnormalities in terms of processes determining normal behaviour. An example is research into learning mechanisms as causes of neuroses (see Chapter 6).

A second characteristic of the psychological approach is its concern with the interaction between the person and his environment. The psychological approach differs from the social approach in being concerned less with environmental variables, and more with the person's ways of processing information coming from the external environment and from his own body. Some of these ideas will become clearer when coping mechanisms are discussed later in this section.

A third characteristic of psychological research into mental illness is an emphasis on factors maintaining abnormal behaviour. Psychologists are less likely to regard behaviour disorders as resulting from internal disease processes, and more likely to assume that persisting behaviour is maintained by reinforcement. This has led, for example, to research findings suggesting that some abnormal behaviour of chronic schizophrenic patients is maintained by social reinforcement, and that some anxiety neuroses are maintained by avoidance of situations that provoke anxiety.

Experimental psychology, more than neurochemistry or neurophysiology, makes use of broad theoretical schemes. Familiar examples are operant and Pavlovian conditioning. Such schemes are useful in providing a framework for experimental work, and can be used to construct plausible explanations of neurotic disorders (for example, Mowrer 1950). So far these schemes have not proved particularly useful.

Experimental studies using the methods of psychological research are well exemplified by studies linking depressive mood change in normal subjects and depressive disorder in patients. These studies use standard tests of memory to investigate recall during different mood states. In normal people, if an unhappy mood is induced experimentally, unhappy events are recalled more easily than happy events; the reverse is true when a happy mood is induced (Teasdale *et al.* 1980). Similarly, among depressed patients, the ease of recall of unhappy events relative to happy events increases with increasing severity of depression (Clarke and Teasdale 1983). Given that thinking about unhappy events increases depressive mood, this series of experiments suggests that a vicious circle might be set up in depressive disorders. Such a process might prolong the mood disorder most in patients whose memory of past experience included an excess of unhappy events.

Coping mechanisms

This term is applied to certain aspects of the ways in which people deal with changes in their environment. It is used in a narrow sense and a wide sense. Thus, some psychologists limit the word to those responses to a stressor that reduce any stress reaction that might otherwise ensue. Others apply it more widely to any response whether or not it reduces stress.

Coping mechanisms have two components: internal events and observable behaviour. After bereavement a person's coping mechanisms might be: first, a return to former religious beliefs (an internal mechanism) and second, joining a social club to combat loneliness (an observable behaviour). Research into coping mechanisms is much concerned with the ways in which meaning is attached to events. The same event, for example a change of job, can be seen as a threat by one person and as a challenge by another. It is presumed that the meaning attached to an event by a person is an important determinant of his response to it.

Ethology

Ethology is concerned with the observation and description of behaviour, particularly behaviour that appears to be innate. Ethology has contributed indirectly to psychiatric aetiology by suggesting simple techniques of observation that have been valuable in studying the behaviour of children. Another contribution has been the study of critical periods of development, during which the learning of a particular behaviour takes place more readily than at any other time.

Ethological studies of primates have examined the effects of separating infants from their mothers. When the primate mother is removed and the environment remains otherwise unchanged, the infant first makes frequent distress calls, and then becomes active, apparently searching for her. Soon this activity decreases and the infant shuffles about in a hunched posture, calling less often. If the mother is returned to the infant, the two usually unite immediately. The infant's hunched posture soon disappears, and within two weeks he is as active as before the separation. When the separation is longer, the infant takes longer to readjust after its mother returns. Comparable methods of observation have been used to study human infants and young children (see for example Blurton-Jones 1972). Not surprisingly, there appear to be both parallels and important differences between monkey and man.

Psychoanalysis

The method of investigation used in psychoanalysis differs from the methods considered so far in that it was developed specifically for the study of psychiatric disorders. It arose from clinical experience and not from work in the basic sciences. Psychoanalysis is characterized by a particularly elaborate and comprehensive theory of both normal and abnormal mental functioning. Compared with experimental psychology, it is much more concerned with the irrational parts of mental activity. Because psychoanalytic theory provides a comprehensive range of explanations for clinical phenomena, it has a wide appeal. However, the features that make it all-embracing also make it impervious to scientific testing.

Freud originated psychoanalytic theory, but many other workers contributed to it or constructed alternative theories. This section refers only to Freud's theory and not to the contributions of these other analysts, which are described elsewhere in the book. This section also focuses on the basic ideas of psychoanalysis; hypotheses about particular syndromes are discussed in other chapters.

It is recommended that this account be supplemented by reading some of Freud's original writings, for example the New Introductory Lectures or the volume on Psychopathology (both published in the Pelican Freud Library). It is also valuable to study a critical evaluation of psychoanalytic theory (for example Farrell 1981 or Dalbiez 1941).

Most of the data of psychoanalytic enquiry are obtained in the course of psychoanalytic treatment. They consist of an account given by the patient of his thoughts, fantasies, and dreams, together with his memories of childhood experiences. By adopting a passive role, the analyst tries to ensure that the material of the interviews is the result of the patient's free associations, and not of his own preconceptions. The analyst also interprets some of the patient's statements and behaviour in terms of analytic theory. In analytic writings it is sometimes difficult to distinguish clearly between the patient's statements and the analyst's interpretations.

As pointed out earlier in this chapter, an important distinction can be made between understanding and explanation. In the sense of this distinction psychoanalysis is a highly elaborate form of understanding which makes psychiatric disorders more intelligible. It does not lead to explanatory hypotheses that can be tested experimentally – although attempts have been made to test some of the low-level hypotheses (see Fisher and Greenberg 1977).

Farrell (1981) has pointed out that psychoanalysis is an example of a broad theory of a kind found in other branches of knowledge. Such theories can be useful in science by providing a framework within which other ideas can be developed. Darwin's theory of evolution is an example of a useful theory of this kind. To be useful, such theories must be able to incorporate new observations as they come along. Darwinian theory survives partly because it has proved compatible with later observations from genetics and from work on the fossil record. On the other hand, psychoanalytic theory has not proved compatible with advances in the neurosciences in such a satisfactory way. Its present status is more akin to that of the insights into human nature provided by great creative writers. These insights succeed in deepening our understanding of man, but they are not part of scientific knowledge. Psychiatrists need a wide understanding of human nature. They can achieve this from some of the ideas of psychoanalysis, but they can also achieve it from great works of literature.

At this point a summary will be presented of the main features of Freud's theory. The summary is too short to do full justice to Freud's ideas, but long in relation to the space devoted to some other methods of enquiry.

Many of the ideas in the theory were current before Freud began his psychological studies (see Sulloway 1979) but he succeeded in combining them ingeniously. A central feature was Freud's elaborate concept of the unconscious mind. He supposed that all mental processes originated there. Some of these processes were allowed to enter the conscious mind freely (for example, sensations), some not at all (the unconscious proper), and some occasionally (most memories, which made up the 'preconscious'). The unconscious mind, according to Freud, had three characteristics that were important in the genesis of neurosis: it was divorced from reality; it was dynamic in that it contained powerful forces; and it was in conflict with the conscious mind. These three characteristics will be discussed in turn.

The unconscious mind was divorced from reality in several ways. It contained flagrant contradictions and paradoxes, and it tended to telescope situations and fantasies that were widely separated in time. These features were well illustrated, in Freud's view, by dream-analysis. He believed that the manifest content of a dream (what the dreamer remembered) could be analysed back to a latent content, which was an infantile wish. The sleeper was thought to perform 'dream work' to translate the latent to the manifest content. He did this by using a series of mechanisms such as: condensation (several images fused into one); displacement (of feelings from an essential to non-essential features of an object); and secondary elaboration (rearrangement of the assembled elements). Freud attached importance to this dream theory because he supposed the composition of neurotic symptoms to be like that of dreams, though with greater secondary elaboration.

Secondly the unconscious mind was dynamic; that is, it contained impulses that were kept in equilibrium by a series of checks and balances. In Freud's early writings, these impulses were regarded as entirely sexual. Later he placed more emphasis on aggressive impulses. Sexual wishes were supposed to be active even in infancy, receding by about the age of four and then remaining latent until re-emergence at puberty. In Freud's view, psychosexual development not only began early but was long and complicated. The first stage of organization was oral; that is, the sexual drive was activated by stimulation of the mouth by sucking and touching with the lips. The second stage was anal, that is the drive was activated by expelling or retaining faeces. Only in the third stage did the genitals become the primary source of sexual energy. Sometimes these stages were not passed through smoothly. The libido (the energy of the sexual instincts) could become fixated (partially arrested) at one of the early stages. When this happened the person would tend to engage in infantile patterns of behaviour or regress to such patterns under stress. In this way the point of fixation determined the nature of any neurosis that developed later in life.

As libido developed, not only was it activated in these three successive ways, but its object was also supposed to change. Self-love came first, to be followed in both boys and girls by love of the mother. Next, still in infancy, boys focused their sexual wishes more intensely upon the mother while developing hostile feelings towards the father (the Oedipus complex). Girls developed the reverse attachments. These attachments came to an end through repression of sexual impulses. As a result the capacity to feel shame and disgust developed and the child passed into the latency period. Finally, at puberty the sexual impulses emerged again, and were directed into relationships with other adults.

The third aspect of the unconscious mind was its struggle against the conscious mind. This conflict was regarded as giving rise to anxiety that could persist throughout life and generate neurotic symptoms. One of Freud's lasting contributions was his idea that anxiety could be reduced by a variety of defence mechanisms, which could be discerned at times in the behaviour of healthy people. These mechanisms are considered on pp. 353–4.

Freud's ideas have had considerable influence in certain countries. In Great Britain most psychiatrists take the view (which is shared by the authors of this book) that some of the basic ideas are useful in understanding patients, for example the ideas about defence mechanisms; but that the details of the theory are generally unhelpful, either as an aetiological explanation of clinical syndromes or as a guide to practice. Much of the theory is expressed in an elaborate series of metaphors which, as explained above, cannot be subjected to verification.

It is stressed again that it is impossible to do justice to Freud's theories in the space of this chapter, and it is important to read some of his original papers.

Relationship of this chapter to the psychiatric syndromes

This chapter has reviewed several diverse approaches to aetiology. It may be easier for the reader to put these approaches in perspective when reading the chapters on the different psychiatric syndromes. A useful first step would be to read the section on the aetiology of depression on pages 202–14, and also the paper on depressive disorders by Akiskal and McKinney (see reading list below).

FURTHER READING

Akiskal, H.S. and McKinney, W.T. (1975). Overview of recent research in depression. *Archives of general Psychiatry* **32**, 285–305.

Farrell, B.A. (1981). *The standing of psychoanalysis.* Oxford University Press.

Freud, S. (1918). *From the history of an infantile neurosis (the 'wolf man').* Reprinted in Penguin Freud Library, Vol. 9, pp. 227–366. Penguin, Harmondsworth.

——(1924a). *Neurosis and psychosis.* Reprinted in Penguin Freud Library. Vol. 10, pp.209–18. Penguin, Harmondsworth.

—— (1924b). *The loss of reality in neurosis and psychosis.* Reprinted in Penguin Freud Library, Vol. 10. pp. 219–29. Penguin, Harmondsworth.

—— (1916–17). *Introductory lectures on psychoanalysis.* Reprinted in Penguin Freud Library, Vol. 1. Penguin, Harmondsworth.

Jaspers, K. (1963). *General psychopathology* (trans. J. Hoenig and M.W. Hamilton) pp. 301–11 (The psychology of meaning); 355–64 (The basic law of psychological understanding); and 383–99 (Pathological psychogenic reactions). Manchester University Press.

5. Personality disorder

The term personality refers to enduring qualities of an individual shown in his ways of behaving in a wide variety of circumstances. All doctors should be able to assess personality so that they can predict how patients are likely to behave when ill. The psychiatrist shares this general concern about the personality of his patients but his interests go further. This is because among psychiatric patients personality not only determines how they react when ill; it can also prepare the ground for illness and can sometimes be mistaken for illness.

Features of personality make some people more vulnerable to develop neurotic illness when experiencing stressful events. Someone who has always worried over minor problems is more likely to develop an anxiety state when faced with difficulties that would not affect another person in the same way. With this degree of vulnerability in the personality, abnormal behaviour only occurs in response to stressful events.

In more abnormal personalities, unusual behaviour occurs even in the absence of stressful events. At times, these anomalies of behaviour may be so great that it is difficult to decide, solely on the patient's state at the time, whether they are due to personality or to mental illness.

The conceptual distinction between personality and illness is valuable in everyday clinical practice, but it is not always easy to make. Central to the concept is the duration of the unusual behaviour in question. If the person previously behaved normally and then begins to behave abnormally, he is said to have an illness. If his behaviour has always been as abnormal as it is now, he is said to have a personality disorder. The distinction is easy when behaviour changes quickly (as in an acute manic illness), but difficult when it changes slowly (as in some cases of schizophrenia).

Some German psychiatrists (for example, Jaspers 1963) added a third criterion, that illness arises from causes within the person and is not a reaction to circumstances. This led, in turn, to the idea that conditions clearly provoked by stressful events should not be regarded as illness but as reactions of the personality. Although there is some merit in this idea, it can no longer be sustained because recent research shows that stressful events also occur before the onset of some conditions (such as schizophrenia) that were regarded as illnesses rather than reactions by the earlier authors.

The assessment of personality

Although this has been discussed in Chapter 2, two points need to be mentioned again. The first is that judgements of personality of the kind made in everyday life should not be applied to patients. If we meet a new colleague at work, we are likely to judge his personality largely from his behaviour in the first few weeks of meeting him. We assume that this represents his habitual way of behaving. Occasionally we are wrong, for example the new colleague may have been exceptionally guarded. Generally, however, this sort of everyday assessment is accurate.

The personality of patients cannot be judged in the same way. It is a common mistake to place too much weight on the pattern of behaviour observed in the ward, or during outpatient visits, for this behaviour is likely to reflect a combination of personality and illness. Personality can only be judged from reliable accounts of past behaviour.

The second point concerns psychological tests. It is tempting to suppose that they give better information about personality than the clinician can obtain from interviews with the patient and informants. This is not so, because most personality tests are affected by the presence of illness, and because they measure traits that are seldom useful in clinical practice. In the assessment of personality there is no substitute for careful interviewing of the patient and other informants.

The concept of abnormal personality

Some personalities are obviously abnormal: for example those of violent and sadistic people who repeatedly harm others and show no remorse. It is, however, impossible to draw a sharp dividing line between the normal and the abnormal. Indeed, it is even difficult to decide what criterion should be used to make this distinction. Two criteria have been suggested, the first statistical and the second social. On the statistical criterion, abnormal personalities are quantitative variations from the normal, and the dividing line is decided by a cut-off score. In principle, this scheme is attractive, as it parallels the approach used successfully in defining abnormalities of intelligence. It has obvious value in research where tests are required to measure personality in groups of patients. However, in clinical work with individual patients it is of limited value.

The second approach can also be applied to a scheme in which abnormal personalities are regarded as quantitative variations from the normal. However, the arbitrary dividing line is determined by social criteria rather than by a statistical cut-off. The criteria are that the individual suffers from his own personality or that other people suffer from it. Thus someone with an abnormally sensitive and gloomy personality suffers himself, while a person who is emotionally cold and aggressive makes other people suffer. Although such criteria are subjective and lack the precision of the first approach, they correspond well with the realities of clinical practice and they have been adopted widely.

Given the conceptual problems involved, it is hardly surprising that it is difficult to frame a satisfactory definition of abnormal personality. The definition in the International Classification of Diseases is not without difficulties but is widely accepted: 'deeply ingrained maladaptive patterns of behaviour recognizable by the time of adolescence or earlier and continuing through most of adult life, although often becoming less obvious in middle or old age. The personality is abnormal either in the balance of its components, their quality and expression or in its total aspect. Because of this . . . the patient suffers or others have to suffer and there is an adverse effect on the individual or on society'.

It is important to recognize that people with abnormal personalities may have favourable as well as unfavourable traits. However abnormal the personality, enquiries should always be made about positive features as well as unfavourable ones. These are particularly important in planning treatment.

How ideas about abnormal personality developed

The concept of abnormal personality in psychiatry can be traced back to the beginning of the nineteenth century when the French psychiatrist Pinel described '*manie sans délire*'. Pinel applied this term to patients who were prone to unexplained outbursts of rage and violence but were not deluded (at that time delusions were regarded as the hallmark of mental illness; and *délire* is the French term for delusion). Presumably this group of patients included not only those who would now be regarded as having antisocial personality, but also mentally ill patients who were not deluded, for example some with mania. (See Kavka (1949) for a translation of the relevant section of the second edition of Pinel's book, first published in 1801.)

Although other writers, such as the American Benjamin Rush (1830), were interested in similar clinical problems, it was an English physician who took the next important step forward. In 1835, J.C. Prichard, senior physician to the Bristol Infirmary, published his *Treatise on insanity and other disorders of the mind*. After referring to Pinel's *manie sans délire*, he suggested a new term, **moral insanity**, which he defined as a 'morbid perversion of the natural feelings, affections, inclinations, temper, habits, moral dispositions and natural impulses without any remarkable disorder or defect of the intellect or knowing or reasoning faculties and in particular without any insane delusion or hallucination' (Prichard 1835, p. 6). Although this description included the violent patients described by Pinel, Prichard clearly had a wider group in mind, since he added: 'a propensity to theft is sometimes a feature of moral insanity and sometimes it is its leading if not its sole characteristic' (p. 27). Prichard's category of moral insanity, like Pinel's *manie sans délire*, may have included affective disorders, for he wrote (p. 18): 'a considerable proportion among the most striking instances of moral insanity are those in which a tendency to gloom or sorrow is the predominant feature', and furthermore: 'a state of gloom and melancholy depression occasionally gives way . . . to the opposite condition of praeternatural excitement' (p. 19).

It is clear that Prichard also included patients who would now be regarded as having antisocial personality disorder. Thus he wrote (p. 23) 'eccentricity of conduct, singular and absurd habits, a propensity to perform the common actions of life in a different way from that usually practised, is a feature of many cases of moral insanity but can hardly be said to contribute sufficient evidence of its existence. When however such phenomena are observed in connection with a wayward and intractable temper with a decay of social affections, an aversion to the nearest relatives and friends formerly beloved – in short, with a change in the moral character of the individual, the case becomes tolerably well marked'.

Later in the nineteenth century, it became understood that mental illness could occur without delusions, and the affective disorders and schizophrenia were recognized as separate entities. Nevertheless, the concept of moral insanity continued, although with a more restricted meaning. Thus it was applied by Henry Maudsley to someone described as having 'no capacity for true moral feeling – all his impulses and desires, to which he yields without check, are egoistic, his conduct appears to be governed by immoral motives, which are cherished and obeyed without any evident desire to resist them' (Maudsley 1885, p. 171). Maudsley commented on the current dissatisfaction with the term, and referred to it as 'a form of mental alienation which has so much the look of vice or crime that many people regard it as an unfounded medical invention' (p. 170).

The next step towards modern ideas was the introduction by Koch (1891) of the term **psychopathic inferiority** to denote this same group of people with marked abnormalities of behaviour in the absence of mental illness or intellectual impairment. Later, the word inferiority was replaced by personality to avoid the judgemental overtones. Kraepelin at first shared the general doubt about the best way to classify these people, and it was not until the 8th edition of his textbook that he finally adopted the term **psychopathic personality** and devoted a long chapter to it. He described seven separate types: excitable, unstable, eccentric, liars, swindlers, antisocial, and quarrelsome.

A further step was taken by another German psychiatrist, Schneider. Whereas Kraepelin's seven types of psychopathic personality included only those causing inconvenience, annoyance or suffering to other people, Schneider extended the concept to include those causing suffering to themselves and not to others. He included for example people with markedly depressive or insecure characters. In Schneider's usage psychopathic personality covered the whole range of abnormal personality, not just antisocial personality. In this way the term came to have two meanings: the wider meaning of all abnormal personality, and the narrower meaning of antisocial personality.

The confusion about the term psychopathic personality does not end with Schneider's broader definition. Two other usages call for attention. The first originates in the work of the Scottish psychiatrist Sir David Henderson, who in 1939 published an influential book *Psychopathic states*. In this he began by defining psychopaths as people who, although not mentally subnormal, 'throughout their lives or from a comparatively early age, have exhibited disorders of conduct of an antisocial or asocial nature, usually of a recurrent or episodic type which in many instances have proved difficult to influence by methods of social, penal and medical care or for whom we have no adequate provision of a preventative or curative nature'. So far this corresponds to the familiar narrow definition of psychopathic personality. However, Henderson extended his definition by referring to three groups of psychopaths: the predominantly aggressive, the predominantly passive or inadequate, and the creative. This division had the effect of widening the concept once again. The predominantly aggressive group includes not only those who are repeatedly aggressive, but also those prone to suicide, drug addiction, and alcohol abuse. The group of passive and inadequate personalities includes unstable, hypo-chondriacal and sensitive people, pathological liars, and schizoid states. The group of creative psychopaths is so wide as to be of little value; thus the examples given by Henderson included T.E. Lawrence and Joan of Arc, who were both creative in different ways but had little in common. In retrospect, Henderson's main contribution was to draw attention to the inadequate personalities.

Yet another variation in the meaning of the term psychopathic was introduced in the 1959 Mental Health Act for England and Wales. In this, psychopathic disorder was defined in Section 4(4) as: 'a persistent disorder or disability of mind (whether or not including subnormality of intelligence) which results in abnormally aggressive or seriously irresponsible conduct on the part of the patient, and requires or is susceptible to medical treatment'. This definition returns to the central idea of aggressive or irresponsible acts that cause suffering to other people. However, it is unsatisfactory because it includes the require-ment for or response to treatment – a requirement that may be administratively convenient but cannot be justified logically. Not surprisingly, many difficulties have attended the use of this definition. (Recent mental health legislation is discussed in the appendix.)

The two meanings of psychopathic personality – the wider meaning of all abnormal personality, and the narrower meaning of antisocial personality – persist to the present day. Because of this ambiguity, this textbook avoids the term, and uses personality disorder and antisocial personality to denote the wide and narrow senses respectively.

The classification of abnormal personalities

Before considering how abnormal personalities can be classified, it is important to realize that each category in any classification scheme represents an ideal

devious, and self-sufficient to a fault. He seems to have little sense of humour or capacity for enjoyment. Such personality traits are fertile grounds for jealousy. (See also Chapter 10).

People with paranoid personalities appear argumentative and stubborn. Presented with a new proposal, they are overcautious and look for ways in which it might be designed to harm their own interests. Some engage in litigation that is prolonged long after any non-paranoid person would have abandoned it.

An important feature of the paranoid personality is a strong sense of self-importance. The person often has a powerful inner conviction that he is unusually talented and capable of great achievements. This idea is maintained, in the face of modest accomplishments, by paranoid beliefs that other people have prevented him from fulfilling his real potential, that he has been let down, tricked, swindled, or deceived. Sometimes, these self-important ideas are crystallized round a central overvalued idea that persists for many years.

Sensitivity is another important aspect of the paranoid personality. People of this kind readily feel shame and humiliation. They take offence easily and see rebuffs where none are intended. As a result, other people find them difficult, prickly and unreasonable. Both Schneider (1950) and Kretschmer (1927) used the term **sensitive** to describe such a person. Kretschmer also described how, when faced with a deeply humiliating experience, such people develop suspicious ideas that can easily be mistaken for persecutory delusions. These 'sensitive ideas of reference' are considered further in Chapter 10.

The affective personality disorder

Some people have life-long disorders of mood regulation. They may be persistently gloomy (depressive personality disorder), or habitually in a state of inappropriate elation (hyperthymic personality disorder). A third group alternate between these two extremes (cycloid or cyclothymic personality disorder). People with **depressive personality disorder** seem always to be in low spirits. They take a persistently gloomy view of life, anticipating the worst outcome of every event. They brood about their misfortunes and worry unduly. They often have a strong sense of duty. They show little capacity for enjoyment and express dissatisfaction with their lives. Some are irritable and bad tempered.

People with **hyperthymic personality disorder** are habitually cheerful and optimistic and show a striking zest for living. They may also show poor judgement, and may be uncritical and hasty in coming to conclusions. Their habitual cheerfulness is often interrupted by periods of irritability, especially when their aims are frustrated. This kind of personality is seldom so extreme as to cause suffering. A few contentious people in this group were called pseudo-querulants by early German authors.

People with **cycloid personality disorder** alternate between the extremes of depressive and hyperthymic described above. This instability of mood is much more disruptive than either of the others. Such people pass through periods in which they are extremely cheerful, active, and productive. At these times they take on additional commitments at work and in their social lives. Eventually the mood changes. Instead of confident optimism, there is a gloomy defeatist approach to life. Energy is reduced. Activities taken up with so much relish in the phase of elated mood, are now felt to be a burden. In this phase, different but equally unwise decisions may be made, and opportunities that could be managed are refused. In time, there is a change either to a normal mood or back to a further state of mild elation.

Schizoid personality disorder

In this disorder, the person is introspective and prone to engage in fantasy rather than take action. He is emotionally cold, self-sufficient, and detached from other people. The name schizoid was suggested by Kretschmer (1936), who held that there is an aetiological relationship between this kind of personality and schizophrenia (see Chapter 9). However, the two are not associated invariably, and the term should be used descriptively without implying any causal relationship with schizophrenia.

The most striking feature is lack of emotional warmth and rapport. People with this disorder appear detached, aloof and humourless, and seem incapable of expressing affection or tenderness. As a result, they do not make intimate friendships and often remain unmarried. They show little concern for the opinions of other people and pursue a lonely course through life. Their hobbies and interests are solitary and more often intellectual than practical.

These people tend to be introspective. Their inner world of fantasy is often extensive but it lacks emotional content. They are more likely to be concerned with intellectual problems than with ideas about other people.

If the disorder is extreme, the individual is seen as cold, callous, seclusive, ill at ease in company, and without friends. Lesser degrees of the same traits, appearing as part of a normal personality, may confer advantages in some ways of life. For example, some forms of academic work may be carried out more effectively by a person who can detach himself from social activities for long periods, and can concentrate in a detached and unemotional way on intellectual problems.

Antisocial personality disorder

In ICD 9 this disorder is called **sociopathic personality disorder** or **asocial personality disorder**. The preference of this book is for the term antisocial, which appears in DSM III. People with this disorder show a bewildering variety of abnormal features. Several attempts have been made to identify an essential core to the disorder. The most useful of these recognizes four features: failure to make loving relationships, impulsive actions, lack of guilt, and failure to learn from adverse experiences.

The failure to make loving relationships is accompanied by self-centredness and heartlessness. In its extreme form there is a degree of callousness that allows the person to inflict cruel, painful, or degrading acts on others. This lack of feeling is often in striking contrast to a superficial charm, which enables the person to make shallow and passing relationships. Sexual activity is carried on without evidence of tender feelings. Marriage is often marked by lack of concern for the partner, and sometimes by physical violence. Many marriages end in separation or divorce.

The characteristic impulsive behaviour is often reflected in an unstable work record marked by frequent dismissals. It is also shown in the whole pattern of life, which seems to lack any plan or persistent striving towards a goal.

This impulsive behaviour, coupled with a lack of guilt or remorse, is often associated with repeated offences against the law. Such offences begin in adolescence with petty acts of delinquency, lying, and vandalism; many of them show a striking indifference to the feelings of other people involved, and some include acts of violence or callous neglect. Often the behaviour is made more extreme by the effects of alcohol or drugs.

People with sociopathic personality make seriously inadequate parents, and may neglect or abuse their children. Some have difficulty in managing their finances or in organizing family life in other ways.

Vivid descriptions of antisocial personality disorder are contained in Cleckley's book *The mask of sanity* first published in 1941. These still make valuable reading (Cleckley 1964.)

The explosive personality disorder

People with this kind of disorder cannot control their emotions adequately, and are subject to sudden and unrestrained outpourings of anger. These outbursts are not always confined to words, but may include physical violence leading at times to serious injury. Unlike people with antisocial personalities, who also exhibit explosions of anger, this group do not have other difficulties in their relationships.

Asthenic personality disorders

This personality disorder has also been called **passive**, and in DSM III the term **dependent personality disorder** is used. People with this disorder appear weak willed and unduly compliant, falling in passively with the wishes of others. They lack vigour and show little capacity for enjoyment. They avoid responsibility and lack self-reliance. Some dependent people are more determined, but achieve their aims by persuading other people to assist them, whilst protesting their own helplessness.

If married, such people may be protected from the full effects of their personality by support from a more energetic and determined spouse who is willing to make decisions and arrange activities. Left to themselves, some drift down the social scale and others are found among the long-term unemployed and the homeless.

Other categories of abnormal personality

This section is concerned with several descriptions of abnormal personality that are included in the American scheme (DSM III) but not in the International Classification of Diseases.

Schizotypal personality disorder

In DSM III this term refers to a group of people characterized by superstitious ideas, an interest in clairvoyance and telepathy, unrealistic thinking, and odd forms of speech. The authors of DSM III (p. 310) state that 'recent evidence suggests a possible relationship between these individuals and a family history of schizophrenia'. Until this evidence is much stronger, there seems to be little advantage in recognizing this as a separate category.

Narcissistic personality disorder

People with this disorder are characterized by a grandiose sense of self-importance and by a preoccupation with fantasies of unlimited success, power, and intellectual brilliance. They crave attention from other people but show few warm feelings in return. They exploit others and seek favours that they do not return. Most people of this kind could be classified as having histrionic personality disorders, and some of the rest seem to fit into the group of antisocial personalities. Intermediate forms are inevitable in any scheme of classification of personality, and there seems to be no strong reason at present for assigning an additional category to people with these characteristics. Moreover, even if the category is used, the problem of transitional states is not solved. Thus in DSM III (p. 316) it is stated that in addition to the features listed above, 'frequently many of the features of histrionic, borderline, and anti-social personalities are present; in some cases more than one diagnosis is warranted'.

Avoidant personality disorder

People with this disorder are hypersensitive to rejection, unwilling to enter into relationships, and characterized by a desire for acceptance coupled with low self-esteem. These people are unlike those with schizoid personalities, because they are not emotionally cold and they crave relationships with other people. Such people cannot be classified easily within the International Classification of Diseases, and the category has some value, although the term 'avoidant' is not entirely satisfactory.

Borderline personality disorder

In DSM III people with this disorder are described as showing 'instability in a variety of areas, including interpersonal behaviours, mood, and self-image'.

This very general description is made even more difficult to apply by the additional statement that 'no single feature is invariably present'. Instead, eight criteria are listed, of which five must be present. These are impulsive behaviour that is damaging to the person, unstable relationships, undue anger, doubts about personal identity, variable moods, intolerance of being left alone, self-injury, and chronic boredom. The examples given in the manual to DSM III show that the category would be properly applied to someone who repeatedly engaged in shop-lifting, showed frequent anger, had made several attempts to harm himself, frequently felt bored, and showed a pattern of unstable relationships. Such a person could equally well be included among antisocial personalities. The manual also indicates that the category could be applied to a person who repeatedly overeats; doubts his own identity; has frequent short-lived episodes of depression, irritability, and anxiety; cannot tolerate being alone; and has chronic feelings of boredom. It is surprising that a category encompassing two such different types of person can be used reliably, but there is some evidence that it can. However, even if it is reliable, the category is not necessarily useful. Indeed the Manual contains a statement (p. 322) suggesting the category may not be useful: 'this disorder can be accompanied by many features of other personality disorders such as schizotypal, histrionic, narcissistic, and antisocial personality disorders'. In short, the category seems to be a broad receptacle for many kinds of abnormal personality that are difficult to classify exactly. To label them all as borderline personalities seems to add little to knowledge (see also p. 244).

Passive–aggressive personality disorder

This term is applied to a person who, when demands are made upon him for adequate performance, responds with some form of passive resistance, such as procrastination, dawdling, stubbornness, deliberate inefficiency, or pretended forgetfulness. Such patterns of behaviour are familiar enough among normal people and in many different kinds of abnormal personality. There is no good reason to make such behaviour the defining feature of a separate category of personality disorder.

Sjobring's classification

Sjobring devised a scheme which has been widely used in Scandinavia but not elsewhere. The reader may encounter this scheme in some of the important Scandinavian monographs published in English. The classification uses three dimensions to characterize personality, adding a fourth for intelligence (which is called **capacity**). The first of the three dimensions is **stability**. This resembles introversion–extraversion. A superstable person is cold, introverted, and interested in ideas, whilst a substable one is warm, sociable, and active. The second dimension is **solidity**. A supersolid person is dependable, deliberate, and self-possessed, whilst a subsolid one is inconstant, quick, and subjective in judgements. The third dimension is **validity**. A supervalid person is venturesome, expansive, and self-confident, whilst a subvalid person is retiring, cautious, and easily worried. The interested reader will find an account of this scheme in English in the paper by Sjobring (1973).

Terms to avoid

Two commonly used terms should be avoided. Both tend to be used when the doctor has not thought clearly enough about the precise nature of his patient's difficulties. The first is **inadequate personality**, a term often employed in a pejorative way. In place of this term, it is better to specify precisely the ways in which the person is inadequate to the demands of life. Such a specification will lead to more constructive ideas about helping the person to cope better.

The second is **immature personality**, a vague term which implies a non-specific discrepancy between the patient's behaviour and his chronological age. In place of this term, it is better to specify the exact nature of this immaturity, whether it is in social relationships, or the control of emotions, or willingness to take responsibility, or elsewhere. This precise description of the patient's problems is more likely to lead to a constructive approach than the mere labelling of the personality as immature.

AETIOLOGY

Since so little is known about the factors accounting for normal variations in personality, it is not surprising that knowledge about the causes of personality disorder should be incomplete. Research is made difficult by the long interval between potentially relevant events in early life, and the time when disorder comes to attention in the adult. It might be expected that the more extreme the disorder, the more obvious its causes would be. In keeping with this expectation, there is more information about antisocial personality disorder than about the other disorders. Nevertheless it is more convenient to begin by considering what is known about these other disorders.

GENERAL CAUSES OF PERSONALITY DISORDER

Genetic causes

Although there is some evidence that normal personality is partly inherited, there is no satisfactory evidence about the genetic contribution to personality disorders. Investigations of normal variations are illustrated by the work of Shields (1962) who studied 44 pairs of monozygotic twins, some of whom had been separated at birth. On personality tests, the scores of twins brought up apart were as similar as those reared together, suggesting a substantial genetic influence. It has been suggested (for example by Mayer Gross *et al.* 1969) that personality disorders are merely extremes of this genetic variation. However, there is no direct evidence to test this hypothesis.

Body build

The idea that body build is related to temperament is illustrated by the common belief that fat men are jolly. Kretschmer (1936) attempted to study the associa- tion scientifically. He described three types of body build: **pyknic** (stocky and rounded), **athletic** (with strong development of muscles and bones), and **asthenic** or **leptosomatic** (lean and narrow). Kretschmer suggested that pyknic build was related to the cyclothymic type of normal personality, and to the cycloid type of abnormal personality (cyclothymes are variable in mood). The asthenic type of body build was thought to be related to the schizothymic type of normal personality and the schizoid type of abnormal personality (schizothymes are cold, aloof, and self-sufficient). Kretschmer's findings must be viewed cautiously because he made subjective judgements of personality and did not use statistics.

Sheldon *et al.* (1940) repeated these studies using more quantitative methods. Instead of assigning physique to one of three types, he rated it along three dimensions. **Endomorphy** signified 'predominance of soft roundness'; **mesomorphy** 'predominance of muscle, bone, and connective tissue', and **ectomorphy** 'predominance of linearity and fragility'. After elaborate measure- ments each person was given a score that indicated his position on the three dimensions: thus 711 indicated extreme endomorphy, whilst 444 indicated the midpoint on all three dimensions. Sheldon also attempted to rate personality objectively, but unfortunately chose dimensions that are no longer in general use. **Viscerotonia** denoted relaxation and enjoyment of comfort, **somatotonia** denoted assertiveness and energy; whilst **cerebrotonia** indicated strong inhibitory controls and a tendency to choose symbolic expression instead of action (Sheldon *et al.* 1942).

Sheldon's efforts at more precise measurement did not reveal any simple relationship between body build and personality. Interest in the subject has declined in recent years. In any case, even if such an association were to be proved, its significance would be difficult to explain. The most likely link would presumably be through genetic causes of both variables.

Relation to mental illness

As already mentioned, Kretschmer suggested not only a relationship between personality and body build, but also an association between personality and mental illness. On this view, some disorders of personality are partial expressions of a process that can cause illness. Schizoid personalities are conceived as halfway to schizophrenia, and cycloid personalities as halfway to manic depressive psychosis. Although this theory is without convincing support, it lingers on in the names cycloid and schizoid, which are still included in the International Classification of Diseases. There could be some less specific connection between mental illness and personality disorder, as suggested by reports of an increased frequency of various kinds of personality abnormality among relatives of schizophrenic patients (see p. 248) and of patients with manic-depressive illness (see p. 204).

Psychological theories

Although it is generally agreed that upbringing must affect the development of normal personality, little is known about the extent and nature of these influences in shaping abnormal personalities. This lack of information has allowed many rival theories of psychological development to flourish. Because none of these offers a satisfactory explanation of disorders of personality, only a brief account will be given of the three widely adopted schemes. For further information on these theories, the reader is referred to Hall and Lindzey (1980).

Psychoanalytic theories: In this scheme, emphasis is placed on events in the first five years of life. It is supposed that crucial stages of development (oral, anal, and genital) must be passed through successfully if personality development is to proceed normally (see Chapter 4). Certain predictions are made about the effects of failure at particular stages; for example, that serious difficulties at the anal stage will result in an obsessional personality disorder. The scheme allows for some modifications of personality at a later age through identification with people other than the parents, but these are thought to be less important than the earlier influences.

The scheme is comprehensive and flexible enough to enable clinicians to construct a retrospective explanation of many of the personality disorders that they encounter among their patients. Some doctors find this more satisfactory than an admission of ignorance, and a proportion of patients are helped by an understandable explanation of their problems. However, the scheme is unsatisfactory as a scientific account of abnormal personality because this same flexibility makes it impossible to generate crucial tests of the hypotheses.

Adler's individual psychology: this rejected the idea of libido development. Instead, it proposed that personality develops through efforts to compensate for feelings of inferiority. Other departures from Freud's ideas were proposed by the neo-Freudians, Fromm, Horney, and Sullivan. Each emphasized social factors in development rather than the biologically determined stages in Freud's scheme, although each took a different view about the details of this social development. Erikson's system was essentially similar to Freud's in its early stages, though the nomenclature was different. However, Erikson put far more emphasis on events in adolescence, to which Freud gave little importance.

Jung's theory: this scheme is difficult to grasp because Jung chose to explain it in a particularly abstruse kind of metaphor. However, the scheme resembles Freud's in placing the greatest emphasis on internal psychic events rather than social influences. Unlike Freud, Jung thought of personality development as a life-long process. Indeed he referred to events in the first part of life as merely 'fulfilling ones' obligations', and applied this term to severing ties with parents, finding a spouse, and starting a family. Jung was more concerned with changes that occur later and reach completion only when a person is ready to face death.

None of these schemes provides a convincing explanation for the personality disorders described in this chapter, so they will not be elaborated further.

Studies of childhood influences on personality development

Even in young infants, marked differences can be seen in such characteristic activities as patterns of sleeping and waking, approach and withdrawal from new situations, the intensity of emotional responses, and span of attention. Although these differences have been shown to persist into the childhood years, they do not seem to be closely related to adult personality traits (see Rutter 1977).

Considerable attention has been given to the effects on personality development of disturbances in parent–child relationships, particularly maternal deprivation. However, although such deprivation has been proposed as a cause of antisocial personality, there is no convincing evidence that it leads to other kinds of personality disorder.

CAUSES OF ANTISOCIAL PERSONALITY

Genetic causes

There are no satisfactory twin studies directly concerned with the inheritance of antisocial personality. Some indirect evidence was provided by Lange (1931) who studied 13 pairs of monozygotic pairs in which one of each pair had committed a criminal offence. Of the 13 co-twins, as many as ten had offended. Moreover in one of the three discordant pairs, the proband had committed his offence after a head injury. On the other hand, among 17 pairs of binovular twins of the same sex, in which the proband was a criminal, only two co-twins had offended. As criminal behaviour cannot itself be inherited, the results of this study presumably reflect the inheritance of certain kinds of personality, including antisocial disorders. Lange reported that the personalities of the MZ twins were usually similar, for example both were explosive and excitable, or both were weak-willed and shy; while DZ twins did not resemble each other so much in their personalities.

These striking findings must be viewed cautiously because the study had methodological shortcomings. The numbers were small and the selection of cases may have been biased. However, similar conclusions were reached in part of a larger study carried out in America by Rosanoff *et al.* (1934). In a study of 340 twin pairs they identified those in which at least one had offended in adult life. Among the 33 monozygous pairs, 22 had co-twins who had offended. Among the 23 dizygous pairs, only three had a criminal co-twin.

Another source of evidence is the study of people separated at birth from antisocial parents by adoption. Conflicting results have been obtained from such investigations, perhaps because the criterion of antisocial behaviour (usually criminal convictions) was subject to many influences other than those of personality.

Cadoret (1978) attempted to study 190 adoptees who had been separated at birth from parents who showed persistent antisocial behaviour. He examined those adoptees who had been reared in a permanent home, and compared them with a control group of adoptees whose parents were not antisocial. The findings must be accepted cautiously because about 30 per cent of the subjects refused to be interviewed. Of the adult descendants of antisocial parents, 22 per cent had been diagnosed as having antisocial personality, while none of the descendents of controls had this diagnosis. This was true irrespective of whether the biological father or mother had shown antisocial behaviour. However, among the offspring, antisocial behaviour disorder was diagnosed more often in men than women. (Cadoret also found an increased rate of hysteria among the women, and suggested that this condition might be an alternative expression of the same genetic endowment.) These findings did not appear to be accounted for by differences in the families of adoption. However, in the sample as a whole, the number of antisocial symptoms in the offspring was related to psychiatric problems in the adoptive parents. Two other investigations support this evidence that the adopted children of antisocial biological parents have an increased rate of antisocial behaviour (Crowe 1974; Cadoret *et al.* 1975).

Other studies start with a group of adoptees who have shown antisocial behaviour. These studies show an excess of antisocial behaviour in the biological parents of the adoptees as compared with the biological parents of children who are not antisocial (Schulsinger 1972). However, the number of cases is not great. Thus in Schulsinger's study of 57 biological parents of antisocial adoptees, only four showed antisocial personality disorders. Even when a wide definition of antisocial personality disorder was adopted which included criminality, alcoholism, and hysterical personality traits, the figure was still only 14.

Chromosomal abnormalities

These have been suggested as an occasional cause of abnormally aggressive behaviour, following the discovery that about 3 per cent of patients in a maximum security hospital had the XYY karyotype (Jacobs *et al.* 1965). Since this report first appeared it has become known that the incidence of the XYY karyotype in the general population is higher than was thought at the time. The number found in the special hospital, though rather high, is much less remarkable than had originally been supposed.

Cerebral pathology and cerebral maturation

Antisocial personality disorders seem so far removed from the normal variations of personality, and so similar to some of the behaviours of people who have suffered brain injuries, that an organic cause has been suggested, which is supposed to operate at the age when personality is still being formed. This idea of minimal brain damage is discussed in Chapter 21. There is no convincing evidence that it is an important cause of antisocial personality disorder among adults.

A related view is that antisocial personality disorder might result from delay in the development of the brain. Electroencephalographic abnormalities consistent with maturational delays have been reported in people with antisocial personalities. For example, Hill (1952) carried out an uncontrolled study of 194 antisocial and aggressive people, none of whom had epilepsy. Three patterns of abnormality were found all of which could have arisen from maturational defects. The most frequent were bilateral excess of slow waves (theta activity) and foci of 3–5 cycles per second activity in the posterior temporal regions. Both kinds of abnormality were usually bilateral but, if not, were more often on the right. The abnormalities were less frequent among the older subjects. Williams (1969) confirmed these findings in a study of 333 men convicted of violent offences, of whom 206 had been habitually aggressive, whilst 127 were known to have had only a single aggressive outburst usually in response to provocation. After exclusion of subjects with mental subnormality, epilepsy, or a previous head injury, 57 per cent of the habitually aggressive group had abnormal EEGs as against only 12 per cent of the single outburst group. Abnormalities were found most often in the anterior temporal region. Williams speculated that these might indicate a primary disorder in the reticular activating system or limbic mechanisms. He concluded that disturbed cerebral physiology was an important predisposing cause of the propensity to seriously aggressive behaviour, though the outbursts were usually provoked by environmental factors.

The idea that cerebral disorder can contribute to repeated aggressive behaviour, especially when there is no adequate provocation, was developed further by Bach-y-Rita *et al.* (1971) who described an **episodic dyscontrol syndrome.** They regarded this as a disorder with more than one organic cause, and in their original series they included some patients with epilepsy. In a further study, Maletzky (1973) studied 22 men, excluding any who had evidence of epilepsy, pathological intoxication, schizophrenia, or acute drug reactions. All had the pattern of episodic violent behaviour described by Bach-y-Rita *et* *al.,* 14 having seriously injured a victim (who was often a family member) and five having killed. A sequence of aura, headache, and drowsiness was often described, and 12 patients reported amnesia for the episode. The frequency of these occurrences varied from one a day to a few in a year, with a median of four a month. Even small amounts of alcohol appeared to make the episodes more likely, and the authors suggested that benzodiazepines might have a similar effect. 'Soft' neurological signs were reported among the patients, and in 14 there were abnormal EEG findings, usually in the temporal regions. No long-term follow up was carried out, but from clinical experience the author suggests the syndrome may improve with age. Maletzky also reported striking improvements during treatment with phenytoin, but no placebo controls were used and so it is impossible to assess this finding. It remains uncertain whether the episodic dyscontrol syndrome is a separate entity, or merely represents a small group of patients with undiagnosed epilepsy coupled with an unusually aggressive personality.

The effects of upbringing

In 1944, Bowlby published a paper in which he suggested, on the basis of an uncontrolled retrospective study of 44 young delinquents, that separation of a young child from its mother leads to a personality characterized by antisocial behaviour and a failure to form close relationships. Two years later these ideas were expanded in the influential book *Forty-four juvenile thieves* (Bowlby 1946). They stimulated a large amount of research into the immediate and long-term effects of separating children from their mothers, and the concepts of 'maternal deprivation' gained wide acceptance. However, the ideas also provoked much controversy. In retrospect, it can be said that the concept of 'maternal deprivation' has been useful in drawing the attention of doctors and others to the importance of maintaining links between mother and child, particularly when either of them goes into hospital. It has also had the unfortunate effect of suggesting a unitary process where, in reality, there is much diversity. The effect of separation depends on many things: the age of the child, his previous relationship with his mother (and father) and the reasons for the separation. For example when a mother separates from her husband there have usually been months of tension and arguments that could themselves affect the child's development. In the light of these problems, Bowlby revised his original view that the effects of maternal deprivation are almost invariable; he acknowledged that the outcome might vary widely amongst children who had undergone the experience of separation. From a review of the literature, it is clear that there is no evidence proving that early separation is an important determinant of antisocial personality (see Rutter 1972).

Childhood behaviour problems and antisocial personality

If the causes of antisocial personality are in early life, behaviour disorders in childhood might be expected to be forerunners of personality disorder in the adult. Robins (1966) followed 524 people who, as children 30 years before, had attended a child guidance clinic. Amongst those who had had serious antisocial behaviour in childhood, in adult life a bad outcome was not invariable but a substantial minority had problems with the law, a poor work record, and evidence of unsatisfactory relationships. This contrasted with the generally good prognosis of neurotic symptoms in childhood. The outcome was particularly poor if in childhood several different antisocial behaviours coexisted and the acts were repeated. Stealing among boys and sexual delinquency among girls also had a poor prognosis. Most of those who later became antisocial had a father who was judged to be antisocial or alcoholic at the time of the child's attendance at the child guidance clinic. This association was not lessened among children whose fathers had left home before the child attended the clinic, and among children who had been adopted. However, this could have reflected persisting social disadvantages as much as genetic factors.

Learning theory

Several authors have suggested that psychopathic personality results from a failure of social learning. Scott (1960) proposed a broad scheme which is based on commonsense considerations rather than experimental evidence, but does provide a useful framework for the clinician. He suggested four ways in which repeated antisocial behaviour could develop. First, a person may learn normally, but acquire behaviour contrary to generally accepted standards through growing up in an antisocial family. Secondly, he may have had no opportunity to learn because not presented with consistent rules of behaviour in the family. Thirdly, he may have learnt antisocial behaviour as a way of overcoming some emotional problem; for example, a young man who feels inferior with women may adopt aggressive behaviour to hide this. Fourthly, the learning process itself may have been abnormal. This last idea has been developed by Eysenck (1970), who suggested that antisocial personality disorder is more likely to develop in people who condition slowly and so fail to learn normal social behaviour. However, this broad explanation takes no account of the complexities of social learning, and cannot explain why people with antisocial personality may learn other behaviour patterns normally.

THE PROGNOSIS OF PERSONALITY DISORDERS

Just as small changes occur in normal personalities with increasing age, so abnormal personalities may become rather less abnormal as the person grows older. There is little factual information about the outcome of personality disorders, and virtually all of it concerns sociopathic disorders. In the American follow-up study by Robins mentioned above, information was collected about people with persistent antisocial behaviour in early adult life. During the later follow-up about a third of them had improved as judged by the number of arrests and contacts with social agencies, but still had problems in relationships as shown by hostility to wives and neighbours. They also had an increased rate of death by suicide. Research in England showed that, amongst offenders with antisocial personalities whose first offences were aggressive, subsequent offences were not predominantly aggressive (Gibbens *et al.* 1959). This accords with a general impression among clinicians that antisocial people over the age of 45 present fewer problems of aggressive behaviour, although their problems of personal relationship tend to persist.

THE MANAGEMENT OF PERSONALITY DISORDERS

It is said that men cannot change their natures, all they can do is change their situations. Although this refers to normal personalities, much the same holds for disordered personality. There has been some progress in finding ways of effecting small changes in disorders of personality, but management still consists largely of helping the person to find a way of life that conflicts less with his character. It is also true that personality does not become fixed in many people until the mid-twenties.

Assessment

As always in psychiatry, thorough assessment is the first step in management. In assessing someone with a personality disorder, it is less useful to attach a single diagnostic label than to describe the main features of his character. This description should refer to his strengths and his weaknesses, because treatment attempts to build on favourable features as well as modify unfavourable ones. The patient's circumstances must be examined with equal care, with particular attention to any that regularly provoke undesirable behaviour. This last step is often overlooked to the patient's detriment. Aggressive people are not aggressive in all circumstances, nor are shy and self-conscious people ill at ease in every social encounter. To find out what provokes undesirable behaviour, there must be detailed observation over several weeks to discover any recurring patterns. This method is often useful for people with antisocial personalities, as they appreciate a practical approach.

Such enquiries may show that specific factors are making abnormal behaviour worse. For example, a man with an anankastic personality may need encouragement to move to a job with less responsibility for the work of other people who have lower standards than his own. A man with an antisocial personality may by provoked into anger when he feels rejected by women. Sometimes the enquiries suggest that attention should be given to a problem which was not apparent at first. For example the man just described may provoke rejection by his own clumsy approach to women. He might be helped by counselling and social skills training directed to this clumsiness.

General measures of treatment

The aims of treatment should be modest, and considerable time should be allowed to achieve them. Drugs have little part to play in the management of personality disorders. Anxiolytic drugs or major tranquillizers may be given for short periods at times of unusual stress, but they should not be maintained for long because their benefits are likely to decline and they may induce dependency.

Psychotherapy is most likely to help young people who lack confidence, have difficulty in making relationships, and are uncertain about the direction their lives should take. Such people must be highly motivated to work at solving their problems by examining their attitudes and emotions. Psychotherapy is least likely to help people with antisocial personality disorders, although some are helped by special forms of large group treatment in a therapeutic community. (This form of treatment is considered below.)

For the majority, psychotherapy is not indicated, but supervision and support are often beneficial. This can be given by a doctor, though many patients can be managed equally well by an experienced social worker or psychiatric nurse. For antisocial personalities several years of supervision may be required. For other kinds of personality disorder useful readjustments can often be effected over a period of months. Some antisocial people are put on probation after breaking the law, and this can sometimes provide useful external control when their motivation for treatment is poor at the start.

Whatever the nature of the disorder, the treatment plan aims to bring about limited changes in the patient's circumstances so that he has less contact with situations that provoke his difficulties, and more opportunity to develop the assets in his personality. It is essential to attempt to build a trusting relationship so that the patient can talk openly and learn from his mistakes. The patient will certainly experience setbacks, and at these times the therapist should avoid any suggestion of failure. Often progress can only be made by a series of small steps whereby the patient gradually moves nearer to a satisfactory adjustment. Often these steps can be taken most effectively when setbacks occur, since it is then most likely that the patient will be willing to face his real problems. The therapist should also help the patient to develop more satisfying relationships, for example by taking part in leisure interests, pursuing further education, or joining clubs.

When the disorder is of the antisocial kind, the patient should be seen over a long period, but not at short intervals. Indeed for some patients frequent visits only lead to undue dependency and a consequent worsening of their difficulties. Even if little progress is made, a supportive and watchful relationship can often prevent the accumulation of additional problems until some fortuitous change in the patient's life brings about some improvement.

It should also be recognized that there is no point in persisting with endless 'supportive' sessions that bring no benefit. No matter how skilful the treatment, some patients will not benefit, and the therapist should not be disheartened by this.

Psychotherapy for personality disorders

General issues

Treatment by dynamic psychotherapy is much the same for personality disorders as for neuroses. It can be carried out individually or in groups (see Chapter 18).

In the individual treatment of personality disorders, there are some differences in emphasis from the treatment of neuroses. There is less emphasis on the reconstruction of past events and more on the analysis of current behaviour. In so-called character analysis there is detailed examination of the ways a person relates to others, copes with external difficulties and deals with his own feelings. The approach is more directive than in the classical methods of analysis for neurotic symptoms, although the analysis of transference remains an important element. To emphasize any discrepancies between the patient's habitual ways of relating to others and his real life situation, the therapist has to reveal more of himself than is usual in classical analysis. At the same time the analysis of countertransference (the therapists' emotional attitudes to the patient) can be an important guide to the likely reactions of other people to the patient.

Hysterical personality disorder

Murphy and Guze (1960) have given an interesting account of the difficulties that can arise in the treatment of hysterical personalities. They describe direct and indirect demands that patients can place on the doctor. Direct demands include unreasonable requests for medication, repeated seeking for assurances of continuing help, telephoning at unreasonable times, and attempts to impose impractical conditions on treatment. Indirect demands include seductive behaviour, threats of dangerous actions such as drug overdoses, and repeated unfavourable comparisons of the present treatment with any received in the past. The doctor has to be alert for the first signs of such demands, and should clearly set limits by indicating how much of the patient's behaviour he is prepared to tolerate. This must be done before the patient's demands become too great.

Obsessional personality disorder

People with obsessional personality disorders often express great eagerness to please the therapist. However, this kind of personality disorder does not, as a rule, respond well to psychotherapy, and unskilled treatment can lead to excessive morbid introspection that leaves the person worse rather than better.

Schizoid personality disorder

The schizoid person's tendency to avoid close personal contacts makes any kind of psychotherapy difficult. A patient of this kind often drops out after a few sessions; if he does stay, he tends to intellectualize his problems, and to question the scientific status of the treatment. The therapist has to try gradually to penetrate these intellectual defences and to help the patient recognize his emotional problems. Only then can the therapist begin to explore ways of dealing with them. At best it is a slow process, and one that often fails.

Psychological treatment for antisocial personality disorder

Individual psychotherapy

Most psychiatrists agree that individual psychotherapy seldom helps patients with antisocial personalities, and that the conduct of the interviews is often made difficult by their behaviour. Schmideberg (1947) is exceptional in reporting good results from a form of psychotherapy in which patients are confronted repeatedly and directly with evidence of their own abnormal behaviour. If such treatment is effective at all, it is only with therapists who have a particularly forceful and robust personality.

Small group therapy

This has also been tried. However, if one person with an antisocial personality disorder joins a conventional therapeutic group, it seldom helps him and often disrupts the treatment of the others. On the other hand, groups composed entirely of antisocial patients can sometimes be run more constructively. This requires skill and experience, together with a determination to set limited goals and to encourage group members to share responsibility and help each other. This kind of treatment should not be undertaken without special training (see Whiteley 1975).

The therapeutic community

The principles of the therapeutic community are outlined in Chapter 18. The method has been used for sociopathic personalities since the work of Jones (1952) at the Social Rehabilitation Unit at Belmont Hospital, later called The Henderson Hospital. In such a unit, sociopathic patients live and work together, and meet several times a day for group discussions in which each person's behaviour and feelings are examined by the other group members. Frank discussion is encouraged and patients are required to consider their own behaviour and the effect it has on other people. These discussions often take place with much outpouring of emotion including anger. It is hoped that, by repeatedly facing these issues, patients will gradually learn to control their antisocial behaviour and adopt more acceptable ways of dealing with their feelings and relationships. Rapoport (1960) has described four aspects of treatment that may be important in bringing about change: permission to act on feelings without the usual social restraints; sharing of tasks and responsibilities; group decision-making to involve patients in making rules as well as breaking them; and confrontation of each person with the effects his actions have on others. No controlled study has been carried out and opinions about the value of this treatment are divergent. One- to two-year follow-up studies have reported improvement rates of 40–60 per cent, depending on whether the criterion for improvement was general social functioning, employment or reconviction (see Taylor 1966).

Other group regimes

In contrast to communities in which patients are given freedom to learn from their mistakes, Craft (1965) has advocated a more authoritarian regime for people who have antisocial personality disorder combined with subnormality of intelligence and who become more disturbed when treated in a therapeutic community.

Stürup (1968) described the application of therapeutic community principles to offenders who had committed violent crimes or serious sexual offences, and were detained on indefinite sentences in the Herstedvester Detention Centre in Denmark. At Grendon Prison in England similar principles have been applied to the care of prisoners who have committed less serious offences and are not serving an indefinite sentence. In neither case has any controlled enquiry been possible. Hence it is difficult to evaluate Sturup's report (1968, p. ix) that 90 per cent of offenders passing through his unit commit no further offences.

FURTHER READING

Hall, C.S. and Lindzey, G. (1978). *Theories of personality*, 3rd edn. John Wiley, New York.

Lewis, A. (1974). Psychopathic personality: a most elusive category. *Psychological Medicine* **4**, 133–40.

Schneider, K. (1950). *Psychopathic personalities* trans. M.W. Hamilton. Cassell, London.

Vaillant, G.E. and Perry, J.C. (1980). Personality disorders. In *Comprehensive textbook of psychiatry*, 3rd edn (ed. H.I. Kaplan, A.M. Freedman, and B.J. Sadock) Vol. 3, Chapter 22. Williams and Wilkins, Baltimore.

6. Neurosis: part I

The modern view of neurosis embodies three ideas. The first is that a neurosis is not caused by any kind of organic brain disorder. The second is that neurotic patients do not lose touch with external reality. The third is that, although neurosis is often associated with a degree of personality disorder, the personality is not grossly abnormal. These features are included in the definition of neurosis in the 9th Edition of the International Classification of Disease, which states that neuroses are: 'mental disorders without any demonstrable organic basis in which the patient may have considerable insight and has unimpaired reality testing, in that he does not usually confuse his morbid subjective experiences and fantasies with external reality. Behaviour may be greatly affected although usually remaining within socially acceptable limits, but personality is not disorganised'.

Neuroses can be thought of as exaggerated forms of the normal reactions to stressful events. Anxiety, depression, occasional short-lived obsessional thoughts, and physical symptoms without an organic cause are experienced by many people in response to the stressful circumstances of everyday life. In the neuroses these symptoms become more intense, and are often out of proportion to the severity of the stressors.

These minor symptoms of everyday life often occur together. Distressed people may feel both anxious and despondent, and may experience occasional obsessional thoughts at the same time. In its mildest form, a neurosis is usually much the same: anxiety, depression, and other neurotic symptoms develop together, and it is often difficult to pick out one major feature.

Among the more severe neuroses, specific syndromes can be discerned. A particular symptom predominates and the syndrome is named after it – for example, obsessional neurosis. Even when the neurosis is mild, in some people it takes the form of a specific syndrome. It seems that some people have a vulnerable personality that predisposes them to react to minor stress in this way, whereas most people would show a less differentiated reaction.

It is partly because the less severe forms have much in common, that it is useful to put these disorders together under the collective term neurosis. This is in marked contrast to the term psychosis which is sometimes used in a parallel way, as a collective term for the severe forms of mental illness – schizophrenia, manic depressive illness, and organic psychosyndromes. Because these latter conditions have little in common, even in their mildest form, it is not particularly useful to refer to them collectively. The term psychosis serves only to obscure differences between severe forms of mental illness, whereas the term neurosis draws attention to important common features of the milder disorders.

In this book the neuroses are presented in two chapters. This chapter discusses classification of neuroses, describes the less severe forms, and reviews certain issues about aetiology, prognosis, and treatment that apply to all forms. In the following chapter specific syndromes are discussed in turn, with reference to aspects of aetiology, prognosis, and treatment particular to each.

Terminology

Readers who are studying the neuroses for the first time may be confused by the terms neurosis, functional nervous illness, character neurosis, psycho-neurosis, and abnormal emotional reaction. The term **neurosis** was used in 1772 by the Edinburgh physician Cullen to denote conditions arising from a 'generalised affection of the nervous system', that did not seem, at the time, to be caused by either localized disease or febrile illness. In other words, neuroses were regarded as disorders of the nervous system for which no physical lesion could be found. The term necessarily included conditions such as migraine that are now within the subject matter of neurology (see Tuke 1892), as well as the disorders now regarded as neuroses. Used in this sense, neurosis was synonymous with the term **functional nervous illness** which persisted until the 1930s.

Freud did not accept this negative view of neuroses as disorders of unknown aetiology. Like many other physicians of his time, he held that many forms of neurosis had clear psychological causes. He therefore called them **psycho-neuroses**, a grouping that included hysteria, anxiety hysteria (roughly equivalent to the modern concept of agoraphobia), and obsessional neuroses. At first anxiety states were excluded from the psychoneuroses but were later added, so that the term psychoneurosis became synonymous with neurosis. As Freud tried to find causes for the psychoneuroses, he concluded that many originated in the processes that determine the development of personality. This line of reasoning led to the term **character neurosis** to denote personalities that appeared to have origins similar to those presumed for the neuroses, even though the person might have no neurotic symptoms at the time. The term character neurosis is confusing and its use is not recommended.

Psychoanalysts were not the only clinicians to notice a clear relationship between neuroses and personality. Some German psychiatrists, notably Jaspers and Schneider, thought of neuroses as reactions to stress occurring in people with abnormal personalities. If this view is accepted, there is no need to think of neuroses as separate entities; it is only necessary to describe the personality from which the reaction arises. This approach led to the term **abnormal emotional reaction**, as a synonym for neurosis. As will be explained later, it is generally useful to think of neurosis as a reaction of a particular kind of personality to stress. However, the relationship between the type of personality and the type of reaction is not simple. Thus obsessional personalities may react with an anxiety neurosis or a depressive neurosis as much as with an obsessional neurosis. Conversely hysteria may occur in people who do not have a hysterical personality.

It is important to make a clear distinction between individual neurotic symptoms such as anxiety or obsessions, and neurotic syndromes such as anxiety neuroses or obsessional neurosis. Individual neurotic symptoms occur in many psychiatric disorders, but the syndromes are unique combinations of symptoms. This distinction is reasonably clear for the main neurotic syndromes – anxiety neurosis, obsessional neurosis, and hysteria. It is much less clear for hypochondriasis and depersonalization; some psychiatrists believe that these occur only as symptoms of another psychiatric syndrome, and that there is no primary hypochondriacal neurosis or depersonalization neurosis. These controversial issues are taken up in the next chapter.

The classification of neurosis

In the 9th Edition of the International Classification of Diseases (ICD 9), the different neuroses are listed as anxiety states, hysteria, phobic states, neurotic depression, obsessive compulsive disorder, neurasthenia, depersonalization and hypochondriasis (Table 6.1). The American system DSM III groups the syndromes differently. To avoid confusion the differences in DSM III will be pointed out here (Table 6.2). Two variations are not particularly controversial. The first is that neurotic depression is classified with the affective disorders, (a classification adopted in this book). The second is that anxiety neurosis and phobic neurosis are classified together, which is logical; but obsessional states are also included in this group even though they have distinct features.

The most radical differences in DSM III concern the syndrome of hysteria. Three categories are used for this. The first, somatoform disorder, contains cases of hysteria with mainly physical symptoms, together with hypochondriasis. The second, dissociative disorder, includes cases of hysteria with mainly psychological symptoms, and also depersonalization disorder which has little in common with hysteria. The third, factitious disorders, is a potentially useful addition to the classification, in which uncommon self-inflicted disorders can be placed.

In the first half of Table 6.1 the DSM III categories have been gathered together for comparison with those of ICD 9. In DSM III the separation of phobic states into agoraphobia, social phobia, and simple phobia is useful, but the division of agorophobia into cases with and without panic attacks, is of doubtful value. It is also uncertain whether the proliferation of subcategories of hysteria can be used reliably by either clinicians or research workers. For these reasons, this chapter is based mainly on the ICD 9 scheme.

It is important to remember that transitional forms of neurosis are common, especially those between anxiety states and neurotic depression. Moreover,

Table 6.1. *Classification of neuroses in ICD 9 and DSM III**

ICD 9	DSM III
300.0 Anxiety state	300.01 Panic disorder
	300.02 Generalized anxiety disorder
300.1 Hysteria	300.11 Conversion disorder
	300.12 Psychogenic disorder
	300.13 Psychogenic fugue
	300.14 Multiple personality
	300.15 Atypical dissociative disorder
	300.16 Factitious disorder with physical symptoms
	300.17 Atypical factitious disorder with physical symptoms
300.2 Phobic state	300.2 Phobic state
	300.21 Agoraphobia without panic attacks
	300.22 Agoraphobia with panic attacks
	300.23 Social phobia
	300.29 Simple phobia
300.3 Obsessive compulsive disorder	300.3 Obsessive–compulsive disorder
300.4 Neurotic depression	300.4 Dysthymic disorder (depressive neurosis)
300.5 Neurasthenia	300.5 Chronic factitious disorder
300.6 Depersonalization syndrome	300.6 Depersonalization disorder
300.7 Hypochondriasis	300.7 Hypochondriasis; atypical somatoform disorder
300.8 Other	300.8 Other
	300.81 Somatization disorder

*DSM III does not include a formal category of neurosis – but instead divides them as in Table 6.2.

many neuroses are not differentiated clearly into specific syndromes. They are often referred to as minor emotional disorders, or else can be classified under one of two headings to be discussed next.

ICD 9 contains two categories for emotional reactions that do not clearly meet the criteria for neurosis. **Acute reactions to stress** (308.0) are 'very transient disorders of any severity or nature which occur in individuals without any apparent mental disorder in response to exceptional physical or mental stress, such as natural catastrophe or battle, and which usually subside within hours or days'. **Adjustment reactions** (309) are 'mild or transient disorders lasting longer than acute stress reactions which occur in individuals of any age without apparent pre-existing mental disorder. Such disorders are often relatively circumscribed or situation-specific, are generally reversible, and

Table 6.2. *Categories in which neurotic syndromes appear in DSM III*

Affective disorders	296	Bipolar disorder
		Major depression
		Atypical affective disorder
	301.1	Cyclothymic disorder
	300.4	*Dysthymic disorder* (depressive neurosis)
Anxiety disorders	300.21/2	*Agoraphobia*
	300.23	*Social phobia*
	300.29	*Simple phobia*
	300.01	*Panic disorder*
	300.02	*Generalized anxiety disorder*
	300.30	*Obsessive compulsive disorder*
	308.30	Acute post-traumatic stress disorder
	309.81	Chronic or delayed post traumatic stress disorder
Somatoform disorders	300.81	*Somatization disorder*
	300.11	*Conversion disorder*
	307.80	*Psychogenic pain disorder*
	300.70	*Hypochondriasis*
	300.70	Atypical somatoform disorder
Dissociative disorders*	300.81	Psychogenic amnesia
	300.13	Psychogenic fugue
	300.14	Multiple personality
	300.60	*Depersonalization disorder*
	300.70	Atypical dissociative disorder
Factitious disorders* (hysterical neuroses, dissociative type)	300.16	Factitious disorder with psychological symptoms
	300.51	Chronic factitious disorder with physical symptoms

*All the subcategories in these groups except 300.60 are subsumed in ICD under the single category of hysteria (300.1).

Conditions in each group which are listed under Neuroses in the International Classification of Disease are shown in italics.

usually last only a few months. They are usually closely related in time and content to stresses such as bereavement, migration or separation experiences. Reactions to major stress that last longer than a few days are also included here'. This diagnosis can be applied usefully to emotional reactions to major disablement, such as those that follow strokes or road accidents and seem to be understandable and in proportion to the severity of the stressful experience.

The problem of depressive neurosis

Some of the less severe forms of depressive disorder have features that meet the criteria for neurosis. They have no organic basis, seem to result from stressors acting on a predisposed personality, and do not include features (often called psychotic) such as hallucinations and delusions. Moreover, many of them include prominent anxiety symptoms, and some have other kinds of neurotic symptom as well. For this reason, minor depressive disorders are sometimes classified as depressive neuroses (DSM III) or neurotic depression (ICD 9).

This has led some psychiatrists, notably Mapother (1926) and Lewis (1956) to the view that all depressive disorders should be classified together, and others to the equally firm conviction that they should not. These opposing views have been debated at length and with some passion, but without any clear result. Because it has not been possible to settle the matter by ordinary clinical observation, some research workers have tried to find an answer by using statistical methods. Techniques such as cluster analysis and principal component analysis might be expected to show whether there is one group of depressive disorders or two. However, statistical methods can only do this if the original data are unbiased, which is doubtful. The data are mostly derived from clinical interviews carried out by psychiatrists whose preconceived ideas about depressive states could have influenced their observations. (That this can occur was shown clearly by Kendell (1968).) At present, the findings are rather evenly balanced, some supporting the theory that depressive disorders are a single entity, and some that there are two separate groups. In this book all degrees and types of depression are considered together in Chapter 8, in which these issues are discussed further.

Before leaving the subject of minor depressive disorders two other points need to be made. The first was referred to by Mapother and Lewis, who considered that anxiety neuroses cannot be separated clearly from depressive disorders. Most psychiatrists now accept that this distinction can be made among the more severe forms seen in psychiatric practice. However, the distinction cannot be made easily among the mild and transient disorders seen in general practice. The second issue is whether conditions presenting initially as undoubted anxiety neuroses or depressive disorders remain distinct as time passes. Information about this is incomplete but it appears that definite anxiety neuroses seldom turn into depressive disorders (Shapira *et al.* 1972), even though their course is often interspersed with brief episodes of depressive symptoms lasting for weeks or months (Clancy *et al.* 1978). There is no comparable information about the long-term course of the minor depressive disorders that could be diagnosed as neurotic depression, but clinical experience suggests that they too continue in the same original pattern.

Neurasthenia and psychasthenia

Although it is still in the International Classification of Diseases, neurasthenia does not appear to be a distinct syndrome separate from neurotic depression and anxiety neurosis. However, the term is important in the history of psychiatry, and a brief account is appropriate here.

The term was first employed in 1869 by Beard in America to describe a syndrome of mental and physical fatigue, poor appetite, irritability, insomnia, poor concentration, and headache in the absence of specific disease. Beard recognized that similar symptoms could arise from chronic disease, wasting fevers, and parturition, and the term came to be used in a wide sense. Neurasthenia was discussed at length in many textbooks of the late nineteenth and early twentieth century. It is interesting that Ross included the term in the first edition of his well known book *The common neuroses* published in 1923; by the time the second edition was prepared in 1937, Ross had discarded the term on the grounds that most cases were anxiety states.

Originally the cause of neurasthenia was thought to be nervous exhaustion resulting from overwork, and treatment included a sequence of rest and planned activity, usually coupled with tonics and sometimes with electrical stimulation applied to the feet and head. Later, overwork was discounted as an important cause, and constitutional factors and psychological precipitants were emphasized instead.

Recent investigations in general practice (see Goldberg and Huxley 1980) have shown that complaints of fatigue and irritability commonly accompany anxiety and mild depression. Whilst it is no longer fashionable to call this pattern of symptoms neurasthenia, these recent observations show that the clinical phenomena described by Beard can still be detected today.

Janet put forward the related term psychasthenia to emphasize that the disorder was psychological and not neurological (see Janet 1909). He used the term in a wide sense to include anxiety states, obsessional neuroses, and phobic disorder, leaving aside only hysteria as a separate neurotic syndrome.

THE EPIDEMIOLOGY OF THE NEUROSES

As pointed out above, neurotic disorders can occur at three 'levels' – individual symptoms; the undifferentiated neurotic syndrome; and specific neurotic syndromes. Individual symptoms may be experienced by normal people from time to time. In the undifferentiated neurotic syndrome (sometimes called minor emotional disorder) a variety of neurotic symptoms occur together without any one predominating; this is commonly seen in general practice. In specific neurotic syndromes, one type of symptom predominates; they are more often seen in psychiatric practice.

Epidemiological methods have been used to estimate the frequency of disorder at each of these levels. In such studies, it is important to use standardized methods of observation. Thus, if general practitioners are simply asked to report the frequency of minor emotional disorders among their patients, their estimates vary as much as ninefold (Shepherd *et al.* 1966). Objective estimates reveal that this is not mainly due to any real difference in frequency. Instead it relates to differences in the doctors' ability to detect such disorders, and to variation in diagnostic practices especially when physical and emotional symptoms occur together. In general, family doctors detect emotional disorders more readily among women, the middle aged, separated, and widowed (Goldberg and Huxley 1980).

At the first 'level', epidemiological studies show that **individual neurotic symptoms** are exceedingly common in the general population; for example, 815 in every 1000 people in New York reported some neurotic symptoms (Srole *et al.* 1962).

Estimates of the frequency of **undifferentiated neuroses** show wide variation, ranging from lifetime prevalence rates of 18 per 1000 for men and 27 per 1000 for women (in a Danish survey by Fremming 1951); to 79 per 1000 for men and 165 per 1000 for women (in a Swedish investigation by Hagnell 1966). One-year prevalence rates vary even more (see Carey *et al.* 1980). Looked at in another way, neuroses probably form about two-thirds of the psychiatric cases seen in general practice (Shepherd *et al.* 1966). Among chronic neuroses inception rates are greater in the first half of life, exceeding recovery rates up to the age of 35 (Shepherd and Gruenberg 1957). There is also general agreement that the most frequent symptoms of these undifferentiated neuroses are anxiety, depression, irritability, insomnia, and fatigue (see Goldberg and Huxley (1980) for a review of the evidence).

There have been few estimates of the true prevalence of **individual neurotic syndromes**, and their findings differ considerably. However, there is more agreement about the relative frequency of these syndromes: anxiety neuroses and mild depressive states are generally found to be more common than either hysteria or obsessional neuroses; and mild depression is especially common amongst women (see for example Bille and Juel-Nielsen 1968).

The population of neurotic patients consists of some who experience brief reactions to stress and others who have chronic disorders. Although it is not possible to draw a sharp dividing line between the two, it appears that amongst new cases of undifferentiated mild neurosis about two-thirds recover within six months (Goldberg and Blackwell 1970; Hagnell 1970) while only about 4 per cent last as long as three years (Hagnell 1970). (The question of prognosis will be taken up again later.)

It is not surprising that in developing countries the incidence and prevalence of the neuroses is even more difficult to estimate. The few reported investigations suggest that rates in the community are comparable to those found in Britain and the United States. However, fewer patients reach general practitioners and psychiatric clinics (see German (1972) for a review, and the study of African students by German and Arya (1969)).

UNDIFFERENTIATED NEUROSES

These **minor emotional reactions** are met commonly in general practice but seldom referred to psychiatrists (see Goldberg and Huxley 1980). Whilst the psychiatric literature contains many descriptions of differentiated neurotic syndromes, there are few accounts of these minor states. One of the best descriptions has been given by Goldberg *et al.* (1976) who studied 88 patients from a general practice in Philadelphia. As shown in Table 6.3, they found that complaints of anxiety and worry were most frequent, but that despondency and sadness were almost as common. Mostly these complaints occurred together, and it was not possible to assign primacy to one or the other.

Somatic symptoms were present in about half the cases and excessive concern with bodily functions in about a quarter. Some of these somatic complaints are autonomic features of anxiety, but it is not fully understood why these and other bodily sensations should so often be the focus of the patients' concern when consulting practitioners. Some patients may emphasize somatic complaints because they expect them to be received more sympathetically than emotional complaints. Understandably some patients may also want

Table 6.3. *Relative frequency of 12 common symptoms in 88 patients diagnosed as mental illness in general practice*

Anxiety and worry	82
Despondency, sadness	71
Fatigue	71 †
Somatic symptoms*	52
Sleep disturbance	50
Irritability	38
Excessive concern with bodily function	27
Depressive thoughts, inability to concentrate	21
Obsessions and compulsions	19
Phobias	11
Depersonalization	6

*Only those precipitated, exacerbated, or maintained by psychological factors.
† Not all the same patients who complain of despondency and sadness.
Source: Goldberg *et al.* (1976).

to ensure that the doctor makes a thorough search for physical illness before their symptoms are regarded as psychological. Whatever the reason, it is no new phenomenon, as shown by the lengthy coverage of physical symptoms of neurosis in many older textbooks on neuroses (see, for example Déjerine and Gauckler 1913).

In the patients studied by Goldberg *et al.* (1976), complaints of sleep disturbance were also common, particularly difficulty in getting off to sleep and restlessness during the night. (Complaints of early waking suggest that the condition may be the early stage of a depressive illness requiring antidepressant medication, rather than a neurosis.) About a fifth of the patients complained of obsessional thoughts and mild compulsions. Definite phobic symptoms were less common then either of these although mild phobias are of course very common among normal people.

Complaints of fatigue and irritability were also frequent (Table 6.3), and often accompanied by poor concentration and lack of enjoyment. As mentioned earlier, these symptoms were grouped together as neurasthenia in the past. Because they are so common, some of the main complaints are listed here (they will be mentioned again when anxiety neuroses are described in the next chapter). Complaints related to the digestive system include feelings of abdominal discomfort or distension, and preoccupations with the effects of certain foods in producing indigestion or flatulence. There may also be complaints of poor appetite, nausea, epigastric pain, weight loss or difficulty in swallowing, but all of these require a particularly thorough search for physical disease. Other complaints in the neuroses are discomfort in the left iliac fossa, and excessive concern about minor degrees of constipation; these too require that physical disease be carefully excluded. Complaints related to the cardiovascular system include palpitations, precordial discomfort, and unfounded worries about heart disease; once again it is important to take appropriate steps to exclude physical disease before concluding that the symptoms are neurotic. Other frequent complaints include aching in the neck, shoulders, and back. Headaches are commonly described as tightness and pressure, or a dull constant ache, or throbbing. Pain may have other regional localization, especially in the face, precordium, and abdomen.

The nature of complaints differs among people from different cultures, and in the same society at different times. Interested readers should consult Déjerine and Gauckler (1913) for an account of the somatic symptoms presented by neurotic patients in France at the beginning of the century; and Ndetei and Muhangi (1979) for a description of the frequent complaints of physical symptoms among Africans with minor psychiatric disorder.

THE AETIOLOGY OF THE NEUROSES

This section deals with the question why some people develop a neurosis when others do not. In the next chapter, the aetiology of specific neurotic syndromes is discussed. In general, the causes of neurosis can be divided into three groups: precipitating factors, predisposing factors, and maintaining factors. In the following pages, different methods of investigation are reviewed in turn, and this means that the three groups of causal factors cannot be kept completely apart. Nevertheless, the three groups should be borne in mind throughout the discussion (and whenever the causes of neurosis are being assessed in practice).

Environmental causes

Conditions of living and work

It might be expected that the amount of neuroses would decrease amongst people moving to better living conditions. However, this was not confirmed in investigations of people moving from poor urban conditions to a new town (Taylor and Chave 1964) or from an old housing estate to a new one (Hare and Shaw 1965). The explanation may be that such moves entail exchanging poor physical conditions in the old housing for social isolation in the new. This multiplicity of potential social causes of neurosis makes it difficult to study the effect of any one.

Noise is an environmental stress, and people who report most annoyance from noise tend to have more neurotic symptoms than other people. However, when comparisons were made between populations of districts exposed to different levels of aircraft noise, no simple relationship could be found between rates of neurosis and the amount of noise. Some individual symptoms were associated with high noise levels, notably irritability and mild depression (Tarnopolsky *et al.* 1980). However, around London airport the admission rates for neurotic syndromes were not increased (Jenkins *et al.* 1981). A contradictory finding that admission rates were increased round Los Angeles airport (Meecham and Smith 1977) could be explained by the fact that the authors did not allow for confounding variables such as age, race, and sex. Again this illustrates the great difficulties of the epidemiological study of potential causes of neurosis.

The stress of industrial work has also been suggested as a cause of neurosis. This was studied extensively during the Second World War, when it was concluded (Fraser 1947) that work requiring constant attention but little initiative or responsibility (such as repetitive machine work) could lead to neurosis. More recent studies have confirmed that men on assembly lines report more neurotic symptoms than do comparable men who have more control over their rate of work (Broadbent and Gath 1979; Broadbent 1981). Taken alone, this finding could be due to the selective movement of healthy individuals away from the unpleasant environment. However, it has also been shown that the same person reports more symptoms under difficult than under easy working conditions. When changing from medical to surgical wards, student nurses reported more symptoms when working in the conditions that they judged more stressful and less satisfying (Parkes 1982). From this, it seems fair to conclude that stressful conditions of work can play a part in causing neurotic syndromes, even when allowance has been made for the tendency of neurotic patients to complain more about their surroundings.

Life events

Another approach is to assess the frequency and severity of potentially stressful events in the patient's life ('life events') and to relate these to the onset of neurosis. Examples of such events are childbirth, marriage, loss of job, retirement, and moving home. They can be divided conveniently into **dependent** events that might be the result rather than the cause of illness, for example losing a job through poor work; and **independent** events that could not be the result of illness, for example losing a job because the firm closes down. It has been found that, compared with controls, patients seen in general practice experience more independent life events in the three months before the onset of undifferentiated neuroses (Cooper and Sylph 1973). While studies of this kind indicate that life events are important, they also show that many people experience comparable events without developing a neurosis. This may be explained by the personality and early experience of the person encountering the events (this will be discussed below). It is also possible that **vulnerability factors** such as those identified by Brown and Harris (1978) in depressed women, are important for the neuroses generally. These are discussed in Chapter 8, here attention is drawn to the idea that certain circumstances in a person's life can make him more vulnerable to stressors. Among young women, Brown and his colleagues identified the following as increasing vulnerability to depression: having the care of children under the age of five; not going out to work; lack of close friends; and a poor relationship with the husband.

Although some of these ideas are still controversial (see, for example Tennant and Bebbington 1978), Brown's approach is better than that of considering social class, type of work or housing conditions as if they were unitary variables.

The family as a source of stress and support

It is widely held that neuroses often result from emotional problems involving other family members. It has also been suggested that the emotional difficulties of other family members are often greater than those of the person coming for treatment (the 'identified' patient). Although there can be little doubt that family problems are common sources of stress, this formulation almost certainly overstates their importance. Some of the emotional difficulties experienced by other family members are the result of the patient's neurosis rather than its cause. This was well illustrated in a study by Kreitman *et al.* (1970) in which the wives of neurotic men were compared with the wives of controls. It was found that the former had more neurotic symptoms and higher neuroticism scores. It was also found that the longer the marriage the more symptoms were recorded; this suggests that the wife's symptoms had resulted from living with the neurotic husband. Such an interaction was probably made worse by the tendency of neurotic men to spend more time with their wives and less in outside social activities (Kreitman *et al.* 1970; Henderson *et al.* 1978).

Personality

In the aetiology of neurosis, abnormalities of personality have an importance that is, generally speaking, inversely proportional to the severity of stressful events. Among fighting soldiers, the extreme stress of battle has been observed to provoke anxiety states and hysterical neuroses in men of normal personality (Sargant and Slater 1940). On the other hand, among patients who develop symptoms of comparable severity in response to everyday problems, disorder of personality is usually detectable.

Psychologists have attempted to measure the personality attributes that predispose to neurosis. Eysenck (1957) has taken this a step further with a questionnaire designed to measure both neuroticism and extraversion. He has proposed that neuroticism determines the readiness to develop a neurosis, while the degree of extraversion or introversion determines the type. Thus extraverted neurotics are supposed to develop hysteria, and introverted neurotics to develop anxiety or obsessional neurosis. This attractively simple theory has some support from measurements of these personality dimensions in 'dysthymic' patients, but the findings among hysterics are less clear. The main success of the theory has been in linking the study of personality to the laws of learning. This work is reviewed in a later section, when learning explanations of neurosis are discussed.

Genetic influences

Among early studies suggesting increased rates of neurosis in relatives of neurotic patients, those of Brown (1942) and Slater (1943) were particularly influential. This approach is of limited value because it cannot separate the effects of heredity from those of early environment. To achieve this, twin studies are needed. The largest twin study, reported by Slater and Shields (1969) involved 62 monozygotic and 84 dizygotic pairs. The overall concordance for neurosis was 40 per cent in the monozygotic pairs and 15 per cent in the dizygotics, suggesting a moderate genetic influence. Other smaller investigations have broadly confirmed this conclusion. There appears to be a degree of genetic influence on neuroticism as measured by personality tests (see Shields 1976 for a review), and also on the reactivity of the autonomic nervous system as measured by the rate of habituation of galvanic skin responses (Lader and Wing 1966).

Neurosis in childhood and in adult life

If the tendency to develop neurosis is laid down before birth by genetic mechanisms or in childhood by learning, it might be expected that people experiencing neurotic symptoms in childhood would also develop them in adult life. In an important study, Robins (1966) followed up 500 people who had attended a child guidance clinic 30 years previously; as adults, they had no more neuroses than a suitably chosen control group. Other follow-up investigations have confirmed that most neurotic children grow up to be normal, and that most neurotic adults have not been treated for neurosis in childhood (see Robins 1970 for a review).

On the other hand, when emotional disorders do persist from childhood into adult life, they usually develop into neuroses or depressive states (Pritchard and Graham 1966). It is not known why a minority continue in this way, but it is possible that persistent neuroses have a greater genetic component, while the others are reactions to circumstances at the time.

'Neurotic' traits

'Neurotic' traits in childhood include thumb sucking, nail biting, faddiness about food, stammering, and bed wetting. Some of these can be regarded as delays in maturation. None, by itself, is of pathological significance. Nail biting and food fads are very common among children. Stammering and bed wetting begin as developmental delays; if bed wetting persists it is as likely to be associated with antisocial behaviour as with neurosis (see Rutter 1972). Childhood fears are of little significance for the child's later development.

There is little value, therefore, in asking about any of these behaviours when taking the history of adult neurotic patients. There is even less reason to treat these problems in childhood with the expectation that this will prevent neuroses in adult life. Most disappear spontaneously; if they do not there is no evidence that treating them lessens the patient's chances of developing neurosis in adult life.

Childhood experiences

There are many theories about the role of childhood experiences in the aetiology of neuroses. However, these are based almost entirely on the recollections of adult neurotic patients about events taking place many years before, and such reports are known to be both unreliable and selective. Prospective studies are the only satisfactory method of enquiry, but are not practical because of the long intervals involved. In the absence of prospective studies, a brief review will be given of psychoanalytic views on the importance of childhood experience.

Psychoanalytic theories of aetiology

These have been referred to already in Chapter 4. They stress the importance of certain key events in childhood, some of which can only be understood in the context of the whole body of psychoanalytic theory. In brief, it is supposed that neuroses represent a failure of the ego to deal on the one hand with instinctual energy reaching it from the id, and on the other with the demands of the superego. Anxiety is supposed to be a direct expression of excessive psychic energy; whilst other neurotic symptoms are thought to arise as the result of defence mechanisms acting to reduce this excessive energy. (The specific ways in which this reduction is supposed to take place are outlined in Chapter 7.) It is suggested that failure of the ego can develop in three circumstances: when id impulses have not been repressed adequately, when the demands of the superego are excessive, and when the ego itself is weak. It is further supposed that neurotic symptoms are more likely to arise when the child has failed to pass normally through the oral, anal, and genital stages of development.

In Freud's scheme, any predisposition to neurosis has been more or less formed by the time the latency period is entered. It leaves little room for influences beyond the child's relationships with his parents. Other analysts, such as Horney, rejected Freud's stages of libido development but retained the idea that anxiety is the central feature of neurosis. She placed the origins of this anxiety in childhood, stressing the importance of a loving relationship with parents. Horney also stressed the importance of repressed hostility as a cause of anxiety, and related this to social influences (rather than to instinct as in Freud's theory). Fromm rejected Freud's ideas even more radically. He held that, unlike animals, man is free to choose whether to follow his drives or to override them. However, there is a conflict between this possibility of freedom and the security of the infant's relationship to the parents. Neurosis results from this conflict, and represents an attempt to avoid feelings of isolation.

Learning theories

Learning theories attempt to explain neuroses in terms of earlier experience, and they make use of learning mechanisms identified in the study of animal behaviour. The theories can be divided into two main groups. The first, exemplified by the writings of Mowrer (1950) and Dollard and Miller (1950), incorporate many Freudian concepts but attempt to account for them in terms of learning mechanisms. For example, the concept of repression is translated into that of avoidance learning, emotional conflict into approach–avoidance conflict, and displacement into association learning.

The second approach rejects Freudian theory and tries to build entirely on experimental findings. Anxiety is regarded as a drive state, and symptoms are explained as learned behaviours that are reinforced by their effects in reducing this drive. This can provide a reasonable explanation of some phobic symptoms but is much less able to account for the symptoms of hysteria and obsessional neurosis.

The principal difficulty of all learning theory explanations of neurosis is that, although learned behaviour is known to extinguish rapidly if not reinforced, neurotic behaviour often persists without any obvious reinforcement. Mowrer (1950) tried to resolve this 'neurotic paradox' by proposing a two-stage theory: first neutral stimuli become able to elicit anxiety through classical conditioning, and afterwards instrumental avoidance responses reduce this anxiety. He further proposed that immediate anxiety reduction is the reinforcer that perpetuates neurotic behaviour. Eysenck (1976) has offered an alternative explanation which he calls the incubation effect: although conditional stimuli that do not produce a drive are subject to extinction (as in Pavlov's bell-salivation experiments), those that do produce a drive are not extinguished by reinforced repetition but enhanced. In explaining neurosis, it is held that the relevant conditioned stimuli usually produce anxiety (a drive) and are therefore subject to incubation. Although these theories have attracted much attention among psychologists, they have not led to substantial advances in factual knowledge about the causes of neurosis.

Eysenck has developed this scheme further by linking it to personality variables. As explained above, he assumes that predisposition to neurosis has two dimensions, both mainly inherited. The first, neuroticism, reflects the readiness of the autonomic system to respond to stress. The second, intro-version–extraversion, is said to reflect the ease with which inhibition builds up during learning. People with little tendency to inhibition are supposed to be more responsive to social conditioning in childhood, and to develop anxiety and obsessional states. People who develop inhibition readily are supposed to learn less well, and to develop hysteria or psychopathic behaviour. The scheme is intellectually satisfying but has not been supported convincingly by investiga-tions of the degree of extraversion or the speed of conditioning in these groups of neurotic patients (see Gossop 1981 for a review).

Conclusion

The aetiology of the neuroses is still not understood clearly. In the most general terms, the evidence is consistent with the idea that neuroses arise when stressful factors in a person's life outweigh both his capacity to deal with them and also his supportive relationships. The capacity to withstand stress – and its converse, the predisposition to neurosis – arise partly from inheritance and partly from upbringing. How upbringing has this effect, and what events in childhood are important, are questions on which there is much speculation but little factual information. However, there is now fairly general agreement that the important period in development is not limited to early childhood, and that relationships outside the family are influential as well as those with parents. Factors determining whether a person develops a particular kind of neurosis, such as an anxiety neurosis or hysteria, will be considered in the next chapter.

THE PROGNOSIS OF NEUROSIS

The neuroses have a variable prognosis. Among neurotic patients aged 20–50, identified in the community by standard methods of assessment, about half recover within three months (Hagnell 1970; Tennant *et al.* 1981). Of those who attend their general practitioners, about half recover within a year (Mann *et al.* 1981), but the rest may remain unchanged for many months. Of those who are referred to psychiatric outpatient or inpatient units, only about half achieve a satisfactory adjustment even after four years (Greer and Cawley 1966). Looking at the problem in another way, Goldberg and Huxley (1980, p. 104) calculated from the data of Harvey Smith and Cooper (1970) that recent-onset cases would have a turnover of about 70 per cent per year, and chronic cases a turnover of only 3 per cent per year.

Turning to the prognosis for physical health, it has been shown among neurotic patients that death rate is increased by a factor of 1.5 to 2.0 among neurotic outpatients and 2.0 to 3.0 among inpatients (Sims 1978). The excess is largely accounted for by suicide and accidental deaths, though there is some contribution from misdiagnosis of cases in which emotional disorder was secondary to physical disease in the first place. This is more likely to happen in cases diagnosed as hysteria.

Although it is difficult to make an accurate prediction of the outcome of an individual neurotic patient, certain factors help to narrow the possibilities. Prognosis tends to be worse when: the initial symptoms are severe; there are social problems that are likely to persist; the patient lacks social support and friendships (Huxley *et al.* 1979; Cooper *et al.* 1969); and the patient's personality is abnormal (Mann *et al.* 1981). Conversely, neuroses related to temporary events and occurring in people of good personality are likely to recover quickly (Tennant *et al.* 1981).

These general factors have emerged from studies of patients in primary care, most of whom have undifferentiated neuroses; in these, the precise pattern of symptoms does not appear to be an important determinant of outcome. Amongst the specific neurotic syndromes, however, there are differences in outcome (see Chapter 7).

ASSESSMENT

When any neurotic patient is assessed it is essential to make sure that no primary cause has been overlooked, such as physical disease, depressive disorder, schizophrenia, and dementia. The relative probability of these varies according to the age of the patient. Even if there is no evidence of a primary cause when the patient is first examined, it should always be considered again if there is no improvement in the neurosis after adequate treatment. In weighing up the likelihood of physical disease, it should always be remembered that stressful events are commonplace, and their presence does not exclude the possibility of primary organic disease. This is particularly important in middle-aged patients who have not had a neurosis before and (as described below) in any patient with symptoms of hysteria.

The search for organic disease requires a thorough history and physical examination, together with appropriate investigations. What is appropriate varies with the age of the patient, the nature of the symptoms, and any clues from the history. If, after appropriate investigation, a degree of uncertainty remains, it is important to make a note of it; the diagnosis should be recorded as provisional and subject to review after a suitable interval. Depression, organic brain syndromes, and schizophrenia should also be excluded by careful enquiry about relevant signs and symptoms (described in the chapters on each of these conditions).

When it is as certain as possible that the patient is free from organic disease, affective disorder, schizophrenia, and dementia, the next step is to assess the need for treatment of the neurosis. In deciding this, attention should be paid to the severity of the symptoms, how long they have been present, the likelihood that any causative stress will persist, and the patient's personality. At one extreme, symptoms are likely to recover quickly without treatment if they are mild, have been present for only two or three weeks, and began when temporary stressful events were present; and if the patient's personality is normal.

MANAGEMENT

The treatment needs of the patient are now considered. These can be thought of in three parts: measures to relieve symptoms, steps to help him solve the problems in his life, and treatment intended to improve his relationships with other people. If the symptoms are mild and appear to be a response to stressful events that are likely to resolve quickly, only supportive measures may be needed. In many cases, however, the patient will need to take more active steps to deal with his problems. To do this effectively, he may need to become less anxious; usually this can be achieved by reassurance and discussion but sometimes an anxiolytic drug is required for a short time. It is not necessary to abolish all anxiety, for a certain amount may motivate the patient to bring about changes in his life. (See Chapter 17 for further advice about the use of anxiolytic drugs.)

Whenever practical, the patient should be encouraged to solve problems himself and, if appropriate, his relatives should be encouraged to play a part. When problems are overwhelming, the help of a doctor, nurse, or social worker may be needed. Even so, the patient should still be encouraged to do what he can by listing problems, considering what can be done about each one, and deciding the order in which they should be tackled. In this way he will be better equipped to help himself in the future. If there seems to be no way to resolve a problem, the patient should be helped to accept it.

At the same time, efforts should be made to build up the patient's social life. Many neurotic patients lack friends in whom they can confide, and they have often given up leisure activities. They should be encouraged to join a club or, in the case of a full-time housewife, take a part-time job. For most patients, such normal social pursuits are better than those involving other people who are ill. However, for a few a psychiatric social club or a weekly visit to a day centre may be the only way of encouraging social contact.

A recent trial in general practice showed that intervention by an attached social worker was effective in two-thirds of cases diagnosed as chronic neurosis (Shepherd *et al.* 1979).

If it seems that the neurosis is partly the result of persistent emotional conflicts or maladaptive ways of dealing with personal relationships, psychotherapy may be helpful. This can vary from simple counselling with limited aims to intensive treatment intended to produce substantial changes in ways of dealing with emotional difficulties (see Chapter 18 for further information about counselling and short-term psychotherapy).

The treatment of specific neurotic syndromes is considered in Chapter 7.

When reading it, the general measures just described should be borne in mind. They are as important in the treatment of specific neuroses as in the treatment of the undifferentiated minor emotional reactions described in this chapter.

FURTHER READING

Fischer-Homberger, E. (1983). Neurosis. In *Handbook of psychiatry* (ed. M. Shepherd and O. Zangwill) Vol. 1. Cambridge University Press.

Goldberg, D. and Huxley, P. (1980). *Mental illness in the community.* Tavistock, London.

Shepherd, M., Cooper, B., Brown, A.C. and Kalton, G. (1981). *Psychiatric illness in general practice* 2nd edn, with new material by M. Shepherd and A. Clare. Oxford University Press.

Slater, E. and Slater, P. (1944). A heuristic theory of neurosis. *Journal of Neurology, Neurosurgery and Psychiatry* **7**, 49–55.

7. Neurosis: part II

In ICD 9, anxiety neuroses are named anxiety states and defined as 'various combinations of physical and mental manifestations of anxiety, not attributable to real danger and occurring either in attacks or as a persisting state. The anxiety is usually diffuse and may extend to panic. Other neurotic features such as obsessional or hysterical symptoms may be present but do not dominate the clinical picture'.

If minor depressive disorders are excluded from the neuroses, it is generally agreed that anxiety neuroses are the most common neurotic syndromes. They are more frequent among women, although absolute estimates of life time prevalence vary considerably, from 3–17 per 1000 among men and from 1–38 per 1000 among women.

Clinical picture

Anxiety neuroses have psychological and physical symptoms. The **psychological symptoms** are the familiar feeling of fearful anticipation that gives the condition its name, irritability, difficulty in concentration, sensitivity to noise, and a feeling of restlessness. Patients often complain of poor memory when they are really experiencing the effects of failure to concentrate; if there is true memory impairment a careful search should be made for an organic syndrome. Repetitive worrying thoughts form an important part of an anxiety neurosis. These are often provoked by awareness of autonomic overactivity; for example, a patient who feels his heart beating fast may worry about having a heart attack. Thoughts of this kind probably prolong the condition.

The **appearance** of a person with an anxiety neurosis is characteristic. His face looks strained, with a furrowed brow; his posture is tense; he is restless and often tremulous. The skin looks pale, and sweating is common especially from the hands, feet, and axillae. Readiness to tears, which may at first suggest depression, reflects a generally apprehensive state.

The **physical symptoms and signs** of an anxiety neurosis result from either over-activity in the sympathetic nervous system or increased tension in skeletal muscles. The list of symptoms is long, and is conveniently grouped by systems of the body. Symptoms related to the gastrointestinal tract include dry mouth, difficulty in swallowing, epigastric discomfort, excessive wind caused by aerophagy, borborygmi, and frequent or loose motions. Common respiratory symptoms include a feeling of constriction in the chest, difficulty in inhaling (which contrasts with the expiratory difficulty in asthma), and overbreathing and its consequences (which are described below). Cardiovascular symptoms include palpitations, a feeling of discomfort or pain over the heart, awareness of missed beats, and throbbing in the neck. Common genito-urinary symptoms are increased frequency and urgency of micturition, failure of erection, and lack of libido. Women may complain of increased menstrual discomfort and sometimes amenorrhoea. Complaints related to the functions of the central nervous system include tinnitus, blurring of vision, prickling sensations, and dizziness (which is not rotational).

It is important to remember that any of these physical symptoms may be the presenting complaint, particularly in general practice. Patients may, for example, complain of palpitations or headaches rather than of anxiety feelings. This presents problems of differential diagnosis that are discussed in the next section.

Other symptoms may be related to muscular tension. In the scalp this is felt as headache, typically in the form of constriction or pressure, which is usually bilateral and often in the frontal or occipital region. Tension in other muscles may be experienced as aching or stiffness, especially in the back and shoulders. The hands may tremble so that delicate movements are impaired. However, the use of the electromyogram has shown that such symptoms are not always a direct result of muscle tension. Scalp muscle tension is not always greater in patients who have 'tension headaches' than in controls who do not; and in the same patient it is not always greater during headaches than at other times (Martin and Mathews 1978).

In anxiety neuroses sleep is disturbed in a characteristic way. On going to bed the patient lies awake worrying; when at last he falls asleep, he wakes intermittently. He often reports unpleasant dreams. Occasionally he experiences 'night terrors', in which he wakes suddenly feeling intensely fearful, sometimes remembering a nightmare, and sometimes uncertain why he is so frightened. In the morning he often feels unrefreshed. Early waking is much less common in the patient with anxiety neurosis than in the patient with depressive illness. Therefore early waking should always suggest the possibility that anxiety symptoms are secondary to a depressive illness.

Some of these symptoms and signs can be studied objectively with physiological recordings. Although often valuable in research, such recordings are of little help to the clinician who can learn all he needs from a careful history. The measures include sweat gland activity measured by galvanic skin responses, pulse rate, muscle blood flow, and electromyographic activity. Further information can be found in the review by Lader (1975).

Overbreathing is breathing in a rapid and shallow way which results in a fall in the concentration of carbon dioxide in the blood. The resultant symptoms include dizziness, tinnitus, headache, a feeling of weakness, faintness, numbness and tingling in the hands and feet and face, carpopedal spasms, and precordial discomfort. There is also a feeling of breathlessness, which may prolong the condition. When a patient has unexplained bodily symptoms, the possibility of persistent overbreathing should always be borne in mind. The diagnosis can usually be made by watching the pattern of breathing. If there is doubt, blood gas analysis should decide the matter in acute cases, though the findings may be normal in chronic cases. A helpful account of the condition is given by Engel *et al.* (1947).

Neurocirculatory asthenia was the name given in the past to an anxiety syndrome in which palpitations and the effects of overbreathing directed attention to the cardiovascular system, and the patient was convinced that he had heart disease. It was originally described among American soldiers under the name of irritable heart or **da Costa's syndrome** (da Costa 1871). In the First World War it was recognized again as disordered action of the heart or **effort syndrome**, and was thought to result from excessive strain on the cardiovascular system. Subsequently the psychological origins became recognized. (Other aspects of 'cardiac neurosis' are considered in Chapter 12.)

Patients with anxiety neuroses are seldom free from **other neurotic symptoms**, which commonly include mild depression, and also obsessional symptoms and depersonalization.

Differential diagnosis

Anxiety neuroses must be distinguished from other psychiatric disorders and from physical illnesses. Anxiety symptoms can occur in all psychiatric illnesses, but in some there are likely to be particular diagnostic difficulties. For example, anxiety is a common symptom of the syndrome of **depressive illness**, but the syndrome of anxiety neurosis often includes some depressive symptoms. The two syndromes can usually be distinguished by the relative severity of the symptoms as well as the order in which these appeared. Information on these two points should be obtained from a relative or other informant as well as from the patient. The more serious diagnostic error is to mistake the agitation of a severe depressive illness for an anxiety neurosis. This mistake will seldom be made if every anxious patient is asked about symptoms of depression including depressive thinking and suicidal ideas.

In **schizophrenia** the patient sometimes complains of anxiety before other symptoms are recognized. However, the correct diagnosis can often be made by asking every anxious patient what he thinks is the cause of his symptoms. In reply, a schizophrenic patient may reveal delusional ideas. **Presenile** or **senile dementia** occasionally comes to notice because the person is complaining of anxiety. When this happens, the clinician may overlook any accompanying memory disorder or dismiss it as the result of poor concentration. Memory should therefore be assessed appropriately in every patient presenting with anxiety. Occasionally a patient dependent on **drugs or alcohol** reports that he is taking these substances to relieve anxiety, either because he wishes to deceive the doctor or because he genuinely mistakes symptoms of drug withdrawal for anxiety. If the patient reports that anxiety is particularly severe on waking in the morning, this should suggest the possibility of alcohol dependence (withdrawal symptoms being most likely at this time).

Some **physical illnesses** present with anxiety symptoms. In making a diagnosis, they should be considered when no obvious psychological cause can be found and when the personality is normal. Again, some diagnoses may be difficult to make. In **thyrotoxicosis** the patient is irritable and restless, and there is tremor and tachycardia. Anxious patients should therefore be examined for an enlarged thyroid, atrial fibrillation, and exophthalmos. If there is any doubt, thyroid function tests should be arranged. **Phaeochromocytoma** and **hypoglycaemia** should be considered when the anxiety symptoms are episodic. In other physical illness, anxiety is sometimes the presenting symptom because the patient fears that the early symptoms portend fatal illness. This is particularly likely when the patient has a special reason to fear a serious illness, for example, because a relative or friend has died after developing similar symptoms. It is good practice to ask an anxious patient whether he knows anyone who has had similar symptoms.

The opposite diagnostic error can also be made. Anxiety neuroses presenting with prominent physical symptoms can easily be mistaken for physical disease. The patient may then be subjected to unnecessary investigations that only make him more anxious. Such mistakes will be less common if the doctor remembers the diversity of anxiety symptoms; palpitations, headache, frequency of micturition, and abdominal discomfort can all be the primary complaint of an anxious patient. The correct diagnosis depends on finding other symptoms of the anxiety neurosis; on enquiring carefully about the order in which symptoms appeared when the illness developed; and on asking about the order in which symptoms are experienced during an attack, for example in a paroxysm of tachycardia, does awareness of rapid heart action come before or after the feelings of anxiety?

Aetiology

Genetics

Anxiety neurosis is more frequent among relatives of patients with anxiety neuroses – about 15 per cent – than in the general population – about 3 per cent (Brown 1942; Noyes *et al.* 1978). However, this could be the result of upbringing rather than inheritance. Stronger evidence for a genetic cause was found by Slater and Shields (1969) in an important study of 17 monozygous and 28 dizygous twin pairs, each containing a twin with an anxiety neurosis. Forty-one per cent of the monozygous co-twins also had an anxiety neurosis, as against only 4 per cent of the dizygous twins.

Biochemical and endocrine investigations

In anxious patients secretions of adrenaline and noradrenaline are increased, but these are accompaniments of anxiety rather than its cause. Lactate levels after exercise are known to be greater in patients with anxiety neurosis than among normal subjects (Pitts and McClure 1967). Also symptoms resembling those of an anxiety neurosis can be provoked by infusions of lactate (Bonn *et al.* 1971). This is unlikely to reveal much about the causes of anxiety, though it may indicate one mechanism by which symptoms can be prolonged.

Psychoanalytic theories

These theories suppose that anxiety is experienced when the ego is overwhelmed by excitation. Freud suggested that this excess energy has three possible sources: the outside world (realistic anxiety), the id (neurotic anxiety), and the superego (moral anxiety). Breakdown is more likely when the ego has been weakened by developmental failures in childhood. Another part of psycho-analytic theory supposes that anxiety is experienced for the first time during the process of birth (primary anxiety). It is thought that the child is overwhelmed by stimulation at the very moment of separation from its mother. It has been suggested that this may explain why separation can provoke anxiety. This idea that separation is an important cause of neurotic anxiety has been elaborated by Bowlby (1969).

Taken literally, ideas of energy flowing between compartments of the mind are impossible to reconcile with modern knowledge from the neurosciences. Viewed as metaphors representing the instinctual part of man in conflict with his social training and his conscience, they reflect everyday experience but add little to it.

Learning theories

In these theories, anxiety is regarded as a fear response that has been attached to another stimulus through conditioning. They seek to explain the tendency to develop excessive anxiety in terms of an inherited predisposition that is reflected in undue lability of the autonomic nervous system, and detected by measures of neuroticism. This idea has some merit as an explanation of the development and spread of anxiety, because it relates to known biological mechanisms (see Gray (1971) for a useful review).

Prognosis

Among anxiety neuroses of recent onset, most recover quickly. Among those lasting for more than six months, however, about 80 per cent are present three years later despite efforts at treatment (Kedward and Cooper 1966). Poor prognosis is associated with severe symptoms and with syncopal episodes, agitation, derealization, hysterical features, and suicidal ideas (Kerr *et al.* 1974). The prognosis of anxiety neurosis with mainly physical symptoms can be judged from a follow-up study of 'effort syndrome' by Wheeler *et al.* (1950). Although most patients had a good social prognosis, nine out of ten still had some symptoms 20 years later. Whilst this finding supports the clinical impression that patients who complain of physical symptoms are less easy to help than those who recognize the emotional basis for their disorder, it may also reflect the limitations of treatment at the time of the study. Thus, in a more recent study of medical patients with anxiety neurosis, two-thirds were found to have improved substantially or recovered within six years (Noyes and Clancy 1976).

Although a considerable proportion of anxiety neuroses persist for several years, they do not change their form. On follow-up, the rates of schizophrenia and manic-depressive illness found in patients with anxiety neurosis are no greater than in the general population (Greer 1969; Kerr *et al.* 1974). On the other hand, brief depressive episodes occur repeatedly among many patients who have long-standing anxiety neuroses (Clancy *et al.* 1978). It is often during one of these episodes that patients seek further treatment.

Treatment

Supportive measures

For most brief anxiety neuroses, anxiolytic drugs need not be prescribed. Discussion with the doctor and reassurance are usually sufficient. Interviews need not be lengthy provided the patient feels that he has the doctor's undivided attention, and that his problems have been understood sympathetically. A clear explanation should be given of any physical symptoms of anxiety; for example, that palpitations are an exaggeration of a normal reaction to stressful events and not a sign of heart disease. Anxiety is prolonged by uncertainty and a clear plan of treatment helps to reduce it.

The immediate treatment of an acute episode of overbreathing is simple. The patient is shown that the paraesthesiae and other symptoms disappear quickly if he breathes from a bag in order to increase the concentration of carbon dioxide in the alveolar air. This demonstration is usually enough to restore normal breathing. It is less easy to prevent the condition from recurring; however, the patient should be made aware of the way he breathes when anxious, and he should be encouraged to control this by practising breathing exercises.

Drugs

The introduction of safe and effective anxiolytic drugs has encouraged doctors to rely on them too much in the treatment of anxiety states. Drugs are sometimes prescribed without adequate assessment of the causes of anxiety. Thorough assessment will often make it clear that drugs are not required, or else should be only one component in a wider plan that encourages the patient to solve the difficulties from which the anxiety neurosis arose.

If an anxiolytic drug is required, one of the **benzodiazepines** should be selected. Diazepam is a suitable drug, given in doses between 5 mg twice daily in mild cases and 10 mg three times a day in the most severe. It is good practice to stop the drug after a few weeks to make certain that it is still required. Barbiturates should no longer be used for anxiety because patients readily become dependent upon them. Some doctors still prescribe barbiturates for a few days to control severe anxiety, but a benzodiazepine is safer and equally effective provided the dose is adequate.

Beta adrenoceptor antagonists have a limited use in treating anxiety neuroses in which palpitations are the most troublesome symptom. Otherwise they are no more effective than benzodiazepines and less safe (see Chapter 17 for further advice on their use).

Antidepressant drugs are also used to treat anxiety states, but there is often misunderstanding about the circumstances in which they are likely to be effective. Tricyclic drugs have two pharmacological properties: antidepressant effects which are appropriate when the anxiety symptoms are secondary to depressive illness; and anxiolytic properties which are sometimes useful in a primary anxiety neurosis when medication has to be prolonged beyond the few weeks for which benzodiazepine should be prescribed.

Monoamine oxidase inhibitors also have anxiolytic effects. They have been reported valuable in both general and phobic anxiety neuroses (Sargant and Dally 1962), but there is no convincing evidence that these effects are superior to those of either benzodiazepines or tricyclic antidepressants. Since monoamine oxidase inhibitors interact in a potentially dangerous way with other drugs and with foodstuffs, they should seldom be used, and then only after other appropriate drugs have been tried without success.

Relaxation training can be as effective as drugs in reducing anxiety of mild or moderate degree, but is of less value when anxiety is severe. Since it takes time to learn the technique, relaxation cannot be used in the early stages of treatment unless the patient knows the method already. A more elaborate form of behavioural treatment known as **anxiety management training (AMT)** may be more effective than simple relaxation. Both methods of training are discussed further in Chapter 18. Yoga and other techniques of meditation give relief to some patients not only because of an element of relaxation, but also by encouraging them to review their values in a way that often leads to a less stressful life.

PHOBIC ANXIETY NEUROSES

In ICD 9 these neuroses are called phobic anxiety states and defined as 'neurotic states with an abnormally intense dread of certain objects or specific situations which would not normally have that effect'. To this definition should be added the important observation that the dread is accompanied by a strong wish to avoid the feared objects or situations. Three main phobic syndromes are usually recognized: simple phobias, agoraphobia, and social phobias. Some less common syndromes will be mentioned briefly later in this section.

The prevalence of phobic disorders in the community is about six per thousand. About two per thousand are seriously disabling and of these half are agoraphobias (Agras *et al.* 1969). Agoraphobia and simple phobias are more common among women but social phobias are equally common in men and women.

Simple phobic neuroses

Many normal people find that some specific object or situation causes them unreasonable anxiety: heights, thunderstorms, spiders, and dogs are common examples. In the past it has been fashionable to invent names for these fears, such as acrophobia (fear of heights), arachnophobia (fear of spiders), and claustrophobia (fear of enclosed spaces). There is nothing to recommend these terms which convey no more information than a description of the fear in every-day language.

Simple phobias are common symptoms among children. When simple phobic neuroses occur in adults, those of animals almost always date from early childhood, while those of heights, darkness, thunderstorms, and other situations more often start in early adult life. A simple phobic neurosis has three components: first, symptoms of anxiety identical to those of any other anxiety state; second, anxious thoughts usually in anticipation of situations the person may have to encounter; and third, the habit of avoiding situations that provoke fear. Specific fears, although narrowly circumscribed, can be intense and cause considerable suffering even when the person is not in direct contact with the feared object. For example a patient with a thunder phobia not only becomes terrified during storms, but also feels intense anxiety whenever there is any possibility of thunder, for example on a cloudy or humid day.

Simple phobic neuroses seldom present difficulties of **differential diagnosis**. It is important to remember that phobic patients sometimes ask for help with the phobia only when they suffer from a depressive illness that makes them less able to tolerate the phobia even though its severity has not altered. In these circumstances it is the depression not the phobia that needs treatment.

Agoraphobia

Agoraphobic patients become anxious when they travel from home, mix with crowds, or are in situations that they cannot easily leave. The symptoms are so diverse that some writers (such as Snaith 1981) have concluded that agoraphobia is not a single syndrome. However, despite the variations in the clinical picture, a central group of symptoms can be identified that characterize a single disorder (see Mathews *et al.* 1981). These can be grouped conveniently into anxiety symptoms, situations that provoke anxiety, and avoidance behaviour. In agoraphobia the anxiety symptoms are no different from those of any other anxiety states. However, the associated anxious thoughts are characteristically centred on ideas of fainting or losing control.

The most characteristic features of agoraphobia are the situations in which anxiety symptoms appear and the pattern of avoidance that develops. The situations include buses and trains, shops and supermarkets, and any place that cannot be left suddenly without attracting attention, such as the hairdresser's chair or a seat in the middle of a row in the theatre or cinema. As the condition progresses, the patient increasingly avoids these places so that eventually only a few local shops can be reached. In the most severe cases, the patient cannot leave the house at all, a condition sometimes called the **housebound housewife syndrome**. Agoraphobic patients become increasingly dependent on the spouse and other relations. The consequent demands on the spouse often lead to arguments, but serious marital problems are no more common among agarophobics than among other people of similar social background (Buglass *et al.* 1977).

There are many other variations in the detailed pattern of the symptoms. Some patients can go by car without symptoms but feel anxious travelling in other ways; some are anxious in a car but not on foot or riding a bicycle. Agoraphobics usually feel less anxious when accompanied by someone trusted; and for some the presence of a child or even a pet dog reduces the symptoms. These peculiarities may suggest a histrionic component to the behaviour, but true hysterical symptoms are not commonly part of the syndrome.

At first agoraphobic patients are anxious only when exposed to situations that provoke their symptoms, but gradually they become anxious even when they contemplate these situations. In severe cases this anticipatory anxiety appears hours before the patient has to go out, thereby adding greatly to the distress.

Certain other symptoms are common among agoraphobic patients. Depression is frequent and obsessional thoughts or depersonalization also occur. Roth (1959) reported that depersonalization is a particularly important symptom and described a **phobic anxiety—depersonalization syndrome**, starting usually after intense stress (hence the alternative name 'calamity syndrome'). Roth also reported EEG changes similar to those found in disorders of the temporal lobe, and suggested that there might be an organic basis to the syndrome. Subsequent work has not confirmed these views, and agoraphobic patients with depersonalization should not be regarded as fundamentally different from agoraphobic patients without depersonalization.

Agoraphobia usually begins in the early or middle twenties, though there is a further period of high incidence in the mid-thirties (Marks and Gelder 1960). The first episode of anxiety is usually clearly recalled by the patient. Typically, while waiting for public transport or shopping in a crowded store, the patient suddenly becomes extremely anxious without knowing why, feels faint and experiences palpitations. She rushes away from the place and goes home or to hospital. Recovery is almost always rapid. When the same or similar surroundings are entered again, anxiety is felt again and a further hurried escape is made. As this sequence recurs over the next weeks or months, the symptoms appear in more and more places, and the habit of avoidance grows. It is unusual to discover any serious stress that could account for the first episode of anxiety, but it is common to find a background of social or emotional problems (such as worry about a sick child), or less often of concurrent physical illness or recent childbirth.

The **differential diagnosis** of agoraphobia includes anxiety neurosis, social phobic neurosis, depressive disorder, and paranoid state. In **anxiety neurosis** the symptoms often increase when the patient is in public places, but the characteristic pattern of avoidance found in agoraphobia is lacking and the patient does not describe situations in which anxiety is wholly absent. In severe cases, this distinction can be difficult but fortunately it is not of great practical importance for treatment. Agoraphobia may be confused with a **social phobic neurosis** (see below) because many agoraphobic patients feel anxious in certain social situations, and some social phobics may avoid buses and shops. However, detailed enquiry into the pattern of avoidance will reveal whether it is typical of agoraphobia. Agoraphobic symptoms can appear as a minor part of a **depressive disorder** but the diagnosis is seldom in doubt after careful history-taking and mental state examination. A common mistake is to overlook the development of a depressive disorder in a patient who has had agoraphobia for many years. Such a patient may complain that the agoraphobia is becoming worse rather than that she feels depressed. Thorough assessment of the history and mental state will usually settle the issue. Occasionally a patient with **a paranoid state** gives a history suggestive of agoraphobia, but careful examination of the mental state will usually reveal persecutory delusions or ideas of reference that account for the avoidance behaviour.

Social phobic neurosis

Patients with social phobias feel anxious in and avoid situations in which they may be observed by other people. These include restaurants, canteens, dinner parties, public transport, the hairdressers, theatres, cinemas, and places where they may have to speak in public. Unlike the paranoid patient, the person with a social phobia realizes that these concerns are exaggerated and does not feel persecuted. The symptoms that develop in these situations are those of any anxiety neurosis, although blushing, trembling, and nausea are particularly common. Patients usually believe that other people notice the symptoms and this belief leads to more anxiety. Like agoraphobics, patients with social phobic neuroses think about the situations in advance and often feel anxious long before encountering them. Depression, obsessions, and depersonalization may occur as part of the syndrome but less frequently than in agoraphobia. Patients often take alcohol to relieve symptoms, and alcohol abuse is more common in this phobia than in the other phobic syndromes.

Social phobic neuroses are equally common in men and women, and usually begin between the ages of 17 and 30. The first episode is often in a restaurant or other public place, the anxiety starting suddenly for no obvious reason. This is followed by a gradual increase of anxiety and avoidance, comparable to that described in agoraphobia. Because the symptoms are so varied, some writers (for example Snaith 1981) have concluded that social phobias do not constitute a distinct psychopathological entity. This view is not supported by clinical experience which shows that the syndrome remains constant over many years and does not change into another neurosis.

The **differential diagnosis** of a social phobic neurosis includes anxiety neurosis, depressive illness, and schizophrenia. For all these conditions, the distinguishing points are the same as those already described under agoraphobia. Social phobic neurosis may also be mistaken for **personality disorder** characterized by shyness and lack of self-confidence. There are, however, two points of distinction: social phobic neurosis begins more abruptly and involves a smaller range of circumstances. Social phobias must also be distinguished from **social inadequacy**, that is primary lack of social skills with secondary anxiety. Social inadequacy is found commonly among schizophrenic patients and people with personality disorders, and is more common in men. Its features include hesitant, dull and inaudible diction, inappropriate use of facial expression and gesture, and failure to look at other people at appropriate times in conversation (see Bryant *et al.* (1976) for a full account).

Other phobic neuroses

(i) Of illness

So-called illness phobias are more closely related to obsessional thoughts than to the other phobic disorders. The patient experiences repeated fearful thoughts that he might have cancer, venereal disease, or some other serious illness. Such fears may be associated with avoidance of hospitals, but are not otherwise specific to situations.

(ii) Of dental treatment

About 5 per cent of adults have fears of the dentist's chair, which can become so severe that all dental treatment is avoided and serious caries develop (see Gale and Ayer 1969; Kleinknecht, Klepac and Alexander 1973).

(iii) Of excretion

Patients with these phobias either become anxious and unable to pass urine in public lavatories, or have frequent urges to pass urine with associated dread of incontinence. Such patients often arrange their lives so as never to be far from a lavatory. A few have comparable symptoms centred around defecation.

(iv) Of vomiting

Some patients fear that they may vomit in a public place, often a bus or train; in these surroundings they feel anxious and nauseated. A smaller group have repeated fears that other people will vomit in such places.

(v) Fear of flying

Anxiety during aeroplane travel is, of course, common. A few people have such intense fear that flying is impossible and they seek treatment. This fear occurs occasionally among pilots who have had an accident while flying.

(vi) Space phobia

In this syndrome described by Marks (1981), the central feature is a fear of falling made worse by the absence of any immediate source of support. It therefore appears especially in open spaces. It has a superficial resemblance to agoraphobia, but starts later (mean age 55 years), is seldom accompanied by anxiety or depression, does not respond to behaviour therapy, and is often accompanied by evidence of neurological or cardiovascular disorder.

Aetiology

Simple phobic neurosis

The simple phobic neuroses of adults are often the remnants of fears that began in childhood; for this reason they almost certainly differ from other neuroses in their aetiology. Phobias of animals and insects are common in childhood, but usually disappear spontaneously by the teenage years. The aetiological problem is, therefore, to explain why a few persist into adult life. There is no satisfactory answer except that, not surprisingly, the most severe phobias last longest. This raises the problem of why some childhood fears are more intense than others. Some may be learnt by imitation of parents or of other children who are afraid. Others may be acquired by conditioning in response to frightening events (for example a fear of dogs after being bitten by one).

The psychoanalytic explanation is that simple phobias represent some other source of anxiety that has been excluded from consciousness by repression and displacement. In other words the manifest fear is the symbolic representation of an unconscious conflict.

Agoraphobia

Neither family studies (Buglass *et al.* 1977) nor investigations of twins (Torgerson 1979) point to specific genetic influences as important. Studies of personality have all been carried out after the onset of agoraphobia, so that it is difficult to interpret reports of increased dependency and high neuroticism (see Mathews *et al.* (1981) for a review of the evidence). Solyom *et al.* 1974 found that agoraphobic patients were more likely than controls to report having been over-protected by their mothers, but Buglass *et al.* (1977) found no difference between agoraphobics and controls in history of separation anxiety or other indices of dependency. Turning to precipitating factors, there is no evidence that a single stressful event usually precedes the first onset of agoraphobia. However, clinical accounts often indicate a source of worry in the patient's life at the time of onset, and this has been broadly confirmed by investigation (Buglass *et al.* 1977).

Against these few facts about the causes of agoraphobia, three main theories have to be considered. According to psychodynamic theory, when unconscious conflicts are not allowed direct expression because of repression, they may be transformed by displacement into phobias. This idea is well expressed in Freud's own words: 'in order to simplify what is very often a complicated business, let us suppose that the agoraphobic patient is invariably afraid of feelings of temptation that are aroused when meeting people in the street. In his phobia he brings about a displacement and is henceforth afraid of an external situation. What he gains from this . . . [is that] one can save oneself from an external danger by flight; fleeing from an internal danger is a difficult enterprise' (Freud 1933, p. 84).

Learning theory attempts to explain agoraphobia as a series of conditioned fear responses with learned avoidance. This theory is only convincing if there is a stimulus for the first episode of anxiety; as mentioned above, such a stimulus is not usually reported.

On the available evidence the best explanation is as follows. Agoraphobia develops when there is a background of stressful events leading to a moderate level of anxiety. A small additional stress then leads to an acute anxiety attack. This leads to avoidance behaviour if the person lacks self-confidence and attributes his anxiety to the circumstances surrounding the first attack, rather than to the antecedent worry about other problems. This conviction, coupled perhaps with a conditioning process, generates further anxiety when the same situation is encountered later. In this way the pattern of anxiety and avoidance becomes established.

When symptoms have begun in one situation, they may spread to others as a result of conditioning coupled with social reinforcement of the tendency to avoid. Some of this reinforcement seems to arise from the family's wishes to spare the patient distress.

Social phobic neuroses

Social phobias presumably have the same general causes as other phobic neuroses. There is, however, no convincing explanation why a patient should develop a social phobia rather than some other kind. The main reason could be the circumstances in which the first episode of acute anxiety was experienced, coupled perhaps with general lack of self-confidence in social encounters.

Prognosis

There is no systematic follow-up study of either simple phobias or agoraphobia. Clinical experience suggests that, among adults, severe simple phobias have usually persisted since childhood and continue for many years. Social phobias that have lasted for more than a year probably change little in the next five years, but many improve gradually over a longer period. Agoraphobia that has lasted for a year usually changes little over the next five years (Marks 1969). This persistence over many years runs counter to the suggestion that agoraphobia is not a specific syndrome. Brief episodes of depression often occur, but when they remit, the original agoraphobic syndrome reappears.

Treatment

Since phobic symptoms are sometimes secondary to a depressive disorder, the first step is always to look for and treat such a primary condition if detected.

Although some immediate relief of phobic symptoms may be gained from **anxiolytic drugs**, lasting improvement requires attention to the accompanying avoidance behaviour. In cases of recent onset, the patient should be encouraged to make determined efforts to go out more. However, once avoidance behaviour has become established, it will usually be necessary to use one of several methods of **behaviour therapy**. If the patient has a simple phobia of an object or situation that he can encounter readily, treatment by exposure usually gives good results. If the feared situation is not readily available (for example thunderstorms) desensitization in imagination can be used instead (see Chapter 18).

For agoraphobia, the treatment of choice is programmed practice (described in Chapter 18). Patients are trained to overcome avoidance behaviour in a planned way, and practice is carried out for at least an hour every day. The therapist takes the role of teacher, encouraging the patient to plan and execute tasks. Substantial and lasting changes in avoidance behaviour usually follow, but after treatment most patients are left with some mild anxiety in situations that originally caused panic (see Mathews *et al.* 1981).

Antidepressant drugs have also been used to treat agoraphobic patients who have no concurrent depressive illness. Presumably such drugs are effective because of their anxiolytic properties. Monoamine oxidase inhibitors reduce agoraphobic symptoms but there is a high rate of relapse when the drugs are stopped (Tyrer and Steinberg 1975). The tricyclic antidepressant imipramine has been shown to have similar effects, but again there is a high relapse rate when the drug is discontinued (Zitrin *et al.* 1978). These drugs can be used to provide temporary relief when the illness is expected to be brief or when behavioural treatment cannot be offered at once. Some clinicians consider that imipramine is the treatment of choice for agoraphobia (e.g. Zitrin *et al.* 1980). The authors do not consider that there is, as yet, strong evidence for this view.

OBSESSIVE COMPULSIVE NEUROSIS

In ICD 9 obsessive–compulsive neurosis is defined as a state in which 'the outstanding symptom is a feeling of subjective compulsion – which must be resisted – to carry out some action, to dwell on an idea, to recall an experience, or to ruminate on an abstract topic. Unwanted thoughts which intrude, the insistency of words or ideas, ruminations or trains of thought are perceived by the patient to be inappropriate or nonsensical. The obsessional urge or idea is recognised as alien to the personality but as coming from within the self. Obsessional actions may be quasi-ritual performances designed to relieve anxiety e.g. washing the hands to deal with contamination. Attempts to dispel the unwelcome thoughts or urges may lead to a severe inner struggle, with intense anxiety.'

Obsessive–compulsive neuroses are considerably less common than anxiety neuroses. Estimates of the one year prevalence vary from 0.1 to 2.3 per 1000 (see Carey *et al.* 1980). Men and women are probably affected about equally.

Clinical picture

Obsessional neuroses are characterized by obsessional thinking, compulsive behaviour, and varying degrees of anxiety, depression, and depersonalization. Obsessional and compulsive symptoms are described in Chapter 4 but the reader may find it helpful if the main features are repeated here.

Obsessional thoughts are words, ideas, beliefs, and images recognized by the patient as his own, that intrude forcibly into his mind. Because they are usually unpleasant, attempts are made to exclude them. It is the combination of an inner sense of compulsion and of efforts at resistance that characterize obsessional symptoms, but the amount of resistance is the more variable of the two. Obsessional thoughts may take the form of single words, phrases, or rhymes; they are usually unpleasant or shocking to the patient, and may be obscene or blasphemous. **Obsessional images** are vividly imagined scenes often of a violent or disgusting kind, involving for example abnormal sexual practices.

Obsessional ruminations are internal debates in which arguments for and against even the simplest everyday action are reviewed endlessly. Some **obsessional doubts** concern actions that may not have been completed adequately, such as turning off a gas tap or securing a door; others concern actions that may have harmed other people, for example, driving a car past a cyclist might have caused him to fall off his bicycle. Sometimes doubts are related to religious convictions or observances ('scruples') – a phenomenon well known to those who hear confession.

Obsessional impulses are urges to perform acts, usually of a violent or embarassing kind; for example, leaping in front of a car, injuring a child, or shouting blasphemies in church.

Obsessional rituals include both mental activities, such as counting repeatedly in a special way or repeating a certain form of words; and repeated but senseless behaviours, such as washing the hands 20 or more times a day. Some of these have an understandable connection with obsessional thoughts that precede them, for example repeated handwashing and thoughts of contamination. Other rituals have no such connection, for example routines concerned with laying out clothes in a complicated way before dressing. Some patients feel compelled to repeat such actions a certain number of times; if this cannot be achieved, they have to start the whole sequence again. Patients are invariably aware that their rituals are illogical, and usually try to hide them. Some fear that their symptoms are a sign of incipient madness, and are greatly helped by reassurance that this is not so.

Both obsessional thoughts and rituals inevitably lead to slow performance of everyday activities. However, a minority of obsessional patients are afflicted by extreme **obsessional slowness** that is out of proportion to other symptoms (Rachman 1974).

Obsessional thoughts and compulsive rituals may worsen in certain situations; for example, obsessional thoughts about harming other people often increase in a kitchen or other place where knives are kept. Because patients often avoid such situations, there may be a superficial resemblance to the characteristic pattern of avoidance found in a phobic anxiety state. It is partly for this reason that obsessional thoughts with fearful content (such as thoughts about knives) have been called obsessional phobias.

Anxiety is an important component of the obsessional neurosis. Some rituals are followed by a diminution of anxiety, whilst others are followed by increased anxiety (Walker and Beech 1969).

Obsessional patients are often **depressed**. In some, this seems to be an understandable reaction to the obsessional symptoms, but others have recurring depressive mood swings that arise independently. A proportion of obsessional patients also report **depersonalization**.

The **obsessional personality** is described in Chapter 5. It is important to realize that obsessional personality and obsessional neurosis do not have a simple one-to-one relationship. Obsessional personality is over-represented among patients who develop obsessional neuroses, but about a third of obsessional neurotics have other types of personality (Lewis 1936). Moreover, people with obsessional personality are more likely to develop depressive disorders than obsessional neurosis (Pollitt 1960).

Differential diagnosis

Obsessional neuroses have to be distinguished from other disorders in which obsessional symptoms occur. The distinction from **anxiety neuroses** or **phobic neuroses** should seldom be difficult provided that a careful history is taken and the mental state is examined thoroughly. The course of obsessional neuroses is often punctuated by periods of **depression** in which the obsessional symptoms increase; when this happens the depressive disorder may be overlooked. **Primary depressive disorder** may also present with obsessional symptoms; it is particularly important to bear this condition in mind because it usually responds well to antidepressant treatment. Obsessional neurosis is occasionally difficult to distinguish from **schizophrenia**, especially when the degree of resistance is doubtful, the obsessional thoughts are peculiar in content (for example mingling sexual and blasphemous themes) or the rituals are exceptionally odd. In such cases it is important to search for schizophrenic symptoms, and to question relatives carefully about other aspects of the patient's behaviour. Obsessional symptoms are found occasionally in **organic cerebral disorders** and were especially common after the encephalitis lethargica epidemic in the 1920s.

Aetiology

Like obsessions, the intrusive thoughts experienced by normal people are concerned with sexual and aggressive themes, and they are increased by stressful events. Unlike obsessions, they occur only occasionally, and do not persist (Rachman and Hodgson 1980). It is the frequency, intensity, and above all the persistence of obsessional phenomena that have to be explained.

Genetics

Obsessional neuroses have been found in about 5–7 per cent of the parents of obsessional neurotics (Rüdin 1953; Brown 1942); although low, this rate is higher than in the general population. These findings could, of course, reflect environmental as well as genetic causes. Twin studies would help to identify the genetic component, but too few cases have been reported to allow firm conclusions. Whilst the evidence for obsessional neuroses is uncertain, obsessional personality traits can be accounted for largely by genetic influences (Murray *et al.* 1980).

Organic factors

The clinical features of some severe obsessional neuroses are so difficult to explain in psychological terms that organic brain disorder has been suggested as the cause. Further evidence for an organic cause was the frequency of obsessional symptoms in patients after the epidemic of encephalitis lethargica mentioned above. However, in most obsessional patients there is no convincing evidence of disease of the central nervous system.

Relation to schizophrenia

The few reported cases of schizophrenia following obsessional neuroses (for example Stengel 1945) can probably be explained by coincidence. Follow up investigations clearly show that typical obsessional neurotics seldom develop features of schizophrenia (Kringlen 1965).

Early experience

It is uncertain what part early experience plays in the aetiology of obsessional neurosis. Obsessional mothers might be expected to transmit symptoms to their children by imitative learning. However, the children of obsessional neurotics have an increased risk of non-specific neurotic symptoms, but not of obsessional symptoms (Cowie 1961).

Psychoanalytic theories

Freud (1895) originally suggested that obsessional symptoms result from repressed impulses of an aggressive or sexual nature. This idea fits with the turbulent sexual fantasies of many obsessional patients, and with their restraints on their own sexual and aggressive impulses. Freud also proposed that obsessional symptoms occur as a result of regression to the anal stage of development. Although this idea has not been confirmed by objective evidence, it is consistent with the obsessional patient's frequent concerns over excretory functions and dirt. It also draws attention to the aggressive quality of many of the symptoms. However, as a causal explanation of obsessional neurosis, it is not convincing.

Learning theory

It has been suggested that obsessional rituals are the equivalent of avoidance responses, but as a general explanation this cannot be sustained because anxiety increases rather than decreases after some rituals (Walker and Beech 1969). A useful review of this and other aspects of aetiology is given by Rachman and Hodgson (1980).

Prognosis

About two-thirds of cases improve by the end of a year. Cases lasting more than a year usually run a fluctuating course, with periods of partial or complete remission lasting a few months to several years (see Pollitt 1957). Prognosis is worse when the personality is obsessional and symptoms severe (Kringlen 1965), and when there are continuing stressful events in the patient's life. Severe cases may be exceedingly persistent; for example, in a study of obsessional patients admitted to hospital, Kringlen (1965) found that three-quarters remained unchanged 13–20 years later.

Treatment

In treatment, it is important to remember that obsessional neuroses often run a fluctuating course with long periods of remission. The patient's evident distress often seems to call for vigorous treatment, but if the natural course of the condition is kept in mind, the doctor will avoid the common error of overtreating it. It is also essential to remember that depressive disorder often accompanies obsessional neurosis, and that effective treatment of the depressive disorder often leads to improvement in the obsessional symptoms.

For this reason, in every patient presenting with obsessional neurosis, a thorough search should be made for depressive illness.

Treatment should begin with an explanation of the symptoms, and if necessary with reassurance that they are not an early sign of madness (a common concern of obsessional patients). Obsessional patients often involve other family members in their rituals, so in planning treatment it is essential to interview relatives and encourage them to adopt a firm but sympathetic attitude to the patient.

Drugs

Anxiolytic drugs give some short-term symptomatic relief but should not be prescribed for more than a few weeks at a time. If anxiolytic treatment is needed for more than a month or two, small doses of a tricyclic antidepressant or a major tranquillizer are sometimes of value. Any coincident depressive illness should be treated with an antidepressant drug in full dosage. It has been reported that one tricyclic antidepressant, clomipramine, has a specific action against obsessional symptoms (Capstick 1975) but a controlled clinical trial (Marks *et al.* 1980) indicated that the drug effects are modest and occur only in patients with definite depressive symptoms.

Behaviour therapy

Obsessional rituals usually improve with a combination of response prevention and exposure to any environmental cues that increase them (see Chapter 18 for a description of these treatments). About two-thirds of patients with moderately severe rituals can be expected to improve substantially but not completely (Boulagouris 1977; Rachman and Hodgson 1980). When rituals are reduced by this treatment, the accompanying obsessional thoughts usually improve as well.

Behavioural treatment is considerably less effective for obsessional thoughts occurring without rituals. The technique of thought stopping has been used for many years but there is no good evidence that it has a specific effect. Indeed Stern *et al.* (1973) found no difference between thought stopping directed to obsessional thoughts, and thought stopping directed to irrelevant thoughts.

Psychotherapy

We have noted that obsessional neuroses run a fluctuating course and may improve eventually whatever treatment is given. Until recovery, supportive interviews can benefit patients by providing continuing hope. Joint interviews with the spouse are indicated when marital problems seem to be aggravating the symptoms. However, exploratory and interpretative psychotherapy seldom help. Indeed some obsessional patients are made worse because these procedures encourage painful and unproductive rumination about the subjects discussed during treatment.

Psychosurgery

The immediate results of psychosurgery for severe obsessional neurosis are often striking, with a marked reduction in tension and distress. It has not been proved, however, that the long-term prognosis is improved, since no prospective controlled trial has been carried out. In a retrospective survey, Tan *et al.* (1971) studied 24 leucotomized patients, of whom 23 had undergone a bimedial operation. Compared with retrospectively chosen controls, the operated patients improved more in obsessional symptoms and social handicap over the next five years; post-operative personality changes were slight. For other forms of operation only uncontrolled assessments were available. Göktepe *et al.* (1975) followed 18 patients for two years after subcaudate tractotomy, and reported that seven recovered and eight improved. Mitchell-Heggs *et al.* (1976) followed 27 patients for 16 months after limbic leucotomy and reported that seven recovered and 11 improved substantially. However, these periods of follow-up are much too short to allow definite conclusions.

In the absence of information from controlled studies, it is only justifiable to consider brain surgery when it has been demonstrated repeatedly in the individual patient that all other methods have failed. Even then surgery should only be considered when the obsessional neurosis has persisted unchanged for many years. Leucotomy should never be used unless there has been a year of vigorous inpatient or day patient treatment including both antidepressant drugs and behavioural treatment. If this practice is followed, the operation will be undertaken very rarely indeed. If the operation is done at all, it should probably be followed by a vigorous programme of behaviour therapy.

HYSTERIA

The essence of hysteria is that there are symptoms and signs of disease with three characteristics – they occur in the absence of physical pathology, they are produced unconsciously, and they are not caused by overactivity of the sympathetic nervous system. Obviously this concept is bound to give rise to difficulties in clinical practice, since physical pathology can seldom be excluded completely when a patient is first seen. It is for this reason that the diagnosis of hysteria must often be provisional when first made – a vital point to grasp. These diagnostic difficulties led Slater (1965) to suggest that hysteria should be abandoned as a diagnostic category. However, the clinical problem still arises, so it seems more useful to consider how diagnosis can be improved, a point to be taken up later. Although hysterical symptoms are fairly common, hysterical neurosis is not. Nevertheless the neurosis gives rise to many errors of diagnosis, and it is therefore discussed here at a length out of proportion to its numerical importance.

Epidemiology

The lifetime prevalence of hysteria in the general population is difficult to determine but is probably between 3–6 per thousand for women, and substantially lower for men (see Carey *et al.* 1980). Clinical experience suggests that most cases of the neurosis begin before the age of 35, and few new cases appear after 40, although hysterical symptoms commonly occur as part of some other disorder well beyond this age.

Clinical picture

General considerations

The variety of symptoms in hysteria is very great. They are sometimes divided into dissociative and conversion symptoms. The term **dissociative** is used to indicate an apparent dissociation between different mental activities. The major dissociative reactions are amnesia, fugue, somnabulism, and multiple personality. The term **conversion** stems from Freud's theory that mental energy can be converted into certain physical symptoms. A less controversial nomenclature divides the symptoms of hysteria into mental and physical. The mental symptoms include amnesia, fugue, behaviour like that of a major mental illness, and 'multiple personality'. The physical symptoms include paralysis, fits, aphonia, disorder of gait, anaesthesia, blindness, deafness, and abdominal pain.

Although hysterical symptoms are not produced deliberately, they are created around the patient's ideas about illness. Sometimes the symptoms imitate those of a relative or friend who has been ill. Sometimes they originate in the patient's own experience of ill health; for example hysterical memory loss may appear in someone who has had a previous head injury. The reproduction of disease will be least accurate in people who know least about it, such as children and the mentally retarded, and most accurate in people with special knowledge, such as those working in hospital. As a rule, there are obvious discrepancies between hysterical signs and symptoms and those of organic disease; for example, the pattern of hysterical anaesthesia does not correspond to the anatomical innervation of the part. Thorough physical examination is therefore essential in every case.

The symptoms of hysteria usually confer some advantage on the patient. For this reason, following Freud, hysteria has been said to produce **secondary gain** (the primary gain is that anxiety arising from a psychological conflict is excluded from the patient's conscious mind). Thus a woman may be spared the care of an elderly relative if she develops hysterical paralysis of the arm. Although characteristic of hysteria, secondary gain is not confined to it; people with physical illness sometimes gain some advantage from their misfortunes. A woman with paralysis of the arm due to organic cause may be pleased to be spared from nursing an elderly relative. Secondary gain is also seen at times in other neuroses; for example, an agoraphobic woman may receive more attention from her husband when she cannot go out. It follows that although secondary gain is an important feature of hysteria, it cannot be used to support the diagnosis.

Patients with hysterical symptoms often show less than the expected amount of distress, a state sometimes called *'belle indifférence'* following French writers of the nineteenth century. This is not the same as the attitude of stoical patients who do not allow themselves to show distress. The patient with hysteria may be unconcerned by his symptoms, but often shows exaggerated emotional reactions in other ways. In keeping with this, in a small series of patients with conversion hysteria, Lader and Sartorius (1968) found exceptionally high levels of autonomic arousal.

Physical symptoms

The **motor symptoms** of hysteria include paralysis of voluntary muscles, tremor, tics, and disorders of gait. When a limb with hysterical **paralysis** is examined, the lack of movement is often seen to result from simultaneous action of flexors and extensors. If no muscle activity follows a request to move the part, other tests usually show that the muscles are capable of reacting when the patient's attention is directed elsewhere. The pattern of paralysis does not conform to the innervation of the part. Appropriate changes in reflexes are not present; in particular the plantar response always remains flexor. Wasting is absent except in chronic cases, when disuse atrophy may occasionally be seen. With this exception, muscle wasting strongly suggests an organic cause. Similarly, although the limbs may be held in the flexed position, true contractures are uncommon. Hysterical disorders of **gait** are usually of a striking kind that draws attention to the patient and is worse when he is observed. The pattern does not resemble any described in known neurological conditions. Although dramatic unsteadiness may appear when balance is tested, it often disappears when the patient's attention is directed elsewhere.

Typically, hysterical **tremor** is coarse and involves the whole limb. It worsens when attention is drawn to it, but so do many tremors with neurological causes. Choreo-athetoid movements with organic cause are easily mistaken for hysterical symptoms. Disease of the nervous system should always be considered carefully before diagnosing any abnormal movement as hysterical.

Hysterical **aphonia** and **mutism** are not accompanied by any disorder of the lips, tongue, palate, or vocal cords, and the patient is able to cough normally. They are usually more extreme than corresponding conditions caused by organic lesions.

Sensory symptoms include anaesthesiae, paraesthesiae, hyperaesthesiae, and pain, as well as deafness and blindness. In general, the sensory changes are distinguished from those in organic disease by a distribution that does not conform to the known innervation of the part, by their varying intensity, and by their response to suggestion. The last point must be used cautiously in diagnosis because, among suggestible patients, sensory symptoms with an organic cause may also respond to suggestion. Hyperaesthesiae are usually felt in the head or abdomen, and may be described as painful or burning. Though extravagant descriptions are often said to support a hysterical origin for such symptoms, this is not a safe diagnostic point because patients with histrionic personalities may describe symptoms of organic disease in equally florid terms. The diagnosis of hysterical pain should be made only after a thorough search for organic causes (psychogenic pain is discussed further in Chapter 12).

Hysterical blindness may take the form of a concentric diminution of the visual field ('tunnel vision') but other patterns of field defect occur as well. The blindness is not accompanied by changes in pupillary reflexes, and there may be indirect evidence that the person can see, for example avoidance of bumping into furniture. The findings of perimetry are variable, whilst visual evoked responses are normal. Similar considerations apply to hysterical deafness.

Gastrointestinal symptoms include complaints of abdominal discomfort, flatulence, and regurgitation. Anorexia nervosa and bulimia nervosa are sometimes classified as hysterical symptoms but in this book are considered separately in Chapter 12. Repeated **vomiting** may be a symptom of emotional disturbance and is sometimes classified as hysterical. This diagnosis should be made only after thorough investigation to exclude physical causes. In any case, functional vomiting is a poorly understood condition, and is sufficiently unlike other manifestations of hysteria as to be appropriately considered separately. **Globus hystericus,** though often classified as hysterical, has been shown by cineradiology to be frequently caused by an abnormality in the physical mechanism of swallowing, or by oesophageal reflux or other disease affecting the oesophagus (Delahunty and Ardran 1976). It is a diagnosis that should be made exceedingly rarely, and then only after thorough physical investigation.

Mental symptoms

Hysterical **amnesia** starts suddenly. Patients are unable to recall long periods of their lives and sometimes deny any knowledge of their previous life or personal identity. A proportion of those who present in this way have concurrent organic disease, especially epilepsy, multiple sclerosis, or the effects of head injury (Kennedy and Neville 1957). These organic cases have similar symptoms to the psychogenic cases, and are also likely to start suddenly. Moreover, patients with organic disease may be as suggestible as those without it, and may recover their memory just as well.

In a hysterical **fugue** the patient not only loses his memory but also wanders away from his usual surroundings. When found he usually denies all memory of his whereabouts during the period of wandering, and may also deny knowledge of his personal identity. Apart from hysteria, fugue states are associated with epilepsy, severe depressive disorders, and alcoholism. They are also associated with suicide attempts. Many patients who present in a fugue state give a history of seriously disturbed relationships with their parents in childhood, and many others are habitual liars (Stengel 1941).

Hysterical pseudodementia is memory loss and behaviour that at first seem to indicate severe generalized intellectual impairment. Simple tests of memory are answered wrongly but in a way that strongly suggests the correct answer is in the patient's mind. In hysterical cases it is often particularly difficult to be certain how much of the behaviour is deliberately produced. Hysterical pseudodementia is often secondary to organic brain disease, epilepsy, or schizophrenia. (The term pseudodementia is also applied in a different sense to the apparent dementia of depressed elderly patients.)

The **Ganser syndrome** is a rare condition that has four features: the giving of 'approximate answers', somatic or mental symptoms of hysteria, hallucinations, and apparent clouding of consciousness. It was first described among prisoners (Ganser 1898) but is not confined to them. The term 'approximate answers' denotes responses to simple questions that are plainly wrong and strongly suggest that the correct reply is known. Thus a patient who is asked how many legs a chicken has, might reply three; or when asked to add two and two might answer five. When hallucinations are present, they are more often visual and may be of an elaborate kind. The obvious advantage that a prisoner can gain from illness, coupled with the approximate answers, often suggests a crude form of malingering. However, the condition is maintained so consistently that hysterical mechanisms are generally thought more likely. Others have suggested that it is an unusual form of psychosis (see Whitlock 1961). An organic psychosyndrome should be excluded, particularly when muddled thinking and visual hallucinations are part of the clinical picture.

The relation of **somnambulism** to other disorders classified under hysteria is less certain. In this condition, the patient, usually a child, wakes from sleep, rises and carries out complex sequences of behaviour without apparently being fully aware of his surroundings at the time or being able to recall the events afterwards. Sleepwalking takes place during non-REM sleep (Jacobson *et al.* 1965). Its similarity to the condition arising through hypnosis suggests it may be a state of dissociation. (One of Charcot's stages of hypnosis was somnabulism, but this began with the hypnoid state, not with normal sleep.)

In **multiple personality** there are sudden alternations between two patterns of behaviour, each of which is forgotten by the patient when the other is present. Each 'personality' is a complex and integrated scheme of emotional responses, attitudes, memories and social behaviour, and the new one usually contrasts strikingly with the patient's normal state. The condition is rare, though in the past it was probably fostered by the interest of doctors. Even rarer are cases in which there are more than two personalities. Striking examples of multiple personality have been described by Morton Prince (1908) and in the book *The three faces of Eve* (Thigpen *et al.* 1957). Like hysterical memory disorder, these cases may have their basis in organic disease of the central nervous system (Lewis 1953).

Hysterical **seizures** can usually be distinguished from epilepsy in several ways. The patient may seem inaccessible but does not become unconscious; the pattern of movements does not show a regular and stereotyped form of seizure; there is no incontinence, cyanosis, or injury, and the tongue is not bitten. Electroencephalographic findings are normal. Occasionally it is difficult to distinguish between complex partial seizures (temporal lobe epilepsy) and hysterical seizures, but the recent introduction of continuous EEG monitoring has made this less difficult. The older term **hystero-epilepsy** should not be used because it is ambiguous. If there is evidence of a true seizure disorder with electrographic abnormality, the diagnosis is epilepsy even if additional hysterical features are present.

In **hysterical psychosis** the symptoms represent the patient's idea of madness. Unless he has seen mental illness at first hand, he usually presents a clinical picture that differs substantially from those of schizophrenia, mania, or depressive illness. However, just as hysterical neurological symptoms sometimes arise in patients who have organic neurological disease, so hysterical psychosis can occasionally be a manifestation of schizophrenia or affective illness.

Variations of the syndrome of hysteria

Epidemic hysteria

Occasionally hysteria spreads within a group of people as an 'epidemic'. This happens occasionally in men, but most often in closed groups of young women, for example in a girls' school, a nurses' home, or a convent. Usually anxiety has been heightened by some threat to the community, such as the possibility of being involved in an epidemic of actual physical disease already present in the neighbourhood. Typically, the epidemic starts in one person who is highly suggestible, histrionic, and a focus of attention in the group. This first case may be provoked by actual physical illness in an acquaintance or by general apprehension. Gradually other cases appear, first in the most suggestible then, as anxiety mounts, among those with less predisposition. The symptoms are variable but fainting and dizziness are common. Outbreaks among schoolchildren have been reported by Benaim *et al.* (1973) and Moss and McEvedy (1966). Some writers believe that the 'dancing manias' of the Middle Ages may have been hysterical epidemics in people aroused by religious fervour.

Briquet's syndrome

This name was suggested by a group of psychiatrists in St. Louis to denote patients who have multiple physical symptoms starting before the age of 30 and lasting for many years, but without evidence of physical disease. The intention is to define patients in whom organic disease is clearly excluded and a psychogenic aetiology is undoubted. To make diagnosis more reliable, there is a list of

37 symptoms from which 15 must be present to make the diagnosis. None of these symptoms should be explained adequately by physical disease, injury, or the effects of medication, alcohol, or other drugs (Perley and Guze 1962). This criterion, together with the requirement of a history lasting many years, can be used to define a restricted group whose prognosis is more certain than the rest, but it excludes many patients for whom the diagnosis of hysteria would still have to be considered. The name is derived from a nineteenth century French physician who wrote an important monograph on hysteria (Briquet 1859), although he did not describe the exact syndrome outlined above.

Culture and variations of hysteria

Certain patterns of behaviour are found in particular cultures. Some writers regard them as variants of hysteria but it is probable that they can have more than one cause. **Latah**, which is found among women in Malaya (Yap 1951), usually begins after a sudden frightening experience. The patient shows echolalia and echopraxia and is abnormally compliant in other ways. **Amok** has been described among men in Malaya (Van Loon 1927). It begins with a period of brooding, which is followed by violent behaviour and sometimes dangerous use of weapons. Amnesia is usually claimed afterwards. Probably such cases are not all of one kind, some being manic, schizophrenic, or post-epileptic. **Arctic hysteria** is seen among the Eskimo (Gussow 1963), more often in the women. The affected person tears off her clothing, screams and cries, runs about wildly, and may endanger her life by exposure to cold. Sometimes the behaviour is violent. The relationship of this syndrome to hysteria is not firmly established, and it may have more than one cause. These and other cultural variations of hysteria have been described by Kiev (1972).

Differential diagnosis

The diagnosis of hysteria can be mistaken in three ways: first, the symptoms may be those of physical disease that has not yet been detected; for example, an undiagnosed tumour of the oesophagus causing difficulty in swallowing. Secondly, undiscovered brain disease may, in some unknown way, 'release' hysterical symptoms; for example a small tumour in the frontal or parietal lobe, or an early dementia. Thirdly, physical disease may provide a non-specific stimulus to hysterical elaboration of symptoms by a patient of histrionic personality. Some of these problems require further discussion.

Hysteria has to be distinguished from the multitude of physical illnesses that produce similar symptoms. The greatest difficulty arises in distinguishing it from **organic disease of the central nervous system**. The first step is to determine the exact form of the symptoms and signs, and to compare them carefully with those arising from known neurological diseases, including GPI, cerebral tumours, and dementias. Such diseases can not only produce specific symptoms (for example of parietal lobe dysfunction) that can be mistaken for those of hysteria; they may also 'release' a hysterical syndrome – especially an amnesia or fugue. Hysteria may also be difficult to distinguish from **partial complex seizures** (temporal lobe epilepsy), in which unusual disorders of behaviour can occur (see Chapter 11). These points should be considered afresh each time hysterical behaviour occurs in a patient who has more than one episode of symptoms.

Many mistakes in diagnosis arise because the neurotic syndrome of hysteria is confused with the **histrionic (or hysterical) personality** (p. 111). People with this kind of personality display emotions readily but without experiencing a corresponding degree of inner feeling. They often make lively company but are essentially self-centred. Whatever the circumstances, they tend to react in a demonstrative way that attracts attention. Such people respond in the same way to physical illness as to other events in their life – by exaggeration. Such over-reaction to organic disease can be mistaken for the wholly psychological disorder of hysterical neurosis. Exaggeration of physical symptoms is sometimes called 'hysterical overlay' or 'functional overlay', though the latter term is best avoided. Similarly the hysterical personality can put its stamp on psychiatric disorder as well, and histrionic behaviour can occur in depressive disorders, anxiety neuroses, and many other conditions. It is important to remember that extravagant reactions to illness are not hysteria.

The distinction between hysteria and **malingering** should be considered particularly among prisoners, military servicemen, or others who may consciously feign illness either to avoid something unpleasant or to gain compensation. The distinction is difficult because some patients add conscious embellishments to the core of unconsciously produced hysterical symptoms. This happens most often when the patient believes his doctor to be sceptical about his complaint. Unlike hysterical symptoms, the complaints of malingerers can rarely be sustained continuously; for this reason, discrete and prolonged observation will usually provide valuable information.

Diagnostic errors will be minimized if four other points are taken into account. First, **age** is important. Hysteria seldom appears for the first time after the age of 40, presumably because most predisposed patients have already encountered problems severe enough to provoke the reaction at an earlier age. Secondly hysteria is **provoked by stress**. If no stress can be found the diagnosis is in serious doubt. It is therefore important to question other informants, since the patient may not reveal stressful circumstances of which he feels ashamed. On the other hand it is essential to remember that finding stressors does not prove the diagnosis of hysteria, because they often precede physical illness as well. The third point concerns **secondary gain**. If none can be found, the diagnosis must be in serious doubt. However, as already noted, secondary gain does not prove the diagnosis, because patients sometimes extract advantage from physical illness as well as from emotional disorder. The fourth point is that hysterical indifference can seldom be judged reliably, and should be given little weight in diagnosis.

Syndromes related to hysteria

Although hysterical symptoms are primarily the result of unconscious mechanisms, some degree of conscious elaboration is often present. There are three syndromes in which the conscious element appears to be relatively more important: compensation neurosis, hospital addiction (Munchausen syndrome) and artefactual lesions of the skin.

Compensation neurosis

This diagnosis is used for psychologically determined physical or mental symptoms occurring in circumstances in which the case is the subject of an unsettled claim for compensation. This material incentive seems to increase or prolong the symptoms, which usually improve when a single final payment is agreed. As long as the claim continues or if compensation is made to depend on regular review of the continuing disability, symptoms are likely to persist. In these cases it is often very difficult to decide to what extent the patient is producing symptoms consciously or experiencing the result of unconscious processes. Miller (1961), in an important paper based on his experience as a neurologist, drew attention to the frequency with which there is a neurotic basis for persistent symptoms after industrial injuries and road accidents. He went on to emphasize the role of the compensation claim in prolonging symptoms. He pointed also to the role of neurotic predisposition, arguing that this is not a reason for denying compensation to the person 'any more than pleading the pre-existence of thin skull in the case of fracture' (p. 995). The subject has been reviewed by Trimble (1981) (see also p. 358).

The Munchausen syndrome

This is the name suggested by Asher (1951) to describe patients who repeatedly present themselves at hospitals with dramatic symptoms suggesting serious physical illness. These symptoms are often of a kind that seems to require urgent surgical treatment or the administration of powerful analgesics. Because the fictional Baron Munchausen, though given to fanciful exaggeration, did not behave in this way, others (e.g. Barker 1962) have suggested the alternative name **'hospital addiction'**. These patients are more often men than women. Their commonest symptoms include acute pain in the abdomen or loin, haematemesis, and haemoptysis. The symptoms and signs appear to have been produced deliberately and there is usually other evidence that the patient is trying to deceive his doctors – for example his account of previous hospital admissions and even his name and address are often incorrect. Asher (1951) suggested that many of these patients harbour a grudge against doctors and they satisfy this by frustrating and deceiving them. However, the extreme lengths to which they go to imitate illness and the frequent history of multiple operations, strongly suggest a profound disorder of personality. How this has arisen is seldom certain, because patients evade efforts to obtain the information which is needed. Treatment is usually ineffective, but in any case patients seldom remain long enough to attempt it (see also p. 358).

Artefactual skin lesions

In **dermatitis artefacta** blisters or excoriations are produced by self-inflicted trauma. Although the lesions are produced deliberately the behaviour usually indicates a degree of psychological abnormality, usually in the form of a disorder of personality which is difficult to treat. Patients at first deny causing the lesions and if they admit this later often refer to an altered state of mind at the time, which resembles a form of dissociation (see also p. 383).

Aetiology

Before reviewing modern ideas about aetiology, it is instructive to consider briefly some of the explanations proposed in the past (more complete accounts are given by Veith (1965) and Ellenberger (1970)).

Hysteria was recognized in the Ancient World. Among the physicians of Ancient Greece, it was thought to result from movement of the uterus from its normal position (hence the name of the condition). By the second century AD Galen rejected this idea, suggesting instead that the abnormality was an undue retention of uterine secretions. The theory of uterine pathology was generally held until the sixteenth century, when Willis (1621–1675) suggested that hysteria arose from a disorder of the brain (see Dewhurst 1980). By the early nineteenth century, although the importance of predisposing constitutional and organic causes was known, strong emotions were recognized as provoking causes. Later Charcot, a distinguished French neurologist, stressed the importance of strong emotions in producing hysteria in predisposed people. He based this belief partly on the observation that in susceptible patients phenomena resembling hysterical symptoms could be induced by hypnosis. He also believed that hysterical attacks went through a characteristic sequence of changes, but this was subsequently recognized as resulting from suggestion brought about by his own powerful personality. Janet continued the interest of the French school in the phenomena of hysteria, especially somnambulism and fugues.

Psychoanalytic theories of hysteria began with Freud's visit to Charcot in the winter of 1895–6. (See Sulloway (1979) for an interesting account of this period in Freud's life.) Freud developed his ideas with Breuer in a paper 'On the psychical mechanisms of hysterical phenomena' (1893). In the subsequent monograph *Studies in hysteria* (1895), Breuer and Freud wrote 'hysterics suffer mainly from reminiscences' (Standard Edition, Vol. 2, p. 7); that is from the effects of emotionally charged ideas lodged in the unconscious at some time in the past. This idea was central to their theory. Symptoms were explained as the combined effects of repression and the 'conversion' of psychic energy into physical channels in some way that was never fully explained. These ideas have been widely accepted, despite the difficulty in testing them directly.

Genetics

The few genetic studies have been inconclusive. Ljungberg (1957) studied the first-degree relatives of 281 patients, of whom almost half had hysterical disturbances of gait and a further fifth had hysterical fits. The rates of hysteria in relatives, 2.4 per cent among males and 6.4 per cent among females, were probably higher than in the general population. A twin study by Slater (1961) did not support a genetic aetiology, since no concordance was found between identical twins one of whom had hysteria.

Organic disease

As already noted, hysteria is sometimes associated with organic disease of the nervous system. However, it can undoubtedly occur in the absence of such pathology.

Hysteria as a reflex mechanism

From experience of treating acute hysterical reactions in wartime, Kretschmer (1961) suggested that they are preformed instinctive reactions of the nervous system to excessive stress. He believed that such reactions normally subside quickly, but can be prolonged in two ways. First, they may be deliberately cultivated by someone who wishes to take advantage of the symptoms. Secondly, by a supposed neurological mechanism behaviours that are frequently repeated become habitual (or 'slip into a groove' to use Kretschmer's phrase). Although these ideas have never been substantiated, they differ from other theories in drawing attention to the apparent mixture of voluntary and involuntary causes in many cases of hysteria.

Prognosis

Most cases of hysteria of recent onset seen in general practice or hospital emergency departments recover quickly. However, those that last longer than a year are likely to persist for many years more. Thus Ljungberg (1957) found that, among patients who still had symptoms after a year, half still had them after ten years.

It has already been noted that organic disease is often missed among patients with hysteria. In a well-known study, Slater and Glithero (1965) followed up a series of patients who had been referred to a specialist neurological hospital and diagnosed as having hysteria (those with 'hysterical overlay' in known physical disease were excluded). They found that about a third of the patients developed a definite organic illness within 7–11 years, and a further third developed depression or schizophrenia. Although this study teaches an important lesson, it must be remembered that the patients were unrepresentative in being referred to a neurological hospital. For this reason, the findings do not justify the investigators' conclusion that the diagnosis of hysteria is so unreliable that it should be abandoned.

Treatment of hysteria

For the acute hysterical neuroses seen in general practice or hospital casualty departments, treatment by reassurance and suggestion is usually appropriate, together with immediate efforts to resolve any stressful circumstances that provoked the reaction. For cases that have lasted more than a few weeks, more active treatment is required. The general approach is to focus on the elimination of factors that are reinforcing the symptoms, and on the encouragement of normal behaviour. It should be explained to the patient that he has a disability (as in remembering, or moving his arm) which is not caused by physical disease but by psychological factors. It is often helpful to explain the disorder as due to a blocking of the psychological process between, for example, the patient's intention to move his arm and the nervous mechanisms that bring about movement. He should then be told that if he tries hard to regain control, he will succeed. If necessary, he can be offered help in doing this, usually in the form of physiotherapy. Attention is then directed away from the symptoms and towards problems that have provoked the neurosis. The hospital staff should show concern to help the patient, whilst making it clear that this is best done by encouraging self-help. It is important not to make undue concessions to the patient's disability; for example, a patient who cannot walk should not be provided with a wheelchair, and a patient who has collapsed on the floor should be encouraged to get up but not assisted to his feet. To achieve these ends, there must be a clear plan so that all members of staff adopt a consistent approach to the patient.

Abreaction

This can be brought about by hypnosis or by intravenous injection of small amounts of amylobarbitone. In the resulting state, the patient is encouraged to relive the stressful events that provoked the hysteria, and to express the accompanying emotions. These methods have been used successfully in the treatment of acute hysterical neuroses arising in soldiers in wartime (see Chapter 18). There are of much less value in civilian life, where more gradual methods will allow the patient to take responsibility for overcoming his symptoms and for finding solutions to problems that evoked them.

Psychotherapy

Patients with hysteria usually appear to respond well to exploratory psycho-therapy concerned with their past life, and they often produce striking memories of childhood sexual behaviour and other problems apparently relevant to dynamic psychotherapy. However, it is seldom fruitful to explore these ideas at length. Usually such exploration serves only to deflect attention from the patient's current difficulties, and may lead to over-dependence and transference reactions that are difficult to manage.

Medication has no part to play in the treatment of hysteria, unless the hysterical symptoms are secondary to a depressive illness or anxiety neurosis requiring treatment in its own right. Specific methods of **behaviour therapy** are also of little value. The use of operant conditioning methods has been reported for example in the treatment of hysterical blindness (Parry Jones *et al.* 1970) but there is no evidence that these or other techniques are more effective than suggestion.

With simple treatment most patients with hysteria improve, unless there is a strong motivation to remain ill, as in compensation cases. Those who do not improve should be reviewed throughly for undiscovered physical illness. All patients, whether improved or not, should be followed carefully for long enough to exclude any organic disease that might not have been detected. Six months to a year will usually be needed, but if a condition such as multiple sclerosis has to be excluded, a much longer follow up may be required. This must be done discreetly and tactfully in order to identify any symptoms suggestive of organic disease, without perpetuating the psychological problems. The general practitioner is often best placed to undertake this.

DEPERSONALIZATION NEUROSIS

Depersonalization neurosis is defined in ICD 9 as 'a neurotic disorder with an unpleasant state of disturbed perception in which external objects or parts of one's own body are experienced as changed in their quality, unreal, remote or automatized. The patient is aware of the subjective nature of the change he experiences'. The symptom of depersonalization is quite common as a minor feature of other syndromes but the primary depersonalization neurosis is uncommon.

Clinical picture

As well as describing feelings of being unreal and experiencing an unreal quality to perceptions, patients say that their emotions are dulled and their actions feel mechanical. They no longer experience strong emotions such as love, hatred, anger, or pleasure; paradoxically they complain that this lack of feeling is extremely unpleasant. Insight is retained into the subjective nature of their experiences.

In the depersonalization neurosis, these symptoms are intense, and are accompanied by lesser degrees of anxiety, mild depression, *déjà vu*, and changes in the experience of passage of time. Some patients complain of sensory distortions affecting not the whole body but a single part, such as the head, the nose, or limbs, which may be described as feeling as if made of cotton wool. Two-thirds of the patients are women. The symptoms usually begin suddenly, often during relaxation, after intense physical exercise or psychological stimulation (Shorvon *et al.* 1946). The onset is often in adolescence or early adult life, the condition starting before the age of 30 in about half the cases (Shorvon *et al.* 1946). Once established, the disorder often persists for years, though with periods of partial complete remission.

Differential diagnosis

Before diagnosing depersonalization neurosis, a primary disorder must be carefully sought, such as an organic syndrome (including temporal lobe epilepsy), schizophrenia, depressive illness, obsessional neurosis, hysteria, and generalized and phobic anxiety states. Severe and persistent depersonalization symptoms also occur with schizoid personality disorder, but there is no agreement whether the neurosis should be regarded as merely secondary to the personality disorder. Most patients who present with depersonalization will be found to have one of these other disorders; the primary syndrome is rare.

Aetiology

The more careful the search for a primary illness, the fewer cases of primary depersonalization neurosis will be identified. Ackner (1954 *a, b*) studied a series of patients and found that all could be allocated to organic, depressive, anxiety, or hysterical syndromes, or to schizoid personality. Apart from the possible association with schizoid personality no definite constitutional factors have been identified. Lader (1969) suggested that the symptoms represent a restriction of sensory input that serves to reduce intolerably high levels of anxiety. He reported a striking example in a patient who was undergoing physiological recordings at the time. Since many cases begin when the patient is relaxed or tired, this mechanism, if it is important, cannot be invariable.

Prognosis

Most cases are secondary, and have the prognosis of the primary condition. The uncommon primary depersonalization syndrome has not been followed systematically; clinical experience indicates that, if it lasts for more than a year, it has a poor long-term prognosis.

Treatment

Since most depersonalization neuroses are secondary, treatment should usually be directed to the primary condition. In the small group of primary depersonalization neuroses, a short trial of an anxiolytic drug is worthwhile because a few patients are helped in this way. Otherwise drugs have no part in treatment. Behavioural treatment is ineffective. Psychotherapy has no specific value, but the patients, who often suffer extreme distress, may be helped by supportive interviews. Commonsense measures are also needed to reduce stressful events in their lives. However, the doctor has to accept that he can do little to relieve the symptoms of primary depersonalization neurosis; for many patients the only help is encouragement to tolerate their symptoms while continuing as normal a life as possible. These patients often make repeated demands for additional treatment, but despite their obvious suffering it is important to resist the temptation to heap one ineffective measure on another.

HYPOCHONDRIASIS

Hypochondriasis is defined in ICD 9 as 'a neurotic disorder in which the conspicuous features are excessive concern with one's health in general, in the integrity and functioning of some part of one's body or, less frequently, one's mind'. Hypochondriasis may co-exist with actual physical disorder; the important feature is that the patient's concern is out of proportion and not justified. The symptom of hypochondriasis occurs commonly in a variety of disorders, especially anxiety and depression. As a primary neurotic syndrome, the condition is rare and some psychiatrists doubt whether it exists at all.

When hypochondriacal tendencies are life long, the condition should be classified as personality disorder rather than neurosis; sometimes there is worsening of life-long tendencies, and this can then be regarded as neurosis.

Gillespie (1928) was the main advocate of a primary neurotic syndrome of hypochondriasis; Kenyon (1964), in a comprehensive study, found no evidence to support Gillespie's view, nor any specific type of personality in all cases. Most patients had an associated depressive illness. Kenyon suggested that hypochondriasis as a syndrome should be abandoned, retaining only the concepts of hypochondriacal symptoms (present in other disorders) and of hypochondriacal personality traits. This view has not been adopted in the main published diagnostic systems. Clinical experience suggests that most cases are, as Kenyon suggests, either secondary disorders or personality disorders. However, patients with a primary syndrome are occasionally encountered.

Clinical picture

Hypochondriacal symptoms take many forms. The important common feature is undue preoccupation with physical ill health despite well-founded reassurance. Pain, the most frequent symptom, occurs in about two-thirds of patients. The common sites are the head, lower lumbar region, and right iliac fossa. The pain is usually described imprecisely and referred to a diffuse area of the body. Gastrointestinal symptoms are also frequent and include nausea, dysphagia, regurgitation of acid, biliousness, a bad taste in the mouth, flatulence, and abdominal pain. In the cardiovascular system, common symptoms are palpitations, left-sided chest pain, complaints of dyspnoea, and worries about blood pressure. Worries about bladder function are also frequent. Some patients complain about their appearance, especially the shape of the nose, ears or breasts, while others complain of body odours or sweating.

Differential diagnosis

Most hypochondriacal complaints are secondary to another illness or to personality disorder. Depression or anxiety states are the most frequent primary disorders. Schizophrenia and dementia must also be searched for carefully.

Aetiology

In the Ancient World hypochondria was thought to be associated with physical disorder of the organs below the costal margin (hence its name). Views about its relationship with hysteria have varied over the years: Willis separated the two, but Sydenham thought that the same disease caused hysteria in women and hypochondriasis in men. An association with depression has long been proposed; by the end of the nineteenth century associations with organic brain disease (including GPI) and the neuroses were also described (see Tuke 1892). A comprehensive historical review has been provided by Kenyon (1965).

Since hypochondriasis is commonly secondary to another illness or to personality disorder, the problem is to explain why, for example, some patients with depressive illness develop hypochondriacal symptoms while others do not. There is little factual information to explain this. Hypochondriasis is somewhat more common among men, the lower social classes, and the elderly. Cross-cultural studies indicate that in depressive illness hypochondriacal symptoms are more common in non-European cultures.

Psychoanalytic explanations of hypochondriasis have ranged widely from it being an expression of anal eroticism to a defence against psychosis. None is convincing.

Prognosis

In secondary cases, the prognosis is that of the primary disorder. Cases associated with depressive illness or brief anxiety neuroses have a better prognosis than the rest. Hypochondriacal personality traits are unlikely to change. The rare cases of primary hypochondriacal neurosis are probably long-lasting.

Treatment

When the condition is secondary, treatment should be directed to the primary condition, which is often depressive. With the small number of primary hypochondriacal syndromes, **supportive measures** are the mainstay of treatment. As far as possible, the doctor should avoid discussion of the symptoms, while making clear that he understands the extent of the patient's suffering. He should gradually deflect discussion from symptoms to other problems in the patient's life and if possible, help to deal with these. Treatment should be cautious with patients who persistently complain that their symptoms are the cause of personal misfortune and who blame doctors for failing to cure them.

At times, their symptoms may be their only defence against overwhelming feelings of personal inadequacy. To make such people aware that their short-comings and failures are due to themselves rather than to illness that doctors cannot treat, may lead at the best to demoralization and at worst to a serious depressive disorder.

Drugs are of no value unless the patient is depressed. Indeed hypochondriacal patients often complain of the side-effects of drugs even when the doses are small, and many refuse to take drugs. No behaviour therapy is reliably effective although programmes of differential reinforcement can sometimes discourage excessive talk about symptoms that so often alienates friends and relatives.

Finally, it must never be forgotten that hypochondriacal patients may develop physical illness as readily as anyone else. Any new symptoms must always be evaluated thoroughly.

For a review of hypochondriasis see Barsky and Klerman 1983.

FURTHER READING

Ackner, B. (1954). Depersonalization: *Journal of Mental Science* **100,** 838–53, 854–72.

Breuer, J. and Freud, S. (1895). *Studies on hysteria.* Reprinted as Vol. 3. of Pelican Freud Library. Penguin Books, Harmondsworth.

Kenyon, F.E. (1976). Hypochondriacal states. *British Journal of Psychiatry* **129,** 1–14.

Lewis, A.J. (1936). Obsessional illness. In *Inquiries in psychiatry,* Chapter 7. Routledge and Kegan Paul, London.

Marks, I.M. (1969). *Fears and phobias.* Heinemann, London.

Merksey, H. (1979). *The analysis of hysteria.* Baillière Tindall, London.

Nemiah, J.C. (1980). Anxiety state (anxiety neurosis). In *Comprehensive textbook of psychiatry,* 3rd edn (ed. H.I. Kaplan, A.M. Freedman, and B.J. Sadock) Vol. 2, pp. 1483–93.

8. Affective disorders

The affective disorders are so called because one of their main features is abnormality of mood. Nowadays the term is usually restricted to disorders in which this mood is depression or elation, but in the past some authors have included states of anxiety as well (for example Lewis 1956). In this book, anxiety states are described with the neuroses (Chapter 7).

It is part of normal experience to feel unhappy at times of adversity. The symptom of depression is a component of many psychiatric syndromes and is also found commonly in certain physical diseases, for example in glandular fever. In this chapter, we are concerned neither with normal feelings of unhappiness nor with depression as a symptom of other disorders, but with the syndromes known as depressive disorders. The central features of these syndromes are depressive mood, pessimistic thinking, lack of enjoyment, reduced energy, and slowness. Of these, depressive mood is usually, but not invariably, the most prominent symptom. The other elements are variable enough to suggest that there is not one disorder but several.

Similar considerations apply to states of elation. A degree of elated mood is part of normal experience at times of good fortune. Elation can also occur as a symptom in several psychiatric syndromes, though it is less widely encountered than depression. In this chapter we are concerned with a *syndrome* in which the central features are overactivity, self-important ideas, and elation. Of these, elation occurs least constantly, and irritability sometimes occurs instead. This syndrome is called mania. In the past it has been usual to restrict the term mania to severe cases, and to give the name hypomania to less severe cases. As there is no agreed dividing line between mania and hypomania, this book uses only the term mania and severity is indicated by adding mild, moderate, or severe.

CLINICAL FEATURES

Depressive syndromes

The clinical picture of depressive syndromes is so varied that they cannot be described fully in a short space. The following account groups the disorders by their severity. First is a description of the clinical features of depressive disorders of moderate severity. This is followed by a description of severe disorders. Certain important variants of these moderate and severe disorders are then described. Finally the special features of the least severe depressive disorders are outlined.

In depression of moderate severity, the central features are low mood, lack of enjoyment, and reduced energy, all of which lead to impaired efficiency. The patient's **appearance** is characteristic. Dress and grooming may be neglected. The facial features are characterized by a turning downwards of the corners of the mouth and by vertical furrowing of the centre of the brow. The rate of blinking may be reduced. The shoulders are bent, and the head inclined forwards so that the direction of gaze is downwards. Gestural movements are reduced. It is important to note that some patients maintain a smiling exterior despite deep feelings of depression.

Psychomotor retardation is frequent, (though as described later some patients are agitated rather than slowed up). The retarded patient walks and acts slowly. Slowing of thought is reflected in the patient's speech; there is a long delay before questions are answered, and pauses in conversation may be so long that they would be intolerable to a non-depressed person.

The **mood** of the patient is one of misery. This mood does not improve substantially in circumstances where ordinary feelings of sadness would be alleviated – for example in pleasant company or after hearing good news. Moreover the mood may be experienced as different from ordinary sadness. Patients sometimes speak of a black cloud pervading all mental activities. Some patients can conceal this mood change from other people, at least for short periods. Some try to hide their low mood during clinical interviews, making it more difficult for the doctor to detect.

Anxiety is also frequent though not invariable in moderately severe depressive disorder. (As described later, it is common in some less severe depressive disorders.) Another common symptom is **irritability** which is the tendency to respond with undue annoyance to minor demands and frustrations. **Agitation** is state of restlessness which is experienced by the patient as inability to relax, and seen by an observer as restless activity. When it is mild the patient is seen to be plucking at his fingers and making restless movements of his legs; when it is severe, he cannot sit for long but paces up and down.

Lack of interest and enjoyment is frequent, though not always complained of spontaneously. The patient shows no enthusiasm for activities and hobbies that he would normally enjoy. He feels no zest for living and no pleasure in everyday things. He often withdraws from social encounters. **Reduced energy** is characteristic (though sometimes associated with a degree of physical restlessness that can mislead the observer). The patient feels lethargic, finds everything an effort, and leaves tasks unfinished. For example, a normally houseproud woman may leave the beds unmade and the dirty plates on the table. Understandably, many patients attribute this lack of energy to physical illness.

A group of symptoms often called **biological** is important. They include sleep disturbance, diurnal variation of mood, loss of appetite, loss of weight, constipation, loss of libido, and, among women, amenorrhoea. These symptoms are frequent but not invariable in depressive disorders of moderate degree. (They are less usual in mild depressive disorders, but particularly common in the severe disorders.) Some of these symptoms require further comment.

Sleep disturbance in depressive disorders is of several kinds. Most characteristic is early morning waking, but delay in falling asleep and waking during the night also occur. Early morning waking occurs two or three hours before the patient's usual time; he does not fall asleep again, but lies awake feeling unrefreshed and often restless and agitated. He thinks about the coming day with pessimism. In depressive disorders he broods about past failures and ponders gloomily about the future. It is this combination of early waking with depressive thinking that is important in diagnosis. It should be noted that some depressed patients sleep excessively rather than waking early, but they still report waking unrefreshed.

In depressive disorders, **weight loss** often seems greater than can be accounted for merely by the patients **lack of appetite**. In some patients the disturbances of eating and weight are towards excess – they eat more and gain weight; usually it seems that eating brings temporary relief to their distressing feelings.

Pessimistic thoughts ('depressive cognitions') are important symptoms, which can be divided into three groups. The first group is concerned with the *present*. The patient sees the unhappy side of every event; he thinks that he is failing in everything he does and that other people see him as a failure; he no longer feels confident, and discounts any success as a chance happening for which he can take no credit.

The second group of thoughts is concerned with the *future*. The depressed patient expects the worst. He foresees failure in his work, the ruin of his finances, misfortune for his family, and an inevitable deterioration in his health. These ideas of hopelessness are often accompanied by the thought that life is no longer worth living and that death would come as a welcome release. These gloomy preoccupations may progress to thoughts of, and plans for, **suicide**. It is important to ask about these ideas in every case. (The assessment of suicidal risk is considered further in Chapter 13.)

The third group of thoughts is concerned with the **past**. They often take the form of unreasonable guilt and self-blame about minor matters; for example, a patient might feel guilty about past trivial acts of dishonesty or of letting someone down. Usually the patient has not thought about these events for years but, when he becomes depressed, they flood back into his memory accompanied by intense feelings. Preoccupations of this kind strongly suggest depressive disorder. Some patients have similar feelings of guilt but do not attach them to any particular event. Other memories are focused on unhappy events; the patient remembers occasions when he was sad, when he failed, or when his fortunes were at a low ebb. These gloomy memories become increasingly frequent as the depression deepens.

Complaints about **physical symptoms** are common in depressive disorders. They take many forms but complaints of constipation and of aching discomfort anywhere in the body are particularly common. Complaints about any pre-existing physical disorder usually increase and hypochondriacal preoccupations are common.

Finally a number of **other psychiatric symptoms** may occur as part of a depressive disorder, and occasionally one of them dominates the clinical picture. They include depersonalization, obsessional symptoms, phobias, and hysterical symptoms such as fugue or loss of function of a limb. Complaints of **poor memory** are also common; they result from poor concentration, and if the patient is encouraged to make a special effort, it can usually be shown that retention and recall are not impaired.

Masked depression

The term 'masked depression' is sometimes used for cases where depressive mood is not conspicuous. Although there is no reason to think that these cases form a separate syndrome, the term is useful in drawing attention to a mode of presentation that is easily missed. Masked depression is discussed in the chapter on general hospital psychiatry. Here it should be noted that diagnosis depends on a careful search for the other features of depressive disorder, especially sleep disturbance, diurnal mood variation, and depressive cognitions. Masking is most likely to occur with mild or moderate disorders, but it occasionally occurs with severe disorders.

Severe depressive disorder

In severe depressive disorder, all the features just described occur with greater intensity. Distinctive additional features may also occur in the form of delusions and hallucinations; the disorder is then sometimes called a **psychotic depression**.

The **delusions** of severe depressive disorders are concerned with the same themes as the non-delusional thinking of moderate depressive disorders. These themes are: worthlessness, guilt, ill-health, and more rarely poverty. Although such delusions have been described in Chapter 1, a few examples may be helpful at this point. A patient with a delusion of guilt may believe that some dishonest act, such as a minor concealment in making a tax return, will be discovered and that he will be punished severely and humiliated. He is likely to believe that such punishment is deserved. A patient with hypochondriacal delusions may be convinced that he has cancer or venereal disease. A patient with a delusion of impoverishment may wrongly believe that he has lost all his money in a business venture. **Persecutory delusions** also occur. The patient may believe that other people are discussing him in a derogatory way, or about to take revenge on him. When such delusions are part of a depressive syndrome, typically the patient accepts the supposed persecution as something he has brought upon himself. In his view, he is ultimately to blame.

Perceptual disturbances may also be found in severe depressive disorders. Sometimes these fall short of true hallucinations ('pseudohallucinations' see Chapter 1). In a minority of cases definite hallucinations occur; they are usually auditory, and take the form of voices addressing repetitive words and phrases to the patient. The voices seem to confirm his ideas of worthlessness (for example 'he is an evil man; he should die'), or to make derisive comments, or urge the patient to take his own life. A few patients experience visual hallucinations, sometimes in the form of scenes of death and destruction.

Cotard's syndrome is a particular form of severe depressive disorder, described by a French psychiatrist (Cotard 1882). The characteristic feature is an extreme kind of nihilistic delusion (sometimes called by the French name *délire de négation—délire* meaning delusion in this context). Patients with this syndrome carry nihilism to its extreme. For example, a patient may complain that his bowels have been destroyed so that he will never pass faeces again. Another may assert that he is penniless and without any prospect of having money again. A third may be convinced that his whole family has ceased to exist. Although the extreme nature of these symptoms is striking, such cases do not appear to differ in important ways from other severe depressive disorders.

Agitated depression

This term is applied to depressive disorders in which agitation is prominent. As already noted, agitation occurs in many severe depressive disorders, but in agitated depression it is particularly severe. Agitated depression is seen more commonly among the middle aged and elderly than among younger patients. However, there is no reason to suppose that agitated depression differs in other important ways from other depressive disorders.

Retarded depression

This name is sometimes applied to cases in which psychomotor retardation is especially prominent. There is no evidence that they represent a separate syndrome. Therefore if the term is used at all, it should be in a purely descriptive sense. In its most severe form, retarded depression shades into depressive stupor.

Depressive stupor

In severe depressive disorder, slowing of movement and poverty of speech may become so extreme that the patient is motionless and mute. Such depressive stupor is rarely seen now that active treatment is available. The description by Kraepelin (1921, p. 80) is of particular interest. 'The patients lie mute in bed, give no answer of any sort, at most withdraw themselves timidly from approaches, but often do not defend themselves from pinpricks . . . They sit helpless before their food, perhaps, however, they let themselves be spoonfed without making any difficulty . . . Now and then periods of excitement may be interpolated.' This description draws attention to an important feature of the condition – interruption by periods of excitement when the patient is overactive and noisy. Kraepelin commented that recall of the events taking place during stupor was sometimes impaired when the patient recovered. Nowadays, the general view is that on recovery patients are able to recall nearly all the events taking place during the period of stupor (see, for example Lishman 1978). It may be that in some of Kraepelin's cases clouding of consciousness was present (possibly related to inadequate fluid intake which is common in these patients).

Mild depressive disorder

It might be expected that mild depressive disorders would present with symptoms similar to those of the depressive disorders described already, but with less intensity. Sometimes this is so, the patient complaining of low mood, lack of energy and enjoyment, and poor sleep. However, in mild depressive disorder there are frequently other symptoms that are found less often in severe disorders than in mild ones. These symptoms can be broadly characterized as 'neurotic', and they include anxiety, phobias, obsessional symptoms, and less often hysterical symptoms. Although anxiety may be a symptom in all degrees of depressive disorder, it can be just as severe in the mild disorders as in the severe ones. This finding has suggested to many people that these mild depressive disorders are not just a minor variant of the moderate and severe cases but a separate syndrome. Because of the nature of the additional symptoms, this syndrome has been called **neurotic depression**.

Apart from the 'neurotic' symptoms found in some cases, mild depressive disorders are characterized by the expected symptoms of low mood, lack of energy and interest, and irritability. There is sleep disturbance, but not the early morning waking that is so characteristic of more severe depressive disorders. Instead there is more often difficulty in falling asleep and periods of waking during the night, followed usually be a period of sleep at the end of the night. 'Biological' features (poor appetite, weight loss, and low libido) are not usually found. Although mood may vary during the day, it is usually worse in the evening than in the morning. The patient may not be obviously dejected in his appearance, and slowed in his movement. Delusions and hallucinations are not encountered.

In their mildest forms these cases shade into the undifferentiated neuroses considered in Chapter 6. As described later, they pose considerable problems of classification. Many of these mild depressive disorders are brief, starting at a time of personal misfortune and subsiding when fortunes have changed or a new adjustment has been achieved. However, some cases persist for months or years causing considerable suffering even though the symptoms do not increase.

Mania

As already mentioned, the central features of the syndrome of mania are elevation of mood, increased activity, and self-important ideas. When the mood is elevated, the patient seems cheerful and optimistic, and he may have a quality described by earlier writers as infectious gaiety. However, other patients are irritable rather than euphoric, and this irritability can easily turn to anger. The mood often varies during the day, though not with the regular rhythm characteristic of many severe depressive disorders. In those who are elated, not uncommonly high spirits are interrupted by brief episodes of depression.

The patient's clothing often reflects his prevailing mood in its bright colours and ill-assorted choice of garments. When the condition is more severe, his appearance is often untidy and dishevelled. Manic patients are **overactive**. Sometimes their persistent overactivity leads to physical exhaustion. Manic patients start many activities but leave them unfinished as new ones catch their fancy. Their **speech** is often rapid and copious as thoughts crowd into their minds in quick succession. When the disorder is more severe, there is flight of ideas (see p. 10) with such rapid changes that it is difficult to follow the train of thought. **Sleep** is often reduced. The patient wakes early feeling lively and energetic; often he gets up and busies himself noisily, to the surprise of other people. **Appetite** is increased and food may be eaten greedily with little attention to conventional manners. **Sexual desires** are increased and behaviour may be uninhibited. Women sometimes neglect precautions against pregnancy, a point calling for particular attention when the patient is of childbearing age.

Expansive ideas are common. The patient believes that his ideas are original, his opinions important, and his work of outstanding quality. Many patients become extravagant, spending more than they can afford on expensive cars or jewellery. Others make reckless decisions to give up good jobs, or embark on plans for hairbrained and risky business ventures.

Sometimes these expansive themes are accompanied by **grandiose delusions**. The patient may believe that he is a religious prophet or destined to advise statesmen about great issues. At times the delusions are persecutory, the patient believing that people are conspiring against him because of his special importance. Delusions of reference and passivity feelings also occur. Schneiderian first-rank symptoms (see Table 8.3) have been reported in about 10–20 per cent of manic patients (Carpenter *et al.* 1973). Neither the delusions nor the first-rank symptoms last long – most disappear or change in content within days.

Hallucinations also occur. They are usually consistent with the mood, taking the form of voices speaking to the patient about his special powers or, occasionally, of visions with a religious content.

Insight is invariably impaired. The patient may see no reason why his grandiose plans should be restrained or his extravagant expenditure curtailed. He seldom thinks himself ill, or in need of treatment.

Most patients can exert some **control** over their symptoms for a short time, and many do so when the question of treatment is being assessed. For this reason it is important to obtain a history from an informant whenever possible. Henry Maudsley expressed the problem well: 'Just as it is with a person who is not too far gone in intoxication, so it is with a person who is not too far gone in acute mania; he may on occasion pull his scattered ideas together by an effort of will, stop his irrational doings and for a short time talk with an appearance of calmness and reasonableness that may well raise false hopes in inexperienced people' (Maudsley (1879), p. 398).

Carlson and Goodwin (1973) have described three stages of mania which, while not in any way distinctly separated from one another, may help the reader to judge the pattern of symptoms in mild, moderate, and severe cases. In **mild** cases there is increased physical activity and speech; mood is labile being mainly euphoric but giving way to irritability at time; ideas are expansive and the patient often spends more than he can afford; sexual drive increases. In **moderate** cases, there is marked overactivity and pressure of speech which seems disorganized; the euphoric mood is increasingly interrupted by periods of irritability, hostility, and depression; grandiose and other preoccupations may pass into delusions. In **severe** cases, there is frenzied overactivity, thinking is incoherent, delusions become increasingly bizarre and hallucinations are experienced. It should be emphasized that this description is merely a guide, and there is no invariable sequence.

Mixed affective states

Depressive and manic symptoms sometimes occur at the same time. Patients who are overactive and overtalkative may be having profoundly depressive thoughts. In other patients mania and depression follow each other in a sequence of rapid changes; for example a manic patient may become intensely depressed for a few hours and then return quickly to his manic state. These changes were mentioned in early descriptions of mania by Griesinger (1867), and have been re-emphasized in recent years, for example by Kotin and Goodwin (1972).

Manic stupor

In this unusual disorder, the patient is mute and immobile. However, his facial expression suggests elation and on recovery he describes having experienced a rapid succession of thoughts typical of mania. The condition is rarely seen now that active treatment is available for mania. Hence an earlier description by Kraepelin (1921, p. 106) is of interest: 'The patients are usually quite inaccessible, do not trouble themselves about their surroundings, give no answer, or at most speak in a low voice . . . smile without recognisable cause, lie perfectly quiet in bed or tidy about at their clothes and bedclothes, decorate themselves in an extraordinary way, all this without any sign of outward excitement.' On recovery, patients can remember the events that occurred during their period of stupor. The condition may begin from a state of manic excitement, but at times it is a stage in the transition between depressive stupor and mania.

Periodic psychoses

Some bipolar affective disorders recur regularly with short intervals of weeks or months between episodes. These disorders are sometimes referred to as periodic psychoses. The term is not entirely satisfactory because some writers use it to include other disorders such as recurrent schizophrenic illnesses, unusual syndromes like periodic catatonia (see Chapter 9), and the recurring atypical psychoses to which Leonhard (1979) gave the name cycloid psychoses (see page 243).

Bereavement

A recently bereaved person experiences symptoms closely resembling those of depressive disorders. Freud's theory of the aetiology of depressive illness was based on this similarity. For this reason it is convenient to describe the clinical features of bereavement here, even though they are usually part of normal experience rather than a pathological reaction. There are three stages. The first is characterized by a lack of emotional reaction ('numbness') and a feeling of unreality that lasts from a few hours to several days. In this stage, the bereaved person does not accept fully that the death has taken place. In the second stage, the person feels sad, weeps, sleeps badly, and loses appetite. He often experiences motor restlessness and difficulty in concentrating and remembering. About a third of bereaved people feel guilty about failures to do enough for the deceased, and about a fifth blame other people. Many have the experience at some time that they are in the presence of the dead person, and brief hallucinations are reported by about one in ten (Clayton 1979). In the third stage, these symptoms subside gradually, and the person accepts the new situation. It is important to note that certain features occur fairly frequently in depressive disorders, but uncommonly after bereavement, they are suicidal thoughts, retardation, and guilt about past actions in general, as opposed to specific failures to do enough for the deceased. However, the bereaved complain more of physical symptoms (Parkes and Brown 1972).

Clayton *et al.* (1974) found that 35 per cent of a sample of recently bereaved widows over the age of 62 met the criteria of Feighner *et al.* (1972) for a depressive disorder. Among men, there is an increased rate of death from cardiovascular causes in the year after the death of the spouse (Rees and Lutkins 1967).

CLASSIFICATION OF DEPRESSIVE DISORDERS

There is no general agreement about the best method of classifying depressive disorders. Three broad approaches have been tried. The first attempts to base classification on aetiology; the second on symptoms; and the third on the course of the disorder. This section describes each of these approaches in turn, before indicating how depressive disorders are classified in ICD 9 and DSM III.

Finally in this section it is suggested that for clinical purposes classifying depressive disorders is less useful than describing them systematically, and a descriptive scheme is proposed.

Classifications based on aetiology

Reactive and endogenous depression

For many years, this classification has had much support. Depressive disorders are divided into those in which symptoms appear to occur independently of environmental causes (endogenous), and those in which symptoms appear to be a response to external stressors (reactive). However, many influential psychiatrists, notably Mapother (1926), Lewis (1934, 1936, 1938), and Curran (1937), have maintained that few patients can be classified usefully by making this distinction. To quote Lewis (1934) 'every illness is a product of two factors – of the environment working on the organism; whether the constitutional factor is the determining influence or the environmental one, is never a question of kind, never a question to be dealt with as either/or'. This opinion is now held by most modern psychiatrists, including the authors. Neither ICD 9 nor DSM III contains categories of reactive or endogenous depression.

The issue about the reactive–endogenous classification is not so straightforward. Many of its supporters maintain that depressive disorders with an endogenous cause also have a characteristic pattern of symptoms: loss of appetite, weight loss, constipation, reduced libido, amenorrhoea, and early morning waking. Reactive depressions are said to have an equally characteristic pattern of anxiety, irritability, and phobias. As already explained, the latter pattern is sometimes called neurotic depression; it will be explained later that another system of classification divides depressive disorders into neurotic and psychotic forms. There is, therefore, some confusion between the neurotic-psychotic classification (based on symptoms) and the reactive–endogenous classification (based on aetiology but incorporating symptoms as well). Indeed some authors do not make a sharp distinction between the two systems (see, for example Kiloh *et al.* 1972).

Primary and secondary depression

This scheme, which is also based on aetiology, was introduced mainly for research purposes. The aim was to exclude cases of depression that might be caused by another disorder. This exclusion was attempted by applying the term 'secondary' to all cases with a history of previous non-affective psychiatric illness (such as schizophrenia or anxiety neurosis), or of alcoholism, medical illnesses or the taking of certain drugs (such as steroids). At first it was suggested (Guze *et al.* 1971) that primary and secondary depressive disorders might differ in prognosis and response to treatment. No such difference has been found, nor is there any convincing evidence for a difference between the two groups in the pattern of symptoms (see, for example Weissman *et al.* 1977). Therefore, although this classification may have some value for research, it has little value for the clinician.

Occasionally clinicians encounter secondary mania, which arises for example after operations or treatment with steroids. In secondary mania, the average age of onset is later than in primary mania, and a family history of bipolar disorder is less likely (see Krauthammer and Klerman (1978) for a review of the evidence).

Classification based on symptoms

Neurotic and psychotic depressions

As already explained, certain symptoms are frequently more intense in the mild depressive disorders than in the severe disorders. This difference in symptom intensity has led to the suggestion that there are two distinct forms of depression, neurotic and psychotic. In recent years, this hypothesis has been pursued by statistical means. Standardized information gathered either from case-notes or by interviewing is subjected to some form of multivariate analysis. The results have been contradictory. In a series of papers, Roth and his colleagues in Newcastle held that two separate syndromes could be distinguished (Kiloh and Garside 1963; Carney *et al.* 1965). However, Kendell (1968) did not confirm this distinction, but found evidence for a unimodal distribution of cases.

The problems surrounding these issues are made more difficult by the imprecise use of the term psychotic. In one sense, this term means a disorder in which there is evidence of loss of contact with reality, usually in the form of hallucinations or delusions. However, in the literature on depressive disorders, the term has been applied to cases with so-called biological symptoms, namely early morning waking, weight loss, poor appetite, impaired libido, and diurnal variation.

Another problem is that it is exceedingly difficult to collect data that could not have been affected by the preconceptions of the doctors assessing the patients. Thus, interviewers who believe that there are two separate syndromes may be more likely to elicit symptoms that confirm this hypothesis and less likely to elicit symptoms that do not. Indeed Kendell (1968) has produced evidence that such a bias does operate. Until this problem is overcome, the case for separate neurotic and psychotic syndromes must remain unproven.

Classification by course and time of life

Unipolar and bipolar disorders

Kraepelin was guided by the course of illness when he brought together mania and depression as a single entity. He found that the course was essentially the same whether the disorder was manic or depressive, so he put the two together in a single category of manic-depressive psychosis. This view was widely accepted until 1962 when Leonhard *et al.* suggested a division into three groups: patients who had had depressive disorder only **(unipolar depression)**; those who had had mania only **(unipolar mania)**; and those who had had both depressive disorder and mania **(bipolar)**. Nowadays it is standard practice not to use the term unipolar mania, but to include all cases of mania in the bipolar group, on the grounds that nearly all patients who have mania eventually experience a depressive disorder.

In support of the distinction between unipolar and bipolar disorders, Leonhard described differences in heredity and personality between the groups. However, it is generally agreed that the two groups differ neither in their symptoms when depressed nor in their response to treatment (with the possible exception of lithium therapy – see p. 219). There must be some overlap between the two groups, because a patient classified as having unipolar depression at one time may have a manic illness later. In other words the unipolar group inevitably contains some bipolar cases that have not yet declared themselves. Despite this limitation, the division into unipolar and bipolar cases is probably the most useful classification proposed so far.

Involutional depression

In the past, depressive disorders starting in middle life were thought to be a separate group, characterized by agitation and hypochondriacal symptoms. It was suggested that they might have a distinct aetiology, such as involution of the sex glands, or some kind of relationship with schizophrenia. Family studies do not support the idea of a separate group. Thus, among the relatives of patients with so-called involutional depression, the frequency of affective disorders is increased but there is no excess of involutional disorders (early onset disorders being just as frequent). Similarly, the rate of schizophrenia among relatives is not increased (see Slater and Cowie 1971, p. 86; Stenstedt 1959).

Senile depression

In the past, elderly patients with depression were also regarded as a separate group. However, there is no evidence that classification by age of onset is useful either in clinical work or research.

Classification in ICD 9 and DSM III

As shown in Table 8.1, ICD 9 and DSM III have adopted different principles of classification for affective disorders. ICD 9 has two main groups: manic depressive psychosis and neurotic depression. Manic depressive psychosis includes severe depressive disorders; mania; and depressive disorder and mania occurring at different times in the same patient (circular type). The latter is also described, according to the current clinical picture for example, circular type

Table 8.1. *The classification of affective disorder*

ICD 9		DSM III
296	Manic depressive psychosis	Major affective disorder
	(Affective psychosis)	bipolar
		(manic or depressed or mixed)
	manic type	
	depressed type	major depression
	circular type	(single or recurrent)
298	Other non organic psychoses of depressive type	Other specific affective disorders cyclothymic disorder dysthymic disorder
300.4	Neurotic depression	
311	Depressive disorder not elsewhere classified	Atypical affective disorders

currently manic. Neurotic depression includes mild depressive disorders in which disproportionate depression has usually followed a distressing experience, there is often a preoccupation with events preceding the illness, and delusions and hallucinations are absent. In addition to this basic division into two main groups, ICD 9 has further subdivisions into no less than ten three-digit categories and 19 four-digit categories. In Britain these subdivisions are seldom used, and most cases are classified under 'depressive disorder, not elsewhere classified'.

In DSM III the terms depressive psychosis and neurotic depression are not used. Instead, major affective disorders are divided into bipolar disorders and major depression (equivalent to unipolar depressive disorder). Mania is not used as a separate category: it is classified under bipolar disorder whether or not there has been an episode of depressive disorder. Bipolar disorders are subdivided into manic, depressed, and mixed types. Major depression is characterized further in three ways: single episode or recurrent; with 'melancholia' or not; and 'psychotic' or not. In DSM III melancholia is used to mean 'a typically severe form of depression, that is particularly responsive to somatic therapy' (p. 205). Psychotic is used to mean 'gross impairment of reality testing, as when there are delusions or hallucinations or grossly bizarre behaviour' (p. 209). These delusions and hallucinations may be congruent with the mood, but the classification allows the inclusion of cases where they are not. The latter provision allows classification under affective disorder of some cases that would have been grouped under schizoaffective disorder in earlier American systems.

In DSM III, mild depression with 'neurotic' symptoms is called 'dysthymic disorder', and put in a group of 'other specific affective disorders'. However, in practice many cases of mild depression are classified under major depression, for which the criteria are not highly restrictive. Thus, most depressed outpatients would qualify for the rubric major depression.

The distinguishing feature of 'other specific affective disorders' is that they have been present for at least two years, though never with sufficient intensity to meet the criteria for major depressive disorder. Apart from dysthymic disorders, they include 'cyclothymic disorder', which resembles the bipolar disorders but is much less severe.

Both ICD 9 and DSM III have a category for cases that do not fit any of the other categories.

Classification and description in everyday practice

Although neither ICD 9 nor DSM III is entirely satisfactory, it seems unlikely that any further rearrangements of descriptive categories will be better. The solution will only come when we have a better understanding of aetiology. Meanwhile, either ICD 9 or DSM III should be used for statistical returns. For research, cases are best classified by a standardized scheme such as RDC or PSE CATEGO (see p. 77). For most clinical purposes, it is better to *describe* disorders systematically than classify them. This can be done for every case by referring to the severity, the type of episode, and the course of the disorder, together with an evaluation of the relative importance of endogenous and reactive causation.

This scheme is shown in Table 8.2. The **severity** of the episode is easily described as mild, moderate or severe. The **type** of episode is described as depressive, manic, or mixed. Any **special features** are noted, namely neurotic symptoms, psychotic symptoms, agitation, retardation, or stupor.

The **course** of the disorder is characterized as unipolar or bipolar. If the term bipolar is used descriptively, it is logical to restrict it to cases that have had both manic and depressive episodes. However, it has become conventional to record all cases with a manic episode as bipolar even if there has been no depressive disorder, on the grounds (a) most manic patients develop a

Table 8.2. *A systematic scheme for the description of affective disorders*

The episode	
severity	mild, moderate, or severe
type	depressive, manic, mixed
special features	with neurotic symptoms
	with psychotic symptoms
	with agitation
	with retardation or stupor
The course	unipolar or bipolar
Aetiology	predominantly reactive
	predominantly endogenous

depressive disorder eventually; (b) in several important ways manic patients resemble patients who have had both types of episode. This convention is followed in this textbook.

Finally the predominant **aetiology** is noted, remembering that all cases have both endogenous and reactive causes.

DIFFERENTIAL DIAGNOSIS

Depressive disorders have to be distinguished from normal sadness, and from other psychiatric disorders namely neuroses, schizophrenia, and organic brain syndromes. As already explained on page 186, the distinction from normal sadness is made on the presence of other symptoms of the syndrome of depressive disorder.

Mild depressive disorders ('neurotic depression') are sometimes difficult to distinguish from **anxiety neuroses**. This point is also discussed in Chapter 6; here it need only be observed that accurate diagnosis depends on assessment of the relative severity of anxiety and depressive symptoms, and on the order in which they appeared. Similar problems arise when there are prominent **phobic** or **obsessional** symptoms, or when there are hysterical conversion symptoms with or without histrionic behaviour. In each case, the clinician may fail to identify the depressive symptoms and so prescribe the wrong treatment.

As cases with mixed anxiety and depressive symptoms are common, it can be asked whether anxiety and depressive neuroses can really be distinguished from one another. In a follow-up study of 66 patients with anxiety neuroses and 45 patients with depressive disorders, differences were found in the course of the two conditions over an average period of nearly four years (Kerr *et al.* 1972; Schapira *et al.* 1972). Of the 66 patients originally diagnosed as having anxiety neuroses, 24 (40 per cent) relapsed and all but one developed a further anxiety neurosis. Of those originally diagnosed as having depressive neuroses, 12 (26 per cent) relapsed and all but two developed a further depressive neurosis. Moreover features predicting relapse in the two groups were different, a finding that was strongly against the hypothesis that all the cases were really manifestations of the same disorder.

The differential diagnosis from **schizophrenia** depends on a careful search for the characteristic features of this condition (see Chapter 9). Difficult diagnostic problems arise when the patient has persecutory delusions but here again the distinction can usually be made on careful examination of the mental state and on the order in which symptoms appeared. Particular difficulties also arise when symptoms characteristic of depressive disorder and of schizophrenia are found in equal measure in the same patient; these so-called schizoaffective disorders are discussed on page 243.

In middle and late life, depressive disorders are sometimes difficult to distinguish from **dementia** (chronic organic brain syndrome) because some patients with depressive symptoms complain of considerable difficulty in remembering. In depressive disorders, difficulty in remembering occurs because poor concentration leads to inadequate registration. The distinction between the two conditions can often be made by careful memory testing (if necessary by a clinical psychologist), though it can be extremely difficult. If memory disorder does not improve with recovery of normal mood, an organic brain syndrome is probable (see also p. 512).

Manic disorders have to be distinguished from schizophrenia; organic brain disease involving the frontal lobes (including brain tumour and general paralysis of the insane); and states of brief excitement induced by amphetamines. The diagnosis from **schizophrenia** can be most difficult. In manic disorders auditory hallucinations and delusions can occur, including some that are characteristic of schizophrenia such as delusions of reference. However, these symptoms usually change quickly in content, and seldom outlast the phase of overactivity. When there is a more or less equal mixture of features of the two syndromes, the term schizoaffective (sometimes schizomanic) is often used. This term is discussed further in Chapter 9.

An **organic brain lesion** should always by considered, especially in middle-aged or older patients with expansive behaviour and no past history of affective disorder. In the absence of gross mood disorder, extreme social disinhibition (for example urinating in public) strongly suggests frontal lobe pathology. In such cases appropriate neurological investigation is essential.

The distinction between mania and excited behaviour due to **drug abuse** depends on the history and an examination of the urine for drugs before treatment with psychotropic drugs is started. Drug-induced states usually subside quickly once the patient is in hospital (see Chapter 17).

THE EPIDEMIOLOGY OF AFFECTIVE DISORDERS

Depressive disorder

It is difficult to determine the prevalence of depressive disorder partly because different investigators have used different diagnostic definitions. Many studies in the United States have been concerned not with the syndrome of depression, but with depressive symptoms arising in any circumstances (see Weissman and Klerman 1978). Such data are of little value because of the failure to distinguish between depressive symptoms as part of another syndrome (for example schizophrenia), and depressive symptoms as part of a depressive disorder. Recently in both the United States and the United Kingdom the use of standardized diagnostic schedules has led to big advances. These schedules include the Present State Examination (Wing *et al.* 1974), and the Research Diagnostic Criteria (Spitzer *et al.* 1978) with its supplementary Schedule for Affective Disorders and Schizophrenia (Endicott and Spitzer 1979).

Depressive **symptoms** are common, as shown by reported point prevalences of between 13–20 per cent of the population. They are more frequent among women, the lower socioeconomic groups, and the divorced or separated (see Boyd and Weissman 1982).

The information about depressive **syndromes** concerns bipolar cases (in which mania has occurred at some time) and unipolar cases. Bipolar cases are more reliably identified, but even so estimates of their incidence vary substantially. A review of the evidence suggests that the morbid risk for bipolar disorder is less than 1 per cent and the annual incidence between 9 and 15 per 100 000 for men and between 7 and 30 per 100 000 for women (Boyd and Weissman 1981). Estimates of the ratio of women to men differ, but it is generally agreed to lie between 1.3:1 and 2:1 (Krauthammer and Klerman 1979).

For unipolar depressive disorders, the point prevalence is about 3 per cent for men and 5–9 per cent for women. Estimates of their annual incidence vary from about 80 to 200 per 100 000 among men and from 250 to 7800 per 100 000 for women (see Boyd and Weissman 1981). The reasons for increased prevalence among women is uncertain. It could be due in part to a greater readiness in women to admit depressive symptoms, but such selective reporting is unlikely to be the whole explanation. It is possible that some depressed men abuse alcohol and are diagnosed as alcoholic rather than depressed, thus leading to an underestimate of the true number. Misdiagnosis of this kind is unlikely to account for the whole of the difference. Depressive disorders might be inherited disorders with X-linkage, or might be related to the hormonal changes of the reproductive cycle in women, but there is no good evidence that either factor can explain the differences in prevalence. Finally the social role of women might influence prevalence, a point taken up later (p. 206).

Among women the incidence and prevalence of depressive disorders varies with age, the highest rate being between 35–45 years. The rates for men increase with age (see Boyd and Weissman 1981).

THE AETIOLOGY OF AFFECTIVE DISORDERS

There have been many different approaches to the aetiology of affective disorders. In this section, consideration is first given to the role of genetic factors and of childhood experience in laying down a predisposition to affective disorder in adult life. Next an account is given of stressors that may provoke affective disorders. This is followed by a review of psychological and biochemical factors through which predisposing factors and stressors might lead to affective disorders. In all these topics, investigators have paid more attention to depressive disorders than to mania. In this chapter, more space is given to aetiology than in most others in this book; the purpose is to show how several different kinds of enquiry can be used to throw light on the same clinical problem.

Genetic causes

Genetic causes have been studied in moderate to severe cases of affective disorder, but not in milder cases (those called 'neurotic depression' by some investigators). Most family studies have shown that parents, siblings, and children of severely depressed patients have a morbid risk of 10–15 per cent for affective disorder, as against 1–2 per cent in the general population. It is also generally agreed that there is no excess of schizophrenia among the relatives of depressed probands.

Twin studies suggest strongly that these high rates within families are largely due to genetic factors. Thus, from a review of seven twin studies, Price (1968) concluded that the concordance rates for manic-depressive psychosis were 68 per cent for monozygotic twins (97 pairs) reared together, 67 per cent for monozygotic twins reared apart (12 pairs), and 23 per cent for dizygotic twins (119 pairs). Similar percentages were reported in studies from Denmark (Bertelsen *et al.* 1977).

Two small studies of adoptees also point to a genetic aetiology. Cadoret (1978) studied eight children, each born to a parent with an affective disorder and then adopted by a healthy couple. Three of the eight developed an affective disorder, as against only eight of 118 adoptees whose biological parents either suffered from a different psychiatric disorder or were healthy. In a study of 29 adoptees who had suffered from a biopolar affective disorder, Mendlewicz and Rainer (1977) found psychiatric disorder in 31 per cent of their biological parents (mainly but not exclusively affective illnesses), as against only 12 per cent of their adoptive parents.

So far no distinction has been made between cases with depression only (unipolar disorders) and those with a history of mania (bipolar disorders). Leonhard *et al.* (1962) were the first to present evidence that bipolar disorders were more frequent among the families of bipolar probands than among the families of unipolar probands. Several subsequent investigations (reviewed by Nurnberger and Gershon 1982) have confirmed this finding. However, these studies have also shown that unipolar cases are frequent in the families of both unipolar and bipolar probands; it seems that unipolar disorders do not 'breed true' as the bipolar disorders seem to do (see, for example Angst 1966). Bertelsen *et al.* (1977) report higher pair wise concordance rates among bipolar (74 per cent) than among unipolar (43 per cent) monozygotic twins, again suggesting a stronger genetic influence in bipolars.

There are conflicting theories about the **mode of inheritance** because no simple genetic model fits the frequencies of cases observed among family members of different degrees of relationship to the proband.

Attempts to find **genetic markers** for affective disorder have not been successful. Linkages have been reported between affective disorder and colour blindness, Xg blood group, and certain HLA antigens, but none has been confirmed (see Gershon and Bunney 1976; also Nurnberger and Gershon 1982).

Some family studies have shown increased rates of other psychiatric disorders among the families of probands with affective disorder. This finding has led to the hypothesis that these other psychiatric disorders might be aetiologically related to affective disorder, an idea expressed in the name '**depressive spectrum disease**'. So far these claims have not been confirmed. Helzer and Winokur (1974) reported an increase of alcoholism among the relatives of male manic probands, but Morrison (1975) found such an association only when the probands had both alcoholism and depressive disorder. Similarly Winokur *et al.* (1971) reported an increased rate of antisocial personality disorder ('sociopathy') among the male relatives of probands whose depressive disorders had started before the age of 40. This finding was not confirmed by Gershon *et al.* (1975).

Physique and personality

Kretschmer (1936) proposed that patients of **pyknic body build** (thick set and rounded) were particularly prone to affective illness. Subsequent investigations using objective measurements have not shown any strong association of this kind (von Zerssen 1976).

Kraepelin (1921) suggested that people with **cyclothymic personality** (i.e. those with repeated and sustained mood swings) were more prone to develop manic depressive disorder. Subsequently Leonhard *et al.* (1962) reported this association to be stronger among patients with bipolar disorders than among those with unipolar disorders. However, when personality was assessed without knowledge of the type of illness, bipolar patients were not found to have mainly cyclothymic personality traits (Tellenbach 1975).

No single type of personality seems to predispose to unipolar depressive disorders; in particular depressive personality disorder has no such association. Clinical experience suggests that the most relevant personality features are obsessional traits and readiness to develop anxiety. Presumably these features are important because they influence the way in which people respond to stressful life events. Unfortunately most reported investigations of personality in depressed patients are of little value because measurements were made when the patients were depressed. Assessments of patients who are currently depressed may not accurately reflect the premorbid personality.

Early environment

Maternal deprivation

Psychoanalysts have suggested that deprivation of maternal affection through separation or loss predisposes to depressive disorders in adult life. Epidemiologists have attempted to discover what proportion of adults with depressive disorder have experienced parental separation or loss in childhood. Nearly all these studies have methodological defects. Their results are contradictory; of 14 studies reviewed by Paykel (1981), seven confirm the hypothesis and seven do not. Other investigations have shown that the death of a parent is associated with disorders other than depressive disorders, for example psychoneurosis, antisocial personality and alcoholism (see Paykel 1981). At present, therefore, the association between parental loss and depressive disorder is uncertain. If it exists at all, it is weak and may be non-specific.

Relationships with parents

When assessing a depressed patient, it is difficult to determine retrospectively what kind of relationship he had in childhood with his parents. The patient's recollection of the relationship may be distorted by many factors, including the depressive disorder itself. These problems make it difficult to ascribe much aetiological importance to reports that, compared with normal controls or with patients with severe depressive disorders, patients with mild depressive disorders (neurotic depression) remember their parents as having been less caring and more over-protective (Parker 1979).

Precipitating factors

Recent life events

It is an everyday clinical observation that depressive disorders often follow stressful events. However, several other possibilities must be discounted before it can be concluded that stressful events cause depressive disorders that succeed them. First, the association might be coincidental. Secondly, the association might be non-specific; there might be as many stressful events in the weeks preceding other kinds of illness. Thirdly, it might be spurious; the patient might have regarded the events as stressful only in retrospect when seeking an explanation for his illness, or he might have experienced them as stressful only because he was already depressed at the time.

In recent years, research workers have tried to overcome each of these difficulties. The first two problems – whether the events are coincidental or whether any association is non-specific – require the use of control groups suitably chosen from the general population and from people with other illnesses. The third problem – whether the association is spurious – requires two other approaches. The first approach (Brown *et al.* 1973*b*) is to separate events that are undoubtedly independent of illness (such as losing a job because a whole factory closes) from events that may have been secondary to the illness (such as losing a job when no-one else is dismissed). The second approach (Holmes and Rahe 1967) is to assign a rating to each event according to the consensus view of healthy people about its stressful qualities.

By these methods, an excess of life events has been shown in the months before the onset of depressive disorder (Paykel *et al.* 1969; Brown and Harris

1978). However, an excess of similar events has also been shown to precede suicide attempts, and the onset of neurosis and schizophrenia. To estimate the relative importance of life events in each condition, Paykel (1978) applied a modified form of the epidemiological measure of relative risk. He found that the risk of developing depression increased sixfold in the six months after experiencing markedly threatening life events. The comparable increase for schizophrenia was two- to fourfold, and for attempted suicide sevenfold. Brown used another estimate, 'the brought forward time' (Brown *et al.* 1973*a*), and came to similar conclusions.

Are any particular kinds of events more likely to provoke a depressive disorder? Because depressive symptoms are part of the normal response to bereavement, it has been suggested that loss by separation or death might be particularly important. However, research shows that not all people with depressive symptoms report losses. For example, Paykel (1982) reviewed 11 studies that reported specifically on recent separations. In six of these studies depressives reported more separations than the control groups, suggesting some specificity; however, in five studies depressives did not report an excess of separations. Looked at the other way round, amongst people who experience loss events only about 10 per cent develop a depressive disorder (Paykel 1974). So far, therefore, the evidence does not point to any great specificity in the events that can provoke depressive disorder.

It is less certain whether mania is provoked by life events. In the past, mania was thought to arise entirely from endogenous causes. However, clinical experience suggests that a proportion of cases are precipitated, sometimes by events that might have been expected to induce depression, for example bereavement.

Predisposing life events

It is a common clinical impression that events preceding a depressive disorder can act as the 'last straw' for a person who has been subjected to a long period of adverse circumstances, such as an unhappy marriage, problems at work, or unsatisfactory housing. This view is partly supported by the work of Brown and his colleagues who found, among working-class women living in Camberwell in London, that life events are more likely to provoke a depressive disorder in those who are looking after young children, are not working outside the home, and have no one to confide in (see Brown and Harris 1978). Brown refers to these current life circumstances as **vulnerability factors**. He adds a fourth factor from the past – loss of the mother by death or separation before the age of 11. Vulnerability factors are thought to increase the likelihood of depressive disorder in the face of provoking life events, but *not* to produce depression on their own.

This scheme has not been wholly confirmed by subsequent enquiries. When he repeated his work in the Outer Hebrides, Brown could confirm only one of his four vulnerability factors at a statistically significant level – having three children aged under 14 (Brown and Prudo 1981). Also Solomon and Bromet (1982) studied the population living near the nuclear power station at Three Mile Island where a severe accident had occurred. This population was compared with the population who lived near a similar power station but had not been exposed to a stressful accident. Three of Brown's vulnerability factors were examined: lack of employment outside the home, three or more children under 14, and lack of a confiding relationship. There was no evidence that the first two factors acted as vulnerability factors, but there was some evidence that lack of a confiding relationship did so. As a test of Brown's hypothesis this study was not entirely fair because it included not only recent onset cases (to which the model is meant to apply), but also chronic cases (to which it is not meant to apply). At present the evidence for Brown's interesting idea of vulnerability factors must be regarded as incomplete.

The effects of physical illness

The associations between physical illness and depressive disorder are described in Chapter 11. Here it should be noted that some conditions appear particularly likely to be followed by depression. For example influenza, glandular fever, Parkinsonism, and certain endocrine disorders. It has been held that some operations, notably hysterectomy and sterilization, are followed by depression more often than would be expected by chance. However, these clinical impressions have not been confirmed by prospective studies (Gath *et al.* 1982; Cooper *et al.* 1982). It is likely that many physical illnesses can act as non-specific stressors in provoking depressive disorders, but that few have specific effects. Mania has occasionally been reported in association with physical illnesses (for example cerebral neoplasm and virus infections), medication, (notably steroids), and surgery (see Krauthammer and Klerman (1978) for a review of the evidence). However, no aetiological conclusions can be drawn from these diverse associations.

It should be mentioned here that the puerperium (although not an illness) is associated with an increased risk of affective disorder (see p. 390).

Psychological theories of aetiology

These theories are concerned with the psychological mechanisms by which recent and remote life experiences can lead to depressive disorders. Most of the literature on this subject fails to distinguish adequately between the symptom of depression and the syndrome of depressive disorder.

Psychoanalysis

The psychoanalytic theory of depression began with a paper by Abraham in 1911, and was developed by Freud in 1917 in a paper called 'Mourning and melancholia'. Freud drew attention to the resemblance between the phenomena of mourning and the symptoms of depressive disorders, and suggested that their causes might be similar. It is important to note that Freud did not suppose that all severe depressive disorders necessarily had the same cause. Thus he commented that some disorders 'suggest somatic rather than psychogenic affections' and indicated that his ideas were to be applied only to those 'whose psychogenic nature was indisputable' (1917, p. 243). Freud suggested that, just as mourning results from loss by death, so melancholia results from loss of other kinds. Since it was apparent that not every depressed patient had suffered an actual loss, it was necessary to postulate a loss of 'some abstraction' or internal representation, or in Freud's terms the loss of an 'object'.

Freud pointed out that depressed patients often appear critical of themselves, and he proposed that this self-accusation was really a disguised accusation of someone else for whom the patient 'felt affection'. In other words, depression was thought to occur when feelings of love and hostility were present at the same time (ambivalence). When a loved 'object' is lost the patient feels despair; at the same time any hostile feelings attached to this 'object' are redirected against the patient himself, as self-reproach.

In addition to these mechanisms of reaction, Freud also put forward predisposing factors. He proposed that the depressed patient regresses to an earlier stage of development, the oral stage, at which sadistic feelings are powerful. Klein (1934) developed this idea by suggesting that the infant must acquire confidence that, when his mother leaves him, she will return even when he has been angry. This proposed stage of learning was called the 'depressive position'. Klein suggested that, if this stage is not passed through successfully, the child will be more likely to develop depression in adult life.

Further important modifications of Freud's theory were made by Bibring (1953) and Jacobson (1953). They suggested that loss of self-esteem is of central importance in depressive disorders. They also proposed that self-esteem depends not only on experiences at the oral stage, but also on failures at later stages of development. However, although low self-esteem is certainly part of the syndrome of depressive disorders, there is no clear evidence about its frequency before the illness began. Nor has it been shown that low self-esteem is more common among people who subsequently develop depressive disorders than among those who do not.

According to psychodynamic theory, mania is a defence against depression; this is not a convincing explanation of most cases.

For a review of the psychoanalytic literature on depression, see Mendelson (1982).

Learned helplessness

This explanation of depressive disorders is based on experimental work with animals. Seligman (1975) originally suggested that depression develops when reward or punishment is no longer clearly contingent on the actions of the organism. When animals are exposed to experimental situations in which they cannot control punishing stimuli, they develop a behavioural syndrome known as 'learned helplessness'. The features of this syndrome bear some resemblance to those of depressive disorders in man, notably reduced voluntary activity and reduced intake of food. The original hypothesis has been broadened by stating that depression results when 'highly desired outcomes are believed improbable or highly aversive outcomes are believed probable and the individual expects that no response (of his) will change their likelihood' (Abrahamson *et al.* 1978, p. 68). This work has attracted considerable attention, perhaps as a result of the name 'learned helplessness' rather than as a result of scientific strength.

Separation experiments in animals

Arising from the suggestion that the loss of a loved person may be a cause of depressive disorders, there have been numerous experiments on the effects of separation in primates. Most of these experiments are concerned with the separation of infants from their mothers, rather than the separation of adults from one another. As such they are of uncertain relevance to man, since depressive disorders may never occur in young children (see Chapter 20). Nevertheless the studies may be of some importance to understanding the effects of separating human infants from their mothers. In a particularly careful series of experiments, Hinde and his colleagues studied the effects of separating infant rhesus macaques from their mothers (see Hinde 1977). These experiments confirmed earlier observations that separation causes distress to both infant and mother. After an initial period of calling and searching, the infant becomes less active, eats and drinks less, withdraws from encounters with other monkeys, and has an appearance resembling that of a sad human being. Hinde and his co-workers have shown that this response to separation depends on many other variables including the 'relationship' of the pair before separation.

In contrast with these effects of removing infants from their mothers, adolescent monkeys separated from their peer group showed no clear stage of 'despair' but instead greater exploratory behaviour (McKinney *et al.* 1972). Moreover, when five-year-old monkeys were taken away from their family group, reactions were observed only when they were housed alone, and not when they were housed with other monkeys, some of whom they knew already (Suomi *et al.* 1975). Therefore, although much can be learnt by studying separation in primates, it would be unwise to use the available data to support an aetiological theory of depressive disorders in man.

Cognitive theories

Most psychiatrists regard the gloomy thoughts of depressed patients as secondary to a primary disturbance of mood. However, Beck (1967) has suggested that these 'depressive cognitions' may be the primary disorder, or at least powerful factors in aggravating and perpetuating the disorder. Beck divides depressive cognitions into three components. The first is a stream of 'negative' thoughts, for example 'I am a failure as a mother'. The second is a set of expectations, for example that a person cannot be happy unless everyone likes him. The third is a series of 'cognitive distortions', of which four examples can be given: 'arbitrary inference', drawing a conclusion when there is no evidence for it and even some against it; 'selective abstraction', focusing on a detail and ignoring more important features of a situation; 'overgeneralization', drawing a general conclusion on the basis of a single incident; and 'personalization', relating external events to oneself in an unwarranted way.

Beck suggests that a person who habitually adopts such ways of thinking will be more likely to become depressed when faced with minor problems. For example, a rebuff would be more likely to lead to depression in a person who thinks that he needs to be liked by everyone, concludes arbitrarily that the rebuff means he is disliked, focuses on this event despite other evidence that he is generally popular, and draws these general conclusions from this single incident. (It can be seen from this example that the varieties of cognitive distortion are not entirely distinct from one another.)

As yet there is a lack of evidence that these mechanisms are present in people before the onset of depressive disorder; or that these mechanisms are more frequent in people who subsequently develop depressive disorders than in those who do not.

Biochemical theories

The amine hypothesis

In its simple form this hypothesis is that depressive disorders are due to depletion, and mania to excessive provision, of a monoamine neurotransmitter at one or more sites in the brain. More recent elaborations suggest a change in receptor sensitivity as well as a change in the turnover or level of the amines (see, for example Garver and Davis 1979). The monoamine neurotransmitters that have been most studied are noradrenaline, dopamine, and 5-hydroxytryptamine. The hypothesis has been tested by observations of three kinds of phenomena: the pharmacological properties that antidepressant drugs have in common; the metabolism of neurotransmitters in patients with affective disorders; the clinical effects of amine precursors and antagonists.

Of the two main groups of drugs used to treat depressive disorders, monoamine oxidase inhibitors increase monoamine transmitters by reducing their metabolism, while tricyclic antidepressants increase their concentrations in the synaptic cleft by blocking their reuptake into presynaptic neurones (and possibly by other mechanisms as well – see Chapter 17). These actions suggest that the concentration of one of these transmitters may be important in depressive disorders, but they do not indicate which one is involved.

More direct evidence comes from studies of post-mortem brain, though suitable specimens are not easy to obtain. The results are difficult to interpret for three reasons. First the observed changes may have taken place after death.

Secondly, the changes may have been caused just before death by anoxia or the effects of metabolic disturbance. Thirdly they may have been caused by drugs used in treatment, or in some cases to commit suicide. With these reservations in mind, it can be noted that some investigators have reported lowered concentrations of 5HT in the brain stem of depressed patients (for example Lloyd *et al.* 1974), but other investigators have not confirmed this (for example Cochran *et al.* 1976). No significant changes have been reported in concentrations of noradrenaline or dopamine in post-mortem brains of depressed patients. Therefore these findings point to 5HT as the relevant transmitter.

Studies of CSF can yield only indirect evidence about the metabolism of monoamine transmitters in the central nervous system. Measurements have been made of the main metabolites formed in brain: 3-methoxy-4-hydroxy-phenylethylene glycol (MHPG) from noradrenaline; homovanillic acid (HVA) from dopamine; and 5-hydroxyindolacetic acid (5HIAA) from 5-hydroxytrypt-amine (5HT). As it is uncertain what proportions of the metabolites in lumbar CSF originate in the brain rather than in the spinal cord, the interpretation of these investigations is difficult. Moreover, changed concentrations may simply reflect alterations in the transport of metabolites out of the CSF; this possibility can be partly excluded by giving large doses of probenecid which interferes with such transport. On balance, the evidence is that 5HIAA concentrations are reduced in CSF of patients with depressive disorders, suggesting that there is reduced 5HT turnover in brain (for example van Praag and Korf 1971). However, in mania, where raised concentrations would be predicted, normal or low values have been found. A more serious difficulty for the amine hypothesis is that low 5HIAA levels persist after clinical recovery (see Coppen 1972). Evidence about the noradrenaline metabolite MHPG is conflicting, though there is some suggestion that it is reduced in depressive disorders (see van Praag 1982). Evidence about the dopamine metabolite HVA is also inconsistent, although it may be reduced in depressive disorders with retardation.

Studies of urine yield even more indirect evidence about events in the brain. Metabolism of 5-hydroxytryptamine in the brain cannot be inferred from urinary 5HIAA because most of the excreted metabolite arises in peripheral tissues. It is equally unlikely that urinary HVA reflects central dopamine metabolism because it is normal in Parkinsonism (Calne *et al.* 1969). It is supposed that noradrenaline is metabolized to MHPG in the brain, and to vanillylmandelic acid (VMA) in peripheral tissues. However, some MHPG is probably produced peripherally, so reports of its reduced excretion in depressive disorders cannot necessarily be taken as evidence of reduced turnover in brain.

The effects of giving precursors or antagonists of the monoamine transmitters are equally uncertain. L-tryptophan, the precursor of 5HT, has been reported to have antidepressant effects by some workers (for example Coppen *et al.* 1972) but not by others (for example Mendels *et al.* 1975). Concentrations of tryptophan in the brain are known to be partly determined by concentrations of free (as opposed to bound) tryptophan in plasma. For this reason, plasma concentrations of free tryptophan have been measured in depressed patients. Reduced concentrations have been reported by some workers (for example Coppen and Wood 1978) but not confirmed by others (see Green and Costain (1979) for a review). It is generally agreed that L-dopa, a precursor of both dopamine and noradrenaline, has no antidepressant effects.

The conclusion must be that none of these investigations provides strong evidence for the amine hypothesis. There is some evidence from biochemical studies that 5HT concentrations may be low in depressive disorders. Antidepressant drugs seem to raise noradrenaline concentrations. However, this latter evidence is difficult to interpret because even if raised noradrenaline concentrations are associated with a therapeutic effect, this might be due to balancing a change in another transmitter. The finding would not necessarily indicate that noradrenaline concentrations are low in depressive disorders. It is important to remember the analogy of Parkinsonism; in this condition anticholinergic drugs are effective, but the underlying disorder is a deficiency in the dopaminergic system, not an excess of cholinergic function. In any case, the original amine hypothesis is almost certainly based on a considerable oversimplification of the mechanisms occurring at synapses in the central nervous system.

Endocrine abnormalities

These abnormalities are important in aetiology for three reasons. First, some disorders of endocrine function are followed by depressive disorders more often than would be expected by chance, suggesting a causative relationship. Secondly endocrine abnormalities found in depressive disorder suggest that there may be a disorder of the hypothalamic centres controlling the endocrine system. Thirdly endocrine changes are regulated by hypothalamic mechanisms, which in turn are partly controlled by monoamine systems; hence endocrine changes might reflect abnormalities in monoamine systems. These three lines of enquiry will be considered in turn.

Cushing's syndrome is sometimes accompanied by depression or elation; and Addison's disease and hyperparathyroidism by depression. Endocrine changes may possibly account for depressive disorders occurring premenstrually, during the menopause and after childbirth. These clinical associations are discussed further in Chapter 12. Here it need only be noted that none has so far led to a better understanding of the causes of affective disorder.

Much research effort has been concerned with abnormalities in the control of cortisol in depressive disorders. In about half of patients whose depression is at least moderately severe, plasma cortisol secretion is increased. This increase is accompanied by a change in the diurnal pattern of secretion. An increased secretion of cortisol could arise because the experience of being ill acted as a stressor; but such an explanation is unlikely because stressors do not alter the diurnal pattern. In depressed patients cortisol secretion is abnormal in that it remains high throughout the afternoon and evening, whereas in normal subjects it falls to a lower level. Another finding is that between 20 and 40 per cent of depressed patients do not show the normal suppression of cortisol secretion induced by giving the powerful synthetic corticosteroid dexamethasone about midnight. However, not all cortisol hypersecretors are dexamethasone resistant. These abnormalities seem to occur mainly in depressive disorders with 'biological' symptoms, but they are not detected in all such cases, nor are they associated with any single clinical feature.

Attempts have been made to relate these findings to changes in the neurotransmitters involved in the central control of ACTH secretion. It is thought that 5HT and acetylcholine may stimulate, and GABA and noradrenaline inhibit, the production of corticotrophin releasing factor. Acetylcholine and GABA can probably be discounted on the grounds that there is no other evidence to implicate them in depression. This leaves 5HT and noradrenaline for further consideration. The evidence reviewed above suggests that 5HT may be low rather than high in depressive disorders, so increased 5HT could not account for the high output of cortisol. This leaves the possibility that the observed abnormality in cortisol secretion could reflect a deficiency of noradrenergic control. Although such arguments are ingenious, they cannot be accepted as firm evidence for the amine hypothesis. The reader is referred to Sachar (1982) for a review of this complicated subject.

Water and electrolytes

There have been several reports of changes in water and electrolytes in depressive disorders and mania. Thus 'residual sodium' (more or less equivalent to intracellular sodium) has been reported to be increased in both conditions (Coppen and Shaw 1963; Coppen *et al.* 1976). There have also been reports of changes in erythrocyte membrane sodium–potassium ATPase, such that active transport of sodium and potassium increases on recovery from mania and depressive disorders (Naylor *et al.* 1973, 1976). Such findings are of some interest because they could reflect an abnormality of the mechanisms subserving nerve conduction. However, much more needs to be known before aetiological hypotheses can be constructed.

Conclusion

The **predisposition** to develop mania and severe depressive disorders has important genetic determinants. There is no convincing evidence that this inherited predisposition is modified in important ways by specific childhood experiences of the kind postulated by psychoanalysts. Nevertheless, adverse early experience may play a part in shaping features of personality which in turn determine whether, in adult life, certain events are experienced as stressful. If such a predisposition exists, it is not expressed as a single personality type that is invariably associated with affective disorder, but in several different kinds of personality.

The **precipitating** causes are stressful life events and certain kinds of physical illness. Some progress has been made in discovering the types of event that provoke depression and in quantifying their stressful qualities. Such studies show that loss is an important precipitant, but not the only one. The effects of particular events may be modified by a number of background factors that may make a person more vulnerable, for example caring for several small children without help, and not having someone to confide in. As noted in the preceding paragraph the impact of potentially stressful events also depends on personality factors.

Two kinds of **mechanism** have been proposed to explain how precipitating events lead to the phenomena observed in depressive disorders. The first mechanism is psychological and the second biochemical. The two sets of mechanism are not necessarily mutually exclusive, for they may represent different levels of organization of the same pathological process. The psychological studies are at an early stage. Abnormalities have been shown in the thinking of depressed patients, and they may play a part in perpetuating depressive disorder. However, there is no convincing evidence that they induce it. The biochemical theory is based largely on the response of depressive disorders to treatment with drugs. Many studies give some general support to the hypothesis of a biochemical abnormality, but they have not identified it.

COURSE AND PROGNOSIS

In considering course and prognosis it is convenient to deal with bipolar and unipolar disorders separately, because more information is available about the bipolar cases.

Bipolar disorders

As explained earlier, in these disorders there has been at least one episode of mania, irrespective of whether or not there has been a depressive disorder. The mean age of **onset** is about 30 years, though there is wide variation, some cases starting in the late teens, and a few in late life. Angst *et al.* (1973) reported that almost 90 per cent of cases began before the age of 50.

The natural **course** of manic episodes can be judged from reports written before the introduction of modern treatment. According to Kraepelin (1921, p. 73) 'while occasionally attacks run their course within a few weeks or even a few days, the great majority extend over many months. Attacks of two or three years duration are very frequent; isolated cases may last longer, for ten years or more'. In 1945, before phenothiazines had been introduced, Lundquist reported an average duration of 13 months. These estimates contrast with the average duration of under three months reported by Angst *et al.* in 1973.

Among patients who have repeated manic attacks, the length of each episode does not seem to alter systematically in the later attacks (Angst *et al.* 1973).

It is generally agreed that nearly all manic patients **recover** eventually. Before modern treatment was available, about 5 per cent persisted for several years (Lundquist 1945; Stendstedt 1952). Nowadays, many of these lasting cases can be kept under control with prolonged medication. Manic illnesses often recur, and subsequent depressive disorder is frequent. The proportion of patients who have only a single episode of mania is wholly uncertain, estimates varying from as many as 50 per cent (Kraepelin 1921; Lundquist 1945) to as few as 1 per cent (Angst *et al.* 1973). Nowadays it is often difficult to decide whether there is a succession of illnesses or a single illness interrupted by periods of partially successful treatment. According to Angst *et al.* (1973) the length of remission between episodes of illness becomes shorter up to the third attack, but does not change after that.

Unipolar depressive disorders

The age of **onset** varies so widely that a mean is not informative. The **course** of the episode is equally variable. Kraepelin (1921, p. 97) wrote that 'the duration of the attack is usually longer than in mania; but it may likewise fluctuate between a few days and more than a decade. The remission of the morbid phenomena invariably takes place with many fluctuations . . .'. Studies that have included both unipolar and bipolar disorders have not revealed consistent differences between them in rates of **recovery** (see Tsuang *et al.* 1979). It is generally agreed that among unipolar depressives nearly all young patients recover, though not all elderly patients do so.

Depressive disorder and suicide

Of people who have suffered a severe depressive disorder at any time, between 11 and 17 per cent will eventually commit suicide (Fremming 1951; Helgason 1964; Pitts and Winokur 1964). There is not enough information to decide the relative risks of suicide in unipolar and bipolar disorders.

TREATMENT

This section is concerned with the effectiveness of various forms of treatment. *Details of treatment with drugs and ECT are described in Chapter 17* which should be consulted before reading this section. Advice on the selection of treatments and the day-to-day care of patients is given in the section on management.

Antidepressant drugs

In an important study by the Medical Research Council (Clinical Psychiatry Committee 1965), the therapeutic effects of imipramine, phenelzine, ECT, and placebo were compared in 250 patients suffering from moderately severe depression. At the end of four weeks ECT was the most effective of these four treatments. After three months ECT and imipramine were equally effective, about two-thirds of the patients in both treatment groups having improved. Phenelzine was no more effective than placebo, about one-third of the patients in both these groups having improved. Other controlled trials have also shown imipramine to be more effective than placebo in moderately severe depressive disorders (for example Ball and Kiloh 1959). However, controlled trials also indicate that the value of imipramine in less severe 'neurotic' depressive disorders is less certain (Rogers and May 1975). Comparisons between the many tricyclic antidepressant drugs now available have not shown any important difference in their therapeutic effects, although there are some worthwhile differences in their side-effects (see, for example Wechsler *et al.* 1965).

Comparative studies have shown that monoamine oxidase inhibitors are less effective than tricyclic antidepressants for moderate to severe depressive disorders. In mild cases with neurotic symptoms they are probably about as effective as tricyclics, provided that they are given for long enough and in sufficient dose. Thus for phenelzine the effect may take up to six weeks to appear and the dose may need to be increased beyond 45 mg per day to 60 mg or even 75 mg. There is moreover still some doubt whether they have a specific antidepressant rather than an anxiolytic effect. However work by Rowan *et al.* (1982) suggests that in high doses there is. They found that phenelzine given for six weeks at doses increasing progressively to 60–75 mg a day was as effective in the treatment of mild depression as amitryptyline in doses increasing to 150–187.5 mg/day. Moreover both were more effective than placebo. These therapeutic effects have to be balanced against the many interactions of the monoamine oxidase inhibitors with foodstuffs and other drugs (see Chapter 17). It is therefore recommended that MAOI drugs should never be the first choice of treatment for any depressive disorder. If they are used it should only be for less severe chronic depressive disorders with prominent anxiety symptoms which have not responded to a full trial of a cyclic antidepressant drug.

Lithium

This section is concerned with lithium only as a treatment for depressive disorders. Its use in prevention is considered later. Some studies suggest that, for depressive disorder without obvious precipitants ('endogenous depression'), lithium has antidepressant effects comparable to those of a tricyclic drug (for example Mendels *et al.* 1972; Watanabe *et al.* 1975; Worrall *et al.* 1979). However, other studies have not confirmed these effects (for example Fieve *et al.* 1968, Stokes *et al.* 1971) or have obtained equivocal results (Goodwin *et al.* 1969). So it seems that if lithium has a therapeutic effect in the acute stage of depressive disorders, it is not a powerful effect. Hence there is no justification for using lithium in this way except perhaps when other measures have failed. Even the latter use is doubtful; there are few reports that lithium is effective in patients who have not responded to antidepressants (for example Bennie 1975) or that it enhances the effects of tricyclic drugs (for example Lingjaerde *et al.* 1974) or MAOIs (Zall *et al.* 1968); and these reports have yet to be confirmed convincingly.

Electroconvulsive therapy

This treatment is described in Chapter 17, where its unwanted effects are also considered. The present section is concerned with evidence about its therapeutic action in depressive disorders. It is generally agreed that the effects of ECT are best in severe depressive disorders, especially those with marked weight loss, early morning waking, and delusions (Carney *et al.* 1965). Surprisingly few controlled clinical trials have been carried out. As mentioned above, the Medical Research Council Trial showed that the effects of ECT were greater than either imipramine or placebo after four weeks of treatment. Thus marked improvement was found in 71 per cent of ECT-treated patients, 52 per cent of imipramine-treated patients, and 39 per cent of placebo-treated patients. However, at six months follow up marked improvement was found in equal proportions of the ECT- and imipramine-treated groups. Similar results were obtained in the United States by Greenblatt *et al.* (1964), who compared ECT with impramine, placebo, phenelzine, and isocarboxazid. In addition to the severe depressive disorders, these investigators included psychoneurotic depressive reactions and some depressed schizophrenic patients. They also gave more ECT than the MRC trial (nine or more as against 4–8). In this trial the percentages of patients showing marked improvement after eight weeks were: ECT 76 and placebo 46. In the drug groups the percentages were imipramine 49, phenelzine 50, and isocarboxazid 28. The low response in the imipramine group is surprising. Kiloh *et al.* (1960) also found that ECT was more effective (89 per cent improvement) than placebo (11 per cent improvement). An authorative review of the evidence from these and other trials has concluded that, in the treatment of severe depressive disorders, ECT is more effective than placebo, and acts more quickly than tricyclic antidepressants (Royal College of Psychiatrists 1977). In a wide-ranging review, Wechsler *et al.* (1965) reach the same conclusion.

Even if ECT is more effective than placebo tablets, its effects might not be due to the convulsion, but to repeated anaesthesia, the electric current, or other aspects of the procedure. *The evidence on these points is considered on pages 546–5* in the chapter on treatment; it indicates that the therapeutic agent is the convulsion.

What clinical features predict a good response to ECT? Three main studies have been carried out; in general they agree that 'biological' and psychotic features predict a good outcome, whilst neurotic symptoms predict a poor outcome. Thus Carney *et al.* (1965) found that a good response to ECT was related to early waking, weight loss, and somatic and paranoid delusions. Mendels (1965) identified early waking, retardation, and somatic and paranoid delusions. Hobson (1953) identified retardation and marked self-reproach, together with sudden onset, obsessional personality, and illness of less than one year's duration. All three investigations found that an unfavourable outcome was related to hypochondriasis and hysterical features; two of the three studies added poor premorbid adjustment, neurotic traits, and fluctuating course. These predictors are not specific to ECT, for they resemble the predictors of response to imipramine (Kiloh *et al.* 1962). This similarity is in keeping with the evidence that it is mainly speed of action that distinguishes ECT from tricyclic drug treatment.

Psychotherapy

The psychological treatments mainly used for depressive disorders can be divided into supportive methods, dynamic psychotherapy, 'interpersonal' methods, and cognitive therapy. **Supportive treatment** is part of the management of every depressed patient; it is intended to sustain him until other treatments have their effects, or natural recovery occurs. **Dynamic psychotherapy** is intended to have a specific therapeutic effect. Opinions differ about its value. Arieti (1977) suggests that it has a role in the treatment of most cases of depression, including severe cases. Other clinicians restrict the use of dynamic psychotherapy to the less severe cases. There have been few attempts to evaluate treatment, and they have been concerned with group and marital therapy. They suggest that these two forms of psychotherapy may be valuable in reducing social difficulties that might lead to relapse, rather than in bringing about an early resolution of the depressive symptoms. In a comparison of weekly group therapy, imipramine and placebo, Covi *et al.* (1974) found that only the drug produced significantly more symptomatic improvement than the placebo. Friedman (1975) compared weekly marital therapy with amitriptyline, placebo, and minimal contact, over 12 weeks. He found that amitriptyline led to the most change in symptoms, but psychotherapy led to more beneficial changes in marital relationships.

'Interpersonal psychotherapy'

This is a systematic and standardized treatment approach to relationships and life problems. Weissman *et al.* (1979) reported that the effects of interpersonal therapy on the symptoms of moderately severe depressive disorders were equal to those of amitripytline and greater than those of minimal treatment. Drug treatment had more effect on sleep disturbance, appetite, and somatic complaints; while interpersonal therapy had more effect on depressed mood, guilt, suicidal ideas, interests, and work. The drug effects began in the first week, the effects of psychotherapy only after 4–8 weeks (Di Mascio *et al.* 1979). 'Endogenous' depression appeared less likely to respond to psychotherapy alone, while 'situational' depression responded equally well to drugs or psychotherapy (Prussoff *et al.* 1980).

Cognitive therapy

Comparable results have been reported with cognitive therapy – the method is described in Chapter 18. Essentially, it is directed not to life problems but to the patient's way of thinking about these problems, and to other depressive cognitions on described on page 608. Cognitive therapy has been tested against antidepressant drug treatment in two randomized trials with patients suffering from moderately severe depressive disorders (Rush *et al.* 1977; Blackburn *et al.* 1981). In each of these trials, the results of cognitive therapy were as good as those of the drug. These findings require further replication before the treatment is used in everyday practice. They are sufficiently encouraging to demand further investigation, particularly for chronic depressive disorders that begin as a response to life problems but persist long after the problems have resolved.

Sleep deprivation

Several studies suggest that short-term changes can be brought about in a proportion of severe depressive disorders by keeping the patients awake for long periods. This interesting finding seems paradoxical because most depressed patients already sleep badly. At present this procedure cannot be regarded as a practical form of treatment, but rather as a subject for further study (see Roy and Bhanji (1976) for a review).

Preventing relapse

It has been shown convincingly that, if treatment with **tricyclic antidepressants** is prolonged for six months after clinical recovery, it reduces the rate of relapse to about half the rate observed in placebo-treated patients (Mindham *et al.* 1973; Paykel *et al.* 1975). Such prolonged treatment should be considered in all patients whose recovery appears closely related to treatment with an anti-depressant drug.

Lithium has also been used to reduce the rate of relapse. In bipolar disorders, there is convincing evidence that prolonged administration of lithium prevents not only relapses into mania but also relapses into depression (Coppen *et al.* 1971) though the effect may be less marked on depressive than on manic relapses (Prien *et al.* 1973).

There is less convincing evidence that lithium reduces the rate of relapse of unipolar depressive disorders. Coppen *et al.* (1971) reported a significant reduction of periods of depressive disorder during follow up in lithium-treated as compared with placebo-treated patients. In a multi-centre trial, the Medical Research Council Drug Trials Subcommittee (1981) found that amitryptyline and lithium were both more effective than placebo in preventing relapses, and not significantly different from one another. However, Coppen *et al.* (1976) found lithium superior to maprotiline. Coppen *et al.* (1981) found that continuing treatment with lithium reduced the rate of relapse after ECT, but this finding requires confirmation. It seems likely that lithium does reduce the rate of relapse of moderate and severe depressive disorders with mainly endogenous causes; but the effect is not evidently greater than that of the less toxic antidepressant drugs. For bipolar disorders, lithium is more useful because tricyclic drugs may produce manic relapses.

Treatment of mania

Antipsychotic drugs such as chlorpromazine and haloperidol usually bring the symptoms of acute mania under rapid control, although sometimes very large doses are needed (see p. 539). Lithium carbonate is also effective but the therapeutic response usually occurs only in the second week of treatment, and is therefore slower than the response to antipsychotic drugs. Controlled comparisons of lithium carbonate with chlorpromazine (for example Prien *et al.* 1972) and haloperidol (for example Garfinkel *et al.* 1980) indicate that both these drugs are superior to lithium in producing rapid control of overactivity. Otherwise the balance of evidence is that their effects are not obviously different (see Goodwin and Zis 1979).

Prevention of mania

There is convincing evidence that, in the majority of bipolar patients, continued administration of lithium carbonate reduces the rate of relapse into manic illness (for example Coppen *et al.* 1971; Prien *et al.* 1973). Attempts have been made to predict which patients will respond to lithium prophylaxis, but without success. No relationship has been found between response to lithium and age at onset of illness, number of previous episodes, or family history of affective illness. *The practical details of lithium prophylaxis are discussed on pages 556–7.*

ASSESSMENT OF DEPRESSIVE DISORDERS

The steps in assessment are (a) to decide whether the diagnosis is depressive disorder; (b) to judge the severity of the disorder, including the risk of suicide; (c) to form an opinion about the causes; (d) to assess the patient's social resources; and (e) to gauge the effect of the disorder on other people.

Diagnosis depends on thorough history taking and examination of physical and mental state. It has been discussed earlier in this chapter. Particular care should be taken not to overlook a depressive disorder in the patient who does not complain spontaneously of being depressed ('masked depression'). It is equally important not to diagnose a depressive disorder simply on the grounds of prominent depressive symptoms; the latter could be part of another disorder, for example an organic syndrome caused by a cerebral neoplasm.

It should also be remembered that certain drugs can induce depression (see p. 333).

The **severity** of the disorder is judged from the symptoms. Considerable severity is indicated by 'biological' symptoms, and hallucinations and delusion, particularly the latter two. It is also important to assess how the depressive disorder has reduced the patient's capacity to work, or engage in family life and social activities. In this assessment the duration and course of the condition should be taken into account as well as the severity of the present symptoms. Not only does the length of history affect prognosis, it also gives an indication of the patient's capacity to tolerate further distress. A long continued disorder, even if not severe, can bring the patient to the point of desperation. The risk of **suicide** must be judged in every case (the methods of assessment are described on pp. 404-6).

Aetiology is assessed next, with reference to precipitating, predisposing, maintaining, and pathoplastic factors. No attempt need be made to allocate the syndrome to an exclusively endogenous or reactive category; instead the importance of external and internal causes should be evaluated in every case.

Provoking causes may be psychological and social (the 'life events' discussed earlier in this chapter) or they may be physical illness and its treatment. In assessing such cases, it is good practice to enquire routinely into the patient's work, finances, family life, social activities, general living conditions, and physical health. Problems in these areas may be recent and acute, or may take the form of chronic background difficulties such as prolonged marital tension, problems with children, and financial hardship.

The patient's **social resources** are considered next. Enquiries should cover family, friends, and work. A loving family can help to support a patient through a period of depression by providing company, encouraging him when he has lost confidence, and guiding him into suitable activities. For some patients, work is a valuable social resource, providing distraction and comradeship. For others it is a source of stress. A careful assessment is needed in each case.

The **effects** of the disorder **on other people** must be considered carefully. The most obvious problems arise when a severely depressed patient is the mother of young children who depend on her. It is important to consider whether the patient could endanger other people by remaining at work; for example, as a bus driver. When there are depressive delusions, it is necessary to consider what would happen were the patient to act on them. For example, severely depressed mothers may occasionally kill their children because they believe them doomed to suffer if they remain alive.

THE MANAGEMENT OF DEPRESSIVE DISORDERS

This section starts with the management of a patient with a depressive disorder of moderate or greater severity. The first question is whether the patient requires inpatient or day-patient care. The answer depends on the severity of the disorder and the quality of the patient's social resources. In judging severity, particular attention should be paid to the risk of suicide (or any risk to the life or welfare of family members, particularly dependent children) and to any failure to eat or drink that might endanger the patient's life. Provided that these risks are absent most patients with a supportive family can be treated at home, even when severely depressed. Patients who live alone, or whose families cannot care for them during the day, may need in-patient or day-patient care.

If the patient is to remain out of hospital, the next question is whether he should continue to work. If the disorder is mild, work can provide a valuable distraction from depressive thoughts and a source of companionship. When the disorder is more severe, retardation, poor concentration, and lack of drive are likely to impair performance at work, and such failure may add to the patient's feelings of hopelessness. In severe disorders there may be dangers to other people if the patient remains at his job.

The next step is to decide whether physical treatment is required. **ECT** will seldom be the first measure and will usually be considered only for patients already admitted to hospital. The only indication for ECT as a first measure is the need to bring about improvement as rapidly as possible. In practice this applies to two main groups of patients: those who refuse to drink enough to maintain an adequate output of urine (including the rare cases of depressive stupor); and those who present a highly dangerous suicidal risk. Occasionally this indication also applies to a patient who is suffering such extreme distress that the most rapid form of treatment is deemed justifiable. Such cases are rare. It should be remembered that the effects of ECT differ from those of anti-depressant drugs in greater rapidity of action rather than in the final therapeutic result.

The need for **antidepressant drug treatment** should be considered next. This treatment is indicated for most patients with a depressive syndrome of at least moderate severity, and particularly those with 'biological' symptoms. (*The management of antidepressant drug treatment is considered further on page 546*). One of the tricyclic antidepressants should be chosen unless there are special reasons to avoid the cardiovascular and other side-effects, in which case a drug with fewer side-effects such as mianserin may be chosen (see p. 543). *The dosage of these drugs, the precautions to be observed in using them, and the instructions to be given to patients, are described in Chapter 17.* Here it is only necessary to emphasize again the importance of explaining to the patient that, although side-effects will appear quickly, the therapeutic effect is likely to be delayed for up to three weeks. During this time patients should be seen to provide support; those with the more severe disorders may need to be seen every two or three days, and the others once a week. During this time it is important to make sure that the drugs are being taken in the prescribed dose. Patients should be warned about the effects of taking alcohol. They should be advised about driving, particularly that they should not drive while experiencing sedative side-effects or any other effects that might impair their performance in an emergency.

If after a reasonable time antidepressant drug treatment has not succeeded, the dose should be increased gradually to the maximum advised by the manufacturers, provided that there are no severe unwanted effects (see also Chapter 17). If the patient's condition worsens despite adequate treatment as an outpatient, day-hospital or inpatient care should be considered. Such a change is often followed by improvement even though the dose of drugs has not changed, presumably because the patient has been removed from a stressful environment.

For every patient, the need for suitable activity should be considered. Depressed patients give up activities and withdraw from other people. In this way they become deprived of social stimulation and rewarding experiences, and their original feelings of depression are increased. It is important to make sure that the patient is occupied adequately, though he should not be pushed into activities where he is likely to fail because of slowness or poor concentration. Hence there is a fairly narrow range of activity that is appropriate for the individual depressed patient, and the range changes as the illness runs its course. If the patient remains at home, it is important to discuss with relatives how much the patient should be encouraged to do each day. If he is in hospital the question should be decided in collaboration with nurses and occupational therapists. Relatives may also need to be helped to accept the disorder as an illness, and to avoid criticising the patient.

The need for **psychological treatment** should also be decided in every case. All depressed patients require support, encouragement, and a thorough explanation that they are suffering from illness, not moral failure. If the depressive disorder is mainly a reaction to life problems and is not severe, discussion and counselling should be started. However, if the depressive disorder is severe, too much discussion of problems at an early stage only increases the patient's feeling of hopelessness. The more depressed the patient, the more the psychiatrist should take over problems for him in the early days of treatment. Later the psychiatrist should encourage the patient to resume responsibility for his own affairs as he recovers.

Dynamic psychotherapy

Any therapy directed to self-examination rather than to problem solving is seldom appropriate for the acutely depressed patient, as it is likely to make the disorder worse. During intervals between acute episodes, such therapy may be valuable for patients who have recurrent depressive disorders caused largely by their ways of reacting to life events.

Resistant cases

If a depressive disorder does not respond within a reasonable time to a chosen combination of antidepressant drugs, graded activity, and psychological treatment, the plan should be reviewed. The first step is to check once more that the patient has been taking his medication in full amount. If he has not, the reasons should be sought. He may be convinced that no treatment can help, or may find the side-effects unpleasant. The diagnosis should also be reviewed carefully, and a check made that important stressful life events or continuing difficulties have not been overlooked.

If this enquiry reveals nothing, antidepressants should be continued in full dosage: there is no value in changing to another drug unless side-effects are preventing full dosage of the original preparation. Supportive interviews should be continued and the patient reassured that depressive disorders almost invariably recover in the end whether or not treatment can speed up this process. Meanwhile, provided that the patient is not too depressed, any problems that have contributed to his depressed state should be discussed further. In resistant cases it is particularly important to watch carefully for developing suicidal intentions. If serious depression persists, ECT should be considered; clinical experience suggests that ECT is sometimes effective in patients who have not responded to full doses of antidepressant drugs, but this impression has not been tested in an adequate clinical trial. Although vigorous treatment should be given, the doctor should remember that nearly all depressive disorders recover eventually. While he must provide optimal treatment, he should avoid the temptation to overtreat his patient with many drugs.

Less severe cases

Not every depressive disorder requires treatment with antidepressant drugs. If the condition is of mild to moderate severity and clearly a reaction to stressful life events, treatment should be mainly psychological and social. The patient should be encouraged to talk about his feelings and to discuss his problems. If provoking factors can be altered, he should be encouraged to think of suitable means for changing them; if they cannot be altered, he should be helped to come to terms with his new situation. Help towards acceptance is particularly important after bereavement or other kinds of loss. Bereaved patients need time to talk about their ideas and feelings so that they no longer feel the pain of separation but can begin to cherish things of lasting value in the relationship.

Amongst patients with mild depressive disorders of reactive origin, a history of several weeks poor sleep is common. A hypnotic drug, given for a few days, often helps to start the process of recovery, but such treatment should not be prolonged. If the depressive symptoms do not respond to adequate social and psychological measures, and if there are symptoms indicating a likely response to medication (see p. 218), antidepressants should not be withheld. However, a frequent error is to prescribe antidepressants for many months to patients who have symptoms clearly related to life problems, and who did not show any response to medication in the first place.

Prevention of relapse

After recovery, the patient should be followed for several months either by the psychiatrist or by the family doctor. If the recovery appears to have been brought about by an antidepressant drug, the drug should usually be continued at two-thirds to half the therapeutic dose for about six months. At follow up interviews, a careful watch should be kept for signs of relapse. Relatives should be warned of the possibility of relapse and asked to report any signs of returning illness. If the patient has had both manic and depressive illnesses in the past, and if relapses have been frequent, lithium prophylaxis should be considered carefully, weighing possible advantages against the risks (see Chapter 17). If the depressive disorder was related to self-imposed stressors such as overwork, or unduly complicated social relationships, the patient should be encouraged to change to a life style less likely to lead to further episodes of illness. These readjustments may be helped by psychotherapy, which may be individual, marital, or group therapy.

THE ASSESSMENT OF MANIA

In the assessment of mania, the steps are those already outlined for depressive disorders. They are to: (a) decide the diagnosis, (b) assess the severity of the disorder, (c) form an opinion about the causes, (d) assess the patient's social resources, and (e) judge the effect on other people.

Diagnosis depends on a careful history and examination. Whenever possible, the history should be taken from relatives as well as from the patient because the patient may not recognize the extent of his abnormal behaviour. Differential diagnosis has been discussed earlier in this chapter; it is always important to remember that mildly disinhibited behaviour can result from frontal lobe lesions (such as tumours or GPI) as well as from mania.

Severity is judged next. For this purpose it is essential to interview another informant. Manic patients are often able to exert self-control during an interview with a doctor, and then behave in a disinhibited and grandiose way immediately afterwards (see p. 193). At an early stage it is easy to be misled and to miss the opportunity to persuade the patient to enter hospital before he causes long-term difficulties to himself, for example by ill-judged decisions or unjustified extravagance.

Usually the **causes** of a manic disorder are largely endogenous, but it is important to identify any life events that may have provoked the onset. Some cases follow physical illness, treatment by drugs (especially steroids) or operations.

The patient's **resources** and the **effect of the illness** on other people are assessed along the lines already described for depressive disorders. Even for the most supportive family, it is extremely difficult to care for a manic patient at home for more than a few days unless the disorder is exceptionally mild. The patient's responsibilities in the care of dependent children or at work should always be considered carefully.

THE MANAGEMENT OF MANIC PATIENTS

The first decision is whether to admit the patient to hospital. In all but the mildest cases, admission is nearly always advisable to protect the patient from the consequences of his own behaviour. If the disorder is not too severe, the patient will usually agree to enter hospital after some persuasion. When the disorder is more severe, compulsory admission is likely to be needed.

The immediate treatment is usually with an antipsychotic drug. Haloperidol is a suitable choice, chlorpromazine a more sedating alternative. The first dose should be large enough to bring the abnormal behaviour under rapid control. At this stage it is better for the patient to be somewhat over-sedated than to be left overactive, irritable, and interfering with other people. In emergencies, the first dose may need to be given by intramuscular injection (see p. 540 for further advice about the use of antipsychotic drugs in urgent cases).

The subsequent dosage should be adjusted frequently to take account of the degree of overactivity. The doctor should visit the ward repeatedly until the patient's condition has been brought under control. During this early phase, it is important for all staff to avoid angry confrontations which often arise because the patient makes unreasonable demands that cannot be met. It is often possible to avoid an argument by taking advantage of the manic patient's easy distracta- bility; instead of refusing his demands, it is better to delay until his attention turns to another topic that he can be encouraged to pursue.

As soon as the patient is well enough to co-operate, tests of renal and thyroid function are carried out, so that the results are available if lithium treatment should be required later. Practices vary about the use of lithium. Some psychia- trists continue to use haloperidol or chlorpromazine throughout the manic episode, and reserve lithium for prophylactic treatment. Others start lithium as soon as the acute symptoms are under control, though taking precautions not to introduce it when the dose of haloperidol is high (because occasional inter- actions have been reported, see p. 555). The use of lithium rather than haloperidol at an early stage sometimes has the advantage of leaving the patient more alert; possibly it also has the advantage of making a depressive disorder less likely to follow.

Progress can be judged not only by the mental state and general behaviour, but also by the pattern of sleep and by the regaining of any weight lost during the illness. As progress continues, antipsychotic drug treatment is reduced gradually. However, it is important not to discontinue the drug too soon, otherwise relapse may occur with a return of all the original problems of man- agement.

Whatever treatment is adopted, a careful watch should be kept for symptoms of depressive disorder. It should be remembered that transient but profound depressive mood change, accompanied by depressive ideas, is common among manic patients. The clinical picture may also change rapidly to a sustained depressive disorder. If either change happens, the patient may develop suicidal ideas. A sustained change to a depressive syndrome is likely to require anti-depressant drug treatment unless the disorder is mild.

The practical aspects of using lithium to prevent further episodes are discussed on pp. 556–7. There are two aspects of prophylaxis that require emphasis. First, patients should be seen and plasma lithium measured, at regular intervals. Secondly, some patients stop of their own accord because they fear the drug may have harmful long-term effects, or because it makes them feel 'flat'. The risk of stopping lithium is that it may lead to relapse. With carefully supervised follow-ups, the chances of relapse can be reduced substantially, though lesser degrees of mood change often continue.

FURTHER READING

Brown, G.W. and Harris, T. (1978). *Social origins of depression.* Tavistock, London.

Kraepelin, E. (1921). *Manic-depressive insanity and paranoia* (trans. R.M. Barclay), pp. 1–164. Churchill Livingstone, Edinburgh. (Reprinted in 1976 by Arno Press, New York.)

Lewis, A.J. (1930). Melancholia: a clinical survey of depressive states. *Journal of mental science* **80**, 277–378. (Reprinted in Lewis, A.J. (1967) *Inquiries in psychiatry*, pp. 30–117. Routledge and Kegan Paul, London.)

Lewis, A.J. (1938). States of depression: their clinical and aetiological differentiation. *British Medical Journal* **2**, 875–8. (Reprinted in Lewis, A.J. (1967) *Inquiries in psychiatry*, pp. 133–140. Routledge and Kegan Paul, London.)

Paykel, E.S. (ed.) (1982). *Handbook of affective disorders.* Churchill Livingstone, Edinburgh.

9. Schizophrenia

Of all the major psychiatric syndromes, schizophrenia is much the most difficult to define and describe. The main reason for this difficulty is that, over the past 100 years, many widely divergent concepts of schizophrenia have been held in different countries and by different psychiatrists. Radical differences of opinion persist to the present day. If these conflicting ideas are to be made intelligible, it is useful to start with a simple comparison between two basic concepts – acute schizophrenia and chronic schizophrenia. Such a comparison can pave the way for description of the many varieties of clinical picture encountered in clinical practice, and for discussion of the main theories and arguments about schizophrenia. Accordingly, after a brief section on epidemiology, this chapter describes the features of 'typical' acute and chronic syndromes. The reader should bear in mind that these will be idealized descriptions, but it is useful to oversimplify at first before introducing controversial issues.

Essentially, in acute schizophrenia the predominant clinical features are delusions, hallucinations, and interference with thinking. Features of this kind are often called 'positive' symptoms. Some patients recover from the acute illness, whilst others progress to the chronic syndrome. By contrast, the main features of chronic schizophrenia are apathy, lack of drive, slowness, and social withdrawal. These features are often called 'negative' symptoms. Once the chronic syndrome is established, few patients recover completely.

Most of the disagreements about schizophrenia are concerned with the acute syndrome. They arise for many reasons which can be illustrated by two aspects of definition. First, some psychiatrists define schizophrenia solely in terms of symptoms, whilst others define it in terms of symptoms and the course of the illness. Second, where definitions are based on symptoms, they vary between narrow specifications that exclude many clinical conditions, and broad definitions that are much more inclusive. These principles should become clearer later in the chapter.

EPIDEMIOLOGY

In surveys in 12 countries the annual prevalence of schizophrenia was generally estimated as from 2 to 4 per 1000 of the population (Jablensky and Sartorius 1975). Using first contacts with psychiatric services to estimate the annual incidence of schizophrenia, Dunham (1965) found a rate of about 0.22 per 1000 of the population, but other investigations have reported higher rates, such as 0.54 per 1000 in Mannheim (Häfner and Reimann 1970). These variations probably reflect the differences in the definition of schizophrenia more than real differences in the incidence (see Cooper 1978). Data from two British case registers, based on rigorous criteria, gave lower rates of between 0.11 and 0.14 per 1000 for first contact with psychiatric services (Wing and Fryers 1976).

The disease expectancy ('lifetime risk') is about 7.0–9.0 per 1000. Pooled data from 19 studies gave a rate of 8.6 per 1000 (Shields and Slater 1975), while studies of cohorts of people gave rates of 9.0 per 1000 in Denmark (Fremming 1951) and 7.0 per 1000 in Iceland (Helgason 1964).

Generally the rates from various countries are more striking for their similarities than for their differences, but there have been some major discrepancies. In the extreme north of Sweden Böök (1953) reported an annual prevalence of 11 per 1000. A possible explanation for this exceedingly high rate is that people with a predisposition to schizophrenia can tolerate extreme social isolation; in the remote north of Sweden such people might have stayed whilst others moved away. Another explanation might be that the findings reflect Böök's diagnostic criteria.

In contrast, Eaton and Weil (1955) reported a rate as low as 1.1 per 1000 among the Hutterites, an Anabaptist sect in the United States. Here the opposite explanation is possible, that people prone to schizophrenia moved away because the community was too tight knit. Again the findings might have reflected methods of case-finding; this seems more likely since in Canada a recent review showed no difference between Hutterite areas and other areas in admission rates for schizophrenia (Murphy 1968).

There is somewhat better evidence of high prevalence in some other groups, notably inhabitants of North-West Jugoslavia, Canadian Catholics, and the Tamils of Southern India (see Cooper 1978). Increased prevalence does not necessarily reflect increased incidence; it may reflect differences in the duration of illness. Epidemiological studies of the demographic and social correlates of schizophrenia are considered later under aetiology.

CLINICAL FEATURES

The acute syndrome

Some of the main clinical features are illustrated by a short description of a patient. A previously healthy 20-year-old male student had been behaving in an increasingly odd way. At times he appeared angry and told his friends that he was being persecuted; at other times he was seen to be laughing to himself for no apparent reason. For several months he had seemed increasingly preoccupied with his own thoughts. His academic work had deteriorated. When interviewed, he was restless and awkward. He described hearing voices commenting on his actions and abusing him. He said he believed that the police had conspired with his university teachers to harm his brain with poisonous gases and take away his thoughts. He also believed that other people could read his thoughts.

This case history illustrates the following common features of acute schizophrenia: prominent persecutory ideas with accompanying hallucinations; gradual social withdrawal and impaired performance at work; and the odd idea that other people can read one's thoughts. In describing the features of schizophrenia here, it is assumed that the reader has read the description of symptoms and signs in Chapter 1. Reference will be made to that chapter in the following account.

In **appearance and behaviour** some patients with acute schizophrenia are entirely normal. Others seem awkward in their social behaviour, preoccupied and withdrawn, or otherwise odd. Some patients smile or laugh without obvious reason. Some appear to be constantly perplexed. Some are restless and noisy, or show sudden and unexpected changes of behaviour. Others retire from company, spending a long time in their rooms, perhaps lying immobile on the bed apparently preoccupied in thought.

The **speech** often reflects an underlying **thought disorder.** In the early stages, there is vagueness in the patient's talk that makes it difficult to grasp his meaning. Some patients have difficulty in dealing with abstract ideas (a phenomenon called concrete thinking). Other patients become preoccupied with vague pseudoscientific or mystical ideas.

When the disturbance is more severe two characteristic kinds of abnormality may occur. **Disorders of the stream of thought** include pressure of thought, poverty of thought, and thought blocking, which are described on pp. 9–10. Thought withdrawal (the conviction that one's thoughts have been taken away) is sometimes classified as a disorder of the stream of thought, but it is more usefully considered as a form of delusion (see p. 18).

Loosening of association denotes a lack of connection between ideas. This may be detected in illogical thinking ('knight's move') or talking past the point (*Vorbeireden*). In the severest form of loosening the structure and coherence of thinking is lost, so that utterances are jumbled (word salad or verbigeration). Some patients use ordinary words in unusual ways (paraphrasias or metonyms), and a few coin new words (neologisms).

Abnormalities of mood are common, and of three main kinds. First, there may be sustained abnormalities of mood such as anxiety, depression, irritability, or euphoria. Secondly, there may be blunting of affect, sometimes known as flattening of affect. Essentially this is sustained emotional indifference or diminution of emotional response. Thirdly, there is incongruity of affect. Here the emotion is not necessarily diminished, but it is not in keeping with the mood that would ordinarily be expected. For example, a patient may laugh when told about a bereavement. The third abnormality is often said to be highly characteristic of schizophrenia, but different interviewers often disagree about its presence.

Auditory hallucinations are among the most frequent symptoms. They may take the form of noises, music, single words, brief phrases, or whole conversations. They may be unobtrusive or so severe as to cause great distress.

Some voices seem to give commands to the patient. Some patients hear their own thoughts apparently spoken out loud either as they think them (*Gedanken-lautwerden*) or immediately afterwards (*écho de la pensée*). Some voices seem to discuss the patient in the third person. Others comment on his actions. As described later, these last three symptoms have particular diagnostic value.

Visual hallucinations are less frequent and usually occur with other kinds of hallucination. **Tactile, olfactory, gustatory,** and **somatic** hallucinations are reported by some patients; they are often interpreted in a delusional way, for example hallucinated sensations in the lower abdomen are attributed to unwanted sexual interference by a persecutor.

Delusions are characteristic. Primary delusions (see p. 13) are infrequent, and difficult to identify with certainty. Delusions may originate against a background of so-called primary delusional mood – *Wahnstimmung* (see p. 15). Persecutory delusions are common, but not specific to schizophrenia. Less common but of greater diagnostic value are delusions of reference and of control, and delusions about the possession of thought. The latter are delusions that thoughts are being inserted into or withdrawn from one's mind, or 'broadcast' to other people (see p. 16). These important symptoms are considered further on pages 237 and 245.

In acute schizophrenia **orientation** is normal. Impairment of **attention** and **concentration** is common, and may produce apparent difficulties in remembering, though **memory** is not impaired. Delusional memory occurs in a few patients (see p. 15).

Insight is usually impaired. Most patients do not accept that their experiences result from illness, but usually ascribe them to the malevolent actions of other people. This lack of insight is often accompanied by unwillingness to accept treatment.

Schizophrenic patients do not necessarily experience all these symptoms. The clinical picture is variable, as described later in this chapter. At this stage the reader is referred to Table 9.1, which lists the most frequent symptoms found in one large survey.

Table 9.1. *The most frequent symptoms of acute schizophrenia (World Health Organization 1973)*

Symptom	Frequency (%)
Lack of insight	97
Auditory hallucinations	74
Ideas of reference	70
Suspiciousness	66
Flatness of affect	66
Voices speaking to the patient	65
Delusional mood	64
Delusions of persecution	64
Thought alienation	52
Thoughts spoken aloud	50

The chronic syndrome

In contrast to the 'positive' symptoms of the acute syndrome, the **chronic syndrome** is characterized by thought disorder and by 'negative' symptoms of underactivity, lack of drive, social withdrawal, and emotional apathy. The syndrome can be illustrated by a brief example. A middle-aged man lives in a group home and attends a sheltered workshop. He spends most of his time alone. He is usually dishevelled and unshaven, and cares for himself only when encouraged to do so by others. His social behaviour seems odd and stilted. His speech is slow, and its content vague and incoherent. He shows few signs of emotion. For several years this clinical picture has changed little except for brief periods of acute symptoms which are usually related to upsets in the ordered life of the hostel.

This description illustrates several of the negative features of what is sometimes called schizophrenic defect state. The most striking feature is diminished **volition,** that is a lack of drive and initiative. Left to himself, the patient may be inactive for long periods, or may engage in aimless and repeated activity. He withdraws from social encounters and his behaviour may deteriorate in ways that embarrass other people. A few patients neglect themselves to the point of incontinence.

A variety of **motor disturbances** occur, but most are uncommon. They are outlined here because they are the only symptoms of schizophrenia not described in Chapter 1.

Disorders of motor activity are often called **catatonic.** In the past a separate syndrome of catatonia was recognized, but nowadays the symptoms more often occur individually than as a distinct syndrome. **Stupor** and **excitement** are the most striking catatonic symptoms. A patient in stupor is immobile, mute, and unresponsive, although fully conscious. Stupor may change (sometimes quickly) to a state of uncontrolled motor activity and excitement.

Occasionally schizophrenic patients show a disorder of muscle tone called **waxy flexibility** (or flexibilitas cerea). The patient allows himself to be placed in an awkward posture which he then maintains apparently without distress for much longer than most people could achieve without severe discomfort. This phenomenon is also called **catalepsy** (a term that is also used to describe similar phenomena in patients who have been hypnotized). Some patients themselves take up odd and uncomfortable postures and maintain them for long periods. At times these postures have obvious symbolic significance (for example, crucifixion). Occasionally a patient lies for a long period with his head raised a little above the pillow (the so-called psychological pillow). Healthy people would experience extreme discomfort if they tried to do the same.

Various disorders of movement occur in schizophrenia (Manschreck *et al.* 1982). A **stereotypy** is a repeated movement that does not appear to be goal directed. It is more complex than a tic. The movement may be repeated in a regular sequence, for example rocking forwards and backwards or rotating the trunk.

A **mannerism** is a normal goal directed movement that appears to have social significance but is odd in appearance, stilted and out of context; for example a repeated hand movement resembling a military salute. It is often difficult to decide whether an abnormal movement is a stereotypy or a mannerism, but the distinction is of no diagnostic importance.

Ambitendence is a special form of ambivalence in which a patient begins to make a movement but, before completing it, starts the opposite movement; for example putting the hand back and forth to an object but without reaching it. **Mitgehen** is moving a limb in response to slight pressure on it, despite being told to resist the pressure (the last point is important). To elicit this sign, the psychiatrist should distract the patient by talking about another topic and then press gently on the arm with one finger. Mitgehen is often associated with forced grasping, which is repeated grasping (despite instructions to the contrary) at the interviewer's outstretched hand. In **automatic obedience** the patient obeys every command, though he has first been told not to do so. These disorders are described in more detail by Fish (1962).

Social behaviour may deteriorate. For example, some patients collect and hoard objects, so that their surroundings become cluttered and dirty. Others break social conventions by talking intimately to strangers, or shouting obscenities in public.

Speech is often abnormal, showing evidence of **thought disorder** of the kinds found in acute syndrome. **Affect** is generally blunted; when emotion is shown, it is often incongruous. **Hallucinations** are common, again in any of the forms occurring in the acute syndrome described above.

Delusions are often systematized. In chronic schizophrenia, delusions may be held with little emotional response. For example patients may be convinced that they are being persecuted but show neither fear nor anger. Delusions may also be 'encapsulated' from the rest of the patients' beliefs. Thus a patient may be convinced that his private sexual fantasies and practices are widely discussed by strangers; his remaining beliefs may be normal, and his working and social life well preserved.

Orientation is normal. **Attention** and **concentration** are often poor. **Memory** is not generally impaired though some patients have difficulty in giving their age correctly (this is sometimes called 'age disorientation'). **Insight** is impaired; the patient does not recognize that his symptoms are due to illness and is seldom fully convinced of the need for treatment.

The symptoms and signs are combined in many ways so that the clinical picture is variable. The reader is referred to Table 9.2 which shows the range and frequency of the symptoms and behavioural abnormalities found in one survey of chronic schizophrenic patients.

Variations in the clinical picture

As anticipated in the introduction to this chapter, so far an account has been given of the typical features of acute and chronic syndromes. Such an account

Table 9.2. *Behavioural characteristics of chronic schizophrenic patients in rank order of frequency*

Characteristic	Per cent
Social withdrawal	74
Underactivity	56
Lack of conversation	54
Few leisure interests	50
Slowness	48
Overactivity	41
Odd ideas	34
Depression	34
Odd behaviour	34
Neglect of appearance	30
Odd postures and movements	25
Threats or violence	23
Poor mealtime behaviour	13
Socially embarrassing behaviour	8
Sexually unusual behaviour	8
Suicidal attempts	4
Incontinence	4

From Creer and Wing (1975).

makes description easier, but it is an oversimplification. Two points need to be stressed. First, different features may predominate within a syndrome; for example in the acute syndrome, one patient may have predominantly paranoid delusions, and another mainly thought disorder. Secondly, some patients have features of both the acute and the chronic syndromes. Clinicians have attempted to identify various clinical subtypes, and these will be described later in the chapter.

Depressive symptoms in schizophrenia

Depressive symptoms occur commonly in association with schizophrenia (World Health Organization 1973). Brockington and Leff (1979) have reported that schizophrenic and affective symptoms coincide in about 10 per cent of psychotic patients admitted to a psychiatric hospital.

There are several reasons why depressive symptoms may be associated with schizophrenia. First, they may be a side-effect of antipsychotic medication; this is not the full explanation, since depressive symptoms occur in patients not receiving drugs. Secondly, depressive symptoms may be a response to recovery of insight into the nature of the illness and the problems to be faced. Again this may happen at times, but it does not provide a convincing general explanation. Thirdly, depression may be an integral part of schizophrenia. In a study of patients after the acute onset of schizophrenia, Knights and Hirsch (1981) found depression to be most common in the acute phase, decreasing during the following three months. They concluded that depression is a symptom of schizophrenia, although it may be recognized only after more striking symptoms have improved (see Hirsch 1982 for a review).

Factors modifying the clinical features

The amount of **social stimulation** has a considerable effect on the clinical picture. Understimulation increases 'negative' symptoms such as poverty of speech, social withdrawal, apathy, and lack of drive. Overstimulation precipitates 'positive' symptoms such as hallucinations, delusions, and restlessness. Modern treatment is designed to avoid understimulation, and as a result 'negative' features including catatonia are less frequent than in the past.

The **social background** of the patient may affect the content of some symptoms. For example, religious delusions are less common now than a century ago (Klaf and Hamilton 1961). **Age** also seems to modify the clinical features of schizophrenia. In adolescents and young adults, the clinical features often include thought disorder, mood disturbance, and considerable disruption of behaviour. This 'hebephrenic' picture (described on p. 241) has been thought to reflect the effect of the disease process on a personality still developing. With increasing age, paranoid symptomatology is more common and the effects on personality are less marked (the 'paranoid type' of schizophrenia).

Low intelligence also affects the clinical features. Patients of subnormal intelligence usually present with a less complex clinical picture sometimes referred to as 'pfropfschizophrenie' (described in Chapter 21, p. 691).

DIAGNOSTIC PROBLEMS

The development of ideas about schizophrenia

Some of the diagnostic problems encountered today can be understood better with some knowledge of the historical development of ideas about schizophrenia.

In the nineteenth century, one view was that all mental disorders were expressions of a single entity which Griesinger called *Einheitpsychose* (unitary psychosis). The alternative view, which was put forward by Morel in France, was that mental disorders could be separated and classified. Morel searched for specific entities, and argued for a classification based on cause, symptoms, and outcome (Morel 1860). In 1852 he gave the name *démence précoce* to a disorder which he described as starting in adolescence and leading first to withdrawal, odd mannerisms and self-neglect, and eventually to intellectual deterioration. Not long after, Kahlbaum (1874) described the syndrome of catatonia, and Hecker (1871) wrote an account of a condition he called hebephrenia.

Emil Kraepelin (1855–1926) took an intermediate view. On the one hand he argued against the idea of a single psychosis, and proposed a subdivision (which is still used) into organic and functional psychoses, the latter being divided into **dementia praecox** and manic-depression. On the other hand he brought together the separate entities of hebephrenia and catatonia, regarding them as subclasses of dementia praecox. In 1899 Kraepelin published a description of dementia praecox in his textbook, expanding it in later editions. He described the illness as occurring in clear consciousness and consisting of 'a series of states, the common characteristic of which is a peculiar destruction of the internal connections of the psychic personality. The effects of this injury predominate in the emotional and volitional spheres of mental life' (Kraepelin 1919 p. 3). He originally divided the disorder into three subtypes (catatonic, hebephrenic, and paranoid) and later added a fourth (simple). Kraepelin separated paraphrenia from dementia praecox, on the grounds that it started in middle life and was thought to be free from the changes in emotion and volition found in dementia praecox.

It is commonly held that Kraepelin regarded dementia praecox as invariably progressing to chronic deterioration. However he reported that, in his series of cases, 13 per cent recovered completely (though some relapsed later), and 17 per cent were ultimately able to live and work without difficulty.

Eugen Bleuler (1857–1959) was the Director of Burghölzli Clinic and Professor of Psychiatry in Zurich. He based his work on Kraepelin's, and in his own book wrote 'the whole idea of dementia praecox originates with Kraepelin' (Bleuler 1911 p. 1). He also acknowledged the help of his younger colleague, C. G. Jung, in trying to apply some of Freud's ideas to dementia praecox. Compared with Kraepelin, Bleuler was concerned less with prognosis and more with the mechanisms of symptom formation. It was Bleuler who proposed the name **schizophrenia** to denote a 'splitting' of psychic functions which he thought to be of central importance.

Bleuler believed in a distinction between fundamental and accessory symptoms. Fundamental symptoms included disturbances of associations, changes in emotional reactions, a tendency to prefer fantasy to reality, and autism (withdrawal from reality into an inner world of fantasy). It is interesting that, in Bleuler's view, some of the most frequent and striking symptoms were accessory (secondary); for example, hallucinations, delusions, catatonia, and abnormal behaviours. Bleuler was interested in the psychological study of his cases, but did not deny the possibility of a neuropathological cause for schizophrenia. Compared with Kraepelin, Bleuler took a more optimistic view of the outcome, but still held that one should not 'speak of cure but of far reaching improvement'. He also wrote: 'as yet I have never released a schizophrenic in whom I could not still see distinct signs of the disease, indeed there are very few in whom one would have to search for such signs' (Bleuler 1911 pp. 256 and 258). Since Bleuler was more preoccupied with psychopathological mechanisms than with symptoms themselves, his approach to diagnosis was less precise than Kraepelin's approach.

Kurt Schneider (1887–1967) tried to make the diagnosis more reliable by identifying a group of symptoms characteristic of schizophrenia, but rarely found in other disorders. Unlike Bleuler's fundamental symptoms, Schneider's symptoms were not supposed to have any central psychopathological role. Thus Schneider (1959) wrote: 'Among the many abnormal modes of experience that occur in schizophrenia, there are some which we put in the first rank of importance, not because we think of them as basic disturbances, but because they have this special value in helping us to determine the diagnosis of schizophrenia. When any one of these modes of experience is undeniably present and no basic somatic illness can be found, we may make the diagnosis of schizophrenia . . . Symptoms of first rank importance do not always have to be present for a diagnosis to be made'. (The last point is important.) Schneider's first-rank symptoms have had an important influence on diagnostic practices in the United Kingdom. They are listed in Table 9.3.

Table 9.3. *Schneider's symptoms of the first rank*

Hearing thoughts spoken aloud
'Third person' hallucinations (see p. 7)
Hallucinations in the form of a commentary
Somatic hallucinations
Thought withdrawal or insertion
Thought broadcasting
Delusional perception
Feelings or actions experienced as made or influenced by others

Karl Kleist, a pupil of the neurologist Wernicke, looked for associations between brain pathology and different subtypes of psychotic illness. He accepted Kraepelin's main diagnostic framework, but used careful clinical observation in an attempt to distinguish various subdivisions within schizophrenia and other atypical disorders. He then attempted to match these subtypes to specific kinds of brain pathology (Kleist 1928). This attempt was ingenious but not successful.

Leonhard continued this approach of careful clinical observation, but did not pursue Kleist's interest in cerebral pathology. He published a complicated classification which distinguishes schizophrenia from the 'cycloid' psychoses, which are a group of non-affective psychoses of good outcome (Leonhard 1957). Cycloid psychoses are described later in this chapter. Leonhard also divided schizophrenia into two groups. The first group is characterized by a progressive course, and is divided into catatonias, hebephrenias, and paraphrenias. Leonhard gave this group a name which is often translated as 'systematic'. The second group, called **non-systematic,** is divided into affect-laden paraphrenia, schizophasia, and periodic catatonia. **Affect-laden paraphrenia** is characterized by paranoid delusions and the expression of strong emotion about their content. In **schizophasia** speech is grossly disordered and difficult to understand. **Periodic catatonia** is a condition with regular remissions; during an episode akinetic symptoms are sometimes interrupted by hyperkinetic symptoms. Originally Leonhard's views had little impact outside his own country of East Germany, but recently an increasing concern with the heterogeneity of schizophrenia has led to a wider interest in his system of classification and particularly the concept of cycloid psychoses. Further information can be found in the accounts by Fish (1974) and Ban (1982).

Scandinavian psychiatrists have been influenced by Jasper's distinction between process schizophrenia and reactive psychoses. In the late 1930s **Langfeldt,** using follow-up data on patients in Oslo, proposed a distinction between **true schizophrenia,** which had a poor prognosis, and **schizophreniform states,** which had a good prognosis (see Langfeldt 1960). True schizophrenia was defined narrowly and was essentially similar to Kraepelin's dementia praecox. It was characterized by emotional blunting, lack of initiative, paranoid symptoms, and primary delusions. Schizophreniform states were described as often precipitated by stress and frequently accompanied by confusional and affective symptoms. Langfeldt's proposed distinction between good and bad prognosis cases has been influential but, as explained later, other psychiatrists have not found that his criteria predict prognosis accurately (see p. 260).

International differences in diagnostic practices

By the 1960s there were wide divergences in the criteria for the diagnosis of schizophrenia. In Britain and continental Europe, psychiatrists generally employed Schneider's approach, using typical symptoms to identify a narrowly delineated group of cases. In the United States, on the other hand, interest in psychodynamic processes led to diagnosis on the basis of mental mechanisms, and to the inclusion of a much wider group of cases.

First admission rates for schizophrenia were much higher in the United States than in the United Kingdom. This discrepancy prompted two major cross-national studies of diagnostic practice. The **US–UK Diagnostic Project** (Cooper *et al.* 1972) showed that the diagnostic concept of schizophrenia was much wider in New York than in Britain. In New York the concept included cases that were diagnosed as depressive illness, mania, or personality disorder in Britain. The **International Pilot Study of Schizophrenia** (IPSS) was concerned with the diagnosis of schizophrenia in nine countries (World Health Organization 1973). The main finding was that similar criteria were adopted in seven of the nine countries: Colombia, Czechoslovakia, Denmark, India, Nigeria, Taiwan, and the United Kingdom. Broader criteria were used in the United States and the USSR. Despite these differences it was found, by using standard diagnostic techniques, that a core of cases with similar features could be identified in all the countries.

In the USSR an unusually broad concept of schizophrenia has been developed by Snezhnevsky. This concept apparently allows schizophrenia to be diagnosed in people who would be regarded elsewhere as suffering from personality disorder or eccentricity. It is a concept based largely on course of the disorder, and much less on symptoms. Three main subdivisions of schizophrenia are recognized – continuous, periodic, and a mixture of these two ('shift-like'). Such a broad concept is susceptible to political abuse (see Bloch and Chodoff 1981).

Some reasons for diagnostic inconsistencies

Most psychiatrists agree that clinical practice and research would benefit from an improved operational definition of schizophrenia, but they do not agree on how such a definition should be achieved. When there are arguments about the details of definition, it is often because wider conceptual issues have not been resolved. In this section, wider conceptual issues are discussed first, and then specific definitions are examined in detail.

Wider conceptual issues

Some concepts of schizophrenia are based solely on symptoms, such as Schneider's first-rank symptoms. This is sometimes called a cross-sectional approach. Other concepts are based on symptoms and also on the course of the disorder; for example progression to a state of chronic disorder.

Concepts based solely on symptoms may be broad or narrow. Some concepts are so broad as to include cases that most psychiatrists would diagnose as affective disorder, or neurosis, or personality disorder. Narrow concepts can be used more reliably, and are therefore valuable in research. However, in everyday clinical use, they may either leave an undesirably large number of cases without a diagnosis or else may lead to overdiagnosis of another syndrome, usually affective disorder.

When the disorder is conceptualized in terms of course as well as symptoms, the term 'process' schizophrenia is sometimes used.

Some commonly used criteria

Cross sectional definitions

Schneider's first-rank symptoms (Table 9.3) are the usual basis of diagnosis in Britain. They lead to high reliability in diagnosis but not to effective prediction of outcome (Kendell *et al.* 1979). Moreover first-rank symptoms are not completely specific to schizophrenia, since they are occasionally found in mania and depressive disorder. 'Third person' hallucinatory voices (see p. 7) have been found to be the least discriminating of these symptoms (Mellor 1982). Other cross-sectional definitions of schizophrenia are to be found in ICD 9 (see below) and the research diagnostic system CATEGO.

CATEGO is a computer program designed to process data from a standard interview, the Present State Examination (see Wing *et al.* 1974). It incorporates diagnostic rules. The syndrome of schizophrenia is diagnosed mainly on the symptoms of thought intrusion, broadcast or withdrawal; delusions of control; and voices discussing the patient in the third person or commenting on his actions.

Longitudinal criteria

The operational classification developed at Washington University, St. Louis, includes both longitudinal and cross sectional criteria (often referred to as Feighner criteria) designed to identify patients with a poor prognosis. The symptomatic criteria are less precise than those in CATEGO (thought disorder alone being sufficient). The definition also requires the exclusion of affective illness, drug abuse, or alcoholism; and the selection of cases with six months continuous illness. These criteria are reliable but restrictive, leaving a high proportion of cases without a certain diagnosis. Patients with a poor prognosis are identified reasonably well, mainly because six months of continuous illness are required before the diagnosis can be made. Feighner's criteria have been widely used in research (Feigner *et al.* 1972).

The **Research Diagnostic Criteria** (RDC) were developed from the Feighner criteria by Spitzer *et al.* (1978). The two systems differ mainly in emphasis on the course of illness; whereas Feighner requires six months continuous illness, RDC requires only a two week history. A structured interview, the Schedule of Affective Disorders and Schizophrenia (SADS), has been developed for use with the RDC.

The criteria used in **DSM III** were developed from those of the Feighner and Research Diagnostic systems. Schizophrenic disorder is defined by an elaborate set of criteria shown in Table 9.4. It is important to recognize that, whereas in the past the concept of schizophrenia in the United States was exceptionally broad, DSM III now defines it much more narrowly. As shown in Table 9.4, one of the criteria in DSM III stipulates that there must have been continuous signs of illness for at least six months at some time during the patient's life. If an illness meets the other criteria but has lasted less than six months and more than two weeks, it is called a **schizophreniform disorder.** If it has lasted less than two weeks it is either a **brief reactive psychosis** (following obvious stress) or an **atypical psychosis** (no obvious stress).

'Symptomatic schizophrenia'

If the symptoms of schizophrenia occur with organic disease of the central nervous system, the condition is generally referred to as an organic brain syndrome (see p. 299). Alternatively, this combination is sometimes referred to as 'symptomatic schizophrenia'. Certain organic conditions that can produce a secondary schizophrenic syndrome are discussed elsewhere in this book. They include: **temporal lobe epilepsy** (complex partial seizures) (p. 335), **encephalitis** (p. 319), **amphetamine abuse** (p. 451), and **alcohol abuse** (p. 429). In addition,

Table 9.4. *Diagnostic criteria for a schizophrenic disorder in DSM III*

A. At least one of the following during a phase of the illness:

(i) bizarre delusions (content is patently absurd and has *no* possible basis in fact), such as delusions of being controlled, thought broadcasting, thought inserion, or thought withdrawal

(ii) somatic, grandiose, religious, nihilistic, or other delusions without persecutory or jealous content

(iii) delusions with persecutory or jealous content if accompanied by hallucinations of any type

(iv) auditory hallucinations in which either a voice keeps up a running commentary on the individual's behavior or thoughts, or two or more voices converse with each other

(v) auditory hallucinations on several occasions with content of more than one or two words, having no apparent relation to depression or elation

(vi) incoherence, marked loosening of associations, markedly illogical thinking, or marked poverty of content of speech if associated with at least one of the following:

(a) blunted, flat, or inappropriate affect

(b) delusions or hallucinations

(c) catatonic or other grossly disorganized behaviour

B. Deterioration from a previous level of functioning in such areas as work, social relations, and self-care

C. Duration: continuous signs of illness for at least six months at some time during the person's life, with some signs of the illness at present. The six-month period must include an active phase during which there were symptoms from A, with or without prodromal or residual phase, as defined below

E. Onset of prodromal or active phase of the illness before age 45

F. Not due to any Organic Mental Disorder or Mental Retardation

---

a schizophrenic syndrome can occur **post partum** (p. 391) and in the **post-operative** period (p. 394).

ARE THERE SUBGROUPS OF SCHIZOPHRENIA?

The variety of the symptoms and course of schizophrenia has led to several attempts to define subgroups (see Carpenter and Stephens 1979). This section is concerned only with the traditional subgroups of hebephrenic, catatonic, paranoid, and simple schizophrenia.

Patients with **hebephrenic** schizophrenia often appear silly and childish in their behaviour. Affective symptoms and thought disorder are prominent. Delusions are common, and not highly organized. Hallucinations also are common, and not elaborate. **Catatonic schizophrenia** is characterized by motor symptoms of the kind described on page 232 and by changes in activity varying between excitement and stupor. Hallucinations, delusions, and affective symptoms occur but are usually less obvious. In **paranoid schizophrenia** the clinical picture is dominated by well-organized paranoid delusions. Thought processes and mood are relatively spared, and the patient may appear normal until his abnormal beliefs are uncovered. **Simple schizophrenia** is characterized by the insidious development of odd behaviour, social withdrawal, and declining performance at work. Since clear schizophrenic symptoms are absent, simple schizophrenia is difficult to identify reliably, and ICD 9 recommends that 'diagnosis of this form should be made sparingly, if at all'.

With the possible exception of paranoid schizophrenia, these 'subgroups' are of doubtful validity. Some patients present symptoms of one group at one time, and then symptoms of another group later. There is some genetic evidence for separating cases with the paranoid picture (see Kendler and Davis 1981) but not enough to recommend doing so in everyday clinical work. Catatonic symptoms are much less common now than 50 years ago, perhaps because of improvements in the social environment in which patients are treated. Other explanations are possible; for example, organic syndromes may have been included in some earlier series (see Mahendra 1981).

The four subgroups described above cannot be clearly distinguished in clinical practice, and no support was found for them in the International Pilot Study of Schizophrenia (WHO 1974).

Good prognosis schizophrenia and atypical cases

It would be useful if schizophrenic patients could be subdivided according to prognosis. There have been many attempts to do so by means of criteria as diverse as the clinical picture, CAT scan findings, psychological test results, and the immediate response to treatment. No attempt has been wholly successful. Attempts have also been made to subdivide atypical cases that fall between the central syndrome of schizophrenia and the affective disorders, or cases that are atypical in other ways. It turns out that the prognosis is generally better for these atypical cases than for the central syndrome. Hence there is a considerable overlap between groupings based on prognosis and groupings based on clinical features. Some of these subdivisions will now be described, the first being based on prognosis.

Schizophreniform states

As mentioned earlier, this term was applied by Langfeldt (1960) to good prognosis cases as distinct from 'true' schizophrenia. The main features of schizophreniform states were the presence of a precipitating factor; acute onset; clouding of consciousness; and depressive and hysterical features. Although Welner and Strömgren (1958) confirmed the better outcome of schizophreniform cases, recent work has cast considerable doubt on the predictive value of Langfeldt's criteria. It is unfortunate that DSM III uses the term schizophreniform quite differently to describe a condition identical to schizophrenia but with a course of less than six months.

Reactive or psychogenic psychosis

This term is used in Denmark and Norway to denote cases in which psychotic symptoms follow definite stressful events. In their clinical picture the paranoid sub-group of these cases resembles those described by Langfeldt. It has now been shown that many cases of schizophrenia are preceded by stressful, though less striking events (see p. 255), and it no longer seems useful to separate cases on this criterion alone. Readers seeking further information are referred to Strömgren (1968) or Faergeman (1963).

Cycloid psychoses

Kleist introduced the term cycloid marginal psychoses to denote functional psychoses which were neither typically schizophrenic nor manic depressive. Leonhard (1957) developed these ideas by describing three forms of cycloid psychosis which are distinguished by their predominant symptoms: these conditions are all bipolar and are described as having a good prognosis and leaving no chronic defect state. The first is **anxiety elation psychosis** in which the prominent symptom is a mood change. At one 'pole' anxiety is associated with ideas of reference and sometimes with hallucinations. At the other 'pole' the mood is elated, often with an ecstatic quality. The second is **confusion psychosis** in which thought disorder is the prominent symptom, and the clinical picture varies between excitement and a state of underactivity with poverty of speech. The third is **motility psychosis** in which the striking changes are in psychomotor activity. These syndromes are described briefly by Fish (1962) and in detail by Leonhard (1957). In practice, it is difficult to distinguish them from schizophrenia (see Perris 1974).

Schizoaffective disorder

This term has been used in several distinct ways (see Procci 1976). It was first applied by Kasanin (1933) to a small group of young patients with severe mental disorders 'characterised by a very sudden onset in a setting of marked emotional turmoil with a distortion of the outside world. The psychosis lasts a few weeks to a few months and is followed by recovery'. The term continues to be used in this way to describe an acute syndrome, especially in the United States. A second usage is for cases in which there is an alternation of affective and schizophrenic symptoms in successive episodes. A third usage (which is to be strongly preferred) is to describe cases with a more or less equal mixture of the symptoms of schizophrenia and affective disorder. The confusion about the term is now so great that schizoaffective disorder is the only category not defined operationally in DSM III. Instead there is a recommendation that the diagnosis 'should be made whenever the clinician is unable to make a differential diagnosis between schizophrenia and affective disorder'. In ICD 9 on the other hand, schizoaffective disorder is defined as 'a psychosis in which pronounced manic or depressive features are intermingled with schizophrenic features and which tends towards remission without permanent defect, but which is prone to recur. The diagnosis should be made only when both the affective and schizophrenic symptoms are pronounced'.

Conclusion

Family studies provide one argument for the separate classification of the acute illnesses with good prognosis. Among relatives of probands, there is a low incidence of schizophrenia, and a raised incidence of affective disorder. However, in the present state of knowledge, it is still uncertain whether these illnesses are simply unusual manifestations of affective disorder or schizophrenia, or whether they make up a separate third group.

Other notable syndromes

Gjessing's syndrome

Gjessing (1947) described a rare disorder in which catatonic symptoms recurred in phases. He also found changes in nitrogen balance, which were not always in phase with the symptoms. Gjessing believed that there were underlying changes in thyroid function and that the disorder could be treated successfully with thyroid hormone. The condition, if it exists, is exceedingly rare.

Bouffée délirante

This is part of the French classification. It is a syndrome of sudden onset with delusions, prominent mood disturbance, and perplexity. It has a good immediate prognosis, but often relapses (Ey *et al.* 1966; Pichot 1982).

Borderline disorders

In the United States there has been much interest in states intermediate between schizophrenia and the neuroses and personality disorders. The term 'borderline states' is applied to them, but is used in several different ways (see Liebowitz 1979). There are three main usages. In the first, a borderline state is regarded as an independent entity which is wholly distinct from all other diagnostic categories. The main features are vaguely defined, but include anger, difficulty in relationships, and lack of self-identity. In the second usage, a borderline state is a mild expression of schizophrenia. This usage resembles Bleuler's concept of latent schizophrenia; it also covers the 'schizophrenia spectrum' referred to in some genetic studies (see p. 248) and the concept of pseudoneurotic schizophrenia (Hoch and Polatin 1959). In DSM III the corresponding term is **schizotypal personality**, which is characterized by 'magical thinking', ideas of reference, social isolation, odd communication, suspiciousness, and social anxiety. In the third usage, the term 'borderline' is applied to a form of personality abnormality characterized by impulsive, unstable relationships, inappropriate anger, identity disturbance, unstable mood, and chronic boredom. In DSM III this is called **borderline personality** (see Chapter 5).

The lack of precise descriptive criteria makes these diagnostic categories of doubtful value. If patients with so-called borderline states are studied carefully, most can be diagnosed as having personality disorder, schizophrenia, or affective disorder. In doubtful cases, follow-up often strengthens the diagnosis.

THE DIAGNOSIS OF SCHIZOPHRENIA IN EVERDAY CLINICAL PRACTICE

Difficulties in the classification of schizophrenia pose problems for the research worker and the clinician. The research worker will usually choose a restrictive definition (such as those of Feighner, the RDC, or CATEGO), because of the advantages of precision and the possibility of comparison with other work.

In everyday clinical practice, diagnosis is made on a combination of present state and history. Provided that there is no evidence of organic pathology, then definite evidence of persistent first-rank symptoms indicates a diagnosis of **schizophrenia**. It is sometimes said that primary delusions are of diagnostic importance; however, they are not specially helpful in clinical practice because they are difficult to identify with certainty and they may occur in other conditions such as epilepsy (see Gruhle 1936). If there are no first-rank symptoms, and if delusions are not obviously secondary to an affective disorder or explained by cultural factors, it is still possible to make a diagnosis of schizophrenia if there is evidence of a prolonged course together with definite evidence of such characteristic negative symptoms as lack of volition, blunting of affect and thought disorder. If there is any doubt then a provisional diagnosis such as 'possible schizophrenia' should be made. A definite diagnosis will have to wait upon evidence from follow up.

In such doubtful cases, the ICD 9 categories of paranoid state (297) (see Chapter 10) or of unspecified psychosis (298.9) could be used. The foregoing remarks apply to clinical practice in the United Kingdom. In the United States the diagnostic recommendations in DSM III should be used.

Differential diagnosis

Schizophrenia has to be distinguished mainly from organic syndromes, affective disorder, and personality disorder. Among younger patients the most relevant *organic diagnoses* are drug-induced states and temporal lobe epilepsy. Among older patients, various brain diseases must be excluded. For example an acute brain syndrome could be mistaken for schizophrenia; the same holds for dementia, particularly with prominent persecutory delusions. Some diffuse brain diseases can present a schizophrenia-like picture in the absence of neurological disorder; the most important example is General Paralysis of the Insane (see Chapter 11). In seeking to exclude such organic disorders, it is important to obtain a thorough history, mental state examination, and physical examination with particular reference to neurological abnormalities. There must be careful observation for clouding of consciousness, memory deficit, and other symptoms and signs which are not characteristic of schizophrenia. The distinction between **affective disorder** and schizophrenia depends on the degree and persistence of the mood disorder, the relation of any hallucinations or delusions to the prevailing mood, and the nature of the symptoms in any previous episodes. Differential diagnosis from **personality disorder** can be very difficult when insidious changes are reported in a young person. Prolonged lengthy observation for first-rank symptoms may be required.

AETIOLOGY

Before giving a detailed review of evidence on the causation of schizophrenia, it may be helpful to outline the main areas of inquiry. The strongest evidence for **predisposing** factors comes from genetic studies, but it is clear that inheritance cannot be the complete explanation and that environmental factors must be important as well. There are several psychodynamic theories of causation. Recently there has been more interest in the possible causal role of abnormal patterns of communication within families. The difficulty here is that it is impossible to decide retrospectively which came first, schizophrenia in the patient or abnormal communication in the family. Attempts have been made to overcome this limitation by prospective studies of people likely to have an increased risk of schizophrenia; for example, children of schizophrenic patients and people with abnormal psychophysiological responses resembling those of schizophrenic patients. So far the results are inconclusive.

Research on **precipitating factors** has been concerned with life events and physical illnesses. Although these factors seem important, the size of their effect is uncertain. Among **perpetuating factors** social and family influences seem important; they are considered later in the section on course and prognosis (see p. 262).

Investigation of **mediating mechanisms** has concentrated on psychological processes such as arousal, attention, and thinking; and on biochemical disorders, in which interest has been encouraged by advances in psychopharmacology.

Genetics

The genetic study of schizophrenia has been directed towards three questions: (i) is there a genetic basis? (ii) is there a relationship between clinical form and inheritance? (iii) what is the mode of inheritance? These three questions will be considered in turn.

(i) Is there a genetic basis?

Family studies
The first systematic family study of dementia praecox was carried out in Kraepelin's department by Ernst Rüdin, who showed that the rate of dementia praecox was higher among the siblings of probands than in the general population (Rüdin 1916). Another comprehensive study of families was conducted by

Kallmann (1938), whose sample of schizophrenic probands numbered more than a thousand. He found increased rates not only among the probands' siblings but also among their children. The findings of these and subsequent family studies have been summarized by Slater and Cowie (1971) and by Shields (1978), who concluded that morbidity risks vary somewhat from one study to another but that the general pattern is consistent. This pattern can be seen in Table 9.5 which shows the approximate risks for various degrees of kinship to a schizophrenic patient. The explanation for the low risk in patients is probably that patients who develop schizophrenia in early life are less likely to become parents. An important point genetically is that rates of affective disorders are not generally increased in the families of schizophrenic patients (see Shields 1978). The above findings strongly suggest a hereditary aetiology but the effects of the family environment can only be excluded by twin and adoption studies.

Table 9.5. *Approximate life time expectancy of developing schizophrenia for relatives of schizophrenics*

Relationship	Risk (per cent) Definite cases only	Definite and probable cases
Parents	4.4	5.5
All siblings	8.5	10.2
Siblings (one parent schizophrenic)	13.8	17.2
Children	12.3	13.9
Children (both parents schizophrenic)	36.6	46.3
Half siblings	3.2	3.5
Nephews and nieces	2.2	2.6

Adapted from Shields (1980).

Twin studies

These studies compare the concordance rates for schizophrenia in monozygotic (MZ) and dizygotic (DZ) twins. The methodological problems of such studies have been considered already (see p. 93).

The first substantial twin study was carried out in Munich by Luxenberger (1928), who found concordance in 11 of his 19 MZ pairs and none of his 13 DZ pairs. Although this finding for DZ pairs casts doubt on the selection of the sample, other workers (for example Kallmann 1946; Slater 1953) confirmed that concordance was higher among MZ than DZ pairs. Subsequent investigations using improved methods have led to similar results. In these studies concordance rates in MZ pairs have varied considerably, but they have always been higher than the concordance rates in DZ pairs (Gottesman and Shields 1972; Kringlen 1967; Tienari 1968; Fischer 1973). Representative figures for concordance are about 50 per cent for MZ pairs and about 17 per cent for DZ pairs (Shields 1978). It might be expected that studies of MZ twins discordant for schizophrenia would reveal some environmental factors relevant to aetiology. A few such factors have been reported, for example low birth weight and poor family relationships, but no conclusive findings have emerged (see Pollin and Stabenau 1968; Mosher *et al.* 1971).

A more precise estimate of the relative importance of genetic and environmental factors can be obtained by comparing MZ twins reared together with MZ twins separated at birth and reared apart. The concordance rates are quite similar for the two groups, suggesting a major genetic contribution (Shields 1978).

Adoption studies

Heston (1966) studied 47 adults who had been born to schizophrenic mothers and separated from them within three days of birth. As children they had been brought up in a variety of circumstances, though not by the mother's family. At the time of the study their mean age was 36. Heston compared them with controls who were matched for circumstances of upbringing, but whose mothers had not been schizophrenic. Amongst the offspring of schizophrenic mothers, five were diagnosed as schizophrenic, as against none of the controls. There was also an excess of antisocial personality and neurotic disorders among the children of schizophrenic mothers. The age-corrected rate for schizophrenia among the index cases was comparable to that among non-adopted children with one schizophrenic parent. In this investigation, no account was taken of the fathers.

Further evidence has come from a series of studies started in 1965 by a group of Danish and American investigators. The work has been carried out in Denmark, which has national registers of psychiatric cases and adoptions. In a study of children separated from schizophrenic mothers at an average age of six months, the findings confirmed those of Heston described above (Rosenthal *et al.* 1971). The major project (Kety *et al.* 1975) employed a different design. Two groups of adoptees were identified: 33 who had schizophrenia, and a matched group who were free from schizophrenia. Rates of disorder were compared in the biological and adoptive families of the two groups of adoptees. The rate for schizophrenia was greater among the biological relatives of the schizophrenic adoptees, than among the relatives of controls, a finding which supports the genetic hypothesis. Furthermore, the rate for schizophrenia was not increased amongst couples who adopted the schizophrenic adoptees, suggesting that environmental factors were not of substantial importance. The reverse situation was studied by Wender *et al.* (1974), who found no increase in schizophrenia amongst adoptees who had normal biological parents and a schizophrenic adoptive parent.

The Danish investigators viewed schizophrenia as a spectrum of illnesses with four divisions: (i) process schizophrenia; (ii) reactive schizophrenia; (iii) borderline schizophrenia; and (iv) schizoid states. The last three are sometimes referred to collectively as schizophrenia spectrum disease. The adoption-study findings reported above were for process schizophrenia, but the investigators also reported an excess of schizophrenia spectrum disease in biological relatives.

Adoption studies cannot rule out environmental causes in the adoptive family; but they indicate that, if there are such environmental causes, they act only on genetically predisposed children.

(ii) Is there a relationship between clinical form and inheritance?

Early family studies of hebephrenic, catatonic, and paranoid subtypes showed that they did not breed true to type. However, there was a somewhat lower risk of schizophrenia in the relatives of patients with the paranoid form (see Kendler and Davis 1981). There is also a lower risk of schizophrenia among the relatives of probands with 'good-prognosis' illnesses. Shields (1978) suggests that the milder the illness is, the more heterogeneous the aetiology.

It has been suggested that schizoaffective disorder results from a genetic predisposition to both schizophrenia and affective disorder. This idea is not supported by studies of families in which one parent had schizophrenia, and the other an affective illness (Fisher and Gottesman 1980).

(iii) What is the mode of inheritance?

The genetic evidence does not permit definite conclusions about the mode of inheritance. There are three main theories (see Shields 1978):

1. Monogenic
As the ratios of the frequencies of schizophrenia in different relatives do not fit any simple Mendelian pattern, it is necessary to propose modifying factors. Slater (1958) suggested a dominant gene of variable penetrance.

2. Polygenic
This theory proposes a cumulative effect of several genes (see for example Gottesman and Shields 1967). This model is less precise than the monogenic theory and even more difficult to test.

3. Genetic heterogeneity
Monogenic and polygenic theories assume that schizophrenia is a single disease. Heterogeneity theories explain the observed patterns of inheritance by proposing that schizophrenia is a group of disorders.

Several attempts have been made to test these hypotheses, but the results are ambiguous. The problem may be even more complex; there may be a group of disorders each of which is inherited in a different way. These uncertainties are only likely to be overcome when genetic studies can be directed to subgroups defined biochemically rather than symptomatically (see Watt 1982).

Other constitutional factors

Perinatal factors

Investigators have looked for specific associations between rates for schizophrenia and factors such as birth order and season of birth. The results have been contradictory. Schizophrenia has been reported as more frequent among younger members of large sibships (Farina *et al.* 1963) and people born in winter (Hare 1975). In a comparison between children of schizophrenic parents and controls from non-schizophrenic parents, Hanson *et al.* (1976) found no significant differences in the frequency of perinatal complications or of any neurological abnormalities that might have resulted from such complications.

The difficulty of interpreting the effects of factors such as birth order, season of birth, and birth complications is that they may all interact with other factors, such as maternal age and social conditions. Also there are all the usual problems of retrospective enquiry.

'High-risk' research

These problems of method can be partly overcome by prospective studies of young people who are judged to have an increased risk of developing schizophrenia. This approach is now referred to as 'high-risk' research. Two kinds of people have been studied – those with a schizophrenic parent, and those in whom psychophysiological measures indicate increased arousal (which is a characteristic of some patients with established schizophrenia). So far the results have been inconclusive (see Parnas *et al.* (1982) for further information).

Personality

Several early writers including Bleuler (1911) commented on the frequency of abnormalities of personality preceding the onset of illness. Kretschmer (1936) proposed that both personality type and schizophrenia were related to the asthenic type of body build. He suggested a continuous variation between normal personality, schizoid personality (see p. 114), and schizophrenia. He regarded schizoid personality as a partial expression of the psychological abnormalities that manifest in their full form in schizophrenia. Such ideas must be treated with caution since it is difficult to distinguish between premorbid personality and the prodromal phase of a slowly developing illness.

Despite these reservations it seems probable that abnormal personality is common among people who later become schizophrenic. This may indicate a specific aetiological relationship, or a non-specific vulnerability to stressful events. It is emphasized that many schizophrenics have no obvious disorder of personality before the onset of the illness, and that only a minority of people with schizoid personalities develop schizophrenia.

Neurological abnormalities

Clinicians have often detected signs of minor neurological abnormality in schizophrenic patients. It is possible that some of these signs resulted from coincidental neurological disease. In the past, investigators searched for gross pathological changes in the brains of schizophrenics, but found none. Recent research is concerned with four issues: non-localizing ('soft') neurological signs; possible abnormalities of the corpus callosum; evidence of ventricular enlargement; and changes in the EEG. Each will be considered in turn.

'Soft signs' (neurological signs without localizing significance) have been reported in many studies. Rochford *et al.* (1970) found them in about 65 patients examined before starting drug treatment. Pollin and Stabenau (1968) found at least one sign in nearly three-quarters of a series of schizophrenics. It is generally found that the commonest abnormalities are in stereognosis, graphaesthesia, balance, and proprioception. It has been suggested that these abnormalities reflect defects in the integration of proprioceptive and other sensory information (see Cox and Ludwid 1979; Quitkin *et al.* 1976).

Thickening of the corpus callosum has been reported in brains from a small number of schizophrenic patients (Rosenthal and Bigelow 1972). There have also been reports of functional abnormalities suggesting impairment of inter-hemispheric transfer in schizophrenics (for example Carr 1980). This work needs to be replicated (see Wyke (1982) for a review of evidence on how function is integrated between the two hemispheres).

Ventricular enlargement in schizophrenia was first reported from studies using air encephalography (Haug 1962). The introduction of CT scanning has provided a non-invasive method for investigating the brain size in schizophrenic patients. Johnstone *et al.* (1976) reported that the ventricles were significantly larger in 17 elderly institutionalized schizophrenics than in eight normal controls. Weinberger *et al.* (1980) found evidence in schizophrenics of significant ventricular enlargement, widening of sulci, and atrophy of the cerebellar vermis. These changes were not correlated with length of hospital stay, length of illness, or current or past dosage of antipsychotic drugs. There is some evidence that patients with enlarged ventricles have more 'negative' symptoms such as affective flattening, lack of drive, and poverty of speech (Andreasen *et al.* 1982). It has also been reported that such patients perform poorly on tests of intellectual function (Johnstone *et al.* 1976). In chronic schizophrenics there is some evidence of poorer premorbid educational and social adjustment among those with cerebral atrophy than among those without cerebral atrophy (Weinberger *et al.* 1980). This finding raises the possibility of a long-standing process predating the onset of symptoms. It is of interest that Weinberger *et al.* (1981) found somewhat larger ventricles among the siblings of schizophrenics than among normal controls. The significance of this finding cannot be assessed without further data.

EEG abnormalities in schizophrenic patients have often been reported, including increased theta activity, fast activity, and paroxysmal activity. Recent studies using computerized analysis and evoked potentials have confirmed that there are more abnormalities among schizophrenics than normal subjects; but these studies have not pointed to a single abnormality present in all patients.

Psychodynamic theories

Freud's theory of schizophrenia was stated most clearly in his 1911 analysis of the Schreber case (see p. 274) and in his 1914 paper 'On narcissism: an introduction'. According to Freud, in the first stage libido was withdrawn from external objects and attached to the ego. The result was exaggerated self-importance. Since the withdrawal of libido made the external world meaningless, the patient attempted to restore meaning by developing abnormal beliefs. Because of libidinal withdrawal, the patient could not form a transference, and therefore could not be treated by psychoanalysis. Whilst Freud developed his general ideas considerably after 1914, he elaborated his original theory of schizophrenia but did not replace it.

Melanie Klein believed that the origins of schizophrenia were in infancy. In the 'paranoid–schizoid position' the infant was thought to deal with innate aggressive impulses by splitting both his own ego and his representation of his mother into two incompatible parts, one wholly bad and the other wholly good. Only later did the child realize that the same person could be good at one time and bad at another. Failure to pass through this stage adequately was the basis for the later development of schizophrenia.

Hartmann (1964) and other writers developed Freudian ideas about schizophrenia in another way. They took the view that defects in the ego result in problems in the defence and 'neutralization' of libido and aggression. Yet a different approach was taken by Sullivan, who explained schizophrenia in terms not of a withdrawal of libido but rather of interpersonal difficulties. Recent psychodynamic views on aetiology and treatment have been discussed by Arieti (1974).

The family as a cause of schizophrenia

Two kinds of theory have been proposed about the family as a cause of the onset of schizophrenia: deviant role relationships, and disordered communication (see Liem 1980). The different role of the family in determining the *course* of established schizophrenia is discussed later (p. 262).

Deviant role relationships

The concept of the 'schizophrenogenic' mother was suggested by the analyst Fromm-Reichmann in 1948. In a comparison of the mothers of schizophrenic patients, neurotic patients, and normal controls, Alanen (1958, 1970) found that the mothers of schizophrenics showed an excess of psychological abnormalities. He suggested that these abnormalities might be an important cause of the child's schizophrenia. Lidz and his colleagues (Lidz and Lidz 1949; Lidz, Fleck and Cornelison 1968) used intensive psychoanalytic methods to study the families of 17 schizophrenic patients, of whom 14 were in social classes I or II. There was no control group. Two types of abnormal family pattern were reported: (i) 'marital skew', in which one parent yielded to the other's (usually the mother's) eccentricities, which dominated the family; (ii) 'marital schism' in which the parents maintained contrary views so that the child had divided loyalties. It was suggested that these abnormalities were the cause rather than the result of the schizophrenia. Investigations by other clinicians have not confirmed these findings (see Sharan 1965; Ferreira and Winter 1965). Even if they were confirmed, the abnormalities in the parents could be an expression of genetic causes or secondary to the disorder in the patient. These and other speculations about the causative role of family relationships have had the unfortunate consequence of inducing unjustified guilt in parents.

Disordered family communication

Research on disordered communication in families originated from the idea of the **double bind** (Bateson *et al.* 1956). A double bind occurs when an instruction is given overtly, but contradicted by a second, more covert instruction. For example, a mother may overtly tell her child to come to her, whilst conveying by manner and tone of voice that she rejects him. A further element is that there is no escape from the situation in which the contradictory injunctions are received. According to Bateson, double binds leave the child able to make only ambiguous or meaningless responses. Bateson further supposes that schizophrenia develops when this process persists. The theory is ingenious but not supported by evidence (see Leff (1978) for a more detailed discussion).

Wynne and his colleagues suggested that different patterns of disordered communication occurred among the parents of schizophrenics (Wynne *et al.* 1958). These investigators first gave projective tests to such parents, and identified 'amorphous communications' ('vague, indefinite, and loose') and 'fragmented communications' ('easily disrupted, poorly integrated, and lacking closure'). In a further study using blind interpretation of these tests, the investigators found more of these disordered communications in parents of schizophrenics than in parents of neurotics (Singer and Wynne 1965). In an independent replication, Hirsch and Leff (1975) found a similar but smaller difference between schizophrenic parents and others. These workers pointed out that such differences might simply be explained by a tendency for the parents of the schizophrenic patients to make more utterances in response to the projective tests. However, when Singer and Wynne's data were re-analysed to allow for number of utterances, some significant differences still remained between parents of schizophrenics and controls.

Subsequent attempts to test Wynne's hypothesis have used more elaborate methods such as observing family communication during the performance of a task (see Liem 1980; Wynne 1981). So far the hypothesis must be judged as not proven. Even if Wynne's findings are substantiated, it remains possible that the abnormalities are a reaction to, rather than the cause of, schizophrenia in the family member. Neither Wynne's theory nor any other theory of disordered communication can give a satisfactory explanation why it is unusual for more than one child in a family to develop schizophrenia.

Social factors

Occupation and social class

Schizophrenia is over-represented amongst people of low socioeconomic status (see Cooper 1978). At first these findings were thought to be of aetiological significance, but more recent evidence suggests that they could be a consequence of illness. For instance, Goldberg and Morrison (1963) found that schizophrenics were of lower social status than their fathers and that the change had usually occurred after the illness began.

Place of residence

Faris and Dunham (1939) studied the place of residence of mentally ill people in Chicago, and found that schizophrenics were over-represented in the disadvantaged inner city areas. This distribution has been confirmed in other cities, including Bristol (Hare 1956) and Mannheim (Häfner and Reimann 1970). Faris and Dunham suggested that unsatisfactory living conditions caused the schizophrenia. However, the findings can be explained equally plausibly by the occupational and social decline described above, or by a search for social isolation by people about to develop schizophrenia. A search for isolation would be consistent with the finding that schizophrenics in disadvantaged areas usually live alone, not with their families (Hare 1956).

Migration

High rates of schizophrenia have been reported among migrants (see, for example Malzberg and Lee 1956). The reasons for these high rates are not clear, but they are probably due mainly to a disproportionate migration of people who are unsettled because they are becoming mentally ill. The effects of a new environment may also play a part in provoking illness in predisposed people. Thus 'social selection' and 'social causation' may both contribute to an excess of schizophrenia among migrants (see Murphy (1977) for a review).

Social isolation

Schizophrenics often live alone, unmarried, and with few friends (see, for example Hare 1956). A retrospective study comparing schizophrenics with controls (Clausen and Kohn 1959) suggested that the pattern of isolation began before the illness, sometimes in early childhood. Schizophrenics who were not isolated in early life, were not isolated as adults.

Conclusion

From the epidemiological evidence, it is uncertain whether schizophrenia is evoked by living in a disadvantaged neighbourhood. On balance it seems more likely that people who are developing schizophrenia tend to move into areas providing solitary and unsatisfactory accommodation.

Precipitating factors

Physical illness and childbirth

The onset of schizophrenia after infectious illness or childbirth is probably a non-specific effect of psychological and physiological stress. More specific aetiological associations with brain disease have been suggested, especially disorders of the temporal lobe (see Davison and Bagley 1969). Recently it has been proposed that virus infection may be a major cause of schizophrenia, and it has been reported that virus-like material can be isolated from the cerebro-spinal fluid of schizophrenics (Tyrell *et al.* 1979). Confirmation by further research is awaited.

Psychosocial stresses

Life stresses have often been put forward as precipitants of schizophrenia, but few entirely satisfactory studies have been carried out. In one of the most convincing studies, Brown and Birley (1968) used a standardized procedure to collect information from 50 patients newly admitted with a first onset or relapse of schizophrenia. By comparison with a control group, the rate of 'independent' events in the schizophrenics was increased in the three weeks before the onset of the acute symptoms. (Independent events are those that could not be the result of illness – see p. 91.) When the events (which included moving house, starting or losing a job, and domestic crises) were compared with events preceding depression, neurosis, and suicide attempts, they were found to be non-specific. Other workers have confirmed these findings both for first episodes and for relapse of schizophrenia (Jacobs *et al.* 1974; Jacobs and Myers 1976).

Mediating mechanisms

In research on the aetiology of schizophrenia, much attention has been given to mediating mechanisms. These are not 'ultimate' causes of schizophrenia in the same sense that genetic predisposition or early environment might be; nor are they precipitating factors. They are best thought of as central abnormalities that form a link between such causal factors and the phenomena of schizophrenia. They can be divided into a psychological group, and a biochemical and pharmacological group.

Psychological mediating mechanisms

'Arousal'

Much attention has been paid to autonomic measures such as skin conductance and pulse rate in schizophrenic patients. The results have been inconsistent, some workers reporting increased activity, and others reporting no differences from normal subjects (see Neale and Oltmans (1980) for a review). The results of studies of autonomic activity and of EEG activity have been interpreted as indicating arousal in the central nervous system. Viewed in this way the results suggest that some but not all schizophrenics are overaroused, and that this abnormality is more frequent among the more socially withdrawn chronic patients (see Lader 1975; also Venables and Wing 1962). Venables and his colleagues have reported asymmetries in autonomic responses which they interpret as evidence for a disorder of left hemispheric function possibly related to the hippocampus (see Venables 1977).

The literature on arousal in schizophrenia is difficult to interpret, because different investigators work with different subgroups of patients (or do not specify the characteristics of patients), and because some of the reported effects could be due to medication.

Attention and perception

Many schizophrenics describe their perceptions as either more vivid or less real than usual. Objects may also seem unusual in shape or size. Some schizophrenics perform badly on tests of attention, for example picking out a signal from a noisy background. There have been attempts to explain these deficits in terms of current models of information processing in the nervous system, but they have not led to any significant advances in knowledge of the aetiology of schizophrenia (see Helmsley (1975) for a review). In general terms it seems that schizophrenics cannot concentrate selectively on the important aspects of sensory input. One theory is that an overwhelming input of stimuli may provide a basis for some of the perceptual abnormalities described by these patients.

Thought disorder

Schizophrenic patients tend to use language in a literal way. They are unable to handle alternative or ambiguous meanings and have difficulty in generalizing. Goldstein and Scheerer (1941) introduced tests to demonstrate this 'concrete thinking' more objectively. For example, these tests require patients to discern similarities between common objects.

Other research has used the concept of 'over inclusiveness', which has been defined as 'the inability to conserve conceptual boundaries with the result that there is an incorporation of irrelevant ideas' (Cameron 1938). Payne and his colleagues, using object sorting tests, have shown that schizophrenics classify objects in unusual and idiosyncratic ways (see Payne 1962).

A third approach to schizophrenic thought disorder uses Kelly's personal construct theory (Kelly 1955). Bannister (1962) suggested that schizophrenics had an abnormally loose construct system which could be measured with the repertory grid. He also suggested that abnormal constructs might have developed through repeated invalidations of the patient's previous attempts to make sense of the world, perhaps as a result of disordered family communication experienced in childhood. The available evidence does not support this theory.

Current research is more concerned with the nature of the disorders in schizophrenic language (see Wyke 1980). Small but significant differences have been found between the speech of schizophrenics and that of normal people. This is an interesting approach but so far it has not increased knowledge about aetiology.

Biochemistry and psychopharmacological factors

Many findings of early biochemical investigations turned out to be the result of unusual diet or medication rather than of schizophrenia itself. Recent studies have usually attempted to control these extraneous variables. Several hypotheses have been suggested, but most attention has been paid to those concerned with **serotonergic** transmission, **transmethylation**, and **dopaminergic** transmission.

Woolley and Shaw (1954) suggested that serotonergic transmission in the brain might be diminished in schizophrenia. However, subsequent post-mortem brain studies have not revealed any consistent abnormality of serotonin or its metabolite 5-hydroxyindolacetic acid (Crow *et al.* 1979*a*).

Transmethylation

Mescaline, a hallucinogen, is a methylated substance with a chemical relationship to dopamine and noradrenaline. Osmond *et al.* (1952) suggested that abnormal methylated metabolites might be formed in the brain and produce the psychological symptoms of schizophrenia. A basic weakness of the theory is that the effects of mescaline do not closely resemble schizophrenia. Nevertheless, some supporting evidence appeared to come from two sources. According to Pollin *et al.* (1961), when chronic schizophrenics were given a methyl donor such as methionine (with or without a monoamine oxidase inhibitor) their schizophrenic symptoms appeared to increase. However, as Pollin *et al.* point out, it is difficult to know whether the effect is an exacerbation of schizophrenia, or 'a toxic delirium superimposed upon chronic schizophrenia'. The second evidence was the finding of a methylated substance in the urine of some schizophrenics (Friedhoff and van Winkle 1962), which appeared as a pink area on a chromatogram, (the so-called 'pink spot'). However, this compound (3,4-dimethoxyphenylethylamine) proved to be inactive in human beings, and was subsequently found to be excreted by normal subjects living in the same conditions as the schizophrenic patients, and to be dietary in origin (see Green and Costain 1981).

Recent attempts to identify methylated metabolites have centred on the indoleamine *N*-dimethyltryptamine, which can be identified in the tissues, blood, and urine of schizophrenic patients. This substance is also present in people with other mental disorders, so any specific relationship to schizophrenia is doubtful (see Rodnight *et al.* 1977).

The dopamine hypothesis

Two lines of research have converged on the transmitter dopamine. The first concerns amphetamine which, among other actions, releases dopamine at central synapses. Amphetamine also induces a disorder indistinguishable from schizophrenia in some normal people, and worsens schizophrenic symptoms. The second approach starts from the finding that the various antipsychotic drugs share dopamine blocking effects. Carlsson and Lindqvist (1963) showed that such drugs increase dopamine turnover. This effect was interpreted as a feedback response of the presynaptic neurone to blockade of postsynaptic dopamine receptors. There is now much additional evidence that antipsychotic drugs block postsynaptic dopamine receptors. They also antagonize dopamine-sensitive adenylcyclase; and the extent to which this effect is produced *in vitro* by the different antipsychotic drugs correlates closely with their clinical potency (Miller *et al.* 1974). Further it has been shown that α-flupenthixol, an effective dopamine antagonist, has significant antipsychotic activity; whilst the β-isomer, which lacks receptor-blocking properties, is therapeutically inert (Johnstone *et al.* 1978).

Although this evidence is strong that dopamine is central to the action of antipsychotic drugs, evidence for the corollary – that dopamine metabolism is abnormal in schizophrenia – is weak. The antipsychotic drugs do not have effects specific to schizophrenia; they are equally effective in mania. Also, it is important to recall the analogy of Parkinsonism (mentioned on page 96). In this condition, anticholinergic drugs have therapeutic effects even though the biochemical lesion is not an excess of acetylcholine but a deficiency in dopaminergic neurones due to selective degeneration.

Because of these difficulties of interpretation, more direct evidence has been sought by biochemical studies of post-mortem brains from schizophrenic patients. Owen *et al.* (1978) found an increase in dopamine receptor density in the caudate, putamen, and nucleus accumbens of schizophrenics. Such findings are difficult to interpret because they might result from antipsychotic medication taken by nearly all schizophrenic patients at some time. Moreover, the same workers found no increase of dopamine turnover. Further studies of unmedicated patients are needed before definite conclusions can be reached.

Conclusion

There is strong evidence for genetic causes. There is good reason to think that stressful life events often provoke the disorder; the events appear to be non-specific and are similar to those which precede affective disorders. There have been several attempts to find factors in early life that might increase vulnerability to schizophrenia in later years. One set of observations concerns minor neurological disorder, possibly secondary to birth injury. Another set concerns the way parents communicate with their children. Neither set is convincing. Psychological studies have succeeded in characterizing some of the abnormalities found in schizophrenia but so far they have not increased knowledge of causation. In established cases of schizophrenia, it is possible that exacerbations are related to events that increase an already high level of arousal. Although a biochemical disorder has long been suspected, no convincing evidence has been found. Dopamine receptors are blocked by drugs that control schizophrenic symptoms, but there is no compelling evidence that activity of dopaminergic systems is the central disorder in schizophrenia.

COURSE AND PROGNOSIS

Although it is generally agreed that the outcome of schizophrenia is worse than that of most psychiatric disorders, there have been surprisingly few long-term follow-up studies of schizophrenic patients. Fewer still have included satisfactory criteria for diagnosis, samples of adequate size, and outcome measures that distinguish between symptoms and social adjustment. It is generally accepted that there are wide variations in outcome. This variation can be explained in three ways: first schizophrenia may be a single condition whose course is modified by extraneous factors; secondly, schizophrenia may consist of separate subtypes with different prognoses; thirdly, the good prognosis cases may not be schizophrenia but some other condition. The second and third explanations have already been discussed; the rest of this section is concerned with the first explanation.

When successive reports are studied, it appears that prognosis may have improved since the beginning of the century. Kraepelin (1919) concluded that only 17 per cent of his patients in Heidelberg were socially well-adjusted many years later. In 1932, from the same clinic Mayer-Gross reported social recovery in about 30 per cent of patients after 16 years. By 1966, Brown *et al.* reported social recovery in 56 per cent of patients after five years. Against this, in a study of patients identified as schizophrenic in a single centre between the early years of the century and 1962, Ciompi (1980) found little change in the proportion with a good or fair social outcome. All studies with prolonged follow-up report that up to 10 per cent of schizophrenics die by suicide (see Roy 1982).

An important long-term study was carried out by Manfred Bleuler (1972, 1974) who personally followed up 208 patients who had been admitted to hospital in Switzerland between 1942 and 1943. Twenty years after admission, 20 per cent had a complete remission of symptoms and 24 per cent were severely disturbed. Bleuler considered that these proportions had changed little since the introduction of modern treatments. When social adjustment was examined, a good outcome was found in about 30 per cent of the whole group, and in 40 per cent of those who had originally been first admissions. When full recovery had occurred, it was usually in the first two years and seldom after five years of continuous illness. Bleuler's diagnostic criteria were narrow, and his findings suggest that the traditional view of schizophrenia as a generally progressive and disabling condition must be reconsidered. Nevertheless, 10 per cent of his patients suffered an illness of such severity that they required long-term sheltered care. When the illness was recurrent, usually each subsequent episode resembled the first in its clinical features.

Bleuler's conclusions are broadly supported by Ciompi's larger but less detailed study of long-term outcome in Lausanne (Ciompi 1980). The study was based on the well-kept records of 1642 patients diagnosed as schizophrenic from the beginning of the century to 1962. The average follow-up was 37 years. A third of the patients were found to have a good or fair social outcome. Symptoms often became less severe in the later years of life.

There have been several attempts to find satisfactory predictors of the outcome of schizophrenia (see Stephens 1978). Langfeldt (1960) identified a set of criteria and reported them to be successful. However, in the International Pilot Study of Schizophrenia, tests were made of the predictive value of several sets of criteria based on symptoms, including Langfeldt's criteria, Feighner's diagnostic criteria, and others. All these symptom criteria proved to be largely unsuccessful at predicting outcome at two years (Strauss and Carpenter 1974), or five years (Strauss and Carpenter 1977). Brockington *et al.* (1978) made similar tests of a range of symptom criteria, and reached a similar conclusion.

In the IPSS study, the investigators went on to test other clinical and social criteria. When the 15 best predictors were combined, they accounted for less than a third of the variance of the two-year outcome.

Clinicians should therefore be cautious when asked to predict the outcome of individual cases. The factors listed in Table 9.6 are generally agreed to be a moderately useful guide.

So far this discussion has been concerned with factors operating before or at the onset of schizophrenia. An account will now be given of factors acting after the illness has become established.

Social environment and course

Cultural background

Recent international studies suggest that the incidence of schizophrenia is similar in different countries, but that the course and outcome are not similar. In a 12 year follow-up study of 90 patients in Mauritius, Murphy and Raman

Table 9.6. *Factors predicting the outcome of schizophrenia*

Good prognosis	Poor prognosis
Sudden onset	Insidious onset
Short episode	Long episode
No previous psychiatric history	Previous psychiatric history
Prominent affective symptoms	Blunted affect
Older age at onset	Younger age at onset
Married	Single, separated, widowed, divorced
Good psychosexual adjustment	Poor psychosexual adjustment
Good previous personality	Abnormal previous personality
Good work record	Poor work record
Good social relationships	Social isolation

(1971) observed a better prognosis than that reported in the United Kingdom by Brown *et al.* (1966). More Mauritian patients were able to leave hospital and return to a normal way of life. Nearly two-thirds were classified as socially independent and symptom free at follow-up as compared with only half of the English sample.

Comparable differences were reported at two year follow-up in the International Pilot Study of Schizophrenia (World Health Organization 1979). Outcome was better in India, Columbia, and Nigeria than in the other centres. This finding could not be explained by any recorded differences in the initial characteristics of the patients. There remains the possibility of selection bias; for example, in these three countries it may be that patients with acute illness are more likely to be taken to hospital than patients with illness of insidious onset (see Leff 1981).

Life events

As explained above (p. 255), patients experience an excess of life events in the three weeks before the onset of acute symptoms of schizophrenia. This applies not only to first illnesses but also to relapses (Brown and Birley 1968). It seems likely therefore that patients exposed to many life events would have a less favourable course.

Social stimulation

In the 1940s and 1950s clinicians recognized that among schizophrenics living in institutions many clinical features were associated with an unstimulating environment. Wing and Brown (1970) investigated patients at three mental hospitals. One was a traditional institution, another had an active rehabilitation programme, and the third had a reputation for progressive policies and short admissions. The research team devised a measure of 'poverty of the social milieu' which took into account: little contact with the outside world, few personal possessions, lack of constructive occupation, and pessimistic expectations on the part of ward staff. Poverty of social milieu was found to be closely related to three aspects of the patients' clinical condition: social withdrawal, blunting of affect, and poverty of speech. The causal significance of these social conditions was strongly supported by a further survey of the same hospitals four years later. Improvements had taken place in the environment of the hospitals, and these changes were accompanied by corresponding improvements in the three aspects of the patients' clinical state.

While an understimulating hospital environment is associated with worsening of the so-called clinical poverty syndrome, an overstimulating environment can precipitate florid symptoms and lead to relapse. Since factors in a hospital environment play an important part in determining prognosis, it seems likely that similar factors are important to patients living in the community. The use of social measures is reviewed in Chapter 19 (see also the reviews edited by Wing (1982) and Watts and Bennett (1983).

Family life

Brown *et al.* (1958) found that, on discharge from hospital, schizophrenics returning to their families generally had a worse prognosis than those entering hostels. Brown *et al.* (1962) found that relapse rates were greater in families where relatives showed 'high expressed emotion' by making critical comments, expressing hostility, and showing signs of emotional over-involvement. In such families the risk of relapse was greater if the patients were in contact with their close relatives for more than 35 hours a week. The work was confirmed and extended when Leff and Vaughn (1981) investigated the interaction between 'expressed emotion' in relatives and life events in the three months before relapse. The onset of illness was associated either with a high level of expressed emotion or with an independent life event. In an investigation using psychophysiological methods Sturgeon *et al.* (1980) reported an association between expressed emotion in a close relative and the level of autonomic arousal recorded in the patient, suggesting that such arousal may be a mediating variable.

Vaughn and Leff (1976) have suggested an association between expressed emotion in relatives and the patient's response to antipsychotic medication. Among patients who were spending more than 35 hours a week in contact with relatives showing high emotional expression, the relapse rate was 92 per cent for those not taking antipsychotic medication, and only 53 per cent for those taking antipsychotic medication. Among patients taking antipsychotic drugs and spending less than 35 hours in contact with high emotional expression relatives, the relapse rate was as low as 15 per cent. In this study patients had not been allocated randomly to the treatment conditions. However, a further study (Leff *et al.* 1982) strongly suggests that high emotional expression has a causal role. Twenty-four families were selected in which a schizophrenic patient had high contact with high emotional expression relatives. All patients were on maintenance neuroleptic drugs. Half of the families were randomly assigned to routine outpatient care. The other half took part in a programme including education about schizophrenia, relatives' groups, and family sessions for relatives and patients. The relapse rate was significantly lower in this group than in the controls. Apart from providing further evidence of the importance of relatives' expressed emotion in relapse, this study showed the effectiveness of combined social intervention and drug treatment.

Conclusion

Degree of social stimulation may be a common factor explaining the relationships between outcome of schizophrenia and different cultures, life events, changes in the social environment, and the emotional involvement of relatives. Too much stimulation appears to precipitate relapse into positive symptoms, while understimulation leads to worsening of negative symptoms. An intervening mechanism could be the degree of autonomic arousal.

EFFECTS OF SCHIZOPHRENIA ON THE FAMILY

With the increasing care of patients in the community rather than in hospital, difficulties have arisen for some families. Relatives of schizophrenics describe two main groups of problems (Creer 1978). The first group relates to social withdrawal: schizophrenic patients do not interact with other family members; they seem slow, lack conversation, have few interests, and neglect themselves. The second group relates to more obviously disturbed and socially embarassing behaviour, such as restlessness, odd or uninhibited social behaviour, and threats of violence.

Creer found that relatives often felt anxious, depressed, guilty, or bewildered. Many were uncertain how to deal with difficult and odd behaviour. Further difficulties arose from differences in opinion between family members, and more commonly from a lack of understanding and sympathy among neighbours and friends. The effects on the lives of such relatives were often serious.

TREATMENT

The treatment of schizophrenia is concerned with both the acute illness and chronic disability. In general, the best results are obtained by combining drug and social treatments, while methods aimed at providing psychodynamic insight are unhelpful.

This section is concerned with the evidence from clinical trials about the efficacy of various forms of treatment. A later section on management deals with the use of these treatments in everyday clinical practice.

The history of insulin-coma therapy is a warning that clinical impressions about the value of treatment can be misleading. Insulin-coma therapy was widely used for many years until Ackner and Oldham (1962) showed that coma induced by barbiturates produced equally good results. This finding indicated that the therapeutic benefits were probably due to non-specific factors including intensive care by enthusiastic staff.

Antipsychotic drugs

Treatment of acute schizophrenia

The effectiveness of antipsychotic medication in the treatment of acute schizophrenia has been established by several well-controlled, double-blind studies. For example the NIMH collaborative project (Cole *et al.* 1964) compared chlorpromazine, fluphenazine, and thioridazine with placebo. Three-quarters of the patients receiving antipsychotic treatment for six weeks improved, whatever the drug, whilst a half of those receiving placebo worsened. Drug treatment has most effect on the positive symptoms of schizophrenia, such as hallucinations and delusions, and least effect on the negative symptoms.

The various antipsychotic drugs do not differ in therapeutic effectiveness, although their side-effects vary (see p. 533). There is generally little to be gained by exceeding maximum dose equivalent to about 900 mg of chlorpromazine a day (see Davis *et al.* 1980; a table of dose equivalents appears on page 539). The exception to this rule is that higher dosages are sometimes required to achieve a sedative effect in acutely ill patients. For the acute illness there is no proven way of distinguishing patients who require medication if they are to improve from those who would improve without medication (Davis *et al.* 1980).

Treatment after the acute phase

Since the original demonstration by Pasamanick *et al.* (1964), many controlled trials have shown the effectiveness of continued oral and depot therapy in preventing relapse (see Hirsch *et al.* 1973; Leff and Wing 1971). It has also become clear that some chronic schizophrenics do not respond even to long-term medication, and that others remain well without drugs. Unfortunately there has been no success in predicting which patients benefit from such treatment. Since long-continued antipsychotic medication may lead to irreversible dyskinesias (see pp. 380 and 536), it is important to know how long such treatment needs to be given. There is still no clear answer to this question, but Hogarty and Ulrich (1977) reported that, over a three-year period, maintenance anti-psychotic medication was 2½ to 3 times better than the placebo in preventing relapse. There is a widespread clinical impression that, in preventing relapses of schizophrenia, depot injections are more successful than continued oral medication. However, Schooler *et al.* (1980) found that depot injections offered no such advantage. According to Davis *et al.* (1980), in the long-term management of schizophrenia there is no difference in the usefulness of the various antipsychotic drugs available.

Interaction of maintenance treatment and social treatment

Since both medication and social casework appear effective in the management of schizophrenia, it is reasonable to enquire whether the two kinds of treatment interact. Hogarty *et al.* (1974) studied the use of 'major role therapy' (i.e. social casework) with and without drugs. Given alone, social casework had only a small effect in reducing relapse rate; combined with medication, it had a larger effect. This difference may have occurred partly because patients took their drugs more regularly when seeing social workers, but such an effect seems unlikely to be the whole explanation. In a study of the effect of adding day hospital treatment to continued medication, Linn *et al.* (1980) found that day care conferred extra benefit on patients when it was of low intensity and based on occupational therapy, but not when it included more active treatments such as group therapy.

Antidepressants and lithium

As already explained, symptoms of depression occur commonly in the syndrome of schizophrenia (p. 234). Since it is not easy to distinguish between depressive symptoms and apathy, it is difficult to assess the effects of antidepressant medication in chronic schizophrenia. As yet there has been no satisfactory clinical trial (see *British Medical Journal* (1980*a*) for a review).

The value of lithium in treating schizophrenia is uncertain. Occasional beneficial effects could be due to the treatment of schizoaffective cases. There is some evidence that lithium has a therapeutic action in this diagnostic group. In two small trials, Brockington *et al.* (1978) found that chlorpromazine was more effective than lithium for schizodepressive patients (that is, those satisfying criteria for both depressive disorder and schizophrenia). However, lithium and chlorpromazine were equally effective for patients with 'schizomania'. (For a review of the evidence in favour of the value of lithium see Delva and Letemendia 1982.)

ECT

In the treatment of schizophrenia, the traditional indications for ECT are catatonic stupor and severe depressive symptoms accompanying schizophrenia. The effects of ECT are often rapid and striking in both these conditions. Nowadays ECT is seldom used for other presentations of schizophrenia, although there is some evidence that it is rapidly effective in acute episodes (Taylor and Fleminger 1980).

Psychotherapy

In the past, individual psychotherapy was used quite commonly for schizophrenia, though much more in the United States than in Britain. Evidence from clinical trials is scanty but it does not support the use of psychotherapy. An investigation by May (1968) found that psychotherapy had little benefit, but the treatment was short and provided by relatively inexperienced psychiatrists. Apart from the lack of convincing evidence that intensive individual psychotherapy is effective in schizophrenia, there may be some danger of the treatment causing over-stimulation and consequent relapse (see Mosher and Keith 1979).

Many kinds of group therapy have been used to treat schizophrenia. When the results have been compared with routine hospital treatment, the general finding in the better controlled evaluations has been that group therapy is of little benefit in the acute stage of the disorder (see Mosher and Keith 1979). Indeed clinical experience strongly suggests that small group therapy is likely to make some acutely ill patients worse, and to confer little or no benefit after the acute stage.

Work with relatives

There have been few controlled studies of intensive family therapy in the treatment of schizophrenia. They were all concerned with short interventions for acute illness, and all found slight benefits from the treatment (see Mosher and Keith 1979).

The work on emotional expression reviewed above (see p. 262) suggests that counselling should be beneficial to families, especially when directed to reducing specific problems. It also seems sensible to offer advice to families about practical matters, although it would be difficult to evaluate the effectiveness of such advice.

Behavioural treatment

The results of behavioural treatment for schizophrenia have not been fully evaluated. Most of the reported results could be due to increased attention. **Individual methods** include social skills training (see p. 606) and programmes of operant conditioning directed to specific symptoms (see p. 610). These procedures have been reviewed by Matson (1980).

Token economies also use positive and negative reinforcement to alter behaviour but they are applied to all the patients in a ward rather than to a single patient. Rewards may be praise and interest, but it is usual to give tokens that can be used to purchase goods or privileges (hence the name of the treatment). Such systems can change the behaviour of regressed chronic patients. However, a clinical trial showed that the effects are due mainly to the graded and systematic approach rather than to the use of reinforcers (Baker *et al.* 1974). Unfortunately many patients relapse when they move from a token economy to a new environment in which there is not the same system of rewards. For this reason, and because there are potential ethical problems about the use of reward systems of this kind, the methods are not used widely.

ASSESSMENT

Assessment begins with differential diagnosis, which is particularly concerned with the exclusion of organic disorder (especially a drug-induced state), affective disorder, and personality disorder. In practice, the main difficulty is often to elicit all the symptoms from a withdrawn or suspicious patient. This procedure may require several psychiatric interviews as well as careful observations by the nursing staff. The differential diagnosis from affective disorder can be particularly difficult and may require prolonged observation for discriminating symptoms of schizophrenia.

While the psychiatric diagnosis is being confirmed, a social assessment should be carried out. This includes assessment of the patient's previous personality, work record, accommodation and leisure pursuits, and especially the attitudes to the patient of relatives and any close friends. The doctor or social worker can proceed with this enquiry while an evaluation of the patient's social functioning in the ward is made by nurses and occupational therapists.

Psychological testing

In the assessment of schizophrenia, formal psychological testing seldom adds much to clinical observation. In the past, projective tests such as the Rorschach and Thematic Apperception Tests were used to examine thought processes, but they are unreliable and lack validity. More recent tests using the repertory grid and sorting procedures are more reliable but rarely help much if the mental state has been carefully examined. Standardized tests of personality are less useful than a thorough history from an informant who knows the patient well.

While there is little place for psychometric assessment in diagnosing schizo-phrenia, the clinical psychologist has a valuable role in making quantitative assessments of specific abnormalities of behaviour as a basis for planning and evaluating social rehabilitation.

MANAGEMENT

Success in management depends on establishing a good relationship with the patient so that his co-operation is enlisted. It is often difficult to establish a working relationship with chronic patients who are paranoid or emotionally unresponsive, but with skill and patience progress can usually be made. It is important to make plans that are realistic, especially for the more handicapped patient. Over-enthusiastic schemes of rehabilitation may increase the patient's symptoms and (if he lives in the community) place unacceptable burdens on relatives.

The acute illness

Treatment in hospital is usually needed both for first episodes of schizophrenia and for acute relapses. Hospital admission allows a thorough assessment, provides a secure environment for the patient, and gives a period of relief to the family.

There are important advantages in a few days of observation without drugs, although some acutely disturbed patients may require immediate treatment. A drug-free period allows thorough assessment of the patient's mental state and behavior as described above. It also shows whether mental abnormalities and disturbed behaviour are likely to improve simply with change of environment. If they do not improve, an antipsychotic drug should be prescribed, the dose depending on the severity of the symptoms. There is a wide choice of drugs (see p. 535) but the clinician should become thoroughly familiar with a few. For acutely disturbed patients, the sedating effects of chlorpromazine are valuable. For less overactive patients, trifluoperazine is an alternative with less sedative action. Although these drugs need be given only once a day for their (delayed) antipsychotic effects, it is often appropriate to prescribe them in divided doses. In this way their immediate sedating effects can operate at the times when the patient is most disturbed. The timing and dosage should be reviewed frequently with the ward staff, and adjusted to changes in the patient's condition. At this stage, oral medication is usually given, although occasional intramuscular doses may be needed for acutely disturbed behaviour. If there are doubts whether the patient is swallowing tablets, the drug can be given as a syrup. Other phenothiazines are equally effective, but have no particular advantages unless there are problems with individual sensitivities or side-effects (see page 538 for further advice about the use of antipsychotic drugs).

After the first few days, medication is continued at a constant daily amount for several weeks, with a gradual transfer to twice daily dosage or a single dose at night. Anti-Parkinsonian drugs should be prescribed if Parkinsonian side-effects are troublesome, but they need not be given routinely. Symptoms of excitement, restlessness, irritability, and insomnia can be expected to improve within days. Affective and psychotic symptoms respond more slowly, often persisting for six to eight weeks. Lack of improvement at this stage suggests inadequate dosage or failure to take the drugs prescribed, but a few cases resist all efforts at treatment. Once there is undoubted evidence of sustained improvement, dosage can be reduced cautiously while careful watch is kept for any return of symptoms. This reduced dose is continued for a further period (see below).

During the early days of treatment, the doctor will have taken histories from the patient, relatives, and other informants, so as to build up a picture of the patient's previous personality, premorbid adjustment and social circumstances, and any precipitants of illness. By the time symptomatic improvement has taken place, the doctor should have formulated a provisional plan for continuing care. Although it is difficult to predict the long-term prognosis at this stage, a judgement has to be made about the likely immediate outcome. This judgement is based on the degree and speed of response to treatment, and on the factors listed in Table 9.6. The aim is to decide how much aftercare patients will require, and to make realistic plans accordingly.

Aftercare of 'good prognosis' patients

After a first episode of schizophrenia, patients judged to have a good immediate prognosis have two principal needs for treatment following discharge from hospital. The first is to take medication in reducing dosage for at least three months. The second is to be given advice about avoiding obviously stressful events. The patient should be seen regularly as an outpatient until a few months after medication has been stopped and symptoms have ceased. Thereafter, a cautiously optimistic prognosis can be given, but the patient and his family should be warned to consult a doctor immediately if there is any suggestion of the condition returning.

The aftercare of the 'poor prognosis' patients without major social handicaps

When it is judged that further relapse is likely, continuing care will be required, and this will probably include prophylactic medication. It is often better to give such medication by injection (for example as fluphenazine decanoate or flupenthixol), since some patients fail to take oral medication regularly over long periods. The dosage, which should be the minimum required to suppress symptoms, can be determined by cautiously varying its size and frequency while observing the patient's clinical state (see p. 541). Some patients show little response to continued antipsychotic medication even in high doses. For such patients medication should not be given continuously, but only for acute relapses (for which it generally remains active).

It is uncertain how long such prophylactic treatment with neuroleptics should be continued. The treatment should be reviewed at least once a year, taking into account side-effects as well as symptoms. Medication should be withdrawn if tardive dyskinesia occurs (see p. 537), otherwise a balance has to be struck between benefits and adverse effects.

Whether maintenance drug therapy is given or not, the patient should be seen regularly to review his mental state and social adjustment. When necessary he should be advised to avoid stressful situations and helped to reduce the amount of time spent with an emotionally arousing family. Help may also be required in finding a suitable occupation. Community psychiatric nurses can undertake most of treatment of this kind, and social workers can help with those measures not involving the administration of medication. The most difficult problem in continuing management is likely to be the patient's tendency to withdraw from treatment.

Patients with chronic handicap

When patients have poor social adjustment and behavioural defects characteristic of chronic schizophrenia, they require more elaborate aftercare. They should be identified as early as possible so that long-term plans can be made for both rehabilitation in hospital and resettlement outside hospital. Maintenance drug therapy plays an important part, but the main emphasis is on a programme of rehabilitation tailored to the needs of the individual patient.

It can be expected that the least handicapped patients will live more or less independently. For the rest, sheltered work and accommodation are likely to be needed. The essential requirements are a management plan that focuses on one or two aspects of behaviour disorder at any one time, and a consistent approach between the members of staff carrying it out.

Despite the present emphasis on treatment outside hospital, early rehabilitation in hospital has significant advantages because it allows greater consistency of approach over the whole of the patient's day. Wards organized mainly for the treatment of acute illness are often too stimulating for chronic schizophrenics in need of rehabilitation. Hence it is appropriate to set aside a special area for rehabilitation. Treatment can be based either on the principles of a therapeutic community or on those of behavioural management. These two approaches produce similar results, and are compatible with one another (Hall 1983).

Most handicapped patients are able to live outside hospital albeit in sheltered provisions. A minority require long-term care in hospital. The components of a community service for these patients are described in Chapter 19. Success depends less on physical provisions than on well-trained staff who have tolerant attitudes and the capacity to obtain satisfaction from work that produces small improvements over long periods.

When a patient has persisting abnormalities of behaviour, particular attention needs to be given to the problems of his family. Relatives may be helped by joining a voluntary group and meeting others who have learnt to deal with similar problems. They also need to know that professional help will be provided whenever problems become too great. Advice is needed about the best ways of responding to abnormal behaviour, and about the expectations they should have of the patient. Such advice is often given best by community nurses who have experience of treating chronic schizophrenic patients in hospital as well as in the community. Social workers also have a part to play in advising and helping relatives.

The violent patient

Overactivity and disturbances of behaviour are common in schizophrenia. Though often feared by laymen, major violence towards others is uncommon. Homicide is rare. Self-mutilation is more frequent, and about one schizophrenic patient in ten dies by suicide. These self-harmful behaviours may be associated with delusions of control, persecutory delusions or auditory hallucinations.

General management for the potentially violent patient is the same as for any other schizophrenic, although a compulsory order is more likely to be needed. While medication is often needed to bring disturbed behaviour under immediate control, much can be done by providing a calm, reassuring, and consistent environment in which provocation is avoided. A special ward area with an adequate number of experienced staff is much better than the use of heavy medication.

Threats of violence should be taken seriously, especially if there is a history of such behaviour in the past, whether or not the patient was ill at the time. The danger usually resolves as acute symptoms are brought under control, but a few patients pose a continuing threat. The management of violence is considered further in Chapter 22.

FURTHER READING

Bleuler, E. (1911). (English edition 1950) *Dementia praecox or the group of schizophrenias.* International University Press, New York.

Fish, F.J. (1962). *Schizophrenia.* John Wright, Bristol.

Kraepelin, E. (1919). *Dementia praecox and paraphrenia.* Churchill Livingstone, Edinburgh.

Schneider, K. (1959). *Clinical psychopathology.* Grune and Stratton, New York.

Strauss, J.S. and Carpenter, W.T. (1981). *Schizophrenia.* Plenum, New York.

Watts, F.N. and Bennett, D.H. (1983). *Theory and practice of psychiatric rehabilitation.* John Wiley, Chichester.

Wing, J.K. and Brown, G.W. (1970). *Institutionalism and schizophrenia.* Cambridge University Press.

—— and Wing, L.L. (Eds.) (1983). Psychoses of uncertain origin (part I schizophrenia and paranoid psychoses). In *Handbook of psychiatry,* Vol. 3. Cambridge University Press.

10. Paranoid symptoms and paranoid states

INTRODUCTION

The term 'paranoid' can be applied to symptoms, syndromes, or personality-types. Paranoid symptoms are delusional beliefs which are most commonly persecutory but not always so. Paranoid syndromes are those syndromes in which paranoid symptoms form part of a characteristic constellation of symptoms, such as pathological jealousy or erotomania (described later). Paranoid personalities are those personalities in which there is excessive self-reference and undue sensitiveness to real or imaginary humiliations and rebuffs, often combined with self-importance, combativeness, and aggressiveness. The term paranoid is descriptive and not diagnostic. If we recognize a symptom or syndrome as paranoid, this is not making a diagnosis, but it is a preliminary to doing so. In this respect it is like recognizing stupor or depersonalization.

Paranoid syndromes present considerable problems of classification and diagnosis. The reasons for this can be understood by dividing them into two groups. In the first group, paranoid features occur in association with a primary mental illness, such as schizophrenia, affective disorder, or an organic mental disorder. In the second group, paranoid features occur, but no primary disorder can be detected – the paranoid features appear to have arisen independently. In this book, following the ICD 9 system of classification, the term 'paranoid states' is applied to this second group (DSM III refers to them as 'paranoid disorders'). It is this second group that has given rise to difficulties and confusion over classification and diagnosis. For example, there has been much argument as to whether these conditions are an alternative form of schizophrenia, or a stage in the evolution of schizophrenia, or a quite separate entity. It is because these problems arise frequently in clinical practice that a whole chapter is devoted to them.

This chapter begins with definitions of the commonest paranoid symptoms, and then reviews the causes of such symptoms. Next comes a short account of paranoid personality. This is followed by discussion of primary psychiatric disorders, such as organic mental states, affective disorders, and schizophrenia, with which paranoid features are frequently associated. These primary illnesses are dealt with elsewhere in the book, but the focus here is on differentiating them from paranoid states. Paranoid states are then reviewed, with particular reference to paranoia and paraphrenia. These latter terms are considered against their historical background. Next, an account is given of a number of distinctive paranoid symptoms and syndromes, some of which are fairly common and some exceedingly rare. The chapter finishes with a description of the assessment and treatment of patients with paranoid features.

PARANOID SYMPTOMS

In the introduction it was pointed out that the commonest paranoid delusions are persecutory. The term paranoid is also applied to the less common delusions of grandeur and of jealousy, and sometimes to delusions concerning love, litigation, or religion. It may seem puzzling that such varied delusions should be grouped together. The reason is that the central abnormality implied by the term paranoid is a morbid distortion of beliefs or attitudes concerning relationships between oneself and other people. If someone believes falsely or on inadequate grounds that he is being victimized, or exalted, or deceived, or loved by a famous person, then in each case he is construing the relationship between himself and other people in a morbidly distorted way.

The varieties of paranoid symptom are discussed in Chapter 1, but the main ones are outlined here for convenience. The following definitions are derived from those in the glossary to the *Present State Examination* (see Wing *et al.* 1974). **Ideas of reference** are held by people who are unduly self-conscious. The subject cannot help feeling that people take notice of him in buses, restaurants, or other public places, and that they observe things about him that he would prefer not to be seen. He realizes that this feeling originates with himself and that he is no more noticed than other people, but he cannot help the feeling all the same, quite out of proportion to any possible cause. **Delusions of reference** consist of a further elaboration of simple ideas of self-reference, and the person does not recognize that the ideas are false. The whole neighbourhood may seem to be gossiping about the subject, far beyond the bounds of possibility, or he may see references to himself on the television or in newspapers. The subject may hear someone on the radio say something connected with some topic that he has just been thinking about, or he may seem to be followed, his movements observed, and what he says tape-recorded.

Delusions of persecution. The subject believes that someone, or some organization, or some force or power is trying to harm him in some way; to damage his reputation, to cause him bodily injury, to drive him mad or to bring about his death.

The symptom may take many forms from the direct belief that people are hunting him down, to complex and bizarre plots with every kind of science fiction elaboration.

Delusions of grandeur. The glossary of the PSE proposes a division into delusions of grandiose ability, and delusions of grandiose identity.

The subject with delusions of *grandiose ability* thinks he is chosen by some power, or by destiny, for a special mission or purpose, because of his unusual talents. He thinks he is able to read people's thoughts, or that he is particularly good at helping them, that he is much cleverer than anyone else, that he has invented machines, composed music, or solved mathematical problems beyond most people's comprehension.

The subject with delusions of *grandiose identity* believes that he is famous, rich, titled, or related to prominent people. He may believe that he is a changeling and that his real parents are royalty.

The causes of paranoid symptoms

When paranoid symptoms occur in association with a primary organic, affective, or schizophrenic illness, the main aetiological factors are those determining this primary illness. The question still arises as to why some people develop paranoid symptoms, whilst others do not. It has usually been answered in terms of premorbid personality and of factors causing social isolation.

Many writers including Kraepelin have held that paranoid symptoms are most likely to occur in patients with premorbid personalities of a paranoid type (see next section). Modern studies of so-called late onset paraphrenia have supported these views (see Chapter 16, p. 514). Thus Kay and Roth (1961) found paranoid or hypersensitive personalities in over half of their group of 99 such patients, whilst Herbert and Jacobsen (1967) found similar personality features in all but four of their 45 patients.

Freud (1911) proposed that, in predisposed people, paranoid symptoms could arise through the defence mechanisms of denial and projection. He held that a person does not consciously admit his own inadequacy and self-distrust, but projects them on to the outside world. Clinical experience generally confirms this idea. If one examines paranoid patients, one often finds an inner dissatisfaction associated with a sense of inferiority, and self-esteem and ambition which are inconsistent with achievement.

Freud also held that paranoid symptoms could arise when denial and projection were being used as defences against unconscious homosexual tendencies. These ideas were derived from his study of Daniel Schreber, the presiding judge of the Dresden appeal court (see Freud 1911). Freud never met Schreber, but read the latter's autobiographical account of his paranoid illness (now generally accepted to be paranoid schizophrenia), together with a report by Weber, the physician in charge. Freud held that Schreber could not consciously admit his homosexuality, so the idea 'I love him' was dealt with by denial and changed by a reaction formation to 'I hate him'; this was further changed by projection into 'it is not I who hate him, but he who hates me', and this in turn becomes transformed to 'I am persecuted by him'. Freud believed that all paranoid delusions could be represented as contradictions of the idea 'I (a man) love him (a man)'. He went so far as to argue that delusions of jealousy could be explained in terms of unconscious homosexuality; the jealous husband was unconsciously attracted to the man whom he accused his wife of loving. In this case the formulation was 'it is not I who love him; it is she who loves him'. At one time these ideas were widely taken up, particularly in the USA, but nowadays they gain little acceptance. They are certainly not supported by clinical experience.

Kretschmer (1927) also believed that paranoid disorders were more likely in people with predisposed or 'sensitive' personalities. In such people a precipitating event could induce what Kretschmer called sensitive delusions of reference (*sensitive Beziehungswahn*), occurring as an understandable psychological reaction.

Apart from psychological factors within the patient, social isolation may also lead to the emergence of paranoid symptoms. As mentioned later in this chapter, prisoners in solitary confinement, refugees, and migrants may be prone to paranoid developments, although the evidence on this is conflicting.

Social isolation can also be produced by deafness. In 1915, Kraepelin pointed out that chronic deafness could lead to paranoid attitudes. Houston and Royse (1954) found an association between deafness and paranoid schizophrenia, whilst Kay and Roth (1961) found hearing impairment in 40 per cent of late onset paraphrenics. However, it should be remembered that the great majority of deaf people do not become paranoid.

PARANOID PERSONALITY DISORDER

The concept of personality disorder was discussed in Chapter 5, and paranoid personality disorder was briefly described there. In ICD 9 the category paranoid personality disorder (301.0) is defined as follows:

there is excessive sensitiveness to set-backs or to what are taken to be humiliations and rebuffs, a tendency to distort experience by misconstruing the neutral or friendly actions of others as hostile or contemptuous, and a combative and tenacious sense of personal rights. There may be a proneness to jealousy or excessive self-importance. Such persons may feel helplessly humiliated and put upon; others, likewise excessively sensitive, are aggressive and insistent. In all cases there is excessive self-reference.

As implied in this definition (and in the similar DSM III definition), paranoid personality embraces a wide range of types. At one extreme is the painfully shy, timid youth who shrinks from social encounters and thinks everyone disapproves of him. At the other is the assertive and challenging man who flares up at the least provocation. Many grades lie between these two extremes.

Because of the implications for treatment, it is important to distinguish these paranoid personalities from the paranoid syndromes to be described later. The distinction can be very difficult to make. Sometimes the one shades into the other in the course of a single life history, as exemplified by the life of the philosopher Jean Jaques Rousseau. The basis for making the distinction is that in paranoid personalities there are no delusions but only dominant ideas, and no hallucinations. Separating paranoid ideas from delusions calls for considerable skill. The criteria for doing so are given in Chapter 1.

PRIMARY PSYCHIATRIC DISORDERS WITH PARANOID FEATURES

As mentioned in the introduction to this chapter, paranoid features occur in association with primary mental disorders. This association occurs commonly in clinical practice. As the primary disorders are described at length in other chapters, they are mentioned only briefly here.

Organic mental states

Paranoid symptoms are common in the acute organic syndrome. Impaired grasp of what is going on around the patient may give rise to apprehension and mis-interpretation, and so to suspicion. Delusions may then emerge which are usually transient and disorganized; they may lead to disturbed behaviour, such as querulousness or aggression. Examples are drug-induced states. Similarly, paranoid delusions may occur in dementia (chronic brain syndrome), arising from any cause, including trauma, degenerations, infections, metabolic and endocrine disorders (see Chapter 11).

In clinical practice it is important to remember that in elderly patients with senile dementia, paranoid delusions may appear before any intellectual deterioration is detectable.

Affective disorders

Paranoid delusions not uncommonly occur in patients with severe depressive illness. The latter is often characterized by guilt and retardation, and by 'biological' features such as loss of appetite and weight, sleep disturbance, and reduced sex drive. These disorders are commoner in middle or later life. In depressive illness, the patient typically accepts the supposed activities of the persecutors as justified by his own guilt or wickedness, but in schizophrenia he often resents them bitterly. It is sometimes difficult to determine whether the paranoid features are secondary to depressive illness, or whether depressed mood is secondary to paranoid symptoms arising from another cause. Primary depression is likely if the mood changes have occurred earlier and are of greater intensity than the paranoid features. The distinction is important, as it may indicate whether anti-depressant medication or phenothiazines should be prescribed.

Paranoid delusions also occur in manic patients. Often the delusions are grandiose rather than persecutory – the patient claiming to be extremely wealthy or of exalted rank or importance.

Paranoid schizophrenia

Paranoid schizophrenia has been described in Chapter 9. In contrast with the hebephrenic and catatonic forms of schizophrenia, the paranoid form usually begins later in life – in the thirties rather than in the twenties. The dominant feature of paranoid schizophrenia is delusions that are relatively stable over time. The delusions are frequently of persecution, but may also be of jealousy, exalted birth, Messianic mission, or bodily change. They may be accompanied by hallucinatory voices which sometimes but not invariably have a persecutory or grandiose content.

It is important to consider the differential diagnosis of paranoid schizophrenia from other paranoid conditions. As explained in the chapter on schizophrenia (p. 245) the authors of this book take the view that the diagnosis of schizophrenia can only be made with complete confidence if any of Schneider's first rank symptoms are detected. (In the United States the DSM III definition will be used.) In the absence of first rank symptoms, schizophrenia may be suggested if the paranoid delusions are particularly odd in content (often referred to by psychiatrists as bizarre delusions). Here the ground is much less certain. If the delusions are grotesque, then there may be no room for doubt. For example, a middle-aged woman became convinced that a Cabinet Minister was taking a special interest in her, and was promoting her well-being. She believed that he was the pilot of an aeroplane that flew over her house shortly after noon each day. She therefore waited in her garden each day, and threw a large red beach-ball into the sky when the plane flew over. She maintained that the pilot always acknowledged this action by 'waggling the wings' of the plane. When the delusions are less extreme than this, a judgement as to how bizarre they are must be arbitrary.

There are two other diagnostic points. First, in schizophrenia delusions are more likely to be fragmented and multiple, rather than systematized and unitary. Secondly, paranoid schizophrenics often have hallucinations that seem to be totally unrelated to their delusions; whereas patients with paranoid conditions other than schizophrenia frequently have no hallucinations, or else hallucinations that are closely connected with their delusions. These criteria would help to support the diagnosis of paranoid schizophrenia, but would not in themselves justify a confident diagnosis.

PARANOID STATES

As mentioned in the introduction to this chapter, the term 'paranoid states' is applied to paranoid conditions that are not associated with a primary organic, affective, or schizophrenic disorder. This is the nomenclature adopted by the ICD 9 system of classification in which 'category 297.0 paranoid state, simple' is defined as follows:

a psychosis, acute or chronic, not classifiable as schizophrenia or affective psychosis, in which delusions, especially of being influenced, persecuted or treated in some special way, are the main symptoms. The delusions are of a fairly fixed, elaborate and systematised kind.

In DSM III, the corresponding category is '297, paranoid disorder', which is much the same as the ICD 9 category. Apart from the absence of features of schizophrenia, manic–depressive disorder, or organic mental disorder, the DSM III diagnostic criteria for paranoid disorder are as follows: persistent persecutory delusions or delusional jealousy; emotion and behaviour appropriate to the content of the delusional system; duration of illness of at least one week; no prominent hallucinations.

The broad correspondence between ICD 9 and DSM III can be seen in Table 10.1. The few differences are: first, only ICD 9 has the subcategory of paraphrenia; second, ICD 9 has the additional main category, 298, other non-organic psychoses; and third, this additional category includes an extra sub-category, 298.4, psychogenic paranoid psychosis.

Table 10.1.

ICD 9	DSM III
297 Paranoid states	**Paranoid disorders**
297.0 Paranoid state, simple	
297.1 Paranoia	297.10 Paranoia
297.2 Paraphrenia	
297.3 Induced psychosis (*folie à deux*)	297.30 Shared paranoid disorder
297.8 Other	297.90 Atypical paranoid disorder
297.9 Unspecified	
298 Other non-organic psychoses	
298.3 Acute paranoid reaction	298.30 Acute paranoid disorder
298.4 Psychogenic paranoid psychosis	

It was pointed out earlier that the classification of paranoid states has given rise to controversy and confusion of thought. It is clear that these difficulties persist to the present day, since the DSM III manual states that 'the boundaries of this group of disorders (Paranoid Disorders) and their differentiation from such other disorders as severe paranoid personality disorder and schizophrenia, are unclear'.

In view of so much uncertainty, it is important to be clear about the usage of paranoid states. The authors of this book recommend that the term should be applied (as recommended by ICD 9) to paranoid conditions that are not associated with a primary organic, affective, or schizophrenic disorder. In this usage, paranoid state is a noncommittal category for cases that do not at the time meet the criteria for another disorder. The term implies that, with observation over time, the diagnosis may be revised to another category. The diagnosis of the primary disorders (organic, affective, schizophrenic) is dealt with in the corresponding chapters.

Paranoia and paraphrenia

These two terms have played a prominent part in psychiatric thought, and paranoia is still included in ICD 9 and DSM III. The authors of this book take the view that both terms are not only unsatisfactory but also unnecessary (as explained later), and therefore recommend that neither term should be used. However, much can be learnt from reviewing the conceptual difficulties associated with these terms. For this reason, their history will be traced in some detail, starting with paranoia.

The term **paranoia**, from which the modern adjective paranoid is derived, has a long and chequered history. It has probably given rise to more controversy and confusion of thought than any other term used in psychiatry. A comprehensive review of the large literature, which is mostly German, has been provided by Lewis (1970).

The term paranoia came into special prominence in the last quarter of the nineteenth century, but its origins are much older. The word paranoia is derived from the Greek *para* (beside) and *nous* (mind). It was used in ancient Greek literature to mean 'out of mind', that is, of unsound mind or insane. This broad usage was revived in the eighteenth century. However, in the mid-nineteenth century, German psychiatrists became interested in conditions that were particularly characterized by delusions of persecution and grandeur. The German term '*verrücktheit*' was often applied to these conditions, but eventually was superseded by paranoia. There were many different conceptions of these disorders. The main issues can be summarized as follows:

1. Did these conditions constitute a primary disorder, or were they secondary to a mood disorder or other disorder?
2. Did they persist unchanged for many years, or were they a stage in an illness which later manifested deterioration of intellect and personality?
3. Did they sometimes occur in the absence of hallucinations, or were hallucinations an invariable accompaniment?

As early as 1863 Kahlbaum raised these issues, when he classified paranoia as an independent or primary delusional condition, which would remain unchanged over the years.

Kraepelin had a strong influence on the conceptual history of paranoia, although he was never comfortable with the term, and his views changed strikingly over the years (see Kendler and Tsuang 1981). Eventually (Kraepelin 1912) he proposed paranoia as the insidious and permanent development of an unshakable delusional system, the personality remaining intact. It differed from dementia praecox in the preservation of clear and orderly thinking, of normal volition and normal social behaviour. In his final account, Kraepelin (1919) developed these ideas by distinguishing between dementia praecox, paranoia, and paraphrenia. Dementia praecox has an early onset and a poor outcome ending in mental deterioration, and was fundamentally a disturbance of affect and volition. Paranoia was restricted to patients with the late onset of completely systematized delusions, and a prolonged course usually without recovery but not inevitably deteriorating. An important point was that the patients did not have hallucinations. Kraepelin regarded paraphrenia as lying between dementia praecox and paranoia; in paraphrenia, the patient had unremitting systematized delusions, but did not progress to dementia. The main difference from paranoia was that the patient with paraphrenia had hallucinations.

Bleuler's concept of the paranoid form of dementia praecox (which he later called paranoia schizophrenia) was broader than Kraepelin's (Bleuler 1906, 1911). Thus Bleuler did not regard paraphrenia as a separate condition, but as part of dementia praecox. On the other hand he accepted Kraepelin's view of paranoia as a separate entity, but he differed from Kraepelin in maintaining that hallucinations could occur in many cases. Bleuler was particularly interested in the psychological development of paranoia; at the same time he left open the question of whether paranoia had a somatic pathology.

From this time, two main themes were prominent in the history of paranoia. The first theme was that paranoia was distinct from schizophrenia, and mainly psychogenic in origin. The second theme was that paranoia was part of schizophrenia.

Two celebrated studies of individual cases supported the first theme, the psychogenic origins of paranoid delusions. Gaupp (1914) made an intensive study of the diaries and mental state of the mass murderer Wagner who murdered his wife, four children, and eight other people, as part of a careful plan to revenge himself on his supposed enemies. Gaupp concluded that Wagner suffered from paranoia in the sense described by Kraepelin, as described above. At the same time, he believed that Wagner's first recognizable delusion developed as a psychogenic reaction. The second study, mentioned earlier in the chapter, was Freud's analysis of the memoirs of Schreber. Freud called this a case of paranoia, although Schreber's illness conformed much more to the clinical picture of schizophrenia than to any of the prevailing notions of paranoia.

The most detailed argument for psychogenesis was put forward by Kretschmer (1927) in his monograph, *Der Sensitive Beziehungwahn*. Kretschmer believed that paranoia should not be regarded as a disease, but as a psychogenic reaction occurring in people with particularly sensitive personalities. Many of Kretschmer's cases would nowadays be classified as suffering from schizophrenia.

In 1931, Kolle put forward evidence for the second theme, that paranoia is part of schizophrenia. He analysed a series of 66 patients, with so-called paranoia, including those diagnosed by Kraepelin in his Munich clinic. For several reasons, both symptomatic and genetic, Kolle came to the conclusion that so-called paranoia was really a mild form of schizophrenia.

Considerably less has been written about **paraphrenia**. However, it is interesting that Mayer (1921), following up Kraepelin's series of 78 paraphrenic patients, found that 50 of them had become schizophrenic. He found no difference in original clinical presentation between those who became schizophrenic and those who did not. Since then paraphrenia has usually been regarded as late onset schizophrenia of good prognosis. Kay and Roth (1961) used the term 'late paraphrenia' to denote paranoid conditions in the elderly which were not due to primary organic or affective illnesses. These authors found that a large majority of their 99 patients had the characteristic features of schizophrenia. Late paraphrenia is further discussed in the chapter on the elderly.

Modern usage

In ICD 9, **Paranoia** (297.1) is defined as follows:

a rare chronic psychosis in which logically constructed systematised delusions have developed gradually without concomitant hallucinations or the schizophrenic type of disordered thinking. The delusions are mostly of grandeur (the paranoiac prophet or inventor), persecution or somatic abnormality.

In DSM III, the definition is in similar terms, although hallucinations are specified as not prominent rather than absent. Clearly these modern definitions are much the same as those put forward by Kraepelin in 1912 and 1919, as outlined above.

The essence of the modern concept of paranoia is that of a permanent and unshakable delusional system, developing insidiously in a person in middle or late life. This delusional system is encapsulated, and there is no impairment of other mental functions. The patient can often go on working, and his social life may sometimes by maintained fairly well. It is interesting that this concept of paranoia has been preserved in the two main contemporary systems of classification, since in clinical practice cases conforming strictly to their definitions are never, or extremely rarely, encountered. It is for this reason that the authors of this book recommend that the term paranoia should not be retained.

The term **paraphrenia** does not appear in DSM III. According to ICD 9, Paraphrenia (297.2) is a 'paranoid psychosis in which there are conspicuous hallucinations, often in several modalities. Affective symptoms and disordered thinking, if present, do not dominate the clinical picture and the personality is well preserved'. This category includes involutional paranoid state, and **late paraphrenia**. Here again, the ICD 9 definition closely resembles Kraepelin's concept of paraphrenia as described above – that is, the late onset of systematized delusions, with preservation of personality and intellect, and with prominent hallucinations. The term is little used in modern psychiatric practice. The authors of this book do not recommend its use because it appears to denote a condition which can best be regarded as paranoid schizophrenia of late onset and good prognosis.

Other categories in ICD 9 and DSM III

ICD 9 category 297.3, **induced psychosis** is often referred to as *folie à deux*. In DSM III the corresponding category is 297.30, **shared paranoid disorder**. This rare condition is described in the next section.

The ICD has two categories for paranoid conditions that appear to be psychogenic in origin. The first category is 298.3 **acute paranoid reaction**, which is to be applied to paranoid conditions that occur acutely and apparently in response to a stressful situation, which is often construed as a threat or attack. The second category is 298.4, **psychogenic paranoid psychosis** which is to be applied to a paranoid reaction of any type which is more prolonged than the acute reaction just described. These two categories correspond to the paranoid subgroup of the reactive or psychogenic psychoses that are widely diagnosed in Scandinavia. Clinical experience shows that paranoid conditions sometimes appear to be reactions to stressful situations. However, there is nothing to be gained by classifying them on the basis of presumed aetiology rather than symptoms and course, and the authors do not recommend this practice.

Acute paranoid reactions (and the corresponding DSM III category of acute paranoid disorders) are said to be particularly likely in people experiencing drastic changes in their environment, such as migration or imprisonment. However, as explained in the next section, it has not been established that these life changes are specially associated with paranoid developments.

SPECIAL PARANOID CONDITIONS

Certain paranoid conditions are recognizable by their distinctive features. They can be divided into two groups – those with special symptoms and those occurring in special situations. The special symptoms include jealous, erotic, and querulant delusions and also the delusions associated with the names of Capgras and Fregoli. The special situations include intimate relationships (*folie à deux*), migration, and imprisonment. Many of these symptoms have been of particular interest to French psychiatrists (see Pichot 1982).

Among the conditions with special symptoms, pathological jealousy will be described first and in the greatest detail because of its importance in clinical practice. It is probably the most common, and is often dangerous.

Pathological jealousy

In pathological (or morbid) jealousy, the essential feature is a delusional belief that the marital partner is being unfaithful. The condition is called pathological because the belief is held on inadequate grounds and is unaffected by rational argument.

The delusion is often accompanied by strong emotions and characteristic behaviour, but these do not in themselves constitute pathological jealousy. A man who finds his wife in bed with a lover may experience extreme jealousy and may behave in an uncontrolled way, but this should not be called pathological jealousy. The term should only be used when the jealousy is based on unsound evidence and reasoning.

Pathological jealousy has often been described in the literature, generally in reports of one or two cases. Various names have been given to it, including sexual jealousy, erotic jealousy, morbid jealousy, psychotic jealousy, and the Othello syndrome. The main sources of information are surveys of patients with pathological jealousy carried out by Shepherd (1961), Langfeldt (1960), and Vauhkonen (1968). Shepherd examined hospital case notes of 81 patients in London, and Langfeldt did the same for 66 patients in Norway. Vauhkonen made an interview study of 55 patients in Finland.

The frequency of pathological jealousy in the general population is unknown. However the condition is not uncommon in psychiatric practice and most full-time clinicians probably see one or two cases a year. They merit careful attention, not only because of the great distress they cause within marriages and families, but also because they may be highly dangerous.

All the evidence suggests that pathological jealousy is commoner in men than women. In the three surveys mentioned above, the male to female ratios were: 3.76:1 (Shepherd); 1.46:1 (Langfeldt); and 2.05:1 (Vauhkonen).

Clinical features

As indicated above, the main feature is a delusional belief in the partner's infidelity. This may be accompanied by other delusions; for example, that the spouse is plotting against the patient, trying to poison him, taking away his sexual capacities, or infecting him with venereal disease.

The mood of the pathologically jealous patient may vary with the underlying disorder, but often it is a mixture of misery, apprehension, irritability, and anger.

The behaviour of the patient is often characteristic. Commonly there is intensive seeking for evidence of the partner's infidelity, for example by searching in diaries and correspondence, and by examining bed-linen and underwear for signs of sexual secretions. The patient may follow the spouse about, or engage a private detective to spy on her. Typically the jealous person cross-questions the spouse incessantly. This may lead to violent quarrelling and paroxysms of rage in the patient. Sometimes the partner becomes exasperated and worn out, and is finally goaded into making a false confession. If this happens, the jealousy is inflamed rather than assuaged.

An interesting feature is that the jealous person often has no idea as to who the supposed lover may be, or what kind of person he may be. Moreover, he may avoid taking steps that could produce unequivocal proof one way or the other.

The behaviour of patients with pathological jealousy may be strikingly abnormal. A successful City businessman carried a brief case that contained not only his financial documents but also a machette for use against any lover who might be detected. A carpenter installed an elaborate system of mirrors in his house so that he could watch his wife from another room. A third patient avoided waiting alongside another car at traffic lights, in case his wife in the passenger seat might surreptitiously make an assignation with the other driver.

Aetiology

In the three surveys described above, pathological jealousy was found to be associated with a range of primary disorders. The frequencies varied, depending on the population studied and the diagnostic scheme used. For example paranoid schizophrenia (or paranoia or paraphrenia) was reported in 17–44 per cent of patients; depressive illness in 3–16 per cent; neurosis and personality disorder in 38–57 per cent; alcoholism in 5–7 per cent; and organic disorders in 6–20 per cent. Primary organic causes include exogenous substances such as amphetamine and cocaine, but more commonly a wide range of brain disorders, including infections, neoplasms, metabolic and endocrine disorders, and degenerative conditions.

The role of personality in the genesis of pathological jealousy should be stressed. It is often found that the patient has a pervasive sense of his own inadequacy. There is a discrepancy between his ambitions and his attainments. Such a personality is particularly vulnerable to anything that may threaten this sense of inadequacy, such as loss of status or advancing age. In the face of such threats, the person may project the blame on to others, and this may take the form of jealous accusations of infidelity. As mentioned earlier, Freud believed that unconscious homosexual urges played a part in all jealousy, particularly the delusional kind. He held that this could occur when such urges were dealt with by repression, denial, and reaction formation. However, none of the three surveys mentioned above found any association between homosexuality and pathological jealousy.

Many writers have held that pathological jealousy may be induced by the onset of erectile difficulties in men or sexual dysfunction in women. In their surveys, Langfeldt and Shepherd found little or no evidence of such associations. Vauhkonen however reported sexual difficulties in over half the men and women in his series, but his sample was drawn partly from a marriage guidance clinic.

The prognosis depends on a number of factors, including the nature of any underlying psychiatric disorder, and the patient's premorbid personality. There is little statistical evidence on prognosis. Langfeldt followed up 27 of his patients after 17 years, and found that over half of them still had persistent or recurrent jealousy. This confirms a general clinical impression that the prognosis is often poor.

Risk of violence

Although there is no direct statistical evidence of the risks of violence in cases of pathological jealousy, there is no doubt that it can be highly dangerous. Mowat (1966) made a survey of homicidal patients admitted to Broadmoor hospital over several years, and found pathological jealousy amongst 12 per cent of men and 15 per cent of women. In Shepherd's series of 81 patients with pathological jealousy, three had shown homicidal tendencies. In addition to homicide, the risk of physical injury inflicted by jealous patients is undoubtedly considerable.

Assessment

The assessment of a patient with pathological jealousy should be painstaking and thorough. Full psychiatric assessment of the patient is essential and the spouse should be seen alone at first, and with the patient afterwards.

The spouse may give a much more detailed account of the patient's morbid beliefs and actions than can be elicited from the patient. The doctor should try to find out tactfully how firmly the patient believes in the partner's infidelity, how much resentment he feels, and whether he has contemplated any vengeful action. What factors provoke outbursts of resentment, accusation, and cross-questioning? How does the partner respond to such outbursts by the patient? How does the patient respond in turn to the partner's behaviour? Has there been any violence so far? If so, how was it inflicted? Has there been any serious injury?

In addition to these enquiries, the doctor should take a detailed marital and sexual history from both partners. It is also important to diagnose any underlying psychiatric disorder, as this will have implications for treatment.

Treatment

The treatment of pathological jealousy is often difficult, because the jealous person may regard it as obtrusive, and may show little compliance. Adequate treatment of any underlying disorder such as schizophrenia or affective illness is a first requisite. In cases where the underlying diagnosis is uncertain, a pheno-thiazine such as chlorpromazine may be beneficial.

Psychotherapy may be given to patients with neurotic or personality disorders. The aims may be to reduce tensions by allowing the patient (and spouse) to ventilate feelings. Behavioural methods have also been advocated (Cobb and Marks 1977). These include encouraging the partner to produce behaviour that reduces jealousy, for example by counter-aggression or refusal to argue, depending on the individual case.

If there is no response to out-patient treatment, or if the risk of violence is high, inpatient care may be necessary. Not uncommonly, however, the patient appears to improve as an inpatient, only to relapse on discharge.

If there appears to be a risk of violence, the doctor should warn the spouse. In some cases, the safest procedure is to advise separation. This is embodied in an old axiom that the best treatment for pathological jealousy is geographical.

Erotic delusions (De Clerambault's syndrome)

De Clerambault (1921) proposed that a distinction should be made between paranoid delusions and delusions of passion. The latter differed in their pathogenesis and in being accompanied by excitement. They also had a sense of purpose: 'patients in this category whether they display erotomania, litigious behaviour, or morbid jealousy all have a precise aim in view from the onset of the illness, which brings the will into play from the beginning. This constitutes a distinguishing feature of the illness'. This distinction is of historical interest only, as it is not made nowadays. However, the syndrome of erotomania is still known as de Clerambault's syndrome. It is exceedingly rare (see Enoch and Trethowan 1979 for further information).

In erotomania, the subject, usually a single woman, believes that an exalted person is in love with her. The supposed lover is usually inaccessible, being already married, of much higher social status, or famous as an entertainer or public figure. According to De Clerambault, the infatuated woman believes that it is the 'object' who first fell in love with her, that he is the more in love, or even the only one who is in love. She believes that she has been specially chosen by this man of high standing, and that it was not she who had made the initial advances. She derives satisfaction and pride from this belief. She is convinced that the 'object' cannot be happy or a complete person without her.

The patient often believes that the 'object' is unable to reveal his love for various reasons, that he is withheld from her, has difficulties in approaching her, has indirect conversations with her, and has to behave in a paradoxical and contradictory way. The woman may be a considerable nuisance to the 'object' who may complain to the police and the courts. Sometimes the patient's delusion remains unshakable, and she invents explanations for the 'object's' paradoxical behaviour. She may be extremely tenacious and impervious to reality. Other patients turn from a delusion of love to a delusion of persecution. They become abusive, and make public complaints about the 'object'. This was described by de Clerambault as two phases, hope followed by resentment.

Probably most patients with erotic delusions are suffering from paranoid schizophrenia; sometimes there is insufficient evidence to make a final diagnosis at the time.

Querulant delusions and reformist delusions

Querulant delusions were the subject of a special study by Krafft-Ebing in 1878. Patients with this kind of delusion indulge in a series of complaints and claims lodged against the authorities. Closely related to querulant patients are paranoid litigants who undertake a succession of lawsuits; they become involved in numerous court hearings, in which they may become passionately angry and make threats against the magistrates. Baruk (1959) described 'reformist delusions', which are centred on religious, philosophical, or political themes. People with these delusions constantly criticize society, and sometimes embark on elaborate courses of action. Their behaviour may be violent, particularly when the delusions are political. Some political assassins fall within this group. It is extremely important that this diagnosis is made on clear psychiatric grounds rather than political grounds (see Bloch and Chodoff 1981).

Capgras delusion

Although there had been previous case reports, the condition now known as Capgras syndrome was well described by Capgras and Reboul-Lachaux in 1923, who called it *l'illusion des sosies* (illusion of doubles). Strictly speaking it is not a syndrome but a single symptom, and it is better termed the *delusion* (rather than illusion) of doubles. The patient believes that a person closely related to him has been replaced by a double. He accepts that the misidentified person has a great resemblance to the familiar person, but still believes they are different people. It is an extremely rare condition. It is more common in women than in men and is usually associated with schizophrenia or affective disorder. A history of depersonalization, derealization or *déjà vu* is common. The misidentified person is usually the patient's spouse or another relative. It is said that in most cases there is strong evidence of an organic component as shown by the clinical features, psychological testing, and radiological studies of the brain (see Christodoulou 1977).

Fregoli delusion

This is usually referred to as the Fregoli syndrome, and derives its name from an actor called Fregoli who had remarkable skill in changing his facial appearance. The condition is even rarer than the Capgras delusion. It was originally described by Courbon and Fail in 1927. The patient identifies a familiar person (usually someone he believes to be his persecutor) in various other people he encounters. He maintains that, although there is no physical resemblance between the familiar person and the others, nevertheless they are psychologically identical. This symptom is usually associated with schizophrenia. Here again the clinical features, psychological testing, and radiological examination of the brain suggest an organic component in the aetiology (Christodoulou 1976).

PARANOID CONDITIONS OCCURRING IN SPECIAL SITUATIONS

An account will now be given of these conditions, beginning with induced psychosis.

Induced psychosis (*folie à deux*)

An induced psychosis is a paranoid delusional system which appears to have developed in a person as a result of a close relationship with another person who already has an established and similar delusional system. The delusions are nearly always persecutory. The frequency of induced psychosis is not known, but it is rare. Sometimes more than two people are involved, but this is exceedingly rare.

The condition has occasionally been described in two people who are not family relations, but 90 per cent or more of reported cases are members of the same family. Usually there is a dominant partner with fixed delusions who appears to induce similar delusions in a dependent or suggestible partner, sometimes after initial resistance. Generally the two have lived together for a long time in close intimacy, often in isolation from the outside world. Once established, the condition runs a chronic course.

Induced psychosis is more common in women than in men. Gralnick (1942) studied a series of patients with *folie à deux* and found the following combinations in order of frequency: two sisters, 40; husband and wife, 26; mother and child, 24; two brothers, 11; brother and sister, 6; father and child, 2; not related, 9.

The principles of treatment are the same as for other paranoid conditions (p. 290). It is usually necessary to advise separation of the affected people. This sometimes leads to disappearance of the delusional state but not invariably, improvement being more likely in the recipient than in the inducer. Induced psychosis is comprehensively reviewed by Enoch and Trethowan (1979).

Migration psychoses

It might be expected that people migrating to foreign countries would be likely to develop paranoid symptoms because their appearance, speech, and behaviour attract attention to them. Ødegaard (1932) found that rates for schizophrenia (including paranoid schizophrenia) were twice as high amongst Norwegian-born immigrants to the United States as amongst the general population of Norway. However, the explanation of the finding appeared to be not so much that emigration was a pathogenic experience as that pre-psychotic Norwegians were more likely than others to emigrate. Astrup and Ødegaard (1960) later found that hospital first admission rates for psychotic illness in general were significantly lower amongst people who had migrated inside their own country than amongst those who stayed where they were born. The authors suggested that migration within one's own country might be a natural step for enterprising young people, whilst migrating abroad was likely to be a much more stressful experience. To this extent they favoured the environmental hypothesis.

Studies of immigrants are difficult to interpret. If one controls for factors such as age, social class, occupational status, and ethnic group, it becomes doubtful whether there is a significant association between migration and rates of mental illness (Murphy 1977). The highest rates of mental disorder have been reported in refugees whose migration was enforced (Eitinger 1960). However, such people may have been exposed to persecution, in addition to the experiences of losing their homeland and readjusting to another country.

Prison psychosis

The evidence about imprisonment is conflicting. The work of Birnbaum (1908) suggests that isolation in prison and especially solitary confinement may lead to paranoid disorders that clear up when the prisoners are allowed to mix with others. Eitinger (1960) reported that paranoid states were not uncommon in prisoners of war. However, Faergeman (1963) concluded that such developments were rare even amongst the inmates of concentration camps.

Cultural psychoses

It appears that in some developing countries there is a high incidence of transient and acute psychotic states, in which paranoid features commonly occur. Some of these acute states may be due to organic causes, such as tropical infections. Because of the conditions of observation, information about these disorders is incomplete. A useful review has been provided by Leff (1981).

PARANOID SYMPTOMS: ASSESSMENT AND DIAGNOSIS

In the assessment of paranoid symptoms there are two stages, the recognition of the symptoms themselves and the diagnosis of the underlying condition.

Sometimes it is obvious to everyone that the patient has persecutory ideas or delusions. At other times recognition of paranoid symptoms may be exceedingly difficult. The patient may be suspicious or angry. He may offer little speech, simply staring silently at the interviewer, or he may talk fluently and convincingly about other things, whilst steering away from delusional ideas or beliefs, or denying them completely. Considerable skill may be needed to elicit the false beliefs. The psychiatrist should be tolerant and impartial. He should present himself as a detached but interested listener, who wants to understand the patient's point of view. He should show compassion and ask how he can help, but without colluding in the delusions or giving promises that cannot be fulfilled. Tact is required to avoid any argument which may cause the patient to take offence. Despite skill and tact, experienced psychiatrists may interview a patient for a long time without detecting the morbid thoughts.

If apparently false beliefs are disclosed, before concluding that they are delusions, it may be necessary to check the patient's statements against those of an informant and to ensure that the patient has had an opportunity to recognize the falsity of his beliefs. As with all apparent delusions, they must be judged against the cultural background, since the patient may hold a false belief which is generally held by his own group.

If paranoid delusions are detected, the next step is to diagnose the underlying psychiatric disorder. This means looking for the diagnostic features of organic mental states, schizophrenia and affective disorders, which are described in other chapters.

It is important to determine whether any persecutory or jealous delusions are likely to make the patient behave dangerously, by trying to kill or injure his supposed persecutor. This calls for close study of the patient's personality and the characteristics of his delusions and any associated hallucinations. Hints or threats of homicide should be taken seriously, in the same way as for suicide. The doctor should be prepared to ask tactfully about possible homicidal plans and preparations to enact them. In many ways the method of enquiry resembles the assessment of suicide risk, 'have you ever thought of doing anything about it?' 'Have you made any plans?' 'What might prompt you to do it?'

Sometimes a patient with persecutory delusions does not know the identity of a supposed persecutor, but may still be dangerous. For example an overseas visitor in his early twenties was seen in a psychiatric emergency clinic. Careful enquiry revealed that he believed that unidentified conspirators were trying to kill him, and that his life was in imminent danger. When asked if he had taken any steps to protect himself, he said he had made a brief trip to Brussels to buy a pistol, which he was now carrying. When asked what he might do with the gun, he said he was waiting until 'the voices' told him to shoot someone.

The assessment of dangerousness is further discussed in Chapter 22. The most reliable guideline is that the risk of violence is greatest in patients with a history of previous violence.

THE TREATMENT OF PATIENTS WITH PARANOID SYMPTOMS

In the management of patients with paranoid symptoms, both psychological and physical measures should be considered.

Psychological management is frequently difficult. The patient may be suspicious and distrustful, and may believe that psychiatric treatment is intended to harm him. Even if he is not suspicious, he is likely to regard his delusional beliefs as justified, and to see no need for treatment. Considerable tact and skill are needed to persuade patients with paranoid symptoms to accept treatment. Sometimes this can be done by offering to help non-specific symptoms, such as anxiety or insomnia. Thus a patient who believes that he is surrounded by persecutors may agree that his nerves are being strained as a result, and that this nervous strain needs treatment.

It is usually necessary at an early stage to decide whether to admit the patient for in-patient care. This may be indicated if the delusions are causing aggressive behaviour or social difficulties. In assessing such factors, it is usually best to consult other informants, and to obtain a history of the patient's behaviour in the past. If voluntary admission is refused, compulsory admission is often justified to protect the patient or other people, although this is likely to add to the patient's resentment.

During treatment the psychiatrist should strive to maintain a good relationship. He should be dependable, and should avoid provoking resentment by letting the patient down. He should show compassionate interest in the patient's beliefs, but without condemning them or colluding in them.

Patients with paranoid delusions may be helped by psychological support, encouragement, and assurance. Interpretative psychotherapy and group psychotherapy are unsuitable because suspiciousness and hypersensitivity may easily lead the patient to misinterpret what is being said.

Treatment by medication may be indicated for a primary psychiatric illness, such as schizophrenia, affective disorder, or an organic mental state. In paranoid states with no detectable primary disorder, symptoms are sometimes relieved by antipsychotic medication, such as trifluoperazine, chlorpromazine, thioridazine, or haloperidol, the choice of drug and dosage depending on the patient's age, physical condition, degree of agitation, and response to previous medication. Probably the commonest reason for failure of treatment is that patients do not take their medication because they suspect it will harm them. It may then be necessary to prescribe a long-acting preparation such as fluphenazine decanoate. In some patients the dosage can be reduced or stopped later without ill-effects, whilst in others it must be maintained for long periods of time. This can only be discovered by trial and error.

FURTHER READING

Hirsch, S.R. and Shepherd, M. (eds) (1974). *Themes and variations in European psychiatry.* John Wright, Bristol. See following sections: Strömgren, E. Psychogenic psychoses; Gaup, R. The scientific significance of the case of Ernst Wagner; and The illness and death of the paranoid mass murderer schoolmaster Wagner: a case history; Kretschmer, E. The sensitive delusion of reference; Baruk, H. Delusions of passion; Ey, H., Barnard, P. and Brisset, C. Acute delusional psychoses (Bouffées délirantes).

Kendler, K.S. and Tsuang, M.T. (1981). Nosology of paranoid schizophrenia and other paranoid psychoses. *Schizophrenia Bulletin* 7, 594–610.

Lewis, A. (1970). Paranoia and paranoid: a historical perspective. *Psychological Medicine* **1**, 2–12.
Shepherd, M. (1961). Morbid jealousy: some clinical and social aspects of a psychiatric symptom. *Journal of Mental Science* **107**, 687–753.

11. Organic psychiatry

The term 'organic psychiatry' is applied to a diverse group of topics that are only loosely related to one another. First and foremost, the term is used to denote psychiatric disorders that arise from demonstrable structural disease of the brain, such as brain tumours, injuries, or degenerations. Secondly, it is applied to psychiatric disorders that arise from brain dysfunction which is clearly caused by disease outside the brain, such as myxoedema. By convention, the term also includes epilepsy, which is sometimes but not always associated with psychiatric disorder, and which may or may not be associated with a structural lesion in the brain. Finally, sleep disorders are generally included in organic psychiatry.

By convention, organic psychiatry excludes mental retardation, even though the latter is sometimes associated with demonstrable brain disease. Also excluded are the various biochemical disorders, such as disturbances of catecholamine metabolism, which may be present in a number of psychiatric syndromes. These biochemical disorders are referred to elsewhere in this book as mediating mechanisms.

This chapter is divided into three main parts. The first part describes the main organic psychiatric syndromes encountered in psychiatric practice and outlines the principles of assessment and treatment of these syndromes. It is recommended that the reader give detailed attention to this part of the chapter at an early stage.

The second part reviews the specific physical conditions that give rise to the psychiatric syndromes described in part one. Inevitably these conditions are numerous and diverse. It may be advisable for the reader to cover them quickly at a first reading, and to refer to them again in detail as they are met in clinical practice.

Part three deals with epilepsy and sleep disorders.

Additional information on all these topics can be found in the valuable textbook on organic psychiatry by Lishman (1978a). Reference to a textbook of neurology is also recommended (for example Walton 1977, or Matthews and Miller 1977).

I. Organic psychiatric syndromes

Organic psychiatric syndromes can be subdivided on three criteria. The first criterion is whether the impairment of psychological functioning is generalized or specific. Generalized impairment affects cognition, mood, and behaviour globally. Specific impairment affects just one or two functions, such as memory, thinking, perception, or mood.

The second criterion is whether the syndrome is acute or chronic. As explained below, the clinical features of an acute syndrome may differ radically from those of a chronic syndrome.

The third criterion is whether the underlying dysfunction of the brain is generalized or focal. Generalized dysfunction of the brain may result, for example, from raised intra-cranial pressure, whereas focal dysfunction may arise from a tumour in the temporal lobe (though such a lesion may also cause generalized dysfunction).

In this chapter, organic psychiatric syndromes are divided into three simple groups: acute generalized psychological impairment; chronic generalized psychological impairment; and specific psychological impairment. It can be seen that these groups are based on the first two criteria above.

The first group (acute generalized psychological impairment) is usually referred to as the *acute organic psychiatric syndrome* (or some similar term). In the United States it is called delirium. The most important clinical feature is impairment of consciousness. The underlying brain dysfunction is generalized, and the primary cause is often outside the brain; for example, anoxia due to respiratory failure.

The second group (chronic generalized psychological impairment) is often referred to as the *chronic organic psychiatric syndrome*, or as *dementia*. The main clinical feature is generalized intellectual impairment, but there are also changes in mood and behaviour. The underlying brain dysfunction is generalized. The primary cause is usually within the brain, and often a degenerative condition, such as Alzheimer's disease.

The third group (specific psychological impairment) may take the form of a specific impairment of memory, thinking, perception, or mood. It may also include personality change or a schizophrenia-like picture. In some of these conditions, but not all, focal lesions in the brain can be demonstrated.

Each of these three groups will be described in turn. Afterwards, an outline will be given of the ICD-9 and DSM III classifications of organic disorders, which are more complicated than the simple grouping given here.

ACUTE ORGANIC PSYCHIATRIC SYNDROMES

These syndromes are characterized by impairment of consciousness. They are common accompaniments of physical illness, occurring in about 5 to 15 per cent of patients in general medical or surgical wards, and about 20 to 30 per cent of patients in surgical intensive care units (Lipowski 1980). Most cases recover quickly, so despite their frequency only a few are seen by psychiatrists.

Historical background

In the past the word 'delirium' was used in two ways. Until the early nineteenth century it was generally used to denote a disorder of thinking. Later it was used to denote an organic brain disorder with impaired consciousness and the associated symptoms (see Berrios 1981 for a review).

In 1909 Karl Bonhoeffer, professor of psychiatry in Berlin, defined delirium as the stereotyped manifestation of acute brain failure. He proposed several different 'exogenous reactions' – or distinct psychiatric syndromes resulting from the effects of agents or disorders outside the brain. These proposed reactions included delirium, hallucinosis, epileptic excitement, twilight state, and amentia (which in Bonhoeffer's scheme meant a syndrome of incoherent thinking). Since the early part of the twentieth century, the last three syndromes have been discarded; the first two have been retained, but are now applied to the effects of both cerebral and extracerebral disorders.

Nowadays the term delirium is unsatisfactory because it is ambiguous. Some writers, including the authors of DSM III, use it as a synonym for an acute organic psychiatric syndrome, whilst others use it more narrowly to denote a particular combination of impaired consciousness and intrusive abnormalities of mood and perception (see for example Lishman 1978*a*). For this reason, the authors avoid the term.

The term confusional state has also been applied to acute organic psychiatric syndromes. This term is also unsatisfactory because the word confusion properly refers to muddled thinking. The latter is an important symptom of acute organic disorders, but is not confined to them. It is unsatisfactory to name a syndrome by a symptom of low specificity.

Clinical features

The most important feature is impairment of consciousness, though it is not always the most obvious. It often varies in intensity through the day and is usually worse at night. It is recognized by slowness, poor concentration, and uncertainty about the time of day. Lishman (1978*a*) has summarized the main features as: 'slight impairment of thinking, attending, perceiving, and remembering, in other words as mild global impairment of cognitive processes in association with reduced awareness of the environment'. Occasionally it is difficult to establish whether consciousness is impaired. After recovery, memory is poor for the period of impaired consciousness, a point which may allow retrospective diagnosis in previously doubtful cases.

Apart from impaired consciousness, the other features vary widely between different patients, and in the same patient at different times. The features are often influenced by the patient's personality; for example, ideas of persecution are more likely in a person who is habitually suspicious and touchy. Lipowski (1980) distinguished two patterns of presentation: in the first, the patient is restless and oversensitive to stimuli, and has psychotic symptoms; in the second, he is lethargic and quiet, and has few psychotic symptoms.

The patient's **behaviour,** as Lipowski's distinction implies, may take the form of overactivity, irritability, and noisiness; or else of inactivity, slowness, reduced speech, and perseveration. In either case, repetitive purposeless movements are common.

Thinking is slow and muddled but often rich in content. Ideas of reference and delusions (often persecutory) are common, but are usually transient and poorly elaborated.

Visual perception may be distorted. Illusions, misinterpretations, and visual hallucinations are frequent, and may have a fantastic content. Tactile and auditory hallucinations also occur.

Changes in **mood** such as anxiety, depression, or lability are common. Some patients are perplexed, whilst others are frightened and agitated. Experiences of depersonalization and derealization are also reported by some patients. **Disorientation** in time and place is an invariable and important feature. Disturbance of **memory** affects registration, retention, and recall, and new learning is impaired. As mentioned above, on recovery there is usually amnesia for most of the illness. **Insight** is impaired.

Aetiology

The main causes of the acute organic syndrome are shown in Table 11.1. The condition appears particularly in association with: increasing age; anxiety; sensory under- or overstimulation; drug dependence; and brain damage of any kind. Wolff and Curran (1935) showed that the clinical picture, as noted above, is much influenced by previous experience and personality. Engel and Romano (1959) showed that the severity of the clinical state was related to the degree of impairment of brain function as reflected by abnormal rhythms in the EEG.

Table 11.1. *Some causes of the acute organic syndrome*

1. Drug intoxication
   e.g. anticholinergic, anxiolytic-hypnotic, anticonvulsant, digitalis, opiates, laevo-dopa, also some industrial poisons

2. Withdrawal of alcohol and drugs
   alcohol; anxiolytic-sedatives

3. Metabolic failures
   uraemia, liver failure, respiratory failure, cardiac failure; disorders of electrolyte balance

4. Endocrine causes: hypoglycaemia

5. Systemic infection:
   e.g. exanthemata, septicaemia, pneumonia

6. Intracranial infection
   encephalitis, meningitis

7. Other intracranial causes
   space occupying lesions, raised intracranial pressure

8. Head injury

9. Nutritional and viatamin deficiency
   thiamine, nicotinic acid, B_{12}

10. Epileptic:
    epileptic status, post-ictal states

The assessment, diagnosis, and treatment of acute organic psychiatric syndromes are described later in this chapter.

DEMENTIA

Dementia is a generalized impairment of intellect, memory, and personality, with no impairment of consciousness. It is an acquired disorder, as distinct from amentia which is present from birth. Although most cases of dementia are irreversible, a small but important group are remediable.

Clinical features

Dementia usually presents with impairment of memory. Other features include change in personality, mood disorder, hallucinations, and delusions. Though dementia generally develops gradually, it often comes to notice after an exacerbation caused by either a change in social circumstances or an intercurrent illness.

Again the clinical picture is much determined by the patient's premorbid personality. For example, in some patients, neurotic traits become exaggerated. People with good social skills may maintain a social facade despite severe intellectual deterioration, whilst those who are socially isolated or deaf are less likely to compensate for failing intellectual abilities.

Behaviour is often muddled, inappropriate, distractable, and restless. There are few signs of interest or initiative. Changes in personality may manifest as antisocial behaviour, which sometimes includes sexual disinhibition or shoplifting. In middle aged or elderly people any social lapse that is out of character should always suggest an organic cause.

Goldstein (see 1975) described the ways in which behaviour can be affected by the cognitive defects. Typically there is a reduction of interests ('shrinkage of the milieu'), rigid and stereotyped routines ('organic orderliness') and, when the person is taxed beyond restricted abilities, a sudden explosion of anger or other emotion ('catastrophic reaction').

As dementia worsens patients care for themselves less well and neglect social conventions. Behaviour becomes aimless, and stereotypies and mannerisms may appear. Eventually, the patient becomes disorientated, incoherent, and incontinent of urine and faeces.

Thinking slows and becomes impoverished in content. There may be concrete thinking, reduced flexibility, and perseveration. Judgement is impaired. False ideas, often of a persecutory kind, gain ground easily. In the later stages thinking becomes grossly fragmented and incoherent. Disturbed thinking is reflected in the quality of **speech**, in which syntactical errors and nominal dysphasia are common. Eventually the patient may utter only meaningless noises or become mute.

In the early stages, changes of **mood** may include anxiety, irritability, and depression. As dementia progresses emotions and responses to events become blunted, and sudden mood changes may occur without apparent cause.

Disorders of **cognitive function** are salient features. Forgetfulness is usually early and prominent, but may sometimes be difficult to detect in the early stages. Difficulty in new learning is generally the most conspicuous sign. Memory loss is more obvious for recent than for remote events. Patients often make excuses to hide these memory defects, and some confabulate. Other cognitive defects include impaired attention and concentration. Disorientation for time, and at a later stage for place and person, is almost invariable once dementia is well established.

Insight is lacking into the degree and nature of the disorder.

Aetiology

Dementia has many causes, of which the most important are listed in Table 11.2. The aetiology of dementia in the elderly is discussed separately in Chapter 16. Among elderly patients degenerative and vascular causes predominate, but at

Table 11.2. *Some causes of dementia*

Degenerative	Senile dementia,* Alzheimer's disease, Pick's disease, Huntington's chorea, Parkinson's disease, Jacob–Creutzfeld disease, † normal pressure hydrocephalus, ‡ multiple sclerosis
Intracranial space occupying lesions	Tumour, subdural haematoma
Traumatic	Severe single head injuries, repeated head injury in boxers and others
Infections and related conditions	Encephalitis of any cause, neurosyphilis, cerebral sarcoidosis
Vascular	Multi-infarct dementia, occlusion of the carotid artery, cranial arteritis
Metabolic	Sustained uraemia, liver failure, remote effects of carcinoma or lymphoma; renal dialysis
Toxic	Alcohol, poisoning with heavy metals (lead, arsenic, thallium)
Anoxia	Anaemia, post-anaesthesia, carbon monoxide, cardiac arrest, chronic respiratory failure
Vitamin lack	Sustained lack of B_{12}, folic acid, thiamine

*See Chapter 16.
†Possibly infective, see p. 314.
‡Cause uncertain, see text.

other ages no sub-groups predominate. The clinician should therefore keep in mind the whole range of causes when assessing a patient, and should take care not to miss any that might be partly or wholly arrested by treatment, such as an operable cerebral neoplasm, cerebral syphilis, or normal pressure hydrocephalus.

Individual causes in the list should be familiar to the reader from general medical training. If necessary, a textbook of medicine should be consulted. Several of the conditions listed (including Alzheimer's disease) are described in detail later in this chapter.

The assessment, diagnosis and treatment of dementia are also discussed later.

So far the two main generalized organic psychiatric syndromes (acute and chronic) have been described. An account will now be given of the third group of syndromes, in which there is impairment of specific psychological functions.

ORGANIC PSYCHIATRIC SYNDROMES WITH SPECIFIC PSYCHOLOGICAL DYSFUNCTIONS

In this group, as explained earlier, psychological impairment is partial rather than general; that is, a limited number of specific functions are affected, such as memory, thinking, perception, or mood. Affective syndromes occur, depressive disorders being more common than mania. A schizophrenia-like syndrome can arise in association with brain disease (described later in this chapter). Personality disorder is another highly important complication, (also described later).

In some of these conditions, but not all, focal lesions in the brain are demonstrable. Examples will now be given of syndromes due to focal brain damage, starting with the amnesic syndrome, which is the most distinctive.

The amnesic syndrome

The amnesic (or amnestic) syndrome is characterized by a prominent disorder of recent memory and by disordered time-sense, in the absence of generalized intellectual impairment. The psychological disorder has been reviewed by Hirst (1982). The condition usually results from lesions in the posterior hypothalamus and nearby midline structures, but occasionally it is due to bilateral hippocampal lesions.

Korsakov, a Russian neuropsychiatrist, described a chronic syndrome in which memory deficit was accompanied by confabulation and irritability (Korsakov 1889). His patients also suffered from peripheral neuropathy. They either abused alcohol or developed the syndrome in association with puerperal sepsis or an infection causing persistent vomiting. It is therefore likely that they were suffering from thiamine deficiency. Nowadays peripheral neuropathy is not regarded as an essential feature of the amnesic syndrome, and vitamin deficiency is not regarded as the only cause.

The term Korsakov's syndrome is often used. This term is used in two ways: first, in a narrower sense, to describe cases associated with thiamine deficiency; secondly, in a wider sense, to include all cases with a pathology similar to that of thiamine deficiency cases, irrespective of cause. It is not generally used for cases with bilateral hippocampal lesions. To add to the complexity of the nomenclature, the term Wernicke-Korsakov syndrome is sometimes used, for example by Victor *et al.* (1971). This term is used because the chronic amnesic syndrome often follows an acute neurological syndrome described by Wernicke in 1881. The main features of this acute syndrome are impairment of consciousness, memory defect, disorientation, ataxia, and opthalmoplegia. At post-mortem examination Wernicke found haemorrhagic lesions in the grey matter around the third and fourth ventricles and the aqueduct. More recent investigation has shown that lesions occur in these same anatomical sites in both the acute Wernicke syndrome and the chronic Korsakov syndrome.

In ICD 9, the term Korsakov's psychosis (rather than Korsakov's syndrome) is used to denote 'a prominent and lasting reduction of memory span, including striking loss of recent memory, disordered time appreciation and confabulation'. The condition is coded as either alcoholic (291.1) or non-alcoholic (294.0), and ICD 9 states that the alcoholic form is usually accompanied by peripheral neuropathy. In DSM III the term Korsakov's disease (rather than Korsakov's syndrome) is used for the amnesic syndrome associated with alcoholism; whilst the term amnestic syndrome is used for any other amnesic syndrome.

The authors recommend that the eponym is best avoided. The term amnesic syndrome should be used, because less ambiguous. If there is confabulation, this can be specified additionally. Similarly, there is no need for a special nomenclature based on aetiology, such as alcoholism; the latter can be specified additionally.

Clinical features

The central feature of the amnesic syndrome is a profound impairment of recent memory. The patient can recall events immediately after they occur, but cannot do so a few minutes or hours afterwards. Thus on a test of digit span, recall is good in the first few seconds, but impaired ten minutes later. New learning is grossly defective, but remote memory is relatively preserved. There is some evidence that the disorder may not be entirely an inability to lay down memories, but may also be a failure to recall established memories – possibly because of interference from irrelevant memories (Warrington and Weiskrantz 1970). One consequence of this profound disorder of memory is an associated disorientation in time.

Gaps in memory are often filled by confabulating. The patient may give a vivid and detailed account of recent activities all of which, on checking, turn out to be inaccurate. It is as though he cannot distinguish between true memories and the products of his imagination or the recollection of events from times other than those he is trying to recall. Such a patient is often suggestible; in response to a few cues from the interviewer, he may give an elaborate account of taking part in events that never happened. Confabulation is not a feature of the amnesic syndrome associated with bilateral hippocampal lesions.

Other cognitive functions are relatively well preserved. The patient seems alert and able to reason or hold an ordinary conversation, so that the interviewer is often surprised when the extent of the memory disorder is revealed. However, the disorder is not limited entirely to memory; some emotional blunting and lack of volition are often observed as well.

The diagnosis of amnesic syndrome tends to be made wrongly in cases that are really alcoholic dementia – which is of course a generalized impairment of cognitive function (Cutting 1979).

Aetiology and pathology

Alcohol abuse, the most frequent cause, seems to act by causing a deficiency of thiamine. Several other causes also seem to act through thiamine deficiency; for example, gastric carcinoma and severe dietary deficiency. As mentioned above, Korsakov described cases due to persistent vomiting in puerperal sepsis and typhoid fever, but these diseases are rarely seen today. At post mortem such cases generally have haemorrhagic lesions in the mamillary bodies, the region of the third ventricle, the periaqueductal grey matter, and parts of certain thalamic nuclei. The mamillary bodies (Brierly 1966) or the medial dorsal nucleus of the thalamus (Victor 1964) are the structures most often involved.

Other causes involve the brain directly and not through thiamine deficiency. The brain areas listed above may be damaged by vascular lesions, carbon monoxide poisoning, or encephalitis; and by tumours in the third ventricle. Another cause is bilateral hippocampal damage due to surgery. When the syndrome is due to causes other than thiamine deficiency, patients seem less likely to show confabulation and more likely to retain insight into the memory disorder.

Course and prognosis

Victor *et al.* (1971) studied 245 patients who had developed an acute Wernicke–Korsakov syndrome, most of whom had histories of many years of alcohol abuse. There was a 17 per cent death rate in the acute stage. All except 4 per cent of cases presented with Wernicke's encephalopathy. Eighty four per cent of those who were followed up developed a typical amnesic syndrome. Once established there was no improvement in a half, complete recovery in a quarter and partial recovery in the rest (see also Cutting 1978 *a, b*).

Rarely an improvement occurs in cases due to causes other than alcoholism; for example carbon monoxide poisoning or thiamine deficiency due to simple malnutrition. Sometimes the amnesia is progressive, as in cases with slowly expanding brain tumours.

Other psychiatric syndromes due to focal brain damage

An account will now be given of other 'focal' syndromes that are relevant to psychiatry. The many forms of dysphasia, agnosia and dyspraxia will not be described, as they are part of neurology; they are to be found in the textbook on organic psychiatry by Lishman (1978) or one of the standard textbooks of neurology.

Frontal lobe syndrome

Frontal lobe damage has distinctive effects on temperament and behaviour which are generally referred to as personality change. In **behaviour** the patient is disinhibited, over-familiar, tactless, and over-talkative. He makes jokes and engages in pranks (a feature sometimes referred to in the literature by the German word *Witzelsucht*). He may make errors of judgement, commit sexual indiscretions, and disregard the feelings of others. The **mood** is generally one of fatuous euphoria. **Concentration** and **attention** are reduced. Measures of formal intelligence are generally unimpaired, but special testing may show deficits in abstract reasoning. **Insight** is impaired.

Encroachment of a frontal lobe lesion on the motor cortex or deep projections may result in contra-lateral spastic paresis or dysphasia. Other possible signs are optic atrophy on the same side as the frontal lobe lesion, anosmia, a grasp reflex, and, if the lesion is bilateral, incontinence of urine (see Blumer and Benson 1975 for further information about personality change after frontal lobe injury).

Parietal lobe

Compared with lesions of the frontal or temporal lobe, lesions of the parietal lobe are less likely to induce psychiatric changes (Lishman 1978), but they do cause various neuropsychological disturbances which are easily mistaken for hysteria. Lesions of the non-dominant parietal lobe cause visuo-spatial difficulties. Lesions of the dominant lobe are associated with dysphasia, motor and dressing apraxias, right–left disorientation, finger agnosia, and agraphia (see p. 26). These clinical features present in various combinations, some of which are designated as syndromes (see a textbook of neurology). If these conditions are not to be misdiagnosed, thorough neurological assessment is required. Important signs may include cortical sensory loss and sensory inattention and agraphaesthesia. There may also be evidence of a mild contra-lateral hemiparesis.

Temporal lobe

Although some temporal lobe lesions are asymptomatic, there is usually impairment of intellectual function especially with a lesion on the dominant side. There may be personality change resembling that of frontal lobe lesions, though more often accompanied by intellectual deficits and neurological signs. With chronic temporal lobe lesions another kind of personality change is characterized by emotional instability and aggressive behaviour.

Temporal lobe lesions may cause epilepsy, and also an increased risk of a schizophrenia-like psychosis (see p. 341). Unilateral temporal lobe lesions produce specific learning impairments (in right-handed people verbal on the left, non-verbal on the right). Rare bilateral lesions of medial temporal lobe structures can produce an amnesic syndrome. An important neurological sign of a deep temporal lobe lesion is a contra-lateral homonymous upper quandrantic visual field defect due to interference with the visual radiation. Sometimes a deep lesion causes a mild contralateral hemiparesis. Dominant lesions may produce language difficulties.

Occipital lobe

Occipital lobe lesions may cause complex disturbances of visual recognition which are easily misdiagnosed as hysterical. Complex visual hallucinations can also occur and may be mistaken for signs of non-organic mental illness. The visual fields should be examined thoroughly and tests carried out for visual agnosias.

The corpus callosum

Corpus callosum lesions typically extend laterally into both hemispheres. They then produce a picture of severe and rapid intellectual deterioration, with localized neurological signs varying with the degree of extension into the frontal or occipital lobes or the diencephalon.

Diencephalon and brain stem

With lesions of mid-line structures, the most characteristic features are the amnesic syndrome, hypersomnia and the syndrome of 'akinetic mutism'. There may also be progressive intellectual deterioration; emotional lability with euphoria and abrupt outbursts of temper; excessive eating; and endocrine signs of pituitary disorder.

INTERNATIONAL CLASSIFICATIONS OF ORGANIC PSYCHIATRIC DISORDERS

In ICD 9, four main categories are used, as shown in Table 11.3. Category 290, Senile and presenile organic psychotic conditions, corresponds approximately to the chronic organic psychiatric syndrome described above. Similarly Category 293, Transient organic psychotic conditions, corresponds broadly to the acute organic psychiatric syndrome described earlier. Category 294, Other organic psychotic conditions, includes Korsakov's psychosis or syndrome (reviewed above under the amnesic syndrome), together with dementia secondary to known causes. Finally Category 310, Specific nonpsychotic mental disorders following organic brain damage, includes the frontal lobe syndrome, cognitive or personality change of other type, and the postconcussional syndrome.

In DSM III the approach is substantially different. First a distinction is made between **organic brain syndromes** and **organic mental disorders**. The first term is used to refer to a group of symptoms and signs without any reference to

Table 11.3. *Classification of organic psychiatric disorders*

(a) **ICD 9**

    290   Senile and presenile organic psychotic conditions
    293   Transient organic psychotic conditions
    294   Other chronic organic psychotic conditions
    310   Specific non-psychotic mental disorders following organic brain damage

(b) **DSM III**

    Organic brain syndromes
    Delirium and dementia
    Amnestic syndrome and organic hallucinosis
    Organic delusional syndrome and organic affective syndrome
    Organic personality syndrome
    Intoxication with and withdrawal of drugs

    Organic mental disorders
    Dementia arising in the senium and presenium
    Primary degenerative dementia
    Multi-infarct dementia
    Substance induced mental disorder

aetiology; the second term designates a particular organic brain syndrome in which the aetiology is 'known or presumed'. The two terms do not imply any difference in clinical features, but only in what is known about aetiology.

Within the organic brain syndromes (those of unknown aetiology) several groups are recognized. The first group includes cases with **global** cognitive impairment. It is divided further into brief conditions (delirium) and lasting ones (dementia). The second group is for conditions with **selective** impairment, which may affect memory (the amnestic syndrome); perception (organic hallucinosis); thinking (organic delusional syndrome); mood (organic affective syndrome); or personality (organic personality syndrome). A final group is for the effects of drug intoxication and withdrawal (which are described in Chapter 14).

Within the organic mental disorders (those of known or presumed aetiology), there is a further subdivision into: senile and presenile dementia, primary degenerative dementia, and multi-infarct dementia. A group for substance induced mental disorder is further divided into sub-groups for alcohol, barbiturates, amphetamines, opioids, cocaine, and hallucinogens.

It remains to be seen whether this complicated scheme will prove more useful than the simpler ICD 9 scheme.

THE ASSESSMENT OF SUSPECTED ORGANIC PSYCHIATRIC DISORDER

Any suspicion of an organic disorder should lead to detailed questioning about intellectual function and neurological symptoms. It is particularly important to interview other informants. The mode of onset and progression of symptoms should be determined in detail. An appropriate physical examination is essential.

Special investigations

With every patient the psychiatrist should use his judgement about the extent of the special investigations required. The aim should be to perform the minimum of investigations that will allow accurate diagnosis. A common basic routine for every patient is: haemoglobin and ESR; blood urea and electrolytes; urinary sugar and protein. Serology for syphilis used to be routine, but in the recent past was often omitted because of the decrease in cerebral syphilis. Its current use is discussed on page 318. No single serological test is wholly satisfactory. The best combination is a reagin test together with the *Treponema pallidum* haemagglutination assay test.

Automated biochemistry now makes more extensive screening of blood samples possible, though experience is needed to interpret the results. If on clinical grounds there is the least suspicion of physical disorder or if any of the screening tests is abnormal, the clinician should judge what further investigations are required. They are likely to include: MSU microscopy; urine analysis for drugs and porphyrins; liver function tests; serum calcium and phosphate; thyroid function (T_4, T_3, TSH); serum B_{12}; and red cell folate. Also chest and lateral skull X-rays should be taken.

Further investigations

A review of the clinical findings and the results of this first round of investigations will usually indicate whether organic disorder can be excluded or special investigations are needed. The latter may include antero-posterior and basal skull X-rays, CT scan, EEG, and further laboratory investigations. Psychological tests may be required at this stage. Some of these investigations will now be considered in more detail.

Skull X-ray

As already noted, in the absence of physical signs a single lateral film is usually adequate. When indicated antero-posterior and basal views should be added. Possible findings include: abnormalities of the vault (such as overgrowth, osteolysis, abnormal vascular markings), intracranial calcification, changes in the sella turcica, the shift of a calcified pineal and unsuspected fractures.

Computerized axial tomography

This technique has greatly improved the diagnosis of cerebral lesions. In psychiatric patients it has increasing importance in the diagnosis of both focal and diffuse cerebral pathology. Although easy to arrange, CAT scans are expensive and the results require skilled interpretation. In the United Kingdom the current practice is that CAT scans are not requested routinely for all psychiatric patients. Instead they are requested if there is any suspicion of organic brain disease in patients up to late middle age, or if there is any suggestion of a focal brain lesion in the elderly (radiological investigation of the elderly is further discussed in Chapter 16). Jacoby (1981) has reviewed the value of CAT scanning in dementia and depressive disorders.

Electroencephalography

The EEG has an important but limited role in diagnosis. It must be interpreted skilfully. Apart from standard recordings, there are more elaborate techniques such as recordings during sleep or sleep deprivation, and ambulatory monitoring over 24 hours (Stores and Brankin 1982). The value of the EEG in diagnosis is limited by its sensitivity to minor physiological changes (such as level of wakefulness, blood sugar and acid-base fluctuations) and to most psychotropic drugs. The EEG may be abnormal in some disorders generally thought to be without any organic pathology, namely anti-social personality disorder and some cases of schizophrenia. Conversely, normal records do not exclude cerebral pathology. Despite these problems, the EEG is sometimes helpful in localising a space occupying or other focal lesion. Now that these aims can generally be achieved better with the CAT scan, the main use of the EEG is in the management of epilepsy.

Further physical investigation

Psychiatrists who have the appropriate neurological skills may go on to perform a lumbar puncture or order further special radiology. However it is usually more appropriate to seek the opinion of a neurologist or general physician before doing either.

Psychological testing

Psychometric tests depend on the patient's co-operation but can be valuable when given by an experienced tester. They may help in localizing lesions in certain sites, for example the parietal lobe. Even when interpreted skilfully, they discriminate poorly between organic and functional disorders. They are of more value in monitoring changes in psychological functioning over time, and in assessing patterns of disability as a basis for planning rehabilitation. Some of the most frequently used tests will now be considered briefly.

(1) *Wechsler Adult Intelligence Scale* (WAIS). This is a well standardized test providing a profile of verbal and non-verbal abilities. Analysis of subscores can provide useful information for diagnosis. It is often said that organic impairment is indicated by a discrepancy between performance IQ (as an estimate of current capacity) and verbal IQ (as an estimate of previous capacity), but there is no strong evidence to support this view. Usually the more specific tests mentioned below are more helpful in diagnosis, but the WAIS is useful for screening.

(2) *Perceptual functions, especially spatial relationships.* This kind of test is exemplified by the Benton Revised Visual Retention Test, which requires the

patient to study and reproduce ten designs. Parallel versions of the test are available, thus allowing serial testing.

(3) *New learning as a test of memory.* There are many new word learning tasks, for example the Walton–Black Modified Word Learning Test and the Paired Associate Learning Test, both of which give a useful quantitative estimate of memory impairment.

(4) *Specific tests.* Examples of specific tests are the Wisconsin Card Sorting Test for frontal lobe damage, and the Token Test for receptive language disturbance.

(5) *Dementia scales.* Strictly speaking these are not single psychometric tests but combinations of several tests. Examples are the Kendrick Battery and the Clifton Assessment Procedures for the Elderly (CAPE). Further information about the use of psychological tests in neuropsychiatry is provided by Mittler (1973) and Lishman (1978*a*).

ASPECTS OF DIFFERENTIAL DIAGNOSIS

Organic or functional?

Usually there is little difficulty in distinguishing between organic and functional disorders, but occasionally the one may be mistaken for the other. Thus an organic disorder may sometimes be misdiagnosed as functional if the patient has abnormalities of personality that modify the clinical presentation; for example, by adding prominent depressive or paranoid features. Conversely, a functional disorder may be misdiagnosed as organic if there is apparent cognitive impairment; for example, a patient with a depressive disorder may complain of poor memory and 'confusion'. Of the two kinds of misdiagnosis, to miss an organic disorder is of course more serious. It is therefore vital that the psychiatrist should be constantly vigilant to the possibility of an organic psychiatric disorder. The first requirement is to take a full history and make a thorough examination of the physical and mental state. Certain features call for alertness. For example, complaints of physical symptoms should always be taken seriously, and suitable questions should be asked about their nature and time of onset. If psychiatric symptoms are not psychologically understandable, enquiry should always be directed to a possible primary organic disorder.

In making the distinction between organic and functional disorders, several principles should be borne in mind. The first concerns three modes of presentation – as hysteria, as episodic disturbed behaviour, and as depression. Hysteria should not be diagnosed unless there is an adequate psychological explanation for it, and unless every symptom has been adequately investigated. This principle holds even for patients with a previous history of hysteria. Brain disease may present with symptoms that resemble those of hysteria; this is likely for example with the parietal lobe lesions described above. Another point is that hysterical symptoms (such as global amnesia) may be 'released' by organic brain disease (see p. 176).

In a patient with a previously stable personality unexplained episodes of disturbed behaviour suggest organic brain disease. Possible causes include epilepsy, early dementia, and transient global amnesia; and extracerebral conditions such as hypoglycaemia, porphyria, or other metabolic disorders.

A second principle is that certain symptoms need to be analysed with particular care. For example, muscular weakness must be differentiated from the psychological experience of 'feeling weak', a distinction that is important in the diagnosis of myasthenia gravis. Another principle is that certain symptoms should arouse suspicion of an organic lesion; for example visual hallucinations, or complaints of 'confusion', or any complaint that would be unusual in a functional disorder, such as ataxia and incontinence. Finally depressed mood is sometimes the first manifestation of organic brain disease.

As mentioned above, a functional disorder may be misdiagnosed as organic if there is apparent cognitive impairment. The term 'pseudodementia' is applied to patients who have a functional disorder and show intellectual impairment resembling that of organic disease. Pseudodementia is most common in elderly depressed patients (see p. 511). In diagnosing pseudodementia from true dementia, it is important to know which symptoms developed first, since in functional disorders other psychological symptoms precede the apparent intellectual defects. Hence it is important to interview other informants to determine the precise mode of onset.

Acute or chronic?

In making the differential diagnosis, it is sometimes difficult to distinguish between an acute and a chronic organic psychiatric syndrome. This difficulty usually arises because a clear history is lacking. It should be remembered that an acute syndrome may be superimposed on a long-standing dementia; such an event may obscure the diagnosis, or alternatively may draw attention to the underlying chronic disorder. The characteristic features of the acute and chronic syndromes have been described above. In distinguishing the acute syndrome, the most helpful features are: impairment of consciousness, perceptual abnormalities, disturbed attention, poor sleep, and thinking that is disorganized but rich in content.

Differential diagnosis of stupor

This symptom, which is discussed on p. 29, requires specific mention. The main psychiatric causes are severe depression, schizophrenia, and rarely hysteria and mania. Organic causes are relatively uncommon in cases seen in psychiatric practice (Joyson-Bechal 1966). They include focal lesions in the posterior diencephalon or upper midbrain (e.g. tumours, especially craniopharyngiomas; infarction, meningitis, and epilepsy) and a number of extracerebral causes (e.g. uraemia, hypoglycaemia, electrolyte and fluid disturbance, endocrine disorder, alcohol and drug intoxication). Diagnosis can usually be made on the history and examination. An EEG can be helpful in distinguishing between organic and psychogenic causes. (See Lishman (1978*a*) for a review of the differential diagnosis of stupor and Berrios (1981) for a history of the concept of stupor.)

Diagnosis of the cause

A final aspect of differential diagnosis is to identify the cause of an organic psychiatric syndrome. If the cause is not readily apparent, the history and findings on physical and mental examination should be reviewed. Careful enquiry should be made about any history of head injuries, fits, alcohol or drug abuse, and recent physical illness. Dietary deficiency should be considered if the patient is elderly or of low intelligence. It is important to enquire about the symptoms of raised intracranial pressure (headaches, vomiting, and visual disturbance), as well as those suggesting a focal lesion in the brain. Physical examination should be directed towards signs of disease in other systems as well as the nervous system. Any appropriate investigations should then be arranged.

THE MANAGEMENT OF ACUTE ORGANIC SYNDROMES

The fundamental treatment is directed to the physical cause. General measures are necessary to relieve distress, and to prevent behaviour that might lead to accidents or other difficulties affecting the patient or other people. Amongst these general measures, the most important are to reduce the patient's anxiety, and to avoid too much or too little sensory stimulation.

Apart from good nursing care, the patient should be given repeated explanations of his condition. Disorientation and misinterpretation of the environment can be reduced by a calm and consistent approach, and by avoiding too many changes in the staff caring for the patient. If possible relatives and friends should visit the patient frequently; it is good practice to explain the patient's condition to them, and to advise them how to reassure and orientate the patient. There are many advantages in nursing the patient in a quiet single room. At night, the room should have enough light to enable him to know where he is; on the other hand it is desirable to avoid the high levels of illumination found in some intensive care units.

Drug treatment

In general it is important to give as few drugs as possible, and to avoid any that may increase impairment of consciousness. Nevertheless, medication often has an important role. Overactive, frightened, and disturbed patients may require medication to control distress and prevent accidents. There are two main requirements. First, during the daytime it may be necessary to calm the patient without inducing drowsiness. Second, at night it may be necessary to help him to sleep. For the first purpose (calming by day), the drug of choice is an anti-psychotic drug such as haloperidol, which calms without causing drowsiness, hypotension, or cardiac side effects. The effective daily dose usually varies between 10 and 60 mg. If necessary, the first dose of 2 mg to 10 mg can be given intramuscularly. Chlorpromazine and other phenothiazines are also widely used, but their usefulness is limited by their side effects, such as hypotension and sedation. For the second purpose (promoting sleep), a sedative anxiolytic drug such as one of the benzodiazepines is suitable. Whilst in general benzo-diazepines should be avoided during the daytime because of their sedative effects, they may be used by day if there is liver failure since they are less likely to precipitate coma. In the special case of alcohol withdrawal, chlormethiazole is a suitable drug (see p. 438).

THE MANAGEMENT OF DEMENTIA

If possible the cause should be treated. Otherwise management begins with an assessment of the degree of disability and the social circumstances of the patient. The plan of treatment should seek to improve functional ability as far as possible, relieve distressing symptoms, make practical provisions for the patient and support his family.

Plans for long-term care should make clear the part to be played by the doctors, nurses, and social workers. This applies whether the patient is living in hospital or outside. For certain conditions there are some benefits from carrying out the first stage of rehabilitation in special units; for example, dementia caused by head injury or by a stroke. It should be remembered that personality change and restlessness at night cause particular difficulties for the family.

Drugs

There is no specific drug treatment for dementia, and medication can only be used to alleviate certain symptoms. For example, anxiety may be treated by a benzodiazepine or a phenothiazine such as chlorpromazine or thioridazine. At night a benzodiazepine or a sedating phenothiazine may be useful. Patients with cognitive impairment may be unusually sensitive to anti-psychotic drugs, so the first doses should be small. If the patient is overactive or deluded or halluci-nated, a phenothiazine may be appropriate, but care is needed to find the optimal dose. If the patient has depressive symptoms, a trial of antidepressant medi-cation is worthwhile even in the presence of dementia.

Behavioural methods

Much rehabilitation is based on the analysis of problems and the setting of goals. Behavioural methods share these principles but add specific procedures to modify particular aspects of behaviour. (Sand *et al.* 1970). Recently these methods have been directed to improving deficits of memory, for example by the use of lists and reminders, and by practice (Miller 1980). There is insufficient evidence on which to judge their value.

2. Specific physical conditions giving rise to mental disorders

PRIMARY DEMENTIA

Among the important causes of dementia are intrinsic degenerative diseases of the central nervous system presenting in middle or late life. The dementias arising from these diseases are sometimes called primary dementias. The commonest examples are those occurring in old age, namely senile dementia and multi-infarct dementia, which are discussed in Chapter 16.

The category of **presenile dementia** was introduced in 1898 by Binswanger and later included in Kraepelin's classification. Nowadays the term presenile is usually taken to mean younger than 65 years of age. It includes Alzheimer's and Pick's diseases and Huntington's chorea. One of these conditions, Alzheimer's disease, is closely similar to the commonest form of dementia in old age; a point to be taken up in the chapter on old age psychiatry.

Two follow-up studies have shown that it is not easy to make an accurate diagnosis of presenile dementia. Marsden and Harrison (1972) found that, among 106 patients with a presumptive diagnosis of presenile dementia, 14 per cent were subsequently rediagnosed as suffering from another illness, usually a depressive disorder. Ron *et al.* (1979) studied 51 patients aged between 5 and 15 years after a confident diagnosis of presenile dementia had been made. Follow-up information led to rejection of the original diagnosis in almost a third of the cases. Accurate diagnosis depends on careful history taking together with mental and physical examination. In doubtful cases, admission for observation is often informative. A non-organic diagnosis is suggested by a history of affective disturbance, ability to learn in everyday activities or in psychological tests, and marked inconsistencies in performance.

Alzheimer's disease

The clinical features and pathology of this condition were first fully described in 1906 by Alzheimer in a case report of a 51 year old woman (see Alzheimer 1967). It is the commonest form of presenile dementia, and is more common in women than in men in a ratio of 3 to 1. The onset is insidious and occurs from middle age onwards. The course is progressive with death occurring usually in 3–7 years. In the early stages, failing memory, perplexity, and mood disturbance (usually agitation) are most obvious. After a year or so, there is more rapid deterioration followed by parietal and extrapyramidal symptoms and eventually by 'primitive' reflexes (sucking, glabella tap, tonic grasp) and generalized bodily wasting. *The pathology, aetiology, and treatment of this condition are discussed in the section on senile dementia on p. 504.*

Pick's disease

This disease, which was described by Pick in 1892, is much less common than Alzheimer's disease. It appears to be inherited as an autosomal dominant (Sjögren *et al.* 1952). The gross pathology is circumscribed asymmetrical atrophy of the frontal or temporal lobes accompanied by a lesser degree of general atrophy. The gyri are said to have a characteristic brownish 'knife blade' atrophy. There is severe neuronal loss in the outer layers of the atrophic cortex with proliferation of astrocytes and fibrous gliosis.

Although the onset may be at any adult age, most cases start between 50 and 60 years. Women are affected twice as often as men. There are no specific clinical features to separate Pick's disease from Alzheimer's, and the distinction is generally made at autopsy, not in life. None the less it is sometimes said that the presenting symptoms of Pick's disease are changes in character and social behaviour more often than memory disturbance. There is loss of inhibition (sometimes affecting sexual behaviour), deterioration of conventional manners, and sometimes marked loss of drive. These features correspond to the predominant pathology in the frontal lobes, and to a less extent temporal lobes. Parietal lobe features and extrapyramidal symptoms are less common. The condition is progressive with death after 2–10 years.

Huntington's chorea

This was described in 1872 by George Huntington, a New England physician. Since then epidemiological studies have shown that the condition occurs in many countries; the estimated prevalence varies widely, the average being about 4–7 per 100000 (see for example Oliver 1970). Men and women are affected in equal numbers. The pathological changes mainly affect the frontal lobes and the caudate nucleus. Neuronal loss, which is most marked in the frontal lobes, is accompanied by gliosis. The basal ganglia are strikingly atrophied.

Clinical features

Huntington's chorea usually begins at an age between 25 and 50, the mean being in the forties (Minski and Guttman 1938). A rare juvenile form has been reported. The onset of neurological and psychiatric symptoms may be several years apart. Usually neurological signs precede dementia but the reverse sequence can occur. The early neurological signs are choreiform movements of the face, hands, and shoulders. These movements are sudden, unexpected, aimless, and forceful. They are associated with dysarthria and changes in gait. Patients often attempt to disguise an involuntary movement by following it with a voluntary movement in the same direction. Gradually abnormal movements become increasingly obvious with gross writhing contortions and ataxia. Patients begin to drop objects and later to fall over. Extrapyramidal rigidity and epilepsy also occur, especially in younger patients (see Lishman 1978*a*). Eventually walking, eating, and even sitting become difficult or impossible.

Memory is less affected than other aspects of cognitive function and insight is often retained until a late stage. In the early stage distractability is characteristic, and in the later stages apathy. Psychiatric symptoms of all types occur at an early stage, but depression is particularly frequent. Some patients develop a depressive disorder, and others develop a schizophrenia-like picture with persecutory delusions. The dementia usually progresses slowly. The expectation of life is variable but the average is probably 13–16 years. When the onset is late patients often survive for many years and may die of other causes. Suicide is a frequent cause of death; among Huntington's chorea patients living in the community the suicide rate is 7 per cent (Reed and Chandler 1958).

Interviews with wives (Hans and Koeppen 1980) and a postal survey of relatives (Barette and Marsden 1979) have confirmed that family members suffer much personal distress and many social problems. Their first reaction is usually disbelief, followed by resentment and hostility. Most family members say they would prefer to have known the diagnosis earlier and to have had an opportunity for genetic counselling.

Aetiology

Huntington's chorea is normally inherited as an autosomal dominant although sporadic cases have been described. It appears to develop about ten years earlier in the children of affected males than in the children of affected females, suggesting an inherited sex-related modifying factor (see Bird 1978).

The dominant inheritance suggests an inborn error of metabolism. Perry *et al.* (1973) were the first to report decreased concentrations of gamma-aminobutyric acid (GABA), a neuro-inhibitory transmitter, in the caudate nucleus. Later work (Bird 1978) has shown decreased GABA biosynthesis and increased dopamine concentrations in parts of the basal ganglia (see Perry and Perry 1982).

Management

Surveys have shown that the first diagnosis is wrong in at least a third of cases. Common wrong diagnoses are various psychiatric disorders especially schizophrenia, Alzheimer's dementia, and various disorders of movement including chorea.

In general, the treatment is similar to that of other dementing disorders. For the specific control of choreiform movements, phenothiazines and butyrophenones have been reported as effective (see Lishman 1978*a*). It is uncertain whether they act as non-specific tranquillizers or through their specific effect on the dopamine systems. Pallidectomy and thalamotomy have also been used for the involuntary movements; some success has been reported in younger patients, but there is a risk of worsening the dementia or causing neurological side-effects (see Heathfield 1967).

Prevention

Many attempts have been made to detect Huntington's chorea before symptoms develop. The methods include EEG recording, a search for biochemical abnormalities that might act as markers for the genes, and attempts to provoke chorea with L-dopa. No test is satisfactory.

From surveys of family members it appears that, at a time of life when they are likely to become parents, only a few know about the risks of any future children being affected. There is disagreement as to how far families should be told and how strongly they should be advised against having children. Carter and Evans (1979) found a considerable decline in births after non-directive genetic counselling.

Creutzfeld-Jacob disease

This uncommon disorder was described by Creutzfeld in 1920 and independently by Jakob in 1921. It is a rapidly progressive degenerative disease of the nervous system characterized by intellectual deterioration and various neurological deficits including cerebellar ataxia, spasticity, and extrapyramidal signs. Evidence for an infective agent followed the discovery that the rare neurological disease Kuru, which is pathologically similar, can be transmitted. In 1968 Gibbs *et al.* were able to transmit Creutzfeld–Jakob disease by inoculation of brain biopsy homogenate to a chimpanzee, an observation that has been frequently repeated (for example Beck *et al.* 1969). The nature of the transmissible agent remains uncertain but it is often referred to as a 'slow virus'. It could provide a model for other chronic neurological diseases.

Precautions should be taken to avoid contamination with blood from these patients. These precautions have been described by Matthews (1982) and the Advisory Group on the Management of Patients with Spongiform Encephalopathy (Creutzfeld–Jakob disease) (1981). Essentially they involve extra care in handling samples of blood or tissue from these patients.

Normal pressure hydrocephalus

In this variety of hydrocephalus there is no block within the ventricular system (Hakim and Adams 1965). Instead there is an obstruction in the sub-arachnoid space such that cerebral spinal fluid can escape from the ventricles but is prevented from flowing up over the surface of the hemispheres. There is marked hydrocephalus with a generally normal or even low ventricular pressure (though sometimes with episodes of high pressure).

The characteristic features are progressive memory impairment, slowness, marked unsteadiness of gait, and later urinary incontinence. The condition is more common in the elderly but sometimes occurs in middle life. Often, no cause for the obstruction can be discovered although there may be a history of sub-arachnoid haemorrhage, head injury, or meningitis. It is most important to differentiate the condition from the primary dementias, or possibly from depressive disorder with mental slowness. Treatment is a shunt operation to lower the pressure in the ventricles. The results are difficult to predict. The dementia may improve but generally it does not.

HEAD INJURY

The psychiatrist is likely to encounter two main kinds of patients who have suffered a head injury. First there is a small number of patients with serious and lasting psychological sequelae, such as persistent defect of memory. Second there is a larger group with emotional symptoms and anergia; these symptoms are less obvious and may be easily overlooked, but they often cause persistent disability.

Acute psychological effects

Impairment of consciousness

This occurs after all but the mildest closed injuries, but is less common after penetrating injuries. The cause is uncertain but is probably related to rotational stresses within the brain.

Memory disorders

On recovery of consciousness, defects of memory are usually apparent. The period of **post traumatic amnesia** is the time between the injury and the resumption of normal continuous memory. The duration of post traumatic amnesia is closely correlated with: first, neurological complications such as motor disorder and dysphasia, and persistent deficits in memory and calculation (Russell and Smith 1961; Smith 1961); second, psychiatric disability and generalized intellectual impairment (Lishman 1968); and third, change of personality after head injury (Steadman and Graham 1970). The period of **retrograde amnesia** is the time between the injury and the last clearly recalled memory *before* the injury. It is not a good predictor of outcome.

Acute post-traumatic psychosis

After severe injury there is often a prolonged phase of confusion, and sometimes disordered behaviour, mood disturbance, hallucinations, delusions, and disorientation.

Chronic psychological effects

Damage to the brain is of central importance in determining chronic psychological effects. Other factors are important (see Lishman 1978), particularly the premorbid personality, and also environmental factors such as type of job, amount of social support available, and whether there is a compensation claim.

Lishman (1968) found that the site and extent of brain damage after penetrating injuries were related to the mental state one to five years later. The amount of tissue destruction was related both to intellectual impairment and 'organic' psychological symptoms such as apathy, euphoria, poor judgement, and disinhibition. Neurotic symptoms were not related to the amount of damage.

Lishman's study suggested that cognitive disorder was particularly associated with parietal and temporal damage (especially on the left side). Affective disorders were more common after frontal lobe injury.

Lasting cognitive impairment

When head injuries are followed by post-traumatic amnesia of more than 24 hours, they are likely to give rise to persisting cognitive impairment proportional to the amount of damage to the brain. After a closed injury, the impairment is usually global, and varies in severity from obvious dementia to slight defects that only become apparent during intellectually demanding activities. After a penetrating or other localized injury, there may be only focal cognitive defects but some evidence of general impairment is usually found.

Slow improvement usually takes place over months or years. For example Miller and Stern (1965) followed 100 patients with severe head injuries for an average of 11 years and found substantial improvement over this period. Some patients had improved greatly despite pessimistic medical reports written 3 years after the injury. Presumably these findings reflect the slow education of intact brain tissue. Dementia out of keeping with the severity of the injury should suggest subdural haematoma, normal pressure hydrocephalus, or a coincidental degenerative process.

Personality change

This is particularly likely after frontal lobe damage. There may be irritability, loss of spontaneity and drive, some coarsening of behaviour, and occasionally reduced control of aggressive impulses. These changes may improve gradually, but when present often cause serious difficulties for the patient and his family.

Neurosis

This may follow any kind of injury. It is uncertain whether neurosis after head injury is a non-specific response or a specific result of brain damage.

The main features of chronic neurosis developing after head injury are headache, dizziness, fatigue, irritability, poor concentration, and insomnia. Lewis (1942) examined prolonged neurotic reactions among soldiers with head injuries, and concluded that they occurred in 'much the same person as develops a psychiatric syndrome anyway'. Denker (1958) studied 37 monozygotic and 81 dizygotic twin pairs in each of which a single twin had received a head injury. The incidence of headache, dizziness, and sensitivity to noise was more similar within MZ twins than within DZ pairs, suggesting that these symptoms were related more to constitution than to head injury. In a study of patients who were making claims for compensation, Miller (1961) found no relation between the severity of head injury and the extent of neurotic symptoms. In his study of penetrating injuries, Lishman (1968) found no demonstrable relationship between extent of brain damage and the main symptoms of the post-traumatic syndrome. It can be concluded that neurotic predisposition is the main aetiological factor in the chronic neuroses after head injury (see Trimble 1981 for a review).

Schizophrenia-like syndromes

Achté *et al.* (1967) studied 3552 Finnish soldiers aged 22–26 years after a head injury, and found that the rate of schizophrenia-like syndromes was well above expectation. In an extensive review of schizophrenia-like syndromes associated with organic disorders of the central nervous system, Davison and Bagley (1969) confirmed this finding and concluded that it could not be explained by chance. These authors suggested that trauma can sometimes be of direct aetiological significance, and not merely a precipitating factor. There is some evidence (for example Achté *et al.* 1967) that head injury is associated with paranoid and affective psychoses, but it is less convincing. It is generally agreed that the risk of suicide is substantially increased among head-injured patients, though the reason is not clear.

Social consequences of head injury

Family life is particularly affected by personality change, but it appears that most patients and relatives eventually adapt to their altered circumstances (see Bond 1975 or Weddell *et al.* 1980 for further information about social consequences).

Treatment

A plan for long-term treatment should be made as early as possible after head injury. Planning begins with a careful assessment of three aspects of the problem. The first is the degree of physical disability. It has been shown by prospective study that early assessment of the extent of neurological signs provides a useful guide to the likely pattern of long-term physical disability (Bond 1975). Second any neuropsychiatric problems should be assessed and their future course anticipated. Third, a social assessment should be made.

Treatment includes physical rehabilitation, to which the clinical psychologist can sometimes contribute behavioural techniques. If there are associated psychiatric disorders, the psychiatrist has an occasional role in treatment. Practical and social support may be needed for the family. Any problems of compensation and litigation should be settled as quickly as possible.

Boxing and head injury

For many years there has been dispute about the significance of 'punch drunk' states after repeated minor head injury in the boxing ring. There have been numerous published reports of a characteristic syndrome, but most of the findings could be due to biased selection of cases with coincidental neurological disease. However, in an important study of a random sample of 224 retired professional boxers, Roberts (1969) found that 37 had a characteristic syndrome related to the extent of exposure to head-injury during boxing. The principal features were dysarthria, slowness of movement, unsteadiness of gait, intellectual impairment and personality change in the form of irritability and lack of drive. Johnson (1969) reported that morbid jealousy occurred in some cases. When the syndrome is fully developed, there are cerebellar, pyramidal, and extrapyramidal signs as well as intellectual disorientation. The condition usually progresses until retirement from the ring, but only occasionally progresses afterwards. Cerebral atrophy has been shown radiologically. Corsellis *et al.* (1973) examined the post-mortem brains of ex-boxers and found excessive loss of cortical neurones and neurofibrillary degeneration. The psychiatrist should bear this condition in mind as an occasional cause of dementia.

INTRA-CRANIAL INFECTIONS

Neurosyphilis

So far the recent increase in primary and secondary syphilis has not been accompanied by an increase in neurosyphilis. Although uncommon, neuro-syphilis is important to recognize as a cause of mental symptoms because it is treatable. Of every twelve patients with neurosyphilis approximately five have general paresis, four meningovascular syphilis, and three tabes dorsalis. Of these groups general paresis (General Paralysis of the Insane; GPI) is the most important to psychiatrists. Neurosyphilis is so variable in presentation that there is a good case for testing the serology of all patients admitted to psychiatric wards. If this practice is not followed, serological tests should certainly be performed for all psychiatric patients with symptoms or signs suggesting organic brain disease. If serology is positive, treatment with penicillin is required. The administration of such treatment is complicated for several reasons, including the risk of Herxheimer reactions. It is therefore advisable to obtain a neurologist's collaboration in management.

General paresis

The identification of general paresis and the discovery of its cause were important landmarks in the history of psychiatry because they stimulated a search for organic causes of other psychiatric syndromes. A further important discovery was that one cause could give rise to many different kinds of clinical picture (see Hare 1959 for a historical review).

General paresis is three times more common in men than women. It usually starts between the ages of 30 and 50. The time from infection to symptoms is generally thought to be between 5 and 25 years, with an average of 10 to 15 years. General paresis often presents with minor emotional symptoms or evidence of personality changes such as moodiness, irritability, or apathy, which precede evidence of intellectual impairment. About half the patients present more urgently, often with a striking lapse of social conduct such as indecent exposure, or sometimes with a seizure.

In the past, an expansive and grandiose clinical picture was frequently described. Nowadays, the most striking symptoms are usually those of dementia. Since the condition was first described, patients with a depressive clinical picture seem to have become relatively more common; they were found, for example, in about a quarter of one series (Dewhurst 1969). Such patients have the symptoms of a depressive disorder, evidence of dementia, and delusions that may be of an extreme melancholic content. Less common presentations resemble mania or schizophrenia. Many other combinations of psychiatric symptoms can occur, so it is important to keep the diagnosis in mind when assessing any unusual psychiatric state. Neurological examination usually reveals abnormalities, most often Argyll Robertson pupils, tremor, and dysarthria. As the disease progresses there is increasing dementia, spastic paralysis, ataxia, and seizures. In untreated cases death usually occurs within four to five years. If treatment is given early, the condition usually remits; if treatment is given in established cases, progression of the disease can generally be halted (see Hahn *et al.* 1959).

Encephalitis

Encephalitis may be due either to a primary viral disease of the brain or to a complication of bacterial meningitis, septicaemia, or a brain abscess. Many viral causes have been identified, of which herpes simplex is the most common in the United Kingdom. Encephalitis sometimes occurs after influenza, measles, rubella, and other infectious diseases, and also after vaccination.

In the acute stage headache, vomiting, and impaired consciousness are usual, and seizures are common. There may be an acute organic psychiatric syndrome. Rarely encephalitis presents with predominant psychiatric symptoms; for example, Misra and Hay (1971) reported three cases resembling acute schizophrenia. However the psychiatrist is more likely to see the complications that follow the acute episode; these may include prolonged anxiety and depression, dementia, personality change, or epilepsy. In childhood encephalitis may be followed by behaviour disorders.

Encephalitis lethargica (epidemic encephalitis)

A small outbreak of encephalitis lethargica was first reported in 1917 by von Economo at the Vienna Psychiatric Clinic. The condition increased in the 1920s. By the 1930s it had largely disappeared, although possibly rare sporadic cases still occur. The acute stage was usually characterized by somnolence and opthalmoplegia. The chronic sequelae were of most interest to the psychiatrist. Parkinsonism was a disabling complication, and oculogyric crises were particularly striking. Another disabling sequel was personality change towards more antisocial behaviour. Some patients developed a clinical state resembling schizophrenia. Davison and Bagley (1969) analysed 40 of these schizophrenia-like cases from the literature, and found that they had fewer schizophrenic family members than did schizophrenic probands.

Mental symptoms were commonly associated with Parkinsonism. Some Parkinsonian patients had marked slowing and apathy. Sacks (1973) has given a vivid description of such cases, and the striking but temporary improvements brought about in some by L-dopa.

Benign myalgic encephalomyelitis

This is a rare condition which occurs in epidemics. It is sometimes called Royal Free Disease because of a notable outbreak in 1955 at the Royal Free Hospital in London. Acheson (1959) summarized the common features of the various outbreaks as headache, myalgia, paresis, mental symptoms, low or absent fever, and no mortality; there may also be sore throat and gastro-intestinal symptoms. The severity of the symptoms contrasts with the lack of neurological signs and lack of evidence for an infective agent. The sequelae include prominent psychological symptoms.

McEvedy and Beard (1970) suggested that most if not all the cases in the Royal Free epidemic were examples of epidemic hysteria. Against this view, it has been argued that common features occurring in widely dispersed outbreaks suggest an organic basis, even if some cases have hysterical features (Acheson 1959; Ramsay 1973). At present, there is insufficient evidence to settle the argument.

Cerebral abscess

A cerebral abscess may present rapidly and obviously with headache, epileptic seizures, papilloedema, and focal signs. On the other hand, a cerebral abscess may develop insidiously, and may then be mistaken for a psychiatric disorder. It is vital that the psychiatrist should always be alert to such a possibility. For example, the diagnosis of cerebral abscess should always be considered when depressive symptoms are accompanied by mild confusion and fever, especially when the patient seems generally ill. In such cases papilloedema often appears late and there may be few other neurological signs. Radiological studies using CAT scan are likely to be important. The primary focus of infection is usually outside the brain and difficult to detect; common sites include the mastoid, middle ear and nasal sinuses, and chronic suppurative lung disease. Penetrating head injury is another cause.

Tuberculous meningitis

Nowadays, tuberculous meningitis is uncommon and notoriously difficult to diagnose. The psychiatrist occasionally encounters the condition when it presents with apathy, irritability, and 'personality change'. Pyrexia, neck stiffness, and clouding of consciousness are often late to appear, and should therefore be looked for repeatedly.

CEREBROVASCULAR DISEASE

Cerebrovascular accident

Amongst people who survive a cerebrovascular accident, just over half return to a fully independent life. The rest suffer some loss of independence because of disabilities that may be psychological as well as physical. The psychological changes are often the more significant (see Adams and Hurwitz 1963), and many patients do not return to normal life even after physical disability has ceased to be a serious obstacle (Gresham *et al.* 1979).

Cognitive defects

A single stroke can cause deficits of higher cortical function such as dysphasia and dyspraxia, which may handicap the patient to a degree that is often under-estimated by doctors. After a first stroke repeated small strokes may lead to progressive dementia.

Personality change

Irritability, apathy, or lability of mood may occur. Inflexibility in coping with problems is common and may be seen in extreme form as a 'catastrophic reaction'. Such changes are probably due more to associated widespread arteriosclerotic vascular disease than to a single stroke; they may continue to worsen even though the focal signs of a stroke are improving.

Mood disturbance

Depressive mood is a common reaction to the handicap caused by a stroke, and is often an important obstacle to rehabilitation (Adams and Hurwitz 1963). A more profound depressive disorder with biological features is much less common; if found it should be treated with antidepressants. It is important not to mistake lethargy and low mood due to hypotensive drugs for a depressive disorder.

Other psychological problems

These include denial, excessive invalidism, lack of motivation, and disturbed behaviour.

Treatment

Although rehabilitation is used widely, it probably has little effect on the physical recovery of most stroke patients (Lind 1982). However, for all except the mildest strokes, rehabilitation can improve psychological wellbeing (Feigenson 1980).

Sub-arachnoid haemorrhage

A high incidence of mental disorder has been reported after sub-arachnoid haemorrhage. In a study of 261 patients after sub-arachnoid haemorrhage, Storey (1967; 1970) found that 40 per cent had organic psychiatric defects on simple clinical testing. Adverse personality changes were also common, although surprisingly relatives reported personality improvement in 13 per cent of patients with bleeds from anterior aneurysms. Significant depressive symptoms were reported in 14 per cent.

Subdural haematoma

The psychiatrist should remember that subdural haematoma is not uncommon after falls associated with chronic alcoholism. The symptoms may then be easily overlooked or misdiagnosed. Acute haematomas may cause coma or fluctuating impairment of consciousness, and are often associated with hemi-paresis and oculomotor signs. The psychiatrist is more likely to see the chronic syndromes, in which patients present with headache, vague physical complaints, and fluctuating consciousness, but often few localizing neurological signs. If there is any suspicion of a subdural haematoma, radiological investigation is required. Treatment is by surgical evacuation, which may reverse the symptoms in some chronic cases, but leaves many others with continuing deficits.

OTHER NEUROLOGICAL CONDITIONS

Cerebral tumours

Many cerebral tumours cause psychological symptoms at some stage, and a significant minority first present with such symptoms. Psychiatrists are most concerned with slow growing tumours in brain areas that produce psychological effects but few neurological signs, for example frontal meningiomas. The nature of the psychological symptoms depends not only on the site of the tumour but also on the presence or absence of raised intracranial pressure. The rate of tumour growth is also important; fast growing tumours with raised intra-cranial pressure can present as an acute organic syndrome, whilst less rapidly growing tumours are more likely to cause cognitive defects. The nature of the psychological symptoms is also much affected by the patient's personality. It should be remembered that focal lesions can give rise to one of the specific syndromes discussed already (p. 299); these may take the form of personality change or may be mistaken for neurotic symptoms.

In psychiatric practice, cerebral tumours are easily overlooked unless the psychiatrist is constantly alert. Unexplained 'changes in personality' are particularly suspicious.

Transient global amnesia

This syndrome is important in the differential diagnosis of episodes of unusual behaviour. It occurs in middle or late life. It is characterized by abrupt episodes, lasting several hours, in which there is a global loss of recent memory. The patient apparently remains alert and responsive but usually appears bewildered by his inability to understand his experience. There is impairment of new learning but not of other cognitive functions, and the patient may be able to continue a set task or find his way around. There is complete recovery, but with amnesia for the episode. The aetiology is obscure but the prognosis good (see Fisher and Adams 1964).

Patients with this condition often present as emergencies to general practitioners and casualty officers. Doctors who are not familiar with the syndrome may misdiagnose it as a hysterical fugue.

Multiple sclerosis

In its early stages, multiple sclerosis is often difficult to diagnose, and may be mistaken for hysteria or anxiety neurosis. When the disease is established, the main psychiatric issue is how far it affects mood and intellectual function. Surridge (1969) compared 108 multiple sclerosis patients with a control group suffering from muscular dystrophy. Three-quarters of the multiple sclerosis group suffered from a psychiatric abnormality, as against less than half the controls. Intellectual deterioration was detected in about 60 per cent of the multiple sclerosis patients, and was of at least moderate severity in 20 per cent. The predominant changes were loss of memory for recent events and impairment of conceptual thinking. Psychometric testing of these patients showed both general and specific intellectual impairments (Jambor 1969).

Surridge found abnormalities of mood in 53 per cent of the multiple sclerosis patients as against 13 per cent of controls. Half were depressed and half euphoric. Depression seemed to occur early as a reaction to the neurological symptoms, whilst euphoria was more frequent in those with intellectual deterioration. Denial of disability was found in about 10 per cent of patients, and again was more frequent as cognitive impairment progressed. The illness places a burden on patients' families (see Miles 1979).

Systemic lupus erythematosus

Psychiatric symptoms are common in the course of systemic lupus erythematosus, though seldom the first manifestation. They include acute and chronic organic syndromes, other psychoses, changes of personality, and various neurotic symptoms. Most of these disturbances last less than six weeks but some recur. Seizures are common. Possible neurological findings include cranial nerve palsies, peripheral neuropathy, and motor disorders. The course of the psychiatric symptoms usually parallels that of other features of the condition. The treatment of the psychiatric symptoms is mainly that of the primary condition. Treatment with prolonged high dosage steroid therapy is a further cause of psychiatric symptoms in some patients (see Lishman 1978a and Gurland *et al.* 1972, for further information).

Parkinson's disease

Some patients with Parkinson's disease show obvious mental slowing and memory difficulties, while others remain mentally intact. It is not certain whether the cognitive impairments are a feature of Parkinson's disease or a separate and coincidental dementia. The work of Mindham (1970) and Loranger *et al.* (1972) indicates that the expectation of dementia is probably greater than chance. It has been suggested that the dementia is 'sub-cortical'; that is, due to a lack of activated inputs to the cortex from lower centres, rather than to primary cortical pathology. However, recent evidence suggests that the pathological changes associated with the dementia in Parkinson's disease resemble those in Alzheimer's disease (Hakim and Mathieson 1978).

The association of Parkinson's disease with depression is well established. The depression can often be understood as an appropriate response to the limitations of an unpleasant disease. Mindham (1970) found a highly significant correlation between the severity of the signs of Parkinson's disease and the intensity of the depressive symptoms. However the depression is not always a reaction to disability because it sometimes precedes physical symptoms. Moreover it is more frequent in Parkinsonism than in other disabling conditions. These findings point to a specific association but the cause is not known. Tune *et al.* (1982) have reviewed the psychiatric aspects of Parkinson's disease.

The drugs used to treat Parkinsonism may cause organic mental disorders. Anticholinergic drugs may cause excitement, agitation, delusions, and hallucinations. Levodopa is also associated with an acute organic syndrome and with depressive symptoms. Stereotactic surgery for the treatment of tremor often produces transient deficits in cognitive function and rarely more permanent damage. The relief of physical symptoms can have a highly beneficial effect on the mental state.

ENDOCRINE DISORDERS

Hyperthyroidism

In hyperthyroidism, there are always some psychological symptoms, including restlessness, irritability, and distractability, which may be so marked as to resemble anxiety neurosis. In the past, acute organic psychiatric syndromes were observed as part of a 'thyroid crisis', but with modern treatment they are rare. Schizophrenia or affective psychoses occur in a few patients, but may be coincidental.

The differential diagnosis between thyrotoxicosis and anxiety neurosis depends on a history of distinctive symptoms and on physical examination. Discriminating symptoms of thyrotoxicosis are preference for cold weather and weight loss despite increased appetite. The most discriminating signs of thyrotoxicosis are: a palpable thyroid, sleeping pulse above 90 beats per minute, atrial fibrillation, and tremor. T_4 and T_3 should be measured.

As mentioned above, an acute organic psychiatric syndrome is now uncommon, but mild degrees of memory impairment can often be demonstrated if specially looked for (Whybrow and Hurwitz (1976)). MacCrimmon *et al.* (1979) found that these memory deficits correlated with serum T_4 concentration.

Occasionally a functional psychosis begins in association with thyrotoxicosis. The nature of the association between the two conditions has long been of interest. As long ago as 1909, Packard studied 82 cases reported in the literature and concluded that thyrotoxicosis was a precipitant rather than a fundamental cause. Packard's conclusion is generally held today. It is also suggested that there is no specific psychosis associated with thyrotoxicosis; the clinical picture may be of depressive disorder, mania, or schizophrenia, although modified at times by the psychological effects of hyperthyroidism.

Alexander (1950) considered that thyrotoxicosis was a psychomatic disorder (in the sense of a physical disorder induced by psychological factors) but this is not supported by evidence (see Weiner 1977).

Hypothyroidism

Lack of thyroid hormones invariably produces mental effects. In early life, it leads to retardation of mental development (see Chapter 21). When thyroid deficiency begins in adult life, it leads to mental slowness, apathy, and complaints of poor memory. These effects are important to psychiatrists because they easily lead to a mistaken diagnosis of dementia or a depressive disorder.

The symptoms of hypothyroidism are less distinctive than those of thyrotoxicosis. They include poor appetite and constipation, generalized aches and pains, and sometimes angina. On psychiatric examination, actions and speech are found to be slow, and thinking may be slow and muddled. Since these features are non-specific, myxoedema must be differentiated from dementia on the basis of its physical signs: distinctive facial appearance with non-pitting oedematous swelling and receding hair line; deep coarse voice; dry rough skin and lank hair; slow pulse, and delayed tendon reflexes.

In determining the cause of hypothyroidism, it is important to remember that lithium therapy may be a cause (see p. 554). Measurements of TSH help to distinguish primary thyroid disease (in which TSH is high) from pituitary causes (in which TSH is low). Further information is given by Whybrow and Hurwitz (1976).

Asher (1949) coined the phrase 'myxoedematous madness' to denote serious mental disorders associated with thyroid deficiency in adult life. There is no single form of psychiatric disorder specific to hypothyroidism. The commonest is an acute or subacute organic psychosis. Other patients develop a slowly progressive dementia or more rarely there may be serious depression or schizophrenia. Paranoid features are said to be common in all the conditions.

Replacement therapy usually reverses the organic features provided that the diagnosis has not been long delayed. A severe depressive disorder may also require antidepressant medication or ECT. Tonks (1964) reported that patients with organic psychoses have a better prognosis than those with the clinical picture of an affective or schizophrenic disorder.

Addison's disease (hypoadrenalism)

Psychological symptoms of withdrawal, apathy, fatigue, and mood disturbance are frequent and appear early. Hence, Addison's disease may be misdiagnosed as dementia. When he first described the disease in 1868, Thomas Addison commented that memory disorder was common. Modern observation confirms this view. Michael and Gibbons (1963) reported memory disorder in three quarters of a series of patients. Addisonian crises are accompanied by the features of an acute organic psychiatric syndrome. The diagnosis is usually apparent because the patient is obviously unwell, cold, and dehydrated, with low blood pressure and signs of failing circulation. Occasionally a depressive or schizophrenic picture coincides with Addison's disease, but less commonly than in Cushing's syndrome (see Lishman 1978a).

Cushing's syndrome (hyperadrenalism)

Emotional disorder is common, as Cushing noted in his original description. Michael and Gibbons (1963) reported emotional disorder in about half their cases. Cushing's disease usually comes to attention because of physical symptoms and signs, and any psychiatric disorders are usually encountered as complications in known cases. The physical signs include moon-face, 'buffalo hump', purple striae of the thighs and abdomen, hirsutes, and hypertension. Women are usually amenorrhoeic and men often impotent.

Depressive symptoms are the most frequent psychiatric manifestations of Cushing's syndrome. Paranoid symptoms are less common and appear mainly in patients with severe physical illness (Cohen 1980; Starkman and Schteingart 1981). The psychological symptoms usually improve quickly when the medical condition has been controlled. A few patients develop a severe depressive disorder with retardation, delusions, and hallucinations. Even these severe disorders generally improve when the endocrine disorder is brought under control. A textbook of medicine should be consulted for information about endocrine treatment.

Corticosteroid treatment

The psychiatric symptoms induced by corticosteroid treatment might be expected to be identical to those of Cushing's syndrome, but they are not entirely the same. When the symptoms are not severe, euphoria or a mild manic syndrome is more common than depressive symptoms. When they are severe, they take the form of depressive disorder, as in Cushing's syndrome (see Ling *et al.* 1981).

Sometimes corticosteroid treatment induces an acute organic syndrome in which paranoid symptoms may be prominent. The severity of the mental disorder is not associated with the dosage. It appears that patients with a history of previous mental disorder are not specially prone to develop the psychological complications of cortisone treatment (Lewis and Fleminger 1954).

Less severe symptoms usually improve when the dose is reduced. A severe depressive disorder may require treatment with antidepressant medication, or a manic disorder with antipsychotic drugs. Lithium prophylaxis should be considered for patients who need to continue steroid treatment after an affective disorder has been brought under control.

Phaeochromocytoma

Phaeochromocytomas are a rare and easily overlooked cause of episodic attacks of anxiety. They are tumours, usually benign, arising from the chromaffin cells of the adrenal medulla or ectopically in relation to the sympathetic ganglia. They secrete adrenaline and noradrenaline either continuously or paroxysmally, causing attacks characterized by palpitations, blushing, sweating, tremulousness, and violent headaches, together with hypertension and tachycardia. Intense anxiety is usual in the attacks. Occasionally there is an episode of confusion. Between attacks blood pressure is usually continuously raised. The attacks may be precipitated by physical exertion or occasionally by emotion.

Diagnosis depends on the demonstration of increased concentrations of catecholamines in the blood or urine, or of their metabolites in the urine. For further information about the syndrome and its treatment the reader should consult a textbook of medicine.

Acromegaly

In acromegaly, apathy and lack of initiative are common, but other psychiatric symptoms are uncommon. Depression sometimes occurs, but it may be a psychological reaction to the physical symptoms rather than a direct effect of the hormonal disturbance.

Hypopituitarism

Psychological symptoms are usual. From a survey of the literature, including his own series of cases, Kind (1958) concluded that 90 per cent of patients with hypopituitarism had some psychological symptoms, whilst half had severe symptoms. The main symptoms were depression, apathy, lack of initiative, and somnolence. Sometimes cognitive impairment is severe enough for hypopituitarism to be misdiagnosed as dementia. Another possible misdiagnosis is mild depressive disorder or non-specific neurosis. In the differential diagnosis from anorexia nervosa, hypopituitarism is distinguished by loss of bodily hair and by the absence of a weight phobia. Psychological symptoms usually respond well when hypopituitarism is treated by replacement therapy.

Hyperparathyroidism

Psychological symptoms are common and apparently related to the raised blood level of calcium (see Crammer 1977). In two reported series (Petersen 1968; Karpati and Frame 1964) depression, anergia, and irritability were the most frequent symptoms. Cognitive impairment also occurs. An acute organic psychiatric syndrome may develop as part of a 'parathyroid crisis'. A few patients first present with psychiatric symptoms, whilst many patients report, in retrospect, that they experienced mild anergia and low spirits for years before definite symptoms appeared.

Hyperparathyroidism should be considered when prolonged neurotic or minor intellectual symptoms are accompanied by thirst and polyuria. Mental symptoms usually recover after removal of a parathyroid adenoma, but there may be episodes of hypocalcaemia after the operation, giving rise to anxiety and sometimes tetany.

Hypoparathyroidism

Hypoparathyroidism is usually due to removal of or damage to the parathyroid glands at thyroidectomy, but a few cases are idiopathic. The main symptoms are tetany, ocular cataracts and epilepsy. Denko and Kaelbling (1962) reviewed the literature on hypoparathyroidism and concluded that at least half the cases attributable to surgery had psychiatric symptoms, usually in the form of acute organic psychiatric syndromes. In idiopathic cases of hypoparathyroidism chronic psychiatric syndromes are more common. Less frequent complications are depression, irritability and nervousness ('pseudo neurosis'). Manic depressive and schizophrenic disorders are rare (see Lishman 1978*a*) and may be coincidental. The diagnosis is made on the characteristic physical symptoms and measurement of serum calcium.

Insulinomas

These usually present between the ages of 20 and 50. There is generally a long history of transient but recurrent attacks, in which the patient behaves out of character, often in an aggressive and uninhibited way. At times the clinical features may resemble those of almost any psychiatric syndrome. The important diagnostic clue is the recurrence of attacks. Usually the patient cannot remember what happened during an attack.

Diagnosis depends on demonstrating a low blood glucose concentration during or immediately after an attack. In doubtful cases, the advice of a physician should be obtained (see Marks and Rose 1965, and Lishman 1978*a* for further information).

METABOLIC DISORDERS

Liver disease

The psychiatric features of liver failure are sometimes known as hepatic encephalopathy. The clinical picture is an acute organic psychiatric syndrome (Summerskill *et al.* 1956), together with flapping tremor of the outstretched hands, facial grimacing and foetor hepaticus. As in other acute organic syndromes, there may be hallucinations and confabulation. The condition may progress to coma, and there is a substantial mortality.

Acute porphyria

The classification of the porphyrias is complex and need not be detailed here (for a full account, the reader should consult a textbook of medicine). In Britain, the commonest form is the acute intermittent type, which is an inborn error of metabolism inherited through a dominant autosomal gene with incomplete penetrance. Acute porphyria is important to the psychiatrist because it may resemble hysteria, an acute organic reaction, or a functional psychosis. McAlpine and Hunter (1966) suggested that acute porphyria caused the madness of George III; although their arguments were scholarly and ingenious, they are open to substantial doubt.

Acute intermittent porphyria occurs at any age from puberty onwards, but is most common in the third decade. The clinical picture is variable (Stein and Tschudy 1970), but the typical symptoms are: acute abdominal pain, pain in limbs or back, nausea and vomiting, tachycardia, headaches, and severe constipation. Seizures occur in 20 per cent of cases. There may be a peripheral neuropathy which is predominantly motor. There is often a history of laparotomies without abnormal findings.

Psychiatric symptoms occur during the attack in a quarter to three-quarters of cases, and at times dominate the clinical picture (Ackner *et al.* 1962). They include depression, restlessness, and disturbed behaviour. Emotions are often labile. There may be an acute organic syndrome with impaired consciousness or eventually coma. Psychotic symptoms often occur.

Attacks may be precipitated by acute infection, alcohol, anaesthesia, and certain drugs, notably barbiturates, the contraceptive pill, dichloralphenazone, and methyldopa.

The **diagnosis** is made by the detection of porphobilinogen and d-amino laevulinic acid in the urine. Porphyria is not common, but is often missed when it presents in psychiatric practice. It should be considered whenever there is a long history of intermittent physical and psychological complaints.

There is no specific **treatment.** The main aim is prevention of attacks by avoiding precipitants. Most attacks improve without residual defects. A few patients are handicapped by persistent peripheral neuropathy or muscular wasting. Occasionally abnormal mental states are prolonged.

Cerebral anoxia

Cerebral anoxia can be divided into four categories: **anoxic** (respiratory failure, asphyxia, the effects of high altitude); **anaemic** (blood loss and carbon monoxide poisoning); **stagnant** (cerebral vascular disease, peripheral circulatory failure, cardiac failure, cardiac arrest and arrythmias); and **metabolic** (hypoglycaemia, cyanide poisoning). The clinical picture depends substantially on the cause, but most forms of anoxia are temporary and present with impairment of consciousness which may be accompanied by muscular twitching or tremor and epileptic fits. Afterwards there is a dense amnesic gap but usually no permanent consequences. In a small proportion of patients who have had severe anoxia, there may be permanent memory deficits and neurological symptoms.

Carbon monoxide poisoning

The psychiatrist has an interest in both the causes and the effects of carbon monoxide poisoning. In the past carbon monoxide poisoning was usually the result of deliberate self harm with domestic gas supplies. Household gas no longer contains substantial amounts of carbon monoxide, but car exhaust fumes do so and are sometimes used for self-poisoning.

After carbon monoxide poisoning, the course is variable. Milder cases recover over days or weeks. Recovery of consciousness is often followed by an organic psychiatric syndrome; this clears up leaving an amnesic syndrome, which in turn gradually improves. Extrapyramidal and other neurological signs occur at an early stage, and then resolve. In more severe cases there is a characteristic period of partial recovery, followed by relapse with a return of an acute organic syndrome and extrapyramidal symptoms. Occasionally death occurs at this stage. Some patients are left with permanent extrapyramidal symptoms, or become demented.

The frequency of these complications is uncertain. Shillito *et al.* (1936) surveyed 21 000 cases of carbon monoxide poisoning in New York City and found few lasting problems. In contrast Smith and Brandon (1973) made a detailed study of 206 cases from a defined area. They followed up 74 patients for an average of three years; 8 patients had sustained gross neurological damage; 8 patients had died; of those alive at follow-up, 8 had improved, 21 had shown personality deterioration, and 27 reported memory impairment.

VITAMIN DEFICIENCY

Severe chronic malnutrition is accompanied by psychological changes such as apathy, emotional instability, cognitive impairment, and occasional delusions or hallucinations. These symptoms are well-known among prisoners of war (see for example Helweg-Larsen *et al.* 1952). In peace time severe malnutrition with deficiency of several vitamins as well as protein and calories is unusual in developed countries. Even so there are groups of people who lack balanced diets and are at special risk of deficiency; they include the aged, the chronically mentally ill, the mentally handicapped, alcoholics, and patients with chronic gastro-intestinal diseases.

Vitamin B deficiency

Thiamine deficiency

Chronic depletion of thiamine leads first to fatigue, weakness, and emotional disturbance. Eventually it causes beri-beri, which is characterized by peripheral neuropathy, cardiac failure, and peripheral oedema. More acute and severe depletion of thiamine may lead to Wernicke's encephalopathy and thereby to the amnesic syndrome (see p. 299).

Nicotinic acid deficiency

In established pellagra, disorientation and confusion may progress to outbursts of excitement and violence. Depression is often conspicuous and a paranoid hallucinatory state is sometimes seen. In these cases response to treatment with nicotinic acid is often dramatic.

More acute and severe nicotinic acid depletion leads to an acute organic psychiatric syndrome. Cogwheel rigidity and grasping and sucking reflexes are said to be characteristic. This clinical picture may occur in elderly malnourished patients and in alcoholics.

Vitamin B_{12} deficiency

Severe pernicious anaemia due to deficiency of gastric intrinsic factor causes the classical picture of sub-acute combined degeneration of the cord accompanied by anaemia (macrocytic and megaloblastic) and a progressive dementia. In less advanced cases there is depression and lethargy. There may also be impairment of memory which improves after treatment with B_{12} (Shulman 1967).

It has been suggested that the dementia and other psychological symptoms may occur before the characteristic physical features. Surveys have often shown that low serum B_{12} levels are common among psychiatric patients (Edwin *et al.* 1965). However it is highly likely that such findings can be explained by a poor diet consequent upon psychiatric disorder, rather than by B_{12} deficiency as a causal factor. Clinical experience indicates that it is unusual to diagnose B_{12} deficiency for the first time in a patient with early dementia. When B_{12} deficiency is found, replacement therapy rarely leads to improvement in dementia. It is reasonable to measure serum B_{12} in any unexplained acute or chronic organic psychiatric syndrome, but there is no justification for its routine estimation in all psychiatric patients.

Folic acid deficiency

Among the elderly and among psychiatric patients of all ages, it is common to find folic acid deficiency of dietary origin, but it is difficult to assess its causal significance, if any. Low serum concentrations of folate and low red cell levels are unusually common in epileptic patients, probably as a result of anti-convulsant medication. It has been suggested that these deficiencies may account for some of the psychological symptoms of epileptic patients (see for example Reynolds *et al.* 1969), but at present the evidence is not convincing.

Overall there is little evidence that folate deficiency is an important cause of psychiatric disorder. Routine screening is not justified, although measurement of red cell folate may occasionally be appropriate when investigating an unexplained organic psychiatric disorder. If the folate is low, replacement therapy can be tried, though without great expectation of success.

TOXIC DISORDERS AND SIDE EFFECTS OF DRUGS

Table 11.4 lists drugs that are most likely to give rise to psychiatric side effects. In addition to this list it is important to remember alcohol, drugs of addiction, psychotropic medication, and steroid therapy (all discussed elsewhere in this

Table 11.4. *Drugs with psychological side effects*

Antiparkinsonian agents	
Anticholinergic (benzhexol, benztropine, procyclidine)	Disorientation, agitation, confusion, visual hallucinations
Laevodopa	Acute organic syndrome, depression, psychotic symptoms
Antihypertensive drugs	
Reserpine	Depression
Methyldopa	Tiredness, weakness, depression
Sympathetic blockers	Impotence, mild depression
Digitalis	Disorientation, confusion, and mood disturbance
Diuretics	Weakness, apathy, and depression (due to electrolyte depletion)
Analgesics	
Salicylamide	Confusion, agitation, amnesia
Phenacetin	Dementia with chronic abuse
Antituberculous therapy	
Isoniazid	Acute organic syndrome and mania
Cycloserine	Confusion, schizophrenia-like syndrome

book). The rare syndromes associated with heavy metals, such as lead, arsenic, and mercury are reviewed by Lishman (1978*a*), and in the larger medical text-books.

ELECTROLYTE AND BODY FLUID DISORDERS

Various electrolyte and fluid disorders can cause mental symptoms, usually but not invariably in the form of an acute organic syndrome. In Table 11.5 the

Table 11.5. *Psychological symptoms of electrolyte disorders*

Sodium depletion	Weakness, dizziness, sweating Lassitude or apathy and weakness Progression to an acute organic syndrome and coma (low blood pressure, abdominal pain)
Potassium depletion	Lethargy, apathy, anorexia, constipation, depression, anxiety Rarely an acute organic syndrome (Paralytic ileus, muscle weakness, ECG changes)
Potassium excess	Weakness, lethargy and confusion (cardiac arrhythmia)
Hypercalcaemia	Depression and acute organic syndrome
Hypocalcaemia	Depression and acute organic syndrome (cramps, tetany)
Alkalosis	Apathy, disorientation, acute organic syndrome (paraesthesia; tetany)
Acidosis	Impaired consciousness (rapid respiration)

main psychological disturbances are listed, and certain important physical symptoms and signs are shown in brackets. (Other physical features of the various disorders will be found in a textbook of medicine). The role of hypo-magnesaemia is at present uncertain. Calcium metabolism was mentioned earlier in relation to parathyroid conditions (p. 328); it is of particular interest because there seems to be a close relationship between the concentration of serum calcium and the extent of the mental changes (Crammer 1977; Petersen 1968).

3: Epilepsy and sleep disorders

EPILEPSY

Epilepsy has long been held to be associated with mental disorder (see Temkin 1971). In the nineteenth century, it was thought that personality deterioration and dementia were inevitable in epileptic patients, a belief that continued well into the present century. It is now known that most people with epilepsy can lead full and almost normal lives, and over two-thirds of them are free from psychiatric problems.

The psychiatrist is likely to meet three kinds of problem in relation to epilepsy: the treatment of the psychiatric and social complications of epilepsy; the treatment of epilepsy itself in patients who consult him; and the psycho-logical side effects of anti-convulsant drugs.

Types of epilepsy

To understand the psychiatric aspects of epilepsy, it is necessary to know how epilepsy is classified and what the clinical features are of its common forms. Views on these subjects have changed in recent years, and detailed up to date accounts can be found in the texts by Laidlaw and Richens 1982, or Reynolds and Trimble 1981.

The International League against Epilepsy has drawn up the classification of seizures which is now in general use (Gastaut 1969). Traditional terms such as **petit mal** and **grand mal** are not used. The scheme is elaborate, and the outline shown in Table 11.6 is much simplified. The principal distinction is between partial seizures which start focally, and generalized seizures which are generalized from the beginning. Since focal seizures often become generalized, a description of the initial stages of the attack is of the greatest importance in the use of this diagnostic scheme. For the description of seizures, it is useful to remember that the term **ictus** refers to the period of abnormal electrical activity; the first stage of a seizure may be an **aura;** and the latter must be distinguished from the **prodromata** which sometimes precede the ictus.

Table 11.6. *Classification of epilepsy*

1. *Partial seizures* or seizures beginning focally
   (a) *Elementary:* motor or sensory usually without impaired consciousness
   (b) *Complex*

2. *Generalized seizures* without focal onset
   Tonic–clonic convulsion
   Myoclonic, atonic, or akinetic
   Absences

3. *Unclassified*

Elementary partial seizures

This group includes Jacksonian motor seizures and a variety of sensory fits in which the phenomena are relatively unformed. Consciousness is usually not impaired.

Complex partial seizures

This category replaces the earlier categories of 'psychomotor' seizures and 'temporal lobe epilepsy'. These seizures arise most commonly in the temporal lobe but may have other focal origins. The ictus is usually preceded by an aura which lasts for a few seconds and may take the form of hallucinations of smell, taste, vision, hearing, or bodily sensation. The patient may also experience intense disturbances of thinking, perception, or emotion. Consciousness is usually impaired.

The clinical features of complex partial seizures are summarized in Table 11.7. (A detailed description is given by Daly 1975.) An important point is that in an individual patient the sequence of events in the seizure tends to be the same on each occasion. A particularly common feature is the 'epigastric aura', a sensation of churning felt in the stomach and spreading towards the neck. Patients often have great difficulty in describing these phenomena.

Table 11.7. *Clinical features of complex partial seizures*

Autonomic and visceral	'Epigastric aura', dizziness, flushing, tachycardia, and other bodily sensations
Perceptual	Distorted perceptions, *déjà vu*, visual, auditory, olfactory, and somatic hallucinations
Cognitive	Disturbances of speech, thought, and memory
Affective	Fear and anxiety
Psychomotor	Automatisms, grimacing and other bodily movements, repetitive or more complex stereotyped behaviour, changes in breathing, autonomic symptoms

The whole ictal phase lasts up to one or two minutes. During this phase and the post-ictal phase the subject appears out of touch with his surroundings and may show automatisms. After recovery, only the aura may be recalled. Sometimes complex partial seizures follow one another as a form of status epilepticus. In such cases a prolonged period of automatic behaviour and amnesia may be mistaken for a hysterical fugue or transient global amnesia.

Generalized tonic–clonic seizure

This is the familiar epileptic seizure with a sudden onset, tonic and clonic phases, and a final period of several minutes in which the patient is unrousable.

Myoclonic, atonic, or akinetic

There are several types of generalized epilepsy with predominantly motor symptoms, such as widespread myoclonic jerks or drop attacks. They are unlikely to present problems to the psychiatrist.

Absences

There are several clinical types, all of which have impaired consciousness as the cardinal feature. The attack starts suddenly without an aura, lasts for seconds, and ends abruptly. Motor symptoms or simple automatisms are often present. The simple absence seizure ('*petit mal*') is rather less common. For a number of purposes including treatment, it is important to distinguish between absence seizures and the less florid forms of complex partial seizures. The latter begin with an aura, last longer, and are followed by slow return to recovery. An EEG is required to make the distinction with certainty.

Epidemiology

In the United Kingdom, surveys in general practice have shown the prevalence of epilepsy to be 4–6 per 1000 (for example Pond *et al.* 1960). The inception rate is highest in early childhood, and there are further peaks at adolescence and over the age of 65. In a few cases starting in childhood, epilepsy is associated with mental handicap.

Aetiology

Many causes of epilepsy are recognized and their frequency varies with age. In the newborn, birth injury, congenital malformations, metabolic disorders, and infections are the most common. In the elderly, the most common causes are cerebrovascular disease, head injury, and degenerative cerebral disorder. In two-thirds of patients no cause is found after full investigation; in such cases genetic factors appear to be of greater significance than in those with demonstrable pathology.

Seizures often occur as a result of drug therapy, but many neurologists would not diagnose them as epilepsy. Amongst the psychotropic drugs chlorpromazine is implicated most often, and amitriptyline and imipramine less often. Sudden withdrawal of substantial doses of any drug with anticonvulsant properties may be followed by seizures. The withdrawal of large doses of diazepam and alcohol are the commonest examples among psychiatric patients.

The diagnosis of epilepsy

Epilepsy is essentially a clinical diagnosis which depends upon detailed accounts of the attacks given by witnesses as well as by the patient. The rest of the history, the physical examination, and special investigations are concerned with aetiology. The extent of investigation is guided by the initial findings, the type of attack, and the patient's age. Only an outline can be given here; for a full account the reader is referred to a textbook of neurology.

An EEG may confirm but cannot exclude the diagnosis of epilepsy. It is more useful in determining the type of epilepsy and site of origin. The standard recording may be supplemented by sleep recording, ambulatory recording, and split-screen video techniques.

Table 11.8 lists the differential diagnoses. Particular difficulty may be experienced in distinguishing complex forms of epilepsy from certain kinds of psychiatric disorder, of which hysteria is the most important and difficult. Features that suggest hysteria are an unusual or variable pattern of attacks, occurrence only in public, and absence of autonomic signs or changes in reflexes. Factors that point strongly to epilepsy are tongue biting, incontinence, definite loss of consciousness, and sustaining injury during the attack. If the diagnosis remains uncertain, closer observation in hospital should be considered (though seizures often stop when the patient is in hospital).

If an epileptic patient has an abnormal personality and shows aggressive

Table 11.8. *Differential diagnosis of epilepsy*

Organic
  Syncope
  Hypoglycaemia
  Transient ischaemic attacks
  Migraine
  Sleep disorders

Non-organic
  Temper tantrums
  Breath holding
  Hyperventilation
  Hysteria
  Panic attacks
  Schizophrenia
  Aggressive outburst in unstable personality
  Night terrors

outbursts, it is sometimes difficult to decide whether the latter are due to epileptic automatism or simply an expression of personality disorder (see p. 341).

Social aspects of epilepsy

The person with epilepsy is often at a social disadvantage. In a survey of epileptic patients in general practice, Pond and Bidwell (1960) found that half had experienced serious difficulties with work. Many patients suffer more from the misconceptions and prejudices of other people about epilepsy than from the condition itself. Problems arise in school, at work, and in the course of family life. Marriage prospects may be affected. In the care of epileptic patients, it is important to attempt to reduce these misunderstandings, and to support the patient and his family (see Laidlaw and Richens 1982).

In Britain legislation about driving is less restrictive than it used to be. To obtain a driving licence the patient must have had at least two years with no fits whilst awake, whether or not he is still taking anticonvulsants. Those who suffer fits only whilst asleep may have a licence if this pattern has been present for at least three years.

Psychiatric consequences of epilepsy

As mentioned already, it used to be thought that epileptic patients suffered an inevitable deterioration of personality. This belief has been repeatedly disproved, but it continues as a popular misconception that causes much unnecessary distress. However, there are several important ways in which epilepsy predisposes to psychiatric disturbance.

Prevalence

In their survey of epileptic patients in general practice, Pond and Bidwell (1960) found that nearly 30 per cent had conspicuous psychological difficulties, 7 per cent had had inpatient psychiatric care, and 10 per cent were educationally subnormal. Temporal lobe disorders were especially associated with psychological disability. In their Isle of Wight survey of schoolchildren aged between 5 and 14, Graham and Rutter (1968) diagnosed psychiatric disorder in 7 per cent of non-epileptic children, 30 per cent of those with uncomplicated epilepsy, and nearly 60 per cent of those with epilepsy complicated by evidence of brain damage.

Clinical features

A classification of the psychiatric consequences of epilepsy is shown in Table 11.9.

Table 11.9. *Associations between epilepsy and psychological disturbance*

1. Psychiatric disorder associated with the underlying cause

2. Behavioural disturbance associated with the seizure
    Pre-ictal
    Ictal
    ·Post-ictal

3. Interictal disorders
    Cognitive
    Personality
    Sexual behaviour
    Crime
    Neurosis
    Psychoses

Psychiatric disorder associated with the underlying cause

The underlying cause of epilepsy may contribute to intellectual impairment or personality problems, especially if there is extensive brain damage. Epilepsy is common in the mentally retarded (see Chapter 21).

Behavioural disturbance associated with the seizure

Increasing tension, irritability, and depression are sometimes apparent for several days before a seizure. Transient confusional states and automatisms may occur during seizures (especially those associated with temporal lobe disorders) and after seizures (usually those involving generalized convulsions). Less commonly, non-convulsive seizures may continue for days or even weeks (absence status or complex partial status).

Interictal disorders

There is no convincing evidence of a direct relationship between epilepsy and psychiatric disturbance occurring between seizures (see Tizard, 1962 for a review; also Hermann and Stevens 1981). However there are several indirect associations.

Cognitive function

In the nineteenth century it was widely believed that epilepsy was associated with an inevitable decline in intellectual functioning. Subsequently, investigations tended to support this belief, but the findings were misleading because they were based on epileptics resident in institutions. Early research was also unsatisfactory because it was retrospective, and therefore unable to distinguish between dementia that progressed over time, and dementia that had remained unchanged (see Brown and Reynolds 1981). Nowadays it is established that relatively few epileptic patients show cognitive changes.

When intellectual changes do occur the significant aetiological factors are likely to be: brain damage; poor concentration and memory during periods of abnormal electrical activity; and the adverse effects of anti-epileptic drugs given in high doses or even in doses optimal for the control of seizures (especially barbiturates).

A few epileptic patients show a progressive decline in cognitive function. In such cases careful investigation is required to exclude the progression of an underlying neurological disorder, toxic drug levels, and repeated non-convulsive epileptic status.

Learning problems are more common in epileptic children than in non-epileptic children (Stores 1981). Apart from the factors listed above, possible causes include poor school attendance and the general social difficulties of being epileptic.

Personality

As already explained, nineteenth-century writers suggested that fits cause personality deterioration. Early in the twentieth century, it was held that epilepsy and personality changes resulted from some common underlying abnormality (see Guerrant *et al.* 1962). The 'epileptic personality' was said to be characterized by egocentricity, irritability, religiosity, quarrelsomeness, and 'sticky' thought processes. It is now recognized that these ideas arose from observations of patients living in institutions. Surveys of epileptics living in the community have shown that only a minority have serious personality difficulties. Even when they occur, such personality problems show no distinctive pattern (see Tizard 1962). It is generally accepted that abnormalities of personality are mainly associated with temporal lobe lesions (see for example Pond and Bidwell 1960; Guerrant *et al.* 1962). There are only clinical impressions to support an association between epilepsy and aggressiveness.

When personality disorder does occur, social factors probably play an important part in aetiology. These factors include the social limitations imposed on the epileptic, his own embarrassment, and the reactions of other people. It is also possible that brain damage sometimes contributes to the development of personality disorder.

Sexual dysfunction

Sexual dysfunction is probably more common in epileptics than in non-epileptics. This is thought to apply particularly to patients with temporal lobe foci. Possible causes include the general social maladjustment of some epileptics and the effects of anticonvulsant medication.

Epilepsy and crime

Nineteenth-century writers such as Lombroso thought that crime was far more common among epileptics than among non-epileptic people. It is now well established that there is no such close association between epilepsy and crime.

However, Gunn (see 1977) surveyed the prison population of England and Wales, and found that it contained a somewhat greater proportion of epileptics (7–8 per thousand) than did the general population. Epileptic prisoners were no more aggressive than other prisoners, but they had a greater rate of psychiatric disturbance. There was no relationship between epilepsy and the type of crime. The explanation for the disproportionate number of epileptics in prison is not known; it may be that the social difficulties of epileptics lead them into more conflict with the law. For a general review see Gunn (1976).

Gunn and Fenton (1971) carried out a survey of special hospitals and concluded that crimes committed during epileptic automatisms are extremely rare. This conclusion, which has important medico-legal implications, is supported by evidence from other countries (see *Lancet* editorial 1981).

Neurosis

In Pond and Bidwell's (1960) general practice survey, half the epileptic patients with psychological problems (15 per cent of the total number) were thought to suffer from neuroses. There was no evidence that these neuroses had a distinctive pattern. Since this survey was carried out before the introduction of standardized diagnostic methods it is not possible to compare the findings with the prevalence of neuroses in the general population.

Interictal psychoses

The nature of the interictal psychoses is controversial. Some writers have suggested that psychotic disorder is less common in people who suffer from epilepsy than in the general population (the antagonism hypothesis); others have argued the opposite view, that such illnesses are more common in epilepsy (the affinity hypothesis) (see Toone 1981 for a review). It is still not possible to reach definite conclusions but most recent research has concentrated on possible associations between certain forms of epilepsy and schizophrenia-like disorders.

Interictal disorders resembling schizophrenia

Hill (1953) and Pond (1957) defined a 'chronic paranoid hallucinatory psychosis' associated with temporal lobe epilepsy. The clinical picture closely resembled that of schizophrenia except that affective responses were preserved. Slater and his colleagues (1963) collected 69 patients with unequivocal epilepsy who developed an illness diagnosed as schizophrenia. Almost all these patients suffered from temporal lobe epilepsy, and although there was no control group, the authors argued that this association was unlikely to have been due to chance. Like Hill and Pond, these authors reported that normal affective responses were usually preserved. They also found that some cases progressed towards a more 'organic' clinical picture. A family history of schizophrenia was usually lacking. The psychosis usually began many years after the onset of epilepsy, in patients with a normal premorbid personality.

There is continuing dispute as to whether or not there is a specific association between temporal lobe epilepsy and schizophrenia. For example, Hermann and Stevens (1966) challenged such an association, while Davison and Bagley (1969) supported it. A complicating factor is that epilepsy arising in the temporal lobe could be due to damage elsewhere in the brain. Sometimes a patient's history suggests widespread brain damage involving areas other than the temporal lobe. On the other hand pathological studies more often show discrete focal lesions in the temporal lobes (see Toone 1981).

Interictal affective disorders

The relationship of epilepsy to affective disorder has been studied less thoroughly than its relationship to schizophrenia. Few attempts have been made to separate the syndrome of depressive disorder from the depressive symptoms that are encountered commonly. Pond (1957) suggested that post-ictal confusional states are sometimes misdiagnosed as affective disorders. Flor-Henry (1969) studied a group of 50 patients with temporal lobe epilepsy, who included 9 diagnosed as manic depressive, 11 as schizoaffective, 21 as schizophrenic, and the rest as suffering from organic psychiatric syndromes. He reported associations between affective disorder and non-dominant temporal lobe epilepsy, and between schizophrenia and dominant temporal lobe epilepsy. These findings require confirmation in a larger independent series before a final conclusion can be reached. Betts (1981) has reviewed the evidence for an association between epilepsy and affective disorder.

Treatment

The drug treatment of epilepsy is summarized in Chapter 17. For a more detailed account of the care of epileptic patients a textbook of epilepsy should be consulted (for example Laidlaw and Richens 1982). Here it is only necessary to emphasize the importance of distinguishing between peri-ictal and inter-ictal psychiatric disorders. For peri-ictal psychiatric disorders, treatment is aimed at control of the seizures. For inter-ictal psychiatric disorders, the treatment is the same as it would be for a non-epileptic patient, though it should be remembered that many psychotropic drugs can increase fit frequency. Emotional arousal can do the same.

SLEEP DISORDERS

Psychiatrists may be asked to see patients whose main problem is either difficulty in sleeping or, less often, excessive sleep. Many patients who sleep badly complain of tiredness during the day and mood disturbance. Although prolonged sleep deprivation leads to some impairment of intellectual performance and disturbance of mood, loss of sleep on occasional nights is of little significance. The daytime symptoms of people who sleep badly are

Table 11.10. *Classification of sleep disorders*

Insomnia
    Primary
    Painful physical conditions
    Psychiatric disorder
    Abuse of alcohol and caffeine
    Structural and metabolic disorders affecting CNS

Hypersomnia
    Narcolepsy
      idiopathic
    Secondary (structural and metabolic disorders affecting CNS)
    Nocturnal hyperkinesis
    Sleep apnoea
    Long cycle hypersomnia (including Kleine–Levin syndrome)

Table adapted from Roth, B. (1980) and the Association of Sleep Disorder Centres (1979).

probably related more to the cause of their insomnia (often a depressive disorder or anxiety neurosis) than to the insomnia itself.

Table 11.10 shows a shortened version of the current classification of sleep disorders. The two main classes are insomnia and hypersomnia (see Parkes 1981; Roth 1980).

Insomnia

There is a wide range of variation in reported estimates of the prevalence of insomnia, depending on the definition of insomnia and on the population studied. Rates of 10 per cent to 20 per cent are usual, but rates of 30 per cent are also reported (see for example Bixler *et al.* 1979). Insomnia is mostly secondary to other disorders, notably painful physical conditions, depressive disorders, and anxiety neuroses. It also occurs with excessive use of alcohol or caffeine, and in dementia. Sleep may be disturbed for several weeks after stopping heavy drinking. In about 15 per cent of cases of insomnia, no cause can be found ('primary insomnia'). People vary in the amount of sleep they require, and many who complain of insomnia are probably having enough sleep without realizing it.

Usually the diagnosis of insomnia has to be based on the account given by the patient. EEG recordings made in a sleep laboratory are occasionally helpful when there is continuing doubt about the extent and nature of the insomnia (Oswald 1981). These observations sometimes show that, despite the patient's complaint, sleeping time is within the normal range.

If insomnia is secondary to another condition, the latter should be treated. When no cause can be found it is important to encourage regular habits and discourage over indulgence in alcohol or caffeine. Although it may sometimes be justifiable to give a hypnotic for a few nights, demands for prolonged medication should be resisted. This is because withdrawal of hypnotics may lead to insomnia as distressing as the original sleep disturbance. Continuation of hypnotics may be associated with impaired performance during the day, tolerance to the sedative effects, and dependency. The use of hypnotic drugs is described further on page 529.

The hypersomnias

Narcolepsy

Narcolepsy is an uncommon syndrome characterized by day-time attacks of irresistible sleep. The attacks are often associated with cataplexy, in which muscle tone is abruptly lost and the patient may fall to the ground. Other features are sleep paralysis and hypnagogic hallucinations that are usually auditory. The syndrome was originally described by the French physician Gelineau in 1880 and his name is sometimes still attached to it.

Narcolepsy usually begins between the ages of 10 and 20, and rarely begins after middle age. It is more common in males. Narcolepsy is accompanied by cataplexy in most cases, but sleep paralysis and hypnagogic hallucinations occur in only a quarter of patients. Narcolepsy and cataplexy may start together, or the narcoleptic attacks may come first; it is rare for cataplexy to precede the sleep disorder. There is a family history of the disorder in about a third of patients. In occasional families, the disorder appears to be transmitted as an autosomal dominant. Yoss (1970) has suggested that the tendency to narcolepsy may be polygenically determined and distributed in the population in a graded manner. Many aetiological theories have been advanced (see Lishman 1978a) but none is convincing. The condition usually persists for life, though it may become less severe in middle age.

Psychiatric aspects

Strong emotions sometimes precipitate cataplexy, but apparently not narcolepsy. It has been reported that patients with narcolepsy have a particular type of personality, but the personality features described could be the effects rather than the cause of the condition. Schizophrenia-like psychoses appear to be more common than chance expectation, often without evidence of familial predisposition (Davison and Bagley 1969). The reason for this association is not known.

Management

The EEG is helpful in diagnosis. Night-time sleep is often abnormal with an unusually early onset of REM sleep, frequent periods of wakefulness, and many shifts of phase. Narcoleptic attacks by day are sometimes accompanied by REM sleep, though not always.

There is no really satisfactory treatment. Patients should be encouraged to follow a regular routine with planned short periods of sleep during the day. If stressful events seem to provoke attacks, efforts should be made to avoid them. Regular dosage with amphetamine or methylphenidate has some effect in reducing narcoleptic attacks but little effect on cataplexy. These drugs have to be given in high doses that lead to side-effects and problems of dependency. (These problems are discussed on p. 558.) Tricyclic antidepressants do not affect the sleep disorder but may reduce the frequency of cataplexy. Some authors suggest the combined use of tricyclics and amphetamines, but this combination is better avoided if possible because of the risk of hypertensive effects. (See Lishman 1978*a* for further information about narcolepsy and its treatment.)

Other hypersomnias

In other hypersomnias episodes of sleep are more gradual in onset and usually longer lasting than attacks of narcolepsy. The daytime drowsiness causes difficulties at work (see Parkes 1981). The more common causes are idiopathic hypersomnolence and sleep apnoea. Kleine–Levin syndrome is another rare cause.

Idiopathic hypersomnolence

This is the most prevalent of the primary hypersomnias. Patients complain that they are unable to wake completely until several hours after getting up. During this time they feel confused and may be disorientated ('sleep drunkenness'). They usually report prolonged and deep night-time sleep. Almost half have periods of daytime automatic behaviour, the aetiology of which is obscure. Most patients respond well to small doses of CNS stimulant drugs (see Roth *et al.* 1972).

Sleep apnoea

This syndrome consists of daytime drowsiness together with periodic respiration and excessive snoring at night. It is usually associated with upper airways obstruction. Another uncommon cause is the Pickwickian syndrome, in which hypoventilation is associated with extreme obesity. Treatment consists of relieving the cause of the respiratory obstruction or obesity.

The Kleine–Levin syndrome

This consists of episodes of somnolence and increased appetite, often lasting for days or weeks and with long intervals between them. Patients can always be roused from the day-time sleep, but are irritable on waking and occasionally aggressive; some are muddled and experience depression, hallucinations, and disorientation. Although the combination of appetite disorder and sleep disturbance suggests a hypothalamic disorder, there is no convincing evidence about the aetiology.

FURTHER READING

Benson, D.F. and Blumer, D. (eds.) (1982). *Psychiatric aspects of neurological disease,* Vol. 2. Grune and Stratton, New York.

Bleuler, M. (1951). Psychiatry of cerebral disease. *British Medical Journal* **2**, 1233–8.

Bonhoeffer, K. (1909). Exogenous psychoses. In Hirsch, S.R. and Shepherd, M. (ed.) (1974). *Themes and variations in European psychiatry.* John Wright, Bristol.

Laidlaw, J. and Richens, A. (eds.) (1982). *A textbook of epilepsy.* Churchill Livingstone, Edinburgh.

Lipowski, Z.J. (1980). Organic mental disorders: Introduction and review of syndromes. In *Comprehensive textbook of psychiatry* (ed. H.I. Kaplan, A.M. Freedman, and B.J. Sadock) 3rd edn. Williams and Wilkins, Baltimore.

Lishman, W.A. (1978) *Organic psychiatry.* Blackwell, Oxford.

Wolff, H.G. and Curran, D. (1935). Nature of delirium and allied states. *Archives of Neurology and Psychiatry* **35**, 1175–1215.

Zangwill, O.L. (1983). Disorders of memory. In *Handbook of psychiatry,* Vol. I (ed. O.L. Zangwill and M. Shepherd). Cambridge University Press.

12. Psychiatry and medicine

INTRODUCTION

The psychiatrist commonly encounters physical disorders in psychiatric out-patient clinics and inpatient wards, especially amongst middle-aged and elderly patients. He is also likely to see physically ill patients if he visits general practices or provides a consultation service to medical wards in general hospitals.

Surveys have confirmed that physical disorders and psychiatric disorders commonly occur together in clinical practice. In a study of 100 consecutive patients attending a psychiatric outpatient clinic in Canada, 49 patients were found to have 'significant physical illness', which in many cases had not been previously diagnosed (Koryani 1972). Physical illness was thought to be the cause of psychiatric disorder in 12 of the 49 patients, and to be aggravating it in 23.

Similar findings have been reported amongst psychiatric inpatients. For example, in a study of 200 consecutive patients admitted to a general hospital psychiatric inpatient unit with district responsibilities, Maguire and Granville-Grossman (1968) found that 67 had a concurrent physical illness. Of these 67 patients, 33 had not been previously diagnosed as physically ill, and 18 had to be transferred to specialist medical care. The incidence of physical disorder increased with increasing age.

The association between psychiatric and physical disorders was clearly shown in a survey of over 14 000 patients registered with general practitioners in London (Shepherd *et al.* 1966). First, patients identified as suffering from psychiatric illness attended the general practice surgery more frequently and exhibited higher rates of physical morbidity than the remainder of the patients consulting their doctors. Secondly, a group of established chronic psychiatric patients were found at interview to have a high incidence of chronic physical illness, often closely interwoven with their psychiatric symptoms. Thirdly, a sample of chronic neurotic female patients followed up by the keeping of health diaries reported more episodes of ill health than a control group. In a later study of a randomly chosen sample of the general population, Eastwood (1975) likewise found a positive association between psychiatric and physical disorder.

Several studies have drawn attention to the association between physical and psychiatric disorders in medical clinics and wards. For example, amongst patients referred to a medical outpatient department in south-east London, 51 per cent were diagnosed as having a psychiatric disorder (Culpan and Davies 1960). In medical inpatient wards in an English hospital, Maguire *et al.* (1974)

found psychiatric disorders in about a quarter of the patients (excluding those admitted after deliberately harming themselves). In other surveys high rates of psychiatric disorder have been found among elderly patients in general medical wards (see Chapter 16 on old age psychiatry, p. 426).

The findings of all the surveys reviewed above are consistent with an idea originally proposed by Hinkle and Wolff (1957). This idea was that illnesses of all types, both psychiatric and physical, tend to 'cluster' in some people, whilst other people remain largely free from illnesses.

In recent years psychiatrists have been increasingly working in general hospitals, a practice sometimes known as consultation-liaison psychiatry. Practical aspects of this work are discussed later in the chapter (p. 361). At this point the patterns of psychiatric morbidity in medical and surgical patients will be examined in more detail.

In their study of general medical wards in an English hospital, Maguire *et al.* (1974) found that affective disorders and acute organic syndromes were the most frequent psychiatric disorders. Other studies have shown that alcohol-related disorders are also common in general hospital wards. Different surveys indicate that between 10 per cent and 30 per cent of patients in such wards have been diagnosed as problem drinkers, the rates being highest in accident and emergency wards, and especially in cities where excessive drinking is frequent (Holt *et al.* 1980; Jarman and Kellett 1979).

An important finding has been that psychiatric disorder in medical and surgical wards often goes undetected. In their survey of medical wards in an English Hospital, Maguire *et al.* (1974) found that half the psychiatric morbidity was not recognized by the physicians or nurses. Similarly, in the general medical clinics of an American university hospital, Brody (1980) found that about one-third of the psychiatric morbidity was missed by the medical residents.

It is important that psychiatric disorders should not be missed on such a large scale. This is because the more severe conditions are likely to need specialist psychiatric treatment, and may carry a risk of suicide. The moderately severe disturbances may be less dangerous, but they may require treatment, and if they persist they may seriously delay recovery from the physical illness. Even the mild disorders may cause suffering which could be alleviated.

Evidence that psychiatric disorder may interfere with recovery from physical illness was provided by Querido (1959), who studied 1630 general hospital patients and found that the medical outcome seven months later was significantly better in patients who had had fewer psychiatric symptoms at the time of the original illness.

Whether psychiatric treatment should be provided by a specialist or non-specialist depends on the severity of the psychiatric disorder. As indicated above, severe disorders are likely to require treatment by a psychiatrist. The moderate and mild disorders are usually straightforward and can be treated by a physician, surgeon or general practitioner with a sound knowledge of psychiatry.

In this introductory section, attention has been drawn to the frequent association between physical disorders and psychiatric disorders. The next part of the chapter discusses certain general issues concerning this association. It begins with two important themes concerning aetiology – the possible role of psychological factors in the aetiology of physical illness, and the psychological consequences of physical illnesses. This is followed by a discussion of the psychological care of the dying, and a review of consultation and liaison psychiatry.

After these general themes, the rest of the chapter is concerned with individual medical and surgical syndromes and procedures. It is recommended that this part be read rapidly at first, and then referred to subsequently as the different conditions are encountered in practice. Topics have been selected for this part of the chapter according to their clinical importance and also the extent and reliability of psychiatric information about them. The sections on heart disease (p. 373) and cancer (p. 385) provide examples of the general issues underlying the individual syndromes.

PSYCHOLOGICAL FACTORS AS CAUSES OF PHYSICAL ILLNESS

In the nineteenth century there was wide acceptance of the idea that psychological factors may play a part in the aetiology of physical illness (Tuke 1872). In the twentieth century this idea was elaborated by Freud and his followers, including Ferenczi, Groddeck, and Adler, who presented case studies of physical illnesses for which they proposed psychological causes. From these beginnings there emerged a body of theory and practice known as **psychosomatic medicine**, which was developed largely be psychoanalysts. Two of the foremost exponents of this subject were Flanders Dunbar and Franz Alexander. Dunbar founded the American Psychosomatic Society, and published a substantial survey of her own and other clinicians' observations in the book *Emotion and bodily changes* (Dunbar 1938). Alexander, a German psychoanalyst who migrated to the USA, put forward some of the basic concepts of psychosomatic medicine, and proposed that there were seven psychosomatic diseases: bronchial asthma, rheumatoid arthritis, ulcerative colitis, essential hypertension, neurodermatitis, thyrotoxicosis, and peptic ulcer. These ideas gained some prominence from the 1930s to the 1960s, but in recent years there has been a marked switch from traditional psychosomatic medicine to a more general approach to psychological causation in physical illness (see below).

The central theme of psychosomatic medicine was that psychological factors, particularly emotional conflicts, could play an important part in causing the onset of certain physical diseases; once these physical diseases were established, psychological factors could contribute to maintaining or aggravating them, or to triggering relapses. A large body of doctrine was built round this theme. Its tenets were complicated, but they can be summarized in five examples:

1. A particular emotional disturbance or conflict can evoke a particular form of physical pathology.
2. A characteristic type of personality is associated with a particular condition of the body. For example, a driving, independent, competitive, and ambitious personality is associated with peptic ulcer; an egocentric impulsive, and affection-seeking personality is associated with bronchial asthma.
3. Stressful events commonly occur before the onset of certain physical pathological conditions.
4. There are certain 'target organs'. That is, a particular organ or function in a particular individual is especially liable to respond to psychological stress by exhibiting pathological changes.
5. The pathological physical condition improves if the psychological disturbance improves either spontaneously or as a result of psychological treatment.

The theoretical underpining of these ideas was derived from early work by psychologists and neurophysiologists on the effects of emotion on the autonomic nervous system and the viscera. For example, Pavlov and Cannon showed that responses in animals which could be regarded as rage or fear were associated with visceral changes. On this basis psychosomatic theorists held that emotional changes in human beings are accompanied by physiological changes (which is undoubted); and if the emotional changes persist or are repeated frequently, then *pathological* physical changes may follow (which is open to doubt).

The early ideas of psychosomatic medicine were taken up enthusiastically in some centres, notably in the United States. However, many clinicians were sceptical on the grounds that they could not detect associations between the onset of particular physical diseases and specific emotional conflicts, or personality types, or stressful events. Findings reported in the psychosomatic literature were difficult to sustain because based on faulty research. Observations were often based on biased samples (patients selected by physicians for referral to psychiatrists), and often there were no control groups. Methods of psychological assessment were subjective and unstandardized. Above all, most of the work was retrospective in so far as the clinician saw patients with established physical diseases, and tried to determine whether certain emotional conflicts, personality characteristics, or stressful events had preceded the onset of those diseases.

In the past twenty years, researchers have tried to develop psychosomatic ideas along various lines. Engel and his colleagues have continued to postulate a particular emotional disturbance that could induce physical pathology, but they apply it to a wider group of physical diseases than the seven psychosomatic diseases proposed by Alexander (Engel 1962). They believe that people are particularly likely to become physically ill if they develop a 'giving-up given-up complex' in response to actual or threatened 'object loss'. This complex is a combination of depressive mood, 'helplessness' and 'hopelessness'. Engel maintains that 'helplessness' and 'hopelessness' indicate 'the greatest degree of disorganization in response to stress'. In helplessness, there are feelings 'of being left out, let down and deserted, but the individual considers himself neither responsible nor capable of doing anything about it, instead feeling that help must be provided from an outside source'. On the other hand, in hopelessness, the feeling of giving up includes 'more despair, futility, "nothing left", the self judgement that one is completely responsible for the situation leads to the feeling that there is nothing he or anyone can do to overcome the feelings or change the situation' (Engel 1962, pp. 174–5). These ideas have been quoted at length because they are well-known concepts in psychosomatic medicine, but it is emphasized that many psychiatrists do not find them useful.

Modern research has also focused on more objective study of the role of stressful events in precipitating physical illness. Most workers have used the Schedule of Recent Experience (Holmes and Rahe 1967) or modifications of it to measure life events. At present there is little or no firm evidence on the significance of stressful events in physical illness (see Brown (1979) for a review).

Other work has been concerned with the physiological mechanisms through which emotions might induce physical changes. Originally Wolf and Wolff (1947) studied a patient with a gastric fistula and found that emotional changes were accompanied by characteristic changes in the colour, motility, and secretory activity of the stomach mucosa. Subsequent research by other workers has focused on neuroendocrine mechanisms and immune processes (see Weiner 1977; Henry 1982). Such investigations show that emotion can be accompanied by anatomical and physiological changes in viscera, but they do not show whether these changes can proceed to pathological conditions (see Weiner, (1977), and Lipowski (1977) for reviews of the extensive literature on this subject).

As mentioned earlier, nowadays most psychiatrists do not accept the principles of traditional psychosomatic medicine. They see no point in separating a subgroup of so-called psychosomatic disorders, but consider that psychological factors may have some aetiological influences on a much wider range of physical disorders. It remains highly doubtful whether psychological factors can lead to the initial onset of physical disease, but there is growing evidence that they may influence the course of a disease, once it has occurred. As indicated in the introduction to this chapter, psychiatric symptoms may be associated with delays in recovery from physical illness.

Franz Alexander believed that the psychosomatic diseases would clear up or improve in response to psychological treatment. There have been numerous reports of individual patients with asthma, peptic ulcer, or ulcerative colitis who appeared to get better physically after supportive psychotherapy. These reports do not prove that psychiatric treatment affected the outcome, and are not supported by the few clinical trials that have been completed (see Karasu

1979). A more rewarding application of psychological techniques may be the modification of behaviours that predispose to physical disease, for example over-eating, smoking, and excessive drinking (see Houpt *et al.* 1980).

Some patients with physical disorders will of course need psychiatric treatment for psychological disorders arising in response to physical illnesses. This is the subject of the next section.

PSYCHOLOGICAL CONSEQUENCES OF PHYSICAL ILLNESS

The psychological consequences of physical illness can be divided into three groups. First, psychological symptoms may be directly induced by physical illnesses or drugs used to treat them. Second, psychiatric disorders may occur as psychological reactions to physical illnesses or their treatment. Third, psychological defence mechanisms (such as denial) and certain kinds of behaviour (coping behaviour) may be evoked by physical illnesses. In addition to these psychological consequences, social adjustment can be affected by physical illness. Each of these groups will be discussed in turn.

Psychological symptoms directly induced by physical illness

The main psychological symptoms are shown in Table 12.1 along with some physical disorders that can induce them. All the symptoms are commonly encountered in ordinary psychiatric practice: depression, anxiety, fatigue, weakness, episodes of disturbed behaviour, headache, and weight loss. It follows that the psychiatrist must always be on the look-out for undetected physical illness in his patients. The physical conditions listed in Table 12.1 are

Table 12.1. *Some organic causes of common psychiatric symptoms*

Depression	Drug side effects, carcinoma, infections, neurological disorders including dementias, diabetes, thyroid disorders, Addison's disease, SLE
Anxiety	Hyperthyroidism, hyperventilation, phaeochromocytoma, hypoglycaemia, neurological disorders, drug withdrawal
Fatigue	Anaemia, drug side effects, sleep disorders, chronic infection, diabetes, hypothyroidism, Addison's disease, carcinoma, Cushing's syndrome, radiotherapy
Weakness	Myasthenia gravis, McArdle's disease and primary muscle disorders, peripheral neuropathy, other neurological disorders
Episodes of disturbed behaviour	Epilepsy, hypoglycaemia, phaeochromocytoma, porphyria, early dementia, toxic states, transient global amnesia
Headache	Migraine, giant cell arteritis, space occupying lesion
Loss of weight	Carcinoma, diabetes, tuberculosis, hyperthyroidism, malabsorbtion

discussed in more detail in the later part of this chapter dealing with individual syndromes.

Drug effects are mentioned several times in Table 12.1. Whenever psychological disorder is found in a medical or surgical patient, the possibility should be considered that it has been induced by medication. For example, depression may be caused by reserpine, laevodopa, the atropine group, and some antituberculous drugs.

Psychological reactions to physical illness

It is not surprising that physically ill people should respond to their illness by feeling anxious or depressed, or (in some cases) angry. These emotional reactions are often transient, but sometimes they persist after the acute stage of physical illness has passed. In some patients emotional reactions are intense, and sometimes psychiatric illnesses appear to be provoked by physical illness (see Cutting 1980). The most common psychiatric illnesses are depressive disorders, anxiety neuroses, and actue organic syndromes, but mania and schizophrenia also occur. In all these conditions the clinical picture is much the same as in physically healthy people.

Certain factors increase the risk of serious psychiatric disorders developing in the physically ill. Patients are more vulnerable if they have a history of previous psychiatric disorder or of life-long inability to deal with adversity, or if they have a disturbed home life or otherwise unsatisfactory background. Certain kinds of physical illness are more likely to provoke serious psychiatric consequences. They include life-threatening illnesses such as cancer, and illnesses requiring lengthy and unpleasant treatment such as radiotherapy or renal dialysis, or mutilating treatment such as mastectomy. A physical illness is likely to have a greater psychological impact if it has a special effect on the patient's life; for example arthritis of the hands in a pianist.

Particular psychological problems have been described in patients in intensive care units (Kornfeld 1980), coronary care units (Hackett and Cassem 1978), and renal dialysis units (Pritchard 1982).

The treatment of emotional reactions is the same in the physically ill as in the physically healthy, except that drugs should only be prescribed after making careful allowance for their interaction with the physical illness and its treatment. Usually it is important to give the patient a clear and adequate explanation of the nature of his physical illness and its treatment (see Ley (1982) for a review of the methods of giving advice and information). Explanations should be consistent when given on different occasions and by different members of staff. This subject is discussed further in the section on cancer (p. 385).

Defence mechanisms and coping behaviour

Physical illnesses may activate various psychological **defence mechanisms** (see p. 30). Probably the commonest mechanism is denial, which can be a valuable defence against overwhelming anxiety; for example, shortly after diagnosis of a fatal illness, denial of the prognosis may allow a patient to continue with everyday life. On the other hand excessive or prolonged denial may be maladaptive; it may lead to delay in seeking treatment, lack of collaboration in treatment, or failure to safeguard the financial interests of the family. Whenever a physically ill patient appears to behave irrationally, the clinician should consider whether the behaviour can be understood in terms of denial or another defence mechanism (see p. 30 for a list of the common defence mechanisms).

Coping. This is a term applied to behaviours that people use when faced by stressful events. Such behaviours are sometimes adaptive, at other times maladaptive. On the evidence of clinical observations (see for example Hamburg and Adams 1967), the common types of response were divided by Lipowski (see 1975) into denial, vigilance, avoidance, and tackling. Certain kinds of behaviour are sometimes referred to as coping strategies; they include seeking information, social withdrawal, and looking for alternative sources of satisfaction. Such terms are now widely used in clinical practice and research, but their value is limited by lack of precise definitions (Cohen and Lazarus 1979).

Social adjustment. Physical illness and disability may have widespread effects upon a patient's adjustment in work, leisure, and family life. Patients vary in their capacity to adjust socially; most manage well but a few develop social handicaps out of proportion to the severity of physical illness. Some patients find that physical illness has advantages; for example, they may use it as an excuse to avoid responsibilities, or as an opportunity to reconsider their way of life and improve its quality.

Sociologists have pointed out that the impact of physical illness on a person may be affected by social forces. According to Parsons (1951) society bestows a **'sick role'** on people who are accepted as ill. Parsons holds that this role has four components: exemption from normal responsibilities; exemption from responsibility for certain aspects of behaviour; responsibility to try to recover; and responsibility to seek appropriate help.

Whilst Parsons put forward a theoretical formulation of the sick role, Mechanic (1978) suggested the descriptive term **illness behaviour** for the actions that people take when ill. These actions include consulting doctors, taking medicines, seeking help from relatives and friends, and giving up various activities. Such behaviours depend more on the conviction of being ill than on the presence of disease. These concepts may be of some value in understanding patients whose invalidism is excessive in relation to their physical pathology. (A critique of some of these ideas is given by Twaddle (1972).)

PSYCHIATRIC DISORDERS PRESENTING WITH PHYSICAL SYMPTOMS

Earlier in the chapter it was pointed out that psychiatric outpatients and inpatients not uncommonly have unsuspected physical disorders, whilst patients with medical and surgical disorders often have unsuspected psychiatric disorders. It is important to recognize a third group of patients, those who complain of physical symptoms for which no organic explanation can be found, and for which there is good evidence of a psychological cause. Typical symptoms of this kind are fatigue, headache, backache, anorexia, abdominal discomfort, and the many symptoms associated with autonomic arousal.

These patients with physical complaints but without evidence of organic disease are commonly seen in general practice (Goldberg and Huxley 1980). They are also encountered in hospital practice. In an investigation of 96 unselected patients referred to a specialist clinic for recurrent or persistent abdominal pain, only 15 were found to have organic disease; among the rest, 31 had a depressive disorder and 21 an anxiety neurosis, 17 had symptoms arising through hysterical mechanisms, and 12 had alcoholism that had not been detected by doctors until the survey (Dally and Gomez 1977). Although it is likely that patients with abdominal complaints of this kind are particularly prone to psychiatric problems, the psychiatric disorders found in this series are no different from those found in other patients with physical complaints but without evidence of organic disease. These psychiatric disorders will now be reviewed in turn.

Depressive disorders

Depressive disorders give rise to physical complaints in several ways. First some physical symptoms are part of the depressive syndrome; for example, constipation, aching muscles, poor sleep, lack of sexual drive, and a general feeling of malaise. Some patients may complain more of the physical symptoms than of the mental symptoms of the syndrome. Secondly, patients with gloomy thoughts may focus on ordinary bodily sensations and become convinced that these sensations have a serious cause such as cancer. Thirdly, depressive disorders may present with increased complaints about pre-existing physical illness. This occurs because lowered mood makes the patient less able to tolerate symptoms and disability that were previously tolerated with little or no complaint. This effect is common with, for example, chronic bronchitis, low back pain, chronic arthritis, and menstrual disorders.

In all these cases diagnosis of depressive disorder depends on a careful examination of the patient's mental state and a description of the patient's behaviour from another informant. The main difficulty is to decide whether depressive disorder is primary, or secondary to physical symptoms. This judgement requires a clear history of the sequence in which symptoms appeared. It also depends on the clinician's experience in gauging what is a normal reaction to illness.

Anxiety neurosis

When patients with anxiety neurosis present with physical symptoms, they usually complain of one or more features of autonomic overactivity such as palpitations or diarrhoea. Other common symptoms are related to increased muscle tension, and include headache, backache, and chest pain. Some patients present with symptoms related to overbreathing, such as dizziness, para-aesthesiae, and faintness. Until its true cause was discovered, a combination of aching in the chest, palpitations, and the effects of overbreathing used to be known as **disorderly action of the heart** or **effort syndrome** (see p. 375). When anxiety symptoms are episodic they may resemble paroxysmal tachycardia or epilepsy.

Patients with long-standing anxiety symptoms may seek advice after hearing about serious illness in a person with similar symptoms; for example, the sudden death of a relative who had experienced headaches. For this reason it is appropriate to ask whether the patient knows anyone with similar symptoms.

Hysteria

Although hysterical symptoms are common in medical practice, the primary syndrome of hysteria is uncommon. The reader is referred to p. 171 for an account of the main ways in which the syndrome presents with physical symptoms; and to p. 175 for a discussion of the dangers of diagnosing hysteria.

Alcoholism

Alcohol dependence and its physical concomitants are discussed in Chapter 14. In this condition there may be physical complaints without evidence of physical pathology, but such complaints may also be the symptoms of actual physical disease induced by the patient's excessive drinking.

Schizophrenia and paranoid states

Rarely the first evidence of these conditions is a physical complaint arising from somatic hallucinations or persecutory delusions. For example, a patient experiencing unusual sensations in the abdomen may be convinced he is being poisoned. He may seek help for his supposed physical disorder without giving any hint of his hallucinations or delusions. The diagnosis is often revealed if the patient is asked what he thinks the cause of his symptoms may be. If the answer is evasive, the question should be pursued.

Other psychiatric disorders

Amongst patients with physical complaints but without evidence of organic disease, some have so-called illness phobias, that is, morbid fears that they have a serious physical disease such as cancer or heart disease. Not all patients with such morbid fears complain of physical symptoms.

As explained on p. 183, the authors regard hypochondriasis as a symptom of another psychiatric disorder and not as a primary syndrome.

One further point about diagnosis needs to be emphasized. In a patient with unexplained physical symptoms a psychiatric diagnosis should only be made on positive grounds. It should not be assumed that such symptoms are of psychogenic origin merely because they occur in relation to stressful events. The latter are common and may coincide with physical disease which is not yet detectable but is far enough advanced to produce symptoms. For the diagnosis of psychiatric disorder, the same strict criteria should be used in the physically ill as in the physically healthy.

When physical symptoms can be confidently diagnosed as psychologically determined, the treatment is that of the underlying psychological disorder. Patients with fears of serious physical illness should be given strong reassurance. Often such patients are easily reassured, but a few become persistently dissatisfied attenders at general practice surgeries and hospital clinics. Patients with a firm conviction of being seriously ill are difficult to reassure. They often remain convinced that doctors have failed to find the cause of their illness. Such patients should not only be reassured on this point; they should be given a positive explanation of the psychological nature of their problem.

OTHER ASPECTS OF PSYCHOLOGICAL CAUSATION IN MEDICINE

Pain

Pain is the commonest symptom in medical practice. It is also common in psychiatric practice; in several surveys it was reported as a symptom by about one-fifth of psychiatric inpatients and over half of psychiatric outpatients (Mersky and Spear 1967).

Pain may cause psychological distress, or may itself arise from psychological causes. It is for example a major cause of emotional distress in the severely ill and dying. On the other hand it may be a feature of any of the psychiatric conditions described in the previous section, particularly depression (see Blumer and Heilbronn 1982). Pain is a common complaint of people with a hypochondriacal personality, an association that led Engel to suggest the term 'pain-prone' personality.

The main sites of psychologically determined pain are the head and neck, the abdomen in both adults (Dally and Gomez 1977) and children (see p. 677), the lower back (see Wolkind 1976; Crown 1980), the limbs, and the genitals. The pain is often continuous for long periods and unresponsive to analgesics, but does not wake the patient from sleep. The patient often describes the pain as being clearly associated with emotional factors.

Atypical facial pain is of particular interest. It is a poorly located pain that has no segmental or cranial nerve distribution. In a study of 93 patients attending a special clinic for facial pain, Lascelles (1969) found that they all had depressive symptoms, and many had depressive disorders that were often atypical. When 53 of these patients were given physical treatment (ECT or antidepressant medication), 29 were completely relieved of pain, and most of the others had some relief. When the other 40 patients entered a double blind trial of antidepressant or placebo, those on antidepressants had more relief from pain than did those on placebo.

Complaints of pain should always be taken seriously and treated appropriately. Adequate medical treatment is essential especially in the chronically ill and the dying (see Reuler *et al.* 1980). The treatment of psychological pain is that of the underlying condition (see Merskey 1980). Behavioural treatment of chronic pain has been reviewed by Fordyce (1982).

Compensation neurosis

In this condition, which is also known as accident or traumatic neurosis, symptoms or disabilities are prolonged or elaborated pending settlement of claims for compensation for injury, or pending settlement of a pension that depends on the extent of continuing disability. There is an inverse relation between the severity of injury and the frequency of compensation neurosis. Psychiatric treatment is seldom effective, but a single final settlement of the claim is often followed by an improvement in symptoms or disability. The condition is discussed in Chapter 7 (p. 177). For a review see Trimble (1981).

Munchausen syndrome

This syndrome is described on p. 177. The main features can be summarized by quoting Asher's (1951) original description of a patient:

admitted to hospital with apparent acute illness supported by a plausible or dramatic history. Usually his story is largely made up of falsehoods; he is found to have attended and deceived an astounding number of hospitals; and he nearly always discharges himself against advice after quarrelling violently with both doctors and nurses. A large number of scars is particularly characteristic of this condition.

The patient is usually a vagrant moving from one part of the country to another. Blackwell (1968) and Pankratz (1981) have reviewed the condition.

Dysmorphophobia

Dysmorphophobia is the name given to a condition in which the patient thinks that he has a deformity of some part of the body, and that this is noticeable to other people, although in reality there is no such deformity. The term was originally proposed in 1886 by Morselli, who grouped the condition with phobias and obsessional disorders. In fact it belongs to neither of the categories, since the symptom is either an overvalued idea or a delusion (see Chapter 1).

Typically the patient is convinced that some part of the body is too large, too small, or misshapen. To other people the appearance is normal, or there is a trivial abnormality. The common sites for complaint are the nose, ears, mouth, breasts, buttocks, and penis, but any part of the body may be complained of. The patient may be constantly preoccupied and tormented by his mistaken belief. It seems to him that other people notice and talk about his supposed deformity. He may blame all his other difficulties on to it – if only his nose were a better shape, he would be much more successful in work, social life, and sexual relationships. Such patients usually present in clinical practice with repeated requests to be referred to a plastic surgeon.

This symptom may be an overvalued idea occurring in association with severe personality disorder of the 'sensitive' kind described by Kretschmer. Alternatively it may be a delusion, and this is usually found in patients with schizophrenia. Hay (1970 *b*) reported a series of 12 men and five women with dysmorphophobia. Of these 11 had severe personality disorder, five had schizophrenia, and one depressive illness.

The treatment of dysmorphophobia is not easy. Cosmetic surgery is usually unhelpful, and often leaves the patient with a greater sense of grievance. It is generally best to explain to the patient that nothing would be gained by such surgery.

Treatment is basically that of the underlying condition. If schizophrenia is diagnosed, a phenothiazine drug in appropriate dosage may help. If there is personality disorder, the doctor should try to help the patient to cope with occupational, social, and sexual difficulties. He should explain to the patient tactfully that there is no real deformity, and that mistaken beliefs about one's own appearance may develop through overhearing chance remarks, or in other ways. Some patients are helped by reassurance, encouragement, and support, but many are resistant to change.

THE PSYCHOLOGICAL CARE OF THE DYING PATIENT

This section is mainly concerned with patients who are dying slowly, especially from cancer. Surveys have shown that these patients often have significant depressive or anxiety symptoms; among patients dying in hospital, for example, it has been reported that up to a half have such symptoms. Guilt and anger are also common, either in association with depressive symptoms or without them. Guilty ideas are often concerned with the demands that the patient must inevitably make on the family. Anger may be obvious or hidden; although evoked by the patient's plight, it is often displaced on to doctors, nurses, and relatives who are trying to help him. Acute organic syndromes are also common.

These symptoms have both physical and psychological causes. The physical causes are important and include dyspnoea, nausea, vomiting, and pain. There is a particularly strong association between dyspnoea and anxiety. Some of the drugs used to treat physical illness may cause depression (see p. 333). The psychological causes are obvious but often overlooked. Depression can be understood as a form of mourning for the impending loss of friends and family. Anxiety is an understandable reaction to the uncertainties ahead and the possibility of pain, disfigurement, and incontinence. Patients are often made anxious by the thought that they may be abandoned by their friends, relatives, or doctors.

These reactions are more common among dying patients who are young, and less frequent in those who are elderly. They depend on the patient's personality and his beliefs about an afterlife. They are also increased when the patient has poor communication with the staff looking after him, or with his relatives. Poor communication is more common than it need be because staff or relatives are often uncertain how to speak to the dying. Such uncertainty is greater if the patient, relatives, and staff do not know exactly who has been told what about the diagnosis and prognosis. In these circumstances, relatives may draw back from the patient, so increasing his feelings of fear and despair.

Kubler Ross (1969) has described five phases of psychological adjustment to impending death. Although the phases do not always occur in the same sequence, and some may not be experienced at all, they are a useful guide to reactions that may be met. The phases are: denial and isolation; anger, 'bargaining' (partial acceptance but immediate problems still denied); depression; and acceptance.

Dying patients use various psychological defence mechanisms against over-whelming emotion. The three commonest mechanisms are denial, dependency, and displacement. **Denial** is usually the first reaction to being told that the illness is fatal. This reaction may lead to an initial period of calm. Afterwards denial usually diminishes and the patient gradually comes to terms with the problems facing him. Even so, denial may return at times when there are signs that the disease is progressing. As a result, a patient may behave for a time as if he understands the nature of his illness, and may later behave as if unaware of it. A degree of **dependency** is appropriate at certain stages of treatment, but it may be exaggerated to the point of giving up responsibility and making undue demands on other people. As mentioned above, **displacement** occurs when the dying patient directs anger inappropriately at other people.

Management

The aim is to bring about what Hackett and Weissman called an appropriate death, which means that 'the person should be relatively free from pain, should operate on as effective a level as possible, should recognise and resolve remaining conflicts, should satisfy as far as possible remaining wishes and should be able to yield control to others in whom he has confidence' (Hackett and Weissman 1962, p. 121).

For success in these aims the first requirement is adequate treatment of physical symptoms. The second requirement is to make a good relationship with the patient so that he feels able to talk freely about the illness and his feelings (see Hinton 1972; Cassem and Stewart 1978; Kubler-Ross 1969). If the doctor encourages the patient to lead the discussion, it is seldom difficult to know how much to say about diagnosis and prognosis. If the patient does not indicate a desire to be given information about approaching death, it is usually better to withold it until he is more prepared to receive it. On the other hand if he wants to know the prognosis, prevarication will only make him feel that he cannot trust those who are caring for him. The decision as to what should be said is less difficult than is usually supposed. It is useful to remember that most patients become aware that they are dying whether they are told or not (Hinton 1972).

Psychotropic medication has a limited but important part in the treatment of the dying. Anxiolytic drugs may be given for short periods to relieve extreme distress. Antidepressant drugs should be prescribed when there is a persistent depressive disorder that does not respond to psychological measures.

It should not be forgotten that relatives also need information, advice, and an opportunity to talk about their feelings. They should be helped to understand the reasons for the patient's anger or other reactions that may cause them distress.

Most problems of the dying are better dealt with by hospital staff or the general practitioner than by a psychiatrist. Referral to a psychiatrist is appropriate for patients with severe psychiatric symptoms or disturbed behaviour (usually due to an acute organic syndrome). In one terminal care unit about a sixth of admissions were referred to a psychiatrist (Stedeford and Bloch 1979). The referred patients had four main types of problem: (i) difficulty in talking to relatives and doctors about the illness; (ii) difficulties in accepting social restrictions, making appropriate plans, and taking decisions about their illness and everyday lives; (iii) difficulties in accepting the effects of the illness on the pattern of family life; (iv) long-term problems (personality and family problems) that had been present long before the physical illness (Stedeford 1981).

CONSULTATION AND LIAISON PSYCHIATRY

These terms refer to two separate ways of conducting psychiatric work in a general hospital. In consultation work, the psychiatrist is available to give an opinion on patients referred to him by physicians and surgeons. In liaison work he becomes a member of a medical or surgical team, takes part in ward rounds and clinical meetings and offers advice about any patient to whose care he feels able to contribute. The liaison psychiatrist also tries to help other staff to deal with day to day psychological problems encountered in their work, including the problems of patients whom he does not interview himself. Although it is generally accepted that close personal contact between psychiatrist and physician can be of considerable value, it is also widely held that regular participation in medical ward rounds and the activities of the medical team is of much less value (Lipowski 1979; Greenhill 1977).

Lipowski and Wolsten (1981) have described the characteristics of 2000 referrals to a typical American consultation unit. The main reasons for referral were: help with diagnosis (52 per cent), advice on management (51 per cent); and 'disposal' (15 per cent). The patients represented 4 per cent of all admissions to the hospital. Referral was determined not so much by the severity of psychiatric disorder as by management difficulties and the attitudes of the physicians and surgeons towards psychiatry. Similar findings have been reported from other American consultation services. In Britain the majority of referrals to consultation units are for deliberate self harm (see p. 408).

Consultation-liaison units vary considerably in their size and organization. In some the staff is permanent, whilst in others the staff is rotating through a psychiatric training programme. Some units have multidisciplinary teams including psychiatrists, clinical psychologists, and nurses. Lipowski (1981) found that the attachment of a liaison nurse to his unit resulted in fewer referrals to psychiatrists and fewer management difficulties on the wards.

Consultation

Consultation has two parts: assessment of the patient and communication with the doctor making the referral. Assessment is not essentially different from that of any other patient referred for a psychiatric opinion. On receiving the referral request the psychiatrist makes sure that the referring doctor has discussed psychiatric referral with the patient. Before interviewing the patient the psychiatrist reads the relevant medical notes and asks the nursing staff about the patient's mental state and behaviour. He finds out what treatment the patient is receiving, and if necessary consults the *British national formulary* about the side-effects of any drugs not well known to him.

When starting to interview the patient, the psychiatrist makes clear the purpose of the consultation. It may be necessary to discuss the patient's anxieties about seeing a psychiatrist and to explain how the interview may contribute to the treatment plan. Next an appropriately detailed history is obtained and the mental state examined. Usually the physical state is already recorded in the notes, but occasionally it will be necessary to extend the examination of the nervous system. It is essential for the psychiatrist to have a full understanding of the patient's physical condition. At this stage it may be necessary to ask further questions of the ward staff or social worker, to interview relatives, or to telephone the family doctor and enquire about the patient's social background and any previous psychiatric disorder.

The psychiatrist should keep separate full notes of the examination of the patient and of interviews with informants. His entry in the medical notes should differ from conventional psychiatric case-notes (see Garrick and Stotland 1982). The entry should be brief. It should omit confidential information as far as possible and should concentrate on answering the questions raised by the referring doctor. When an opinion is entered in the medical notes, the principles are similar to those adopted in writing to the general practitioner (see p. 65). It is important to make clear the nature of any immediate treatment that is recommended, and who is to carry it out. If the assessment is provisional until other informants have been interviewed, the psychiatrist should state when the final opinion will be given. It is often appropriate to discuss the proposed plan of management with the consultant, ward doctor, or nurse in charge, before writing a final option. In this way the psychiatrist can make sure that his recommendations are feasible and that he has answered the relevant questions about the patient. The note should be signed legibly, and indicate the psychiatrist's professional grade (for example, registrar). The psychiatrist should tell the ward staff where he or a deputy can be found should further help be required.

Recommendations about treatment are similar to those for a similar psychiatric disorder in a physically well patient. When psychiatric drugs are prescribed, attention should be paid to the possible effects of the patient's physical state on their metabolism and excretion; and to any possible interactions with other drugs prescribed for the physical illness. A realistic assessment should be made of the amount of supervision available on a medical or surgical ward; for example, for a depressed patient with suicidal ideas. No undue demands should be made, but with support from a psychiatrist the nursing staff can manage most brief psychiatric disorders that arise in a general hospital. (For reviews of the methods of consultation see Lipowski 1974; Glickman 1980).

A review of syndromes

INTRODUCTION

Of the endocrine disorders, only diabetes will be discussed here; the rest are considered in Chapter 11. Similarly, of the neurological syndromes, only movement disorders are discussed here; the rest are also reviewed in Chapter 11. The reasons for this separation are explained on p. 295. Before turning to the individual syndromes, some problems of classification need to be considered.

When a psychiatric disorder arises in the course of physical illness, both are recorded: for example, coronary thrombosis and depressive disorder. When the psychiatric disturbance is not severe enough to be diagnosed as a syndrome, it is recorded as an adjustment reaction.

Occasionally there may be good evidence that psychological factors have contributed to the aetiology of a physical disorder. Code 316 of ICD 9 can then be used, which is called 'psychic factors associated with diseases classified elsewhere'. This name is rather unsatisfactory but the category is defined as follows:

mental disturbances or psychic factors of any type thought to have played a major part in the aetiology of physical conditions, usually involving tissue damage, classified elsewhere. The mental disturbance is usually mild and nonspecific and psychic factors (worry, fear, conflict, etc.) may be present without any overt psychiatric disorder.

ICD 9 recommends that, in the rare instance where a psychiatric disorder is thought to have caused a physical condition, a second additional code should be used to record the psychiatric diagnosis.

When physical symptoms arise from a psychiatric disorder, only the latter is recorded. If the psychiatric disorder falls short of a syndrome, code 306 can be used, namely: 'physiological malfunction arising from mental factors'. This code might be applied, for example, to episodes of hyperventilation in a patient who does not have a definite anxiety neurosis.

Finally, some specific disorders are classified under 307: 'special symptoms or syndromes not classified elsewhere'. Examples of disorders classified under this heading are anorexia nervosa, tics, and specific disorders of sleep.

DSM III has an additional category, 'factitious disorders'. The word factitious means not real or genuine. According to DSM III, factitious disorders are characterized by physical or psychological symptoms that are produced by the individual and are under voluntary control. Whether or not symptoms are under voluntary control can only be inferred by the outside observer, and this is clearly a difficult judgement to make.

DSM has separate categories of factitious disorder with psychological symptoms, and factitious disorder with physical symptoms. However, the essential characteristic of both is that there is no apparent goal other than to assume the patient role. Factitious disorders are to be distinguished from malingering, in which symptoms are also under voluntary control, but the goal 'is obviously recognisable with a knowledge of the environmental circumstances'. According to DSM III, an example of factitious disorder is the Munchausen syndrome (see p. 177), whilst examples of malingering are feigning illness to avoid trial in court or military conscription.

DISORDERS OF EATING

Anorexia nervosa

Anorexia nervosa was described and named in 1868 by the physician William Gull, who emphasized psychological causes, the need to restore weight, and the role of the family.

The main clinical features are a body weight more than 25 per cent below the standard weight, an intense wish to be thin and, in women, amenorrhoea. Most patients are young women (see epidemiology below). The condition usually begins in adolescence, most often between the ages of 16 and 17. It generally begins with ordinary efforts at dieting in a girl who is somewhat overweight at the time. The central psychological features are a fear of being fat and a relentless pursuit of a low body weight. The patient has a distorted image of her body, believing herself to be too fat even when severely underweight. This distorted image has been confirmed by measurements of the actual and perceived size of the body (see Garner 1981). It explains why many patients do not want to be helped to gain weight.

The pursuit of thinness may take several forms. Patients generally eat little and show a particular avoidance of carbohydrates, and some try to achieve weight loss by induced vomiting, excessive exercise, and purging. Patients are often preoccupied with thoughts of food, and sometimes enjoy cooking elaborate meals for other people. Ten to 20 per cent of patients with anorexia nervosa admit to stealing food, either by shop-lifting or in other ways. In various series reported by British psychiatrists, up to half the patients had episodes of uncontrollable overeating, sometimes called binge eating or bulimia. This behaviour becomes more frequent with increasing age. During binges, the patients may eat large amounts of foods usually avoided, such as a whole loaf of bread with jam and butter. After overeating they feel bloated and may induce vomiting. Binges are followed by remorse and intensified efforts to lose weight. If other people encourage them to eat more, patients are often resentful; they may hide food or vomit secretly as soon as the meal is over.

Amenorrhoea is an important feature. It occurs early in the development of the condition and in about a fifth of cases it precedes obvious weight loss. Some cases first come to medical attention with amenorrhoea rather than eating disorder. In women and men lack of sexual interest is usual. (Anorexia nervosa is reviewed in the book by Garfinkel and Garner 1982.)

Physical consequences

A number of important symptoms and signs are secondary to starvation, including sensitivity to cold, constipation, low blood pressure, bradycardia, and hypothermia. In most cases, amenorrhoea is probably secondary to weight loss but as mentioned above in a few cases amenorrhoea is the first symptom. Investigations may show leucopenia, and abnormalities of water regulation. Vomiting and abuse of laxatives may lead to hypokalaemia and alkalosis. These abnormalities may cause epilepsy or, rarely, death from cardiac arrhythmia. Hormonal abnormalities also occur: growth hormone levels are raised; plasma cortisol is increased and its normal diurnal variation lost; levels of gonadotrophin are reduced. Thyroxine and TSH are usually normal but tri-iodothyronine (T_3) may be reduced (see Beumont and Russell 1982).

Epidemiology

Using data from three psychiatric case registers, Kendell *et al.* (1973) found that the average incidence of anorexia nervosa varied from 0.37 per 100 000 population per year in Monroe County, to 1.6 per 100 000 in north-east Scotland. For females aged 15 to 34, the rates per 100 000 per year ranged from 0.8 in Monroe County to 10.8 in north-east Scotland.

It is difficult to determine the true prevalence of anorexia nervosa because many people with the condition deny their symptoms. Surveys have suggested prevalence rates of 1–2 per cent among schoolgirls and female university students. Many more young women may have amennorhoea and less weight loss than the 25 per cent required for the diagnosis of anorexia nervosa (Crisp *et al.* 1976). Anorexia nervosa is certainly much less common among men, although the ratios reported in various European and American studies range from one male in four patients to one in twenty. The onset of anorexia nervosa in females is usually between the ages of 16 and 17, and seldom after the age of 30; in males the peak onset is earlier, about the age of 12. The condition is more common in the upper than the lower social classes.

Aetiology

Anorexia nervosa appears to result from a combination of individual predisposition and social factors that encourage dieting. Once the disorder is started, the response of the family may help to perpetuate it.

Genetics

Among the female siblings of patients with established anorexia nervosa, 6 to 10 per cent suffer from the condition (Theander 1970), as against the 1 to 2 per cent found in the general population of the same age (see above). This increase might be due to family environment or to genetic influences. There is no study of monozygotic twins large enough to give a reliable estimate of concordance.

Hypothalamic dysfunction

In anorexia nervosa there is profound disturbance of weight regulation. In some cases amenorrhoea begins before weight loss. This combination suggests a primary disorder of hypothalamic function, since it can occur with structural lesions of the hypothalamus. However post-mortem studies have not revealed any regular occurrence of hypothalamic lesions in anorexia nervosa, despite occasional reports of hypothalamic tumours in patients originally diagnosed as having anorexia nervosa (Lewin *et al.* 1972).

The occasional occurrence of amenorrhoea before weight loss strongly suggests a disorder of hypothalamic–pituitary function. However, according to Beumont *et al.* (1979) menstrual disorder nearly always follows dieting even if substantial weight loss has not occurred.

The endocrine disturbance in anorexia nervosa also suggests a hypothalamic–pituitary abnormality. Luteinizing hormone levels are low and show an impaired response to LH-releasing factor and to clomiphene. When weight is restored, LH levels rise but often fail to show the phasic pattern found in normal menstruating women. This abnormal pattern suggests a persisting abnormality of hypothalamic–pituitary function, but it could simply be secondary to prolonged starvation. (See Beumont and Russell (1982) for a review of the endocrine abnormalities in anorexia nervosa.)

Social factors

Surveys show that many schoolchildren and college students diet at one time or another. Concern about body weight is more frequent, and anorexia nervosa more prevalent, in the middle and upper social classes. There is also a high prevalence of anorexia nervosa in occupational groups who are particularly concerned with weight, such as ballet students (Garner and Garfinkel 1980).

Individual psychological causes

Bruch (1974) was one of the first writers to suggest that a disturbance of body image is of central importance in anorexia nervosa. She supposed that patients are engaged in 'a struggle for control, for a sense of identity and effectiveness with the relentless pursuit of thinness as a final step in this effort'. She also suggested three predisposing factors: dietary problems in early life; parents who are preoccupied with food; and family relationships that leave the child without a sense of identity. Crisp (1977) proposed that, while anorexia is at one level a 'weight phobia', the consequent changes in body shape and menstruation can be regarded as a regression to childhood and an escape from the emotional problems of adolescence. It is often said that psychosexual immaturity is characteristic of patients with anorexia nervosa. In a study of the sexual attitudes and knowledge of 31 female anorexics aged 15–33, Beumont *et al.* (1981) found that a considerable number were anxious or uninformed about sexual matters, but others appeared normal or near normal. These findings are difficult to evaluate in the absence of a control group, but psychosexual problems did not appear to be characteristic of the group as a whole.

Causes within the family

Disturbed relationships are often found in the families of patients with anorexia nervosa, and some authors have suggested that they have an important causal role. Minuchin *et al.* (1978) held that a specific pattern of relationships could be identified consisting of 'enmeshment, overprotectiveness, rigidity and lack of conflict resolution'. They also suggested that the development of anorexia nervosa in the patient served to prevent dissention within the family. From a study of 56 families in which one member had anorexia nervosa, Kalucy *et al.* (1977) concluded that the other family members had an unusual interest in food and physical appearance, and that the families were unusually close knit to an extent that might impede the patient's adolescent development. Neither these studies nor others in the literature have shown convincingly that such patterns of behaviour precede the illness or differ significantly from the patterns in families of normal adolescents.

Course and prognosis

In its early stages, anorexia nervosa often runs a fluctuating course with exacerbations and periods of partial remission. The long-term prognosis is difficult to judge because most published series are either based on selected cases or incomplete in their follow-up (see Hsu (1980) or Schwarz and

Thompson (1981) for a review). An example of an informative survey is a four-to eight-year follow-up of 102 female patients with anorexia nervosa who had attended a hospital in London (see Hsu 1980). At follow-up, two of the women had died of starvation. Of the remaining 100, as many as 65 had a normal weight; two were obese; 16 were seriously underweight (less than 75 per cent of ideal body weight), and 19 were moderately underweight. Amenorrhoea was still reported by 29 patients, and sporadic menstruation by 17. Food intake was normal in 37 patients; the rest had restricted diets, bulimia, or both. Purgative abuse was reported by 36 patients, and anxiety when eating with other people was reported by 33. The distribution of psychiatric symptomatology was: nil, 47; depression, 40; social phobia, 25; obsessive–compulsive, 22; and schizophrenic, 3. Psychosexual attitudes and behaviour appeared normal in 60 women, and clearly abnormal in 21. In a study at another London hospital Morgan and Russell (1975) followed up 41 patients (38 women and 3 men) after four to ten years. The findings were similar to those given above. The indicators of a poor outcome are: long illness; great weight loss; bulimia; vomiting or purging; and difficulties in relationships. The prognosis is generally worse in men than women (see Hsu 1980; Schwartz and Thompson 1981). It is generally said that late age of onset is associated with a bad prognosis. However, it is evident that many patients whose illness begins in early adolescence also have a poor outcome (see Smith 1982).

Assessment

Most patients with anorexia nervosa are reluctant to see a psychiatrist, so it is important to try to establish a good relationship. A thorough history should be taken of the development of the disorder, the present pattern of eating, and the patient's ideas about body weight. In the mental state examination, particular attention should be given to depressive symptoms. More than one interview may be needed to obtain this information and gain the patient's confidence. The parents or other informants should be interviewed whenever possible. It is essential to perform a physical examination, with particular attention to the distribution of body hair (normal in anorexia nervosa, abnormal in pituitary failure), the degree of emaciation, signs of vitamin deficiency, and the state of the peripheral circulation. A search should also be made for evidence of any other wasting disease, such as malabsorption, endocrine disorder, or cancer. Electrolytes should be measured if there is any possibility that the patient has been inducing vomiting or abusing purgatives.

Management

Starting treatment

Success largely depends on making a good relationship with the patient so that a firm approach is possible. It should be made clear that the maintenance of an adequate weight is an essential first priority. It is important to agree a definite dietary plan but not to become involved in wrangles about it. At the same time, help should be offered with psychological problems. Admission to hospital is often needed to re-establish an appropriate weight, but less serious cases may be treated as outpatients.

Restoring weight

The patient's admission should be on the understanding that she will stay in hospital until her agreed target weight has been reached. The target usually has to be a compromise between the ideal weight (from height and weight tables) and the patient's idea of what her weight should be. A balanced daily diet of at least 3000 calories is provided as three or four meals per day. Eating must be supervised by a nurse, who has two important roles: to reassure the patient that she can eat without the risk of losing control over her weight; and to be firm about agreed targets and ensure that the patient does not induce vomiting or take purgatives. In the early stages, it is often best for the patient to remain in bed in a single room while nurses maintain close observation. It is reasonable to aim for a weight gain of between a half and one kilogram each week. Treatment usually lasts between 8 and 12 weeks. Some patients demand to leave hospital before their treatment is finished, but with patience the staff can usually persuade them to stay.

Rarely the patient's weight loss is so severe as to pose an immediate threat to life. If such a patient cannot be persuaded to enter hospital, compulsory admission has to be used.

In addition to the general measures described above, chlorpromazine in high dosage is sometimes used, and has been reported to reduce anxiety and stimulate eating (Dally *et al.* 1979). However it may produce hypotension, and there is no convincing evidence that its use improves the outcome.

Behavioural principles are sometimes used. The usual approach is to remove privileges when the patient enters hospital, and to restore them gradually as rewards for weight gain. Suitable privileges include having visitors, newspapers, books, radio, or television for agreed periods of time. It is essential that the patient should agree freely to the programme before it starts, and should feel free to withdraw whenever she wishes. These methods have been described more fully by Garfinkel *et al.* (1977). They have not been shown convincingly to give better results than a general programme of the kind described above (which leads to satisfactory weight gain in hospital in about four patients out of five).

The role of psychotherapy

Many forms of psychotherapy have been tried. It is generally agreed that intensive psychoanalytic methods are not helpful. Clinical experience suggests that there is some value in simpler measures directed to improving personal relationships and increasing the patient's sense of personal effectiveness. In recent years, family therapy has been advocated (for example by Minuchin *et al.* 1978). Although problems in family relationships are common in anorexia nervosa, there is no convincing evidence that the general use of family therapy improves the outcome. If this therapy is used, it should be for selected cases in which family problems seem particularly relevant and the family members are willing to join in treatment.

Bulimia nervosa

Bulimia refers to episodes of uncontrolled excessive eating, sometimes called 'binges'. As mentioned above, bulimia is a symptom of anorexia nervosa but not in all cases. The syndrome of bulimia nervosa was described by Russell (1979) as an 'ominous variant' of anorexia nervosa. The syndrome has two principal components. The first is an intractable urge to overeat. The second is self-induced vomiting to prevent weight gain, sometimes accompanied by the abuse of purgatives. Patients with this syndrome are usually of normal weight and the women often have normal menses. Most patients are female. The prevalence of bulimia nervosa is not known, but surveys indicate that self-inducing vomiting is commonly used as a way of controlling weight (Fairburn and Cooper 1982). In a survey of college students, Halmi *et al.* (1981) found that 13 per cent met the DSM III definition of bulimia nervosa.

Clinical features

The patients experience an overwhelming urge to overeat. They then consume enormous amounts of food, for example a loaf of bread, a whole pot of jam, a cake, and biscuits. This voracious eating is done without any companion. At first it brings relief from tension, but relief is soon followed by guilt and disgust. The patient then induces vomiting, which at first is often done by putting fingers in the throat, but later can usually be done at will. Repeated vomiting leads to several complications. Potassium depletion is particularly serious, resulting in weakness, cardiac arrythmia, and renal damage. Urinary infections, tetany, and epileptic fits may occur. The teeth become pitted in a characteristic way by the acid gastric contents. In contrast to anorexia nervosa, bodyweight is usually within normal limits and menstrual abnormalities occur in less than half the patients. Another difference from anorexia nervosa is that the patients are usually eager for help. Bulimia nervosa should be distinguished from recurrent involuntary vomiting (psychogenic vomiting), and should be diagnosed only after the most careful investigation to exclude a physical cause (see Hill 1972).

Prognosis

This is uncertain. When bulimia is preceded by anorexia nervosa the prognosis is generally poor (Hsu 1980). The outcome of cases arising *de novo* may be better (see Fairburn 1982).

Management

As the syndrome has been recognized only in recent years, there is uncertainty about the most effective treatment. Russell (1979) advocates admission to hospital with careful control over the patients' eating. Fairburn (1981*a*) has developed an outpatient treatment which makes patients responsible for controlling their own eating. The patients attend as outpatients several times a week, keep records of their food intake and episodes of vomiting, and attempt to identify and avoid any environmental stimuli or emotional changes that regularly precede the urge to overeat. The preliminary results are promising.

Obesity

By convention, obesity is diagnosed when bodyweight exceeds standard weight by 20 per cent. When weight excess is greater than 30 per cent, the risk of cardiovascular disorder is increased. Most obesity is probably caused by a combination of constitutional factors and social factors that encourage overeating.

Psychological causes do not seem to be of great importance in most cases, but psychiatrists are sometimes asked to see obese people whose excessive eating seems to be determined by emotional factors. Even when obesity is not due to definite psychological causes, the psychological problems may result from being overweight and from attempts at weight reduction (see Stunkard 1980).

Treatment

Mildly obese people may need nothing more than advice about diet. The moderately obese require closer supervision (see Garrow 1981). The long-term results of all kinds of reducing diet are disappointing, whether supervised by a doctor or not (Stunkard and McLaren-Hume 1959). Weight groups, whether commercial or self-help, produce short-term benefit but do not improve long-term results. The same holds for appetite-suppressing drugs (see Stunkard 1980). Behavioural methods make use of positive rewards for weight loss or for behaviour that reduces the likelihood of overeating, such as eating exceptionally slowly. In controlled trials it has been found that regaining weight is less frequent after these methods than after other treatment (see Stunkard 1980; Forreyt *et al.* 1981).

For the grossly obese, surgical procedures are sometimes used, including jaw-wiring and by-pass operations. Jaw-wiring is often followed by rapid weight gain when the wiring is removed. Jejuno-ileal bypass results in sustained weight loss which seems to be due to reduced food intake rather than continued malabsorption. Metabolic complications are common after the operation, but psychological benefits seem to be considerable (Castelnuovo-Tedesco *et al.* 1982). Gastric reduction operations have fewer complications but are technically more difficult. The psychological and social outcomes of surgery are good but careful selection and prolonged follow-up are required (see Garrow 1981).

DIABETES MELLITUS

Because diabetes is a chronic condition requiring prolonged medical supervision and informed self-care, it is hardly surprising that physicians emphasize the psychological aspects of treatment (Tattersall 1981). However psychiatrists have taken relatively little interest in the disease. For reviews of the psychiatric literature see Johnson (1980) and Wilkinson (1981).

Psychological factors and diabetic control

Diabetes mellitus has sometimes been included among the so-called psychosomatic disorders, but there is no convincing evidence that psychological factors evoke the disease. There is much more reason to suppose that psychological factors influence the control of established diabetes. Such influences are likely to be highly important, since it is now generally accepted that good control of blood glucose is the single most important factor in preventing long-term complications. Hinkle and Wolf (1952) suggested that endocrine changes evoked by stressful life events could directly produce metabolic changes, including coma, in diabetic patients. They also recognized that failures of self-care could lead to failures of diabetic control.

Problems of being diabetic

Potential causes of psychological problems include restrictions of diet and activity, the need for careful self-care, and the possibility of serious physical complications such as vascular disease and impaired vision. At all stages of life, and especially in childhood, (see Johnson 1980) diabetes affects the family as well as the patient (see Tattersall 1981).

Sexual problems are believed to be common among diabetics. Two kinds of impotence occur in the men. First there is psychogenic impotence of the kind found in all chronic debilitating diseases. The second kind is more common in diabetes and is said to be characteristic of it. It may predate other features of the disease and is thought to be associated with pelvic autonomic neuropathy, although vascular and endocrine factors may also contribute (see Fairburn *et al.* 1982; Tattersall 1982).

Organic psychiatric syndromes

An **acute organic syndrome** is a prodromal sign of diabetic (hyperglycaemic) coma. It may present as an episode of disturbed behaviour, and the onset may be abrupt or insidious. The prodromal physical symptoms include thirst, headaches, abdominal pain, nausea, and vomiting. The pulse is rapid and blood pressure low. Dehydration is marked and acetone may be smelt on the breath. Another cause of an acute organic syndrome is hypoglycaemia (see below).

Mild **cognitive impairment** is not uncommon among chronic diabetics (Bale 1973). It may be caused by recurrent attacks of hypoglycaemia or cerebral arteriosclerosis. A more severe dementia is sometimes associated with cerebro-vascular disease.

Hypoglycaemia

This condition is usually induced by therapeutic insulin (when the patient has too much insulin or not enough food). Other syndromes occur as a result of an insulin secreting tumour of the pancreas (see p. 329), or of alcoholism or liver diseases (Marks and Rose 1965). Common psychological features of acute hypoglycaemia include anxiety and other abnormalities of mood, restlessness, irritability, aggressiveness, and behaving as if drunk. Physical symptoms include hunger and palpitations. Common physical signs are flushing, sweating, tremor, tachycardia, and ataxic gait. Occasionally other neurological signs occur. Severe episodes may proceed to hypoglycaemic coma. Hypoglycaemia is important in the differential diagnosis of psychiatric disorders, but it is easily missed.

CARDIOVASCULAR DISORDERS

Ischaemic heart disease

For many years, it has been assumed that emotional disorder predisposes to ischaemic heart disease (Osler 1910). Dunbar (1935) described a 'coronary personality'. Such ideas are difficult to test because only prospective studies can separate psychological factors present before the heart disease from the psychological effects of being ill. Recent research has concentrated on several groups of possible risk factors including chronic emotional disturbance, social and economic disadvantage, overwork or other chronic stress, and the Type A behaviour pattern (see Jenkins 1982). The best established of these factors is the Type A behaviour pattern, which is defined as hostility, excessive competitive drive, ambitiousness, a chronic sense of urgency, and a preoccupation with deadlines (Friedman and Rosenman 1959). There have been two large prospective studies of the Type A behaviour pattern. The Western Collaborative Group studied over 3000 men aged 29 to 59 working in ten Californian companies, and followed them up for eight to nine years (Rosenman *et al.* 1975). The other study was based on a sample from over 5000 men and women aged 29–62 living in the town of Framingham, Massachusetts (Haynes *et al.* 1980). These subjects were initially free from cardiovascular disease, and were followed up for eight years. In both studies rates of ischaemic heart disease proved to be twice as high in Type A subjects as in other subjects. These results are important, though it is not known how they might be brought about; whether, for example by hormonal changes or by alterations in blood lipids (see Stamler 1980; Marmot 1980; Steptoe 1981).

Trials of primary and secondary prevention have largely concentrated on changing risk factors such as smoking, diet, and lack of physical activity (see *Lancet* 1982*c*). Attempts have also been made to alter Type A behaviour. Thus the Stanford Heart Disease Prevention Programme attempted to alter two behavioural characteristics: 'hostility' and 'time urgency'. The study was based on male volunteers who had experienced a heart attack. An experimental group of 600 patients received monthly group therapy, and a control group of 600 were simply seen by a cardiologist. In the experimental group, the frequency of Type A behaviour was reduced, and the re-infarction rate was 7 per cent compared with 14 per cent among the controls (Friedman *et al.* 1982). It is not known whether at the end of the treatment there were differences between the two groups in exercise, smoking or other risk factors that might have mediated these effects (see Johnston 1982).

Patients often meet the early symptoms of myocardial infarction with denial and consequent delay in seeking treatment. In a coronary care unit, acute organic syndromes and anxiety symptoms are common (see Hackett and Cassem 1977), and emotional distress may be an important cause of arrhythmias and sudden death (Lown 1982). When the patient leaves the unit, depressive symptoms, excessive caution and uncertainty are common. Most patients overcome early discouragements and return to a fully active life, but a minority suffer persistent emotional distress and social disability out of proportion to their physical state (see Doehreman 1977). Such problems are more common in patients with the following features: long-standing psychiatric or social problems; overprotective families; a myocardial infarction that ran a complicated course (Mayou 1979).

Attempts have been made to reduce these psychological sequelae with various forms of rehabilitation (see Garrity 1981; Razin 1982). The most important component is probably early mobilization. Other components include exercise training, education programmes, and group therapy. Exercise training has been used most, but research has not confirmed the early assumption that it improves morale (Mayou *et al.* 1981; Stern and Cleary 1982). Individual and group psychotherapy seem to have only a limited value (see Blanchard and Miller 1977). It is important to provide appropriate care for the small minority of patients with persistent depression or other emotional or social problems.

Essential hypertension

Brief changes in blood pressure occur in the course of temporary emotional states. It has been suggested that prolonged emotional changes can lead to sustained hypertension (for example Alexander 1950) but the evidence is unconvincing (see Weiner 1977). There is some indirect evidence from animal experiments. For example, Henry *et al.* (1967) found that rats became hypertensive if kept in crowded cages in the first few weeks of life. In man, there have been studies of people working in stressful occupations. Thus, Cobb and Rose (1973) found hypertension to be more common among air traffic controllers than in the general population. Theorell and Lind (1973) studied middle-aged men and reported that those with more responsible jobs had higher blood pressure. Attempts have also been made to relate hypertension to neurotic conflicts or personality type, but they have not been convincing (see Steptoe (1981) for a review).

Among patients who know themselves to be hypertensive, complaints of headache, dizziness, and fatigue are common. These complaints probably reflect awareness of being hypertensive, since they are not particularly common in people who are hypertensive without knowing it (Stewart 1953; Kidson 1973). However, awareness does not necessarily lead to such psychological consequences. In a screening programme, Mann (1977) found no adverse effects from telling patients that they had raised blood pressure for which treatment was available.

Some of the drugs used to treat hypertension have psychological side effects. Depression has been reported in association particularly with reserpine, and also with beta-blockers and clonidine.

Psychological treatments have been tried for hypertension. Some have aimed to improve compliance with drug treatment (see Steptoe 1981), whilst others have attempted to provide an alternative to drug treatment. So far the most effective approach seems to be a combination of relaxation, home practice, and encouragement (Patel 1975). This combination leads to modest changes in blood pressure that are not merely the result of improved compliance with drug taking (see Johnston 1982).

Cardiac neurosis

This term has been applied to two conditions; in the first, the patient has heart disease and is disproportionately disabled by it; in the second the patient is free from heart disease but convinced that he has it. This section is concerned only with the second condition. During the American Civil War da Costa (see 1871) described this condition and called it Irritable Heart. Typically the conviction of suffering from heart disease is accompanied by palpitations, breathlessness, fatigue, and inframammary pain. This combination has also been named 'disorderly action of the heart', 'effort syndrome', and 'neurocirculatory asthenia'. The symptoms were originally thought to indicate a functional disorder of the heart. Now they are known to be an expression of an anxiety neurosis with hyperventilation (see p. 152). Beta-blockers have been said to be useful in controlling the symptoms (Fiorentini *et al.* 1981).

RESPIRATORY DISORDERS

Asthma

Alexander (1950) suggested that asthma is caused by unresolved conflicts about dependency, but there is no satisfactory evidence for this idea (see Weiner 1977). Explanations in terms of learning theory are equally unsupported (see King 1980). There is more convincing evidence that emotional factors can provoke individual attacks in patients with established asthma. Among asthmatic children, the prevalence of psychiatric morbidity is little greater than in the general population (Graham and Rutter 1970).

Attempts have been made to treat asthma with psychotherapy and behavioural methods but there is no definite evidence that these treatments are any better than simple advice and support (see King 1980).

Chronic bronchitis

Chronic obstructive airways disease is often associated with depression (McSweeney *et al.* 1982) and with cognitive impairment due to hypoxaemia (Grant *et al.* 1982). Some patients complain of breathlessness which is out of proportion to their physical disorder (Burns and Howell 1969). In everyday clinical practice breathing exercises, general exercise and social support all appear to be useful in improving morale and reducing disability (see Rosser and Guz 1981).

Hyperventilation

This causes alkalosis with vertigo, paraesthesiae, tetany, and mental confusion, and rarely loss of consciousness. Attacks of hyperventilation may occur in anxiety neurosis or hysteria. There may be a syndrome of chronic habitual hyperventilation (see Lum 1981) but this is uncertain. The diagnosis of hyperventilation can usually be made clinically; if not, it can be made by blood gas analysis which shows a low pCO_2. The acute episode can be treated by encouraging the patient to rebreathe his expired air from a paper bag. The general condition can be treated by drawing the patient's attention to his abnormal pattern of breathing and by providing training in normal breathing.

RENAL DISORDERS

Uraemia

This leads to an acute organic psychiatric syndrome. Uraemic patients are often drowsy and show intellectual impairment (see Osberg *et al.* 1982). Consciousness usually fluctuates, and there may be episodes of disturbed behaviour in up to a third of cases. These symptoms are not closely related to the urea concentration in the plasma, probably because electrolyte disturbances and failure to excrete drugs may contribute to the aetiology (see Lishman 1978*a*; Salmons 1980).

Haemodialysis

This procedure is associated with enduring psychological and social problems for the patient and his family (Cramond *et al.* 1967).

Psychological problems in the patient commonly include cognitive deficits associated with uraemia, anaemia, drug toxicity, and other physical complications. Other organic disorders are an acute psychiatric syndrome associated with dialysis disequilibrium, and a rare dialysis dementia probably due to the aluminium content of the perfusion fluid (Burks *et al.* 1967). Depression and anxiety are common (Czakes and De Nour 1978), and there is an increased risk of suicide. Symptoms such as lethargy, insomnia, and poor concentration may be due to either physical or psychological causes. Impotence is common, and often psychologically determined.

The social consequences of haemodialysis are prolonged, largely as a result of decreased physical activity. In a national survey in the United States, Guttman *et al.* (1981) found that 60 per cent of patients could not manage any physical activity beyond self-care. The consequences for family life are substantial; many patients withdraw from their family responsibilities, and the other members of the family often respond with overprotectiveness or resentment. Spouses have a high rate of psychiatric morbidity (Czackes and de Nour 1978).

Psychological and social factors cause difficulties in the management of treatment, particularly dialysis in the patient's home. The patient's capacity to cope may be influenced by his emotional state, general personality characteristics, and understanding of the treatment. Many patients fail to comply consistently with restrictions on diet and fluid intake, and this behaviour occasionally has a suicidal motive. Within the family, the willingness and ability to help in treatment is important, and so is the quality of family relationships. General social and financial circumstances are also relevant. Wai *et al.* (1981) followed up 285 patients on home dialysis for a minimum of 18 months and concluded that psychosocial and demographic variables may be more important that physiological factors for survival.

Renal transplantation

After receiving a kidney transplant, most patients are better physically and psychologically than they were before the operation. There is often a striking improvement in their sense of well-being, both physical and mental, and in their sexual functioning. Such patients are usually much fitter than those on haemodialysis.

Nevertheless psychological problems often occur. Problems of transplant rejection or threatened rejection are common, and frequently associated with considerable depression and anger. Psychological problems may also occur in association with immunosuppressive drugs and steroids in high dosage (see Salmons 1980; and Surman 1981). For these and other reasons, there is probably substantial continuing social and psychological morbidity in renal transplant patients (Procci 1980). It has been reported that such morbidity is greater in patients receiving a kidney from a living donor than in those receiving a cadaver kidney (Cramond *et al.* 1967).

GASTROINTESTINAL DISORDERS

Gastrointestinal symptoms are often an expression of psychiatric disorder. Complaints of poor appetite, abdominal pain, and constipation can all be due to psychological causes, especially depressive disorders and anxiety neuroses. In addition to the conditions reviewed in this section, the following conditions are discussed elsewhere: abdominal pain (p. 355), eating disorders (p. 364), alcoholic gastritis (p. 425), carcinoma of pancreas and bowel (p. 386), and globus hystericus (p. 172).

Peptic ulcer

It has long been held that mental activity can affect the stomach (see Weiner 1977 for a review). Peptic ulcers have been produced in animals by electrical stimulation of the hypothalamus (for example French *et al.* 1957). If rats are allowed varying degrees of control over electric shock, the less control they have the more likely they are to develop ulcers (see Ader 1976). In human subjects, the direct effect of emotion on the gastric mucosa has been observed in patients with gastric fistulae such as the patient Tom who was described by Wolf and Wolff (1947).

Alexander (1950) suggested that 'the repressed longing for love is the unconscious psychological stimulus directly connected with the physiological processes leading finally to ulceration'. The physiological processes were supposed to be hypersecretion of acid. In a prospective study of 2073 US army entrants (see Weiner *et al.* 1957), Mirsky and colleagues identified high and low acid secretors by using serum pepsinogen as an index. Subjects who developed ulceration were found to be hypersecretors, and were said to show 'psychic conflict related to passive and receptive wishes'. These findings are compatible with Alexander's theory, that high acid secretion could be the physiological mechanism through which psychological factors cause ulceration. However, much other evidence is against such a mechanism. For example, high acid secretion appears to be a lifelong characteristic rather than a response to stressors; moreover it appears that some forms of peptic ulceration are not associated with high acid secretion.

There is no evidence that specific psychological treatment is beneficial in the treatment of peptic ulcer.

Ulcerative colitis

In some patients with ulcerative colitis psychological stressors appear to provoke relapses. Because no physical cause has been found for ulcerative colitis, some authors have suggested that psychological factors are important in evoking its initial onset; for example, Alexander (1950) included the disease among the psychosomatic disorders. Theories about psychological causes vary from the suggestion that real or fantasized loss is the essential factor (Engel 1955), to the hypothesis that ulcerative colitis is related to a particular kind of personality characterized by obsessional traits, oversensitivity, and an excessive need for love. These ideas have been derived from clinical observations of selected patients, and have not been confirmed by suitably designed investigations (see Weiner (1977) for a review).

Although many psychological and social problems have been described in association with ulcerative colitis (Engel 1955; Feldman *et al.* 1967) most patients seem to adapt well to this unpleasant disease (Hendriksen and Binder 1980). Karush *et al.* (1977) carried out a controlled trial comparing combined psychotherapy and medical treatment, with medical treatment alone. They reported a better outcome after the combined treatment, but there are serious doubts about their diagnostic criteria, matching of controls, and assessment of outcome. Generally patients benefit from continuing support and encouragement, but it is doubtful whether more elaborate psychological treatment is needed in most cases.

Colostomy and ileostomy

In a survey of patients with a colostomy performed for anorectal cancer, it was found that complications such as depression, sexual problems, and social isolation were frequent and lasting. These complications were less frequent in patients who had undergone surgery without colostomy for anorectal cancer (Devlin *et al.* 1971). Patients undergoing colostomy or ileostomy for ulcerative colitis are generally pleased with the result, but psychological problems are again common. Apart from discomfort, embarrassment and concern about leakage of the bowel contents, sexual problems are common (Burnham *et al.* 1976). Often patients undergoing this kind of surgery are particularly helped by advice from other patients who have already made a good adjustment to it.

Irritable bowel syndrome

This syndrome consists of complaints of abdominal pain, usually over the descending colon, with diarrhoea or alternating diarrhoea and constipation. Some patients describe the passage of mucus (hence the alternative name mucus colitis). The syndrome is commonly seen in gastroenterology clinics. It appears that many people have the symptoms but do not consult a doctor (Thompson and Heaton 1980).

The **aetiology** is not certain. The abnormality is in the motility of the bowel; the mucosa is not inflamed. Chaudhury and Truelove (1962) drew attention to the role of psychological factors in precipitating the condition, but there is no convincing evidence that such factors are the sole cause. Associations have been reported with particular kinds of anxious-histrionic or hypochondriacal personality, but they probably reflect an unrepresentative selection of cases. Speculations about psychodynamic factors are unconvincing (see Latimer 1981; Ford *et al.* 1982). There is no specific medical **treatment**, but advice about diet may be helpful (dietary bulk to be increased, but fibrous food to be avoided). Occasionally anti-spasmodic drugs help (Kirsner 1981). Psychological treatment in the form of simple counselling appears to bring improvement to some patients. There is no evidence that more elaborate psychotherapy leads to better results.

DISORDERS OF MOVEMENT

In Chapter 11 on organic psychiatry, an account was given of several neurological disorders, including those that cause dementia, and some that may be followed by neurotic syndromes. This section is concerned with movement disorders.

Tardive dyskinesia

This condition is usually encountered after antipsychotic medication but rarely it occurs in elderly people who have not been treated with drugs. Tardive dyskinesia includes orolingual dyskinesia, chorea, athetosis, dystonia, and tics. The disorder may affect a single part of the body, or it may be widespread causing interference with feeding and walking. When the disorder is associated with antipsychotic drugs it usually begins after several months or years of treatment, but occasionally sooner. Reduction in drug dosage may precipitate it, and usually worsens it.

Between 10 and 20 per cent of patients taking antipsychotic drugs develop a detectable degree of tardive dyskinesia after a year, but severe symptoms are rare. The review by the American Psychiatric Association Review Task Force (1981) concluded that neither the length of the treatment nor the size of the daily dose was a main determinant. The elderly and women may be most at risk. There is no relationship between the late development of dyskinesia and the early occurrence of extrapyramidal side effects. Most patients eventually improve after medication has been stopped, although symptoms may last for months or years. Among those who initially develop symptoms, the risk of permanent dyskinesia is reported to be about 30 per cent. The biochemical basis is uncertain but dopamine supersensitivity has been suggested.

Treatment is to stop medication but this must be weighed against the dangers of relapse of the schizophrenia. Since tardive dyskinesia does not always progress, continued medication is justified if the psychiatric disorder is disabling and appears to respond to drugs (American Psychiatric Association Task Force 1981). Anti-cholinergic drugs make the condition worse and must therefore be avoided. Dopamine-depleting drugs such as reserpine and tetrabenazine have been tried but there is no generally effective remedy. (For reviews see Marsden and Jenner (1980); American Psychiatric Association Task Force (1981); Kane and Smith (1982)).

Spasmodic torticollis

In this rare condition there are repeated, purposeless movements of the head and neck, or sustained abnormal positions, or both. There is always some element of muscle spasm (a point of distinction from tics). The onset is usually between the ages of 30 and 50 years. The course may vary but it is usually a slow progression over many years. It is not certain whether the causes are organic, psychogenic or a combination of the two (see Lishman 1978*a* and Martin 1982 for reviews of the evidence). Treatment is unsatisfactory. Approaches have ranged from psychotherapy to surgery to the affected muscles, but there is no evidence that any is effective.

Writer's and occupational cramps

In writer's cramp attempts at handwriting are accompanied by painful spasms of the muscles controlling fine movements of the fingers. The spasms often begin as soon as the pen is gripped. The patient can learn to write with the other hand, but sometimes this too becomes affected. Related activities such as holding a paintbrush are not usually affected.

Occupational cramps are similar disorders in which a particular motor skill is impaired. They occur for example in pianists, violinists, telegraphists, and typists. They usually begin in middle life, and the prognosis is poor. Attempts have been made to explain the aetiology in terms of psychodynamic, organic, and learning theories, but without success. The poor response to any psychological treatment suggests an organic element in the aetiology, but so far none has been found.

Whatever the type of cramp, a common-sense approach to treatment is probably as effective as any other. For example, patients with writer's cramp can be taught to relax and then write for gradually increasing periods; first letters, then words and sentences. A form of aversion therapy has been used whereby a special pen delivers a small shock whenever the pressure of the writing fingers is too great. This therapy gives unsatisfactory results and it is not recommended.

Tics

Tics are purposeless, stereotyped, and repetitive jerking movements occurring most commonly in the face and neck. They are much more common in childhood than in adult life, though a few cases begin up to 40 years of age. The peak of onset is about seven years, and the onset is often at a time of emotional disturbance. They are especially common in boys. Most sufferers have just one kind of abnormal movement, but a few people have more than one (multiple tics). Like almost all involuntary movements, tics are worsened by anxiety. Tics can be controlled briefly by voluntary effort, but this results in an increasingly unpleasant feeling of tension. Many tics occurring in childhood last only a few weeks; others last longer, but 80–90 per cent of cases improve within five years (Corbett *et al.* 1969). A few cases become chronic. The subject of tics has been reviewed by Singer (1982).

Gilles de la Tourette syndrome

This condition was described first by Itard in 1825 and subsequently by Gilles de la Tourette in 1895. The main clinical features are multiple tics beginning before the age of 16, together with vocal tics, (grunting, snarling, and similar ejaculations). About half the people affected show coprolalia (uttering obscenities), and a few show echolalia. There may be stereotyped movements such as jumping and dancing. The tics usually precede the other features (Corbett *et al.* 1969). Associated features include overactivity, difficulties in learning, and emotional disturbances.

The frequency of the condition is about 1 to 5 per 10 000 population. It is 3 to 4 times commoner in males, and the mean age of onset is 5–6 years (Shapiro *et al.* 1968).

Studies of families suggest that Gilles de la Tourette syndrome and multiple tics (without vocal tics) are expressions of the same basic condition.

Aetiological explanations have been proposed in terms of psychogenic, developmental, learning, and organic theories, but none of them is convincing. The condition is aggravated by emotional influences, but this does not prove an emotional aetiology. On the other hand, the evidence for an organic cause (Shapiro *et al.* 1968) is only suggestive.

Many treatments have been tried. Haloperidol appears to be the most satisfactory, but the side-effects can be a disadvantage. There is not enough follow-up information to indicate the prognosis, but clinical impressions suggest that the outcome is generally poor (see Singer 1982).

SENSORY DISORDERS

Deafness

Deafness may develop before speech is learnt (prelingual deafness) or afterwards. Prelingual deafness interferes profoundly with speech and language development (see Cooper 1976; Thomas 1981). It affects educational achievement so much that 16-year-old school leavers are generally eight years behind children with normal hearing. Prelingually deaf adults often keep together in their own social groups and communicate by sign language. They appear to develop behaviour problems and social maladjustment more often than emotional disorder.

Deafness of later onset has different effects from those just described (see Thomas 1981). Both depressive disorders and persecutory ideas are common. In a systematic study of consecutive admissions to an ENT ward for stapedectomy, Mahapatra (1974) compared bilaterally with unilaterally deaf patients, and found more psychiatric disorder (predominantly depressive) among the bilaterally deaf.

Kraepelin suggested that deafness was an important aetiological factor in the development of persecutory delusions. This idea was supported by Kay *et al.* (1976), who carried out a large survey of elderly patients with chronic paranoid hallucinatory illnesses, and found a high prevalence of deafness among them, (p. 514). It is not clear whether there is any association between deafness and paranoid disorders in younger patients. This subject has been reviewed by Cooper (1976) and Thomas (1981).

SKIN DISORDERS

Alexander (1950) included 'neurodermatitis' among the psychosomatic disorders. Psychological causes have been suggested for many skin conditions including urticaria, lichen simplex, atopic dermatitis, psoriasis, alopecia areata, and pruritus (see Whitlock 1976). Usually the evidence for psychological causation is not strong, and any emotional problems detected could be the result rather than the cause of the skin disease, especially when the latter is disfiguring or unpleasant. Moreover, anxious or obsessional patients may be specially prone to consult doctors about skin disorders. When planning treatment it is important, as in all other physical illnesses, to take psychological factors into account. There is no convincing evidence, however, that dynamic psychotherapy leads to better results than supportive interviews provided by a physician.

Psychiatric disorders are common among attenders at dermatology clinics (Hall Smith and Norton 1952). The most frequent are illness fears, dermatitis artefacta, delusions of infestation, and depressive disorders (Sneddon 1979). **Dermatitis artefacta** is the name for self-inflicted skin lesions, which are usually areas of superficial necrosis. At first the patient denies responsibility for them. Most of the patients are young women, many of whom have abnormal personalities, though there is no single personality type. The prognosis is poor; the condition persists for many years in about a third of cases. Recovery is usually associated with a change in life circumstances rather than with treatment (see Sneddon and Sneddon 1975).

Some patients present to dermatologists with **delusions** about parasites or other objects in the skin. Most of the patients are middle-aged or elderly women. A few respond to treatment with antipsychotic drugs but generally the prognosis is poor (see Munro 1980).

A less common but important condition is **trichotillomania,** which is the irresistible urge to pull hairs from the scalp. Most cases start in adolescence, though children are occasionally affected. Women are more commonly affected than men. Some cases start at a time of stress and last only a few months, others last for years. Usually the scalp hair is pulled out, but eyelashes, eyebrows, axillary, and pubic hair may also be removed. Hairs may be removed in tufts or one by one. Some patients save the hair and eat it, a practice that can lead to intestinal obstruction. The hair-pulling is often denied by the patient.

No single psychological cause has been found. Many teenage girls habitually twist or pull scalp hairs, and a minority pull so much hair that patches of baldness result. Trichotillomania could be regarded as an extreme variant of this behaviour. Hair-pulling has been interpreted as a tension-reducing habit, a masochistic behaviour, a symbol of fear of castration, an expression of rage, a denial of femininity, and a masturbatory equivalent. None of these explanations is convincing. Hair pulling has also been reported in association with depression. Among the patients studied by Greenberg and Sarner (1965), two-thirds were judged to be depressed, but in the absence of a comparison group it is difficult to assess this finding. Hair pulling also occurs among the mentally retarded.

The prognosis is not known. A few cases have been treated by behavioural methods; for example, patients were rewarded for resisting the urge, required to keep count of the hairs removed, and trained in relaxation. Such treatment has not been shown to be generally effective.

JOINT DISEASE

Rheumatoid arthritis

Although rheumatoid arthritis is one of Alexander's psychosomatic disorders, there is no convincing evidence that psychological factors are important in its **aetiology** (see Weiner 1977). As with other physical illnesses, psychological abnormalities have often been described, but they could be the result rather than the cause of the illness, or simply coincidental. Attempts to describe a characteristic premorbid personality are equally unsatisfactory. Reports that psychological stressors can precipitate the onset or relapse of the disease are also unconvincing.

It is not surprising that this painful chronic disorder is sometimes associated with anxiety and depressive symptoms (Mindham *et al.* 1981). Most of these symptoms can be **treated** with counselling and anxiolytic or antidepressant drugs. Physicians treating rheumatoid arthritis spend much of their time in treating psychological reactions to the illness (Rogers *et al.* 1982).

INFECTIONS

Prolonged depressive disorder is likely to follow certain infectious diseases, particularly infectious hepatitis, infectious mononucleosis, influenza and brucellosis. Investigations of the last two suggest that prolonged depressive disorder is more likely in people who have experienced previous psychological difficulties (see Imboden 1972). In one study, a series of psychological tests was completed by 600 people who subsequently developed Asian influenza. Delayed recovery from the influenza was no more common among people whose initial illness had been severe, but it was more frequent among those who had obtained more abnormal scores on the psychological tests before the illness (Imboden *et al.* 1961).

CANCER

A useful review of psychiatric aspects of cancer has been provided by Greer and Silberfarb (1982).

Aetiology

It is not surprising that cancer patients have emotional reactions to the disease. Some writers have suggested the opposite relationship – that psychological factors play a part in the aetiology of cancer. For example Kissen (1963) studied patients with cancers in various sites, and concluded that those with lung cancer were characterized by 'restricted outlet for emotional discharge'. From this conclusion he drew the retrospective inference that this psychological characteristic had played a part in the aetiology of the lung cancer. Arguments such as this are not convincing, since they are based on investigations with considerable limitations of method. The limitations include reliance on retrospective accounts and on subjective or non-standardized methods of assessment (see Fox 1978). Instead of studying the role of psychological factors in the onset of cancer, other workers have examined the influence of these factors on the course and outcome of cancer. Greer *et al.* (1979) reported that the prognosis of breast cancer was better in patients who reacted to their illness by denial or who had 'a fighting spirit', than in patients who reacted in other ways. Animal research has indicated that the rate of tumour growth may be increased in animals exposed to stressful situations that are only partially under their control (Sklar and Anisman 1981). This finding suggests the possibility that endocrine or immunological mechanisms may be identifiable through which emotion could affect the prognosis of all malignancy.

Psychological symptoms in the early stages of cancer

It has been suggested that depressive symptoms may be a precursor of cancer in various sites. For example, Kerr *et al.* (1969) carried out a four-year follow-up of 135 unselected patients admitted with an affective disorder to psychiatric hospitals in Newcastle-upon-Tyne. Of 28 men diagnosed as having a depressive illness, 5 were found to have died from carcinoma. Compared with the expected figure (0.73) based on national death rates, this incidence was very significantly raised. The authors concluded that 'a form of depressive illness in male patients arising in late middle age without previous psychiatric illness and occurring without apparent cause may be an early and direct manifestation of latent carcinoma'.

However Evans *et al.* (1974) used record linkage data to carry out a standardized four-year follow-up on 823 patients who had been admitted to hospitals in Oxford with a principal diagnosis of depression. No evidence was found of any association between depressive illness and subsequent deaths from cancer in psychiatric inpatients. The issue therefore remains unproved, and there is a need for further studies based on all psychiatric patients (not just inpatients) or community surveys.

One association may be important. In a study of patients with carcinoma of the pancreas, Fras *et al.* (1967) found that 76 per cent had psychiatric symptoms, mainly depressive; in almost half of these patients, depression had preceded the onset of physical symptoms and signs such as abdominal pain, weakness, jaundice, and weight loss.

Psychological consequences of cancer

Generally the psychological consequences of cancer are the same as the psychological reactions to any serious physical illness. Some patients delay seeking medical help because of fear or denial of symptoms. When the diagnosis is known, anxiety and depression are common and the risk of suicide is increased in the early stages (Fox *et al.* 1982). In the later stages, organic mental syndromes are common. Levine *et al.* (1978) found organic syndromes in 40 per cent of cancer patients referred for a psychiatric opinion. The treatment of cancer by chemotherapy or radiotherapy can lead to both cognitive and affective symptoms (Silberfarb *et al.* 1980). An organic syndrome may also arise from brain metastases; these originate most often from carcinoma of the lung, but other common sources include tumours of the breast, alimentary tract, prostate, and pancreas, as well as melanomas. Occasionally brain metastases produce psychiatric symptoms before the primary lesion is discovered. Some forms of cancer produce a brain syndrome in the absence of metastases; this finding has been reported in carcinoma of the lung (16 per cent of cases) and of the ovary and stomach. The mechanism is unknown (see Lishman 1978*a*).

Psychological problems occur not only in the patient with cancer but also in close relatives (Freidenbergs *et al.* 1982). Nevertheless many patients and relatives make a good adjustment to the problems of cancer (see Weissman 1978). Their adjustment depends partly on the information they receive. Some doctors are reluctant to tell patients that the diagnosis is cancer, but most patients prefer to know the diagnosis and how it will affect their lives. The problem is particularly difficult when the patient is a child; even then it is probably better to tell the child the diagnosis unless there are particular reasons against it. Slavin *et al.* (1982) followed 116 survivors of childhood cancer and concluded that good psychological outcome was associated with the child having early knowledge of the diagnosis. Most of the survivors and their parents thought that the diagnosis should be shared with the child.

Although psychological problems in patients with cancer can often be helped, many remain undetected. One solution is to provide all cancer patients with educational programmes (see Harvey *et al.* 1982), counselling (for example Gordon *et al.* 1980), or with group therapy (Spiegel *et al.* 1981). However it seems more appropriate to select patients most in need, particularly as there is some evidence that counselling may increase distress occasionally (Maguire *et al.* 1980). The patients most likely to need psychological treatment include those with a history of previous psychiatric disorder or poor adjustment to other problems and those who lack a supportive family.

Breast cancer

About a quarter of patients undergoing mastectomy develop an affective disorder within eighteen months (Maguire *et al.* 1978). Affective symptoms are especially common after a recurrence, and during radiotherapy (Silberfarb *et al.* 1980) and chemotherapy. Frequent responses to mastectomy are low self-esteem, and embarrassment about disfigurement, and marital and sexual problems (see Morris 1979; Meyerowitz 1980). Careful follow-up to detect patients with psychiatric complications is probably more useful than counselling given routinely (Maguire *et al.* 1980).

Childhood leukaemia

This also presents special problems. Not surprisingly the child often reacts to the illness and its treatment with behaviour problems (Eiser 1979). Many parents react at first with shock and disbelief, taking months to accept the full implications of the diagnosis (see Hamburg and Adams 1967). About one mother in five develops an anxiety neurosis or depressive disorder during the first two years of treatment, and other family members may also be affected (Maguire *et al.* 1979). In the early stages of the illness parents are usually helped by advice about practical matters, and later by information about the disease and the opportunity to discuss their feelings which often include guilt.

PSYCHIATRIC ASPECTS OF OBSTETRICS AND GYNAECOLOGY

Pregnancy

Psychiatric disorder is more common in the first and third trimesters of pregnancy than in the second. In the first trimester, unwanted pregnancies are particularly associated with symptoms of anxiety and depression. In the third trimester there may be fears about the impending delivery or doubts about the normality of the fetus. Psychiatric symptoms in pregnancy are more common in women with a history of previous psychiatric disorder. Although minor affective symptoms are common in pregnancy, serious psychiatric disorders are probably less common than in non-pregnant women of the same age (Puch *et al.* 1963).

About half of all pregnant women experience nausea and vomiting in the first trimester. Some authors have suggested that these symptoms as well as the severe condition of **hyperemesis gravidarum**, have psychological causes related to the rejection of pregnancy. There is no reason to suppose that these conditions do have a psychiatric explanation. (For further information about hyperemesis gravidarum, see Tylden (1968) and Wolkind and Zayicek (1979).)

Pseudocyesis

Pseudocyesis is a rare condition in which a woman believes she is pregnant when she is not, and develops amenorrhoea and abdominal distension. This distension results in most cases from downward pressure of the diaphragm and lordosis of the lumbar spine rather than from the swallowing of air (Trethowan 1979). The condition is commoner in younger women, and appears to be akin to hysteria. It usually resolves quickly once the diagnosis has been made.

Older women occasionally develop a conviction of being pregnant when they have reached the end of their childbearing life. In these women abdominal swelling is less likely, but their morbid convictions are less easy to alter (see Cohen 1982).

The couvade

In this syndrome, the husband of a pregnant woman reports that he is himself experiencing some of the symptoms of pregnancy. The condition may occur in the early months of the woman's pregnancy, when the man complains usually of nausea and morning sickness and often of toothache. These complaints usually resolve after a few weeks, and seem to result from anxiety about the wife's pregnancy. Symptoms may also appear at the time of delivery, mostly in the form of cramp-like abdominal pains which disappear quickly when the woman's labour is over. Trethowan and Conlon (1965) studied 327 men whose wives were pregnant, and compared them with a control group of men whose wives were not pregnant. Individual symptoms of the couvade syndrome were reported more commonly by the expectant fathers, with a peak incidence at 12 weeks. These symptoms were associated with reports of worry about the wife's pregnancy.

Unwanted pregnancy

Until 1967, psychiatrists in Britain were often asked to see pregnant women who were seeking a therapeutic abortion on the grounds of mental illness. Before 1967, the law was restrictive so that a therapeutic abortion could be legally carried out only when there was a serious risk to the mother's life. (In practice, the psychiatrist was usually concerned with the risk of suicide.) Since 1967 the law has allowed therapeutic abortion on the grounds of likely damage to the health of the mother and also of her children. The provisions now make it generally more appropriate for decisions to be made by the family doctor and the gynaecologist, without involving a psychiatrist. However psychiatric opinions are still sought at times, not only about the grounds for termination of pregnancy but also for an assessment of the likely psychological effects of termination in a particular patient.

At the time of referral for a therapeutic abortion, anxiety, depression, and guilt are common. After termination most patients quickly lose these symptoms, and remain in good health without regretting the abortion (e.g. Ekblad 1955). Some patients have more symptoms after abortion, and they have usually had more psychiatric disorder previously (Todd 1972). Because of their previous history, such patients would be most likely to develop psychiatric symptoms if their pregnancy had continued. A serious mental illness is a rare sequel; Brewer (1977) estimated the incidence as 0.3 per 1000 legal abortions. The risks have been well summarized by the report of the Committee on the Working of the Abortion Act (1974), which stated 'the risk of serious mental illness or even any kind of disabling mental disturbance after therapeutic abortion appears to be slight'.

When abortion was less easily obtained than in Britain today, studies were made of aborted women and of those refused an abortion. For example Höök (1963) followed 294 Swedish women whose application for abortion had been rejected in 1948. Seven to twelve years afterwards there were high rates of divorce and emotional problems in these women. Forssman and Thuwe (1966) examined children born after refused applications for abortion and compared them with control children. By the age of 20 the first group showed significantly more psychiatric disorder and delinquency than did the controls.

Post-partum mental disorders

These disorders can be divided into maternity blues, puerperal psychosis, and chronic depressive disorders of moderate severity. (They are well reviewed in the book edited by Brockington and Kumar 1982.)

Maternity blues

Amongst women delivered of a normal child, between a half and two-thirds experience brief episodes of irritability, lability of mood, and episodes of crying. Lability of mood is particularly characteristic, in the form or rapid alternations between euphoria and misery. The symptoms reach their peak on the third or fourth post-partum day. Patients often speak of being 'confused', but tests of cognitive function are normal. Although frequently tearful, patients may not be feeling depressed at the time, but tense and irritable (Yalom *et al.* 1968).

Maternity blues is more frequent among primigravida. It is not related to complications at the time of delivery or to the use of anaesthesia. 'Blues' patients have often experienced depressive symptoms in the last trimester of pregnancy; they are also more likely to give a history of premenstrual tension (see Nott *et al.* 1976; Davidson 1972 for evidence on these points).

Both the frequency of the emotional changes and their timing suggests that maternity blues may be related to readjustments in hormones after delivery. Oestrogens and progesterone both increase greatly during late pregnancy and fall precipitously after childbirth. Changes also occur in adrenal steroids but they are complicated by associated changes in corticosteroid binding globulin. Yalom *et al.* (1968) suggested that changes in oestrogen or progesterone might be related to the blues, but this suggestion has not been confirmed (Nott *et al.* 1976). Bower and Altschule (1956) suggested that changes in corticosteroids might be important, but there is no direct evidence to support this view. At present the cause of maternity blues remains unknown.

No treatment is required because the condition resolves spontaneously in a few days.

Puerperal psychosis

In the nineteenth century, puerperal and lactational psychoses were thought to be specific entities that were distinct from other mental illnesses (for example Prichard 1835; Marcé 1858). Later psychiatrists such as Bleuler and Kraepelin regarded the puerperal psychoses as no different from other mental illnesses. This latter view is widely held today on the grounds that puerperal psychoses generally resemble other psychoses in their clinical picture (see below).

The **incidence** of puerperal psychoses has been estimated in terms of admission rates to psychiatric hospital (for example, Pugh (1963); Kendell *et al.* (1976)). The reported rates vary, but a representative figure is one admission per 500 births. This incidence is substantially above the expected rate for non-puerperal women of the same age. There is no evidence to support the hypothesis that the increased incidence in the puerperium can be explained in terms of delayed admission to hospital of women who developed psychiatric disorder in late pregnancy. The onset of puerperal psychosis is usually within the first one to two weeks after delivery, but only rarely in the first two days.

Three types of **clinical picture** are observed: acute organic, affective, and schizophrenic. Organic syndromes were common in the past, but are now much less frequent since the incidence of puerperal sepsis was reduced by antibiotics. Nowadays affective syndromes predominate. Dean and Kendell (1981) found that 80 per cent of cases were affective, and that the proportion of manic disorders was unusually high. Though less common than affective disorders, schizophrenic illnesses were much more frequent than the expected rate. As mentioned above, the clinical features of these syndromes are generally regarded as being much the same as those of corresponding non-puerperal syndromes. The exceptions are that affective features are probably more common in puerperal schizophrenic disorders; and that disorientation and other organic features are more common in both the schizophrenic and the affective disorders. Although (as noted above) it is generally held that puerperal psychoses are not essentially different from non-puerperal psychoses, some psychiatrists take the view that there may be rare specific puerperal disorders (for example, Brockington *et al.* 1978).

The early onset of puerperal psychoses has led to speculation that they might be caused by hormonal changes such as those discusses above in relation to the blues syndrome. There is no evidence that hormonal changes in women with puerperal psychoses differ from those in other women in the early puerperium. Hence if endocrine factors do play a part, they probably act only as precipitating factors in predisposed women. This suggestion is in keeping with the finding that women who develop post-partum psychoses are more akin to other psychotic women than to normal women in personal and family history of mental disorder (Seager 1960; Protheroe 1969). Attempts to find psychological causes such as conflicts about motherhood (for example Melges 1968) have not been convincing.

In the **assessment** of patients with puerperal psychosis, it is vital to ascertain their ideas concerning the baby. Severely depressed patients may have delusional ideas that the child is malformed or otherwise imperfect. These false ideas may lead to attempts to kill the child to spare it from future suffering. Schizophrenic patients may also have delusional beliefs about the child; they may be convinced for example that the child is abnormal or evil. Again such beliefs may point to the risk of an attempt to kill the child. Depressed or schizophrenic patients may also make suicide attempts.

Treatment is given according to the clinical syndrome. Acute organic syndromes are treated by finding and treating the primary cause. Schizophrenia and affective disorders are treated by the methods described in Chapters 9 and 8 respectively. In general it is better that the baby remain with the mother to help maintain emotional 'bonding' between them. For this purpose special arrangements are required. The ward must have facilities for a separate nursery where the child can be nursed at times when the mother is too ill to care for him. The lay-out of the ward should enable staff to observe the mother closely while she is with the baby. The nursing staff should have experience in the care of small babies as well as in psychiatry. Since the mental state may change quickly in puerperal psychosis, the psychiatrist should visit frequently to re-examine the patient. These arrangements are demanding for a while, but the risk to the child does not usually last long if treatment is vigorous.

For patients with depressive disorders of marked or moderate severity, ECT is usually the best treatment, because it is rapidly effective and enables the mother to resume the care of her baby quickly. For less urgent cases depressive disorders, antidepressant medication may be tried first. If the patient has predominantly schizophrenic features, a phenothiazine may be tried; if there is no definite improvement within a few days, ECT should be given as well as the phenothiazine.

Most patients recover fully from a puerperal psychosis, but a few (mostly schizophrenics) remain chronically ill (Protheroe 1969). After subsequent childbirth the recurrence rate for depressive illness in the puerperium is 15–20 per cent. According to Prothero (1969), amongst women who have suffered a puerperal depressive illness, at least half will later suffer a depressive illness that is not puerperal.

Puerperal depression of mild or moderate severity

Less severe depressive disorders are much more common than the puerperal psychoses. Estimated rates vary, but are mainly within the range 10 to 20 per cent (Pitt 1968; Nilsson *et al.* 1967; Paykel *et al.* 1980). These depressive disorders usually begin after the first two weeks of the puerperium. Tiredness, irritability, and anxiety are often more prominent than depressive mood change, and there may be prominent phobic symptoms.

Clinical observation suggests that these disorders are often determined by the psychological adjustments required after childbirth, as well as by the loss of sleep and hard work involved in the care of the baby. Previous psychiatric history and recent stressful events appear to be important aetiological factors. Paykel *et al.* (1980) assessed a series of women with mild clinical depression about six weeks post-partum, and found that the strongest associated factor was recent stressful life events. Previous history of psychiatric disorder, younger age, early postpartum blues, and a group of variables affecting poor marital relationship and absence of social support were also notable.

Most patients recover after a few months. Pitt (1968) found that about 4 per cent of all delivered women were still depressed twelve months after delivery. Using case register data from south-east London, Kendell *et al.* (1976) found there were two peaks of psychiatric consultation among women after childbirth – one about 3 months and the other 9 to 12 months after delivery.

In treatment, psychological and social measures are usually as important as antidepressant drugs.

MENSTRUAL DISORDERS

Premenstrual tension

This term denotes a group of psychological and physical symptoms starting a few days before the onset, and ending shortly after the onset, of a menstrual period. The psychological symptoms include anxiety, irritability, and depression; the physical symptoms include breast tenderness, abdominal discomfort, and a feeling of distension.

The estimated frequency of premenstrual tension in the general population varies widely from 30 per cent to 80 per cent of women of reproductive age (see Clare 1982). There are several reasons for this wide variation in reported rates. First, there is a problem of definition. Mild and brief symptoms are frequent premenstrually and it is difficult to decide when they should be classified as premenstrual tension. Second, information about symptoms is often collected retrospectively by asking women to recall earlier menstrual periods. Third, description of premenstrual symptoms appears to vary according to whether or not the subject knows that the enquiry is concerned specifically with premenstrual tension.

The aetiology is uncertain (see Osborn 1981; Clare 1982). Physical explanations have been based on ovarian hormones (oestrogen excess; progesterone lack); and pituitary hormones (disturbed fluid and electrolyte balance). None of these theories has been proved. Dalton (1964) has particularly argued that premenstrual tension is caused by oestrogen–progesterone imbalance, but the evidence on this point remains inconclusive. Various psychological explanations have been based on possible associations of premenstrual tension with neuroticism or with individual or public attitudes towards menstruation. These ideas are also unproven.

Premenstrual tension has been widely treated with progesterone, and also with oral contraceptives, bromocriptine, diuretics, and psychotropic drugs. There is no convincing evidence that any of these is effective, and treatment trials suggest a high placebo response (up to 65 per cent). Psychological support and encouragement may be as helpful as medication (see Clare (1982) for a review).

The menopause

In addition to the physical symptoms of flushing, sweating, and vaginal dryness, menopausal women often complain of headache, dizziness, and depression. It is not certain whether depressive symptoms are more common in menopausal women than in non-menopausal women. Weissman and Klerman (1977) concluded that there is no such increase in symptoms at the menopause. Nevertheless, amongst patients who consult general practitioners because of emotional symptoms, a disproportionately large number of women are in the middle age-group that spans the menopausal years (Shepherd *et al.* 1966).

Depressive and anxiety-related symptoms at the time of the menopause could have several causes. Hormonal changes have often been suggested, notably deficiency of oestrogen. In some countries, notably the USA, oestrogen has been used to treat emotional symptoms in women of menopausal age, but the results are uncertain. Psychiatric symptoms at this time of life could equally well reflect changes in the woman's role as her children leave home, her relationship with her husband alters, and her own parents become ill or die.

PSYCHIATRIC ASPECTS OF SURGICAL TREATMENT

Acute organic symptoms are common after major surgery (see Lipowski 1980 *a*). It is also a matter of everyday observation that patients about to undergo surgery are often anxious. Some investigations have looked for relationships between psychological state before surgery and post-operative psychological state or rate of recovery.

For example, Janis (1958) reported that patients who were anxious before surgery were likely to be excessively anxious afterwards; those who were moderately anxious were least anxious afterwards; whilst those who were least anxious before were likely to be inappropriately angry and resentful afterwards. Other investigators have not confirmed these findings, but have found a linear relationship between anxiety before and after surgery.

Johnston and Carpenter (1980) found that measures of anxiety before operation were poor predictors of the amount of post-operative pain or of the rate of return to normal activities. Cohen and Lazarus (1973) compared two groups of patients with different attitudes to forthcoming surgery: a 'vigilant' group who sought information about the operation, and an 'avoidant' group who preferred not to know. Contrary to expectation, the vigilant group fared worse post-operatively as judged by the number of days they stayed in hospital, and by the reporting of minor complications. No convincing relationship has been found between surgical outcome and personality measures, or between surgical outcome and interventions designed to reduce emotional disorders (Cohen and Lazarus 1979; Mathews and Ridgeway 1981).

The psychiatrist is most likely to be consulted about patients who develop post-operative psychoses. These illnesses do not differ from mental disorders encountered at other times; there is no specific post-operative syndrome. Stengel *et al.* (1958) studied 80 patients admitted to a psychiatric unit with post-operative psychoses. Affective disorders were most common, acute organic syndromes less common, and schizophrenia least so. Of the 46 affective disorders, 36 were depressive, 9 manic, and 1 mixed. Of the 21 acute organic syndromes 8 were superimposed on a pre-existing dementia. In the series, 22 post-operative psychoses developed within the first five days after surgery; and the rest up to nine weeks afterwards. Illnesses that began shortly after surgery were mainly organic. Some patients showed mainly the features of an organic syndrome immediately after the operation, and developed a typical affective disorder after a few days. There was no clear relationship between the occurrence of mental illness and the site of the operation, complications of the operation, or the anaesthetic procedure. Stengel *et al.* concluded that, apart from the organic syndromes, the operation acted as a non-specific precipitant. These findings still stand today.

The treatment of post-operative mental disorders is the same as that of similar mental disorders occurring at other times (see Surman 1981). Difficult decisions may have to be taken about the need to move the patient from the surgical ward (in which his post-operative treatment can be managed better) to a psychiatric ward (where any behaviour disturbance can be more easily contained).

Although there is no specific relationship between any particular type of surgery and the occurrence of mental disorder, a few procedures pose special problems. Two procedures may provoke paranoid states – eye surgery followed by prolonged bandaging, and orthopaedic surgery requiring prolonged immobilization. Mastectomy is followed by particular problems of adjustment (see p. 387), but not by an increased rate of major post-operative mental illness. The same holds for renal transplantation (p. 377). Amputations are followed by characteristic psychological problems (see Parkes 1978). Four types of surgery require special mention: hysterectomy, sterilization, plastic surgery, and cardiac surgery.

Hysterectomy

Several retrospective studies have indicated an increased frequency of depressive disorder after hysterectomy (e.g. Barker 1968). A recent prospective investigation using standardized methods showed that patients who are free from psychiatric symptoms before hysterectomy seldom develop them afterwards; some patients with psychiatric symptoms before hysterectomy lose them afterwards, but others do not (Gath *et al.* 1982). It is likely that these persisting cases (those with symptoms before and after surgery) are identified in the retrospective studies, and lead to the erroneous conclusion that hysterectomy causes depressive disorder. This finding provides a general warning about inferring the effects of treatment from the results of retrospective investigations.

Sterilization operations

Similar considerations apply to these procedures. Retrospective studies have suggested that sterilization leads to psychiatric disorder, sexual dysfunction, and frequent regrets after the operation. A recent prospective enquiry has shown that the operation does not lead to significant psychiatric disorder; sexual relationships are more likely to improve than worsen, and definite regrets are reported by fewer than one patient in twenty (Cooper *et al.* 1982).

Plastic surgery

In patients who are psychiatrically healthy, cosmetic plastic surgery generally gives good results irrespective of the degree of deformity (Connolly and Gipson 1978; Hay 1970 *a*). However, the outcome of cosmetic surgery is likely to be poor in patients who have unrealistic expectations, delusions, or a history of dissatisfaction with previous surgery (see Olley 1974). As explained in the section on dysmorphophobia, such patients are likely to be left with a greater sense of grievance after cosmetic surgery.

Cardiac surgery

Major heart operations, especially those involving by-pass procedures, are associated with considerable short-term and long-term psychiatric complications. Acute organic psychiatric syndromes occur in 20 to 40 per cent of patients who have undergone major heart surgery (see Lipowski 1980 *a*; Speidel and Rodewald 1980). Organic psychiatric complications may also arise from brain damage incurred at the time of the operation, particularly in the case of by-pass operations (see *Lancet* 1982*a*). Affective symptoms appear to be common during post-operative recovery and convalescence. It has also been reported that depression before the operation is associated with an increased surgical mortality (Kimball 1976). In some patients the surgical outcome is good, but the psychological and social outcome is poor; for example, after coronary artery surgery there may be persistent work and social difficulties, and psychiatric problems (Gundle *et al.* 1980; National Institute of Health 1981). Further prospective studies are required to determine whether these problems result from the operation, or are simply a continuation of problems that existed before surgery.

BURNS

Psychological and social problems may contribute to the causation of burns in children and adults (see Welch 1981). For example, burns in children are associated with overactivity and mental retardation, and also with child abuse and neglect. In adults, burns are associated with deliberate self-harm, alcohol and drug abuse, and dementia. Severe burns and their protracted treatment may cause severe psychological problems. Hamburg *et al.* (1953) described three stages. In the first, lasting days or weeks, denial is common. The most frequent psychiatric disorders are organic syndromes. At this stage, the relatives often need considerable help. The intermediate stage is prolonged and painful; here denial recedes and emotional disorders are more common. Patients need to be helped to withstand pain, to express their feelings and gradually accept disfigurement. In the final stage the patient leaves hospital and has to make further adjustments to deformity or physical disability and the reaction of other people to his appearance.

There are conflicting reports about the numbers of patients who have persistent emotional difficulties in adjusting after burns. Andreasen and Norris (1972) found persistent difficulties in about a third, but other workers have reported higher figures (see Welch 1981). It is generally agreed that the outcome is worse in patients with burns affecting the appearance of the face. Such patients are likely to withdraw permanently from social activities. These patients need considerable support from the staff of the burns unit, but only a minority require psychiatric referral.

FURTHER READING

Creed, F. and Pfeffer, J.M. (1982). *Psychiatry and Medicine.* Pitman, London.

Kaplan, H.I., Freedman, A.M., and Sadock, B.J. (1980). Section on psychological factors affecting physical conditions (psychosomatic disorders). In *Comprehensive textbook of psychiatry,* 3rd edn, Vol. 2. Williams and Wilkins, Baltimore.

Lipowski, Z.J. (1977). Psychosomatic medicine in the seventies: an overview. *American Journal of Psychiatry* **134**, 3.

Weiner, H. (1977). *Psychobiology and human disease.* Elsevier, New York.

13. Suicide and deliberate self-harm

In recent years a large proportion of admissions to medical wards has been people who have deliberately taken drug overdoses or harmed themselves in other ways. It has become clear that only a small minority of these patients intend to take their lives; the rest have other motives for their actions. Equally, only a minority are suffering from psychiatric disorder; the rest are facing difficult social problems. Psychiatrists are often called upon to identify and treat the minority with suicidal intent or psychiatric disorder, and to provide appropriate help for the rest.

In order to assess such patients properly, the psychiatrist must understand the differences between people who commit suicide (completed suicide), and those who survive after taking an overdose or harming themselves (deliberate self-harm). At this early stage in the chapter, it may be helpful to give a brief outline of the differences between the two.

In general, compared with people who harm themselves and survive, those who commit suicide are more often male, and are usually suffering from a psychiatric disorder. They plan their suicidal acts carefully, take precautions against discovery, and use dangerous methods. By contrast, amongst those who harm themselves and survive, a large proportion carry out their acts impulsively in a way that invites discovery and is unlikely to be dangerous. The two groups are not distinctly separate; they overlap in important ways. This point should be borne in mind throughout this chapter.

The chapter begins with an account of those who die by suicide. After this we describe people whose overdoses of drugs or self injury do not result in death. Each section starts with a description of the behaviour, its epidemiology and its causes. We then consider assessment, management, and prevention.

SUICIDE

The act of suicide

People take their lives in different ways. In England, drug overdoses account for about two-thirds of suicides among women and about a third of those among men (Morgan 1979). The drugs used most often are analgesics and anti-depressants; barbiturates were often used until recently, but are less common now. In the 1978 Registrar General's Report carbon monoxide accounted for about a third of deaths by poisoning among men but less than 5 per cent among

398

women. Nowadays carbon monoxide poisoning arises mainly from car exhaust fumes; until it was made less toxic, domestic gas was a frequent cause.

The remaining deaths are by a variety of physical means: hanging, shooting, wounding, drowning, jumping from high places, and falling in front of moving vehicles. Occasionally people pour petrol on themselves and burn to death; this drastic method is sometimes used in politically motivated suicides, but it occurs in other circumstances as well, for example following a widely publicized case (see Ashton and Donnan 1981).

Most completed suicides have been planned. Some patients save drugs obtained from a series of prescriptions; others use drugs that can be bought without a prescription, such as aspirin. Precautions against discovery are often taken, for example choosing a lonely place or a time when no one is expected.

In most cases a warning is given before committing suicide. In a survey in the United States, interviews were held with relatives and friends of people who had committed suicide. It was found that suicidal ideas had been expressed by over two-thirds of the deceased, and clear suicidal intent by rather more than a third. Often the warning had been given to more than one person (Robins *et al.* 1959).

Amongst people committing suicide, about one in six leaves a suicide note (see Shneidman 1976). The content of the note varies; some ask for forgiveness, whilst others are accusing or vindictive, drawing attention to failings in relatives or friends. Such vindictive notes are more often left by younger people. Older patients often express concern for those who remain alive (Capstick 1960).

The epidemiology of suicide

Accurate statistics about suicide are difficult to obtain. In England and Wales, official figures depend on the verdicts reached in coroners' courts, and comparable procedures are used in other countries. Such figures are affected by several sources of error. Occasionally it is uncertain whether a death is caused by suicide or murder. Much more often it is difficult to decide whether death was by suicide or accident. In many cases of uncertainty, the verdict will depend on legal criteria. In England and Wales there is a strict rule that suicide must be proved by evidence; if there is doubt an open or accidental verdict must be returned. In some other countries, less stringent criteria are used.

For these reasons, it is not surprising that official statistics appear to under-estimate the true rates of suicide. In Dublin, psychiatrists ascertained four times as many suicides as the coroners did (McCarthy and Walsh 1975) and similar discrepancies have been reported from other places (see for example, Litman *et al.* 1963). Amongst people whose deaths are recorded as accidental, many have recently been depressed or dependent on drugs or alcohol, thus resembling people who commit suicide (Holding and Barraclough 1975). For this reason, some investigators try to estimate suicide rates by combining official figures for suicide, accidental poisoning and undetermined causes. For the purpose of comparing suicide rates between different countries, this procedure makes little difference since the rank ordering is not affected significantly by using it (Barraclough 1973).

The suicide rate in the United Kingdom (less than 10 per 100 000 per year) is in the lower range of those reported in Western countries. Recently, the highest rates have been reported in Hungary (about 40 per 100 000 per annum) and the German Democratic Republic (36 per 100 000). Among the lowest rates are those of Spain (3.9 per 100 000) and Greece (2.8 per 100 000). It is not certain how far these variations reflect differences in reporting rather than real differences in the frequency of suicide.

Changes in suicide rates

Over the years since 1900, suicide rates in Great Britain have changed substantially at different times. During both world wars, recorded rates for men and women fell, but it is not certain whether this fall reflected a true change or the difficulties of ascertaining causes of death in war time. There were also two periods when rates were unusually high. The first, 1932–3, was a time of economic depression and high unemployment; the second, between the late 1950s and the early 1960s, was not so. Another unusual period was 1963–74, when rates declined in England and Wales but not in other European countries. The reasons for this fall are not clear. The latest data suggest that since 1975 the rates in England and Wales are rising again. While various reasons have been suggested for these fluctuations since 1900, the factors involved are so complicated that the explanation remains unknown.

Variations with the seasons

In England and Wales, for every decade since 1921–30 suicide rates have been highest in the months of April, May, and June. A similar pattern has been found in other countries in the Northern hemisphere. In the Southern Hemisphere a similar rise occurs during the spring and early summer, even though these seasons are in different months of the year. The reason for these fluctuations is not known.

Variations according to personal characteristics

In both men and women, suicide rates increase with age. At all ages, the rate is higher in men and women. Suicide rates are lowest among the married, and increase progressively through the never married, widowers, widows, and divorced. Rates are higher in social class V (unskilled workers) and social class I (professional) than in the remaining social classes.

Variations according to place of residence

Suicide rates in cities used to be higher than those in the country. In recent years this difference has grown less and for men it has reversed (Adelstein and

Mardon 1975). Within large cities rates vary among different kinds of residential area. The highest rates are reported from areas in which there are many inhabitants of boarding houses, and many immigrants and divorced people. The common factor appears to be social isolation (Sainsbury 1955). Compared with the general population, people who have committed suicide are more likely to have been divorced, unemployed, or living alone. (Sainsbury 1955; Whitlock, 1973 *a, b*).

The causes of suicide

Social causes

In 1897, Durkheim published an important book in which he proposed a relationship between suicide and social conditions (see Durkheim 1951). He divided suicides into three main categories. **Egotistic suicide** occurred in individuals who had lost their sense of integration within their social group, so that they no longer felt subject to its social, family, and religious controls. **Anomic suicide** occurred in individuals who lived in a society that lacked 'collective order' because it was in the midst of major social change or political crisis. **Altruistic suicide** occurred in individuals who sacrificed their lives for the good of the social group, thus reflecting the influence of the group's identity. Durkheim's views have been influential even though it now seems that he overemphasized social factors at the expense of individual causes. Sainsbury's work on social isolation, referred to above, follows directly from Durkheim's ideas.

Medical causes

Mental disorders are a most important cause of suicide. In several studies interviews have been held with doctors, relatives, and friends of people who have committed suicide, and detailed histories have been compiled about the deceased. These studies indicate that, amongst those who die from suicide, about nine in every ten have some form of mental disorder at the time of death (Robins *et al.* 1959; Dorpat and Ripley 1967; Barraclough *et al.* 1974). The most frequent of these mental disorders are depressive disorders and alcoholism.

The importance of **depressive disorders** is confirmed by findings that rates of suicide are increased among depressed patients (Fremming 1951; Helgason 1964). The depressed patients who die by suicide cannot be distinguished from other depressed patients by their symptoms. However, they differ in having made more previous suicide attempts (Barraclough *et al.* 1974), and being more often single, separated, or widowed (Pitts and Winokur 1964) and older (Robins *et al.* 1959). The risk is also greater among men than women (Pitts and Winokur 1964).

Alcoholism is the second most frequent psychiatric disorder among those who die from suicide, being present in about 15 per cent of cases (Robins *et al.* 1959; Dorpat and Ripley 1967; Barraclough *et al.* 1974). Follow-up studies of alcoholics confirm this high risk of suicide. Thus among alcoholics who had received psychiatric treatment in hospital, the incidence of suicide over a five-year follow-up was about 80 times that of the general population (Kessell and Grossman 1961). The risk is greatest among older men with a long history of drinking, a definite depressive illness and previous suicidal attempts. It is also increased among those whose drinking has caused physical complications, marital problems, difficulties at work, or arrests for drunkenness offences (Barraclough *et al.* 1974). **Drug dependent** patients also have an increased suicide risk (James 1967).

Personality disorder is detected in a third to a half of people who commit suicide, (Seager and Flood 1965; McCulloch *et al.* 1967; Ovenstone and Kreitman 1974). This group tends to be younger, to come from broken homes, and to live in a subculture in which violence and alcohol or drug abuse is common. Personality disorder probably combines with other causes to increase the risk of suicide. In their study, Barraclough *et al.* (1974) found personality disorder in about half the alcoholics and a fifth of the depressed patients who had died by suicide. **Schizophrenia** accounts for only about 3 per cent of suicides, but when treating it the risk should always be borne in mind (see Chapter 9).

Chronic painful physical illness is associated with suicide among the elderly (Sainsbury 1962). The risk of suicide among **epileptics** is about four times that in the general population (Barraclough 1981). After **deliberate self-poisoning** the suicide rate is raised (see p. 413).

Conclusion

The associations between suicide and the various factors mentioned above do not, of course, establish causation. Nevertheless they point to the importance of two sets of interacting influences: amongst social factors, social isolation stands out; whilst amongst medical factors, depressive disorders, alcoholism, and abnormal personality are particularly prominent.

'Rational' suicide

Despite the findings reviewed above, there can be no doubt that suicide is occasionally the rational act of a mentally healthy person. Moreover mass suicides have been described among groups of people, and it is unlikely that they were all suffering from mental disorder. A recent example was the religious community at Jonestown, in which a large number of people died together by taking poison (Rosen 1981). Nevertheless, in the clinical assessment of someone who is talking of suicide, it is a good rule to assume that his suicidal inclinations are influenced by an abnormal state of mind. If this assumption is correct – as it usually will be – the patient's urge to suicide is likely to diminish with recovery from the abnormal mental state. Even if the assumption is wrong (that is, if the patient is one of the few who have reached a rational decision to die) the doctor should still try to protect him from harming himself. Given more time for reflection, most people with suicidal intent change their intentions. For example they may discover that death from cancer need not be as painful as they believed. Hence they may change a decision that was made rationally but on false premises.

Special groups

Children and young adolescents

Suicide is rare in childhood. In a survey of all known suicides occurring between 1962 and 1968 amongst children under the age of 14, Shaffer (1974) found none in those under the age of 12. Up to the age of 14 years, official figures show a rate of about one in 800 000 per annum.

In the 12–14 year old group, more boys than girls commit suicide. Boys are more likely to use violent methods such as shooting or hanging, girls to take drug overdoses. Among children seen by child psychiatrists, most of those who threaten suicide do not carry it out. Nevertheless, amongst the group who did commit suicide, Shaffer found that more than 40 per cent had made threats beforehand. So in children, as in adults, threats should be investigated with great care.

Little is known about factors leading to suicide in childhood. Shaffer (1974) reported that suicidal acts and depressive disorders were common among the parents and siblings; and that children who died by suicide had usually shown antisocial behaviour. None of these associations is strong enough for reliable detection of the few children at risk. (Suicide in childhood is discussed further on p. 675).

University students

In the 1950s it was reported that suicide rates were increased among male students in some universities. Rook (1959) reported that the rate was 22 per 100 000 among Cambridge undergraduates compared with 6 per 100 000 in males aged 20–24 in the general population. Rook also presented evidence that the rates were increased in the universities of Oxford and London. The reasons for this increase are uncertain, though it has been suggested that loneliness and pressures of work might be important. Accurate data are difficult to obtain but it seems that the present rates among undergraduates may still be high, though lower than in 1959 (Hawton *et al.* 1978).

Doctors

The suicide rate among doctors is greater than that in the general population, the highest rates being among psychiatrists and anaesthetists. Many reasons have been suggested, such as the ready availability of drugs, increased rates of addiction to alcohol and drugs, the extra stresses of work, reluctance to seek treatment for depressive disorders, and the selection into the medical profession of predisposed personalities (see *British Medical Journal* 1964; also Craig and Pitts 1968). Whatever the true reasons, it is clear that the profession could do useful preventive work within its own ranks.

Suicide pacts

In suicide pacts, two people agree that at the same time each will take his own life. Completed pacts are uncommon. Cohen (1961) reported that completed pacts account for one in 300 of all completed suicides, while Parry-Jones (1973) estimated that there are about twice as many uncompleted suicide pacts as completed ones. Suicide pacts have to be distinguished from cases where murder is followed by suicide (especially when one person dies but the other is revived), or where one person aids another person's suicide without intending to die himself. The law deals with such cases by the provisions of the Homicide Act of 1957 and the Suicide Act of 1961. Under the Suicide Act a survivor who agreed to die himself but took no active part in the death of the other person is guilty of aiding and abetting suicide. Under the Homicide Act, a survivor who took an active part in the death of the other person is guilty of manslaughter. In practice, all cases are reviewed carefully, but not all are followed by prosecution. Of survivors found guilty, many are dealt with by probation (Parry-Jones 1973).

The psychological causes for these pacts are not known. It seems paradoxical that suicide, an act that is so often associated with social isolation, should be carried out with another person. Usually there is a particularly close relationship between the two members of the pact. In Parry-Jones's series, half the pacts were between lovers; however, in this study at least one person from each pair survived and had been prosecuted, so the finding may not be representative.

The subject has been reviewed by Rosen (1981).

The assessment of suicidal risk

General issues

Every doctor should be able to assess the risk of suicide. The first requirement is a willingness to make tactful but direct enquiries about a patient's intentions. The second is an alertness for the general factors that signify an increased risk.

Asking a patient about suicidal inclinations does not make suicidal behaviour more likely. On the contrary, if the patient has already thought of suicide he will feel better understood when the doctor raises the issue, and this feeling may reduce the risk. If a person has not thought of suicide before, tactful questioning will not make him behave suicidally.

Assessing risk

The most obvious warning sign is a **direct statement of intent**. It is now well recognized, but cannot be repeated too often, that there is no truth in the idea that people who talk of suicide do not enact it. On the contrary, two-thirds of those who die by suicide have told someone of their intentions. The greatest difficulty arises with people who talk repeatedly of suicide. In time their statements may no longer be taken seriously but discounted as threats intended to influence other people. However, some of these repeated threateners do kill themselves in the end. Just before the act, there may be a subtle change in their way of talking about dying, sometimes in the form of oblique hints that need to be taken more seriously than the original open statements.

Risk is also assessed by considering the factors that have been found in surveys to be associated with suicide (see p. 400 above). Older patients are more at risk, as are the lonely and those suffering from chronic painful illness. **Depressive disorders** are highly important especially when there is severe mood change, with insomnia, anorexia, and weight loss (Barraclough *et al.* 1974). It is important to remember that suicide may occur during recovery from a depressive disorder in patients who previously, when more severely depressed, had thought of the act but had lacked the energy and initiative to carry it out.

Other associations

As noted earlier there is an increased risk of suicide with alcohol dependence, especially when associated with physical complications or severe social damage; drug dependence; epilepsy; and abnormal personality. Suicidal schizophrenics are difficult to recognize; few give a warning or show any obvious mood change, but a history of previous self-harm is an important pointer.

Completing the history

When these general risk factors have been assessed, the rest of the history should be evaluated. The interview should be conducted in an unhurried and sympathetic way that allows the patient to admit any despair or self-destructive intentions. It is usually appropriate to start by asking about current problems and the patient's reaction to them. Enquiries should cover losses, both personal (such as bereavement or divorce) and financial, as well as loss of status. Information about conflict with other people and social isolation should also be elicited. Physical illness should always be asked about, particularly any painful condition in the elderly.

In assessing previous personality, it should be borne in mind that the patient's self-description may be coloured by depression. Whenever possible, another informant should be interviewed. The important points include mood swings, impulsive or aggressive tendencies, and attitudes towards religion and death.

Mental state examination

The assessment of mood should be particularly thorough and cognitive function must not be overlooked. The interviewer should then assess suicidal intent. It is usually appropriate to begin by asking whether the patient thinks that life is too much for him, or whether he no longer wants to go on. This can lead to more direct questions about thoughts of suicide, specific plans, and actions such as saving tablets. It is important always to remember that severely depressed patients occasionally have homicidal ideas; they may believe that it would be an act of mercy to kill other people, often the spouse or a child, to spare them intolerable suffering. Such homicidal ideas must not be missed, and should always be taken extremely seriously.

The management of the suicidal patient

General issues

Having assessed the suicidal risk, the clinician should make a treatment plan and try to persuade the patient to accept it. The first step is to decide whether the patient should be admitted to hospital or treated as an outpatient or day-patient. This decision depends on the intensity of the suicidal intentions, the severity of any associated psychiatric illness, and the availability of social support outside hospital. If outpatient treatment is chosen, the patient should be given a telephone number with which he can, at all times, obtain help if feeling worse. Frustrated attempts to find a doctor can be the last straw for a patient with suicidal inclinations.

If the suicidal risk is judged to be significant, inpatient care is nearly always required. An occasional exception may be made when the patient lives with reliable relatives, but only if these relatives wish to care for the patient themselves, understand their responsibilities, and are able to fulfill them. Such a decision requires an exceptionally thorough knowledge of the patient and his problems. If hospital treatment is essential but the patient refuses it, admission under a compulsory order will be necessary. The method of arranging this is discussed in the Appendix.

Management in hospital

The obvious first requirement is to prevent the patient from harming himself. This depends on adequate staffing, vigilance, and good communications. At times special nursing arrangements may be required so that the patient is never left alone. It is essential that a clear policy should be stated for each patient and understood by all the staff. For example, it should be clearly specified whether the patient is to be kept in pyjamas, how closely a member of staff is to remain at hand, and whether potentially dangerous objects such as scissors are to be removed. The policy should be drawn up as soon as the patient is admitted, and agreed between the doctor and the nursing staff. It should be carefully reconsidered at frequent intervals until the danger passes. It is especially important that any changes in policy should be made clear when staff change between shifts.

When intensive supervision is needed for more than a few days, increasing difficulties may arise. Patients under constant observation may become irritated and resentful, and may evade supervision. Staff should be aware of such problems, and treatment of any associated mental illness should not be delayed. If the patient has a severe depressive disorder, the rapid action of ECT may be required (see Chapter 8).

Appropriate physical treatment should be accompanied by simple psychotherapy. However determined the patient is to die, there is usually some small remaining wish to go on living. If doctors and nurses adopt a caring and hopeful attitude, these positive feelings can be encouraged and the patient can be helped towards a more realistic and balanced view of his future. At the same time he can be helped to see how an apparently overwhelming accumulation of problems can be dealt with one by one.

However carefully patients are managed, it will happen occasionally that a patient dies by suicide despite all the efforts of the staff. The doctor then has an important role in supporting other staff, particularly any nurses who have come to know the patient well through taking part in constant observation. Although it is essential to review every suicide carefully to determine whether any useful lessions can be learnt, this review should never become a search for a culprit.

The relatives

When a patient has died by suicide, the relatives require not only the support that is appropriate for any bereaved person, but also help with particular difficulties. In a study by Barraclough and Shepherd (1976) the relatives usually reported that the police conducted their enquiries in a considerate way, but nearly all found the public inquest distressing. The subsequent newspaper publicity caused further grief, reactivating the events surrounding the death and increasing any feelings of stigma. Sympathetic counselling is likely to help relatives with these difficulties.

Suicide prevention

As reported above, many people who commit suicide contact their doctors shortly beforehand. Most have a psychiatric illness, and four-fifths are being treated with psychotropic drugs – though not always with the most appropriate drug or the optimal dosage. These findings suggest a need to improve skills of doctors in identifying high risk patients and in planning their treatment. On the other hand, many depressed patients are treated successfully by general practitioners. It would be wrong therefore to suggest that the solution to the problem lies wholly in better training of doctors, though the latter might make a contribution.

Suicide prevention centres

In the United States, suicide prevention centres staffed by clinicians have been developed in many cities, starting in Los Angeles in 1958 (Shneidman *et al.* 1961). It is difficult to assess their efficacy. Kiev (1971) found no evidence that any of the centres had reduced the suicide rates in the areas they served. Moreover, many of the contacts (which are made by telephone) did not relate to suicide; those that did relate to suicide appeared to be of low risk. For these reasons Kiev argued that the centres might be better called crisis intervention centres.

The Samaritan organization

This organization was founded in London in 1953 by the Reverend Chad Varah. People in despair are encouraged to contact a widely publicized telephone number. The help offered ('befriending') is provided by non-professional volunteers who are trained to listen sympathetically without attempting to take on tasks that are in the province of a doctor or social worker. The Samaritans now have over 150 centres in Great Britain, and branches in nine other countries.

There is some evidence that amongst people who phone the Samaritans, the suicide rate in the ensuing year is higher than in the general population (Barraclough and Shea 1970). This suggests that the organization is attracting an appropriate group of people, but it also raises the question of the efficacy of the help offered.

To examine this problem, Bagley (1968) compared suicide rates in 15 pairs of towns in England and Wales. One of each pair was served by the Samaritans, the other was a similar kind of town except that it had no Samaritan branch. The results appeared to show lower rates of suicide in the towns served by the Samaritans. This finding was not confirmed by another study of similar design, but with improved matching of the towns (Jennings *et al.* 1978). It seems therefore that the effectiveness of the Samaritans has not been proved. The methodological problems involved may be too great to allow the issue to be decided conclusively. Even so, whether or not they prevent suicide, the Samaritans appear to perform a useful role by providing for the needs of many lonely and despairing people.

DELIBERATE SELF-HARM

Introduction

Before the 1950s, little distinction was made between people who killed themselves and those who survived after an apparent suicidal act. Stengel (1952) identified epidemiological differences between the two groups, and proposed the terms 'suicide' and 'attempted suicide' to distinguish the two forms of behaviour. He supposed that a degree of suicidal intent was essential in both groups; in other words, those who survived were failed suicides. These ideas were developed in an important monograph (Stengel and Cook 1958).

In the 1960s it was proposed that suicidal intent should no longer be regarded as essential, because it was recognized that most 'attempted suicides' had 'performed their acts in the belief that they were comparatively safe; aware, even in the heat of the moment, that they would survive their overdosage, and be able to disclose what they had done in good time to ensure rescue' (Kessel 1965). For this reason, Kessel proposed that 'attempted suicide' should be replaced by 'deliberate self-poisoning' and 'deliberate self-injury'. These terms were chosen to imply that the behaviour was clearly not accidental, without any assumption whether the desire for death was present. By the end of the 1960s, these ideas were widely accepted.

Kreitman and his colleagues have introduced the term 'parasuicide' to refer to 'a non-fatal act – in which an individual deliberately causes self injury or ingests a substance in excess of any prescribed or generally recognised thera-peutic dose' (Kreitman 1977 p. 3). Thus, the term parasuicide excludes the question whether death was a desired outcome. Although 'parasuicide' has been used quite widely, 'self-poisoning' and 'self-injury' are retained by some workers (for example Bancroft *et al.* 1975; Morgan *et al.* 1975). More recently Morgan (1979) has suggested the term deliberate self-harm (sometimes abbreviated to DSH) to provide a single term covering deliberate self-poisoning and deliberate self-injury. It has been objected that the term deliberate self-harm is sometimes a misnomer because the act is not invariably harmful (even though done in the knowledge that it might cause harm). In fact, no single term is wholly satis-factory. In this chapter, the term deliberate self-harm will be used rather than parasuicide.

The distinction between suicide and deliberate self-harm is not absolute. There is an important overlap. Some people who had no intention of dying succumb to the effects of an overdose. Others who intended to die are revived. Moreover, many patients were ambivalent at the time, uncertain whether they wished to die or live.

It should be remembered that among patients who have been involved in deliberate self-harm, the suicide rate in the subsequent twelve months is about a hundred times greater than in the general population. For this reason and other reasons to be given later, deliberate self-harm should not be regarded lightly.

The act of deliberate self-harm

The drugs used in deliberate self poisoning

In the United Kingdom, about 90 per cent of the cases of deliberate self-harm referred to general hospitals involve a drug overdose, and most of them present no serious threat to life. The most commonly used drugs are **minor tranquillizers** and the **non-opiate analgesics** such as salicylates and paracetamol. In recent years paracetamol has been used increasingly; it is particularly dangerous because it damages the liver (Davidson and Eastham 1966) and may lead to the delayed death of patients who had not intended to die. It is especially worrying that this drug is often taken by younger patients who are usually unaware of the serious risks (Gazzard *et al.* 1976). **Antidepressants** are taken in about a fifth of cases; in large amounts they may cause cardiac arrhythmias or convulsions. In the 1950s **barbiturates** were commonly used in deliberate self-poisoning; such usage is much less frequent nowadays following the general reduction in the prescribing of these drugs. Amongst all cases of deliberate self-harm about half the men and a quarter of the women take alcohol in the six hours before the act (Morgan *et al.* 1975).

Methods of deliberate self-injury

The commonest method of self-injury is laceration, usually of the forearm or wrists; it accounts for about four-fifths of the self-injuries referred to a general hospital (Hawton and Catalan 1982). Self-laceration is discussed separately below. Other forms of self-injury are jumping from heights or in front of a train or motor vehicle, shooting, and drowning. These acts occur mainly among older people who intended to die (Morgan *et al.* 1975).

Deliberate self-laceration

There are three forms of deliberate self-laceration: deep and dangerous wounds inflicted with serious suicidal intent, more often by men; self-mutilation by schizophrenic patients (often in response to hallucinatory voices) or by trans-sexuals; and superficial wounds that do not endanger life. Only the last group will be described here.

The patients are mostly young. Generally they have severe personality problems characterized by low self-esteem, impulsive or aggressive behaviour, unstable moods, difficulty in interpersonal relationships, and a tendency to abuse alcohol and drugs. Sexual identity problems have also been reported (Simpson 1976).

Usually increasing tension and irritability precede self-laceration, and are then relieved by it. Some patients say that the lacerations were inflicted during a state of feeling detached from their surroundings and of experiencing little or no pain. The lacerations are usually multiple, and made with glass or a razor blade on the forearms or wrists. Generally, some blood is drawn and the sight of this is often important to the patient. Some patients cause other injuries as well, for example by burning with cigarettes or by inflicting bruises. After the act, the patient often feels shame and disgust. A useful review is given by Simpson (1976).

The epidemiology of deliberate self-harm

During the 1960s and early 1970s there was a substantial increase in cases of deliberate self-harm admitted to general hospitals. Among women, deliberate self-harm is now the most frequent single reason for admission to a medical ward, and among men it is second only to ischaemic heart disease.

Accuracy of statistics

The official statistics for the incidence of deliberate self-harm are likely to be less than the true rates, because not all cases are referred to hospital. For example, a survey in Edinburgh suggested that hospital referral rates underestimated the frequency of deliberate self-harm by at least 30 per cent (Kennedy and Kreitman 1973).

Trends in the last two decades

In the early 1960s a substantial increase in deliberate self-harm began in most Western countries (see Weissman 1974). In the United Kingdom, the rates of admission to general hospitals increased about fourfold in the ten years up to 1973 (Kreitman 1977; Bancroft *et al.* 1975). The rates continued to increase more slowly in the mid-1970s, but may have been falling since the late 1970s (Gibbons *et al.* 1978). There are reports that the rates in younger teenagers are still rising (see Hawton *et al.* 1982).

Variations according to personal characteristics

Deliberate self-harm is more common among younger people, the rates declining sharply in middle age. In all but the very old, the rates are 1.5–2.5 times higher for **women**; particularly high rates are found among females aged 15–30 years. Deliberate self-harm is more prevalent in the lower **social classes**. There are also differences related to **marital status**; the highest rates for both men and women are among the divorced, and high rates are also found among teenage wives and younger single men and women (Bancroft *et al.* 1975; Holding *et al.* 1977).

Variations according to place of residence

High rates are found in areas characterized by high unemployment, overcrowding, many children in care, and substantial social mobility (Buglass and Duffy 1978; Morgan *et al.* 1975).

Causes of deliberate self-harm

Precipitating factors

Compared with the general population, people who deliberately harm themselves experience four times as many stressful life problems in the six months before the act (Paykel *et al.* 1975). The events are various but a recent quarrel with a spouse, girlfriend, or boyfriend is particularly common (Bancroft *et al.* 1977). Other events include separations from or rejection by a sexual partner, the illness of a family member, recent personal physical illness, and a court appearance.

Predisposing factors

The precipitating events often occur against a background of long-term problems concerning marriage, children, work, and health. In one study (Bancroft *et al.* 1977) about two-thirds of patients had some kind of marital problem; half the men had been involved in an extramarital relationship, and a further quarter said that their wives had been unfaithful. Among the unmarried, a similar proportion have difficulties in their relationships with sexual partners. Among men, unemployment is frequent: in a study in Bristol, one third of men who deliberately harmed themselves were unemployed (Morgan *et al.* 1975), and in Edinburgh the proportion was nearly a half (Holding *et al.* 1977). Generally such findings from interviews with individual patients agree with the findings from epidemiological studies of neighbourhoods, for example that deliberate self-harm is more frequent in areas with high rates of unemployment. Kreitman *et al.* (1969) have suggested that a kind of social contagion may operate in such areas, so that people become more likely to harm themselves if they know someone else who has done so.

A background of poor physical health is common (Bancroft *et al.* 1975). This applies particularly to epileptics, who are found in the deliberate self-harm population about six times more frequently than would be expected (Hawton *et al.* 1980).

Finally, there is some evidence that early parental loss through bereavement is more frequent among cases of deliberate self-harm (Birtchnell 1970 *a, b*).

Psychiatric disorder

Amongst patients who deliberately harm themselves, many have affective symptoms falling short of a full psychiatric syndrome (Newsome-Smith and Hirsch 1979*a*; Urwin and Gibbons 1979), but few have severe or sustained psychiatric disorder. This is in marked contrast to cases of completed suicide (see p. 401). Personality disorder is more common, being found in about a third to a half of self-harm patients (Kreitman 1977).

Dependence on alcohol is common (as in completed suicide), the frequencies in different series varying between 15 and 50 per cent among men, and 5 and 15 per cent among women.

Motivation and deliberate self-harm

The motives for deliberate self-harm are usually mixed and difficult to identify for certain. Even if the patient knows his own motives, he may try to hide them from other people. For example someone who has taken an overdose in frustration and anger may feel ashamed and say instead that he wished to die. In one study, amongst patients who said they had intended to die, only about half were judged by psychiatrists to have had true suicidal intentions (Bancroft *et al.* 1979). Conversely, someone who truly intended to kill himself may deny it. For this reason, more emphasis should be placed on a common sense evaluation of the patient's actions leading up to self-harm, than on his subsequent account of his own motives.

Despite this limitation, useful information has been obtained by questioning groups of patients about their motives. About a quarter say they wished to die. Some say that they are uncertain whether they wanted to die or not; others that they were leaving it to 'fate' to decide; and others that they were seeking unconsciousness as a temporary escape from their problems. Another group admit that they were trying to influence someone; for example that they were seeking to make a relative feel guilty for failing them in some way (Bancroft *et al.* 1979). This motive of influencing other people was first emphasized by Stengel and Cook (1958) who described the act of attempted suicide (as it was then called) as 'calling forth action from the human environment'. This behaviour has since been referred to as 'a cry for help'. Although some acts of deliberate self-harm result in increased help for the patient, others may arouse resentment, particularly if they are repeated.

The outcome of deliberate self-harm

This section deals first with the risk that the act of self-harm will be repeated, and second with the risk that the patient will die by suicide on some later occasion.

The risk of repetition

Repetition rates are based on groups of patients, some of whom have received psychiatric treatment after the act. Reported rates vary between about 15 and 25 per cent in the year after the act (Bancroft and Marsack 1977; Buglass and Horton 1974; Morgan *et al.* 1976). There are three broad patterns. First, some patients repeat only once; secondly some repeat several times but only during a limited period of continuing problems; and thirdly a small group repeat many times over a long period as a habitual response to stressful events.

Several studies agree that the following factors distinguish patients who repeat self-harm from those who do not: previous deliberate self-harm, previous psychiatric treatment, a personality disorder of the antisocial type, a criminal record, and alcohol or drug abuse. Lower social class and unemployment are also predictors (see Buglass and Horton 1974; Kreitman 1977). These factors are summarized in Table 13.3.

The risk of completed suicide

Among people who have intentionally harmed themselves the risk of later suicide is much increased. For example, in the first year afterwards, the risk of suicide is about 1–2 per cent, which is 100 times that of the general population (Kreitman 1977; Morgan *et al.* 1976). Investigations over a long period indicate that, amongst patients who were previously admitted with deliberate self-harm, about 10 per cent eventually take their own lives (Tuckman and Youngman 1963; Dorpat and Ripley 1967). Looked at in another way, in a third to a half of completed suicides, there is a history of previous deliberate self-harm (see Kreitman 1977).

Among people who deliberately harm themselves, the risk of eventual suicide is greater in those with other risk factors for suicide. Thus the risk is greater among older patients who are male, depressed, or alcoholic (see Kreitman 1977). A non-dangerous method of self-harm does not necessarily indicate a low risk of subsequent suicide, but the risk is certainly greater when violence or dangerous drug overdoses have been used.

The assessment of patients after deliberate self-harm

General aims

Assessment is concerned with three main issues: the immediate risk of suicide; the subsequent risks of further deliberate self-harm or suicide; and any current medical or social problems. The assessment should be carried out in a way that encourages the patient to undertake a constructive review of his problems and of the ways he can deal with them himself. This encouragement of self-help is important, because many patients are unwilling to be seen again as out-patients.

Usually the assessment has to be carried out in an accident and emergency department or a ward of a general hospital, in which there may be little privacy. Whenever possible, the interview should be in a side room so that it will not be overheard or interrupted. The interviewer should first make sure that the patient has recovered sufficiently from the overdose to be able to give a satisfactory history. If consciousness is still impaired, the interview should be delayed. Information should also be obtained from relatives or friends, the family doctor, and any other person (such as a social worker) already attempting to help the patient. Wide enquiry is important because sometimes information from other sources differs substantially from the account given by the patient.

Specific enquiries

The interview is directed to five questions: (1) What were the patient's intentions when he harmed himself? (2) Does he still intend to die? (3) What are the patient's current problems? (4) Is there a psychiatric disorder? (5) What helpful resources are available to this patient? Each will be considered in turn.

1. *What were the patient's intentions when he harmed himself?* As mentioned already, patients sometimes misrepresent their intentions. For this reason the interviewer should reconstruct, as fully as possible, the events that led up to the act of self harm. He will need to find the answers to five subsidiary questions (see Table 13.1).

Table 13.1 *Circumstances suggesting high suicidal intent*

Planning in advance
Precautions to avoid discovery
No attempts to obtain help afterwards
Dangerous method
'Final acts'

(i) Was the act **planned** or carried out on impulse? The longer and more carefully the plans have been made, the greater the risk of a fatal repetition.

(ii) Were **precautions** taken against being found? The more thorough the precautions, the greater the risk of fatal repetition. Of course, events do not always take place as the patient expected; for example a husband may arrive home later than usual because of an unexpected delay. In such circumstances, it is the patient's reasonable expectations that count.

(iii) **Did the patient seek help?** Serious intent can be inferred if there were no attempts to obtain help after the act.

(iv) **Was the method dangerous?** If drugs were used, what were they and what amount was taken? Did the patient take all the drugs available to him? If self-injury was used, what form did it take? (As noted above, the more dangerous the method the greater the risk of a further suicide attempt.) Not only should the actual risk be assessed, but also the risk anticipated by the patient, which may be inaccurate. For example some people wrongly believe that paracetamol overdose is harmless or that benzodiazepines are dangerous.

(v) **Was there a 'final act'** such as writing a suicide note or making a will? If so, the risk of further fatal attempt is greater.

By reviewing the answers to these questions, the interviewer makes a judgement of the patient's intentions at the time of the act. A similar approach has been formalized in Beck's suicide intent scale (Beck *et al.* 1974) which gives a score for the degree of intent.

2. *Does the patient still intend to die?* The interviewer should ask directly whether the patient is pleased to have recovered or wishes that he had died. If the act suggested serious suicidal intent, and if the patient now denies such intent, the interviewer should try to find out by tactful questioning whether there has been a genuine change of resolve.

3. *What are the current problems?* Many patients will have experienced a mounting series of difficulties in the weeks or months leading up to the act. Some of these difficulties may have been resolved by the time the patient is interviewed; for example, a husband who has planned to leave his wife may now have agreed to stay. The more that serious problems remain, the greater the risk of a fatal repetition. This risk is particularly strong if there are problems of loneliness or ill-health. The review of problems should be systematic and should cover the following: intimate relationships with the spouse or another

person; relations with children and other relatives; employment, finance, and housing; legal problems; social isolation, bereavement, and other losses. Drug and alcohol problems can be considered at this stage or when the psychiatric state is reviewed.

4.   *Is there a psychiatric disorder?* It should be possible to answer this question from the history and from a brief but systematic examination of the mental state. Particular attention should be directed to depressive disorder, alcoholism, and personality disorder. Schizophrenia and dementia should also be considered though they will be found less often.

5.   *What are the patient's resources?* These include his capacity to solve his own problems; his material resources; and the help that others may provide. The best guide to the patient's ability to solve future problems is his record of dealing with difficulties in the past, for example the loss of a job, or a broken relationship. The availability of help should be assessed by asking about the patient's friends and confidants, and about any support he may be receiving from his general practitioner, social workers or voluntary agencies.

Is there a continuing risk of suicide?

The interviewer now has the information required to answer this important question. In summary, he reviews the answers to the first four questions outlined above, namely: (a) Did the patient originally intend to die? (b) Does he intend it now? (c) Are the problems which provoked the act still present? and (d) Is he suffering from a mental disorder? He also decides what help other people are likely to provide after the patient leaves hospital (question 5 above). Having reviewed the individual factors in this way, the interviewer compares the patient's characteristics with those found in groups of people who have died by suicide. These characteristics are summarized in Table 13.2.

Table 13.2 *Factors predicting suicide after deliberate self-poisoning*

Evidence of serious intent*

Depressive disorder
Alcoholism or drug abuse
Antisocial personality disorder

Previous suicide attempt(s)

Social isolation
Unemployment
Older age group
Male sex

*see Table 13.1.

Is there a risk of further non-fatal self-harm?

The predictive factors which have been outlined already (see p. 413), are summarized in Table 13.3. The interviewer should consider all the points in turn

Table 13.3. *Factors predicting the repetition of deliberate self-poisoning**

Previous deliberate self-harm
Previous psychiatric treatment
Antisocial personality disorder
Alcohol or drug abuse
Criminal record
Low social class
Unemployment

*See Kreitman and Dyer (1980).

before making a judgement about the risk. Using their own six item scale (slightly different from Table 13.3) Buglass and Horton (1974) gave a score according to the number of items that were present in each case. Patients with a score of zero had a five per cent chance of repeating the act in the next year, while those with a score of five or more had an almost 50 per cent chance.

Is treatment required and will the patient agree to it?

If the patient is actively suicidal, the procedures are those outlined in the first part of this chapter (see p. 406). About 10 per cent of deliberate self-harm patients require admission to a psychiatric unit for further treatment; usually they are suffering from a depressive disorder or alcoholism. A further two-thirds of patients appear likely to benefit from outpatient care, mostly in the form of counselling about their problems rather than treatment of psychiatric disorder. Many of these patients refuse the offer of outpatient help; they should be discussed particularly carefully with their general practitioner before being allowed to return home. The remaining 25 per cent do not require special treatment, and are returned to the care of their general practitioners. These patients have a small risk of repetition and few continuing social problems. The proportion dealt with in this way will depend on the resources of the unit and the willingness of local family doctors to supervise such cases.

Special problems

Mothers of young children

Mothers of young children require special consideration because of the known association between deliberate self-harm and child abuse (Roberts and Hawton 1980). It is important to ask about the mother's feelings towards her children, and to enquire about their welfare. In the United Kingdom information about the children can usually be obtained from the general practitioner, who may ask his health visitor to investigate the case.

Young teenagers

Young teenagers also present special problems of assessment. In this group deliberate self-harm usually occurs against a background of serious difficulties within the family. The teenagers are seldom willing to talk about such problems, and the other family members may be equally defensive. It is particularly important to discuss these cases with the family doctor. When there are serious problems, referral to an adolescent psychiatry service may be needed.

Who should assess?

Since a Government report in 1968 it has been official policy that all cases of deliberate self-harm should be assessed by a psychiatrist (Central Health Services Council 1968). The intention was to make sure that patients with depressive and other psychiatric disorders should be identified and treated, and that appropriate assistance should be given for other psychological and social problems. It is likely that a large proportion of the patients at that time were suffering from psychiatric disorder. The increase of cases since then has been made up mainly of younger patients in whom serious psychiatric disorders are less frequent. Such patients usually require assessment and counselling for social problems, rather than diagnosis and treatment of psychiatric disorders. If performed thoroughly, such assessments are time-consuming. It has therefore been suggested that they might be carried out equally well by trained staff other than psychiatrists, provided that psychiatrists make the final decision about the presence of psychiatric disorder. It has been shown that, if they receive appropriate additional training, junior medical staff (Gardner *et al.* 1977), psychiatric nurses (Hawton *et al.* 1979) and social workers (Newsome-Smith and Hirsch 1979*b*) can all assess these patients as well as psychiatrists. It is emphasized that when a nurse or social worker makes the assessment a psychiatrist reviews the question of psychiatric disorder.

For patients admitted to medical beds after deliberate self-harm, the best policy seems to be that the local consultant physicians and psychiatrists should agree who is to make the assessments and who will take the final responsibility for decisions about management. In this way each hospital can adopt the policy that makes the most effective use of the available medical, nursing and social work staff.

Management

As indicated above, the assessment procedure divides patients into three goups. About ten per cent need immediate inpatient treatment in a psychiatric unit, and about a quarter require no special treatment because their self-harm was a response to temporary difficulties and carried little risk of repetition. This section is concerned with the remaining two-thirds for whom some outpatient treatment may be appropriate.

The main aim of such treatment is to enable the patient first to resolve the difficulties that led up to the act of self harm, and second to deal with any future crisis without resorting to further self-harm. The main problem is that, once they have left hospital, many patients are disinclined to take part in any treatment.

The treatment is psychological and social. Drugs are seldom required, but a small minority of patients require anti-depressant medication. It is more often necessary to withdraw drugs for which there is no clear indication. The starting-point of treatment is the list of problems compiled during the assessment procedure. The patient is encouraged to consider what steps he should take to resolve each of these problems, and to formulate a practical plan for tackling them one at a time. Throughout this discussion, the therapist tries to persuade the patient to do as much as possible for himself.

Many cases are associated with interpersonal problems. It is often helpful to interview the other person involved, at first alone, and then in a few joint interviews with the patient. This procedure may help to resolve problems that the couple have been unable to discuss on their own.

When deliberate self-harm follows a bereavement or other kind of loss, a different approach is needed. The first step should be sympathetic listening while the patient expresses his feelings of loss. Then the patient is encouraged to seek ways of gradually rebuilding his life without the lost person. Appropriate measures will depend on the nature of the loss – whether it was through death, or the break-up of a marriage, or the end of another relationship. Again, the emphasis should be on self-help.

Some special problems of management

Frequent repeaters

Some patients take repeated overdoses at times of recurring stress. Often the behaviour seems to become a maladaptive habit released by minor stressful events. By the time this stage is reached, relatives have often become unsympathetic or even overtly hostile. The patients usually have a disordered personality and a multitude of insoluble social problems. Counselling or intensive psychotherapy usually has little effect, and the risk of eventual death by suicide is substantial.

Deliberate self-laceration

The management of self-laceration presents many problems. The patient often has difficulty in expressing his feelings in words, and so formal psychotherapy is seldom helpful. Simple efforts to gain the patient's confidence and increase his self-esteem are more likely to succeed. An attempt should also be made to find an alternative method of relieving tension, for example through vigorous exercise. Anxiolytic drugs are seldom helpful and may produce disinhibition. If drug treatment is needed to reduce tension, a phenothiazine is more likely to be effective.

The results of treatment

As already indicated, the treatment of deliberate self-harm has two aims. The first is to help the patient to deal with the social and emotional problems that led up to the act. The second is to prevent further acts of self-harm.

Two retrospective studies suggested that psychiatric intervention might be effective in reducing the repetition of deliberate self-harm. Greer and Bagley (1971) reported that, if patients received no psychiatric attention before discharge from hospital, they made more attempts at deliberate self-harm in the next 18 months than those who had been assessed or treated by a psychiatrist. These findings held even when allowances were made for characteristics correlated with the risk of repetition. Kennedy (1972) used a general practice survey to identify deliberate self-harm patients who had not been referred to the Edinburgh Regional Poisoning Treatment Centre. At one-year follow-up, he found that his group had repeated deliberate self-harm more often than patients who had been admitted to the Centre where psychiatric assessment and treatment were available. The disadvantages of both studies were that they were retrospective; hence the groups of patients could not be adequately matched, and the treatment provided could not be clearly described.

There have been two prospective studies of the treatment of deliberate self-harm patients. In a study of patients who had made at least two previous attempts, Chowdhury *et al.* (1973) allocated them randomly either to the usual follow-up service, or to an augmented service which included intensive follow-up, home visits for defaulters, and continuous on-call access to the team. At a six-month follow-up, there were no differences between the two groups in repetition rates. The experimental group showed a marginally greater improvement in psychological symptoms, and a significantly greater improvement in problems with finance, housing, and employment. Gibbons *et al.* (1978) compared task-centred social casework with routine treatment; they found no difference in rates of repetition of deliberate self-harm, even though the groups receiving social work improved more in social adjustment.

It seems therefore that additional treatments of the kinds described do not reduce the risk of repeated self-harm. It may still be useful to deal with social problems, since many of them would have required attention even if the patient had not harmed himself.

Primary prevention

If prevention after the first episode of self-harm is so difficult, can primary prevention be achieved? Three main strategies have been suggested: reducing the availability of means of self-harm; encouraging the work of agencies that try to help people with social and emotional problems; and improving health education.

Reducing the means

It has been suggested that psychotropic drugs should be prescribed more cautiously, especially for patients whose affective symptoms are a reaction to life problems. Drugs may not help these patients but may merely provide the opportunity to take an overdose when the problems increase. Two factors should be weighed against this argument: up to a third of people who take deliberate drug overdoses use drugs originally prescribed for a person other than the patient; and another quarter use drugs that can be bought without prescription, notably analgesics some of which are particularly dangerous in overdosage.

This last consideration has led to suggestions that, if any non-prescribed drug is dangerous in overdose, it should be sold in strip or blister packets to prevent people taking large amounts on impulse; or a small quantity of emetic should be added. It has also been suggested that paracetamol, one of the most dangerous analgesics, should be available only on prescription (e.g. Gazzard *et al.* 1976).

Encouraging helping agencies

This at first appears sensible but, on closer enquiry, may be unlikely to help. In one study it was found that about three-quarters of patients taking deliberate overdoses already knew about the Samaritans and many were also aware of the social services provided in their area (Bancroft *et al.* 1977). Their overdoses were taken impulsively without thought about ways of obtaining help.

Education

Education about the dangers of drug overdoses and discussions of common emotional problems might be provided for teenagers. However, in the absence of any evidence that such measures reduce deliberate self-harm, there is an understandable reluctance to introduce them in schools.

FURTHER READING

Hawton, K. and Catalán, J. (1982). *Attempted suicide: a practical guide to its nature and management.* Oxford University Press.

Kessell, N. (1965). Self poisoning. *British Medical Journal* **2**, 1265–70, 1671–2.

Kreitman, N. (ed.) (1967). *Parasuicide.* John Wiley, London.

Morgan, H.G. (1979). *Death wishes? The understanding and management of deliberate self harm.* John Wiley, London.

14. Dependence on alcohol and drugs

DEPENDENCE ON ALCOHOL

Although widely used the term 'alcoholism' is unsatisfactory because it has several different meanings. It can be applied to habitual alcohol consumption that is deemed excessive in amount according to some arbitrary criterion. Alcoholism may also refer to damage, whether mental, physical, or social, resulting from such excessive consumption. In a more specialized sense, alcoholism may imply a specific disease entity that is supposed to require medical treatment. On the other hand, to speak of 'an alcoholic' often has a pejorative meaning, suggesting behaviour that is morally bad.

Although the term alcoholism remains in common use, for most purposes it is better to use four more specific terms: excessive consumption of alcohol; alcohol-related disability; problem drinking; and alcohol dependence. These terms will be explained later, but at this stage they can be defined briefly. Excessive consumption of alcohol refers to a daily or weekly intake of alcohol exceeding a specified amount. Alcohol-related disability refers to any mental, physical, or social harm resulting from excessive consumption. Problem drinking is drinking that incurs alcohol-related disability, but has not yet advanced to alcohol dependence. Alcohol dependence refers to a state in which there is a syndrome of mental or physical disturbance when the drug is withdrawn. The term alcoholism, if it is used at all, should be regarded as a shorthand way of referring to some combination of these four conditions. However, since these specific terms have been introduced recently, the term alcoholism is used when referring to much of the literature. Before explaining these specific terms further, it is appropriate to examine the moral and the medical models of 'alcoholism'.

THE MORAL AND MEDICAL MODELS

According to the **moral model,** if someone drinks too much, he does so of his own free will, and if his drinking causes harm to himself or his family, his actions are morally bad. The corollary of this attitude is that public drunkenness should be punished. In many countries, this is the official practice; public drunks are fined, and if they cannot pay the fine, they go to prison. Many people now believe that this approach is too harsh and unsympathetic. Whatever the humanitarian arguments, there is little practical justification for punishment, since there is little evidence that it influences the behaviour of excessive drinkers.

According to the **medical model,** an alcoholic is sick rather than wicked. Although it had been proposed earlier, this idea was most strongly advocated in 1960, when Jellinek published an influential book, *The disease concept of alcoholism.* The disease concept embodies three basic ideas. The first is that some people have some kind of specific vulnerability to alcoholism. The second idea is that excessive drinking progresses through regular stages, at one of which the person can no longer control his drinking, (Glatt 1976; Keller 1976). The third idea is that excessive drinking may lead to physical and mental disease of several kinds. While this is true, it seems illogical to say that alcoholism is itself a disease because it can lead to other diseases.

One of the main consequences of the disease model is that attitudes towards excessive drinking become more humane. Instead of blame and punishment, medical treatment is provided. The disease model also has certain disadvantages. By implying that only certain people are at risk, it diverts attention from two important facts. First, *anyone* who drinks a great deal for a long time may become dependent on alcohol. Second, the best way to curtail alcoholism may be to limit consumption in the whole population, and not just among a predisposed minority.

THE SYNDROME OF ALCOHOL DEPENDENCE

In 1977, a group of investigators sponsored by the World Health Organization recommended the term **alcohol dependence syndrome** to describe a group of symptoms arising in some people when they stop drinking alcohol (Edwards *et al.* 1977). This syndrome has been well described by Victor and Adams (1953) who found that relative or absolute withdrawal was followed by a state of tremulousness, transient hallucinations, epileptic fits, and delirium tremens. Soon after this, Isbell *et al.* (1955) gave large quantities of ethyl alcohol to 10 healthy ex-morphine addicts for periods of between 7 and 87 days. Four patients who dropped out early in the experiment developed tremulousness, nausea, sweating, and insomnia. Of the six patients who drank over 48 days two had epileptic fits and three had delirium tremens on withdrawal.

As described by Edwards *et al.* (1977), there are seven essential elements in the alcohol dependence syndrome:

(i) *The feeling of being compelled to drink.* The dependent drinker is aware of being unsure that he can stop drinking once started. If he tries to give up alcohol, he experiences craving for it.

(ii) *A stereotyped pattern of drinking.* Whereas the ordinary drinker varies his intake from day to day, the dependent person drinks at regular intervals to relieve or avoid withdrawal symptoms.

(iii) *Primacy of drinking over other activities.* For the dependent drinker alcohol takes priority over everything else, including health, family, home, career, and social life.

(iv) *Altered tolerance to alcohol.* The dependent drinker is relatively unaffected by blood levels of alcohol that would incapacitate a normal drinker. Since he can 'hold his drink', he may persuade himself that alcohol is no problem to him. This is a false argument, because increasing tolerance is an important sign of increasing dependence. In the late stages of dependence, tolerance falls and the dependent drinker becomes incapacitated after only a few drinks.

(v) *Repeated withdrawal symptoms.* Withdrawal symptoms occur in people who have been drinking heavily for years and who maintain a high intake of alcohol for weeks at a time. The symptoms follow a drop in blood concentration. They characteristically appear on waking, after the fall in concentration during sleep.

The earliest and commonest feature is acute tremulousness affecting the hands, legs, and trunk ('the shakes'). The sufferer may be unable to sit still, hold a cup steadily, or do up buttons. He is also agitated and easily startled, and often dreads facing people or crossing the road. Nausea, retching, and sweating are frequent. If alcohol is taken, these symptoms may be relieved quickly; if not, they may last for several days.

As withdrawal progresses, misperceptions and hallucinations may occur, usually only briefly. Objects appear distorted in shape, or shadows seem to move; disorganized voices, shouting, or snatches of music may be heard. Later there may be epileptic seizures, and finally after about 48 hours delirium tremens may develop (see below).

(vi) *Relief drinking.* Since they can only stave off withdrawal symptoms by further drinking, many dependent drinkers take a drink on waking. In most cultures, early morning drinking is diagnostic of dependency.

With increasing need to stave off withdrawal symptoms during the day, the drinker typically becomes secretive about the amount consumed, hides bottles or carries them in a pocket. Rough cider and cheap wines may be drunk regularly to obtain the most alcohol for the least money.

(vii) *Reinstatement after abstinence.* A severely dependent person who drinks again after a period of abstinence is likely to relapse quickly and totally, returning to his old drinking pattern within a few days.

The syndrome becomes established most often in the mid-forties for men, and a few years later for women (Royal College of Psychiatrists 1979). However, it is now occurring increasingly among teenagers, and it is sometimes seen for the first time in elderly people after retirement. Once established, the syndrome usually progresses steadily and destructively, unless the patient stops drinking or manages to bring it under control.

ALCOHOL-RELATED DISABILITIES

This section describes the different types of damage, physical, psychological, and social, that can result from excessive drinking. A person who suffers from these disabilities may or may not be suffering from the dependence syndrome.

Physical damage

Excessive consumption of alcohol may lead to physical damage in several ways. First, it can have a direct toxic effect on certain tissues, notably the brain and liver. Secondly, it is often accompanied by poor diet which may lead to deficiency of protein and B vitamins. Excessive drinkers are also prone to accidents, particularly head-injury. Their general neglect of health can lead to increased susceptibility to infection.

Physical complications of excessive drinking occur in several systems of the body. Alimentary disorders are common, notably cirrhosis of the liver, gastritis, peptic ulcer, oesophageal varices and carcinoma, and acute and chronic pancreatitis. Damage to the liver including fatty infiltration, hepatitis, cirrhosis, and hepatoma is particularly important. The rate of cirrhosis appears to be increasing. Thus, in a 20 year prospective study of cirrhosis in Birmingham, Saunders *et al.* (1981) found that the annual incidence rate for all cases of cirrhosis almost tripled between 1959 and 1975, whilst the proportion due to alcohol rose from one-third to two-thirds.

For a person dependent on alcohol, the risk of dying from liver cirrhosis is almost 10 times greater than the average (Williams and Davies 1977). On the other hand, only about 10 per cent of alcohol-dependent people develop cirrhosis. Recent work suggests that vulnerability to alcohol induced liver disease may be due in part to the histocompatibility antigen HLA B8, which is found in up to a quarter of the population. Conversely, HLA-A28 may have a protective effect (Saunders *et al.* 1981). There is also a suggestion that patterns of drinking may influence the risk of certain forms of liver disease. Thus in Scotland, alcoholic hepatitis occurred in two-thirds of a group of continuous heavy drinkers, as against one-third of binge-drinkers (Brunt *et al.* 1974).

Excess alcohol consumption also damages the **nervous system.** Neuro-psychiatric complications are described later; other neurological conditions include peripheral neuropathy, epilepsy, and cerebellar degeneration. Rare complications are optic atrophy, central pontine myelinolysis, and Marchiafava–Bignami syndrome. The latter syndrome results from widespread demyelination of the corpus callosum, optic tracts, and cerebellar peduncles. Its main features are dysarthria, ataxia, epilepsy, and marked impairment of consciousness; in the more prolonged forms there are dementia and limb paralysis (see Lishman (1981) for a review). Head injury is common in alcohol-dependent people. Thus, in a large series of men arrested for public drunkenness in London, nearly a quarter had a history of head injury resulting in unconsciousness (Gath *et al.* 1968).

Other physical complications of excessive drinking are too numerous to detail here. Examples include anaemia, myopathy, episodic hypoglycaemia, haemochromatosis, cardiomyopathy, vitamin deficiencies, and tuberculosis (see Royal College of Psychiatrists 1979).

Not surprisingly, the **mortality rate** is increased in alcoholic patients. In the United Kingdom the overall rate is about twice the expected level, whilst for women aged between 15 and 39 it is 17 times greater (Adelstein and White 1976). Similar findings have been reported in the United States (Schmidt and de Lindt 1972), and in Sweden (Peterson *et al.* 1980). Even allowing for the fact that heavy drinkers tend to be heavy smokers, alcohol itself is almost certainly responsible for a substantial part of this increased mortality.

Damage to the fetus

Recently evidence has been presented that a fetal **alcohol syndrome** occurs in some children born to mothers who drink excessively. In France, Lemoine *et al.* (1968) described a syndrome of facial abnormality, small stature, low birth-weight, low intelligence, and psychological over-activity. In Seattle, USA, a series of reports confirmed this general clinical picture (Jones and Smith 1973; Hanson *et al.* 1976).

These studies were retrospective. In a large prospective study in France (Kaminski *et al.* 1976), women who drank above 400 ml of wine per day (or equivalent of other drinks) were found to have babies with no higher rates of congenital malformation or neonatal mortality. However the women had more stillbirths, and their babies' birth weights were lower. Mothers who drank more were older, more often unmarried, of lower social status and of greater parity, and they smoked more. They also had more bleeding in early pregnancy. When allowance was made for these factors, the authors still found that alcohol independently affected birth weight, placental weight, and stillbirths.

Other research on this subject has been reviewed by El-Guebaly and Offord (1977), and Kessel (1977). It seems fair to conclude that, among the offspring of some alcoholic mothers, there is a syndrome of the kind mentioned above but that it occurs infrequently and only when the mother has been drinking very heavily indeed during pregnancy. When mothers drink excessively though less heavily than this, their infants appear to have lower birth weights and stature than others, but the differences are not great. Because mothers who drink excessively have more of the other known high-risk factors, such as smoking, malnutrition, and social handicaps, it is not certain that all the effects described are due directly to alcohol.

Psychiatric disorders

Alcohol-related psychiatric disabilities fall into four groups: intoxication phenomena; withdrawal phenomena; chronic or nutritional disorders; and associated psychiatric disorders (see Cutting 1979).

(i) Intoxication phenomena

Pathological drunkenness is defined in ICD 9 (291.4) as 'acute psychotic episodes induced by relatively small amounts of alcohol. These are regarded as individual idiosyncratic reactions to alcohol, not due to excessive consumption and without conspicuous neurological signs of intoxication'. These episodes usually take the form of explosive outbursts of aggression. There is doubt whether behaviour of this kind really is induced by small amounts of alcohol. Maletzky (1976) gave intravenous infusions of alcohol to 23 men who gave a history of pathological drunkenness. Fifteen developed aggressive behaviour but they only did so when the blood alcohol level was substantially raised (see Coid 1979 for a review).

Memory blackouts: or short-term amnesia are frequently reported after heavy drinking. At first the events of the night before are forgotten, even though consciousness was maintained at the time. Such memory losses can occur after a single episode of heavy drinking in people who are not dependent on alcohol; if they recur regularly, they indicate habitual heavy drinking. With sustained excessive drinking, memory losses may become more severe, affecting parts of the daytime or even whole days.

(ii) Withdrawal phenomena

The general **withdrawal syndrome** was described earlier when alcohol dependence was considered. Here we are concerned with the more serious psychiatric syndrome of delirium tremens.

Delirium tremens

This occurs in people whose history of excessive drinking extends over several years. There is a dramatic and rapidly changing picture of disordered mental activity, with clouding of consciousness, disorientation in time and place, and impairment of recent memory. Perceptual disturbances include misinterpretations of sensory stimuli and vivid hallucinations which are usually visual, but sometimes in other modalities. There is severe agitation, with restlessness, shouting, and evident fear. Insomnia is prolonged. The hands are grossly tremulous and sometimes pick up imaginary objects, and truncal ataxia occurs. Autonomic disturbances include sweating, fever, tachycardia, raised blood pressure, and dilatation of pupils. Blood testing shows leucocytosis, a raised ESR and impaired liver function. Dehydration and electrolyte disturbance are characteristic.

The condition lasts three or four days, the symptoms being characteristically worse at night. It often ends with deep prolonged sleep from which the patient awakens with no symptoms and little or no memory of the period of delirium.

(iii) Toxic or nutritional conditions

These include **Korsakov's psychosis** and **Wernicke's encephalopathy,** which are **described in the chapter on organic mental states.** (pp. 299–301).

Alcoholic dementia

There has been considerable disagreement as to whether this occurs as a separate condition. The doubt has probably arisen because in the past many excessive drinkers with general intellectual deficits were wrongly labelled as Korsakov's psychosis (Cutting 1978). The question has been investigated by radiological methods. Early studies using air encephalography (Brewer and Perrett 1971), gave equivocal results because it is difficult to assess volumetric changes by this means. Recently CAT-scanning has provided a technically more satisfactory and ethically more acceptable method. Such studies have shown cortical atrophy in a third to two thirds of alcoholic patients (Fox *et al.* 1976; Cala *et al.* 1978; Bergmann *et al.* 1980). A recent controlled investigation using rigorous methods (Ron *et al.* 1980; Lishman *et al.* 1980) has confirmed this among alcoholics who had been abstinent for 234 days on average before testing.

Studies of this kind suggest that alcoholic dementia is more common than was previously supposed, and it should be searched for carefully in every problem drinker. Older patients appear to be more at risk than younger ones with a similar length of heavy drinking; and those who have been drinking without respite seem to be more at risk than people who have periods in which they reduce their drinking (see Cutting (1982) and Ron (1977) for reviews).

(iv) Associated psychiatric disorders

Personality deterioration
As the patient is concerned more and more with the need to obtain alcohol, there is increasing self-centredness, a lack of consideration for others, and a decline in standards of conduct. Responsibilities at home and work are evaded, and behaviour may become dishonest and deceitful.

Affective disorder
The relationship between alcohol consumption and mood is complex. On the one hand some depressed patients drink excessively in an attempt to improve their mood; on the other hand excess drinking may induce persistent depression or anxiety (Gibson and Becker 1973; Woodruff *et al.* 1973).

Suicidal behaviour
Suicide rates amongst alcoholics are higher than among non-alcoholics of the same age. Kessel and Grossman (1961) found that 8 per cent of alcoholics admitted for treatment killed themselves within a few years of discharge. Reports from a number of countries suggest that 6 per cent to 20 per cent of alcoholics end their lives by suicide (Ritson 1977). Suicide among alcoholics is discussed further on p. 401.

Impaired psychosexual function
Sexual impotence and delayed ejaculation are common. These difficulties may be worsened when drinking leads to marital estrangement, or if the wife develops a revulsion for intercourse with an inebriated partner.

Pathological jealousy
Possibly as a result of sexual dysfunction, excessive drinkers may develop the delusion that the partner is being unfaithful. This syndrome of pathological jealousy is described on p. 282. Although it is a striking complication, delusional

jealousy is less common than a non-delusional suspicious attitude to the spouse.

Alcoholic hallucinosis

This is characterized by auditory hallucinations, usually voices uttering insults or threats, occurring in clear consciousness. The patient is usually distressed by these experiences, appearing anxious and restless.

There has been considerable controversy about the aetiology of the condition. Some follow Kraepelin and Bonhöffer in regarding it as organically determined; others follow Bleuler in supposing that it is related to schizophrenia.

Benedetti (1952) made a retrospective survey of 113 cases of alcoholic hallucinosis and divided them into those of less than six months' duration (acute cases) and the remaining chronic group. Among the former he found no evidence of a link with schizophrenia as judged by family history. However he did find evidence of an organic cause, in that about half had experienced memory disorders. Despite this the condition cleared up without residual defect. Among the cases that had lasted six months, nearly all went on for much longer, despite abstinence. Half developed the typical picture of schizophrenia, and half developed amnesic syndromes or dementia. In their family histories, these chronic patients were intermediate between the acute cases and typical schizophrenic patients. Of course, this study cannot tell us whether these patients would have developed schizophrenia if they had never taken alcohol.

Some authors have held that auditory hallucinosis is not essentially different from the hallucinations occurring in excessive drinkers in the 24–48 hours after alcohol withdrawal (Knott and Beard 1971). It is true that auditory hallucinations may occur in simple withdrawal states (Hershon 1977) and may accompany the visual hallucinations of delirium tremens (Gross *et al.* 1971). However they are fleeting and disorganized, in contrast to the persistent organized voices experienced in alcoholic hallucinosis.

Cutting (1978) has concluded that there is a small group of patients who have a true alcoholic hallucinosis, but that many of those who receive this diagnosis have depressive symptoms or first rank symptoms of schizophrenia. Clinical experience also points to this conclusion.

Social damage

Excessive drinking is liable to cause profound social disruption particularly in the family. Marital and family tension is virtually inevitable (Orford 1979). The divorce rate amongst alcoholics is high; and the wives of heavy drinkers are likely to become anxious, depressed, and socially isolated (Wilkins 1974); the husbands of 'battered wives' frequently drink heavily; and women admitted to hospital because of self-poisoning, often blame their husband's drinking. The home atmosphere is often detrimental to the children, because of quarelling and violence, and a drunken parent provides a poor role model. Children of alcoholics are at risk of developing neurotic or behaviour disorders, and of performing badly at school.

At work, the heavy drinker often progresses through declining efficiency, lower grade jobs, and repeated dismissals to lasting unemployment. There is also a strong association between road accidents and alcohol abuse. In the United Kingdom, a third of drivers killed on the road have blood alcohol levels above the statutory limit; around the hours of midnight the figure rises to 50 per cent; and on Saturday night to 75 per cent (Department of the Environment 1976). This toll of road accident deaths involving alcohol is particularly high in the young (Havard 1977).

Excessive drinking is also associated with crime, mainly petty offences such as larceny, but also fraud, sexual offences, and crimes of violence including murder. Studies of recidivist prisoners in England and Wales have shown that many of them had serious drinking problem before imprisonment. This is particularly so for men on short sentences (Edwards *et al.* 1971). It is not easy to know how far alcohol causes the criminal behaviour and how far it is just part of the life-style of the criminal. This question is discussed further on p. 722.

EXCESSIVE ALCOHOL CONSUMPTION AND PROBLEM DRINKING

Having described alcohol dependence and alcohol-related disabilities, we are now in a position to explain the terms excessive alcohol consumption and problem drinking. The concept of **excessive alcohol consumption** can be defined in relation to the risks of developing alcohol dependence and alcohol-related disability. We have seen that there is reason to suppose that anyone may become dependent on alcohol if he drinks a sufficiently large amount for long enough. Unfortunately no exact threshold can be specified. The Royal College of Psychiatrists (1979) suggests that 'anyone who makes a habit of drinking the equivalent of half a bottle of spirits or eight pints of beer daily is putting himself at very considerable risk of acquiring dependence, and this statement should not be taken as meaning that lower levels are necessarily safe.' The same report proposes a provisional lower level of safe drinking in relation to alcohol-related disability, namely four pints of beer a day, or four doubles of spirits, or one standard-sized bottle of wine, though this does not mean that it is wise to make a habit of drinking even at these levels.

The DHSS Advisory Committee on Alcoholism proposed the term **problem drinkers** to refer to those who cause alcohol-related disability by repeated drinking (Department of Health and Social Security 1978 *a*). Such problem drinkers may or may not be dependent on alcohol. Those who are not dependent may become so and need to be recognized.

EPIDEMIOLOGICAL ASPECTS OF EXCESSIVE DRINKING

Epidemiological methods can be applied to the following questions concerning excessive drinking (i) What is the annual per capita consumption of alcohol for a nation as a whole; how does this vary over the years and between nations? (ii) What are the drinking habits of different groups of people within a defined population? (iii) How many people in a defined population are alcohol-dependent, and how many have related disability? (v) How do alcohol dependence and alcohol-related disability vary with such characteristics as sex, age, occupation, social class, and marital status?

Unfortunately, we lack reliable answers to many of these questions, partly because different investigators have used different methods of defining and identifying heavy drinking and 'alcoholism', and also because excessive drinkers tend to be evasive about the amounts they drink and the symptoms they experience.

The national consumption of alcohol

In Great Britain, consumption of alcohol was exceptionally high between the years 1860–1910, falling until the 1930s, and remaining low until the 1950s. Between 1950 and 1976, the per capita consumption of alcohol rose by 90 per cent in Great Britain. Even so, it is still lower than it was in the late nineteenth century. The recent change has been accompanied by a substantial increase in wine drinking, which is now four times greater then it was in 1900. Despite this, beer still accounts for two thirds of all the alcohol consumed. A similar increase in consumption since the 1950s occurred in 17 out of 18 European countries.

The drinking habits in different groups

Surveys of drinking behaviour generally depend on self-reports, a method that is open to obvious errors. Enquiries of this kind have been conducted in Camberwell (Edwards *et al.* 1972) in Scotland (Dight 1976), and in England and Wales as a special project of the Office of Population and Census Surveys (Wilson 1980).

Such studies show that the highest consumption of alcohol is generally amongst young men who are unmarried, separated, or divorced. Indeed, Dight (1976) found that 3 per cent of the population, mostly single men in their late teens or twenties, were responsible for 30 per cent of all alcohol consumption in Scotland. In recent years alcohol consumption amongst women has risen (Shaw 1980).

The prevalence of problem drinking

This can be estimated in three ways: from hospital admission rates; by the use of Jellinek's formula; and by surveys in the general population.

Hospital admission rates

These give an inadequate measure of prevalence because a large proportion of problem drinkers do not enter hospital. In the United Kingdom psychiatric admissions for alcohol problems account for 10 per cent of all psychiatric admissions. In France, Germany, and Eire the figure is almost 30 per cent. In the United Kingdom there has been a 30-fold increase in psychiatric hospital admission rates for alcoholism in the past 30 years, but this may reflect changes more in the provision of services than in prevalence.

Jellinek's formula

This was proposed to overcome the difficulties in estimating the numbers of alcoholics. Jellinek proposed that the frequency of cirrhosis of the liver should be used as an indirect measure. The formula proposed was $R\,(PD)/K$, in which D is the number of cirrhosis deaths in a given year and place; P is the percentage of such deaths due to alcoholism; K is the percentage of all alcoholics with complications who die from cirrhosis; R is the ratio of all alcoholics to alcoholics with complications. On the basis of long-term trends and mortality rates in different populations, it was assumed that the relationship between alcoholism and cirrhosis was fairly constant (Jolliffe and Jellinek 1941). Using the Jellinek formula, in 1951 the World Health Organization made its well known estimate that there were 350 000 alcoholics in England and Wales.

The Jellinek formula has been much criticized (e.g. Popham 1956; Brenner 1959), mainly on the grounds that the supposed constants K, P, and R are subject to change. Jellinek (1959) himself suggested that the formula should be abandoned, and this is now widely accepted.

General population surveys

One method is to ascertain cases of problem drinking by seeking information from general practitioners, social workers, probation officers, health visitors, and other agents who are likely to come in contact with heavy drinkers (Prys Williams and Glatt 1966). Another approach is the community survey in which samples of people are asked about the amount they drink and whether they experience symptoms. For example, in the London suburb of Camberwell, Edwards *et al.* (1972) questioned 928 people and found 25 'problem drinkers' and five who were alcohol dependent.

Alcohol dependence and population characteristics

Sex

For many years in the United Kingdom, the ratio of male to female 'alcoholics' has been five to one. Recently it seems that alcohol problems have increased substantially, and perhaps disproportionately, amongst women (Shaw 1980). Thus convictions for drunkenness and for drunken driving offences have risen more rapidly in women than men (though this may be due to changes in arrest policy) and so have hospital admissions for alcohol problems (see Smith 1981).

Age

We have seen that the heaviest drinkers are men in their late teens or early twenties. Recently there has been disturbing evidence of increasing drinking and drunkenness amongst adolescents. In England and Wales, convictions for drunkenness in people aged under 16 more than doubled between 1964 and 1976. High levels of drunkenness were found in a study of over 7000 English adolescents (Hawker 1978) whilst evidence of serious drinking problems was found amongst a large proportion of 15–16 year olds in Scotland (Plant *et al.* 1982).

Occupation

The risk of both alcohol dependence and alcohol-related disability is much increased among several occupational groups: chefs, kitchen porters, barmen, and brewery workers, who have easy access to alcohol; executives and salesmen who entertain on expense accounts; actors and entertainers; seamen; printers; and doctors.

THE CAUSES OF EXCESSIVE DRINKING AND ALCOHOL DEPENDENCE

Despite much research, surprisingly little is known about the causes of excessive drinking and alcohol dependence. At one time it was supposed that certain people were particularly predisposed, either through personality or an innate biochemical anomaly. Nowadays this simple notion of specific predisposition is no longer held. Instead alcohol dependence is thought to result from a variety of interacting factors, which can be divided into individual and environmental.

Individual factors

Genetic factors

In a study conducted in Denmark the sons of alcoholics, who had been adopted away from their original home early in life, were nearly four times more likely to develop drinking problems than the adopted away sons of non-alcoholics (Goodwin *et al.* 1973). Similar findings have been reported from America by Cadoret and Gath (1978) and in Sweden by Bohman (1978). Such studies suggest a genetic mechanism but it is not certain how it might act. Recent analyses of the Swedish adoption data led the investigators to suggest two types of inheritance. In one type there appeared to be a large genetic component that was independent of environmental influences. Inheritance appeared to be passed from fathers to sons, and women were seldom affected. Alcoholism was severe in both the probands and the biological fathers. The biological mothers did not differ from the mothers of non-alcoholics. In the other type of inheritance, there appeared to be a smaller genetic and larger environmental component. This type appeared to affect both men and women. Alcoholism was generally mild in the proband and in the parent (father or mother). Severe alcohol abuse was found occasionally in the probands; this was more likely to occur if there were environmental difficulties, especially for men in unskilled jobs (Cloninger *et al.* 1981; Bohman *et al.* 1981). This work needs to be confirmed.

Biochemical factors

Several possible biochemical factors have been suggested, including abnormalities in alcohol dehydrogenase or in neurotransmitter mechanisms. So far there is no firm evidence that any biochemical factors play a causal role.

Learning factors

It has been reported that children tend to follow their parents' drinking patterns (Hawker 1978), and that boys from an early age tend to be encouraged to drink more than girls (Jahoda and Cramond 1972). Nevertheless, it is not uncommon to meet people who are abstainers although their parents drank heavily. It has been suggested that learning processes may contribute in a more specific way to the development of alcohol dependence through the repeated experience of withdrawal symptoms. On this view, relief of withdrawal symptoms by alcohol may act as a reinforcer for further drinking.

Personality factors

Little progress has been made in identifying personality factors that contribute to alcohol dependence. In clinical practice it is common to find that alcohol problems are associated with chronic anxiety, a pervading sense of inferiority, or self-indulgent tendencies. However, many people with personality problems of this kind do not resort to excessive drinking. It seems likely that if personality is important it is because it increases vulnerability to other causal factors.

Psychiatric illness

Although this is not a common cause of problem drinking, it should always be borne in mind, as it may be treatable. Some patients with depressive disorders take to alcohol in the mistaken hope that it will alleviate low mood. Those with anxiety states, including social phobias, are also at risk. Alcohol dependence occasionally occurs in patients with brain disease or schizophrenia.

Alcohol consumption in society

In recent years there has been increasing interest in the idea that rates of alcohol dependence and alcohol-related disability are related to the general level of alcohol consumption in a society. Previously it had been supposed that levels of intake amongst excessive drinkers were independent of the amounts taken by moderate drinkers. The French demographer Ledermann (1956) challenged this idea, proposing instead that the distribution of consumption within a homogeneous population follows a logarithmic normal curve. If this is the case, an increase in the average consumption must inevitably be accompanied by an increase in the number of people who drink an amount that is harmful.

The mathematical details of Ledermann's work have been heavily criticized (for example Miller and Agnew 1974; Duffy 1977). None the less, it is true that there are striking correlations between average annual consumption in a society and several indices of alcohol-related damage among its members (see Smith 1981). For this reason, despite the criticisms of Ledermann's work, it is now widely accepted that the proportion of a population drinking excessively is largely determined by the average consumption of that population.

What then determines the average level of drinking within a nation? Economic, formal, and informal controls must be considered. The **economic** control is the price of alcohol. There is now ample evidence, from the United Kingdom and other countries, that the real price of alcohol profoundly influences a nation's drinking.

The main **formal controls** are the licensing laws. It is difficult to be sure how these affect drinking behaviour, because results in different countries have been conflicting. For example, in Finland in 1969 a new law led to greatly increased availability of alcohol in restaurants, cafés, and shops. This was followed by a 47 per cent increase in consumption. However, in Scotland recent relaxation of licensing hours did not apparently lead to a large increase in consumption.

Informal controls are the customs and moral beliefs in a society that determine who should drink, in what circumstances, at what time of day, and to what extent. Some communities seem to protect their members from alcoholism despite general availability of alcohol; for example, among Jews, drinking problems are uncommon even in countries with high rates in the rest of the community.

RECOGNITION OF THE PROBLEM DRINKER

Only a small proportion of problem drinkers in the community are known to specialized agencies (Edwards *et al.* 1973), and many opportunities to detect problem drinkers are missed. When special efforts are made to screen patients in medical and surgical wards, between 10 and 30 per cent are found to have serious drinking problems, the rates being highest in accident and emergency wards (for example Barcha *et al.* 1968; Jarman and Kellett 1979; Holt *et al.* 1980).

Problem drinking often goes undetected because excessive drinkers conceal their drinking. However doctors and other professionals often do not ask the right questions. It should be a standard practice to ask all patients – medical, surgical, and psychiatric – about their alcohol consumption. A useful question is simply to ask that patient how much he drank in the preceding week. Some patients will give a false answer, but there will be others for whom it provides the opportunity to reveal the problem.

The next requirement is for the doctor to be suspicious about 'at risk' factors. In general practice, problem drinking may come to light as a result of problems in the marriage and family, at work, with finances, or the law (Hore and Wilkins 1976). The wife may complain of the husband's boastfulness, lack of consideration, sexual dysfunction, or aggressiveness towards herself and the children. The problem drinker is likely to have many more days off work than the moderate drinker, and repeated absences on Monday are highly suggestive. The occupations at risk (see p. 433) should also be remembered.

In hospital practice, the problem drinker may be noticed it he develops withdrawal symptoms after admission. Florid delirium tremens is obvious, but milder forms may be mistaken for the acute organic syndrome occurring in pneumonia or post-operatively.

In both general and hospital practice, 'at-risk' factors include physical disorders that may be alcohol-related. Common examples are gastritis, peptic ulcer, and liver disease, but others such as neuropathy and seizures should be borne in mind. Repeated accidents should also arouse suspicion. Psychiatric 'at risk' factors include anxiety, depression, erratic moods, impaired concentration, memory lapses, and sexual dysfunction. In all cases of deliberate self-harm, problem drinking should be considered.

If at-risk factors raise suspicion, or if the patient hints at a drink problem, the next step is tactful but persistent questions to confirm the diagnosis. The doctor should find out how much the patient drinks on a typical 'drinking day', starting with the amount he takes in the second half of the day, and working back to the earlier part of the day. The patient should be asked how he feels if he goes without drink for a day or two and how he feels on waking. Gradually a picture can be built up of what and how much a patient drinks throughout a typical day. Similarly, tactful enquiry should be made about social effects of drinking, such as declining efficiency at work, missed promotion, accidents, lateness, absences, and extended meal breaks. The patient should be asked about any difficulties in relationships with the spouse and children. In this way, the patient may be led step by step to recognize and accept that he has a drinking problem which he has previously denied. Once this stage is reached, the doctor should be in a position to enquire about the typical features of dependency, and the full range of physical, psychological, and social disabilities described in preceding sections.

Laboratory tests

Several laboratory tests can be used to detect heavy drinkers, though none gives an unequivocal answer. This is because the more sensitive tests can give 'false positives' when there is disease of the liver, heart, kidneys, or blood, or if enzyme-inducing drugs have been taken, such as anticonvulsants, steroids, or barbiturates. However, abnormal values point to the possibility of alcohol abuse. Only the three most useful tests are considered here.

Gamma-glutamyl-transpeptidase (GGT)

Estimations of GGT in blood provide a useful screening test (Rosalki *et al.* 1970). The level is raised in about 80 per cent of problem drinkers, both men and women, whether or not there is demonstrable liver damage. The heavier the drinking, the greater the rise in GGT.

Mean corpuscular volume (MCV)

MCV is raised above the normal value in about 60 per cent of alcohol-dependent people, and more commonly in women than in men. If other causes are excluded, a raised MCV is a strong pointer to excessive drinking. Moreover, it takes several weeks to return to normal after abstinence.

Blood alcohol concentration

A high level does not distinguish between an isolated drinking episode and chronic abuse, but if someone does not appear intoxicated at levels above 80 mg/100 ml (the legal limit for driving) he is likely to be a regular heavy drinker. Alcohol is eliminated relatively slowly from the blood, and can be detected in appreciable amounts for 24 hours after a drinking episode.

THE TREATMENT OF THE PROBLEM DRINKER

The treatment plan

The assessment should include a full drinking history and an appraisal of current medical, psychological, and social problems. An intensive and searching enquiry often helps the patient gain a new recognition and under-standing of his problem, and this is the basis of treatment. It is usually desirable to involve the husband or wife in the assessment, both to obtain additional information and to give the spouse a chance to unburden feelings.

An explicit treatment plan should be worked out with the patient (and spouse if appropriate). There should be specific goals and the patient should be required to take responsibility for realizing them. These goals should deal not only with the drinking problem, but also with any accompanying problems in health, marriage, job, and social adjustment. In the early stages they should be short-term and achievable; for example, complete abstinence for two weeks. In this way the patient can be rewarded by early achievement.

Longer term goals can be set as treatment progresses. These will be concerned with trying to change factors that precipitate or maintain excessive drinking, such as tensions in the family. In drawing up this treatment plan, an important decision is whether to aim at total abstinence or at limited consumption of alcohol (controlled drinking).

TOTAL ABSTINENCE VERSUS CONTROLLED DRINKING

The disease model of alcoholism proposes that an alcohol-dependent person must become totally abstinent and remain so, since a single drink would lead to relapse. Alcoholics Anonymous have made this a tenet of their approach to treatment. In 1962 Davies reported that a small number of alcoholics who had failed to abstain when asked to do so, had nevertheless succeeded in drinking in a controlled and moderate way. This finding was confirmed by Orford and Edwards (1977) and in the influential American Rand report (Armor *et al.* 1976). Several writers have suggested that controlled drinking might be a suitable goal for people dependent on alcohol (Pattison 1966; Orford 1973; Clark 1976). In 1973, Sobell and Sobell tested the idea by randomly assigning patients to 'non-drinking' and 'controlled drinking' groups. They found no difference in outcome one year later. However this was not confirmed by Ewing and Rouse (1976).

The issue of abstinence versus controlled drinking remains unresolved. A prevalent view is that controlled drinking may be a feasible goal for people aged under 40, whose problem has been detected early, and who are not heavily dependent or damaged; whilst abstinence is the better goal for those aged over 40, who are heavily dependent and have incurred physical damage, and who have attempted controlled drinking unsuccessfully (Ritson 1982). If controlled drinking is to be attempted, then the doctor should advise the patient clearly about safe limits (see p. 430).

WITHDRAWAL FROM ALCOHOL

For patients with the dependence syndrome, withdrawal from alcohol must be carried out carefully. In the less severe cases, withdrawal may be at home provided there is someone to look after the patient. The general practitioner or health visitor should visit daily to check the patient's physical state and supervise medication. However, any patient likely to have severe withdrawal symptoms should be admitted to hospital.

Sedative drugs are generally prescribed to reduce withdrawal symptoms. Chlormethiazole or chlordiazepoxide are often used. Chlormethiazole may be prescribed in either of two ways: flexibly according to the patient's symptoms, or on a fixed six-hourly regime of gradually decreasing dosage over six to nine days. It should not be prescribed for more that a few days because it can itself become a drug of dependence. Preparations and dosages of chlormethiazole are subject to revision, and before prescribing it the clinician should consult the current edition of the *British National Formulary* or equivalent work of reference. According to the severity of symptoms, chlordiazepoxide maybe given in doses of 50 mg or 100 mg by intramuscuar injection repeated if necessary in two to four hours. Oral dosage may be 40 to 100 mg daily in divided doses. If convulsions occur, large doses of chlordiazepoxide may be used. Vitamin supplements are often given, and in some countries anti-convulsants, glucose, and magnesium infusions are added. During the first five days, there should be a daily check on the patient's temperature, pulse, blood pressure, hydration, level of consciousness, and orientation.

Withdrawal from alcohol is the main purpose of so-called **detoxification units**. In some places these units are used mainly for chronic drunkenness offenders who have little prospect of progressing to a treatment programme. In other places patients come mainly from general practitioners and a substantial proportion move on to further treatment (see Hamilton *et al.* 1977; Arroyave *et al.* 1980).

TREATMENT

Psychological treatment

Group therapy

This is probably the most widely used treatment for problem drinkers. Regular meetings are attended by about 10 patients and one or more members of staff. The aim is to enable patients to observe their own problems mirrored in other problem drinkers and to work out better ways of coping with their problems. They gain confidence as members of the group jointly strive to reorganize their lives without alcohol. Group therapy is further discussed on p. 590.

Supportive therapy

If group therapy is not available or not acceptable to the patient, individual psychological support may be provided by a psychiatrist or social worker. The aim is to help the patient to cope with problems in day-to-day living without drinking to excess. Supportive therapy is discussed on p. 585.

Behaviour therapy

Recently there has been increasing interest in behavioural methods which tackle drinking behaviour itself rather than underlying psychological problems. Patients may be shown films of themselves when drunk; taught to drink without gulping rapidly; and shown how to identify stimuli to drinking and find other ways of dealing with them. In a clinical trial of these methods Sobell and Sobell (1973) found that outcome on many measures was better than with conventional methods. Much more evaluative work needs to be done before these time consuming methods can be accepted into everyday practice.

Medication

Apart from the management of withdrawal discussed above, drug treatment plays only a small part in the management of excessive drinking. None the less drug treatment is described at some length here because it carries certain risks and may cause unpleasant side-effects. **Disulfiram** (antabuse) is sometimes prescribed as a deterrent to impulsive drinking. It acts by blocking the oxidation of alcohol so that acetaldehyde accumulates. If the patient drinks alcohol he experiences unpleasant flushing of the face, headache, choking sensations, rapid pulse, and feelings of anxiety. The drug is not without risk, occasionally causing cardiac irregularities, and rarely cardiovascular collapse. It also has unpleasant side-effects in the absence of alcohol: a metallic taste in the mouth; gastro-intestinal symptoms; dermatitis; peripheral neuropathy; urinary frequency; impotence; and toxic confusional states. Treatment with disulfiram should not be started until at least 12 hours after the last ingestion of alcohol. On the first day the patient is warned carefully about the dangers of drinking alcohol while taking the drug. He is then given four tablets each of 200 mg and told not to take any alcohol whatever. The dosage is then reduced by one tablet a day over three days, the maintenance dose being half to one tablet a day.

Citrated calcium carbimide is used in the same way. Compared with disulfiram, it is more rapidly absorbed and excreted, induces a milder reaction with alcohol, and has fewer side-effects. Details of the dosage will be found in standard works of reference.

Some clinicians find these drugs valuable (see Costello 1975; Armor *et al.* 1976). In our view they have a limited use for a few patients and then only as an adjunct to other treatment. They are most suited to patients who are compliant in treatment, attend regularly, and have high expectations of improvement (Kitson 1977) – just the patients who are most likely to abstain without them.

Treatment by the general practitioner

Recently an Advisory Committee on Alcoholism (Kessel 1978) concluded that the treatment of alcoholism should be undertaken increasingly by primary care teams. General practitioners are well placed to provide early treatment and they are likely to know the patient and his family well. It is often effective if the general practitioner gives simple advice in a frank, matter-of-fact way, but with tact and understanding. This is followed by supportive treatment as described above.

Other agencies concerned with drinking problems

Alcoholics Anonymous (AA)

This is a self-help organization which came to Britain from the USA in 1947. Members attend group meetings usually twice weekly on a long-term basis. In crisis they can obtain immediate help from other members by telephone. The organization works on the firm belief that abstinence must be complete. At present there are about 1200 groups in the United Kingdom.

Alcoholics Anonymous does not appeal to all problem drinkers because the meetings involve an emotional confession of problems. However the organization is of great value to some problem drinkers, and anyone developing a drink problem should be encouraged to try it. The activities of Alcoholics Anonymous are described by Robinson (1979).

Al-Anon

This is a parallel organization providing support for the spouses of excessive drinkers, and *Al-Ateen* does the same for their teenage children.

Councils on alcoholism

These are voluntary bodies that co-ordinate available services in an area and train counsellors. They advise problem drinkers and their families where to obtain help, and provide social activities for those who have recovered.

Hostels

These are intended mainly for homeless problem drinkers. They provide rehabilitation and counselling. Usually abstinence is a condition of residence.

Results of treatment

A number of investigations have combined results from different treatment centres. The Rand Report (Armor *et al.* 1976) describes a prospective study of 45 treatment centres in the USA, of which eight were followed for 18 months. Only a quarter of the patients remained abstinent for six months, and fewer than 10 per cent for 18 months. However, at 18 months 70 per cent of patients had reduced their consumption of alcohol. Patients with a better outcome had received more intensive treatment but the form of treatment made no difference.

In a controlled trial with 100 male alcoholics, Edwards *et al.* (1977) compared simple advice with intensive treatment that included introductions to Alcoholics Anonymous, medication, repeated interviews, counselling for their wives, and, where appropriate, inpatient treatment as well. The advice group received a three-hour assessment together with a single session of counselling with the spouse present. The two groups were well matched. After 12 months there was no significant difference between them in drinking behaviour, subjective ratings, or social adjustment (see also Orford and Edwards 1977).

Probably outcome depends as much upon factors in the patient as upon the particular treatment. There is some disagreement as to what these factors are but the following generally predict a better prognosis whatever treatment is used: good insight into the nature of the problems; social stability in the form of a fixed abode, family support, and ability to keep a job; and ability to control impulsiveness, to defer gratification, and to form deep emotional relationships.

PREVENTION OF ALCOHOL DEPENDENCE

In seeking to prevent problem drinking and alcohol dependence, two approaches are possible. The first is to improve the help and guidance available to the individual as already described. The second is to introduce social changes likely to affect drinking patterns in the population as a whole. It is with this second group that we are concerned here. Consumption in a population might be reduced by four methods:

(i) *The pricing of alcoholic beverages.* Putting up the price of alcohol would probably reduce the consumption.

(ii) *Advertising.* Controlling or abolishing the advertising of alcoholic drinks might be another preventive measure, but there is little evidence that it would work. A total press and television ban in British Columbia made little difference (Smart and Cutler 1976). Moreover, there is a large alcohol problem in the Soviet Union, where there is no advertising in the Western sense.

(iii) *Controls on sale.* Another preventive measure might be to control sales of alcohol by limiting hours or banning sales in supermarkets. It is known that relaxation of restrictions led to increased sales in Finland and some other countries, but it does not follow that increased restrictions would reduce established rates of drinking.

(iv) *Health education.* It is not known whether education about alcohol abuse is effective. Little is known as to how attitudes are formed or changed. Although education about alcohol seems desirable, it cannot be assumed that classroom lectures or mass media propaganda would alter attitudes.

Dependence on drugs

This section is concerned mainly with physical dependence on drugs but some reference is also made to the non-dependent abuse of drugs. The latter is the term used in ICD 9 to refer to the taking of drugs to the detriment of the person's health or social functioning but without evidence of dependence. In DSM III the corresponding term is substance abuse. The pattern of use in dependent patients varies according to the drug and the severity of its withdrawal effects, as described later in this chapter. In this section, the authors have broadly followed the scheme used by Mitcheson (1983).

PREVALENCE OF DRUG DEPENDENCE

Little is known for certain about the prevalence of different types of drug dependence. In the United Kingdom, information comes from several sources: criminal statistics, mainly based on offences involving the misuse of drugs and thefts from chemists shops; hospital admissions; Home Office statistics; and special surveys. Unfortunately none of these sources is satisfactory, since much drug use goes undetected.

Figures given by Edwards (1979) indicate that the proportion of addicts aged under 20 rose steeply in the mid- and late-1960s, and may have declined again in the 1970s. In the early 1980s there is increasing concern that the problem is increasing again. Adolescents are at risk of drug abuse, particularly around school-leaving age. In this group, abuse is often associated with rebelliousness and rejection of authority. Amongst attenders at drug dependence clinics in the big cities, there is a high proportion of unemployed youths who lead disorganized lives and have few stable relationships. On the other hand, in a study of an English town, Plant (1975) found that many younger drug abusers remained in employment, and their drug-taking was a passing phase. The middle-aged and elderly are at risk mainly from dependence on sleeping tablets and, until recently, amphetamines obtained on prescription.

An interesting epidemiological study of heroin abuse in an English new town was carried out by de Alarcon (1969). He estimated incidence rates and studied paths of transmission by establishing the approximate date on which each heroin user had first injected the drug and the identity of the person who had provided it. At first, there were only a few heroin users who had been initiated in other towns. They gradually initiated a small number of new cases in the town. Heroin abuse then spread rapidly from these 'new cases' to others. Two major 'transmission trees' were traced, one including 32 users who could be traced back to one original initiator, the other including 16 users.

CAUSES OF DRUG DEPENDENCE

There is no single cause of drug dependence. It is generally argued that three factors are important, namely availability of drugs, a vulnerable personality, and social pressures. Once regular drug taking is established, pharmacological factors are important in determining dependence.

Many drug users, particularly younger people taking non-prescribed drugs, appear to have some degree of **personality disorder** before taking drugs, as shown by a poor school record, truancy, or delinquency. They often seem to be without resources to cope with the challenges of day to day life, inconsistent in their feelings, and critical of society and authority. Many of those who abuse drugs report depression and anxiety, but it is seldom clear whether these are the causes or the consequences of drug dependence.

Some give a history of mental illness or personality disorder in the family, or come from severely **disorganized backgrounds**. A history of childhood unhappiness is common. However many drug-dependent people show none of these features.

The risk of drug dependence is greater in societies which condone drug taking. Within the immediate peer group, there may be **social pressures** for a young person to take drugs to achieve status.

In addition to these social and personality factors, various **pharmacological mechanisms** have been postulated. For example, it has been suggested that both tolerance and physical withdrawal effects, which usually develop in parallel, can be explained by mechanisms such as an increased amount of neuro-transmitter receptor supersensitivity or hypertrophy of alternative pathways (see Paton 1969).

DIAGNOSIS OF DRUG DEPENDENCE

It is important to diagnose drug dependence early, at a stage when tolerance may be less established and behaviour patterns less fixed, and the complications of intravenous use may not have developed. Before describing the clinical presentations of the different types of drugs, some general principles will be given. The psychiatrist who is not used to treating drug-dependent people should remember that he may be in the unusual position of trying to help a patient who is attempting to deceive him. Patients dependent on heroin may overstate the daily dose to obtain extra supplies for their own use or for sale to others. Also many patients take more than one drug but may not say so. It is important to try to corroborate the patient's account of the amount he takes by asking detailed questions about the duration of drug-taking, and the cost and source of drugs; by checking the story for internal consistency; and by external verification whenever possible.

Certain clinical signs lead to the suspicion that drugs are being injected. These include: needle tracks and thrombosis of veins, especially in the antecubital fossa; the wearing of long sleeves in hot weather; and scars. Intra-venous use should be considered in any patient who presents with subcutaneous abscesses or hepatitis.

Behavioural changes may also suggest drug dependence. These include absence from school or work and occupational decline. The dependent person may also neglect his appearance, isolate himself from his former friends, and adopt new ones in an addict culture. Minor criminal offences, such as petty theft and prostitution, may also be indicators.

Dependent people may come to medical attention in several ways. Some declare that they are dependent on drugs. Others conceal their dependency, asking for controlled drugs for the relief of pain such as renal colic or dysmen-orrhoea. It is important to be especially wary of such requests from temporary patients. Others present with drug-related complications such as cellulitis, pneumonia, serum hepatitis, or accidents; or for the treatment of acute drug effects, overdose, withdrawal symptoms, intoxication, or adverse reactions to hallucinogenic drugs. A few are detected during an admission to hospital for an unrelated illness.

Laboratory diagnosis

Whenever possible, the diagnosis of drug dependence should be confirmed by laboratory tests. Most drugs of abuse can be detected in the urine, the notable exceptions being cannabis and LSD. Urine specimens should be sent to the laboratory as quickly as possible. An indication should be given of the interval between the last admitted drug-dose and the collection of the urine sample. The laboratory should be provided with as complete a list as possible of drugs likely to have been taken, including those prescribed as well as those obtained in other ways.

TREATMENT AND REHABILITATION: GENERAL PRINCIPLES

The main aim of the treatment of the drug-dependent person is the withdrawal of the drug of dependence. If this cannot be achieved, maintenance therapy may be considered. In addition to withdrawal or maintenance, psychological treatment and social support are required. At this point in the chapter, the general principles of treatment are outlined. In later sections, treatment specific to individual drugs will be considered.

In Britain, most drug-dependent patients are treated in clinics based on psychiatric units. In London there are 13 **special treatment centres** mainly for people dependent on narcotics. Inpatient care is usually provided within the psychiatric unit of general hospitals or in psychiatric hospitals.

The principles of withdrawal

Withdrawal from some drugs is best carried out gradually with the patient in hospital under medical and nursing supervision. This applies to the opiates and, more particularly barbiturates, which may present serious problems during and after withdrawal (see below). Amphetamines, on the other hand, can be withdrawn more rapidly – provided that barbiturates are not being taken at the same time. Nevertheless the risk of depression and suicide should always be remembered.

Maintenance therapy

Some clinicians provide maintenance therapy to addicts who are not sufficiently motivated to accept withdrawal treatment. Others use maintenance rarely, preferring to wait until the person's motivation has increased, and then offering withdrawal and rehabilitation. The evidence in support of the first course is not compelling.

If maintenance is used, it should be remembered that some addicts convert tablets or capsules into material for injection, a particularly dangerous practice. Also, some addicts attend a succession of general practitioners in search of supplementary supplies of drugs. They may withhold information about attendance at clinics, or pose as temporary residents.

There is little good information about the outcome of long-term supportive maintenance compared with drug-free programmes. Much seems to depend on the personality of the drug user. Some patients who receive maintenance drugs achieve a degree of social stability, but others continue heavy drug abuse and deteriorate both medically and socially.

Physical complications

The complications of self-injection may need to be treated in a general hospital. Skin infections may need to be dressed, and abscesses drained, while complications of using infected syringes, such as septicaemia and infective hepatitis, require inpatient treatment. Pollard (1973) has reviewed the surgical treatment needed for complications of intravenous drug abuse.

Psychological treatment

Psychological treatment is appropriate when personality factors play a large part. Some dependent patients may be helped by simple measures with outpatient support. In many units group psychotherapy is provided to help patients develop insight into their emotional and personality problems. Some patients have sufficient resources to benefit from treatment in a therapeutic community. This treatment follows the general principles described in Chapter 5, but the group sessions involve more intense confrontation, often with considerable emotional release, than in most other forms of group treatment.

It is difficult to evaluate the efficacy of these treatments, although there have been some suggestive findings. For example, in a study of patients admitted to a therapeutic community for drug dependence, it appeared that longer residence in the community (more than six months) was associated with a better outcome, as judged by subsequent conviction rates for crime (Wilson and Mandelbrote 1978) and frequency of drug injection (Wilson 1978).

Rehabilitation

Many drug takers have great difficulty in establishing themselves in normal society. The aim of rehabilitation is to enable the addict to leave the drug subculture, and develop new social contacts. Unless he can do this, treatment is likely to fail.

Hostel accommodation may be valuable to withdrawn heroin addicts and those still undergoing treatment. These are available mainly in metropolitan London, but also in other centres. Continuing social support is usually required if the addict is to learn to live in society without recourse to drugs.

DEPENDENCE ON SPECIFIC TYPES OF DRUG

Morphine type

This type includes morphine, heroin, and codeine, as well as synthetic and semi-synthetic analgesics such as pethidine and methadone. **Morphine** is the principal active alkaloid in opium. As an analgesic, it is about as potent as heroin, but it is much less effective in producing euphoria. It causes dependence, but less readily than heroin. Signs of morphine dependence and of the withdrawal syndrome resemble those of heroin, which are described below. **Heroin** is diacetyl morphine. It is a powerful analgesic and cough suppressant. Its capacity to produce euphoria gives it the greatest potential of any opiate for producing dependence. Such dependence develops rapidly. The immediate effect of injected heroin is often described as one of intense pleasure, with a feeling of warmth and tingling. However for some addicts the first sensations are not pleasant. This first stage is followed by a detached feeling of relaxation. Appetite and sexual desire are decreased and constipation is common. As tolerance develops, more of the drug has to be taken to produce these effects.

Withdrawal symptoms rarely threaten the life of someone in reasonable health, though they cause great distress and so drive the person to seek further supplies. The withdrawal symptoms include restlessness and insomnia; pain in muscles and joints; running nose and eyes; sweating; abdominal cramps, vomiting and diarrhoea; pilo-erection; dilated pupils; raised pulse rate, and disturbance of temperature control. These features usually begin about six hours after the last dose, reach a peak after 36–48 hours, and then wane.

Methadone is an analgesic which is approximately as potent, weight for weight, as morphine. It causes cough suppression, constipation, and depression of the central nervous system and of respiration. Pupillary constriction is less marked than with morphine. The withdrawal syndrome is similar to that of heroin and morphine, but slower and less severe. Thus symptoms may only begin after 36 hours, and reach a peak after three to five days. For this reason, methadone is often used to replace heroin in patients dependent on the latter drug.

The natural course of opiate dependence

Follow-up studies of opiate dependent people indicate that after seven years only about a quarter to a third appear to be abstinent while between 10 and 20 per cent have died from causes related to drug taking (for example Stimson *et al.* 1978; Chapple *et al.* 1972). Deaths are usually due to accidental overdosage, often related to loss of tolerance after a period of enforced abstinence (Gardner 1970). Abstinence is often related to changed circumstances of life; a point that is reflected in the report of 95 per cent abstinence among returning soldiers who had become addicted during the Vietnam war (Robins *et al.* 1974).

Management of opiate dependence

Restriction on prescribing of opiates

In the United Kingdom (in 1982) only specially licensed doctors may legally prescribe heroin, and cocaine, to an addict for maintenance of addiction. Opiates other than heroin, cocaine, as well as stimulants or barbiturates, may be prescribed to addicts by doctors who are not specially licensed. However, it is unwise for unlicensed doctors to prescribe these substances to addicts except in an emergency. The list of drugs requiring a licence is being reviewed at the time of writing and may be extended.

In the United Kingdom, there is a central register of opiate addicts, but there is no formal procedure of registration. Any doctor attending an opiate addict is required to notify the latter's name to: The Drugs Branch, Home Office, 50 Queen Anne Gate, London. SW1.

Planned withdrawal

Planned withdrawal of opiates under medical supervision need not be very uncomfortable. In a well motivated person, withdrawal may be achieved by prescribing any of the opiate drugs and reducing the dose over two to four weeks. Methadone Mixture Drug Tariff Formula is convenient and the least likely to be abused. It is given in an initial dose of 20 to 70 mg, depending upon the patient's usual consumption; in the case of exceptionally heavy use, a first dose of 100 mg may be needed. The dose should be reduced by between 20 per cent and 30 per cent every two or three days, according to the patient's response. For outpatient withdrawal, dose reduction should be smaller and the intervals longer, to minimize the patient's temptation to seek additional supplies. None the less, a clear time-limit should be set from the start.

When the daily intake of heroin is not great, patients can be withdrawn by using a combination of lomotil (diphenloxylate hydrochloride 2.5 mg with atrophine sulphate 0.025 mg) and chlormethiazole. The usual regime lasts three days. Lomotil is given in a dosage of two tablets six hourly for 24 hours, followed by one tablet six hourly for 48 hours. Chlormethiazole is given twice daily, at morning and night for three days. As explained earlier in the chapter (p. 438) dosages of this drug are subject to revision, and before prescribing it the clinician should consult the current edition of the British National Formulary or equivalent work of reference. Since chlormethiazole can be abused, this treatment should be carried out during inpatient care.

Maintenance treatment for opiate dependence

If possible, patients should be withdrawn from drugs. If they refuse, maintenance treatment can be considered. A few patients still receive a maintenance prescription of injectable drugs but new patients are likely to be offered oral methadone instead. This is prescribed as Methadone Mixture Drug Tariff Formula, containing 5 mg methadone hydrochloride per 5 ml, which is a liquid preparation formulated to discourage attempts to inject it. It is not to be confused with the cough mixture properly referred to as methadone linctus. The maintenance dose is from 20 to 70 mg per day. Great care is needed in deciding the amount and the higher dosage should never be given on the first occasion except to someone known to be heavily addicted.

Although some patients seem to acquire some social stability while taking maintenance methadone, the general value of this form of treatment has not been demonstrated convincingly, and is being increasingly questioned (see Gossop (1978) for a review).

Barbiturate type

This 'type' includes various kinds of sedatives, tranquillizers, and hypnotic drugs. Most problems are presented by the barbiturates, although more careful prescribing has reduced their extent. Other drugs currently abused include chlormethiazole, glutethimide, and benzodiazepines.

Barbiturates

Although tolerance develops less rapidly to barbiturates than to opiates, none the less barbiturates present particular dangers. This is because tolerance to the sedating effects occurs to a greater extent than it does to the depressant effects on vital centres, so increasing the risk of inadvertent fatal overdose. Most people dependent on barbiturates take them by mouth. They are usually middle-aged or elderly, and may be tolerant of large doses. Most began taking the drug because it had been prescribed as a hypnotic. However in recent years some young people have been using barbiturates intravenously, by dissolving capsules. These addicts are usually multiple drug users. Short-acting barbiturates are favoured for injection, for example pentobarbitone or 'Tuinal' (a mixture of quinalbarbitone and amylobarbitone). In aqueous solution these drugs are highly irritant to tissues, causing periphlebitis, indolent abscesses, sloughing ulcers, and even gangrene. Patients with such complications not infrequently need surgical treatment varying from skin grafting to amputation. Overdosage amongst users is common, and difficult to treat.

Recognition of the abuser of barbiturates depends on a number of features. He may appear to be drunk, with slurred speech and incoherence. Dullness and drowsiness are common, and so is depression. Nystagmus is a valuable sign, which should always be sought. Pupillary size is not helpful. Younger needle users tend to be unkempt and dirty, and often appear malnourished. Blood levels are generally only useful in acute poisoning. Urine should be examined to investigate the possible simultaneous abuse of other drugs.

Withdrawal

Abrupt withdrawal of barbiturates from a dependent person is highly dangerous. It may result in a mental disorder like that after alcohol withdrawal, and may lead to seizures and sometimes to death (see Isbell *et al.* 1950). The withdrawal syndrome may not appear at its severest for several days.

The syndrome begins with anxiety, restlessness, disturbed sleep, anorexia, and nausea. These may progress to vomiting, hypotension, pyrexia, tremulousness, major seizures, disorientation, and hallucinations – a picture similar to delirium tremens.

Withdrawal should nearly always be an inpatient procedure. If the patient has been taking a small dose of barbiturate, outpatient withdrawal may be considered but only if there is no history of epilepsy before drug abuse, or recent antiepileptic medication.

In the management of withdrawal, phenothiazines should be avoided as they may lower the fit threshold. Instead withdrawal can be initiated by giving enough pentobarbital in divided doses to maintain the patient between intoxication and withdrawal. Following this, dosage is reduced from 50 to 100 mg a day so long as withdrawal symptoms do not occur. An alternative is to use a short-acting benzodiazepine.

If slow withdrawal is to be attempted outside hospital, short-acting substitutes should be avoided because of the risk of abuse. Instead phenobarbitone should be given. An attempt should be made to calculate the patient's usual daily dosage allowing for all drugs with similar actions such as alcohol and benzodiazepines. For every 100 mg of a shorter acting barbiturate or its equivalent, a daily dose of 30 mg phenobarbitone should be given in divided dose, up to a maximum of 300 mg daily (exceptionally 400 mg). This is reduced progressively over 10–20 days, the patient being assessed every second or third day.

Management of long-term dependence
Patients who have been taking drugs of this kind for a long period may be transferred to the safer benzodiazepines. In most well-motivated patients, withdrawal can eventually be achieved provided enough time is allowed.

Prevention of dependence
It is essential that dependence is avoided by restricting prescribing of sedatives and hypnotics to small amounts and short periods. It should be explained to the patient why long-term consumption is to be avoided.

Cannabis

Cannabis is derived from the plant *Cannabis sativa*. It is consumed either as the dried vegetative parts in the form known as marijuana or 'grass', or as the resin secreted by the flowering tops of the female plant. In some parts of North Africa and Asia, cannabis products are consumed in a similar way to alcohol in Western society. In North America and Britain the intermittent use of cannabis is quite widespread among young people (Kosviner 1976). It appears that most users do not take any other illegal drug, but some are given to high consumption of alcohol.

The effects of the drug vary with the dose, the person's expectations and mood, and the social setting. Users sometimes describe themselves as 'high' but, like alcohol, cannabis seems to exaggerate the pre-existing mood, whether exhiliration, depression, or anxiety. Users sometimes report an increased enjoyment of aesthetic experiences and distortion of time and space. There may be reddening of the eyes, dry mouth, irritation of the respiratory tract, and coughing.

There is no definite withdrawal syndrome in man nor any convincing evidence of tolerance. For this reason the detection of cannabis use can be very difficult. No serious side-effects have been proved amongst intermittent users. There is no evidence of teratogenicity, but cannabis has not been proved to be safe in the first three months of pregnancy. Inhaled cannabis smoke irritates the respiratory tract and is potentially carcinogenic.

There is some disagreement whether cannabis can lead to a psychosis. Acute effects have been reported in volunteers given the drug (Isbell *et al.* 1967), but the evidence for a lasting syndrome is not convincing (see Edwards 1976).

It is often said that chronic use of cannabis leads to a state of apathy and indolence. However an objective study of chronic cannabis users failed to demonstrate this (Beaubrun and Knight 1973). Campbell *et al.* (1971) reported that such usage may result in cerebral atrophy demonstrable by air-encephalography, but this has not been confirmed.

For a review of the pharmacological and medical aspects of cannabis taking see Graham (1976). The social and legal aspects are well reviewed in the report of the Advisory Committee on Drug Dependence (1968).

Amphetamine type

This type includes: the amphetamines; related drugs such as phenmetrazine and methylphenidate; and fenfluramine.

Dexamphetamine is the drug most often abused, either alone or in conjunction with the barbiturates as in Drinamyl. In 1968 in the United Kingdom there was a marked increase of methylamphetamine injection, which stopped when the drug was withdrawn from the retail pharmaceutical market.

Amphetamines have temporary stimulant and euphoriant effects, which are followed by depression, anxiety, irritability, and anergia. Hence psychological dependence can develop quickly. Some people can take amphetamines in controlled dosage, whilst others (especially those repeatedly seeking a 'high') rapidly increase the dosage. Amphetamines have therefore been largely abandoned in medical practice. They are still used for the hyperkinetic syndrome of childhood and narcolepsy in adults. It is therefore good practice to be wary of new patients who purport to suffer from this latter condition.

The clinical picture of dependence upon amphetamines is ill-defined except in those who take large doses. A common feature is a tendency to be over-talkative and over-active for an hour or two, afterwards becoming quiet, sleepy, or depressed. Amphetamines cause insomnia, and barbiturates or other hypnotics may be taken to overcome this. The nose, lips, and mouth may be dry, and licking of the lips may be frequent. Reduced hunger may lead to evident malnutrition. There may be dilatation of the pupils, sweating, temporary high blood pressure, tachycardia and perhaps cardiac arrhythmia, over-brisk tendon reflexes, shallow respiration and occasionally high fever and circulatory collapse. Regular high dose users may exhibit repetitive stereotyped behaviour such as obsessive tidying.

A paranoid psychosis indistinguishable from acute paranoid schizophrenia may be induced by high doses, whether taken by mouth or intravenously. The features include persecutory delusions, auditory and visual hallucinations, and sometimes hostile and dangerously aggressive behaviour (Connell 1958). Usually the condition subsides over about a week, but a few cases continue for months. It is not certain whether these are cases of schizophrenia provoked by amphetamine, or true drug-induced psychoses.

Whenever amphetamine abuse is at all likely, a urine sample should be taken within 24 hours of admission and analysed for the drugs before any phenothiazines are given.

Occasional chronic amphetamine users are found among older patients, who originally had the drug prescribed in the 1950s and 1960s and cannot tolerate the withdrawal depression. For these patients, maintenance therapy may occasionally be justifiable, but prescriptions should be for short periods.

Treatment of acute overdose requires sedation, and management of hyperpyrexia and cardiac arrhythmias. Most toxic symptoms, including paranoid psychosis, resolve rapidly as the drug is eliminated. The use of major tranquillizers may be necessary, but if they can be avoided the differential diagnosis from acute paranoid schizophrenia will be less difficult.

Cocaine

Cocaine is a central nervous system stimulant with effects similar to those of amphetamines described above. It causes strong psychological dependence. In the past it was used by injection, and also by sniffing into the nostrils for more rapid mucosal absorption. The latter practice sometimes caused perforation of the nasal septum.

The classical clinical picture is of excitation, dilated pupils, and tremulousness. Dizziness and convulsions sometimes occur. Psychological effects, apart from excitement, include confusion and depression. A paranoid psychosis may also occur, similar to that induced by amphetamines. Formication ('cocaine bugs'), a feeling as though insects are crawling under the skin, is characteristic of cocaine dependence. It can also occur in intoxication with alcohol or amphetamine.

Hallucinogens

Drugs of this type are sometimes known as psychedelics, because they produce alterations in mood and perception. The term psychotomimetic is also used, although the drugs seldom produce states closely resembling schizophrenia. The synthetic hallucinogens include lysergic acid diethylamide (LSD), dimethyltryptamine (DMT), diethyltryptamine and methyldimethoxyamphetamine. The commonest drug encountered at present in the United Kingdom is LSD. People who believe they are consuming DMT may have been sold lysergide in disguised form. Hallucinogenic mushrooms containing psilocylin are sometimes consumed.

The physical actions of LSD are variable. There are some sympathomimetic effects: heart rate may be increased, and pupils dilated. However overdosage does not appear to result in severe physiological reactions. Conventional doses do not seem to be associated with chromosomal or teratogenic abnormalities.

The mental effects develop during the two hours after LSD consumption, and generally last from eight to 14 hours. The most remarkable experiences are distortions or intensifications of sensory perception. There may be confusion between sensory modalities (synaesthesia), sounds being perceived as visual, or movements experienced as if heard. Objects may seem to merge with one another or move rhythmically. A distressing experience may be distortion of the body image, the person sometimes feeling that he is outside his own body. These experiences may lead to panic with fears of insanity. The mood may be exhilaration, distress, or acute anxiety. According to early reports, behaviour could be unpredictable and extremely dangerous, the user sometimes injuring or killing himself through behaving as if he were invulnerable. Recently there may have been some reduction in such adverse reactions, possibly because users are more aware of the dangers and take precautions to ensure support from other people during a 'trip'.

Whenever possible, adverse reactions should be managed by 'talking down' the user, explaining that the alarming experiences are due to the drug. If there is not time for this, a minor tranquillizer such as diazepam should be given. For severe intoxication, phenothiazines may be given, but are contraindicated if anti-cholinergic drugs (atropine or phencyclidine PCP) have been taken as well.

It has been argued that abuse of lysergide can cause long term abnormalities in thinking or behaviour (Blacker *et al.* 1968), or even schizophrenia. The evidence for any such association is extremely dubious. However, the 'flashback' is a recognized event; that is, the recurrence of psychedelic experience a considerable time after the drug was last taken. This experience may be distressing and occasionally requires treatment with minor tranquillizers.

Phencyclidine

Phencyclidine (otherwise known as PCP or 'angel dust') is a widely abused street drug in North America but is used only sporadically in Britain. It was introduced in 1960 as an analgesic and general anaesthetic, but quickly given up because of side-effects. Its use in veterinary medicine continued for some years, but legal manufacture stopped in 1979. It is easy to synthesize cheaply, and at least six analogues have been reported to be sold illicitly in America. It may be sniffed, smoked, eaten, or injected, and is often consumed mixed with LSD, cannabis, amphetamine, or cocaine (*British Medical Journal* 1980b).

Small doses produce drunkenness, with analgesia of fingers and toes, and even anaesthesia. Intoxication with the drug is prolonged, the common features being: agitation, depressed consciousness, aggressiveness and schizophrenia-like psychosis, nystagmus and raised blood pressure. With high doses there may be ataxia, muscle rigidity, convulsions, and unresponsiveness to the environment even though the eyes are wide open. Characteristic EEG changes may be seen. Phencyclidine can be detected in the urine for 72 hours after it was last taken.

With serious overdoses, an adrenergic crisis may occur with hypertensive heart failure, cerebro-vascular accident, or malignant hyperthermia. Status epilepticus may appear. Fatalities have been reported due mainly to hypertensive crisis but also to respiratory failure, or suicide. Chronic use of phencyclidine may lead to aggressive behaviour accompanied by memory loss.

A phencyclidine withdrawal syndrome has been described, consisting of extreme craving, anergia, depression, and physical discomfort. These symptoms can be relieved by desimipramine (Tennant *et al.* 1981).

Treatment of acute intoxication is symptomatic, according to the features listed above. Haloperidol, or diazepam, or both may be given. Chlorpromazine should be avoided because considerably less safe: it may cause severe postural hypotension or increased muscle rigidity, and may also increase the anti-cholinergic effects of phencyclidine or any other drugs that may have been taken. For a discussion of clinical management see Walker *et al.* 1981.

Solvent abuse

Solvent abuse started amongst adolescents in the USA in the 1950s. It came to attention in the United Kingdom in the early 1970s and is now causing serious concern in some areas (*Lancet* 1982; Watson 1982).

The prevalence of solvent abuse in the United Kingdom is uncertain, but there is no doubt that it occurs mainly in boys aged 8–19, with a peak in those aged 13–15. Most of the young people known to abuse solvents do so as a group activity, and only about five per cent are solitary abusers. In most of these cases, abuse is occasional and experimental, but in about ten per cent it is daily and sustained over months or years (Watson 1982).

The substances abused are mainly solvents and adhesives (hence the name 'glue sniffing'), but also include many other substances such as petrol, cleaning fluid, aerosols of all kinds, agents used in fire extinguishers, and butane. Abuse is often associated with taking other illicit drugs, or with tobacco or alcohol consumption which can be heavy. The methods of ingestion depend on the substance; they include inhalation from tops of bottles, beer cans, cloths held over the mouth, plastic bags, and sprays.

If abuse is regular, psychological dependence can develop, but physical withdrawal symptoms are rare. With sustained use over 6–12 months, tolerance can develop.

The clinical effects of these substances were studied in over 400 cases seen in the West of Scotland between 1975 and 1981 (Watson 1982). Regardless of the solvent used, the early effects are similar to those of alcohol consumption. The central nervous system is first stimulated and then depressed. The stages of intoxication are similar to those of alcohol: euphoria, blurring of vision, slurring of speech, inco-ordination, staggering gait, and coma. Compared with alcohol intoxication, solvent intoxication develops and wanes rapidly (within a few minutes, or up to 2 hours). There is early disorientation, and two-fifths of cases may develop hallucinations, which are mainly visual and often frightening. This combination of symptoms may lead to serious accidents.

From a survey of young people referred to a child psychiatry clinic in London, Skuse and Burrell (1982) found that many chronic users reported transient symptoms of a toxic psychosis, which often had an affective component. These authors also reported that physical symptoms were common in chronic users, notably weight loss, nausea and vomiting, acute bronchospasm, and cardiac arrhythmias.

Certain substances have neurotoxic effects. Peripheral neuropathy is a frequently described consequence of some hexacarbons. For example, n-hexane and methylbutylketone are both metabolized to 2,5 hexanedione, which causes neuropathy. Severe and disabling peripheral neuropathy has been described in teenagers abusing glues containing these substances (Korobkin *et al.* 1975). Abuse of toluene can result in impaired cerebellar function (Boor and Hurtig 1977).

Solvent abuse can be fatal. Anderson *et al.* (1982) identified 140 deaths from volatile substance abuse in the United Kingdom over the period 1971–81. As many as 39 deaths were identified in 1981; these accounted for over 1 per cent of all deaths from all causes in males aged 10–19 years. The male–female ratio was 13 to 1. About half the deaths were due to the direct toxic effects of the solvent. The rest were due to trauma, asphyxia (plastic bag over head) or inhalation of stomach contents.

The diagnosis of acute solvent intoxication is suggested by several features: glue on the hands, face or clothes; chemical smell of the breath; rapid onset and waning of intoxication; disorientation in time and space. Chronic abuse is diagnosed mainly on an admitted history of habitual consumption, increasing tolerance, and psychological dependence. A suggestive feature is a facial rash ('glue-sniffer's rash') caused by repeated inhalation from a bag.

There is no specific treatment for solvent abuse. Favourable results have been reported in chronic or periodic abusers treated by means of family and individual work at a psychiatric hospital (Skuse and Burrell 1982). Some people advocate a strong publicity campaign against solvent abuse, but others maintain this might only make matters worse (*Lancet* 1982).

FURTHER READING

Edwards, G. (1982). *The treatment of drinking problems.* Grant McIntyre, London.

Edwards, G. and Busch, C. (eds) (1981). *Drug problems in Britain: a review of ten years*. Academic Press, New York.

Hore, B.D. (1976). *Alcohol dependence*. Butterworths, London.

Royal College of Psychiatrists (1979). *Alcohol and alcoholism: report of a special committee*. Tavistock, London.

Schecter, A. (1978). *Treatment aspects of drug dependence*. CRC Press, Florida.

15. Sexual problems

Human sexual behaviour does not conform to any single pattern. People vary in the strength of their sexual drives and in the kind of sexual activity they prefer. Societies differ in their attitudes to practices such as homosexuality. Many of these social attitudes reflect the moral codes of the major religions of the world, and they are being modified as the influence of religion on society changes. These variations in sexual attitudes and behaviour cannot be documented in detail here, but a useful account of them can be found in the book by Ford and Beach (1952).

There are two reasons why the doctor should be aware of these variations. First he should be careful not to impose his own values upon his patients. Instead he should find out their values and those of their sexual partners, and try to work within that framework (assuming it is acceptable to him). Secondly, he should remember that some forms of behaviour are generally regarded as abnormal when regularly preferred to heterosexual intercourse, but are quite common as occasional variations of the sexual act; sexual fetishism or masochism are examples.

Difficulties with heterosexual intercourse (sexual dysfunction) are common. Gross departures from the usual pattern of heterosexual intercourse (sexual deviations) are rare; however, they present in a wide variety of syndromes, and are therefore allotted more space in this chapter than would otherwise be appropriate.

CLASSIFICATION

In the ninth edition of the International Classification of Disease (ICD 9) sexual dysfunction and sexual deviations are put together in section 302 (as shown in Table 15.1). This grouping is not entirely appropriate because the two kinds of problem differ in many ways. Another limitation is that, while section 302 has eight categories for sexual deviations, it has only one for sexual dysfunction (302.7). The American Diagnostic and Statistical Manual (DSM III) subdivides 302.7 (Psychosexual Dysfunctions) into six sub-groups (302.71 to 302.76) as follows: inhibited sexual desire; inhibited sexual excitement; inhibited female orgasm; inhibited male orgasm; premature ejaculation; and functional dyspareunia. DSM III generally follows ICD 9, but there are several minor differences. For example, under 302.8 (Other), subgroups are coded in DSM III as follows: fetishism (302.81), voyeurism (302.82), sexual masochism (302.83),

Table 15.1. *Classification of sexual disorders and deviations in ICD 9 and DSM III*

(a) ICD 9
302.0 Homosexuality
302.1 Bestiality
302.2 Paedophilia
302.3 Transvestism
302.4 Exhibitionism
302.5 Transsexualism
302.6 Disorders of psychosexual identity
302.7 Frigidity and impotence
302.8 Other (fetishism, masochism, sadism)
302.9 Unspecified

(b) Differences in DSM III
302.0 Ego-dystonic homosexuality
302.1 Zoophilia
302.6 Gender identity disorder of childhood
302.8 Other (for subdivisions see text)

and sexual sadism (302.84). Category 302.1 is designated zoophilia rather than bestiality. Category 302.00 is called ego-dystonic homosexuality, implying that homosexuality is only to be considered a disorder if it is a persistent source of distress. Any reader interested in the other features distinctive of DSM III should consult the manual.

This chapter adopts a different scheme of classification from those in ICD 9 and DSM III. The scheme divides sexual disorders into sexual dysfunctions, homosexuality, sexual deviations and gender role disorders, as shown in Table 15.2. Homosexuality is classified separately to take account of the widely held view that it is an alternative form of sexual behaviour, and not abnormal in the sense that conditions listed under sexual deviations are abnormal. The deviations are divided into those where the sexual act is abnormal, and those where the 'object' of the act is anomalous (for example, children or inanimate objects). The category of gender role disorders includes cross-gender behaviour among children and transsexualism among adults.

SEXUAL DYSFUNCTION

In men, sexual dysfunction refers to repeated inability to achieve normal sexual intercourse. In women, it refers more often to a repeated unsatisfactory quality to the experience; sexual intercourse can be completed, but without enjoyment (Bancroft *et al.* 1982). What is regarded as normal sexual intercourse, and therefore what is thought to be inadequate, depends in part on the expectations of the two people concerned. For example, when the woman is regularly unable to achieve orgasm, one couple may regard it as normal, whilst another may ask for treatment. Problems of sexual dysfunction can be usefully classi-

Table 15.2. *Alternative classification of sexual disorders*

I.	*Sexual dysfunction*	
	1. Affecting sexual desire	Low libido
	2. Impaired sexual arousal	Erectile impotence
		Failure of arousal in women
	3. Affecting orgasm	Premature ejaculation
		Retarded ejaculation
		Orgasmic dysfunction in women
	4. Other	Vaginismus
		Dyspareunia
		Pain on ejaculation
II.	*Homosexuality*	
III.	*Sexual deviations*	
	Variations of the sexual 'object'	Fetishism
		Transvestism
		Paedophilia
		Bestiality
		Necrophilia
	Variations of the sexual act	Exhibitionism
		Voyeurism
		Sadism
		Masochism
		Frotteurism
IV.	*Disorders of gender role*	
	Transsexualism	
	Gender disturbance in children	

fied into these affecting (1) sexual desire, (2) sexual arousal – erectile impotence in men, failure of arousal in women, (3) orgasm – premature or retarded ejaculation in men, orgasmic dysfunction in women. A fourth category contains other problems such as pain on ejaculation or vaginismus. Sexual dysfunction is sometimes disclosed when the patient consults the doctor about another complaint. This presentation is more likely among women who complain of symptoms such as depression or poor sleep, and gynaecological symptoms such as vaginal discharge.

Prevalence of sexual dysfunction

Erectile impotence that is partial and temporary, rather than complete and permanent, is not uncommon, especially with increasing age. In a population survey, total and apparently permanent erectile impotence was reported by 1.3 per cent of American men aged under 35, 6.7 per cent aged under 50, and 18.4 per cent aged under 60 (cumulative figures from Kinsey *et al.* 1948). Among men presenting for treatment of sexual dysfunction, impotence is the most frequent complaint. The prevalence of premature ejaculation is not known exactly because it depends in part on the partner's speed of response. Ejaculatory failure appears to be rare; it was reported to Kinsey *et al.* (1948) by only six of 4108 men interviewed.

Among women seeking help for sexual disorders, lack of sexual enjoyment is the most common complaint. In about a third of couples seen for treatment, both partners have a problem, usually low libido in the woman and premature ejaculation in the man. Sexual dysfunction is found in about 10 per cent of psychiatric outpatients (Swan and Wilson 1979).

Disorders of sexual desire

Complaints of low libido are much more common among women than men. They often reflect general problems in the relationship between the partners. Sometimes there is a specific sexual problem, which may be due to longstanding inhibitions about sex, or to an apparent biological variation of sexual drive that cannot be modified.

Disorders of sexual arousal

Erectile impotence

This is the inability to reach an erection or to sustain it long enough for satisfactory coitus. It may be present from the first attempt at intercourse (primary) or develop after a period of normal function (secondary). In contrast to premature ejaculation, it is more common among older men. If a man has had more than one sexual partner, he should be asked whether the failure occurs with each partner or only with one. It is also important to find out whether erections occur on waking or in response to masturbation.

Failure of genital response among women

Failure of vaginal lubrication is often secondary to lack of sexual interest. Other causes are anxiety about intercourse and inadequate sexual foreplay by the partner. From the time of the menopause, hormonal changes often lead to reduced vaginal secretions.

Disorders of orgasm

Premature ejaculation

This is habitual ejaculation before penetration or so shortly afterwards that the woman has not gained pleasure. It is more common among younger men, especially during their first sexual encounters.

Retarded ejaculation

This is less common. It refers to serious delay in ejaculation, or complete absence of it. Usually the delay occurs only during coitus, but may also occur in masturbation. It is usually associated with a general psychological inhibition about sexual relations.

Orgasmic dysfunction

Orgasmic dysfunction in women depends on the man's experience as well as the woman's capacity to reach orgasm. Whether it is regarded as a disorder depends on social attitudes and the expectations of the individual. Many women do not regularly achieve orgasm during intercourse. About 25 per cent of women have no orgasm during intercourse for the first year of marriage (Gebhard *et al.* 1970). In the past, absence of orgasm was not generally thought abnormal. More recently attitudes have changed, so that some women may now regard themselves as abnormal although previously they would have been content with the intimacy of sexual relations without regular orgasm.

Other disorders

Vaginismus

This is spasm of the vaginal muscles which causes pain when intercourse is attempted. The spasm is usually associated with fears about penetration, but occasionally it is associated with painful scarring after episiotomy. It is made worse by an inexperienced partner. The woman often reports that spasms start as soon as the man attempts to enter the vagina, and in severe cases it occurs when the woman attempts to introduce her own finger. Extreme cases of vaginismus may lead to non-consummation of marriage. So-called 'virgin wives' sometimes have extreme fears and guilt about sexual relationships rather than a specific fear of penetration. Some women with vaginismus are married to passive and undemanding men who have low libido and who seem at times to be colluding with their wives' refusal to permit full sexual relations (see Dawkins 1961; Friedman 1962).

Dyspareunia

This is the term for pain on intercourse. It has many causes. Pain after partial penetration may result from impaired lubrication of the vagina, from scars or other painful lesions, or (as described above) from the muscle spasm of vaginismus. Pain on deep penetration strongly suggests pelvic pathology such as endometriosis, ovarian cysts and tumours, or pelvic infection.

Pain on ejaculation

This is an uncommon complaint, whose cause is unknown.

Specific sexual fears

A few women are made extremely anxious by specific aspects of the sexual act, such as being touched on the genitalia, the sight or smell of seminal fluid, or even kissing. Despite these specific fears, they may still enjoy other parts of sexual intercourse.

AETIOLOGY OF SEXUAL DYSFUNCTION

Factors common to many forms of sexual dysfunction

Sexual inadequacy arises from a varying combination of a poor general relationship with the partner, low sexual drive, ignorance about sexual technique, and anxiety about sexual performance. The effects of physical illness and associated medication are important. As with other disorders, the aetiology can also be considered as due to predisposing causes, precipitating factors, and influences that maintain the problem. (Nowadays treatment is usually concerned with the last.)

Sexual drive varies considerably between different people, but it is not known how far this variation is determined by constitutional factors. At puberty, the increasing sexual drive of the male is related to an increased output of androgens. Castration, treatment with oestrogens, or the administration of anti-androgenic drugs reduce drive. Cooper *et al.* (1970) reported low urinary testosterone levels in patients whose impotence began gradually and whose sexual drive had always been low. However, there is no convincing evidence that treatment with androgens increases sexual drive in men with normal endocrine function. By contrast, small doses of androgens increase the sexual drive of women.

Ignorance about sexual technique is a cause of sexual inadequacy. It is often accompanied by anxiety about social aspects of relationships with the opposite sex.

Anxiety is an important cause of sexual disorders. Sometimes such anxiety can be understood in terms of an earlier frightening experience. For example, anxiety may stem from a man's failure in his first attempt at intercourse or a girl's experience of sexual assault, or from frightening accounts of sexual relationships given by parents or other people. Psychoanalysts believe that such anxiety often originates from early childhood experiences, which they regard as generally more important than more obvious problems occurring in adult life. Psychoanalysts particularly emphasize failure to resolve the Oedipus complex in boys and the corresponding attachment of the girl to her father. There is no convincing evidence that such early experiences are more influential than later experiences. Undoubtedly, many sexual problems persist because of fears that a previous failure will be repeated.

Physical illnesses and the measures used to treat them can both affect sexual performance. Many effects of treatment are obvious (for example those of colostomy) but others such as the side effects of drugs are not. Sexual disorders sometimes appear to date from a period of abstinence associated with minor physical illness, pregnancy and childbirth, or from the debilitating effects of physical illness. Of the diseases that have a direct effect on sexual performance, diabetes is particularly important. Between a third and a half of **diabetic** men experience erectile impotence, probably as a result of neuropathy affecting the autonomic nerves mediating erection. Impaired ejaculation also occurs. Some diabetic women may be affected in a corresponding way although this is less certain (see Fairburn 1981). Sexual dysfunction is reported after **myocardial infarction** but it may result from anxiety rather than from physical causes. Most of the other physical causes are self-evident. Nevertheless, doctors often fail to think of the sexual consequences of disease and the (often unexpressed) problems that result. For this reason the causes are listed in Table 15.3, despite their obviousness. A comprehensive account of the effects of physical illness on sexual function has been written by Kolodny *et al.* (1979).

Table 15.3. *Medical and surgical conditions commonly associated with sexual dysfunction**

Medical	
Endocrine	diabetes, hyperthyroidism, myxoedema, Addison's disease
Gynaecological	vaginitis, endometriosis, pelvic infections
Cardiovascular	angina pectoris, previous myocardial infarction
Respiratory	asthma, obstructive airways disease
Arthritic	arthritis from any cause
Renal	renal failure with or without dialysis
Neurological	pelvic autonomic neuropathy, spinal cord lesions
Surgical	mastectomy
	colostomy; ileostomy
	oophorectomy
	episiotomy; operations for prolapse
	amputation

*Modified from Hawton and Oppenheimer (1982).

Table 15.4. *Some drugs that may impair sexual function**

Alcohol	
Antihypertensives:	guanethidine, beta-adrenoceptor antagonists, methyl dopa
Antidepressants:	tricyclics, monoamine oxidase inhibitors
Anxiolytics and hypnotics:	benzodiazepines, barbiturates
Antipsychotics:	especially thioridazine
Anti-inflammatory drugs:	indomethacin
Anticholinergics:	e.g. probanthine
Diuretics:	bendrofluazide
Hormones:	steroids, possibly oral contraceptives

*Modified from Hawton (1982).

Several **drugs** have side effects that involve sexual function (see Table 15.4). The most important drugs are antihypertensives (especially andrenoceptor antagonists), and major tranquillizers (especially thioridazine). The role of oral contraceptives is still uncertain (see Hawton and Oppenheimer 1982). If they cause dysfunction, it is probably only in a minority. Anxiolytics, sedatives, and hormones, have more effect on the sexual activity of men than of women. Apart from these prescribed drugs the excessive use of **alcohol** impairs sexual performance.

The aetiology of particular conditions

Erectile impotence

Primary cases may occur through a combination of low sexual drive and anxiety about sexual performance. Secondary cases arise from diminishing sexual drive in the middle aged or elderly; loss of interest in the sexual partner; anxiety; depressive illness; organic disease and its treatment.

Premature ejaculation

This is so common in sexually inexperienced young men that it may be regarded as a normal variation. When it persists, it is often because of fear of failure.

Orgasmic dysfunction

This arises from normal variations in sexual drive; poor sexual technique by the partner; lack of affection for him; tiredness, depression, physical illness, and the effects of medication.

Vaginismus

This has the psychological causes described above (p. 461).

Dyspareunia

This generally has physical causes (though it may result from vaginismus, or from failure of arousal and consequent lack of vaginal lubrication).

The assessment of a patient who presents with sexual dysfunction

Whenever possible the sexual partner should be interviewed as well as the patient. The two should be seen separately, and then together. The first step is to define clearly the **nature of the problem** as it appears to each partner. Details must not be omitted because the interviewer is too embarrassed to make full enquiries. Each of the partners must be asked, separately, whether the problem has occurred with other partners. The origin and the course of the disorder is recorded next. It is especially important to discover whether the problem has always been present or whether it started after a period of normal function. The general strength of the sexual drive is assessed by asking about frequency of intercourse and masturbation, and about feelings of sexual arousal.

An assessment is next made of knowledge of sexual techniques, and then of anxieties about sex. At the same time, possible sources of misinformation and anxiety are considered by asking about the family's attitude to sex, the kind of sex education received by each partner, and the extent of sexual experience with other partners. Each partner should be asked about the sexual technique of the other.

Social relationships

Social relationships with the opposite sex are considered next. The interviewer should find out whether either partner is shy and socially inhibited. If the couple are husband and wife, or otherwise cohabiting, disharmony in their relationship should be enquired into carefully. If the couple lack a loving relationship in their everyday life, it is unlikely that they will achieve a fully satisfying sexual relationship. It is important to remember that some couples ask for help with sexual problems which are the result and not the cause of marital conflict. The interviewer should also find out why the patient has come for treatment at this time. The reason may be that the sexual problem has increased, but there may be another reason such as the spouse's threatening to leave.

Careful enquiry must also be made for evidence of psychiatric disorder in either partner, especially depressive illness, which might account for the sexual problem. Finally questions are asked about **physical illness** and its **treatment** and about abuse of alcohol or drugs. If the general practitioner or another specialist has not already done so, a physical examination should be carried out. Appropriate laboratory tests should be arranged, for example fasting blood sugar, testosterone, and gonadotrophin levels in men with erectile impotence.

TREATMENT OF SEXUAL DYSFUNCTION

Before directing treatment to the sexual problem, it is important to consider whether the couple need marital therapy instead. If sex therapy is appropriate it should be directed to both partners whenever possible. The usual approach, which owes much to the work of Masters and Johnson (1970), has four characteristic features. First, the partners are treated together. Second, they are helped to communicate better, through words and actions, about their sexual relationship. Third, they are taught the anatomy and physiology of sexual intercourse. Fourth, they are given a graded series of 'sexual tasks'. Masters and Johnson held that two other factors were important. The first was that treatment should be intensive; for example, seeing both partners every day for up to three weeks. The second was that treatment should be carried out by a man and a woman working as co-therapists. It has been shown that neither of these measures is essential. Bancroft and Coles (1976) found that good results were obtained when only one therapist saw couples, and when treatment was given once a week. Although the best results are obtained with the treatment of couples, useful help can often be given to a patient who has no regular partner. Such a patient can at least discuss his difficulties and possible ways of overcoming them. Discussion of this kind can sometimes help to overcome social inhibitions and so develop a relationship with someone of the opposite sex.

Communication is not only talking more freely about the problems each partner is experiencing; it is also concerned with increasing understanding of the other person's wishes and feelings. Some women believe that all men know instinctively how to please the female during intercourse. They interpret failure to please as due to lack of concern or affection rather than to ignorance. They do not realize that such failure might be overcome by a more frank expression of their own desires.

Education stresses the physiology of the sexual response. The doctor explains the longer time needed for a woman to reach sexual arousal, and he emphasizes the importance of foreplay, including clitoral stimulation, in bringing about vaginal lubrication. Suitably chosen sex education books can reinforce the therapist's advice. Such counselling is often the most important part of the treatment of sexual dysfunctions.

Graded tasks begin with simple, tender physical contact. The couples are encouraged to caress any part of the other person's body except the genitalia, in order to give enjoyment (Masters and Johnson call this the 'sensate focus'). At a later stage, the couple are allowed to engage in mutual masturbation. Penetration is prohibited until the early stages have been completed. At every stage, both partners are encouraged to provide the experience most enjoyed by the other person, and they are strongly discouraged from checking on their own state of sexual arousal. Such checking is a common habit of people with sexual disorder, and has been called the 'spectator role'. Graded tasks are not only therapeutic on their own; they also help to uncover hidden fears or areas of ignorance that need to be discussed with the couple.

Special methods have been devised for certain problems. The so-called squeeze technique is used for premature ejaculation. When the man indicates that he is about to have an orgasm, the woman grips the penis for a few seconds and then releases it suddenly. Intercourse is then continued. A somewhat similar 'start–stop' method has been described in which the woman attempts to regulate the amount of sexual stimulation during intercourse.

Dynamic psychotherapy is used by some psychiatrists as their main method of treatment. The results are discussed in the next section.

Results of treatment

Clinical experience suggests that most patients can be treated effectively with directive methods of the kind described above. For unselected patients referred for treatment in the Health Service, such directive methods are followed by a successful outcome in about a third of cases, and by worthwhile improvement in a further third (Bancroft and Coles 1976). The best results are obtained with vaginismus and premature ejaculation. Results are less good if sexual problems have been present for many years, or if they are accompanied by serious marital disorder or psychiatric problems (Hawton 1980). However, these methods have not been subjected to adequate controlled trials. Similarly, psychotherapy has not been evaluated by controlled methods. Wright *et al.* (1977) concluded that, in the few studies of psychotherapy, patients were so highly selected that no general conclusions could be reached.

The use of **hormones** is not recommended, except for the occasional use of testosterone in hypogonadism. There is no convincing evidence that testosterone improves impotence unless there is a gross endocrine disorder. Bromocryptine has been prescribed for impotence on the doubtful premise that hyperprolactinaemia is associated with low libido and impotence. There is no convincing evidence that it is generally effective (for review see Hawton 1980).

Sexual dysfunction among the physically handicapped

Physically handicapped people have sexual problems arising from several sources: direct effects on sexual function, for example disease of the nervous system affecting the autonomic nerve supply; the general effects of tiredness and pain; fears about the effects of intercourse on the handicapping condition; and lack of information about the sexual activities of other people with the same disability. Much can be done to help disabled people by discussing the forms of sexual activity that are possible despite their disability; and, if appropriate, by adapting the methods already described for treating sexual dysfunction. (See Stewart (1978) and Crown (1978) for accounts of sexual problems among the disabled.)

HOMOSEXUALITY AND SEXUAL DEVIATIONS

The study of homosexuality and sexual deviations in the past

For centuries, variations in the sexual act were regarded as offences against the laws of religion rather than disorders that doctors should study and treat. The systematic study of sexual pathology began in the 1870s with the work of Krafft-Ebing, Hirschfeld, Schrenck-Notzing, and Havelock Ellis. Krafft-Ebing (1840–1902), a Professor of Psychiatry in Vienna, compiled an important systematic account of the sexual deviations in his book *Psychopathia sexualis,* which was first published in 1886 and later achieved twelve editions and translation into seven languages. In 1899 Magnus Hirschfeld founded a journal (*Jahrbuch für sexuelle Zwichenstufen*) devoted to the study of sexual deviations. Krafft-Ebing considered that sexual deviations were due mainly to hereditary causes, though the latter could be modified by social and psychological factors.

About the same time, Schrenck-Notzing developed psychological treatments for both sexual inadequacy and sexual deviations, and reported striking successes from the use of therapeutic suggestion (Schrenk-Notzing 1892). In England, the study of sexual disorders was particularly associated with the name of Havelock Ellis (1859–1939), whose book *Sexual inversion* was published in 1897.

Freud attempted to explain sexual deviations as failures of the developmental processes that he believed himself to have identified in normal children. Following this contribution, psychoanalysts have devoted much attention to sexual deviancy. As a result, most of the literature on sexual deviations is still in the psychoanalytic tradition; and until recently treatment of both sexual deviations and sexual dysfunction has been largely centred on psychoanalytic principles. As described later, these approaches have not been successful either in explaining the conditions or in modifying them.

Current views of the concept of sexual deviance

Nowadays, the concept of sexual deviance has three aspects. The first aspect is social: the behaviour does not conform to some generally accepted view of what is normal. The accepted view is not the same in every society or at every period of history. For example, regular masturbation was included among the sexual deviations by many medical writers in Victorian England. The second aspect concerns the harm that might be done to the other person involved in the sexual behaviour. Intercourse with young children or extreme forms of sexual sadism are examples. The third aspect is the suffering experienced by the person himself. This suffering is related to the attitudes of the society in which the person lives (for example attitudes to homosexuality); to conflict between his sexual urges and his own moral standards; and to his awareness of distress caused to another person by his sexual practices (for example a man's transsexual activities might distress his wife).

It is difficult to know how far doctors should attempt to alter unusual sexual behaviour, particularly at present when public attitudes are changing. For example, many people now believe that homosexuality is an alternative form of sexual behaviour that is not an appropriate concern for doctors. Whether unusual forms of sexual behaviour are regarded as illness depends on how illness is defined. Nowadays it is generally accepted as more appropriate to regard them simply as unusual forms of behaviour. There is no reason why doctors should not help people who wish to alter their own unusual patterns of behaviour, but doctors should not try to impose treatment on people who do not want it. How to decide who really wants help is a difficult point which is taken up later in the chapter.

HOMOSEXUALITY

The term homosexuality denotes erotic thoughts and feelings towards a person of the same sex, whether or not they are associated with overt sexual behaviour.

Using a six-point scale to rate degree of homosexuality, Kinsey *et al.* (1948) estimated that 10 per cent of men were 'more or less exclusively homosexual' (rating 5 or 6) for at least three years, and that 4 per cent of men were exclusively homosexual throughout their lives. Kinsey *et al.* (1953) reported that four per cent of single women were persistently homosexual from the ages of 20 to 35, while Kenyon (1980) concluded that about one in 45 of the adult female population was predominantly homosexual.

People cannot be divided sharply into those who are homosexual and those who are heterosexual. There is a continuum, with exclusively heterosexual people at one extreme, and exclusively homosexual people at the other; between them are people who engage in varying degrees of both homosexual and heterosexual relationships.

Homosexual men

In men homosexual behaviour includes oral–genital contact, mutual masturbation, and, less often, anal intercourse. In these acts, the partners usually change roles; but with some couples one partner is always passive and the other always active. Relationships between homosexual men do not usually last as long as those between men and women, or those between lesbian couples.

Some exclusively homosexual men experience strong feelings of identity with other homosexuals and adopt the corresponding **social behaviour,** for example seeking the company of homosexual acquaintances in clubs or bars. A promiscuous minority seeks for a series of sexual partners in such places, or frequents public lavatories where it is known that other homosexuals will be found. A few homosexual men adopt an effeminate style of life, preferring work and leisure activities that would usually be undertaken by a woman. Some adopt exaggerated feminine mannerisms, and a small number like to dress in women's clothes (in which they may be mistaken for transsexuals or transvestists). However most homosexual men do not behave in this way, and some are notably masculine in their social behaviour.

Homosexual men vary in **personality** as much as do other men. However, when homosexuality is combined with a disorder of personality, the individual is particularly likely to run into difficulties with other people or with the law, and therefore more likely to be referred to a psychiatrist. Scott (1957) has suggested that homosexual men referred to psychiatrists can be divided into five groups. The first group comprises adolescents or mentally immature adults whose homosexual behaviour may be temporary. The second contains adults with normal personalities whose social adjustment is normal. The third is made up of those with disordered personalities, such as the effeminate and self-advertising, the inadequate and socially isolated, the resentful and antisocial (the latter may be aggressive and often exploit other homosexuals). The fourth group includes latent homosexuals whose overt sexual behaviour appears only at times of stress or depression, particulary in middle or later life. The fifth group contains those homosexuals who have severe sociopathic personality disorder, brain damage, or schizophrenia, and who may injure or otherwise damage their partners. Although anal intercourse is often the cause of marked social disapproval, it is not particularly associated with abnormal personality; Saghir and Robins (1973) report that most persistently homosexual men have experienced anal intercourse at some time.

Many homosexual men live as happily as those who are heterosexual, forming stable and rewarding relationships with a partner. For others, homosexuality leads to difficulties which change with increasing age. In adolescence there is often distress as sexual orientation is recognized for the first time, and a decision has to be made whether to follow or suppress homosexual feelings. As the person grows older, social stigma may increase and sexual partnerships may become more difficult to arrange. With the approach of middle age there may be loneliness, isolation, and depression, particularly if the man has not previously established stable relationships built on friendships as well as sexual attraction. A few middle-aged homosexuals, finding it increasingly difficult to obtain sexual partners of their own age, turn towards teenage homosexual prostitutes. It is exceptional for these men to turn to prepubertal children; paedophiles are a separate group to be considered later in this chapter.

Homosexual women

In women homosexual practices include mutual masturbation, oral–genital contacts (cunnilingus); caressing, and breast stimulation. A small minority of women practice full body contact with genital friction or pressure (tribadism), or insertion of a vibrator or artificial penis into the vagina. Active and passive roles are usually exchanged, but one partner may prefer to take the more active role habitually. Other sexual practices such as sexual sadism occasionally occur with female homosexual practices. The **social behaviour** of lesbians is usually unremarkable, but some prefer a dominant sexual role and seek the kind of work and leisure activities usually associated with men. A few lesbians dress and behave in a masculine way. Lesbians are less likely than male homosexuals to frequent bars and public places.

All kinds of **personality** are represented among female homosexuals. As with males, there is a continuum between the exclusively heterosexual and the exclusively homosexual. Most lesbians engage in heterosexual relationships at some time, even though they obtain little satisfaction from them, and some marry. As a group, lesbians are less promiscuous than homosexual men, more likely to form lasting relationships, and correspondingly less likely to suffer loneliness and depression in middle life (see Saghir and Robins 1973.)

Legal aspects of homosexuality

There are no laws specifically concerning homosexual behaviour between women. In England and Wales, homosexual behaviour between consenting males over the age of 21 in private is not an offence, but to attempt to obtain a partner in a public place breaks the law. The age for legal consent for homo-

sexual intercourse is 21, whereas for the female partner in heterosexual intercourse it is 16.

Aetiology

It has long been supposed that homosexual behaviour is determined by
heredity. This view was apparently confirmed when Kallmann (1952) reported
100 per cent concordance for homosexuality in 40 monozygotic twin pairs, as
against only 12 per cent concordance in 26 dizygotic twin pairs. Although this
report of complete concordance between monozygotic pairs has not been
confirmed, other investigators have found that monozygotic twins are more
often alike in respect of homosexuality than are dizygotics (for example Heston
and Shields 1968). Reports of female identical twins with a homosexual proband
have been too few to allow any conclusions about inheritance of homosexuality
among women. In neither male nor female homosexuals is there convincing
evidence of abnormality in **sex chromosomes** or the **neuroendocrine system** (see
Bancroft 1975 and Kenyon 1980 for reviews of this and other aspects of
aetiology). There have been studies of variations in body build that might
reflect constitutional differences between homosexual and heterosexual people,
but no convincing differences have been found among men (Coppen 1959) or
women (Kenyon 1968; Eisinger *et al.* 1972). It is interesting that although many
animals engage in sexual activity with members of the same sex, there is
apparently no evidence of exclusive homosexual behaviour in species other than
man.

Psychological and social causes have also been investigated. Social anth-
ropologists point out that the acceptance of homosexual behaviour varies widely
in different societies. Ford and Beach (1972) reported that among 76 societies
described in the literature, homosexuality was socially acceptable – at least for
certain people – in 49 of them (64 per cent). Observations such as these suggest
that social influences may play a part in determining how far homosexual
impulses are expressed.

Many studies have been made of the **upbringing** of homosexuals. Bieber
(1962) was amongst those who have concluded, on the basis of the patients'
memories of childhood events, that homosexuals have commonly had a poor
relationship with the father, or experienced prolonged absence of the father.
Other psychoanalysts report that the mothers of homosexuals are overprotective
or unduly intimate. Little weight can be placed on such retrospective accounts
of the relationships of homosexuals with their parents. Similar descriptions
have been given of the parents of men with sexual deviations. If there is any
association with upbringing it is more likely to reflect some inhibition of the
development of heterosexual behaviour than a specific cause of homosexuality.
In any case the reports were all based on patients seeking treatment. When
Siegelman (1974) compared homosexual and heterosexual men all of whom

had normal neuroticism scores, he found no evidence of abnormal parental behaviour.

In a study of lesbians, Wolff (1971) concluded that their mothers were rejecting or indifferent. Kenyon (1968) found that, compared with heterosexual women, more lesbians reported a poor relationship with both mother and father; also a quarter of their parents had divorced (compared with 5 per cent in the controls). Some psychoanalysts suggest that lesbianism results from failure to resolve unduly close relationships with the parents in early childhood, with the result that intimate involvement with men is frightening and women become the only possible object of love. There is no single convincing view on this question.

A useful way of uniting these different ideas is to suppose that young people develop with the capacity for both heterosexual and homosexual behaviour, and that various factors determine which behaviour develops more strongly. Heterosexual development might be impeded by repressive family attitudes towards sex, or by a general lack of self-confidence. Freudians suggest that it could also be impeded by unresolved castration anxiety. On the other hand, homosexual development might be encouraged by unusually close relationships with a friend of the same sex, especially when other social relationships have not developed well (see Bancroft 1975 for a full account of this scheme). None of these ideas is founded on convincing research evidence, but the general framework has some value in the assessment of a homosexual who is seeking treatment.

Prognosis

In the absence of data from adequate follow-up studies, clinical experience must be used to predict whether homosexual behaviour will persist. Persistence appears to depend on the patient's age, the extent to which he has any heterosexual interests, his own wish to change, and the external pressures acting upon him. People who have reached adult life without experiencing heterosexual feelings are unlikely to develop them later. For the rest, in estimating the likelihood of persistent homosexual behaviour, the first step is to weigh up the factors mentioned in the preceding paragraph. The second step is to add an assessment of personality, bearing in mind that a worse outcome is suggested by anti-social traits or by any evidence of effeminate social behaviour. In general, the older the person, the less likely he is to change his sexual orientation.

Treating the homosexual

In practice, four kinds of treatment problem are encountered by doctors. The first concerns shy and sexually inexperienced young men who fear that they may be homosexual but in fact are not. The second is presented by young men who have realized, correctly, that they are predominantly homosexual, and are bewildered about the implications for their lives. The third concerns men who have bisexual inclinations and want to discuss ways of arranging their lives appropriately. The fourth is the problem of the established homosexual who becomes depressed or anxious because of personal or social difficulties arising from sexual relationships. In all of these groups, the doctor's principal role is to help the patient to clarify his thoughts. More elaborate treatment is seldom required.

Occasionally it is appropriate to attempt to modify the patient's homosexual impulses and behaviour. The patient should be told that he can assist this process by avoiding situations that stimulate his homosexual feelings, while at the same time seeking opportunities for social encounters with women. The patient should pay attention to his mental preoccupations when alone; and also to his fantasies during masturbation, since they are thought to be powerful reinforcers of sexual behaviour. Although psychoanalysis (Bieber 1962) and psychotherapy have been used in attempts to change sexual orientation, there is no convincing evidence that either has worthwhile effects. Aversion therapy has been used to suppress homosexual mental imagery but the results are not satisfactory (Bancroft 1974). Nowadays, behavioural treatment is concerned mainly with reducing anxiety, and with developing heterosexual behaviour patterns by methods similar to those for the treatment of sexual dysfunction (described earlier).

Masters and Johnson (1979) have offered treatment to both male and female homosexual couples who have stable social relationships but complain of inability to achieve a satisfactory sexual performance.

SEXUAL DEVIATIONS

There are many forms of sexual deviation, all uncommon, and some extremely rare. The reader need not be concerned with all the details in this section at the first reading, though he will need to refer to them when he encounters a case in clinical practice. Such a case may come to medical attention in various ways, and the doctor should be aware of the different modes of presentation.

A doctor may be consulted directly by the person with the deviant behaviour. He may also be asked to help by the spouse or other sexual partner, possibly because behaviour accepted in the past has now become so frequent that it can be tolerated no longer. Sometimes the problem is presented as sexual inadequacy, and the deviant sexual interests are discovered only in the course of history taking.

A doctor may also be asked for an opinion about a patient charged with an offence arising from deviant sexual interests. Offences of this kind include indecent exposure, the behaviour of a 'peeping Tom', the stealing of clothes by fetishists, appearing in public in clothes of the opposite sex, rape and assaults upon children, intercourse with willing children who are under age, and incest. With two exceptions these offences are discussed in the following paragraphs in relation to the corresponding deviations. The exceptions are rape and incest, which are considered at the end of this section, together with the problem of pornography.

DISORDERS OF SEXUAL OBJECT

Fetishism

In sexual fetishism, inanimate objects are the preferred or only means of achieving sexual excitement. The disorder shades into normal sexual behaviour; it is not uncommon for men to be aroused by particular items of clothing, such as stockings, or by parts of the female body that do not usually have sexual associations.

Prevalence

As the sole or preferred means of sexual arousal, sexual fetishism is uncommon but no exact figures are available.

Description

Fetishism usually begins in adolescence. It occurs almost exclusively among men, although a few cases have been described among women (see for example Odlum 1955). Most fetishists are heterosexual. The objects that can evoke sexual arousal are many and varied, but for each person there is usually a small number of objects or classes of objects. Among the more frequent are rubber garments, women's underclothes, and high-heeled shoes. Sometimes the object is an attribute of a person, for example lameness or deformity in a woman; or a part of the human body, such as the hair or foot. The texture and smell of objects is often as important as their appearance; for example furs, velvet, rubber garments, and polished leather are often preferred. Contact with the object causes sexual excitement, which may be followed by solitary masturbation or by sexual intercourse incorporating the fetish if a willing partner is available. Occasionally fetishism also occurs in homosexual men.

Fetishists may spend much time seeking their desired objects. Some buy them, and others steal – for example underclothes from a washing line. A few men engage in fetishistic behaviour with a prostitute. When the object is a particular attribute of a woman, many hours may be spent in searching for and following a suitable woman. Inanimate fetish objects are often hoarded; Hirschfeld recorded a striking example, the hoarding by one man of 31 pigtails of hair, each cut with scissors from women he had followed, and each labelled with the date and hour when it had been cut (Hirschfeld 1944).

Aetiology

There are several theories of fetishism but few facts. Fetishism has occasionally been reported in association with EEG evidence of temporal lobe dysfunction

(Epstein 1961) or with frank epilepsy (Mitchell *et al.* 1954). There is no evidence of such associations in the majority of cases. Fetishism was the first sexual disorder for which a theory of association learning was put forward. Thus Binet (1877) suggested that it arose by a chance coming together of sexual excitation and the object that becomes the fetish object. Some experimental evidence for such a mechanism has been reported by Rachman (1966). Male volunteers were repeatedly shown pictures of boots followed immediately by sexually arousing pictures of women. After several pairings, the pictures of boots were also followed by sexual arousal. The suggestion that fetishism results from faulty imprinting (Wilson 1981) rests entirely on analogy. Imprinting apparently affects the sexual behaviour of birds, but there is no evidence that it does so in man.

Psychoanalysts suggest that sexual fetishism arises when castration anxiety is not resolved in childhood, and the man attempts to ward off this anxiety by maintaining in his unconscious mind the idea that women have a penis (Freud 1927). In Freud's words it is 'a token of triumph against the threat of castration and a protection against it'. In this view, each fetish is a symbolic representation of a phallus. Although some fetishes can be interpreted in this way, others require tortuous interpretations if the general hypothesis is to be sustained (see for example Stekel 1953). In any case the general idea does not convincingly explain the majority of cases.

The explanation that best fits clinical observations is that sexual fetishism arises when the expression of heterosexual impulses has been inhibited in some way. This inhibition might arise in a number of ways; for example, through shyness with women or irrational fears about sexual intercourse. Sexual arousal might then become associated by chance with something other than heterosexual ideas, and in this way conditioned responses could arise. This kind of explanation is not supported by direct evidence, but it is at least consistent with what facts are available.

Prognosis

In the absence of reliable follow-up data, the prognosis has to be based on clinical experience. In adolescents and young adults, fetishism is often transient, disappearing when satisfying heterosexual relationships have been established. The prognosis at all ages depends crucially on the extent of other friendships and sexual activities. Solitary single men without a sexual partner have a worse prognosis. The prognosis also depends on the frequency of the behaviour and the extent to which it has already broken social conventions and legal barriers.

Treatment

There are case-reports of treatment by psychoanalysis (see Nagler 1957) and by aversion therapy (for example Marks and Gelder 1967) but no controlled trials. Clinical experience indicates that the general measures outlined later in the chapter are as effective as any psychoanalytic or specific behavioural treatment.

Transvestism

Transvestism is repeated dressing in the clothes of the opposite sex. It varies from the occasional wearing of a few articles of clothing to complete cross-dressing. When a person experiences sexual excitement while dressed in clothes of the opposite sex, the condition is called fetishistic transvestism. Some men who cross-dress are effeminate homosexuals or transsexuals, and almost all women who cross-dress are lesbian or transsexual.

Prevalence

The prevalence of transvestism is not known.

Description

Cross-dressing usually begins at about the time of puberty. The person usually starts by putting on only a few garments, but as time goes by, he adds more until he is eventually dressed entirely in clothes of the other sex. Transvestists experience erections when cross-dressing and may masturbate. Later the clothes may be worn in public, at first underneath male outer garments but eventually without such precautions against discovery.

Most transvestists are heterosexual. Unlike the transsexuals described later, they have no doubt that they are really men. Exceptionally, after many years of cross-dressing, a few transvestists may begin to believe that they are women. Despite these transitional cases, transvestists differ in important ways from transsexualists. Transvestists are sexually aroused by cross-dressing and convinced they are of the correct gender; transsexuals experience no erotic pleasure from cross-dressing and are convinced that they are trapped in a body that is of the opposite sex to their real nature. Many transvestists are married; most of them hide the behaviour from their wives, but a few reveal it and persuade their wives to assist in obtaining clothes. Wives usually express distress and disgust if they discover their husband dressed as a woman, but a few appear to collude with the behaviour.

Aetiology

There is no evidence that the chromosomal sex or hormonal make up of transvestists is abnormal (see Lukianowicz 1959). Despite a report of three cases in one family (Liakos 1967) transvestism is not familial and there is no evidence that it is inherited. Although occasional associations with temporal lobe dysfunction have been reported (Epstein 1960; Davies and Morgenstern 1960) there is no evidence of such an association in the majority. Suggestions (for example Allen 1969) that tranvestism is an expression of repressed homosexuality do not accord with the clinical evidence that transvestists continue to have heterosexual interests for many years. Transvestism develops gradually from puberty, and since it is associated with sexual arousal, the aetiology is likely to resemble that proposed above for fetishism, namely an impediment to normal sexual development coupled perhaps with association learning. Some psychoanalysts (for example Fenichel 1945) have suggested that the transvestist is creating a 'phallic woman' (himself in women's clothes) to allay castration anxiety. The theory is not convincing.

Prognosis

In the absence of reliable information from follow-up of a representative group of transvestists, statements about prognosis must be based on clinical experience. Most cases appear to continue for years, becoming less severe as sexual drives decline in middle age or later. However there are wide variations in outcome, and the comments made earlier about the prognosis of fetishism apply here as well. As already noted, a minority of persistent transvestists develop the idea that they are women and continue to cross-dress without sexual arousal.

Treatment

There are some reports of psychoanalytic treatment (Rosen 1979) and aversion therapy (Marks and Gelder 1967) but no clinical trials. Cross-dressing can sometimes be supressed rapidly by aversion therapy. In the long term, however, general measures (described at the end of this chapter) are probably as effective as psychoanalysis or aversion therapy.

Paedophilia

Paedophilia is repeated sexual activity (or fantasy of such activity) with pre-pubertal children, as a preferred or exclusive method of obtaining sexual excitement. Males who have intercourse with young girls can be divided into two groups. An adolescent group have intercourse with girls who are only a few years younger than themselves and who are often at an age when sexual behaviour would be permitted in some other societies. With few exceptions, such adolescent males are of normal intelligence and background. The second group are older men who deliberately choose a sexual partner who is still a child.

The law on sexual intercourse with young people is complicated. Girls under 16 cannot give legal consent to sexual intercourse; and young men under 21 cannot, as the law stands at present, consent to homosexual practices. However if a girl is between 13 and 16 years old and the man is less than 24, and if he believes her to be over 16, then the girl's consent is a defence against a charge of unlawful sexual intercourse brought against the man. Paedophilia involves relationships between an adult and a prepubertal child, rather than these borderlines of the legal age of consent.

Prevalence

Paedophilia is almost invariably a disorder of men. There is no reliable information about its prevalence. From the existence of child prostitution in some countries and the ready sale of pornographic material depicting sex with children, it appears that interest in sexual relationships with children is not rare. Nevertheless paedophilia, defined as an exclusive form of sexual behaviour, is probably uncommon.

Description

The paedophile usually chooses a child aged between 9 years and puberty. The child may be of the opposite sex (heterosexual paedophilia) or the same sex (homosexual paedophilia). Although the condition can begin at any age, most paedophiles seen by doctors are men of middle age. There is no evidence that paedophiles change their interests from adult to child partners as they grow older; usually the preference seems established from the start.

Paedophilia has to be distinguished from exhibitionism towards young girls (in which no attempt is made to engage in direct sexual contact). Sexual contact with children may also be sought by people with subnormal intelligence, dementia, and alcoholism. With younger children fondling or masturbation is more likely than full coitus, but some young children are injured by forcible attempts at penetration.Rare and tragic cases of sexual sadism occur.

The child

Of the children involved in paedophilia, two-thirds have co-operated in sexual activity more than once with the same or another adult (Gibbens and Prince 1963). However, some of these children have apparently co-operated through fear rather than interest. A minority of the children are also promiscuous and steal, truant, or run away from home, but most are not delinquent and come from well organized families. Gibbens and Prince thought that the mothers often showed an ambivalent attitude both to discipline and to the child's sexual development. The long-term effects of paedophilia on the child are not certain. In a follow-up of children who had experienced sexual activity with an adult, Bender and Grugett (1952) found there was no lasting maladjustment provided that the child had developed normally up to the time of the sexual experience. The effect on the child is probably much influenced by the reaction of the parents, and by how far the child is involved in legal proceedings (Mohr *et al.* 1964).

Aetiology

This is unknown. Paedophiles often have a marked incapacity for relationships with adults, and fears of relationships with women. The various aetiological theories are reviewed by Mohr *et al.* (1964).

Prognosis

In the absence of reliable information from follow-up studies, prognosis has to be judged in individual patients by the length of the history, the frequency of the behaviour, the absence of other social and sexual relationships and the strengths and weaknesses of the personality. Behaviour that has been frequently repeated is likely to persist despite efforts at treatment.

Treatment

Both group treatment (Hartman 1965) and behaviour therapy (Beech *et al.* 1971) have been tried, but there is no convincing evidence that either leads to good results in the majority of paedophiles. The general measures described at the end of this chapter should be tried, although good results should not be expected.

Other variations of the sexual object

Bestiality

Bestiality, otherwise called zoophilia or bestiosexuality, is the use of an animal as a repeated and preferred or exclusive method of achieving sexual excitement. It is uncommon, and rarely encountered by doctors.

Necrophilia

In this extremely rare condition sexual arousal is obtained through intercourse with a dead body. Occasionally there are legal trials of men who murder and then attempt intercourse with the victim. No reliable information is available about the causes or prognosis of this extreme form of sexual deviation.

VARIATIONS IN THE SEXUAL ACT

Exhibitionism

Exhibitionism is the repeated exposing of the genitals to unprepared strangers for the purposes of achieving sexual excitement but without any attempt at further sexual activity with the other person. The name exhibitionism was suggested by Lasègue (1877) and further clinical observations were reported by Krafft-Ebing in 1886 (see Krafft-Ebing 1924). The use of the term in this technical sense is to be distinguished from its everyday sense of extravagant behaviour to draw attention to oneself.

Prevalence

This is not known. Exhibitionists make up about one-third of sexual offenders referred for psychiatric treatment, and about a quarter of sexual offenders dealt with in the courts (Rosen 1979). Almost all are men, though there are rare women exhibitionists who repeatedly expose the breasts, or, even rarer, those who expose the genitalia.

Descriptions

The act of exposure is usually preceded by a feeling of mounting tension. Exhibitionists characteristically seek to evoke a strong emotional reaction from the other person, generally surprise and shock. Some are satisfied by any evidence of being noticed, even laughter. Most exhibitionists choose places from which escape is easy, though a few choose places where they risk detection. Whatever the exact pattern of behaviour, the experience is one of intense excitement and exhilaration at the same time. In some exhibitionists the preoccupation is persistent, in others it is episodic. As a broad generalization, two groups can be described. The first group includes men of inhibited temperament who struggle against their urges and feel much guilt after the act; they sometimes expose a flaccid penis. The second group includes men who have aggressive traits, sometimes accompanied by features of antisocial personality disorder. They usually expose an erect penis, often while masturbating. They gain pleasure from any distress they cause and often feel little guilt.

Women often fear that the act of exposure will be followed by rape, but this is not usual. It has been suggested that exhibitionism and voyeurism are related aetiologically, but exhibitionists seldom practise voyeurism (Rooth 1971). There is uncertainty about the relationship between exhibitionism and the making of obscene phone calls by men who talk to women about sexual activities while masturbating. It has been suggested (Tollison and Adams 1979) that these obscene callers are also exhibitionists, but it is not easy to identify them in order to study their psychopathology.

In Britain, if a man is brought to court because of exhibitionism, he is charged with the offence of indecent exposure (see Chapter 22, p. 735, for the definition of indecent exposure). About four-fifths of men charged with indecent exposure are exhibitionists (as defined at the beginning of this section).

Aetiology

There are several theories, all unsubstantiated. As in other sexual deviations, the first step must be to explain why heterosexual development has been inhibited. The same explanations have been put forward for this disorder as for the others we have described earlier in the chapter; namely, failure to resolve Oedipal conflict or a general inhibition of social relationships. The relationship between exhibitionists and their parents has been investigated retrospectively. Some exhibitionists describe unduly close relationships with their mothers and a poor relationship with ineffectual fathers (see Rickles 1950). As always with retrospective accounts, it is not certain how far these memories reflect the actual circumstances of the patient's upbringing. Also, many people describe similar experiences in childhood, but do not grow up to be exhibitionists. To the clinician, the most striking feature of many exhibitionists is a personality characterized by lack of assertion and a striking degree of passivity in everyday relationships.

Whatever the original cause of exhibitionism, it has been suggested that the behaviour is perpetuated by the reinforcing effects of sexual release during masturbation that often follows (Evans 1970). Exhibitionism may be self perpetuating in this way, but it is not a form of obsessive–compulsive behaviour as suggested by Rickles (1950). Although the exhibitionist may feel compelled to carry out his act, the phenomenon is not a compulsion in the technical sense of the term, nor is there any evidence that it is associated with obsessive compulsive neurosis. In middle-aged or elderly people, the onset of exhibitionism should always suggest organic brain disease. Such organic disease presumably releases a reaction pattern that is preformed but has been previously inhibited.

Prognosis

There is no reliable information about prognosis. Clinical experience suggests a variable outcome. Men who exhibit only once do not fall within the definition of the disorder. In men who exhibit repeatedly but only at times of stress the prognosis depends on the likelihood of the stressors returning. Exhibitionists who repeat often are likely to persist for years despite treatment by psychiatrists or punishment by the courts. In keeping with these clinical impressions, the evidence from the courts is that the reconviction rate for indecent exposure is low after a first conviction but high after a second conviction. Although a history of exhibitionism is sometimes given by men who commit rape, the majority of exhibitionists do not go on to commit violent sexual acts nor do they interfere with children (Rooth 1973). A full account of exhibitionism is given by Rooth (1971).

Treatment

Exhibitionism has been treated by psychoanalysis, individual psychotherapy, and group psychotherapy (Witzig 1970) but there is no satisfactory evidence about their value. Among behavioural techniques, electrical aversion therapy has been found to be more effective than a self-control therapy (Rooth and Marks 1974). Maletzky (1974, 1977) has reported good results with covert sensitization. However, none of these methods offers a reliable treatment for the majority of exhibitionists. Feminizing hormones have been used, but are not recommended because the results are uncertain and there are risks from long-term use. It is always important to search for depressive illness, dementia, or alcoholism and to treat them if possible.

Voyeurism

Many men are sexually excited by observing others engaged in intercourse. Voyeurism (occasionally called scopophilia), is observing the sexual activity of others repeatedly as a preferred means of sexual arousal. The voyeur also spies on women who are undressing or without clothes, but does not attempt sexual activity with them. Voyeurism is usually accompanied or followed by masturbation.

Voyeurism is a disorder of heterosexual men, whose heterosexual activities are usually inadequate. Although the voyeur usually takes great care to hide from the woman he is watching, he often takes considerable risks of discovery by other people. Hence most voyeurs are reported by passers-by, not by the victim.

Aetiology

Among adolescents voyeuristic activities are not uncommon as an expression of sexual curiosity, but they are usually replaced by direct sexual experience. The voyeur continues to watch because he is shy, socially awkward with girls, or prevented from normal sexual expression by some other obstacle. Psychoanalytic explanations follow the general lines described above for other sexual disorders. Behavioural theories seek an explanation in terms of chance associations between a first experience of peeping and sexual arousal.

Prognosis

No reliable information is available.

Treatment

Psychoanalysis, group therapy (Witzig 1968) and counter-conditioning (Jackson 1969) have been used but, as no systematic trials have been reported, no conclusions can be drawn. It is doubtful whether any treatment is effective, but it is reasonable to try the general measures described later in this chapter.

Sexual sadism

Sadism is named after the Marquis de Sade (1774–1814) who inflicted extreme cruelty on women for sexual purposes. Sexual sadism is achieving sexual arousal, habitually and in preference to heterosexual intercourse, by inflicting pain on another person.

Prevalence

Inflicting pain or restraint in fantasy or practice is a not uncommon accompaniment of other forms of sexual behaviour. Sex-shops sell chains, whips, and shackles, while some pornographic magazines provide pictures and descriptions of sadistic sexual practices. Sexual sadism as a predominant sexual practice is probably uncommon but its frequency is not known.

Description

Beating, whipping, and tying are common forms of sadistic activity. Repeated acts are usually with a partner who is a masochist, or a prostitute who is paid to take part. Sadism may be a component of homosexual as well as heterosexual acts. Rare cases of sexual sadism towards animals have been reported (see Allen

1969). The acts may be symbolic with little actual damage, some involving humiliation rather than injury. Sometimes serious and permanent injuries are caused. Extreme examples are 'lust murders', in which the killer inflicts serious and often ritually repeated injuries – usually stabbings and mutilations – on the genitalia of his victim. In these rare cases, ejaculation may occur during the sadistic act or later by intercourse with the dead body (necrophilia). Further information is given by Hirschfeld (1944).

Aetiology

This is not known. Psychoanalytical explanations draw attention to the association of loving and aggressive feelings that is supposed to exist in the young child's early relationship with his parents. Behavioural formulations rely on association learning. The two explanations are equally unsatisfactory.

Prognosis

There is no reliable information, but clinical experience suggests that once established the behaviour is likely to persist for many years.

Treatment

There are case reports of the use of behaviour therapy (for example Davison 1968) but no evidence from adequate clinical trials. In the absence of any proven treatment, men who have committed serious injury must be dealt with by legal means if there is risk of another offence. In deciding this issue it is wise to assume that treatment of any kind is unlikely to alter an established pattern of sadistic sexual behaviour. The risks must not be underestimated when potentially dangerous behaviour has been planned or has already occurred.

Sexual masochism

Sexual masochism is achieving sexual excitement, as a preferred or exclusive practice, through the experience of suffering. As a predominant activity, it differs from the common use of minor painful practices as an accompaniment to sexual intercourse. The condition is named after Leopold von Sacher-Masoch (1836–1905), an Austrian novelist, who described sexual gratification from the experience of pain.

Prevalence

Fantasies of being beaten or raped are common enough among males to create a demand for pornographic literature, and also for prostitutes who will help the man act out his fantasies. Established sexual masochism is probably uncommon though no exact information is available.

Description

The suffering may take the form of being beaten, trodden upon, bound or chained, or the enactment of various symbolic forms of humiliation, for example dressing as a child and being punished. Masochism, unlike most other sexual deviations, occurs in women as well as in men, perhaps as a reflection of the more submissive role of the woman in normal sexual relationships. It may occur in homosexual as well as heterosexual relationships.

At times, the masochist may allow dangerous forms of assault upon himself, including strangulation, a practice that can increase sexual excitation through the resulting partial anoxia. Some solitary people seek sexual arousal from anoxia by covering the head with a plastic bag. This act is sometimes accompanied by fetishistic practices or cross-dressing. Occasionally this behaviour has resulted in death (see for example Johnstone *et al.* 1960).

Aetiology

This is not known. One theory is that, as a result of beatings delivered to pubertal children, sexual arousal becomes associated by chance with the experience of pain and humiliation. Psychoanalytic theory suggests that masochism is sadism turned inwards, and therefore explicable in the same way as sadism (see above).

Prognosis

There is no reliable information about prognosis. Clinical experience suggests that, once established as a preferred form of sexual behaviour, masochism is likely to persist for many years.

Treatment

There are case reports of treatment by psychoanalysis (Stekel 1953) and behavioural treatment (Marks *et al.* 1965) but no satisfactory evidence from which to judge the effects of either.

Other variations of the sexual act

In **frotteurism** the preferred form of sexual excitement is applying or rubbing the male genitalia against another person, usually a stranger and an unwilling participant, in a crowded place such as an underground train. In **coprophilia**, sexual arousal is induced by thinking about or watching the act of defecation and this is the preferred sexual activity; in **coprophagia** arousal follows the eating of faeces. In **sexual urethism,** which occurs mainly in women, erotic arousal is obtained by stimulation of the urethra. **Urophilia** refers to sexual arousal obtained by watching the act of urination, being urinated upon, or drinking urine. It was described at length by Havelock Ellis (1928) who named it **undinism**. The prevalence of these disorders is not known, but some are sufficiently common to demand provision from prostitutes. Further information will be found in Allen (1969) and Tollison and Adams (1979).

ASSESSMENT AND MANAGEMENT OF SEXUAL DEVIATIONS

In assessment, the first step is to **exclude mental illness**. Deviant sexual behaviour is sometimes secondary to dementia, alcoholism, depressive illness, or mania. These illnesses probably release the behaviour in a person who has previously experienced the corresponding sexual fantasies but not acted on them. It is particularly important to look for mental illness when the sexual deviation comes to notice for the first time in middle age or later.

Motives for seeking treatment

People who request treatment for sexual disorders often have mixed motives. Many consult a doctor because their sexual behaviour has become known to the spouse, another relative, or the police. Such people may have little wish to change and many prefer to be told that no treatment will help, so as to justify the continuation of their sexual practices. Sometimes people with sexual deviations seek help when they become depressed and feel guilty about the behaviour and its effects on other people. At these times of low mood, strong wishes for change may be expressed only to fade quickly as normal mood returns. Strong motivation is known to be important whether treatment is by psychoanalysis (Bieber 1962), psychotherapy (Ellis 1956), or behaviour therapy (Feldman and McCulloch 1971). It is therefore important to assess whether the expressed wishes for change will be maintained.

Detailed enquiry is then made about the patient's sexual practices. It should be borne in mind that patients not uncommonly have more than one form of deviant behaviour. The extent and vigour of normal heterosexual interests, both in the present and in the past, are determined. Whenever possible, an interview should be arranged with the patient's regular sexual partner.

It is always important to find out what part the deviant sexual behaviour is playing in the patient's life. Apart from being a source of sexual arousal, it may be a comforting activity that helps to ward off feelings of loneliness, anxiety, or depression. Unless other means are found to deal with such feelings, treatment may reduce the patient's deviant sexual behaviour but worsen his emotional state.

Planning treatment

The aim of treatment must be discussed with the patient: whether it is to control, or if possible give up, the behaviour; or to adapt better to the behaviour so that less guilt and distress are felt. In considering these aims, the doctor will sometimes have to take into account whether any psychological or even physical harm is being caused to other people, although his first concern must be for his patient. At this early stage it is important to make clear that, whatever the aim, treatment will require considerable effort on the part of the patient.

If the agreed aim is better adjustment, treatment will be by counselling designed to explore the patient's feelings, and to help him to identify the problems caused by his sexual practices and to find ways of reducing them. If the agreed aim is change, the first step is to find ways of encouraging ordinary heterosexual relationships. For this purpose, treatment is directed first to any anxieties that are impeding social relationships with the opposite sex. Attention is then directed to any detected sexual inadequacy using the methods outlined earlier in this chapter. In most cases, these two steps are the most important part of treatment.

The problems likely to arise from giving up the deviant practices are considered next. Some patients occupy much of their time in preparing for the sexual act (for example fetishists may spend many hours searching for a particular kind of women's underclothes). As already noted, the behaviour often becomes a way of warding off feelings of loneliness or despair. To safeguard against distress, the patient must be helped to develop leisure activities, seek new friends, and find other ways of coping with unpleasant emotions.

Only when these steps have been taken should attention be directed to ways of suppressing the unwanted sexual behaviour. Sometimes the preceding steps are enough to strengthen the patient's capacity to control himself, but additional help is often needed.

Masturbation fantasies appear to play an important part in perpetuating deviant sexual behaviour. It is therefore important to encourage the patient to keep any deviant fantasies out of mind during masturbation. If he cannot rid his mind of fantasies, he should be encouraged to modify them progressively, so that the themes become less and less sexually deviant, and increasingly concerned with ordinary heterosexual intercourse.

For men, antiandrogens have been used in an attempt to reduce sexual drive but this approach has limited value. Oestrogens may be tried if libido is strong, and if the continuation of the behaviour is likely to have serious consequences outweighing the risks of treatment. Oestrogens may be given as depot injections such as oestradiol undecylenate, or as an oestradiol implant. The therapy can cause breast enlargement and nodules, testicular atrophy, osteoporosis, and, rarely, breast tumours. For this reason antiandrogen drugs such as cyproterone acetate are sometimes used although it is still not clear how far their effects exceed the placebo response (see Wakeling 1979 for further information). Cyproterone can produce a reversible atrophy of the seminiferous tubules and its side effects include gynaecomastia, sedation, and depression.

Behavioural treatment may also be tried. Aversion therapy is no longer recommended, except to produce a temporary suppression of strong mental imagery while other steps are taken to enable the patient to suppress such imagery himself. Used in this way, aversion therapy is most effective for fetishism and transvestism. The main value of behaviour therapy is to encourage normal heterosexual behaviour, although the general methods described earlier in this chapter seem to be equally effective.

Many people with sexual deviations appear before the courts. Sanctions such as a suspended sentence or probation order can sometimes help the patient to gain control of his own behaviour. However, no doctor should agree to treat patients who are sent to him against their wishes.

GENDER ROLE DISTURBANCE

Transsexualism

A transsexualist is convinced that he is of the sex opposite to that indicated by his normal external genitalia. In addition, he feels estranged from his body, has an overpowering wish to live as a member of the opposite sex, and seeks to alter his bodily appearance and genitalia to conform to those of the opposite sex. Most transsexuals are men. In the past the condition was called **eonism** because it was exemplified by the Chevalier d'Eon de Beaumont. In psychiatric literature, the condition was mentioned by Esquirol in 1838 and described in more detail by Kraft-Ebbing (1886). More recently the description by Benjamin (1966) has directed the attention of doctors and the public to the condition.

Prevalence

Epidemiological data are understandably difficult to obtain. Wålinder (1968) estimated the prevalence among Swedish males to be 1 in 37 000 and among Swedish females to be 1 in 103 000. Hoenig and Kenna (1974) reported similar figures (1:34 000 and 1:108 000) in Great Britain. Most of those seeking medical help are men.

Description

(a) Among men. Patients report a strong conviction of belonging to the other sex, usually dating from before puberty. It is sometimes reported by the parents that in childhood the patients preferred the company and pursuits of girls, although such a history is not invariable (gender disturbance in children is considered later).

By the time medical help is requested, most transsexuals have started dressing as women. In contrast to transvestists, they cross-dress to feel more like women, not to produce sexual arousal. (They also differ from those homosexuals who dress as women to attract other homosexuals.) For this purpose, make-up is worn and the hair is arranged in a feminine style; facial and body hair is usually removed by electrolysis. Transsexuals try to adopt feminine gestures and to alter the pitch of their voice, but few succeed wholly convincingly. Transsexuals also seek changes in social role. They apply for the kind of work that is usually done by women and they enjoy cooking and sewing.

They do not show maternal interests. Sex drive is usually low and unlike transvestists, these patients do not masturbate when cross-dressed. As Benjamin has written (1966 p. 21) 'the transvestist looks on his sex organ as an organ of pleasure, and the transsexual turns from it in disgust'.

There is no characteristic type of **personality**, but some transsexuals are self-centred, demanding, and attention-seeking; they are often particularly difficult to treat.

Many transsexual patients are greatly distressed by their predicament. Depression is common, and in one series 16 per cent had made suicide attempts (Wålinder 1967). About a third marry but, not surprisingly, about half of these become divorced (Roth and Ball 1964).

Transsexuals often ask the doctor for help in altering the appearance of the breasts and external genitalia. Usually the first requests are for oestrogens to enlarge the breasts. These requests are often followed by increasingly insistent demands for surgery to the breasts, for surgical castration and removal of the penis, and even for operations to create an artificial vagina. Such demands are usually made in a determined and persistent way, and are sometimes accompanied by threats of self-mutilation or suicide. Some patients do attempt to castrate themselves, and may maintain afterwards that the injury was accidental.

(b) Among women. Many women who appear to be transsexuals are really homosexuals. Transsexual women resemble transsexual men in having held since childhood a strong conviction that they 'occupy' a body of the wrong sex. Some seek to alter their body by mastectomy or hysterectomy, and a few hope for plastic surgery to create an artificial penis. Transsexual women strive to be like men in dress, voice, gestures, and social behaviour, and in their choice of work and hobbies. They wish to have intercourse not with a lesbian, but in the role of male with a heterosexual partner.

Aetiology

Many ideas have been put forward to explain this puzzling condition but its cause remains unknown. Transsexuals have normal sex chromosomes, and there is no convincing evidence of a genetic cause. It has been suggested that abnormal acquisition of gender role might be relevant. However, there is no convincing evidence that transsexuals have been brought up in the wrong gender role.

It has been suggested that transsexualism might result from hormonal abnormalities during intrauterine development. There is some evidence that when large doses of androgens are given to pregnant rhesus monkeys, their female infants behave more like males during play (Young *et al.* 1964). There is no direct parallel in man but it may be relevant that female children with the adrenogenital syndrome (who are exposed to large amounts of androgen before and after birth) have been reported to show rather boyish behaviour in childhood (Ehrhardt *et al.* 1968). Despite this, they have not been reported to grow up as transsexuals. Endocrine disorders have also been sought in adult transsexuals but no definite abnormality has been found. Wålinder (1967) found abnormal EEGs in 28 per cent of his patients. There is no other evidence of organic brain disorder among transsexuals.

In an interesting minority of patients, transsexualism begins after many years of transvestism. These patients start by cross-dressing to obtain sexual excitement, but the resultant arousal gradually diminishes. At the same time the patients gradually become convinced that they are women.

Prognosis

There is no reliable information about the prognosis of untreated transsexuals. Clinical experience suggests that once established the condition persists for many years, though it is not known whether it lasts beyond middle age. The rate of suicide among transsexuals is probably increased.

Treatment

Although transsexualism is undoubtedly a psychological disorder in a person whose body is normal, patients usually demand treatment directed to the body not the mind. The most rational treatment would be to alter the patient's conviction that he is of the wrong sex, but attempts to do so by psychotherapy rarely succeed. If treatment involving physical changes is offered, it should be done by carefully planned stages. The evident distress of these patients and their insistent demands should not be allowed to interfere with this plan. Many psychiatrists, including the authors, consider that physical changes are seldom appropriate and that in most cases it is better to use supportive psychotherapy. When other treatment is used it generally passes through the stages described in the following paragraphs.

A male transsexual usually has three aims: to take on a woman's appearance, to live as a woman, and to change his genitalia. For the first the beard is often removed by electrolysis. He can learn to speak like a woman; and practise appropriate gestures and ways of walking and sitting. These changes in speech and movement are often particularly difficult, but social skills training with video-feedback may possibly aid them (Yardley 1976). Male patients usually seek breast enlargement, at first by oestrogens and later by mammoplasty. Neither treatment should be provided at an early stage, since suitable clothing can be used instead and the drugs are not without danger (see below).

If the patient persists in his intentions, he may try to live as a woman. During this some patients become sufficiently impressed by the problems of living as a woman that they modify their aims. If after a year the patient persists in demanding surgery and his personality is stable, he may be given a full explanation of what the operation entails. He must understand that no surgery can make a man into a woman; at best it can provide only a poor copy of the female body.

Oestrogen is sometimes given at this stage or earlier to produce some enlargement of the breasts and deposition of fat around hips and thighs.

Minor side-effects include nausea and dizziness, while more serious risks are thrombosis and malignant breast tumours (Symmers 1968). Methyl testosterone has been prescribed to women transsexuals who wish to become male, but it carries the risk of liver damage.

If after these preliminaries the psychiatrist considers that the patient is one of the few who might benefit from surgery, the opinion of an experienced consultant surgeon can be sought. He will make the final decision about the indications for surgery and the type of operation, though with the psychiatrist's advice. In giving this it should be remembered that the late results of such surgery are unknown. The publicity given to a few successful cases should not be accorded undue weight in reaching a decision. More information about these controversial forms of surgical treatment is given in the book edited by Green and Money (1969) and the review by Schapira *et al.* (1979).

Gender identity disorders in children

Parents more often seek advice about effeminate behaviour in boys than about masculine behaviour in small girls, (it is not clear whether such behaviour in girls is less frequent or more socially acceptable). Effeminate boys prefer girlish games and enjoy wearing female clothing. The outcome amongst these boys is variable (Green and Money 1961); some develop normal male interests and activities, others continue their effeminate ways into adolescence. Further information is given by Green (1974).

SOME OTHER ASPECTS OF SEXUAL BEHAVIOUR

Rape

The legal definition of rape is considered on page 736. Men convicted of rape are mainly young, and most of them are not convicted a second time (Gibbens *et al.* 1977). The offender has often taken alcohol. In nearly a third of convictions, one or more other people took part in the offence (Gibbens *et al.* 1977). The act differs widely from a clumsy misunderstanding of the woman's intentions to brutal acts carried out in a drunken state. A few acts of rape are carried out by men with aggressive personalities who have a deep hatred of women. There is an important minority who commit rape repeatedly; they are difficult to treat by any means. (See Tollison and Adams (1979) for a review of the evidence.)

A raped woman needs sympathetic help, preferably from her general practitioner. In the United States and increasingly in Great Britain, special counselling services provide additional help to enable the victims to overcome the adverse psychological effects of the assault. These adverse effects include anxiety and depression, feelings of humiliation, disgust about sex with consequent problems in relationships, and phobic responses to circumstances resembling those of the rape.

Doctors may be asked to examine patients to determine whether rape has taken place and how much physical damage has been done. Other measures required are to determine whether a venereal infection has been transmitted and whether the woman has become pregnant. An account of the medical examination of rape victims is given by Barnes (1967) (see also page 736).

Incest

In their interviews about sexual behaviour, Kinsey *et al.* (1948) received few reports of incest. This finding is hardly surprising, because incestuous behaviour is particularly unlikely to be revealed to an interviewer. Clinical experience suggests that such statistics underestimate the frequency of incest, particularly between men who have taken alcohol and their teenage daughters, or between siblings as part of adolescent experimentation.

Although incest violates social rules, the main question for the doctor is whether it causes psychological harm, particularly to a young daughter involved in sexual activity with her father. On this important problem there is no reliable general information. The clinician must therefore judge each case on a common-sense appraisal of the circumstances of the incest, the emotional atmosphere of the family, and the personality of the patient. Sometimes it seems that more psychological harm is caused to the girl by legal proceedings than by incestuous experience. In England and Wales, if a child is thought to be in continuing danger, a report should be made to the Social Services whose duty is to investigate such cases. Incest is punishable by imprisonment; offenders sentenced in 1975 received terms varying from two to ten years (Freeman 1979). Imprisonment prevents further acts of incest, but it also prevents the working through of any family problems arising before or after the act. From the psychiatrist's point of view, imprisonment should be considered only if there is no more constructive way of dealing with the case.

Pornography

It is not known whether pornographic publications merely provide a harmless outlet for deviant sexual impulses that might otherwise be inflicted on another person; or whether they encourage such impulses and so increase sexual offences. Epidemiological studies have attempted to relate the numbers of sexual offences to changes in the law about pornography (as in Denmark), but they have given inconclusive results. Clinical studies of sexual deviations suggest that fantasies experienced during sexual arousal and orgasm are reinforced by pornographic literature. This evidence is inconclusive because it is not known whether a person who has strong sexual fantasies is more likely to enact them. Moreover, for sexual deviants it is possible that pictorial material promotes solitary sexual release and so reduces the involvement of other people.

Without more definite evidence the following restriction seems appropriate: pornographic material relating sexual activity to violence or to children should not be available to young people whose sexual development is incomplete. The arguments for more general restrictions are that pornographic publications debase women, and possibly put children at risk of exploitation. These are important matters of public policy. In his dealings with his patients and their families, the doctor is more likely to be asked what effect pornographic material, discovered by a wife or parent, is likely to have on a husband or adolescent son. He should explain the different points of view, and indicate that the effects are likely to differ in different people. If the doctor can interview the person concerned and review his sexual life thoroughly, he will usually be able to give some useful advice. Such advice should, if possible, extend to broader aspects of personal relationships and not merely to the effects of the pornographic material.

FURTHER READING

Caplan, H.I., Freedman, A.M., and Sadock, B.J. (eds.) (1980). Normal human sexuality and psychosexual disorders. In *Comprehensive textbook of psychiatry,* Vol. 3, 3rd edn. Chapter 24. Williams and Wilkins, Baltimore.

Felstein, M. (1980). Sexual medicine. *Clinics in obstetrics and gynaecology,* Vol. 7, No. 2. Saunders, London.

Ford, C.S. and Beach, F.A. (1952). *Patterns of sexual behaviour.* Methuen, London.

Lo Piccolo, J. and Lo Piccolo, K. (eds.) (1978). *Handbook of sex therapy.* Plenum Press, New York.

16. Psychiatry of the elderly

INTRODUCTION

It is only in the past thirty years that the psychiatric care of the elderly has attracted special interest. This change of interest largely reflects the increasing numbers of old people in the population. In Western Europe at the beginning of this century only 5 per cent of the population were aged over 65; now the figure is about 15 per cent, a third of whom are aged over 75. It is expected that the proportion of elderly people will continue to rise well into the next century. Since the prevalence of mental disorder and particularly dementia increases with age, there has been a disproportionate increase in the demand for psychiatric care for the elderly. People aged over 65 now make up half of all long-stay psychiatric patients, and about a fifth of all first admissions to psychiatric wards.

Although the psychiatric disorders of the elderly have some special features, they do not differ substantially from the psychiatric disorders of younger adults. It is the needs of elderly psychiatric patients that set them apart from others. Indeed the practice of psychogeriatrics requires special psychiatric skills. It is for this reason that a separate chapter is devoted to the subject.

The chapter begins with a brief account of normal aging. General principles of psychogeriatric care are discussed next, and then an account is given of different psychiatric syndromes in the aged.

Normal aging

The aging brain

The weight of the human brain decreases by approximately 5 per cent between the ages of 30 and 70 years, 10 per cent by the age of 80, and 20 per cent by the age of 90. Along with these changes, the ventricles enlarge and the meninges thicken. There is some loss of nerve cells, but this is minor and selective; more important is a decline in quantity of nerve processes. Senile plaques are increasingly common with advancing age. They are present in 80 per cent of healthy people aged 70 or more. In a smaller number there are neurofibrillary tangles and granulovacuolar degeneration. Ischaemic lesions are present in brains from half of normal subjects aged over 65. Biochemically there is evidence of decline in some neurotransmitter systems. Unfortunately the significance of many of these findings is not understood because of the difficulty of

493

studying the relationships between post-mortem histology and brain function in life (see Bondareff 1980).

The psychology of aging

Because old people are often unwell and have sensory impairments, it is difficult to decide what is psychologically normal in old age. It is commonly accepted that intellectual functions as measured with standard intelligence tests decline from mid-life, but the significance of the changes is uncertain. This is partly because the tests focus on new learning tasks, which tend to under-represent the value of experience. Deterioration of short-term memory is an obvious feature of aging but the true nature and extent of the defect is not clear. Slowness is another obvious characteristic of aging, and it partly explains impaired performance on cognitive tests. Impairment of psychomotor tasks, which has been demonstrated repeatedly, appears to be due to changes in central rather than peripheral mechanisms. As well as these cognitive and motor changes there are important alterations in personality and attitudes, such as increasing cautiousness, rigidity, and 'disengagement' from the outside world. (See Birren and Sloane (1980) for further information about the psychology of normal aging.)

Physical health

In addition to a general decline in functional capacity and adaptability with aging, chronic degenerative conditions are common. As a result, the elderly consult their family doctors frequently and occupy a half of all general hospital beds. Medical management is often made more difficult by the presence of more than one disorder, by increased sensitivity to the side effects of treatment, and by the frequency of psychiatric and social problems.

Social circumstances

Almost all the elderly live at home; about a third are alone, about half are with their spouse, and about 10 per cent with their children. Many see families, friends, and neighbours regularly, but a quarter of those over 65 have no children to help them and a considerable number rarely have visitors. In an aging population in which more middle-aged women work, there are fewer people to visit and help the elderly. The aged have poorer accommodation and lower incomes than younger people. A half of the aged are believed to be near the official definition of poverty, and many lack basic amenities such as adequate bathrooms and inside lavatories. Although this picture of unsatisfactory social circumstances is typical of most western countries it is not so everywhere. In some cultures, for example the Chinese, the elderly are esteemed and most can expect to live with their children.

GENERAL CONSIDERATIONS

Until the mid-1950s understanding of the mental disorders of later life was largely based upon accounts written at the beginning of the century, when Kraepelin, Bleuler, and others described the presenile, senile, and arterio-sclerotic psychoses. At that time disorders with a predominantly affective picture were usually ascribed to a supposed underlying organic cause. Doubts about the evidence for such an organic cause, together with the success of new physical treatments led to a re-examination of the problem. Using information from case-notes, Roth (1955) divided patients into five diagnostic groups, and assessed their outcome six months and two years after admission. He found that affective psychosis, late paraphrenia, and acute confusion had better prognoses than arteriosclerotic or senile psychoses. Roth also found that organic states appeared to be diagnosed more often in the United States than in Britain, and this finding was subsequently confirmed in a systematic comparison between the two countries (Copeland *et al.* 1975). Roth's investigation provided the basis for many subsequent studies of the epidemiology, clinical features, prognosis, and treatment of mental disorder in old age. The subject is reviewed in the textbook by Birren and Sloane (1980).

Epidemiology

In an area of Newcastle-upon-Tyne, Kay *et al.* (1964) examined the prevalence of psychiatric disorder amongst elderly people in the general population, including those living at home as well as those living in institutions. The findings, which are shown in Table 16.1, have been broadly replicated in subsequent surveys in Britain, North America, and Europe. In particular there is agreement that 5 to 10 per cent of those over the age of 65 suffer from dementia and that the prevalence rises to around 20 per cent of those aged over 80. Follow-up of the Newcastle group confirmed that patients with dementia had a

Table 16.1. *Estimated prevalence of psychiatric disorder**

Disorder	Prevalence in people aged 65 and over (%)	Ratio of patients living at home to those in institutions
Dementia (severe)	5.6	6:1
Dementia (mild)	5.7	10:1
Manic depressive	1.4	18:1
Schizophrenia (excluding long-stay hospital patients)	1.1	9:1
Neurosis and personality disorder	12.5	51:1
All disorder	26.3	14:1

*Adapted from Kay *et al.* (1964).

poor prognosis; they were three times more likely than those in the other diagnostic groups to require admission to a hospital or an institution.

Other surveys have shown a high prevalence of psychiatric disorder among elderly people in sheltered accommodation and in hospital. A third of the residents in old people's homes have significant cognitive impairment. In general hospital wards (medical and geriatric) Bergmann and Eastham (1974) found that about half of the patients aged 65 or over suffered from some form of psychiatric illness.

It has frequently been reported that general practitioners are unaware of most of the psychiatric problems amongst elderly people living in the community. Williamson *et al.* (1964) found that general practitioners were unaware of 60 per cent of elderly patients with neurosis, 76 per cent with depression, and 87 per cent with slight to moderate dementia. Such findings presumably reflect both the difficulties of early diagnosis and unawareness by doctors of the benefits of early identification of mental disorder in the elderly. Moreover, the presentation of such disorders to general practitioners and psychiatrists is determined as much by social factors as by a change in the patient's mental state. For example, there may be a sudden alteration in the patient's environment, such as illness of a relative or a bereavement. Sometimes, an increasingly exhausted or frustrated family decide they can no longer continue to care for the old person. At other times there is an element of manipulation by relatives who are trying to rid themselves of an unwanted responsibility.

Epidemiology is discussed further when individual syndromes are considered later in this chapter. A review of epidemiological methods and findings has been provided by Kay and Bergmann (1980).

Services for the elderly

After the Second World War, legislation was enacted in the United Kingdom making local authorities responsible for domiciliary, day, and residential services for the elderly. In the National Health Service a new medical specialty of geriatric medicine was established to develop the special interest and skill necessary to provide adequate community and hospital care for old people. Specialist psychiatric services soon followed.

The government policy document *Services for Mental Illness Related to Old Age* (Department of Health and Social Security 1972) divided elderly patients with psychiatric problems into three broad groups: 1. Patients who entered hospitals for the mentally ill before modern methods of treatment were available, and who have grown old in them; 2. Elderly patients with functional mental illness; 3. Elderly patients with dementia. ('Elderly' is usually taken to mean over 65 years of age.) The first group of old long-stay patients are mostly schizophrenics; they are usually cared for by general psychiatrists. Their numbers are being increased by the 'new long-stay' who, in their turn, will require some form of institutional care as they grow old (see Chapter 19). With the exception of these patients who have grown old in hospital, the specialist psychogeriatric services are usually responsible for all elderly psychiatric patients, whether their illness is functional or organic. The case for defining the speciality in this way, rather than confining it to the elderly demented, is twofold. First, there are special problems in the diagnosis and management of functional illness in the elderly; second, staff morale can be maintained better if a proportion of recoverable cases is seen.

Government policy in Britain, more than in some other countries, emphasizes the importance of treatment in the community rather than in hospital (Department of Health and Social Security 1972, 1978*b*). In trying to achieve this goal, obstacles arise because of the administrative separation of health services which are provided by central government, from social services and community facilities which are the responsibility of local authorities.

Table 16.2 lists the official recommendations for provision of hospital places and residential care. In most areas there are shortages of hospital beds, special accommodation, and staff. Also many elderly people require practical services, such as home help or day care, but are not receiving them. For example, among

Table 16.2. *Recommended provisions for the elderly per 1000 total population over the age of 65**

Psychiatric beds for severe dementia	2.5–3.0
Psychiatric beds for functional illness	included in general adult provision
Psychiatric day hospital places	2.3
Geriatric hospital beds	10
Geriatric day hospital places	2
Residential care (Local Authority)	25

*See Department of Health and Social Security 1972.

a random sample of 477 people aged 65 and over living at home, only about 10 per cent were receiving domiciliary services, although almost three times as many appeared to need them (Foster *et al.* 1976).

The organization of psychiatric services varies in different places, since it reflects the personal style of doctors in addition to local needs and national policies. Nevertheless there are some general principles for the planning of services (see Jolley and Arie 1978). The aims of the service should be defined in relation to the age distribution of the population living in the catchment area, and also in relation to the service provided by general adult psychiatry. There should be close liaison with the medical geriatric department as well as the local authority social services. A multi-disciplinary approach should be adopted by a clinical team that includes psychiatrists, community nurses, and social workers. Some members of the team will spend more of their working day in patients' homes and in general practices than in the hospital. The contributions of the several parts of the service will now be considered.

Primary care

In the United Kingdom, general practitioners deal with most of the problems of mentally ill old people without referring them to specialists. As already mentioned, general practitioners do not always detect psychiatric problems at an early stage (Williamson 1974). It also appears that they do not always provide necessary long term medical supervision. A recent review (Royal College of Physicians 1981) suggests that these problems are due in part to doctors' unawareness of the significance of psychiatric illness and in part to the organization of general practice as a 'patient-initiated service'. Nevertheless, general practitioners and their primary care teams are the most important group in the care of the elderly.

The psychiatric hospital

Most wards for elderly psychiatric patients are in large mental hospitals. They exemplify the problems of two classes of care, which have resulted from the policy of developing psychiatric units in District Hospitals (see Chapter 19). Even so, the more active psychogeriatric units have been able to overcome the disadvantages of old-fashioned buildings by providing good basic amenities such as privacy, the use of personal possessions, and adequate occupational and social therapy. Hospitals are used for assessment and short-term treatment as well as for long-term care. This policy has resulted in some reduction in bed numbers, despite a substantial increase in the numbers of patients admitted and discharged.

Psychogeriatric assessment units

From a study in Belfast, Kidd (1962) concluded that extensive 'misplacement' of patients between geriatric and psychiatric hospitals led to poor treatment, prolonged stay, and unnecessary mortality. Subsequent studies have not confirmed this conclusion. For example, Copeland *et al.* (1975) found that 64 per cent of patients admitted to a geriatric hospital were psychiatrically ill, but only 12 per cent appeared to be wrongly placed and their outcome did not appear to be affected adversely. It seems that many patients can be cared for equally well in either type of hospital. Although the original findings of 'misplacement' have not been confirmed, they aroused concern that led to an official policy of developing joint psychogeriatric assessment units. These are short-stay units staffed by a multidisciplinary team and directed jointly by a psychiatrist and geriatrician. Such units can be valuable when there is a diagnostic difficulty or when medical and psychiatric problems coexist. Some units have been unable to function effectively as short-term assessment units, because of lack of suitable accommodation to which patients could be discharged. Others have worked well.

Day and outpatient care

Day care in geriatric hospitals began in the 1950s, and the first psychiatric day hospitals for the elderly were opened a few years later. Psychiatric day care affords social support and treatment for patients with organic or functional illnesses, provided that adequate transport is available. Government policy in Britain is to provide a substantial number of day places, though in many hospitals the intended numbers have not been reached. Local authorities provide social clubs and day centres for the infirm elderly, many of whom suffer from dementia. For severely ill patients, outpatient clinics play only a small part because of transport difficulties and because home assessment has many advantages. Outpatient clinics are convenient for the assessment and follow-up of patients who are younger and more mobile.

Residential care

In Britain, under Part III of the National Assistance Act of 1948, local authorities are responsible for providing old people's homes and other sheltered accommodation. When the 1948 Act was passed, there was a legacy of large impersonal institutions (see Townsend 1962). Since then, accommodation has been provided in small units, but it has still proved difficult to achieve an acceptable standard of privacy, while encouraging independence and involvement in outside activities. In some homes there is no security of tenure, and residents who have to be admitted to hospital may find themselves homeless if discharged.

The average age of residents has risen steadily. They are more disabled physically and mentally than was originally intended, and about a third are forgetful and disorientated. It has been argued that the most severely ill should be cared for in separate specialist homes. However, as Meacher (1972) has pointed out, such segregation can have harmful effects. Problems have sometimes arisen from the inappropriate use of specialist homes for the most 'difficult' patients rather than for those who would benefit most (see Wilkin *et al.* 1982).

Apart from old people's homes, there is a need for special housing, conveniently sited and easy to run. Ideally an old person should be able to transfer to more sheltered accommodation if he becomes more disabled, without losing all independence or moving away from friends and familiar places.

Other countries have different systems of care. Gurland *et al.* (1979) compared two random samples of patients living in institutions in New York and London. Both cities provided residential care for about 4 per cent of their elderly population. However in New York 60 per cent of the places for the elderly were in large nursing homes staffed by nurses, whereas in London nearly two-thirds were in small residential units staffed by a warden and domestic helpers. Thus many elderly people with similar problems were receiving different forms of care in the two cities. For the elderly in Sweden there are three times as many hospital beds and residential places per unit of population as there are in Britain.

Domiciliary services

These services include home helps, meals at home, laundry, telephones, and emergency call systems. Such provisions have been increasing in the United Kingdom, but more are needed. In a random sample of nearly 500 people aged 65 and over living at home, Foster *et al.* (1976) found that 12 per cent were receiving domiciliary services but a further 20 per cent still needed them. Bergmann *et al.* (1978) have argued that if resources are limited, more should be directed to patients living with their families than to those living alone. This is because the former can often remain at home if they receive such help, while many of the latter require admission before long even when extra help is given.

Some general principles of assessment

In Britain most psychogeriatricians believe that the first assessment should normally take place in the elderly patient's home, where other informants can be interviewed and social conditions observed. Since less than half of the patients assessed in this way are admitted to hospital, the home visit is an important opportunity to plan treatment with all those concerned. The answers to three general questions should be sought: (1) Can the patient be managed at home? (2) If so what additional help does the family need? (3) Can the patient manage his financial affairs?

During the assessment, emphasis should be put on the medical history and physical examination as well as a thorough formulation of social problems. Whenever possible the clinician should interview close relatives or friends, who can give information about the patient and may be involved in his continuing care. Such interviews are specially helpful when the patient has cognitive impairment. In every case, the reasons for the referral should be considered carefully, since many emergencies reflect changes in the attitudes of the family and neighbours to the patient's longstanding problems, rather than a change in his psychiatric state. In order to answer the three questions listed above, the clinician will need to elicit the following information:

1. The time and mode of onset of symptoms and their subsequent course.
2. Any previous medical and psychiatric history.
3. The patient's living conditions and financial position.
4. The patient's ability to look after himself. Any odd or undesirable behaviour that may cause difficulties with his neighbours.
5. The attitudes of family and friends, and their ability to help.
6. Other services already involved in the patient's care.

Usually a diagnosis can be made and provisional plans formulated during the first home visit. Hospital admission may be required, either for investigation and treatment, or for social reasons. More often it is possible to arrange extra social or medical care in the patient's normal surroundings.

With these general points in mind, consideration can now be given to specific aspects of history-taking, physical and mental examination, and psychological assessment.

History taking

Normally the problem should be discussed with the general practitioner before the patient is seen. If there is any likelihood of intellectual impairment in the patient, it is usually best to speak to relatives or other informants first. Details of the onset and time course of the symptoms are of particular value in differential diagnosis. Since a social formulation is important, the history should cover information about the patient's financial state and social circumstances, and about people who may be willing to help him. A description of the patient's behaviour over a typical 24-hour period is often helpful in eliciting symptoms and obtaining a detailed picture of the patient's way of life.

Examination

A thorough physical examination should be carried out, including an appropriately detailed neurological assessment with particular attention to vision and hearing. The mental state examination should include a systematic assessment of cognitive functions. It may be necessary to test linguistic, visuospatial, and other higher cortical functions.

If the patient is admitted to hospital, systematic observations should be made of his behaviour on the ward. The Gresham Ward Questionnaire (Post 1965) provides a scheme for assessing memory for general events, past personal events, and recent personal events; a simple score for correct answers gives a useful indication of the severity of intellectual handicap.

Physical investigations

On admission to hospital, the minimum routine investigations are a full blood count, blood urea and electrolytes, urine analysis and culture, and chest X-ray. If physical illness is suspected, additional investigations may be required. In the case of very old patients with dementia, the clinician should use his judgement in deciding how far to pursue physical investigations when there are no clinical signs. If an organic diagnosis is suspected the following may be required: blood count and film, ESR, syphilis serology, thyroid function, electrolytes, urea and liver function, plasma calcium, vitamin B_{12}, chest X-ray, skull X-ray, ECG, and EEG. A CT scan is often recommended as a routine (see for example Wells 1978), but it is probably only justified when there are specific indications. With older patients, especially when a reasonably confident clinical diagnosis can be made, elaborate investigations are seldom necessary.

Psychological assessment

In skilled hands psychometric testing has a limited but important role (see Miller 1980). Common obstacles to testing are the patient's confusion, lack of motivation, sensory handicaps, and his need for adequate time to become accustomed to the procedure. The two main uses of psychological assessment are to measure decline in cognitive function, and to differentiate between organic and functional illness. Measuring cognitive decline is difficult because there is seldom enough information about the patient's premorbid state. There is doubt about the common assumption that verbal tests indicate the premorbid level. Also reliance on previous educational and other achievement can be misleading. Serial measurements can provide better evidence of decline, but the assessor must be aware of the test-retest reliability of his methods.

In making the diagnosis between organic and functional illness, verbal learning tests are the most helpful and design copying is also useful. In addition, the demonstration of focal abnormalities of higher cortical functions strongly suggests an organic disorder. It can be helpful to use a battery of tests, such as those introduced by Kendrick, which combine an object learning test and a motor task (see Gibson *et al.* 1980). For demented patients already in hospital, a careful description of their behaviour can also contribute to the assessment of disability and remaining skills (see Patterson and Jackson 1980).

Treatment

Essentially the psychiatric treatment of the elderly resembles that of other adults, but there are differences in emphasis. If practicable, treatment is generally preferable at home rather than in hospital, not only because most elderly people want to be at home, but also because they function best there. Home treatment requires a willingness on the part of the doctor to arrange a plan with the family, to organize appropriate day care or help, and to admit to hospital should it become necessary.

General care and the use of drugs

Whenever possible, it is essential to treat the underlying cause of an organic mental disorder. Other physical disorders, however minor, should be actively treated, since in this way the mental state can often be improved. Mobility should be encouraged, and physiotherapy is often helpful. A good diet should be provided.

In prescribing drugs to the elderly, special attention must be given to several points. Slow degradation and delayed excretion of drugs may lead to undesirably high blood levels. In the elderly, side effects are more common, especially impairement of consciousness (which may be caused by psychotropic and anticholinergic drugs, digoxin, and diuretics). Barbiturates may cause agitation. For these reasons it is essential to restrict the number of drugs and to start with small doses. The patient's response should be watched carefully. Since older patients may be unreliable in taking drugs, the regime should be simple, bottles should be labelled clearly, memory aids should be provided, and if possible drug taking should be supervised. In these aspects of treatment, as in many others, domiciliary nursing plays a vital part.

Despite the need for caution in prescribing, patients should not be denied effective drug treatment. This is particularly required for depressive disorders. Antidepressant medication should be started cautiously and increased gradually. If patients do not respond to antidepressants, the measurement of plasma concentrations is sometimes helpful before increasing the dose. ECT can be remarkably successful in treating serious depressive illness in the elderly. However, if there is cognitive impairment, ECT may be complicated by temporary memory impairment and confusion, hence longer intervals between treatments are advisable. Before receiving ECT, physically frail patients should be assessed by an experienced anaesthetist.

Psychological treatment

Interpretative psychotherapy is seldom appropriate for the elderly. However, supportive therapy with clearly defined aims may be required, and joint interviews with the spouse are sometimes helpful.

There has been increasing interest in behavioural treatment of demented patients. Methods have been developed for training patients with problems in eating, continence, or social skills (see Patterson and Jackson 1980) and it can be useful to encourage patients with memory disorder to use memory aids such as notebooks and alarm clocks. Folsom (1967) described reality orientation therapy, which is intended to reduce confusion and improve behaviour. In this approach, basic information is given about orientation in time and place, and repeated on every contact with the patient. This technique is widely practised, though evaluative studies suggest that its benefits are modest (see Powell-Proctor and Miller 1982).

Social treatment

Some patients can achieve independence through measures to encourage self-care, social contacts, and domestic skills. More severely impaired patients can benefit from a humane, dignified environment in which individual needs are respected and each person retains some personal possessions. Disorientation can be reduced by the general design of the ward and the use of simple aids such as colour codes on doors. For those living at home, domiciliary occupational therapy may be helpful.

Support for relatives

Time should be spent with the family in discussion of problems and advice about care. Such support can help families to avoid some of the frustrations and anxieties of caring for elderly relatives. Practical help should include the organization of day-care or holiday admissions, and a laundry and meal service to the home. If these steps are taken, many patients can remain in their own homes without imposing an unreasonable burden on their families. Community psychiatric nurses play essential roles in co-ordinating these services, supporting relatives, and providing practical nursing care. The first two roles can also be undertaken by social workers.

ACUTE ORGANIC SYNDROMES

Because acute organic syndromes have physical causes, the patients are usually under the care of physicians or general practitioners. In a survey of patients admitted to medical geriatric wards, about a tenth were found to have acute organic psychiatric syndromes (Hodkinson 1973). The main predisposing factors were pre-existing dementia, defective hearing and vision, Parkinson's disease, and advanced age. The most frequent precipitating causes were pneumonia, cardiac failure, urinary infection, carcinomatosis, and hypokalaemia.

The **clinical features** of acute organic syndromes are discussed on p. 294. It should be remembered that when elderly patients suffer from an acute organic syndrome, impairment of consciousness although invariable, is not always obvious – especially when the onset is gradual. In patients who have a preceding dementia, cognitive function can sometimes be affected by minor physical upsets, such as constipation, dehydration, or mild bronchitis. Since many of the causes of acute organic syndromes are a threat to life, mortality is high. In a Newcastle survey of patients admitted to hospital with such syndromes, half were found to have died within two years of admission (Roth 1955).

The basic requirement in management is to search for and treat the under-lying cause. Meanwhile, psychotropic drugs can provide valuable symptomatic relief. Benzodiazepines may increase confusion. Small doses of a phenothia-zine, such as promazine, thioridazine, or haloperidol are usually effective without increasing confusion. The amount and timing of the dosage should be carefully determined for each patient, by reference to the British National Formulary or a similar source. If a hypnotic is needed, chloral hydrate and dichloralphenazine are safe and effective.

DEMENTIA IN THE ELDERLY

In this book, the main account of dementia is given in Chapter 11, p. 294. The reader is referred to that chapter for a definition of dementia, and a description of its clinical features and treatment. This section is concerned only with dementia in the elderly.

Dementia in the elderly has been recognized since Esquirol described 'démence senile' in his textbook *Des maladies mentales* (see Esquirol 1845).

Esquirol described the disorder in general terms, but it can be recognized as similar to the present day concept. Kraepelin distinguished dementia from psychoses due to other organic causes, such as neurosyphilis; and he divided dementia into pre-senile, senile, and arteriosclerotic forms. In 1955, in an important follow-up study, Roth showed that in the elderly dementia differed from affective disorders and paranoid disorders in its poorer prognosis.

Dementia in old age can be divided into three groups according to aetiology and pathology:

1. Senile dementia of the Alzheimer type (SDAT). This has the same pathological changes in the brain as pre-senile dementia of the Alzheimer type (pre-senile dementia is described in Chapter 11). SDAT is known to be the commonest kind of dementia in old age.

2. Multi-infarct dementia. As the name implies, this is due to multiple infarcts in the brain, resulting from vascular occlusions. It corresponds to the older category of arteriosclerotic dementia.

3. Dementia due to other causes. This group includes dementia resulting from a wide range of causes, such as neoplasms, infections, toxins, and metabolic disorders, some of which are reversible (see Perry and Perry 1982).

This chapter is concerned only with groups 1 and 2. Group 3 is discussed in Chapter 11.

The clinical picture of dementia is much the same in all three groups. Some minor differences in clinical features are found fairly consistently, but they cannot always be relied on to differentiate between the three groups.

It is only recently that pathologists have distinguished these sub-groups of dementia outlined above. For many years it was believed that vascular disease was the commonest cause of dementia. Doubt was cast on this belief when Corsellis (1962) reported that pathological changes of the Alzheimer type were more common. This finding was subsequently confirmed by several workers. For example, in a careful clinicopathological study based on 50 successive postmortems of demented patients, Tomlinson *et al.* (1970) found the following distribution of changes: definite Alzheimer type, 50 per cent; probable Alzheimer type, 16 per cent; definite arteriosclerotic, 12 per cent; probable arteriosclerotic, 6 per cent; both Alzheimer and arteriosclerotic, 8 per cent; no evident pathology, 8 per cent.

Senile dementia of the Alzheimer type (SDAT)

Although the clinical features of dementia have been described in Chapter 11, the features of SDAT are reviewed here briefly. This is because SDAT is common and important, and because some of its features are characteristic (though not discriminating for diagnostic purposes).

Clinical features

SDAT usually begins after the age of 70. In one large study, the mean age of onset was found to be 73 for men, and 75 for women (Larsson *et al.* 1963). It occurs mainly in women.

In the early stages there is minor forgetfulness. Doctors are seldom consulted until a later stage of chronic deterioration, or a sudden worsening in relation to some other physical illness. Memory becomes increasingly impaired, and there is general intellectual deterioration. The personality alters, usually in the form of declining social behaviour, though some patients maintain a good social facade despite severe cognitive impairment. In the early stages, the clinical features are modified by the premorbid personality, and any personality defects tend to be exaggerated. Patients are often restless and wake at night, disorientated and perplexed. The mood may be predominantly depressed, euphoric, flattened, or labile. Fragmentary persecutory delusions and hallucinations are common. Focal signs of parietal lobe dysfunction (such as dysphasia or dyspraxia) may occur, but are less common than in presenile Alzheimer's disease. In the advanced stages, there is progressive physical frailty and loss of sphincter control.

The course of the illness is usually progressive deterioration. In the early stages episodic depressive or paranoid symptoms may be conspicuous. An incidental physical illness may cause a superimposed acute brain syndrome and also a sudden deterioration in cognitive function which is sometimes permanent.

From the time when the first signs of the disease appear, death generally occurs within four to five years. From the time of diagnosis, the mean expectation of life is 2.6 years for men and 2.3 years for women (Kay 1962). According to Roth (1955), 60 per cent of patients die within six months of admission to hospital, and 80 per cent within two years.

If there are specific symptoms of parietal lobe dysfunction, the prognosis is worse (McDonald 1969; Naguib and Levy 1982).

Pathology of SDAT

As mentioned above, the pathological changes are the same in presenile and senile Alzheimer's disease. Grossly the brain is shrunken with widened sulci and enlarged ventricles. Histologically, there is some cell loss, particularly in the three outer cortical layers, together with proliferation of astrocytes, increased fibrous gliosis, and shrinkage of the dendritic tree. Silver staining shows senile plaques throughout the cortical and subcortical grey matter, and also neurofibrillary tangles and granulovacuolar degeneration. Electronmicroscopy shows that the senile plaques have a central core of amyloid surrounded by abnormal neurites; and that the neurofibrillary tangles are helically paired twisted filaments (see Schneck, *et al.* 1982; Tomlinson 1982; Perry and Perry 1982).

It has been reported that the degree of cognitive impairment is closely related to the number of senile plaques, and less closely related to the number of neuro-fibrillary tangles (see Roth 1971).

Neurophysiological abnormalities have been found in the peripheral nerves as well as in the cerebral hemispheres, suggesting a possible widespread involve-ment of the nervous system (Levy *et al.* 1970; Schneck *et al.* 1982).

Biochemistry of SDAT

Several studies have indicated that in SDAT there is impaired synaptic function which probably differs from that of normal aging. Davies and Maloney (1976) found reduced levels of choline acetyl transferase and of acetylcholinesterase in patients with SDAT; they suggested a selective loss of the cholinergic neurones involved in memory. Perry *et al.* (1978) found that levels of choline acetyl trans-ferase were directly related to the numbers of senile plaques, and inversely related to intellectual performance before death.

Does SDAT differ from presenile Alzheimer's disease?

As already mentioned, the brain pathology is the same in SDAT and presenile Alzheimer's disease. The same holds for the neurochemical changes. Similar clinical features probably occur in both conditions, although some parietal lobe symptoms (such as dyspraxias) are less common in the elderly (see for example Lauter and Meyer 1968). It has been suggested that the two conditions differ genetically, since no case of presenile Alzheimer's disease was found amongst 2000 relatives of probands with SDAT (Larrson *et al.* 1963). This evidence is not convincing, because presenile dementia is so rare that a sample of 2000 is too small to allow any firm conclusions. More recent research (for example Heston *et al.* 1981) indicates that there are no grounds for regarding SDAT and presenile Alzheimer's as separate diseases (see Schneck *et al.* 1982).

Does SDAT differ from normal aging?

In SDAT the pathological changes in the brain are much more pronounced than in the brains of normal old people, but they do not differ in kind. In other words, the differences between the Alzheimer brain and the normal aging brain are quantitative, but not qualitative. The main evidence for a difference between the disease and normal aging is genetic, as described in the section on aetiology (below).

Kral (1962) described a syndrome of 'benign senescent forgetfulness', which he regarded as distinct from SDAT. Patients with this syndrome were said to have difficulty in remembering which was not progressive. Their life expectancy was unchanged. At present the status of this syndrome is uncertain; some clinicians find it useful to distinguish between progressive and non-progressive memory disturbance, whilst others do not.

Aetiology of SDAT

In the large study mentioned above, Larsson *et al.* (1963) found evidence of a genetic basis for SDAT. This finding was confirmed by Heston *et al.* (1981) in a rigorous study of the relatives of 125 probands with senile dementia proved by post-mortem histology. In this study, the relatives also had an excess of Down's syndrome, lymphoma, and immune diathesis. If proven, an association with immune diathesis would have important aetiological implications. However, such an association was not found by Whalley *et al.* (1982).

For relatives the risk of SDAT (and presenile Alzheimer's disease) is much greater if the disease started in the proband before the age of 65, or if another relative apart from the proband is affected (Heston *et al.* 1981). The mechanism of inheritance is uncertain. A specific link with chromosome 21 is suggested by the observation that surviving Down's syndrome patients eventually develop Alzheimer's disease.

Other aetiological hypotheses have been proposed. For example, it has been reported that aluminium (which is neurotoxic in animals) is found in excess in the brains of patients with Alzheimer's disease (Crapper *et al.* 1973). This finding has not been convincingly confirmed. Another hypothesis is that the disease is caused by a slow virus of the type implicated in Kuru and Creutzfeld–Jacob disease (see for example Gibbs *et al.* 1968). At present an infective cause is unproven (see Schneck *et al.* 1982).

Multi-infarct dementia

In this condition, dementia is associated with multiple infarcts of varying size, mostly caused by thromboembolism from extracranial arteries (Hachinski *et al.* 1974). The term 'multi-infarct' has largely replaced the older term 'arteriosclerotic'. The condition is slightly more common in men than in women. The onset, which is usually in the late sixties or the seventies, may follow a cerebrovascular accident and is often more acute than in SDAT. Emotional and personality changes may appear first, followed by impairments of memory and intellect that are characteristically fluctuating. Episodes of emotional lability and confusion are common, especially at night. Fits or minor episodes of cerebral ischaemia are usual at some stage.

The diagnosis is difficult to make with certainty unless there is a clear history of strokes or else definite localizing signs. Suggestive features are patchy psychological deficits, erratic progression, and relative preservation of the personality. On physical examination there are usually signs of hypertension and of arteriosclerosis in peripheral and retinal vessels, and neurological signs may also be present.

The course of multi-infarct dementia is usually a stepwise progression, with periods of deterioration that are sometimes followed by partial recovery for a few months. About half the patients die from ischaemic heart disease, and others from cerebral infarction or renal complications. From the time of diagnosis the life-span varies widely but averages about four to five years – perhaps slightly longer than for SDAT (Roth 1955).

In multi-infarct dementia the gross pathology is distinctive. There is localized or generalized brain atrophy and ventricular dilatation, with areas of cerebral infarction and evidence of arteriosclerosis in major vessels. On microscopy, multiple areas of infarction and ischaemia are evident. Tomlinson *et al.* (1970) found that the volume of damaged cerebral cortex at post-mortem was related to the degree of intellectual impairment shortly before death; usually no cognitive impairment was detectable until at least 50 ml of brain tissue had been affected.

In multi-infarct dementia biochemical studies have shown that there is no association between cognitive impairment and levels of choline acetyltransferase (Perry *et al.* 1978) – a distinguishing feature from dementia of the Alzheimer type. (For a review of the pathology see Perry and Perry 1982.)

The assessment of dementia in the elderly

The assessment of dementia in general is discussed in the chapter on organic psychiatry (p. 304). In the elderly, assessment follows the same principles.

Dementia has to be differentiated from acute organic syndromes, depressive disorders, and paranoid disorders. An acute organic syndrome is suggested by impaired and fluctuating consciousness, and by symptoms such as perceptual misinterpretations and hallucinations (see p. 308). Differentiation from affective disorders and paranoid states is discussed later in this chapter. It should be remembered that hypothyroidism may be mistaken for dementia.

In the assessment of dementia it is important to look for the treatable causes, although they are rare. They include, for example, deficiency of vitamin B_{12}, neurosyphilis and operable tumours (see Chapter 11). The investigations listed earlier in this chapter are usually sufficient. As already mentioned, the intensity of investigation must be judged in relation to the patient's age and general debility.

The assessment should also include a thorough search for treatable, often minor, medical conditions that are associated rather than primary causes. Treatment of these conditions can reduce distress and disability (Wells 1978).

The principles of social assessment have been described earlier in the chapter (p. 500).

The treatment of dementia in the elderly

As implied above, the first concern must be to treat any treatable physical disorder. If the latter is the primary cause, the dementia may sometimes be reversible. If an acute organic mental state is superimposed on the dementia, the mental state may improve considerably with treatment of any associated physical disorder.

Whatever the cause of dementia, restlessness by day or night may be reduced by drugs such as promazine, thioridazine, or haloperidol, without causing serious side-effects. Reducing restlessness is an important first step when a family is worn down by caring for a confused and wandering patient. Antipsychotic drugs may also be required for paranoid delusions, and antidepressants for severe depressive symptoms.

For SDAT it has been reported that drugs such as anticoagulants and the so-called vasodilators are of specific benefit, but the evidence is not convincing. The same holds for hyperbaric oxygen. Hydergine, an ergot derivative, seems more promising. Other groups under investigation include piracetam, a GABA derivative, and substances that might improve cholinergic function. There have been no adequate clinical trials of any of these substances, and at present there is no good reason to use any of them (see Reisberg *et al.* for a review of the evidence about the use of all these substances).

For multi-infarct dementia there are no specific measures apart from the control of blood pressure and, if indicated, surgical treatment of carotid artery stenosis.

Psychological and social treatment

For elderly demented patients the principles of psychological and social treatment follow those outlined earlier in the chapter (p. 502). Whenever feasible, patients should continue to live in their own homes, particularly if they have someone to live with. Social care should be planned with all concerned, – family, friends, general practitioner, and in most cases a community psychiatric nurse or social worker. Day-care may be needed for the patient not only to provide supervision, occupation, and training, but also to relieve the family. Occasional hospital admissions may be indicated, to provide a holiday or tide over a crisis.

If the patient cannot be managed at home, residential care may be appropriate in an old people's home or other sheltered accommodation. Failing this, long-term care in hospital will be needed.

AFFECTIVE DISORDER

Depressive disorder

Depressive disorders are common in late life. For first depressive disorders of a severe kind, the highest incidence is between the ages of 50 and 65. First depressive illnesses only become rare after the age of 80. The incidence of suicide increases steadily with age, and in the elderly suicide is usually associated with depressive disorder. There is evidence from population surveys that many depressive disorders in elderly patients are not detected by their general practitioners (Foster *et al.* 1976). In medical wards, too, depressive disorder in the elderly is frequently unrecognized (Bergmann and Eastham 1974).

Clinical features

There is no clear distinction between depressive disorders in the elderly and those in younger people, but symptoms are often more striking in the elderly. Post (1972) reported that a third of his depressed elderly patients had severe retardation and agitation. Depressive delusions concerning poverty and physical illness are common, and occasionally there are nihilistic delusions, such as beliefs that the body is empty, non-existent, or not functioning (see Cotard's syndrome, p. 190). Hallucinations of an accusing or obscene kind are frequent. A small proportion of retarded patients present with 'pseudo-dementia'; that is, they have conspicuous difficulty in concentration and remembering, but careful clinical testing shows there is no defect of memory function.

Course and prognosis

From accounts of depressive disorders written before the introduction of ECT, it is clear that many lasted for years. Nowadays considerable improvement within a few months can be expected in about 85 per cent of admitted patients; the remaining 15 per cent never completely recover. Long-term follow-up shows a less encouraging picture. Post (1972) reported that patients who recovered in the first few months fell into three groups: one-third remained completely well for three years; another third suffered further depressive disorder with complete remissions; while the remaining third developed a state of chronic invalidism punctuated by depressive disorders. Despite this poor outlook for affective symptoms, only a small number of patients develop dementia (Roth 1955; Post 1972). Factors predicting a good prognosis are: onset before the age of 70, short duration of illness, good previous adjustment, absence of disabling physical illness, and good recovery from previous episodes.

Aetiology

In general the aetiology of depressive disorders in late life almost certainly resembles the aetiology of similar disorders in early life. Genetic factors are of less significance. For first degree relatives the risk is 4–5 per cent with elderly probands, as against 10–12 per cent with young and middle-aged probands (Stenstedt 1959). It might be expected that the loneliness and hardship of old age would be important predisposing factors for depression. Surprisingly, there is no convincing evidence for such an association (see Murphy 1982). Indeed Parkes *et al.* (1969) even found that the association between bereavement and mental illness no longer held in the aged.

Although neurological and other physical illnesses may have a slightly raised prevalence among depressed as against non-depressed elderly patients, there is no evidence that they have a specific aetiological role. Instead such illnesses appear to act as non-specific precipitants.

Differential diagnosis

The most difficult differential diagnosis is between depressive pseudodementia and dementia. It is essential to obtain a detailed history from other informants, and to make careful observations of mental state and behaviour. In depressive pseudodementia usually a history of mood disturbance precedes the other symptoms. On examination of mental state, the depressed patient's unwillingness to answer questions can usually be distinguished from the demented patient's failure of memory. Psychological testing is often said to be useful, but it requires experienced interpretation and it usually adds little to skilful clinical assessment (Miller 1980). At times, dementia and depressive illness coexist. If there is real doubt there is no harm in a trial of antidepressant treatment.

Less frequently, depressive disorder has to be differentiated from a paranoid disorder. When persecutory ideas occur in a depressive disorder, the patient usually believes that the supposed persecution is justified by his wickedness (see p. 276). Particular difficulty may occur with the small group of patients who suffer schizoaffective illness in old age (see below).

Treatment

The general principles of the treatment of depressive disorders are the same for adults of all ages. They are described in Chapter 8. With elderly patients it is especially important to be aware of the risk of suicide. Any intercurrent physical disorder should be treated thoroughly. Antidepressants are effective, but should be used cautiously (perhaps starting with half the normal dosage) and adjusted in relation to side effects and response. It is probably wise to avoid the once daily dosage now commonly used for younger patients; instead the drugs should be given two or three times a day. Although it is appropriate to start cautiously, it is equally important to avoid under-medication. For severe and distressing agitation, life-threatening stupor, or failure to respond to drugs, ECT is usually appropriate. If the patient is unduly confused after ECT, applications should be given at longer intervals. If a patient has previously responded to antidepressants or ECT, but does not respond in the present episode, undetected physical illness is a likely cause. After recovery, antidepressant medication should be reduced slowly and then continued in a reduced dose for several months as in younger patients (see p. 225). A minority of patients require more prolonged maintenance treatment.

Mania

Mania accounts for between 5 and 10 per cent of affective illnesses in old age. Unlike depressive disorder, mania does not increase in incidence with age. The clinical picture nearly always combines depressive and manic symptoms, and the condition is frequently recurrent. Management is similar to that described for younger patients (p. 220). Lithium prophylaxis is valuable but the blood level should be monitored with special care, and should be kept at the lower end of the therapeutic range used for younger patients. Shulmann and Post (1980) have reviewed mania in old age.

Schizo-affective disorder

In a study of patients aged over 60 admitted to hospital, Post (1971) found that 4 per cent had schizo-affective disorders (that is, disorders with a more or less equal mixture of the symptoms of schizophrenia and affective disorder), or they had a schizophrenic illness followed by an affective illness or vice versa. For these conditions, intermediate and long-term outcome were less favourable than for depressive disorder.

NEUROSIS, PERSONALITY DISORDER, AND ALCOHOLISM

In later life, neurosis is seldom a cause for referral to a psychiatrist. In a survey in general practice, Shepherd *et al.* (1966) found that, after the age of 55, the incidence of new cases of neurosis declined; however, the frequency of consultations with the general practitioner for neurosis did not fall – presumably as a result of chronic or recurrent cases. From surveys in the community, it appears that after the age of 65 new cases of neurosis still appear (see Kay and Bergmann 1980). Probably many of these new cases do not present to general practitioners or psychiatrists.

Among the elderly, neurotic syndromes are usually of the non-specific kind with symptoms of both anxiety and depression. Hypochondriacal symptoms are often prominent. Hysteria, obsessional neurosis, and phobic neurosis are less common. Most patients presenting with neurosis have a personality disorder, and physical illness is a frequent precipitant.

Personality disorder causes many problems for elderly patients and their families. Paranoid traits may become accentuated with the social isolation of old age, sometimes to the extent of being mistaken for a paranoid state (see p. 275). Abnormal personality is one of the causes of the so-called 'senile squalor syndrome', in which elderly people become isolated and neglect themselves in filthy conditions.

Alcoholism is an increasingly common cause of psychiatric and social problems among old people (see Simon 1980).

The treatment of neuroses and personality disorders in old age is generally similar to that in younger adult life. It is essential to treat any physical disorder. Social measures are usually more important than psychological treatments, but psychotherapy should not be ruled out because of age alone. The treatment of alcoholism is similar to that in younger people.

SCHIZOPHRENIA AND PARANOID STATES IN THE ELDERLY

In the assessment and management of schizophrenia and paranoid states, the same principles apply to elderly as to younger adult patients (see Chapters 9 and 10). In this book, paranoid syndromes are divided into those due to primary disorders (organic, schizophrenic, or affective) and a separate group called paranoid states which appear to be unrelated to any primary disorder (see p. 272). Schizophrenia in this book is defined mainly in terms of first rank symptoms (p. 245). Since similar principles of treatment apply to schizophrenia and paranoid states in the elderly, the two conditions are dealt with together here.

All the paranoid syndromes outlined above occur in elderly patients, the commonest being those secondary to organic or affective disorders. In some patients, schizophrenia starts in mid-life and persists into old age. In a few patients schizophrenia or a paranoid state occurs for the first time in late life. Many clinicians combine these two conditions (late onset schizophrenia and paranoid state), into a single group. For example, the term 'late paraphrenia' has been used for all paranoid syndromes of the elderly in which there is no evidence of organic or affective disorder.

Late paraphrenia was described by Kay and Roth (1961) on the basis of a clinical follow-up and genetic study of 99 patients. Females predominated over males in a ratio of about 7:1, and unmarried patients were significantly more common than in the general population. The clinical picture was characterized by many schizophrenia-like disorders of thought, mood, and volition; by relatively good preservation of intellect, personality and memory, and by conspicuous hallucinations. The course of the illness tended to be chronic, and the changes of schizophrenic type usually became more prominent. The authors concluded that late paraphrenia must be regarded as the mode of manifestation of schizophrenia in old age. The condition is uncommon, accounting for less than 5 per cent of first admissions among the elderly (Kay and Bergmann 1980), though possibly some less severe cases are regarded as eccentricity and not brought to medical attention.

Post (1966) did not use the term paraphrenia, but divided paranoid conditions of the elderly into the following groups: (a) schizophrenia with typical first rank symptoms; (b) schizophrenia with more understandable paranoid symptoms; (c) paranoid hallucinosis in which paranoid beliefs are based solely on pathological perceptions. These clinical groups are not specially useful because they do not differ in aetiology, social characteristics, or outcome.

Aetiology

In schizophrenia and paranoid states of the elderly, the same aetiological factors apply as in younger adults (pp. 246 and 274). However, certain causal factors may apply particularly in old age. Thus Kay and Roth (1961) found that, compared with patients with affective disorder, significantly more late paraphrenics were living alone at the onset of illness, and were 'socially isolated' as a result of deafness, abnormalities of personality, and lack of surviving relatives.

Differential diagnosis

Schizophrenia is diagnosed by the same criteria as in younger patients (see p. 245). In paranoid states, there are persecutory delusions, but no demonstrable underlying primary disorder. Both conditions have to be differentiated from organic mental disorders, affective disorders, and paranoid personality. In organic mental disorder, cognitive impairment is detectable and visual hallucinations are more likely. In affective disorder, the mood disturbance is more profound, and the persecutory delusions are usually associated with ideas of guilt. In paranoid personality there are lifelong suspiciousness and distrust, with sensitive ideas but no delusions (p. 275).

Treatment

In old age, the general principles of treatment are as described in Chapters 9 and 10. Outpatient treatment is sometimes suitable, but for adequate assessment an inpatient admission is usually required. Compulsory admission may be indicated at times. A few patients improve on admission, and remain well on discharge if social help is provided. Most patients require anti-psychotic medication, usually with a phenothiazine, occasionally with a butyrophenone. The dosage should be about half that for younger adults. If there are doubts about a patient's likelihood of continuing medication, and if there is no one to supervise, a depot preparation should be considered. Attendance at a day hospital or centre may be needed to ensure adequate supervision.

FURTHER READING

Birren, J.E. and Sloane, R.B. (1980). *Handbook of mental health and ageing.* Prentice Hall, Englewood Cliffs, New Jersey.

Levy, R. and Post, F. (1982). *The psychiatry of late life.* Blackwell Scientific Publications, Oxford.

Roth, M. (1955). The natural history of mental disorder in old age. *Journal of Mental Science* **101**, 281–301.

Royal College of Physicians (1981). Organic mental impairment in the elderly. Report of the College Committee on Geriatrics. *Journal of the Royal College of Physicians* **15**, 141–67.

17. Drugs and other physical treatments

This chapter is concerned with the use of drugs, electroconvulsive therapy, and psychosurgical procedures. Psychological treatments are the subject of the next chapter. This separation, although convenient when treatments are described, does not imply that the two kinds of therapy are to be thought of as alternatives when an individual patient is considered; on the contrary many patients require both. In this book, the ways of combining treatments are considered in other chapters where the treatment of individual syndromes is discussed. It is important to keep this point in mind when reading this chapter and the next.

Our concern is with clinical therapeutics rather than basic psychopharmacology which the reader is assumed to have studied already. An adequate knowledge of the mechanisms of drug action is essential if drugs are to be used in a rational way, but some words of caution are appropriate. The clinician should not assume that the therapeutic effects of psychotropic drugs are necessarily explained by the pharmacological actions that have been discovered so far. The substantial delay in the effects of antidepressant and antipsychotic drugs suggests that their actions on transmitters, which occur rapidly, may turn out to be only the first steps in a chain of biochemical changes. Moreover, if a drug is known to have a particular action (such as blocking dopamine receptors) it cannot be assumed that a disease controlled by this drug necessarily results from an opposite effect (such as excessive dopaminergic function). Thus Parkinson's disease is relieved by anticholinergic drugs even though the primary disorder is one of dopaminergic rather than cholinergic function. Equally, because a drug acts at a particular site in the nervous system, it cannot be assumed that the disease process lies there: diuretics, which improve heart failure, act on the kidney not on the heart.

These cautions do not imply that a knowledge of pharmacological mechanisms has no bearing on psychiatric therapeutics. On the contrary, there have been substantial advances in pharmacological knowledge since the first psychotropic drugs were introduced in the 1950s, and it is increasingly important for the clinician to relate this knowledge to his use of drugs.

GENERAL CONSIDERATIONS

The pharmacokinetics of psychotropic drugs

Before psychotropic drugs can produce their therapeutic effects, they must reach the brain in adequate amounts. How far they do so depends on their absorption, metabolism, excretion, and passage across the blood–brain barrier. A short review of these processes is given here. The reader who has not studied them before should consult the monograph by Goldstein *et al.* (1974).

In general, psychotropic drugs are easily **absorbed** from the gut because most are lipophilic and are not highly ionized at physiological pH. Like other drugs, they are absorbed faster from an empty stomach, and in smaller amounts by patients suffering from intestinal hurry, malabsorption syndrome, or the effects of a previous partial gastrectomy.

Most psychotropic drugs are **metabolized** in the liver. This process begins as the drugs pass through the liver in the portal circulation on their way from the gut. This 'first-pass' metabolism reduces the amount of available drug, and is one of the reasons why smaller doses are needed when a drug such as chlorpromazine is given intramuscularly. The extent of this liver metabolism differs from one person to another. It is altered by certain other drugs which, if taken at the same time, induce liver enzymes (for example barbiturates) or inhibit them (for example monoamine oxidase inhibitors). Some drugs, such as chlorpromazine, actually induce their own metabolism, especially after being taken for a long time. Not all drug metabolites are inactive: for example chlorpromazine is metabolized to a 7-hydroxy derivative which has therapeutic properties, as well as to a sulphoxide which is inactive. Because chlorpromazine, diazepam, and many other psychotropic drugs give rise to many metabolites, measurements of plasma concentrations of the parent drug are a poor guide to therapeutic activity.

Psychotropic drugs are **distributed** in the plasma, where most are largely bound to proteins; thus diazepam, chlorpromazine, and amitriptyline are about 95 per cent bound. They pass easily from the plasma to the brain because they are highly lipophilic. For the same reason they enter fat stores, from which they are released slowly long after the patient has ceased to take the drug.

The **excretion** of most psychotropic drugs and their metabolites is mainly through the kidney. When kidney function is impaired, excretion is reduced and a lower dose of drug should be given. For basic or acidic drugs, renal excretion depends on the pH of the urine: for example amphetamine, a weak base, is excreted more rapidly when the urine is acid rather than alkaline. Lithium is filtered passively and then partly reabsorbed by the same mechanism that absorbs sodium. The two ions compete for this mechanism; hence reabsorption of lithium increases when that of sodium is reduced. Certain fractions of lipophilic drugs such as chlorpromazine are partly excreted in the bile, enter the intestine for the second time, and are then partly reabsorbed; that is, a proportion of the drug is recycled between intestine and liver.

Measurement of circulating drug concentrations

As a result of the mechanisms described above, plasma concentrations after standard doses of psychotropic drugs vary substantially from one patient to another. Tenfold differences have been observed with the antidepressant drug nortriptyline. It might be expected, therefore, that measurements of the plasma concentration of circulating drugs would help the clinician. There are several reasons why this is seldom the case. The most important reason is that the relationship between plasma concentration and clinical effects is variable. The second reason is that, as already noted, most psychotropic drugs are substantially bound to plasma proteins. Assays measure the total drug concentration but the free fraction is more important; and the ratio of free to bound drug varies in different patients. The third reason has also been mentioned above: many drugs have metabolites, some of which have therapeutic effects while others do not. Some assays are too specific, measuring only the parent drug but not its active derivatives; others are too general, measuring active and inactive metabolites alike.

As an alternative to these assays, measurements can be made of the pharmacological property thought to be responsible for the therapeutic effect. This has been tried with the neuroleptics by measuring dopamine receptor blocking activity. Such methods are still experimental. Indeed it is only with the simplest psychotropic agent, lithium, that plasma concentrations are sufficiently useful to be measured routinely, and then only to avoid toxic effects.

Plasma concentrations vary throughout the day, rising immediately after the dose and falling at a rate that differs between individual drugs and people. The rate at which a drug level declines after a single dose varies from hours with lithium carbonate to weeks with slow release preparations of injectable neuroleptics. Knowledge of these differences allows more rational decisions about appropriate intervals between doses.

Drug interactions

When two psychotropic drugs are given together, one may interfere with the actions of the other. This interference may arise through alterations in absorption, binding, metabolism, or excretion; or by interference between pharmacodynamic effects.

For psychotropic drugs, interactions affecting drug absorption are seldom important, although absorption of chlorpromazine is reduced by antacids. Likewise interactions due to protein binding are uncommon, although the chloral metabolite trichloracetic acid may displace warfarin from albumin. Interactions affecting drug metabolism are of considerable importance. Examples include the inhibition of the metabolism of sympathomimetic amines by monoamine oxidase inhibitors, and the increase in metabolism of chlorpromazine and tricyclic antidepressants by barbiturates which induce the relevant enzymes. Interactions affecting renal excretion are mainly important for lithium, the elimination of which is increased by acetazolamide, aminophylline, and sodium bicarbonate. Pharmacodynamic interactions are exemplified by the antagonism of guanethidine and tricyclic antidepressants.

As a rule, a single drug can be used to produce all the effects required of a combination; for example many tricyclic antidepressants have anti-anxiety effects. It is desirable to avoid combinations of psychotropic drugs whenever possible; if a combination is to be used, it is essential to know about possible interactions.

Drug withdrawal

Many psychotropic drugs do not achieve their full effects for several days and antidepressants may take up to three weeks. After drugs have been stopped there is often a comparable delay before their effects are lost. With some drugs, tissues have to readjust when treatment is stopped; this appears clinically as a withdrawal syndrome. Among the psychotropic drugs, the hypnotics and anxiolytics are most likely to induce this kind of effect. After withdrawal of hypnotic drugs, readjustments are shown clinically in the experience of poor sleep, and physiologically in an increase in rapid eye movement (REM) sleep. These changes occur, for example, when large doses of nitrazepam are stopped; withdrawal from smaller doses results in sleep disturbance without a rebound of REM (Adam *et al.* 1976). Unless the symptoms are recognized as due to drug withdrawal, it may be wrongly concluded from the sleep disturbance that the patient still needs a hypnotic. There is less certainty about the frequency of withdrawal symptoms when benzodiazepines are used as daytime anxiolytics. Anxiety, apprehension, tremor, insomnia, nausea, and vomiting have all been reported three to ten days after stopping the drug, but it is difficult to decide whether these are withdrawal symptoms or the residue of an anxiety neurosis. It is best to follow the advice of the Committee on the Review of Medicines (1980): all benzodiazepines should be withdrawn gradually; and whenever a prescription is about to be repeated, the possibility should be considered that remaining symptoms are those of drug withdrawal. The Committee also recommended that treatment with benzodiazepines should not exceed six weeks.

General advice about prescribing psychotropic drugs

It is good practice to use well-tried drugs with therapeutic actions and side effects that are thoroughly understood. The clinician should become familiar with a small number of drugs from each of the main groups – two or three antidepressants, two or three antipsychotics, and so on. In this way he can become used to adjusting the dosage and recognizing side effects. (Advice about drugs of choice will be found in the later part of this chapter.) Well-tried drugs are usually less expensive than new preparations.

Having chosen a suitable drug, the doctor should prescribe it in adequate doses. He should not change the drug or add others without a good reason. In general, if there is no therapeutic response to one established drug, there is no likelihood of a better response to another from the same therapeutic group (provided that the first drug has been taken in adequate amounts). However, since the main obstacle to adequate dosage is usually side effects, it is sometimes appropriate to change to a drug with a different pattern of side effects – for example, from one tricyclic antidepressant to another with fewer anticholinergic effects.

Some drug companies market tablets that contain a mixture of drugs: for example, tricyclic antidepressants with a small dose of a phenothiazine. These mixtures have little value. In the few cases when two drugs are really required, it is better to give them separately so that the dose of each can be adjusted independently.

Occasionally, drug combinations are given deliberately in the hope of producing interactions that will be more potent than the effects of either drug taken alone in full dosage (for example a tricyclic antidepressant with a mono-amine oxidase inhibitor). This practice, if it is to be used at all, should only be carried out by specialists because the adverse effects of combinations are much less easy to predict than those of single drugs. In any case, as explained later, there is little or no evidence that such combinations of psychotropic drugs are more effective than a single drug given in full dosage.

When a drug is prescribed, it is necessary to determine the dose, the interval between doses, and the likely duration of treatment. The dose-ranges for commonly used drugs are indicated later in this chapter. Ranges for others will be found in the manufacturers' literature, the British National Formulary or another work of reference. Within the therapeutic range, the correct dose for an individual patient should be decided after considering the severity of symptoms, and the patient's age, weight, and any factors that may affect drug metabolism (for example other drugs being taken; or renal disease).

Next the interval between doses must be decided. Psychotropic drugs are often given three times a day, even though their duration of action is such that most can be taken once or twice a day without any undesirable fall in plasma concentrations between doses. Outpatients are more likely to be reliable in taking drugs that have to be taken once or twice instead of three or four times a day. In hospital, less frequent drug rounds mean that nurses have more time for psychological aspects of treatment. Some anxiolytic drugs are required for immediate effects rather than continuous action; it is then usually best to give them shortly before occasions on which symptoms are expected to be at their worst.

Before giving a patient a first prescription for a drug, the doctor should explain several points. He should make clear what effects are likely to be experienced on first taking the drug – for example drowsiness or dry mouth. He should also explain how long it will be before therapeutic effects appear and what the first signs are likely to be – for example improved sleep after a tricyclic antidepressant. He should name any serious effects that must be reported by the patient, such as coarse tremor after taking lithium. Finally he should indicate how long the patient will need to take the drug. For some drugs such as anxio-lytics, the latter information is given to discourage the patient from taking them for too long; for others, such as antidepressants, it is given to deter the patient from stopping too soon.

Compliance with treatment

Many patients do not take the drugs prescribed for them. This problem is greater when treating outpatients, but it also occurs in hospital where some patients find ways of avoiding drugs administered by nurses.

If a patient is to comply with medication of any kind, he must be convinced that he needs it, free from unfounded fears about its dangers, and informed how to take it. Each of these requirements presents particular problems when the patient has a psychiatric disorder. Thus, schizophrenic or seriously depressed patients may not be convinced that they are ill or they may not wish to recover. Deluded patients may distrust their doctors, and hypochondriacal patients may fear dangerous side-effects. Anxious patients often forget the prescribed dosage and frequency of their drugs. It is not surprising, therefore, that many psychiatric patients do not take their drugs in the prescribed way. It is important for the clinician to give attention to this problem. Time spent in discussing the patient's concerns is time well spent, for it often increases compliance (For a comprehensive review of patients' compliance with treatment, see Haynes *et al.* 1979.)

The overprescribing of psychotropic drugs

In the last thirty years, many safe and effective drugs have been produced for the treatment of psychiatric disorders. Unfortunately, their proven value in severe conditions has led to unnecessary prescribing for mild cases that would recover without medication. Similarly, the safety of these drugs has sometimes encouraged prolonged prescribing when brief treatment would be more appropriate. These problems have arisen most often with drugs prescribed for insomnia, anxiety, and depression. All three symptoms are important components of psychiatric illness, but in their mildest form they are also part of everyday life. The extent of usage of anxiolytic and antidepressant drugs was shown by a survey of all prescriptions issued in general practices serving 40 000 people (Skegg *et al.* 1977). It was found that psychotropic drugs were prescribed more often than any others. Amongst patients registered in the practices, nearly 10 per cent of men and over 20 per cent of women received at least one prescription for a psychotropic drug during the course of a year. In women aged 45–49, one-third received such a prescription.

While there are important implications about the amount of drugs consumed through these high rates of prescribing, it is equally important to remember that many prescribed drugs are not taken. Nicholson (1967) collected unused drugs from about 500 patients' houses in the course of six days. He recovered 36 000 tablets, of which nearly 5000 were sedatives and tranquillizers, over 2000 were hypnotics and 750 were antidepressants. Unused drugs are a danger to children and a potential source of supply for self-poisoning either by the patient or by other people. For these reasons patients should not be given more drugs than they need, and care should be taken to enquire whether existing supplies have been used before prescribing more.

Prescribing for special groups

The psychiatric problems of **children** seldom require medication. When they do, doses must be adjusted appropriately (advice on this is given in the British National Formulary). It is also important to start with low doses for **elderly** patients, who are often sensitive to side-effects and may have impaired renal or hepatic function. It is prudent to avoid drug treatment in the first trimester of **pregnancy** even with drugs that have not been shown conclusively to increase the incidence of fetal abnormalities in human beings. The medication of mothers who are **breast-feeding** should be reviewed, especially if the baby appears drowsy or unwell. Little information is available about the passage of individual drugs into breast milk. Lithium concentrations are probably up to half those in plasma. Diazepam, chloral, and chlorpromazine have been found in amounts sufficient to cause drowsiness (see Savage (1976) and *Drugs and Therapeutics Bulletin* (1983)).

What to do if there is no therapeutic response

The first step is to find out whether the patient has been taking the drug in the correct dose. He may not have understood the original instructions, or may be worried that a full dose will produce unpleasant effects. Some patients fear they will become dependent if they take the drug regularly. Other patients have little wish to take drugs because they do not regard themselves as ill – a problem presented by many schizophrenics. If the doctor is satisfied that the drug has been taken correctly, he should find out whether the patient is taking any other drug (such as a barbiturate) which could affect the metabolism of the psychotropic agent. Finally, he should review the diagnosis to make sure that the treatment is appropriate before deciding whether to increase the dose.

The evaluation of psychotropic drugs

After being tested in animals, new drugs have to be evaluated for clinical use. This requires two stages. First, the drug is used cautiously at doses sufficient to give a therapeutic effect without unwanted effects. Then, controlled clinical trials are carried out in which the drug is compared, under double-blind conditions, with a placebo or standard drug. The methodology of clinical trials should be familiar to readers; those seeking information should consult Harris and Fitzgerald (1970). This chapter is concerned only with a few essential points that need to be kept in mind when reading a report of a trial of a new psychotropic drug. These points concern patients, treatments, and measurements.

Patients

In any clinical trial the patients have been selected, and the clinician has to decide how far they are typical of the disorder as a whole (for example schizophrenia) and how far they resemble patients he wishes to treat (for example chronic schizophrenics undergoing rehabilitation). Part of the selection procedure will have been reported by the research workers, but often other parts are not stated explicitly. Thus if a trial is restricted to hospital outpatients, it is necessary to consider what kinds of patients are likely to be referred to the particular hospital by the local general practitioners. For example, it might be important to know whether most depressed patients are referred, or only those who have not responded to adequate antidepressant treatment. If the latter, a hospital-based trial will be dealing with drug-resistant patients.

The reader should next consider how diagnoses have been made and whether a standard and generally accepted method has been used. The next questions are: how many of the patients originally referred to the trial were rejected; of those accepted, how many dropped out; and were they replaced? Another important issue is how the patients would have fared without treatment. This applies particularly to any trial not including a placebo condition. In these circumstances, if patients treated with the new drug improve as much as those treated with a standard preparation, this may merely indicate that the patients selected for the investigation have a high rate of spontaneous recovery. A final point to check is whether allocation of patients to the various treatments has been random.

The treatments

The first questions concern dosage, intervals between doses, whether the same quantity of drugs was given to every patients, and whether additional drugs were allowed. It is important to decide whether the treatments were given for long enough. Nearly all clinical trials include precautions to ensure that neither patients nor staff can tell which treatment any one patient is receiving (the 'double-blind' trial). Identical tablets do not always achieve this aim because side effects, such as dry mouth, tremor, or postural hypotension, can provide clues to the identity of one or more treatments. The reader should therefore study the frequency and pattern of side effects reported by each group of patients.

It is also important to know what precautions have been taken to ensure that patients took the drugs prescribed for them. These precautions include counting any tablets remaining at the end of each treatment period; measuring blood plasma levels; and incorporating in the tablets a marker substance, such as riboflavine, that can be detected in urine more easily than the drug itself.

The measurements

When assessment methods are chosen for a clinical trial, a balance has to be struck between precision and reliability on the one hand, and clinical relevance on the other. Psychological test scores may be reliable and precise, but they seldom relate in a simple way to judgements made in everday clinical work. Psychiatric rating scales are less precise and reliable but more relevant. The reader should also consider whether the assessments are sensitive within the range of changes to be expected in the trial: thus measures developed for use with severely depressed patients treated in hospital may not be appropriate for a study of minor depressive disorders in general practice. The timing of assessments should also be considered; for example, whether they began sufficiently early and were continued long enough. Finally the appropriateness of the statistical methods should be reviewed. If statistically significant changes are reported, it is important to decide whether they are big enough to justify a change to new treatment.

THE CLASSIFICATION OF DRUGS USED IN PSYCHIATRY

Drugs that have effects mainly on mental symptoms are called psychotropic. Psychiatrists often use two other groups of drugs: anti-parkinsonian agents, which are employed to control the side effects of some psychotropic drugs, and anti-epileptic drugs.

The psychotropic drugs are divided into five groups (Table 17.1). **Anxiolytic** drugs reduce anxiety. They are sometimes called minor tranquillizers because

Table 17.1. *Classification of drugs used commonly in psychiatry*

(a) *Psychotropic*
  Anxiolytic
  Hypnotic
  Antipsychotic
  Antidepressant
  Stimulant

(b) *Others*
  Anti-parkinsonian
  Anti-epileptic

they have a calming effect, though not powerful enough to calm severely ill schizophrenic or manic patients (drugs that calm such patients are sometimes called major tranquillizers). In large doses anxiolytics produce drowsiness; hence they were formerly called sedatives. In still larger doses they promote sleep, so that the anxiolytic group overlaps with the **hypnotic group.** The next group comprises **antidepressant** drugs, which relieve the symptoms of depressive illness, although they do not affect the mood of healthy people. Drugs with the latter effect are called central nervous **stimulants;** they have little use in psychiatric practice. **Antipsychotic** agents control some of the symptoms of schizophrenia, mania, and organic psychoses. As already noted, they are sometimes called major tranquillizers; and because of their side effects they are also referred to as neuroleptics.

Not all the drugs used in psychiatry fit into this scheme. Lithium carbonate has some effect against depression and controls the symptoms of mania, but its main use is to prevent relapses of these conditions. Disulfiram and citrated calcium carbimide are used in the treatment of alcoholism; hormones and vitamins have some special uses; and antibiotics are used for cerebral syphilis and other bacterial infections of the brain. However the scheme of classification is useful, not least because it corresponds to that in the British National Formulary which is a standard source of information about specific drugs.

The five main groups of drugs will now be reviewed in turn. For each group, an account will be given of therapeutic effects, pharmacology, principal compounds available, pharmacokinetics, unwanted effects (both those appearing with ordinary doses and the toxic effects of unduly high doses) and contraindications. General advice will also be given about the use of each group in everday clinical practice, but specific applications to the treatment of individual disorders will be found in the chapters dealing with these conditions. Drugs that have a limited use in the treatment of a single disorder, for example disulfiram for alcohol problems, are discussed in the chapters dealing with the relevant clinical syndromes.

ANXIOLYTIC DRUGS

Drugs that are anxiolytic in small doses produce drowsiness and sleep when given in large amounts. They are prescribed widely and often inappropriately. Before prescribing these drugs it is always important to seek the causes of anxiety and to try to modify them. It is also essential to recognize that a degree of anxiety can motivate patients to take steps to reduce problems that are causing it. Hence removing all anxiety is not always beneficial to the patient in the long run. Anxiolytics are most useful when given for a short time either to tide the patient over a crisis or to help him tackle a specific problem. Tolerance probably develops sooner or later to all anxiolytic sedatives. Because the benzodiazepines are now the most widely used anxiolytics, they will be considered first. Other compounds will then be described in less detail.

Benzodiazepines

Pharmacology

Benzodiazepines are anxiolytic, sedative, and, in large doses, hypnotic. They also have muscle relaxant and anticonvulsant properties. They appear to act mainly on the reticular and limbic system and have less effect on the cortex. These actions may be related to their property of potentiating the inhibitory neurotransmitter gamma-aminobutyric acid (GABA) although they also affect 5-hydroxytryptamine and dopamine mechanisms.

Compounds available

Research in commercial laboratories has produced many variants on the basic benzodiazepine structure, but the resulting drugs are similar in their actions. The clinician needs only two compounds: one with a short action and one with a long action. The short-acting compounds, which include oxazepam, lorazepam, temazepam, and triazolam, are more appropriate when a brief action is required. Long-acting compounds, which include diazepam, chlordiazepoxide, nitrazepam, clobazam, and chlorazepate, are more appropriate when a sustained action is needed. An appropriate pair of drugs is lorazepam 3–10 mg per day in divided doses, and diazepam 6–30 mg per day in divided doses. It is conventional to use nitrazepam as a hypnotic, but it is generally more rational to use a shorter acting drug to avoid residual effects next day.

Pharmacokinetics

Benzodiazepines are rapidly absorbed. They are highly bound to plasma proteins but, because they are lipophilic, pass rapidly into the brain. They are metabolized to a large number of compounds, many of which have therapeutic effects of their own: for example, temazepam and oxazepam are among the metabolic products of diazepam. Excretion is mainly as conjugates in the urine (see Schwartz (1973) for a review).

Unwanted effects

Benzodiazepines are well tolerated. When they are given as anxiolytics, their main side effects are due to the sedative properties of large doses, which can lead to ataxia and drowsiness (especially in the elderly) and occasionally to confused thinking. Minor degrees of drowsiness and of impaired co-ordination and judgement can affect driving skills and the operation of potentially dangerous machinery; moreover people affected in this way are not always aware of it (Betts *et al.* 1972). For this reason, when benzodiazepines are prescribed, especially those with a longer action, patients should be advised about these dangers and about the potentiating effects of alcohol. The prescriber should remember that these effects are more common among elderly patients and those with impaired renal or liver function. Although in some circumstances benzodiazepines reduce tension and aggression, in certain doses they lead to a release of aggression by reducing inhibitions in people with a tendency to aggressive behaviour (DiMascio 1973). In this they resemble alcohol. This possible effect should be remembered when prescribing to women judged to be at risk of child abuse.

Toxic effects

Benzodiazepines have few toxic effects. Patients recover from large overdosages because these drugs do not depress respiration and blood pressure as barbiturates do. No convincing evidence of teratogenic effects has been reported, but it is wise to avoid prescribing in the first trimester of pregnancy unless there is a strong indication.

Drug interactions

Benzodiazepines, like other sedative-anxiolytics, potentiate the effects of alcohol and of drugs that depress the central nervous system.

Effects of withdrawal

It is not certain whether physical dependence develops after prolonged use of benzodiazepines, but there is increasing evidence that it may do so (Committee on the Review of Medicines 1980). About 24 hours after stopping short-acting compounds and three to ten days after stopping long acting ones, some patients experience apprehension, tremor, nausea, and insomnia for a few days. Although these symptoms strongly suggest withdrawal effects, they could be the residue of the original anxiety state at least in some patients. Nevertheless it is wise to withdraw the drugs gradually if they have been used for a long time.

Other drugs used to treat anxiety

Beta-adrenoceptor antagonists

These drugs relieve some of the autonomic symptoms of anxiety, such as tachycardia, almost certainly by a peripheral effect (see Bonn *et al.* 1972). They are best reserved for anxious patients whose main complaint is of tachycardia or tremor that does not respond to benzodiazepines. An appropriate drug is propranolol in a dose of 40 mg three times a day. Contraindications are heart block, systolic blood pressure below 90 mm Hg, or a pulse rate less than 60 per minute; history of bronchospasm; metabolic acidosis, for example in diabetes; and after prolonged fasting, as in anorexia nervosa. Great caution is needed if there are signs of poor cardiac reserve. Beta-adrenoceptor antagonists precipitate heart failure in a few patients and should not be given to those with atrioventricular node block as they decrease conduction in the A–V node and bundle of His. They can cause severe bronchospasm and exacerbate both Raynaud's phenomenon and intermittent claudication. In diabetics they may cause hypoglycaemia.

Phenothiazines

These are sometimes prescribed for their anxiolytic effects. In doses that do not lead to side effects, they are generally no more effective than benzodiazepines. Nevertheless, as anxiolytics phenothiazines have a small place in the treatment of two groups of patients – those with persistent anxiety who have become dependent on other drugs, and those with aggressive personalities who respond badly to the disinhibiting effects of other anxiolytics.

Tricyclic antidepressants

These drugs are appropriate treatment for the anxiety that often accompanies a depressive disorder. Sometimes sedative tricyclics are used for their anxiolytic effects in patients who are not suffering from depressive illness. These drugs are also worth trying for patients whose chronic anxiety states have not responded to benzodiazepines.

Barbiturates and other sedative anxiolytics

In the past barbiturates were widely used as anxiolytics. Although effective, they readily cause dependency. They should now be used only for the rare cases in which extremely severe anxiety does not respond to a benzodiazepine, and even then they should be given for a few days only. Amylobarbitone sodium, 60 mg two or three times a day, is a suitable drug for this occasional use. Phenobarbitone was much used against anxiety in the past, but has now been completely superseded by the benzodiazepines. The **sedative antihistamine** hydroxyzine is sometimes used in geriatric practice but has no obvious general advantage as an anxiolytic agent. It has powerful antihistaminic and weak anticholinergic effects, and is antiemetic. **Propanediols** such as meprobamate have no advantages over benzodiazepines, and are more sedative in the doses needed to relieve anxiety.

Unwanted effects

These resemble those of the benzodiazepines and generally appear at doses nearer to the anxiolytic dose. Barbiturates may produce irritability, drowsiness, and ataxia.

Toxic effects

In large doses sedative anxiolytics depress respiration and reduce blood pressure. This is particularly a problem with the barbiturates.

Drug interactions

These resemble those of the benzodiazepines. In addition, barbiturates interact with coumarin drugs and reduce their anticoagulant action. They also increase the metabolism of tricyclic antidepressants and tetracycline.

Effects of withdrawal

These resemble the effects of withdrawing benzodiazepines, described above. After stopping barbiturates the effects are particularly marked in the form of psychological tension, sweating, tremor, irritability, and, after large doses, seizures. Hence barbiturates should not be stopped suddenly if the dose has been substantial.

Advice on management

Before prescribing an anxiolytic drug, the cause of the anxiety should always be sought. For most patients, attention to life problems, an opportunity to talk about their feelings, and reassurance from the doctor are enough to reduce anxiety to tolerable levels. If an anxiolytic is needed, it should be given for a short time – seldom more than three weeks – and withdrawn gradually. It is important to remember that dependency is particularly likely to develop among people with alcohol problems. If the drug has been taken for several weeks, the patient should be warned that he may feel tense for a few days when it is stopped.

The drug of choice is a benzodiazepine. A short-acting compound should be chosen if anxiety is intermittent, a long-acting one if it lasts throughout the day. The prescriber should become familiar with one preparation from each group, preferably the least expensive, and should thoroughly understand its effects. The other drugs should be kept for the specific purposes outlined above: beta adrenoceptor antagonists for control of palpitations and tremor caused by anxiety and not responding to benzodiazepines; phenothiazines for patients who respond badly to the disinhibiting effects of sedative-anxiolytics (for example abnormally aggressive patients), or for patients who have become dependent upon them; and sedative tricyclics in small doses for persistent chronic anxiety unresponsive to other drugs. Monoamine oxidase inhibitors are anxiolytic, but should not be used as such because of the risks of interactions with other drugs and foodstuffs (see p. 549).

HYPNOTICS

Hypnotics are drugs used to improve sleep. Many anxiolytic sedatives also act as hypnotics, and they have been reviewed in the previous section. Hypnotic drugs are prescribed widely and often continued for too long. This reflects the frequency of insomnia as a complaint. Mendelson (1980) found that about a third of American adults reported disturbed sleep, and a third of these described it as a major problem. Insomnia is reported more often by women and by the elderly.

Pharmacology

The ideal hypnotic would increase the length and quality of sleep without residual effects the next morning. It would do so without altering the pattern of sleep and without any withdrawal effects when the patient ceased to take it. Unfortunately, no drug meets these exacting criteria. It is not easy to produce drugs that affect the whole night's sleep and yet have been eliminated sufficiently by morning to leave behind no sedative effects. Moreover most drugs alter the electrophysiological characteristics of sleep while they are being taken and for some nights after they have been stopped. Thus hypnotic drugs affect the pattern of the EEG; they suppress rapid eye movement (REM) sleep while they are taken, and lead to an increase of REM sleep up to several weeks after they have been stopped. These latter changes are often reflected in reports of disturbed sleep.

Compounds available

Nowadays the most commonly used hypnotics are benzodiazepines. In the past, barbiturates were prescribed most frequently, but are very rarely used now. Among the many other drugs available, chloral hydrate, chlormethiazole, and glutethimide are the commonest.

Of the **benzodiazepines**, nitrazepam, flurazepam, temazepam, and triazolam are commonly used as hypnotics. The first two are long-acting and more liable to produce hangover effects. The last two are short-acting drugs appropriate for initial insomnia. Any of the other benzodiazepines can be used as a hypnotic taken as a single dose at night.

Barbiturates are conveniently divided into long-, medium-, and short-acting drugs. Only the second group is appropriate for insomnia, the long-acting compounds being used for epilepsy and anaesthesia. Except in rare cases when other drugs have failed, barbiturates should not be used to treat insomnia. Amylobarbitone, amylobarbitone sodium, butobarbitone, and quinalbarbitone are examples of compounds used as hypnotics.

Other hypnotic drugs include **chloral hydrate**, which is sometimes prescribed for children and old people. It is a gastric irritant and should be diluted adequately. **Dichloralphenazone** is related to chloral but is less irritant. **Chlormethiazole edisylate** is a hypnotic drug with anticonvulsant properties. It is often used to prevent withdrawal symptoms in patients dependent on alcohol. For this reason it is sometimes thought, mistakenly, to be a suitable hypnotic for alcoholic patients. This belief is wrong because the drug is as likely to cause dependency as any other hypnotic drug. Although an effective hypnotic, **glutethimide** is toxic in overdosage and for this reason should not be prescribed except in small amounts (see *British Medical Journal* 1976).

Pharmacokinetics

The metabolism and excretion of benzodiazepines has been described already. Barbiturates, the other important group of hypnotics, vary somewhat in their patterns of metabolism and excretion. Long-acting barbiturates are more water-soluble and less lipid-soluble than the medium-acting compounds, and are therefore largely excreted unchanged through the kidneys. Medium-acting compounds are largely metabolized in the liver and subsequently excreted as conjugated hydroxyl compounds. Barbiturates induce the enzymes by which they are themselves metabolized; they also induce liver enzymes that metabolize other drugs (see below).

Unwanted effects

The most important unwanted effects of hypnotics are their residual effects. These are experienced by the patient on the next day as feelings of being slow and drowsy. Psychological tests of reaction time have shown deficits in the afternoon after a single bed-time dose of a barbiturate or long-acting benzodiazepine (e.g. Bond and Lader 1973). The subject is not always aware of these impairments, which may be serious for work involving potentially dangerous machinery or for driving motor vehicles, trains, or aeroplanes. People who sleep badly often make similar complaints after a poor night in which they did not take hypnotics; but these subjective feelings are not accompanied by comparable impairments of performance on psychological tests. The complaints may reflect the cause of insomnia (for example depression, or over indulgence in alcohol on the previous day) rather than the loss of sleep itself.

Contraindications

Barbiturates and dichloralphenazone should not be given to patients suffering from acute intermittent porphyria.

Drug interactions

The most important interaction is with alcohol. At first the two potentiate one another, sometimes to a dangerous extent. After prolonged usage, a degree of cross-tolerance develops; however, persistent abuse of alcohol may damage the liver and so increase sensitivity to hypnotic drugs by reducing their metabolism. With the longer-acting benzodiazepines the alcohol-potentiating effect may last well into the day after the drug was taken (Saario *et al.* 1975). Barbiturates increase the metabolism of other drugs including anticoagulants, tricyclic antidepressants, and tetracycline.

Advice on management

Before prescribing hypnotic drugs it is important to find out whether the patient is really sleeping badly and if so, why. Many people have unrealistic ideas about the number of hours they should sleep. For example, they may not know that length of sleep often becomes shorter in middle and late life. Others take 'cat naps' in the daytime, perhaps through boredom, and still expect to sleep as long at night. Some people ask for sleeping tablets in anticipation of poor sleep for one or two nights, for example when travelling. Such temporary loss of sleep is soon compensated by increased sleep on subsequent nights; and any supposed advantage in alertness after a full night's sleep is likely to be offset by the residual effects of the drugs. If a drug is justifiable in these circumstances it should be a short-acting benzodiazepine.

Among the common causes of disturbed sleep are excessive caffeine or alcohol; pain, cough, pruritus, and dyspnoea; anxiety and depression. When any primary cause is present, this should be treated, not the insomnia. If, after careful enquiry, a hypnotic appears to be essential, it should be prescribed for a few days only. The clinician should explain this to the patient, and should warn him that a few nights of restless sleep may occur when the drugs are stopped, but this will not be a reason for prolonging the prescription.

For children the prescription of hypnotics is not justified, except for the occasional treatment of night terrors and somnambulism. Hypnotics should also be prescribed with particular care for the elderly, who may become confused and get out of bed in the night perhaps injuring themselves. Many patients are started on long periods of dependency on hypnotics by the prescribing of 'routine night sedation' in hospital. Prescription of these drugs should *not* be routine; it should only be a response to a real need, and should be stopped before the patient goes home.

ANTIPSYCHOTIC DRUGS

This term is applied to drugs that reduce psychomotor excitement and control some symptoms of schizophrenia without causing disinhibition, confusion, or sleep. Alternative terms for these drugs are **neuroleptic, anti-schizophrenic,** and **major tranquillizer.** None of these names is wholly satisfactory. Neuroleptic refers to the side-effects of the drugs rather than their therapeutic effects; major tranquillizer does not refer to the most important clinical action; and anti-schizophrenic suggests a more specific action than the drugs really possess. The term antipsychotic is used here because it appears in the *British National Formulary.*

The main therapeutic uses of antipsychotic drugs are to reduce hallucinations, delusions, agitation and psychomotor excitement in schizophrenia, organic psychosis, or mania. They are also used prophylactically to prevent relapses of schizophrenia. In 1952 the introduction of chlorpromazine led to substantial improvements in the treatment of schizophrenia, and paved the way to the discovery of the many psychotropic drugs now available.

Pharmacology

Antipsychotic drugs share the property of blocking dopamine receptors. This may account for their therapeutic action, a suggestion supported by the close relationship between their potency in blocking dopaminergic mechanisms *in vitro* and their therapeutic strength. It is also supported by the finding that, of the two stereo-isomers of flupenthixol, the alpha isomer blocks dopamine receptors and is therapeutic, while the beta isomer does not block dopamine receptors and is not therapeutic. Both alpha and beta isomers block noradrenergic and cholinergic receptors. These anti-adrenergic and anti-cholinergic actions account for many of the side effects of the drugs, while the antidopaminergic actions on basal ganglia are responsible for the extra-pyramidal side effects. Drugs that lead to fewer extrapyramidal side effects have anticholinergic actions which appear to exert an 'in-built' antiparkinsonian activity.

Compounds available

A large number of antipsychotic compounds have been developed. Some, like chlorpromazine, are phenothiazines. They differ from one another in the nature of the side chain and the radical in the 2 position (see Table 17.2 for examples). Others are thioxanthenes (thiothixine, flupenthixol), butyro-phenones (haloperidol) (Table 17.3) or diphenylbutylpiperidines (pimozide). The various compounds differ more in their side effects than in their therapeutic properties. An account of the relations between structure and function is given by Shepherd *et al.* (1968).

Phenothiazines fall into three groups, according to the side-chain attached to the 10 position (R_1 in Table 17.2). Aminoalkyl compounds such as chlorproma-

Table 17.2.

The basic phenothiazine structure

Type of compound	Example	R_1	R_2
Aliphatic	Chlorpromazine	$-Cl$	$-(CH_2)_3-N\begin{smallmatrix}CH_3\\CH_3\end{smallmatrix}$
Piperidine	Thioridazine	$-SCH_3$	$-CH_2-CH_2-\bigcirc$ (N-CH$_3$ piperidine)
Piperazine	Trifluoperazine	$-CF_3$	$-(CH_2)_3-N\bigcirc N-CH_3$
	Fluphenazine	$-CF_3$	$-(CH_2)_3-N\bigcirc N-CH_2-CH_2OH$

Table 17.3. *Two other antipsychotic drugs*

Flupenthixol
a thioxanthine

Haloperidol
a butyrophenone

zine are the most sedative and have moderate extrapyramidal side effects.
Piperidine compounds such as thioridazine have fewer extrapyramidal effects
than this first group. **Piperazine** compounds such as trifluoperazine or
fluphenazine are the least sedating and the most likely to produce extrapyramidal effects. They are also the most potent therapeutically.

Thioxanthines are similar in structure to the phenothiazines (Table 17.2 and
17.3) differing only in the presence of a carbon rather than a nitrogen atom in
the 10 position. Their properties are also similar to those of phenothiazines.
Butyrophenones have a different basic structure (Table 17.3). They have
powerful antipsychotic effects and are highly likely to cause extrapyramidal
side effects, but have relatively little sedative effect. The **butylpiperidines,** of
which pimozide is most often used in clinical work, are related in structure to
the butyrophenones. Their most important difference is a longer half life which
allows once daily dosage.

The wide range of drugs now available can be seen from Table 17.4, which is
not an exhaustive list. Fortunately, the clinician need acquaint himself with
only a few of these drugs, as explained below.

A more recent development has been the introduction of **slow-release depot
preparations** for patients who need to take drugs to prevent relapse and cannot
be relied on to take them regularly. These preparations include the esters
fluphenazine enanthate, fluphenazine decanoate, flupenthixol decanoate, and
clopenthixol decanoate; as well as fluspiriline. All except the latter are given in
an oily medium. Fluspiriline is an aqueous suspension and has a shorter action
than the others. Flupenthixol has been reported to have a mood-elevating
effect, but this has not been proved.

Choice of drug

Of the many compounds available, the following are appropriate: chlorpromazine when a more sedating drug is required; trifluoperazine or haloperidol when
sedation is undesirable; and fluphenazine decanoate when a depot preparation
is required. Promazine or thioridazine is useful for elderly patients when it is
desirable to reduce the risk of extrapyramidal and anticholinergic side-effects.
For the treatment of mania, haloperidol is often preferred because it is less
sedative than most phenothiazines. Chlorpromazine and haloperidol can be

Table 17.4. *A list of antipsychotic drugs*

Phenothiazines with:	Butyrophenones
(a) *Aliphatic side-chain*	Haloperidol
Chlorpromazine	Trifluperidol
Promazine	Spiroperidol
	Droperidol
(b) *Piperidine side-chain*	
Thioridazine	
Mesoridazine	*Diphenylbutylpiperidines*
Pericyazine	Penfluridol
Fluspiriline	
(c) *Piperazine side-chain*	
Trifluoperazine	
Perphenazine	*Azepines*
Fluphenazine	Clozapine
Prochlorperazine	
Thiopropazate	
	Indoles
	Oxypertine
Thioxanthines	Molindone
Thiothixene	
Flupenthixol	
Clopenthixol	*Substituted benzamides*
Chlorprothixene	Sulpiride
	Amine depletors
	Reserpine
	Tetrabenazine

given by intramuscular injection to produce a rapid calming effect in severely disturbed patients.

Pharmacokinetics

Antipsychotic drugs are well absorbed, mainly from the jejunum. They are largely metabolized in the liver. When they are taken by mouth, part of this metabolism is completed as they pass through the portal system on their way to the systemic circulation (first pass metabolism). With chlorpromazine 75 per cent of the drug is metabolized in this way; with fluphenazine the proportion is even greater; while with haloperidol and pimozide it is less. The breakdown of chlorpromazine is complicated, about 75 metabolites having been detected in the blood or urine. The two principal metabolites are 7-hydroxychlorpromazine which is still therapeutically active, and chlorpromazine sulphoxide which is not. Combinations of active and inactive metabolites also occur with other antipsychotic drugs. They make it difficult to interpret the clinical significance of plasma concentrations; hence the latter are seldom used in everyday clinical work. Chlorpromazine induces liver enzymes that increase its own metabolism; the latter is also increased by barbiturates and some antiparkinsonian drugs

536 *Drugs and other physical treatments*

(notably orphenadrine). Other drugs (particularly imipramine and amitriptyline) reduce the metabolism of chlorpromazine by competing for relevant enzymes.

Unwanted effects

The many different antipsychotic drugs share a broad pattern of unwanted effects that are mainly related to their antidopaminergic, anti-adrenergic, and anticholinergic properties. Details of the effects of individual drugs will be found in the *British National Formulary* or a similar work of reference. Here an account is given of the general pattern, with examples of the side effects associated with a few commonly used drugs.

Extrapyramidal effects

These are related to the anti-dopaminergic action of the drugs on the basal ganglia. As already noted, the therapeutic effects may also derive from their anti-dopaminergic action, though presumably at a site other than the basal ganglia. It is not surprising, therefore, that it has so far proved impossible to produce active psychotic drugs with no extrapyramidal side effects.

The effects on the extrapyramidal system fall into four groups. **Acute dystonia** occurs soon after treatment begins, especially in young men. It is observed most often with butyrophenones and with the piperazine group of phenothiazines. The main features are torticollis, tongue protrusion, grimacing and opisthotonus, an odd clinical picture which can easily be mistaken for histrionic behaviour. It can be controlled by biperiden lactate 2–5 mg given carefully by intramuscular injection, or in the most severe cases by slow intravenous injection. **Akathisia** is uncontrollable physical restlessness with an unpleasant feeling of being unable to keep still. It occurs usually in the first two weeks of treatment. It is not usually controlled by antiparkinsonian agents, and requires a reduction in the dose of antipsychotic drug.

The common side effect is a **parkinsonian syndrome** characterized by akinesia, an expressionless face, and lack of associated movements when walking, together with rigidity, coarse tremor, stooped posture, and in severe cases a festinant gait. This syndrome often takes a few weeks to appear and then sometimes diminishes even though the dose has not been reduced. The symptoms can be controlled with antiparkinsonian drugs. However, it is not good practice to prescribe antiparkinsonian drugs prophylactically as a routine, because not all patients will need them. Moreover, they have undesirable effects of their own in some patients; for example they occasionally cause an acute organic syndrome, and possibly increase the incidence of tardive dyskinesia.

This last syndrome, **tardive dyskinesia**, is particularly serious because, unlike the others, it does not always recover when the drugs are stopped. It is characterized by chewing and sucking movements, grimacing, and choreo-athetoid movements. The latter usually affect the face but the limbs and the muscles of respiration may also be involved. The syndrome is seen occasionally among patients who have not taken antipsychotic drugs, but it is much more common among those who have taken high doses of antipsychotic drugs for many years. It is more common among women, and among patients who have diffuse brain pathology. In about half the cases it disappears when drugs are stopped. Estimates of the frequency of the syndrome vary in different series, but it seems to develop in 20–40 per cent of schizophrenic patients treated with long-term antipsychotic drugs (see Marsden and Jenner 1980). Whatever the exact incidence, the existence of this syndrome should be a deterrent to the long-term prescribing of antipsychotic drugs in large doses.

The cause of the syndrome is uncertain but it could possibly be supersensitivity to dopamine resulting from prolonged dopaminergic blockade. This explanation is consistent with the observations that tardive dyskinesia may be aggravated in three ways: frequently by stopping the antipsychotic drugs; by the action of anticholinergic antiparkinsonian drugs (presumably by upsetting further the balance between cholinergic and dopaminergic systems in the basal ganglia); and by l-dopa and apomorphine in some patients. However, there are other observations that do not readily fit this explanation.

Many treatments for tardive dyskinesia have been tried but none is universally effective. It is important, therefore, to reduce its incidence as far as possible by limiting long-term treatment and high doses to patients who really need them. At the same time, a careful watch should be kept for abnormal movements in all patients who have taken antipsychotic drugs for a long time. If the dyskinesia persists, a cautious trial can be made of a drug from each of the groups that have been reported, on the basis of controlled trials, to reduce the abnormal movements. These groups include dopamine receptorant agonists such as haloperidol and pimozide, and dopamine-depleting agents such as tetrabenazine. The reader should consult MacKay and Sheppard 1979 for a review of the treatment of tardive dyskinesia; and Marsden and Jenner 1980 for further information about the pathophysiology of this and other extrapyramidal side effects of antipsychotic drugs.

Anti-adrenergic effects

These include postural hypotension with reflex tachycardia, nasal congestion, and inhibition of ejaculation. The effects on blood pressure are particularly likely to appear after intramuscular administration, and in the elderly whatever the route of administration.

Anticholinergic effects

These include dry mouth, urinary hesitancy and retention, constipation, reduced sweating, blurred vision, and rarely the precipitation of glaucoma.

Other effects

Cardiac arrhythmias are sometimes reported. ECG changes are more common in the form of prolongation of the QT interval and T wave blurring. Depression of mood has been said to occur, but this is difficult to evaluate because untreated schizophrenic patients may have periods of depression. Some patients gain weight when taking antipsychotic drugs, especially chlorpromazine. Galactorrhoea and amenorrhoea are induced in some women. In the elderly, hypothermia is an important unwanted effect. Some phenothiazines, especially chlorpromazine, increase the frequency of seizures in epileptic patients. Prolonged chlorpromazine treatment can lead to photosensitivity and to accumulation of pigment in the skin, cornea, and lens. Thioridazine in exceptionally high dose (more than 800 mg/day) may cause retinal degeneration. Rare adverse reactions include cholestatic jaundice and agranulocytosis.

These drugs have not been shown to be teratogenic but nevertheless they should be used cautiously in early pregnancy.

Contraindications

There are few contraindications and they vary with individual drugs. Before any of these drugs is used, it is important to consult the *British National Formulary* or a comparable work of reference. Contraindications include myasthenia gravis, Addison's disease, glaucoma, and evidence of present or past bone marrow depression; all of these conditions can be exacerbated by these drugs. In patients with liver disease chlorpromazine should be avoided and other drugs used with caution. Caution is also required when there is renal disease, cardiovascular disorder, parkinsonism, epilepsy, or serious infection.

Dosage

Doses of antipsychotic drugs need to be adjusted for the individual patient and changes should be made gradually. Doses should be lower for children, the elderly, patients with brain damage or epilepsy, and the physically ill. The dosage of individual drugs can be found in the *British National Formulary* or a comparable work of reference or in the manufacturer's literature. An indication of the relative dosage of some commonly used drugs, taken by mouth, is given in Table 17.5. Some practical guidance on the most commonly used drugs is given in the next section.

Table 17.5. *Approximate relative dosage of some antipsychotic drugs**

Taken by mouth	
chlorpromazine	100
thioridazine	100
trifluoperazine	5
fluphenazine	2
haloperidol	2

*See Davis (1976).

Advice on management

Use in emergencies

Antipsychotic drugs are used to control psychomotor excitement, hostility, and other abnormal behaviour resulting from schizophrenia, mania, or organic psychosis. If the patient is very excited and particularly if he is abnormally aggressive, the first dose should be large enough to bring his behaviour under control. Chlorpromazine is useful because it has sedative side effects and is less likely to result in an acute dystonic reaction than drugs such as haloperidol. An appropriate dose for a healthy young adult is chlorpromazine 100–200 mg by mouth; or if a rapid action is essential, an intramuscular injection of 50 to 100 mg according to the weight of the patient and the degree of danger. An appropriate dose of haloperidol is 10–30 mg by intramuscular injection. When larger doses are given, a careful watch must be kept for hypotensive effects, and antiparkinsonian agents may be needed to prevent extra-pyramidal effects. The doses stated above must be reduced appropriately for children and adolescents, older patients, the physically ill, people of small body size, and those who have taken too much alcohol. Thus for an elderly agitated patient 25 mg of chlorpromazine by mouth may be enough. The *British National Formulary* or the maker's literature should be consulted before deciding the dose.

In the **management of the acutely disturbed patient**, there are several other practical points that can be dealt with conveniently here. Although it may not be easy in the early stages to differentiate between mania and schizophrenia as causes of the disturbed behaviour, it is necessary to try to distinguish them from organic mental states and from outbursts of aggression in abnormal personalities. Among organic causes it is important to think of post-epileptic states, the effects of head injury, transient global amnesia, and hypoglycaemia. People with abnormal personalities may act highly abnormally when subjected to stressful events, especially if they have taken alcohol or other drugs. When overactive behaviour is secondary to an organic cause, it may be necessary to treat it symptomatically; but any drugs must be given cautiously, and the primary disorder should be treated whenever possible. If the patient has been drinking alcohol, the danger of potentiating the sedative effects of antipsychotic drugs should be remembered. Similarly antipsychotic drugs that may provoke seizures (for example chlorpromazine) should not be used for post-epileptic states.

In order to make a diagnosis, a careful history should be taken from an informant as well as from the patient. It is unwise to be alone with a patient who has already been violent, at least until a diagnosis has been made. The interviewer should do his best to calm the patient. Provided that it seems safe and help remains at hand, he should disengage anyone who is restraining the patient physically. If medication is essential and the patient refuses to accept it, compulsory powers must be acquired by invoking the relevant part of the Mental Health Act (p. 745) before applying treatment. If, having obtained the and help remains at hand, he should disengage anyone who is restraining the patient physically. If medication is essential and the patient refuses to accept it, compulsory powers must be acquired by invoking the relevant part of the Mental Health Act (p. 745) before applying treatment. If, having obtained the necessary legal authority, a calming injection is required, the doctor should assemble enough helpers to restrain the patient effectively. They should act in a swift and determined way to secure the patient; half measures are likely to make him more aggressive. After the patient has become calmer, blood pressure should be monitored, particularly when the antipsychotic drug has been given by intramuscular injection.

The treatment of acute episodes of psychosis

When any necessary emergency measures have been taken, or from the beginning in less urgent cases, treatment with moderate doses of a less sedating antipsychotic drug should be started. An appropriate prescription would be trifluoperazine 15 mg to 30 mg per day in divided doses, or haloperidol 10–15 mg per day in divided doses. The latter drug is often used for manic patients because it has less sedative side-effects. In the early stages of treatment the amount and timing of doses should be adjusted if necessary from one day to the next, until the most acute symptoms have been brought under control. Thereafter, regular twice-daily dosage is usually appropriate. A careful watch should be kept for acute dystonic reactions in the early days of treatment, especially when large doses are being used. Watch should also be kept for parkinsonian side-effects as treatment progresses; if they appear, an antiparkinsonian drug should be given (see next section). In the elderly or physically ill, appropriate observations of temperature and blood pressure should be made to detect hypothermia or postural hypotension.

If the disorder does not respond within a week to ten days, the dose should be increased progressively until either a therapeutic effect is obtained or troublesome side-effects appear. If the latter, it may be necessary to change to another drug with a different pattern of unwanted effects; for example from chlorpromazine to haloperidol if the former has caused serious postural hypotension. Unwanted effects are the only reason for changing from one antipsychotic drug to another. If a full dose of one drug does not produce a therapeutic effect, it is unlikely that another drug will be more effective.

Treatment after the acute episode

Episodes of mania and acute organic psychoses usually subside within weeks. On the other hand, schizophrenic patients often require treatment for many months or years. Such maintenance treatment can be a continuation, in a smaller dose, of the oral medication used to bring the condition under control. However, schizophrenic patients frequently fail to take their drugs regularly, and so delayed release depot preparations are often used. These are given by is given to find out whether serious side effects are likely with the full dose; for fluphenazine decanoate 12.5 mg is appropriate. The maintenance dose is then established by trial and error. It is likely to be between 25 and 50 mg every 2–4 weeks, and it is appropriate to begin with fluphenazine decanoate 25 mg every three weeks. It is important to find the smallest dose that will control the symptoms; since this may diminish with time, regular reassessment is needed of the remaining symptoms of illness and the extent of side effects. It is not necessary to give antiparkinsonian drugs routinely; if they are needed it may be only for a few days after injection of the depot preparation (when the drug plasma concentrations are highest).

Alternative sustained-action injectable preparations are flupenthixol decanoate and clopenthixol decanoate. It has been reported that the former leads to less depression of mood than fluphenazine preparations, but this has not been substantiated.

An informative review of the use of long-term antipsychotic treatment in psychiatry has been provided by Shepherd and Watt (1977).

ANTI-PARKINSONIAN DRUGS

Although these drugs have no direct therapeutic use in psychiatry, they are often required to control the extrapyramidal side effects of antipsychotic drugs.

Pharmacology

Of the drugs used to treat idiopathic Parkinsonism, the anticholinergic compounds are used for drug-induced extrapyramidal syndromes.

Preparations available

Many anticholinergic drugs are available and there is no rational reason for choosing any particular compound. Those most often used in psychiatric practice are the synthetic anticholinergics, benzhexol, benztropine mesylate, and procyclidine; and the antihistaminic, orphenadrine. Orphenadrine is said to have a mood-elevating effect. An injectable preparation of biperiden is useful for the treatment of acute dystonias.

Unwanted effects

In larger doses, these drugs may cause an acute organic syndrome especially in the elderly. Their anticholinergic activity can summate with those of antipsychotic drugs, so that glaucoma may be precipitated, or retention of urine in men with enlarged prostates. Drowsiness, dry mouth, and constipation also occur. These effects tend to diminish as the drug is continued. There is some evidence that these drugs increase the likelihood of tardive dyskinesia with prolonged antipsychotic treatment.

Drug interactions

Antiparkinsonian drugs can induce drug metabolizing enzymes in the liver, so that plasma concentrations of antipsychotic drugs are sometimes reduced.

Advice on management

As noted already, anticholinergic drugs should not be given routinely because they may increase the risk of tardive dyskinesia. It has also been pointed out that patients receiving injectable long-acting preparations usually require anticholinergic drugs for only a few days after the injection, if at all. There have been a few reports of dependence on benzhexol, possibly resulting from a mood-elevating effect (Harrison 1980). Benzhexol 5–15 mg per day in divided doses or orphenadrine 50–100 mg three times a day is appropriate for routine use.

ANTIDEPRESSANTS

Antidepressant drugs have therapeutic effects in depressive illness, but they do not have immediate mood-stimulating effects of the kind produced by amphetamine. Two groups of drugs have been reported to have antidepressant properties. One consists of the tricyclic antidepressants and related compounds, the first of which, imipramine, was tested in clinical practice by Kuhn (1957). The second consists of the monoamine oxidase inhibitors; despite many years of use, their antidepressant effects are still debated. In this chapter tricyclic and related drugs are considered first; then the monoamine oxidase inhibitors; and finally l-tryptophan, a compound with even more uncertain antidepressant properties.

Tricyclic and tetracyclic antidepressants

Pharmacology

Tricyclic antidepressants are so called because they have three linked rings to which a side-chain is attached. Their antidepressant properties depend on this central ring structure; variations in the side-chain alter their potency and sedative properties. When a fourth ring is attached the compound is called tetracyclic. For the clinician these tetracyclic drugs can be regarded as further variants on the tricyclic structure rather than a separate group. Many tricyclic and tetracyclic drugs have been produced, mainly for commercial reasons. They do not differ importantly in their therapeutic effects although their different range of side effects is sometimes useful for the clinician. The therapeutic effect is thought to depend on their common property of increasing the availability of catecholamines at central receptor sites by blocking the reuptake of these transmitters into the presynaptic nerve terminals. However two facts indicate the need for caution in accepting this explanation. The first is that some of the newer drugs do not fit this model: thus iprindole and mianserin have only a weak effect on the reuptake of either 5-hydroxytryptamine or noradrenaline – and yet they appear to have antidepressant actions. The second is that a two to three weeks delay occurs before therapeutic effects appear, even though the effect of blocking amine re-uptake appears much sooner (see Green and Costain 1981 for a discussion of these issues).

Compounds available

The many compounds available are classified into tricyclics, tetracyclics, and other compounds. The tricyclics are divided further into aminobenzyls, dibenzylcycloheptanes, and aminostilbenes. However the clinician is more concerned with pharmacological differences than with variations in structure, and the former are few in number. Despite some claims by manufacturers, there is no evidence that any drug acts more quickly than the rest.

'Standard' antidepressants

Amitriptyline has marked sedative effects as well as its antidepressent properties. It is therefore an appropriate drug for the treatment of depressive illness accompanied by anxiety or agitation. A sustained release preparation ('Lentizol') is available for use once a day, but amitriptyline is itself long-acting and can be given once a day. For this reason the use of sustained release formulations is not advised. **Imipramine** is a suitable alternative for retarded depression because it is less sedating than amitriptyline.

Other sedative antidepressants

These include dothiepin, doxepin, mianserin, iprindole, and trimipramine. Of these **mianserin** has fewer anticholinergic effects than amitriptyline and is less toxic to the heart; it is therefore appropriate for the treatment of depression in patients with cardiac disease (though the strength of the antidepressant effect of this drug has not yet been established beyond doubt). Iprindole and doxepin also have fewer cardiotoxic effects than amitripyline, and may be used more safely for patients with heart disease.

The less sedative compounds include clomipramine, desipramine, maprotiline, nomifensine, and nortriptyline. Of these **clomipramine** has been reported to have a specific effect on obsessional symptoms but the evidence for this is not convincing. It can be given by intravenous infusion, but this is generally inadvisable because it may produce dangerous cardiac dysrhythmias. **Nomifensine** has milder anticholinergic cardiovascular side effects than imipramine.

Pharmacokinetics

Antidepressant drugs are rapidly absorbed, and extensively metabolized in the liver. They have a long action and need to be given only once a day. The only peak plasma concentrations soon after ingestion. Patients differ widely in the extent to which they absorb and metabolize antidepressants; with nortriptyline tenfold differences in blood concentration have been reported after giving the same dose to different people. For this reason, dosage should always be adjusted according to the individual's clinical response and to the side-effects of the drug. Measurements of plasma levels are of some value in patients who have not responded to the usual dosage. With nortriptyline there is some evidence that too high a dose as well as too low a dose is associated with poor response (Asberg *et al.* 1973). However, this 'therapeutic window' has not been confirmed with amitriptyline (Coppen *et al.* 1978) and it may not apply generally.

Unwanted effects

These are numerous and important (see Table 17.6). They can be divided conveniently into five groups. **Autonomic:** dry mouth, disturbance of accommodation, difficulty in micturition leading to retention, constipation leading rarely to ileus, postural hypotension, tachycardia, increased sweating. Of these, retention of urine, especially in elderly men with enlarged prostates, and worsening of glaucoma are the most serious; dry mouth and accommodation difficulties are the most common. Iprindole and mianserin are least likely to produce these anticholinergic side effects. **Psychiatric:** tiredness and drowsiness with amitryptyline and other sedative compounds; insomnia with imipramine; acute organic syndromes; mania may be provoked in manic-depressive patients. **Cardiovascular effects:** Tachycardia and hypotension occur commonly. The electrocardiogram frequently shows prolongation of PR and

Table 17.6. *Some unwanted effects of tricyclic antidepressant drugs*

Autonomic (excluding cardiovascular)	dry mouth impaired accommodation difficulty in micturition increased sweating
Cardiovascular	tachycardia hypotension ECG changes ventricular arrythmias
Neurological	fine tremor inco-ordination headache muscle twitching epileptic seizures peripheral neuropathy
Other	skin rashes cholestatic jaundice agranulocytosis

QT intervals, depressed ST segments and flattened T waves. Ventricular arrhythmias develop occasionally, more often in patients with pre-existing heart disease. These effects are less marked with mianserin, iprindole and doxepin. **Neurological:** fine tremor (commonly), inco-ordination, headache, muscle twitching, epileptic seizures in predisposed patients and, rarely, peripheral neuropathy. Nomifensine seems least likely to induce seizures and may be a suitable drug for depressed epileptics. **Other:** allergic skin rashes, mild chole-static jaundice, and rarely agranulocytosis. Mianserin has been associated, rarely, with depression of white blood cells (Committee on Safety of Medicines 1981). Teratogenic effects have not been recorded in human beings but the drugs should nevertheless be used cautiously in the first trimester of pregnancy.

Antidepressants should be withdrawn slowly. Sudden cessation may be followed by nausea, sweating, and insomnia.

Toxic effects

In overdosage, tricyclic antidepressants produce a large number of effects, some extremely serious. Urgent expert treatment in a general hospital is therefore required, but the psychiatrist should know the main signs of overdosage. These can be listed as follows. The **cardiovascular** effects include ventricular fibrillation, conduction disturbances, and low blood pressure. Heart rate may be increased or decreased depending partly on the degree of conduction disturbance. The **respiratory** effects lead to respiratory depression. The resulting hypoxia increases the likelihood of cardiac complications. Aspiration pneumonia may develop. The **central nervous system** complications include agitation, twitching, convulsions, hallucinations, delirium, and coma. Pyramidal and extrapyramidal signs may develop. **Parasympathetic** effects include dry mouth, dilated pupils, blurred vision, retention of urine, and pyrexia. Most patients need only supportive care, but cardiac monitoring is important and arrhythmias require urgent treatment by a physician in an intensive care unit. Tricyclic antidepressants delay gastric emptying, and so gastric lavage is valuable for several hours after the overdose. Lavage must be carried out with particular care to prevent aspiration of gastric contents, if necessary by the insertion of a cuffed endotracheal tube before lavage is attempted.

Interactions with other drugs

The metabolism of tricyclic drugs is reduced competitively by phenothiazines and increased by barbiturates (though not by benzodiazepines). Tricyclic compounds potentiate the pressor effects of noradrenaline, adrenalin, and phenylephrine by preventing re-uptake (Boakes *et al.* 1973) and this is a potential hazard when local anaesthetics are used for dental surgery or other purposes. These drugs also interfere with the effects of the antihypertensive agents bethanidine, clonidine, debrisoquine, and guanethidine. They do not, however, interact with the beta-adrenoceptor antagonists used to treat hypertension. Alternatively, mianserin can be used to treat depressed hypertensives for it interacts only with clonidine. Interactions of tricyclic drugs with monoamine oxidase inhibitors are considered later.

Contraindications include agranulocytosis, severe liver damage, glaucoma, and prostatic hypertrophy. The drugs must be used cautiously in epileptic patients, in the elderly, and after coronary thrombosis.

Management

The clinician should become familiar with two 'standard' drugs, one of which is more sedating than the other. Amitriptyline (more sedating) and imipramine (less sedating) fulfil these requirements and have been thoroughly tested in clinical trials. The doctor should also be familiar with a drug that has few anticholinergic side effects and is less cardiotoxic than the rest; mianserin is one choice, although it is not yet certain whether its antidepressant properties are as great as those of amitriptyline. There is no value in changing from one tricyclic to another in the hope of producing a therapeutic effect when the first has failed, nor is there any value in giving more than one antidepressant drug at the same time (combinations of antidepressants and mono-aminoxidase inhibitors are considered later). Equally there is nothing to be gained by using proprietary preparations containing a mixture of an antidepressant and a phenothiazine. Agitation can usually be controlled equally well by choosing a sedative antidepressant. If it is necessary to supplement the latter with a phenothiazine, it is better to give the drugs separately so that doses can be adjusted independently.

If a depressed patient needs antihypertensive drugs, management is easier if the anti-hypertensive treatment can be a diuretic, a suitable beta adrenoreceptor antagonist such as propranolol, or a combination of the two. If this cannot be done, blood pressure should be measured carefully at least once a week because tricyclics may interfere with the actions of other antihypertensives (see above). If necessary, the dose of the antihypertensive drugs should be adjusted. It is also important to continue measuring blood pressure and to be ready to readjust the antihypertensive dosage after the antidepressant drugs have been stopped.

Having selected a suitable antidepressant drug, it is most important to tell the patient that the therapeutic effect is likely to be delayed for up to two or three weeks although sleep may improve sooner. He should be told that side effects will appear earlier than this, and that he may notice dry mouth, difficulty in accommodation, and constipation. An older patient should be warned about the effects of postural hypotension. Reassurance should be given that most of these effects are likely to grow less as the drug is taken for longer. Since the patient may feel worse from the side effects of the drug before feeling any benefits from its therapeutic effects, he should be seen again within a week (or less if he is severely depressed). At this interview the doctor should find out what side effects have appeared, and explain any of them that were not discussed on the first occasion. He should encourage the patient to continue taking the drug, and should reassess the severity of the depression.

The starting dose should be moderate; for example amitriptyline 100–150 mg/day according to the urgency of the case. If necessary this dose can be increased after about a week when the extent of side effects will have been observed. The whole dose of the antidepressant drug can usually be given at night, so that any sedative side effects help the patient to sleep and the peak of other side effects is less likely to be noticed. Doses must be reduced for elderly patients, those with cardiac disease, prostatism, or other conditions that may be exacerbated by the drugs, and those with disease of the liver or kidneys.

If after two or three weeks the depression has not responded, the drug should not be changed for another. Instead the doctor should try to find out why there has been no response. In doing this he should consider whether the patient has been taking the drugs in the correct dose, whether the diagnosis is correct, and what part social factors are playing in maintaining the condition. Poor compliance with antidepressant drug treatment is common. It often results from the depressed person's gloomy conviction that nothing can help him, from an unwillingness to suffer unpleasant side effects, or from a fear that once started the drug will have to be taken indefinitely.

When a therapeutic effect has been achieved, the drug should be continued in full dose for at least six weeks. After this treatment a reduced dosage should be usually continued for a further six months (Mindham *et al.* 1973). If a relapse occurs when the dose is reduced, the former dosage should be reinstated for at least a further three months before lowering it cautiously for a second time.

MONOAMINE OXIDASE INHIBITORS

Although monoamine oxidase inhibitors have been used in psychiatry for many years, the exact nature of their therapeutic actions has not been established beyond doubt. They certainly have anxiolytic properties. They may have a weak antidepressant action as well, but if so it is restricted to less severe depressive disorders. An antidepressant action has not been proved conclusively, and any improvement experienced by the patient could result from the anxiolytic effects of the drugs. Monoamine oxidase inhibitors have also been reported to have therapeutic actions in phobic anxiety states (Sargant and Dally 1962). One of these drugs, tranylcypromine, has a stimulant effect similar to that of amphetamine; this may account in part for the reputation gained by the whole group in the treatment of mild depressive disorders.

Against these modest therapeutic effects must be set a wide range of dangerous interactions with certain drugs and foodstuffs. These interactions are sufficiently serious that we recommend that monoamine oxidase inhibitors should never be used as a drug of first choice, but only after failure of adequate treatment with one of the tricyclic or similar antidepressant drugs. Even in these circumstances, the drugs should be used infrequently. The reader should understand, however, that these issues are still somewhat controversial.

Pharmacological actions

Monoamine oxidase inhibitors (MAOIs) inactivate enzymes that oxidize noradrenaline, 5-hydroxytryptamine, tyramine, and other amines which are widely distributed in the body as transmitters, or taken in food and drink, or as drugs. Monoamine oxidase exists in a number of forms that differ in their substrate and inhibitor specificities. The action of the drugs is not confined to the monoamine oxidases. They also inhibit the hydroxylases in the liver which metabolize barbiturates, tricyclic antidepressants, phenytoin, and antiparkinsonian drugs. Inhibition of monoamine oxidase occurs rapidly, but when MAOIs are withdrawn it can take two weeks before the enzyme recovers its previous level of activity, so that dangers of drug interactions persist for this time. A full account of these important actions of the monoamine oxidase inhibitors will be found in a standard textbook of pharmacology.

Compounds available

Several compounds are available but, with the exception of tranylcypromine, there are few therapeutic differences between them. **Iproniazid** is the prototype of this group of drugs but its hepatotoxic effects make it unsuitable for general use in psychiatry. **Phenelzine** is the most widely used compound being less toxic to the liver than the others. **Isocarboxazid** has no advantage over phenelzine. **Tranylcypromine** differs from the others in combining the ability to inhibit monoamine oxidase with an amphetamine-like stimulating effect which many patients welcome. Indeed the drug is partly metabolized to amphetamine. It is sometimes used in combination with trifluoperazine as the proprietary preparation 'Parstelin' (tranylcypromine 10 mg plus trifluoperazine 1 mg in each tablet) but there is no good reason to use this mixture. Some patients become dependent on the stimulant effect of tranylcypromine (see for example Griffin *et al.* 1981). Moreover, compared with phenelzine, it is more likely to give rise to hypertensive crises, though less likely to damage the liver. For these reasons, tranylcypromine should be prescribed with particular caution.

Pharmacokinetics

Monoamine oxidase inhibitors are absorbed quickly and distributed widely. Most are hydrazine derivatives and these are inactivated by acetylation of their side-chain in the liver. The speed of this acetylation varies between individuals in a way that is genetically determined. It has been reported that people who are slow acetylators respond better to the antidepressant effects of the drugs (Johnstone and Marsh 1973). The non-hydrazine compound of clinical interest, tranylcypromine, is metabolized rapidly and largely eliminated within 24 hours.

Unwanted effects

These include dry mouth, difficulty in micturition, postural hypotension, headache, dizziness, tremor, paraesthesiae of the hands and feet, constipation, and oedema of the ankles. Hydrazine compounds can give rise to hepatocellular jaundice.

Interactions with foodstuffs and drugs

Foods and drink

Some foods contain tyramine, a substance that is normally inactivated by monoamine oxidases, mainly by those in the intestine and liver. When these enzymes are inhibited, tyramine is not broken down and is free to exert its hypertensive effects. These effects are due to the release of noradrenaline with consequent elevation of blood pressure. This may reach dangerous levels and occasionally result in subarachnoid haemorrhage. Important early symptoms of such a crisis include a severe, usually throbbing, headache. The main foodstuffs to be avoided are extracts of meat and yeast, pickled herrings, chicken liver, cheeses – especially camembert, brie, stilton, gorgonzola, and some American processed cheeses. Chianti, some other red wines and beers may also cause reactions. Hypertensive crises are treated by blocking alpha adrenoceptors by parenteral administration of phentolamine, or if this drug is not available by intramuscular chlorpromazine. Blood pressure must be followed carefully.

Drugs

Patients taking monoamine oxidase inhibitors must not be given drugs whose metabolism depends on enzymes that are affected by the MAOI. These drugs include sympathomimetic amines such as adrenaline, noradrenaline, amphetamine, and fenfluramine, as well as phenylpropanolamine and ephedrine (which may be present in proprietary cold cures). Antihypertensive drugs, such as methyldopa and guanethidine, and antihistamines are also affected. Local anaesthetics often contain a sympathomimetic amine and should also be avoided. Morphine, pethidine, procaine, cocaine, alcohol, barbiturates, and insulin can also be involved in dangerous interactions. Sensitivity to oral anti-diabetic drugs is increased, with consequent risk of hypoglycaemia. The metabolism of barbiturates, phenytoin, and other drugs broken down in the liver may be slowed.

Tricyclic drugs also interact with monoamine oxidase inhibitors. Some clinicians make use of this combination believing it to be more effective than either drug used alone. However, the evidence to support this practice is far from convincing and the potential risks of drug interactions are probably not justified (see *British National Formulary,* 1981 p. 119). If administered at all, combinations should only be prescribed by clinicians with extensive experience of their use, and then only for patients who can be relied on to adhere strictly to dosage schedules and report side effects. The combination of tranylcypromine with clomipramine is particularly dangerous (*British National Formulary* 1981).

The possibility of interactions must also be remembered when changing between tricyclic antidepressants and monoamine oxidase inhibitors. Tricyclics should not be given for two weeks after stopping a MAOI, otherwise interactions may occur. If tricyclics are given first (as is done in combined treatment) no drug-free interval is required. This adds to the other reasons for always using tricyclics as the first drug for depressive illness.

Contraindications

These include liver disease, congestive cardiac failure, and conditions which require the patient to take any of the drugs that react with MAOI.

Management

As explained earlier, monoamine oxidase inhibitors should not be prescribed as the first drug for the treatment of depressive disorders. If they are prescribed, the dangers of interactions with foods and other drugs must be explained carefully to the patient. A warning card should also be given because few patients remember the essential facts when given by word of mouth. A suitable card published in the *British National Formulary,* is shown in Figure 17.1. Patients should be told to show this card to any doctor or dentist who is treating them. They also should be told not to buy proprietary drugs, except from a qualified pharmacist, to whom the card should always be shown. If an MAOI has to be used, phenelzine is probably the best choice, starting in a dose of 15 mg twice a day and increasing cautiously to 15 mg four times a day. Although patients are often impressed by the amphetamine-like effects of tranylcypromine, we do not recommend its use because some patients become dependent on this stimulant action.

If the drugs do not have a therapeutic effect, an interval of at least two weeks must be allowed before tricyclic antidepressants are substituted. MAOIs should be discontinued slowly.

L-TRYPTOPHAN

The hypothesis that the cerebral content of 5-hydroxytryptamine (5HT) is lowered in depression has led to the therapeutic use of L-tryptophan, a 5HT

TREATMENT CARD
Carry this card with you at all times. Show it to any doctor who may treat you other than the doctor who prescribed this medicine, and to your dentist if you require dental treatment.

INSTRUCTIONS TO PATIENTS
Please read carefully
While taking this medicine and for 10 days after your treatment finishes you must observe the following simple instructions: –
1 Do not eat CHEESE, PICKLED HERRING OR BROAD BEAN PODS.
2 Do not eat or drink BOVRIL, OXO, MAR-MITE or ANY SIMILAR MEAT OR YEAST EXTRACT.
3 Do not take any other MEDICINES (including tablets, capsules, nose drops, inhalations or suppositories) whether purchased by you or previously prescribed by your doctor, without first consulting your doctor or your pharmacist.
NB *Treatment for coughs and colds, pain relievers and tonics are medicines.*
4 Drink ALCOHOL only in moderation and avoid CHIANTI WINE completely.
Report any severe symptoms to your doctor and follow any other advice given by him.

M.A.O.I.   Prepared by The Pharmaceutical Society and the British Medical Association on behalf of the Health Departments of the United Kingdom.

Fig. 17.1. Treatment card. (Reproduced from *British National Formulary.* Copyright BNF.)

precursor capable of crossing the blood–brain barrier. L-tryptophan is sometimes administered alone, but it has also been used in combination with a monoamine oxidase inhibitor, given to reduce its metabolism and thereby increase the amount reaching the brain. Even with these additional steps, the evidence for an antidepressant effect is equivocal. If L-tryptophan is used, it must be regarded as a therapeutic experiment with each patient. The evidence about its actions has been reviewed by Mindham (1979).

Pharmacology

5-Hydroxytryptamine is synthesized from tryptophan by hydroxylation to 5-hydroxytryptophan (5HTP) and then by decarboxylation. It is broken down by monoamine oxidase. L-Tryptophan is an essential amino acid which probably has no important pharmacological actions of its own. In particular it does not elevate mood in normal people. 5HTP has also been tried as a treatment for depressive disorders but without benefit (Pare and Sandler 1959).

Pharmacokinetics

Tryptophan is readily absorbed. It enters many metabolic reactions and is rapidly broken down by a pyrrolase in the liver to kynurenine and eventually nicotinic acid. The activity of this pyrrolase is increased by cortisol and oestrogens and by the inducing effect of L-tryptophan itself.

Compounds available

Tryptophan is available as a tablet containing 0.5 g of the drug together with 5 mg pyridoxine hydrochloride and 10 mg ascorbic acid (which are respectively cofactors in the decarboxylation and hydroxylation reactions). It has also been made up as a chocolate flavoured powder, intended to disguise the unpleasant taste of the large quantities of L-tryptophan.

Unwanted effects

L-Tryptophan has few unwanted effects except nausea and anorexia occurring soon after it is taken. It causes daytime drowsiness and can improve night time sleep if taken in the evening.

Advice on management

The lack of convincing evidence for a therapeutic effect indicates that the drug should not be used as the treatment of first choice for depressive illness. Its use may occasionally be worth considering for patients who have not responded to other treatments, but the clinician should not expect substantial effects.

LITHIUM

Lithium salts have been used in medicine for over a century, originally in the treatment of gout. In the 1940s they were employed as a substitute for sodium chloride for cardiac patients taking a salt free diet. Toxic effects were frequent and the practice was abandoned. As a treatment for mania, lithium salts were first employed in 1949 by Cade in Australia. It was the work of Schou in Denmark that established the use of lithium carbonate in the treatment and prophylaxis of affective disorders.

The principal use of lithium is to prevent recurrence of mania and depressive disorders. It is also used as a treatment for acute episodes of mania. It may have an antidepressant effect but this is less sure; any such effect is certainly no greater than that of tricyclic drugs which are less toxic. Lithium carbonate has also been claimed on inadequate evidence, to reduce premenstrual tension. The evidence for the general therapeutic effectiveness of lithium is examined in the chapter dealing with the affective disorders (p. 219).

In animals lithium affects a number of transmitters and enzymes, although some of these actions have only been observed at lithium concentrations greater than those used in man. It is not clear which of the many pharmacological actions of the lithium ion explains its therapeutic effects.

Pharmacokinetics

Lithium is rapidly absorbed from the gut and diffuses quickly throughout the body fluids and cells, displacing sodium and potassium and interfering with magnesium and calcium. Lithium moves out of cells more slowly than sodium. It is removed from plasma by renal excretion and by entering cells and other body compartments. There is therefore a rapid excretion of lithium from the plasma, and a slower phase reflecting its removal from the whole body pool. Lithium, like sodium, is filtered and partly reabsorbed in the kidney. When the proximal tubule absorbs more water, lithium absorption increases. Therefore dehydration causes plasma lithium concentrations to rise. Because lithium is transported in competition with sodium, more is reabsorbed when sodium concentrations fall. Thiazide diuretics increase sodium excretion without increasing that of lithium; hence they can lead to toxic concentrations of lithium in the blood.

Dosage and plasma concentrations

Because the therapeutic and toxic doses are close together, it is essential to measure plasma concentrations of lithium during treatment. Measurements should first be made after four to seven days; then weekly for three weeks; and then, provided that a satisfactory steady state has been achieved, once every six weeks. After an oral dose, plasma lithium levels rise by a factor of two or three within about four hours. For this reason, concentrations are normally measured twelve hours after the last dose, usually just before the morning dose which can be delayed if necessary for an hour or two. It is important to follow this routine because published information about lithium concentrations refers to the level twelve hours after the last dose, and not to the 'peak' reached in the four hours after that dose. If an unexpectedly high concentration is found it is important to find out whether the patient has inadvertently taken the morning dose before the blood sample was taken.

The usually accepted range for prophylaxis is 0.7–1.2 mmol/l measured 12 hours after the last dose. However Srinivasan and Hullin (1980) have suggested that these levels are unnecessarily high. They believe that concentrations in the range 0.5–0.8 mmol/l are sufficient for prophylaxis, and that higher levels are required only for treatment of acute illness. This point has not been settled finally. In the treatment of acute mania, plasma concentrations below 0.9 mmol/l appear to be ineffective and a range of 0.9–1.4 mmol/l is probably required (Prien *et al.* 1972). Serious toxic effects appear with concentrations above 2.0 mmol/l though early symptoms may appear between 1.5–2.0 mmol/l.

Although it is conventional to measure concentrations 12 hours after the last dose, it is plausible to assume that any damage caused by the drug may depend on the highest level reached. For this reason, delayed release tablets have been introduced in an attempt to reduce the peak concentrations. However, it appears that the time-course of plasma levels resulting from these tablets is no different from that of lithium carbonate (see Srinivasan and Hullin 1980). It is prudent to give lithium in two doses a day rather than one, so that peak concentrations are less. An exception must be made for patients who take one dose reliably but consistently forget to take a second on the same day.

Unwanted effects

Early effects: A mild diuresis due to sodium excretion occurs soon after the drug is started. Other common effects include tremor of the hands, dry mouth, a metallic taste, feelings of muscular weakness, and fatigue. **Later effects:** After the initial sodium diuresis, about 10 per cent of patients develop persistent polyuria and polydipsia. A few patients develop a diabetes insipidus syndrome which does not respond to antidiuretic hormone but reverses within a week or two of stopping lithium. Some patients, especially women, gain some weight when taking the drug. Persistent fine tremor mainly affecting the hands is common; but coarse tremor suggests that the plasma concentration of lithium has reached toxic levels. Most patients adapt to the fine tremor; for those who do not, propranolol 10 mg t.d.s. often reduces the symptom.

Thyroid gland enlargement occurs in about 5 per cent of patients taking lithium. The thyroid shrinks again if thyroxine is given while lithium is continued; and it returns to normal a month or two after lithium has been stopped (Schou *et al.* 1968). Lithium interferes with thyroid production and **hypothyroidism** occurs in up to 20 per cent of women patients (Lindstedt *et al.* 1977) with a compensatory rise in thyroid stimulating hormone. Tests of thyroid function should be performed every six months to help in detecting these changes, but these intermittent tests are no substitute for a continuous watch for suggestive clinical signs particularly lethargy and substantial weight gain. If hypothyroidism develops and the reasons for lithium treatment are still strong, thyroxine treatment should be added.

Reversible **ECG changes** also occur. These may be due to displacement of potassium in the myocardium by lithium, for they resemble those of hypo-kalaemia, with T wave flattening and inversion or widening of the QRS. Other changes include a reversible **leucocytosis** and occasional papular or maculo-papular rashes. There is some uncertain evidence that prolonged treatment may lead to osteoporosis in women.

Long-term effects on the kidney: In 10 per cent of cases there is a persistent impairment of concentrating ability, and in a small number the syndrome of nephrogenic diabetes insipidus develops due to interference with the effect of antidiuretic hormone. This usually recovers when the drug is stopped though there are reports of persisting cases (Simon *et al.* 1977). Structural changes have been reported in the kidneys of animals receiving toxic doses of lithium (Radomski *et al.* 1950) but these are much higher doses than the equivalent in man. There have also been reports of a chronic nephropathy in patients on prolonged treatment (e.g. Herstbech *et al.* 1977) but these reports were not confirmed by other groups of research workers (see *Lancet* Editorial 1979). Moreover, Glen *et al.* (1979) found no increased mortality from renal disease in 784 patients who had taken lithium for many years. Hence it seems that, provided doses are kept below 1.2 mml/l, there is no reason to expect renal damage in patients whose renal function is normal at the start. Nevertheless in the present state of knowledge it is wise to perform simple tests of renal function every six months (see below). Readers who require further information about the effects of lithium on the kidney should consult Myers *et al.* (1980).

Toxic effects

These are related to dose. They include ataxia, poor co-ordination of limb movements, muscle twitching, slurred speech, and confusion. They constitute a serious medical emergency for they can progress through coma and fits to death. If these symptoms appear, lithium must be stopped at once and a high intake of fluid provided, with extra sodium chloride to stimulate an osmotic diuresis. In severe cases renal dialysis may be needed. Lithium is rapidly cleared if renal function is normal so that most cases either recover completely or die. However, a few cases have been reported of permanent neurological damage despite haemodialysis (von Hartitzsch *et al.* 1972).

Lithium in pregnancy and the puerperium

Lithium crosses the placenta. There are reports of an increased rate of abnormalities in the babies of mothers receiving lithium in pregnancy; hence it is wise to avoid the drug in the first trimester of pregnancy (Weinstein 1980). Lithium is secreted into breast milk to the extent that plasma lithium concentrations of breast-fed infants can be one third to a half that in the maternal blood. Bottle-feeding is a wise precaution in such cases.

Drug interactions

There have been several reports of serious toxic reactions when lithium is given with large doses of haloperidol in the treatment of acute mania (for example Cohen and Cohen 1974; Loudon and Waring 1976). These reactions consist of confusion, tremor, and signs of extrapyramidal and cerebellar dysfunction. Of the four cases reported by Cohen and Cohen, two were left with dementia and two with persistent dyskinesia. Other investigators have not found evidence of this syndrome among patients taking the two drugs. It has been suggested that the cases reported by Cohen and Cohen may have been due to coincidental encephalitis. However Loudon and Waring conclude that there must be special caution when doses of haloperidol above 40 mg/day are combined with lithium concentrations greater than 1 mmol/l. Until more evidence is available this is a sensible precaution.

Thiazide diuretics can precipitate lithium toxicity, so they should not be given with lithium. If a patient taking lithium requires surgery involving a muscle relaxant, the anaesthetist should be informed in advance and lithium should be stopped 48–72 hours before the operation (*Drugs and Therapeutics Bulletin* 1981; Havdala *et al.* 1979).

Contraindications

These include renal failure or recent renal disease, current cardiac failure or recent myocardial infarction, and chronic diarrhoea sufficient to alter electrolytes. It is advisable not to use lithium for children or in early pregnancy. It should not be prescribed if the patient is judged unlikely to observe the precautions required for its safe use.

The management of patients on lithium

A careful routine of management is essential because of the effects of therapeutic doses of lithium on the thyroid and kidney, and the toxic effects of excessive dosage. The following routine is one of several that have been proposed and can be adopted safely. Successful treatment requires attention to detail, so the steps are set out below at some length.

Before starting lithium, a physical examination should be carried out including the measurement of blood pressure. It is also useful to weigh the patient. The urine should be examined for protein, sugar, and casts. Blood should be taken for estimation of electrolytes, urea, serum creatinine, haemoglobin, ESR, and a full blood count. When a particularly thorough evaluation is indicated, creatinine clearance is carried out, an 18-hour collection usually being adequate. Thyroid function tests are also necessary: T_4 as a screening test, followed by T_3, TSH and FTI as indicated. (It is sensible to find out from a clinical pathologist or consultant endocrinologist, what tests are preferred locally.) If indicated, ECG, pregnancy tests, or lithium clearance should be done as well.

If these tests show no contraindication to lithium treatment, the doctor should check that the patient is not taking a thiazide diuretic. A careful explanation should then be given to the patient. He should understand the possible early toxic effects of an unduly high blood level; and also the circumstances in which this can arise – for example during intercurrent gastroenteritis, renal infection, or the dehydration secondary to fever. He should be advised that if any of these arise, he should stop the drug and seek medical advice. It is usually appropriate to include another member of the family in these discussions. Providing printed guidelines on these points is often appropriate (either written by the doctor, or in one of the forms provided by pharmaceutical firms). In these discussions a sensible balance must be struck between alarming the patient by over emphasizing the risks, and failing to give him the information he needs to take a responsible part in the treatment.

Starting treatment: Lithium should normally be prescribed as the carbonate. Treatment should begin and continue with two doses 12 hours apart. The only exception is that, if the patient persistently forgets one of the doses, a single evening dose can be tried. If the drug is being used for prophylaxis, it is appropriate to begin with 750–1000 mg per day in divided doses, taking blood for lithium estimations every week and adjusting the dose until an appropriate concentration is achieved. For prophylaxis, a lithium level of 0.4–0.8 mmol/l (in a sample taken 12 hours after the last dose) may be adequate, as explained above; if this is not effective, the previously accepted higher range of 0.7–1.2 mmol/l should be used. In judging response, it should be remembered that it may take several months before lithium achieves its full effect.

As treatment continues lithium estimations should be carried out every six weeks. It is important to have some means of reminding patients and doctors about the times at which repeat investigations are required. If a doctor is treating many patients with lithium it is useful to keep a card index arranged in order of date to ensure that tests are not overlooked. Every six months, blood samples should be taken for electrolytes, urea, and creatinine, a full blood count, and the thyroid function tests listed above. The results should be recorded in tabular form in the patient's notes so that results of successive estimations can be compared easily. If two consecutive thyroid function tests a month apart show hypothyroidism, lithium should be stopped or l-thyroxine prescribed. Troublesome polyuria is a reason for attempting a reduction in dose, while severe persistent polyuria is an indication for specialist renal investigation including tests of concentrating ability. A persistent leucocytosis is not uncommon and apparently harmless. It reverses soon after the drug is stopped.

While lithium is given, the doctor must keep in mind the rare interactions that have been reported with haloperidol (see above). It is also prudent to watch for toxic effects with extra care if other antipsychotic drugs are being taken or ECT is being given. If the patient requires an anaesthetic for any reason, the anaesthetist should be told that the patient is taking lithium; this is because there is some evidence that the effects of muscle relaxant may be potentiated.

Lithium is usually continued for at least a year, and often for much longer. The need for the drug should be reviewed once a year, taking into account any persistence of mild mood fluctuations which suggest the possibility of relapse if treatment is stopped. Continuing medication is more likely to be needed if the patient has previously had several episodes of affective disorder within a short time, or if previous affective disorders were so severe that even a small risk of recurrence should be avoided. Some patients have taken lithium continuously for 15 years or more, but there should always be compelling reasons for continuing treatment for more than five years. It is not certain whether lithium should be reduced gradually or can be stopped abruptly. A few patients relapse within two weeks after stopping the drug and this has been interpreted as a 'rebound'. Until more is known, it is probably wise to reduce the drug gradually after prolonged use.

CENTRAL NERVOUS STIMULANTS

This class of drugs includes mild stimulants, of which the best known is caffeine, and more powerful stimulants such as amphetamine. Other mild stimulants include fencamfamin, meclofenoxate, and pemoline. These drugs have been advocated for the treatment of states of fatigue and senility, but their value for these purposes is doubtful. They are not suitable for the treatment of depressive disorders.

The most important of the powerful stimulants are the amphetamines. Although these drugs were much used in the past, they are no longer recommended because they readily give rise to dependence. They are certainly not appropriate for the treatment of depressive disorders. They have been used as appetite suppressants, but this is no longer appropriate. Their only remaining indication in adult patients is in the treatment of narcolepsy. (Their use in the hyperkinetic syndrome of childhood is discussed on p. 659.)

The remaining central nervous stimulant, cocaine, has even more potential for addiction. It has no uses in psychiatry but is still prescribed occasionally for terminally ill patients, often in combination with diamorphine or morphine.

The main **preparations** are dexamphetamine sulphate, given for narcolepsy in divided doses of 10 mg per day increased to a maximum of 50 mg per day by steps of 10 mg each week; and methylamphetamine hydrochloride which has similar effects.

Unwanted effects: These include restlessness, insomnia, poor appetite, dizziness, tremor, palpitations, and cardiac arrhythmias. **Toxic effects** from large doses include disorientation and aggressive behaviour, hallucinations, convulsions, and coma. Persistent abuse can lead to a paranoid state similar to paranoid schizophrenia (Connell 1958). Amphetamines **interact** dangerously with monoamine oxidase inhibitors. They are **contraindicated** in cardiovascular disease and thyrotoxicosis.

ANTIEPILEPTIC DRUGS

Antiepileptic drugs are sometimes called anticonvulsants, a name that is less appropriate because not all epileptic seizures are convulsive. The drugs are usually given prophylactically; a single fit is not treated. However when seizures are continuous (status epilepticus) or frequently repeated (serial seizures) drugs are needed to arrest the condition. The psychiatrist should know about these drugs, not only because he may be called upon to treat patients with epilepsy but also because some of the drugs may cause behavioural disturbance.

Compounds available

A large number of compounds are used to treat epilepsy. The drugs in most common use can be classified on the basis of their chemical structure into hydantoins, barbiturates, succinimides, benzodiazepines, carbamazepine, and sodium valproate. Sulthiame is no longer used widely because it has doubtful antiepileptic effects and it may impair performance on intellectual tasks and social functioning (Green *et al.* 1974; Dodrill 1975). However, these chemical differences are of little interest to the clinician, who will find it more useful to classify the drugs according to the type of epilepsy against which they are most effective. Before considering such a classification, some comments are required on the main groups of drugs.

Hydantoins have been widely used since their introduction in 1938. Phenytoin is the only one in general use today.

Barbiturates, introduced in 1912, were until recently the most widely prescribed antiepileptic drugs. Those used most often to treat seizure disorders are phenobarbitone and the closely related drug primidone.

Other compounds: Carbamazepine is chemically similar to the tricyclic anti-depressant drugs, differing from imipramine only in its shorter side chain. This structure suggests that it might have antidepressant actions as well, but this has not been shown convincingly (see Stores 1978). Sodium valproate has a structure that is different from the other antiepileptics, being a branched chain carboxylic acid salt. Sulthiame is a sulphonamide derivitive.

Choice of drug and type of seizure (Table 17.7)

In treating epilepsy, the choice of drug is based more on freedom from adverse effects than on any differences in effectiveness in controlling seizures. For partial (otherwise called focal) seizures, whether complex or simple in type, carbamazepine is the drug of choice and phenytoin the main alternative. Phenytoin has a narrow therapeutic range and is more likely than carbamazepine to give rise to adverse effects. For tonic–clonic generalized seizures, the

Table 17.7. *Classification of seizures and Drugs of choice*

Type of seizure	First choice	Others
(a) Partial or focal (whether simple or complex)	Carbamazepine	Phenytoin
(b) Generalized Tonic–clonic	Carbamazepine or sodium valproate	Phenytoin
Absence seizures	Sodium valproate	Ethosuximide
Myoclonic and atonic	Sodium valproate	Clonazepam

first choice lies between carbamazepine and sodium valproate. For absence seizures, sodium valproate is the first choice with ethosuximide as the alternative. Until recently myoclonic and atonic seizures did not respond well to antiepileptic drugs, but some can now be controlled with the newer drugs sodium valproate or clonazepam.

Drugs used in status epilepticus

Diazepam, given intravenously, is the drug of first choice. Care must be taken to avoid respiratory depression and venous thrombophlebitis. As a rule, diazepam is not effective in status epilepticus when injected intramuscularly, but it can be given effectively by rectal infusion when entry to a vein is difficult (Munthe-Kaas 1980). If diazepam fails, an intravenous infusion of chlormethiazole should be used. In the past paraldehyde was the mainstay of treatment, but until recently was out of fashion. It is now being used increasingly when diazepam fails. It can be given intramuscularly, rectally, or by intravenous infusion. If a plastic syringe is used, the drug must be given as soon as it has been drawn up. If status persists despite these measures, intravenous phenytoin, with EEG monitoring, or phenobarbitone may be tried. These latter measures should not be taken without advice from a neurologist unless the circumstances are exceptional. Details of dosage will be found in the *British National Formulary* (1981) or comparable handbooks; a useful discussion of the treatment of status epilepticus is given by Richens (1976).

Pharmacodynamics

It appears that antiepileptic drugs do not have a single common pharmacological action that accounts for their therapeutic effects. Presumably they act in different ways and perhaps at different stages in the development of seizure activity; for example, phenobarbitone increases seizure threshold, whereas phenytoin appears to limit the propagation of the discharge. Until more is known about the mechanisms involved, the clinician gains little of practical value from a review of the pharmacodynamics of these drugs.

Pharmacokinetics

There are so many different antiepileptic drugs that many exceptions can be made to any generalization about them. Most are readily absorbed, the exception being phenytoin which is not very soluble in water and is absorbed in different amounts from different proprietary preparations. Most antiepileptic drugs are metabolized in the liver and excreted in the urine as the conjugated or free compound. Most have long actions. They can therefore be given once or twice a day provided that the dose is not so big that side effects result from the peak level after a single dose. Carbamazepine is an exception and has to be given three times a day to many patients.

It is often useful to measure plasma concentrations because they are not always closely related to dose. Although this can be done for most of the commonly used drugs, it is most useful with phenytoin since the relationship between its dose and plasma concentration is particularly variable. Whichever drug is measured, it is necessary to find out how long after the last dose the sample should be taken – otherwise there may be difficulty in the interpretation of the results.

Unwanted effects

All antiepileptic drugs are potentially harmful and must be used with care. Because adverse effects differ between the many compounds in use, only general guidance can be given here. Before prescribing, it is important to study carefully the *British National Formulary* (1981), another appropriate work of reference, or the review paper by Jeavons (1970).

Phenytoin has many adverse effects. It commonly causes gum hypertrophy. Acne, hirsutism, and coarsening of the skin are sufficiently frequent to demand caution in its use. In the nervous system cerebellar signs occur (ataxia, dysarthria, nystagmus) and indicate overdosage; among children intoxication may occur without these signs, and may therefore be missed. High plasma concentrations (above 40 mg/ml) may result in an acute organic state. According to Glaser (1972) phenytoin can cause an encephalopathy, of which one feature is an increase in seizure frequency. Haematological effects include a megaloblastic anaemia related to folate deficiency, leucopenia, thrombocytopenia, and agranulocytosis. Serum calcium may be lowered. Reynolds (1968) has suggested that mental side effects of phenytoin are due to folate deficiency. However the evicence for this is not convincing (see Richens 1976).

Carbamazepine has fewer unwanted effects. Drowsiness, ataxia, and diplopia develop if the plasma concentrations are too high; idiosyncratic effects include an erythematous rash and, rarely, visual disturbance, drowsiness, and ataxia, and in higher doses an acute organic state. **Sodium valproate** has few adverse effects, the more common including potentiation of the effects of sedative drugs, gastrointestinal disturbance (often prevented by taking the drug with food, or by taking an enteric coated preparation), and obesity. Thrombocytopenia, tremor, transient hair loss, and serious impairment of liver function have occurred occasionally. It has been recommended that liver function tests should be carried out before starting treatment (see *Drugs and Therapeutics Bulletin* 1981) but this is still controversial. The unwanted effects of **phenobarbitone** in the treatment of epilepsy include drowsiness, irritability, and in larger doses slurred speech and ataxia. In children hyperactivity, tearfulness, impaired learning, and skin rashes occur so often that the drug should be avoided whenever possible.

The infants born to epileptic mothers appear to have a slightly increased incidence of congenital malformations including hare lip and cleft palate. These may result from the use of anticonvulsants in pregnancy, but could perhaps be more related in some unknown way to the epilepsy itself. These possible risks have to be balanced against the risk of stopping the drugs in each patient.

Drug interactions

With so many different compounds in use it is difficult to make useful general statements about the interactions of antiepileptic drugs. It is important to remember that liver metabolism may play a major role in the elimination of these drugs, and this is increased by some compounds (notably phenobarbitone, phenytoin, primidone, and carbamazepine). Sulthiame inhibits the metabolism of phenytoin, phenobarbitone, and primidone. Also, some antiepileptic drugs accelerate the metabolism of other drugs, including the contraceptive pill (it may therefore be advisable to use another form of contraception). Antidepressants, anticoagulants, folic acid, vitamin D, and steroids are also affected, and in each case it may be necessary to increase the dose. For this reason, if the clinician is using an antiepileptic drug and is not already fully familiar with its effects, it is important to refer to a textbook of clinical pharmacology.

Contraindications

These are few in number and depend on the particular drug. They should be checked carefully before prescribing a compound with which the doctor is not already familiar. It should be noted especially that phenobarbitone has a limited place in treating epilepsy, especially among children and psychiatric patients, because it frequently leads to disturbed behaviour. In patients who have renal or hepatic disease, antiepileptic drugs must be given cautiously.

Management

The psychiatrist is more likely to be involved in maintaining established treatment for a patient with epilepsy than in starting treatment for a newly diagnosed case. In some patients the epilepsy and the psychiatric disorder will be unrelated. Other patients will have psychiatric symptoms that are secondary to the epilepsy or its treatment. Adverse behavioural effects of treatment occur particularly with barbiturates but also with overdosage of any antiepileptic drug. The psychiatrist will usually be taking over treatment of an established condition from a general practitioner or neurologist, and he should normally discuss the case with them before making any changes. If the psychiatrist initiates treatment of a new case he should remember that the treatment is likely to continue for years; hence discussion with a specialist as well as the family doctor will usually be appropriate. Drug treatment is not indicated for a single seizure (though the cause must be investigated).

It is good practice to prescribe only one antiepileptic drug at a time and adjust its dose carefully. Sudden changes in dosage are potentially hazardous, for they may cause status epilepticus. The drug chosen should be known to be effective for the particular type of epilepsy presented by the patient (see above). If this first choice fails, a second can be tried, again given on its own. With the range of preparations now available it should be uncommon to combine two drugs, and most exceptional to use more than two. Whenever combinations are used, careful consideration must be given to possible interactions. It is particularly important to avoid the following combinations: sulthiame with phenytoin since the former may increase phenytoin concentrations to toxic levels; phenobarbitone and primidone because the latter is broken down to phenobarbitone; sodium valproate, and drugs such as clonazepam which are also sedative. Similarly it is important to review any drugs that are being prescribed for other purposes, and to decide whether they might interact with the antiepileptic drug.

Throughout treatment a careful watch must be kept for the particular side effects of the drug in use. At the same time the doctor must make sure that the patient is continuing to comply with the dosage schedule. He should warn the patient about the dangers of suddenly stopping taking the tablets (an important cause of status epilepticus). If it becomes necessary to change from one drug to another, the new drug should be introduced gradually until its full dosage is reached. Only then should the old one be phased out.

Once an effective regime is established it should be continued until there has been freedom from fits for at least two years. Blood levels should be measured if there is poor control of seizures (since this may be the result of too little drug or too much), or any change in neurological or behavioural state, or other signs suggesting drug intoxication. When drugs are eventually withdrawn this should be done gradually. In the United Kingdom epileptic patients may drive a private motor vehicle but not a public service or heavy goods vehicle, provided they have experienced no fits while awake for at least three years. However patients whose fits can only be controlled at the expense of drowsiness should not drive. If there is doubt, advice should be obtained from a consultant with special experience in the treatment of epilepsy.

ELECTROCONVULSIVE THERAPY

Convulsive therapy was introduced in the late 1930s on the basis of the mistaken idea that epilepsy and schizophrenia do not occur together. It seemed to follow that induced fits should lead to improvement in schizophrenia. However when the treatment was tried it became apparent that the most striking changes occurred not in schizophrenia but in severe depressive disorders, in which it brought about a substantial reduction in chronicity and mortality (Slater 1951). At first, fits were produced either by using cardiazol (Meduna 1938) or by passing an electric current through the brain (Cerletti and Bini 1938). As time went by, electrical stimulation became the rule. The subsequent addition of brief anaesthesia and muscle relaxants made the treatment safe and acceptable.

Indications

ECT is a rapid and effective treatment for severe **depressive disorders.** In the Medical Research Council trial (*Clinical Psychiatry Committee* 1965) it acted faster than imipramine or phenelzine, and was more effective than imipramine in women and more effective than phenelzine in both sexes. (However Greenblatt *et al.* 1964 did not find sex differences in response.) These findings accord with the impression of many clinicians, and with the recommendation of this book that ECT should be mainly used when it is essential to bring about improvement quickly.

The strongest indications are therefore an immediate high risk of suicide, depressive stupor, or danger to physical health because the patient is not drinking enough to maintain adequate renal function. Less strong indications are persistent severe depressive disorder despite an adequate trial of antidepressant drugs; and a depressive disorder causing extreme distress requiring rapid relief. ECT is also appropriate for some **puerperal depressive disorders** when it is important that the mother should return quickly to the care of her baby. In the past, ECT was used to control the symptoms of **mania,** but no convincing controlled trial has demonstrated its value for this condition; moreover, effective drug treatment is now available. Clinical experience suggests that ECT can produce rapid changes in acute **catatonic schizophrenia** (though there have been no clinical trials to test this) and in the depressive form of **schizoaffective psychosis**. It is not indicated in other forms of schizophrenia. The evidence for the efficacy of ECT in these conditions is considered further in other chapters of this book. The reader will find a useful short account in the memorandum of the Royal College of Psychiatrists (1977) and a longer account in the review by Kendell (1981).

Mode of action

The specific therapeutic effects of ECT must presumably be brought about through physiological and biochemical changes in the brain. The first step in identifying the mode of action must be to find out whether the therapeutic effect depends on the convulsion; or whether other features of the treatment are sufficient, such as the passage of the current through the brain and the use of anaesthesia and muscle relaxants. Clinicians have generally been convinced that the patient does not improve unless a seizure is produced during the ECT procedure. This impression is strongly supported, though not proved beyond doubt, by the evidence of clinical trials. Thus less improvement is observed when the seizure is shortened by lidocaine (Cronholm and Ottosson 1960) or when subconvulsive shocks are given (Miller *et al.* 1953). There is also less improvement when the shock is left out but the anaesthesia and all other aspects of the procedure remain the same (Brill *et al.* 1959; Robin and Harris 1962; Freeman *et al.* 1978). Slight reservations must remain because each of these investigations had some methodological problem. For example, in the study by Cronholm and Ottosson patients were not randomly allocated; whilst Robin and Harris used rating methods that were not wholly satisfactory. Taken together, however, the general weight of evidence points to the importance of the convulsion. This conclusion is supported by the apparent therapeutic effectiveness of convulsions produced by the drug flurothyl, or 'Indoklon'. (Laurell 1970, 1968).

Recently, experiments have been carried out with animals to identify changes that parallel those in man. In rats, Grahame-Smith *et al.* (1978) identified changes that occur only when electric shocks are given to the head to produce a fit and only when the shocks are spaced over several days as in ECT. These changes do not occur when several shocks are given in one day, or when they are spaced widely. The findings can be interpreted as showing that postsynaptic sensitivity to noradrenaline and dopamine are increased by ECT. If this work can be confirmed and extended, it might be possible eventually to produce changes in post-synaptic sensitivity by methods that do not involve giving electric shocks.

Physiological changes during ECT

If ECT is given without atropine premedication, the pulse slows at first and then rises quickly to 130–190 beats/minute, falling again towards the end of the seizure before a final less marked tachycardia lasting several minutes. It is generally agreed that atropine abolishes both these periods of slowing, although a controlled trial by Wyant and MacDonald (1980) did not confirm this. If no muscle relaxant is given, there are corresponding changes in blood pressure; if a relaxant is given, blood pressure changes are less although systolic pressure can still rise to 200 mm Hg. Cerebral blood flow also increases by up to 200 per cent. If no atropine is given, transient cardiac arrhythmias occur during ECT in up to 70 per cent of patients; adequate doses of atropine reduce this substantially provided that the heart is healthy. More details of these physiological changes are given by Perrin (1961).

Unilateral ECT

For many years the electric current used in ECT was always given through electrodes placed on opposite sides of the head. More recently it has been found that memory loss following ECT is less if both electrodes are placed over the non-dominant hemisphere. A review of 29 relevant studies by d'Elia and Raotma (1975) suggests that unilateral ECT has the same antidepressant effect as bilateral electrode placement. Handedness is used as a guide to cerebral dominance; it should be determined at least by asking the patient which hand he uses to catch and throw, as well as which foot to kick. In right-handed people, the left hemisphere is nearly always dominant. In left-handed people the left or right hemisphere may be dominant. Hence if there is an indication that the patient is not right-handed, it is usually better to give bilateral ECT. In any case the patient should be observed carefully after the first application of ECT. If there is marked confusion, especially with dysphasia, for more than five minutes after consciousness is regained, the dominant side may have been chosen inadvertently. In that case, the opposite side can be chosen for the second application, or bilateral placement can be adopted.

Unwanted effects after ECT

Subconvulsive shock may be followed by anxiety and headache. ECT can cause a brief retrograde amnesia as well as loss of memory for up to 30 minutes after the fit. If ECT is repeated at short intervals, this amnesia builds up; this does not usually happen when treatments are given two or three times a week. Some patients complain of confusion, headache, nausea, and vertigo for a few hours after the treatment, but with modern methods these unwanted effects are mild and brief (Gomez 1975). These effects are less marked after unilateral ECT. A few patients complain of muscle pain, especially in the jaws, which is probably attributable to the relaxant. There have been a few reports of sporadic major seizures in the months after ECT (for example Blumenthal 1955) but these seizures may have had other causes. If they occur at all it is only during the first year after treatment.

Occasional damage to the teeth, tongue, or lips can occur if there have been problems in positioning the gag or airway. Poor application of the electrodes can lead to small electrical burns. Fractures, including crush fractures of the vertebrae, occurred occasionally when ECT was given without muscle relaxants. All these physical consequences are rare provided that a good technique of anesthesia is used and the fit is modified adequately.

Memory disorder after ECT

As already mentioned, the immediate effects of ECT include loss of memory for events shortly before the treatment, and impaired retention of information acquired soon after the treatment. These effects are less after unilateral than after bilateral ECT, and the type of effect depends on the side of the head through which the current passes: electrode placement on the non-dominant side leads to selective impairment of non-verbal learning. These memory changes are experienced by nearly all patients receiving ECT, and they disappear within a few weeks of the end of the treatment.

Many patients fear that there will be lasting memory change, and some complain of it after ECT. However studies have revealed no differences in performance on tests of memory given before ECT and a few weeks afterwards (Cronholm and Molander 1964). Also several studies have found no significant differences in memory tests between ECT treated patients and controls who had not received ECT (for example Weeks *et al.* 1980; Johnstone *et al.* 1980). However in a study of former patients who were complaining that they had suffered permanent harm to memory from ECT given in the past, Freeman *et al.* (1980) found that these patients did worse than controls on some tests in a battery designed to test memory. These patients also had residual depressive symptoms, so it is possible that continuing depressive disorder accounted for the memory problems. It seems reasonable to conclude that, when used in the usual way, ECT is not followed by permanent memory disorder except perhaps in a small minority; and that even in this group, it is still uncertain whether the impairment is due to the effects of ECT or to a continuation of the original depressive illness.

The mortality of ECT

The death rate attributable to ECT was estimated to be 3–4 per 100 000 treatments by Barker and Barker in 1959. A recent survey of all ECT treatments given with anaesthesia in Denmark, found a similar rate of one death in 22 210 treatments, i.e. 4 to 5 per 100 000 treatments (Heshe and Roeder 1976). The risks are related to the anaesthetic procedure and are greatest in patients with cardiovascular disease. When death occurs it is usually due to ventricular fibrillation or myocardial infarction.

Contraindications

The contraindications to ECT are any medical illnesses that increase the risk of anaesthetic procedure by an unacceptable amount; for example respiratory infections, serious heart disease, and serious pyrexial illness. Other contraindications are diseases likely to be made worse by the changes in blood pressure and cardiac rhythm that occur even in a well modified fit; these include serious heart disease, recent coronary thrombosis, cerebral aneurysm, and raised intracranial pressure. Patients of African stock who might have sickle cell trait need additional care that oxygen tension does not fall. Extra care is also required with diabetic patients who take insulin. Although risks rise somewhat in old age, so do the risks of untreated depression and of drug treatment.

ECT should not be given to patients taking reserpine, but it is not contraindicated by any other psychiatric medication. The anaesthetist must know when the patient is taking a monoamine oxidase inhibitor or lithium. It is, of course, wise to inform the anaesthetist of all the drugs taken by any patient who is to be anaesthetized.

Technique of administration

In this section we outline the technical procedures used at the time of treatment. Although the information in this account should be known, it is important to remember that ECT is a practical procedure that must be learnt by apprenticeship as well as by reading. Much useful information is contained in a report to the Royal College of Psychiatrists by Pippard and Ellam (1981).

ECT should be given in pleasant, safe surroundings. Patients should not have to wait where they can see or hear treatment given to others. There should be a recovery area separate from the room in which treatment is given, and adequate emergency equipment should be available including a sucker, endotracheal tubes, adequate supplies of oxygen, and, ideally, a defibrillator. The nursing and medical staff who give ECT should receive special training.

The first step in giving ECT is to put the patient at ease, and to check his identity. The case-notes should then be seen to make sure that there is a valid consent form. The drug sheet should be checked to ensure that the patient is not receiving any drugs, such as MAOIs, that might interfere with anaesthetic procedures. It is also important to check for evidence of drug allergy or adverse effects of previous general anaesthetics. The drug sheet should be available for the anaesthetist to see. If the patient is not well known to the psychiatrist and anaesthetist who are giving ECT, one or other should check for evidence of physical illness, especially recent cardiac disease. The next step is to make sure that nothing has been taken by mouth for at least five hours; then with the anaesthetist, to remove dentures and check for loose or broken teeth. Finally the record of any previous ECTs should be examined for evidence of delayed recovery from the relaxant (due to deficiency in pseudocholinesterase) or other complications.

Except in exceptional circumstances an anaesthetist should be present when ECT is given (though this cannot always be achieved in developing countries). Suction apparatus, a positive pressure oxygen supply, and emergency drugs should always be available. If possible, there should be a telephone in the room or nearby. A cardiac defibrillator is an added precaution (though it is very rarely required – see Pippard and Ellam (1981)); the anaesthetist's opinion should be sought about its provision. A tilting trolley is also valuable. As well as the psychiatrist and anaesthetist at least one nurse should be present.

Premedication with atropine is generally used to dry secretions and lessen the incidence of arrhythmias and vagal overstimulation. It is often given intravenously in a dose of 0.3–0.6 mg at the time of the anaesthetic. Sometimes it is given subcutaneously beforehand. In any case, the decision about the use of atropine and its route, timing, and dose should be decided by the anaesthetist. (The American Psychiatric Association's Task Force recommends methscopolamine instead of atropine for ECT because it does not pass the blood–brain barrier. However, the evidence that the use of atropine increases confusion after ECT is not compelling.) The anaesthetist then administers an ultra-short-acting anaesthetic agent (often methohexitone) followed immediately by a muscle relaxant (often suxamethonium chloride). The anaesthetist is responsible for the choice of drugs. He ensures that the lungs are well oxygenated before a mouth gag is inserted.

While the anaesthetic is being given, the psychiatrist checks whether unilateral or bilateral electrode placement has been prescribed for the patient. If there is any doubt about handedness, bilateral positioning should be chosen. The skin is cleaned in the appropriate areas and moistened electrodes are applied. (If good electrical contact is to be obtained it is also important that grease and hair lacquer are removed by ward staff before the patient is sent for ECT.) While dry electrodes can cause skin burns, it is also important to remember that excessive moisture causes shorting and may prevent a seizure response. (This can happen more readily with unilateral placement because the electrodes are closer to one another.) Although enough muscle relaxant should have been given to ensure that convulsive movements are minimal, a nurse or other assistant should stand ready to restrain the patient gently if necessary. The electrodes are now secured firmly. For unilateral ECT the first electrode is placed on the non-dominant side, 4 cm above the mid-point between the external angle of the orbit and the external auditory meatus. The second is 10 cm away from the first, vertically above the meatus of the same side (see Fig. 17.2). For bilateral ECT, electrodes are on opposite sides of the head, each

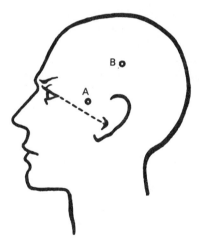

Fig. 17.2. Unilateral ECT. Electrodes are placed: A: 4 cm above midpoint between ear-hole and angle of eye; B: 10 cm further away above ear. (From Crammer, J., Barraclough, B., and Heine, B. *The use of drugs in psychiatry.* Gaskell, London (1978).)

4 cm above the mid-point of the line joining the external angle of the orbit to the external auditory meatus – usually just above the hairline. The shock is now given.

Various types of machine are available to give the electric shock. In Great

Britain about half of all ECT is given with a bidirectional sinusoidal or modified sinusoidal waveform, and most of the rest with unidirectional stimuli (Pippard and Ellam 1981). There is, so far, no evidence that any one method is better than the rest. Indeed, it is not certain whether it is the quantity of electricity delivered (the charge), the energy (work done), or the peak initial current that is important. It is important to study the manufacturer's instructions for the use of each machine. Useful information will also be found in Appendix 6 to the monograph by Pippard and Ellam. ECT machines should be tested and serviced regularly to ensure that they are safe and that the correct amount of current is being delivered. A recent survey found that 40 per cent of clinics did not maintain the machines regularly and only half had an up-to-date reserve machine (Pippard and Ellam 1981).

If a satisfactory degree of relaxation has been achieved, the seizure will take the following form. First, the muscles of the face begin to twitch, the mouth drops open, then the big toes, thumbs, and upper eyelids jerk rhythmically for about half a minute. After the seizure, the lungs are oxygenated thoroughly with an airway in place. The patient remains in the care of the anaesthetist and under close nursing observation until breathing resumes and consciousness is restored. During recovery, the patient should be turned on his side and cared for in the usual way for anyone recovering from an anaesthetic after a minor surgical procedure. A qualified nurse should be in attendance to supervise the patient and reassure him. Meanwhile the psychiatrist makes a note of the date, type of electrode placement, drugs used, and amount of current, together with a brief description of the fit and any problems that have arisen. When the patient is awake and orientated, he should rest for an hour or so on his bed or in a chair.

If ECT is ever given to a day patient, it is especially important to make certain that no food or drink has been taken before the patient arrives at the hospital. He should rest for several hours and should not leave until it is certain that his recovery is complete; he should leave in the company of a responsible adult, preferably by ambulance, and certainly not riding a bicycle or driving a car. The viewpoint of this book is that it is always preferable to admit patients to hospital for ECT.

The most important problem, apart from those relating to the anaesthetic procedure, is failure to produce a clonic convulsion (a tonic jerk produced by the current must not be mistaken for a seizure). If it is certain that no seizure has appeared, checks should be made of the machine, electrodes, and contact with the skin. Also the possibility of shorting due to excess moisture on the scalp should be considered. If all these are excluded, the patient may have either an unusually high resistance to the passage of current through the extra-cranial tissues and skull, or a high convulsive threshold. The charge can then be increased by five joules. (It is not good practice to 'play safe' by giving larger doses to all patients because the degree of memory impairment after treatment depends on the current used.)

Patterns of use

In Great Britain bilateral ECT is usually given twice a week, although in urgent cases three applications may be used in the first and perhaps the second week. If treatment is to be three times a week unilateral ECT is preferable because it leads to less memory disorder. In the past, 'maintenance' ECT was given every two to four weeks in an attempt to maintain the improvement of patients who otherwise tended to relapse. Nowadays antidepressant drugs can be used for the same purpose and maintenance ECT is no longer needed.

ECT is usually given as a course of about six treatments administered twice a week. There is usually little response until two or three treatments have been given. After this, increasing change takes place up to about the sixth. If response is more rapid than this, fewer ECT may be given; if it is slower more may be required. Progress should be reviewed once a week, and after six treatments the need for further ECT should be considered carefully. As some patients relapse after ECT, antidepressants should be started towards the end of the course to reduce the risk of this happening.

Medicolegal issues including consent to ECT

Before a patient is asked to agree to ECT, it is essential to explain the procedure and indicate its expected benefits and possible risks (especially the possible effects on memory). The importance of this step is underlined by the finding (Freeman and Kendell 1980) that only one-fifth of patients receiving ECT thought that they had received adequate explanation. Many patients expect severe and permanent memory impairment after treatment and some even expect to receive unmodified fits. Once the doctor is sure that the patient understands what he has been told, the latter is asked to sign a standard form of consent. The patient should understand that consent is being sought for the whole course of ECT and not just for one treatment (although he can of course withdraw consent at any time). All this is the doctor's job – he should not delegate it to other staff.

If a patient refuses consent or is unable to give it because he is in a stupor, and if – and only if – the procedure is essential to save life, further steps must be considered. The first is to decide whether there are grounds for invoking the appropriate section of the Mental Health Act (see Appendix). The section does not allow anyone to give consent on behalf of the patient, but it does establish formally that he is mentally ill and in need of treatment. In England and Wales the opinion of a second independent consultant is required by the Mental Health Act 1983. The requirements of the Act are outlined on page 752. Readers working elsewhere should find out the relevant legal requirements. If the decision is made in this careful way, it is rare for patients to question the need for treatment once they have recovered. Instead most acknowledge that treatment has helped, and they understand why it was necessary to give it without their expressed consent.

PSYCHOSURGERY

Psychosurgery refers to the use of neurosurgical procedures to modify the symptoms of psychiatric illness, by operating either on the nuclei of the brain or on the white matter. Psychosurgery began in 1936 with the work of Moniz whose operation consisted of an extensive cut in the white matter of the frontal lobes (**frontal leucotomy**). This extensive operation was modified by Freeman and Watts (1942) who made smaller coronal incisions in the frontal lobes through lateral burr holes. Although their so-called **standard leucotomy** was far from standardized anatomically, and although it produced unacceptable side effects (see below), the procedure was widely used in Great Britain and other countries. There was enthusiasm for the initial improvements observed in patients, but this was followed by growing evidence of adverse effects including intellectual impairment, emotional lability, disinhibition, apathy, incontinence, obesity and epilepsy. This led to a search for more restricted lesions capable of producing the same therapeutic benefits without these adverse consequences. Some progress was made but at the same time advances in pharmacology made it possible to use drugs to treat the disorders for which surgery was intended.

There have been no controlled trials to test the value of these operations. If such surgery is used at all, it should be only after the most thorough and persistent attempts to produce improvement with other forms of treatment. If this is done, the requirement for psychosurgery will be extremely small. It is not easy to judge how widely the operations are used. A survey of the 44 neurological units in the British Isles showed that the number of these operations had declined from 158 per annum in 1974 to 119 in 1976, and that they had been performed for persistent depression, anxiety states, and obsessive compulsive neurosis (Barraclough and Mitchell-Heggs 1978). The numbers have probably fallen further since this survey.

Types of operation

As operations on the frontal lobe became anatomically less extensive, the most commonly used procedures in Great Britain became restricted undercutting of the medial third of the orbital cortex, and a bimedial operation aimed at the fronto-thalamic bundle. At the same time it became clear that the frontal cortex has complex connections with the hypothalamus, temporal cortex, hippocampus, amygdala, and mamillary bodies. The surgical approach was therefore directed to some of these connections as well as to the frontal lobe.

Nowadays the older 'blind' operations have been replaced by stereotactic procedures that allow the lesions to be placed more accurately. These stereotactic operations are tractotomy, limbic leucotomy, and amygdalotomy. In **stereotactic tractotomy**, the target is the posterior part of the area incised in orbital undercutting. The lesion is produced by implanting radioactive yttrium 'seeds' (see Knight 1972). In **stereotactic limbic leucotomy** small bilateral lesions are placed in the lower medial quadrant of the frontal lobe to interrupt two of the fronto-limbic pathways, and in the cingulum (Richardson 1973). In **amygdalotomy** bilateral lesions are placed in the amygdala, usually in an attempt to control aggressive behaviour (see Small *et al.* 1977).

After the operation, there is usually a decline in anxiety and tension; other symptoms recover more slowly. If the treatment is used at all, it is important to carry out appropriate rehabilitation during the post-operative period. This will vary according to the condition being treated; for obsessional neurosis, a behavioural treatment is appropriate, while for depressive disorder a gradual programme of social rehabilitation is required.

Indications

There is no general agreement about these. Some clinicians consider that psychosurgery should never be used, others regard it as the treatment of choice for a few intractable disorders. Because no satisfactory controlled evaluation has been carried out, judgements have to be made on the uncertain basis of follow-up studies of patients subjected to one procedure. Patients treated by stereotactic subcaudate tractotomy have been followed by Ström-Olsen and Carlisle (1971) who reported on 210 patients, and by Göktepe *et al.* (1975) who reported on a further 208. In these two series the few schizophrenics changed little, while improvement rates were about 70 per cent for depressive disorders, 60 per cent for anxiety states, and 50 per cent for obsessional neuroses. However the criteria of improvement were far from rigorous, and the lack of controls makes it impossible to decide how much improvement would have taken place without the operations.

Sixty-six patients treated with **stereotactic limbic leucotomy** were followed by Mitchell-Heggs *et al.* (1976) who concluded that this operation could benefit chronic schizophrenic patients as well as others. They reported improvement rates of 78 per cent for depressive disorders, 66 per cent for chronic anxiety neuroses, and 89 per cent for obsessional disorders. Again methodological shortcomings make it difficult to interpret the significance of these findings.

Unwanted effects

The serious adverse effects of the early operations have been mentioned already. With modern stereotactic procedures, residual effects are far fewer but when they do occur they follow the same pattern of apathy, excessive weight gain, disinhibition, and epilepsy.

Management

In our experience, vigorous and persistent treatment with drugs and behavioural methods almost always leads to an acceptable remission in patients who might be considered for psychosurgery. A good rule is that the operation should never be carried out until the effects of at least a year of vigorous inpatient treatment have been observed. If this rule is followed, the operation will hardly be used. If the operation is to be considered at all, it should only be for chronic intractable obsessional disorder and severe chronic depressive disorders in older patients. There is no clear justification for psychosurgery for anxiety neuroses or schizophrenia. For an account of a less conservative view the reader should consult Bartlett *et al.* (1981).

OBSOLETE TREATMENTS

Continuous narcosis

Many psychiatric patients report sleeping badly for months, and some say that they desire a prolonged period of sleep. In continuous narcosis, this is provided by heavy and repeated sedation continued for several days at a time. The patient is kept asleep throughout the day as well as the night, being wakened only to eat and to evacuate the bladder and bowels. This procedure has been used for severe and chronic anxiety and obsessional neuroses, and it is often followed by a temporary period of relief. There is no evidence that the longer effects are better than those of less intensive treatment, and the method has fallen from general use. Sargant and Slater (1963) provide a detailed account.

Insulin coma therapy

This was introduced in the late 1930s by Sakel (1938) as a treatment for schizophrenia, and for many years was used extensively without controlled evaluation. Eventually Ackner and Oldham (1962) found that insulin coma therapy had no more therapeutic effect than repeated periods of unconsciousness produced by sedative hypnotics. In any case the antipsychotic drugs were being introduced at the same time and proved to have powerful therapeutic effects. Insulin coma soon ceased to be used. The procedure was, essentially, to produce repeated hypoglycaemic comas with insulin and then reverse them after an interval by giving glucose. An account of the methods is given by Sargant and Slater (1963).

Modified insulin therapy

Many psychiatric patients lose weight during their illness. It has always been part of treatment to attempt to restore weight as psychological improvement occurs. During and after the Second World War a treatment became popular in which small doses of insulin were given to improve the appetite of patients with chronic anxiety neuroses with the hope that this would also improve their anxiety. Today it is considered more logical to bring about weight gain by treating the primary psychological disorder. Modified insulin treatment is no longer in general use, and is not recommended in this book. Those who wish to find out more should consult Sargant and Slater (1963).

FURTHER READING

Barchas, J.D., Berger, P.A., Ciaranello, R.D. and Elliot, G.R. (1977). *Psychopharmacology.* Oxford University Press, New York.

Crammer, J., Barraclough, B. and Heine, B. (1982). *Use of drugs in psychiatry,* 2nd edn. Gaskell, London.

Green A.R. and Costain, D. (1981). *Pharmacology and biochemistry of psychiatric disorders.* John Wiley, Chichester.

Royal College of Psychiatrists (1977). Memorandum on the use of electroconvulsive therapy. *British Journal of Psychiatry* **131,** 261–72.

Silverstone, T. and Turner, P. (1982). *Drug treatment in psychiatry,* 2nd edn. Routledge and Kegan Paul. London.

18. Psychological treatment

This chapter is concerned with the various kinds of psychotherapy and behaviour therapy and with some related treatments such as relaxation. The subject is large, and it will be easier to follow if the reader's attention is drawn to certain points about the organization of the chapter and its relation to other parts of the book. First, this account should be read in conjunction with the general advice about planning treatment in the previous chapter and about the provision of services in Chapter 19. Secondly, although this chapter includes general comments about the value of the different treatments, advice about their specific use will be found in the chapters concerned with particular syndromes. Thirdly, because the chapter has to cover many different techniques of treatment, it is not possible to consider each in detail. For this reason suggestions for further reading are given. Finally, and most important, it should be remembered that psychological treatments cannot be learnt by reading alone; it is also necessary to obtain appropriate and adequately supervised experience of some of the methods.

The first part of this chapter deals with psychotherapy, and the second with behaviour therapy. The account of psychotherapy begins with some general considerations. First the main types of psychotherapy are listed, then an outline is given of simple psychotherapy of the kind that might be carried out by a psychiatrist early in his training. Next comes a review of features that are common to this simple kind of treatment and to other forms of psychotherapy. A historical outline is then given of the main influences that have led to the kinds of psychotherapy employed today. This general section is followed by a systematic account of the most important kinds of psychotherapy, and by a brief review of research on this subject. Next comes a similar review of the principal kinds of behaviour therapy; and finally a brief reference to some other forms of psychological treatment such as relaxation, autogenic training, abreaction, and hypnosis.

GENERAL CONSIDERATIONS

Types of psychotherapy and general indications for their use

It is helpful to have a broad framework in which to place the many forms of psychotherapy. One practical scheme divides psychotherapy along two dimensions, the first concerned with the complexity of the procedures, and the second with the number of patients taking part. On the first dimension treatments can be divided into: simple psychotherapy which is appropriate in general practice; short or long-term supportive psychotherapy which can be provided by all psychiatrists; and special methods which are best provided by specialists in psychotherapy (see Skynner and Brown 1981). On the second dimension, treatments can be divided into psychotherapy with a single patient (individual psychotherapy), psychotherapy with couples, small group therapy, and large group therapy.

In general practice, psychotherapy may be considered either for patients with emotional problems of short duration, or for patients who need help in coming to terms with the effects of incurable illness, whether physical or mental. Some general practitioners with a special interest may undertake psychotherapy with other groups of patients, but most will consider referring patients with more difficult problems to a psychiatrist.

Psychiatrists are likely to use psychotherapy as the main treatment for young patients with personality disorders of a moderate degree (other than the anti-social type), and for patients with neuroses in which anxiety and depressive symptoms are the main features. (Phobic, obsessional, and general anxiety neuroses are more likely to require behavioural methods.) Psychiatrists are likely to refer certain problems to a specialist psychotherapist, such as severe personality disorders in young people, especially those with marked schizoid or histrionic features, together with other cases exceptionally complicated. (In practice, many patients suitable for treatment by a general psychiatrist are given psychotherapy by trainee psychiatrists under the supervision of a specialist psychotherapist.)

On the choice between individual, group, marital, or family therapy, it can be said at this stage that individual therapy is more suitable for specific problems that can be the focus of short-term treatment. It is also appropriate for people who would feel unduly awkward in a group, either through shyness or through the nature of their problems (for example a sexual deviation). Otherwise, for patients whose problems mainly concern their relationships with other people, individual and group therapy are usually equally effective.

Marital therapy is appropriate when the emotional problems mainly reside in the relationship between the two partners of a marriage. Family therapy may be employed when the difficulties of an older child or adolescent reflect those of his parents. These preliminary generalizations are provided as a background to the chapter, but it will become evident that they frequently need to be modified.

What happens in psychotherapy?

It is difficult to give a concise answer to this question, because there are many different forms of psychotherapy. The basic elements can be illustrated in an outline of brief therapy of the kind that might be carried out by a psychiatrist over a few months with a patient whose problems are mainly in personal relationships.

After taking a full psychiatric history, the therapist discusses with the patient what aspects of his problems are to be dealt with in treatment, what aims are realistic, and how long treatment will last. In this sort of treatment, between five and twenty sessions might be allocated depending on the complexity of the problems. The therapist emphasizes that the patient will be helped to find his own solutions to his problems; the therapist's role is not to provide the solutions but to help the patient towards them.

The patient is then asked to talk about one of the problems selected for consideration. He is encouraged to give specific examples of events that can be examined in detail with the intention of finding out how he thought, felt, and acted at the time. Various prompts and other interviewing techniques are required for this, but they are essentially similar to those described in Chapter 2. To encourage the patient to think aloud about his difficulties, the therapist says little. He encourages the patient to talk about emotionally painful subjects rather than avoid them, to review his own part in any difficulties that he ascribes to other people, and to look for common themes in what he is describing. At times the therapist helps the patient to look back on his life to see how present patterns of behaviour began. He asks him to consider whether behaviour that served a purpose in the past is continuing to the present, although no longer appropriate. Finally, he encourages the patient to consider alternative ways of thinking and behaving in situations that cause difficulties.

Throughout treatment, the therapist pays as much attention to the patient's non-verbal behaviour as to his words, because discrepancies between the two often point to problems that have not yet been expressed directly. He also watches for behaviour that suggests undue emotional attachment to the therapist. If such attachment is suspected, it is discussed with the patient. At the same time the therapist must be sensitive to his own emotional reactions to the patient, and make sure that he is neither over-involved nor rejecting. If he does have such feelings, he should try to find out why – if necessary through discussion with a colleague.

In the middle phase of treatment, the patient continues to talk about the problems he identified at the start and examines current examples. The therapist points out any patterns of behaviour that are being repeated, and relates them to the patient's account of childhood experiences. He also comments on the patient's emotional reactions during the interview.

As the end of treatment approaches, the patient should feel that he has a better understanding of the problems selected at the beginning, and should be more confident of dealing with them himself. At this stage the patient should no longer feel too dependent on the therapist, but it is often useful to ease the separation by arranging a few follow-up appointments spaced over two or three months.

Other forms of psychotherapy differ from this basic procedure in several ways. First, many long-term treatments begin in an unstructured way; the patient is simply asked to talk about anything that occurs to him, with the expectation that themes and goals will emerge later. Secondly, treatments differ in the number and kind of explanations offered by the therapist. In the simple kind of treatment just described, explanations are based mainly on common sense. In more intensive treatments, they are based on some theory of psychological development – for example that of psychoanalysis. As a rule, formulations based on a theoretical framework are not presented to the patient *in toto*, but revealed piecemeal in the form of comments about the origins of his behaviour and feelings as they gradually emerge during the interviews. (These comments are one form of interpretation.) Thirdly, treatments differ in how far attention is given to matters other than day-to-day experiences. In some treatments, fantasies in the form of dreams, paintings, and poetry are used extensively to encourage the patient to examine aspects of his personality of which he was previously unaware. Fourthly, treatments differ in the extent to which the relationship between patient and therapist is encouraged to develop into a transference, which can then be utilized to put the patient more in touch with his own feelings and reactions.

Common factors in psychotherapy

In all forms of psychotherapy, the therapist tries to help the patient to overcome emotional problems by a combination of *listening* and *talking*. In this process, listening is generally more important than talking because the main purpose is to help the patient to understand himself more clearly. For the patient, part of this process is thinking aloud, which is a good way to clarify ideas that have not been put into words before. It also helps the patient to become aware of links between aspects of feelings and behaviour that have previously been unrecognized.

Most people receiving psychotherapy have tried to deal with their problems without success, and are demoralized. *Restoration of morale* is an important part of treatment. Similarly, patients receiving psychological treatment usually need encouragement to believe that they can solve their own difficulties without depending on others. People seeking treatment are also emotionally aroused. All forms of psychotherapy provide for the *release of emotion*, some rapidly, some slowly. Rapid release, which is sometimes called abreaction, may be helpful in acute neuroses, but it is not generally useful to repeat the process unless the discharge of emotion is coupled with a rethinking of problems.

All forms of psychological treatment include a *rationale* that makes the patient's disorder more intelligible. This rationale may be described in detail by the therapist (as in the behaviour therapies or short-term psychotherapy), or the patient may have to piece it together from partial explanations and interpretations (as in psychoanalytically-oriented treatments). Whatever the method of imparting the rationale, it has the effect of making problems more understandable and therefore gives the patient more confidence that he can solve his problems.

All psychotherapy contains an element of *suggestion*. In hypnosis this is deliberately cultivated as the main agent of change. In other treatments suggestion is removed as much as possible because its effects are generally not lasting.

Tranference and countertransference

Another component of psychotherapy, the relationship between patient and therapist, is present from the start and grows more important as treatment lasts longer or is carried out more frequently. Even in the shortest forms of psycho-therapy this relationship forms the cornerstone of treatment, helping to sustain the patient through his difficulties and to motivate him to overcome his problems. As treatment progresses, the realistic relationship or 'treatment alliance' becomes more intense, and unrealistic elements are superimposed on it. These arise largely because the therapist listens more than he talks. As a result, the patient reveals personal problems that in other circumstances would not be revealed at all, or only to an intimate friend or close relation. The psychotherapist, on the other hand, tells the patient little about his own back-ground or personal beliefs. The intimacy of the situation causes the patient to react to the therapist as if he were a close relation – usually a parent. The patient cannot correct his fantasies about the therapist by knowing what he is really like. As a result, the patient transfers to the therapist feelings and attitudes that were originally experienced in relation to other significant persons with whom he experienced a comparable intimacy in earlier life – usually the parents. It is for this reason that the process is called the transference.

The therapist's role is unlike that of his everyday relationships. He has to remain an impartial professional adviser and yet be genuinely concerned with his patient's most intimate problems. Despite his training, the therapist cannot always achieve this. As treatment progresses he may begin to respond to the patient in a way that reflects not only the latter's emotional make-up but also the therapist's own emotional reaction. This is called counter-transference.

Both transference and counter-transference can be impediments to treatment, but both can be turned to advantage. One disadvantage of transference is that it may induce behaviour that distracts from the main plan of treatment; for example, there may be attempts to prolong interviews, requests for extra appointments, and dramatic behaviours demanding urgent action such as threats of suicide. Transference may also make it difficult to bring treatment to an end; there may be a recrudescence of symptoms that had improved, and demands for further treatment. If these behaviours are noticed early and discussed, difficulties can be prevented with the added advantage that the patient learns more about himself.

Counter-transference causes difficulties when the therapist becomes inappro-priately involved in the patient's problems or is inappropriately angry with him. It too can be turned to advantage. If the therapist recognizes these feelings and examines how they have arisen, he will learn more about his patient and – equally important – about himself.

Transference and counter-transference are most developed in the intensive forms of treatment based on psychoanalysis, where transference is encouraged in order to use it therapeutically. However, it is important to realize that transference and counter-transference occur to some degree in every form of psychological treatment.

How modern psychotherapy developed

The use of psychological healing must be as old as the practice of medicine itself. Parallels are often drawn between aspects of modern psychotherapy and the ceremonials carried out in some of the ancient Greek temples of healing. However, the history of formal psychotherapy starts in the mid-nineteenth century. At that time, the most important developments concerned hypnosis, which came to the attention of doctors in Great Britain and France through the activities of Anton Mesmer. In England, it was a Manchester doctor, James Braid, who first properly detached hypnosis from mystical and superstitious practices. Braid suggested the name hypnosis in a book (Braid 1843) in which he attempted a physiological explanation drawing parallels between hypnosis and sleep. In contrast Alexander Bertrand, who worked in France, was more concerned with the psychological determinants of the hypnotic state.

The main alternative form of psychotherapy was called persuasion, a treatment that relied on argument rather than suggestion. In contrast to hypnosis it did not set out to impress the patient and make him suggestible. Instead it relied on discussion of symptoms and other problems in ways that might help the patient to control them and become more self-reliant. The treatment was not based on any special theory of psychological development, but rather on the physician's good sense and understanding of people and disease.

Freud's interest in psychological treatment began with hypnosis. In Paris in 1886 he saw Charcot's demonstrations of hypnosis with hysterical patients. He tried the method with some of his own neurotic patients and at first was pleased by its success. He was not a particularly good hypnotist and his early successes were not always repeated. He therefore began to modify the method, and by progressive changes eventually arrived at the technique of psychoanalysis on which most modern forms of psychotherapy are based. At first Freud used hypnosis to suppress symptoms (Greenson 1967) but by 1889, in the case of Emmy von N., he was employing it to release the emotion associated with repressed ideas. Remembering Bernheim's demonstration that patients could recall forgotten events under the influence of waking suggestion, Freud used this method instead, requiring his patients to shut their eyes while he placed his hands on the forehead (Breuer and Freud 1893–5 pp. 109 and 270). He soon found that it was equally effective for the patient to lie on a couch and talk freely while the therapist kept out of sight. This was the origin of *free association.* Freud used various methods to encourage the flow of associations, to comment on them, and to regulate the intensity of the relationship between patient and analyst. These methods made up the basic technique of psychoanalysis and subsequently of much psychotherapy. They are described briefly later in this chapter. The interested reader is recommended to read one of the accounts written by Freud himself (for example, Freud 1923).

As psychoanalysis developed, Freud built up the elaborate theory of mental development mentioned already in Chapter 3. Not all of his colleagues agreed with these developments and some parted from him to start their own 'schools' of psychotherapy. As the years progressed various changes were suggested that were too numerous to describe here. A useful short account is given by Brown (1961) and a longer one by Munroe (1955).

Adler and Jung were the first important figures to leave Freud and develop their own theories. **Adler,** who left Freud in 1910, rejected the libido theory and emphasized instead the influence of social factors in development. In keeping with this, his therapeutic technique known as individual analysis attempts to bring about greater understanding of how the patient's life-style has developed, and also places considerable emphasis on current problems. Adler's theories lacked the ingenuity and interest of Freud's. His methods have never been used widely, although they laid the foundation for the development of the influential dynamic-cultural school of American analysts (see below).

While Adler emphasized the real problems in the patient's life, **Jung** was more concerned with the inner world of fantasy. As a result, his technique of psychotherapy relies more on the interpretation of unconscious material as represented in dreams and artistic production, although contemporary problems are by no means neglected. In interpreting these problems, reference is made not only to the past experience of the individual but also to aspects of the 'collective' unconscious which Jung believed to be common to all mankind (the archetypes). In contrast with Freudian analysis, in Jungian analysis the relationship between therapist and patient is less one-sided because the therapist is more willing to be active and to reveal information about himself.

Several other developments followed which were important in the evolution of psychotherapy. All shared the basic analytic technique; they differed mainly in their theories of mental development, and consequently in the kind of response made by the therapist to the patient's account of himself.

The so-called **dynamic-cultural** methods of analysis share some of Adler's concerns with social causes of neurosis. The most important figures in this movement were Erich Fromm and Karen Horney, two refugees from Nazi Germany who settled in the United States in the 1930s, and the American Harry Stack Sullivan. All three emphasized social factors in the development of personality and in the aetiology of neurosis; and all three considered that the stages of development, which Freud attributed to the unfolding of biological influences, were determined to a much greater extent by influences within the family.

Fromm emphasized the need to help patients to understand irrational aspects of their reactions to authority as a way of releasing their potential and developing other relationships. **Horney's** theories were more optimistic than the classical psychoanalytical view of man as a creature led by instinctual forces. In treatment she emphasized the importance in early childhood of the infant's need to feel loved, and of the 'basic anxiety' which she believed to be experienced at this time.

Sullivan on the other hand was more concerned with the patient's relationships with other people in adult life. For him, sexual problems were only one aspect of the patient's problems; they lacked the central importance ascribed to them in psychoanalysis. His treatment centred on the relationship between analyst and patient, and the discussion of everyday social encounters. In this process, patient and therapist were more equal than in Freudian analysis, and Sullivan preferred pointed questions and provocative statements to interpretations based on theory.

Melanie Klein enlarged on some of the biological and psychoanalytical aspects of Freud's theories. Her work has been influential among analysts in Britain, where it has grown into the **'object-relations'** school. Her developments of technique were particularly related to play therapy with children, in which she made extensive use of interpretations. Her ideas have also been applied to the treatment by psychotherapy of schizophrenia and severe ('psychotic') depression, but such a usage is not to be recommended – indeed it is generally contraindicated. An essential concept in Klein's theory is the 'object', a term that refers to a person who is emotionally important to the patient (for example a parent), and to an internal psychological representation of such a person. Klein's theory of personality is much concerned with the earliest development of the infant, with the way in which 'objects' are dealt with at this time, and with the instinctual feelings of love and hatred that accompany them. The theory has been described as 'fanciful projections of a theoretically based therapist' (Wolberg 1977 p. 186). However, a substantial group of psychotherapists use interpretations about object relations whilst employing a technique broadly similar to psychoanalysis.

A further line of development can be traced to **Ferenczi**. By the early 1920s psychoanalysis, which began as a brief treatment, had grown increasingly long. Ferenczi tried to shorten it again while keeping broadly within Freud's methods. He set time-limits to treatment, adopted a less passive role as therapist, and planned the way in which the main themes were to be dealt with in treatment. Many of these innovations have found their way into the brief psychotherapy used today.

The value of psychotherapy

Although in the practice of medicine our aim must be to use only treatments that have proved valuable in clinical trials, there are still many treatments that have not been evaluated in this way. Many surgical procedures in common use can only be judged on clinical grounds because they have not been subjected to comparative trial.

There are several reasons why a treatment continues to be used without a complete evaluation. Sometimes the treatment has been used for so long with such obvious benefit that it seems unethical to test it – for example appendicectomy. In other cases, the desired outcome of treatment is so complicated that it is difficult to devise valid and reliable ways of assessing it objectively; the use of physiotherapy for rheumatoid arthritis is an example. Psychotherapy is used largely on the basis of clinical opinion rather than scientific evaluation. One reason for this is the real problem of measuring the changes aimed at by psychotherapists (this and other research problems are discussed in a later section). Another reason is the belief, held by some clinicians, that the treatments are obviously beneficial. In reading this chapter, it is important to remember that many recommendations about the indications for various kinds of psychotherapy are based on clinical experience and therefore subject to revision when evaluative studies are carried out.

INDIVIDUAL PSYCHOTHERAPY

Brief psychotherapy

This is psychotherapy that aims to produce limited but definite changes in the patient's ways of dealing with situations that cause him distress. It depends mainly on non-specific elements common to all forms of therapy rather than on methods derived from any one 'school' of psychotherapy. It seldom lasts for more than six months and is often much shorter.

The basic procedures of brief psychotherapy have been described already (see p. 577).

Indications

Brief psychotherapy is mainly helpful for patients who have difficulties in personal relationships but are free from serious disorder of personality. Suitable patients are interested in gaining psychological understanding of their own behaviour, reasonably intelligent, and well motivated to change by their own efforts. Particularly suitable are those who have problems in relationships leading to unhappiness and anguish in the absence of a specific neurotic syndrome. Patients with obsessional or hypochondriacal neurosis are much less likely to respond to such brief treatment.

An account of the eclectic type of brief psychotherapy is given by Garfield (1980), while accounts of brief psychoanalytical methods are given by Malan (1963) and Sifneos (1972).

Counselling

This is a particular form of brief psychotherapy. The term is used in a specific sense to refer to methods developed by Carl Rogers. In these the therapist takes a passive role, largely restricting his interventions to comments on the emotional significance of the client's utterances ('reflection of feelings'). Rogers believed that this procedure, together with the relationship between patient and therapist, was therapeutic.

The term counselling is also applied less specifically to other kinds of brief therapy with limited objectives, especially when carried out by social workers.

Supportive psychotherapy

Supportive psychotherapy is used to help a person through a time-limited crisis caused either by social problems or by physical illness. It is also employed to relieve the distress caused by prolonged physical or mental illness or physical handicap. It is often useful with patients who have serious disorders of personality that are unlikely to change with any treatment.

Patients are encouraged to talk about their problems while the therapist listens sympathetically. The therapist offers advice, and may use suggestion deliberately in order to help the patient through a short-lived worsening of the symptoms. He may also arrange practical help. When the problem is insoluble or the illness chronic, he helps the patient to accept inevitable disability and to live as well as possible despite it.

Listening is an important part of supportive therapy. The patient should feel that he has the doctor's undivided attention and concern, and that his worries are being taken seriously. This can be far more valuable than lengthy reassurance. When supportive treatment is used in conditions of acute crisis, patients may be helped by the opportunity to express emotions. However, as noted above, it is not usually helpful to repeat this process frequently.

Prestige suggestion: in supportive treatment, patients should be encouraged to take responsibility for their own actions and to work out solutions to their problems. Nevertheless there are times when it is appropriate for the doctor to use his authority as an expert to persuade the patient to take some necessary first step – for example an anxious patient might be told confidently that he will be able to cope with a frightening social encounter. This kind of persuasion is called prestige suggestion. It is important to discuss the outcome in such a way that the patient sees himself rather than the doctor as having mastered the problem. Suggestion should be used sparingly; if the patient tries and fails, he may lose confidence not only in himself but also in his doctor.

Explanation and advice is important, but it should be borne in mind that distressed patients often remember little of what they are told. Doctors often give information in language that is too complicated. Important points should be put simply and repeated often, and sometimes put in writing so that the patient can study them at home.

Reassurance is valuable but premature reassurance can destroy the patient's confidence in the doctor. It should only be offered when the patient's concerns have been fully understood. Reassurance must be truthful, but if a patient asks about prognosis, it may be appropriate to give the most optimistic outcome of those that can be foreseen. If a patient finds he has been deceived, he will lose the basic trust on which all treatment depends. Even in the most difficult cases a positive approach can often be maintained by encouraging patients to build on their few remaining assets and opportunities.

The regulation of the **relationship** between patient and therapist is important in supportive therapy. Intense relationships develop easily when the patient has a dependent personality and the treatment is prolonged. If there is a real need for lengthy treatment, dependency should be directed to the staff of the hospital or general practice rather than to an individual member. In general practice, dependency may be shown by demands for repeat prescriptions long after any real need for the drugs has ceased, and by a dramatic increase in symptoms whenever the doctor tries to change the medication. (A useful account of these problems has been given by Balint *et al.* (1970).)

Supportive treatment is often mistakenly given to patients who do not benefit from it, or to those who would gain as much from the support of friends and relatives as from the time given by the doctor. It is essential not to abandon people with incurable illness, but support in a self-help group or at a day centre is often more appropriate than individual supportive psychotherapy given by a doctor. A useful account of supportive treatment is given by Bloch (1979*a*).

Crisis intervention

The supportive treatment just described may help people to pass through a crisis unchanged. Crisis intervention attempts to use the crisis to bring about change and to impart better ways of dealing with future stress. It may be used when there is an acute disruption of personal affairs such as the break-up of a marriage, or the sudden death of someone who is loved; or after natural disasters such as floods and earthquakes. The ideas of crisis intervention originated in the work of Lindemann (1944) and of Caplan (1961). Much has since been written about the subject and about the related idea of coping behaviour (see for example Lazarus 1966). The literature is made difficult by a rather obscure terminology, but the essential notions are straightforward. **Coping** refers to behaviour used to deal with a difficulty or threatened difficulty, and it can take four forms: **problem-solving behaviour** which is the satisfactory, adaptive form; **regression** which is the use of behaviours that were appropriate at an earlier time of life but no longer adaptive; and **denial** and **inertia** which are self-explanatory. Viewed in another way, the response to a crisis can be thought of as passing through four stages: emotional arousal with efforts to solve the problem; if these fail, greater arousal and distress accompanied by disorganization of behaviour; then trials of alternative ways of dealing with the problem; finally, if there is still no resolution, exhaustion and abnormal behaviour called 'decompensation' (see Caplan 1961).

Although no two problems are exactly alike, it is useful to recognize four groups according to their themes (Bancroft 1979): **loss problems** which include the loss of a person through bereavement or separation, and the loss of a body-part or the function of an organ; **role changes** such as marriage, parenthood, or a new job with added responsibilities: **problems in relationships** such as those between sexual partners, or between parent and child; and **conflict problems,** usually difficulties in choosing between two equally undesirable alternatives.

Treatment starts by attempting to restore emotional arousal to a near normal level. This is because, if emotional arousal is too high, problem-solving is interfered with; and if it is too low there is little motivation for change. To achieve an optimal level, reassurance and an opportunity to express emotions are usually enough, although anxiolytic drugs may be required for a few days. Patients are encouraged to help themselves, but early in treatment arrangements sometimes have to be made for them – for example, over the care of children.

The patient's problems and his assests are assessed carefully. He is encouraged to suggest alternative solutions and choose the most promising. The therapist's role is to encourage, prompt, and question. He does not formulate problems or suggest solutions directly but helps the patient to do so himself. One way of providing such help is to divide the patient's task into seven stages as suggested by Goldfried and Goldfried (1975): identify the problem, propose alternative solutions, rehearse each alternative until its implications are clear, choose one solution, define the steps needed to carry it out, do this, check the result. In crisis intervention, an important aim is that the patient should recognize that he has learnt a general method that can be used for solving future problems. Treatment is usually short but intensive.

Indications

Clinical experience suggests that crisis intervention may be most valuable for well-motivated people with stable personalities who are facing major but transitory difficulties; in other words, those who are most likely to cope eventually on their own. The generally accepted indications are: deliberate self-harm and other disturbed behaviour resulting from social crisis; and severe responses to major disruptions in life such as unexpected bereavement or natural disaster.

Brief psychotherapy and the general practitioner

In countries with well developed systems of primary care, most patients with neurotic or personality problems are treated by general practitioners. There are many opportunities for psychological treatment in general practice, but little time to carry it out. Treatment must therefore be brief. There are other limitations on the kinds of psychotherapy that are practicable. For example, the general practitioner should avoid the development of a relationship so intense that it will cause problems if the patient has to be treated for physical illness, or if other members of the same family need treatment.

The best known attempt to adapt psychotherapy to the conditions of general practice is the work of Balint and his colleagues, whose ideas have been influential in the training of family doctors in Great Britain. These ideas were based on psychoanalysis, which is perhaps least suited to the special conditions of general practice. In recent years, more attention has been rightly given to an eclectic approach that is not based on psychoanalytic theory (see Sowerby 1977).

INDIVIDUAL LONG-TERM PSYCHOTHERAPY

There are many different methods of long-term psychotherapy, each derived from a different theory of psychological development. All these treatments attempt to bring about lasting changes in the patient's emotions and habitual patterns of responding to people, a process often referred to as personality change. The indications for all the long-term psychotherapies are discussed at the end of this section, after the procedures themselves have been described. Since most of the procedures originate from it, psychoanalysis will be examined first.

Psychoanalysis

Psychoanalysis requires lengthy training which involves prolonged personal analysis as well as supervised experience in treating patients. It is the most time-consuming and therefore the most expensive form of psychotherapy. For this reason, and because its results are not yet known to be better than those of shorter forms of treatment, it is not available in the British Health Service except in a small number of special centres.

In the basic psychoanalytic technique, the analyst tries to reveal as little as possible about himself, while encouraging the patient to talk freely about his own thoughts and feelings ('free association'). This is the 'basic rule' of analysis which, with dream analysis, is thought to allow access to unconscious processes. The analyst asks questions to make the material clearer, confronts the patient with any contradictions, and makes interpretations. Otherwise he remains relatively passive. As this procedure continues, the patient usually begins to avoid certain topics and may show other forms of **resistance** to treatment.

Gradually the patient's behaviour and talk begin to give direct or indirect evidence that he is developing intense but distorted ideas and feelings about the analyst. These distortions result from the **transference** to the analyst of feelings and ideas related to earlier experiences in the patient's life. At the same time a **treatment alliance** develops, that is, a realistic approach between the patient and analyst reflecting the former's wish to recover. The development of transference is deliberately encouraged by the use of a couch and by seeing the patient frequently, sometimes as often as five days a week. At times the patient presents his ideas and feelings not in words (as he is supposed to do) but in his behaviour within or outside the therapeutic sessions (**acting out**). Interpretations are made about this behaviour, and about other issues in treatment. At first interpretations are frequently rejected, sometimes because they are inaccurate, but more often because ingrained habits of thought can be changed only slowly – they require repeated **working through**. As interpretations begin to be accepted the patient is said to gain **insight**. As treatment progresses the analyst's feelings towards the patient change in ways that are partly realistic and partly distorted by his own previous experiences (**counter transference**).

Two of the concepts mentioned above will now be explained further. For a full account of other basic concepts in psychoanalysis the reader is referred to Sandler *et al.* (1970 *a–e*) or Greenson (1967).

Negative transference denotes the patient's hostile feelings to the therapist; whilst positive transference denotes the opposite feelings to the therapist, such as dependency, idealization, or erotic feelings. If transference develops to such an extent that many of the patient's neurotic problems are re-experienced in relation to the analyst, this is called the **transference neurosis.** The analysis of the latter is an essential part of treatment.

As already described, **counter transference** refers to feelings of the therapist towards the patient that are unrealistic, and so an interference in treatment. In recent years the term has been extended to all the analyst's feelings towards the patient, whether unrealistic or not. According to Heimann (1950), some of these feelings provide the analyst with valuable insights into the patient's problems.

Psychoanalytically orientated brief psychotherapy

This employs the basic concepts and methods of psychoanalysis but generally puts less emphasis on the development and analysis of the transference neurosis.

Treatment is shorter and less intensive than psychoanalysis (sessions are usually once a week) and aims to bring about less profound changes. The couch is used less often and the therapist takes a more active part. Some therapists set specific goals (which is not done in psychoanalysis), but otherwise the strategies of treatment are those of psychoanalysis. Readers who require a detailed account are referred to Wolberg (1977).

Other forms of long-term psychotherapy

These vary in the nature of the interpretations, in the relative emphasis put on present problems and early experience, and in the attention given to dreams. The variants of treatment proposed by Jung, Klein, and the neo-Freudians were discussed in the historical section earlier in this chapter. Readers who wish to obtain further information are referred to Munroe (1955).

Existential psychotherapy

This stems originally from the existential movement in philosophy. It is concerned with patients' ways of dealing with the fundamental issues of human existence – the meaning and purpose of life, isolation, freedom, and the inevitability of death. In this method of treatment, increased awareness of the self is more important than exploration of the unconscious, but many of the techniques are borrowed from brief psychoanaltyic therapy. An account of existential psychotherapy has been written by Yalom (1980).

Results and indications

It is still uncertain how far the results of long-term psychotherapy are superior to those of shorter methods. In general the research literature supports the impression of experienced clinicians that patients who respond well to long-term therapy are motivated, at least of average intelligence, and free from schizophrenia, manic–depressive illness, or antisocial personality. (For a summary of the research literature, see Bloch 1979*b*). Clinical experience suggests that long-term therapy is more appropriate than shorter treatment for patients who have long lasting and complicated emotional difficulties, or delays in their personal development. In general, specific neurotic syndromes respond less well than disorders primarily affecting personal relationships. Some therapists have devised special techniques claimed to be suitable for schizophrenia (see Arieti 1974), but these are not generally recommended. Contraindications to long-term therapy include marked paranoid personality traits, and severe depressive personality disorder. Hysterical and schizoid personality disorders, while not contraindications, are particularly difficult to treat.

SMALL GROUP PSYCHOTHERAPY

This section is concerned with psychotherapy carried out with a group of patients, usually about eight in number. Treatment in larger groups is considered later. Small group psychotherapy can be used with the intention of bringing about substantial change in symptoms, personal problems or difficulties in interpersonal relationships; as a form of supportive treatment; or to encourage limited adjustments to specific problems including those of disabling physical or mental illness.

The development of group psychotherapy

Group therapy is often said to originate from the work of Joseph Pratt, an American physician who used 'class methods' to treat patients with pulmonary tuberculosis (Pratt 1908). Pratt's classes had little resemblance to modern group therapy, for they combined supportive conversations with instruction about the effects of disease. A more obvious precursor of modern group psychotherapy is the work of J. L. Moreno, a Romanian who worked in Vienna before emigrating to the United States. Moreno also laid the foundations of psychodrama and sociometry (measurement of the social position of the members of a group). Trigant Burrow, an American, experimented with analysis in small groups (Burrow 1927) and his combination of analytic enquiry and comment on each patient's 'social image' has an obvious similarity to modern group therapy. Despite these developments and others up to the 1940s, it was the experience of treating neuroses in wartime Britain that led to the full development of group therapy.

Pioneering steps were taken in the Northfield Military Hospital, where S. H. Foulkes developed group methods which he had first tried in his civilian practice in 1941 (see Foulkes and Lewis 1944). His method was based on psychoanalysis; the therapist or group leader was relatively passive, and much use was made of analytic interpretations (see Foulkes 1948 p. 136). A different approach was developed by W. R. Bion, a Kleinian analyst whose interest in groups also grew from wartime experience at the Northfield Hospital. His theory of group dynamics (see Bion 1961) was more elaborate than that of Foulkes. It has been criticized as being 'more interested in understanding the dynamics of groups than in elaborating an effective system of therapy' (Yalom 1975, p. 179). After the 1939–45 war, group therapy grew vigorously. Particularly in the United States many new methods were tried with an enthusiasm that was not generally matched by critical appraisal of the results. (A useful account of the history of group therapy is given by Taylor (1958).

General features of small group treatments

Certain psychological processes take place when people meet repeatedly in a small group to discuss their problems. Processes that help people to resolve problems (therapeutic factors) include: the feeling of belonging to the group (**cohesiveness**), learning from the successes and mistakes of others (**interpersonal learning**), discovering that other people have similar problems (**universality**), regaining hope through being valued and helped by others (**altruism**), learning from other members' reactions to the patient's social behaviour, copying the behaviour of others (**modelling**), and the opportunity to express strong emotions (**catharsis**). Accounts of these therapeutic factors are given by Yalom (1975) and by Bloch *et al.* (1981). A general review of the field will be found in Brown and Pedder (1979).

The principal varieties of group treatment

Dynamic-interactional methods

These are now the most widely used small group techniques. They concentrate on present problems in relationships, and how these are reflected within the group. The past is discussed only in so far as it helps to make sense of present problems. The therapist seeks to capitalize on the therapeutic factors mentioned in the preceding paragraph, and to help each person to correct false assumptions about other people's views of him.

Group therapy of this kind goes through predictable stages. At first the group tends to depend too much on the therapist, asking for expert advice about everyday problems and about appropriate ways of behaving within the group. Before long, some patients miss meetings or come late, either because they are anxious about talking in the group, or because they are angry and resentful about lack of immediate progress. The second stage begins as the members get to know each other better and become used to discussing each other's problems. This is the stage in which most change can be expected. The therapist encourages the examination of current problems and relationships, and he comments on the dynamics of the group. In the last stage of treatment the problems of the most dependent members tend to dominate the rest. To avoid this imbalance, discussion of problems of termination should begin several weeks before the group is due to end. A full account of these methods is given by Yalom (1975).

Analytic group therapy is essentially an adaptation of psychoanalysis to treatment in a group. Several varieties have been described. In the most important, **group analytic treatment,** each patient is considered as the meeting-point of relationships with other group members. Interpretations are made about these relationships and how they become intensified into transferences. Reference is also made to unconscious material that is inferred from the talk and behaviour of the individual members. The method has been described by Foulkes and Anthony (1957) and by de Maré and Kreeger (1974).

Transactional group therapy, which derives mainly from the work of Berne (1966), attempts to increase the patients' understanding of their ways of relating to other people. Berne suggests that relationships have three compon-ents: remains of earlier relationships with parents, residues of childhood behaviour, and an adult level of interaction. Berne has written about these ideas in a popular style which has undoubtedly added to the appeal of the method. For example, in *Games people play* (1966) he describes patterns of interaction under titles such as 'see what you made me do' and 'if it weren't for you'. Each encapsulates a recurrent situation which most readers could recognize in their own lives or those of the people they know. Treatment passes through four stages: **structural analysis** designed to encourage each member of the group to recognize the three levels in himself; **transactional analysis** dealing with the ways in which group members relate to one another – for example like adult to adult, or parent to child; **game analysis** examining transactions between several people; and **script analysis,** a 'script' being a consistent pattern of interaction laid down in childhood and persisting into adult life.

Experiential group methods include encounter and sensitivity groups. There are many variations most of which originate from charismatic leaders. Indeed they often have the aura of a cult rather than a form of medical treatment. All these methods can be traced back to the **sensitivity groups** which began in the National Training Laboratories in the United States, and were intended to teach community workers about group process by direct experience in the short term. Another source of ideas was the work of Carl Rogers in the University of Chicago. From these beginnings, training groups (T groups) developed, in which people seeking 'personal awareness' (rather than treatment) are required to talk about their own experiences. The other forms of experiential group share this basic requirement of unrestrained self-disclosure and a willingness to receive frank comments from other members of the group.

Encounter groups are essentially intense forms of experiential group. In some the 'encounter' is entirely verbal, though the words are usually very direct and emotive. Some forms include physical contact as well, for example touching, massage, and rearrangements of the body position of other participants. Other methods seek to intensify the group-members' experience by prolonging it (**'marathon'** groups) for a whole day or even longer without interruption except for meals and sleep. Another well-publicized variant is the **Gestalt therapy** of Perls (see Perls *et al.* 1951; and Fagan and Shepherd 1971). This is a complex method, but one characteristic procedure is to encourage each individual to personify parts of his mind and body in order to arrange an artificial dialogue between them. It is hoped that this will improve the person's self-knowledge.

Many people taking part in such encounter groups report finding them helpful, but it appears that emotional problems are increased in a minority of participants, notably those who had substantial emotional disorders at the start. Not surprisingly, the most direct and attacking methods seem the most likely to have these adverse effects (see Lieberman *et al.* 1973). Although these effects are most serious with encounter methods, it is possible that even the less intense experience of sensitivity training can have adverse effects on a minority of those taking part (Stone and Tieger 1971).

Action techniques

These overlap with some of the procedures used in encounter groups. In **psychodrama,** the group enacts scenes taken from the life of one of its members. These scenes usually reflect either current relationships or those of the family in which the person grew up. The enactment usually provokes strong feelings in the person represented, whilst other members often see a reflection of their own problems. Treatment usually begins with a 'warm up' to help participants feel less self-conscious. It ends with a discussion in which everyone takes part. The therapist often has one or more assistants who try to keep the action going without taking the lead. One technique, role-reversal, can sometimes be used profitably in other psychotherapy. Here the patient and another person enact an event from the patient's experience, but the role of the patient is played by the other person. In this way the patient may be helped to see his own behaviour more objectively and to understand other people's points of view.

Action techniques are used most often in combination with other group methods. For example, a few sessions of psychodrama can provide topics for discussion when a group using other methods is failing to make progress. Instead of building a drama round the personal experiences of one member, the action can be concerned with problems that the participants share, for example how to deal with authority. (An account of action techniques is given by Lewis and Streitfield (1970).)

Indications

There is no evidence that the results of group therapy in general differ from those of long-term individual psychotherapy, or that the results of any one form of group therapy differ from those of the rest. In particular there is no evidence that encounter groups or action techniques are superior to other methods.

There are no specific proven indications for long-term group therapy (as opposed to long-term individual psychotherapy), but it is generally thought to be well suited to patients whose problems are mainly in relationships with other people rather than in specific symptoms. As in individual psychotherapy, results are better in patients who are young, well-motivated, able to express themselves fluently in words, and free from severe personality disorder. Groups are often suitable for patients with moderate degrees of social anxiety, presumably because they benefit from the opportunity to rehearse social behaviour. The contraindications are similar to those for long-term individual psychotherapy, with the additional point that a group should never include a solitary patient whose problem may cause him to be made an outsider (for example deviant sexual behaviour).

PSYCHOTHERAPY WITH COUPLES AND FAMILIES

Marital therapy

In marital therapy, treatment is given to both partners in a marriage. The term **'couple therapy'** is sometimes used to include people living in common law cohabitation. Such treatment is chosen either because marital conflict appears to be the cause of emotional disorder in one of the partners, or because the marriage appears likely to break up and both partners wish to save it. (Family therapy, which is discussed later, differs in including one or more other family members, usually children.)

In the apparently simple step from treating an individual to treating a couple, there is an important conceptual issue. This is the idea that the problem is not confined to one person but shared between marriage partners. The problem then centres on the way the partners interact, and treatment is directed to this interaction. It is generally assumed that a good marriage includes the sharing of values, concern for the welfare and personal development of the spouse, tolerance of differences, and an agreed balance of dominance and decision-making. However, to avoid imposing values, the clinician often adopts a 'target problem' approach, whereby the couple are required to identify the difficulties that they would like to put right. It is also helpful to the clinician in discussion with the patients to bear in mind the stages through which a marriage passes: the adjustments on first living together, and then of bringing up children, and the readjustments needed when the children leave home.

The development of marital therapy

This therapy is a relatively recent development which, in Britain, owes much to the work of Henry Dicks. In his book *Marital tensions* Dicks (1967) proposed that psychoanalytic ideas were useful in understanding and treating marital problems. In the United States, an important influence was that of Bateson's group in Palo Alto who studied indirect modes of communication within families (see Haley 1963 and Watzlawick *et al.* 1968). Another development was the introduction of behavioural principles (see Stuart 1969).

Description of marital therapies

Analytic methods

These employ concepts from psychoanalysis. A central idea is that the behaviour of a married couple is largely determined, from the moment they choose each other, by unconscious forces. Each person selects a spouse who is perceived as completing unfulfilled parts of himself. When the selection is successful the couple complement one another, but sometimes one partner fails to live up to the (unconscious) expectations of the other. For example, a wife may criticize her husband for failing to show the independence and self-reliance that she lacks herself.

The aim of this kind of treatment is therefore to help each person to understand his own emotional needs and how they relate to those of the partner. Various combinations of patient and therapist are used. One therapist may see the two partners together; two therapists may see them together (each therapist having a primary concern with one of them); or separate therapists may see the patients separately, but meet regularly to co-ordinate their treatments. Opinions differ about the value of and indications for each of these methods. In marital therapy of this kind, the therapist takes a more active part than he would in the analytic treatment of a single patient. The therapist is also less likely to make interpretations about transferences towards himself, and more likely to comment on the relationship between the partners and how it reflects the childhood experience of each.

Transactional methods

In these methods, one or two therapists may take part but the partners are always seen together. The focus of treatment is on the hidden rules that govern the behaviour of the couple towards one another, on disagreements about who makes these rules, and on inconsistencies between these two 'levels' of interaction. These issues are discussed around conflicts arising in the everyday life of the couple, for example who decides where to go on holiday, and who decides who is to decide this. In this way it is hoped to arrive at a more balanced and co-operative relationship. A lively account of the method has been given by Haley (1963).

Behavioural methods

These use so-called operant–interpersonal techniques. The therapist first identifies the ways in which undesired behaviour between the couple is reinforced. He then asks each partner to say what alternative behaviours would be preferable in the other person. These behaviours must be described in specific terms; for example, 'talk to me for half an hour when you come in from work', rather than 'take more notice of me'. Each partner then has to agree a way of rewarding the other when the desired behaviour is carried out. This may simply be through the expression of approval and affection, or it may be by carrying out a behaviour that the partner desires. The latter is often called 'give to get'. Described as briefly as this, the treatment may seem a crude form of bargaining that is remote from a loving relationship. In practice it can enable a couple to co-operate and give up old habits of criticism and nagging, with a consequent improvement in their feelings for one another. The method has been described by Stuart (1969).

Eclectic methods

As well as these formal methods, there is an important place for simple treatment directed to specific problems, as part of a wider plan of treatment. For example, many depressed patients have some marital difficulties that are contributing to their problems. A few sessions can then be undertaken with the couple, with attention to specific and limited goals. Often a social worker joins the doctor in such interviews.

Results and indications

Gurman (1979) reviewed the literature and found fairly strong evidence that marital therapy is better than no treatment, and that the behavioural form of marital therapy is followed by improvement in about 60 per cent of cases. Crowe (1973) compared a behavioural form of marital treatment with two other methods, one combining elements of systems theory and interpretation, the other a non-directive approach. The non-directive approach was followed by least improvement, but the other two did not differ in their effects. Clinical experience supports the value of the simple eclectic methods just described, particularly if incorporated in a wider plan of treatment.

Family therapy

Several family members take part in this treatment. Both parents are involved, together with one of the children whose problems brought the family to treatment in the first place. At times they are joined by other children or grandparents. The aim of treatment is to alleviate the problems that led to the disorder in the identified patient, rather than to achieve some ideal state of a healthy family.

Family therapy is a recent development dating from the 1950s. It can be traced to two sources: an influential book by Ackerman (1958) on *The psychodynamics of family life*, and the work on communication by Bateson and his colleagues (mentioned above).

Classification

According to Madanes and Haley (1977), a useful way of distinguishing between different forms of family therapy is as follows: some forms are concerned mainly with past events, others with the present; in some the therapist relies on interpretation, in others he suggests actions to be taken by the family; some have a general strategy of treatment whatever the presenting problem, others apply flexible tactics to the particular disorder; some insist that all members of the family have equal rights in treatment, others accept the usual divisions of authority between parents and children. It will be apparent that these differences lead to many different forms of therapy. Only four will be described here. The interested reader should consult Skynner (1976).

Psychodynamic methods

These use concepts taken from the psychoanalytical treatment of individual patients. It is assumed that current problems in the family originate in the separate past experiences of its individual members, particularly those of the parents. The therapist's role is to give interpretations linking present behaviour with past experience. He also uses aspects of the relationship between himself and the different family members to throw light on their unconscious ideas and feelings. In keeping with psychoanalytical practices he is not directive. Ackerman's work is an important example of this form of treatment.

Communication and systems methods

These owe much to the work of Haley (1963), Satir (1967), and Minuchin (1974). These methods attempt to change the present, rather than explore the past. They assume that family problems can be traced to unspoken rules of behaviour, to disagreements about who makes these rules, and to distorted communication. The therapist's role is to expose the rules, to help the family to modify them, and to improve communication.

The three authors describe somewhat different roles for the therapist. Satir's role is that of a teacher who instructs the members how to communicate. For Minuchin the role is that of a director of a play, who helps the family to try out ways of communicating with one another, thereby bringing to light the unspoken rules by which they interact. These rules are called the family structure, and the method is called **structural family therapy**. Haley sees the role more in terms of provoking the family into desirable actions and of helping them to set goals. He calls this approach **strategic therapy**. The interested reader should refer to the book by Minuchin and Fishman (1981) or the article by Madanes and Haley (1977).

Behavioural methods

These are based on the idea that the behaviour of each individual in the family is maintained by continuing social reinforcement from the others. It also assumes that problems arise either when undesirable behaviour is unwittingly reinforced or when desirable behaviour is not rewarded. The therapist's role is to encourage family members first to specify desirable behaviours, and then to make contact with the others to organize more appropriate systems of reinforcement.

Eclectic approaches

In everyday clinical practice, especially with adolescents, there is a place for a simple short-term method designed to bring about limited changes in the family. For this purpose, it is appropriate to concentrate on the present situation of the family and to examine how the members communicate with one another. The number of family members who are to take part should be decided on practical rather than theoretical grounds; for example some of the children may be too young, others may be away as students for much of the time. Sessions can be at varying intervals, perhaps weekly at first, and then every three weeks to allow the family time to work at the problems raised in treatment.

Indications and contraindications

The **indications** for family therapy, as for other forms of psychotherapy, must be judged mainly on clinical grounds. Its principal use is in the treatment of adolescents. Beyond this, criteria for selection are not easy to define. Skynner (1969) suggests that conjoint family therapy is most useful when the parents cannot cope with the behaviour of a child or adolescent, or when the family makes one member a scapegoat for its problems. Among the **contraindications** are families in which one member has a serious condition requiring treatment in its own right (for example schizophrenia), and families with little motivation to face the true nature of their problems. However, when one member of the family is seriously ill, a few family interviews can occasionally be a useful addition to treatment, either to deal with sources of stress that may prevent or delay recovery, or to help the family to adjust to the illness.

OTHER FORMS OF PSYCHOTHERAPY

Therapy in large groups

This form of therapy is characteristic of therapeutic communities and also part of the daily programme of many psychiatric wards. Large groups usually include all the patients in a treatment unit together with some or all of the staff, the number varying from 20 to 50. At the simplest level, these groups allow patients to express problems of living together. At a more ambitious level, they can attempt to change their members. Change is attempted by presenting each member with examples of his disordered behaviour or irrational responses. At the same time support is provided by other members who share similar problems and opportunities for social learning. The group is sometimes made into a kind of governing body which formulates rules and seeks to enforce them. Because large groups can evoke much anxiety in patients and staff, care should be taken to prepare new members for the experience. It is also important to protect vulnerable people from attacks by other group members and to decide when patients are too unwell to participate.

Self-help groups

All the groups described so far are led by a professional therapist. Self-help groups are organized and led by patients or ex-patients who have learnt ways of overcoming or adjusting to their difficulties. The other group members benefit from this experience and from mutual support. There are self-help groups for people who suffer from many kinds of disorder; among the best known are Alcoholics Anonymous and Weight Watchers. Other self-help groups are helpful to patients with chronic illness, such as colostomy; to people facing special problems, such as single parents or those with a handicapped child; and to widows (Cruse Clubs). If they are well run, such self-help groups can be of considerable value.

Psychotherapy for children

The kinds of psychotherapy discussed so far do not lend themselves to the treatment of young children who lack the necessary verbal skills. In practice there are fewer difficulties than might be expected because many emotional problems of younger children are secondary to those of their parents, and it is often appropriate to direct psychotherapy mainly to the parents.

Some psychotherapists believe that it is possible to use the child's play as equivalent to the words of the adult in psychotherapy. Klein developed this approach extensively by making frequent analytic interpretations of the child's actions during play, and by attempting to relate these actions to the child's feelings towards his parents. Although ingenious, this approach is highly speculative since there is almost no evidence against which the interpretations can be checked. Anna Freud also developed child psychotherapy, by a less extreme adaptation of her father's techniques to the needs of a child. In Britain most psychotherapy for children is eclectic; the therapist tries to establish a good relationship with the child and to learn about his feelings and thoughts, partly through the medium of play and partly by talking and listening.

So far the discussion has been concerned with the treatment of the parents alone or of the child alone. It is often appropriate to see them together at some stage, particularly if the patient is an adolescent. Problems often centre on the adolescent's need to become independent, and on the parents' difficulties in coping with his rebelliousness and changing moods. A description has already been given of the various forms of family therapy that can be used.

RESEARCH IN PSYCHOTHERAPY

Although many investigations of psychotherapy have been carried out, definite results are few. This account is therefore brief. Further information on the extensive research literature can be found in the review edited by Garfield and Bergin (1978).

Until recently, psychotherapy research suffered from over-ambitious attempts to investigate complex problems, although the available methods of assessment were only suited to simple issues. An understandable wish to establish the value of psychoanalytically based treatments was provoked in part by Eysenck's challenging assertion that they had none (Eysenck 1952). This problem cannot be answered until there are valid and reliable methods for the assessment of basic psychodynamic variables. Moreover, there is no unambiguous specification of psychoanalytical method that would allow one study to be replicated by another research team. No amount of complicated experimental design or elaborate statistics can overcome these fundamental problems.

For these reasons, psychotherapy research has been most informative when applied to simple forms of treatment. Work by two groups of investigators stands out as particularly successful: Carl Rogers's investigation of client-centred therapy (see for example Rogers and Dymond 1954), and enquiries into short-term therapies by a group at Johns Hopkins Hospital led by Jerome Frank (see Frank *et al.* 1978). These investigations and others in psychotherapy can be divided into studies of outcome and studies of the processes occurring in the therapy sessions.

Few well-conducted studies of the **outcome** of psychotherapy have been reported, and even they are often difficult to interpret. Untreated control groups are required if treatment effects are to be separated from spontaneous recovery. When a lengthy technique is being studied, controls are difficult to find because patients seeking treatment are unlikely to be willing to wait for a long time. Two approaches have been taken to the evaluation of completed studies of outcome. The first, exemplified by the work of Luborsky *et al.* (1975), is to accept only investigations that reach certain minimal scientific standards. The second, adopted by Smith and Glass (1977), is to include all studies having a comparison group, and to subject them to a statistical analysis designed to yield a composite estimate of change. It turns out that the two approaches give similar results. In general, psychotherapy leads to greater change than is found in comparable patients who are untreated, but no differences can be detected between the results of different forms of psycho-therapy.

Even this finding has to be qualified. Frank's research group found that the difference between treated and control groups grew less with the passage of time after treatment had ended, so that five years later no differences existed. The explanation appeared to be that the control groups continued to improve slowly for several years and eventually caught up with the treated patients. This suggested that psychotherapy had merely accelerated natural processes of change (Stone *et al.* 1961). This finding must be treated cautiously because the patients studied by Frank's group had disorders that were not severe or long-standing. For this reason, their results may not apply to all patients treated with psychotherapy.

An important point in assessing any outcome study is that hidden selection processes operate before a patient is accepted for psychotherapy. This applies particularly to comparisons between American and British studies. As Goldberg and Huxley (1980) point out, in Britain a patient with a psychiatric disorder has to pass through three 'filters' before he can be treated with psycho-therapy. First, the patient has to decide that his problems are appropriate to take to a general practitioner. Secondly, the general practitioner must recognize that the problem requires treatment from a psychiatrist. Thirdly, the psychiatrist must decide to use psychotherapy rather than some other treatment. In the United States, one of these filters is often removed because patients refer themselves directly to psychiatrists. In England Shepherd *et al.* (1966) have shown that general practitioners refer to psychiatrists only about 5 per cent of their patients with identified psychiatric disorder. This difference in referral methods is likely to alter substantially the types of patient receiving psycho-therapy in the two countries, possibly resulting in less severe disorders reaching psychotherapists in the USA.

The investigations reviewed so far were designed to measure possible beneficial effects of psychotherapy. The idea that psychotherapy could harm some patients was first discussed fully in the book *Psychotherapy for better or worse* by Strupp, Hadley, and Gomes-Schwartz (1977) and soon afterwards in the review by Bergin and Lambert (1978). The latter authors found nine well-conducted investigations in which some worsening of symptoms seemed to have occurred in some patients. Clinical experience indicates that, when harm results from psychotherapy, it is usually in the form of excessive preoccupation with emotional problems, increase of symptoms, and 'acting out'.

Research into the **process** of psychotherapy has added little to the results of outcome studies. There have been several attempts to find which techniques and what aspects of the therapist's personality are associated with good results. Amongst investigators concerned with the personality of the therapist, Whitehorn and Betz (1954) reported that they could identify two types of therapist whose results differed when treating schizophrenic patients with psychotherapy. However, other workers have not confirmed these claims consistently (see Parloff *et al.* 1978). It has also been argued that the results of treatment vary with measurable qualities of empathy, warmth, and genuineness in the therapist (Truax and Carkhuff 1967). This notion too was not confirmed by others (see Shapiro 1976).

The study of patients who **drop-out** from treatment has been more fruitful. Dropping-out depends on factors in the patient, the therapist and the treatment (Frank *et al.* 1957). Patients who drop out are more likely to be of lower social class, less educated, less integrated into society, and less ready to talk about their feelings; to have persevered less in any previous treatment, and to be receiving a treatment that does not match their expectations.

The factors that determine whether patients stay in treatment are not necessarily the same as the factors that lead to improvement in patients who remain. Every psychiatrist knows of patients who have persisted for years with a treatment that has not helped them at all. According to Frank's group, the likelihood of patients dropping out of psychotherapy can be reduced by making their expectations about treatment more realistic (Hoehn-Sarik *et al.* 1964). Although such methods are attractive, their value is not firmly established. When Yalom *et al.* (1967) prepared patients in a similar way for group therapy, attendance did not improve, although the patients learnt more quickly what was required of them during group sessions.

BEHAVIOUR THERAPY

The term **behaviour therapy** is applied to psychological treatments based on experimental psychology and intended to change symptoms and behaviour. Two other terms are used to describe these methods: **behaviour modification** is employed both as a synonym for behaviour therapy, and to refer to a particular group of procedures based on operant conditioning. **Behavioural psychotherapy** generally refers to behaviour therapies other than operant methods.

How behaviour therapy developed

Behaviour therapy can be traced to Janet's (1925) methods of **re-education**, which were used for disorders with a behavioural element. These early methods arose from practical experience rather than from any formal theory. It was the well-known experiments on conditioning by Pavlov and on reward learning by Thorndike and others (Thorndike 1913) that provided a theoretical basis for a treatment based on experimental psychology. The practical application of these findings can be traced to the experiments of Watson and Rayner (1920). These workers showed for example that, in a healthy child, fear responses could become associated with a previously neutral stimulus by Pavlovian conditioning. This experiment suggested that naturally occurring fears might be removed by comparable methods. However, although behaviourism continued as a dominant force in psychology throughout the 1920s and 1930s, especially in the United States, there were few applications to treatment except in the use of aversion therapy for alcoholism (see page 607).

The development of modern behaviour therapy dates from the 1950s when it grew from three separate beginnings. In England, psychologists working at the Maudsley Hospital applied learning principles to the treatment of individual patients, especially those with phobic disorders. In South Africa, Wolpe developed a treatment based on his experimental work with animals. He subsequently described it in an influential book *Psychotherapy by reciprocal inhibition* (Wolpe 1958). This book was a landmark because, for the first time, the clinician was offered a practical treatment procedure backed by a reasonably convincing theory and supported by results. The third strand of development began with Skinner's *Science and human behaviour* (1953) in which he argued that normal and abnormal behaviours are governed by the laws of operant conditioning and that similar principles could be used to change them. These beginnings explain the subsequent course of development of behaviour therapy in Britain and the United States. Wolpe's ideas were introduced to Britain by Eysenck (1960) and were soon adopted because they were easily assimilated to the methods which the Maudsley Hospital psychologists had started. In the United States, on the other hand, there was a vigorous development of methods based on operant conditioning.

Exposure treatments for phobias

Phobias can be treated by focusing on the avoidance behaviour, or on the anxiety felt in phobic situations, or on the anticipatory anxiety experienced before meeting these situations. All of these treatments require the patient to return to situations that are being avoided ('exposure'). They vary in the methods of exposure, and in how far they deal with anxiety symptoms felt during or before exposure.

In **desensitization**, treatment is concerned mainly with anticipatory anxiety. Patients are required to imagine the fear-provoking situations vividly, starting with those that evoke little fear and progressing through carefully planned steps (a 'hierarchy'). At each stage anxiety is neutralized as far as possible, usually by relaxation. Short-acting anxiolytic drugs have been used intravenously as another way of reducing anxiety (Friedman 1966) but this method is no more effective than relaxation. Graduated return to actual situations is also practised, but this is generally subsidiary to treatment in imagination.

Improvement in phobias is greater after desensitization than after group or individual psychotherapy (Gelder *et al.* 1967), but treatment is lengthy (an average of 24 weekly sessions of 50 minutes for severe phobias) and improvement is partial. Nowadays the main indication for desensitization is phobia of objects that cannot be encountered in a planned way because they occur infrequently and unpredictably (e.g. thunderstorms).

Flooding treatment is based on experimental evidence that conditioned fear responses dissipate when animals are prevented from running away from fear-provoking situations; if the animals are kept in the situation, fear eventually dies away. In flooding treatment patients are required either to imagine or to enter feared situations in a way that produces maximum anxiety. They continue to do this until the fear exhausts itself. In a variant of the treatment, anxiety is increased further by requiring the patient to imagine fantastically exaggerated scenes (for example a person afraid of spiders might have to imagine hundreds of spiders crawling over his naked body). This procedure is called **implosion**. Because flooding and implosion both cause distress, and because their results are no better than those of desensitization (Gelder *et al.* 1973) their use is not recommended.

Programmed practice is now the treatment of choice for agoraphobia. It combines exposure to actual (rather than imagined) anxiety-provoking situations with measures to control any anxiety felt in these situations. The patient is strongly encouraged to take an active role, and this contrasts with the rather passive role of the person treated with desensitization or flooding. The therapist teaches the patient how best to return to the feared situation, and what to do when feeling anxious. At the same time the spouse or a close friend helps the patient in planning these activities, and encourages him to persist with treatment.

The return to feared and avoided situations (exposure) is carried out for at least one hour every day. Situations are chosen that give rise to moderate anxiety, thus ensuring that patients gain experience of bringing anxiety under control (by using the anxiety management techniques described below). To make sure the patient understands what he has to do, written instructions are used. Emphasis is placed on equipping the patient with the knowledge required to plan his own treatment.

With this procedure, the therapist need spend only about four hours with each patient. (The technique is described fully in Matthews *et al.* 1981.) For agoraphobia, programmed practice gives results comparable to those of much longer periods of desensitization or flooding, and significantly greater than those of non-specific treatment (Jannoun *et al.* 1980).

Techniques for general anxiety states

Anxiety reduction methods derive from Jacobson's (1938) **progressive relaxation**. This procedure uses an elaborate system of exercises intended to bring about relaxation of individual groups of skeletal muscles and to regulate breathing. Jacobson reported that this method was highly successful, but it has not been subjected to any properly controlled clinical trial. Clinical experience suggests that the method is not specially effective. In behaviour therapy, use is made of less elaborate methods of relaxation, which avoid the long training required in progressive relaxation (see Bernstein and Borkovek 1973). There is no evidence that any one technique of relaxation is superior to the rest.

There is a surprising lack of controlled investigations of relaxation methods for anxious patients, although there are studies of their effects with mildly anxious volunteers. Moreover no satisfactory study has compared the effects of relaxation with those of anxiolytic drugs. In the absence of such evidence, clinical experience suggests that the anxiolytic effects of relaxation properly carried out are roughly equivalent to those of a moderate dose of a benzodiazepine drug. However, amongst patients who willingly take drugs, many refuse to practise relaxation diligently enough to produce useful effects. For those who are prepared to practise, there is the advantage that the effects of relaxation increase with practice, while those of anxiolytic drugs almost certainly diminish with time.

Anxiety management training was originally described by Suinn and Richardson (1971). It has two stages. In the first, verbal cues and mental imagery are used to arouse anxiety. In the second, the patient is trained to reduce this anxiety by relaxation, distraction, and reassuring self-statements. In the absence of satisfactory evidence from comparative clinical trials, clinical experience suggests that anxiety management training can produce worthwhile changes in those who persist with it, but many patients fail to carry it out regularly. In those who improve it is not known whether the changes are due to specific elements in the treatment or to placebo effects.

Response prevention and other methods for obsessional neurosis

Obsessional neuroses do not respond well to relaxation or desensitization (see Rachman and Hodgson 1980). For obsessional rituals the best method of treatment is **response prevention**, which derives from the work of Meyer and Levy (1971). When the latter persuaded patients to refrain from carrying out rituals, at first there was an increase in distress, but with persistance the rituals and the distress subsequently diminished. The method of Meyer and Levy required continuous supervision over the whole day. Subsequent work has shown that such intense supervision is unnecessary, except perhaps in the early treatment of the most severe cases. Once rituals have been brought under some degree of control in this way, patients are encouraged to practise keeping them under control whilst returning to environmental situations that usually make them worse. It is sometimes helpful to demonstrate what is required and encourage the patient to follow the example. In the case of hand-washing rituals, this might consist of holding a 'contaminated' object and then carrying out other activities without washing. This procedure is called **modelling** (see p. 611). Treatment often begins in hospital with much help from the therapist, but it is important that the patient should soon practise in his own home and take increasing responsibility for the procedure. Clomipramine has been recommended as an adjunct to response prevention, but there is no good evidence that it improves the results except for patients with depressive symptoms (Marks *et al.* 1980).

When obsessional thoughts accompany rituals, they usually subside as the rituals improve. Obsessional thoughts occurring without rituals are more difficult to treat. **Thought stopping** is sometimes advocated. In this procedure the patient arrests the obsessional thoughts by arranging a sudden intrusion (for example, snapping an elastic band on the wrist). The results are uncertain. Stern *et al.* (1973) found that the effects on obsessional thoughts were no less when the patient practised stopping irrelevant thoughts rather than obsessional thoughts. This suggests that the effects were merely those of distraction. For further information about behaviour therapy for obsessional disorders and about related psychological research, a comprehensive account is given by Rachman and Hodgson (1980). Some further discussion will also be found in Chapter 7.

Assertive training

Assertive training is designed to encourage the direct but socially appropriate expression of thoughts and feelings. It was described by Wolpe (1958) in his book *Psychotherapy by reciprocal inhibition*, and similar methods were reported independently by Salter (1949). Wolpe recommended assertive training as one means of inhibiting neurotic anxiety, but in the United States it has also been used for shy or socially awkward people. In Britain it has not had the same vogue, possibly because the culture places less value on self-assertion. The essence of the treatment is that patients enact social encounters in which a degree of self-assertion would be appropriate, for example being ignored by a gossiping shop assistant. By a combination of coaching, modelling, and role-reversal, patients are encouraged to practise appropriate verbal and non-verbal behaviour. (The latter might take into account eye contact, facial expression, and posture.) An account of these methods has been given by Rimm and Masters (1979).

Social skills training

This form of training derives from the work of Argyle and his colleagues (for example Trower *et al.* 1978), who regard social behaviour as a set of learnt skills that can be assessed and improved in certain ways. Video recordings are used to define and rate elements of the patient's behaviour in standard social encounters. The patient is then taught more appropriate behaviour by a combination of direct instruction, modelling, video-feedback, and role reversal. Trower *et al.* have devised a procedure suitable for patients particularly lacking in social skills. The procedure can be applied to socially inadequate people and to patients with social deficits consequent upon schizophrenia.

The only controlled trial with socially anxious patients showed no difference between social skills training and a much less elaborate procedure using desensitization (Shaw 1979). However, socially anxious patients do not usually lack social skills; rather they are too anxious to put into practice the skills that they already possess. Therefore this research finding does not necessarily reflect the value of social skills training for schizophrenic and inadequate patients. Clinical experience suggests that, for these patients, simple methods of social skills training using video feedback can sometimes be a useful part of a more general programme of treatment.

Aversion therapy

Behaviour therapy is often used to control inappropriate or otherwise undesirable behaviour. Mild punishment is known to suppress behaviour and several attempts have been made to base a treatment (aversion therapy) on this observation. There are two problems about such an approach, one technical and the other ethical. The technical problem is that punishment usually has only temporary effects. The ethical problem is obvious: punishment as treatment can easily shade into punishment given with other intentions. These are reasons enough for not recommending aversion therapy, but research findings also indicate that methods other than aversion therapy can bring about comparable changes in behaviour. For these reasons the account of aversion methods here will be brief. Longer accounts are given by Rachman and Teasdale (1969) and in the book by Rimm and Masters (1979).

In the 1940s, aversion therapy was used for alcoholism. The sight, smell, and taste of alcohol were linked by classical conditioning with nausea and vomiting induced by apomorphine. Despite early enthusiasm (Lemere *et al.* 1942) the method fell into disuse because its long-term effects were uncertain and the procedures were extremely unpleasant.

Later aversion therapy was modified by using mild electric shock instead of apomorphine as the aversive stimulus. This new procedure was introduced to make it easier to associate conditioned and unconditioned stimuli at precise intervals (which are known to be crucial for the development of conditioned responses). However, shock has the additional advantage that it can be given repeatedly, so making possible the use of operant rather than classical conditioning. The former produces longer lasting changes in behaviour.

Used in this way aversion has been applied mainly to sexual fetishism and related forms of deviant sexual behaviour. At first aversion was used to suppress behaviour such as dressing in a fetish object. Later it was used to suppress thoughts and imagery about sexual activities that precede overt behaviour, for example thinking about being dressed in a fetish object. Treatment of this kind has lasting effects in some patients provided it is combined with efforts to encourage normal sexual behaviour (Bancroft and Marks 1968). However subsequent clinical experience indicates that comparable results can usually be obtained without shock simply by encouraging normal behaviour.

An alternative to aversion therapy is provided by **covert sensitization** (Cautela 1967). Mental images of the unwanted behaviour (for example fantasies about cross-dressing) are associated with mental images of situations that the patient finds unpleasant or disgusting. The results of this method have never been established in an adequate clinical trial. Clinical experience suggests that it has little, if any, specific effect.

Cognitive behaviour therapy

Behaviour therapy was developed when experimental psychology was dominated by a form of behaviourism that took little account of cognitive processes. As a starting-point for clinical applications, this emphasis had the advantage of simplicity and it allowed investigators to explore the limits of a behavioural approach. It turned out that treatment directed to behaviour also produced changes in cognitions; in other words, people think differently when they find themselves behaving differently. In some disorders such as depressive disorder, cognitive disturbance is marked with little abnormality in outward behaviour. The question then arises of whether cognitive change can be effected without first altering behaviour.

Cognitive behaviour therapy derives from the ideas of Meichenbaum (1977) and the treatment studies of Beck (1976). It also has some similarities to the work of Ellis (1979) who identified certain self-defeating ideas held by neurotic patients and tried to change them by rational argument. Beck has devised a comprehensive system of treatment (Beck *et al.* 1979) which combines behavioural tasks with questioning and argument designed to alter cognitions directly. The treatment is directed to some of the ideas that are common among depressed patients and appear to exaggerate and prolong their depression. Among these are: negative interpretations of events – if a friend passes without a greeting the patient does not assume that the friend was preoccupied but rather that he was being hostile; overgeneralization – a woman who has cooked one meal badly assumes that she is a poor wife and mother; and maladaptive assumptions – believing that people can only be happy if they are successful at work. In treatment, Beck requires patients to record such ideas and examine the evidence for and against them. Patients are also encouraged to undertake some of the pleasurable activities that they gave up when they became depressed.

At present Beck's treatment for depression is the most fully documented form of cognitive therapy, and there is some evidence that its effects with moderately depressed patients are about the same as those of antidepressant drugs (Rush *et al.* 1977; Blackburn 1981).

Self-control

All behavioural treatments encourage patients to learn to control their own behaviour and feelings. In self-control techniques such learning is the principal aim. The methods can be traced on the one hand to Goldiamond (1965) who suggested that operant conditioning methods should be used for this purpose, and on the other to Bandura (1969) who pointed out the importance of self-reward. Self-control treatments lack specific procedures directed to individual symptoms. Instead they attempt to increase the patient's ability to make common-sense efforts at altering his behaviour. For this reason they have usually been employed when the goals of treatment are obvious but the effort required to achieve them are great. Over-eating and excessive smoking are examples.

Two stages of treatment can be recognized: self-monitoring and self-reinforcement. **Self-monitoring** refers to keeping daily records of the problem behaviour and the circumstances in which it appears. Thus a patient with bulimia nervosa would be asked to record the frequency of binge eating and subsequent vomiting, and to note any association between overeating and events experienced as stressful (see Fairburn 1981*a*). Keeping such records can itself act as a powerful stimulus to self-control, because patients often avoid facing the true extent of their problem and the factors that make it worse. Once the problem behaviour has been documented in this way the patient is required to start '**self-reinforcement**'; that is, he rewards himself in some way when he has controlled behaviour successfully. Thus a woman who is trying to diet might buy herself new shoes on reaching her target weight for the month. **Self-evaluation** refers to making records of progress, and this also helps to bring about change.

In self-control treatment the patient takes responsibility for his own treatment, and the therapist merely advises him. If the behaviour is found to be under the control of particular environmental stimuli, the patient is at first encouraged to avoid them. Thereafter he returns to them progressively in order to extend his control over his behaviour.

Biofeedback

In biofeedback, patients are trained to gain control of a bodily function, such as blood pressure, over which they normally have little or no control. The techniques are generally applied to autonomic functions, mostly in the cardio-vascular system. Attempts have been made to control electroencephalographic activity but the results are not convincing.

The essentials of treatment are simple. Physiological devices are used to measure the function to be controlled, and information is presented to the subject in a simplified form, usually as a tone of varying pitch or a visual display. Even without this information subjects can learn some control over autonomic activity, for example by relaxing or tensing muscles, and it does not appear that feedback adds much in most cases. There are two exceptions. The first is when normal sensory feedback has been interrupted, for example after a spinal injury (Brudny *et al.* 1974). The second is when the task is not merely to alter activity but to change it by a precise amount, for example to lower pulse rate by 10 beats per minute (see Johnstone and Letham 1981). Neither of these requirements is common, and since feedback apparatus is often expensive and cumbersome, the method cannot be recommended for general use at present. Attempts to treat tension headache have been generally unsuccessful (Martin and Matthews 1978).

Contingency management

This group of procedures is based on the principle that, if behaviour persists, it is being reinforced by certain of its consequences, and if these consequences can be altered the behaviour should change. Likewise if some aspect of behaviour needs to be strengthened or made more frequent, this should be possible by increasing its reinforcing consequences. It is assumed in treatment that the relevant positive reinforcers are usually social. They include expressions of approval and disapproval from other people, and actions that are enjoyable and rewarding for the patient.

Contingency management has four stages. First, the behaviour to be changed is defined, and another person (for example a nurse, spouse, or parent) is trained to record it; for example a nurse might count the number of times a schizophrenic patient shouts obscene phrases in the ward. Secondly, the events that immediately follow (and presumably reinforce) the behaviour are identified. For example, nurses may be unwittingly reinforcing the behaviour by paying more attention to the patient when he shouts than when he is quiet. Thirdly, alternative reinforcements are devised; these may be tokens that can be exchanged for privileges, signs of approval by other people, or some activity that the patient enjoys. Lastly staff or relatives must be trained to provide these reinforcements immediately after the desired behaviour and to withold them at other times. As treatment progresses, records are kept of the frequency of the problem behaviours and of the behaviours to be encouraged. Although treatment is mainly concerned with the consequences of behaviour, some attention is also given to events that might be provoking it. For example, in a ward the abnormal behaviour of one patient may be provoked on each occasion by the actions of another patient. A good account of the practical details of contingency management is given by Rimm and Masters (1979).

Contingency management can be arranged for individual patients, for couples or families (as in behavioural, marital, and family therapy), or for a group of patients living together in a ward or hostel. When reinforcement is mainly by tokens to be exchanged for privileges, the system is called a **token**

economy. Ethical problems arise with token economies because it is often necessary to deprive patients of some amenity which can then be earned with tokens. If this amenity is something that the patient should have by right, there is ethical difficulty. It is sometimes difficult to decide whether a particular amenity is a right or privilege – for example the opportunity to watch television.

Token economies often bring about useful changes in behaviour which tend to disappear when the patient moves to new surroundings, at work or in the family. Relapse probably occurs because the patient starts meeting people who respond to him just as the staff originally did in hospital, taking more notice of him when his behaviour is abnormal. Such a setback can sometimes be avoided by training the other people to respond appropriately. More information about the problems of achieving long-term changes is given by Keeley *et al.* (1976) and by Rimm and Masters (1979, Chapter 6).

A further problem about token economy treatment is whether tokens have any specific effect. With chronic schizophrenic patients, Baker *et al.* (1974) found that the treatment was equally effective when the tokens were withheld. Hence it is likely that other features of the programme, particularly the careful planning of graduated goals, must be useful in themselves. If tokens have an effect it may be by encouraging staff to observe behaviour systematically, and not be acting as reinforcers for the patient's behaviour.

Contingency management has proved to be valuable as one component of treatment for mentally handicapped adults. It has also been used effectively for patients with schizophrenic defect states. Behaviour disorders in children have been treated by training parents to act as therapists; this approach has some value in improving the social behaviour of autistic children.

Other techniques

Behaviour therapy methods devised specifically for **sexual disorders** are considered in Chapter 15.

Modelling is a method which requires the patient to imitate behaviour demonstrated by the therapist. Although given prominence in many books on behaviour therapy, it is not reviewed here. The reason is that, whilst it is an important aspect of learning especially in childhood (see Bandura 1962), modelling alone has not proved to be an effective treatment for adult psychiatric patients. It may however encourage some patients to begin using other more specific techniques. Readers who wish to review the evidence should consult the more optimistic account by Bandura (1971).

Negative practice derives from the work of Dunlap (1932) who suggested that tics, stammering, thumb-sucking, and nail-biting could be reduced when the patient deliberately repeated the behaviour. Some theoretical support for this idea is provided by experiments showing that inhibition accumulates during massed practice (Hull 1943); on repetition, reactive inhibition becomes associated with the behaviour which is then reduced. Negative practice has been used mainly to treat tics. Although short-term improvement has been reported (for example Walton 1961), there is no convincing evidence of sustained improvement.

The pad and bell method has been used to treat enuresis since the late 1930s. Two metal plates separated by a pad are placed under the sheets of the bed. If the child passes urine in his sleep, the pad becomes moist and its resistance falls, allowing electric contact between the metal plates which are wired to a battery and a bell. The noise of the bell wakes the child, who must then go to the lavatory to empty his bladder. After this has been repeated on several nights, the child does not pass urine in his sleep but wakens to empty the bladder. Eventually he sleeps through the night without being enuretic. The waking from sleep before passing urine can be understood as the result of classical conditioning. It is less easy to understand how the treatment leads to the child passing an uninterrupted dry night. Readers who wish to know more about this treatment and its rationale should consult Lovibond and Coote (1970). The method is referred to again on p. 669.

Some problems in the use of behaviour therapy

Multiple disorders

Patients often have more than one problem behaviour – for example generalized anxiety with poor social skills. It is usually best to treat such problems one at a time. If improvement can be brought about in one aspect of behaviour, the patient usually feels more confident, and may be able to deal with the remaining problems without further help.

Combinations of behaviour therapy with psychotherapy

Although it might appear in theory that psychodynamic treatments could not be combined with behaviour therapy, in practice such a combination presents little difficulty. The patient must understand the purpose of each approach; for example psychotherapy is given for his problems in intimate relationships, and behaviour therapy for an associated phobia. If the psychotherapy needs to be intensive, it may be difficult for one clinician to change from the more passive role of psychotherapist to the more directive role of behaviour therapist. Hence it is often appropriate to appoint two therapists.

Symptom substitution

Psychoanalytical theory predicts that direct treatment of symptoms will lead to the eruption of other symptoms because the underlying psychodynamic problems have not been affected. Clinical experience and the results of many follow up studies show that, when behaviour therapy is used, such symptom substitution does not occur.

Other forms of psychological treatment

Hypnosis

The technique of hypnosis is intended to induce relaxation and a heightened state of suggestibility. Other characteristic phenomena include relative analgesia, vivid imagery and hallucinations, failure of memory, and 'age regression' (behaving as the person might have done when younger). The hypnotic state is also accompanied by an intense emotional relationship with the hypnotist. There is evidence (for example Barber 1962) that susceptible subjects can be made equally suggestible without hypnosis, and there seem to be no physiological changes peculiar to the trance.

Hypnosis can be induced in many ways. The main requirements are that the subject should be willing to be hypnotized and convinced that hypnosis will occur. Most procedures contain some combination of the following elements: relaxation and slowed respiration, a fixation point for attention (such as watching a moving object), rhythmic monotonous instructions, and the use of a graduated series of suggestions, for example that the arm will rise from the patient's side. The therapist uses the suggestible state either to implant direct suggestions of improvement or to encourage recall of previously repressed memories.

Indications

In psychiatry, hypnosis can be used in several ways. The first and simplest use, which requires only a light trance, is as a form of relaxation. For this purpose, it has not been shown to be better than methods that leave patients with more control over their actions. The second use, which requires a deeper trance, is to enhance suggestion in order to relieve symptoms, especially those of hysteria. Although this procedure is often effective, at least in the short-term, it has not been proved better than more gradual forms of suggestion with no trance. Moreover the sudden removal of symptoms by hypnosis is sometimes followed by an intense emotional reaction of anxiety or depression. The third use of hypnosis is as an aid to psychotherapy, by bringing about the recall of repressed memories, but there is no evidence that this improves the effects of treatment. For all these reasons this book does not recommend the use of hypnosis in clinical psychiatry. Readers seeking more information about hypnosis should consult Wolberg (1977) for a brief account or Wolberg (1948) for an extended one.

Autogenic training

This derives from the work of Oskar Vogt who, at the turn of the century, studied the psychophysiological changes brought about by hypnosis and auto-suggestion. Shortly afterwards, in 1905, Schultz developed from this work a clinical procedure known as autogenic training and used it to treat physical symptoms caused by emotional disorder (Schultz 1932).

In autogenic training, 'standard exercises' are used to induce feelings of heaviness, warmth, or cooling in parts of the body and to slow respiration. 'Meditative exercises' follow, in which colours or objects are imagined as vividly as possible. Practising these two kinds of exercise is supposed to induce changes in autonomic nervous activity that benefit patients with diverse disorders of the cardiovascular, endocrine, and urogenital system as well as neuroses and habit disorders. It has not been established that autonomic changes after autogenic training differ substantially from those following simple relaxation, nor is there any good evidence about the therapeutic effects of the procedure. These methods have not been used widely in Britain or the United States, though they are employed more in Europe and Canada. The interested reader should consult the short account by Schultz and Luthe (1959).

Techniques of meditation

In recent years a number of techniques of meditation have attracted popular attention, and some have been used to treat neurotic patients. Although the individual methods are based on different systems of belief, they have certain common features. First, they include some kind of instruction about relaxation and about the regulation of the speed and depth of breathing. Secondly they include some activity to direct the person's attention away from the external world and from the stream of thoughts that would otherwise occupy his mind. Often this activity requires concentration on a repeated word or phrase (a mantra). Thirdly emphasis is placed on setting aside from the day's activities periods when calm can be restored. Fourthly the person joins a group of people who believe strongly in the method and encourage each other to practise it. Such group pressure is often lacking from hospital-based programmes of relaxation or meditation, and this may explain why many hospital patients fail to persist with the exercises.

There is no satisfactory evidence about the value of these methods. Clinical experience indicates that the less extreme forms have some value for patients whose neurotic symptoms result from a style of life that is too stressful and hurried.

Abreaction

It has long been known that the unrestrained expression of emotion often leads to temporary relief of mental disorder. Such abreaction is part of many forms of religious healing and it has also been used in medicine. Since it is of most value in acute neuroses caused by extreme stress, its main use has been for war neuroses. After Sargant and Slater (1940) used abreaction in the treatment of acute neurosis in soldiers evacuated from Dunkirk, the method was widely employed in the front line of battle to bring rapid relief and so enable soldiers to return quickly to combat. In civilian practice, abreaction has much less value because comparable cases are seldom encountered in which acute symptoms are seen a few hours after emotional trauma. Abreaction can be brought about by strong encouragement to relive the traumatic events. This procedure can be facilitated by giving a sedative drug intravenously. The use of abreaction in peacetime is not recommended. Those who are interested in the details of the procedure should consult Sargant and Slater (1963).

FURTHER READING

Suggestions for further reading about specific methods of psychological treatment have been given in the course of this chapter. The following reading list concerns general issues about psychotherapy.

Bloch, S. (ed.) (1979). *An introduction to the psychotherapies.* Oxford University Press.

Brown, D. and Pedder, J. (1979). *Introduction to psychotherapy: an outline of psychodynamic principles and practice.* Tavistock Publications, London.

Frank, J.D. (1967). *Persuasion and healing.* Johns Hopkins Press, Baltimore.

Malan, D.H. (1979). *Individual psychotherapy and the science of psychodynamics.* Butterworths, London.

Storr, A. (1979). *The art of psychotherapy.* Secker and Warburg with Heinemann Medical Books, London.

Wolberg, L.R. (1977). *The technique of psychotherapy.* Secker and Warburg with Heinemann Medical Books, London.

Yalom, I. (1975). *The theory and practice of group psychotherapy*, 2nd edn. Basic Books, New York.

19. Psychiatric services

The last two chapters have dealt with the treatment of individual patients by physical and psychological methods. This chapter deals with the provision of psychiatric and social services for whole populations. In the United Kingdom these specialist facilities are provided by the hospital services and by the local government authorities, but it should be remembered that the majority of patients with psychiatric disorder are treated by general practitioners. Amongst psychiatrically disturbed patients seen in general practice, only about five per cent are referred to psychiatrists (Shepherd *et al.* 1966); the proportion of neurotic patients referred is particularly small.

Apart from the division of administrative responsibility (hospital and local authority), psychiatric and social services can be divided into two basic groups – those required by acute, and those by chronic patients. It is the chronic patients who pose the major problems in providing services. Some of these problems are discussed in the chapters dealing with dementia (p. 504), mental handicap (p. 686), and childhood disorders (p. 627). This chapter therefore focuses more on patients with chronic schizophrenia.

Before describing the present services, it will be helpful to give a historical outline of methods of caring for psychiatric patients in the past.

THE HISTORICAL BACKGROUND

Until the middle of the eighteenth century, there were hardly any special provisions for the mentally ill. In England, for example, the only hospital for the mentally ill was the Bethlem Hospital, founded in 1247. In continental Europe there was a similar lack, although in the Middle Ages hospitals in Spain were a notable exception (Chamberlain 1966). Nearly all mentally ill people lived in the community with some help from poor law provisions, or else they were in prison. In England the Vagrancy Act of 1744 made the first legal distinction between lunatics and paupers. In the eighteenth century private 'madhouses' (that is, places for the mentally ill) were developed mainly for mentally disordered people who could afford to pay, but also for some who were paupers supported by their parishes (Parry-Jones 1972). About the same time, a few hospitals or wards were established through private benefaction and public subscription. The lunatic ward at Guy's Hospital was founded in 1728, and this was followed by St Luke's Hospital (1751) which was founded as an alternative to the overcrowded Bethlem Hospital. In those days, just as nowadays, there were debates about the value of psychiatric wards in general hospitals (Allderidge 1979).

At the end of the eighteenth century, in Britain and other countries public concern led to renewed efforts to improve the care of the mentally ill. In Paris Pinel gave an important lead in 1793, when he released patients who had previously been restrained in chains. Pinel went on to introduce other reforms leading to more humane care. In Britain William Tuke, a Quaker philanthropist, founded the Retreat at York in 1792. This provided 'moral' (that is, psychological) management based on respect for the patient, rather than the bleeding and purging favoured by most doctors at that time. At the Retreat there were pleasant surroundings, and adequate facilities for occupation and recreation. These enlightened principles were later described by William Tuke's grandson, Samuel, in *A description of the Retreat*, published in 1813.

Despite such pioneering efforts, in the early nineteenth century there were still too few mental hospitals. Many mentally ill people lived as vagrants or as inmates of workhouses and gaols. Public concern was increased by reports of scandalously low standards of care in some of the private madhouses – though many continued to provide good care (see Parry-Jones 1972). In 1808 the County Asylum Act provided for the building of mental hospitals in each of the English counties, but little progress was made. In 1845 it was necessary to enact the Lunatics Act, this time requiring each county to build an asylum. When the first new asylums were built, they provided enough space for their patients, and their staff attempted to base treatment on moral management. This liberal approach was encouraged by the **non-restraint movement**, which began with the work of Gardiner Hill at the Lincoln Asylum in 1837, and was taken further at the Middlesex County Asylum, Hanwell, by John Conolly. In 1856 John Conolly published a significant book *The treatment of the insane without medical restraints*.

Unfortunately these liberal steps were soon followed by a new restrictive approach. More and more patients were being transferred to the new asylums from the community. Under the pressures of overcrowding and staff shortages, moral management gave way to a custodial approach. This change was endorsed by the 1890 Lunacy Act, which amongst other things imposed restrictions on discharge from hospital. These custodial provisions continued into the twentieth century, and their legacy is still to be seen in the architecture of the large Victorian hospitals in which much modern psychiatry is practised. (See Jones (1972) and Rothman (1970) for an account of psychiatric hospitals in Britain and the United States in the nineteenth century.)

In England an early indication of the return to liberal policies was the opening in 1923 of the Maudsley hospital. This provided an outpatient service and voluntary inpatient treatment in a hospital where teaching and research were pursued. In 1930, the Mental Treatment Act repealed many of the restrictions imposed by the Lunacy Act of 1890, and allowed county asylums to accept patients for voluntary treatment. This 1930 Act also encouraged local government authorities to set up outpatient clinics and after-care facilities. Not long after, the new optimism was encouraged by the introduction of treatments such as insulin coma (later abandoned) and ECT. At the same time, efforts were made to improve conditions in hospital and to unlock previously locked wards.

After the 1939–45 war, several influences led to major changes in psychiatric hospitals. Social attitudes had become more sympathetic towards disadvantaged people. Amongst psychiatrists, wartime experience of treating battle neuroses had encouraged interest in the general treatment of neuroses. The advent of the National Health Service paved the way for a reorganization of medical services. In 1952 the introduction of chlorpromazine made it easier to control disturbed behaviour, and therefore easier to open wards which had been locked, and discharge more patients into the community. Vigorous efforts at rehabilitation helped patients by improving handicaps which resulted as much from years of institutional living as from mental illness. Day hospitals were set up, and hostels began to provide alternative accommodation in the community. As a result, the numbers of patients in psychiatric hospitals began to fall substantially.

Whilst a large reduction in mental hospital beds was achieved, not all the early aims were realized in Britain or in other countries. Some patients simply could not manage in the community; of these, a proportion became vagrants or prison inmates. Others survived outside hospital but could not progress through the rehabilitation services. In many day hospital and rehabilitation services, patients attended for years without advancing further (see Jones 1972; Cross *et al.* 1972).

Much of the planning of psychiatric services focuses on the need to provide rehabilitation for patients with chronic schizophrenia. The principles of rehabilitation will therefore be outlined before discussing the provision of services (for a review see Watts and Bennett (1983)).

PRINCIPLES OF REHABILITATION

Rehabilitation aims to remedy three kinds of problem: (i) impairments of function directly due to psychiatric illness; for example, persistent hallucinations, social withdrawal, underactivity and slowness; (ii) secondary social disadvantages, such as unemployment, poverty, and homelessness, as well as the stigma still attached to psychiatric illness; (iii) adverse personal reactions, such as low self-esteem, expectations of failure and helplessness. Problems of the second and third kinds do not result from illness alone, but from the effects of living in hospital for many years. These latter effects are sometimes called institutionalization, or occasionally (following Barton 1959) institutional neurosis. The relative contributions of illness and institutionalization depend on the type of illness and on how far life in hospital has been regimented and socially deprived. It also seems that these two factors interact; for example, patients with schizophrenia seem to be more than usually sensitive to the effects of institutional living (see p. 261).

When rehabilitation programmes began in the 1950s, probably most of the patients were suffering from handicaps that were largely due to years of institutional living, and therefore responsive to the vigorous new methods. In modern psychiatric hospitals, where the social environment is much improved, the disabilities of chronic patients are probably due more to illness than to institutionalization. If this supposition is correct, it could partly explain why recent experience has not sustained some of the earlier optimism about the value of rehabilitation. It has to be accepted that some handicapped patients require lifelong help from the psychiatric services.

Assessment of patients' needs

Rehabilitation should not be regarded as the same for all patients, but should be tailored to individual needs. It is therefore important to assess each patient in relation to six items:

(1) persistent symptoms, both positive (such as hallucinations) and negative (such as lack of drive);
(2) unusual behaviour, especially if likely to be socially disapproved; for example, shouting obscenities;
(3) activities of daily living, such as the capacity to wash and dress;
(4) occupational skills; or domestic skills, such as shopping and cooking;
(5) personal attitudes and expectations;
(6) the social circumstances to which the patient is likely to return.

After these six items have been assessed, a rehabilitation plan can be drawn up to suit the individual patient. The plan should specify the following: the order in which disabilities will be attended to; the responsibilities of each member of the clinical team; the methods and facilities to be used; and ways of encouraging the patient to take part, and of rewarding him for doing so.

Facilities required

Several facilities are required for a rehabilitation programme. They can be divided broadly into social, occupational, and residential. These facilities are partly described later in this chapter, and partly in the chapter on psychological treatment. At this stage only some examples will be given. Social facilities include small and large group psychotherapy, behaviour therapy, and social case-work with relatives or friends. Occupational facilities include occupational therapy and work rehabilitation in hospital; and sheltered workshops, day centres, and day hospitals in the community. Residential facilities include hostels, group homes, and boarding houses.

Occupational rehabilitation confers several benefits. It can prepare patients for simple industrial work (Carstairs *et al.* 1956; Wing *et al.* 1964). It also helps to structure the day, and provide an opportunity to work with other people (Bennett 1970). Payment for work can be an incentive and a source of self-esteem. In recent years, as unemployment has increased among healthy people, chances of employment have fallen for the handicapped. It is therefore less appropriate to direct rehabilitation mainly towards employment in industry. Instead activities such as gardening, home repairs, and cooking can provide a sense of achievement in shared occupation, with less risk of eventual failure.

Further information on practical aspects of rehabilitation is given by Wing and Morris (1981), and by Watts and Bennett (1983).

THE PROVISION OF PSYCHIATRIC SERVICES

As mentioned at the beginning of this chapter, there is a basic functional division of psychiatric services into those for acute and those for chronic patients. Administratively, in the United Kingdom the specialist services are divided into hospital services and local authority services. Hospital services include facilities for inpatients, day-patients, and outpatients. Local authority services include day activities and residential accommodation, such as hostels and group homes. Each of the facilities will be discussed in turn. While the general principles apply to any developed country, there are many differences between nations in the details of the arrangements for rehabilitation.

Hospital services

Nowadays there are two main kinds of psychiatric hospital service – traditional large mental hospitals, and the new psychiatric units in general hospitals. Before this, traditional hospitals were the only hospital provision. Some of these hospitals were built at a time when the aim of treatment was long-term asylum rather than return to the community. All the services were concentrated on a single site, which was often remote from centres of population. These large old mental hospitals have considerable disadvantages, mainly arising from their size and their isolation. (These disadvantages, have been documented by Goffman (1961) and Wing and Brown (1970).) The new district general hospital units have the advantages of modern buildings, closeness to the area they serve, and lack of stigma; in addition, they enable psychiatrists and other staff to mix with colleagues in other branches of medicine. They do have certain disadvantages, including the difficulties of providing adequate work rehabilitation and of creating an informal environment suitable for psychiatric patients, in a hospital catering for the different needs of medical and surgical patients. In many areas there are no general hospital units, and psychiatry continues to be practised in the old mental hospitals. It is often possible for these hospitals to modernize their buildings and create a satisfactory environment. Indeed it was in such large hospitals that many modern approaches to treatment originated, such as the therapeutic community, rehabilitation, and early return to the outside world.

Since hospitals serve populations of different sizes, service needs are conveniently expressed in relation to a notional population of 100 000. In Table 19.1 are shown estimates of service needs provided by the Department of Health and Social Security. In interpreting these estimates, it should be borne in mind, as already mentioned, that in the United Kingdom general practitioners make a major contribution to the psychiatric care of their patients.

Inpatient facilities

From Table 19.1 it can be seen that 50 beds per 100 000 population are the estimated requirement for a district general hospital psychiatric unit. Most of these beds would be for patients with severe acute disorders or exacerbations of chronic disorders. A further 30–40 beds would be required for the 'elderly

Table 19.1. *Summary of guidelines for services at district level Rates per 100 000 population*

	Facility	Beds	Day places
Hospital services	District general hospital psychiatric unit	50	65
	Accommodation for the elderly severely mental infirm	30–40	25–40
	Units for the 'new' long-stay	*	
Local authority services	Hostels	4–6	
	Long-stay accommodation	15–24	
	Day centres		60

*Still to be determined.
From *Better services for the mentally ill.* Department of Health and Social Security (1975).

severely mentally infirm'; most of these would be demented patients. A third category of patients requiring hospital accommodation is the 'new' long-stay; that is, patients who have begun to accumulate in long-stay wards in recent years, despite the advent of community care and anti-psychotic drugs. The number of hospital beds required for such patients is still undecided; it depends in part on the extent of provision of supervised hostels in the community.

Demented patients and schizophrenic patients make up the bulk of the chronic patients mentioned earlier. The two groups have different needs. For example, demented patients are more likely to require supporting medical and surgical services, whilst schizophrenic patients are more likely to require occupational rehabilitation.

Psychiatric day hospitals

Day care is essential if inpatient places are to be limited to the numbers just given. As shown in Table 19.1, the Department of Health and Social Security estimates that, for a population of 100 000, the requirement would be 65 day hospital places for general psychiatry, and 25–40 for psychogeriatrics, depending on the age structure of the population in the area (these numbers assume an appropriate provision of places in day centres – see below).

Day hospitals vary considerably in their selection of patients and the range of treatments they provide. Some day hospitals accept mainly patients with disorders requiring treatment of an intensity midway between outpatient and inpatient care; for example, depressive disorders of moderate severity. Other day hospitals are more concerned with the care of patients handicapped by chronic illness, particularly schizophrenia. Some day hospitals were intended to treat acute patients, but gradually became filled with chronic patients (Cross *et al.* 1972).

Day care is often provided in an area separate from the inpatient unit, sometimes in a different building in the same hospital, sometimes in a converted house in the neighbourhood. Effective day care can also be achieved in a unit providing overnight accommodation for inpatients; such an arrangement can have the advantage of providing continuity of care for patients who go on to day-patient care after an inpatient admission.

Hospital outpatient and domiciliary services

These are an essential part of any comprehensive psychiatric service. If an area is sparsely populated, an effective arrangement is to hold outpatient clinics in towns away from the base hospital, either in the local general hospital or in general practice premises. Apart from the obvious advantage of reducing travelling for patients and relatives, this arrangement enables psychiatrists to meet general practitioners and discuss the management of referred and non-referred patients.

Psychiatrists also meet local general practitioners on domiciliary visits. Such visits may be valuable for assessing the alternative merits of admission to hospital and care at home, particularly if the patient is elderly (see Chapter 16). Also, when compulsory admission is appropriate, the psychiatrist is often required to visit the patient's home.

Hospital-based psychiatric nurses and clinical psychologists can profitably work with general practitioners. Administrative arrangements usually result in separate social work teams in hospital and the community.

Regional hospital services

Sometimes the requirements for a specialist service do not justify separate provision for each hospital district. Instead a regional hospital unit can provide specialist inpatient and outpatient services for a larger population, and serve as a specialist advice centre for doctors working in other places. Regional units can usefully cater for groups such as adolescents, drug-dependent patients, and potentially violent patients requiring specially secure accommodation.

Local authority services

These services include day centres and various kinds of residential accommodation. Local authorities also provide domiciliary services such as home help, meals, laundry, and social support.

Day centres

These complement day hospitals, but have more restricted aims. Instead of psychiatric treatment, they provide company for the lonely, occupation for the handicapped, and meals for people who have difficulty in shopping or cooking. Their staff is non-medical. As shown in Table 19.1, the Department of Health and Social Security recommends a provision of 60 day centre places for a population of 100 000.

Residential accommodation

In a comprehensive service it is important to provide sheltered accommodation, both short-term and long-term, for mentally disordered people. Such accommodation is needed for patients who are well enough to live outside hospital but too handicapped to live with their families or on their own. At present there are many long-stay hospital inpatients who could transfer to suitable **hostels** if available. In a survey of long-stay patients aged under 65 in 15 mental hospitals, Mann and Cree (1976) found that about a fifth of the total could be discharged to supervised hostels. It is also likely that there are many mentally disordered people destitute in the community, in prison, or causing considerable problems to their families, who would be better accommodated in hostels.

Basically there are two kinds of hostel: short-stay hostels, otherwise known as half-way houses, which are intended for rehabilitation; and long-stay hostels for people who are unlikely to improve further (see Ryan 1979). As shown in Table 19.1, the Department of Health and Social Security recommends that, for a population of 100 000, there should be 4–6 short-stay places and 15–24 long-stay places.

In the 1950s the first hostels for psychiatric patients were intended to be half-way houses. Experience showed that many residents continued to need the hostel in the long-term, so half-way houses often became long-term hostels (see Wing and Hailey 1972). This process should not be interpreted as a failure, since long-term hostels undoubtedly serve a useful purpose. Thus, in a study of hostel residents, Hewett and Ryan (1975) found that half of them had remained in the hostel over two years and had reached a plateau in recovery; nevertheless most were working and had little behavioural impairment.

The intensity of supervision varies in different kinds of residential accommodation. In the hostels just described, there may be supervision by medical and nursing staff, or by a resident warden. For patients needing more supervision, experimental hostel wards are being developed. These are hostels within or close to hospitals, in which severely handicapped patients are encouraged to learn to care for themselves, with close supervision available. It is hoped that this experience will enable the same patients to graduate to ordinary staffed hostels (see Wing 1982).

Group homes provide accommodation for patients who need little supervision. They are particularly suitable for chronic schizophrenics who have become independent of the hospital. Group homes are ordinary houses in residential areas. Five or six patients live together, sharing domestic tasks according to their abilities. Community nurses visit regularly as overseers, but as much responsibility as possible is left to the residents. Success depends on discreet supervision and careful selection of the patients who have to live closely together.

Another form of residential accommodation is **boarding out** in a lodging-house or with a family. As early as the thirteenth century, at Gheel in Belgium arrangements were made for mentally disordered people to stay with local families. Nowadays the practice works well in many parts of Europe and the United States, but it has not been widely adopted in Britain (Olsen 1979). See Wing and Olsen (1979) for further information about the use of residential care for patients with chronic mental disorders.

The relative roles of hospital care and community care

As explained in the historical review earlier in this chapter, the development of community psychiatric services has been accompanied by a substantial reduction in the numbers of long-stay patients in hospitals. Since the early 1950s, the number of such patients in British psychiatric hospitals has been approximately halved. However, there is an increasing number of 'new' long-stay patients. In a survey cited earlier, Mann and Cree (1976) studied 400 patients aged under 65, who had been resident for one to three years in 15 randomly selected hospitals. Almost half of the patients were chronic schizophrenics. The group as a whole was severely disabled. Almost a third were judged to need further inpatient care, and half of these seemed likely to need such care permanently.

Amongst chronically handicapped patients resident outside hospital, many receive care in the community, by attending day hospitals or day centres, and by living in hostels or with family or friends. A small but important group of mentally disordered people are reluctant to use such provisions. Instead they find their way into common lodging houses, reception centres, or prisons. Studies of destitute people in such places have shown that a substantial proportion are mentally ill or alcoholic, or have personality disorders. Many of these people move repeatedly from one form of accommodation to another, and some sleep rough at times (Leach and Wing 1979). The plight of such people, psychiatrically ill and destitute, suggests that the drive to discharge long-stay patients from hospitals has gone too far. Some would have better lives in a well-run hospital.

It seems that, when estimates were originally made of the likely benefits of community care, over-optimistic assumptions were made about several key issues: the natural course of chronic mental illness; the quality of life in many urban communities; the burden on the patient's family; and the effectiveness of social work.

For each patient with chronic handicap, it is important to weigh the advantages and disadvantages if he lives outside hospital, both for him and his family. Community care will be the better alternative for many patients, but not all. Doctrinaire insistence on community care at all costs is undesirable (see Bennett 1978; World Health Organization 1980; Wing and Olsen 1979).

Evaluation of psychiatric services

It is obviously desirable that the effectiveness of the different forms of psychiatric service should be evaluated by research, or at least by statistics showing the utilization of services.

Comparative trials of different types of care are time-consuming and difficult to carry out properly. As in clinical trials in general, there must be careful selection and allocation of patients, clearly specified alternative treatments, and dependable measures of outcome. Some trials have shown that various forms of day-care can be as effective as inpatient care for some patients, without imposing excessive burdens on families. Others have shown that brief inpatient care followed by day-care or support at home can be as effective as prolonged inpatient care, for certain patients (see Braun *et al.* 1981; Stein and Test 1980).

The evaluation of an area service as a whole is more difficult. In a well-known study, Grad and Sainsbury (1963) compared two areas, one served by a traditional psychiatric hospital, the other by a new service including outpatient clinics, a day hospital, and domiciliary visiting by psychiatrists. In the area with the new service, there were reductions in both hospital admissions and length of stay in hospital; families reported an increased burden of care, but most of them were willing to accept it.

Wing and Hailey (1972) have suggested that an area service should be assessed by asking six questions:
1. How many patients are in contact with the service?
2. What are their needs and those of their relatives?
3. Are the services at present meeting these needs?
4. How many others, not in contact with the service, also have needs?
5. What new services, or modifications to existing services, are required to cater for unmet needs?
6. Having introduced them, are the needs met?

A full answer to these questions poses many problems of method. The most accurate answers can be obtained by the appropriate use of a case register, as shown by a series of reports describing the services in Camberwell, South London (Wing and Hailey 1972). In areas without a register, much useful information on the efficacy of services can be obtained by a combination of good records and simple operational research.

FURTHER READING

Jones, K. (1972). *A history of the mental health services.* Routledge & Kegan Paul, London.

Watts, F.N. and Bennett, D.H. (1983). *Theory and practice of psychiatric rehabilitation.* John Wiley, Chichester.

Wing, J.K. (ed.) (1982). Long term community care: experience in a London Borough. *Psychological Medicine Supplement* No. 2.

Wing, J.K. and Olsen, R. (1979). *Community care for the mentally disabled.* Oxford University Press.

20. Child psychiatry

The practice of child psychiatry differs from that of adult psychiatry in several important ways. It is seldom that the child initiates the consultation with the clinician. Instead he is brought by adults – usually the parents – who think that some aspect of behaviour or development is abnormal. Much depends on the attitudes and tolerance of these adults, and how they perceive the child's behaviour. Healthy children may be brought to the doctor by over-anxious and solicitous parents or teachers, whilst in other circumstances severely disturbed children may be left to themselves.

A related factor is that psychiatric problems in a child may be a manifestation of disturbance in other members of his family. For example, it has been shown that the mothers of children attending child guidance clinics are more likely to suffer from 'nerves', irritability, and bad temper, than the mothers of similar children not attending such clinics (Shepherd *et al.* 1971).

Another difference from adult psychiatry is that, in deciding what is normal and what is abnormal, greater attention must be paid to the stage of development of the patient and the duration of the disorder. For example repeated bed-wetting would be regarded as normal in a three-year-old child but abnormal in a child aged seven.

The practice of child psychiatry differs from adult psychiatry in two other ways. First children are generally less able to express themselves in words. Evidence of disturbance is therefore based more on observations of behaviour made by parents, teachers, and others. The assessment of these accounts requires skills in taking a developmental history, assessing behaviour, evaluating the emotional involvement of informants, and understanding the home and school background. Secondly, in the treatment of children less use is made of medication than in adult psychiatry. Instead the main emphasis is on changing the attitudes of parents, reassuring and retraining the child, and co-ordinating the efforts of others who can help him.

The first part of this chapter is concerned with a number of general issues concerning psychiatric disorder in childhood including its frequency, causes, assessment, and management. The second part of the chapter contains information about the principal syndromes encountered in the practice of child psychiatry. The chapter does not provide a comprehensive account of child psychiatry. It is an introduction to the main themes for the psychiatrist who is starting his specialist general training. It is expected that he will follow it by reading a specialist text, for example one of those listed in the further reading at the end of the chapter. In this book, childhood mental retardation is dealt with in Chapter 21. This is a convenient arrangement but the reader should remember that many aspects of the study and care of mentally retarded children are closely related to child psychiatry.

NORMAL DEVELOPMENT

The practice of child psychiatry calls for knowledge of the normal process of development from a helpless infant to an independent adult. In order to judge whether any observed emotional, social, or intellectual functioning is abnormal, it has to be compared with the corresponding normal range for the age group. This section provides a summary of the main aspects of development that concern the psychiatrist. A textbook of paediatrics should be consulted for details of these developmental phases (for example Illingworth 1980). A useful review of psychological and social development has been provided by Rutter (1980).

The first year of life

This is a period of rapid development of motor and social functioning. Three weeks after birth, the baby smiles at faces; selective smiling appears by six months, fear of strangers by eight months, and anxiety on separation from the mother shortly after.

Bowlby (1980) has emphasized the importance in the early years of life of a general process of **attachment** of the infant to the parents and of more selective emotional **bonding**. Although bonding to the mother is most significant, important attachments are also made to the father and other people who are close to the infant. Recent research has stressed the reciprocal nature of this process and the probable importance of the very early contacts between mother and newborn infant in initiating bonding (Rutter 1980).

By the end of the first year, the child should have formed a close and secure relationship with the mother. There should be an ordered pattern of sleeping and feeding; and weaning has usually been accomplished. The child has begun to learn about objects outside himself, simple causal relationships, and spatial relationships. By the end of the first year, the child enjoys making sounds and may say 'mama', 'dada', and perhaps one or two other words.

Year two

This is also a period of rapid development. The child begins to wish to please the parents, and appears anxious when they disapprove. He begins to learn to control his behaviour. By now, attachment behaviour should be well established. Temper tantrums occur, particularly if exploratory wishes are frustrated. These do not last long, and should lessen as the child learns to accept constraints. By the end of the second year, he should be able to put two or three words together as a simple sentence.

Pre-school years (2 to 5 years)

This phase brings a rapid increase in intellectual abilities, especially in the complexity of language. Social development occurs as the child learns to live within the family. He begins to identify with the parents and to adopt their standards in matters of conscience. Social life develops rapidly as he learns to interact with siblings, other children, and adults. Temper tantrums continue, but diminish and should disappear before the child starts school. At this age, the child has much curiosity about the environment, and may ask a great number of questions.

In children aged two to five, fantasy life is rich and vivid. It is capable of forming a temporary substitute for the real world, enabling desires to be fulfilled regardless of reality. Special objects, such as teddy bears or pieces of blanket become important to the child. They appear to comfort and reassure the child, and help sleep. They have been called 'transitional objects'.

The child begins to learn about his own sexual identity. He realizes the differences between males and females in their appearance, clothes, behaviour, and anatomy. Sexual play and exploration are quite common at this stage.

According to psychodynamic theory, at this stage defence mechanisms develop to enable the child to cope with anxiety arising from unacceptable emotions. These defence mechanisms have been described on p. 30. They include repression, rationalization, compensation, and displacement.

Middle childhood (5 to 10 years)

By the age of five, the child should understand his or her identity as boy or girl, and his position in the family. He has to learn to cope with school, and to read, write, and acquire numerical concepts. The teacher becomes an important person in the child's life. At this stage, the child gradually learns what he can achieve and what are his limitations. Defence mechanisms, conscience, and standards of social behaviour develop further. According to psychoanalytic theory, this is a period in which psychosexual development is quiescent (the latent period). This notion has been questioned by Rutter (1971) among others. It now seems that in the five to ten year old period sexual interests and activities are present, although these may be concealed from adults.

Adolescence

Adolescence is the growing up period between childhood and maturity. Among the most obvious features are the physical changes of puberty. The age at which these occur is quite variable, usually between 11 and 13 in girls, and 13 and 17 in boys. The production of sex hormones precedes this, starting to change in both sexes between the ages of eight and ten. Adolescence is a time of increased awareness of personal identity and individual characteristics. At this age, young people are concerned to know who they are, and begin to consider where they want to go in life. It is popularly but wrongly believed that emotional turmoil and alienation from the family are characteristic of adolescence (see p. 678).

Peer group relationships are important and close friendships often develop, especially amongst girls. Membership of a group is common, and this can help the adolescent in moving towards autonomy. Adolescence brings a marked increase in heterosexual interest and activity. At first, tentative approaches are made to the opposite sex. Gradually these become more direct and confident. In late adolescence, there is a capacity for affection towards the opposite sex, as well as sexual feelings. How far and in what way sexual feelings are expressed depends greatly on the standards of society and rules in the family.

THE CLASSIFICATION OF PSYCHIATRIC DISORDERS IN CHILDREN AND ADOLESCENTS

Both ICD 9 and DSM III contain a scheme for classifying the psychiatric disorders of childhood. Disorders of adolescence are classified partly with this scheme, and partly with the categories used in adult psychiatry.

Six main groups of childhood psychiatric disorders are generally recognized by clinicians. Recently multivariate analysis has supported this classification (see Quay and Werry 1979). The groups are:

(1) neurotic (or emotional);
(2) conduct (or antisocial);
(3) hyperkinetic (or attention deficit);
(4) psychoses of childhood;
(5) specific delays in development;
(6) symptomatic (e.g. enuresis, tics, eating disorders).

Table 20.1 shows the main categories in ICD 9 and DSM III. The latter differs from ICD 9 in containing further subgroupings. These have not been shown in the table because they have not, as yet, been strongly supported by evidence (Quay and Werry 1979).

Recently another classificatory system has been developed for the WHO. This resembles ICD 9 in the categories used, but differs in two ways. First operational definitions are provided. Secondly, diagnoses are recorded on different axes. The most recent version proposes five axes. (i) clinical psychiatric syndrome; (ii) specific delays in development; (iii) intellectual level; (iv) medical conditions; (v) abnormal psycho-social situations. (Further information is given by Rutter *et al.* 1975). Although this system is not in official use it has already been tested and most clinicians have found that it is easy to use. It allows them to record systematically the different kinds of information required in the description of children's problems.

Table 20.1. *Classification of childhood psychiatry disorders in ICD 9 and DSM III**

ICD 9	DSM III
299 Psychoses with origin specific to childhood	Pervasive developmental disorder
309 Adjustment reaction	Adjustment disorder
312 Disturbance of conduct not elsewhere classified	Conduct disorder
313 Disturbance of emotions specific to childhood and adolescence	Anxiety disorders of childhood; other disorders of infancy, childhood and adolescence
314 Hyperkinetic syndrome of childhood	Attention deficit disorder
315 Specific delays in development	Specific developmental disorders (coded on axis 2)

*Only the main headings of the specific disorders of children are shown. Both systems have additional categories for special syndromes such as tics, encopresis, and eating disorders.

EPIDEMIOLOGY

Prevalence studies of children in the general population have shown that isolated problems, such as fears and disturbed sleep, are common (see Shepherd *et al.* 1971). Estimates vary with the criteria that are adopted, but it seems that between 5 and 10 per cent of these problems are severe and persistent, causing distress or limitation to an extent that they can be regarded as psychiatric disorders (see Graham (1979) for a review).

The frequency and nature of the problems change with age. Up to the age of three, it is not possible to diagnose any specific syndrome except childhood autism. Instead, estimates have to be made of the frequency of individual symptoms and the extent to which they cause distress. Richman *et al.* (1975) found that 7 per cent of three year olds had symptoms severe enough to be considered moderate to severe problems, while 14 per cent had mild problems such as overactivity or disobedience. (These findings are considered further on p. 643.)

The most detailed findings about the middle years of childhood come from a study of physical health, intelligence, education, and psychological difficulties in all the 10 and 11 year olds in the Isle of Wight – a total of 2199 children (Rutter *et al.* 1970). Screening questionnaires were completed by parents and teachers. Children identified in this way were given psychological and educational tests and their parents were interviewed. The one year prevalence rate of psychiatric disorder was about 7 per cent, the rate in boys being twice that in girls. There was no correlation with social class, but prevalence increased as intelligence decreased. There were associations with physical handicap and especially with evidence of organic brain damage. There was also a strong association between reading retardation and conduct disorder. Several years later the same methods were used to survey an inner London borough (Rutter *et al.* 1975). It was found that the rates of all types of disorder were twice those in the Isle of Wight.

Evidence about mid-adolescence was provided by a four-year follow-up of the Isle of Wight children (Rutter *et al.* 1976). At the age of 14 the one year prevalence rate of handicapping psychiatric disorders was about 8 per cent. This figure increased to 20 per cent if children who expressed less severe anxiety and depression were included.

Referral to specialists

General practitioners spend much of their time advising and reassuring parents about their children. Only a small proportion of these consultations lead to referral to paediatric or child psychiatry clinics (Bailey *et al.* 1978; Goldberg *et al.* 1979). General practitioners are more likely to refer to a paediatrician developmental difficulties, physical symptoms with a probable psychological cause, and psychological complications of physical illness. Emotional and conduct disorders are more likely to be referred to a child psychiatry clinic. However, the cases referred are no more severe than those which the general practitioner deals with himself (see Gath *et al.* 1977). This is because the reasons for referral often lie in the family rather than the child. Thus Shepherd *et al.* (1971) found greater emotional disturbance in mothers whose children had been referred to a child psychiatric clinic than in those whose similar children had been treated by the family doctor.

Prognosis

Mild symptoms and behavioural or developmental problems are usually short lived. However this is not so for the 5–15 per cent of children with symptoms severe enough to be diagnosed as a childhood psychiatric disorder. Their difficulties often persist for several years. Thus in the Isle of Wight study three-quarters of children with conduct disorder and half of those with emotional disorders at age ten, were still handicapped by these problems four years later (Rutter *et al.* 1976).

The prognosis for adult life can only be established by long follow-up, which is difficult to arrange. The outstanding study is that of Robins (1966) who followed children who had attended a child guidance clinic 30 years previously, and compared them with a control group who had attended the same schools but had not been referred to the clinic. She found that emotional (i.e. neurotic) disorders had a good prognosis. Also when these disorders did continue they usually took the form, in the adult, of neurosis or depression. By contrast, children with conduct disorder had a poor outcome. As adults they were likely to develop antisocial personality disorder or alcoholism, have problems with employment or marriage, or commit offences. More recent research has confirmed that the outcomes of neurotic and conduct disorders are very different. It has also shown that definite overactivity syndromes have a poor prognosis and psychoses a worse one (see Robins 1979*a*).

AETIOLOGY

In discussing the causes of child psychiatric disorders, much the same principles apply as those described in the earlier chapter on the aetiology of adult disorders. In child psychiatry, there are fewer disease entities and more reactions to environmental factors, notably those in the family, school, and neighbourhood. Even more than in adult life, the determinants of childhood disturbance are usually multiple. In the paragraphs which follow four inter-acting groups of factors will be considered briefly. These are: inheritance; temperament; physical impairment, with special reference to brain damage; and environmental, family, social, and cultural causes.

Inheritance

The hereditary factors of importance in child psychiatry are polygenic. They do not seem to control the disorders directly but rather the predisposition to develop them. In part this seems to be through polygenic control of intelligence; in part through a similar influence on temperament – though the evidence for this is less strong. For a review of genetic factors in child psychiatry, the reader should consult Shields (1980).

Temperament

In a longitudinal study in New York, Thomas *et al.* (1968) found that certain temperamental factors detected before the age of two might predispose to later psychiatric disorder. In the first two years, one group of children ('difficult children') tended to respond to new environmental stimuli by withdrawal, slow adaptation, and an intense behavioural response. Another group ('easy children') responded to new stimuli with positive approach, rapid adaptation, and a mild behavioural response. This group was less likely than the first to develop behavioural disorders later in childhood. The investigators thought that these early temperamental differences were determined both genetically and by environmental factors.

Physical disease

Although serious physical disease of any kind can predispose to psychological problems in childhood, brain disorders are the most important. In the Isle of Wight study about 12 per cent of physically ill children aged 10–11 years were classified as having psychiatric problems compared with about 7 per cent in the general population of the same age (Rutter *et al.* 1976). The prevalence was 34 per cent in children with brain disorders. This could not be accounted for by any known association between brain disorder and adverse social factors. Nor is it likely to have been due to physical disability as such because rates of psychiatric disorder are less in children equally disabled by muscular disorders (Seidel *et al.* 1975). The rate of psychiatric disorder among children with brain damage is related to the severity of the damage, though not closely to the site (see Rutter 1981*a*). It is as common among brain-injured girls as boys (Rutter *et al.* 1970) a finding which contrasts with the higher rate of psychiatric disorder among boys in the general population.

Minimal brain dysfunction

The observation that major brain damage to children can cause definite psychiatric disorder led to the hypothesis that smaller amounts of damage could account for otherwise unexplained disorders. This idea has a long history but recent ideas date from the studies of brain-injured children by Strauss and Lehtinen (1974). At first the supposed condition was referred to as minimal brain damage. When it became accepted that there were no demonstrable structural changes in the brain the name was changed to minimal brain dysfunction (see Bax and MacKeith 1963). Later Pasamanick and Knobloch (1966) suggested that there is 'a continuum of reproductive casualty'. By this they meant that reading disability, behaviour disorders, epilepsy, and mental handicap, might result from increasing degrees of brain disorder resulting from abnormalities of pregnancy or childbirth. These ideas were based in part on the observation that abnormal pregnancy, prematurity, and asphyxia at birth are common among children attending psychiatrists (Pasamanick and Knobloch 1966). Such evidence is difficult to interpret because these factors are related to social disadvantage which might be the real cause of any psychiatric problems. The balance of evidence does not support the idea that minimal brain disorder is the cause of childhood psychiatric disorders (see Rutter (1982*a*) for a review).

It has also been suggested that overactivity and poor concentration (the 'hyperkinetic syndrome') are specific consequences of brain injury. This idea, which is also poorly supported by evidence, is considered on p. 658.

Environmental factors

Family

As a child progresses from complete dependence on others to independence, he needs a stable and secure family background, with a consistent pattern of emotional warmth, acceptance, help, and constructive discipline. Prolonged separation from or loss of parents can have a profound effect on psychological development in infancy and childhood. Poor relationships in the family may have similar adverse effects.

The well-known work of Bowlby (1951) led to widespread concern with the effects of 'maternal deprivation'. Bowlby originally suggested that prolonged separation from the mother was a major cause of juvenile delinquency. Subsequently he argued that the experience or threat of separation is associated with anxiety or depression in later years (Bowlby 1973, 1980). Since the original formulation of the consequences of maternal deprivation, it has become apparent that the effect of separation depends on many factors. These include: the age of the child at the time of separation, his previous relationship with his mother and father, and the reasons for the separation. It is also apparent that the various consequences of parental deprivation have different long-term effects. An unstimulating environment and lack of encouragement to learn in infancy is associated with educational underachievement in later years. Poor emotional attachments in early life may result in difficulties in social relationships (see Rutter 1981*b*).

The family factors most strongly associated with psychiatric disorder in the child include: discordant relationships, the illness or personality deviance of a parent, and large family size. Patterns of child rearing are not clearly related to psychiatric disturbance in the child except where they involve child abuse (see Rutter 1981*b*; Rutter and Madge 1976).

Social and cultural factors

Although the family is undoubtedly the part of the child's environment with most effect on his development, wider social influences are important as well. In the early years of childhood these act indirectly through their influence on the patterns of family life. As the child grows older and spends more time outside the family, they have a direct effect as well. These factors have been studied by examining the associations between psychiatric disorder and type of neighbourhood, and school.

Rates of childhood psychiatric disorder are higher in areas of social disadvantage. For example, as already noted (p. 632) the rates of both emotional and conduct disorder were found to be higher in a poor inner London borough than in the Isle of Wight. The important features of inner city life may be lack of play space, inadequate social amenities for teenagers, overcrowded living conditions, and lack of community involvement (see Rutter and Hersov 1977). Rates of child psychiatric referral and delinquency also vary between schools (Power *et al.* 1972; Gath *et al.* 1977). These differences do not seem to be due to the size of the school or the age of its buildings but rather to its social environment.

It has been suggested that immigrant children have high rates of psychiatric disorder. In Britain, most studies have been of West Indian children. The only clear and consistent difference from the local population is the equal sex ratio due to an excess of psychiatric disorder among immigrant girls. Thus a careful study of West Indian children in an inner London borough (Rutter *et al.* 1974) showed that the girls had an increased rate of conduct disorder. Otherwise the rates and types of disorder were similar to those among the English controls (see Kolvin and Nicol (1979) for a review).

PSYCHIATRIC ASSESSMENT OF CHILDREN AND THEIR FAMILIES

The aim of the assessment is to obtain a clear account of the problem supposedly present in the child, and how this is related to his past development and his present life in its psychological and social context. The psychiatric assessment of children differs in several ways from that of adults. In child psychiatry it is often difficult to follow a set routine, and a flexible approach is required. However, it is still important that information and observations be recorded accurately and systematically. Psychological assessment is used more often than in adult psychiatry. Information from teachers about behaviour and educational achievement is generally of great value.

In child psychiatry, the main informants are usually the parents. With younger children there are advantages in seeing them before the child. However many adolescents resent this arrangement so that it is often appropriate to interview them first (see p. 680). With very young children, it is a common practice to see the child in the presence of his parents. This may reassure the child and has the added advantage that the doctor can observe the way in which the child and parents react to one another. Some child psychiatrists prefer to see the whole family together from the start. Although such joint interviews are a useful way of observing family interactions, they are seldom the best way to obtain a clear history. In general it is better to interview the parents and child separately, before seeing the family together.

Interviewing the parents

They should be allowed to talk spontaneously before systematic questions are asked. The methods of interviewing are similar to those used in adult psychiatry (see Chapter 2). The items to be included in the history are listed in the Appendix to this chapter (p. 681). The main areas to be covered are: a detailed description of the present problem; systematic enquiry about the child's recent health, behaviour, and emotional state; the developmental history; temperament; and information about the family – the history, personality, and mental state of the parents and other members, and their relationships with one another.

The child

Because younger children may not be able or willing to express ideas and feelings in words, observations of their behaviour and interaction with the interviewer are especially important. With older children, it may be possible to follow a procedure similar to that used with adults.

It is essential to begin by establishing a friendly atmosphere and winning the child's confidence. It is usually better to begin with a discussion of neutral topics such as pets, games, or birthdays before turning to the presenting problem. When a friendly relationship has been established, the child can be asked about the problem, his likes and dislikes, and his hopes for the future. It is often informative to ask what he would request if given three wishes. He may also be given the opportunity to express his concerns and feelings in paintings or play.

Observations of the child's behaviour and mental state should be recorded systematically. The items to be included are listed in the Appendix (p. 683). The main areas are: general behaviour; mood; talk; attention and persistence; activity level; and intellectual functioning. At some stage, preferably late in the interview, a physical examination should be performed, with particular attention to the nervous system (see Appendix p. 684). An assessment should also be made of the child's development relative to other children of his age.

Psychological assessment

Measures of intelligence and educational achievement are often useful. Some of the more commonly used procedures are listed in Table 20.2. (Further information is given in Mittler (1973)). Some psychologists also use one or more of the many projective techniques. These are difficult to score and their validity has not been established. However, they sometimes provide a useful way of discovering the child's feelings about the members of his family and about other matters. Used in this way, they resemble clinical methods (for example, asking the child to make up a story) rather than psychological tests.

Other information

The most important additional informants are the child's teachers. They can describe his classroom behaviour, educational achievements, and relationships with other children. They may also make useful comments about the family and home circumstances. It is often helpful for a social worker to visit the home. This can provide useful information about material circumstances in the home, the relationships of family members, and the pattern of their life together.

Formulation

A formulation should be made in every case. This starts with a brief statement of the current problem. The diagnosis and differential diagnosis are discussed next. Aetiological factors are often considered under the headings: genetic; physical; temperamental; family; and other environmental. Alternatively these can be grouped into predisposing, precipitating, and perpetuating factors. Any further assessment should be specified, a treatment plan drawn up, and the expected outcome recorded.

Table 20.2. *Notes on some psychological measures in use with children and the mentally retarded*

(a) *Intelligence tests*	
Stanford–Binet Intelligence Scale	A revision of the original intelligence test; now seldom used. Provides mental age. Weighted to verbal abilities and this may result in cultural bias. More useful for middle class patients and for low ability.
Weschler Intelligence Scale for Children (WISC)	Provides a profile of specific verbal and performance ability as well as IQ. Widely used and well standardized. Cannot be used for IQ below 40.
Weschler Pre-School and Primary Scale of Intelligence (WPPSI)	A version of WISC for use with younger children (4–6½ years) and with the mentally retarded.
British Ability Scales	Twenty-three sub-scales suitable for 2½ to 17 years, and covering six areas: speed of information processing, reasoning, spatial imagery, perceptual matching, short-term memory, retrieval and application of knowledge. Analysis can be general or specific.
(b) *Social development assessments*	
Vineland Social Maturity Scale	The original development scale, which has psycho-metric limitations. Covers general self-help, self-help in dressing, self-help in eating, locomotion, communication, self-direction, social isolation and occupation. Provides 'Social Age'.
Adaptive Behaviour Scales (Nihira)	Rating scales to evaluate abilities and habits in ten behavioural areas.
Gunzburg Progress Assessment Charts	Provides a clear visual display of self-help, communication, social, and occupational abilities.
(c) *Other developmental assessments*	
Denver Development Scale	Assessments of gross and fine motor, language, and social development.
Griffiths Mental Development Scale	Tests of locomotor, social, language, eye–hand performance, and practical reasoning abilities.
(d) *Personality*	
Rotter Sentence Completion	Projective personality test. Also used to encourage children to talk about attitudes and feelings
Junior Eysenck Personality Inventory	An adaptation of the adult Eysenck Personality Inventory for use for age 7–13.
(e) *Reading*	
Neale Analysis of Reading Difficulty	Graded test of reading ability and comprehension.

TREATMENT

In the past, the usual practice in child guidance clinics was for a social worker to see the parents while a doctor treated the child by psychotherapy. Nowadays, treatment is likely to be shorter and more varied in its content. Also, although the members of the treatment team (doctor, social worker, and psychologist) have special skills, they do not confine themselves to their traditional professional roles when they work with children and families. Instead they take whatever part seems most likely to be helpful in the particular case. (For a review of current methods see Rutter (1982*b*).)

There are usually two main themes: a family approach, and close liaison with other agencies involved with the child or his family. To an increasing extent, a family approach is fundamental whatever the method of treatment. In this the child, his parents, and on some occasions his siblings, are involved in a discussion of the problems. The parents receive advice and are given an opportunity to express their concerns. The second theme, liaison with others, is discussed in the next section. At this stage it is sufficient to note that it usually involves school, medical, and social services. Its aim is to co-ordinate their efforts in a way that is most likely to help the child and his family.

The sections which follow contain general descriptions of the main kinds of treatment. In the second part of the chapter further information is given about the management of individual disorders. When reading both accounts it should be remembered that few treatments in child psychiatry have been evaluated adequately.

Liaison

The importance of liaison with other agencies dealing with the child has been referred to already. The child psychiatrist works closely with hospital paediatricians, the child health and social services, teachers and educational psychologists. Since many childhood problems are either most obvious at school or show themselves as educational difficulties, the child's teachers usually need to be involved in his treatment (see Kolvin *et al.* 1981). They may require advice about the best way to manage behavioural disturbance; remedial teaching may be indicated; or some other change may be needed in the child's school timetable. Occasionally a change of school is indicated. A few patients need to be transferred to a special day or boarding school for maladjusted children.

Drug treatment

Drugs are of limited value in child psychiatry. The main indications, which are discussed later in this chapter, are epilepsy, depressive disorders, overactivity syndromes and, occasionally, nocturnal enuresis. In all cases dosages should be checked carefully in a standard reference book such as the *British National Formulary,* paying attention to allowances required for the child's age and body weight (see also Werry 1982).

Psychotherapy with the child

This originated in the separate methods developed by Anna Freud and Melanie Klein. These differed especially in the emphasis placed by the latter on the psychodynamic interpretation of the child's play. Nowadays lengthy intensive treatment of this kind is not used commonly in Britain. Instead most psychotherapy with children is brief and aims to help with current problems. The psychotherapist tries to make a warm and accepting relationship with the child. He uses this to encourage the child to express feelings and to find alternative ways of behaving. Acceptance is important and criticism should be avoided, although this does not, of course, imply approval of every aspect of the child's behaviour. At first, the child often perceives the psychotherapist as an agent of his parents and expects him to share their attitudes. For this reason, it is advisable to delay discussion of the presenting problems until the child's confidence has been gained by talking about neutral things that interest him. The techniques of child therapy have been summarized by Dare (1977). A fuller understanding of child psychotherapy is acquired most effectively through supervised experience.

There has been little adequate evaluation of psychotherapy for children. An exception is the trial reported by Eisenberg *et al.* (1965) in which it was found that brief therapy was superior to a single consultation interview in the treatment of neurotic disorders.

Family therapy

This is a specific form of treatment which should be distinguished from the general family approach to treatment described above. In family therapy the child's symptoms are considered as an expression of the functioning of the family, which is the primary focus of treatment. The techniques employed to do this are beyond the scope of this account. They have been described by Glick and Kessler (1980). The indications for family therapy are still debated. Glick and Kessler (1980) suggest that family therapy is appropriate when: (1) the child's symptoms appear to be manifestations of a disturbance of the whole family; (2) individual therapy is not proving effective; (3) family difficulties arise during treatment of the patient. On the other hand, family therapy is contraindicated when the marriage is breaking up, or the patient's problems do not appear closely related to family function.

Group therapy

Group therapy can be used for the child or the parents. Older children and adolescents may be helped through the sharing of problems, discussion, and modelling that form part of group therapy. Parents may be helped by the opportunity to discuss shared problems of child management or other difficulties. The principles of group therapy are described in Chapter 18.

Behaviour therapy

These methods have several applications in child psychiatry. They can be used to encourage new behaviour by positive reinforcement and modelling. This is often done by first rewarding behaviour that approximates to the desired behaviour (shaping), before using reinforcement in a more discriminating way. Behaviour therapy can also be used to reduce inappropriate behaviour. This should not be done by punishment which, apart from ethical objections, has only temporary effects. Instead a search is made for the factors in the child's environment that are helping to reinforce the unwanted behaviour and efforts are made to remove these. It is often found that undesired behaviour is being reinforced unwittingly by the extra attention given to the child when it is present. If the child is ignored at these times and attended to when his behaviour is more normal, beneficial changes often take place. More specific forms of behaviour therapy can be used for enuresis (see p. 669), or phobias. The principles resemble those which apply in adult psychiatry (see Chapter 18).

Education and occupational therapy

Children attending as outpatients, as well as the smaller number who are day or inpatients, often benefit from additional educational arrangements. Special teaching may be needed to remedy backwardness in writing, reading, and arithmetic which are common among children with conduct disorders. In occupational therapy, social interaction can be encouraged and practical or artistic skills developed.

Residential care including fostering

This can be valuable for children whose symptoms result from a severely unstable home background, or extreme parental rejection. The children considered for residential placement often have conduct disorder and severe educational problems. Removal from home should only be considered after every practical effort has been made to improve the circumstances of the family. Residential care can be arranged in a foster home; a children's home in which a group of about ten children live in circumstances as close as possible to those of a large family; or a boarding school.

Hospital units

Admission to an inpatient unit is usually arranged for one of three reasons. First, the behaviour disorder may be too severe to treat in any other way: examples include severe hyperactivity, childhood psychosis, and school refusal resistant to outpatient treatment. Second, the child may be admitted for observation when the diagnosis is uncertain. Third, inpatient treatment is one way of providing a period away from a disturbing home environment, for example when there is gross over-protection.

Sometimes the mother is admitted as well as the child. This allows close observation of the way in which she responds to the child, for example in cases of child abuse. Once the nature of the problem is clear, the mother can be helped to overcome it by taking an increasing part in the child's care while both remain in hospital (see Ounsted *et al.* 1974).

Day hospital treatment for children was introduced in Great Britain by Connell (1961). It provides many of the advantages of inpatient care without removing the child from home. Unless there is any danger that the child may be abused if he remains at home, this has the advantage that relationships with other family members are maintained. Day care can also relieve the family from some of the stressful effects of managing an overactive or autistic child.

Review of syndromes

The remaining part of this chapter contains a review of the main clinical syndromes encountered in the practice of child psychiatry. It may help the reader at this stage to see the overall scheme, which broadly follows the international scheme considered already (see p. 631). The following groups of disorders will be considered in turn.

1. Problems of pre-school children
2. Neurotic disorders
   Anxiety neurosis
   Phobic disorder
   Hysteria
   Obsessive compulsive neurosis
   Depressive disorder
   School refusal
3. Conduct disorders (and juvenile delinquency – see below)
4. Overactivity syndromes
5. Psychotic disorders
   Infantile autism
   Disintegrative psychoses
   Other childhood psychoses
   Schizophrenia
   Manic depressive disorder
6. Specific delays in development
   Specific reading retardation
   Specific arithmetic disorders
   Specific motor retardation
   Speech and language disorder
7. Other disorders of speech
8. Enuresis and encopresis
9. Child abuse
10. Suicide and deliberate self-harm
11. Psychiatric aspects of paediatric medicine
12. Disorders of adolescence

Juvenile delinquency is not of course a psychiatric syndrome, but an administrative category. However, it is included in this part of the chapter because child psychiatrists are often called upon to give opinions about juvenile delinquents, some of whom have conduct disorders.

PROBLEMS OF PRE-SCHOOL CHILDREN AND THEIR FAMILIES

It has been noted already that in the pre-school years, children are learning several kinds of social behaviour. They are acquiring sphincter control. They are learning how to behave at mealtimes, to go to bed at an appropriate time, and to control angry feelings. They are also becoming less dependent. All these things are being learnt within the family. The psychiatric problems of pre-school children centre round these behaviours and they often reflect factors in the family as well as factors in the child. Most of the psychological problems at this age are short lived: they can be thought of as delays in normal development. However, a small but important proportion persist into later childhood.

Prevalence

Richman *et al.* (1975) studied a sample of 705 families with a three-year-old in a London borough. The most frequent individual abnormal behavioural items in these three-year-olds were: bed wetting at least 3 times a week (present in 37 per cent); wetting by day at least once a week (17 per cent); overactivity (14 per cent); soiling at least once a week (13 per cent); difficulty in settling at night (13 per cent); fears (13 per cent); disobedience (11 per cent); attention-seeking (10 per cent); and temper tantrums (5 per cent).

Whether these behaviours are reported as problems depends on the attitudes of the parents as well as on the nature, severity and frequency of the behaviour. Richman *et al.* (1975) overcame this difficulty by making their own ratings of the extent to which there was a problem. They based this on the effects on the child's wellbeing and the consequences for the other members of the family. They used common-sense criteria to decide whether the problems were mild, moderate, or severe. Seven per cent of the three-year-olds in their survey had behaviour problems of marked severity and 15 per cent had mild problems. The behaviours most often rated as problems were temper tantrums, attention-seeking, and disobedience.

Prognosis

It is not known whether children who have persistent problems of this kind in the pre-school years are more likely to have other psychiatric problems in later childhood. Wolff (1961) followed children under five years of age referred to a psychiatric clinic. Three to six years later, a substantial number still had their original symptoms: for example almost a third of those with temper tantrums and two-thirds of those with fears or enuresis. There was some evidence that prognosis was worse when there was marital strife, a parent had suffered a psychiatric illness, or when the home was broken. Prognosis is also worse for children who have associated brain damage and for those in care.

Aetiology

Aetiological factors are related to the stage of development, the child's temperament, and influences in the family. There are wide individual variations in the rate at which normal development proceeds, particularly in sphincter control and language acquisition. As noted above (p. 633) differences in the child's temperament are evident from the earliest weeks. These are capable of affecting the mother's response – how much time she spends with him, how often she picks him up, and so on. These maternal responses may in turn affect the child's development. Behaviour problems at this age are also associated with poor marital relationships, maternal depression, rivalry with siblings, and inadequate parental behaviour. (See Richman (1976) for a review of the evidence.)

Some common problems

Temper trantrums

It is usual for toddlers to have occasional temper tantrums. Only when they are persistent or very severe are they abnormal. The immediate cause is often unwitting reinforcement by excessive attention and inconsistent discipline on the part of the parents. When this arises it is often because the parents have emotional problems of their own or their relationship is unsatisfactory. Temper tantrums usually respond to kindly but firm and consistent setting of limits. In treatment it is first necessary to discover why the parents have been unable to set limits in this way. They should be helped with any problems of their own and also advised how to respond to the tantrums.

Sleep problems

Difficulties in getting to sleep, nightmares, and night terrors are quite common among healthy toddlers but they seldom persist for long. In a night terror the child wakes apparently terrified and at first seems unresponsive to reassurance. He may appear to be hallucinated, for example talking to people who are not there. The disturbance may last up to fifteen minutes, but eventually subsides. The child then goes back to sleep, and usually does not remember the incident. Nightmares or night terrors are sometimes accompanied by sleep-walking.

When sleep disturbances are severe or persistent, two reasons should be considered. First they may have been made worse by physical or emotional disorders. Second, they may have been exacerbated by the parents' over-concern or inability to provide reassurance. If either of these causes is found, it should be treated. Otherwise it is usually sufficient to reassure the parents and the child.

Feeding problems

Minor food fads or food refusal are common in pre-school children, but do not usually last long. In a minority, the behaviour is severe or persistent, although not accompanied by signs of poor nourishment. When this happens it is often because the parents are over-attentive and obsessional, and unwittingly reinforce the child's behaviour. Treatment is directed to the parents' management of the problem. They should be encouraged to ignore the feeding problem and refrain from offering the child special foods or otherwise attempting to do anything unusual to persuade him to eat. Instead he should be offered a normal meal and left to decide whether to eat it or not.

Pica

This is the eating of items generally regarded as inedible, for example, soil, paint, and paper. It is often associated with other behaviour problems. These cases should be investigated carefully because some are due to brain damage and mental retardation. Some are associated with emotional distress, which should be reduced if possible. Otherwise, treatment consists of commonsense precautions to keep the child away from the abnormal items of diet. Pica usually diminishes as the child grows older. The subject has been reviewed by Bicknell (1975).

Assessment and treatment

In assessing problems in pre-school children, the psychiatrist usually has to rely largely on information from the parents. As noted already, it is important to distinguish between a primary disorder in the child, and one that reflects the difficulties of the mother or the entire family. It is necessary to make a careful assessment of the particular behaviour, the child's general level of develop-ment and the functioning of the family as a whole.

Apart from particular points noted already under the specific disorders, treatment includes counselling for the mother – and sometimes other family members as well – and advice about child-rearing. It is often helpful to arrange for the child to spend some time away from the family in a playgroup or nursery school.

NEUROTIC DISORDERS

The diagnosis of neurotic disorder is widely used in child psychiatry, where it has much the same meaning as in adult psychiatry. In this account, it includes anxiety neurosis, hysteria, obsessive compulsive neurosis, depressive disorder, and school refusal as well as non-specific neuroses. Some psychiatrists prefer the term 'emotional disorder' to 'neurotic disorder' because these conditions of childhood are generally less differentiated than adult neuroses.

Prevalence

Neurotic disorders are the second most frequent psychiatric disorders of childhood being exceeded only by conduct disorders. In their survey of 10 and 11 year old children on the Isle of Wight, Rutter *et al.* (1970) found a prevalence of 2.5 per cent in both boys and girls. This was about half the rate for conduct disorders. In their community survey of an Inner London Borough, the prevalence rate was twice as high for both conditions (Rutter 1975). In another survey of over 1000 children referred to a child psychiatric clinic in south-east London, one-third were diagnosed as having neurotic disorders (Gath *et al.* 1977).

Of the individual neurotic syndromes, anxiety disorders are the most common disorders in mid-childhood. Depressive disorders are more common in adolescence than in younger children. Hysterical and obsessional disorders are infrequent at both ages.

Prognosis

The prognosis for all forms of neurotic disorder in childhood is generally favourable. Even severe neurotic disorders usually clear up without treatment leaving no residual symptoms. As noted already (p. 632), when childhood neurotic disorder does persist into adult life, it is usually as one of the neuroses or an affective disorder.

Treatment

This is usually a form of brief intervention involving the family. In some cases individual psychotherapy is also carried out with the child. Behavioural methods have some part in the treatment of specific syndromes, as will be apparent in the sections which follow. Drugs have little part in the treatment of neuroses in childhood.

Anxiety neurosis

This is called an anxiety state by some authors, and anxiety disorder in DSM III. These children are abnormally fearful. They cling to their parents, on whom they are over-dependent, and are timid with other children. They often have disturbed sleep with frequent nightmares. They may concentrate badly. Various bodily symptoms may be experienced, notably headaches and symptoms related to the alimentary system such as nausea, vomiting, abdominal pain, and bowel disturbance. Phobias and obsessional symptoms also occur.

Sometimes an anxiety neurosis is precipitated by a frightening experience. This may be short-lived, such as admission to hospital, or prolonged – for example, conflict between the parents. In other cases it may be a response to chronically anxious parents (Eisenberg 1958), or a reflection of an anxiety-prone temperament in the child. Particularly in pre-school children, separation from the parents is an important cause of anxiety. (In DSM III these latter cases are recognized as a separate subgroup – Separation Anxiety Disorder.) Children with separation anxiety cling to their parents and demand attention. They may also worry that an accident or illness may befall their parents. Separation anxiety is one cause of school refusal (see p. 650).

DSM III also contains the category Overanxious Disorder. This is for children with an anxious temperament who worry excessively about stressful events such as examinations, or about taking part in activities with other children.

In treatment account should be taken of possible aetiological factors, e.g. stressful events, separation, and anxiety-prone temperament. Any continuing stress should be reduced if possible, for example by seeking to improve the relationship between the parents. The child should be helped to talk over his worries. Also the parents' management of the child may need to be reviewed. Anxiolytic drugs should be avoided except for temporary relief of extreme anxiety.

Phobic disorders

Minor phobic symptoms are common in childhood. They usually concern animals, insects, the dark, school, and death. The prevalence of more severe phobias varies with age. Severe and persistent fears of animals usually begin before the age of five, and nearly all have declined by the early teenage years. Persistent fears of social situations begin around early adolescence and often last into early adult life. In DSM III, these fears of social encounters are classified as Avoidant Disorder. These children shy away from contact with strangers, and are embarrassed in company, blushing and remaining silent. Agoraphobia seldom begins before late adolescence. School phobia is considered separately below under School Refusal (p. 650).

Most childhood phobias improve without specific treatment provided the parents adopt a firm and reassuring approach. For those that do not, simple behavioural treatment can be combined with reassurance and support. The child is encouraged to encounter more of the situations which frighten him, doing so in a graded way as in the treatment of phobias in adult life. Psychotherapy has also been used but is not obviously more effective than simple behavioural treatment. A fuller account of childhood phobias can be found in Marks (1969).

Hysteria

Hysteria is more common in adolescence than in childhood both as an individual illness and in its epidemic form (see p. 174). In childhood, symptoms of hysteria are usually mild and they seldom last long. The most frequent symptoms include paralyses, abnormalities of gait, and inability to see or hear normally. As in adults, such symptoms can occur in the course of organic illness as well as in the primary syndrome of hysteria. Also as in adult psychiatry, physical symptoms are sometimes misdiagnosed as hysteria. For these reasons, the diagnosis of hysteria should be made only after the most careful search for organic disease.

Hysteria was encountered rarely in the Isle of Wight study of children in the community (Rutter *et al.* 1970). Among children referred to paediatricians hysteria has been reported in 3–13 per cent (see Rae 1977). In a survey of prepubertal children, Caplan (1970) found that hysteria was diagnosed in about 2 per cent of those referred to the Maudsley Hospital. In almost half of this 2 per cent, organic illness was eventually detected either near the time or during the four to eleven years' follow-up. Amblyopia was the symptom of organic disorder most likely to be misdiagnosed as hysterical. As in adults, physical illness was more likely to be misdiagnosed as hysteria when physical signs were absent and an obvious emotional upset coincided with the onset of symptoms.

Hysteria should be treated as early as possible. Delay may allow symptoms to become entrenched as secondary gains accumulate. Treatment is directed mainly to reducing any stressful circumstances and encouraging the child to talk about the problems. Symptoms may subside with these measures, or may need management comparable to that used for hysteria in adults (see p. 180). See Kolvin and Goodyer (1982) for further information about hysteria in childhood.

Obsessive-compulsive neurosis

Obsessive–compulsive neuroses are rare in childhood. However several forms of repetitive behaviour are common, particularly between the ages of four and ten. These repetitive behaviours include preoccupation with numbers and counting, the repeated handling of certain objects, and hoarding. Much of this behaviour cannot strictly be called compulsive, because the child does not struggle against it (see p. 20 for the definition of obsessional and compulsive symptoms). However, it is not certain how crucial this distinction is in childhood. It is also common for children to adopt rituals, such as avoiding cracks in the pavement or touching lamp posts. Many children's games contain elements of shared ritual, and some of these short-lived solitary ritual behaviours also seem to be part of normal development. However in some children they take up an increasing amount of the child's time – for example rechecking school work many times or repeated handwashing.

When severe and persistent obsessional thoughts or compulsive symptoms occur in childhood, they are often part of an anxiety neurosis. True obsessional neurosis is less common, and seldom appears in full form before late childhood, though the first symptoms may appear as early as six years of age

(Adams 1973). These children often involve their parents by asking them to take part in the rituals or give repeated reassurance about the obsessional thoughts.

Clinical observations suggest that severe obsessional neuroses of childhood have a poor prognosis. However there is no satisfactory follow-up investigation of patients of this age. Warren (1965) studied 15 adolescents with severe obsessional neuroses, in nine of whom the disorder began before 10 years of age. At follow-up, six or more years later, nine still had symptoms of at least moderate severity. It is not certain whether the prognosis of less severe obsessional disorders is more favourable. When obsessional symptoms occur as part of an anxiety neurosis, treatment is directed to this primary disorder. True obsessional neuroses of later childhood are treated along similar lines to an anxiety neurosis but with the addition of behavioural methods like those used with adults (see p. 604).

Depressive disorder

Many children appear miserable in unhappy circumstances, such as the serious illness of a parent, the death of a family member, or parental disharmony. Some of these children are tearful and lose interest and concentration. They may eat and sleep badly. The same symptoms are seen quite often in the course of neurotic or conduct disorders. However, depressive disorders of the adult type seldom occur before puberty and they are not common even at that age (see Graham 1974). Thus Rutter *et al.* (1970) found depressive disorders in only three of the girls and none of the boys among 2000 ten to eleven year olds – though depressive symptoms were common as part of another disorder. Among 2303 fourteen-year-olds, 35 had depressive disorders (Rutter *et al.* 1976).

In contrast to the view that depressive disorders rarely occur before puberty, some psychiatrists, for example Frommer (1968) and Cytryn and McKnew (1972), have argued that depressive disorders are common in childhood, although appearing in a 'masked' form. These authors suggest that depressive disorders can present with a wide variety of symptoms including unexplained abdominal pain, headache, anorexia, and enuresis. It has sometimes been maintained that an even wider range of behaviours can be 'depressive equivalents'. These include boredom, truancy, running away from home, bullying, or promiscuity.

It is not unreasonable to suggest that in childhood, as in adult life, depressive disorders can come to light because of associated physical or behavioural symptoms (see Kashani *et al.* 1982). However, as in adult life, the diagnosis of depressive disorder in children should only be made when there is clear evidence of the principal features of the syndrome. Depressive mood change is particularly important even though it may not be obvious at first. Depressive disorder should also be distinguished clearly from depressive symptoms occurring as a component of a neurotic or conduct disorder. If these distinctions are made, depressive disorders can occasionally be diagnosed in children although they are uncommon before puberty (see Puig-Antich and Gittleman 1982).

Depressive disorders in childhood are treated by reducing unhappy circumstances, and helping the child to talk about his feelings. Antidepressant drugs have been used to treat depressive symptoms in childhood but as yet no satisfactory clinical trial has been carried out (see Rapoport 1977). In general, these drugs should be reserved for older children with definite symptoms of a severe depressive disorder.

School refusal

There are many causes of repeated absence from school. Physical illness is the commonest. A small number of children are deliberately kept at home by parents to help with domestic work or for company. Some are truants who could go to school but choose not to, often as a form of rebellion. An important group stay away from school because they are anxious or miserable when there. These are the school-refusers. The important distinction between truancy and school refusal was first made by Broadwin in 1932. Later, Hersov (1960) studied 50 school-refusers and 50 truants, all referred to a child psychiatric clinic. Compared with the truants, the school-refusers came from more neurotic families, were more depressed, passive, and overprotected, and had better records of school work and behaviour.

Prevalence

Although cases of school refusal are common among children referred to psychiatric clinics, the prevalence in the general population is uncertain. In the Isle of Wight it was reported in rather less than 3 per cent of 10 and 11 year olds with psychiatric disorder (Rutter *et al.* 1970). It is commonest at three periods of school life, between 5 and 7 years, at 11 years with the change of school, and at 14 years and older.

Clinical picture

At times, the first sign to the parents that something is wrong is the child's sudden and complete refusal to attend school. More often there is an increasing reluctance to set out with signs of unhappiness and anxiety when it is time to go. Some of the children complain of somatic symptoms of anxiety such as headache, abdominal pain, diarrhoea, sickness, or vague complaints of feeling ill. Some children appear to want to go to school but become increasingly distressed as they get nearer to it. The final refusal can arise in several ways. It may follow a period of gradually increasing difficulty of the kind just described. It may appear after an enforced absence for another reason, such as a respiratory tract infection. It may follow an event at school such as a change of class. It may occur when there is a problem in the family such as the illness of a grandparent to whom the child is attached. Whatever the final sequence of events, the child is extremely resistant to efforts to return him to school and his evident distress makes it hard for the parents to insist that he goes.

Aetiology

Several causes have been suggested. Johnson *et al.* (1941) emphasized the general role of separation anxiety, a mechanism also stressed by Eisenberg (1958). More recent observations suggest that separation anxiety is particularly important in younger children. In older children there may be a true school phobia, that is a fear of certain aspects of school life, or fears of failure and rejection, often associated with depression (see Smith 1970).

Prognosis

Clinical experience suggests that most younger children eventually return to school. However a proportion of the most severely affected adolescents do not return before the end of the time for compulsory school attendance. There have been a few studies of the longer prognosis. Tyrer and Tyrer (1974) in a retrospective enquiry suggested that a third of all school refusers later develop an adult neurosis. Berg (1982) concluded, on the basis of his own and other studies, that up to a fifth of hospital treated school refusers are left with continuing neurotic symptoms and social disability ten years later. These studies were concerned with more severe cases and the general prognosis may be rather better than they suggest.

Treatment

Except in the most severe cases, arrangements should be made for an early return to school. This is discussed with the schoolteachers, who should be given advice about any difficulties that are likely to be encountered. It is often more satisfactory for someone other than the mother – for example a social worker – to accompany the child to school in the first place. In a minority of cases a more elaborate graded behavioural plan is necessary. In the most severe cases admission to hospital may be required to reduce anxiety before a return to school can be arranged. If depressive disorder is present in older children, this should be treated. In all cases, the child is encouraged to talk about his feelings while support and reassurance are needed for the parents. (See Hersov and Berg (1980) for a review of school refusal and truancy.)

CONDUCT DISORDERS

Conduct disorders are characterized by severe and persistent antisocial behaviour. They form the largest single group of psychiatric disorders in older children and adolescents. In their survey of 10- and 11-year old children on the Isle of Wight, Rutter *et al.* (1976) found that nearly two-thirds of those with psychiatric disorder had conduct disorders. In a study of over 1000 children referred to a child guidance clinic in south-east London (a sample which excluded children referred for a court report) Gath *et al.* (1977) reported that conduct disorders made up one third of the sample. Studies in the community, in psychiatric practice, and in the juvenile courts, all indicate that conduct disorders are more common in boys than girls (Rutter *et al.* 1970; Gath *et al.* 1977).

The wide variety of clinical features of conduct disorders has led to attempts to divide them into socialized, unsocialized, and overinhibited groups (Hewett and Jenkins 1946). These are similar to the subdivisions of the ICD 9 category 312, which are: unsocialized, socialized, and compulsive conduct disorder, and mixed disturbance of conduct and emotions. DSM III has a similar scheme in which conduct disorders are divided into socialized, under-socialized, aggressive, and non-aggressive. Multivariate analyses of symptoms and follow-up results (Robins 1979*a*) do not support these subdivisions of conduct disorder. In this book a single category of conduct disorder is used.

Clinical features

The essential feature is persistent abnormal conduct which is more serious than ordinary childish mischief. It is usually first evident in the home as stealing, lying, and disobedience, together with verbal or physical aggression. Later, the disturbance is often evident outside the home as well, especially at school, as truanting, delinquency, vandalism, and poor school work, as well as reckless behaviour or alcohol and drug abuse.

In children above the age of seven years persistent stealing is abnormal. Below that age, children seldom have a real appreciation of other people's property. Many children steal occasionally, so that minor or isolated instances need not be taken seriously. A small proportion of children with conduct disorders present with sexual behaviour which incurs the disapproval of adults. In younger children, masturbation and sexual curiosity may be frequent and obtrusive. In adolescent girls, promiscuity is a particular problem. Although fire-setting is rare, it is obviously a dangerous form of antisocial behaviour (see p. 738).

Aetiology

Conduct disorders are found commonly in children from unstable, insecure, and rejecting families. Thus Wolkind and Rutter (1973) found that antisocial behaviour is frequent amongst children from broken homes and those who have been in residential care in their early childhood. Others have shown associations with large family size and lower social class. Conduct disorders are also related to adverse factors in the wider social environment of the neighbourhood and school (Power *et al.* 1972; Rutter *et al.* 1975; Gath *et al.* 1977).

As well as these environmental causes, certain factors in the child may predispose to conduct disorder. As mentioned earlier (p. 633), some children have 'difficult' temperaments from an early age (Thomas *et al.* 1968) These difficulties may be aggravated by incompatibility of temperament between child and parents. Children with brain-damage and epilepsy are prone to conduct disorder, as they are to other psychiatric disorders. An important finding in the Isle of Wight survey was a strong association between antisocial behaviour and specific reading retardation (see p. 664). It is not known whether the antisocial behaviour and reading retardation result from common predisposing factors, or whether either one causes the other (see Sturge 1982).

Prognosis

Conduct disorders usually run a prolonged course in childhood (West and Farrington 1973; Rutter *et al.* 1976). As noted already (p. 632) they also have a poor long-term prognosis. Among people who had had conduct disorders in adolescence, Robins (1970) found that almost a half had some form of anti-social behaviour in adult life. Few of those diagnosed in childhood as having conduct disorder are entirely free of antisocial traits when they become adults. There are no good indicators of the long-term outcome of individual cases. The best available predictor seems to be the extent of the childhood antisocial behaviour. There is no convincing evidence that treatment affects the long-term outlook (see Robins 1970). However it is unfortunate that awareness of the poor long-term prognosis often leads to half-hearted attention to the immediate problems. It is reasonable to believe that in many cases immediate distress can be reduced. Moreover in some cases it is possible to modify adverse social and family factors which might worsen the long-term outlook.

Treatment

Mild conduct disorders often subside without treatment other than common-sense advice to the parents. For more severe disorders, treatment is mainly directed to the family. It usually takes the form of social case-work or family therapy. Some families are difficult to help, especially where there is material deprivation, chaotic relationships, and poorly educated parents. A simple form of behaviour therapy is sometimes used in treatment. In this, desirable behaviour is rewarded while reinforcement is withheld from undesirable behaviour. Group therapy, in which peer pressures are utilized, is sometimes helpful. If there are associated reading difficulties remedial teaching should be arranged. Medication is of little value.

The treatment of **truancy** requires separate consideration. A direct and energetic approach is called for. Pressure should be brought to bear upon the child to return to school, and if possible, support from the family should be enlisted. If other steps fail, court proceedings may need to be initiated. At the same time, an attempt should be made to resolve any educational or other problems at school. In all this it is essential to maintain good communications between clinician, parents, and teachers.

When the conduct disorder is intractable, residential placement may be necessary in a foster home, group home, or special school. This should only be done for compelling reasons, for example the failure of other ways of treating a child from a disorganized family, or when the child has been severely deprived of affection and cannot form satisfactory emotional relationships within the family.

JUVENILE DELINQUENCY

Delinquency is not a psychiatric diagnosis but a legal category. However, juvenile delinquency may be associated with psychiatric disorder, especially conduct disorder. For this reason it is appropriate to interrupt this review of the syndromes of child psychiatry to consider juvenile delinquency. The majority of adolescent boys asked to report their own behaviour admit to offences against the law and a fifth are convicted at some time (West and Farrington 1973); most of the offences are trivial, and only a half of those who are convicted are reconvicted. Few continue to offend in adult life. Many more boys than girls are delinquent and the peak age of contact with the police is 15–16 years. (In considering these figures it has to be remembered that crime statistics may be misleading. Nevertheless there seems to be substantial agreement between the characteristics of self-reported offenders and those convicted (West and Farrington 1973).)

Delinquency is often equated with conduct disorder. This is wrong, for although the two categories overlap, they are not the same. Many delinquents do not suffer from conduct disorders or any other psychological disorder. Equally, many of those with conduct disorder do not offend. Nevertheless in an important group, persistent law-breaking is frequently preceded and accompanied by abnormalities of conduct, such as truancy, aggressiveness, attention-seeking, and poor concentration (Glueck and Glueck 1950; West and Farrington 1973). Also high rates of criminality and antisocial behaviour in adult life have been reported in long-term follow-up studies of children with conduct disorders (Robins 1966).

Classification

Criminologists have tried to classify offenders as a basis for choosing the most effective treatment. One scheme follows that used for conduct disorders (see p. 652). It has three categories: socialized, unsocialized, and overinhibited. It has poor predictive value (Field 1967). A more complex but possibly more useful scheme is based on the concept of 'interpersonal maturity'. This was originally described by Sullivan *et al.* (1959), and further developed by Warren (1969, 1973) in a large evaluative study of the treatment of delinquents in California. The categories in this scheme are defined in terms of quality of the delinquent's relationships with adults and peers and his attitudes to rules and authority. The ratings were originally made from a taped interview, but a simplified assessment can be made using the Jesness Inventory (Jesness 1962).

Aetiology

The aetiology of juvenile delinquency overlaps with that of conduct disorder. However, greater emphasis must necessarily be given to social explanations since delinquency is a form of behaviour disorder which is defined by the provisions of the law and by the way it is operated.

Social factors

Delinquency is related to low social class, poverty, poor housing, and poor education. There are marked differences in delinquency rates between adjacent neighbourhoods which differ in these respects. Rates also differ between schools (Power *et al.* 1972; Gath *et al.* 1977). Many social theories have been put forward to explain the origins of crime but none offers a completely adequate explanation. The interested reader should consult West and Farrington (1973), West (1976), or Radzinowicz and King (1979).

Family factors

Many studies have found that crime runs in families. For example about half the boys with criminal fathers are convicted as compared with a fifth of those with fathers who are not criminals (see West and Farrington 1977). The reasons for this are poorly understood. They may include poor parenting and shared attitudes to the law.

Bowlby (1946) examined the characteristics of 'juvenile thieves' and argued that prolonged separation from the mother during childhood was a major cause of their problems. More recent work has not confirmed such a precise link (see p. 635). Although delinquency is particularly common among those who come from broken homes, this seems to be largely because separation often reflects family discord in early and mid-childhood (see Rutter and Madge 1976).

Other family factors correlated with delinquency are large family size and child rearing practices. In neither case is it clear which aspects of a complex situation are the most important in predisposing to delinquency (see Rutter and Madge 1976).

Factors in the child

Genetic factors appear to be of only minor importance in the aetiology of delinquency (see Shields 1980). They are certainly less significant than in the more serious criminal behaviour of adult life (see p. 720). The association with conduct disorder has been noted already. There are also important relationships between delinquency and slightly below average IQ as well as educational and reading difficulties (Rutter *et al.* 1976). As noted above, there are at least two possible explanations for the latter finding. Temperament or social factors may predispose to both delinquency and the reading failure. Alternatively it is possible that reading difficulties result in frustration and loss of self-esteem at school and that these predispose to antisocial behaviour (see Sturge 1982).

Physical abnormalities probably play only a minor role among the causes of delinquency even though brain-damage and epilepsy predispose to conduct disorder.

Assessment

When the child is seen as part of an ordinary referral and his delinquency is related to a psychiatric syndrome, the latter should be assessed in the usual way. Sometimes the child psychiatrist is asked to see a delinquent specifically to prepare a court report. In these circumstances as well as making enquiries with the parents and teachers, it is essential to consult any social worker or probation officer who has been involved with the child. Psychological testing of intelligence and educational achievements can also be useful. The form of the report is similar to that described in Chapter 22. It should include a summary of the history and present state together with recommendations about treatment.

Treatment

When considering the treatment of delinquent children and adolescents, the psychiatrist needs to know how the legal system works. In England and Wales the provisions are largely covered by the Children and Young Persons Act of 1969. This contains a wide range of provisions: fines, the requirement that the parent or guardian take proper control (see p. 754), supervision by a probation officer, a period at an attendance centre, or an order committing the child to the care of the local authority. It is also possible to make orders for compulsory treatment or to send older delinquents for fixed periods to detention centres or to Borstals for custodial training. Since the main aim of the law as it applies to children and young persons is treatment rather than punishment or even deterrence, there has been extensive criminological research to determine the effectiveness of the measures used. The general conclusions are not encouraging. Any appearance in court or period of detention seems to be associated with a greater risk of reconviction than that of children who have committed similar offences without any official action having been taken (e.g. West and Farrington 1977). There have been many attempts to establish and evaluate forms of treatment that might be effective. One of the earliest, the Highfields Project, compared group treatment in a small well-staffed unit with the usual custodial sentence. Modest benefits were found for the former (Weeks 1958). A larger study, the PICO (Pilot Intensive Counselling Organization) project found some evidence that 9 months' counselling is of more benefit to 'amenable' boys in a medium security unit than to more difficult and uncooperative boys (called 'non-amenable'). These and other studies suggest the need to match the type of treatment to the type of offender. Some delinquents seem to respond better to authoritative supervision, others to more permissive counselling. Unfortunately it is not yet possible to provide any satisfactory practical guidelines about the choice of treatment for the individual delinquent. The results of an elaborate investigation known as the Community Treatment Project of the Californian Youth Authority (Warren 1973) showed that community treatment was generally at least as effective as institutional care.

OVERACTIVITY SYNDROMES

About a third of children are described by their parents as 'overactive' but usually this means no more than normal high spirits. Much less commonly the child displays a particular syndrome of abnormal behaviour. This includes extreme restlessness, impulsiveness, uncontrolled activity, and poor concentration. In Britain, the term hyperkinetic syndrome is reserved for this latter group. The overactivity in the other group is thought to arise either as a normal variant or as a symptom of another psychiatric syndrome. In America, the diagnosis of hyperkinetic syndrome covers a much wider group of overactive children. As a consequence the diagnosis is made more frequently in the United States than in Britain.

This difference is reflected in epidemiological findings. Thus Rutter *et al.* (1970) reported the hyperkinetic syndrome in only 1 per 1000 of the children in the Isle of Wight. In the United States the hyperkinetic syndrome (called in DSM III Attention Deficit Disorder with Hyperactivity) is diagnosed in up to 40 per thousand of children.

This difference between Britain and the United States is not limited to the definition of the syndrome. Opinions about aetiology are also divergent. It is widely believed in the United States that the hyperkinetic syndrome (in the wide definition used there) is usually caused by minimal brain dysfunction perhaps with a partial genetic aetiology as well (Wender 1971). Moreover, it is widely believed in the United States that the hyperkinetic syndrome can be treated with amphetamine or related drugs. There are three important objections to these views (see Rutter 1982a). First, if a wide definition of the hyperkinetic syndrome is used, the symptoms are very varied and do not correlate well with one another. Second, the same symptoms are common in conduct disorders. Third, no sharp dividing line can be drawn between the hyperkinetic syndrome, defined in this broad way, and active normal behaviour.

These are reasons for preferring the view that overactivity has many causes, and for adopting a narrow definition of the hyperkinetic syndrome. It is particularly important to remember that considerable variations of activity occur as part of normal differences in physical make-up and temperament. Other causes of overactive behaviour include anxiety neurosis, conduct disorder, the effects of institutional living, and, occasionally, mania, or autism. When overactivity occurs in the course of another disorder, the prognosis is that of the primary condition. The prognosis of the rare hyperkinetic syndrome is discussed below.

The hyperkinetic syndrome

This section is about the narrowly defined syndrome, not the broader North American concept. The hyperkinetic syndrome occurs more often in boys than girls. It is diagnosed in about 1.5 per cent of children referred to psychiatric hospitals (Sandberg *et al.* 1978). It may be associated with epilepsy, other neurological disorders, and intellectual retardation. It is also said to be associated with a higher prevalence of non-localizing neurological abnormalities ('soft signs') than is found among controls (e.g. Werry *et al.* 1972). The significance of this finding is uncertain.

Clinical features

The cardinal features of the syndrome are extreme restlessness and sustained and prolonged motor overactivity. The child concentrates badly and is distractable. There are several associated features. Learning difficulties may occur, due in part to impaired attention. Minor forms of antisocial behaviour are common, particularly disobedience and aggression. These antisocial behaviours do not appear early, neither are they prominent. (If they are, the diagnosis conduct disorder is made.) Mood fluctuates and is often one of depression. Temper tantrums are common.

Some children with this disorder have been overactive as babies, but more often the significant problems begin when the child starts to walk. He is constantly on the move, interfering with furniture and other objects and exhausting his parents. A fuller description of the syndrome has been given by Cantwell (1977).

Prognosis

The overactivity usually lessens as the child grows older, especially when it is mild and not present in every situation. It usually ceases by puberty. The prognosis for any associated learning difficulties is less good, while antisocial behaviour has the worst prognosis. When the overactivity is severe, pervasive, and associated with low intelligence the prognosis is poor, and the condition may persist into adult life.

Treatment

A hyperactive child exhausts his parents who need support from the start of treatment, particularly as it may be difficult to reduce the child's behaviour.

The child's teachers also need advice and remedial teaching may be required. Behaviour modification may help to reduce the inadvertent reinforcement of overactivity by parents and teachers. Especially when attention deficits are severe, stimulant drugs may be tried. The usual drug is methyl phenidate. Dosage which should be related to body weight is given in the *British National Formulary* or a comparable work of reference. Amphetamines have been shown, in short-term clinical trials, to be effective in about two-thirds of children (see Cantwell 1977; Barkley 1977) though their long-term value is less certain. There are significant side effects, including suppression of appetite, mood disturbance, and, with high doses, growth retardation (see Barkley 1977). Careful monitoring is therefore essential. Surprisingly, it has not been reported that children treated in this way become abusers of amphetamine.

Phenobarbitone and benzodiazepines should not be used because they can have the paradoxical effect of increasing overactivity. If drug treatment is to be used at all for these children it should be supervised by a child psychiatrist who is familiar with its effects. Further information about treatment is given by Laufer and Shetty (1980). The nature and management of the hyperkinetic syndrome has been reviewed by Kolvin and Goodyer (1982).

PSYCHOTIC DISORDERS

In the chapter on classification reference was made to the problems associated with the use of the term psychosis in adult psychiatry (see p. 71). There are similar problems in the use of the term in child psychiatry. It is generally employed in a loose way as a collective term for several serious disorders not seen in adult life. These are: infantile autism, disintegrative psychosis, and a group of poorly understood conditions known as childhood psychoses. In addition, two adult psychoses are seen occasionally in older children, namely schizophrenia and manic–depressive disorder. In DSM III the term 'Pervasive Developmental Disorder of Childhood' is used instead of childhood psychosis.

The prevalence of early childhood psychosis in the general population is about 40 per 100 000 children. Probably half of all cases have the specific syndrome of autism (see Rutter 1976). Childhood psychoses occur twice as commonly in boys as girls.

Infantile autism

This condition was described by Kanner (1943). He also suggested the name which has remained in use, though not always with the meaning intended by him. Other names for the condition include childhood schizophrenia and schizophrenic syndrome of childhood. It is better to avoid these latter terms, since there is no evidence for a link between this childhood disorder and schizophrenia in adult life.

As noted above, the prevalence of infantile autism is probably about 20 per 100 000 children. It is more frequent in the upper socio-economic classes (see the book edited by Rutter and Schopler (1978) for a comprehensive review of this and other aspects of the condition).

Clinical features

In his original description, Kanner (1943) identified four main features which are still used to make the diagnosis. The first was onset within the first two years of life (now usually extended to two and a half years) after a period of normal early development. The other three features which form the so-called autistic triad, are described below.

Autistic aloneness is the inability to make warm emotional relationships with people. Autistic children do not respond to their parents' affectionate behaviour by smiling or cuddling. Instead they appear to dislike being picked up or kissed. They are no more responsive to their parents than to strangers and they behave towards people and inanimate objects in a similar way. A characteristic sign is gaze avoidance, that is the absence of eye to eye contact.

Speech and language disorder is the second feature of the autistic triad. Speech may develop late or never appear. Occasionally, it develops normally until about the age of two years, and then disappears in part or completely. This lack of speech is a manifestation of a severe cognitive defect, which affects non-verbal communication as well. It is also shown in play; autistic children do not take part in the imitative games of the first year of life and later they do not use toys in an appropriate way. They also show little imagination or creative play. As autistic children grow up, about half acquire some useful speech, although serious impairments usually remain, such as the misuse of pronouns and the inappropriate repeating of words spoken by other people (echolalia).

Obsessive desire for sameness is the third part of Kanner's triad. Although this term is unsatisfactory it is still used widely. It describes stereotyped behaviour together with evidence of distress if there is any change in the environment. For example, autistic children may prefer the same food repeatedly, insist on wearing exactly the same clothes or engage in repetitive games. Autistic children are often fascinated by spinning toys.

There are other abnormalities as well as the autistic triad. These children may be overactive and distractable. Some engage in odd motor behaviour such as whirling round and round, twiddling their fingers repeatedly, flapping their hands, or rocking. Others do not differ obviously in motor behaviour from normal children. Autistic children may suddenly show anger or fear without apparent reason.

Kanner originally believed that the intelligence of autistic children was normal. Subsequent research has shown that three-quarters have IQ scores in the retarded range and that this appears to be due to true intellectual impairment (Rutter and Lockyer 1967).

Aetiology

There is some evidence suggesting a genetic component in aetiology. The risk of autism in the siblings of autistic children is three or four times higher than in the general population. Although this does not of course prove a genetic basis, it points to the need for twin studies. A small series has been reported by Folstein and Rutter (1976) who found that four of eleven pairs of monozygotic twins were concordant for autism, as against none of ten pairs of dizygotic twins. Until further evidence has been collected, no definite conclusion can be reached about genetic causes.

An organic cause is suggested by the development of seizures in some of these children when they reach adolescence (see below). Moreover some have non-localizing neurological abnormalities ('soft signs').

Kanner (1943) originally suggested that the behaviour of the autistic child was a response to abnormalities in the parents who were characterized as cold, detached, and 'obsessive'. These ideas have not been substantiated by subsequent research (see Cox *et al.* (1975) for a review).

It is possible that the basic disorder in infantile autism is one of language or perception. However language is itself a complex skill the acquisition of which depends on many individual psychological processes as well as interaction with other people. At present, it seems appropriate to regard infantile autism as a behavioural syndrome that may have more than one cause.

Prognosis

Between 10 and 20 per cent of children with infantile autism begin to improve between the ages of about four to six years and are eventually able to attend an ordinary school and obtain work. A further 10 to 20 per cent can live at home but need to attend a special school or training centre and cannot work. The remainder, at least 60 per cent, improve little and are unable to lead an independent life, most needing long-term residential care (Rutter 1970). Those who improve may continue to show language problems, emotional coldness, and odd behaviour. As noted already, a substantial minority develop epilepsy in adolescence (28 per cent of Rutter's series). For further information about follow-up see Creak (1963) and Eisenberg (1957).

Differential diagnosis

It is more usual to encounter partial syndromes which fail to meet all four of Kanner's criteria, than the full syndrome described by him. These partial syndromes must be distinguished from **other psychoses of childhood** arising after the age of 30 months (see below). Some psychiatrists also recognize a rare syndrome of **'autistic psychopathy'** (Asperger 1944). These children show abnormal social behaviour and 'obsessive' preoccupations with routine like those of autistic children. Some also have poor visuo-spatial perception. The condition begins in the third year of life and is said to have a good social prognosis. It is not certain whether this clinical picture does in fact indicate a condition separate from autism (see van Krevelin (1971) and Kolvin and Goodyer (1982) for further information).

Deafness should be excluded by appropriate tests of hearing. **Developmental language disorder** (see p. 666) differs from autism in that the child usually responds normally to people, and has good non-verbal communication. **Mental handicap** can be differentiated because although the child has general intellectual retardation he usually responds to other people in a more normal way than the autistic child. Compared with a mentally handicapped child of the same age the autistic child has more impairment of language relative to other skills (Hermelin and O'Connor 1970).

Treatment

This has three main aspects: management of the abnormal behaviour, arrangements for social and educational services, and help for the family. Individual psychotherapy has been used in the hope of effecting more fundamental changes but there is no evidence that it achieves this (see Rutter 1967). Neither is there evidence that any form of medication is effective in infantile autism.

Behavioural methods, using contingency management (see p. 610) may control some of the abnormal behaviour of autistic children. This treatment is often carried out at home by the parents, instructed and supervised by a clinical psychologist (see for example Howlin *et al.* 1973). It is not known whether these methods have any lasting benefit, but in autism even temporary changes are often worthwhile for the patient and the family.

Most autistic children require special schooling. It is generally thought better for them to live at home and to attend special day schools. If the condition is so severe that the child cannot stay in the family, residential schooling is necessary, even though the characteristic social withdrawal may be increased by an institutional atmosphere. Educational and residential provisions are often best arranged through the services for the mentally retarded.

The family of an autistic child needs considerable help to cope with the child's behaviour which is often bewildering and distressing. Although little can be done to treat many of these patients, the doctor must not withdraw from the family. They need continuing support and repeated encouragement in their efforts to help their child develop his remaining potential for normal development. Many parents find it helpful to join a voluntary organization in which they can meet other parents of autistic children and discuss common problems. A general review of treatment is given by Wing (1981) and in Rutter and Schopler (1978).

Disintegrative psychoses

Disintegrative psychoses are defined in ICD 9 as disorders in which 'normal or near-normal development for the first few years is followed by loss of social skills and speech, together with a severe disorder of emotions, behaviour and relationships'. This loss usually occurs over a few months. Overactivity and intellectual impairment are frequent, though not invariable. There is no corresponding category in DSM III, which states that such cases should be diagnosed as dementia.

These disorders are rare. It seems that they are almost always the result of an organic brain disease such as a lipoidosis or leucodystrophy. The prognosis is variable. Many cases are progressive, ending in death; others are left with profound mental retardation.

Other childhood psychoses

This term is used for serious mental disorders of early childhood which do not show the features required to make the diagnosis of infantile autism or disintegrative psychosis (nor of schizophrenia or manic–depressive psychosis, which are discussed next). There is no single picture, but rather a group of disorders which are poorly understood. Some occur in children who are mentally retarded or have organic brain disease (see Rutter and Hersov (1977) for further information).

Schizophrenia

Schizophrenia is almost unknown before seven years of age and seldom begins before late adolescence. Kolvin (1971) found that schizophrenia in childhood could be distinguished clearly from the other childhood psychoses on the basis of its symptoms. He observed in childhood schizophrenia the whole range of clinical features that characterize schizophrenia in adults (see Chapter 9). Before the schizophrenic symptoms appeared, four-fifths of the affected children were odd, timid, and sensitive. In nearly half the cases there was a history of delayed speech development. Diagnosis is difficult in the early stages, especially when these non-specific abnormalities have preceded the characteristic symptoms.

Manic–depressive disorder

Depressive disorders in childhood have been considered already (p. 649). The typical picture of mania is rarely seen until late adolescence. It is possible that mania appears occasionally in a disguised form in younger adolescents, causing episodes of overactive and disturbed behaviour.

SPECIFIC DELAYS IN DEVELOPMENT

ICD 9 contains a special coding 'Specific Delays in Development'. In DSM III there is a corresponding category of 'Specific Development Disorders'. These are for circumscribed developmental delays which cannot be accounted for by another disorder. For example, a delay in language development, in an otherwise normal child, would be classified under one of these headings; a delay in language development in a child with infantile autism would not. Similarly, the child with *general* delays in development would receive a diagnosis of mental retardation, not of a specific delay of development. Despite these conventions, it is debatable whether these circumscribed disorders should be classified as mental disorders at all, since many of the children have no other signs of psychopathology. Also identical developmental disorders often accompany psychiatric disorders. For these reasons, both the WHO multi-axial system and DSM III code specific delays of development on a separate axis from that used to code psychiatric disorders.

An example of the association between circumscribed delays in development and other disorders is provided by reading retardation. In the Isle of Wight study, a third of children with conduct disorder had reading retardation compared with 4 per cent in the general population of the same age (Rutter *et al.* 1970). It is not certain why the two are associated. In some cases the reading and conduct problems may have a common (unknown) cause, in others the reading difficulties may have contributed to the psychiatric problems.

In this section, the following conditions are considered in turn: specific reading retardation, arithmetic disorders, specific motor retardation, and speech and language disorders.

Specific reading retardation

This is sometimes defined by a reading age for 10 year olds of 28 months or more below the level expected from the child's age and IQ (see Yule 1967). Defined in this way, it was present in 4 per cent of 10–11 year olds in the Isle of Wight (see Rutter and Yule 1975). Specific reading disorder should be clearly distinguished from general backwardness in scholastic achievements due to low intelligence or inadequate education.

Clinical features

The child presents with a history of serious delay in learning to read, sometimes preceded by delayed acquisition of speech and language. Writing and spelling are also impaired, but development in other areas is not. Compared with children with general backwardness at school, those with specific reading retardation are more often boys. They are also more likely to have minor neurological abnormalities. On the other hand, they are less likely to come from socially disadvantaged homes.

Aetiology

This is not known. The frequent occurrence of other cases in the family suggests a genetic cause but definite evidence is lacking. Because children with cerebral palsy and epilepsy have increased rates of reading retardation, it has been suggested that those without any obvious neurological disease might have minor neurological abnormalities. The evidence does not support this idea. The most likely cause appears to be a disorder of brain maturation affecting one or more of the skills required in reading. This is in keeping with the finding of difficulties in verbal coding and sequencing in many cases and of confusion between right and left – and with the general improvement with age (see Rutter and Yule 1975).

Social factors may add to these psychological problems. Presumably, some children have borderline difficulties that lead to reading retardation if they are brought up in a large family in which they receive less personal attention, or in a poor school, but do not do so in better circumstances. Frequent changes of school and an illiterate home background are also associated with specific reading disorder, and could act in a similar way.

Assessment and treatment

Assessment is carried out by an educational or clinical psychologist. Treatment is given by remedial teachers. There are several approaches but whatever scheme is used, it is most important to reawaken the interest of the child who has a long experience of failure. There is so far no good evidence that any method of treatment has long-term benefits (see Hewison 1982).

Prognosis

This varies with the severity of the condition. About a quarter of those with a mild problem in mid-childhood achieve normal reading skills by adolescence. However, very few of those with severe problems overcome them by adolescence. There is insufficient evidence to be certain what happens to these people as adults but it is likely that those with substantial difficulties in adolescence, retain them (see Watson *et al.* 1982 for a review of the evidence).

Specific arithmetic disorders

Difficulty with arithmetic is probably the second most common specific learning disorder that cannot be explained in terms of generally low IQ. Little is known about it. There has been no study of its epidemiology although it is thought to be quite common. Although it causes a less severe handicap in everyday life than reading difficulties, it can lead to secondary emotional difficulties while the child is at school.

The **causes** are uncertain. The existence of mathematical prodigies suggests that some of the abilities needed for mathematics might be inherited. If so, arithmetical difficulties might also be determined by heredity. However it seems unlikely that there is a single cause. **Assessment** is usually based on the arithmetic sub-tests of the WISC and the WAIS and on specific tests. **Treatment** is by remedial teaching but it is not known whether it is effective. The **prognosis** is not known. For further information, the reader should consult Cantwell (1980).

Specific motor retardation

Some children have delayed motor development, which results in clumsiness in school-work or play. The condition used to be called 'developmental apraxia'. Now paediatricians more often use the simpler term 'clumsiness'. These children can carry out all normal movements, but their co-ordination is poor. They are late in developing skills such as dressing, walking, and feeding. They tend to break things and are poor at handicrafts and organized games. They may also have difficulty in writing, drawing, and copying. IQ testing usually shows good verbal but poor performance scores.

These children are sometimes referred to a psychiatrist because of a secondary emotional disorder. An explanation of the nature of the problem should be given to the child, the family, and the teachers. Special teaching can be tried though without great hope of success. It may be necessary to exempt the child from organized games or other school activities involving motor co-ordination. Further information is given by Cantwell and Baker (1980).

Developmental speech and language disorders

Half of all children use words with meaning by 12.5 months and 97 per cent do so by 21 months. Half form words into simple sentences by 23 months (Neligan and Prudham 1969). Vocabulary and complexity of language develop rapidly during the pre-school years. However, when they start school, 1 per cent of children are seriously retarded in speech and 5 per cent have difficulty in making themselves understood by strangers. The process by which language is acquired is complex, and still not fully understood. It cannot be adequately described here but the interested reader can consult Howlin (1980).

Children with developmental speech and language disorder have a marked delay in acquiring normal speech, in the absence of any of the primary causes considered in the next section. Many speak freely and appear to understand speech, but their own speech is hard to understand because the words are ill-formed. They have greater difficulty with longer words and tend to omit the ends of words. Consonants are usually more difficult than vowels. Speech therapy is the usual treatment and there is some evidence that it is beneficial (Cooper *et al.* 1979). Language disorders are reviewed in Hersov *et al.* (1980).

OTHER DISORDERS OF SPEECH

This section is concerned with causes of delayed speech other than the specific developmental delays considered at the end of the previous section. It also contains a description of elective mutism and stammering.

Speech delay

The most common cause of delay in the development of normal speech is mental retardation. Other important causes are deafness and cerebral palsy.

Social deprivation can cause mild delays in speaking. Infantile autism is an important but infrequent cause. The remaining cases are attributed to the specific developmental speech and language delay described above.

Serious speech delay is often accompanied by other problems of development. It has obvious and important consequences for education and social development. Thorough early investigation is essential and should include both a detailed assessment of speech and language and a search for one of the causes mentioned above (see Rutter and Hersov 1977). Treatment depends partly on the cause but usually includes a programme of speech training carried out through play and social interaction. In milder cases this help is best provided at home by the parents who are instructed what to do. More severe difficulties are likely to require specialized help in a remedial class or a special school. The prognosis depends on the cause.

Elective mutism

In this condition, a child refuses to speak in certain circumstances although he does so normally in others. Usually speech is normal in the home but lacking in school. There is no defect of speech or language, only a refusal to speak in certain situations. Often there is other negative behaviour such as refusing to sit down or to play when invited to do so. The condition usually begins between three and five years of age, after normal speech has been acquired.

Elective mutism is rare, being diagnosed in less than 1 per cent of children referred to child psychiatric clinics. The cause is unknown. In some cases, the elective mutism lasts for months or years but the long-term prognosis is good. Assessment is difficult because the child often refuses to speak at the clinic so that diagnosis depends to a large extent on the parents' account. In questioning them it is important to ask whether speech and comprehension are normal at home. Although psychotherapy, behaviour modification, and speech therapy have all been tried, there is no evidence that any treatment is effective (Kolvin and Fundudis 1981).

Stammering

Stammering (or stuttering) is a disturbance of the rhythm and fluency of speech. It may take the form of repetitions of syllables or words, or of blocks in the production of speech. Stammering is four times more frequent in boys than girls. It is usually a short-lived disorder in the early stages of language development. However, 1 per cent of children suffer from stammering after they have entered school.

The cause of stammering is not known, although many theories exist. Genetic factors, brain damage, and anxiety may all play a part in certain cases: it seems unlikely that all are caused in the same way. Stammering is not usually associated with a psychiatric disorder even though it can cause distress and embarrassment. Most children improve whether treated or not. Many kinds of treatment have been tried including psychotherapy and behaviour therapy, but none has been shown to be effective. The usual treatment is speech therapy. Further information about stammering is given by Silver (1980).

ENURESIS

Functional nocturnal enuresis is the repeated involuntary voiding of urine during sleep occurring after an age at which continence is usual, in the absence of any identified physical disorder. Enuresis may be **nocturnal** (bed wetting) or **diurnal** (during waking hours), or both. Most children achieve day and night time continence by three or four years of age. Persistent enuresis after the age of five is generally regarded as abnormal. Nocturnal enuresis is often referred to as **primary** if there has been no preceding period of urinary continence for at least one year. It is called **secondary** if there has been a preceding period of urinary continence for this period. This distinction is not particularly useful in practice.

In Great Britain, the prevalence of nocturnal enuresis is about 10 per cent at five years of age. It increases somewhat between 5–7 years as secondary cases begin. It then falls to 5 per cent at the age of ten years and 1 to 2 per cent in the teenage years. Similar figures have been reported from the United States. Nocturnal enuresis occurs more frequently in boys. Daytime enuresis has a lower prevalence. It has been estimated to occur at least once a week in 2 per cent of five-year-old children (de Jonge 1973) and it becomes progressively less frequent after that age. Unlike nocturnal enuresis, it is more common in girls than boys (see Shaffer 1977). Most children who wet during the day also do so during sleep. On the other hand, only a few of those who have nocturnal enuresis have diurnal enuresis as well.

Nocturnal enuresis is a symptom that can cause great unhappiness and distress, particularly if the parents blame or punish the child. This unhappiness may be made worse by limitations imposed by enuresis on activities such as staying with friends or going on holiday.

Aetiology

The aetiology of functional nocturnal enuresis is uncertain. Probably not all have the same cause. There is some evidence for a genetic basis. About 70 per cent of children with enuresis have a first-degree relative who has been enuretic (Bakwin 1961). Also, concordance rates are twice as high in monozygotic as in dizygotic twins (Hallgren 1960). If genetic influences are present, they might act through delayed maturation of part of the nervous system. It has been suggested that children with nocturnal enuresis have abnormally deep sleep. However this was not supported in a controlled investigation by Boyd (1960).

Five per cent of enuretic children have urinary infections, compared with about 1 per cent of children of comparable age in the general population (Shaffer *et al.* 1968). Infection is more frequent in girls than boys. In some cases the infection is causing enuresis, in others bedwetting has led to an ascending urinary infection.

It has also been claimed that the bladder capacity of enuretic children is smaller than usual or alternatively that their bladders function abnormally. Neither claim has been supported by convincing evidence (see Shaffer 1977).

Most enuretic children are free from psychiatric disorder. Nevertheless the proportion of enuretic children who are psychiatrically disordered is greater than that of dry children (Rutter *et al.* 1973). It is not known whether this association indicates that enuresis causes psychiatric disorder, or that psychiatric disorder is a cause of enuresis, or that they share a common cause such as disturbed family circumstances. The observation that enuresis sometimes starts or worsens after a stressful event, suggests that psychological causes may play a part in some cases.

Assessment and treatment

The first step is to make sure that the wetting is really due to functional nocturnal enuresis rather than an as yet undetected physical disorder, particularly urinary infection, diabetes, or epilepsy.

Psychiatric disorder should be looked for. If none is found, an assessment should be made of the extent of the distress caused to the child. Finally an evaluation is made of the attitudes to the bedwetting of the parents and siblings.

If a physical disorder is found, it should be treated. If the enuresis is functional, the child and parents should be told that this is a common problem, for which the child is not to blame. It should be explained to the parents that punishment and disapproval are inappropriate and likely to be ineffective. They should be encouraged to focus less attention on the problem and to reward success without drawing attention to failure. Many enuretic children improve spontaneously soon after an explanation of this kind.

Children who do not improve with these simple measures may be treated with enuresis alarm methods (otherwise called the pad and bell method). Two perforated metal plates are separated by a cotton sheet. The plates of metal are incorporated in a low voltage circuit including a battery, a switch, and a bell or buzzer. The resistance of the cotton sheet prevents current from flowing in the circuit. When the bed is made, the plates are placed under the position in which the child's pelvis will rest. When the child begins to pass urine, the circuit is completed and the bell or buzzer sounds. The child turns off the switch, and rises to complete the emptying of the bladder. The bed is remade and a dry sheet is put between the metal plates before the child returns. Successful results probably depend on conditioning mechanisms, but they cannot be fully explained by classical conditioning; other learning mechanisms may play a part, including social reinforcement from the parents for the child's successes (see Turner 1973).

The enuresis alarm seldom works with children under the age of six, or those who are unco-operative. For the rest it is effective within a month in about 70–80 per cent of cases (see Shaffer *et al.* 1968), although about a third relapse within a year (Turner 1973). It is often difficult to persuade families to persist long enough with the treatment. It has been suggested that, even if they persist with the treatment, children with associated psychiatric disorder do less well than the rest (see Berg 1981).

Drug treatment is with a tricyclic antidepressant, usually imipramine or amitriptyline. These are given in a dose of 25 mg at night increasing to 50 mg if necessary. Their beneficial effect has been demonstrated in clinical trials (see Shaffer *et al.* 1968). Most bed-wetters improve initially with complete relief in about a third. However, most also relapse when the drug is stopped. Because of this high relapse rate, the side effects of tricyclics and the danger of accidental overdose, the drugs have a limited value in treating enuresis. They are most useful when it is important to control the enuresis for a short time – for example when the child goes on holiday (see Berg (1981), and Schaefer (1979) for a review of enuresis and its treatment).

ENCOPRESIS

Encopresis is the voluntary or involuntary passing of faeces into clothing after the age at which bowel control is usual, in the absence of a known organic cause. Children usually achieve bowel control by about the age of three, and soiling after the age of four is generally regarded as abnormal. Encopresis may be present continuously from birth (primary) or appear after a period of continence (secondary).

A prevalence of about 1 per cent amongst five-year-olds is quoted in the manual DSM III. In the Isle of Wight survey of 10 to 11-year-old children, encopresis was found in 1.3 per cent of boys, and 0.3 per cent of girls. Other studies have confirmed that the condition is more common among boys.

Aetiology

In some cases of encopresis, bowel control has never been established, in others it has been achieved but lost. The latter may have physical or emotional causes.

Failure to establish bowel control

This may be due to poor toilet training in a disorganized family or an understaffed institution. It may also be due to mental retardation.

Emotional causes

Emotional disorder is common among encopretic children and in some cases it is thought to play a causal role. Cases of this kind are usually divided into regressive or aggressive types. 'Regressive' soiling is thought of as a return to an earlier stage of development. It often follows an upsetting family event, such as the arrival of a new sibling, or the illness of a parent. It is often accompanied by evident emotional symptoms. 'Aggressive' soiling may develop when there is a poor relationship between the child and one of the parents. Often the mother is controlling and is preoccupied with bowel function. She has started toilet training unusually early. The child appears to be rebelling against these controls. He is often excessively clean in other ways and inhibited in his emotions. He is usually reluctant to discuss the soiling and may deny it. The clinical picture of encopresis has been described by Anthony (1957) and Hersov (1977). Further information about the condition is given by Schaefer (1979).

Assessment

The first step is to make sure that the faecal soiling is due to encopresis and not a sign of an undiagnosed physical disorder. Soiling may be caused by faecal impaction with overflow incontinence. It can also be a sign of Hirschsprung's disease. A psychiatric examination should also be performed.

It is always important to find out whether there is any retention of faeces. Whenever this is prolonged it can lead to secondary enlargement of the large bowel even in cases of functional encopresis. It then becomes difficult to decide whether the original cause was physical or not. The assessment of cases with large bowel enlargement requires close co-operation with a paediatrician, who will advise whether investigation by barium enema is indicated.

Treatment

This depends on the cause, the child's age, and the presence of faecal retention. If there is faecal retention with soiling, the bowel should be cleared. When the cause is inadequate toilet training, this should be provided in hospital. Children with regressive soiling require help with the causative emotional problems. In cases of aggressive soiling, attention should be paid to the parents' restrictive attitudes while the child is encouraged to express his feelings in a form of psychotherapy appropriate to his age. Aggressive soiling can be explained to the parents as a form of protest in a child who is unable to express his feelings in other ways.

Prognosis

Regressive soiling usually improves quickly. Aggressive soiling is more difficult to treat. Cases with retention present particular difficulties. Whatever the cause it is unusual for encopresis to persist beyond the middle teenage years (see Hersov 1976).

CHILD ABUSE

Child abuse refers to the inflicting of physical harm on, or serious neglect of a child by one or both parents or others who have the responsibility for his care. Although child abuse is primarily a disorder of the parents, it is considered here because the treatment of these adults is undertaken by child psychiatrists who are also called upon to help with the emotional consequences for the child. Child abuse was first identified from radiological findings of unexplained multiple fractures (Caffey 1946). Among the subsequent clinical accounts that of Kempe *et al.* (1962) is noteworthy not only for the clinical descriptions which it contains but also for the introduction of the term 'the battered baby syndrome' which helped to arouse public concern.

In recent years there have been attempts to widen the concept of child abuse to include emotional abuse and neglect as well as physical abuse. However with the doubtful exception of 'deprivation dwarfism' (see below p. 675), no clear syndrome of emotional abuse has been described (see Kavanagh 1982). It seems better, therefore, to limit the term to cases in which physical abuse has taken place.

Prevalence

It has been estimated that about 3 per 1000 children under the age of 18 are physically abused each year and another 7 per 1000 severely neglected or sexually abused (see Graham 1979). Baldwin and Oliver (1975) studied the prevalence of abuse of such severity that there was evidence of a bone fracture or bleeding around the brain. They found a rate of 1 per 1000 in children under four years of age over a seven-year period in an English county.

Clinical features

Often the abused child is first brought to a doctor with an injury that is alleged to have been caused accidentally. In fact it has been inflicted by the parents. These children may be slapped or punched, thrown to the floor or against a wall, or burnt. On closer examination, evidence is often found of previous injuries including multiple fractures. The child may show general abnormalities as well. The latter may be physical—dehydration and malnourishment—or psychological – the alert but inhibited appearance that has been called 'frozen watchfulness'. The injuries may be very serious: dislocation of joints, multiple fractures, subdural haematoma and retinal haemorrhage, injuries to the abdominal viscera including ruptures of organs, severe burns and lacerations.

The parents characteristically persist in maintaining that these injuries are accidental. Although usually only one parent is responsible, the other colludes in the denial. When the parents eventually admit their involvement, it often appears that there has been a period of increasing tension, often at a time when the child's crying cannot be quietened, followed by an outburst of aggressive behaviour. Some parents inflict deliberate painful injuries with burning cigarettes or in other ways.

Prognosis

Severe abuse has a serious prognosis. Baldwin and Oliver (1975) reported that 10 per cent of severely abused children died and a quarter of those who survived were intellectually impaired. The consequences of less severe abuse and neglect have not been studied so thoroughly but are likely to be substantial. Adults who have been abused as children probably have more psychiatric problems and social difficulties than the general population, and perform poorly as parents (see Scott 1977*b*; Rutter and Madge 1976).

Aetiology

Aetiology can be considered in terms of factors in the parents and those in the child (see Baldwin and Oliver 1975; Smith *et al.* 1973). Factors in the parents associated with child abuse include: extreme youth, abnormal personality, psychiatric disorder, low social class, criminal record, marital disharmony and breakdown of marriage, a high rate of illegitimacy, and social isolation (see Friedrich and Wheeler 1982). Many of the parents give a history of themselves having suffered abuse or deprivation in childhood (see Oliver and Buchanan 1979). Child abuse is more common in families in which there are other forms of social pathology, but it is certainly not limited to such families – a point that should be remembered if cases are to be detected early.

Abused children are usually under two years of age. Many are illegitimate or for other reasons unwanted. Some are premature and some have congenital defects. Some are temperamentally difficult, and persistent crying is particularly likely to evoke battering. Lynch (1975) studied 25 abused children each of whom had at least one sibling who had not been abused. Compared with the siblings, the history of the abused children more often had one or more of the following features: an abnormal pregnancy, labour, or delivery; separation from the mother in the neonatal period; and illness of the mother in the first year of life. It is possible that the common theme in these various factors is a failure of the mother to establish normal emotional bonds with her child (see also Rutter 1981*b*).

Assessment and treatment

Doctors and others involved in the care of children should always be alert to the possibility that a child's injuries may have been caused by the parents. It is easy to be deceived by plausible excuses especially if the doctor is unwilling to risk upsetting the parents by questioning them closely. Suspicion should be aroused by an evasive or contradictory account of an accident to the child; by repeated injuries; by delay in seeking help; by evidence of general neglect; and by a watchful or fearful attitude of the child to the parents. Full skeletal X-rays and examination of the retina for haemorrhages are important in diagnosis. When there is a definite suspicion of abuse the injured child should be admitted to hospital for further assessment. It is essential that all findings are fully documented. The records should include a detailed clinical description, photographs of injuries and full skeletal X-rays.

After the diagnosis has been made, it is first necessary to consider what emergency action is needed to ensure the safety of the child. After this, a long-term plan must be made. The most difficult decision is whether to separate the child from the parents, and if so for how long. This decision should involve all the doctors and social workers concerned with the case. Otherwise mistakes can arise because some important aspects of the case are not taken into account. The decision can only be reached after a full assessment of the extent and frequency of the injuries, and the family background. If separation is judged to be necessary and the parents are unwilling to agree to it, an urgent application should be made to a magistrate for a Place of Safety Order. Thereafter a longer term Care Order can be sought by the Social Services Department if the need for separation is confirmed by the results of the further assessment (see p. 754).

When the abuse is severe, permanent separation may be necessary. In some cases, the parents will face criminal charges. In less severe cases, it may be more satisfactory for the child to return home after appropriate help has been given to the parents than to suffer the disadvantages of long-term residential care. Nevertheless the death or repeated severe injury of some children returned to their parents indicates the need for great caution and close supervision in every case. By putting the child's name on an 'at risk' register, the Social Services Department takes on a statutory responsibility for continuing supervision.

Usually, several agencies are involved in the management of these problems and success depends on the effective co-ordination of medical, social, and voluntary services. In this the general practitioner plays an essential part. The family of a child who is 'at risk' requires support and regular supervision by an experienced social worker who is alert to the dangers of further injury or neglect. In addition, some parents are helped by psychiatric treatment. This may take several forms, depending on the nature of the parent's difficulties. Family therapy is often indicated. Ounsted *et al.* (1974) have described an in-patient unit in which the parents and child can be admitted for intensive treatment.

Prevention

Attempts to prevent child abuse have concentrated on early detection and upon the identification of those at risk. Lynch and Roberts (1977) studied 50 cases of children who had been abused or were thought to be at serious risk of abuse. They concluded that many of the children at risk could be identified by taking into account three kinds of evidence which was available by the time the mother left the maternity ward with her new baby. The first was evidence of emotional disorder or serious social problems affecting the mother in the course of the pregnancy, sufficient to have required referral to a social worker. The second was evidence of a period of separation of the mother from her baby during the first few days of life (often by admission to a special care baby unit). The third was evidence of concern by hospital staff about the woman's ability to mother her baby immediately after delivery. Although these findings require confirmation, they provide useful guidelines in clinical work.

Families identified as being at risk in this or other ways should be supervised carefully and given extra support by the general practitioner and his team, in collaboration with a social worker (see Beswick *et al.* 1976).

Deprivation dwarfism

In 1967 Powell *et al.* described 13 children of abnormally short stature who also showed unusual eating patterns, retarded speech development, and temper tantrums. Growth hormone levels were low. These abnormalities receded rapidly when the child was moved to a different environment. Since this original account, the syndrome has been widely recognized. The children come from disturbed families and some have been physically abused. It has been suggested that the failure to grow is related to emotional deprivation. However, although the cause of the dwarfism is not wholly understood, it seems that it only occurs when the children have been fed inadequately (see Kavanagh 1982).

SUICIDE AND DELIBERATE SELF-HARM

Both deliberate self-harm and suicide are rare among children less than 12 years of age. Shaffer (1974) searched official records in England and Wales over a seven-year period for evidence of suicides among children aged 10 to 14 years. The rate was one in 800 000 for this four-year span of age, and all cases were in children older than 12. This study was based on official records and it is probable that these under report suicide in childhood because of the wish, in doubtful cases, to spare parents additional suffering.

Of the children who died by suicide in Shaffer's series, almost half had previously talked about, threatened, or attempted suicide. He distinguished two groups of children. The first comprised children of superior intelligence who seemed to be isolated from their less educated parents. Many of the mothers were mentally ill. Before death, these children had seemed depressed and withdrawn, and some had stayed away from school. The second group contained children who were impetuous, prone to violence, and resentful of criticism.

Deliberate self-harm that is not fatal, and threats of suicide without any act of self-harm are increasingly common after the age of 12, especially among girls. Most of these acts of self-harm follow some disturbance of a close relationship. Psychiatric disorder is seldom found. The prognosis for life is usually good but at least a tenth harm themselves again within a year. There also appears to be an increased risk of suicide in later years. Threats or acts of deliberate self-harm by children should always be taken seriously and careful psychiatric assessment should be carried out (see Hawton (1982) and Garfinkel *et al.* (1982) for reviews of suicide and deliberate self-harm in adolescence).

PSYCHIATRIC ASPECTS OF PHYSICAL ILLNESS

The associations between physical and psychiatric disorders in children resemble those in adults (see Chapters 11 and 12). There are three main groups each of which is at least as common in general paediatric practice as among children referred to child psychiatrists. The first group comprises the psychological and social consequences of physical illness. The second consists of psychiatric disorders presenting with physical symptoms, for example abdominal pain and multiple tics. The third consists of physical complications of psychiatric disorders, for example eating disorders (p. 364 and 645), child abuse (p. 672), and encopresis (p. 670). In this section, the first two are considered.

Children in hospital

Apart from the specific consequences of particular illnesses, admission to hospital has important psychological consequences of its own. Until recent years most hospitals discouraged families from visiting children. Bowlby (1951) was influential in suggesting that separation from the mother on admission to hospital could have immediate and long-term adverse psychological effects. He identified successive stages of protest, despair, and detachment during the admission. He also suggested that these were followed by long-term adverse effects on emotional development. Subsequent investigations have shown that neither immediate nor long-term adverse consequences need occur if the child is prepared for the experience, if the parents are involved in his care in hospital, and if nurses are aware of the potential problems (see Rutter 1981*b*).

These findings have brought about beneficial changes in attitudes of the staff of paediatric units which have reduced the amount of emotional disturbance among children admitted to hospital. The child psychiatrist still has a part to play in helping the minority of those in whom emotional problems arise and their families. For most wards he can do this by providing a consultation service (see Froese 1977). In units in which emotional problems are especially likely to arise, a more regular liaison arrangement is often appropriate. Examples include special care baby units, wards caring for dying children, and clinics dealing with chronic disorders such as diabetes, epilepsy, and cystic fibrosis.

Psychiatric consequences of physical illness

Children are more likely than adults to develop an acute organic syndrome when they are physically ill. A familiar example is that caused by febrile illness. When a chronic brain disorder occurs it can result in mental retardation, a disintegrative psychosis (p. 662), or dementia according to the age of the child. Children with organic brain disease have a high prevalence of psychiatric disorder which is greater than that found among children with other kinds of physical illness. In the Isle of Wight study, Rutter *et al.* (1970) and Seidel *et al.* (1975) found that the prevalence of psychiatric disorder was only slightly increased with a physical illness such as asthma or diabetes which do not affect the brain. This investigation also showed that physically ill children, whether brain damaged or not, had an increased prevalence of reading retardation (Rutter *et al.* 1970). Physical illnesses, particularly when life-threatening or chronically disabling, are associated with psychiatric symptoms in the parents (Breslau *et al.* 1982).

As well as these general associations between physical illness and psychological problems, several specific associations have been reported. Those involving asthma, epilepsy, diabetes, and leukaemia are discussed in Chapters 11 and 12. Spina bifida (Dorner 1976) and cerebral palsy (Rutter *et al.* 1970) are other examples of physical illnesses particularly likely to give rise to psychological problems for the child and his parents.

Psychological disorders presenting with physical symptoms

Children often complain of somatic symptoms when they are suffering from a psychiatric disorder. These complaints include abdominal pain, headache, and limb pains. Most of the children are treated by family doctors and the minority who are referred to specialists are more likely to be sent to paediatricians than child psychiatrists.

Of these symptoms, abdominal pain has been studied most thoroughly (see Kolvin and Nichol 1979). Estimates of prevalence vary between 4 and 17 per cent of all children. The symptom is a common reason for referral to a paediatrician. In most cases, abdominal pain is associated with headache, limb pains, and sickness (Apley and Hale 1973). Physical causes are seldom found and psychological ones are often suspected. Some are related to anxiety and, as discussed on p. 649, others have been ascribed to 'masked' depressive disorders. Follow-up suggests that about a quarter of cases severe enough to require investigation by a paediatrician develop chronic psychiatric problems.

ADOLESCENCE

There are no specific disorders of adolescence. However, special experience and skill are required to apply the general principles of psychiatric diagnosis and treatment to patients who are at this time of transition between childhood and adult life. It is often particularly difficult to distinguish psychiatric disorder from the normal emotional reactions of the teenage years. For this reason, this section begins by discussing how far emotional disorder is an inevitable part of adolescence.

Considerable changes – physical, psychosexual, emotional, and social – take place in adolescence. In the 1950s and 1960s it was widely assumed that these changes were commonly accompanied by emotional upset of such a degree that it could be considered a psychiatric disorder. Indeed, Anna Freud (1958) regarded 'disharmony within the psychic structure' as a 'basic' fact of adolescence. Others described alienation, inner turmoil, adjustment reactions, and identity crises as common features of this time of life. Recently a more cautious view has prevailed. Rutter *et al.* (1976) have reviewed the evidence, including their own findings in 14-year-olds on the Isle of Wight. They concluded that rebellion and parental alienation are uncommon among adolescents although inner turmoil, as indicated by reports of misery, self-depreciation, and ideas of reference, is present in about half of all adolescents. However this turmoil seldom lasts for long and it usually goes unnoticed by adults. Among older adolescents rebellious behaviour is rather common and many become estranged from school during their last year of compulsory attendance.

Psychiatric disorders

Although psychiatric disorders are only a little more common in adolescence than in the middle years of childhood (see Graham 1979) the pattern of disorder is markedly different, being closer to that of adults. In adolescence, the sexes are affected equally; anxiety is less common than in earlier years, while depression and school refusal are more frequent.

Some psychiatrists believe that there is a specific 'identity disorder' at this age. In DSM III this is defined as severe subjective distress over an inability to reconcile aspects of the self into a relatively coherent and acceptable sense of self. The disturbance is manifested by uncertainty about a variety of issues relating to identity including three or more of the following: long-term goals, career choice, friendship patterns, sexual orientation and behaviour, religious identification, values and loyalties. These problems must have been present for more than three months and be accompanied by impairment of social, academic, or occupational functioning. It is apparent that the category is defined by the focus of the adolescent's preoccupations. Most of the same cases can be classified equally well by symptoms – that is as emotional disorders or conduct disorders. Thus Rutter *et al.* (1976) reported that two-fifths of adolescent psychiatric cases meet the criteria for emotional disorders and two-fifths for conduct disorders. The idea of identity disorders can be questioned for another reason. It implies that the symptoms began in adolescence. In fact many started in childhood, suggesting that they were not caused mainly by adolescent alienation. Indeed, the reverse sequence is more likely, for example feelings of depression causing alienation.

The remaining fifth of adolescent disorders that are neither emotional disorders nor conduct disorders are largely made up of conditions of adult life, seldom seen at younger ages. These are: manic–depressive disorder, schizophrenia, anorexia nervosa, deliberate self-harm, sexual disorders, and drug or alcohol problems.

Clinical features of psychiatric disorders in adolescence

Emotional disorders

Generalized anxiety states are less common than in childhood. Social phobias begin to appear in early adolescence, agoraphobia in the later teenage years. School refusal is common between 14 years of age and the end of compulsory schooling, and at this age it is often associated with other psychiatric disorders. Depressive symptoms are more common in adolescence than in childhood. In the Isle of Wight survey they were ten times more frequent among 14-year-olds than 10-year-olds. In adolescence, depressive mood is often less immediately obvious than anergy, 'alienation' from parents, withdrawal from social contacts with peers and underachievement at school.

Conduct disorders

About half the cases of conduct disorder seen in adolescents have started in childhood. Those which begin in adolescence differ in being less strongly associated with reading retardation and family pathology. Among younger children aggressive behaviour is generally more evident in the home or at school. Among adolescents it is more likely to appear outside these settings as offences against property. Truancy also forms part of the conduct disorders occurring at this age.

Manic–depressive disorders

These occur occasionally in older adolescents. If mild, they may be difficult to distinguish from the emotional lability that is common at this time of life.

Schizophrenia

This is also seen occasionally in adolescence. In its early stages it may be difficult to distinguish from emotional disorder. The characteristic symptoms at this age are similar to those of adults (Kolvin 1971).

Assessment

There are special skills in interviewing adolescents. In general, the younger adolescents require an approach similar to that used for children, while with older adolescents it is more appropriate to employ that used with adults. It must always be remembered that a large proportion of adolescents are attending a psychiatrist somewhat unwillingly and also that most have difficulty in expressing their feelings in adult terms. The psychiatrist must therefore be willing to spend considerable time establishing a relationship with an adolescent patient. To do this, he must show interest in the adolescent, respecting his point of view and talking in terms he can understand. As in adult psychiatry it is important to collect systematic information and describe symptoms in detail, but with adolescents the psychiatrist must be prepared to adopt a more flexible approach to the interview.

It is usually better to see the adolescent before interviewing the parents. In this way, the psychiatrist makes it clear that he regards the adolescent as an independent person. Later, other members of the family may be interviewed, and the family seen as a whole. As well as the usual psychiatric history, particular attention should be paid to information about the adolescent's functioning at home, in school, or at work; and about his relationships with peers. A physical examination should be carried out unless the general practitioner has performed one recently and reported the results.

Such an assessment should allow allocation of the problem to one of three classes. In the first, no psychiatric diagnosis can be made and reassurance is all that is required. In the second, there is no psychiatric diagnosis but anxious parents or a disturbed family need additional help. In the third, there is a psychiatric disorder requiring treatment.

Treatment

Treatment methods are intermediate between those employed in child and adult psychiatry. As in the former, it is important to work with relatives and teachers. It is usually necessary to help, reassure, and support the parents and sometimes necessary to extend this to other members of the family. However it is also important to treat the adolescent as an individual who is gradually becoming independent of the family. In these circumstances, family therapy as practised in child psychiatry is usually inappropriate and may at times be harmful.

Services for adolescents

The proportion of adolescents in the population who are seen in psychiatric clinics is less than the proportion of other age groups. Of those referred, some of the less mature adolescents can be helped more in a child psychiatry clinic. Some of the older and more mature adolescents are better treated in a clinic for adults. Nevertheless for the majority the care can be provided most appropriately by a specialized adolescent service. There is no generally agreed model for this. Most units accept outpatient referrals not only from doctors, but also from senior teachers, social workers, and the courts. When this is done the general practitioner should be informed of the referral and the case discussed with him. All work with schools and social services although there is no one agreed way of arranging this. Inpatient facilities are usually limited in extent. It is uncertain how many beds are required: in the 1960s the official guidance suggested 25 per million but many now consider that this provision is excessive (see Steinberg 1982).

Appendix

History taking and examination in child psychiatry*

HISTORY

I Reason for referral

The problems as seen from various points of view i.e. parents, teachers, referring doctor, and child. Expectations about the referral.

II Detailed description of present problem

Onset, course, consequences including effect on family, help given to date.

III Systematic questioning on recent behaviour and emotional state

1. General health: eating, sleeping, elimination, physical complaints, fits or faints.
2. Interests, activities, hobbies.
3. Social relationships: with siblings, peers, adults, opposite sex; reactions to new people or situations.
4. Emotions: happy, miserable, fearful, worried at home or at school.
5. Rituals, tics, or mannerisms.
6. Antisocial behaviour.
7. Attention and persistence, activity levels, co-ordination.
8. Schooling.

IV Family structure and history

1. Draw a family tree indicating the patient by an arrow. Note also consanguity and whether left handed.
2. Sibs: dates of birth, weights. Also note any miscarriages of the mother's pregnancies.
3. Family occurrence of developmental disorders, and illnesses. Causes of death.
4. Personality, education, and occupation of each family member and relationships with patient.
5. Home circumstances, finances, and character of the neighbourhood.

*This scheme is adapted from that developed by Dr C. Ounsted and used at the Park Hospital for Children, Oxford.

V Family life and relationships

1. Parental relationship – how do the parents get on? What do they enjoy doing together? Father's involvement with child care and household tasks.
2. Parent–child interaction – things done with child. Going out together and playing together. Help with homework.
3. Child's participation in family activities – child's help with washing up, errands, and shopping.
4. Pattern of family relationships – mother or father's child? Who does the child confide in? More like father or mother?
5. Discipline – amount of freedom or restriction, methods of punishment. Who reprimands?

VI Personal history

1. Pregnancy: was it wanted? Complications, duration.
2. Delivery: route, complications, birth weight (compare with sibs).
3. Neonatal problems: breathing, feeding, jaundice, seizures.
4. Early development (compare with sibs), temperament, emotional relationships, motor milestones, speech, and toilet training.
5. Medical history (obtain details of referrals and treatment): immunizations, illnesses or disabilities, seizures or behavioural problems.
6. Separations from parents.
7. Schools attended, progress.

VII Temperamental or personality attributes

1. Meeting new people, e.g. adults, children, approach to strangers.
2. New situations – places, foods, toys.
3. Emotional expression – how vigorous in expression of feelings, how happy or miserable before present problem.
4. Affections and relationships: how are feelings shown? Affectionate? Confiding? Quality of relationships?
5. Regularity of functions – sleeping, bowels, appetite.
6. Sensitivity – Response to the injury of another person or an animal. Reaction when something is wrong.

EXAMINATION

It may be possible with older children to follow something like the same procedure used to examine an adult's mental state but, particularly in young children, formal examination of the mental state may be impossible. Every opportunity should be taken to observe the child's behaviour and this should be recorded systematically and objectively. Avoid global clinical impressions. Do not forget to obtain the child's view of the situation including his likes, dislikes, and hopes for the future.

MENTAL STATE

General behaviour

1. Dress, appearance.
2. Parent–child interaction and separation.
3. Emotional responsiveness and relationship with the doctor.
4. Restless, disinhibited, assertive, or aggressive.

Mood

1. Signs of tension and sadness including facial expression, tearfulness, and apprehension.
2. Preoccupation with fears, worries, depressing thoughts.
3. Apathetic, withdrawn, shy.

Talk (form)

1. Spontaneity, flow.
2. Defects of articulation or sentence structure.
3. Coherence.

Attention and persistence

1. Degree and duration of interest in topics, activities, or objects.
2. Whether easily distracted.
3. Unexplained interruptions of attention.

Activity levels

1. General activity.
2. Fidgeting.

Intellectual function

1. Rough assessment of reading level, spelling, arithmetic, writing, general knowledge.
2. Write name and address, draw a man, copy triangle, diamond, cross, and circle (according to age).
3. If possible, testing by **clinical or educational psychologist** should be arranged including assessment of basic intellectual ability, educational attainments, and specific learning problems.

   (A **school report** about progress and general behaviour should always be obtained or, for younger children, an account from nursery school or playgroup.)

PHYSICAL STATE

General

1. Physique, sexual maturity.
2. Height, weight, head circumference (use percentile charts).
3. Congenital abnormalities.
4. Developmental abnormalities, e.g. asymmetry or other physical abnormality.

Neurological

1. Head; size and shape of skull.
2. Vision and hearing. Other cranial nerves.
3. Preferred hand, eye, foot.
4. Posture, involuntary movements.
5. Co-ordination of fingers and limbs.
6. Limb tone, power, reflexes.
7. Constructional skills.
8. Right–left differentiation.
9. Speech and language.

THE PERSONALITY AND MENTAL STATE OF THE PARENTS

Note in particular

1. Affection for child.
2. Excessive indulgence or anxiety.
3. Degree, type, and consistency of discipline and control of child.
4. Negligence.
5. Lack of self-confidence in parental ability, fear of the child.
6. Understanding of previous diagnoses and management.

(Home visits by **social workers** are a valuable way of collecting this type of information.)

FURTHER READING

Kaplan, H.I., Freedman, A.M., and Sadock, B.J. (1980). *Comprehensive textbook of psychiatry*, Vol. 3, 3rd edn. Williams and Wilkins, Baltimore.

Schwartz, S. and Johnson, J.H. (1981). *Psychopathology of childhood. A clinical experimental approach.* Pergamon General Psychology Series. Pergamon, Oxford.

Hersov, L. and Rutter, M. (1982), *Child psychiatry: modern approaches*, 2nd edn. Blackwell, Oxford.

Quay, H.C. and Werry, J.S. (1970). *Psychopathological disorders of childhood.* John Wiley, New York.

Steinberg, D. (1982). *The clinical psychiatry of adolescence.* John Wiley, Chichester.

Rutter, M. (1981). *Maternal deprivation reassessed.* Penguin, Harmondsworth.

Wing, J.K. and Wing, L. (eds.) (1983). Psychoses of uncertain aetiology: part 3, psychoses of early childhood. *Handbook of psychiatry,* Vol. 3. Cambridge University Press.

21. Mental retardation

Until recent years, most mentally retarded people lived in large hospitals under the care of doctors and nurses. Nowadays the educational and social care of the mentally retarded is generally undertaken by teachers and social workers, and most of the medical care by paediatricians and family doctors. Nevertheless the psychiatrist still has an important role, both in the organization of services and in the assessment and treatment of psychiatric disorders in mentally retarded children and adults. This chapter is therefore concerned with the organization of services and with psychiatric disorder in both children and adults. Many of the psychiatric problems of mentally retarded children are similar to those of children of normal intelligence; they will not be dealt with here but references will be made to the corresponding sections of the chapter on child psychiatry.

TERMINOLOGY

Over the years several terms have been applied to people who have intellectual impairment from early life. In the nineteenth and early twentieth centuries the word idiot was used for people with severe intellectual impairment, and imbecile for those with moderate impairment. The special study and care of such people was known as the field of mental deficiency. When these words came to carry stigma, they were replaced by the terms mental subnormality and mental retardation. In Great Britain the term mental handicap has recently been used increasingly and has been adopted by the Department of Health.

In this chapter the term mental retardation is used. This term is preferred because it is used in ICD 9 and DSM III, and also because the term mental handicap can lead to confusion between the different handicaps of the mentally retarded and of chronic schizophrenics.

THE CONCEPT OF MENTAL RETARDATION

An important distinction has to be made between intellectual impairment starting in early childhood (mental retardation), and intellectual impairment developing later in life (dementia). In 1845 Esquirol made this distinction when he wrote:

idiocy is not a disease, but a condition in which the intellectual faculties are never manifested; or have never been developed sufficiently to enable the idiot to acquire such an amount of knowledge as persons of his own age and placed in similar circumstances with himself are capable of receiving (Esquirol 1845, pp. 446–7).

At the end of the nineteenth century a significant advance was made when methods of measuring intellectual capacity became available. Early in the twentieth century Binet's celebrated tests of intelligence provided quantitative criteria for ascertaining mental retardation. These tests also made it possible to identify mild intellectual retardation that might not be obvious otherwise (see Binet and Simon 1905). Unfortunately, those responsible for the mentally retarded began to assume that people with such mild degrees of intellectual impairment were socially incompetent and required institutional care (see Corbett 1978).

Similar views were reflected in the legislation of the time. In 1886 the Idiots Act had made a simple distinction between idiocy (more severe) and imbecility (less severe). In 1913 the Mental Deficiency Act added a third category for people who 'from an early age display some permanent mental defect coupled with strong vicious or criminal propensities in which punishment has had little or no effect'. As a result of this legislation, people of normal or near normal intelligence were admitted to hospital for long periods simply because their behaviour offended against the values of society. Although some of these people had 'strong vicious' propensities, others were girls whose repeated illegitimate pregnancies were interpreted as a sign of the 'criminal' propensities mentioned in the Act.

In the past the use of social criteria clearly led to abuse. Nevertheless, it is unsatisfactory to define mental retardation in terms of intelligence quotient alone. Social criteria must be included, since a distinction must be made between people who can lead a normal or near-normal life, and those who cannot. This requirement is recognized by ICD 9, in which mental retardation is defined as 'a condition of incomplete development of mind which is especially characterized by subnormality of intelligence'. ICD 9 emphasizes that intellectual assessment should be based not only on psychometrics, but on all available information including clinical observations. The ICD 9 scheme provides definitions in terms of IQ levels, but warns that the latter are 'provided only as a guide and should not be used rigidly'. The ICD 9 classification is shown in Table 21.1.

Table 21.1. *The classification of mental retardation in ICD 9*

317	MILD MENTAL RETARDATION IQ 50–70 (Synonyms include feeble-minded, moron, highgrade defect, and mild mental subnormality)
318	OTHER SPECIFIED MENTAL RETARDATION
318.0	*Moderate mental retardation* IQ 35–49 (Synonyms: imbecile; moderate mental subnormality)
318.1	*Severe mental retardation* IQ 20–34 (Synonym: Severe mental subnormality)
318.2	*Profound mental retardation* IQ under 20 (Synonyms: idiocy; profound mental subnormality)

In DSM III, categories similar to those of ICD 9 are adopted, with the additional specification that all require 'concurrent deficits or impairments in adaptive behaviour, taking age into account'. Educationalists use other terms and these differ between Britain and the United States. In Britain, the terms are Educationally Subnormal (ESN) and Severely Educationally Subnormal (ESN(S)). In the United States, three groups are recognized: Educable Mentally Retarded (EMR), Trainable Mentally Retarded (TMR), and Severely Mentally Retarded (SMR).

EPIDEMIOLOGY

In 1929, in an important survey of schoolchildren in six areas of Britain, E.O. Lewis found that the total prevalence of mental retardation was 27 per 1000, and the prevalence of moderate and severe retardation (IQ less than 50) was 3.7 per 1000. Subsequent studies have generally shown that, in the population aged 15–19, the prevalence of moderate and severe retardation is between 3.5 and 4.0 per 1000. Tizard (1964) pointed out that, although the prevalence of moderate and severe retardation changed little between the 1930s and the 1960s, the incidence of severe retardation fell by about a third. The explanation for the prevalence not changing was that patients were living longer, particularly those with Down's syndrome.

Tizard drew attention to the distinction between 'administrative' prevalence and 'true' prevalence. He defined administrative prevalence as 'the numbers for whom services would be required in a community which made provision for all who needed them'. If the true prevalence of all levels of retardation (IQ less than 70) is taken to be 20–30 per thousand of the population of all ages, then the administrative prevalence is about 10 per thousand of all ages. In other words, less than half of all retarded people require special provision. Administrative prevalence is greater in childhood and falls after the age of 16. This reduction results from continuing slow intellectual development and gradual social adjustment.

The prevalence of **psychiatric disorder** among the mentally retarded is less certain, but it is undoubtedly greater than in the general population (see James and Snaith 1979). Rates of psychiatric disorder are particularly high among mentally retarded people in hospital, presumably because psychiatric disorder is a common reason for admission. Even so, there is good evidence that the mentally retarded have high rates of psychiatric disorder and disturbed behaviour. In a survey of intellectually retarded children aged 9–11 years, Rutter *et al.* (1970) found that almost a third were rated as 'disturbed' by their parents, whilst about 40 per cent were so rated by their teachers. These rates were three to four times higher than the rates among intellectually normal children. Corbett *et al.* (1975) found that rates for psychiatric disorder were particularly high among children with severe retardation; disturbed behaviour was detected in 43 per cent, childhood psychosis in 13 per cent, hyperkinetic syndrome in 12 per cent, severe stereotypies in 5 per cent, neurosis in 3 per cent, and conduct disorder in 9 per cent. In the United States, rather similar findings have been reported by Eaton and Menolascino (1982).

Among people with mild mental retardation the relative frequencies of psychiatric symptoms and syndromes do not differ significantly from those in people of normal intelligence. Among people with severe retardation, certain kinds of abnormal behaviour are unexpectedly frequent, including autism, hyperkinetic syndromes, stereotyped movements, pica, and self-mutilation.

CLINICAL FEATURES OF MENTAL RETARDATION

General description

The most frequent manifestation of mental retardation is uniformly low performance on all kinds of intellectual task, including learning, short-term memory, the use of concepts, and problem-solving. Specific abnormalities may lead to particular difficulties. For example lack of visuospatial skills may cause many practical difficulties such as inability to dress; or there may be disproportionate difficulties with language or social interaction, both of which are strongly associated with behaviour disorder. In the retarded child, the common behaviour problems of childhood tend to occur when he is older and more physically developed than the normal child and they last longer. Such behaviour problems usually improve slowly as the child grows older. At the same time, there is often some catching up in performance on intelligence tests.

Mild mental retardation (IQ 50–70)

People with mild retardation account for about four-fifths of the mentally retarded. Usually their appearance is unremarkable and any sensory or motor deficits are slight. Most people in this group develop more or less normal language abilities and social behaviour during the pre-school years, and their mental retardation may not be identified until the start of schooling. In adult life most of them can live independently in ordinary surroundings, though they may need help when under some unusual stress.

Moderate retardation (IQ 35–49)

People in this group account for about 12 per cent of the mentally retarded. Most of them can talk or at least learn to communicate, and most can learn to care for themselves albeit with some supervision. As adults, they can usually undertake simple routine work and find their way about.

Severe retardation (IQ 20–34)

People with severe retardation account for about 7 per cent of the mentally retarded. In the pre-school years their development is usually greatly slowed. Eventually many of them can be trained to look after themselves under close supervision and to communicate in a simple way. As adults they can undertake simple tasks and engage in limited social activities.

Profound retardation (IQ below 20)

People in this group account for less than 1 per cent of the mentally retarded. Few of them learn to care for themselves completely. Some eventually achieve some simple speech and social behaviour.

Physical disorders among the mentally retarded

The most important physical disorders in the mentally retarded are sensory and motor disabilities, epilepsy, and incontinence. Any **sensory disorders** add an important additional obstacle to normal cognitive development. It is known that about a fifth of mentally retarded children living in hospital have some defect of vision or hearing (see Department of Health and Social Security 1971). **Motor disabilities** are frequent, and include spasticity, ataxia and athetosis.

Epilepsy is common among the mentally retarded, especially the severely retarded. Corbett *et al.* (1975) surveyed all the severely retarded children (whether in hospital or outside) originating from a London suburb. One-third of these children had experienced seizures at some time, and one-fifth had had at least one seizure in the year before the enquiry. Epilepsy is most common when mental retardation is due to cerebral damage, and uncommon when the retardation is due to chromosomal abnormalities. Epilepsy becomes less prevalent with increasing age, partly because those with severe cortical damage tend to die early, and partly because epilepsy tends to improve with age irrespective of intelligence level.

The types of epilepsy found in the mentally retarded are usually the same as those found in people of normal intelligence. However certain rare syndromes are particularly associated with mental retardation. An example is infantile spasms in which seizures start in the first year and take the form of so-called salaam attacks with tonic flexion of the neck and body and movement of the arms outward and forward. The episodes last for a few seconds (see Corbett and Pond 1979). The condition has also been reported in association with autism.

Psychiatric disorders among the mentally retarded

All varieties of psychiatric disorder occur in the mentally retarded, but the symptoms are often greatly modified by low intelligence. Certain symptoms, such as delusions, hallucinations, and obsessions seem to be different in people of low intelligence and limited language development. It is also difficult to detect symptoms when they are present, because the patient needs a minimum verbal fluency (probably at an IQ level of about 50) if he is to describe his experiences. Hence in diagnosing psychiatric disorder among the mentally retarded, more emphasis has to be given to behaviour and less to reports of mental phenomena than would be the case in people of normal intelligence. A short account will now be given of the major syndromes. The reader who wishes to supplement this should consult the review by Reid (1982).

Schizophrenia

In the mentally retarded the clinical picture of schizophrenia is especially characterized by poverty of thinking. Delusions are less elaborate than in schizophrenics of normal intelligence. Hallucinations have a simple and repetitive content. It may be difficult to distinguish between the motor disorders of schizophrenia and the motor disturbances common among the retarded. It is difficult to make a definite diagnosis of schizophrenia when the IQ is below 45, but the diagnosis should be considered if there is a distinct worsening of intellectual or social functioning without evidence of an organic cause, especially if any new behaviour is odd and out of keeping with the patient's previous behaviour. When there is continuing doubt, a trial of antipsychotic drugs is often appropriate.

Some earlier psychiatrists (including Kraepelin) described a syndrome called '*Pfropfschizophrenie*'. This disorder was said to begin in mentally retarded children and adolescents and to be characterized by mannerisms and stereotypies. It now appears that these features were related more to severe mental retardation than to schizophrenia.

In mentally retarded patients the treatment of schizophrenia is essentially the same as in patients of normal intelligence.

Affective disorder

When suffering from a **depressive disorder**, mentally retarded people are less likely than those of normal intelligence to complain of mood changes or to express depressive ideas. Diagnosis has to be made mainly on an appearance of sadness and on behavioural changes of retardation or agitation. Severely depressed patients with adequate verbal abilities may describe hallucinations or delusions. A few make attempts at suicide (which are usually poorly planned). **Mania** has to be diagnosed mainly on overactivity and behavioural signs suggesting elevation of mood. The treatment of affective disorders among the mentally retarded is essentially the same as among people of normal intelligence.

Neurosis

Neurotic disorders occur commonly among the less severely retarded, especially when they are facing changes in the routine of their lives. The clinical picture is often mixed. Treatment is usually directed more to bringing about adjustments in the patient's environment than to discussion of his problems.

Personality disorder

This is common among the mentally retarded. Sometimes it leads to greater problems in management than those caused by the retardation itself. The general approach is as described on p. 127, though with more emphasis on finding an environment to match the patient's temperament and less on attempts to bring about self-understanding.

Organic psychiatric disorders

These are common among mentally retarded people. Disturbed behaviour due to an acute organic psychiatric syndrome is sometimes the first indication of physical illness. Similarly a progressive decline in functioning may be the first indication of a chronic syndrome. Both syndromes are more common at the extremes of life. The syndrome known as childhood disintegrative psychosis (p. 662) is a form of dementia occurring in early life, often associated with lipoidoses or other progressive brain pathology. As the life expectation of mentally retarded patients is increasing, dementia in late life is becoming more common. It is possible that there is a particular association between Alzheimer's disease and Down's syndrome (see p. 701).

Autism and overactivity syndromes

Both are common among the mentally retarded. They are discussed in the chapter on child psychiatry (pp. 659 and 657) and will not be considered further here.

Behaviour disorders

Stereotyped or repetitive and apparently purposeless activities such as mannerisms, head banging and rocking are common in the severely retarded, occurring in about 40 per cent of children and about 20 per cent of adults. Repeated self-injurious behaviour is less frequent but may be even more persistent (see Corbett 1977). Many severely retarded children are overactive, distractable, and impulsive, but not to an extent that would indicate a diagnosis of overactivity syndrome. Other common disturbances are emotional lability (including temper tantrums), self-stimulation, pica, and undue dependency. When these problems are severe admission to hospital may be required, although institutional surroundings may make them worse. Offences against the law are seldom a serious problem (see p. 722, also Hunter 1979).

Sexual problems

Public masturbation is the most frequent problem. Some of the mentally retarded show a child-like curiosity about other people's bodies which can be misunderstood as sexual. In the past, much concern was expressed about the risk that mentally retarded people would have sexual intercourse and produce mentally handicapped children. It is now apparent that most kinds of mental handicap are not inherited; and those which are inherited are often associated with infertility. A more important concern is that, even if their children are of average intelligence, the severely mentally retarded are unlikely to make good parents. With modern contraceptive methods, the risk of unplanned pregnancy is much reduced (see Craft and Craft (1981) for further information).

EFFECTS OF MENTAL RETARDATION ON THE FAMILY

When a new-born child is found to be mentally retarded, the parents are inevitably distressed. Feelings of rejection are common but seldom last long. More often the diagnosis of mental retardation is not made until after the first year of life. The parents then have to make even greater changes in their hopes and expectations for the child. They often experience prolonged depression, guilt, shame, or anger. A few reject the child, while others become over-involved in its care, sacrificing other important aspects of family life. The majority achieve a satisfactory adjustment although the temptation to over-indulge the child remains. However well they adjust psychologically, the parents are still faced with a long prospect of hard work, frustration, and social problems. If the child also has a physical handicap, these problems are increased.

Ann Gath (1978) compared two groups of families, those with a Down's syndrome child at home, and matched controls with a normal child of the same age. Both were studied from the time of the child's birth. There were only small differences between the two groups of families in mental or physical health. Among the parents of the young children with Down's syndrome, a significant proportion gave evidence of marital disharmony but others felt that their relationship had been strengthened by looking after the affected child. It was concluded that 'despite the understandable emotional reaction to the fact of the baby's abnormality, most of the families in this study have adjusted well and two years later are providing a home environment that is stable and enriching for both the normal and handicapped children' (Gath 1978, p. 116). However it seemed likely that the siblings were often at some disadvantage because of the time and effort that had to be devoted to the retarded child.

Other investigators have surveyed the needs of the mothers of older mentally retarded children. Tizard and Grad (1961) compared two groups of families, those with a mentally retarded child living at home and those with a comparable child in an institution. The former were found to be preoccupied with the 'burden of care' for their child, while the latter were living nearly normal lives. Wilkin (1979) found that most mothers with a mentally retarded child living at home were much helped by their husbands but received little assistance from other people. Generally the mothers were pleased with the educational services provided for their retarded child, but were more critical of what they saw as lack of interest and expertise in doctors and social workers. Most of the mothers reported problems of a practical kind: two-thirds wanted help in looking after the child during the school holidays, and large proportions (about half) wanted day care during the week-end, baby sitting in the evening, or help with transport. Brimblecombe (1979) also found that mothers were dissatisfied with the medical services and with the amount of practical help they received from hospitals and social services. Voluntary organizations were often judged more helpful. Bicknell (1982) has reviewed the problems of families with a mentally retarded member.

AETIOLOGY OF MENTAL RETARDATION

Introduction

Lewis (1929) distinguished two kinds of mental retardation: **subcultural** (the lower end of the normal distribution curve of intelligence in the population) and **pathological** (due to specific disease processes). In a study of the 1280 mentally retarded people living in the Colchester Asylum, Penrose (1938) found that most cases were due not to a single cause but to an interaction of inherited and environmental factors.

Subsequent evidence has confirmed that mental retardation has multiple causes (see MacKay 1982). This finding applies particularly to mild mental retardation, in which it is unusual to find a single specific cause. Among the severely retarded however, post-mortem examination shows pathological conditions in the majority (Crome and Stern 1972) although not all these can be identified in life. The relative frequency of the various causes is indicated in surveys of the mentally retarded in hospitals (e.g. Angeli and Kirman 1975) and assessment centres (e.g. Optiz *et al.* 1978). These show environmental causes in about 20 per cent, chromosomal in about 15 per cent, and single gene disorders in about 10 per cent. In about 60 per cent no cause is found. Surveys of the community are more representative but the diagnoses are less certain.
Corbett *et al.* (1975) studied all the severely mentally retarded children living in a defined area of London. They were able to make a diagnosis in 85 per cent. The distribution of the diagnoses is shown in Table 21.2.

It should be noted that increasing success in identifying specific causes does not remove the need to consider all the additional social and other factors in each case.

Table 21.2. *Causes of mental retardation in a community survey**

	Per cent
Down's syndrome	26
Other inherited conditions or associated congenital malformations	19
Perinatal injury	18
Infections	14
Inherited biochemical errors	4
Others	4
Undiagnosable	15

*Corbett *et al.* (1975).

Table 21.3. *The aetiology of mental retardation*

Genetic
Chromosome abnormalities
> Down's syndrome
> Klinefelter's syndrome
> Turner's syndrome

Metabolic disorders affecting:
> amino acids (e.g. phenylketonuria, homocystinuria, Hartnup disease)
>
> the urea cycle (e.g. citrullinuria, aminosuccinic aciduria)
>
> lipids (Tay Sachs, Gaucher's, and Niemann–Pick diseases)
>
> carbohydrate (galactosaemia)
>
> purines (Lesch–Nyhan syndrome)
>
> mucopolysaccahrides (Hurler's, Hunter's, Sanfillipo's, and Morquio's syndromes)

Gross disease of the brain
> Tuberous sclerosis
> Neurofibromatosis

Cranial malformations
> Hydrocephaly
> Microcephaly

Perinatal damage
> Infections (rubella, cytomegalo virus, syphilis, toxoplasmosis)
> Intoxications (lead, certain drugs)
> Physical damage (injury, radiation, hypoxia)
> Placental dysfunction (toxaemia, nutritional growth retardation)
> Endocrine disorders (hypothyroidism; hypoparathyroidism)

Perinatal
> Birth asphyxia
> Complications of prematurity
> Kernicterus
> Intraventricular haemorrhage

Post-natal damage
> Injury (accidental, child abuse)
> Lead intoxication
> Infections (encephalitis, meningitis)

Inheritance

There is good evidence from family, twin, and adoption studies that polygenic inheritance is important in determining intelligence within the normal range, and that much mild mental retardation represents the lower end of the distribution curve of intelligence (see Rutter 1980). In a few cases, genetic abnormalities are responsible for metabolic disorders and other anomalies that cause mental disorder (see Tables 21.3 and 21.4).

Social factors

Studies of the general population suggest that factors in the social environment may account for variation in IQ of as much as 20 points. The evidence comes from two kinds of enquiry (see Clarke and Clarke 1978; Rutter 1980). The first is epidemiological. Low IQ is related to lower social class, poverty, poor housing, and an unstable family environment. Such correlations might reflect

Table 21.4. *Notes on some causes of mental retardation*

Syndrome	Aetiology	Clinical features	Comments
Chromosome abnormalities (For Down's syndrome and X-linked retardation see text)			
Triple X	Trisomy X	No characteristic feature	Mild retardation
Cri du chat	Deletion in chromosome 5	Microcephaly, hyperteleroism, typical cat like cry, failure to thrive	
Inborn errors of metabolism			
Phenylketonuria	Autosomal recessive causing lack of liver phenylalanine hydroxylase Commonest inborn error of metabolism	Lack of pigment (fair hair, blue eyes) Retarded growth. Associated epilepsy microcephaly, eczema, and hyperactivity	Detectable by post-natal screening of blood or urine. Treated by exclusion of phenylalanine from during early years of life
Homocystinuria	Autosomal recessive causing lack of cystathione synthetases	Ectopia lentis, fine and fair hair, joint enlargement, skeletal abnormalities similar to Marfan's syndrome. Associated with thromboembolic episodes	Retardation variable. Sometimes treatable by methionine restriction
Galactosaemia	Autosomal recessive causing lack of galactose 1-phosphate uridyl transferase	Presents following introduction of milk into diet. Failure to thrive, hepatosplenomegaly, cataracts	Detectable by post-natal screening for the enzymic defect. Treatable by galactose-free diet. Toluidine blue test on urine
Tay–Sachs disease	Autosomal recessive resulting in increased lipid storage (the earliest form of the cerebro-macular degeneration)	Progressive loss of vision and hearing Spastic paralysis. Cherry red spot at macula of retina. Epilepsy	Death at 2–4 years
Inborn errors of metabolism			
Hurler's syndrome (gargoylism)	Autosomal recessive affecting mucopolysaccharide storage	Grotesque features. Protuberant abdomen. Hepatosplenomegaly. Associated cardiac abnormalities	Death before adolescence

Lesch–Nyhan syndrome	X-linked recessive leading to enzyme defect affecting purine metabolism. Excessive uric acid production and excretion	Normal at birth. Development of choreo-athetoid movements, scissoring position of legs and self-mutilation	Can be diagnosed prenatally by culture of amniotic fluid and estimation of relevant enzyme. Post-natal diagnosis on enzyme of single hair root. Death in second or third decade from infection or renal failure. Self-mutilation may be reduced by treatment with hydroxy trytophan
Other inherited disorders			
Neurofibromatosis (Von Recklinghausen's syndrome)	Autosomal dominant inheritance	Neurofibromata, *café au lait* spots, vitiligo. Associated with symptoms determined by site of neurofibromata. Astrocytomas, menigioma	Retardation in a minority
Tuberous sclerosis (Epiloia)	Autosomal dominant (very variable penetrance)	Epilepsy, ademona sebaceum on face white skin patches, shagreen skin, retinal phakoma, subungual fibromata. Associated multiple tumours in kidney, spleen, and lungs	Retardation in about 70 per cent
Lawrence–Moon–Biedl syndrome	Autosomal recessive	Retinitis pigmentosa, polydactyly, sometimes with obesity and impaired genital function	Retardation usually not severe
Infection			
Rubella embryopathy	Viral infection of mother in first trimester	Cataract, microphthalmia, deafness, microcephaly, congenital heart disease	If mother infected in first trimester, 10–15 per cent infants are affected (infection may be subclinical)
Toxoplasmosis	Protozoal infection of mother	Hydrocephaly, microcephaly, intra-cerebral calcification retinal damage, hepatosplenomegaly, jaundice, epilepsy	Wide variation in severity
Cytomegalo virus	Virus infection of mother	Brain damage. Only severe cases are apparent at birth	
Congenital syphilis	Syphilitic infection of mother	Many die at birth. Variable neurological signs. 'Stigmata', (Hutchinson teeth and rhagades often absent)	Uncommon since routine testing of pregnant women. Infant's WR positive at first but may become negative

Table 21.4. *continued*

Syndrome	Aetiology	Clinical features	Comments
Cranial malformations			
Hydrocephalus	Sex-limited recessive Inherited developmental abnormality, e.g. atresia of aqueduct, Arnold–Chiari malformation. Meningitis. Spina bifida	Rapid enlargement of head In early infancy, symptoms of raised csf pressure. Other features depend on aetiology	Mild cases may arrest spontaneously. May be symptomatically treated by CSF shunt. Intelligence can be normal
Microcephaly	Recessive inheritance, X-rays, maternal infections	Features depend upon aetiology	Evident in up to a fifth of institutionalized mentally retarded patients
Miscellaneous			
Spina bifida	Aetiology multiple and complex	Failure of vertical fusion. *Spina bifida cystica* is associated with meningocele or, in 15–20%, myelomeningocele. Latter causes spinal cord damage, with lower limb paralysis, incontinence, etc.	Hydrocephalus in four-fifths of those with myelomeningocele. Retardation in this group
Cerebral palsy	Perinatal brain damage. Strong association with prematurity. (Commonest cause childhood brain damage)	Spastic (commonest), Athetoid and ataxic types. Variable in severity	Majority are below average intelligence. Athetoid are more likely to be of normal IQ
Hypothyroidism (cretinism)	Iodine deficiency or (rarely) atrophic thyroid	Appearance normal at birth. Abnormalities appear at 6 months. Growth failure, puffy skin, lethargy	Now rare in Britain. Responds to early replacement treatment
Hyperbilirubinaemia	Haemolysis, rhesus incompatibility, and prematurity	Kernicterus (choreoathetosis), opisthotonus, spasticity, convulsions	Prevention by anti-Rhesus globulin. Neonatal treatment by exchange transfusion

the effects of low intelligence and do not necessarily exclude a genetic cause. Thus mentally retarded people might drift into an adverse social environment and bring up their children there.

The second source of evidence is from attempts to enrich the environment of deprived children in special residential care (see O'Connor 1968) and to provide special education. In one experiment, children from large and unsatisfactory institutions were transferred to small well-staffed children's homes or given more stimulating education. Twenty years later they were found to have higher IQs than those who remained in their original institutions as children (see Skeels 1966). This evidence is interesting but it reveals more about the adverse effects of understaffed hospitals than about the causes of retardation.

Other environmental factors

These include intrauterine infection (such as rubella), environmental pollutants (such as lead), maternal alcoholism in pregnancy (see p. 426), severe malnutrition, and excessive irradiation to the womb (see Birch *et al.* 1970). There seem to be vulnerable periods of brain development during which damage is particularly likely to follow exposure to such environmental hazards (see Davison 1977; Cowie 1980). Malnutrition in the first two years of life is probably the most common cause of retardation in the world as a whole, but is much less frequent in developed countries.

There is no doubt that severe **lead intoxication** can cause an encephalopathy with consequent intellectual impairment. It is less certain whether small amounts of lead taken over longer periods (especially as a result of air pollution from lead additives in petrol) can cause intellectual retardation. It is known that children absorb lead more readily than adults and are therefore at greater risk from environmental pollution. However, most of the studies have been of children from poor homes, and it is impossible to be certain how far findings of low intelligence (compared with children in other areas) are due to slightly raised lead levels in their blood, and how far to social influences (see Needleman 1982 for a review).

Birth injury

This is also important. Birch *et al.* (1970) estimated that clinically recognizable birth injuries accounted for about 10 per cent of mental retardation. Pasamanick and Knobloch (1966) extended this observation, by suggesting a 'continuum of reproductive casualty' in which mild subnormality is assumed to result from less obvious brain lesions sustained *in utero* or perinatally (see p. 634). Although this last idea is controversial, there is good evidence that prematurity and low birth weight are associated with mental retardation.

Specific causes of mental handicap

Many syndromes have been identified which are caused by single genes or chromosomal abnormalities. A large number of specific biochemical abnormalities have now been identified which account for the mental retardation. Table 21.3 summarises many of the main causes, but is not exhaustive. The purpose of the table is to draw attention to the broad categories of disorder and the large number of rare conditions that can lead to mental retardation. Since these causes are rare, they will not be described in this chapter. Useful information about some of the less rare conditions is summarized in Table 21.4. Although these syndromes are still discussed in some textbooks of psychiatry, they are more likely to be dealt with by paediatricians than by psychiatrists. If the psychiatrist takes over the care of a patient suffering from any of these rare syndromes, he should work closely with the paediatrician and family doctor, and should acquaint himself with the up-to-date knowledge of the particular syndrome. It is assumed here that the reader has a basic understanding of these conditions from general medical education. Further information can be found in a standard textbook of paediatrics.

The **specific genetic syndromes** are sufficiently varied to require separate comment. Five groups may be recognized.

1. **Dominant conditions.** These are rare. Examples include the phakomatoses, including neurofibromatosis.

2. **Recessive conditions.** This is the largest group of specific gene disorders. It includes most of the inherited metabolic conditions, such as phenylketonuria, homocystinuria, and galactosaemia.

3. **Sex-linked conditions.** The prevalence of intellectual retardation is 25 per cent greater in males than in females. Lehrke (1971) was the first to suggest that the excess among males might be due to X-chromosome-linked causes. Recent research has shown that about a fifth of intellectual handicap in males is due to X-linked causes (see Turner 1982). Several rare specific syndromes have been identified, for example – glucose dehydrogenase deficiency and the Lesch–Nyhan syndrome. However, in most cases there is no metabolic abnormality. In many of these, usually referred to as cases of 'X linked retardation', the only clinical sign is enlargement of the testes. A marker is visible in the X chromosome in lymphocyte culture. Although the intelligence of most of the carrier females is normal, many have learning difficulties and about 10 per cent have mild mental retardation (Turner 1982).

4. **Chromosome abnormalities.** The most common is Down's syndrome. Sex-chromosome abnormalities, such as Klinefelter's syndrome (XXY), and Turner's syndrome (XO), may also cause retardation (see Ratcliffe 1982).

5. **Conditions with partial and complex inheritance** such as anencephaly. This group is poorly understood.

In this chapter, only the common condition of Down's syndrome will be described further.

Down's syndrome

In 1866, Langdon Down tried to relate the appearance of certain groups of patients to the physical features of ethnic groups. One of the groups had the condition originally called Mongolism, and now generally known as Down's syndrome. This condition is a frequent cause of mental retardation occurring in one in every 600–700 births. The retardation is usually mild or moderate but can occasionally be severe.

The **clinical picture** is made up of a number of features any one of which can occur in a normal person. Four of these features together are generally accepted as strong evidence for the syndrome. The most characteristic signs are: (a) mouth – small mouth and teeth, furrowed tongue, high-arched palate; (b) eyes – oblique palpebral fissures, epicanthic folds; (c) head – flat occiput; (d) hands – short and broad, curved fifth finger, single transverse palmar crease; (e) joints – hyperextensibility or hyperflexibility, hypotonia.

There are often other associated abnormalities. Congenital heart disease (especially septal defects) occurs in about 20 per cent. Intestinal abnormalities are common, especially duodenal obstruction. Hearing may be impaired.

There is considerable variation in the degree of mental retardation, the IQ generally being between 20 and 50. Mental abilities usually develop fairly quickly in the first six to twelve months of life but then increase more slowly. The temperament of children with Down's syndrome is usually described as lovable and easy going. Many of them show an interest in music. Although these features are not found in all cases, patients with Down's syndrome generally present fewer temperamental difficulties than other mentally retarded people.

In the past the infant mortality of Down's syndrome was high, but with improved medical care survival into adult life is more common. Nevertheless, few people with Down's syndrome live beyond 40; signs of premature aging appear and Alzheimer-like changes in the brain develop in middle life.

Aetiology

In 1959, Down's syndrome was found to be associated with the chromosomal disorder of trisomy (three chromosomes instead of the usual two). About 95 per cent of cases are due to trisomy 21. These result from failure of disjunction during meiosis and are associated with increasing maternal age. The risk of recurrence in a subsequent child is about 1 in 100. The remaining five per cent of cases of Down's syndrome are attributable either to translocation involving chromosome 21 or to mozaicism. The disorder leading to translocation is often inherited and the risk of recurrence is about 1 in 10. Mozaicism occurs when non-disjunction takes place in any cell division after fertilization. Normal and trisomic cells occur in the same person and the effects on cognitive development are particularly variable.

CAUSES OF PSYCHIATRIC DISORDER AND BEHAVIOUR PROBLEMS IN THE MENTALLY RETARDED

The diversity of psychiatric disorders among the mentally retarded makes it unlikely that they have a single aetiology. Several causes have to be considered: genetic, organic pathology, psychological, and social (see Corbett 1977).

There is no evidence that the same **genetic** abnormality causes mental retardation and psychiatric disorder. As noted already, most severely retarded people have some **organic brain pathology,** and so do a smaller number of those with moderate and mild retardation. As mentioned in the chapter on child psychiatry, in children of normal intelligence psychiatric disorder is associated with brain damage (see Rutter *et al.* 1970). There is also a known association between cerebral pathology on the one hand and schizophrenia and affective disorders on the other (see Davison and Bagley 1969). In mentally retarded patients, therefore, it is likely that some psychiatric disorders (including major psychiatric illnesses) are related to brain pathology. There is an especially close association between **epilepsy** and behaviour disorder in the mentally retarded. This applies particularly to hyperkinetic behaviour (see Corbett and Pond 1979). Such behaviour disorder may be due not only to the direct effects of epilepsy but also to the side effects of anticonvulsant drugs (see p. 340).

Organic disorder cannot be the whole explanation, because the rate of mental disorder is increased in mentally handicapped people with no brain pathology. Other causes include **psychological** factors associated with mental handicap, particularly abnormalities of temperament, language difficulty, inability to acquire social skills, and educational failure. **Social** factors such as a disrupted family are important in causing mental disorder and behaviour problems in the mentally retarded just as they are in patients of normal intelligence (see Rutter and Madge 1976).

It should not be forgotten that **iatrogenic** factors can contribute to the causes of psychiatric disorder among the mentally retarded. As mentioned above, these include the side effects of drugs, especially those used to treat epilepsy, and also over- or understimulating environments within an institution.

THE ASSESSMENT OF THE MENTALLY RETARDED

Severe retardation can usually be diagnosed in infancy, especially as it is often associated with detectable physical abnormalities or with retardation of motor development. The clinician should be cautious in diagnosing less severe mental retardation on the basis of delays in development. Although routine examination of a child may reveal signs of developmental delay suggesting possible mental retardation (see Illingworth 1980), confident diagnosis often requires a second opinion from a specialist. Full assessment has several stages: history taking, physical examination, developmental testing, behavioural assessment, and examination of the mental state. These will be considered in turn. Although this section is concerned mainly with the assessment of children, similar principles apply in adolescence and adult life.

History taking

In the course of obtaining a full history, particular attention should be given to any family history suggesting an inherited disorder, and to abnormalities in the pregnancy or delivery of the child. Dates of passing developmental milestones should be ascertained (see p. 682). A full account of any behaviour disorders should be obtained.

Physical examination

A systematic physical examination should include the recording of weight, height, and head circumference. It is important to be alert for the physical signs of the many specific syndromes (see Table 21.4). The neurological examination should include particular attention to vision and hearing.

Developmental assessment

This assessment is based on a combination of clinical experience and standardized methods of measuring intelligence, language, motor performance, and social skills. Although the IQ is the best general index of intellectual development, it is not reliable in the very young. Table 20.2 lists some commonly used developmental tests (see p. 638).

Behavioural assessment

This is based on the observations by the clinical team of the patient's ability to care for himself, his social abilities including his ability to communicate, his sensory-motor skills and any unusual behaviour.

Psychiatric assessment

This is directed not so much to the making of a diagnosis as to the formulation of relevant medical and social factors including the attitudes of people who might be involved in the patient's care. If the mentally retarded person has reasonable language ability, it is possible to carry out a standard psychiatric interview whilst making appropriate allowance for any difficulty in his concentration. When language is less well developed, an account has to be obtained mainly from informants. It is particularly important to obtain a complete description of any change from the usual pattern of behaviour. It is often necessary to ask teachers, hospital staff, or parents to keep records of behaviours such as eating, sleeping, and general activity. The interviewer should keep in mind the possible causes of psychiatric disorder outlined above, including unrecognized epilepsy.

Differential diagnosis

At the end of the assessment, the main diagnoses to be considered are: delayed maturation; deafness, blindness or other sensory defects; childhood psychosis; childhood autism; and states due to the side effects of drugs. (Childhood psychosis and autism are described on p. 659.)

THE CARE OF THE MENTALLY RETARDED

A historical perspective

In the last few decades the aims and methods of care for the mentally retarded have been transformed. These changes and the remaining unsolved problems can best be understood in relation to the history of the development of services (see Corbett 1978).

The special treatment of the mentally retarded began with the remarkable efforts of Itard, physician-in-chief at the Asylum for the Deaf and Dumb in Paris, to train the 'wild boy' found in Aveyron in 1801. This child was thought to have grown up in the wild, isolated from human beings. Itard made great efforts to educate the boy, but after persisting for six years he concluded that the training had been a failure. Nevertheless his work had important and lasting consequences, one of which was the development of special educational methods for the mentally retarded. These methods were developed by Seguin, director of the School for Idiots at the Bicêtre in Paris, who in 1842 published his *Theory and nature of the education of idiots*. Seguin believed that the mentally retarded had latent abilities which could be encouraged by special training. He therefore devised an educational programme of physical exercises, moral instruction, and graded tasks (Seguin 1866). His ideas were particularly taken up in Switzerland and Germany. Another pioneer was the Swiss physician Guggenbuhl who in 1841 founded at Abendberg the first special residential institution for the mentally retarded. Similar institutions were soon opened in other parts of Europe to provide a training that would enable their pupils to live as independently as possible. However it was recognized that some mentally retarded people needed long-term care.

At the end of the nineteenth century several influences led to a more custodial approach to the care of the mentally retarded. These influences included the development of the science of genetics, the beliefs embodied in the eugenics movement, and a general decrease in public tolerance of abnormal behaviour. In England and Wales, such ideas were reflected in the Mental Deficiency Act of 1913, which empowered local authorities to provide for the confinement of the intellectually and morally defective. As a result the total number of inpatients of this kind rose from 6000 in 1916 to 50 000 in 1939.

In the 1960s, the need for reform was recognized, partly because of changes that had already been effected in psychiatric hospitals (see p. 618), partly because of improved psychological research, and partly because of public concern about the generally poor conditions in which the mentally retarded were housed. Surveys of hospitals for the retarded showed that the mean IQ of their patients was over 70. Many residents had only mild retardation, and many did not need hospital care. About the same time it was shown that simple training could help many patients, both the mildly and severely retarded (see O'Connor 1968). Further investigations showed the advantages of residential care in small homely units (Tizard 1964). However public concern was aroused less by these research findings than by a series of scandals about the conditions in hospitals for the mentally retarded. In the book *Put away*, Morris (1969) reported a survey of 33 subnormality hospitals. She described large isolated hospitals with dilapidated buildings that were overcrowded and squalid. They were poorly organized, and few of them had clear objectives for treatment. There were shortages of nursing and other staff. This report and other influences led to a search for new methods of care.

The last twenty years have seen the acceptance in all developed countries (especially Scandinavia), of the need for methods of care with a less medical approach. Unfortunately there have been divergent views about these methods, and progress has been slow. In Britain the problems and possible solutions were set out in an important policy paper from the Department of Health and Social Security, *Better services for the mentally handicapped* (1971).

Among the new concepts of care the main principle is 'normalization', which was developed in Scandinavia in the 1960s. This term simply means providing a pattern of life as near normal as possible (Nirje 1970). The least handicapped are brought up in their own homes and encouraged to lead almost independent lives as adults. For the few who enter hospital the accommodation and activities are designed to be as close as possible to those of family life. An account will now be given of the provisions required to achieve these aims. They have been described in more detail by Malin *et al.* (1980).

The general provisions

For the care of the mentally retarded in a community the precise model matters less than the detail in which it is planned and the enthusiasm with which it is carried out. Good planning requires an estimate of the needs of the population to be served. Table 21.5 shows the estimated needs of a general population of 100 000 (see Kushlik and Blunden 1974; Tizard 1974). As a guide to the provision of services in any particular area, the figures can be modified in the light of any local information, such as data from a case register.

The team providing the care includes psychiatrists, psychologists, nurses, residential care staff, teachers, occupational therapists, physiotherapists, and speech therapists. Volunteers can often play a valuable part, and it is useful to encourage self-help groups for parents.

The family doctor and paediatrician are now mainly responsible for the early detection of mental retardation, but the child psychiatrist also plays some part in it. Apart from this, the psychiatrist has three roles. The first is to help mentally retarded children and adults who have psychiatric problems. In this role he is most likely to be called upon at times of particular difficulty for the family. These are when the diagnosis is first made, when the child enters school, and when he leaves school. The second role is liaison between the medical, educational, and social services, all of which may be involved in the care of the individual patient. The third role is to give a lead in the planning of services.

Table 21.5. *Facilities required for the mentally retarded in a population of 100 000**

Children (aged 0–14 years)		
(a) *Mildly retarded:* See text		
(b) *Severely retarded:* Total number 90		
Accommodation	At home	60
	Residential care	30
Education	Special pre-school	10
	Special school	60
	Special care unit	10
	No schooling	10
Adults (aged over 14 years)		
Total number requiring care: 375		
Employment	Employable	180
	Sheltered workshop	140
	Neither	55
Accommodation	Employable: home	105
	hostel	75
	Not employable: home	45
	residential	150

*See Kushlik and Blunden (1974); Tizard (1974).

The mildly retarded

The number of mildly retarded people in the population is not known accurately. Few need specialist services. Most are able to live with their families and to remain under the care of the family doctor. Some have additional problems, such as physical disability, minor emotional disorders, and psychiatric illness. A few mildly retarded children require fostering, boarding school placements, or residential care, either because of such additional problems or because of difficulties in the family. Mildly retarded adults may need support when they are facing extra problems; otherwise most can live at home or in a hostel and carry out sheltered work.

Severely retarded children

There are about 90 severely retarded children in a population of 100 000. Some require special services throughout their lives, and appropriate planning should begin as soon as the diagnosis is certain. About two-thirds can remain at home provided that their parents are taught how to care for them and are given appropriate practical assistance and emotional support. The practical help may include day care, or short stays in hospital or residential care when the parents need a holiday or when another family member is ill. About a quarter of severely retarded children living at home have behavioural problems, difficulty in walking, or incontinence. When the time comes for the child to attend school, account should be taken of such practical matters as the need for transport and for provisions in the holidays.

About one third of severely retarded children need residential care. About half of these have physical or behavioural problems or incontinence too great for the parents or hostel staff to manage. Most of the others come from families that are in some ways unsatisfactory, and they may be helped by fostering or adoption. Even though these children need to live in hospital many can still attend a special school in the community.

Severely retarded adults

In the care of the mentally retarded it is often particularly difficult to arrange a smooth transition during adolescence from children's services to adult services. Care at home becomes less easy to manage and residential provision may be needed (which should be outside hospital if possible). At this stage the co-ordination of services passes from the school to the social services department. Provisions are required for sheltered work, day centres, and hostel accommodation. Some severely retarded people will continue to need treatment for behaviour disorders, psychiatric illness, epilepsy, or physical disability. A few will need to remain in hospital.

Specific services

An account will now be given of the main elements in a service for the mentally retarded. Use will be made of the following headings from the Department of Health Report *Better services for the mentally handicapped* (1972).

(1) The prevention or early detection of mental handicap.
(2) The assessment of the mentally handicapped person's assets and disabilities, and their periodic re-assessment.
(3) Advice, support, and practical measures for families.
(4) Provision for education, training, occupation, or work appropriate for each handicapped person.
(5) Residential accommodation appropriate to the individual's needs.
(6) Medical, nursing, and other services for those who require them, either as outpatients, day-patients, or inpatients.

(1) Preventive services

In the United States, the President's Panel on Mental Retardation (1972) concluded that it would be possible to reduce the occurrence of mental retardation by 50 per cent before the end of the century. Recent experience suggests that this estimate is much too optimistic. Moreover such an aim could be achieved only for severe retardation, and then only in developed countries. For mild retardation, which has less discrete causes, reduction on such a scale is highly unlikely (see Clarke and Clarke 1978).

Primary prevention depends largely on genetic counselling, early detection of fetal abnormalities during pregnancy, and safe childbirth. Secondary prevention aims to prevent the progression of disability by either medical or psychological means. The latter includes 'enriching' education and early attempts to reduce behavioural problems.

Genetic counselling

This begins with assessment of the risk of an abnormal child being born. Such an assessment is based on study of the family history and knowledge of the genetics of conditions that give rise to mental defect. The parents are then given an explanation of the risks and encouraged to discuss them. Most parents seek advice only after a first abnormal child has been born. Some do so before starting to have children because there is a mentally retarded person on one or other side of the family. Although much counselling is carried out, its preventive effects are uncertain (see Haan (1979) and Giller *et al.* (1981) for reviews).

Prenatal care

This begins before conception by providing immunization against rubella for girls who lack immunity. Some causes of mental retardation can now be diagnosed *in utero*. Amniocentesis, fetoscopy and ultrasound scanning of the fetus in the second trimester can reveal chromosomal abnormalities, most open neural tube defects, and about 60 per cent of inborn errors of metabolism (Crawfurd 1982). The procedure carries a small but definite risk, and so is usually offered only to women who have carried a previous abnormal fetus, women with a family history of congenital disorder, and those over 35 years of age.

Rhesus incompatibility is now largely preventable. Sensitization of a rhesus negative mother can usually be avoided by giving anti-D antibody. An affected fetus can be detected by amniocentesis and treated if necessary by exchange transfusion. Further information about these aspects of care will be found in up to date textbooks of obstetrics and paediatrics.

Postnatal prevention

In Britain, all infants are routinely tested for phenylketonuria, and routine testing for hypothyroidism and galactosaemia is becoming increasingly common. Improved methods of care for premature and low birth weight infants can prevent mental retardation in some infants who previously would have suffered brain damage. However the methods also bring about the survival of some retarded children who would otherwise have died.

'Compensatory' education

This is intended to provide optimal conditions for the mental development of the retarded child. Such was the aim of the 'Head Start' programme in the United States, which provided extra education for deprived children. Its methods varied from nursery schooling to attempts to teach specific skills (see Rutter and Madge 1976). The results were disappointing. In retrospect, it seems to have been unduly optimistic to expect good results from a brief programme of education carried out largely by unskilled people, with no attempt at changing the children's homes. A more intensive programme with similar aims has been carried out in Milwaukee (Heber and Garber 1975). Skilled teachers educated children living in slum areas whose mothers had a low IQ (under 75). This additional education started when the child was three months old and continued until school age. At the same time, the mothers were trained in a variety of domestic skills. These children were compared with control children of the same age who came from similar families but who had not received additional education and whose mothers had not been trained. At the age of four and a half, the trained children had a mean IQ 27 points higher than that of the controls. Although this study can be faulted because the selection of children was not strictly random, and because some of the changes in test scores could have been due to practice, the main findings probably stand. The findings show that substantial effort by trained staff can produce worthwhile improvement in children of low intelligence born to socially disadvantaged mothers. The findings also indicate a need to train the parents as well as the children.

(2) Assessment

Severe retardation is usually obvious from an early age. Lesser degrees may become apparent only when the child starts school. Family doctors and teachers should be able to detect possible retardation, but a full assessment requires expert knowledge. Full assessment is often carried out in an assessment centre where the child can be observed in many different activities. The methods have been described earlier (p. 702).

Once mental retardation has been diagnosed, regular reviews are required. For the mentally retarded living in the community, these reviews will usually be carried out by paediatricians, teachers, and social workers. The psychiatrist's main responsibility is for patients resident in hospital or attending as outpatients.

It is important to arrange a thorough review when the child leaves school. This review should assess his need for further education, prospects for employment, suitability for a training centre, and requirements for day care. Mentally retarded adults also need to be assessed regularly to make sure that they are continuing to achieve their potential and still receiving appropriate care.

(3) Help for families

Help for families is needed most when the diagnosis is first made. For worried parents it is not enough to give an explanation on just one occasion. They may need to be given an explanation repeatedly before they can absorb all its implications. Adequate time must be provided to explain the prognosis, indicate what help can be provided, and discuss the part the parents can play in helping their child to achieve his full potential.

Afterwards the parents need continuing support. When the child starts school, they should be kept informed about his progress. They should be given help with practical matters such as day care for the child during school holidays, baby-sitting, or arrangements for family holidays. In addition to practical matters, the parents need continuing psychological support.

Families are likely to need extra help when their mentally retarded child is approaching puberty or leaving school (see Brimblecombe (1979) for a more detailed account of these matters).

(4) Education, training, and occupation

In 1929, the Mental Deficiency Committee made the following comment on schools for the mentally retarded:

If the majority of children for whom these schools are intended are to lead the lives of ordinary citizens . . . these schools must be brought into close relation with the public elementary school system and presented to parents not as something distinct and humiliating but as a helpful variation of an ordinary school.

Progress in achieving this aim has been slow. In 1970 the Education of Handicapped Children Act required Local Education Authorities to provide for the education and training of all mentally retarded children whether living in hospitals or in their own homes. In 1978 the Warnock Committee (Committee of Enquiry into the Education of Handicapped Children and Young People) recommended increased provisions for the special education of pre-school and school-age children. This Committee also emphasized the need for as many mentally retarded children as possible to be educated in ordinary schools.

Research has consistently shown the value of an early start. Such a start can be made in a special pre-school or playgroup, or occasionally in day care at a hospital. When normal school age is reached, the least handicapped children can attend remedial classes in ordinary schools. The others need to attend special schools 'for children with learning difficulties' (formerly called schools for the Educationally Subnormal). It is still not certain which retarded children benefit most from ordinary schooling. Education in an ordinary school offers the advantages of more normal social surroundings and the expectation of progress; but it carries the disadvantage of lack of special teaching skills and equipment, and the risk of the child not being accepted by the more able children.

Traditionally, education for the more severely retarded has been based on the sensory training methods started by Itard and Seguin (see p. 704). It is only recently that the content of the curriculum has been reconsidered. The first change was to an approach similar to that of an ordinary primary school with an emphasis on self expression. However there is some reason to think that methods of this kind are sometimes inappropriate for the retarded. There is now an increasing use of a more structured approach to teaching and of behavioural methods in training.

Before retarded children leave school, they need reassessment and vocational guidance. Most of the mildly retarded are able to take normal jobs or enter sheltered employment. The severely retarded are likely to transfer to Adult Training Centres. For some this transfer will be a stage in the progression towards normal employment, but for the majority it will be permanent. Adult Training Centres were originally intended to provide sheltered industrial work. It is now apparent that they should provide a wider range of activities if the abilities of each attender are to be developed as much as possible. Even for the minority of severely retarded people who require intensive supervision, care is usually provided better in a Training Centre than in a hospital.

(5) Residential care

It is now widely held that the mentally retarded should be looked after by their parents or, failing that, in small homely residential units. Support for this view came from an important study by Tizard (1964), who compared two groups of children who had moderate or severe mental retardation but no serious additional physical handicaps. One group was reared in a large hospital, and the other in a small residential unit where care was provided in small family-like groups. The children brought up in this small unit developed better verbal abilities, emotional relationships, and personal independence. Subsequently King *et al.* (1971) showed that local authority hostels (which are somewhat larger than the small units) had similar advantages over hospitals for the mentally retarded. King *et al.* suggested that the advantage of the hostels was due not merely to smaller size and better staffing, but also to their 'child-centred' approach.

These findings are reflected in the report of the Committee of Enquiry into Mental Handicap Nursing and Care (the 'Jay Report', 1979). The report suggests that conventional nursing training is not an appropriate preparation for the general care of mentally retarded children. However, contrary to the views of many other writers, the authors believe that trained hospital staff still have a role to play in the care of the mentally retarded. This role is to treat the mentally retarded who have accompanying mental illness, severe behaviour disorder, epilepsy, or important sensory defect or language impairment.

In Britain, official policy is to replace existing large and isolated hospitals by smaller units in the community they serve. Various alternatives have been proposed. According to Kushlick (1980), all severely retarded children and most severely retarded adults who would otherwise need institutional care, can be looked after in 25-bedded residential units by people who have not received special nursing training. Evaluation of children's units of this kind suggests that they are as good or better than the traditional large hospital. Other alternatives to hospital include group homes, adoption and fostering (see Udall and Corbett 1979).

(6) Specialist medical services

Retarded children and adults often have physical handicaps or epilepsy for which continuing medical care is needed. In Britain, such medical care is obtained from the ordinary medical services. Sometimes this arrangement works well, but there may be difficulties for the patient and his family because doctors and nurses are unaware how to deal with an uncomprehending patient.

In some countries, such as Denmark, a special medical service is available for the retarded.

TREATMENT OF PSYCHIATRIC PROBLEMS IN THE MENTALLY RETARDED

As explained above, psychiatric disorder in the mentally retarded usually comes to notice through changes in behaviour. It should be remembered that behavioural change can also result from physical illness or from stressful events, both of which should be carefully excluded. In the most retarded and especially those with sensory deficits, behavioural disturbance may be due to understimulation rather than excessive stress. Once the cause is clear, the treatment follows. Physical illness should be treated promptly, stressful events reduced if possible, or a more stimulating environment provided when appropriate. If the disturbed behaviour results from a psychiatric disorder, the treatment is similar in many ways to that for a patient of normal intelligence with the same disorder (see below). It is important to advise and support the parents or others who are caring for the patient during the period of treatment. In the more serious and persistent cases, admission to hospital may be needed.

Drugs

Although antispychotic drugs are used widely to control abnormal behaviour in the mentally retarded, there have been few controlled trials of their effects. The indications for these drugs are similar to those in patients of normal intelligence. Chlorpromazine or haloperidol are suitable preparations. A particularly careful watch should be kept for side effects because the patient may not be able to draw attention to them himself. Although antipsychotic drugs may be used for the short-term control of behaviour problems, whenever possible social measures or behavioural treatment should be used for long-term management.

Many mentally retarded patients suffer from epilepsy and require anticonvulsant treatment. Special care is needed in arriving at a drug and dosage that controls seizures without producing unwanted effects (see p. 561 for the side effects of anticonvulsant drugs).

Counselling

The patients' limited understanding of language sets obvious limitations to the use of psychotherapy. However, simple discussion can help. As noted already, counselling for parents is an important part of treatment.

Behaviour modification

This method has become widely used since it was first introduced in the United States in the 1960s. It can be used to encourage basic skills such as washing, toilet training, and dressing. Often parents and teachers are taught to carry out the training so that it can be maintained in the patient's everyday environment (see Yule and Carr 1980). The behaviour to be modified is first specified. If the problem is an undesired behaviour a search is made for any environmental factors that seem regularly to provoke it or reinforce it. If possible these environmental factors are changed. In this way problem behaviours are eliminated by ensuring that they are not rewarded inadvertently, and by reinforcing alternative responses. Aggressive behaviour is sometimes dealt with by withdrawing all reinforcement; in so-called 'time out' the patient is ignored or secluded until the behaviour subsides. If the problem is the lack of some socially desirable behaviour, attempts are made to reinforce any such behaviour from material or social rewards, if necessary by 'shaping' the final behaviour from simpler components. Reward should be given immediately after the desired behaviour has taken place (for example using the toilet). For training in skills such as dressing, it is often necessary to provide modelling and prompting in the early stages, and to reduce them gradually later.

Compulsory admission

The relevant provisions of the legislation in England and Wales are referred to in the appendix.

FURTHER READING

Clarke, A.M. and Clarke, A.D.B. (1978). *Readings from mental deficiency.* Methuen, London.
Cytran, L. and Louries, R.S. (1980). Mental retardation. In *Comprehensive textbook of psychiatry* III (ed. H.J. Kaplan, A.M. Freedman, and B.J. Sadock). Williams and Wilkins, Baltimore.
Ingall, R.P. (1978). *Mental retardation: the changing outlook.* John Wiley, New York.
Malin, N., Race, D., and Jones, G. (1980). *Services for the mentally handicapped in Britain.* Croom Helm, London.
Reid, A.H. (1982). *The psychiatry of mental handicap.* Blackwell Scientific Publications, Oxford.
Taylor, E. (1979). Mental retardation. In *Essentials of postgraduate psychiatry* (ed. P. Hill, R. Murray, and A. Thorley). Academic Press, London.

22. Forensic psychiatry

The clinical psychiatrist needs a working knowledge of two sets of laws, those relating to patients seen in ordinary clinical practice, and those relating to mentally abnormal offenders.

The first set of laws (concerned with ordinary patients) consists of two main groups. First are the laws regulating clinical practice, particularly the compulsory detention of patients in hospital and the giving of treatment without the patient's consent. Second are civil laws dealing with issues such as the patient's capacity to make a will or care for his own property.

The second set of laws deals with mentally abnormal offenders, that is criminal offenders who suffer from mental disorder, or mental retardation, or severe personality disorder. Such offenders are a small minority of all offenders, but they present many difficult problems in psychiatry and the law. These problems include issues such as criminal responsibility and fitness to plead; and practical questions such as whether an offender needs psychiatric treatment, and whether such treatment should be provided in the community, in a psychiatric hospital or special hospital, or in prison. For the management of such problems the psychiatrist needs knowledge not only of the law, but also of the relationship between particular kinds of crime and particular kinds of psychiatric disorder.

The term forensic psychiatry is used in two different senses, one narrow and one broad. In its narrow sense the term is applied only to the branch of psychiatry that deals with the assessment and treatment of mentally abnormal offenders. In its broad sense the term is applied to all legal aspects of psychiatry, including the civil law and laws regulating psychiatric practice, as well as the sub-specialty concerned with mentally abnormal offenders. In the title of this chapter the term is used in the broad sense.

The chapter begins with a brief discussion of the law in relation to ordinary psychiatric practice, with particular reference to confidentiality, informed consent, and compulsory admission to hospital. Next comes a short section dealing with the civil law in relation to issues such as fitness to drive and the care and disposal of patients' property.

The main part of the chapter is concerned with the mentally abnormal offender. A brief review of the general causes of crime is followed by discussion of the relationship between crime and the various psychiatric diagnostic categories. Next the role of the psychiatrist is described, with particular reference to the offender's fitness to plead, mental state at the time of the offence, diminished responsibility, and the psychiatric treatment of mentally abnormal offenders. An account is then given of the types of offence (violence, sexual offences, and property offences) most likely to be associated with psychological factors. This is followed by some guidelines for the psychiatrist on the work of the courts, and on interviewing defendants and preparing psychiatric court reports. Dangerousness and violence are then discussed, and finally there is an appendix outlining the main provisions of the Mental Health Act.

In reading this chapter, two important points need to be borne in mind. First, there are substantial differences between the laws of different countries. For this reason, the chapter deals with general principles rather than the details of the law. Second, there are differences between the legal and the psychiatric concepts of mental abnormality. These differences are made more complicated because the concept of mental abnormality varies between different parts of the law. In this chapter it is not possible to review all these diverse concepts, but a few examples will be given in relation to such issues as fitness to plead, testamentary capacity (fitness to make a will), and the legal defence of insanity. If a psychiatrist is called upon to give a psychiatric opinion on a legal issue, he should acquaint himself with whichever legal concept of abnormal state of mind is relevant.

There are few textbooks of forensic psychiatry, but the recent textbook by Trick and Tennent (1981) provides much useful further information on most topics in this chapter.

THE LAW IN RELATION TO ORDINARY PSYCHIATRIC PRACTICE

At this stage the reader is reminded of two aspects of medical ethics; *confidentiality* and *informed consent to treatment.* Both of these ethical issues should be familiar to the reader from medical practice. In psychiatry the principles are the same as in general medicine, but certain points need to be stressed.

Confidentiality

This is particularly important in psychiatry because information is collected about private and highly sensitive matters. In general, the psychiatrist should not collect information from other informants without the patient's consent. If the patient is too mentally disturbed to give an account of himself, the psychiatrist should use his own discretion about seeking information from someone else. Sometimes such information is of vital importance to assessment and management. The guiding principle should be to try to act in the patient's best interests, and to obtain information as far as possible from close relatives rather than employers. The same principles apply when the psychiatrist needs to give information or an opinion to relatives or other people.

Informed consent to treatment

This means that the patient has a clear and full understanding of the nature of a treatment procedure and its probable side-effects, and that he freely agrees to receive the treatment. For most treatments, such as established forms of medication, it is sufficient for the psychiatrist to explain the nature of the treatment and probable side-effects. For ECT, a special consent form must be signed (see p. 571). If there is any doubt about a voluntary patient's capacity to give informed consent to any treatment, a close relative should be consulted wherever possible. Sometimes there is the possibility that doubts or arguments will arise at a later stage; for example, if the patient is too ill to give consent, or if the patient or his relatives are critical or litigious. In such cases it is good practice to keep a careful written note of what has been said.

Compulsory admission and treatment

In all developed countries there are laws to protect a mentally disordered person and to protect society from the consequences of his mental disorder. In a particular society the laws vary with the political system, and with public attitudes towards lawyers and doctors. Generally the need for compulsory psychiatric treatment is smaller in societies that provide good psychiatric treatment which is respected by the community.

Special legal provision is needed for people who are a danger to themselves or others because of mental disorder, and who refuse to accept the treatment they require. Such people usually have little or no insight into their own psychiatric condition. They present a difficult ethical dilemma; on the one hand they have a right to be at liberty; on the other hand they need care and treatment, and society has a right to be protected. Countries vary widely in their approach to this dilemma. In some Scandinavian countries, for example, procedures for compulsory care are simple; whilst in some states of the USA, a court hearing may be required.

In England and Wales, provisions for compulsory admission and treatment are embodied in the Mental Health Act (1983). The relevant sections of this Act are explained in the appendix, and at this stage only a few practical aspects of patient management will be mentioned. An experienced psychiatrist can often avoid the use of compulsory admission by patiently and tactfully persuading the patient to accept care voluntarily. If persuasion fails and compulsory treatment is inevitable, family members are often called upon to support the patient's admission to hospital. The doctor should consult the family closely and do his best to minimize their anxiety and guilt. Once the patient is in hospital, restrictions should be kept to the minimum required for safety and adequate treatment. Frequently the patient and his family soon realize that compulsory hospital care is virtually the same as that of a voluntary patient. If the hospital staff is patient and adaptable, it is usually possible to maintain treatment without causing lasting harm to relationships between staff, patient, and relatives.

Sometimes the patient admitted under compulsory order refuses to accept restrictions or medication. Such refusal calls for considerable nursing skill, and the exercise of firmness and flexibility, patience and sympathy.

Another problem is that of the voluntary patient who is judged to need ECT for a severe psychiatric illness (for example, extreme depression with dangerous refusal of food and drink), but who refuses to consent to ECT. Such a problem should be discussed fully with the relatives; an independent psychiatric opinion should be sought; and a compulsory treatment order should be completed with the relatives' collaboration.

In most legal systems, safeguards against unnecessary detention are provided, and patients are entitled to easy access to appeal procedures. The type of safeguard varies from country to country. The system in England and Wales is reviewed in the appendix (p. 745).

CIVIL LAW

As explained in the introduction, civil law deals with laws concerning property and inheritance, and also with contracts. In other words, it deals with the rights and obligations of individuals to one another. In this respect it differs from criminal law, which is concerned with offences against the state (not necessarily against an individual).

In matters of civil law, psychiatrists have special responsibility in relation to issues such as fitness to drive, testamentary capacity, torts and contracts, receivership, marriage contracts, and guardianship. These matters are outlined below.

The psychiatrist may be asked to submit a written report on a patient's state of mind in relation to these issues, or to proceedings concerning divorce, compensation, or other matters. In preparing such a report, the psychiatrist should follow the same principles as in writing a court report (see below, p. 740). He should prepare the report only after full discussion with the patient, and only with the patient's full consent. As with all psychiatric reports for legal purposes, the report should be concise and factual, and should give the reasons for any opinions. Finally, the law on these issues is complicated, and it is often advisable for the psychiatrist to seek legal guidance on them, particularly in relation to the legal concept of abnormal mental state relevant to the issue in question.

Fitness to drive

Questions of fitness to drive may arise in relation to most psychiatric disorders, particularly the major mental illnesses. Reckless driving may result from suicidal inclinations or manic disinhibition; panicky or aggressive driving may result from persecutory delusions; and indecisive or inaccurate driving from dementia.

Fitness to drive also arises in relation to psychiatric drugs, particularly those affecting concentration, such as anxiolytic or antipsychotic drugs in high dosage.

Testamentary capacity

This term refers to the capacity to make a valid will. If someone is suffering from mental disorder at the time of making a will, the validity of the will may be in doubt, and other people may challenge that validity. However, the will may still be legally valid if the testator is of 'sound disposing mind' at the time of making it.

In order to decide whether or not a testator is of sound disposing mind, the doctor should use four legal criteria:

(1) whether the testator understands what a will is, and what its consequences are;

(2) whether he knows the nature and extent of his property, though not in detail;

(3) whether he knows the names of close relatives, and can assess their claims to his property; and

(4) whether he is free from an abnormal state of mind that might distort feelings or judgements relevant to making the will. (A deluded person may legitimately make a will, provided that the delusions are unlikely to influence it.)

In conducting an examination, the doctor should see the testator alone, but should also see relatives and friends to check the accuracy of factual statements.

Torts and contracts

Torts are wrongs for which a person is liable in civil law as opposed to criminal law. They include, for example, negligence, libel, slander, trespass, and nuisance. If such a wrong is committed by a person of unsound mind, then any damages awarded in a court of law are usually only nominal. In this context the legal definition of unsound mind is restrictive, and it is advisable for a psychiatrist to take the advice of a lawyer on it.

If a person makes a contract and later develops a mental disorder, then the contract is binding. If a person makes a contract and is of unsound mind at the time, then a distinction is made between the 'necessaries' and 'non-necessaries' of life. Necessaries are legally defined as goods (or services) 'suitable to the condition in life of such person and to his actual requirements at the time' (Sale of Goods Act 1893). In a particular case, it is for the court to decide whether any goods or services are necessaries within this definition. Any contract made for necessaries is always binding. In the case of a contract for non-necessaries made by a person of unsound mind, the contract is also binding unless it can be shown both (a) that he did not understand what he was doing, and (b) that the other person was aware of the incapacity.

Power of attorney and receivership

If a patient is incapable of managing his possessions by reason of mental disorder, alternative arrangements must be made, particularly if the incapacity is likely to last a long time. Such arrangements may be required for patients living in the community as well as those in hospital. Two methods are available – power of attorney and receivership.

Power of attorney is the simpler method, only requiring the patient to give written authorization for someone else to act for him during his illness. In signing such authorization, the patient must be able to understand what he is doing. He may revoke at at any time.

Receivership is the more formal procedure, and likely to be more in the patient's interests. In England and Wales an application is made to the Court of Protection, which may decide to appoint a receiver (see p. 752). The procedure is most commonly required for the elderly. The question of receivership is one that places special responsibility on the psychiatrist. If a patient is capable of managing his affairs on admission to hospital, but later becomes incapable by reason of intellectual deterioration, then it is the doctor's duty to advise the patient's relatives about the risks to property. If the relatives are unwilling to take action, then it is the doctor's duty to make an application to the Court of Protection. The doctor may feel reluctant to act in this way; but any actions taken subsequently are the Court's responsibility and not the doctor's.

Family law

A marriage contract is not valid if at the time of marriage either party was so mentally disordered as not to understand the nature of the contract. If mental disorder of this degree can be proved, a marriage may be decreed null and void by a divorce court. If a marriage partner becomes of 'incurably unsound mind' later in a marriage, this may be grounds for divorce.

A doctor may be asked for an opinion about the capacity of parents or a guardian to care adequately for a child. This issue is discussed on page 674, and the law in England and Wales is summarized in the Appendix.

THE MENTALLY ABNORMAL OFFENDER

It is possible here to give only a brief outline of patterns of crime. In England and Wales, as in other countries, crime is predominantly an activity of young men. A half of all indictable offences are committed by males aged under 21, and a quarter by males aged under 17. In recent decades crime has increased in amount; since the 1939–45 war there has been a steady rise in the rates of crimes against property and violent crimes. This rise has included a sharp increase in the numbers of offences committed by women. Four-fifths of all crimes are against property. Only a quarter of first offenders are charged with a further offence. Readers requiring further information on criminology are referred to Walker (1965), and Radzinowicz and King (1977).

The causes of crime

In the nineteenth century criminologists were interested in the idea that criminals were degenerate. For example, in 1876 Lombroso published his book *L'Uomo delinquente*, in which he described characteristic physical stigmata in criminals.

In the present century, there has been some interest in a possible genetic basis for antisocial behaviour and criminality. Twin studies have suggested that concordance rates for criminality are two to three times greater in monozygotic twins than in dizygotic twins (Rosanoff *et al.* 1941). Adoption studies in Denmark have suggested a marked genetic influence, particularly for severe and persistent criminality (Hutchings and Mednick 1974). Chromosomal abnormality has also been studied. It was originally reported that the XYY chromosomal abnormality was more frequent in patients in maximum security hospitals than in the general population (for example Jacobs *et al.* 1965), but recent surveys suggest that the XYY constitution is only weakly associated with criminal behaviour and with aggression in particular (for example Witkin *et al.* 1976).

Social studies have drawn attention to numerous social and economic correlates of crime, such as local cultural influences, poverty, and unemployment (Hood and Sparks 1970; Radzinowicz and King 1977).

Nowadays it is generally held that social causes of crime are much more important than psychological causes. Nevertheless, there is a small but important group of offenders whose criminal behaviour seems to be partly explicable by psychological factors (see West 1974). It is this group that particularly concerns the psychiatrist.

Crime and psychiatric disorder

It is difficult to obtain a reliable estimate of the numbers of mentally abnormal offenders. As Walker and McCabe (1973) have pointed out, an unknown but considerable number of mentally abnormal offenders 'by-pass' the courts. This group includes offenders whose offences are known to their doctors but not to the police, and those whose offences are known to the police but not prosecuted. The police have considerable discretion as to whether to prosecute, and it is not uncommon for offences to be dealt with unofficially.

Nevertheless it is known that the prisons contain considerable numbers of psychiatrically disturbed people. In a recent survey of prisons in the south-east region of England, Gunn (1977) found that 31 per cent of prisoners were psychiatrically disturbed.

A brief review will now be given of the associations between crime and the various psychiatric diagnostic categories. It should be borne in mind that such associations are not necessarily causal. Moreover, if an association of this kind is to have any potential significance, the psychiatric diagnoses must be based on independent evidence and must not be deduced solely from the criminal behaviour, however bizarre.

The psychiatric disorders most likely to be associated with crime are personality disorders, alcohol and drug dependence, and mental retardation. In addition to these categories, there is a sizeable group of recidivist offenders who are socially isolated, and often homeless and unemployed. The are often of low intelligence, and some have chronic schizophrenia. In this group, criminality is just one manifestation of all round incompetence.

Personality disorder

There are close associations between crime and personality disorder, particularly antisocial personality disorder. Gunn (see 1977*a, b*) diagnosed abnormal personality in 20 per cent of prisoners in prisons in south-east England; Bluglass (see Gunn 1977*a*) found psychopathic personality disorder in 40 per cent of newly convicted prisoners in a Scottish prison; and Guze (1976) described 70 per cent of prisoners discharged from American prisons as 'sociopathic'. The features, aetiology, and treatment of antisocial personality disorders are discussed in Chapter 5. Offenders with such personality problems are often more susceptible to social than to psychiatric care, but there are sometimes indications for psychological treatment (see Gunn 1979), such as therapeutic community techniques, or treatment for sexual problems or anxiety neurosis.

In this book the term antisocial personality disorder is used in preference to 'psychopathic disorder'. However, the latter term is in current legal use, and when working with the courts the psychiatrist is required to use it. In the Mental Health Amendment Act (1982), psychopathic disorder is defined as a 'persistent disorder or disability of mind (whether or not including significant impairment of intelligence) which results in abnormally aggressive or seriously irresponsible conduct'. If a compulsory order is to be made on the grounds of psychopathy, then the Act requires that there be evidence that treatment is 'likely to alleviate or prevent a deterioration of (the patient's) condition' as well as the requirement 'that it is necessary for the health and safety of the patient, or the protection of other persons'.

It is widely held that the legal concept of psychopathy is unsatisfactory (see Gunn 1979; Walker and McCabe 1973). The legal definition is difficult to apply in practice. There is a danger that the diagnosis will be based on the nature of the crime rather than on any independent evidence of psychiatric disorder (Wootton 1959), and that it will be used as a label for people whose behaviour is not acceptable to conventional society (see West 1974). A further criticism is that the stipulation concerning psychiatric treatment is unrealistic, since most patients with psychopathic disorder are not susceptible to psychiatric treatment.

Abnormal personality may contribute substantially to the causes of crime in people with other psychiatric diagnoses. For example violent crimes are more likely amongst schizophrenics who had antisocial personality traits before the onset of the mental illness (see Rollin 1969).

Eysenck (1970) has suggested that there is an association between crime and personality which depends on the rapidity of 'conditioning'. The evidence is contradictory and a single explanation of this kind appears unlikely (see Farrington *et al.* 1982).

Alcohol and drug dependence

There are close links between alcohol and crime. Alcohol intoxication may lead to charges related to public drunkenness, or to driving offences. Intoxication reduces inhibitions and is strongly associated with crimes of violence, including murder. The neuro-psychiatric complications of alcoholism (see Chapter 14) may also be linked with crime. For example, offences may be committed during alcoholic amnesias or 'blackouts' (periods of several hours or days which the heavy drinker cannot subsequently recall, although at the time he appeared normally conscious to other people and was able to carry out complicated actions).

Drug intoxication may also lead to criminal behaviour. This may happen for example with cocaine or LSD. A more important link with crime is that drug dependent people may be driven to theft or violence in order to obtain drugs. The relationship between drug dependence and crime is discussed further in Chapter 14.

Mental retardation

Contrary to early beliefs, there is no evidence that most criminals are of markedly low intelligence. Recent surveys have shown that most delinquent youths are within the lower part of the normal range of intelligence, and only about 3 per cent are mentally retarded. There is no reason to suppose that the distribution of intelligence is any different amongst adult criminals.

Mentally retarded people may commit offences because they do not understand the implications of their behaviour, or because they are susceptible to exploitation by other people. Compared with other offenders, the mentally retarded are more likely to be caught. The closest association between mental retardation and crime is a high incidence of sexual offences, particularly indecent exposure by males (Power 1969; Hunter 1979). The exposer is often known to the victim, and the rate of detection is therefore high. There is also an association between mental retardation and arson. The motive for fire-setting may be excitement or revenge on someone in authority (see Reid 1982). Apart from sexual offences and arson, no other crimes are closely associated with mental retardation.

The rest of this section is concerned with the major mental illnesses – organic syndromes, affective disorders, and schizophrenia, none of which is closely related to crime.

Organic mental disorders

Acute organic mental disorders may occasionally be associated with criminal behaviour. Diagnostic problems may arise if the mental disturbance improves before the offender is examined by a doctor.

Senile dementia may sometimes be associated with offences, though crime in general is uncommon among the elderly (see Roth 1968). Violent offences are rare. Occasionally elderly men commit sexual offences, usually in the form of indecency with children. Such men have usually had life-long sexual difficulties, but no previous offences of any kind. Whenever an elderly man is charged with a sexual offence, it is essential to consider the possibility of dementia.

Epilepsy

It is uncertain whether criminality is more common among epileptics than non-epileptics. The uncertainty results from the use of selected populations and different definitions of epilepsy in different surveys.

It is known that there are more epileptics in prison than would be expected in relation to the general population (see Gunn 1977 *a, b*). One explanation for the finding may be that epileptics are more likely to be given custodial sentences. On the other hand, some epileptics may suffer from brain disorder that induces both seizures and criminal behaviour; or they may resort to anti-social acts because of general social difficulties. It has often been said that temporal lobe epilepsy is associated with aggression, but the evidence is not wholly convincing (see p. 341). It is possible that epileptic automatisms are an extremely rare cause of crime.

Affective disorder

Depressive disorder

This disorder is sometimes associated with shop-lifting (see p. 737). Much more seriously, severe depressive disorder may lead to homicide. When this happens, the depressed person usually has delusions, for example that the world is too dreadful a place for him and his family to live in; he then kills his spouse or children to spare them from the horrors of the world. The killer often commits suicide afterwards. A mother suffering from post-natal depression may sometimes kill her new-born child or her older children. Rarely, a person with severe depressive disorder may commit homicide because of a persecutory belief; for example, that the victim is responsible for the patient's misery.

Not uncommonly, ideas of guilt and unworthiness may lead depressed patients to confess to crimes that they did not commit.

Mania

Manic patients may spend excessively. They may buy jewellery, fur coats, or cars that they cannot pay for. They may hire cars and fail to return them, or steal other people's cars. They may be charged with fraud or false pretences. Manic patients are also prone to irritability and aggression; this may lead to offences of violence, though seldom to severe violence.

Schizophrenia

The relationship between schizophrenia and crime is still uncertain. According to Taylor (1982), schizophrenia is the psychiatric diagnostic category most associated with violent offences. However, in a large study in West Germany, the risk of homicide was found to be the same in schizophrenics as in the general population (Böker and Häfner 1977).

As mentioned earlier, in some schizophrenics crime is one expression of all-round incompetence. These patients are usually apathetic and lacking in judgement. In the past they were often permanent residents in mental hospitals; nowadays they live mostly in the community, and they sometimes become destitute. Their crimes are usually petty, but their repeated offences may lead to many short prison sentences.

In a second group of schizophrenics, criminality results from delusions and hallucinations. Clinical experience suggests that violence is particularly associated with paranoid schizophrenia, and commoner in the later stages of the illness. According to Planansky and Johnston (1977), violence in schizophrenics may be associated with any of the following features: great fear and loss of self-control in association with non-systematized delusions; irresistible urges; instructions from hallucinatory voices; unaccountable frenzy; and systematized paranoid delusions including the conviction that enemies must be defended against. As mentioned in the section on dangerousness (p. 742), homicidal threats in schizophrenics should be taken very seriously.

THE ROLE OF THE PSYCHIATRIST

Although mentally abnormal offenders are only a small minority of all offenders, both the forensic psychiatrist and the general psychiatrist can play an important role by helping to identify, assess, and manage them. The psychiatrist may be asked to give advice in relation to the following issues: fitness to plead; mental state at the time of the offence; diminished criminal responsibility; and the psychiatric management of offenders.

Each of these issues will be discussed in turn. The discussion will be based on the law in England and Wales, but the principles apply to varying extents in other countries. For further information on the criminal law of England and Wales, the reader is referred to the standard legal text by Smith and Hogan (1978).

Fitness to plead

English law requires that the defendant must be in a fit condition to defend himself. The issue may be raised by the defence, the prosecution, or the judge. It cannot be decided in a magistrates' court, but only by a jury. If the accused is found unfit to plead, an order is made committing him to any hospital specified by the Home Secretary, where he may be detained without limit of time and can only be discharged at the discretion of the Home Secretary.

In determining fitness to plead, it is necessary to determine how far the defendant can: (i) understand the nature of the charge; (ii) understand the difference between pleading guilty and not guilty; (iii) instruct Counsel; (iv) challenge jurors; (v) follow the evidence presented in court.

A person may be suffering from severe mental disorder but still fit to stand trial. An interesting problem arises if the accused has amnesia for the time of the offence; such amnesia has been held to have no bearing on fitness to plead, though it might point to an underlying disorder that could affect the issue.

Mental state at the time of the offence

Mentally abnormal offenders usually stand trial in the same way as other offenders, but when sentence is passed consideration is given to their mental state and to the possibility of psychiatric treatment. In some cases, however, the issue of criminal responsibility is raised at the trial. Underlying this issue is the principle that a person should not be regarded as culpable unless he was able to control his own behaviour and to choose whether to commit an unlawful act or not. It follows from this principle that, in determining whether or not a person is guilty, it is necessary to consider his mental state at the time of the act (see Whitlock 1963; Maher 1981).

Before anyone can be convicted of a crime, the prosecution must prove: (i) that he carried out an unlawful act (actus reus); (ii) that he had a certain guilty state of mind at the time, namely mens rea. The latter is a technical term which is often loosely translated as meaning 'a guilty mind'. However, this translation can be misleading since a person may commit a legal offence whilst completely confident that he is morally right.

The various categories of mens rea are not precisely defined. They vary from crime to crime and are interpreted in the light of the precedents of case law. The categories are:

1. *Intent.* Intent has a varying meaning but the main principle is that the person perceives and intends that his act or omission will produce unlawful consequences.

The three following definitions are from Smith and Hogan 1978:

2. *Recklessness.* 'Recklessness is the deliberate taking of an unjustifiable risk. A man is reckless with respect to the consequence of his act, when he foresees it may occur but does not desire it. Recklessness with respect to circumstances means the realisation that the circumstances may exist, without either knowing or hoping that they do. D points a gun at P and pulls the trigger; if he does not know that it is loaded, but realises that it may be, he is reckless with respect to that circumstance, whether he hopes it is unloaded or just does not care'.

3. *Negligence.* 'A man acts negligently when he brings about a consequence which a reasonable and prudent man would have foreseen and avoided'.

4. *Blameless inadvertence.* 'A man may reasonably fail to foresee a consequence of his act, as when a slight slap causes the death of an apparently healthy person: or reasonably fail to consider the possibility of the existence of a circumstance, as when goods, which are in fact stolen, are bought in the normal course of business from a trader of high repute.'

Children under 10 are excluded because they are deemed incapable of criminal intent (doli incapax). Children aged over 10 and under 14 are excluded unless it can be proved that they knew the nature of their act and knew it to be morally and legally wrong (mischievous discretion); in other words; the law assumes that children in this age group do not have mens rea unless it can be proved otherwise.

The degree of mens rea required for a conviction varies from crime to crime. For murder, it is necessary to establish 'specific intent'; for manslaughter it is sufficient to establish gross negligence; and for some types of traffic offences, it is not necessary to establish any degree of mens rea at all. For most offences it is necessary to establish some degree of intent.

When a person is charged with an offence, the defence can be made that he is not culpable because he did not have a sufficient degree of mens rea. This defence can be raised in several ways:

(1) not guilty by reason of insanity (under the McNaughton rules);

(2) diminished responsibility (not guilty of murder, but guilty of manslaughter, which requires a lesser degree of criminal intent);

(3) incapacity to form an intent because of an automatism.

A further example is that if a mother kills her child in the first year of its life she is not usually held legally responsible for murder but only for the less serious crime of infanticide (see p. 732).

The types of defence listed above will now be considered in turn. For further information the reader is referred to: Walker (1967); Walker and McCabe

(1973); the Committee on Mentally Abnormal Offenders (1975); and Bluglass (1979).

Not guilty by reason of insanity

This concept is embodied in the McNaughton Rules.

In 1843 Daniel McNaughton, a wood turner from Glasgow, shot and killed Edward Drummond, private secretary to the Prime Minister, Sir Robert Peel. In the trial at the Old Bailey, a defence of insanity was presented on the grounds that McNaughton had suffered from delusions for many years. He believed he was persecuted by spies, and had gone to the police and other public figures seeking help. His delusional system gradually focused on the Tory Party, and he decided to kill their leader, Sir Robert Peel. He killed Peel's secretary but was prevented from firing a second shot at the Prime Minister (see West 1974). In accordance with suggestions made by the judge in summing up, McNaughton was found not guilty on the grounds of insanity, and was admitted to Bethlem Hospital. This verdict outraged public opinion and was debated urgently in the House of Lords. At the request of the Lords, the judges drew up rules which were not enacted in the law but provided guidance as follows:

To establish a defence on the ground of insanity, it must be clearly proved that, at the time of committing the act, the party accused was labouring under such a defect of reason, from disease of the mind, as not to know the nature and quality of the act he was doing, or, if he did know it, that he did not know what he was doing was wrong.

The McNaughton Rules have no statutory basis, but they are accepted by the courts as having the same status as statutory law. If an offender is found 'not guilty by reason of insanity', the court must order his admission to a hospital specified by the Home Secretary (Criminal Procedure (Insanity) Act 1964).

The rules are more restrictive than the summing up in the McNaughton trial. They have been strongly criticized as providing a concept of insanity that is much too narrow. Critics have argued that insanity affects not only cognitive faculties, but also emotions and will power. Both for this reason and because of the increasing concern about capital punishment, the defence of diminished responsibility for murder was introduced in 1957. Since then a defence of insanity in terms of the McNaughton Rules is seldom raised.

Diminished responsibility

Diminished responsibility may be pleaded as a defence to the charge of murder. If the defence is upheld, the accused is found guilty only of manslaughter. The concept of diminished responsibility is based on a definition of mental abnormality that is much wider than that embodied in the McNaughton Rules. This point is illustrated by the following extract from the Homicide Act 1957 (section 2):

where a person kills or is party to a killing of another, he shall not be convicted of murder if he was suffering from such abnormality of mind (whether arising from a condition of arrested or retarded development of mind or any inherent causes or induced by disease or injury) as substantially impaired his mental responsibility for his acts and omissions in doing or being party to the killing.

In practice, if a person is charged with murder, he may plead that he is not guilty of murder but guilty of manslaughter on the grounds of diminished responsibility. If this plea is acceptable to the prosecution and to the judge, there is no trial and a sentence for manslaughter is passed. If on the other hand the plea is not acceptable to the prosecution or the judge, a trial is held. The jury must then consider the evidence, both medical and non-medical, to decide whether at the material time the accused was suffering from abnormality of mind, and if so, whether the abnormality was such as *substantially* to impair his responsibility. If the accused is convicted of manslaughter, the judge may pass whatever sentence he deems appropriate; if there is a conviction of murder, there is a statutory sentence of life imprisonment.

Diminished responsibility has been widely interpreted. Successful pleas have been based on conditions such as 'emotional immaturity', 'mental instability', 'psychopathic personality', 'reactive depressed state', 'mixed emotions of depression, disappointment and exasperation' (Wootton 1959). Recently, premenstrual tension has been added to the list.

Automatism

If a person has no control over an act, he cannot be held responsible for it. For this reason verdicts of not guilty have been returned when acts of violence were judged to be committed as automatisms. Such circumstances are rare, but have occurred in association with hypoglycaemia, epileptic seizures, concussion, and sleep walking. If automatism is thought to arise from 'a disease of the mind', then the appropriate defence is insanity, and the McNaughton Rules apply. In legal practice there have been varying interpretations of 'disease of the mind' in this context.

The law relating to alcohol and drug addiction is complicated. It can be summarized as follows: (1) Involuntary intoxication (as when someone unwittingly takes a drink to which a drug has been added), or automatism occurring as a side-effect of medical treatment, constitutes a valid defence. (2) Self-induced intoxication is not a defence unless (a) it is itself evidence of 'disease of the mind' under the McNaughton Rules; or (b) it is evidence of lack of intent in relation to those crimes for which 'specific intent' must be proved (for example murder, theft, burglary). Self-induced intoxication is not a defence to those crimes for which evidence of 'specific intent' is not required (for example manslaughter, rape, indecent assault, common assault).

Treatment of the mentally abnormal offender

When sentence is passed in court, the need for psychiatric treatment may be taken into account. After conviction an offender may be treated on a compulsory or voluntary basis.

When a **custodial** sentence is passed, psychiatric treatment may be given in prison or hospital. Some prisons have offered psychiatric treatment as a main part of their work; for example, Herstedvester prison in Denmark (Stürup 1957) and Grendon Underwood in England (Gunn and Robertson 1982). Generally only limited psychiatric facilities are provided within prison services. Thus the British prison medical service can provide adequate psychiatric treatment for only a small minority of mentally abnormal prisoners (see Gunn and Farrington 1982).

In England and Wales a convicted offender may be committed to hospital for compulsory psychiatric treatment under a Mental Health Act Hospital Order (see Appendix). Commital is usually to a local psychiatric hospital, but it can be to one of the four high security hospitals (Broadmoor, Moss Side, Park Lane, and Rampton). There is also legal provision for a prisoner to be transferred from prison to a psychiatric hospital. An important point is that hospital orders have no time limit, while most prison sentences which are of fixed length. The length of stay in a psychiatric hospital may therefore be substantially shorter or longer than a prison sentence.

When a **non-custodial** sentence is passed, psychiatric treatment may be given on an inpatient or outpatient basis. Psychiatric treatment may be made a condition of probation under the Powers of the Criminal Courts Act (1973), which superseded the Criminal Justice Act (1948). When treatment is made a condition of probation, the offender must state that he is willing to comply.

The principles of psychiatric treatment are the same for mentally abnormal offenders as for other psychiatric patients.

Offenders in hospital

The reform of the mental hospitals in the 1950s and following years has had unforeseen consequences for the care of the mentally abnormal offender. There has been a growing emphasis on acute treatment; at the same time there has been less physical security in psychiatric hospitals, and less willingness by hospital staff to tolerate severely disturbed behaviour. As a result it has become increasingly difficult to arrange admission to hospital for offenders, particularly those who are severely disturbed or have chronic handicaps. For severely disturbed offenders, there are several alternatives. One is to provide well-staffed secure areas in ordinary psychiatric hospitals; such an arrangement carries the risk of adverse public attitudes towards the hospital. Another alternative is to set up the special regional units, often referred to as Medium Secure Units, which were recommended in the 'Butler' Report (Committee on Mentally Abnormal Offenders 1975). In England and Wales it is official government policy to establish such units. A potential disadvantage of such units is that they may become custodial ghettoes rather than active treatment units. A third alternative is to improve psychiatric treatment in the prison service, but it seems that any significant improvement would call for major changes in present attitudes within the prison system (see Gunn 1979).

Among offenders with chronic psychiatric handicaps, those who commit repeated petty offences often lack adequate care. In the past they would have been long-stay hospital inpatients, but now they revolve between hospital, prison and destitution (Rollin 1969). If such people are to lead a better life outside hospital, then the quality of community care must be improved.

TYPES OF OFFENCE

This section is concerned with offences of the types that are most likely to be associated with psychological factors. These offences can be divided into crimes of violence, sexual offences, and offences against property.

CRIMES OF VIOLENCE

Amongst mentally abnormal offenders, violence is associated much more with personality disorder than with psychiatric illness. Violence is particularly common in people of antisocial personality who abuse alcohol or drugs, or who have marked paranoid or sadistic traits (see Fottrell 1981). Generally violence is part of a persistent pattern of impulsive and aggressive behaviour, but it may be a sporadic response to stressful events in 'overcontrolled' personalities (Megargee 1966). The assessment of dangerousness and the management of violence are discussed in a later section.

Homicide

Homicide can be divided into several legal categories. The main ones are murder, manslaughter, and infanticide, and these are the subject of this section of the chapter. Murder and manslaughter are defined by historical precedent (common law offences) and not by statute (see Smith and Hogan 1978).

According to a widely quoted definition put forward by Lord Coke in 1797, **murder** occurs:

when a man of sound memory and of the age of discretion unlawfully killeth within any county of the realm any reasonable creature in rerum natura under the King's peace with malice aforethought, either expressed by the party or implied by law, so as the party wounded or hit, etc. die of the wound or hit within a year and a day after the same.

The phrase 'malice aforethought' is important, although it has no statutory definition and can only be interpreted from case law.

According to Smith and Hogan (1978), **manslaughter:**

is a diverse crime covering all unlawful homicides which are not murder. A wide variety of types of homicide fall within this category, but it is customary and useful to divide manslaughter into two main groups which are designated 'voluntary' and 'involuntary' manslaughter respectively. The distinction is that in voluntary manslaughter the defendant may have malice aforethought of murder but the presence of some defined mitigating circumstances reduces his crime to a less serious grade of criminal homicide.

In involuntary manslaughter, there is no malice aforethought; it includes for example causing death by gross negligence.

As mentioned earlier in this chapter the category of manslaughter resulting from diminished responsibility is defined not by common law but by statute, viz. the Homicide Act (1957). This act also provides that the survivor of a genuine suicide pact should be guilty only of manslaughter.

It is common practice to divide homicide into 'normal' and 'abnormal', according to the legal outcome. Homicide is 'normal' if there is a conviction of murder or common law manslaughter; it is 'abnormal' if there is a finding of insane murder, suicide murder, diminished responsibility, or infanticide. This distinction is useful for the interpretation of statistics (see Gibson 1975).

'*Normal*' *homicide* accounts for about two-thirds of all homicides occurring in Britain. In countries such as the USA where the overall homicide rate is much higher than in Britain, the excess is largely made up of 'normal' homicide. 'Normal' homicide is most likely to be committed by young men of low social class. In Britain the victims are mainly family members or close acquaintances, and they are seldom killed in the course of a robbery or sexual offence. In countries with high homicide rates, there is a greater proportion of killings associated with robbery or sexual offences. When sexual homicide does occur it may result from panic during a sexual offence. Alternatively it may be a sadistic killing, often committed by a shy man with bizarre sadistic and other violent fantasies (Brittain 1970).

'*Abnormal*' *homicide* accounts for about a third of all homicides in Britain. It is usually committed by older people. Homicide by women is much rarer than by men; when it does occur, it is nearly always 'abnormal', and the commonest category is infanticide. The victims are usually family members. In 'abnormal' homicide, the commonest psychiatric diagnosis is depressive disorder, especially in killers who afterwards kill themselves. Other associated diagnoses are schizophrenia (especially the paranoid form), personality disorder, and alcoholism. The syndrome of morbid jealousy may be associated with any of the above diagnoses; it has been identified in 12 per cent of insane male murderers and 3 per cent of insane women murderers. It is particularly dangerous because of the risk of the offence being repeated (see the section on morbid jealousy, p. 282).

A large proportion of all murderers are under the influence of alcohol at the time of the crime (Virkunnen 1974). In a survey of 400 people charged with murder in Scotland, 58 per cent of the men and 30 per cent of the women were found to have been intoxicated at the time of the offence (Gillies 1976).

The statistics about the victims of homicide are also of interest. A quarter of all homicide victims are aged under 16; their deaths usually result from 'abnormal' homicide or repeated child abuse by the parents. Amongst adult victims, women outnumber men by three to two. Nearly half of the women victims are killed by their husbands, and the rest mainly by relatives or intimate friends. By contrast, nearly half of the male victims are killed by strangers or chance associates. Bluglass (1979*b*) studied 70 murders, and in over half found that the victim had played a part in the events leading up to death. It has also been shown that about a third of homicide victims were probably intoxicated with alcohol at the time of the crime (Gillies 1976; Bluglass 1979).

Homicide is followed by suicide in about 10 per cent of homicides in England and Wales. West (1965) studied 78 cases occurring in the London area over the years 1954–61. The offenders were strikingly different from homicide offenders in general. They were much more likely to be women, were of higher social class, and had fewer previous convictions than convicted homicide offenders. The victims were usually children. Half the homicides were 'abnormal' in the sense defined above; in most cases the offender was severely depressed at the time of the offence. In most of the 'normal' offences, the killer appeared to have felt 'driven to suicide by illness or distressing circumstances, the victim being an innocent party involved by virtue of a close relationship'.

Psychiatric assessment in cases of homicide

In England and Wales everyone charged with murder is assessed psychiatrically by a prison doctor. The latter often asks for a second psychiatric opinion, and the defence lawyers often seek independent psychiatric advice. It is good practice for all the doctors involved, whether engaged by the prosecution or defence lawyers, to discuss the case together. If this is done, disagreement is unusual. Copies of the reports are distributed to the judge, and to the prosecution and defence lawyers.

The psychiatric report should be based on full psychiatric and physical examination. It is essential that the psychiatrist read all the depositions by witnesses, statements by the accused, and any previous medical notes and social reports. Family members should be interviewed. The writing of the court report follows the usual format (see p. 740) and should include a discussion of mental state at the time of the alleged offence and of fitness to plead.

Parents who kill their children

In Britain a quarter of all victims of murder or manslaughter are under the age of 16. Most of them are killed by a parent who is mentally ill, especially the mother (d'Orban 1979). Classification of child murder is difficult; useful categories suggested by Scott (1973) are mercy killing, psychotic murder, and killing as the end result of battering or neglect. This last category is discussed further on page 672.

Infanticide

A woman who kills her child may be charged with murder or manslaughter, but under special circumstances the charge may be infanticide. The Infanticide Act

(1922), afterwards amended by the Infanticide Act (1938), defined a category of offence which can now be seen as a special case of the later and wider concept of diminished responsibility. Section 1 of the Act provides that:

where a woman causes the death of her child under the age of 12 months, but at the time the balance of her mind was disturbed by reason of her not having fully recovered from the effects of childbirth or lactation consequent upon the birth of the child, she shall be guilty not of murder but infanticide.

The judge has the same freedom of sentencing for a conviction of infanticide as for a conviction of manslaughter. The legal concept of infanticide is unusual in that the accused is required to show only that her mind was disturbed as a result of birth or lactation, but not that the killing was a consequence of her mental disturbance.

Resnick (1969) found that two types of infanticide could be discerned. When the killing occurred within the first 24 hours after birth, in most cases the child was unwanted, and the mother was young and unequipped to care for the child, but not psychiatrically ill. When the killing occurred more than 24 hours after childbirth, in most cases the mother had a depressive disorder and killed the child to save it from the suffering she anticipated for it; about a third of the mothers also tried to take their own lives.

In an analysis of court disposals for infanticide, Walker and McCabe (1973) found that the great majority of the women were either committed to hospital or put on probation; about 1 per cent were sent to prison.

Violence within the family

This subject has received increasing attention in recent years. Several features require emphasis. First, some people are violent within their family, whilst others are violent outside the family as well. Second, and of particular importance, family violence is strongly associated with excessive drinking. Third, violence in the family can have long-term deleterious effects on the psychological and social development of the children (see Rutter and Madge 1976).

Of the various forms of violence in the family, homicide has been described earlier in this chapter, and child abuse is reviewed in Chapter 20. Attention has recently been drawn to a third aspect of family violence, 'wife battering'. It is difficult to obtain information on this subject, since the husband is usually difficult to interview unless he is in custody. It appears that the perpetrators of wife-battering are mainly men with aggressive personalities, whilst a few are violent only when suffering from psychiatric illness, usually a depressive disorder (see Gayford 1979; Goodstein and Page 1981). Other common features in the men are morbid jealousy and heavy drinking. In the management of wife-battering, marital therapy and family therapy are sometimes helpful. In some cases a frightened wife may need practical help to leave the home.

It is important to keep in mind that family homicide is sometimes a sequel to family violence.

Child stealing

There has been no psychiatric study of men who steal children, although, according to Trick and Tennant (1981, p. 28) the majority of people charged with the offence are males. In a study of 24 women charged with child stealing, d'Orban (1976) recognized three types of stealing: comforting; manipulative with the intention of influencing someone else; and impulsive stealing in psychiatrically disturbed women.

SEXUAL OFFENCES

In Britain sexual offences account for less than 1 per cent of all indictable offences recorded by the police. However, among the various kinds of offenders referred to psychiatrists, sexual offenders make up a relatively large proportion. Apart from soliciting for purposes of prostitution, women seldom commit sexual offences. Men commit sexual offences much more frequently, and this section therefore applies almost entirely to men. As a group, sexual offenders are older than other offenders, and they usually have records of non-sexual offences. Reconviction rates are generally lower in sexual offenders than in other offenders, but there is a minority of recidivist sexual offenders who are extremely difficult to manage.

Some sexual offences do not involve violence (for example indecent exposure; voyeurism; most sexual offences involving children); whilst others may involve substantial violence (for example rape). The nature and treatment of non-violent sexual offences are discussed in Chapter 15, but their forensic aspects are considered here.

Sexual offences against children

It is illegal to have any heterosexual activity with a person aged under 16, or homosexual activity with people aged under 21. Known sexual offences involving children are common, amounting to over half of all reported sexual offences in Britain. It is probable that many more offences are not reported, particularly those occurring within families. The offences vary in severity from mild indecency to seriously aggressive behaviour, but the latter is uncommon.

Adults who commit sexual offences against children are known as paedophiles. They are almost always male. As with other kinds of offender, they are difficult to classify. Some of them are timid and sexually inexperienced; some are mentally retarded and untrained; others have experienced normal sexual relationships but still prefer sexual activity with children.

The victims are known to the offender in four-fifths of cases, and belong to the offender's family in a third (see Mohr 1964). Girl victims outnumber boys by about two to one. It has been reported that up to two-thirds of child victims suffer emotional difficulties later. Court proceedings are likely to be particularly disturbing to child victims (Weiss and Berg 1982).

The prognosis for sexual offenders against children is generally good. The reconviction rate is low. Most offenders do not progress from less serious to more serious activities; but a few may start with indecent exposure and progress to violent sexual offences later. It is for this reason that psychiatrists are often asked to give an opinion on an offender's dangerousness.

In trying to decide whether the offence is likely to be repeated, and whether there is likely to be a progression to more serious offences, the psychiatrist should consider the duration and frequency of the particular sexual activity in the past; and the offender's predominant sexual orientation (exclusively paedophile inclinations and behaviour indicate greater risk of repetition). Older paedophiles, as mentioned above, are less likely to be aggressive. It is important to determine whether alcohol or drugs played any part in the offence, and whether the offender feels any regret or guilt. Relevant environmental factors include any stressful circumstances, and the degree of access to children. Finally evidence should be sought of any psychiatric disorder, or personality defects such as lack of self-control.

Indecent exposure

In England and Wales, indecent exposure is one of the commonest sexual offences. It is most common in men aged between 25 and 35. The term indecent exposure is the legal name for the offence of indecently exposing the genitals to other people. It is applied to all forms of exposure; exhibitionism is by far the most frequent form, but exposure may also occur as an invitation to intercourse, as a prelude to sexual assault, or as an insulting gesture. Exhibitionism, as explained on page 479, is the medical name for the behaviour of men who gain sexual satisfaction from repeatedly exposing to women.

Indecent exposers rarely have a history of psychiatric disorder or of other criminal behaviour. The reconviction rate is low, and few offenders proceed to more serious offences.

Indecent assault

Indecent assault embraces a wide range of behaviour from attempting to touch a stranger's buttocks, to sexual assault without attempted penetration. The psychiatrist is most commonly asked to give a psychiatric opinion on adolescent boys, and on men who have assaulted children. Many adolescent boys behave in ways that could be construed as 'indecent'. More serious indecent behaviour is associated with aggressive personality, ignorance and lack of social skill, personal unattractiveness, and occasionally subnormal intelligence. Treatment may include advice and social skill training.

Rape

The Sexual Offences Act 1956 states 'a man commits rape if (a) he has unlawful sexual intercourse with a woman who at the time of the intercourse does not consent to it and (b) at the time he knows that she does not consent to the intercourse or he is reckless as to whether she consents to it.' Rape does not necessarily include the use of violence. It ranges from the use of deception without violence, to extreme brutality (see also p. 490).

Rapists have been classified in various ways (see Gibbens *et al.* 1977; Bowden 1978; McDonald 1971). Most rapists are young and sexually frustrated with little experience of sexual intercourse, and most have a record of previous criminal offences. Psychiatric disorder is rare among rapists. Some of the main behavioural types are: (i) aggressive antisocial men who have a history of general criminal behaviour; these are probably the most common; (ii) aggressive sadistic men who wish to humiliate and hurt women; (iii) so-called explosive rapists who are often timid and inhibited, and who carry out the act as a deliberate plan to relieve their frustration; (iv) mentally ill rapists, who most often suffer from mania; this is the least common group.

The reconviction rate is low. Gibbens *et al.* (1977) found that, among men charged with rape, 12 per cent of those convicted and 14 per cent of those acquitted were convicted of a further sexual offence during a 12-year follow up. In interpreting these findings it should be remembered that most of the convicted men were in prison and therefore not at risk during part of the follow-up period.

In about a third of cases the victim is an acquaintance of the rapist, and in a fifth she appears to have participated initially in the events leading up to the offence. It is sometimes said that women who are raped have frequently 'asked for it' or else submitted without much resistance. There is little justification for this view. Amir (1971) found that a half of rape victims were threatened with injury either verbally or with weapons; and about a third were handled roughly or violently. In such a dangerous situation submission without much physical resistance is understandable. There is evidence that rape victims may suffer long-term psychological effects. Nadelson *et al.* (1982) interviewed 41 women who attended a clinic in a general hospital shortly after being raped. At follow up one to two and a half years later it was found that half the women were afraid of being alone, and three-quarters were still suspicious of other people. Many women reported depression and sexual difficulties which they attributed to the rape.

Incest

It is widely held that incest is fairly common, although many cases are not officially reported. Most reported cases involve a father and daughter, but brother–sister relationships are probably more common. Incest between father and daughter often starts as the girl reaches puberty. Several social factors may contribute. There is often a history of marital breakdown and the daughter replaces the mother. The family is often socially isolated and sharing bedrooms in crowded accommodation. About a third of the fathers have antisocial personalities, and many of them drink excessively (see Bluglass 1979).

It is likely that many cases are known to the medical or social services but not to the police. Even when cases are known to the police, only half of them are prosecuted. When the girl is a relatively young child, most prosecutions result in imprisonment of the father. Generally the family needs considerable psychological and social support, particularly if the father is imprisoned.

The long-term consequences of incest on the family are uncertain. If there is a prosecution, any resulting publicity or punishment of the father is likely to have serious repercussions in the family (for reviews of incest see Henderson 1972; Bluglass 1979*b*).

OFFENCES AGAINST PROPERTY

Shoplifting

Many adolescents admit occasional shop-lifting, but few admit persistent shoplifting. Among adults in England and Wales, the number of recorded offences of shop-lifting increased substantially in the 1970s, reaching a figure well over 200 000 per annum. The reasons for this increase are uncertain, but it is generally accepted that most shop-lifters are simply covetous rather than psychiatrically disturbed. In a study of shop-lifters, Gibbens *et al.* (1971) found that nearly two-thirds of those appearing in courts in central London were young foreign girls who appeared to be usually honest but shop-lifted because they were short of money. By contrast, male shop-lifters were likely to have had previous convictions for offences of all kinds, and a third of them had previously been in prison.

In a follow-up study of over 500 women who had been convicted of shop-lifting ten years previously, Gibbens *et al.* (1971) found that the reconviction rate was 11 per cent for first offenders, and 20 per cent for the whole group. Most reconvictions were for further shop-lifting. During the follow-up period the admission rate to mental hospital was three times the expected figure of 2.5 per cent for middle-aged women. The authors distinguished two sub-groups of women. One consisted of 51 women who were persistently and widely deviant; they had committed numerous previous and subsequent offences, and two-fifths of them had committed other offences such as theft, violence, and drunkenness. The other sub-group, comprising 10 to 20 per cent of the total, had suffered from a depressive disorder at the time of the original offence, which was often associated with medical symptoms, or chronic background difficulties, or recent severe life events. These women had generally been of good previous character. Most of these women had no further conviction, but a small minority persisted in shop-lifting.

Apart from depressive disorders, various other psychiatric diagnoses may be associated with shop-lifting. Patients with chronic schizophrenia or alcoholism may steal because of economic necessity. In those with acute schizophrenia, mania or anorexia nervosa, shop-lifting may be a symptom of the psychiatric disorder. In other conditions, shop-lifting may result from distractability; examples are organic mental states, phobic anxiety (especially when occurring in supermarkets), and the effects of psychotropic drugs.

When called upon to assess a person charged with shop-lifting, the psychiatrist should carry out a thorough physical and psychiatric enquiry. It is important to obtain detailed information about the following: physical health, past and present; psychiatric health, past and present; how the offence was carried out, and whether any drugs or alcohol were consumed at the time; events leading up to the offence; any chronic background difficulties; any recent stressful events, such as a bereavement or other loss. If the accused has a depressive disorder at the time of the examination, the psychiatrist should try to establish whether the disorder was present at the time of the offence, or whether it developed after the charge was brought.

Arson

This offence is generally regarded extremely seriously, because it threatens life, and also because it can result in great damage to property. Most arsonists are males. Although the courts refer a large proportion of arsonists for psychiatric assessment, the psychiatric literature on arson is small (see Scott 1978). As often occurs in forensic psychiatry, it is difficult to make a behavioural classification, but certain fairly clear-cut groups can be recognized. First, there are arsonists who are free from psychiatric disorder, and who start fires for financial or political reasons; they are sometimes referred to as **motivated** arsonists, though the term is unsatisfactory because non-specific. Second, there are so-called **pathological** arsonists, who suffer from mental retardation, mental illness, or alcoholism. A third group is sometimes said to have **pyromania**, but this is another unsatisfactory term that is best avoided. This group includes people who are not psychiatrically ill, but who raise fires from motives that appear unreasonable; for example, the desire to help the fire brigade in a heroic way, or to obtain sexual arousal by watching a fire (this last practice being associated with particularly dangerous fires).

It is clearly important to obtain information about the risks of further offences. In a 20 year follow-up, Soothill and Pope found that only 4 per cent of arsonists were reconvicted for arson, but about half of them were charged with offences of other kinds. An important guideline is that a person convicted of arson a second time is at a much greater risk of further offences.

Apart from this guideline, certain other factors point to an increased risk of a further offence: antisocial personality disorder; mental retardation; persistent social isolation; and evidence that fire-raising was done for sexual gratification or relief of tension.

Children also present problems of fire-raising. Sometimes the behaviour represents extreme mischievousness in psychologically normal children, and sometimes it springs from psychiatric disturbance. The fire-setting often occurs as a group activity. Among children charged with fire-setting, the recurrence rate in the following two years is under 10 per cent (Strachan 1981).

VICTIMS OF CRIME

As mentioned earlier in this chapter, it sometimes appears that the victim of an offence has helped to provoke it. This applies to homicide, some cases of rape (Amir 1971), and many paedophilic offences (Gibbens and Prince 1963).

For the victim, the psychological consequences of crime include immediate distress and the subsequent distress associated with investigation and court hearings. Long-term adverse consequences can occur, but their frequency is unknown. Recently there has been growing concern for the victims of rape, and in the USA there are advisory centres to help such victims (see Nadelson *et al.* 1982).

THE PSYCHIATRIST AND THE COURT

The psychiatrist needs some knowledge about the workings of magistrates' courts and crown courts. He must also be familiar with the role of the psychiatrist in relation to the courts; the psychiatric examination of a defendant; and the preparation of the court report. Helpful accounts of these topics can be found in the textbook by Trick and Tennent (1981).

The workings of the courts

In England and Wales, **Magistrates' Courts** deal with 98 per cent of all criminal prosecutions. They also deal with civil cases. Magistrates are non-stipendiary laymen, who receive some basic legal training, and are advised on legal points by the Clerk to the Justices.

Indictable offences are those that may be tried by a judge and jury in a Crown Court. The Magistrates' Court tries non-indictable offences. Some indictable offences can be tried in a Magistrates' Court; others must go to a Crown Court. Magistrates may impose a sentence, or else (if the offence seems to merit a more severe penalty than can be imposed by a magistrate) refer the case to the Crown Court for sentencing. If a defendant is charged with a serious indictable offence, and even if he chooses to be tried in a Crown Court, the magistrates must first decide whether the prosecution has established a prima facie case.

In the **Crown Courts**, indictable offences are tried by jury and the sentence is passed by a judge.

Appeals against conviction in a Magistrates' Court are heard either in the Crown Court or the Appeal Court; and appeals against convictions in Crown Court are heard in the Appeal Court.

The role of the psychiatrist in relation to the court

The psychiatrist's role is to draw on his special knowledge to help the court. He should not attempt to tell the court what to do. In Britain, an expert medical witness is expected to remain neutral, and not to favour either the accused or the defendant.

The psychiatrist's interview with the defendant

The psychiatrist should prepare himself as thoroughly as possible before the interview. He should have a clear idea as to the purpose of the examination, and particularly as to any question of fitness to plead. He should have details of the present charge and past convictions, together with copies of any statements made by the defendant and witnesses. The psychiatrist should also study any available report of the defendant's social history but during the subsequent interview it is essential to work through the report with the defendant and check its accuracy.

The psychiatrist should begin by explaining to the client the source of the referral, and why the referral was made. He should explain that the psychiatrist's opinion may be given in court and that the defendant is under no obligation to answer any questions if he chooses not to. The interview should be carried out in strict confidence. Detailed notes should be made, recording any significant comments in the defendant's own words.

At some stage in the interview (not necessarily at the start) the alleged crime should be discussed. The defendant may or may not admit guilt. A detailed history of physical illnesses should be taken; particular attention should be paid to neurological disorders including head injury and epilepsy. A careful history of previous psychiatric disorder and treatment should be obtained. If there has been a previous psychiatric opinion or treatment, further information should be sought. Full examination of the present mental state is made in the usual way. Special investigations should be requested if suitable. If the defendant's intelligence level is under question, an assessment should be made by a clinical psychologist who normally submits a separate report.

It is important to obtain further information from relatives and other informants. If the defendant is remanded in custody, the staff may have long periods of contact with the prisoner and may be able to give particularly useful information.

Preparing a psychiatric court report

This section follows the scheme used by Trick and Tennent (1981). The reader is also referred to the valuable earlier guidelines by Scott (1953) and Gibbens (1974).

In preparing a court report, the psychiatrist should remember that it will be read by non-medical people. The report should therefore be written in simple English and should avoid jargon. If technical terms are used, they should be defined as accurately as possible. The report should be concise and set out as follows:

1. A *statement* of the psychiatrist's full name, qualifications, present appointment, and whether approved under Section 12 of the Mental Health Act.

2. *Where and when the interview was conducted,* and whether any third person was present.

3. *Sources of information.* Including documents that have been examined.

4. *Family and personal history of the defendant.* Usually this need not be given in great detail, particularly if a social report is available to the court. The focus should be on information relevant to the diagnosis and disposal.

5. *The account of the crime given by the accused.* This will depend on whether the defendant is pleading guilty or not guilty. If the accused admits to the crime, comment may be made on his attitude to it, such as degree of remorse. If he is pleading not guilty any reference to the alleged crime is inadmissible.

6. *Other behaviour.* It may be relevant to mention other items of behaviour, even if not directly involved in the crime, such as: alcohol or drug abuse; quality of relationships with other people; tolerance of frustration; general social competence.

7. *Present mental state.* Only the salient positive findings should be stated and negative findings should be omitted. A general diagnosis should be given in the terms of the Mental Health Act (mental illness; mental impairment; or psychopathic disorder). A more specific diagnosis can then be given, but the court will be interested in a categorical statement rather than the finer nuances of diagnosis.

8. *Mental state at the time of the crime.* This is often a highly important issue, and yet it can only be based on retrospective speculation. The assessment can be helped by accounts given by eye-witnesses who saw the offender at the time of the crime or soon after. A current psychiatric diagnosis may suggest the likely mental state at the time of the crime. For example, if the accused suffers from chronic schizophrenia or a chronic organic mental syndrome, the mental state may well have been the same at the time of the crime as at the examination. On the other hand, if the accused suffers from a depressive disorder (now or recently) or from an episodic disorder such as epilepsy, it is more difficult to infer what the mental state is likely to have been at the material time. To add to the difficulty, even if it is judged that the defendant was suffering from a mental disorder, a further judgement is needed as to his mens rea at the time of the crime.

9. *Fitness to plead.* It is often helpful for the psychiatrist to include a statement of fitness to plead. (The criteria for deciding this are given on p. 725).

Advice on medical treatment

One of the psychiatrist's main functions is to give an opinion as to whether or not psychiatric treatment is indicated. The psychiatrist should make sure that his recommendations on treatment are feasible, if necessary by consulting colleagues, social workers, or others. If he recommends hospital treatment, he should let the court know whether or not a suitable placement is available. The assessment of dangerousness is important here (see next section).

The psychiatrist should not recommend any form of disposal other than medical treatment. However, the court often welcomes tactfully worded comments on the suitability of possible sentences, particularly in the case of young offenders.

The psychiatrist appearing in court

The psychiatrist appearing in court should be fully prepared and should have well organized copies of all reports and necessary documents. It is helpful to speak beforehand to the lawyer involved, in order to clarify any points that may be raised in court. When replying to any questions in court, it is important to be brief and clear, to restrict the answers to the psychiatric evidence, and to avoid speculation.

DANGEROUSNESS

The psychiatrist may need to assess dangerousness in everday psychiatric practice, and also in forensic work. In everyday practice, both outpatients and inpatients may appear to be dangerous, and careful assessment may be required so that the most appropriate steps can be taken in the interests of the patient and of other people. Dangerousness is an important criterion for recommending compulsory detention in hospital. In forensic work, the court may ask for the psychiatrist's advice on the defendant's dangerousness so that a suitable sentence can be passed. The psychiatrist may also be asked to comment on offenders who are detained in institutions and who are being considered for release.

There are no fixed rules for assessing dangerousness. Psychiatrists have tried to identify factors associated with dangerousness, but no reliable predictors of violence have been established. The assessment of dangerousness remains difficult. There are a few guidelines, as shown in Table 22.1; these guidelines apply to offenders, but the same principles hold for non-offenders. A thorough review should be made of the history of previous violence, characteristics of the current offence, and the circumstances in which it occurred, and of the mental state. In making the review, it is helpful to consider certain key questions; whether any consistent pattern of behaviour can be discerned; whether any circumstances have provoked violence in the past and are likely to occur again

Table 22.1. *Factors associated with dangerousness*

History
>One or more previous episodes of violence
>Repeated impulsive behaviour
>Evidence of difficulty in coping with stress
>Previous unwillingness to delay gratification
>Sadistic or paranoid traits

Offence
>Bizarre violence
>Lack of provocation
>Lack of regret
>Continuing major denial

Mental state
>Morbid jealousy
>Paranoid beliefs plus a wish to harm others
>Deceptiveness
>Lack of self control
>Threats to repeat violence
>Attitude to treatment

Circumstances
>Provocation or precipitant likely to recur
>Alcohol or drug abuse
>Social difficulties and lack of support

in the future; whether there is any good evidence that the defendant is willing to change his behaviour; and whether there is likely to be any response to treatment.

Difficulties may arise in the assessment of dangerousness in people of anti-social personality or in the mentally retarded, both of whom may be poorly motivated to comply with care. Another difficult problem is presented by the person who threatens to commit a violent act such as homicide. Here the assessment is much the same as for suicide threats (Gunn 1979). The psychiatrist should ask the threatener about his intent, motivation, and potential victim, and should make a full assessment of mental state. Patients who make threats can often be helped by outpatient support and treatment, but sometimes hospital admission is required. It may be necessary to warn potential victims.

It is a valuable principle for the psychiatrist not to rely entirely on his own evaluation of dangerousness, but to discuss the problem with other colleagues, including psychiatrists, general practitioners, social workers, and relatives.

In the difficult task of trying to gauge whether a person is likely to show violence, probably the best criterion is whether or not he has been violent in the past. (For a review see Scott 1977a.)

Violent incidents

Violent incidents are not common in hospitals (Fottrell 1980), but it is important that the staff have a clear policy for managing any incidents that do occur. Such a policy calls for attention to the design of wards, arrangements for summoning assistance, and suitable training for the staff.

When violence occurs or is threatened, staff should be available in adequate numbers, and emergency medication such as intramuscular chlorpromazine should be unobtrusively available. Dangerous people can often be calmed by sympathetic discussion and reassurance, preferably given by someone whom the patient knows and trusts. It is important not to challenge the patient. It is inappropriate to reward violent or threatening behaviour by making concessions in treatment or ward rules, but every effort should be made to allow the patient to withdraw from confrontation without loss of face.

After an incident has occurred, the clinical team should meet to consider the future care of the patient, and also any possible changes in the general policy of the ward (see Gunn 1979). For mentally ill patients, there should be a review of the drugs prescribed and their dosage. When violence occurs in a person with a primary personality disorder, medication may be required in an emergency, but it is usually best to avoid maintenance medication. Other measures include trying to reduce factors that provoke violence, or to provide the patient with more constructive ways of managing tension, such as taking physical exercise or asking a member of staff for help.

FURTHER READING

Hood, R. and Sparks, R. (1970). *Key issues in criminology*. Weidenfeld and Nicholson, London.

Kaplan, H.I., Freedman, A.M., and Sadock, B.J. (1980). Chap. 54, 'Forensic psychiatry'. Slovenko, R., 'Law and psychiatry', Adler, G., 'Correctional (Prison) psychiatry' In *Comprehensive textbook of psychiatry* III, Vol. 3. Williams and Wilkins, Baltimore.

Martin, C.R. (1979). *The law relating to medical practice*, 2nd edn. Pitman, London.

Smith, J.C. and Hogan, B. (1978). *Criminal law*, 4th edn. Butterworths, London.

Trick, K.L.K. and Tennent, T.G. (1981). *Forensic psychiatry: an introductory text*. Pitman, London.

Walker, N. and McCabe, S. (1968). *Crime and insanity in England*, Vol. i. Edinburgh Univeristy Press.

Walker, N. and McCabe, S. (1973). *Crime and insanity in England*, Vol. ii. Edinburgh University Press.

Appendix: The law in England and Wales

This appendix is an introduction to the principal sections of the law of England and Wales relating to psychiatric practice. It begins with a review of the Mental Health Act and then outlines the law in relation to child and adolescent psychiatry. More detailed information can be obtained from the works listed under further reading (p. 755). Psychiatrists practising elsewhere than in England and Wales will need to consult guides to their local legislation and its application in clinical practice.

THE MENTAL HEALTH ACT

The Mental Health Act 1983 regulates the care of mentally abnormal persons. It consolidates the Mental Health Act 1959 and the Mental Health (Amendment) Act 1982. The latter set up the Mental Health Act Commission, which is an independent multidisciplinary body appointed by the Secretary of State. The Commission has powers to safeguard the interests of detained patients. Its duties are to visit such patients, investigate complaints, receive reports on patients' treatment, and appoint doctors and others to give opinions on consent to treatment.

Parts IV and V of the Mental Health Act provide the legal basis for compulsory admission and detention of psychiatric patients. Provision for compulsory detention is also made by the Criminal Procedure (Insanity) Act 1964, which relates to people found 'not guilty by reason of insanity' or 'unfit to plead' (see pp. 727 and 725).

Under the Mental Health Act there are three main groups of compulsory order for assessment and treatment:

(a) admission for assessment (sections 2, 4, 5, 135, 136),

(b) treatment orders (section 3, guardianship);

(c) admission and transfer of patients concerned with criminal proceedings (sections 37, 41, 47, 49).

The short-term orders listed in (a) above apply to any mental disorder, which need not be specified. For the long-term orders listed under (b) and (c), it must be stated that the patient suffers from one of four types of mental disorder: mental illness, psychopathic disorder, mental impairment, and severe mental impairment.

745

The Act does not define 'mental illness', but it states that no one should be 'treated as suffering from mental disorder by reason only of promiscuity, or other immoral conduct, sexual deviancy or dependence on alcohol or drugs'. When the Act is applied in practice the term 'mental illness' is used in the same general way as in this book.

The Act gives the following definitions of the three other types of mental disorder:

(a) **severe mental impairment** means a state of arrested or incomplete development of mind which includes severe impairment of intelligence and social functioning and is associated with abnormally aggressive or seriously irresponsible conduct on the part of the person concerned.

(b) **mental impairment** means a state of arrested or incomplete development of mind (not amounting to severe mental impairment) which includes significant impairment of intelligence and social functioning and is associated with abnormally aggressive or seriously irresponsible conduct on the part of the person concerned.

(c) **psychopathic disorder** means a persistent disorder or disability of mind (whether or not including significant impairment of intelligence) which results in abnormally aggressive conduct on the part of the person concerned.

The Act also specifies the various people who may be involved in procedures for admission and treatment:

Responsible medical officer. The doctor in charge of treatment.

Nearest relative. Nearest adult relative (in the order of spouse, son or daughter, father, mother, sibling, grandparent, grandchild, uncle or aunt, nephew or niece), excepting that preference is given to a relative who lives with or cares for the patient. The definition includes cohabitees (who may be of the same sex as the patient) who have lived with the patient for a specified time. However, they come last on the list of relatives and cannot claim precedence over a husband or wife other than through agreement, desertion, or a court order.

Approved social worker (formerly mental welfare officer). Social worker approved by the local authority as having appropriate competence in dealing with mentally disordered persons.

Approved doctor. A doctor approved under Section 12 of the Act by the Secretary of State as having special experience in the diagnosis or treatment of mental disorder.

The three main groups of compulsory order will now be reviewed in turn.

ADMISSION FOR ASSESSMENT

Whilst a full understanding of the proper use of compulsory admission can be gained only from clinical experience, the clinician needs to be aware of the following general conditions governing compulsory detention:

Section 2: Application for admission for assessment (28 days)

The usual procedure for compulsory admission when informal admission is not appropriate in the circumstances. Detention is for assessment, or for assessment followed by medical treatment. The following grounds must be satisfied:

1. The patient suffers from a mental disorder.
2. Admission is necessary in the interests of the patient's own health and safety or for the protection of others.

The procedure requires:

(i) *application* by the patient's nearest relative, *or* an approved social worker who must have seen the patient within the last 14 days.

(ii) *medical recommendation* by two doctors, one of whom must be approved under Section 12 of the Act. The two doctors should not be on the staff of the same hospital unless it would cause undesirable delay to find a doctor from elsewhere.

Section 4: Emergency order for assessment (72 hours)

This section allows a simpler procedure than Section 2 and provides power to detain patients in emergencies. It is usually completed in the patient's home by the family doctor but is also occasionally used in general hospital casualty departments. Section 4 should be used only when there is insufficient time to obtain the opinion of an approved doctor who could complete Section 2. The grounds are the same as for Section 2. It is expected that a Section 4 order will be converted into a Section 2 order as soon as possible after the patient has arrived in hospital. The procedure for a Section 4 order requires:

(i) *application* by the nearest relative *or* an approved social worker.

(ii) *medical recommendation* by one doctor, who must have examined the patient within the previous 24 hours. The doctor need not be approved under Section 12 of the Act.

Section 5: Change to compulsory detention (72 hours)

This is an order for the emergency detention of a patient who is already in hospital as a voluntary patient but wishes to leave. It requires a single *medical recommendation* by the doctor in charge of the patient's care or by another doctor who is on the staff of the hospital and nominated by the doctor in charge. (This power applies to a patient in any hospital).

If a Section 5 order cannot be obtained immediately, a registered mental nurse or registered nurse for the mentally subnormal may invoke a 6 hour **holding order.** The nurse must record that the patient is suffering from mental disorder such that, in the interests of the patient's health and safety or for the protection of others, the patient should be restrained from leaving the hospital. The holding order applies only when the patient is already under treatment for a mental disorder. It lapses as soon as the doctor signs Section 5. (This power applies only to a patient in a psychiatric ward.)

Section 136: Mentally disordered person found in a public place

Any police officer who finds in a public place someone who appears to be suffering from a mental disorder and to be in immediate need of care and control may take that person to a place of safety, which usually means a police station or a hospital. The person is detained so that he can be examined by a doctor and any necessary arrangements can be made for his treatment and care. The authority under Section 136 expires when these arrangements have been completed or within 72 hours, whichever is shorter.

Section 135: Warrant to search for and remove patients

Any approved social worker who believes that someone is suffering from a mental disorder and is unable to care for himself or is being ill-treated or neglected may apply to a magistrate for a warrant for that person's removal to a place of safety.

An approved social worker has power to inspect any premises where a mentally disordered person is living if he has reasonable cause to believe that that person is not being properly cared for; anyone who obstructs him commits an offence.

TREATMENT ORDERS

Section 3: Admission for treatment (6 months)

The grounds for this longer-term order are that the patient:

(a) is suffering from mental illness, severe mental impairment, psychopathic disorder or mental impairment, being a mental disorder of a nature or degree which makes it appropriate for him to receive medical treatment in a hospital; and
(b) in the case of psychopathic disorder or mental impairment, that such treatment is likely to alleviate or prevent a deterioration of his condition; and
(c) that it is necessary for the health and safety of the patient or for the protection of other persons that he should receive such treatment and that it cannot be provided unless he is detained under this section.

The procedure requires:
1. *Application.* Is made by the patient's nearest relative or an approved social worker. The latter must, if practicable, consult the nearest relative before making an application and cannot proceed if the nearest relative objects.
2. *Medical recommendation.* As for Section 2. In addition the recommendations must state the particular grounds for the doctor's opinion, specifying whether any other methods of dealing with the patient are available and, if so, why they are not appropriate. The doctor must specify one of the four forms of mental disorder.
3. *Renewal.* The order may be renewed on the first occasion for a further six months and subsequently for a year at a time.

Sections 7 and 8. Reception into guardianship

Guardianship is more appropriate than the provisions of Section 3 for the long-term treatment of patients living in the community. The application, medical recommendation, duration, and renewal procedure are similar to those for Section 3. The guardian who is usually but not always the local Social Services Department is given authority for supervision in the community, including power to:

(a) require the patient to live at a place specified by the guardian;
(b) require the patient to attend places specified by the guardian for medical treatment, occupation, training, or education.
(c) ensure that a doctor, social worker, or other person specified by the guardian can see the patient at his home.

ADMISSION TO HOSPITAL OF THOSE APPEARING BEFORE THE COURTS

These sections of the Mental Health Act allow the Courts to order psychiatric care for those charged with or convicted of an offence punishable by imprisonment. Medical recommendations are required together with an assurance that a hospital place is available.

Remands to hospital and interim hospital orders

Persons on remand (but not in custody) may be treated as voluntary patients. Sometimes psychiatric care may be made a condition of the granting of bail. In addition, the Mental Health (Amendment) Act 1982 gave the courts powers to:

(a) remand an accused person to a hospital for medical reports;
(b) remand an accused person to hospital for treatment (except for murder cases);
(c) make an interim hospital order on a convicted person to assess suitability for a hospital order.

Procedure (a) requires a medical recommendation by an approved doctor that there is reason to suspect mental disorder. Procedures (b) and (c) require medical recommendations by two doctors (one of whom must be approved), that the person is suffering from mental disorder.

Section 37: Hospital order

A court may impose a hospital order, which commits an offender to hospital on a similar basis to that of a patient admitted for treatment under the civil provisions of Section 3 of the Act (see above). The duration of the order is 6 months.

Medical recommendation: two doctors one of whom must be approved.

Section 41: Restriction order

When a Section 37 hospital order is made by a Crown Court, the Court may also make an order under Section 41 of the Act restricting the person's discharge from hospital. The restriction order may be either without limit of time or for a specified period. If it is for a fixed term, once that term expires or otherwise ceases to have effect, the patient will still be detained under a hospital order but without restriction, i.e. Section 37.

Section 47: transfer to hospital from prison

This section authorizes the Home Secretary to transfer a person serving a sentence of imprisonment to a local NHS hospital or special hospital. A direction for transfer has the same effect as a hospital order. The patient's status changes to that of a notional Section 37 at the time of the 'earliest date of release'.

The Home Secretary can make the direction with or without special restriction on discharge (section 49).

Medical recommendation: two doctors one of whom must be approved.

DISCHARGE OF PATIENTS

Patients on emergency orders (sections 4, 5, 135, 136) can be discharged by the responsible medical officer. Patients on a section 2 order can be discharged by the responsible medical officer, the hospital managers, the nearest relative, or a Mental Health Review Tribunal. The same applies to patients on Section 3, except that the responsible medical officer may register an objection to discharge by relatives if he considers that the patient is a danger to himself or others. Patients under guardianship are in the same position as patients on Section 3 except that the local health authority replaces the hospital managers.

The nearest relative has no rights to discharge patients on Section 37 or Section 47 orders. Patients on Section 41 and Section 49 restriction orders can be discharged only by the responsible medical officer with the consent of the Secretary of State for Home Affairs, or by a Mental Health Review Tribunal.

Mental Health Review Tribunals

These are regional tribunals that provide an appeal procedure for patients subject to longer-term orders. They hear appeals against compulsory orders and automatically review certain patients under Sections 3 and 37 (see list on next page). Review Tribunals may order immediate or delayed discharge. The members of a panel are appointed by the Lord Chancellor and include a lay member, a doctor, and a lawyer who is the chairman. When the patient is subject to a restriction order, the chairman of the panel is a judge. Patients are entitled to be provided with legal representation.

For the various sections of the Act, the timing of application for appeal is specified:

Section 4 and 5:	No appeal
Section 2:	Application must be made within 14 days.
Section 3:	Application can be made in the first six months, second six months, and then annually. Review is automatic if there has been no appeal either in the first 6 months or in any 3 year period.
Section 37 (with or without Section 41)	Application can be made in the second 6 months, then annually. Review is automatic if there has been no appeal in any 3-year period.
Guardianship	An application can be made in each period of detention. No automatic review.

CONSENT TO TREATMENT

The Mental Health (Amendment) Act 1982 introduced provisions to serve two purposes – to safeguard patients' interests in relation to treatment procedures, and to give authority for certain treatments to be given without consent. This part of the chapter is concerned with the section of the Act that deals with consent to treatment. At the time of writing, the detailed implementation of this section is still to be decided by the Mental Health Act Commission, and then to be approved by the Secretary of State for Health and Social Security.

The Act specifies certain emergency conditions under which treatment can be given without consent to a detained patient. Any treatment (provided it is not irreversible or hazardous) can be given to such a patient without his consent, if it is immediately necessary to save the patient's life, to prevent a serious deterioration in his condition, to alleviate serious suffering, or to prevent violence or danger to the patient himself or to others.

Under Common Law, with the exception of emergency conditions, no treatment can be given to a voluntary patient without his consent. Even if a voluntary patient gives his consent to certain treatments listed in the Act a second psychiatric opinion is required (see below).

The Mental Health (Amendment) Act 1982 defines various groups of treatments according to the type of consent required for them. The allocations of particular treatments to these groups are to be specified in Regulations (which are compulsory) and in a Code of Practice (which is advisory). Certain patients are excluded from the stipulations concerning consent to treatment, namely those detained under Sections 4, 5, 135, and 136, and those remanded to hospital for reports or those subject to Section 41 orders but conditionally discharged by the Home Secretary. For these patients the doctor has only 'common-law' rights and duties when giving treatment.

For other patients, three groups of treatments are stipulated, of which all three apply to detained patients, and only the first to voluntary patients.

(1) Treatments which give rise to special concern

This group applies to both voluntary and detained patients. It includes psycho-surgery and other treatments which are yet to be specified but will probably include hormone implants though not ordinary medication or ECT. For treatments included in this group the patient must consent, and there must be a second opinion. The second opinion must be provided by an independent doctor who will be required to consult two people (one a nurse, one neither a doctor nor a nurse) who have been professionally concerned with the patient's treatment. He considers both the tretment proposed and the patient's ability to give consent. In addition two independent people must certify as to the patient's ability to give consent.

Approval of treatment by the second opinion procedure may cover a plan of care including more than one form of treatment.

(2) Other treatments listed in Regulations

This group applies to detained patients. It consists of other treatments specified in the Act or in Regulations. It includes medication and ECT. For these treatments, a second opinion must be obtained as in 1 (a) above if the patient does not consent, cannot give consent, or withdraws consent. Again the second opinion may cover a plan of treatment. However, for most forms of medication these procedures will not apply during the first three months of treatment.

(3) Other forms of treatment

Treatments not referred to in 1 or 2 above can be given to detained patients without their consent. It should be noted that, according to the act, medical treatment 'includes nursing and also includes care, habilitation and rehabilitation under medical supervision'.

The Court of Protection

This court was set up for the protection and management of the property of the mentally ill or impaired. Application may be made by the nearest relative or any interested party and two medical recommendations are also required. After considering the evidence the judge may appoint a receiver to administer the patients' affairs and also to 'do or secure the doing of all such things as appears necessary or expedient'.

CHILDREN AND THE LAW

Parental consent is normally required for the medical care of children under the age of sixteen. There are some uncertainties about whether parents must always be notified when children aged 15 or 16 consult doctors. Such uncertainty arises for example over the prescribing of contraceptives. When in doubt it is sensible to seek further advice from an experienced child psychiatrist, a medical defence society, or other authority.

When parents (or guardians) are unwilling or unable to give consent to admission or treatment of their children it may be necessary to take Care Proceedings (see below). It is occasionally necessary, especially with older adolescents, to use the provisions of the Mental Health Act.

Apart from the legal provisions discussed below, a psychiatric opinion may be sought in various types of Civil proceedings, for instance adoption, wardship, divorce, and custody. According to the circumstances it is wise to obtain advice from those with knowledge and experience, such as child psychiatrists, social workers, and lawyers.

Children convicted of a criminal offence

Children below the age of 10 are not regarded as capable of criminal responsibility (see p. 726). Between the ages of 10 and 14 responsibility must be proved in court. The range of penalties can be summarized:

(1) *Absolute or conditional discharge.*

(2) *Fine and compensation.* There are maximum limits to the fines that can be imposed on a child or a young person.

(3) *Binding over parents or guardian.* If the child is found guilty of an offence the Court may order the parent or guardian (with their consent) to enter into recognisance to take proper care of him and exercise proper control.

(4) *Supervision order.* This provides for supervision by a probation officer or social worker for a specified period of 1 to 3 years. Where appropriate, psychiatric treatment may be made a condition of the order under Section 12, Children and Young Persons Act 1969. The offender must consent to this condition.

(5) *Care order* (see below).

(6) *Attendance centre order.* Regular attendance is required for a specified number of hours at a daytime centre for training and constructive occupation.

(7) *Hospital order* (Mental Health Act, 1983) (see above p. 749).

(8) *Detention Centre order.* This provides disciplined custodial training lasting three months for offenders aged 14–16 and three to six months for those aged 17–20. Remission of one month is usual for both age groups.

(9) *Borstal training* provides remedial training for young offenders (aged 15–20) who are unsuitable or too old for residential care. The emphasis is intended to be educational rather than punitive. The duration is from 6–24 months.

(10) *Imprisonment.* As specified in section 53 of the Children and Young Persons Act (1933) the court may sentence a child or young person to be detained during Her Majesty's Pleasure when found guilty of an offence which

in the case of an adult would carry a long sentence or life imprisonment. Her Majesty's Pleasure may be determinate or indeterminate length of time.

Child and Young Persons Act (1969)

This is the most significant legislation affecting the care of children (aged 0–14) and young persons (15–17). It reduces earlier distinctions between those who commit criminal offences and those who are in need of help for other reasons.

Care order

A care order commits a child or young person (up to the age of 17) to the care of the local authority social services department. The order can be made if any of the following conditions are met:

(a) his proper development is being avoidably prevented or neglected or his health is being avoidably impaired or neglected or he is being ill-treated; or
(b) it is probable that the condition set out in the preceding paragraph will be satisfied in his case, having regard to the fact that the court or another court has found that condition is or was satisfied in the case of another child or young person who is or was a member of the household in which he belongs; or
(c) he is exposed to moral danger; or
(d) he is beyond the control of his parent or guardian; or
(e) he is of compulsory school age within the meaning of the Education Act 1944 and is not receiving efficient full time education suitable to his age, ability, and aptitude; or
(f) he is guilty of an offence, excluding homicide.

Child Care Act (1980)

This act covers 'voluntary care' and specifies the duties of local authorities to care for children under the age of 17 who have no one to care for them because of death, desertion, illness, or any other reason.

HOSPITALS AND THE POLICE

The police are entitled to question any person, whether suspected or not, who they think may be able to provide useful information. The person need not say anything and cannot be compelled to go to a police station except by arrest. If the police wish to interview a psychiatric patient, it may sometimes be necessary for the doctor to give a medical opinion that the patient's mental condition is such that it would be inappropriate for him to be interviewed.

The Judges' Rules state that, as far as practicable, children and young persons under the age of 17 (whether suspected of a crime or not) should be interviewed only in the presence of a parent or guardian or, in their absence, some person who is not a police officer and who is of the same sex as the child. This recommendation applies to juveniles who are hospital patients. If the parents or guardians cannot be present, the hospital should act *in loco parentis* and an appropriate member of hospital staff of the same sex as the child should be present.

FURTHER READING

Blueglass, R.S. (1983). *A guide to the Mental Health Act 1983*. Churchill Livingstone, Edinburgh.
Martin, C.R.A. (1979). *The law relating to medical practice,* 2nd edn. Pitman, London.

References

Abraham, K. (1911). Notes on the psychoanalytic investigation and treatment of manic-depressive insanity and allied conditions. In *Selected papers on psychoanalysis,* pp. 137–56. Hogarth Press and Institute of Psychoanalysis, London (1927).

Abrahamson, L.Y., Seligman, M.E.P., and Teasdale, J. (1978). Learned helplessness in humans: critique and reformulation. *Journal of Abnormal Psychology* **87**, 49–74.

Acheson, E.D. (1959). The clinical syndrome variously called benign myalgic encephalo-myelitis, Iceland disease and epidemic neuromyasthenia. *American Journal of Medicine* **26**, 569–95.

Ackerman, N.W. (1958). *The psychodynamics of family life.* Basic Books, New York.

Achté, K.A., Hillbom, E., and Aalberg, V. (1969). Psychoses following war brain injuries. *Acta Psychiatrica Scandinavica* **45**, 1–18.

Ackner, B. (1954a). Depersonalization: I Aetiology and phenomenology. *Journal of Mental Science* **100**, 939–53.

—— (1954b). Depersonalization II. The clinical syndromes. *Journal of Mental Science* **100**, 954–72.

—— Cooper, J.E., Gray, C.H., and Kelly, M. (1962). Acute porphyria, a neuro-psychiatric and biochemical study. *Journal of Psychosomatic Research* **6**, 1–24.

—— and Oldham, A.J. (1962). Insulin treatment of schizophrenia. A three year follow up of a controlled study. *Lancet* **i**, 504–6.

Adam, K., Adamson, L., Brezinová, V., Hunter, W.M., and Oswald, I. (1976). Nitrazepam: lastingly effective but trouble on withdrawal. *British Medical Journal* **i**, 1558–60.

Adams, G.F. and Hurwitz, L.J. (1963). Mental barriers to recovery from strokes. *Lancet* **ii**, 533–7.

Adams, P.L. (1973). *Obsessive children; a sociopsychiatric study.* Butterworth, London.

Adelstein, A. and Mardon, C. (1975). Suicide 1961–1974: an analysis of trends follow-ing the Suicide Act of 1961. *Population Trends* **2**, 13–19.

—— and White, G. (1976). Alcoholism and mortality. *Population Trends* **6**, 7–13.

Ader, R. (1976). Psychosomatic research in animals. In *Modern trends in psychosomatic medicine* (ed. O.W. Hill). Butterworth, London.

Advisory Committee on Drug Dependence (1968). *Cannabis.* HMSO, London.

Advisory Group on the Management of Patients with Spongiform Encephalopathy (Creutzfeldt–Jacob Disease CJD) (1981). *Report of the Chief Medical Officers of the Department of Health and Social Security, The Scottish Home and Health Department and Health Department and the Welsh Office.* HMSO, London.

Agras, S., Sylvester, D., and Oliveau, D. (1969). The epidemiology of common fears and phobias. *Comprehensive psychiatry* **10**, 151–6.

Alanen, Y.O. (1958). The mothers of schizophrenic patients. *Acta Psychiatrica Neurologica Scandinavia* **33**, Suppl., 124.

—— (1970). The families of schizophrenic patients. *Proceedings of the Royal Society of Medicine* **63**, 227–30.

de Alarcón, R. (1969). The spread of heroin abuse in a community. *WHO Bulletin on Narcotics* **21**, 17–22.

Alexander, F. (1950). *Psychosomatic medicine.* W.W. Norton, New York.

Allderidge, P. (1979). Hospitals, madhouses and asylums: cycles in the care of the insane. *British Journal of Psychiatry* **134**, 321–4.

Allen, C. (1969). *A textbook of psychosexual disorders,* 2nd ed. Oxford University Press, London.

Alzheimer, A. (1907). Über eine eigenartige Erkrankung der Hirnrinde. *Allgemeine Zeitschrift für Psychiatrie* **64**, 146–8.

American Psychiatric Association (1980). *Diagnostic and statistical manual of mental disorders,* 3rd edn. American Psychiatric Association, Washington.

Amir, M. (1971). *Patterns in forcible rape.* Chicago University Press.

Anderson, E.W. (1933). A study of the sexual life in psychoses associated with child-bearing. *Journal of Mental Science* **79**, 137–49.

Anderson, H.R., Dick, B., MacNair, R.S., Palmer, J.C., and Ramsey, J.D. (1982). An investigation of 140 deaths associated with volatile substance abuse in the United Kingdom (1971–1981). *Human Toxicology* **1**, 207–21.

Andreason, N.J.C. and Norris, A.S. (1972). Management of emotional reactions in severely burned adults. *Journal of Nervous and Mental Disease* **154**, 352–62.

—— Olsen, S.A., Dennant, J.W., and Smith, M.R. (1982). Ventricular enlargement in schizophrenia: relationship to positive and negative symptoms. *American Journal of Psychiatry* **139**, 297–302.

Angeli, E. and Kirman, B. (1975). Genetic prognosis in severe mental handicap. *Journal of Mental Deficiency Research* **19**, 173–93.

Angst, J. (1966). *Zur Aetiologie und Nosologie endogener depressiver Psychosen.* Monographien aus dem Gesamtgebiete der Neurologie und Psychiatrie 112. Springer, Berlin.

—— Baastrup, P., Grof, P., Hippius, H., Pöldinger, W., and Weiss, P. (1973). The course of monopolar depression and bipolar psychosis. *Psychiatrica, Neurologica, Neurochirurgia* **76**, 489–500.

Anthony, E.J. (1957). An experimental approach to the psychopathology of childhood encopresis. *British Journal of Medical Psychology* **30**, 146–75.

Apley, J. and Hale, B. (1973). Children with recurrent abdominal pain: how do they grow up? *British Medical Journal* **ii**, 7–9.

Arieti, S. (1974). Individual psychotherapy for schizophrenia. In *American handbook of psychiatry* (ed. S. Arieti), Vol. III, Chapter 27. Basic Books, New York.

—— (1977). Psychotherapy of severe depression. *American Journal of Psychiatry* **134**, 864–8.

Armstrong, C.N. (1966). Treatment of wrongly assigned sex. *British Medical Journal* **ii**, 1225–6.

Armor, D.J., Polich, J.M., and Stambul, H.B. (1976). *Alcoholism and treatment.* Rand Corporation and Wiley Interscience, Santa Monica.

Arroyave, F., Cooper, S.E., and Harris, A.D. (1980). The role of detoxification in alcoholism: three years' results from the Oxford unit. *Health Trends* **12**, 36–8.

Arthur, A.Z. (1964). Theories and explanations of delusions: a review. *American Journal of Psychiatry* **121**, 105–15.

Asberg, M., Crönholm, B., Sjöqvist, F., and Tuck, D. (1971). Relationship between plasma level and therapeutic effect of nortriptyline. *British Medical Journal* **iii**, 331–4.

Asher, R. (1949). Myxoedematous madness. *British Medical Journal* **ii**, 555–62.

—— (1951). Munchausen's syndrome. *Lancet* **i**, 339–41.

Ashton, J.R. and Donnan, S. (1981). Suicide by burning as an epidemic phenomenon: an analysis of 82 deaths and inquests in England and Wales 1978–1979. *Psychological Medicine* **11**, 735–9.

Asperger, H. (1944). Die 'Autistischen Psychopathien' Kindesalter. *Archives für Psychiatrie und Nervenkrankheiten* **117**, 76–136.

Association of Sleep Disorder Centers (1979). Diagnostic classification of sleep and arousal disorders. *Sleep* 2, 1–137.

Astrup, C. and Ødegaard, Ø. (1960). Internal migration and mental disease in Norway. *Psychiatric Quarterly* 34, supp. 116.

Avni, J. (1980) The severe burns. In *Advances in psychosomatic medicine* (ed. H. Freyburger), Vol. 10, Karger, Basel.

Aylon, T. and Azrin, N.H. (1968). *The token economy: a motivational system for therapy and rehabilitation.* Appleton-Century-Crofts, New York.

Babcock, H. (1930). An experiment in the measurement of mental deterioration. *Archives of Psychology* 117, 5–105.

Bach-y-Rita, G., Lion, J.R., Climent, C.E., and Ervin, F.R. (1971). Episodic dyscontrol: a study of 130 violent patients. *American Journal of Psychiatry* 127, 1473–8.

Baddeley, A.D. (1976). *The psychology of memory.* Harper & Row, New York.

Bagley, C. (1968). The evaluation of a suicide prevention scheme by an ecological method. *Social Science and Medicine* 2, 1–14.

Bailey, V., Graham, P., and Boniface, D. (1978). How much child psychiatry does a general practitioner do? *Journal of the Royal College of General Practitioners* 28, 621–6.

Baker, R., Hall, J.N., and Hutchinson, K. (1974). A token economy project with chronic schizophrenic patients. *British Journal of Psychiatry* 124, 367–84.

Bakwin, H. (1961). Enuresis in children. *Journal of Paediatrics* 58, 806–19.

Baldwin, J.A. and Oliver, J.E. (1975). Epidemiology and family characteristics of severely abused children. *British Journal of Preventive and Social Medicine* 29, 205–21.

Bale, R.N. (1973). Brain damage in diabetes mellitus. *British Journal of Psychiatry* 122, 337–41.

Balint, M. (1957). *The doctor, his patient and the illness.* Pitman Medical, London.

—— Hunt, J., Joyce, D., Marinker, M., and Woodcock, J. (1970). *Treatment or diagnosis: a study of repeat prescriptions in general practice.* Tavistock, London.

Ball, J.R.B. and Kiloh, L.G. (1959). A controlled trial of imipramine in the treatment of depressive states. *British Medical Journal* ii, 1052–5.

Ballinger, C.B. (1977). Psychiatric morbidity and the menopause: survey of a gynaecological out-patient clinic. *British Journal of Psychiatry* 131, 83–9.

Ban, T.A. (1982). Chronic schizophrenias: a guide to Leonhard's classification. *Comprehensive Psychiatry* 23, 155–69.

Bancroft, J.H.J. (1974). *Deviant sexual behaviour: modification and assessment.* Oxford University Press.

—— (1975). Homosexuality in the male. In *Contemporary psychiatry* (ed. T. Silverstone and B. Barraclough). *British Journal of Psychiatry* Special Publication No. 9.

—— (1979). Crisis intervention. In *Introduction to the psychotherapies* (ed. S. Bloch). Oxford University Press.

—— and Coles, L. (1976). Three years experience in a sexual problems clinic. *British Medical Journal* i, 1575–7.

—— Hawton, K., Simkin, S., Kingston, B., Cumming, C., and Whitwell, D. (1979). The reasons people give for taking overdoses: a further inquiry. *British Journal of Medical Psychology* 52, 353–65.

—— and Marks, M. (1968). Electric aversion therapy for sexual deviations. *Proceedings of the Royal Society of Medicine* 61, 796–9.

—— Skrimshire, A.M., Casson, J., Harvard-Watts, O., and Reynolds, F. (1977). People who deliberately poison or injure themselves: their problems and their contacts with helping agencies. *Psychological Medicine* 7, 289–303.

—— Reynolds, F., Simkin, S., and Smith, J. (1975). Self-poisoning and self-injury in the Oxford area. *British Journal of Preventive and Social Medicine* 29, 170–7.

—— Tyrer, G., and Warner, P. (1982). The classification of sexual problems in women. *British Journal of Sexual Medicine* 9, 30–7.

Bandura, A. (1962). Social learning through imitation. In *Nebraska symposium on motivation* (ed. M.R. Jones). University of Nebraska Press, Lincoln.

—— (1969). *Principles of behaviour modification.* Holt, Rinehart and Winston, New York.

—— (1971). Psychotherapy based on modelling principles. In *Handbook of psychotherapy and behaviour change* (ed. A.E. Bergin and S. Garfield). Wiley, New York.

Bannister, D. (1960). Conceptual structure in thought disordered schizophrenics. *Journal of Mental science* 106, 1236–49.

—— (1962). The nature and measurement of schizophrenic thought disorder. *Journal of Mental Science* 108, 825–42.

—— and Fransella, F. (1966). A grid test of schizophrenic thought disorder. *British Journal of Social and Clinical Psychology* 5, 95–102.

Barber, T.X. (1962). Towards a theory of hypnosis: posthypnotic behaviour. *Archives of General Psychiatry* 1, 321–42.

Barcha, R., Stewart, M.A., and Guze, S.B. (1968). The prevalence of alcoholism among general hospital ward patients. *American Journal of Psychiatry* 125, 681–4.

Barette, J. and Marsden, C.D. (1979). Attitudes of families to some aspects of Huntington's chorea. *Psychological Medicine* 9, 327–36.

Barker, J.C. (1962). The hospital addiction syndrome (Munchausen syndrome). *Journal of Mental Science* 108, 167–82.

—— and Barker, A.A. (1959). Deaths associated with electroplexy. *Journal of Mental Science* 105, 339–48.

Barker, M.G. (1968). Psychiatric illness after hysterectomy. *British Medical Journal* ii, 91–95.

Barker, P. (1971). *Basic child psychiatry.* Staples Press, London.

Barkley, R.A. (1977). A review of stimulant drug research with hyperactive children. *Journal of Child Psychology and Psychiatry* 128, 127–65.

Barnes, J. (1967). Rape and other sexual offences. *British Medical Journal* i, 293–4.

Barraclough, B.M. (1973). Differences between national suicide rates. *British Journal of Psychiatry* 122, 95–6.

—— (1981). Suicide and epilepsy. In *Epilepsy and psychiatry* (ed. E.H. Reynolds and M.R. Trimble). Churchill Livingstone, Edinburgh.

—— Bunch, J., Nelson, B., and Sainsbury, P. (1974). A hundred cases of suicide: clinical aspects. *British Journal of Psychiatry* 125, 355–73.

—— and Mitchell-Heggs, N.A. (1978). Use of neurosurgery for psychological disorder in the British Isles during 1974–6. *British Medical Journal* ii, 1591–3.

—— and Shea, M. (1970). Suicide and Samaritan Clients. *Lancet* ii, 868–70.

—— and Shepherd, D.M. (1976). Public interest: private grief. *British Journal of Psychiatry* 129, 109–13.

Barsky, A.J. and Klerman, G.L. (1983). Overview: hypochondriasis, bodily complaints and somatic styles. *American Journal of Psychiatry* 140, 273–83.

Bartlett, J., Bridges, P., and Kelly, D. (1981). Contemporary indications for psychosurgery. *British Journal of Psychiatry* 138, 507–11.

Barton, R. (1966). *Institutional neurosis,* 2nd edn. John Wright, Bristol.

Baruk, H. (1959). Delusions of passion. Reprinted in *Themes and variations in European psychiatry* (ed. S.R. Hirsch and M. Shepherd) pp. 375–84. Wright, Bristol. (1974).

Bateson, G., Jackson, D., Haley, J., and Weakland, J. (1956). Towards a theory of schizophrenia. *Behavioral Science* 1, 251–64.

Bax, M. and MacKeith, R. (1963). *Minimal cerebral dysfunction.* Spastics International Medical Publications and Heinemann, London.

Beaubrun, M.H. and Knight, F. (1973). Psychiatric assessment of 30 chronic users of cannabis and 30 matched controls. *American Journal of Psychiatry* 130, 309–11.

Beck, A.T. (1967). *Depression: clinical experimental and theoretical aspects.* Harper & Row, New York.

—— (1976). *Cognitive therapy and the emotional disorders.* International Universities Press, New York.

—— Rush, A.J., Shaw, B.F., and Emery, G. (1979). *Cognitive therapy of depression.* Guildford Press, New York.

—— Schuyler, D., and Herman, I. (1974). Development of suicide intent scales. In *The prediction of suicide* (ed. A.T. Beck, H.L.P. Resaik, and D.J. Lettie). Charles Press, Maryland.

Beck, E., Daniel, P.M., Mathews, W.D., Stevens, D.L., Alpers, M.P., Asher, D.M., Gajdusek, D.C., and Gibbs, C.J. (1969). Creutzfeld–Jakob disease: the neuropathology of a transmission experiment. *Brain* **92**, 699–716.

Beech, H.R., Watts, F., and Poole, A.D. (1971). Classical conditioning of a sexual deviation: a preliminary note. *Behaviour Therapy* **2**, 400–2.

Beecher, H.K. (1956). Relationship of significance of wound to the pain experienced. *Journal of the American Medical Association* **161**, 1609–13.

Bender, L., and Grugett, A.A. (1952). A follow up report on children who had atypical sexual experiences. *American Journal of Orthopsychiatry* **22**, 825–37.

Benedetti, G. (1952). *Die Alkoholhalluzinosen.* Thieme, Stuttgart.

Benaim, S., Horder, J., and Anderson, J. (1973). Hysterical episode in a classroom. *Psychological Medicine* **3**, 366–73.

Benjamin, H. (1966). *The transsexual phenomenon.* Julian Press, New York.

Bennie, E.H. (1975). Lithium in depression. *Lancet* **i**, 216.

Berg, I. (1981). Child psychiatry and enuresis. *British Journal of Psychiatry* **139**, 247–8.

—— (1982). When truants and school refusers grow up. *British Journal of Psychiatry* **141**, 208–10.

Berg, J.M. (1965). Aetiological aspects of mental subnormality: pathological factors. In *Mental deficiency: the changing outlook,* 2nd ed. (ed. A.D.B.Clarke and A.M. Clarke) Methuen, London.

Bergin, A.E. and Lambert, M.J. (1978). The evaluation of therapeutic outcomes. In *Handbook of psychotherapy and behaviour change,* 2nd edn. (ed. S.L. Garfield and A.E. Bergin). John Wiley, New York.

Bergman, H., Borg, S., Hindmarsh, T., Idestrom, C.-M., and Mutzell, S. (1980). Computed tomography of the brain and neuropsychological assessment of male alcoholic patients. In *Addiction and brain damage* (ed. D. Richter) pp. 201–14. Croom Helm, London.

Bergmann, K. and Eastham, E. (1974). Psychogeriatric ascertainment and assessment for treatment in an acute medical ward setting. *Age and Ageing* **3**, 174–88.

—— Foster, E.M., Justice, A.W., and Matthews, V. (1978). Management of the demented patient in the community. *British Journal of Psychiatry* **132**, 441–9.

Berne, E. (1966). *Games people play.* André Deutsch, London.

Bernstein, D.A. and Borkovec, T.D. (1973). *Progressive relaxation training: a manual for the helping professions.* Research Press, Champaign, Illinois.

Berrios, G.E. (1981). Stupor: a conceptual history. *Psychological Medicine* **11**, 677–88.

—— (1981). Delirium and confusion in the 19th century. *British Journal of Psychiatry* **139**, 439–49.

Bertelsen, A., Harvald, B., and Hauge, M., (1977). A Danish twin study of manic depressive disorders. *British Journal of Psychiatry* **130**, 330–51.

Beskow, J., Gottfries, C.G., Roos, B.-E., and Winblad, B. (1976). Determination of monoamines and monoamine metabolites in human brain: post mortem studies in a group of suicides and a control group. *Acta Psychiatrica Scandinavica* **53**, 7–20.

Beswick, K., Lynch, M.A., and Roberts, J. (1976). Child abuse and general practice. *British Medical Journal* **ii**, 800–2.

Betts, T.A. (1981). Depression, anxiety and epilepsy. In *Epilepsy and psychiatry* (ed. E.H. Reynolds and M.R. Trimble) pp. 60–71. Churchill Livingstone, London.

―― Clayton, A.B., and Mackay, G.M. (1972). Effects of four commonly-used tranquillizers on low-speed driving performance tests. *British Medical Journal* iv, 580–4.

Beumont, P.J.V., Abraham, S.F., Argall, W.J., George, G.C.W., and Glaun, D.E. (1979). The onset of anorexia nervosa. *Australian and New Zealand Journal of Psychiatry* 12, 145–9.

―― ―― and Simson, J.G. (1981). The psychosexual histories of adolescent girls and young women with anorexia nervosa. *Psychological Medicine* 11, 131–40.

―― George G.C.W., and Smart, D.E. (1976). 'Dieters' and 'vomiters and purgers' in anorexia nervosa. *Psychological Medicine* 6, 617–22.

―― and Russell, J. (1982). Anorexia nervosa. In *Handbook of psychiatry and endocrinology* (ed. P.J.V. Beumont and G. Burrows). Elsevier Biomedical Press, Amsterdam.

Bianchi, G.N. (1971). Patterns of hypochondriasis: a principal components analysis. *British Journal of Psychiatry* 122, 541–8.

Bibring, E. (1953). The mechanism of depression. In *Affective disorders* (ed. P. Greenacre) pp. 14–47. International Universities Press, New York.

Bicknell, J. (1982). Living with a mentally handicapped member of the family. *Postgraduate Medical Journal* 58, 597–605.

Bicknell, J. (1975). *Pica: a childhood symptom.* Institute for Research into Mental and Multiple Handicap. Monograph 3. Butterworth, London.

Bieber, I. (1962). *Homosexuality: a psychoanalytic study of male homosexuals.* Basic Books, New York.

Bille, M. and Juel-Nielsen, N. (1968). Incidence of neurosis in psychiatric and other medical services in a Danish county. *Danish Medical Bulletin* 10, 172–6.

Billings, E.G. (1936). Teaching psychiatry in the medical school general hospital. *Journal of the American Medical Association* 107, 635–9.

Bilodeau, C.B. and O'Connor, S.O. (1978). Role of nurse clinicians in liaison psychiatry. In *Handbook of general hospital psychiatry* (ed. T.P. Hackett and N.H. Cassem). Mosby, St. Louis.

Binet, A. (1877). Le fetishisme dans l'amour. *Revue Philosophique* 24, 143.

―― and Simon, T. (1905). Methodes nouvelles pour le diagnostic du niveau intellectuel des normaux. *L'Année Psychologique* 11, 193–244.

Binswanger, O. (1894). *Münchener Medizinische Wochenschrift* 52, 252. 252.

Bion, W.R. (1961). *Experiences in groups.* Tavistock Publications, London.

Birch, H.G., Richardson, S.Á., Baird, D., Horobin, G., and Illsley, R. (1970). *Mental subnormality in the community.* Williams & Wilkins, Baltimore.

Bird, E. (1978). The brain in Huntington's chorea. *Psychological Medicine* 8, 357–60.

Birnbaum, K. (1908). *Psychosen mit Wahnbildung und wahnhafte Einbildungen bei Degenerativen.* Marhold, Halle.

Birren, J.E. and Sloane, R.B. (1980). *Handbook of mental health and ageing.* Prentice Hall, Englewood Cliffs.

Birtchnell, J. (1970a). Early parent death and mental illness. *British Journal of Psychiatry* 116, 281–8.

―― (1970b). The relationship between attempted suicide, depression and parent death. *British Journal of Psychiatry* 116, 307–13.

Bixler, E.O., Kales, A., Soldates, C.R., Kales, J.D., and Healey, J. (1979). Prevalence of sleep disorder in the Los Angeles metropolitan area. *American Journal of Psychiatry* 136, 1257–62.

Blackburn, I.M., Bishop, S., Glen, A.I.M., Whalley, L.J., and Christie, J.E. (1981). The efficacy of cognitive therapy on depression: a treatment trial using cognitive therapy and pharmacotherapy, each alone and in combination. *British Journal of Psychiatry* **139**, 181–9.

Blacker, K.H., Jones, R.T., Stone, G.C., and Pfefferbaum, D. (1968). Chronic users of LSD: the 'acid heads'. *American Journal of Psychiatry* **125**, 341–8.

Blackwell, B. (1968). The Munchausen syndrome. *British Journal of Hospital Medicine* **1**, 98–102.

Blanchard, E.B., Ahles, T.A., and Shaw, E.R. (1979). Behavioural treatment of headaches. *Progress in Behaviour Modification* **8**, 207–48.

—— and Miller, S.T. (1977). Psychological treatment of cardiovascular disease. *Archives of General Psychiatry* **34**, 1402–13.

Bleuler, E. (1906). *Affektivität, Suggestibilität, und Paranoia.* Marhold, Halle.

—— (1911). (English edition 1950). *Dementia praecox or the group of schizophrenias.* International University Press, New York.

—— (1924). *Textbook of psychiatry* (translated by A.A. Brill). Macmillan, New York.

Bleuler, M. (1951). Psychiatry of cerebral disease. *British Medical Journal* **ii**, 1233–8.

—— (1972). (English edition 1978). *The schizophrenic disorders: long term patient and family studies.* Yale Universities Press, New Haven.

—— (1974). The long term course of the schizophrenic psychoses. *Psychological medicine* **4**, 244–54.

Bliss, E.L., Clark, L.D., and West, C.D. (1959). Studies of sleep deprivation: relationship to schizophrenia. *Archives of Neurology and Psychiatry* **81**, 348–59.

Bloch, S. (1979a). Supportive psychotherapy. In *An introduction to the psychotherapies* (ed. S. Bloch). Oxford University Press.

—— (1979b). Assessment of patients for psychotherapy. *British Journal of Psychiatry* **135**, 193–208.

—— and Chodoff, P. (1981). *Psychiatric ethics.* Oxford University Press.

—— Crouch, E., and Rebstein, J. (1981). Therapeutic factors in group psychotherapy: a review. *Archives of General Psychiatry* **38**, 519–26.

Blueglass, R. (1979a). The psychiatric assessment of homicide. *British Journal of Hospital Medicine* **22**, 366–77.

—— (1979b). Incest. *British Journal of Hospital Medicine* **22**, 152–6.

—— (1978). Regional secure units and interim security for psychiatric patients. *British Medical Journal* **i**, 489–93.

Blumenthal, E.J. (1955). Spontaneous seizures and related electroencephalographic findings following shock therapy. *Journal of Nervous Mental Disease* **122**, 581–8.

Blumer, D. and Benson, D.F. (1975). Personality changes with frontal and temporal lobe lesions. In *Psychiatric aspects of neurological disease* (ed. D. Benson and D. Blumer). Grune and Stratton, New York.

—— and Heilbronn, M. (1982). Chronic pain as a variant of depressive disease. The pain prone disorder. *Journal of Nervous and Mental Disease* **170**, 381–406.

Blurton-Jones, N.G. (1972). Non-verbal communication in children. In *Non verbal communication* (ed. R.A. Hinde). Cambridge University Press.

Boakes, A.J., Laurence, D.R., Teoh, P.C., Barar, F.S.K., Benedikter, L.T., and Prichard, B.N.C. (1973). Interactions between sympathomimetic amines and antidepressant agents in man. *British Medical Journal* **i**, 311–15.

Bohman, M. (1978). Some genetic aspects of alcoholism and criminality. *Archives of General Psychiatry* **35**, 269–76.

—— Sigvardsson, S., and Cloninger, C.R. (1981). Maternal inheritance of alcohol abuse: cross fostering analysis of adopted women. *Archives of General Psychiatry* **38**, 965–9.

Böker, W. and Häfner, H. (1977). Crimes of violence by mentally disordered offenders in Germany. *Psychological Medicine* **7**, 733–6.

Bond, A.J. and Lader, M.H. (1973). Residual effects of flurazepam. *Psychopharmacologia* **32**, 223–35.

Bond, M.R. (1975). Assessment of the psychological outcome after severe head injury. In *Outcome of severe damage to the C.N.S.* Symposium 34. Ciba Foundation, London.

Bondareff, W. (1980). Neurobiology of ageing. In *Handbook of mental health and ageing* (ed. J.E. Birren and R.B. Sloane). Prentice Hall, Englewood Cliffs.

Bonhoeffer, K. (1909). Exogenous psychoses. *Zentralblatt für Nervenheilkunde* **32**, 499–505. Translated by H. Marshall in *Themes and variations in European psychiatry* (ed. S.R. Hirsch and M. Shepherd). Wright, Bristol (1974).

Bonn, J., Turner, P., and Hicks, D.C. (1972). Beta-adrenergic receptor blockade with practolol in the treatment of anxiety. *Lancet* **i**, 814–15.

Bonn, J.A., Harrison, J., and Rees, W.L. (1971). Lactate-induced anxiety: therapeutic implications. *British Journal of Psychiatry* **119**, 468–71.

Böök, J.A. (1953). A genetic and neuropsychiatric investigation of a North-Swedish population with special regard to schizophrenia and mental deficiencies. *Acta Genetica et Statistica Medica* **4**, 1–100.

Boor, J.W. and Hurtig, W.I. (1977). Persistent cerebellar ataxia after exposure to toluene. *Annals of Neurology* **2**, 440–42.

Boulagouris, J.C. (1977). Variables affecting the behaviour of obsessive–compulsive patients treated by flooding. In *Studies in phobic and obsessive compulsive disorders* (ed. J.C. Boulagouris and A. Rabavilas). Pergamon Press, Oxford.

Bowden, P. (1978). Rape. *British Journal of Hospital Medicine* **20**, 286–90.

Bower, W.H. and Altschule, M.D. (1956). Use of progesterone in the treatment of postpartum psychosis. *New England Journal of Medicine* **254**, 157–60.

Bowlby, J. (1944). Forty-four juvenile thieves. Their characters and home life. *International Journal of Psychoanalysis* **25**, 19–53.

—— (1951). *Maternal care and maternal health.* World Health Organization, Geneva.

—— (1969). Psychopathology of anxiety: the role of affectional bonds. In *Studies in anxiety* (ed. M.H. Lader). *British Journal of Psychiatry* Special Publication No. 3, London.

—— (1973). *Attachment and loss,* Vol. 2. *Separation, anxiety and anger.* Hogarth Press, London.

—— (1980). *Attachment and loss,* Vol. 3. *Loss, sadness and depression.* Basic Books, New York.

Boyd, J.H. and Weissman, M.M. (1982). Epidemiology. In *Handbook of affective disorders* (ed. E.S. Paykel). Churchill Livingstone, Edinburgh.

Boyd, M.M. (1960). The depth of sleep in enuretic school children and non-enuretic controls. *Journal of Psychosomatic Research* **4**, 274–81.

Braid, J. (1843). *Neurypnology: or the rationale of nervous sleep, considered in relation with animal magnetism.* Churchill, London.

Brain, W.R. (1977). *Diseases of the nervous system,* 8th edn (revised by J.N. Walton). Oxford University Press.

Braun, P., Kuchansky, G., Shapiro, R., Greenberg, S., Gudeman, J.E., Johnson, S., and Shore, M.F. (1981). Overview; reinstitutionalization of psychiatric patients, a critical review of outcome studies. *American Journal of Psychiatry* **138**, 736–49.

Breuer, J. and Freud, S. (1893–5). *Studies on hysteria.* The Standard edition of the complete psychological works. Vol. 2 (1955). Hogarth Press, London.

Brenner, B. (1959). Estimating the prevalence of alcoholism: towards a modification of the Jellinek formula. *Quarterly Journal on Studies of Alcoholism* **20**, 255–69.

Brewer, C. (1977). Incidence of post abortion psychosis: a prospective study. *British Medical Journal* **i**, 476–7.

—— and Perrett, L. (1971). Brain damage due to alcohol consumption: an air-encephalographic, psychometric, and electro-encephalographic study. *British Journal of Addiction* **66**, 170–82.

Breslau, W., Starich, K.S., and Mortimer, E.A. (1982). Psychiatric disorders in the mothers of disabled children. *American Journal of Diseases of Childhood* **136**, 682–6.

Brierley, J.B. (1966). The neuropathology of amnesic states. In: *Amnesia* (ed. C.W.M. Whitty and O.L. Zangwill). Butterworth, London.

Brimblecombe, F.S.W. (1979). A new approach to the care of handicapped children. *Journal of the Royal College of Physicians London* **13**, 231–6.

Brill, N.Q., Crumpton, E., Edisuon, S., Grayson, H.M., Hellman, L.I., and Richards, R.A. (1959). Relative effectiveness of various components of electroconvulsive therapy. *Archives of Neurology and Psychiatry* **81**, 627–35.

Briquet, P. (1859). *Traité clinique et thérapeutique de l'hysterie*. Baillière, Paris.

British National Formulary (1981). British Medical Association and the Pharmaceutical Society of Great Britain.

British Medical Journal (1964). Suicide among doctors. (Editorial.) *British Medical Journal* **i**, 789–90.

—— (1980*a*). The use of antidepressants in schizophrenia. (Editorial.) *British Medical Journal* **i**, 1037–8.

—— (1980*b*). Phencyclidine: the new American street drug. (Editorial.) *British Medical Journal* **281**, 1511–12.

—— (1976). Glutethamide – an unsafe alternative to barbiturate hypnotics. (Editorial.) *British Medical Journal* **ii**, 1426–7.

Brittain, R.P. (1970). The sadistic murderer. *Medicine, Science and the Law* **10**, 198–207.

Broadbent, D.E. (1981). Chronic effects from the physical nature of work. In *Working life: a social science contribution to work reform* (ed. B. Gardell and G. Johansson). Wiley, London.

—— and Gath, D.H. (1979). Chronic effects of repetitive and non-repetitive work. In *Response to stress: occupational aspects* (ed. C.G. McKay and T.R. Cox). Independent Publishing Company, London.

Broadwin, I.T. (1932). A contribution to the study of truancy. *American Journal of Orthopsychiatry* **2**, 253–9.

Brockington, I.F., Kendell, R.E., Kellett, J.M., Curry, S.H., and Wainwright, S. (1978). Trials of lithium, chlorpromazine and amitriptyline on schizoaffective patients. *British Journal of Psychiatry* **133**, 162–8.

—— and Leff, J.P. (1978). Definitions of schizophrenia: concordance and prediction of outcome. *Psychological Medicine* **8**, 387–98.

—— and Kumar, R. (eds.) (1980). *Motherhood and mental illness*. Academic Press, New York.

—— and Leff, J.P. (1979). Schizo-affective psychosis: definitions and incidence. *Psychological Medicine* **9**, 91–9.

—— Schofield, E.M., Donnelly, P., and Hyde, C. (1978). A clinical study of puerperal psychosis. In *Mental illness in pregnancy and the puerperium* (ed. M. Sandler). Oxford University Press, New York.

Brody, D.S. (1980). Physician recognition of behavioural, psychological, and social aspects of medical care. *Archives of Internal Medicine* **140**, 1286–9.

Brown, D. and Pedder, J. (1979). *Introduction to psychotherapy: an outline of psychodynamic principles and practice*. Tavistock, London.

Brown, F.W. (1942). Heredity in the psychoneuroses. *Proceedings of the Royal Society of Medicine* **35**, 785–90.

Brown, G.M. (1976). Endocrine aspects of psychosocial deviation. In *Hormones, behaviour and psychopathology* (ed. E.J. Sachar). Raven, New York.

Brown, G.W., (1979). Life events, psychiatric disorder and physical illness. *Journal Psychosomatic Research* **23**, 461–73.

—— and Birley, J.L.T. (1968). Crisis and life changes at the onset of schizophrenia. *Journal of Health and Social Behaviour* **9**, 203–24.

—— Bone, M., Dalison, B., and Wing, J.K. (1966). *Schizophrenia and social care*. Maudsley Monograph 17. Oxford University Press, London.

—— Carstairs, G.M., and Topping, G.G. (1958). *Lancet* **ii**, 685–9.

—— and Harris, T.O. (1978). *Social origins of depression*. Tavistock, London.

—— —— and Peto, J. (1973). Life events and psychiatric disorders: the nature of the causal link. *Psychological Medicine* **3**, 159–76.

—— Monck, E.M., Carstairs, G.M., and Wing, J.K. (1962). Influence of family life on the cause of schizophrenic illness. *British Journal of Preventive and Social Medicine* **16**, 55–68.

—— and Prudo, R. (1981). Psychiatric disorder in a rural and urban population. 1. Aetiology of depression. *Psychological Medicine* **11**, 581–99.

—— Sklair, F., Harris, T.O., and Birley, J.L.T. (1973). Life events and psychiatric disorder: some methodological issues. *Psychological Medicine* **3**, 74–87.

Brown, J.A.C. (1961). *Freud and the post Freudians*. Penguin, Harmondsworth.

Brown, S.W. and Reynolds, E.M. (1981). Cognitive impairment in epileptic patients. In *Epilepsy and psychiatry* (ed. E.H. Reynolds and R. Trimble). Churchill Livingstone, Edinburgh.

Bruch, H. (1974). *Eating disorders: anorexia nervosa and the person within*. Routledge and Kegan Paul, London.

Brudny, J., Korein, J., Levidow, A., and Friedman, L.W. (1974). Sensory feedback therapy as a modality of treatment in central nervous system disorders of voluntary movement. *Neurology* **24**, 925–32.

Brunt, P.W., Kew, M.C.,Scheuer, P.J., and Sherlock, S. (1974). Studies in alcoholic liver disease in Britain. *Gut* **15**, 52–8.

Bryant, B., Trower, P., Yardley, K., Urbieta, H., and Letemendia, F.J.J. (1976). A survey of social inadequacy among psychiatric outpatients. *Psychological Medicine* **6**, 101–12.

Buglass, D., Clarke, J., Henderson, A.S., Kreitman, N., and Presley, A.S. (1977). A study of agoraphobic housewives. *Psychological Medicine* **7**, 73–86.

—— and Duffy, J.C. (1978). The ecological pattern of suicide and parasuicide in Edinburgh. *Social Science and Medicine* **12**, 241–53.

—— and Horton, J. (1974). The repetition of parasuicide: a comparison of three cohorts. *British Journal of Psychiatry* **125**, 168–74.

Burks, J.S., Alfrey, A.C., Huddlestone, J., Norenburg, M.D., and Lewin, E. (1976). A fatal encephalopathy in chronic haemodialysis patients. *Lancet* **i**, 764–8.

Burnham, W.R., Leonard-Jones, J.E., and Brooke, B.N. (1977). Sexual problems among married ileostomists. *Gut* **18**, 673–7.

Burns, B.H. and Howell, J.B. (1969). Disproportionately severe breathlessness in chronic bronchitis. *Quarterly Journal of Medicine* **38**, 277–94.

Burrow, T. (1927). The group method of analysis. *Psychoanalytic Review* **14**, 268–80.

Bynum, W.F. (1983). Psychiatry in its historical context. In: *Handbook of psychiatry* Vol. I (ed. M. Shepherd and O.L. Zangwill). Cambridge University Press.

Cadoret, R.J. (1978). Evidence of genetic inheritance of primary affective disorder in adoptees. *American Journal of Psychiatry* **135**, 463–6.

—— (1978). Psychopathology in adopted-away offspring of biologic parents with antisocial behaviour. *Archives of General Psychiatry* **35**, 176–84.

—— Cunningham, L., Loftus, R., and Edwards, J. (1975). Studies of adoptees from psychiatrically disturbed biologic parents – II temperament, hyperactive, antisocial and developmental variables. *Journal of Pediatrics* **87**, 301–6.

—— and Gath, A. (1978). Inheritance of alcoholism in adoptees. *British Journal of Psychiatry* **132**, 252–8.

Caffey, J. (1946). Multiple fractures in long bones of children suffering from chronic subdural haematomata. *American Journal of Radiology* **56**, 163–73.

Caine, E.D. (1981). Pseudodementia. *Archives of General Psychiatry* **38**, 1359–64.

Cala, L.A., Jones, B., Masatglia, F.L., and Wiley, B. (1978). Brain atrophy and intellectual impairment in heavy drinkers – a clinical, psychosomatic and computerised tomography study. *Australian and New Zealand Medical Journal* **8**, 147–53.

Caldwell, T. and Weiner, M.F. (1981). Stresses and coping in ICU nursing: a review. *General Hospital Psychiatry* **3**, 119–27.

Calne, D.B., Karoum, F., Ruthven, C.R.J., and Sandler, M. (1969). The metabolism of orally administered L-dopa in Parkinsonism. *British Journal of Pharmacology* **37**, 57–68.

Cameron, N. (1938). Reasoning, regression and communication in schizophrenia. *Psychological Monographs* **50**, 1–34.

Campbell, A.M.G., Thomson, J.L.G., Evans, M., and Williams, M.J. (1971). Cerebral atrophy in young cannabis smokers. *Lancet* **ii**, 1219–24.

Cantwell, D.P. (1977). Hyperkinetic syndrome. In *Child psychiatry: modern approaches* (ed. M.L. Rutter and L. Hersov). Blackwell, Oxford.

—— (1980). Developmental arithmetic disorder. In *Comprehensive textbook of psychiatry,* 3rd edn (ed. H.I. Kaplan, A.M. Freedman, and B.J. Sadock). Williams and Wilkins, Baltimore.

—— and Baker, L. (1980). Coordination disorder. In *Comprehensive textbook of psychiatry,* 3rd edn (ed. H.I. Kaplan, A.M. Freedman, and B.J. Sadock). Williams and Wilkins, Baltimore.

Capgras, J. and Reboul-Lachaux, J. (1923). L'Illusion des sosies dans un délire systématisé chronique. *Bulletin de la Société Clinique de Médicine Mentale* **11**, 6–16.

Caplan, G. (1961). *An approach to community mental health.* Tavistock, London.

Caplan, H.L. (1970). Hysterical conversion symptoms in childhood. M.Phil. Dissertation, University of London. (See the account in *Child psychiatry: modern approaches* (ed. M.L. Rutter and L. Hersov). Blackwell, Oxford (1977).)

Capstick, A. (1960). Recognition of emotional disturbance and the prevention of suicide. *British Medical Journal* **i**, 1179–82.

Capstick, N. (1975). Clomipramine in the treatment of the true obsessional state: a report on four patients. *Psychosomatics* **16**, 21–5.

Carey, G., Gottesman, I.I., and Robins, E. (1980). Prevalence rates among neuroses, pitfalls in the evaluation of familiarity. *Psychological Medicine* **10**, 437–43.

Carlson, G.A. and Goodwin, F.K. (1973). The stages of mania: a longitudinal analysis of the manic episode. *Archives of General Psychiatry* **28**, 221–8.

Carlsson, A. and Lindquist, M. (1963). Effect of chlorpromazine and haloperidol on formation of methoxytyramine and normetanephrine in mouse brain. *Acta Pharmacologia et Toxicologia* **20**, 140–4.

Carney, M.W.P., Roth, M., and Garside, R.F. (1965). The diagnosis of depressive syndromes and the prediction of ECT response. *British Journal of Psychiatry* **111**, 659–74.

Carpenter, W.T. and Stephens, J.H. (1979). An attempted integration of information relevant to schizophrenic subtypes. *Schizophrenia Bulletin* **5**, 490–506.

—— Strauss, J.S., and Muleh, S. (1973). Are there pathognomonic symptoms of schizophrenia? An empiric investigation of Schneider's first rank symptoms. *Archives of General Psychiatry* **28**, 847–52.

Carr, S.A. (1980). Interhemispheric transfer of stereognostic information in chronic schizophrenia. *British Journal of Psychiatry* **136**, 53–8.

Carstairs, G.M., O'Connor, N., and Rawnsley, K. (1956). Organisation of a hospital workshop for chronic psychiatric patients. *British Journal of Preventive and Social Medicine* **10**, 136–40.

Carter, C.O. and Evans, K. (1979). Counselling and Huntington's chorea. *Lancet* ii, 470–1.

Cartwright, A. (1964). *Human relations and hospital care.* Routledge and Kegan Paul, London.

Cassem, N.H. and Stewart, R.S. (1978). Management of the dying patient. In *Psychosomatic medicine* (ed. Z.J. Lipowski, D.R. Lipsitt, and P.C. Whybrow). Oxford University Press, New York.

Castelnuovo-Tedesco, P., Weinberg, J., Buchanan, C.D., and Scott, H.W. (1982). Long term outcome of jejuno-ileal bypass surgery for super-obesity: a psychiatric assessment. *American Journal of Psychiatry* **139**, 1248–52.

Cautela, J.R. (1967). Covert sensitization. *Psychological Reports* **74**, 459–68.

Central Health Services Council (1968). *Hospital treatment of acute poisoning.* HMSO, London.

Cerletti, U. and Bini, L. (1938). Un nuovo metodo di shokterapia; 'l'elettroshock'. *Bulletin Accademia Medica di Roma* **64**, 136–8.

Chamberlain, A.S. (1966). Early mental hospitals in Spain. *American Journal of Psychiatry* **123**, 143–9.

Chapple, P.A.L., Somekh, D.E., and Taylor, M.E. (1972). Follow-up cases of opiate addiction from the time of notification to the Home Office. *British Medical Journal* ii, 680–3.

Chaudhury, N.A. and Truelove, S.C. (1962). The irritable colon syndrome: a study of the clinical features, predisposing causes and progress in 130 cases. *Quarterly Journal of Medicine* **31**, 307–22.

Chowdhury, N., Hicks, R.C., and Kreitman, N. (1973). Evaluation of an after-care service for parasuicide ('attempted suicide') patients. *Social Psychiatry* **8**, 67–81.

Christodoulou, G.N. (1976). Delusional hyper-identifications of the Frégoli type. *Acta Psychiatrica Scandinavica* **54**, 305–14.

—— (1977). The syndrome of Capgras. *British Journal of Psychiatry* **130**, 556–64.

Ciompi, L. (1980). The natural history of schizophrenia in the long term. *British Journal of Psychiatry* **136**, 413–20.

Clancy, J., Noyes, R., Noenk, P.R., and Slymen, D.J. (1978). Secondary depression in anxiety neurosis. *Journal of Nervous and Mental Disease* **166**, 846–50.

Clare, A. (1980). Controversial issues in thought and practice. In: *Psychiatry in dissent* 2nd ed. Tavistock, London.

Clare, A.W. (1978). The treatment of premenstrual symptoms. *British Journal of Psychiatry* **135**, 576–9.

—— (1982). Psychiatric aspects of premenstrual complaint. *Journal of Psychosomatic Obstetrics and Gynaecology* **1**, 22–31.

Clark, W.B. (1976). Loss of control, heavy drinking, and drinking problems in a longitudinal study. *Journal of Studies on Alcoholism* **37**, 1256–90.

Clarke, A.M. and Clarke, A.D.B. (1978). *Readings from mental deficiency.* Methuen, London.

Clarke, D.M. and Teasdale, J.D. (1982). Diurnal variation in clinical depression and accessibility of memories of positive and negative experiences. *Journal of Abnormal Psychology* **91**, 87–95.

Clausen, J.A. and Kohn, M.L. (1950). Relation of schizophrenia to the social structure of a small town. In *Epidemiology of mental disorder* (ed. B. Panamanick). American Association for the Advancement of Science, Washington DC.

Clayton, P.J. (1979). The sequelae and non-sequelae of conjugal bereavement. *American Journal of Psychiatry* **136**, 1530–4.

—— (1981). Bereavement. In *Handbook of affective disorders* (ed. E.S. Paykel). Churchill Livingstone, Edinburgh.

—— Herjanic, M., Murphy, G.E., and Woodruff, R. (1974). Mourning and depression: their similarities and differences. *Canadian Psychiatric Association Journal* **19**, 309–12.

Cleckley, H.M. (1964). *The mask of sanity: an attempt to clarify issues about the so-called psychopathic personality,* 4th edn. Mosby, St. Louis.

Clérambault, G. de (1921). Les délires passionels. Erotomanie, revendication, jalousie. *Bulletin de la Société clinique de Médicine Mentale* 61–71.

Clinical Psychiatry Committee (1965). Clinical trials of the treatment of depressive illness: report to the Medical Research Council. *British Medical Journal* i, 881–6.

Cloninger, C.R., Bohman, M., and Sigvardsson, S. (1981). Inheritance of alcohol abuse: cross fostering analysis of adopted men. *Archives of General Psychiatry* **38**, 861–8.

Cobb, J.P. and Marks, I.M. (1979). Morbid jealousy featuring as obsessive compulsive neurosis. Treatment by behavioural psychotherapy. *British Journal of Psychiatry* **134**, 301–5.

Cobb, S. and Rose, R.M. (1973). Hypertension, peptic ulcer and diabetes in air traffic controllers. *Journal of the American Medical Association* **224**, 489–92.

Cochran, E., Robins, E., and Grote, S. (1976). Regional serotonin levels in the brain: comparison of depressive suicides and alcoholic suicides with controls. *Biological Psychiatry* **11**, 283–94.

Cohen, F. (1980). Cushing's syndrome: a psychiatric study of 29 patients. *British Journal of Psychiatry* **136**, 120–4.

—— and Lazarus, R. (1973). Active coping processes, coping dispositions and recovery from surgery. *Psychosomatic Medicine* **35**, 375–89.

—— —— (1979). Coping with stresses of illness. In *Health psychology* (ed. G.C. Stone, F. Cohen, and N. Adler). Jossey Bass, San Francisco.

Cohen, J. (1961). A study of suicide pacts. *Medicolegal Journal* **29**, 144–51.

Cohen, L.M. (1982). A current perspective of pseudocyesis. *American Journal of Psychiatry* **139**, 1140–4.

Cohen, W.J. and Cohen, N.H. (1974). Lithium carbonate, haloperidol and irreversible brain damage. *Journal of the American Medical Association* **230**, 1283–7.

Cohen-Cole, S. (1980). Training outcome in liaison psychiatry. *General Hospital Psychiatry* **2**, 282–8.

Coid, J. (1979). Mania a potu: a critical review of pathological intoxication. *Psychological Medicine* **9**, 709–19.

Cole, J.D., Goldberg, S.C., and Klerman, G.L. (1964). Phenothiazine treatment in acute schizophrenia. *Archives of General Psychiatry* **10**, 246–61.

Committee on the Child Health Services (1976). (Court Committee.) *Fit for the future.* HMSO, London.

Committee into the Education of Handicapped Children and Young People (1978). (Warnock Committee.) *Special educational needs.* HMSO, London.

Committee of Enquiry into Mental Handicap Nursing and Care (1979). (Jay Committee.) HMSO, London.

Committee on Mentally Abnormal Offenders (1975). (Butler Committee.) HMSO, London.

Committee on the Review of Medicines (1980). Systematic review of the benzodiazepines: guidelines for data sheets on diazepam, chlordiazepoxide, medazepam, temazepam, triazolam, nitrazepam and flurazepam. *British Medical Journal* i, 910–12.

Committee on the Safety of Medicines (1981). Mianserin and blood dyscrasia. *Current Problems* No. 7.

Committee on the Working of the Abortion Act (1974). (Report of the Lane Committee.) HMSO, London.

Connell, P.H. (1958). *Amphetamine psychosis. Maudsley Monograph* No. 5. Oxford University Press, London.

—— (1961). The day hospital approach in child psychiatry. *Journal of Mental Science* **107**, 969–77.

Connolly, F.H. and Gipson, M. (1978). Dysmorphophobia: a long term study. *British Journal of Psychiatry* **132**, 568–70.

Conrad, K. (1958). *Die beginnende Schizophrenie: versuch einer gestaltanalyse des Wahns.* Thieme, Stuttgart.

Conte, H.R. and Karasu, T.B. (1981). Psychotherapy for medically ill patients: review and critique of controlled studies. *Psychosomatics* **22**, 285–315.

Cooper, A.F. (1976). Deafness and psychiatric illness. *British Journal of Psychiatry* **129**, 216–26.

—— Garside, R.F., and Kay, D.W.K. (1976). A comparison of deaf and non-deaf patients with paranoid and affective psychoses. *British Journal of Psychiatry* **129**, 532–8.

Cooper, A.J., Ismail, A.A.A., Smith, C.G., and Loraine, J.A. (1970). Androgen function in 'psychogenic' and 'constitutional' types of impotence. *British Medical Journal* **iii**, 17–20.

Cooper, B. (1978). Epidemiology. In *Schizophrenia. Towards a new synthesis* (ed. J.K: Wing). Academic Press, London.

—— Fry, J., and Kalt, G.W. (1969). A longitudinal study of psychiatric morbidity in a general practice population. *British Journal of Preventive and Social Medicine* **23**, 210–17.

—— and Sylph, J. (1973). Life events and the onset of neurotic illness: an investigation in general practice. *Psychological Medicine* **3**, 421–35.

Cooper, J., Moodley, M., and Reynell, J. (1979). The developmental language programme. Results from a five year study. *British Journal of Disordered Communication* **14**, 57–69.

Cooper, J.E., Kendell, R.E., Gurland, B.J., Sharpe, L., Copeland, J.R.M., and Simon, R. (1972). *Psychiatric diagnosis in New York and London.* Maudsley Monograph No. 20. Oxford University Press, London.

Cooper, P., Gath, D., Rose, N., and Fieldsend, R. (1982). Psychological sequelae to elective sterilisation: a prospective study. *British Medical Journal* **284**, 461–3.

Copeland, J.R.M., Kelleher, M.J., and Kellett, J.M. (1975). Cross-national study of diagnosis of the mental disorders: a comparison of the diagnoses of elderly psychiatric patients admitted to mental hospitals serving Queens County, New York and the former Borough of Camberwell, London. *British Journal of Psychiatry* **126**, 11–20.

—— —— —— Barron, G., Cowan, D., and Gourlay, A.J. (1975). Evaluation of a psychogeriatric service: the distinction between psychogeriatric and geriatric patients. *British Journal of Psychiatry* **126**, 21–9.

Coppen, A. (1972). Indoleamines and the affective disorders. *Journal of Psychiatric Research* **9**, 163–71.

—— Abou-Saleh, M.T., Milln, P., Bailey, J., Metacalfe, M., Burns, B.H., and Armond, A. (1981). Lithium continuation therapy following electroconvulsive therapy. *British Journal of Psychiatry* **139**, 284–7.

—— Ghose, L., Montgomery, S., Rao, V.A.R., Bailey, J., Christiansen, J., Mikkleson, P.L., Van Praag, H.M., Van de Poel, F., Minsker, E.J., Kozulja, V.G., Matussek, N., Kungkunz, G., and Jorgensen, A. (1978). Amitryptyline plasma concentration and clinical effect: a World Health Organiation Collaborative Study. *Lancet* **i**, 63–6.

—— Montgomery, S.A., Gupta, R.K., and Bailey, J. (1976). A double blind comparison of lithium carbonate or maprotiline in the prophylaxis of affective disorder. *British Journal of Psychiatry* **128**, 479–85.

—— Noguera, R., Bailey, J., Burns, B.H., Swani, M.S., Hare, E.H., Gardner, R., and Maggs, R. (1971). Prophylactic lithium in affective disorders: controlled trial. *Lancet* **i**, 275–9.

770   References

—— Prange, A.J., Whybrow, P.C., Noguera, R., and Praez, J.M. (1969). Methysergide in mania. *Lancet* **ii**, 338–40.

—— Whybrow, P.C., Noguera, R., Maggs, R., and Prange, A.J. (1972). The comparative antidepressant value of 1-tryptophan and imipramine with and without attempted potentiation by liothyronine. *Archives of General Psychiatry* **26**, 234–41.

—— and Wood, K. (1978). Tryptophan and depressive illness. *Psychological Medicine* **8**, 49–57.

Coppen, A.J. (1959). Body-build of male homosexuals. *British Medical Journal* **ii**, 1443–5.

—— and Shaw, D.M. (1963). Mineral metabolism in melancholia. *British Medical Journal* **ii**, 1439–44.

Corbett, J. (1978). The development of services for the mentally handicapped: a historical and national review. In *The care of the handicapped child* (ed. J. Apley). Heineman, London.

Corbett, J.A. (1977). Mental retardation – psychiatric aspects. In *Child psychiatry: modern approaches* (ed. M. Rutter and L. Hersov). Blackwell, Oxford.

—— Harris, R., and Robinson, R.G. (1975). Epilepsy. In *Mental retardation and developmental disabilities: an annual review,* Vol. VII (ed. J. Wortis). Brunner-Mazel, New York.

—— Matthews, A.M., Connell, P.M., and Shapiro, D.A. (1969). Tics and Gilles de la Tourette syndrome: a follow-up study and a critical review. *British Journal of Psychiatry* **115**, 1229–41.

—— and Pond, D.A. (1979). Epilepsy and behaviour disorder in the mentally handicapped. In *Psychiatric illness and mental handicap* (ed. F.F. James and R.P. Snaith). Gaskell, Ashford, Kent.

Corsellis, J.A.N. (1962). *Mental illness and the ageing brain.* Maudsley Monographs No. 9. Oxford University Press, London.

—— Bruton, C.J., and Freeman-Browne, D. (1973). The aftermath of boxing. *Psychological Medicine* **3**, 270–303.

Costello, R.M. (1975). Alcoholism treatment and evaluation. *International Journal of the Addictions* **10**, 251–75.

Cotard, M. (1882). Du délire de négations. *Archives de Neurologie, Paris* **4**, 152–70 and 282–96. (Translated into English by M. Rohde in S.R. Hirsch and M. Shepherd (eds.) *Themes and variations in European psychiatry,* pp. 353–73.   Wright, Bristol.

Courbon, P. and Fail, G. (1927). Syndrome d''Illusion de Frégoli' et schizophrénie *Bulletin de la Société Clinique de Médicine Mentale* **15**, 121–4.

Covi, L., Lipman, R., and Derogatis, L. (1974). Drugs and group psychotherapy in neurotic depression. *American Journal of Psychiatry* **131**, 191–8.

Cowie, V. (1961). The incidence of neurosis in the children of psychotics. *Acta Psychiatrica Scandinavica* **37**, 37–71.

—— (1980). Injury and insult – considerations of the neuropathological aetiology of mental subnormality. *British Journal of Psychiatry* **137**, 305–12.

Cox, A., Rutter, M., Newman, S., and Bartak, L. (1975). A comparative study of infantile autism and specific developmental receptive language disorder II. Parental characteristics. *British Journal of Psychiatry* **126**, 146–59.

Cox, S.M. and Ludwig, A. (1979). Neurological soft signs and psychopathology: 1. Findings in schizophrenia. *Journal of Nervous and Mental Disease* **167**, 161–5.

Craft, A. and Craft, M. (1981). Sexuality and mental handicap: a review. *British Journal of Psychiatry* **139**, 494–505.

Craft, M. (1965). *Ten studies in psychopathic personality.* Wright, Bristol.

Craig, A.G. and Pitts, F.N. (1968). Suicide by physicians. *Diseases of the Nervous System* **29**, 763–72.

Craig, T.J. (1982). An epidemiologic study of problems associated with violence among psychiatric inpatients. *American Journal of Psychiatry* **139**, 1262-6.

Crammer, J.L. (1977). Calcium metabolism and mental disorder. *Psychological Medicine* **7**, 557-60.

Cramond, W.A., Knight, P.R., and Lawrence, J.R. (1967). The psychiatric contribution to a renal unit undertaking chronic haemodialysis and renal homotransplantation. *British Journal of Psychiatry* **113**, 1201-12.

Crapper, D., Kirschnan, S.S., and Dalton, A.J. (1973). Brain aluminium distribution in Alzheimer's disease and experimental neurofibrillary degeneration. *Science* **180**, 511-13.

Crawfurd, M. d'A. (1982). Severe mental handicap: pathogenesis, treatment and prevention. *British Medical Journal* **285**, 762-6.

Creak, M. (1963). Childhood psychosis: a review of 100 cases. *British Journal of Psychiatry* **109**, 84-9.

Creer, C. (1978). Social work with patients and their families. In *Schizophrenia: towards a new synthesis* (ed. J.K. Wing). Academic Press, London.

—— and Wing, J.K. (1975). Living with a schizophrenic patient. *British Journal of Hospital Medicine* **14**, 73-82.

Crisp, A.H. (1977). Diagnosis and outcome of anorexia nervosa: the St. Georges view. *Proceedings of the Royal Society of Medicine* **70**, 464-70.

—— Palmer, R.L., and Kalucy, R.S. (1976). How common is anorexia nervosa? A prevalence study. *British Journal of Psychiatry* **128**, 549-54.

Critchley, M. (1953). *The parietal lobes.* Edward Arnold, London.

Crome, L. and Stern, J. (1972). *Pathology of mental retardation,* 2nd ed. Churchill Livingstone, London.

Cronholm, B. and Molander, L. (1964). Memory disturbance after electroconvulsive therapy. *Acta Psychiatrica Scandinavica* **40**, 211-16.

—— and Ottosson, J.-O. (1960). Experimental studies of the therapeutic action of electroconvulsive therapy in endogenous depression. *Acta Psychiatrica Scandinavica* Suppl. 145, 69-101.

Cross, K.W., Hassall, C., and Gath, D. (1972). Psychiatric day care, the new chronic population? *British Journal of Preventive and Social Medicine* **26**, 199-204.

Crow, T.J. (1980). Molecular pathology of schizophrenia; more than one disease process? *British Medical Journal* **280**, 66-8.

—— Baker, H.F., Cross, A.J., Joseph, M.H., Lofthouse, R., Longden, A., Owen, F., Riley, G.J., Glover, V., and Killpack, W.S. (1979). Monoamine mechanisms in chronic schizophrenia: post mortem neurochemical findings. *British Journal of Psychiatry* **134**, 249-56.

—— Johnstone, E.C., and Owen, F. (1979). Research on schizophrenia. In *Recent advances in clinical psychiatry,* Vol. 3 (ed. K. Granville Grossman) pp. 1-36. Churchill Livingstone, Edinburgh.

Crowe, M.J. (1973). Conjoint marital therapy: advice or interpretation. *Journal of Psychosomatic Research* **17**, 309-15.

Crowe, R.R. (1974). An adoption study of antisocial personality. *Archives of General Psychiatry* **31**, 785-91.

Crown, S. (1978). *Psychosexual counselling.* Academic Press, London.

—— (1980). Psychosocial factors in low back pain. *Clinics in Rheumatic Diseases* **6**, 77-92.

Cullen, W. (1772). Nosology. See extracts in I. McAlpine and R. Hunter. *Three hundred years of psychiatry,* pp. 473-9. Oxford University Press, London.

Culpan, R., Davies, R.M., and Oppenheim, A.N. (1960). Incidence of psychiatric illness among hospital outpatients: an application of the Cornell Medical Index. *British Medical Journal* **i**, 855-7.

Cunningham, J., Strassberg, D., and Roback, H. (1978). Group psychotherapy for medical patients. *Comprehensive Psychiatry* **19**, 135–40.

Curran, D. (1937). The differentiation of neuroses and manic-depressive psychosis. *Journal of Mental Science* **83**, 156–74.

Cutting, J. (1978*a*). The relationship between Korsakov's syndrome and 'alcoholic dementia'. *British Journal of Psychiatry* **132**, 240–51.

—— (1978*b*). A reappraisal of alcoholic psychoses. *Psychological Medicine* **8**, 285–95.

—— (1979). Alcohol dependence and alcohol related disabilities. In *Recent advances in clinical psychiatry,* Vol. 3 (ed. K. Granville-Grossman) pp. 225–250. Churchill Livingstone, Edinburgh.

—— (1980). Physical illness and psychosis. *British Journal of Psychiatry* **136**, 109–19.

—— (1982). Neuropsychiatric complications of alcoholism. *British Journal of Hospital Medicine* **27**, 335–42.

Cytryn, L. and McKnew, D.J. (1972). Proposed classification of childhood depression. *American Journal of Psychiatry* **137**, 22–5.

Czackes, J. W. and DeNour, A.K. (1978). *Chronic haemodialysis as a way of life.* Brunner Mazel, New York.

Dalbiez, R. (1941). *Psychoanalytic method and the doctrine of Freud* (2 vols.). Longmans Green, London.

Da Costa, J.M. (1871). An irritable heart: a clinical study of functional cardiac disorder and its consequences. *American Journal of Medical Science* **61**, 17–52. (See extracts in Jarcho, S. (1959). On irritable heart. *American Journal of Cardiology* **4**, 809–17.)

Dally, P. (1981). Treatment of anorexia nervosa. *British Journal of Hospital Medicine* **25**, 434–40.

—— Gomez, J., and Isaccs, A.J. (1979). *Anorexia nervosa.* Heinemann, London.

Dalton, K. (1964). *The premenstrual syndrome.* Heinemann, London.

—— (1977). *The premenstrual syndrome and progesterone therapy.* Heinemann, London.

Daly, D.D. (1975). Ictal clinical manifestations of complex partial seizures. In *Advances in neurology* (ed. J.K. Penry and D. Daly) Vol. 11. Raven Press, New York.

Danford, D.E. and Huber, A.M. (1982). Pica among mentally retarded adults. *American Journal of Mental Deficiency* **87**, 141–6.

Dare, C. (1977). Dynamic treatments. In *Child psychiatry: modern approaches* (ed. M.L. Rutter and L. Hersov). Blackwell, Oxford.

Davidson, D.G.D. and Eastham, W.N. (1966). Acute hepatic necrosis following overdose of paracetamol. *British Medical Journal* **ii**, 497–9.

Davidson, J.R.T. (1972). Postpartum mood change in Jamaican women: a description and a discussion of its significance. *British Journal of Psychiatry* **121**, 659–64.

Davies, B.M. and Morgenstern, F.S. (1960). A case of cysticercosis, temporal lobe epilepsy and transvestism. *Journal of Neurology, Neurosurgery and Psychiatry* **23**, 247–9.

Davies, D.L. (1962). Normal drinking in recovered alcohol addicts. *Quarterly Journal of Studies on Alcohol* **23**, 94–104.

—— and Maloney, A.J.F. (1976). Selective loss of central cholinergic neurones in Alzheimer's disease. *Lancet* **ii**, 1403.

Davis, J.M. (1976). Comparative doses and costs of antipsychotic medication. *Archives of General Psychiatry* **33**, 858–61.

—— Schaffer, C.B., Killian, G.A., Kinard, C., and Chan, C. (1980). Important issues in the drug treatment of schizophrenia. *Schizophrenia Bulletin* **6**, 70–87.

Davison, A. (1977). The biochemistry of brain development and mental retardation. *British Journal Psychiatry* **131**, 565–74.

Davison, G. (1968). Elimination of a sadistic fantasy by a client-controlled counterconditioning technique: a case study. *Journal of Abnormal Psychology* **73**, 84–90.

Davison, K. and Bagley, C.R. (1969). Schizophrenia-like psychoses associated with organic disorders of the central nervous system: a review of the literature. In *Current problems in neuropsychiatry. British Journal of Psychiatry, Special Publication 4* (ed. R.N. Herrington). Headley Brothers, Ashford, Kent.

Dawkins, S. (1961). Non-consummation of marriage. *Lancet* ii, 1029–33.

Dean, C. and Kendell, R.E. (1981). The symptomatology of puerperal illnesses. *British Journal of Psychiatry* 139, 128–33.

Déjerine, J. and Gauckler, E. (1913). *Psychoneurosis and psychotherapy.* (Translated by S.E. Jelliffe and J.B. Lippincott. Reissued by Arno Press, New York.)

De Jonge, G.A. (1973). Epidemiology of enuresis. In *Bladder control and enuresis* (ed. I. Kolvin, R. MacKeith, and S.R. Meadow). Clinics in Developmental Medicine 48/49. Heinemann, London.

Delahunty, J.E. and Ardran, G.M. (1970). Globus hystericus: a manifestation of reflux oesophagitis. *Journal of Laryngology and Otology* 84, 1049–54.

D'Elia, G. and Raotma, H. (1975). Is unilateral ECT less effective than bilateral ECT? *British Journal of Psychiatry* 126, 83–9.

Delva, N.J. and Letemendia, F.J.J. (1982). Lithium treatment in schizophrenia and schizoaffective disorders. *British Journal of Psychiatry* 141, 387–400.

de Maré, P.B. and Kreeger, L.C. (1974). *Introduction to group treatments in psychiatry.* Butterworth, London.

Denker, S.J. (1958). A follow-up study of 128 closed head injuries in twins using co-twins as controls. *Acta Psychiatrica Scandinavica* Suppl. 123, 1–125.

Denko, J.D. and Kaelbling, R. (1962). The psychiatric aspects of hypoparathyroidism. *Acta Psychiatrica Scandinavica* Suppl. 164, 1–70.

Department of the Environment (1976). *Drinking and driving. Report of the Departmental Committee.* (Blennerhassett Report.) HMSO, London.

Department of Health and Social Security (1971). *Better services for the mentally handicapped.* HMSO, London.

—— (1972). *Services for mental illness related to old age.* HMSO, London.

—— (1978a). *Advisory committee on alcoholism: report on prevention.* HMSO, London.

—— (1978b). *A happier old age.* HMSO, London.

Devlin, H.B., Plant, J.A., and Griffin, M. (1971). Aftermath of surgery for anorectal cancer. *British Medical Journal* iii, 413–18.

Dewhurst, D. (1969). The neurosyphilitic psychoses today: a survey of 91 cases. *British Journal of Psychiatry* 115, 31–8.

Dewhurst, K. (1980). *Thomas Willis's Oxford lectures.* Sandford Publications, Oxford.

Dewhurst, W.G. (1968). Methysergide in mania. *Nature* 219, 506–7.

Dicks, H. (1967). *Marital tensions: clinical studies towards a psychological theory of interaction.* Routledge and Kegan Paul, London.

Dight, S.E. (1976). Scottish drinking habits: a survey of Scottish drinking habits and attitudes towards alcohol. *Office of Population Censuses and Surveys.* HMSO, London.

DiMascio, A. (1973). The effects of benzodiazepines on aggression: reduced or increased? In *The benzodiazepines* (ed. S. Grattini, E. Mussini and L.O. Randall). Raven Press, London.

—— Weissman, M.M., Prusoff, B.A., Neu, C., Zwiling, M., and Klerman, G.L. (1979). Differential symptom reduction by drugs and psychotherapy in acute depression. *Archives of General Psychiatry* 36, 1450–6.

Dodrill, C.B. (1975). Effects of sulthiame upon intellectual, neuro-psychological and social function abilities of adult epileptics: comparison with diphenylhydantoin. *Epilepsia* 16, 627–5.

Doehrman, S.R. (1977). Psychosocial aspects of recovery from coronary heart disease: a review. *Social Science and Medicine* 11, 199–218.

Dollard, J. and Miller, N.E. (1950). *Personality and psychotherapy.* McGraw Hill, New York.

d'Orban, P.T. (1976). Child stealing: a typology of female offenders. *British Journal of Criminology* 16, 275–9.

—— (1979). Women who kill their children. *British Journal of Psychiatry* 134, 560–71.

Dorner, S. (1976). Adolescents with spina bifida: how they see the situation. *Archives of Disease in Childhood* 51, 439–44.

Dorpat, T.L. and Ripley, H.S. (1967). The relationship between attempted suicide and completed suicide. *Comprehensive Psychiatry* 8, 74–9.

Douglas, J.W.B. and Blomfield, J.M. (1958). *Children Under Five.* George Allen, London.

Drugs and Therapeutics Bulletin (1981*a*). Lithium updated. *Drugs and Therapeutics Bulletin* 19, 21–4.

—— (1981*b*). Sodium valproate reassessed. *Drugs and Therapeutics Bulletin* 19, 93–5.

—— (1983). Drugs which can be given to nursing mothers. *Drugs and Therapeutics Bulletin* 21, 5–8.

Duffy, J. (1977). Estimating the proportion of heavy drinkers. In *The Ledermann curve* (ed. D.L. Davies). Alcohol Education Centre, London.

Dunbar, H.F. (1935). *Emotions and bodily changes.* Columbia University Press, New York.

Dunham, H.W. (1965). *Community and schizophrenia: an epidemiological analysis.* Wayne State University Press, Detroit.

Dunlap, K. (1932). *Habits: their making and unmaking.* Liverheight Publishing Corporation, New York.

Durkheim, E. (1951). *Suicide: a study in sociology* (translated by J.A. Spaulding and G. Simpson). Free Press, Glencoe, Illinois.

Eastwood, M.R. (1975). *The relation between physical and mental illness.* University of Toronto Press.

Eastwood, R. and Trevelyan, M.H. (1972). Relationship between physical and psychiatric disorder. *Psychological Medicine* 2, 363–72.

Eaton, J.W. and Weil, R.J. (1955). *Culture and mental disorders: a comparative study of the Hutterites and other populations.* Free Press, Glencoe, Illinois.

Eaton, L.F. and Menolascino, F.J. (1982). Psychiatric disorders in the mentally retarded: types, problems and challenges. *American Journal of Psychiatry* 139, 1297–303.

Edwards, G. (1976). Cannabis and the psychiatric position. In *Cannabis and health* (ed. J.D.P. Graham). Academic Press, London.

—— (1979). British policies on opiate addiction. *British Journal of Psychiatry* 134, 1–13.

—— Chandler, J., and Hensman, C. (1972). Drinking in a London suburb. *Quarterly Journal of Studies on Alcoholism* Suppl. No. 6, 69–128.

—— Grossman, M.M., Keller, M., Moser, J., and Room, R. (1977). *Alcohol related disabilities.* World Health Organization, Geneva.

—— Hawker, A., Hensman, C., Peto, J., and Williamson, V. (1973). Alcoholics known or unknown to agencies: epidemiological studies in a London suburb. *British Journal of Psychiatry* 123, 169–83.

—— Hensman, C., and Peto, J. (1971). Drinking problems among recidivist prisoners. *Psychological Medicine* 1, 388–99.

—— Orford, J., Egert, S., Guthrie, S., Hawker, A., Hensman, C., Mitcheson, M., Oppenheimer, E., and Taylor, C. (1977). Alcoholism: a controlled trial of 'treatment' and 'advice'. *Journal of Studies on Alcohol* 38, 1004–31.

Edwin, E., Holten, K., Norum, K.R., Schrumpf, A., and Skaug, O.E. (1965). Vitamin B$_{12}$ hypovitaminosis in mental diseases. *Acta Medica Scandinavica* 177, 689–99.

Ehrhardt, A.A., Epstein, R., and Money, J. (1968). Fetal androgens and female gender identity in the early-treated adrenogenital syndrome. *Johns Hopkins Medical Journal* 122, 160–7.

Eisenberg, L. (1957). The course of childhood schizophrenia. *Archives of Neurology and Psychiatry* **78**, 69–83.

—— (1958). School phobia – a study in the communication of anxiety. *American Journal of Psychiatry* **114**, 712–18.

—— Connors, C.K., and Sharpe, L. (1965). A controlled study of the differential application of outpatient psychiatric treatment for children. *Japanese Journal of Psychiatry* **6**, 125–132.

Eiser, C. (1979). Psychological development of the child with leukaemia: a review. *Journal of Behavioral Medicine* **2**, 141–57.

Eisinger, A.J., Huntsman, R.G., Lord, J., Merry, J., Polani, P., Tanner, J.M., Whitehouse, R.H., and Griffiths, P.D. (1972). Female homosexuality. *Nature* **238**, 157.

Eitinger, L. (1960). The symptomatology of mental disease among refugees in Norway. *Journal of Mental Science* **106**, 947–66.

Ekblad, M. (1955). Induced abortion on psychiatric grounds. *Acta Neurologica Psychiatrica Scandinavica* Suppl. 99.

El-Guebaly, N. and Offord, D.R. (1977). The offspring of alcoholics: a critical review. *American Journal of Psychiatry* **134**, 357–65.

Ellenberger, H.F. (1970). *The discovery of the unconscious.* Basic Books, New York.

Ellis, A. (1956). The effectiveness of psychotherapy in individuals who have severe homosexual problems. *Journal of Consulting Psychology* **20**, 191–5.

—— (1979). *Reasons and emotion in psychotherapy.* Citadel Press, Syracuse, NJ.

—— and Brancale, R. (1956). *The physiology of sex offenders.* Thomas, Springfield, Ill.

Ellis, H. (1901). *Studies in the psychology of sex,* Vol. 2. *Sexual inversion.* Davis, Philadelphia.

—— (1928). *Studies in the psychology of sex,* Vol. 7. *Eonism and other supplementary Studies.* Davis, Philadelphia.

Endicott, J. and Spitzer, R.L. (1978). A diagnostic interview: the schedule for affective disorders and schizophrenia. *Archives of General Psychiatry* **35**, 837–44.

—— —— (1979). Use of the research diagnostic criteria and the schedule for affective disorders and schizophrenia to study affective disorders. *American Journal of Psychiatry* **136**, 52–6.

Engel, G. (1955). Studies of ulcerative colitis III. The nature of the psychological processes. *American Journal of Medicine* **16**, 416–37.

—— (1958). Psychogenic pain and the pain prone person. *American Journal of Medicine* **26**, 899–918.

—— (1962). *Psychological development in health and disease.* Saunders, Philadelphia.

—— (1967). Medical education and the psychosomatic approach: a report on the Rochester experience. *Journal of Psychosomatic Research* **11**, 77–83.

—— (1980). The clinical application of the biopsychosocial model. *American Journal of Psychiatry* **137**, 535–44.

—— Logan, M., and Ferris, E.B. (1947). Hyperventilation: analysis of clinical symptomatology. *Annals of Internal Medicine* **27**, 683–704.

—— and Romano, J. (1959). Delirium, a syndrome of cerebral insufficiency. *Journal of Chronic Diseases* **9**, 260–77.

Enoch, M.D. and Trethowan, W.H. (1979). *Uncommon psychiatric syndromes.* Wright, Bristol.

Epstein, A.W. (1960). Fetishism: a study of its psychopathology with particular reference to a proposed disorder in brain mechanisms as an aetiological factor. *Journal of Nervous and Mental Disease* **130**, 107–19.

—— (1961). Relationship of fetishism and transvestism to brain and particularly to temporal lobe dysfunction. *Journal of Nervous and Mental Disease* **133**, 247–53.

Errera, P. (1962). Some historical aspects of the concept, Phobia. *Psychiatric Quarterly* **36**, 325–36.

Esquirol, E. (1838). *Des maladies mentales.* Baillière, Paris. (Reprinted in 1976 by Arno Press, New York.)

—— (1845). *Mental maladies: a treatise on insanity.* Lea and Blanchard, Philadelphia.

Essen-Moller, E. (1971). Suggestions for further improvement of the international classification of mental disorders. *Psychological Medicine* **1**, 308–11.

Evans, D.R. (1970). Exhibitionism. In *Symptoms of psychopathology* (ed. C.G. Costello) pp. 7–59. Wiley, New York.

Evans, N.J.R., Baldwin, J.A., and Gath, D.H. (1974). The incidence of cancer among patients with affective disorder. *British Journal of Psychiatry* **124**, 518–25.

Ewing, J.A. and Rouse, B.A. (1976). Failure of an experimental treatment program to inculcate controlled drinking in alcoholics. *British Journal of Addiction* **71**, 123–34.

Ey, H., Bernard, P., and Brisset, C. (1960). Acute delusional psychoses. In *Themes and variations in European psychiatry* (1974). (ed. S.R. Hirsch and M. Shepherd). Wright, Bristol.

Eysenck, H.J. (1952). The effects of psychotherapy: an evaluation. *Journal of Consulting Psychology* **16**, 319–24.

—— (1957). *The dynamics of anxiety and hysteria.* Routledge and Kegan Paul, London.

—— (1960). *Behaviour therapy and the neuroses.* Pergamon Press, Oxford.

—— (1970*a*). *Crime and personality.* Paladin Press, London.

—— (1970*b*). A dimensional system of psycho-diagnosis. In *New approaches to personality classification* (ed. A.R. Mahrer) pp. 169–207. Columbia University Press, New York.

—— (1976). The learning theory model of neurosis: a new approach. *Behaviour Research and Therapy* **14**, 251–67.

Faergeman, P.M. (1963). *Psychogenic psychoses.* Butterworth, London.

Fagan, J. and Shepherd, I.L. (eds.) (1971). *Gestalt therapy now.* Harper Colophon, New York.

Fairburn, C. (1981*a*). A cognitive behavioural approach to the treatment of bulimia. *Psychological Medicine* **11**, 707–11.

—— (1981*b*). The sexual problems of diabetic men. *British Journal of Hospital Medicine* **25**, 484–91.

—— (1983). Eating disorders. In *Companion to psychiatric studies,* 3rd edn. (ed. R.E. Kendell and A.K. Zealley). Churchill Livingstone, Edinburgh.

—— and Cooper, P.J. (1982). Self-induced vomiting and bulimia nervosa: an undetected problem. *British Medical Journal* **284**, 1153–5.

—— Wu, F.C., and McCullock, D.K. (1982). The clinical features of diabetic impotence: a preliminary study. *British Journal of Psychiatry* **140**, 447–52.

Farina, A., Barry, H., and Garmezy, N. (1963). Birth order of recovered and non-recovered schizophrenics. *Archives of General Psychiatry* **9**, 224–8.

Faris, R.E.L. and H.W. Dunham (1950). *Mental disorders in urban areas.* Chicago University Press.

Farrell, B.A. (1979). Mental illness: a conceptual analysis. *Psychological Medicine* **9**, 21–35.

—— (1981). *The standing of psychoanalysis.* Oxford University Press.

Farrington, D.P., Biron, L., and Lerblue, M. (1982). Personality and delinquency. In *Abnormal offenders, delinquency and the criminal justice system* (ed. J. Gunn and D.P. Farrington). Wiley, Chichester.

Feigenson, J.S. (1980). Stroke rehabilitation. Outcome studies and guidelines for alternative levels of care. *Stroke* **12**, 372–5.

Feighner, J.P., Robins, E., Guze, S.B., Woodruff, R.A., Winokur, G., and Munoz, R. (1972). Diagnostic criteria for use in psychiatric research. *Archives of General Psychiatry* **26**, 57–63.

Feldman, F., Cantor, D., Soll, S., and Bachrach, W. (1967). Psychiatric study of a consecutive series of 34 patients with ulcerative colitis. *British Medical Journal* **iii**, 711–14.

Feldman, M.P. and McCulloch, M.J. (1979). *Homosexual behaviour, therapy and assessment*. Pergamon, Oxford.

Fenichel, O. (1945). *The psychoanalytic theory of neurosis*. Kegan Paul, Trench and Trubner, London.

Fenton, W.S., Mosher, L.R., and Matthews, S.M. (1981). Diagnosis of schizophrenia: a critical review of current diagnostic systems. *Schizophrenia Bulletin* **7**, 452–76.

Ferdijae, W.E. (1978). Learning processes in pain. In *The psychology of pain* (ed. R.A. Steinback). Raven Press, New York.

Ferreira, A.J. and Winter, W.D. (1965). Family interaction and decision making. *Archives of General Psychiatry* **13**, 214–23.

Field, E. (1967). *A validation of Hewitt and Jenkins' hypothesis*. Home Office Research Unit Publication No. 10. HMSO, London.

Fieve, R.R., Platman, S.R., and Plutchik, R.R. (1968). The use of lithium in affective disorders: I. Acute endogenous depression. *American Journal of Psychiatry* **125**, 487–91.

Fiorentini, C., Olivarai, M.T., Moruzzi, P., and Guazzi, M.D. (1981). Long term follow up of the primary hyperkinetic heart. *American Journal of Medicine* **71**, 221–7.

Fischer, M. (1973). Genetic and environmental factors in schizophrenia: a study of twins and their families. *Acta Psychiatrica Scandinavica* Suppl. 238.

Fish, F.J. (1962). *Schizophrenia*. Wright, Bristol.

—— (1974). *Clinical psychopathology* (revised by M. Hamilton). Wright, Bristol.

Fisher, C.M. and Adams, R.D. (1958). Transient global amnesia. *Transactions of the American Neurological Association* 143–6.

—— —— (1964). Transient global amnesia. *Acta Neurologica Scandinavica* Suppl. 9, 7–83.

Fisher, S. and Greenberg, R.P. (1977). *The scientific credibility of Freud's theories and therapy*. Basic Books, New York.

Flor-Henry, P. (1969). Psychosis and temporal lobe epilepsy: a controlled investigation. *Epilepsia* **10**, 363–95.

Folsom, J.C. (1967). Intensive hospital therapy for psychogeriatric patients. *Current Psychiatric Therapy* **7**, 209–15.

Folstein, S. and Rutter, M. (1971). Infantile autism: a genetic study of 21 twin pairs. *Journal of Child Psychology and Psychiatry* **18**, 297–321.

Ford, C.S. and Beach, F.A. (1952). *Patterns of sexual behaviour*. Eyre and Spottiswoode, London.

Ford, M.J., Eastwood, J., and Eastwood, M.A. (1982). The irritable bowel syndrome: soma and psyche. *Psychological Medicine* **12**, 705–8.

Fordyce, W.E. (1982). A behavioural perspective on chronic pain. *British Journal of Clinical Psychology* **21**, 313–20.

Forreyt, J.P., Goodrick, G.K., and Gotto, A.M. (1981). Limitations of behaviour treatment of obesity: review and analysis. *Journal of Behavioral Medicine* **4**, 159–74.

Forssman, H. and Thuwe, I. (1966). One hundred and twenty children born after application for therapeutic abortion refused: their mental health, social adjustment and educational level up to age 21. *Acta Psychiatrica Scandinavica* **42**, 71–88.

Foster, E.M., Kay, D.W.K., and Bergmann, K. (1976). The characteristics of old people receiving and needing domiciliary services. *Age and Ageing* **5**, 345–55.

Fottrell, E. (1980). A study of violent behaviour among patients in psychiatric hospitals. *British Journal of Psychiatry* **136**, 216–21.

Foundeur, M., Fixsen, C., Triebel, W.A., and White, M.A. (1957). Post-partum mental illness. *Archives of Neurology and Psychiatry* **77**, 503–12.

Foulds, G.A. (1965). *Personality and personal illness.* Tavistock, London.
—— (1976). *The hierarchical nature of personal illness.* Academic Press, London.
Foulkes, S.H. (1948). *Introduction to group-analytic psychotherapy.* Heinemann, London.
—— and Anthony, E.J. (1957). *Group psychotherapy: the psychoanalytic approach.* Penguin, Harmondsworth.
—— and Lewis, E. (1944). Group analysis: a study in the treatment of groups on psychoanalytic lines. *British Journal of Medical Psychology* **20**, 175–82.
Fox, B.H. (1978). Premorbid psychological factors as related to cancer incidence. *Journal of Behavioural Medicine* **1,**, 45–133.
—— Stenet, E.J., Boyd, S.C., and Flannery, J.T. (1982). Suicide rates among cancer patients in Connecticut. *Journal of Chronic Disease* **35**, 89–100.
Fox, J.H., Ramsey, R.G., Huckman, M.S., and Proske, A.E. (1976). Cerebral ventricular enlargement. Chronic alcoholics examined by computerised tomography. *Journal of the American Medical Association* **236**, 365–8.
Frank, D.J., Bliedman, L.H., Imber, S.D., Nash, E.H., and Stone, A.R. (1957). Why patients leave psychotherapy. *Archives of Neurology and Psychiatry* **77**, 283–99.
—— Hoehn-Sarik, R., Imber, S.D., Liberman, B.L., and Stone, A.R. (1978). *Effective ingredients of successful psychotherapy.* Brunner-Mazel, New York.
Fras, I., Litin, E.M., and Pearson, J.S. (1967). Comparison of psychiatric symptoms in carcinoma of the pancreas with those in some other intra-abdominal neoplasms. *American Journal of Psychiatry* **123**, 1553–62.
Fraser, R. (1947). The incidence of neurosis among factory workers. *Industrial Health Research Board Report* Number 90. HMSO, London.
Frederiks, J.A.M. (1969). Disorders of the body schema. In *Handbook of clinical neurology* (ed. P.J. Vinken and G.W. Bruyn) Vol. 4, chapter 11, pp., 207–40. North Holland, Amsterdam.
Freeman, C.P.L., Basson, J.V., and Crighton, A. (1978). Double blind controlled trial of electroconvulsive therapy (ECT) and simulated ECT in depressive illness. *Lancet* **i**, 738–40.
—— and Kendell, R.E. (1980). ECT: patients' experiences and attitudes. *British Journal of Psychiatry* **137**, 8–16.
—— Weeks, D., and Kendell, R.E. (1980). ECT: II patients who complain. *British Journal of Psychiatry* **137**, 17–25.
Freeman, M.D.A. (1979). The law and sexual deviation. In *Sexual deviation,* 2nd edn. (ed. I. Rosen). Oxford University Press.
Freeman, W. and Watts, J.W. (1942). *Psychosurgery.* Thomas, Springfield, Ill.
Freidenbergs, I., Gordon, W., Hibbard, M., Leune, L., Wolf, C., and Dille, L. (1982). Psychological aspects of living with cancer. *International Journal of Psychiatry in Medicine* **11**, 303–29.
Fremming, K.H. (1951). The expectation of mental infirmity in a sample of the Danish population. *Occasional Papers on Eugenics,* No. 7. Cassell, London.
French, M.D., Porter, R.W., Cavanaugh, E.B., and Langmire, R.L. (1957). Experimental gastroduodenal lesion induced by stimulation of the brain. *Psychosomatic Medicine* **3**, 209–20.
Freud, A. (1936). *The ego and the mechanisms of defence.* Hogarth Press, London.
—— (1958). Adolescence. I. Adolescence in the psychoanalytic theory. In *The psychoanalytic study of the child* (ed. A. Freud) Vol. XIII. International University Press, New York.
Freud, S. (1893). On the psychical mechanisms of hysterical phenomena. *The standard edition of the complete psychological works* (ed. J. Strachey), Vol. 3, pp. 25–42. Hogarth Press, London.

—— (1895). Obsessions and phobias, their psychical mechanisms and their aetiology. In *The standard edition of the complete psychological works* (ed. J. Strachey) Vol. 3. Hogarth Press, London.

—— (1911). Psychoanalytic notes upon an autobiographical account of cases of paranoia. (Schreber.) In *The standard edition of the complete psychological works* (1958) Vol. 12, pp. 1–82. Hogarth Press, London.

—— (1914). *Psychopathology of everyday life.* Fisher Unwin, London.

—— (1917). Mourning and melancholia. *The standard edition of the complete psychological works,* Vol. 14, pp. 243–58. Hogarth Press, London.

—— (1923). Psychoanalysis. In *The standard edition of the complete psychological works,* Vol. 18, pp. 235–54. Hogarth Press, London.

—— (1927). Fetishism. *International Journal of Psychoanalysis* 9, 161–6. Also in *The standard edition of the complete psychological works,* Vol. 21, pp. 147–57. Hogarth Press, London.

—— (1933). Anxiety and instinctual life. In *The standard edition of the complete psychological works,* Vol. 22 (ed. J. Strachey). Hogarth Press, London.

Friedhoff, A. and van Winkle, E. (1962). The characteristics of an amine found in the urine of schizophrenic patients. *Journal of Nervous and Mental Disease* 135, 550–5.

Friedman, A.S. (1975). Interaction of drug therapy with marital therapy for depressed patients. *Archives of General Psychiatry* 32, 619–37.

Friedman, D.E.L. (1966). A new technique for the systematic desensitization of phobic symptoms. *Behaviour Research and Therapy* 4, 139–40.

Friedman, L.J. (1962). *Virgin wives: a study of unconsummated marriage.* Tavistock, London.

Friedman, M. and Rosenman, R.H. (1959). Association of specific behaviour pattern with blood and cardiovascular findings. *Journal of the American Medical Association* 169, 1286–96.

—— Thoresen, C.E., Gill, J.E., Ulmer, D., Thompson, L., Powell, L., Price, V., Elek, D.R., Rabin, D.D., Breall, W.S., Piaget, G., Dixon, T., Bourg, E., Levy, R.A. and Tasto, D.L. (1982). Feasibility of altering type A behaviour pattern after myocardial infarction. Recurrent coronary prevention project study: methods, baseline results and preliminary findings. *Circulation* 66, 83–92.

Friedman, S.B., Chodoff, P., Mason, J.W., and Hamburg, D.A. (1963). Behaviour observations on patients anticipating the death of a child. *Pediatrics* 32, 610–25.

Friedrich, W.N. and Wheeler, K.K. (1982). The abusing parent revisited: a decade of psychological research. *Journal of Nervous and Mental Disease* 170, 577–87.

Froese, A.P. (1977). Pediatric referrals to psychiatry. 1. Comparison of referrals and non-referrals. *International Journal of Psychiatry in Medicine* 7, 241–7.

Frommer, E. (1968). Depressive illness in children. In *British Journal of Psychiatry* Special Publication No. 2 (ed. A. Coppen and A. Walk). Headley Brothers, Ashford.

Fromm-Reichman, F. (1948). Notes on the development of treatment of schizophrenia by psychoanalytic psychotherapy. *Psychiatry* 11, 263–73.

Gale, E. and Ayer, W.A. (1969). Treatment of dental phobias. *Journal of the American Dental Association* 78, 1304–7.

Ganser, S.J. (1898). Über einen eigenartigen hysterischen Dämmerzustand. *Archiv für Psychiatrie und Nervenkrankheiten* 30, 633–40. (Translated by Schorer, C.E. in *British Journal of Criminology* 5, 120–6 (1965).

Gardner, R. (1970). Deaths in United Kingdom opioid users 1965–1969. *Lancet* ii, 650–3.

—— Hanka, R., O'Brien, V.C., Page, A.J.F., and Rees, R. (1977). Psychological and social evaluation in cases of deliberate self-poisoning admitted to a general hospital. *British Medical Journal* ii, 1567–70.

Garfield, S. (1980). *Psychotherapy: an eclectic approach.* Wiley, New York.

—— and Bergin, A.E. (eds.) (1978). *Handbook of psychotherapy and behaviour change: an empirical analysis,* 2nd ed. Wiley, New York.

Garfinkel, B.D., Froese, A., and Hood, J. (1982). Suicide attempts in children and adolescents. *American Journal of Psychiatry* 139, 1257–61.

Garfinkel, P.E. and Garner, D.N. (1982). *Anorexia nervosa: a multidimensional perspective.* Brunner Mazel, New York.

—— Moldofsky, H., and Garner, D.N. (1977). The outcome of anorexia nervosa: significance of clinical features, body image and behaviour modification. In *Anorexia nervosa* (ed. R.A. Vigersky). Raven, New York.

—— —— —— (1980). The heterogeneity of anorexia nervosa. *Archives of General Psychiatry* 37, 1036–40.

—— Stancer, H.C., and Persad, E. (1980). A comparison of haloperidol, lithium carbonate and their combination in the treatment of mania. *Journal of Affective Disorders* 2, 279–88.

Garner, D.M. (1981). Body image in anorexia nervosa. *Canadian Journal of Psychiatry* 26, 224–7.

—— and Garfinkel, P.E. (1980). Socio-cultural factors in the development of anorexia nervosa. *Psychological Medicine* 10, 647–56.

Garrick, T.R. and Stottard, N.L. (1982). How to write a psychiatric consultation. *American Journal of Psychiatry* 139, 849–55.

Garrity, T.F. (1981). Behavioral adjustment after myocardial infarction: a selective review of recent descriptive, correlational and intervention research. In *Perspectives on behavioral medicine* (ed. S.M. Weiss, J.A. Herd, and B.H. Fox). Academic Press, New York.

Garrow, J.S. (1981). *Treat obesity seriously: a clinical manual.* Churchill Livingstone, Edinburgh.

Garver, D.E. and Davis, L.M. (1979). Biogenic amine hypothesis of affective disorders. *Life Science* 24, 383–94.

Gastaut, M. (1969). Clinical and electroencephalographic classification of epileptic seizures. *Epilepsia* Suppl. 10, 2–21.

Gath, A. (1978). *Down's syndrome and the family.* Academic Press, London.

Gath, D. (1980). Psychiatric aspects of hysterectomy. In *The social consequences of psychiatric illness* (ed. L. Bosin *et al.*). Brunner-Mazel, New York.

—— and Cooper, P. (1982). Psychiatric aspects of hysterectomy and female sterilisation. In *Recent advances in psychiatry,* Vol. 4 (ed. K. Granville-Grossman). Churchill Livingstone, Edinburgh.

—— —— Bond, A., and Edmonds, G. (1982). Hysterectomy and psychiatric disorder: II. Demographic psychiatric and physical factors in relation to psychiatric outcome. *British Journal of Psychiatry* 140, 343–50.

—— —— and Day, A. (1982). Hysterectomy and psychiatric disorder: I. Levels of psychiatric morbidity before and after hysterectomy. *British Journal of Psychiatry* 140, 335–42.

—— —— Gattoni, F., and Rockett, D. (1977). *Child guidance and delinquency in a London Borough.* Maudsley Monograph No. 24. Oxford University Press, London.

—— Hensman, C., Hawker, A., Kelly, M., and Edwards, G. (1968). The drunk in court: survey of drunkenness offenders from two London courts. *British Medical Journal* iv, 808–11.

Gaupp, R. (1914). The scientific significance of the case of Ernst Wagner. In *Themes and variations in European psychiatry* (ed. S.R. Hirsch and M. Shepherd) pp. 121–33 (1974).

Gayford, J.J. (1979). Battered wives. *British Journal of Hospital Medicine* 22, 496–503.

Gazzard, R.G., Davis, M., Spooner, J., and Williams, R. (1976). Why do people use paracetamol for suicide? *British Medical Journal* i, 212 – 13.

Gebhard, P.H., Raboch, J., and Giese, H. (1970). *The sexuality of women* (translated by C. Bearne). Deutsch, London.

Gelder, M.G. (1978). Hormones and post partum depression. In *Mental illness in pregnancy and the puerperium* (ed. M. Sandler). Oxford University Press.

—— Bancroft, J.H.J., Gath, D.H., Johnston, D.W., Matthews, A.M., and Shaw, P.M. (1973). Specific and non-specific factors in behaviour therapy. *British Journal of Psychiatry* **123**, 445–62.

—— Marks, I.M., and Wolff, H. (1967). Desensitization and psychotherapy in phobic states: a controlled enquiry. *British Journal of Psychiatry* **113**, 53–73.

General Register Office (1968). A glossary of mental disorders. *Studies on Medical and Population Subjects 22.* HMSO, London.

Gerbert, B. (1980). Psychological aspects of Crohn's disease. *Journal of Behavioral Medicine* **3**, 41–58.

German, G.A. (1972). Aspects of clinical psychiatry in Sub-Saharan Africa. *British Journal of Psychiatry* **121**, 461–79.

—— and Arya, O.P. (1969). Psychiatric morbidity amongst a Uganda student population. *British Journal of Psychiatry* **115**, 1323–9.

Gershon, E.S. and Bunney, W.E. (1976). The question of linkage in manic depressive illness. *Journal of Psychiatric Research* **13**, 99–117.

—— Mark, A., Cohen, N., Belizon, N., Barron, M., and Knobe, K.E. (1975). Transmitted factors in the morbidity of affective disorders: a controlled study. *Journal of Psychiatric Research* **12**, 283–99.

Gibbens, T.C.N. (1974). Preparing psychiatric court reports. *British Journal of Hospital Medicine* **11**, 278–84.

—— Palmer, C., and Prince, J. (1971). Mental health aspects of shoplifting. *British Medical Journal* iii, 612–15.

—— Pond, D.A., and Stafford Clark, D.A. (1959). A follow-up study of criminal psychopaths. *Journal of Mental Science* **105**, 108–15.

—— and Prince, J. (1965). *Child victims of sex offences.* Institute for the Study and Treatment of Delinquency, London.

—— Way, C., and Soothill, K.L. (1977). Behavioural types of rape. *British Journal of Psychiatry* **130**, 32–42.

Gibbons, J.S., Butler, J., Urwin, P., and Gibbons, J.L. (1978). Evaluation of a social work service for self-poisoning patients. *British Journal of Psychiatry* **133**, 111–18.

Gibbs, CJ., Gajdusek, D.C., Asher, D.M., Alpers, M.P., Beck, E., Daniel, P.M., and Matthews, W.B. (1968). Creutzfeldt–Jacob disease (spongiform encephalopathy): transmission to the chimpanzee. *Science* **161**, 388–9.

Gibson, A.J., Moyes, I.C.A., and Kendrick, D. (1980). Cognitive assessment of the elderly long stay patient. *British Journal of Psychiatry* **137**, 551–7.

Gibson, E. (1975). Homicide in Enland and Wales. 1967–71. *Home Office Research Study* No. 31. HMSO, London.

Gibson, S. and Becker, J. (1973). Changes in alcoholics' self-reported depression. *Quarterly Journal of Studies on Alcohol* **34**, 829–36.

Giller, E.L., Rotnem, D., Hsia, Y.E., and Leigh, H. (1981). Psychosocial care in a medical genetics clinic. *General Hospital Psychiatry* **3**, 171–8.

Gillespie, R.D. (1928). Hypochondria: definition, nosology and psychopathology. *Guy's Hospital Reports* **78**, 408–60.

—— (1929). Clinical differentiation of types of depression. *Guy's Hospital Reports* **79**, 306–44.

Gillies, N. (1976). Homicide in the west of Scotland. *British Journal of Psychiatry* **128**, 105–27.

Gittelson, N.L., Eacott, S.E., and Mehta, B.M. (1978). Victims of indecent exposure. *British Journal of Psychiatry* 132, 61–6.

Gjessing, R. (1947). Biological investigations in endogenous psychoses. *Acta Psychiatrica* (Kbh) Suppl. 47

Glaser, G.H. (1972). Diphenylhydantoin toxicity. In *Antiepileptic drugs* (ed. M. Dixon, J. Woodbury, J. Kiffin Penry, and R.P. Schmidt) Chapter 20. Raven Press, London.

Glatt, M.M. (1976). Alcoholism: disease concept and lack of control revisited. *British Journal of Addiction* 71, 135–44.

Glen, A.I.M., Dogg, M., Hulme, E.B., and Kreitman, N. (1979). Mortality on lithium. *Neuropsychobiology* 5, 167–73.

Glick, I.D. and Kessler, D.R. (1980). *Marital and family therapy,* 2nd edn. Grune and Stratten, New York.

Glickman, L.S. (1980). *Psychiatric consultation in the general hospital.* Marcel Dekker, New York.

Glueck, S. and Glueck, E. (1960). *Predicting delinquency and crime.* Harvard University Press, Cambridge, Mass.

Goffman, E. (1961). *Asylums: essays on the social situation of mental patients and other inmates.* Doubleday, New York.

Göktepe, E.O., Young, L.B., and Bridges, P.K. (1975). A further review of the results of stereotactic tractotomy. *British Journal of Psychiatry* 126, 270–81.

Goldberg, D. and Blackwell, B. (1970). Psychiatric illness in general practice. A detailed study using a new method of case identification. *British Medical Journal* ii, 439–43.

—— and Huxley, P. (1980). *Mental illness in the community.* Tavistock, London.

—— Richels, J., Downing, R., and Hesbacher, P. (1976). A comparison of two psychiatric screening tests. *British Journal of Psychiatry* 129, 61–7.

Goldberg, E.M. and Morrison, S.L. (1963). Schizophrenia and social class. *British Journal of Psychiatry* 109, 785–802.

Goldberg, I., Reglier, D., and McInery, T.K. (1929). The role of the pediatrician in the delivery of the mental health services to children. *Pediatrics* 63, 898–909.

Goldfried, M.R. and Goldfried, A.P. (1975). Cognitive change methods. In *Helping people change* (ed. F.H. Kafner and A.P. Goldstein). Pergamon, London.

Goldiamond, I. (1965). Self-control procedures in personal behaviour problems. *Psychological Reports* 17, 851–68.

Goldstein, A., Aronow, L., and Kalman, S.M. (1974). *Principles of drug action: the basis of pharmacology,* 2nd edn. Wiley, New York.

Goldstein, K. (1944). Methodological approach to the study of schizophrenic thought disorder. In *Language and thought in schizophrenia* (ed. J.S. Kasanin). University of California Press, Berkeley.

—— and Scheerer, M. (1941). Abstract and concrete behaviour: an experimental study with special tests. *Psychological Monographs* 53 No. 239.

—— (1975). Functional disturbance in brain damage. In *American handbook of psychiatry,* 2nd edn (Ed. S. Arieti and M.F. Reisser) Vol. 4. Basic Books, New York.

Gomez, J. (1975). Subjective side-effects of E.C.T. *British Journal of Psychiatry* 127, 609–11.

—— and Dally, P. (1977). Psychologically mediated abdominal pain in surgical and medical out-patient clinics. *British Medical Journal* i, 1451–3.

Goodstein, R.K. and Page, A.W. (1981). Battered wife syndrome: overview of dynamics and treatment. *American Journal of Psychiatry* 1387, 1036–44.

Goodwin, D.W. (1971). Is alcoholism hereditary? *Archives of General Psychiatry* 25, 545–9.

—— Schulsinger, F., Hermansen, L., Guze, S.B., and Winokur, G. (1973). Alcohol problems in adoptees raised apart from alcoholic biological parents. *Archives of General Psychiatry* **28**, 238–43.

Goodwin, F.K., Murphy, D.L., and Bunney, W.E. (1969). Lithium carbonate treatment in depression and mania: a longitudinal double blind study. *Archives of General Psychiatry* **21**, 486–96.

—— and Zis, A.P. (1979). Lithium in the treatment of mania: comparisons with neuroleptics. *Archives of General Psychiatry* **36**, 840–4.

Gordon, W.A., Freidenbergs, I., Diller, L., Hibbard, M., Wolf, C., Levine, L., Lipkins, R., Ezrachi, O., and Lucido, D. (1980). Efficacy of psychosocial intervention with cancer patients. *Journal of Consulting and Clinical Psychology* **48**, 743–59.

Gossop, M. (1978). A review of the evidence for methadone maintenance as a treatment for narcotic addiction. *Lancet* **i**, 812–15.

—— (1981). *Theories of neurosis.* Springer, Berlin.

Gottesman, I. and Shields, J.A. (1967). A polygenic theory of schizophrenia. *Proceedings of the National Academy of Science* **58**, 199–205.

—— —— (1972). *Schizophrenia and genetics; a twin study vantage point.* Academic Press, New York.

Grad, J. and Sainsbury, P. (1966). Evaluating the community psychiatric service in Chichester: results. *Millbank Research Fund Quarterly* **44**, 246–77.

Graham, J.D.P. (ed.) (1976). *Cannabis and health.* Academic Press, London.

Graham, P. (1974). Depression in prepubertal children. *Developmental Medicine and Child Neurology* **16**, 340–9.

—— (1979). Epidemiological studies. In *Psychological disorders of childhood* (ed. H.C. Quay and J.S. Werry). Wiley, New York.

—— and Rutter, M. (1968). Organic brain dysfunction and child psychiatric disorder. *British Medical Journal* **iii**, 695–700.

—— —— (1973). Psychiatric disorder in the young adolescent: a follow-up study. *Proceedings of the Royal Society of Medicine* **66**, 1226–9.

—— —— (1970). Psychiatric aspects of physical disorder. In *Education, health and behaviour* (ed. M. Rutter, J. Tizard, and K. Whitmore). Longman, London.

Graham, P.S. (1982). Late paraphrenia. *British Journal of Hospital Medicine* **27**, 522–8.

Grahame-Smith, D.G., Green, A.R., and Costain, D.W. (1978). Mechanisms of the antidepressant action of electroconvulsive therapy. *Lancet* **i**, 254–6.

Gralnick, A. (1942). Folie à deux. The psychosis of association. *Psychiatric Quarterly* **16**, 230–63.

Grant, I., Heaton, R.K., McSweeny, J., Adams, K.M., and Timms, R.M. (1982). Neuropsychological findings in hypoxemic chronic obstructive pulmonary disease. *Archives of Internal Medicine* **142**, 1470–6.

Gray, J.A. (1971). *The psychology of fear and stress.* Weidenfeld and Nicholson, London.

Green, A.R. and Costain, D.W. (1979). The biochemistry of depression. In *Psychopharmacology of affective disorders* (ed. E.S. Paykel and A. Coppen). Oxford University Press.

—— —— (1981). *Pharmacology and biochemistry of psychiatric disorders.* Wiley, Chichester.

Green, J.R., Troupin, A.S., Halpern, L.M., Friel, P., and Kanarek, P. (1974). Sulthiame: evaluation as an anticonvulsant. *Epilepsia* **15**, 329–49.

Green, R. (1974). *Sexual identity conflict in children and adults.* Duckworth, London.

—— and Costain, D.W. (1981). *Pharmacology and biochemistry of psychiatric disorders.* Wiley, Chichester.

—— and Money, J. (1961). Effeminacy in prepubertal boys: summary of eleven cases and recommendations for case management. *Pediatrics* **27**, 286–91.

———— (1969). *Transsexualism and sex reassignment.* Johns Hopkins Press, Baltimore.

Greenblatt, M., Grosser, G.H., and Wechsler, H. (1964). Differential response of hospitalized patients to somatic therapy. *American Journal of Psychiatry* **120**, 935–43.

Greenhill, M.H. (1977). The development of liaison programs. In *Psychiatric medicine* (ed. G. Usdin) pp. 115–91. Brunner Mazel, New York.

Greenson, R.R. (1967). *The techniques and practice of psychoanalysis.* Hogarth Press, London.

Greer, S. (1969). The prognosis of anxiety states. In *Studies in Anxiety* (ed. M.H. Lader) pp. 151–7. Royal Medicopsychological Association, London.

——— and Bagley, C. (1971). Effects of psychiatric intervention in attempted suicide: a controlled study. *British Medical Journal* **i**, 310–12.

——— and Cawley, R.H. (1966). *Some observations on the natural history of neurotic illness.* Australian Medical Association. Mervyn Archdall Medical Monograph No. 3. Australasian Medical Publishing Company.

——— Marcus, T., and Pettingale, K. W. (1979). Psychological response to breast cancer: effect on outcome. *Lancet* **ii**, 785–7.

——— and Silberfarb, P.M. (1982). Psychological concomitants of cancer: current state of research. *Psychological Medicine* **12**, 563–73.

Gresham, G.E., Phillips, T.F., and Wolf, P.A. (1979). Epidemiologic profile of long term stroke disability: the Framingham study. *Archives of Physical and Medical Rehabilitation* **60**, 487–91.

Griesinger, W. (1867). *Mental pathology and therapeutics* (translated from the German 2nd edn by C. Lockhart Robertson and J. Rutherford). New Sydenham Society, London.

Griffin, N., Draper, R.J., and Webb, M.G.T. (1981). Addiction to tranylcypromine. *British Medical Journal* **283**, 346.

Gross, M.M., Rosenblatt, S.M., Lewis, E., Malenowski, B., and Broman, M. (1971). Hallucinations and clouding of sensorium during alcohol withdrawal. *Quarterly Journal of Studies on Alcohol* **32**, 1061–9.

Gruhle, H.W. (1936). Uber dem Wahn bei Epilepsie. *Zeitschrift für die gesamte Neurologie und Psychiatrie* **154**, 395–9.

Guerrant, J., Anderson, W.W., Fischer, A., Weinstein, M.R., Jaros, R.M., and Deskins, A. (1962). *Personality in epilepsy.* Thomas, Springfield, Ill.

Gundle, M.J., Bozman, R.R., Tate, S., Raft, D., and McLaurin, L.P. (1980). Psychosocial outcome after coronary artery surgery. *American Journal of Psychiatry* **137**, 1591–4.

Gunn, J. (1976). *Epileptics in prison.* Academic Press, London.

——— (1977). Criminal behaviour and mental disorder. *British Journal of Psychiatry* **130**, 317–29.

——— (1979). Forensic psychiatry. In *Recent advances in clinical psychiatry* Vol. 3 (ed. K. Granville-Grossman). Churchill Livingstone, Edinburgh.

——— and Farrington, D.P. (1982). *Abnormal offenders: delinquency and the criminal justice system.* Wiley, Chichester.

——— and Fenton, G.W. (1971). Epilepsy, automatism and crime. *Lancet* **i**, 1173–6.

——— and Robertson, G. (1982). An evaluation of Grendon Prison. In *Abnormal offenders, delinquency and the criminal justice system* (ed. J. Gunn and D.P. Farrington). Wiley, Chichester.

Gurland, B., Cross, P., Defiguerido, J., Shannon, M., Mann, A.H., Jenkins, R., Bennett, R., Wilder, D., Wright, H., Kileffer, E., Godlove, C., Thompson, P., Ross, M., and Deming, W.E. (1979). A cross-national comparison of the institutionalised elderly in the cities of New York and London. *Psychological Medicine* **9**, 781–8.

—— Ganz, V.F., Fleiss, J.L., and Zubin, J. (1972). The study of psychiatric symptoms of systemic lupus erythematosus: a critical review. *Psychosomatic Medicine* **34**, 199–206.

Gurman, A. (1979). Research on marital and family therapy: progress, perspective and prospect. In *Handbook of psychotherapy and behaviour change,* 2nd. Edn (ed. S.L. Garfield and A.E. Bergin). Wiley, New York.

Gussow, Z. (1963). A preliminary report of Kayak-Angst among the Eskimo of West Greenland: a study in sensory deprivation. *International Journal of Social Psychiatry* **9**, 18–26.

Guttman, E. and Maclay, W.S. (1936). Mescalin and depersonalization; therapeutic experiments. *Journal of Neurology and Psychopathology* **16**, 193–212.

Guttman, R.A., Stead, W.W., and Robinson, R.R. (1981). Physical activity and employment status of patients on maintenance dialysis. *New England Journal of Medicine* **304**, 309–13.

Guze, S.B. (1976). *Criminality and psychiatric disorders.* Oxford University Press, New York.

—— Woodruff, R.A., and Clayton, P.J. (1971). 'Secondary' affective disorder: a study of 95 cases. *Psychological Medicine* **1**, 426–8.

Haan, N.G. (1979). Psychological meanings of unfavourable forecasts. In *Health psychology—a handbook* (ed. G.C. Stone, F. Cohen, and N.E. Adler). Joss Bassey, San Francisco.

Hachinski, V., Lassen, N.A., and Marshall, J. (1974). Multi-infarct dementia. *Lancet* **ii**, 207–9.

Hackett, T.P. and Cassem, N.H. (1978*a*). Psychological aspects of rehabilitation after myocardial infarction. In *Rehabilitation of the coronary patient.* (ed. N.K. Wenger and H.K. Hetherstein). Wiley, New York.

—— —— (1978*b*). *Handbook of general hospital psychiatry.* Mosby, St. Louis.

—— and Weissman, A. (1962). The treatment of the dying. *Current Psychiatric Therapy* **2**, 121–6.

Häfner, H. and Reimann, H. (1970). Spatial distribution of mental disorders in Mannheim. In *Psychiatric epidemiology* (ed. E.H. Hare and J.K. Wing). Oxford University Press, London.

Hagnell, O. (1966). *A prospective study of the incidence of mental disorder.* Scandinavian University Books, Denmark.

—— (1970). Incidence and duration of episodes of mental illness in a total population. In *Psychiatric epidemiology* (ed. E.H. Hare and J.K. Wing). Oxford University Press, London.

Hahn, R.D., Webster, B., Weickhardt, G., Thomas, E., Timberlake, W., Solomon, H., Stokes, J.H., Moore, J.E., Heyman, A., Gammon, G., Gleeson, G.A., Curtis, A.C., and Cutler, J.C. (1959). Penicillin treatment of general paresis (dementia paralytica). *Archives of Neurology and Psychiatry* **81**, 557–90.

Hakim, A.M. and Mathieson, G. (1978). Basis of dementia in Parkinson's disease. *Lancet* **ii**, 729.

Hakim, S. and Adams, R.D. (1965). The special problem of symptomatic hydrocephalus with normal cerebrospinal fluid pressures: observations on cerebrospinal fluid hydrodynamics. *Journal of Neurological Sciences* **2**, 307–27.

Haley, J. (1963). *Strategies of psychotherapy.* Grune and Stratton, New York.

Hall, G.S. and Lindzey, G. (1980). *Theories of personality,* 3rd edn. Wiley, Chichester.

Hall, J. (1983). Ward based rehabilitation programmes. In *Theory and practice of psychiatric rehabilitation* (ed. F.N. Watts and D.H. Bennett). Wiley, Chichester.

Hall, R.C.W. (1980). *Psychiatric presentation of medical illness: somatopsychic disorders.* MTP, Lancaster.

Hall-Smith, S.P. and Norton, A. (1951). Psychiatric survey of a random sample of skin out-patients. *British Medical Journal* **ii**, 417–21.

Hallgren, B. (1960). Nocturnal enuresis in twins. *Acta Psychiatrica Scandinavica* **35**, 73–90.

Halliday, J.L. (1937). Epidemiology and the psychosomatic affections: a study in social medicine. *Lancet* **ii**, 185–91.

Halmi, K.A., Falk, J.R., and Schwartz, E. (1981). Binge-eating and vomiting: a survey of a college population. *Psychological Medicine* **11**, 697–706.

Hamburg, D.A. and Adams, J.E. (1967). A perspective on coping behaviour. *Archives of General Psychiatry* **17**, 277–84.

—— Artz, P., Reiss, E., Amspacker, W., and Chambers, R.E. (1953). Clinical importance of emotional problems in the care of patients with burns. *New England Journal of Medicine* **248**, 355–9.

Hamilton, J.A. (1962). *Post partum psychiatric problems.* Mosby, St. Louis.

Hamilton, J.R. and Freeman, H. (1982). *Dangerousness: psychiatric assessment and management.* Gaskell, London.

—— Griffith, A., Ritson, E.B., and Aitken, R.C.B. (1977). A detoxification unit for habitual drunken offenders. *Health Bulletin* **35**, 146–54.

Hampson, J.L. and Hampson, J.G. (1961). The ontogenesis of sexual behaviour in man. In *Sex and internal secretions,* 3rd edn (ed. W.C. Young). John Hopkins Press, Baltimore.

Hans, M. and Koeppen, A.H. (1980). Huntington's chorea: its impact on the spouse. *Journal of Nervous and Mental Disease* **168**, 209–14.

Hanson, D.R., Gottesman, I.I., and Heston, L.L. (1976). Some possible childhood indications of adult schizophrenia inferred from children of schizophrenics. *British Journal of Psychiatry* **129**, 142–54.

Hanson, J.W., Jones, K.L., and Smith, D.W. (1976). Fetal alcohol syndrome: an experiment with 41 patients. *Journal of the American Medical Association* **235**, 1458–60.

Hare, E.H. (1956). Mental illness and social conditions in Bristol. *Journal of Mental Science* **102**, 349–57.

—— (1956). Family setting and the urban distribution of schizophrenia. *Journal of Mental Science* **102**, 753–60.

—— (1959). The origin and spread of dementia paralytica. *Journal of Mental Science* **105**, 594–626.

—— (1973). A short note on pseudo-hallucinations. *British Journal of Psychiatry* **122**, 469–76.

—— (1975). Season of birth in schizophrenia and neurosis. *American Journal of Psychiatry* **132**, 1168–71.

—— and Shaw, G.K. (1965). *Mental health on a new housing estate: a comparative study of two districts of Croydon.* Maudsley Monographs No. 12. Oxford University Press, London.

Harris, A.I., Cox, E., and Smith, C.R.W. (1971). Handicapped and impaired in Great Britain, Part 1. London. *Office of Population Censuses and Surveys.* HMSO, London.

Harris, E.L. and Fitzgerald, J.D. (1970). *The principles and practice of clinical trials.* Livingstone, Edinburgh.

Harrison, G. (1980). The abuse of anti-cholinergic drugs in adolescents. *British Journal of Psychiatry* **137**, 494–6.

Hartmann, H. (1964). *Essays on ego psychology.* Hogarth Press, London.

Hartman, V. (1965). Notes on group therapy with pedophiles. *Canadian Psychiatric Association Journal* **10**, 283–8.

Harvey, R.F., Jellinek, H.M., and Marteck, R.U. (1982). Cancer rehabilitation: an analysis of 36 program approaches. *Journal of the American Medical Association* **247**, 2127–31.

Harvey Smith, E.A. and Cooper, B. (1970). Patterns of neurotic illness in the community. *Journal of the Royal College of General Practitioners* **19**, 132–9.

Haug, J.O. (1962). Pneumoencephalographic studies in mental disease. *Acta Psychiatrica Scandinavica* Suppl. **165**, 1–114.

Havdala, H.S., Borison, R.L., and Diamond, B.T. (1979). Potential hazards and applications of lithium in anesthesiology. *Anesthesiology* **50**, 534–7.

Havard, J.D.J. (1977). Alcohol and road accidents in *Alcoholism: new knowledge and new responses* (ed. G. Edwards and M. Grant). Croom Helm, London.

Hawker, A. (1978). *Adolescents and alcohol.* Edsall, London.

Hawton, K. (1980). Current trends in sex therapy. In *Current trends in treatment in psychiatry* (ed. T.G. Tennant). Pitman Medical, Tunbridge Wells.

——(1982). Attempted suicide in children and adolescents. *Journal of Child Psychology and Psychiatry* **23**, 497–503.

—— and Catalan, J. (1982). *Attempted suicide: a practical guide to its nature and management.* Oxford University Press.

—— Crowle, J., Simkin, S., and Bancroft, J.H.J. (1978). Attempted suicide and suicide among Oxford University students. *British Journal of Psychiatry* **132**, 506–9.

—— Fagg, J., and Marsack, P. (1980). Association between epilepsy and attempted suicide. *Journal of Neurology, Neurosurgery and Psychiatry* **43**, 168–70.

—— Gath, D., and Smith, E. (1979). Management of attempted suicide in Oxford. *British Medical Journal* **ii**, 1040–2.

—— O'Grady, J. Osborn, M., and Cole, D. (1982). Adolescents who take overdoses: their characteristics, problems and contacts with helping agencies. *British Journal of Psychiatry* **140**, 118–23.

—— and Oppenheimer, C. (1983). Women's sexual problems. In *Women's problems in general practice* (ed. A. Anderson and A. McPherson). Oxford University Press.

Hay, G.G. (1970*a*). Psychiatric aspects of cosmetic nasal operations. *British Journal of Psychiatry* **116**, 85–97.

——(1970*b*). Dysmorphophobia. *British Journal of Psychiatry* **116**, 399–406.

Haynes, R.B., Taylor, D.W., and Sackett, D.L. (eds.) (1979). *Compliance in health care.* Johns Hopkins University Press, Baltimore.

Haynes, S.G., Feinleib, M., and Kannel, W.B. (1980). The relationship of psycho-social factors to coronary heart disease in the Framingham study. III: Eight year incidence of coronary heart disease. *American Journal of Epidemiology* **111**, 37–58.

Head, H. (1920). *Studies in neurology,* Vol. 2. Oxford University Press.

Heathfield, K.W.G. (1967). Huntington's chorea. *Brain* **90**, 203–32.

Heber, R. and Garber, H. (1975). The Milwaukee project: a study of the use of family intervention to prevent cultural familial retardation. In *The exceptional infant* (ed. B.Z. Friedlander, G.M. Sternt, and C.E. Kirk) Vol. 3. Brunner-Mazel, New York.

Hecker, E. (1871). Die Hebephrenie. *Virchows Archiv für Pathologie und Anatomie* **52**, 394–429.

Heimann, P. (1950). On countertransference. *International Journal of Psychoanalysis* **31**, 81–4.

Helgason, T. (1964). Epidemiology of mental disorders in Iceland. A psychiatric and demographic investigation of 5395 Icelanders. *Acta Psychiatrica Scandinavica.* Suppl. 173.

Helmsley, D.R. (1975). A two stage model of attention in schizophrenia research. *British Journal of Social and Clinical Psychology* **14**, 81–9.

Helweg-Larsen, P., Hoffmeyer, H., Kieler, J., Thaysen, E.H., Thaysen, J.H., Thygesen, P., and Wulff, M.H. (1952). Famine disease in German concentration camps: complications and sequels. *Acta Psychiatrica et Neurologica Scandinavica* Suppl. 83, 1–460.

Helzer, J.E. and Winokur, G. (1974). A family interview study of male manic depressives. *Archives of General Psychiatry* **31**, 73–7.

Hempel, C.G. (1961). Introduction to problems of taxonomy. In *Field studies in the mental disorders* (ed. J. Zubin). Grune and Stratton, New York.

Hemphill, R.E. (1952). Puerperal psychiatric illness. *British Medical Journal* ii, 1232–5.
Henderson, A.S., Krapowski, J., and Stoller, A. (1971). Epidemiological aspects of adolescent psychiatry. In *Modern perspectives in adolescent psychiatry* (ed. J.G. Howells). Oliver & Boyd, Edinburgh.
Henderson, D.K. (1939). *Psychopathic states.* Chapman and Hall, London.
Henderson, S., Duncan-Jones, P., McAuley, H., and Ritchie, K. (1978). The patient's primary group. *British Journal of Psychiatry* 132, 74–86.
Hendriksen, C. and Binder, V. (1980). Social prognosis in patients with ulcerative colitis. *British Medical Journal* ii, 581–3.
Henry, G.W. (1929). Some modern aspects of psychiatry in general hospital practice. *American Journal of Psychiatry* 86, 623–30.
Henry, J.P. (1982). The relation of social to biological processes in disease. *Social Science and Medicine* 16, 369–80.
—— Meehan, J.P. and Stephens, P.M. (1967). Use of psychosocial stimuli to induce prolonged systolic hypertension in mice. *Psychosomatic Medicine* 29, 408–32.
Herbert, M. and Jacobson, S. (1967). Late paraphrenia. *British Journal of Psychiatry* 113, 461–9.
Hermann, B.P. and Stevens, J.R. (1981). Interictal behaviour correlates of the epilepsies. In *A multidisciplinary handbook of epilepsy* (ed. B.P. Hermann). Thomas, Springfield, Ill.
Hermelin, B. and O'Connor, N. (1970). *Psychological experiments with autistic children.* Pergamon, Oxford.
Hershon, H.I. (1977). Alcohol withdrawal symptoms and drinking behaviour. *Journal of Studies on Alcoholism* 38, 953–71.
Hersov, L. (1960). Refusal to go to school. *Journal of Child Psychology and Psychiatry* 1, 137–45.
—— (1977). Encopresis. In *Child psychiatry: modern approaches* (ed. L. Hersov and M. Rutter). Blackwell, Oxford.
—— and Berg, I. (eds.) (1980). *Out of school.* Wiley, Chichester.
—— Berger, M., and Nicol, A.R. (eds.) (1980). *Language and language disorders in children.* Pergamon, Oxford.
Herstbech, S., Hansea, H.E., Amdisen, A., and Olsen, S. (1977). Chronic renal lesions following long term treatment with lithium. *Kidney International* 12, 205–13.
Herzog, A. and Detre, T., (1967). Psychotic reaction associated with childbirth. *Diseases of the Nervous System* 37, 229–35.
Heshe, J. and Roeder, E. (1976). Electroconvulsive therapy in Denmark. *British Journal of Psychiatry* 128, 241–5.
Hesse, K.A.F. (1975). Meeting the psychosocial needs of pacemaker patients. *International Journal of Psychiatry in Medicine* 6, 359–72.
Heston, L.J. (1966). Psychiatric disorders in foster home reared children of schizophrenic mothers. *British Journal of Psychiatry* 112, 819–25.
—— Mastri, A.R., Anderson, V.E., and White, J. (1981). Dementia of the Alzheimer type. Clinical genetics, natural history and associated conditions. *Archives of General Psychiatry* 38, 1085–90.
—— and Shields, J. (1968). Homosexuality in twins: a family study and a registry study. *Archives of General Psychiatry* 18, 149–60.
Hewett, L.E. and Jenkins, R.L. (1946). *Fundamental patterns of maladjustment: the dynamics of their origin.* Thomas, Springfield, Ill.
Hewett, S.H. and Ryan, P.J. (1975). Alternatives to living in psychiatric hospitals – a pilot study. *British Journal of Hospital Medicine* 14, 65–70.
Hewison, J. (1982]. The current states of remedial intervention for children with reading problems. *Developmental Medicine and Child Neurology* 24, 183–93.
Hill, D. (1952). EEG in episodic psychotic and psychopathic behaviour: a classification of data. *Electroencephalography and Clinical Neurophysiology* 4, 419–42.

—— (1953). Psychiatric disorders of epilepsy. *Medical Press* **229**, 473–5.

—— (1981). Historical review. In *Epilepsy and psychiatry* (ed. E.M. Reynolds and M.R. Trimble). Churchill Livingstone, Edinburgh.

Hill, O.W. (1972). Functional vomiting. *British Journal of Hospital Medicine* **7**, 755–8.

Hinde, R.A. (1977). Mother–infant separation and the nature of inter-individual relationships: experiments with rhesus monkeys. *Proceedings of the Royal Society of London* (Series B) **196**, 29–50.

—— and Spencer Booth, Y. (1970). Individual differences in the responses of rhesus monkeys to a period of separation from their mothers. *Journal of Child Psychology and Psychiatry* **11**, 159–76.

Hinkle, L.E. and Wolf, S. (1952). Importance of life stress in the course and management of diabetes mellitus. *Journal of the American Medical Association* **148**, 513–20.

Hinton, J. (1972). *Dying*, 2nd edn. Penguin, Harmondsworth.

—— (1979). Comparison of places and policies for terminal care. *Lancet* **i**, 29–32.

Hirsch, S.R. (1982). Depression revealed in schizophrenia. *British Journal of Psychiatry* **140**, 421–3.

—— Gaind, R., Rohde, P.D., Stevens, B.C., and Wing, J.K. (1973). Outpatient maintenance of chronic schizophrenic patients with long acting fluphenazine: double blind placebo trial. *British Medical Journal* **i**, 633–7.

—— and Leff, J. (1975). *Abnormalities in parents of schizophrenics.* Maudsley Monograph No. 22. Oxford University Press, London.

Hirschfeld, M. (1936). *Sexual anomalies and perversions.* Aldor, London.

—— (1944). *Sexual anomalies and perversions: physical and psychological development and treatment.* Aldor, London.

Hirst, W. (1982). The amnesic syndrome: descriptions and explanation. *Psychological Bulletin* **91**, 435–66.

Hobson, R.F. (1953). Prognostic factors in electric convulsive therapy. *Journal of Neurology, Neurosurgery and Psychiatry* **16**, 275–81.

Hoch, P.H. and Polantin, P. (1949). Pseudoneurotic forms of schizophrenia. *Psychiatric Quarterly* **23**, 249–96.

Hodkinson, H.M. (1973). Mental impairment in the elderly. *Journal of the Royal College of Physicians* **7**, 305–17.

Hoehn-Sarik, R., Frank, J.D., Imber, S.D., Nash, E.H., Stone, A.R., and Battle, C.R. (1964). Systematic preparation of patients for psychotherapy I: Effect on therapy behaviour and outcome. *Journal of Psychiatric Research* **2**, 267–81.

Hoenig, J. and Kenna, J.C. (1974). The prevalence of transsexualism in England and Wales. *British Journal of Psychiatry* **124**, 181–90.

Hogarty, G.E., Goldberg, S.C., and Schooler, N. (1974). Drugs and sociotherapy in the aftercare of schizophrenic patients II. Two years relapse rates. *Archives of General Psychiatry* **31**, 603–8.

—— and Ulrich, R. (1977). Temporal effects of drug and placebo in delaying relapse in schizophrenic out-patients. *Archives of General Psychiatry* **34**, 297–301.

Holding, T.A. and Barraclough, B.M. (1975). Psychiatric morbidity in a sample of a London coroner's open verdicts. *British Journal of Psychiatry* **127**, 133–43.

—— Buglass, D., Duffy, J.C., and Kreitman, N. (1977). Parasuicide in Edinburgh – a seven year review, 1968–1974. *British Journal of Psychiatry* **130**, 534–43.

Hollingshead, A.B. and Redlich, F.C. (1958). *Social class and mental illness: a community study.* Wiley, New York.

Holmes, T.H., Hawkins, N.G., Bowerman, E., Clarke, R., and Joffe, J.R. (1957). Psychosocial and psychophysiologic studies of tuberculosis. *Psychosomatic Medicine* **19**, 134–43.

—— and Rahe, R.H. (1967). The social adjustment rating scale. *Journal of Psychosomatic Research* **11**, 213–18.

Holt, S., Stewart, I.C., Dixon, J.M., Elton, R.A., Taylor, T.V., and Little, K. (1980). Alcohol and the emergency service patient. *British Medical Journal* **281**, 638–40.

Hood, R. and Sparks, R. (1980). *Key issues in criminology*. Weidenfeld and Nicholson, London.

Höök, K. (1963). Refused abortion: a follow-up study of 249 women whose applications were refused by the National Board of Health in Sweden. *Acta Psychiatrica Scandinavica* Suppl. 168.

Hore, B.D. and Wilkins, R.H. (1976). A general-practice study of the commonest presenting symptoms of alcoholism. *Journal of the Royal College of General Practitioners* **26**, 140–2.

Houpt, J.L., Orleans, C.S., George, L.K., and Brodie, K.H. (1980). The role of psychiatric behavioural factors in the practice of medicine. *American Journal of Psychiatry* **137**, 37–47.

Houston, F. and Royse, A.B. (1954). Relationship between deafness and psychotic illness. *Journal of Mental Science* **100**, 990–3.

Howlin, P. (1980). Language. In *Scientific foundation of developmental psychology* (ed. M. Rutter). Heinemann, London.

—— Marchant, R., Rutter, M., Berger, M., Hersov, L., and Yule, W. (1973). A home based approach to the treatment of autistic children. *Journal of Autism and Child Schizophrenia* **3**, 308–6.

Hsu, L.K.G. (1980). Outcome of anorexia nervosa. *Archives of General Psychiatry* **37**, 1041–6.

Hull, C.L. (1943). *Principles of behaviour*. Appleton, New York.

Hume, D. (1958). *A treatise of human nature* (ed. L.A. Selby-Bigge). Oxford University Press.

Hunter, M. (1979). Forensic psychiatry and mental handicap. In *Psychiatric illness and mental handicap* (ed. F.E. James and R.P. Snaith). Gaskell, Ashford.

Huntington, G. (1872). On chorea. *Medical and Surgical Reporter. Philadelphia* **26**, 317–21.

Hutchings, B. and Mednick, S.A. (1974). Registered criminality in the adopted and biological parents of registered male criminal adoptees. In *Genetic researches in psychiatry* (ed. R.R. Fieve *et al.*). Johns Hopkins University Press, Baltimore.

Huxley, P.J., Goldberg, D.P., Maguire, E.P., and Kincey, V. (1979). The prediction of the course of minor psychiatric disorders. *British Journal of Psychiatry* **135**, 535–43.

Illingworth, R.S. (1980). *Development of the infant and young child*. Churchill Livingstone, Edinburgh.

Imboden, J.B. (1972). Psychosocial determinants of recovery. In *Psychosocial aspects of physical illness* (ed. Z.J. Lipowski). Karger, Basel.

—— Canter, A., and Cluff, L.E. (1959). Brucellosis III. Psychological aspects of delayed convalescence. *Archives of Internal Medicine* **103**, 406–14.

—— —— —— (1961). Convalescence from influenza: a study of the psychological and clinical determinants. *Archives of Internal Medicine* **108**, 393–9.

Isbell, H., Altschul, S., Kornetsky, C.H., Eisenman, A.J., Flanary, H.G., and Graser, H.F. (1950). Chronic barbiturate intoxication. *Archives of Neurology and Psychiatry* **64**, 416–18.

—— Fraser, H.F., Wikler, A., Belleville, R., and Eisenman, A.J. (1955). An experimental study of the etiology of 'rum fits' and 'delirium tremens'. *Quarterly Journal of Studies on Alcoholism* **16**, 1–33.

—— Gorodetsky, G.W., Jasinski, D., Claussen, U., Spulack, F., and Korte, F. (1967). Effects of delta-9-transtetrahydrocannibinol in man. *Psychopharmacology* **2**, 184–8.

Jablensky, A. and Sartorius, N. (1975). Culture and schizophrenia. *Psychological Medicine* **5**, 113–34.

Jackson, B.M. (1969). A case of voyeurism treated by counterconditioning. *Behaviour Research and Therapy* **7**, 133–4.

Jacobs, P.A., Brunton, M., Melville, M.M., Brittain, R.P., and McClemont, W.F. (1965). Aggressive behaviour and subnormality. *Nature* **208**, 1351–2.

Jacobs, S. and Myers, J. (1976). Recent life events and acute schizophrenic psychosis: a controlled study. *Journal of Nervous and Mental Disease* **162**, 75–87.

—— Prusoff, B.A., and Paykel, E.S. (1974). Recent life events in schizophrenia and depression. *Psychological Medicine* **4**, 444–52.

Jacobson, E. (1938). *Progressive relaxation*. Chicago University Press.

—— (1953). Contribution to the metapsychology of cyclothymic depression. In *Affective disorders* (ed. P. Greenacre). International Universities Press, New York.

—— Kales, A., Lehmann, D., and Zweizig, J.R. (1965). Somnambulism: all night electroencephalographic studies. *Science* **148**, 975–7.

Jacoby, R. (1981). Dementia, depression and the CT scan. *Psychological Medicine* **11**, 673–6.

—— and Levy, R. (1980). Computed tomography in the elderly II: Senile dementia: diagnosis and functional impariment. *British Journal of Psychiatry* **136**, 256–69.

Jahoda, G. and Cramond, J. (1972). *Children and alcohol. A developmental study in Glasgow*, Vol. 1. HMSO, London.

Jakob, A. (1921). Über eingenarte Erkrankungen des Zentralnervensystems mit bemerkenswerten anatomischen Befunde. *Zeitschrift für die gesamte Neurologie und Psychiatrie* **64**, 147–228.

Jambor, K.L. (1969). Cognitive functioning in multiple sclerosis. *British Journal of Psychiatry* **115**, 765–75.

James, F.E. and Snaith, R.P. (1979). *Psychiatric illness and mental handicap*. Gaskell, Ashford.

James, I.P. (1967). Suicide and mortality among heroin addicts in Britain. *British Journal of Addictions* **62**, 391–8.

Janet, P. (1909). *Les névroses*. Flammarion, Paris.

—— (1925). *Psychological healing*. Allen and Unwin, London.

Janis, I.L. (1958). *Psychological stress: psychoanalytic and behavioural studies of surgical patients*. Wiley, New York.

Jannoun, L., Munby, M., Catalan, J., and Gelder, M.G. (1980). A home based treatment program for agoraphobia. *Behaviour Therapy* **11**, 294–305.

Jarman, C.M.B. and Kellet, J.M. (1979). Alcoholism in the general hospital. *British Medical Journal* **ii**, 469–71.

Jaspers, K. (1913). *Allgemeine Psychopathologie*. Springer, Berlin.

—— (1963). *General psychopathology* (translated by J. Hoenig and M.W. Hamilton). Manchester University Press.

Jeavons, P.M. (1970). Choice of drug therapy in epilepsy. *Practitioner* **219**, 542–56.

Jellinek, E.M. (1959). Estimating the prevalence of alcoholism: modified values in the Jellinek formula and an alternative approach. *Quarterly Journal of Studies on Alcohol* **20**, 261–9.

—— (1960). *The disease concept of alcoholism*. Hillhouse Press, New Brunswick.

Jenkins, C.D. (1976). Recent evidence supporting psychologic and social risk factors for coronary disease. *New England Journal of Medicine* **294**, 987–94 and 1033–8.

—— (1982). Psychosocial risk factors for coronary heart disease. *Acta Medica Scandinavica* Suppl. 660, 123–36.

Jenkins, L., Tarnopolsky, A., and Hand, D. (1981). Psychiatric admissions and aircraft noise from London Airport: four year, three-hospitals' study. *Psychological Medicine* **11**, 765–82.

Jennings, C., Barraclough, B.M., and Moss, J.R. (1978). Have the Samaritans lowered the suicide rate? A controlled study. *Psychological Medicine* **8**, 413–22.

Jesness, C.F. (1962). *The Jesness inventory: development and validation*. Research report no. 29. California Youth Authority, Sacramento.

Johnson, A.M., Falstein, E.K., Szorek, S.A., and Svendsen, M. (1941). School phobia. *American Journal of Orthopsychiatry* **11**, 702–11.

Johnson, J. (1969). Organic psychosyndromes due to boxing. *British Journal of Psychiatry* **115**, 45–53.

Johnson, S.B. (1980). Psychosocial factors in juvenile diabetes: a review. *Journal of Behavioural Medicine* **3**, 95–116.

Johnston, D.W. (1982). Behavioural treatment in the reduction of coronary risk factors: type A behaviour and blood pressure. *British Journal of Clinical Psychology* **21**, 281–94.

—— and Letham, J. (1981). The production of specific decrease in interbeat interval and the motor skills analogy. *Psychophysiology* **18**, 288–300.

Johnston, M. and Carpenter, L. (1980). Relationship between pre-operative anxiety and post-operative state. *Psychological Medicine* **10**, 361–7.

Johnstone, E.C., Crow, T.J., Frith, C.D., Carney, M.W.P., and Price, J.S. (1978). Mechanism of the antipsychotic effect in the treatment of acute schizophrenia. *Lancet* **i**, 848–51.

—— Crow, T.J., Firth, C.D., Husband, J., and Kreel, L. (1976). Cerebral ventricular size and cognitive impairment in chronic schizophrenia. *Lancet* **ii**, 924–6.

—— —— and Masheter, K. (1977). Anterior pituitary hormone secretion in chronic schizophrenia – an approach to neurohormonal mechanisms. *Psychological Medicine* **7**, 223–8.

—— Cunningham-Owens, D.G., Gold, A., Crow, T.J., and Macmillan, J.F. (1981). Institutionalisation and the defects of schizophrenia. *British Journal of Psychiatry* **139**, 195–203.

—— Deakin, J.F.W., Lawler, P., Frith, C.D., Stevens, M., McPherson, K., and Crow, T.J. (1980). The Northwick Park electroconvulsive therapy trial. *Lancet* **ii**, 1317–20.

—— and Marsh, W. (1973). Acetylator status and response to phenelzine in depressed patients. *Lancet* **i**, 567–70.

Johnstone, J.M., Hunt, A.C., and Ward, E.M. (1960). Plastic bag asphyxia in adults. *British Medical Journal* **ii**, 1714–15.

Jolley, D.J. and Arie, T. (1978). Organisation of psychogeriatric services. *British Journal of Psychiatry* **132**, 1–11.

Jolliffe, N. and Jellinek, E.M. (1941). Vitamins and liver cirrhosis in alcoholism: VII cirrhosis of the liver. *Quarterly Journal of Studies on Alcohol* **2**, 544–83.

Jones, K. (1972). *A history of the mental health services.* Routledge & Kegan Paul, London.

—— and Smith, D.W. (1973). Recognition of the fetal alcohol syndrome in early infancy. *Lancet* **ii**, 999–1001.

Jones, M. (1952). *Social psychiatry: a study of therapeutic communities.* Tavistock, London.

Joyston-Bechal, M.P. (1966). The clinical features and outcome of stupor. *British Journal of Psychiatry* **112**, 967–81.

Kahlbaum, K. (1863). *Die Gruppirung der psychichen Krankheiten.* Kafemann, Danzig.

Kahn, E. (1928). Die psychopäthischen Persönlichkeiten. In *Handbuch der Geisteskrankheiten,* Vol. 5, p. 227. Springer, Berlin.

Kallmann, F.J. (1932). Study on the genetic affects of male homosexuality. *Journal of Nervous and Mental Disease* **115**, 1283–98.

—— (1938). *The genetics of schizophrenia.* Augustin, New York.

—— (1946). The genetic theory of schizophrenia: an analysis of 691 schizophrenic twin index families. *American Journal of Psychiatry* **103**, 309–22.

Kalucy, R.S., Crisp, A.H., and Harding, B. (1977). A study of 56 families with anorexia nervosa. *British Journal of Medical Psychology* **50**, 381–95.

Kaminski, M., Rumeau-Rouquette, C., and Schwartz, D. (1976). Consommation d'alcool chez les femmes enceintes et issue de la grossesse. *Revue d'Epidemiologie et de Santé Publique* **24**, 27–40.

Kane, J.M. and Smith, J.M. (1982). Tardive dyskinesia: prevalence and risk factors, 1959–1979. *Archives of General Psychiatry* **39**, 473–81.

Kanner, L. (1943). Autistic disturbance of affective contact. *Nervous Child* **2**, 217–50.

Kaplan, H.I., Freedman, A.M., and Sadock, B.J. (eds.) (1980). *Comprehensive textbook of psychiatry*, 3rd edn. Williams and Wilkins, Baltimore.

Karasu, T.B. (1979). Psychotherapy of the medically ill. *American Journal of Psychiatry* **136**. 1–11.

Karpati, G. and Frame, B. (1964). Neuropsychiatric disorders in primary hyperparathyroidism: clinical analysis with review of the literature. *Archives of Neurology* **10**, 387–97.

Karush, A., Daniels, G.E., O'Connor, J.F., and Stern, L.O. (1977). *Psychotherapy in chronic ulcerative colitis*. Saunders, Philadelphia.

Kasanin, J. (1933). The acute schizoaffective psychoses. *American Journal of Psychiatry* **13**, 97–126.

Kashani, J.H., Husain, A., Shekin, W.O., Hodges, K.K., Cytryn, L., and McKnew, D.M. (1982). Current perspectives of childhood depression: an overview. *American Journal of Psychiatry* **138**, 143–53.

Katon, W., Kleinman, A., and Rosen, G. (1982). Depression and somatization: a review. Part I. *American Journal of Medicine* **72**, 127–35.

Kavanagh, C. (1982). Emotional abuse and mental injury. *Journal of the American Academy of Child Psychiatry* **21**, 171–7.

Kavka, J. (1949). Pinel's conception of the psychopathic state. *Bulletin of the History of Medicine* **23**, 461–8.

Kay, D.W.K. (1962). Outcome and cause of death in mental disorders of old age. *Acta Psychiatrica Scandinavica* **38**, 249–76.

—— (1963). Late paraphrenia and its bearing on the aetiology of schizophrenia. *Acta Psychiatrica Scandinavica* **39**, 159–69.

—— Beamish, P., and Roth, M. (1964). Old age mental disorders in Newcastle-upon-Tyne: 1: a study in prevalence. *British Journal of Psychiatry* **110**, 146–58.

—— Bergmann, K. (1980). Epidemiology of mental disorder among the aged in the community. In *Handbook of mental health and ageing* (ed. J.E. Birren and R.B. Sloane). Prentice Hall, Englewood Cliffs.

—— —— Foster, E.M., McKechnie, A.A., and Roth, M. (1970). Mental illness and hospital usage in the elderly: a random sample followed up. *Comprehensive Psychiatry* **11**, 26–35.

—— Cooper, A.F., Garside, R.F., and Roth, M. (1976). The differentiation of paranoid and affective psychoses by patients' premorbid characteristics. *British Journal of Psychiatry* **129**, 207–15.

—— and Roth, M. (1961). Environmental and hereditary factors in the schizophrenias of old age ('late paraphrenia') and their bearing on the general problem of causation in schizophrenia. *Journal of Mental Science* **107**, 649–86.

Kedward, H.B. and Cooper, B. (1966). Neurotic disorders in urban practice: a 3 year follow-up. *Journal of the Royal College of General Practitioners* **12**, 148–63.

Keeley, S.M., Shemberg, K.M., and Carbonell, J. (1976). Operant clinical intervention: behaviour management or beyond? Where are the data? *Behaviour Therapy* **7**, 292–305.

Keller, M. (1976). The disease concept of alcoholism revisited. *Journal of Studies on Alcohol* **37**, 1694–717.

Kelly, G.A. (1955). *The psychology of personal constructs,* Vols. 1 and 2. Norton, New York.

Kemp, N.J. (1981). Social-psychological aspects of blindness: a review. *Current Psychological Reviews* 1, 69–89.

Kempe, C.H., Silverman, F.N., Steele, B.F., Droegemueller, W., and Silver, H.K. (1962). The battered child syndrome. *Journal of the American Medical Association* 181, 17–24.

Kendell, R.E. (1968). *The classification of depressive illness.* Maudsley Monograph No. 18. Oxford University Press, London.

—— (1975). *The role of diagnosis in psychiatry.* Blackwell, Oxford.

—— (1981). The present status of electroconvulsive therapy. *British Journal of Psychiatry* 139, 265–83.

—— Brockington, I.F., and Leff, J.P. (1979). Prognostic implications of six alternative definitions of schizophrenia. *Archives of General Psychiatry* 36, 25–31.

—— Hall, D.J., Hailey, A., and Babigian, H.M. (1973). The epidemiology of anorexia nervosa. *Psychological Medicine* 3, 200–3.

—— Pichot, P., and von Cranach, M. (1974). Diagnostic criteria of English, French and German psychiatrists. *Psychological Medicine* 4, 187–95.

—— Rennie, D., Clarke, J.A., and Dean, C. (1981). The social and obstetric correlates of psychiatric admission in the puerperium. *Psychological Medicine* 11, 341–50.

—— Wainwright, S., Hailey, A., and Shannon, B. (1976). The influence of childbirth on psychiatric morbidity. *Psychological Medicine* 6, 297–302.

Kendler, K.S. and Davis, K.L. (1981). The genetics and biochemistry of paranoid schizophrenia and other paranoid psychoses. *Schizophrenia Bulletin* 7, 689–769.

—— and Tsuang, M.T. (1981). Nosology of paranoid schizophrenia and other paranoid psychoses. *Schizophrenia Bulletin* 7, 594–610.

Kennedy, A. and Neville, J. (1957). Sudden loss of memory. *British Medical Journal* ii, 428–33.

Kennedy, P. (1972). Efficacy of a regional poisoning treatment centre in preventing further suicidal behaviour. *British Medical Journal* iv, 255–7.

—— and Kreitman, N. (1973). An epidemiological survey of parasuicide ('attempted suicide') in general practice. *British Journal of Psychiatry* 123, 23–34.

Kennedy, W.A. (1965). School phobia: a rapid treatment of 50 cases. *Journal of Abnormal Psychology* 70, 285–9.

Kenyon, F.E. (1964). Hypochondriasis: a clinical study. *British Journal of Psychiatry* 110, 478–88.

—— (1965). Hypochondriasis: a survey of some historical, clinical and social aspects. *British Journal of Medical Psychology* 38, 117–33.

—— (1968). Studies in female homosexuality: social and psychiatric aspects: sexual development, attitudes and experience. *British Journal of Psychiatry* 114, 1337–50.

—— (1976). Hypochondriacal states. *British Journal of Psychiatry* 129, 1–14.

—— (1980). Homosexuality in gynaecological practice. *Clinics in Obstetrics and Gynaecology* I, 363–86.

Kerr, T.A., Roth, M., and Shapira, K. (1974). Prediction of outcome in anxiety states and depressive illness. *British Journal of Psychiatry* 124, 125–31.

—— —— —— and Gurney, C. (1972). The assessment and prediction of outcome in affective disorders. *British Journal of Psychiatry* 121, 167–74.

Kerr, T.A., Shapira, K., and Roth, M. (1969). The relationship between premature death and affective disorders. *British Journal of Psychiatry* 115, 1277–82.

Kessel, N. (1977a). Self-poisoning. *British Medical Journal* ii, 1265–70 and 1336–40.

—— (1977b). The foetal alcohol syndrome from the public health standpoint. *Health Trends* 9, 86–9.

—— (1978). Report of the Advisory committee on alcoholism. HMSO, London.

—— and Grossman, G. (1961). Suicide in alcoholics. *British Medical Journal* ii, 1671–2.

Kessler, S. (1980). The genetics of schizophrenia: a review. *Schizophrenia Bulletin* 6, 404–16.

Kety, S. (1980). The syndrome of schizophrenia. *British Journal of Psychiatry* **136**, 421–36.

—— Rosenthal, D., Wender, P.H., Schulsinger, F., and Jacobsen, B. (1975). Mental illness in the biological and adoptive families of adopted individuals who have become schizophrenic. In *Genetic research in psychiatry* (ed. R.R. Fieve, D. Rosenthal, and H. Bull). Johns Hopkins University Press, Baltimore.

Kidd, C.B. (1962). Misplacement of the elderly in hospital. *British Medical Journal* **ii**, 1491–5.

Kidson, M.A. (1973). Personality and hypertension. *Journal of Psychosomatic Research* **17**, 35–41.

Kiev, A. (1971). Suicide prevention. In *Identifying suicide potential* (ed. D.B. Anderson and L.J. McClean) pp. 3–13. Behaviour Publications, New York.

—— (1972). *Transcultural psychiatry*. Penguin, Harmondsworth.

Kiloh, L.G., Andrews, G., Nielson, M., and Bianchi, G.N. (1972). The relationship between the syndromes called endogenous and neurotic depression. *British Journal of Psychiatry* **121**, 183–96.

—— Ball, J.R.B., and Garside, R.F. (1962). Prognostic factors in treatment of depressive states with imipramine. *British Medical Journal* **i**, 1225–7.

—— Child, J.P., and Latner, G. (1960). A controlled trial in the treatment of endogenous depression. *Journal of Mental Science* **106**, 1139–44.

—— and Garside, R.F. (1963). The independence of neurotic depression and endogenous depression. *British Journal of Psychiatry* **109**, 451–63.

Kimball, C.P. (1976). The experience of cardiac surgery and cardiac transplant. In *Modern perspectives in the psychiatric aspects of surgery* (ed. J.G. Howells). Brunner Mazel, New York.

Kind, D. (1958). Die psychiatrie der hypophyseninsuffizienz speziell der Simmondsschen Krankheit. *Forschritte der Neurologie-Psychiatrie* **26**, 501–63.

King, N.J. (1980). The behavioral management of asthma and asthma-related problems in children: a critical review of the literature. *Journal of Behavioral Medicine* **3**, 169–89.

King, R., Raynes, N., and Tizard, J.A. (1971). *Patterns of residential care*. Routledge and Kegan Paul, London.

Kinsey, A.C., Pomeroy, W.B., and Martin, C.E. (1948). *Sexual behavior in the human male*. Saunders, Philadelphia.

—— —— —— and Gebhard, P.H. (1953). *Sexual behaviour in the human female*. Saunders, Philadelphia.

Kirsner, J.B. (1981). The irritable bowel syndrome: a clinical review and ethical consideration. *Archives of Internal Medicine* **141**, 635–9.

Kissen, D.M. (1963). Personality characteristics in males conducive to lung cancer. *British Journal of Medical Psychology* **36**, 27–36.

Kitson, T.M. (1977). The disulfiram–ethanol reaction. *Journal of Studies on Alcoholism* **38**, 96–113.

Klaf, F.S. and Hamilton, J.G. (1961). Schizophrenia – a hundred years ago and today. *Journal of Mental Science* **107**, 819–28.

Klein, M. (1934). A contribution to the psychogenesis of manic-depressive states. Reprinted in *Contributions to psychoanalysis 1921–1945: developments in child and adolescent psychology*, pp. 282–310. Hogarth Press, London (1948).

Kleinknecht, R.A., Klepac, R.K., and Alexander, L.D. (1973). Origin and characteristics of fear of dentistry. *Journal of the American Dental Association* **86**, 842–8.

Kleist, K. (1928). Cycloid paranoid and epileptoid psychoses and the problem of the degenerative psychosis. Reprinted in *Themes and variations in European psychiatry* (ed. S.R. Hirsch and M. Shepherd). Wright, Bristol (1974).

Knight, G. (1972). Neurosurgical aspects of psychosurgery. *Proceedings of the Royal Society of Medicine* **65**, 1099–104.

796   *References*

Knights, A and Hirsch, S.R. (1981). Revealed depression and drug treatment for schizophrenia. *Archives of General Psychiatry* **38**, 806–11.

Knights, E.B. and Folstein, M.F. (1977). Unsuspected emotional and cognitive disturbance in medical patients. *Annals of Internal Medicine* **87**, 723–4.

Knott, D.G. and Beard, J.D. (1971). In *Treatment of the alcohol withdrawal syndrome* (ed. F.A. Seixas) p. 29. National Council on Alcoholism, New York.

Koch, J.L.A. (1891). *Die Psychopathischen Minderwertigkeiter.* Dorn, Ravensburg.

Kolle, K. (1931). *Die primare Verrucktheit: psychopathologishe, klinische und genealogische Untersuchungen.* Thieme, Leipzig.

Kolodny, R.C., Master, W.H., and Johnson, V.E. (1979). *Textbook of sexual medicine.* Little Brown, Boston.

Kolvin, I. (1971). Studies in the childhood psychoses: I. Diagnostic criteria and classification. *British Journal of Psychiatry* **118**, 381–4.

—— and Fundudis, T. (1981). Elective mute children: psychological development and background factors. *Journal of Child Psychology and Psychiatry* **22**, 219–32.

—— Garside, R.F., and Nichol, A.R. (1981). *Help starts here: the maladjusted child in the ordinary school.* Tavistock, London.

—— and Goodyer, I. (1982). Child psychiatry. In *Recent advances in clinical psychiatry,* Vol. 4 (ed. K. Granville-Grossman) pp. 1–24. Churchill Livingstone, London.

—— and Nicol, R. (1979). Child Psychiatry. In *Recent advances in psychiatry,* Vol. 3 (ed. K. Granville-Grossman). Churchill Livingstone, Edinburgh.

Kornfeld, D.S. (1980). The intensive care unit in adults: coronary care and general medical/surgical. *Advances in Psychosomatic Medicine* **10**, 1–29.

Korobkin, R., Asbury, A.K., Sumner, A.J., and Nielsen, M.D. (1975). Glue-sniffing neuropathy. *Archives of Neurology* **32**, 158–62.

Korsakov, S.S. (1889). Translated and reprinted as Psychic disorder in conjunction with multiple neuritis. *Neurology* **5**, 394–406.

Koryani, E.K. (1972). Physical health and illness in a psychiatric outpatient department population. *Canadian Psychiatric Association Journal* **17**, 109–16.

Kosviner, A. (1976). Social science and cannabis use. In *Cannabis and health* (ed. J.D.P: Graham). Academic Press, London.

Kotin, J. and Goodwin, F.K. (1972). Depression during mania. Clinical observations and theoretical implications. *American Journal of Psychiatry* **129**, 679–86.

Kraepelin, E. (1912). Über paranoide Erkrankungen. *Zentralblatt für die gesamte Neurologie und Psychiatrie* **11**, 617–38.

—— (1915). Der Verfolgungswahn der Schwerhörigen. *Psychiatrie* Auflage 8 Band IV. Barth, Leipzig.

—— (1919). *Dementia praecox and paraphrenia.* Livingstone, Edinburgh.

—— (1920). Patterns of mental disorder. Reprinted in *Themes and variations in European psychiatry* (ed. S.R. Hirsch and M. Shepherd). Wright, Bristol (1974).

—— (1921). *Manic depressive insanity and paranoia* (translated by R.M. Barclay from the 8th Edition of *Lehrbuch der Psychiatrie,* Vols. III and IV). E. and S. Livingstone Edinburgh.

Krafft-Ebing, R. (1888). *Lehrbuch der Psychiatrie.* Enke, Stuttgart.

—— (1924). *Psychopathic sexuality with special reference to contrary sexual instinct.* Authorized translation of the 7th German edition by C.G. Chaddock, Philadelphia.

Kral, A.A. (1978). Benign senescent forgetfulness. In *Alzheimer's disease: senile dementia and related disorders* (ed. R. Katzman, R.D. Terry, and K.L. Bick). Raven Press, New York.

Krauthammer, C. and Klerman, G.L. (1978). Secondary mania. *Archives of General Psychiatry* **35**, 1333–9.

—— —— (1979). The epidemiology of mania. In *Manic illness* (ed. B. Shopsin) pp. 11–28. Raven Press, New York.

Kreitman, N. (ed.) (1977). *Parasuicide.* Wiley, London.
—— Collins, J., Nelson, B., and Troop, J. (1970). Neurosis and marital interaction. *British Journal of Psychiatry* **117**, 33–46 and 47–58.
—— and Dyer, J.A.T. (1980). Suicide in relation to parasuicide. *Medicine* 2nd series, 1826–30.
—— Sainsbury, P., Pearce, K., and Costain, W.R. (1965). Hypochondriasis and depression in out-patients at a general hospital. *British Journal of Psychiatry* **111**, 607–15.
—— Smith, P., and Tan, E.S. (1969). Attempted suicide in social networks. *British Journal of Preventive and Social Medicine* **23**, 116–23.
Kretschmer, E. (1924). *Physique and character.* Kegan Paul, London.
—— (1927). Der sensitive Beziehungswahn. Reprinted and translated as Chapter 8 in *Themes and variations in European psychiatry* (ed. S.R. Hirsch and M. Shepherd). Wright, Bristol (1974).
—— (1921). *Physique and character.* Translated from the original German. Harcourt Brace, New York.
—— (1936). *Physique and character,* 2nd edn (translated by W.J.H. Sproff and K. Paul Trench). Trubner, New York.
—— (1961). *Hysteria, reflex and instinct* (translated into English by V. and W. Baskin from the German). Peter Owen, London.
Kringlen, E. (1965). Obsessional neurosis: a long term follow up. *British Journal of Psychiatry* **111**, 709–22.
—— (1967). *Heredity and environment in the functional psychoses.* Heinemann, London.
—— (1980). Schizophrenia: research in Nordic countries. *Schizophrenia Bulletin* **6**, 566–78.
Kroll, J. (1979). Philosophical foundation of French and U.S. nosology. *American Journal of Psychiatry* **136**, 1135–8.
Kubler-Ross, E. (1969). *On death and dying.* Macmillan, New York.
Kuhn, R. (1957). Über die Behandlung depressiver Zustände mit einem Iminodibenzyl-derivat. *Schweizerische medizinische Wochenschrift* **36**, 1135–40.
Kushlick, A. (1980). Evaluation of residential facilities for the severely mentally handicapped. *Advances in Behaviour, Research and Therapy* **3**, No. 1.
—— and Blunden, R. (1974). The epidemiology of mental subnormality. In *Mental deficiency: the changing outlook,* 3rd edn (ed. A.M. Clarke and A.D.B. Clarke). Methuen, London.
Lacey, J.I. and Lacey, B.C. (1958). Verification and extension of autonomic response stereotype. *American Journal of Psychology* **71**, 50–75.
Lader, M.H. (1969). Psychophysiological aspects of anxiety. In *Studies of anxiety* (ed. M.H. Lader) *British Journal of Psychiatry* Special Publication, No. 3.
—— (1975). *The psychophysiology of mental illness.* Routledge and Kegan Paul, London.
—— and Sartorius, N. (1968). Anxiety in patients with hysterical conversion symptoms. *Journal of Neurology, Neurosurgery and Psychiatry* **31**, 490–7.
—— and Wing, L. (1966). *Physiological measures, sedative drugs and morbid anxiety.* Maudsley Monograph No. 14. Oxford University Press, London.
Laidlaw, J. and Richens, A. (eds.) (1982). *A textbook of epilepsy,* 2nd edn. Churchill Livingstone, Edinburgh.
Laing, R. (1965). *The divided self.* Penguin, Harmondsworth.
The Lancet (1979). Lithium and the kidney. Grounds for cautious optimism. (Editorial.) *Lancet* **ii**, 1056–7.
—— (1981). Epilepsy and violence. (Editorial.) *Lancet* **ii**, 966–7.
—— (1982*a*). Brain damage after open-heart surgery. (Editorial.) *Lancet* **i**, 1161–2.

798   References

—— (1982*b*). Solvent abuse. (Editorial.) *Lancet* ii, 1139–40.

—— (1982*c*). Trials of coronary heart disease prevention. (Editorial.) *Lancet* ii, 803–4.

Lange, J. (1929). *Verbrechen als Schicksal: Studien kriminellen Zwillingen.* Thieme, Leipzig.

—— (1931). *Crime as destiny* (translated by C. Haldane). George Allen, London.

Langfeldt, G. (1938). The prognosis in schizophrenia and the factors influencing the course of the disease. *Acta Psychiatrica Neurologica Scandinavica* Suppl. 13.

—— (1939). *The schizophreniform states.* Munksgaard, Copenhagen.

—— (1960). Diagnosis and prognosis of schizophrenia. *Proceedings of the Royal Society of Medicine* 53, 1047–51.

Larsson, T., Sjögren, T., Jacobson, G. with the assistance of Sjögren, G. (1963). Senile dementia. A clinical, socio-medical and genetic study. *Acta Psychiatrica Scandinavica* Suppl. 167, 1–259.

Lascelles, R.G. (1966). Atypical facial pain and depression. *British Journal of Psychiatry* 112, 651–9.

Lasègue, C. (1877). Les exhibitionnistes. *Union Medicale* 23, 709–14.

Latimer, P.R. (1978). Crohn's disease: a review of the psychological and social outcome. *Psychological Medicine* 8, 649–56.

—— (1981). Irritable bowel syndrome: a behavioural model. *Behaviour Research and Therapy* 19, 475–83.

Laufer, M.W. and Shetty, T. (1980). Attention deficit disorders. In *Comprehensive textbook of psychiatry* (ed. H.I. Kaplan, A.M. Freedman, and B.J. Sadock). Williams and Wilkins, Baltimore.

Laurell, B. (1970). Comparison of electric and flurothyl convulsive therapy. II antidepressive effect. *Acta Psychiatric Scandinavica* Suppl. 145, 22–35.

Lauter, I.H. and Meyer, J.E. (1968). Clinical and nosological concepts of dementia. In *Senile dementias* (ed. C. Müller and L. Ciompi). Hans Huber, Bern.

Lazarus, R.S. (1966). *Psychological stress and the coping processes.* McGraw-Hill, New York.

Leach, J. and Wing, J.K. (1979). *Helping destitute men.* Tavistock, London.

Ledermann, S. (1956). *Alcool, alcoolisme, alcoolisation.* Presses Universitaires de Paris.

Leff, J. (1977). International variation in diagnosis of psychiatric illness. *British Journal of Psychiatry* 131, 329–38.

—— (1978). Social and psychological causes of the acute attack. In *Schizophrenia: towards a new synthesis* (ed. J.K. Wing). Academic Press, London.

—— (1981). *Psychiatry around the globe: a transcultural view.* Marcel Dekker, New York.

—— and Isaacs, A.D. (1978). *Psychiatric examination in clinical practice.* Blackwell, Oxford.

—— Kuipers, L., Berkowitz, R., Everlein-Vries, R., and Sturgeon, D.A. (1982). A controlled trial of social intervention in the families of schizophrenic patients. *British Journal of Psychiatry* 141, 121–34.

—— and Vaughn, C. (1972). Psychiatric patients in contact and out of contact with services; a clinical and social assessment. In *Evaluating a community psychiatric service* (ed. J.K. Wing and A.M. Hailey). Oxford University Press, London.

—— —— (1981). The role of maintenance therapy and relative expressed emotion in relapse of schizophrenia: a two year follow up. *British Journal of Psychiatry* 139, 102–4.

—— and Wing, J.K. (1971). Trial of maintenance therapy in schizophrenia. *British Medical Journal* iii, 599–604.

Lehrke, R. (1972). A theory of x-linkage of major intellectual traits. *American Journal of Mental Deficiency* 76, 611–19.

Lemere, F., Voegtlin, W.L., Broz, W.R., O'Hallaren, P., and Tupper, W.E. (1942). Conditioned reflex treatment of chronic alcoholism. VIII: a review of six years experience with this treatment of 1526 patients. *Journal of the American Medical Association* **120**, 269–70.

Lemert, E. (1951). *Social pathology: a systematic approach to the theory of sociopathic behaviour.* McGraw-Hill, New York.

Lemoine, P., Harousseau, H., Borteyru, J.-P., and Menuet, J.-C. (1968). Les enfants de parents alcooliques: anomalies observées à propos de 127 cas. *Ouest Médical* **25**, 477–82.

Leonhard, K. (1957). *The classification of endogenous psychoses.* English translation of the 8th German edition of *Aufteiling der Endogenen Psychosen* by R. Berman. Irvington, New York (1979).

—— Korff, I., and Schulz, H. (1962). Die Temperamente und den Familien der monopolaren und bipolaren phasishen Psychosen. *Psychiatrie und Neurologie* **143**, 416–34.

Levine, P.M., Silberfarb, P.M., and Lipowski, Z.J. (1978). Mental disorders in cancer patients: a study of 100 psychiatric referrals *Cancer* **42**, 1385–91.

Levy, R., Isaacs, A., and Hawks, G. (1970). Neurophysiological correlates of senile dementia: I. Motor and sensory nerve conduction velocity. *Psychological Medicine* **1**, 40–47.

—— and Post, F. (1982). *The psychiatry of late life.* Blackwell, Oxford.

Lewin, K.M., Mattingly, D., and Millis, R.R. (1972). Anorexia nervosa associated with hypothalamic tumour. *British Medical Journal* **ii**, 629–30.

Lewis, A.J. (1934). Melancholia: a clinical survey of depressive states. *Journal of Mental Science* **80**, 277–8.

—— (1936). Melancholia: prognostic study and case material. *Journal of Mental Science* **82**, 488–558.

—— (1936*b*). Problems of obsessional neurosis. *Proceedings of the Royal Society of Medicine* **29**, 325–36.

—— (1938). States of depression: their clinical and aetiological differentiation. *British Medical Journal* **ii**, 875–8.

—— (1942). Discussion on differential diagnosis and treatment of post contusional states. *Proceedings of the Royal Society of Medicine* **35**, 607–14.

—— (1953*a*). Hysterical dissociation in dementia paralytica. *Monatsschrift für Psychiatrie und Neurologie* **125**, 589–604.

—— (1953*b*). Health as a social concept. *British Journal of Sociology* **4**, 109–24.

—— (1956). Psychological medicine. In *Price's textbook of the practice of medicine,* 9th edn (ed. D. Hunter). Oxford University Press, London.

—— (1957). Obsessional illness. *Acta Neuropsiquiàtrica Argentina* **3**, 323–35. Reprinted as chapter 7 in *Inquiries in psychiatry: clinical and social investigations.* Routledge and Kegan Paul, London.

—— (1968). A glossary of mental disorders. Studies on medical and population subjects 22. General Register Office. HMSO, London.

—— (1970). Paranoia and paranoid: a historical perspective. *Psychological Medicine* **I**, 2–12.

—— (1976). A note on classification of phobia. *Psychological Medicine* **6**, 21–2.

—— and Fleminger, J.J. (1954). Psychiatric risk of ACTH and cortisone. *Lancet* **i**, 383.

Lewis, E. (1979). Harming by the family after a stillbirth or neonatal death. *Archives of the Diseases of Childhood* **54**, 303–6.

Lewis, E.O. (1929). Report on an investigation into the incidence of mental deficiency in six areas. 1925–27. In *Report of the mental deficiency committee,* Part IV. HMSO, London.

Lewis, H.R. and Streitfeld, H.S. (1970). *Growth Games.* Harcourt Brace Jovanovich, New York.

Lewis, N.D.S. and Yarnell, P. (1951). Pathological firesetting. *Nervous and Mental Diseases Monograph* No. 82. New York.

Ley, P. (1977). Psychological studies of doctor patient communication. In *Contributions to medical psychology* (ed. S. Rachman). Pergamon, Oxford.

—— (1982). Satisfaction, compliance and communication. *British Journal of Clinical Psychology* 21, 241–54.

Lhermitte, J. (1951). Visual hallucinations of the self. *British Medical Journal* i, 431–4.

Liakos, A. (1967). Familial transvestism. *British Journal of Psychiatry* 113, 49–51.

Lidz, R.W. and Lidz, T. (1949). The family environment of schizophrenic patients. *American Journal of Psychiatry* 106, 332–45.

Lidz, T., Fleck, S., and Cornelison, A. (1965). *Schizophrenia and the family.* International Universities Press, New York.

Lieberman, M.A., Yalom, I.D., and Miles, M.B. (1973). *Encounter groups: first facts.* Basic Books, New York.

Liebowitz, M.R. (1979). Is borderline a distinct entity? *Schizophrenia Bulletin* 5, 23–38.

Liem, J.H. (1980). Family studies of schizophrenia: an update and commentary. *Schizophrenia Bulletin* 6, 429–55.

Lind, K. (1982). A synthesis of studies on stroke rehabilitation. *Journal of Chronic Disorders* 35, 133–49.

Lindemann, E. (1944). Symptomatology and management of acute grief. *American Journal of Psychiatry* 101, 141–8.

Lindstedt, G., Nilsson, L.A., Walinder, J., Skott, A., and Öhman, R. (1977). On the prevalence, diagnosis and management of lithium induced hypothyroidism in psychiatric patients. *British Journal of Psychiatry* 130, 452–8.

Lineberger, H.P. (1981). Social characteristics of a haemophiliac clinic population. *General Hospital Psychiatry* 3, 157–63.

Ling, M.H.M., Perry, P.J., and Tsuang, M.T. (1981). Side effects of corticosteroid therapy. *Archives of General Psychiatry* 38, 471–7.

Lingjaerde, O., Edlund, A.H., Gormsen, C.A., Gottfries, C.G., Haugstad, A., Hermann, I.L., Hollnagel, P., Mäkimattila, A., Rasmussen, K.E., Remvig, J., and Robak, O.H. (1974). The effects of lithium carbonate in combination with tricyclic antidepressants in endogenous depression. *Acta Psychiatrica Scandinavica* 50, 233–42.

Linn, M.W., Caffey, E.M., Klett, J., Hogarty, G.E., and Lamb, R. (1979). Day treatment and psychotropic drugs in the aftercare of schizophrenic patients. *Archives of General Psychiatry* 36, 1055–66.

Lipowski, Z.J. (1975). Physical illness, the patient and his environment: psychosocial foundation of medicine. In *American handbook of psychiatry,* 2nd edn, Vol. 4. Basic Books, New York.

—— (1974). Consultation–liaison psychiatry: an overview. *American Journal of Psychiatry* 131, 623–30.

—— (1977). Psychosomatic medicine in the seventies: an overview. *American Journal of Psychiatry* 134, 233–44.

—— (1979). Consultation–liaison psychiatry, past failures and new opportunities. *General Hospital Psychiatry* 1, 3–10.

—— (1980*a*). *Delirium. Acute brain failure in man.* Thomas, Springfield, Ill.

—— (1980*b*). Organic mental disorders: introduction and review of syndromes. In *Comprehensive textbook of psychiatry,* 3rd edn (ed. H.I. Kaplan, A.M. Freedman, and B.J. Sadock). Williams and Wilkins, Baltimore.

—— (1981*a*). Holistic-medical foundations of American psychiatry: a bicentennial. *American Journal of Psychiatry* 138, 888–95.

—— (1981*b*). Liaison psychiatry, liaison nursing and behavioral medicine. *Comprehensive Psychiatry* 22, 554–61.

—— and Wolston, E. (1981). Liaison psychiatry; referral patterns and their stability over time. *American Journal of Psychiatry* **138**, 1608–11.

Lishman, W.A. (1968). Brain damage in relation to psychiatric disability after head injury. *British Journal of Psychiatry* **114**, 373–410.

—— (1978*a*). *Organic psychiatry.* Blackwell, Oxford.

—— (1978*b*). Research into the dementias. *Psychological Medicine* **8**, 353–6.

—— (1981). Cerebral disorder in alcoholism: syndromes of impairment. *Brain* **104**, 1–20.

—— Ron, M., and Acker, W. (1980). Computed tomography of the brain and psychometric assessment of alcoholic patients – a British study. In *Addiction and brain damage* (ed. D. Richter). Croom Helm, London.

Litman, R.E., Curphey, T., Shneidman, E.S., Farberow, N.C., and Tabachnick, N. (1963). The psychological autopsy of equivocal suicides. *Journal of the American Medical Association* **184**, 924–9.

Ljungberg, L. (1957). Hysteria. *Acta Psychiatrica Scandinavica* Suppl. 12.

Lloyd, G.G. (1980). Whence and whither 'liaison' psychiatry? *Psychological Medicine* **10**, 11–14.

Lloyd, K.G., Farley, I.J., Deck, J.H.N., and Hornykiewicz, O. (1974). Serotonin and 5-hydroxyindolacetic acid in discrete areas of the brain stem of suicide victims and control patients. *Advances in Biochemical Psychopharmacology* **11**, 387–97.

Loranger, A.W., Goodell, H., McDowell, F.H., Lee, J.E., and Sweet, R.D. (1972). Intellectual impairment in Parkinson's syndrome. *Brain* **95**, 405–12.

Loudon, J.B. and Waring, H. (1976). Toxic reactions to lithium and haloperidol. *Lancet* **ii**, 1088.

Lovibond, S.H. (1964). *Conditioning and enuresis.* Pergamon, Oxford.

—— and Coote, M.A. (1970). Enuresis. In *Symptoms of psychopathology* (ed. G.G. Costello). Wiley, New York.

Lown, B. (1982). Mental stress, arrhythmias and sudden death. *American Journal of Medicine* **72**, 177–80.

—— de Silva, R.A., Reich, P., and Murawski, B.J. (1980). Psychophysiologic factors in sudden cardiac death. *American Journal of Psychiatry* **137**, 1325–35.

Luborsky, L., Singer, B., and Luborsky, L. (1975). Comparative studies of psychotherapies. *Archives of General Psychiatry* **31**, 995–1008.

Lukianowicz, N. (1958). Autoscopic phenomena. *Archives of Neurology and Psychiatry* **80**. 199–220.

—— (1959). Survey of various aspects of transvestism in the light of our present knowledge. *Journal of Nervous and Mental Disease* **128**, 36–64.

—— (1967). 'Body image' disturbances in psychiatric disorders. *British Journal of Psychiatry* **113**, 31–47.

Lum, L.C. (1976). The syndrome of chronic habitual hyperventilation. *Modern trends in psychosomatic medicine* (ed. O.W. Hill). Butterworth, London.

Lundquist, G. (1945). Prognosis and course in manic depressive psychosis. A follow-up study of 319 first admissions. *Acta Psychiatrica Scandinavica* Suppl. 35.

Luxenberger, H. (1928). Vorläufiger Bericht über psychiatrische Serienuntersuchungen an Zwillingen. *Zetschrift für die gesamte Neurologie and Psychiatrie* **116**, 297–326.

Lynch, M.A. (1975). Ill-health and child abuse. *Lancet* **ii**, 317–19.

—— and Roberts, J. (1977). Predicting child abuse: signs of bonding failure in the maternity hospital. *British Medical Journal* **i**, 624–6.

MacAlpine, I. and Hunter, R. (1966). The 'insanity' of King George III: a classic case of porphyria. *British Medical Journal* **i**, 65–71.

McCarthy, P.D. and Walsh, D. (1976). Suicide in Dublin: 1. The under-reporting of suicide and the consequences for national statistics. *British Journal of Psychiatry* **126**, 301–8.

McCombie, S.L., Bassuk, E., Savitz, R., and Pell, S. (1976). Development of a medical center rape crisis intervention programme. *American Journal of Psychiatry* **133**, 418–21.

MacCrimmon, D.J., Wallace, J.E., Goldberg, N.M., and Steiner, D.L. (1979). Emotional disturbance and cognitive deficits in hyperthyroidism. *Psychosomatic Medicine* **41**, 331–40.

McCulloch, J., Phillip, A.E., and Carstairs, G.M. (1967). The ecology of suicidal behaviour. *British Journal of Psychiatry* **113**, 313–19.

McDonald, C. (1969). Clinical heterogeneity in senile dementia. *British Journal of Psychiatry* **115**, 267–72.

MacDonald, J.M. (1964). The threat to kill. *American Journal of Psychiatry* **120**, 125–30.

McEvedy, C.P. and Beard, A.W. (1970). Concept of benign myalgic encephalomyelitis. *British Medical Journal* i, 11–15.

MacKay, A.V.P. and Sheppard, G.P. (1979). Pharmacotherapeutic trials in tardive dyskinesia. *British Journal of Psychiatry* **135**, 489–99.

Mackay, R.I. (1982). The causes of severe mental handicap. *Developmental Medicine and Child Neurology* **24**, 386–93.

McKinney, W.T., Suomi, S.J., and Harlow, H.F. (1972). Repetitive peer separation of juvenile-age rhesus moneys. *Archives of General Psychiatry* **27**, 200–3.

Macleod, J. and Walton, H. (1969). Liaison between physicians and psychiatrists in a teaching hospital. *Lancet* ii, 789–92.

McSweeney, A.J., Grant, I., Medlen, R.K., Adams, K.M., and Timms, R.M. (1982). Life quality of patients with chronic obstructive pulmonary disease. *Archives of Internal Medicine* **142**, 473–8.

Madanes, C. and Haley, J. (1977). Dimensions of family therapy. *Journal of Nervous and Mental Disease* **165**, 88–98.

Maguire, G.P., Comoroff, J., Ramsell, P.J., and Morris-Jones, P.H. (1979). Psychological and social problems in the families of children with leukaemia. In *Topics in paediatrics* (ed. P.H. Morris-Jones). Pitman Medical, London.

—— and Granville-Grossman, K.L. (1968). Physical illness in psychiatric patients. *British Journal of Psychiatry* **115**, 1365–9.

—— Julier, D.L., Hawton, K.E., and Bancroft, J.H.J. (1974). Psychiatric morbidity and referral on two general medical wards. *British Medical Journal* i, 268–70.

—— Lee, E.O., Bevington, D.J., Kucheman, C.S., Crabtree, R.J., and Cornell, C.E. (1978). Psychiatric problems in the first year after mastectomy. *British Medical Journal* i, 963–5.

—— Tait, A., Brooke, M., Thomas, C., and Sellwood, R. (1980). Effect of counselling on the psychiatric morbidity associated with mastectomy. *British Medical Journal* **281**, 1454–6.

Mahendra, B. (1981). Where have all the catatonics gone? *Psychological Medicine* **11**, 669–71.

Maher, G. (1981). Sane but normal. In *Legal issues in medicine* (ed. S.A.M. MacLean). Gower, Aldershot.

Mahaptra, S.B. (1974). Deafness and mental health: psychiatric and psychosomatic illness in the deaf. *Acta Psychiatrica Scandinavica* **5**, 596–611.

Mahl, G.F. (1953). Physiological changes during chronic fear. *Annals of the New York Academy of Science* **56**, 240–9.

Malan, D.H. (1963). *A study of brief psychotherapy.* Tavistock, London.

Malmo, R.B. (1962). Activation. In *Experimental foundations of clinical psychology* (ed. A.J. Bachrach). Basic Books, New York.

Maletzky, B.M. (1973). The episodic dyscontrol syndrome. *Diseases of the Nervous System* **34**, 178–84.

—— (1974). 'Assisted' covert sensitization in the treatment of exhibitionism. *Journal of Consulting and Clinical Psychology* **42**, 34–40.

—— (1976). The diagnosis of pathological intoxication. *Journal of Studies on Alcoholism* **37**, 1215–20.

—— (1977). 'Booster' sessions in aversion therapy: the permanency of treatment. *Behaviour Therapy* **11**, 655–7.

Malin, N., Race, D., and Jones, G. (1980). *Services for the mentally handicapped in Britain.* Croom Helm, London.

Malzberg, B. and Lee, E.S. (1956). *Migration and mental disease: a study of first admission to hospitals for mental disease in New York 1939–41.* Social Science Research Council, New York.

Mann, A.H. (1977). The psychological effect of a screening programme and clinical trial for hypertension upon the participants. *Psychological Medicine* **7**, 431–8.

—— Jenkins, R., and Belsey, E. (1981). The twelve-month outcome of patients with neurotic illness in general practice. *Psychological Medicine* **11**, 535–50.

Mann, S.A. and Cree, W. (1976). New long stay patients: a national survey of 15 mental hospitals in England and Wales 1972–3. *Psychological Medicine* **6**, 603–16.

Manschreck, T.C., Maher, B.A., Rucklos, M.E., and Vereen, D.R. (1982). Disturbed voluntary motor activity in schizophrenic disorder. *Psychological Medicine* **12**, 73–84.

Mapother, E. (1926). Manic depressive psychosis. *British Medical Journal* ii, 872–9.

Marcé, L.V. (1858). *Traité de la folie des femmes enceintes, des nouvelles accouchés et des nourrices.* Baillière, Paris.

Marks, I.M. (1969). *Fears and phobias.* Heinemann, London.

—— (1981). Space phobia: a pseudo-agoraphobic syndrome. *Journal of Neurology, Neurosurgery and Psychiatry* **44**, 387–91.

—— and Gelder, M.G. (1966). Different ages of onset of varieties of phobia. *American Journal of Psychiatry* **123**, 218–21.

—— —— (1967). Transvestism and fetishism; clinical and psychological changes during faradic aversion. *British Journal of Psychiatry* **113**, 711–29.

—— Rachman, S., and Gelder, M.G. (1965). Method for the assessment of aversion therapy in fetishism with narcissism. *Behaviour Research and Therapy* **3**, 253–8.

—— Stern, R.S., Mawson, D., Cobb, J., and McDonald, R. (1980). Clomipramine and exposure for obsessive compulsive rituals. *British Journal of Psychiatry* **136**, 1–25.

Marks, V. and Rose, F.C. (1965). *Hypoglycaemia.* Blackwell, Oxford.

Marmot, M. (1980). Type A behaviour and ischaemic heart disease. *Psychological Medicine* **10**, 603–6.

Marsden, C.D. and Harrison, M.J.G. (1972). Outcome of investigation of patients with pre-senile dementia. *British Medical Journal* ii, 249–52.

—— and Jenner, R. (1980). Pathophysiology of extrapyramidal side-effects of neuroleptic drugs. *Psychological Medicine* **10**, 55–72.

Martin, M.E. (1958). Puerperal illness: a follow up study of 75 cases. *British Medical Journal* ii, 773–7.

Martin, P.R. (1982). Spasmodic torticollis: a behavioral perspective. *Journal of Behavioral Medicine* **5**, 249–74.

—— and Mathews, A. (1978). Tension headaches: a physiological investigation. *Journal of Psychosomatic Research* **22**, 389–99.

Masters, W.H. and Johnson, V.E. (1970). *Human sexual inadequacy.* Churchill, London.

—— —— (1979). *Homosexuality in perspective.* Little Brown, Boston.

Mathews, A., Gelder, M.G., and Johnston, D. (1981). *Agoraphobia: nature and treatment.* Tavistock, London.

—— and Ridgeway, V. (1981). Personality and surgical recovery: a review. *British Journal of Clinical Psychology* **20**, 243–60.

Matson, J.L. (1980). Behaviour modification procedures for training chronically institutionalised schizophrenics. *Progress in Behavior Modification* **9**, 167–204.

Matthews, W.B. (1982). Spongiform virus encephalopathy. In *Recent Advances in clinical neurology,* Vol. 3 (ed. W.B. Matthews and G.H.Glaser) pp. 229–39. Churchill Livingstone, Edinburgh.

—— and Miller, M. (1979). *Diseases of the nervous system,* 3rd edn. Blackwell, Oxford.

Maudsley, H. (1879). *The pathology of mind.* Macmillan, London.

—— (1885). *Responsibility in mental disease.* Kegan Paul and Trench, London.

May, P.R.A. (1968). *Treatment of schizophrenia.* Science House, New York.

Mayer, W. (1921). Über paraphrene psychosen. *Zentralblatt für die gesamte Neurologie und Psychiatrie* **71**, 187–206.

Mayer-Gross, W. (1932). Die Schizophrenie. In *Bumke's Handbuch der Geisteskrankheiten,* Vol. 9. Springer, Berlin.

—— (1935). On depersonalization. *British Journal of Medical Psychology* **15**, 103–26.

—— Slater, E., and Roth, M. (1969). *Clinical psychiatry.* Ballière Tindall & Cox, London.

Mayou, R. (1975). Psychological morbidity in a clinic for sexually transmitted disease. *British Journal of Venereal Disease* **51**, 57–60.

—— (1976). The nature of bodily symptoms. *British Journal of Psychiatry* **129**, 55–60.

—— (1979). The course and determinants of reactions to myocardial infarction. *British Journal of Psychiatry* **134**, 588–94.

——Sleight, P. MacMahon, D., and Florencio, M.J. (1981). Early rehabilitation after myocardial infarction. *Lancet* **ii** 1399–401.

Meacher, M. (1982). *Taken for a ride.* Longmans, London.

Mechanic, D. (1962). The concept of illness behaviour. *Journal of Chronic Diseases* **15**, 189–94.

—— (1978). *Medical sociology,* 2nd edn. Free Press, Glencoe.

—— (1979). *Future issues in health care; social policy and the rationing of medical services.* Free Press, New York.

Medical Research Council Drug Trials Subcommittee (1981). Continuation therapy with lithium and amitriptyline in unipolar depressive illness: a controlled clinical trial. *Psychological Medicine* **11**, 409–16.

Mednick, S.A. (1958). A learning theory approach to research in schizophrenia. *Psychological Bulletin* **55**, 316–27.

—— and Schulsinger, F. (1968). In *The transmission of schizophrenia* (ed. D. Rosenthal and S. Kety). Pergamon, Oxford.

Meduna, L. (1938). General discussion of cardiazol therapy. *American Journal of Psychiatry* **94**, Suppl. 40.

Megargee, E.I. (1966). Uncontrolled and overcontrolled personality type in extreme antisocial aggression. *Psychological Monographs* **80**, No. 3.

Meecham, W.C. and Smith, N. (1977). Effects of jet aircraft noise on mental hospital admissions. *British Journal of Audiology* **11**, 81–5.

Meichenbaum, D.H. (1977). *Cognitive-behaviour modification.* Plenum, New York.

Melges, F.T. (1968). Postpartum psychiatric syndromes. *Psychosomatic Medicine* **30**, 95–108.

Mellor, C.S. (1982). The present status of first-rank symptoms. *British Journal of Psychiatry* **140**, 423–4.

Melzack, R. and Wall, P.D. (1965). Pain mechanisms: a new theory. *Science* **130**, 971–9.

Mendels, J. (1965). Electroconvulsive therapy and depression I: the prognostic significance of clinical features. *British Journal of Psychiatry* **111**, 675–81.

—— Secunda, S.K., and Dyson, W.L. (1972). A controlled study of the antidepressant effects of lithium carbonate. *Archives of General Psychiatry* **26**, 154–7.

—— Stinnett, J.L., Burns, D., and Frazer, A. (1975). Amine precursors and depression. *Archives of General Psychiatry* **32**, 22–30.

Mendelson, M. (1982). Psychodynamics of depression. In *Handbook of affective disorders* (ed. E.S. Paykel). Churchill Livingstone, Edinburgh.

Mendelson, W.B. (1980). *The use and misuse of sleeping pills: a clinical guide.* Plenum, New York.

Mendelwicz, J. and Rainer, J.D. (1977). Adoption study supporting genetic transmission of manic depressive illness. *Nature* **268**, 327–9.

Menninger, K. (1948). *Changing concepts of disease.* Viking Press, New York.

Merksey, H. (1980). Psychiatry and the treatment of pain. *British Journal of Psychiatry* **136**, 600–2.

—— and Spear, F.G. (1967). *Pain, psychological and psychiatric aspects.* Baillière, Tindall and Cassell, London.

Meyer, A.J. and Henderson, J.B. (1974). Multiple risk factor reductions in the prevention of cardiovascular disease. *Preventive Medicine* **3**, 225–36.

Meyer, V. and Levy, R. (1971). Treatment of obsessive compulsive neurosis. *Proceedings of the Royal Society of Medicine* **64**, 1115–18.

Meyerowitz, B.E. (1980). Psychological correlates of breast cancer and its treatment. *Psychological Bulletin* **87**, 108–31.

Michael, R.P. and Gibbons, J.L. (1963). Interrelationships between the endocrine system and neuropsychiatry. *International Review of Neurobiology* **5**, 243–302.

Miles, A. (1979). Some psychosocial consequences of multiple sclerosis: problems of social interaction and group identity. *British Medical Journal* **iii**, 321–31.

Miller, D.H., Clancy, J., and Cumming, E. (1953). A comparison between unidirectional current non-convulsive electrical stimulation given with Reiter's machine, standard alternating current electroshock (Cerletti method) and pentothal in chronic schizophrenia. *American Journal of Psychiatry* **109**, 617–20.

Miller, E. (1980). Cognitive assessment of the older adult. In *Handbook of mental health* (ed. J.E. Birren and R.E.Sloane). Prentice Hall, Englewood Cliffs.

—— (1980). Psychological intervention in the management and rehabilitation of neuropsychological impairments. *Behaviour Research and Therapy* **18**, 527–35.

Miller, G.H. and Agnew, N. (1974). The Lederman model of alcohol consumption. *Quarterly Journal of Studies on Alcoholism* **35**, 877–98.

Miller, H. (1961). Accident neurosis. *British Medical Journal* **i**, 919–25 and 992–8.

—— and Stern, G. (1965). The long-term prognosis of severe head injury. *Lancet* **i**, 225–9.

Miller, R.J., Horn, A.S., and Iversen, L.L. (1974). The action of neuroleptic drugs on dopamine-stimulated adenosine cyclic 3'5' monophosphate production in rat neostriatum and limbic forebrain. *Molecular Pharmacology* **10**, 759–66.

Mindham, R.H.S. (1970). Psychiatric symptoms in Parkinsonism. *Journal of Neurology, Neurosurgery and Psychiatry* **33**, 188–91.

—— (1974). Psychiatric aspects of Parkinson's disease. *British Journal of Hospital Medicine* **11**, 411–14.

—— (1979). Tricyclic antidepressants and amine precursors. In *Psychopharmacology of affective disorders* (ed. E.S. Paykel and A. Coppen). Oxford University Press.

—— Bagshaw, A., James, S.A., and Swannell, A.J. (1981). Factors associated with the appearance of psychiatric symptoms in rheumatoid arthritis. *Journal of Psychosomatic Research* **25**, 429–35.

—— Howland, C., and Shepherd, M. (1973). An evaluation of continuation therapy with tricyclic antidepressants in depressive illness. *Psychological Medicine* **3**, 5–17.

Minski, L. and Guttmann, E. (1938). Huntington's chorea: a study of thirty four families. *Journal of Mental Science* **84**, 21–96.

Minuchin, S. (1974). *Families and family therapy.* Tavistock, London.

—— and Fishman, H.C. (1981). *Family therapy techniques.* Harvard University Press, Cambridge, Mass.

—— Rosman, B., and Baker, L. (1978). *Psychosomatic families: anorexia nervosa in context.* Harvard University Press, Cambridge, Mass.

Misra, P.C. and Hay, G.G. (1971). Encephalitis presenting as acute schizophrenia. *British Medical Journal* i, 532–3.

Mitchell, W., Falconer, M.A., and Hill, D. (1954). Epilepsy with fetishism relieved by temporal lobectomy. *Lancet* ii, 626–30.

Mitchell-Heggs, N., Kelly, D., and Richardson, A. (1976). Stereotactic limbic leucotomy – a follow-up after 16 months. *British Journal of Psychiatry* 128, 226–41.

Mitcheson, M.C. (1983). Drug addiction. In *The Oxford textbook of medicine* (ed. D.J. Weatherall, J.G.G. Ledingham, and D.A. Warrell). Oxford University Press.

Mittler, P. (1973). *Psychological assessment of mental and physical handicaps.* Tavistock, London.

Mohr, J.W., Turner, R.E., and Jerry, M.B. (1964). *Pedophilia and exhibitionism.* University Press, Toronto.

Morel, B.A. (1860). *Traité des maladie mentales.* Masson, Paris.

Morgan, H.G. (1979). *Death wishes? The understanding and management of deliberate self-harm.* Wiley, Chichester.

—— Burns-Cox, C.J., Pocock, H., and Pottle, S. (1975). Deliberate self-harm: clinical and socio-economic characteristics of 368 patients. *British Journal of Psychiatry* 127, 564–74.

—— and Russell, G.F.M. (1975). Value of family background and clinical features as predictors of long-term outcome in anorexia nervosa. Four year follow-up study of 41 patients. *Psychological Medicine* 5, 355–71.

Morris, P. (1969). *Put away.* Routledge and Kegan Paul, London.

Morris, T. (1979). Psychological adjustment to mastectomy. *Cancer Treatment Reviews* 6, 41–61.

Morrison, J.R. (1975). The family histories of manic-depressive patients with and without alcoholism. *Journal of Nervous and Mental Diseases* 160, 227–9.

Mosher, L.R. and Keith, S.J. (1979). Research on the psychological treatment of schizophrenia: a summary report. *American Journal of Psychiatry* 136, 623–31.

—— Pollin, W., and Stabenau, J.R. (1971). Families with identifications discordant for schizophrenia: some relationships between identification, thinking styles, psychopathology and dominance-submissiveness. *British Journal of Psychiatry* 118, 29–42.

Moss, P.D. and McEvedy, C.P. (1966). An epidemic of overbreathing among school-girls. *British Medical Journal* ii, 1295–300.

Mowat, R.R. (1966). *Morbid jealousy and murder.* Tavistock, London.

Mowrer, O.H. (1950). *Learning theory and personality dynamics.* Ronald Press, New York.

Munro, A. (1980). Monosymptomatic hypochondriacal psychosis. *British Journal of Hospital Medicine* 24, 34–8.

Munroe, R.L. (1955). *Schools of psychoanalytic thought.* Hutchinson Medical, London.

Munthe-Kaas, A. (1980). Rectal administration of diazepam: theoretical basis and clinical experience. In *Antiepileptic therapy: advances in drug monitoring* (ed. S.L. Johannensen *et al.*). Raven Press, New York.

Murphy, E. (1982). Social origins of depression in old age. *British Journal of Psychiatry* 141, 135–42.

Murphy, G.E. and Guze, S.B. (1960). Setting limits: the management of the manipulative patient. *American Journal of Psychotherapy* 14, 30–47.

Murphy, H.B.M. (1968). Cultural factors in the genesis of schizophrenia. In *The transmission of schizophrenia* (ed. D. Rosenthal and S.S. Kety). Pergamon, Oxford.
—— and Raman, A.C. (1971). The chronicity of schizophrenia in indigenous tropical people. *British Journal of Psychiatry* **118**, 489–97.
—— (1977). Migration, culture and mental health. *Psychological medicine* **7**, 677–84.
Murphy, S.B. and Donderi, D.C. (1980). Predicting the success of cataract surgery. *Journal of Behavioral Medicine* **3**, 1–14.
Murray, R.M. and Reveley, A. (1981). The genetic contribution to the neuroses. *British Journal of Hospital Medicine* **25**, 185–90.
Myers, J.B., Morgan, T.O., Carney, S.L., and Ray, C. (1980). Effects of lithium on the kidney. *Kidney International* **18**, 601–8.
Nadelson, C.C., Notman, M.T., Zackson, H., and Garnick, J. (1982). A follow-up study of rape victims. *American Journal of Psychiatry* **139**, 1266–70.
Nagler, S.H. (1957). Fetishism. *Psychiatric Quarterly* **31**, 713–41.
Naguib, M. and Levy, R. (1982). Prediction of outcome in senile dementia – a computed tomography study. *British Journal of Psychiatry* **140**, 263–7.
Naylor, G.J., Dick, D.A.T., Dick, E.G., Le Poidevin, D., and Whyte, S.F. (1973). Electrolyte membrane cation carrier in depressive illness. *Psychological Medicine* **3**, 502–8.
—— Worrall, E.P., Peet, M., and Dick, P. (1976). Whole blood adenosine triphosphate in manic depressive illness. *British Journal of Psychiatry* **129**, 233–5.
Ndetei, D.M. and Muhangi, J. (1979). The prevalence and clinical presentation of psychiatric illness in a rural setting in Kenya. *British Journal of Psychiatry* **135**, 269–72.
Neale, J.M. and Oltmans, T.F. (1980). *Schizophrenia,* Chapter 6. Wiley, Chichester.
Needleman, H.L. (1982). The neuropsychiatric implications of low level exposure to lead. *Psychological Medicine* **12**, 461–3.
Neligan, G. and Prudham, D. (1969). Norms for four standard developmental milestones by sex, social class and place in the family. *Developmental Medicine and Child Neurology* **11**, 413–22.
Newson-Smith, J.G.B. and Hirsch, S.R. (1979*a*). Psychiatric symptoms in self poisoning patients. *Psychological Medicine* **9**, 493–500.
—— —— (1979*b*). A comparison of social workers and psychiatrists in evaluating suicide. *British Journal of Psychiatry* **134**, 335–42.
Nichols, P.J.R. (1975). Some psychosocial aspects of rehabilitation and their implication in research. *Proceedings Royal Society of Medicine* **68**, 537–44.
Nicholson, W.A. (1967). Collection of unwanted drugs from private homes. *British Medical Journal* **iii**, 730–1.
Nicol, A.R. (1982). Psychogenic abdominal pain in childhood. *British Journal of Hospital Medicine* **27**, 351–3.
Nilsson, A., Kay, L., and Jacobson, L. (1967). Post partum mental disorder in an unselected sample: psychiatric history. *Journal of Psychosomatic Research* **11**, 327–40.
Nirje, B. (1970). Normalisation. *Journal of Mental Subnormality* **31**, 62–70.
Nott, P.N., Franklin, M., Armitage, C., and Gelder, M.G. (1976). Hormonal changes and mood in the puerperium. *British Journal of Psychiatry* **128**, 379–83.
Noyes, R. and Clancy, J. (1976). Anxiety neurosis: a 5 year follow up. *Journal of Nervous and Mental Disease* **162**, 200–5.
—— —— Crowe, R., Hoenk, P.R., and Slymen, D.J. (1978). The familial prevalence of anxiety neurosis. *Archives of General Psychiatry* **35**, 1057–9.
Nurnberger, J.I. and Gershon, E.S. (1982). Genetics. In *Handbook of affective disorders* (ed. E.S. Paykel) pp. 126–45. Churchill Livingstone, Edinburgh.
O'Connor, N. (1968). Psychology and intelligence. In *Studies in psychiatry* (ed. M. Shepherd and D.L. Davis). Oxford University Press, London.

Ødegaard, Ø. (1932). Emigration and insanity. *Acta psychiatrica Scandinavica* Suppl. 4.

Odlum, D. (1955). Fetishism. *British Medical Journal* i, 302.

Oliver, J.E. (1970). Huntington's chorea in Northamptonshire. *British Journal of Psychiatry* 116, 241–53.

Oliver, T.E. and Buchanan, A.H. (1979). Generation of maltreated children and multi-agency care in one kindred. *British Journal of Psychiatry* 135, 289–303.

Olley, P.C. (1974). Psychiatric aspects of referral. *British Medical Journal* iii, 248–9 and 322–4.

Olsen, R. (1979). Services for the elderly and mentally infirm. In *Community care for the mentally disabled* (ed. J.K. Wing and R. Olsen). Oxford University Press.

—— (1979). *Alternative patterns of residential care for discharged psychiatric patients.* British Association of Social Workers, London.

Opitz, J.M., Javeggia, E.G., Durkin-Stamm, M.V., and Pendleton, E. (1978). Diagnostic/genetic studies in severe mental retardation. *Birth Defects* 14, 1–38.

Orford, J. (1973]. A comparison of alcoholics whose drinking is totally uncontrolled and those whose drinking is mainly controlled. *Behaviour Research and Therapy* 11, 565–76.

—— (1979). Alcohol and the family. In *Alcoholism in perspective* (ed. M. Grant and P. Gwinner). Croom Helm, London.

—— and Edwards, G. (1977). *Alcoholism.* Maudsley Monographs No. 26. Oxford University Press, London.

Osberg, J.W., Meares, G.J., McKee, D.C.M., and Burnett, G.B. (1982). Intellectual functioning in renal failure and chronic dialysis. *Journal of Chronic Diseases* 35, 445–57.

Osborn, M. (1981). Physical and psychological determinants of premenstrual tension: research issues and a proposed methodology. *Journal Psychosomatic Research* 25, 363–7.

Osler, W. (1910). Angina pectoris. *Lancet* i, 697–702 and 839–44.

Osmond, H., Smythies, J.R., and Harley-Mason, J. (1965). Schizophrenia: a new approach. *Journal of Mental Science* 98, 309–15.

Oswald, I. (1981). Assessment of insomnia. *British Medical Journal* 283, 874–5.

Ounsted, C., Oppenheimer, R., and Lindsay, J. (1974). Aspects of bonding failure: the psychopathology and psychotherapeutic treatment of families of battered children. *Developmental Medicine and Child Neurology* 16, 447–56.

Ovenstone, I.M.K. and Kreitman, N. (1974). Two syndromes of suicide. *British Journal of Psychiatry* 124, 336–45.

Owen, F., Cross, A.J., Crow, T.J., Longden, A., Pulter, M., and Riley, G.J. (1978). Increased dopamine receptor sensitivity in schizophrenia. *Lancet* ii, 223–5.

Pachalis, A.P., Kimmel, H.D., and Kimmel, E. (1972). Further study of diurnal instrumental conditioning in the treatment of enuresis nocturna. *Journal of Behaviour Research and Experimental Psychiatry* 3, 253–6.

Packard, E.H. (1909). An analysis of the psychoses associated with Graves' disease. *American Journal of Insanity* 66, 189–202.

Paffenberger, R.S. (1964). Epidemiological aspects of post-partum mental illness. *British Journal of Social and Preventive Medicine* 18, *189–95.*

Pankratz, L. (1981). A review of the Munchausen Syndrome. *Clinical Psychology Review* 1, 65–78.

Pare, C.M.B. and Sandler, M.J. (1959). A clinical and biochemical study of a trial of iproniazid in the treatment of depression. *Journal of Neurology, Neurosurgery and Psychiatry* 22, 247–51.

Parker, G. (1979). Parental characteristics in relation to depressive disorders. *British Journal of Psychiatry* 134, 138–47.

Parkes, C.M. (1978). Psychological reactions to loss of a limb. In *Modern perspectives in the psychological aspects of surgery* (ed. J.G. Howells). Macmillan, London.
—— Benjamin, B., and Fitzgerald, R.G. (1969). Broken heart: a statistical study of increased mortality among widowers. *British Medical Journal* i, 740–3.
—— and Brown, R.J. (1972). Health after bereavement: a controlled study of young Boston widows and widowers. *Psychosomatic Medicine* 34, 449–61.
Parkes, J.D. (1981). Day-time drowsiness. *Lancet* ii, 1213–17.
Parkes, K.R. (1982). Occupational stress among student nurses: a natural experiment. *Journal of Applied Psychology* 67, 784–96.
Parloff, M.B., Waskow, I.E., and Wolfe, B.E. (1978). Research on therapist variables in relation to process and outcome. In *Handbook of psychotherapy and behaviour change*, 2nd edn (ed. S.L. Garfield and A.E. Bergin). Wiley, New York.
Parnas, J., Shulsinger, F., Teasdale, T.W., Schulsinger, H., Feldman, P.M., and Mednick, S.A. (1982). Perinatal complications and clinical outcome within the schizophrenia spectrum. *British Journal of Psychiatry* 140, 416–20.
Parry-Jones, W. Ll. (1972). *The trade in lunacy*. Routledge & Kegan Paul, London.
—— (1973). Criminal law and complicity in suicide and attempted suicide. *Medicine, Science and the Law* 13, 110–19.
—— Santer-Westrate, H.C., and Crawley, R.C. (1970). Behaviour therapy in a case of hysterical blindness. *Behaviour Research and Therapy* 8, 79–85.
Parsons, T. (1951). *The social system*. Free Press, Glencoe.
Pasamanick, B. and Knobloch, H. (1966). Retrospective studies on the epidemiology of reproductive casualty: old and new. *Merril-Palmer Quarterly of Behavioral Development* 12, 7–26.
—— Scarpitti, F.R., and Lefton, M. (1964). Home versus hospital care for schizophrenics. *Journal of the American Medical Association* 187, 177–81.
Patel, C. (1975). 12 month follow up of yoga and biofeedback in the management of hypertension. *Lancet* i, 62–4.
Paton, W.D.M. (1969). A pharmacological approach to drug dependence and drug tolerance. In *Scientific basis of drug dependence* (ed. H. Steinberg). Churchill, London.
Patterson, R.L. and Jackson, G.M. (1980). Behaviour modification with the elderly. *Progress in Behaviour Modification* 9, 205–39.
Pattison, E.M. (1966). A critique of alcoholism treatment concepts. *Quarterly Journal of Studies on Alcoholism* 27, 49–71.
Pauls, D.L., Cohen, D.J., Heimbuch, R., Detlor, J., and Kidd, K.K. (1981). Familial pattern and transmission of Gilles de la Tourette syndrome and multiple tics. *Archives of General Psychiatry* 38, 1091–3.
Paykel, E.S. (1974). Recent life events and clinical depression. In *Life stress and illness* (ed. E.G. Gunderson and R.H. Rahe) pp. 134–63. Thomas, Springfield, Ill.
—— (1978). Contribution of life events to causation of psychiatric illness. *Psychological Medicine* 8, 245–53.
—— (1981). Have multivariate statistics contributed to classification? *British Journal of Psychiatry* 139, 357–62.
—— (1982). Life events and environment. In *Handbook of affective disorder* (ed. E.S. Paykel) pp. 146–61. Churchill Livingstone, Edinburgh.
—— DiMascio, A., Haskell, D., and Prusoff, B.A. (1975). Effects of maintenance amitriptyline and psychotherapy on symptoms of depression. *Psychological Medicine* 5, 67–77.
—— Emms, E.M., Fletcher, J., and Rassaby, E.S. (1980). Life events and support in puerperal depression. *British Journal of Psychiatry* 136, 339–46.
—— Myers, J.K., Dienelt, M.N., Klerman, G.L., Lindenthal, J.J., and Pepper, M.P.

(1969). Life events and depression: a controlled study. *Archives of General Psychiatry* **21**, 753–60.

—— Prusoff, B.A., and Myers, J.K. (1975). Suicide attempts and recent life events: a controlled comparison. *Archives of General Psychiatry* **32**, 327–33.

Payne, R.W. (1962). An object classification test as a measure of over-inclusiveness in schizophrenic patients. *British Journal of Social and Clinical Psychology* **1**, 213–21.

—— (1973). Cognitive abnormalities. In *Handbook of abnormal psychology* (ed. H.J Eysenck) 2nd edn. Pitman Medical, London.

—— and Friedlander, D. (1962). A short battery of simple tests for measuring over-inclusive thinking. *Journal of Mental Science* **108**, 362–7.

Penrose, L. (1938). *A clinical and genetic study of 1,280 cases of mental deficiency.* HMSO, London.

Penrose, R.J.J. and Storey, P. (1972). Life events before subarachnoid haemorrhage. *Journal of Psychosomatic Research* **16**, 329–33.

Perley, M.J. and Guze, S.B. (1962). Hysteria – the stability and usefulness of clinical criteria. *New England Journal of Medicine* **266**, 421–6.

Perls, F., Hefferline, R.F., and Goodman, P. (1951). *Gestalt therapy: excitement and growth in human personality.* Penguin, Harmondsworth.

Perrin, G.M. (1961). Cardiovascular aspects of electric shock therapy *Acta Psychiatrica Scandinavica* **36**, Suppl. 152, 1–45.

Perris, C. (1966). A study of bipolar (manic depressive) and unipolar recurrent depressive psychoses. *Acta Psychiatrica Scandinavica* **42**, Suppl. 194.

—— (1974). A study of cycloid psychoses. *Acta Psychiatrica Scandinavica* Suppl. 253.

Perry, E.K., Oakley, A.E., and Candy, J.M. (1981). Neurochemical activities in human temporal lobe related to ageing and Alzheimer-type changes. *Neurobiology of Ageing* **2**, 251–6.

—— Perry, R.H., Blessed, G., and Tomlinson, B.E. (1977). Necropsy evidence of central cholinergic deficits in senile dementia. *Lancet* **i**, 189.

—— Tomlinson, B.E., and Blessed, G. (1978). Correlation of cholinergic abnormalities with senile plaques and mental test scores in senile dementia. *British Medical Journal* **ii**, 1457–9.

Perry, T.L., Hansen, S., and Kloster, M. (1973). Huntington's chorea: deficiency of gamma-aminobutyric acid in brain. *New England Journal of Medicine* **288**, 337–42.

Petersen, P. (1968). Psychiatric disorders in primary hyperparathyroidism. *Journal of Clinical Endocrinology and Metabolism* **28**, 1491–5.

Peterson, B., Kristenson, H., Sternby, N.H., Trell, E., Fex, G., and Hood, B. (1980). Alcohol consumption and premature death in middle-aged men. *British Medical Journal* **i**, 1403–6.

Philippopoulos, G.S., Wittkower, E.D., and Cousineau, A. (1958). The etiologic significance of emotional factors in onset and exacerbations of multiple sclerosis. *Psychosomatic Medicine* **20**, 458–74.

Pichot, P. (1982). The diagnosis and classification of mental disorders in French speaking countries: background, current view and comparison with other nomenclature. *Psychological Medicine* **12**, 475–92.

Pilowsky, I. (1969). A general classification of abnormal illness behaviours. *British Journal of Medical Psychology* **51**, 131–7.

—— (1978). Psychodynamic aspects of pain experience. In *The psychology of pain* (ed. R.A. Sternbach). Raven Press, New York.

Pinel, P. (1806). *A treatise on insanity* (translated by D.D. Davis). Cadell and Davils, Sheffield.

Pippard, J. and Ellam, L. (1981). *Electroconvulsive treatment in Great Britain.* Gaskell, London.

Pitres, A. and Régis, E. (1902). *Les obsessions et les impulsions.* Doin, Paris.

Pitt, B. (1968). 'Atypical' depression following childbirth. *British Journal of Psychiatry* **114**, 1325–35.

Pitts, F.N. and McClure, J.N. (1967). Lactate metabolism in anxiety neurosis. *New England Journal of Medicine* **25**, 1329–36.

—— and Winokur, G. (1964). Affective disorders III: diagnostic correlates and incidence of suicide. *Journal of Nervous and Mental Disease* **139**, 176–81.

Planansky, K. and Johnston, R. (1977). Homicidal aggression in schizophrenic men. *Acta Psychiatrica Scandinavia* **55**, 65–73.

Plant, M.A. (1975). *Drug takers in an English Town.* Tavistock, London.

—— Peck, D.F., and Stuart, R. (1982). Self-reported drinking habits and alcohol-related consequences among a cohort of Scottish teenagers. *British Journal of Addiction* **77**, 75–90.

Pollard, R. (1973). Surgical implications of some types of drug dependence. *British Medical Journal* i, 784–7.

Pollin, W., Cardon, P.V. Jr, and Kety, S.S. (1961). Effects of aminoacid feedings in schizophrenic patients treated with iproniazid. *Science* **133**, 104–5.

—— and Stabenau, J. (1968). Biological, psychological, and historical differences in a series of monozygotic twins discordant for schizophrenia. In *Transmission of schizophrenia* (ed. D. Rosenthal and S. Kety). Pergamon, London.

Pollitt, J. (1957). Natural history of obsessional states. *British Medical Journal* i, 194–8.

—— (1960). Natural history studies in mental illness: a discussion based upon a pilot study of obsessional states. *Journal of Mental Science* **106**, 93–113.

Pond, D.A. (1957). Psychiatric aspects of epilepsy. *Journal of the Indian Medical Profession* **3**, 1441–51.

—— and Bidwell, B.H. (1960). A survey of epilepsy in fourteen general practices. II. Social and psychological aspects. *Epilepsia* **1**, 285–99.

—— —— and Stein, L. (1980). A survey of epilepsy in fourteen general practices. I: Demographic and medical data. *Psychiatrica, Neurologia, et Neurochirurgia* **63**, 217–36.

Popham, R.E. (1956). The Jellinek alcoholism estimation formula and its application to Canadian data. *Quarterly Journal of Studies on Alcohol* **17**, 559–93.

Post, F. (1965). *The clinical psychiatry of late life.* Pergamon, New York.

—— (1966). *Persistent persecutory states in the elderly.* Pergamon, London.

—— (1971). Schizo-affective symptomatology in late life. *British Journal of Psychiatry* **118**, 437–45.

—— (1972). The management and nature of depressive illnesses in late life: a follow-through study. *British Journal of Psychiatry* **121**, 393–404.

Powell, G.F., Brasel, J.A., and Blizzard, R.M. (1967). Emotional deprivation and growth retardation simulating idiopathic hypopituitarism. *New England Journal of Medicine* **276**, 1271–83.

Powell-Proctor, L. and Miller, E. (1982). Reality orientation: a critical appraisal. *British Journal of Psychiatry* **140**, 457–63.

Power, D.J. (1969). Subnormality and crime. *Medicine, Science and the Law* **9**, 82–93 and 162–71.

—— Benn, R.T., and Homes, J.N. (1972). Neighbourhood, school and juveniles before courts. *British Journal of Criminology* **12**, 111–32.

Pratt, J.H. (1908). Results obtained in treatment of pulmonary tuberculosis by the class method. *British Medical Journal* ii, 1070–1.

Pratt, R.T.C. (1951). An investigation of psychiatric aspects of disseminated sclerosis. *Journal of Neurology, Neurosurgery and Psychiatry* **14**, 326–35.

Presidents Panel on Mental Retardation (1972). National action to combat mental retardation. United States Government Printing Office, Washington, DC.

Price, J. (1968). The genetics of depressive behaviour. In *Recent developments in affective disorders. British Journal of Psychiatry* Special Publication No. 2 (ed. A. Coppen and S. Walk).

Prichard, J.C. (1835). *A treatise on insanity.* Sherwood Gilbert and Piper, London.

Prien, R.F., Caffey, E.M., and Glett, C.J. (1972). Comparison of lithium carbonate and chlorpomazine in the treatment of mania. *Archives of General Psychiatry* **26**, 146–53.

—— —— —— (1973). Prophylactic efficacy of lithium carbonate in manic depressive illness. *Archives of General Psychiatry* **28**, 337–41.

Prince, Morton (1908). *Dissociation of a personality: biographical study in abnormal psychology.* Longmans Green, New York.

Pritchard, M. (1982). Psychological problems in a renal unit. *British Journal of Hospital Medicine* **27**, 512–15.

—— and Graham, P. (1966). An investigation of a group of patients who have attended both the child and adult departments of the same psychiatric hospital. *British Journal of Psychiatry* **112**, 603–12.

Procci, W.R. (1976). Schizoaffective psychosis: fact or fiction? *Archives of General Psychiatry* **33**, 1167–78.

—— (1980). A comparison of psychosocial disability in males undergoing maintenance haemodialysis or following cadaver transplantation. *General Hospital Psychiatry* **2**, 255–61.

Protheroe, C. (1969). Puerperal psychoses: a long term study, 1927–1961. *British Journal of Psychiatry* **115**, 9–30.

Prusoff, B.A., Weissman, M.M., Klerman, G.L., and Rounsaville, B.J. (1980). Research diagnostic criteria subtypes of depression as predictors of differential response to psychotherapy and drug treatment. *Archives of General Psychiatry* **37**, 796–801.

Prys-Williams, G. and Glatt, M.M. (1966). The incidence of longstanding alcoholism in England and Wales. *British Journal of Addiction* **61**, 257–68.

Pugh, R., Jerath, B.K., Schimdt, W.M., and Reed, R.B. (1963). Rates of mental disease related to child bearing. *New England Journal of Medicine* **22**, 1224–8.

Puig-Antich, J. and Gittleman, R. (1982). Depression in childhood and adolescence. In *Handbook of affective disorders* (ed. E.S. Paykel). Churchill Livingstone, Edinburgh.

Quay, H.C. and Werry, J.S. (1979). *Psychopathological disorders of childhood.* Wiley, New York.

Querido, A. (1959). Forecast and follow-up. An investigation into the clinical, social and mental factors determining the results of hospital treatment. *British Journal of Preventive and Social Medicine* **13**, 334–9.

Quitkin, F., Rifkin, A., and Klein, D. (1976). Neurologic soft signs in schizophrenia and character disorders. *Archives of General Psychiatry* **33**, 845–53.

Rachman, S. (1966). Sexual fetishism – an experimental analogue. *Psychological Record* **16**, 293–6.

—— (1974). Primary obsessional slowness. *Behaviour Research and Therapy* **11**, 463–71.

—— and Hodgson, R.J. (1980). *Obsessions and compulsions.* Prentice Hall, New Jersey.

—— and Teasdale, J. (1969). *Aversion therapy and behaviour disorders: an analysis.* Pergamon, Oxford.

Radomski, J.K., Fuyat, H.N., Belson, A.A., and Smith, P.K. (1950). The toxic effects, excretion and distribution of lithium chloride. *Journal of Pharmacology and Experimental Therapeutics* **100**, 429–44.

Radzinowicz, L. (1957). *Sexual offences.* Macmillan, London.

—— and King, J. (1979). *The growth of crime.* Penguin, Harmondsworth.

Rae, W. A. (1977). Childhood conversion reactions: a review of incidence in pediatric settings. *Journal of Clinical Child Psychology* **6**, 66–72.

Rahe, R. (1973). Subjects recent life changes and the near future illness reports. *Annals of Clinical Research* **4**, 1–16.

—— Gunderson, E.K.E., and Arthur, R.J. (1970). Demographic and psychosocial factors in acute illness reporting. *Journal of Chronic Diseases* **23**, 245–55.

Ramsay, A.M. (1973). Benign myalgic encephalomyelitis. *British Journal of Psychiatry* **122,,** 618–19.

Rapoport, J.L. (1977). Pediatric psychopharmacology and childhood depression. In *Depression and childhood: diagnosis, treatment and conceptual methods* (ed. J.G. Schuldebrondt and A. Raskin). Raven Press, New York.

Rapoport, R.N. (1960). *Community as doctor.* Tavistock, London.

Ratcliffe, S.G. (1982). Speech and learning disorders in children with sex chromosome abnormalities. *Developmental Medicine and Child Neurology* **24**, 80–4.

Razin, A.M. (1982). Psychosocial intervention in coronary artery disease: a review. *Psychosomatic Medicine* **44**, 363–87.

Reed, G.F. and Sedman, G. (1964). Personality and depersonalization under sensory deprivation conditions. *Perceptual and Motor Skills* **18**, 659–60.

Reed, T.E. and Chandler, J.H. (1958). Huntington's chorea in Michigan. I Demography and genetics. *American Journal of Human Genetics* **10**, 201–25.

Rees, W.D. and Lutkins, S.G. (1967). Mortality of bereavement. *British Medical Journal* **iv**, 13–16.

Reid, A.H. (1982). *The psychiatry of mental handicap.* Blackwell, Oxford.

Reisberg, B., Ferris, S.H., and Gershon, S. (1981). An overview of pharmacologic treatment of cognitive decline in the aged. *American Journal of Psychiatry* **138**, 593–600.

Resnick, P.J. (1969). Child murder by parents. *American Journal of Psychiatry* **126**, 325–34.

Reuler, J.B., Girard, D.E., and Nardone, D.A. (1980). The chronic pain syndrome: misconceptions and management. *Annals of Internal Medicine* **93**, 588–96.

Reynolds, E.H. (1968). Mental effects of anticonvulsants and folic acid metabolism. *Brain* **91**, 197–214.

—— Preece, J., and Chanarin, I. (1969). Folic acid and anticonvulsants. *Lancet* **i**, 1264–5.

—— and Trimble, M.R. (ed.) (1981). *Epilepsy and psychiatry.* Churchill Livingstone, Edinburgh.

Richardson, A. (1973). Stereotactic limbic leucotomy: surgical technique. *Postgraduate Medical Journal* **49**, 860.

Richens, A. (1976). Clinical pharmacology and medical treatment. In *A textbook of epilepsy* (ed. J. Laidlaw and A. Richens). Churchill Livingstone, Edinburgh.

Richman, N., Stevenson, J., and Graham, P. (1975). Prevalence of behaviour problems in 3 year old children: an epidemiological study in a London borough. *Journal of Child Psychology and Psychiatry* **16**, 272–87.

Rickles, N.K. (1950). *Exhibitionism.* Lippincott, Philadelphia.

Ridges, A.P. (1973). Abnormal metabolites in schizophrenia. In *Biochemistry and Mental Illness* (ed. L.L. Iversen and S.P.R. Rose). Biochemical Society Special Publication No. 1, pp. 175–88.

Rimm, D.C. and Masters, J.C. (1974). *Behaviour therapy: techniques and empirical findings.* Academic Press, New York.

Ritson, B. (1977). Alcoholism and suicide. In *Alcoholism: new knowledge and new responses* (ed. G. Edwards and M. Grant). Croom Helm, London.

—— (1982). Helping the problem drinker. *British Medical Journal* **284**, 327–9.

Roberts, A.H. (1969). *Brain damage in boxers.* Pitman, London.

Roberts, J. and Hawton, K. (1980). Child abuse and attempted suicide. *British Journal of Psychiatry* **137**, 319–23.

Robin, A.A. and Harris, J.A. (1962). A controlled comparison of imipramine and electroplexy. *Journal of Mental Science* **108**, 217–19.

Robins, E., Gassner, S., Kayes, J., Wilkinson, R.H., and Murphy, G.E. (1959). The communication of suicidal intent: a study of 134 successful (completed) suicides. *American Journal of Psychiatry* **115**, 724–33.

Robins, L. (1966). *Deviant children grown up*. Williams and Wilkins, Baltimore.

—— (1970). Follow-up studies investigating childhood disorders. In *Psychiatric epidemiology* (ed. E.H. Hare and J.K. Wing). Oxford University Press, London.

—— (1979*a*). Follow-up studies. In *Pathological disorders of childhood* (ed. H.C. Quay and J.S. Werry) pp. 483–513. Wiley, New York.

—— (1979*b*). *N.I.M.H. diagnostic interview*. National Institutes of Mental Health, Bethesda.

——- Davis, D.H., and Goodwin, D.W. (1974). Drug use by the US army enlisted men in Vietnam: a follow-up on their return home. *American Journal of Epidemiology* **99**, 235–49.

Robinson, D. (1978). Self help groups. *British Journal Hospital Medicine* **20**, 306–11.

—— (1979). *Talking out of alcoholism: the self-help process of Alcoholics Anonymous*. Croom Helm, London.

Rochford, J.M., Detre, T., Tucker, G.J., and Harrow, M. (1970). Neuropsychological impairments in functional psychiatric disease. *Archives of General Psychiatry* **22**, 114–19.

Rodnight, R., Murray, R.M., Oon, M.C.H., Brockington, I.F., Nicholls, P., and Birley, J.L.T. (1977). Urinary dimethyltryptamine and psychiatric symptomatology and classification. *Psychological Medicine* **6**, 649–57.

Rogers, C.R. and Dymond, R.F. (eds.) (1954). *Psychotherapy and personality change*. University of Chicago Press.

Rogers, M.P., Liang, M.H., and Partridge, A.J. (1982). Psychological care of adults with rheumatoid arthritis. *Annals of Internal Medicine* **96**, 344–8.

Rogers, S.C. and May, P.M. (1975). A statistical review of controlled trials of imipramine and placebo in the treatment of depressive illness. *British Journal of Psychiatry* **127**, 599–603.

Rollin, H.R. (1969). *The mentally abnormal offender and the law*. Pergamon, Oxford.

Ron, M.A. (1977). Brain damage in chronic alcoholism: a neuropathological, neuro-radiological and psychological review. *Psychological Medicine* **7**, 103–12.

—— Acker, W., and Lishman, W.A. (1980). Morphological abnormalities in the brains of chronic alcoholics. A clinical, psychological and computerised axial tomographic study. *Acta Psychiatrica Scandinavica* Suppl. 286, 51–6.

—— Toone, B.K., Garralda, M.E., and Lishman, W.A. (1979). Diagnostic accuracy in presenile dementia. *British Journal of Psychiatry* **134**, 161–8.

Rook, A. (1959). Student suicides. *British Medical Journal* i, 600–3.

Rooth, F.G. (1971). Indecent exposure and exhibitionism. *British Journal of Hospital Medicine* **5**, 521–33.

—— (1973). Exhibitionism, sexual violence and paedophilia. *British Journal of Psychiatry* **122**, 705–10.

—— and Marks, I.M. (1974). Persistent exhibitionism: short-term response to aversion self regulation and relaxation treatment. *Archives of Sexual Behaviour* **3**, 227–43.

Rosalki, S.B., Rau, D., Lehmann, D., and Prentice, M. (1970). Determination of serum gamma-glutamyl transpeptidase activity and its clinical applications. *American Journal of Clinical Biochemistry* **7**, 143–7.

Rosanoff, A.J., Handy, L.M., and Plesset, I.R. (1941). The ecology and child behaviour difficulties, juvenile delinquency and adult criminality with special reference to the occurrence in twins. *Psychiatric Monograph (California)* No. 1. Department of Institutions, Sacramento.

—— —— and Rosanoff, I.A. (1934). Criminality and delinquency in twins. *Journal of Criminal Law and Criminology* **24**, 923–34.

Rosen, B.K. (1981). Suicide pacts: a review. *Psychological Medicine* **11**, 525–33.

Rosen, I. (1979). Exhibitionism, scopophilia and voyeurism. In *Sexual deviations,* 2nd edn. (ed. I. Rosen). Oxford University Press.

Rosenham, D. (1973). On being sane in insane places. *Science* **179**, 250–8.

Rosenman, R.H., Brand, R.J., Jenkins, C.D., Friedman, H., Straus, R., and Wurner, H. (1975). Coronary heart disease: a western collaborative group study. Final follow up experience of eight and a half years. *Journal of the American Medical Association* **233**, 872–7.

Rosenthal, D., Wender, P.H., Kety, S.S., and Welner, J. (1971). The adopted-away offspring of schizophrenics. *American Journal of Psychiatry* **128**, 307–11.

Rosenthal, R. and Bigelow, L.B. Quantitative brain measurements in chronic schizophrenia. *British Journal of Psychiatry* **121**, 259–64.

Ross, T.A. (1937). *The common neuroses: their treatment by psychotherapy.* 2nd edn. Edward Arnold, London.

Rosser, A.M. and Guz, A. (1981). Psychological approach to breathlessness and its treatment. *Journal of Psychosomatic Research* **25**, 439–47.

Roth, B. (1980). *Narcolepsy and hypersomnia.* Karger, Basel.

—— Nevsimalova, S., and Rechtschaffen, A. (1972). Hypersomnia with sleep drunkeness. *Archives of General Psychiatry* **26**, 456–62.

Roth, M. (1955). The natural history of mental disorder in old age. *Journal of Mental Science* **101**, 281–301.

—— (1959). The phobic anxiety-depersonalization syndrome. *Proceedings of the Royal Society of Medicine* **52**, 587–95.

—— (1971). Classification and aetiology in mental disorders of old age: some recent developments. In *Recent developments in psychogeriatrics* (ed. D.W.K. Kay and A. Walk). Headley Brothers, Ashford.

—— and Ball, J.R.B. (1964). Psychiatric aspects of intersexuality. In *Intersexuality in vertebrates including man* (ed. C.N. Armstrong and A.J. Marshall). Academic Press, London.

Rothman, D. (1971). *The discovery of the asylum.* Little Brown, Boston.

Rothschild, D. (1942). Neuropathological changes in arteriosclerotic psychosis and their psychiatric significance. *Archives of Neurology and Psychiatry, Chicago* **48**, 417–36.

Rowan, P.R., Paykel, E.S., and Parker, R.P. (1982). Phenelzine and amitriptyline effects on symptoms of neurotic depression. *British Journal of Psychiatry* **140**, 475–83.

Roy, A. (1982). Suicide in chronic schizophrenia. *British Journal of Psychiatry* **141**, 171–7.

—— and Bhanji, S. (1976). Sleep deprivation in depression: a review. *Postgraduate Medical Journal* **52**, 50–2.

Royal College of Physicians (1981). Organic mental impairment in the elderly. Report of the College Committee on geriatrics. *Journal of the Royal College of Physicians* **15**, 141–67.

Royal College of Psychiatrists (1977). Memorandum on the use of electroconvulsive therapy. *British Journal of Psychiatry* **131**, 261–72.

—— (1979). *Alcohol and alcoholism. The report of a special committee of the Royal College of Psychiatrists.* Tavistock, London.

Rüdin, E. (1916). Studien über Vererbung und Entstehung geistiger störungen: *I. Zur vererbung und Neuenstehung der Dementia Praecox.* Springer, Berlin.

—— (1953). Ein Beitrag zur Frage der Zwangskrankeit, unsbesondere ihrer hereditaren Beziehungen. *Archiv für Psychiatrie und Nervenkrankheiten* **191**, 14–54.

Rush, A.J., Beck, A.T., Kovacs, M., and Hollon, S. (1977). Comparative efficacy of cognitive therapy and imipramine in the treatment of depressed out-patients. *Cognitive Therapy and Research* **1**, 17–31.

Rush, Benjamin (1830). *Medical inquiries and observations upon the diseases of the mind,* 4th edn. Philadelphia.

Russell, G.F.M. (1977). The present status of anorexia nervosa. *Psychological Medicine* **7**, 363–7.

—— (1979). Bulimia nervosa: an ominous variant of anorexia nervosa. *Psychological Medicine* **9**, 429–48.

—— (1981). The current treatment of anorexia nervosa. *British Journal of Psychiatry* **138**, 164–6.

Russell, W.R. and Smith, A. (1961). Post-traumatic amnesia in closed head injury. *Archives of Neurology* **5**, 4–17.

Rutter, B.M. (1977). Some psychological concomitants of chronic bronchitis. *Psychological Medicine* **7**, 459–64.

Rutter, M. (1967). Psychotic disorders in early childhood. In *Recent developments in schizophrenia. British Journal of Psychiatry* Special publication No. 1. (ed. A. Coppen and W. Walk). Headley Brothers, London.

—— (1970). Autistic children: infancy to adulthood. *Seminars in Psychiatry* **2**, 435–40.

—— (1971). Normal psychosexual development. *Journal of Child Psychology and Psychiatry* **11**, 259–83.

—— (1972). Relationships between child and adult psychiatric disorders. *Acta Psychiatrica Scandinavica* **48**, 3–21.

—— (1977*a*). Sociocultural influences. In *Child psychiatry: modern approaches* (ed. M. Rutter and L. Hersov). Blackwell, Oxford.

—— (1977*b*). Individual differences. In *Child psychiatry: modern approaches* (ed. M. Rutter and L. Hersov). Blackwell, Oxford.

—— (1977*c*). Infantile autism and other child psychoses. In *Child psychiatry: modern approaches* (ed. M. Rutter and L. Hersov). Blackwell, Oxford.

—— (1980). (ed.) *Scientific foundations of developmental psychiatry.* Heinemann, London.

—— (1981*a*). Psychological sequelae of brain damage in children. *American Journal of Psychiatry* **138**, 1533–44.

—— (1981*b*). *Maternal deprivation reassessed.* Penguin, Harmondsworth.

—— (1982*a*). Syndromes attributed to 'minimal brain dysfunction' in childhood. *American Journal of Psychiatry* **139**, 21–33.

—— (1982*b*). Psychological therapies in child psychiatry: issues and prospects. *Psychological Medicine* **12**, 723–40.

—— Graham, P., and Birch, H.G. (1970). *A neuropsychiatric study of childhood.* Clinics in Developmental Medicine No. 35/36. Heinemann, London.

—— —— Chadwick, O., and Yule, W. (1976). Adolescent turmoil: fact or fiction. *Journal of Child Psychology and Psychiatry* **17**, 35–56.

—— and Hersov, L. (eds.) (1977). *Child psychiatry: modern approaches.* Blackwell, Oxford.

—— and Lockyer, L. (1967). A five to fifteen year follow-up study of infantile psychosis: I. Description of sample. *British Journal of Psychiatry* **113**, 1169–82.

—— and Madge, N. (1976). *Cycles of disadvantage: a review of research.* Heinemann, London.

—— and Schopler, E. (1978). *Autism: a reappraisal of concepts and treatment.* Plenum, New York.

—— Shaffer, D., and Shepherd, M. (1975). *A multiaxial classification of child psychiatric disorders.* World Health Organization, Geneva.

—— Tizard, J., and Whitmore, K. (eds.) (1970). *Education, health and behaviour.* Longmans, London.

—— and Yule, W. (1975). The concept of specific reading retardation. *Journal of Child Psychology and Psychiatry* **16**, 181–98.

—— —— Berger, M., Yule, B., Morton, J., and Bagley, C. (1974). Children of West Indian immigrants. I. Rates of behavioural deviance and of psychiatric disorder. *Journal of Child Psychology and Psychiatry* **15**, 241–62.

—— —— and Graham, P. (1973). Enuresis and behaviour deviance: some epidemiological considerations. In *Bladder control and enuresis* (ed. I. Kolvin, R.C. MacKeith, and S.R. Meadow). Little Clinics in Developmental Medicine. Heinemann, London.

—— —— Quinton, D., Rowlands, O., Yule, W., and Berger, M. (1975). Attainment and adjustment in two geographical areas III: some factors accounting for area differences, *British Journal of Psychiatry* **126**, 520–33.

Ryan, P. (1979). Residential care for the mentally disabled. In *Community care for the mentally disabled* (ed. J.K. Wing and R. Olsen). Oxford University Press.

Saario, I., Linnoila, M., and Maki, M. (1975). Interaction of drugs with alcohol on human psychomotor skills related to driving: effects of sleep deprivation or two weeks treatment with hypnotics. *Journal of Clinical Pharmacology* **15**, 52–9.

Sachar, E.J. (1982). Endocrine abnormalities in depression. In *Handbook of affective disorders* (ed. E.S. Paykel). Churchill Livingstone, Edinburgh.

Sacks, O. (1973). *Awakenings.* Duckworth, London.

Saghir, M.T. and Robins, E. (1973). *Male and female homosexuality: a comprehensive investigation.* Williams and Wilkins, Baltimore.

Sainsbury, P. (1955). *Suicide in London.* Maudsley Monograph No. 1. Chapman and Hall, London.

—— (1962). Suicide in later life. *Gerontologia Clinica* **4**, 161–70.

Sakel, M. (1938). *The pharmacological shock treatment of schizophrenia.* Nervous and Mental Diseases Monograph Series No. 62. Nervous and Mental Diseases Publications Co, New York.

Salter, A. (1949). *Conditioned reflex therapy.* Farrar Strauss, New York.

Salmons, P.H. (1980). Psychological aspects of chronic renal failure. *British Journal of Hospital Medicine* **23**, 617–22.

Sand, P.L., Trieschmann, R.B., Rofdyce, W.E., and Fowler, R.S. (1970). Behaviour modification in the medical rehabilitation setting: rationale and some applications. *Rehabilitation and Practice Review* **1**, 11–24.

Sandberg, S.T., Rutter, M., and Taylor, E. (1978). Hyperkinetic disorder in psychiatric clinic attenders. *Developmental Medicine and Child Neurology* **20**, 279–99.

Sanders, S.H. (1979). Behavioural assessment and treatment of clinical pain: appraisal of current status. *Progress in Behaviour Modification* **8**, 249–92.

Sandifer, M.G., Hordern, A., Timbury, G.C., and Green, L.M. (1968). Psychiatric diagnosis: a comparative study in North Carolina. *British Journal of Psychiatry* **114**, 1–9.

Sandler, J., Dare, C., and Holder, A. (1970*a*). Basic psychoanalytic concepts: II. The treatment alliance. *British Journal of Psychiatry* **116**, 555–8.

—— —— —— (1970*b*). Basic psychoanalytic concepts: III. Transference. *British Journal of Psychiatry* **116**, 667–72.

—— —— —— (1970*c*). Basic psychoanalytic concepts: IV. Countertransference. *British Journal of Psychiatry* **117**, 83–8.

—— —— —— (1970*d*). Basic psychoanalytic concepts: V. Resistance *British Journal of Psychiatry* **117**, 215–21.

———————— (1970*e*). Basic psychoanalytic concepts: VI. Acting out. *British Journal of Psychiatry* **117**, 329–35.

Sargant, W. and Dally, P. (1962). Treatment of anxiety state by antidepressant drugs. *British Medical Journal* i, 6–9.

—— and Slater, E. (1940). Acute war neuroses. *Lancet* ii, 1–2.

—— —— (1963). *An introduction to physical methods of treatment in psychiatry.* Livingstone, Edinburgh.

Satir, V. (1967). *Conjoint family therapy.* Science and Behaviour Books, Palo Alto.

Saunders, C. (1969). The moment of truth: care of the dying person. In *Death and dying* (ed. L. Pearson). Case Western Reserve University Press, Cleveland.

Saunders, J.B., Davis, M., and Williams, R. (1981). Do women develop alcoholic liver disease more readily than men? *British Medical Journal* **282**, 1140–3.

Savage, R.L. (1976). Drugs and breast milk. *Adverse Drug Reactions Bulletin* **61**, 212–14.

Scadding, J.G. (1963). Meaning of diagnostic terms in bronchopulmonary disease. *British Medical Journal* ii, 1425–30.

Schaefer, C. (1979). *Childhood encopresis and enuresis.* Van Nostrand, New York.

—— Coyne, J.C., and Lazarus, R.S. (1981). The health-related functions of social support. *Journal of Behavioral Medicine* **4**, 381–406.

Schapira, K., Davison, K., and Brierley, H. (1979). The assessment and management of transsexual problems. *British Journal of Hospital Medicine* **22**, 63–9.

—— Roth, M., Kerr, T.A., and Gurney, C. (1972). The prognosis of affective disorders The differentiation of anxiety states from depressive illness. *British Journal of Psychiatry* **121**, 175–81.

Scharfetter, C. (1980). *General psychopathology: an introduction* (translated from the German by H. Marshall). Cambridge University Press.

Scheff, T.J. (1963). The role of the mentally ill and the dynamics of mental disorder: a research framework. *Sociometry* **26**, 436–53.

Schilder, P. (1935). *The image and appearance of the human body.* International Universities Press, New York.

Schmideberg, M. (1947). The treatment of psychopaths and borderline patients. *American Journal of Psychotherapy* **1**, 45–70.

Schmidt, W. and de Lint, J.E.E. (1972). The causes of death in alcoholics. *Quarterly Journal of Studies on Alcoholism* **33**, 171–85.

Schneck, M.K., Reisberg, B., and Ferris, S.H. (1982). An overview of current concepts of Alzheimer's disease. *American Journal of Psychiatry* **139**, 165–73.

Schneider, K. (1950). *Psychopathic personalities.* Translation of 9th edition by M.W. Hamilton. Cassel, London.

—— (1959). *Clinical psychopathology.* Grune and Stratton, New York.

Schou, M., Amisden, A., Jensen, S.E., and Olsen, T. (1968). Occurrence of goitre during lithium treatment. *British Medical Journal* iii, 710–13.

Schooler, N.R., Levine, J., Severe, J.B., Brauzer, B., diMascio, A., Klerman, G., and Tuason, V.B. (1980). Prevention of relapse in schizophrenia. *Archives of General Psychiatry* **37**, 16–24.

Schulsinger, F. (1982). Psychopathy: heredity and environment. *International Journal of Mental Health* **1**, 190–206.

Schultz, J.H. (1932). *Das autogene training.* Thieme, Liepzig.

—— and Luthe, W. (1959). *Autogenic training: a psychophysiological approach.* Grune and Stratton, New York.

Schwartz, D.M. and Thompson, M.G. (1981). Do anorectics get well? Current research and future needs. *American Journal of Psychiatry* **138**, 319–23.

Schwartz, M.A. (1973). Pathways of metabolism of diazepines. in *The benzodiazepines* (ed. S. Garrattini, E. Mussini, and L.O. Randall). Raven Press, New York.

Scott, D. (1978). The problems of malicious fire raising. *British Journal of Hospital Medicine* 19, 259–63.

Scott, P.D. (1953). Psychiatric reports for magistrates courts. *British Journal of Delinquency* 4, 82–98.

—— (1957). Homosexuality with special reference to classification. *Proceedings of the Royal Society of Medicine* 50, 655–9.

—— (1960). The treatment of psychopaths. *British Medical Journal* i, 1641–6.

—— (1965). The Ganser syndrome. *British Journal of Criminology* 5, 127–34.

—— (1973). Parents who kill their children. *Medicine Science and the Law* 13, 120–6.

—— (1977*a*). Assessing dangerousness in criminals. *British Journal of Psychiatry* 131, 127–42.

—— (1977*b*). Non-accidental injury in children: memorandum of evidence to the Parliamentary select committee on violence in the family. *British Journal of Psychiatry* 131, 366–80.

Seager, C.P. (1960). A controlled study of postpartum mental illness. *Journal of Mental Science* 106, 214–30.

—— and Flood, R.A. (1965). Suicide in Bristol. *British Journal of Psychiatry* 111, 919–32.

Sedman, G. (1966). A phenomenological study of pseudo-hallucinations and related experiences. *British Journal of Psychiatry* 113, 1115–21.

—— (1970). Theories of depersonalization: a reappraisal. *British Journal of Psychiatry* 117, 1–14.

Seguin, E. (1864). Origin of the treatment and training of idiots. In *History of mental retardation,* Vol. 1 (ed. M. Rosen, G.R. Clark, and M.S. Kivitz). University Park Press, Baltimore (1976).

—— (1866). *Idiocy and its treatment by the physiological method.* Brandown, Albany.

Seidel, U., Chadwick, O.F.D., and Rutter, M.L. (1975). Psychological disorder in crippled children: a comparative study of children with and without brain damage. *Developmental Medicine and Child Neurology* 17, 563–73.

Seligman, M.E.P. (1975). *Helplessness: on depression, development and death.* Freeman, San Francisco.

Shaffer, D. (1974). Suicide in childhood and early adolescence. *Journal of Child Psychology and Psychiatry* 15, 275–91.

—— (1977). Enuresis. In *Child psychiatry: modern approaches* (ed. M. Rutter and L. Hersov). Blackwell, Oxford.

—— Costello, A.J., and Hill, I.D. (1968). Control of enuresis with imipramine. *Archives of Diseases of Childhood* 43, 665–71.

Shapiro, A.K., Shapiro, E., Wayne, M., and Clarkin, J. (1968). Organic factors in Gilles de la Tourette's syndrome. *British Journal of Psychiatry* 114, 345–50.

Shapiro, D. (1976). The effects of therapeutic conditions: positive results revisited. *British Journal of Medical Psychology* 49, 315–23.

Sharan, S.N. (1966). Family interaction with schizophrenia and their siblings. *Journal of Abnormal Psychology* 71, 345–53.

Shaw, P.M. (1979). A comparison of three behaviour therapies in the treatment of social phobias. *British Journal of Psychiatry* 134, 620–3.

Shaw, S. (1980). The causes of increasing drinking problems among women. In *Women and alcohol.* Tavistock, London.

Sheldon, W.H., Stevens, S.S., and Tucker, W.B. (1940). *The varieties of human physique*. Harper, London.
—————— (1942). *The varieties of temperament*. Harper, London.
Shepherd, M. (1961). Morbid jealousy: some clinical and social aspects of a psychiatric symptom. *Journal of Mental Science* 107, 687–753.
Shepherd, M. (ed.) (1983). *Handbook of psychiatry*. Vols. 1–5. Cambridge University Press.
—— Cooper, B., Brown, A.C., and Kalton, G.W. (1966). *Psychiatric illness in general practice*. Oxford University Press, London.
—— and Gruenberg, E.M. (1957). The age for neuroses. *Milbank Memorial Fund Quarterly* 35, 258–65.
—— Harwin, B.G., Depla, C., and Cairns, V. (1979). Social work and primary care of mental disorder. *Psychological Medicine* 9, 661–70.
—— Lader, M., and Rodnight, R. (1968). *Clinical psychopharmacology*. English Universities Press, London.
—— Oppenheim, A.N., and Mitchell, S. (1971). *Childhood behaviour and mental health*. University of London Press, London.
—— and Watt, D.C. (1977). Long term treatment with neuroleptics in psychiatry. *Current Developments in Psychopharmacology* 4, 217–47.
Shields, J. (1962). *Monozygotic twins brought up apart and brought up together*. Oxford University Press, London.
—— (1976). Heredity and environment. In *Textbook of human psychology* (ed. H.J. Eysenck and G.D. Wilson). MTP Press, Lancaster.
—— (1978). Genetics. In *Schizophrenia: towards a new synthesis* (ed. J.K. Wing). Academic Press, London.
—— (1980). Genetics and mental development. In *Scientific foundations of developmental psychiatry* (ed. M. Rutter). Heinemann Medical, London.
—— and Slater, E. (1975). Genetic aspects of schizophrenia. In *Contemporary psychiatry* (ed. J. Silverstone and B. Barraclough). *British Journal of Psychiatry* Special Publication No. 9.
Shillito, F.H., Drinker, C.K., and Shaughnessy, T.J. (1936). The problem of nervous and mental sequelae of carbon monoxide poisoning. *Journal American Medical Association* 106, 669–74.
Shneidman, E.S. (1976). Suicide notes reconsidered. In *Suicidology: contemporary developments* (ed. E.S. Shneidman) pp. 253–78. Grune and Stratton, New York.
—— Farberow, N.L., and Litman, R.E. (1961). The suicide prevention centre. In *The cry for help* (ed. N.L. Farberow and E.S. Shneidman) pp. 6–118. McGraw-Hill, New York.
Shorvon, H.J., Hill, J.D.N., Burkitt, E., and Hastead, H. (1946). The depersonalization syndrome. *Proceedings of the Royal Society of Medicine* 39, 779–92.
Shulman, K. and Post, F. (1980). Bipolar affective disorder in old age. *British Journal of Psychiatry* 136, 26–32.
Shulman, R. (1967). Vitamin B_{12} deficiency and psychiatric illness. *British Journal of Psychiatry* 113, 252–6.
Siegelman, M. (1974). Parental background of male homosexuals and heterosexuals. *Archives of Sexual Behaviour* 3, 3–18.
Sifneos, P.E. (1972). *Short-term psychotherapy and emotional crisis*. Harvard University Press, Cambridge, Massachusetts.
Sigurdsson, B. and Gudmundsson, K.B. (1956). Clinical findings six years after an outbreak of Akureyri disease. *Lancet* i, 766–8.
Silberfarb, P., Maurer, L.H., and Crouthamel, C.S. (1980). Psychological aspects of neoplastic disease: I. Functional status of breast cancer patients during different treatment regimens. *American Journal of Psychiatry* 137, 450–5.

—— Philibert, D., and Levine, P.M. (1980). Psychological aspects of neoplastic disease: II. Affective and cognitive effects of chemotherapy in cancer patients. *American Journal of Psychiatry* **137**, 597–601.

Silver, L.B. (1980). Speech disorders. In *Comprehensive textbook of psychiatry*, 3rd edn (ed. H.I. Kaplan, A.M. Freedman, and B.J. Sadock). Williams and Wilkins, Baltimore.

Simon, A. (1980). The neuroses, personality disorders, alcoholism, drug use and misuse, and crime in the aged. In *Handbook of mental health and aging* (ed. J.E. Birren and R.B. Sloane). Prentice-Hall, Englewood Cliffs, New Jersey.

Simon, N.M., Garber, E., and Arieff, A.J. (1977). Persistent nephrogenic diabetes insipidus after lithium carbonate. *Annals of Internal Medicine* **86**, 446–7.

Simpson, M.A. (1976). Self mutilation. *British Journal of Hospital Medicine* **16**, 430–8.

Sims, A.C.P. (1978). Hypotheses linking neuroses with premature mortality. *Psychological Medicine* **8**, 255–63.

Singer, H.S. (1982). Tics and Tourette syndrome. *Johns Hopkins Medical Journal* **151**, 30–5.

Singer, M.T. and Wynne, L.C. (1965). Thought disorder and family relations of schizophrenics: IV. Results and implications. *Archives of General Psychiatry* **12**, 201–12.

Sjöbring, H. (1973). Personality structure and development: a model and its applications. *Acta Psychiatrica Scandinavica* Suppl. 244.

Sjögren, T., Sjögren, H., and Lindgren, A.G.H. (1952). Morbus Alzheimer and morbus Pick. A genetic, clinical and pathoanatomical study. *Acta Psychiatrica Neurologica Scandinavica* Suppl. 82.

Skeels, H. (1966). Adult status of children with contrasting life experiences: a follow-up study. *Monograph of the Society for Research into Child Development* 31. No. 3.

Skegg, D.C.G., Doll, R., and Perry, J. (1977). Use of medicines in general practice. *British Medical Journal* i, 1561–3.

Skinner, B.F. (1953). *Science and human behaviour*. Macmillan, New York.

Sklar, L.S. and Anisman, H. (1981). Stress and cancer. *Psychological Bulletin* **89**, 369–406.

Skuse, D. and Burrell, S. (1982). A review of solvent abusers and their management by a child psychiatric outpatient service. *Human Toxicology* **1**, 321–9.

Skynner, A.C.R. (1969). Indications for and against conjoint family therapy. *International Journal of Social Psychiatry* **15**, 245–9.

—— (1976). *One flesh, separate persons: principles of family and marital psychotherapy*. Constable, London.

—— and Brown, D.G. (1981). Referral of patients for psychotherapy. *British Medical Journal* **282**, 1952–5.

Slater, E. (1943). The neurotic constitution: a statistical study of 2,000 soldiers. *Journal of Neurology and Psychiatry* **6**, 1–16.

—— (1951). Evaluation of electric convulsion therapy as compared with conservative methods in depressive states. *Journal of Mental Science* **97**, 567–9.

—— (1953). *Psychotic and neurotic illness in twins*. HMSO, London.

—— (1958). The monogenic theory of schizophrenia. *Acta Genetica Statistica Medica* **8**, 50–6.

—— (1961). Hysteria 311. *Journal of Mental Science* **107**, 359–81.

—— (1965). The diagnosis of hysteria. *British Medical Journal* i, 1395–9.

—— Beard, A.W., and Glithero, E. (1963). The schizophrenia-like psychoses of epilepsy. *British Journal of Psychiatry* **109**, 95–150.

—— and Cowie, V. (1971). *The genetics of mental disorders*. Oxford University Press, London.

—— and Glithero, E. (1965). A follow-up of patients diagnosed as suffering from hysteria. *Journal of Psychosomatic Research* **9**, 9–13.

—— and Shields, J. (1969). Genetical aspects of anxiety. In *Studies of anxiety* (ed. M.H Lader). *British Journal of Psychiatry* Special Publication No. 3.

Slavin, L.A., O'Malley, J.E., Koocher, G.P., and Foster, D.J. (1982). Communication of the cancer diagnosis to pediatric patients: impact on long-term adjustment. *American Journal of Psychiatry* **139**, 179–83.

Sloan, F.A., Khakoo, R., Cluff, L.E., and Waldman, R.M. (1979). Impact of infection and allergic disease on the quality of life. *Social Science and Medicine* **13**, 473–82.

Small, I.F., Heimburger, R.F., Small, J.G., Milstein, V., and Moore, D.F. (1977). Follow up of stereotaxic amygdalotomy for seizure and behaviour disorders. *Biological Psychiatry* **12**, 401–11.

Smart, R.G. and Cutler, R.E. (1976). The alcohol advertising ban in British Columbia: problems and effects on beverage consumption. *British Journal of Addiction* **71**, 13–21.

Smith, A. (1961). Duration of impaired consciousness as an index of severity of closed head injuries: a review. *Diseases of the Nervous System* **22**, 69–74.

Smith, J.C. and Hogan, B. (1978). *Criminal law*, 4th edn. Butterworth, London.

Smith, J.S. and Brandon, S. (1973). Morbidity from acute carbon monoxide poisoning at 3 year follow up. *British Medical Journal* i, 318–21.

Smith, M.L. and Glass, G.V. (1977). Meta-analysis of psychotherapy outcome studies. *American Psychologist* **32**, 752–60.

Smith, R. (1981). Alcohol, women, and the young: the same old problem? *British Medical Journal* **283**, 1170–2.

Smith, S.L. (1970). School refusal with anxiety: a review of sixty-three cases. *Canadian Psychiatric Association Journal* **15**, 257–64.

Smith, S.M., Hanson, R., and Noble, S. (1973). Parents of battered babies: a controlled study. *British Medical Journal* iv, 388.

Smith, W.J. (1982). Long term outcome of early onset anorexia nervosa. *Journal of American Academy of Child Psychiatry* **21**, 38–46.

Snaith, P. (1981). *Clinical neurosis*. Oxford University Press.

Sneddon, I.B. (1979). The presentation of psychiatric illness to the dermatologist. *Acta Dermatologica Venereologica* **59**, Suppl. 85, 177–9.

—— and Sneddon, J. (1975). Self-inflicted injury: a follow-up study of 43 patients. *British Medical Journal* iii, 527–30.

Sobel, M.B. and Sobell, L.C. (1973). Alcoholics treated by individualized behaviour therapy: one year treatment outcome. *Behaviour Research Therapy* **11**, 599–618.

Sobell, L.C. and Sobell, M.B. (1973). A self-feedback technique to monitor drinking behaviour in alcoholics. *Behaviour Research and Therapy* **11**, 237–8.

Solomon, Z. and Bromet, E. (1982). The role of social factors in affective disorder: an assessment of the vulnerability model of Brown and his colleagues. *Psychological Medicine* **12**, 123–30.

Solyom, L., Beck, P., Solyom, C., and Hugel, R. (1974). Some etological factors in phobic neurosis. *Canadian Psychiatric Association Journal* **19**, 69–78.

Soothill, K.L. and Pope, P.J. (1973). Arson: a twenty-year cohort study. *Medicine, Science and the Law* **13**, 127–38.

Sowerby, P. (1977). Balint reassessed. *Journal of the Royal College of Practitioners* **27**, 583–9.

Sox, G.C. (1979). Quality of care by nurse, practitioner and physician and assistants: a ten year perspective. *Annals of Internal Medicine* **91**, 459–68.

Speidel, H. and Rodewald, G. (eds.) (1980). *Psychic and neurological dysfunctions after open heart surgery*. Thieme, Stuttgart.

Spiegel, D., Bloom, J.R., and Yalom, I. (1981). Group support for patients with metastatic cancer. *Archives of General Psychiatry* **38**, 527–33.

Spitzer, R.L. and Endicott, J. (1968). DIAGNO: a computer programme for psychiatric diagnosis utilizing the differential diagnostic procedures. *Archives of General Psychiatry* 18, 746–56.

—— —— and Gibson, M. (1979). Research diagnostic criteria: rationale and reliability. *Archives of General Psychiatry* 36, 17–24.

—— —— and Robins, E. (1975). Clinical criteria for psychiatric diagnosis and DSM III. *American Journal of Psychiatry* 132, 1187–92.

—— —— —— (1978). Research diagnostic criteria: rationale and reliability. *Archives of General Psychiatry* 35, 773–82.

—— and Williams, J.B.W. (1980). Classification of mental disorders and DSM III. In *Comprehensive textbook of psychiatry,* 3rd edn (ed. H.I. Kaplan, A.M. Freedman, and B.J. Sadok). Williams and Wilkins, Baltimore.

Srinivasan, D.P. and Hullin, R.P. (1980). Current concepts of lithium. *British Journal of Hospital Medicine* 24, 466–75.

Srole, T., Langner, T., Michael, S., Opler, M., and Rennie, T. (1962). *Mental Health in the Metropolis.* McGraw-Hill, New York.

Stamler, J. (1980). Type A behaviour pattern: an established major risk factor for coronary heart disease? The key life-style trait responsible for the coronary epidemic? In *Current controversy in cardiovascular disease* (ed. C. Rappaport). Saunders, Philadelphia.

Stark, O., Atkins, E., Wolff, O.H., and Douglas, J.W.B. (1981). Longitudinal study of obesity in the national survey of health and development. *British Medical Journal* 283, 13–17.

Starkman, M.N. and Schteingart, D.E. (1981). Neuropsychiatric manifestation of patients with Cushing's syndrome. *Archives of Internal Medicine* 141, 215–19.

Steadman, J.H. and Graham, J.G. (1970). Head injuries: an analysis and follow up study. *Proceedings of the Royal Society of Medicine* 63, 23–8.

Stedeford, A. and Bloch, S. (1979). The psychiatrist in the terminal care unit. *British Journal of Psychiatry* 135, 7–14.

Stein, J.A. and Tschudy, D.P. (1970). Acute intermittent porphyria. A clinical and biochemical study of 46 patients. *Medicine* 49, 1–16.

Stein, L.I. and Test, M.A. (1980). An alternative to mental hospital treatment. *Archives of General Psychiatry* 37, 392–7.

Steinberg, D. (1982). Treatment, training, care or control. *British Journal of Psychiatry* 141, 306–9.

Stekel, W. (1952). *Sexual aberrations; the phenomena of fetishism in relation to sex,* 2 Vols (English translation by S. Parker). Vision Press, London.

—— (1953). *Sadism and masochism,* 2 Vols. Liveright, London.

Stengel, E. (1941). On the aetiology of fugue states. *Journal of Mental Science* 87, 572–99.

—— (1945). A study of some clinical aspects of the relationship between obsessional neurosis and psychotic reaction types. *Journal of Mental Science* 91, 166–87.

—— (1952). Enquiries into attempted suicide. *Proceedings of the Royal Society of Medicine* 45, 613–20.

—— (1959). Classification of mental disorders. *Bulletin of the World Health Organization* 21, 601–63.

—— and Cook, N.G. (1958). *Attempted suicide: its social significance and effects.* Maudsley Monograph No. 4. Chapman and Hall, London.

—— Zeitlyn, B.B., and Rayner, E.H. (1958). Post operative psychosis. *Journal of Mental Science* 104, 389–402.

Stenstedt, A. (1952). A study of manic depressive psychosis: clinical, social and genetic investigations. *Acta Psychiatrica et Neurologica Scandinavica* Suppl. 79, 3–85.

—— (1981). Involutional melancholia: an aetiological, clinical and social study of endogenous depression in later life with special reference to genetic factors. *Acta Psychiatrica Scandinavica* Suppl. 127.

Stephens, J.H. (1978). Long term prognosis and follow up in schizophrenia. *Schizophrenia Bulletin* 4, 25–47.

Steptoe, A. (1981). *Psychological factors in cardiovascular disease.* Academic Press, London.

Stern, N.J. and Cleary, P. (1982). The national exercise and heart disease project: long term psychosocial outcome. *Archives of Internal Medicine* 142, 1093–7.

Stern, R.S., Lipsedge, M.A., and Marks, I.M. (1973). Thought-stopping of neutral and obsessional thoughts: a controlled trial. *Behaviour Research and Therapy* 11, 659–62.

Stern, Z.A. and Susser, M. (1977). Recent trends in Down's syndrome. In *Research to practice in mental retardation: biomedical aspects,* Vol. III (ed. P. Mittler). University Park Press, Baltimore.

Sternback, R.A. (1978). *The psychology of pain.* Raven Press, New York.

Stevens, J.R. (1966). Psychiatric implications of psychomotor epilepsy. *Archives of General Psychiatry* 14, 461–71.

Stevenson, J. and Richman, N. (1976). The prevalence of language delay in a population of 3 year old children and its association with general retardation. *Developmental Medicine and Child Neurology* 18, 431–41.

Stewart, I.McD.G. (1953). Headache and hypertension. *Lancet* i, 1261–6.

Stewart, W.F.R. (1978). Sexual fulfillment for the handicapped. *British Journal of Hospital Medicine* 22, 676–80.

Stimson, G.V., Oppenheimer, E., and Thorley, A. (1978). Seven year follow up of heroin addicts. *British Medical Journal* i, 1190–2.

Stokes, P.E., Stoll, P.M., Shamoian, C.A., and Patton, M.J. (1971). Efficacy of lithium as acute treatment of manic depressive illness. *Lancet* i, 1319–25.

Stone, A.R., Frank, J.D., Nash, E.H., and Imber, S.D. (1961). An intensive five year follow up study of treated psychiatric outpatients. *Journal of Nervous and Mental Disease* 133, 410–22.

Stone, W.N. and Tieger, M.E. (1971). Screening for T-groups: the myth of healthy candidates. *American Journal of Psychiatry* 127, 1485–90.

Stores, G. (1978). Antiepileptics (anticonvulsants). In *Paediatric psychopharmacology* (ed. J.S. Werry). Brunner Mazel, New York.

—— (1981). Problems of learning and behaviour in children with epilepsy. In *Epilepsy and psychiatry* (ed. E.H. Reynolds and M.R. Trimble). Churchill Livingstone, Edinburgh.

—— and Brankin, P. (1982). Recent developments in ambulatory EEG monitoring. *British Journal of Clinical Practice* Symposium Suppl. 18, 10–15.

Storey, P.B. (1967). Psychiatric sequelae of subarachnoid haemorrhage. *Journal of Psychosomatic Research* 13, 175–82.

—— (1970). Brain damage and personality change after subarachnoid haemorrhage. *British Journal of Psychiatry* 117, 129–42.

Strachan, J.G. (1981). Conspicuous firesetting in children. *British Journal of Psychiatry* 138, 26–9.

Strain, J.J. and Grossman, S. (1975). *Psychological care of the medically ill.* Appleton-Century-Crofts, New York.

Strauss, A. and Lehtinen, V. (1947). *Psychopathology and education of the brain-injured child,* Vol. 1. Grune and Stratton, New York.

Strauss, J.S. and Carpenter, W.T. (1974). The prediction of outcome of schizophrenia. *Archives of General Psychiatry* 31, 37–42.

—— —— (1977). Prediction of outcome in schizophrenia III. Five-year outcome and its predictors. *Archives of General Psychiatry* **34**, 159–63.

Strömgren, E. (1968). Psychogenic psychoses. In *Themes and variations in European psychiatry* (ed. S.R. Hirsch and M. Shepherd) pp. 97–120. Wright, Bristol (1974).

Ström-Olsen, R. and Carlisle, S. (1971). Bifrontal stereotactic tractotomy. *British Journal of Psychiatry* **118**, 141–54.

Strupp, H.H., Hadley, S.W., and Gomes-Schwartz, B. (1977). *Psychotherapy for better or worse*. Aronson, New York.

Stuart, R.B. (1969). Operant interpersonal treatment for mental disorder. *Journal of Consulting and Clinical Psychology* **33**, 675–82.

Stunkard, A. (1980). Obesity. In *Comprehensive textbook of psychiatry* 3rd edn (ed. M.I. Kaplan, A.M. Freedman, and B.J. Sadock) Vol. 2. Williams and Wilkins, Baltimore.

—— and McLaren-Hume, M. (1959). The results of treatment for obesity. *Archives of Internal Medicine* **103**, 79–85.

Sturge, C.C. (1982). Reading retardation and antisocial behaviour. *Journal of Child Psychology and Psychiatry* **23**, 21–31.

Sturgeon, D., Kuipers, L., Berkowitz, R., Turpin, G., and Leff, J. (1981). Psycho-physiological responses of schizophrenic patients to high and low expressed emotion relatives. *British Journal of Psychiatry* **138**, 40–5.

Stürup, G.K. (1968). *Treating the 'untreatable': chronic criminals at Herstedvester*. Johns Hopkins University Press, Baltimore.

Suinn, R. and Richardson, F. (1971). Anxiety management training: a non-specific behaviour therapy programme for anxiety control. *Behaviour Therapy* **2**, 498–510.

Sullivan, C., Grant, M.Q., and Grant, J.D. (1959). The development of interpersonal maturity: applications to delinquency. *Psychiatry* **20**, 373–85.

Sulloway, F.J. (1979). *Freud: biologist of the mind*. Fontana, London.

Summerskill, W.H.J., Davidson, E.A., Sherlock, S., and Steiner, R.E. (1956). The neuropsychiatric syndrome associated with hepatic cirrhosis and an extensive portal collateral circulation. *Quarterly Journal of Medicine* **25**, 245–66.

Suomi, S.J., Eisele, C.D., Gardy, S.A., and Harlow, H.F. (1975). Depressive behaviour in adult monkeys following separation from family environment. *Journal of Abnormal Psychology* **84**, 576–8.

Surman, O.S. (1978). The surgical patient. In *Massachusetts General Hospital handbook of general hospital psychiatry* (ed. T.P. Hackett and N.H. Cassem). Mosby, St. Louis.

—— (1981). Renal transplantation and the current treatment of end state renal disease: a psychiatric medicine perspective. In *Psychiatric medicine update*. Massachusetts General Hospital Reviews for Physicians (ed. T.C. Manschrek). Mosby, St. Louis.

Surridge, D. (1969). An investigation into some psychiatric aspects of multiple sclerosis. *British Journal of Psychiatry* **115**, 749–64.

Swan, W. and Wilson, L.J. (1979). Sexual and marital problems in a psychiatric out-patient population. *British Journal of Psychiatry* **135**, 310–15.

Swan-Parente, A. (1982). Psychological problems in a neonatal ITU. *British Journal of Hospital Medicine* **27**, 266–8.

Symmers, W. St. C. (1968). Carcinoma of breast in transsexual individuals after surgical and hormonal interference with primary and secondary sex characteristics. *British Medical Journal* **ii**, 83–5.

Szasz, T.S. (1957). *Pain and pleasure. A study in bodily feelings*. Basic Books, New York.

—— (1960). The myth of mental illness. *American Psychologist* **15** 113–18.

—— (1976). *Schizophrenia: the sacred symbol of psychiatry*. Oxford University Press.

Tan, E., Marks, I.M., and Marset, P. (1971). Bimedial leucotomy in obsessive compulsive neurosis: a controlled serial enquiry. *British Journal of Psychiatry* 118, 155–64.

Tarnopolsky, A., Watkins, G.V., and Hand, D.J. (1980). Aircraft noise and mental health: I Prevalence of individual symptoms. *Psychological Medicine* 10, 683–98.

Task Force of the American Psychiatric Association (1980). Tardive dyskinesia. *American Journal of Psychiatry* 137, 163–72.

Tattersall, R.B. (1981). Psychiatric aspects of diabetes – a physicians view. *British Journal of Psychiatry* 139, 485–93.

—— (1982). Sexual problems of diabetic men. *British Medical Journal* 285, 911–12.

Taylor, F.H. (1966). The Henderson therapeutic community. In *Psychopathic disorders*. (ed. M. Craft). Pergamon, Oxford.

Taylor, F.K. (1958). A history of group and administrative therapy in Great Britain. *British Journal of Medical Psychology* 3, 153–73.

—— (1979). *Psychopathology: its causes and symptoms*. Quartermaine House, Sunbury on Thames.

—— (1981). On pseudo-hallucinations. *Psychological Medicine* 11, 265–72.

Taylor, P. (1982). Schizophrenia and violence. In *Abnormal offenders, delinquency, and the criminal justice system* (ed. J. Gunn and D.P. Farrington). Wiley, New York.

Taylor, P.J. and Fleminger, J.J. (1980). ECT for schizophrenia. *Lancet* i, 1380–2.

Taylor, S.J.L. and Chave, S. (1964). *Mental health and environment*. Longman, London.

Teasdale, J.D., Taylor, R., and Fogarty, S.J. (1980). Effects of induced elation-depression on accessibility of memories of happy and unhappy experiences. *Behaviour Research and Therapy* 18, 339–46.

Tellenbach, R. (1975). Typologische untersuchunger zur prämorbiden Persönlichkeit von Psychotikern unter besonderer Berucksichtigung manisch-depressiver. *Confinia Psychiatrica* 18, 1–15.

Temkin, O. (1971). *The falling sickness*. Johns Hopkins Press, Baltimore.

Tennant, C. and Bebbington, P. (1978). The social causation of depression: a critique of the work of Brown and his colleagues. *Psychological Medicine* 8, 565–75.

—— —— and Hurry, J. (1981). The short-term outcome of neurotic disorders in the community: the relation of remission to clinical factors and to 'neutralizing' life events. *British Journal of Psychiatry* 139, 213–20.

Tennant, F.S., Rawson, R.A., and McCann, M. (1981). Withdrawal from chronic phencyclidine (PCP) dependence with desimipramine. *American Journal of Psychiatry* 138, 845–6.

Theander, S. (1970). Anorexia nervosa: a psychiatric investigation of female patients. *Acta Psychiatric Scandinavica* Suppl. 214.

Theorell, T. and Lind, E. (1973). Systolic blood pressure, serum cholesterol, and smoking in relation to sociological factors and myocardial infarctions. *Journal of Psychosomatic Research* 17, 327–32.

Thigpen, C.H., Thigpen, H., and Cleckley, H.M. (1957). *The three faces of Eve*. McGraw-Hill, new York.

Thomas, A., Chess, S., and Birch, H.G. (1968). *Temperament and behaviour disorders in children*. University Press, New York.

Thomas, A.J. (1981). Acquired deafness and mental health. *British Journal of Medical Psychology* 54, 219–29.

Thompson, W.G. and Heaton, K.W. (1980). Functional bowel disorder in apparently healthy people. *Gastroenterology* 79, 283–8.

Thorndike, E.L. (1913). *Educational psychology*, Vol. II. *The psychology of learning*. Teachers College, Columbia University, New York. (Also Kegan Paul, Trench, Trumber, London (1923).)

Tienari, P. (1968). Schizophrenia in monozygotic male twins. In *The transmission of schizophrenia* (ed. D. Rosenthal and S.S. Kety). Pergamon, New York.

Tizard, B. (1962). The personality of epileptics: a discussion of the evidence. *Psychological Bulletin* 59, 196–210.

Tizard, J. (1964). *Community services for the mentally handicapped.* Oxford University Press, London.

—— (1968). Social psychiatry and mental subnormality. In *Studies in psychiatry* (ed. M. Shepherd and D.L. Davies). Oxford University Press, London.

—— (1974). Services and evaluation of services. In *Mental deficiency: the changing outlook* (ed. A.M. Clarke and A.D.M. Clarke). Methuen, London.

—— and Grad, J.C. (1961). *Mentally handicapped children and their families.* Oxford University Press, London.

Todd, N.A. (1972). Follow up of patients recommended for therapeutic abortion. *British Journal of Psychiatry* 120, 645–7.

Tollison, C.D. and Adams, H.E. (1979). *Sexual disorders: treatment, theory and research.* Gardner Press, New York.

Tomlinson, B.E. (1982). Plaques, tangles and Alzheimers disease. *Psychological Medicine* 12, 449–60.

—— Blessed, G., and Roth, M. (1970). Observations on the brains of demented old people. *Journal of the Neurological Sciences* 11, 205–42.

Tonks, C.M. (1964). Mental illness in hypothyroid patients. *British Journal of Psychiatry* 110, 706–10.

Toone, B. (1981). Psychoses of epilepsy. In *Epilepsy and psychiatry* (ed. E.M. Reynolds and M.R. Trimble). Churchill Livingstone, Edinburgh.

Torgerson, S. (1979). The nature and origin of common phobic fears. *British Journal of Psychiatry* 134, 343–51.

Touwen, B.C.L. and Prechtl, H.F.R. (1970). The neurological examination of the child with minor nervous dysfunction. *Clinics in Developmental Medicine* No. 38. Spastics International Medical Publications and William Heinemann Medical, London.

Townsend, P. (1962). *The last refuge.* Routledge and Kegan Paul, London.

Trethowan, W. (1972). The couvade syndrome. In *Modern perspectives in psycho-obstetrics* (ed. J.G. Howells). Oliver and Boyd, Edinburgh.

—— (1979). Some rare psychiatric disorders. In *Current themes in psychiatry,* Vol. 2 (ed. R. Gaind and B. Hudson). Macmillan, London.

—— and Conlon, M.F. (1965). The couvade syndrome. *British Journal of Psychiatry* 111, 57–66.

Trick, K.L.K. and Tennent, T.G. (1981). *Forensic psychiatry: an introductory text.* Pitman, London.

Trimble, M.R. (1981). *Post-traumatic neurosis: from railway spine to the whiplash.* Wiley, Chichester.

Trower, P.E., Bryant, B., and Argyle, M. (1978). *Social skills and mental health.* Methuen, London.

Truax, C.B. and Carkhuff, R.R. (1967). *Towards effective counselling and psychotherapy.* Aldine, Chicago.

Tsuang, M.T. (1978). Suicide in schizophrenics, manics, depressives and surgical controls. *Archives of General Psychiatry* 35, 153–5.

—— (1980). *Genetic issues in epidemiology.* Washington University Press.

—— Woolson, R.F., and Fleming, J.A. (1979). Long-term outcome of major psychosis: I Schizophrenia and affective disorder compared with psychiatrically symptom free surgical controls. *Archives of General Psychiatry* 36, 1295–301.

Tuckman, J. and Youngman, W.F. (1963). Suicide among persons attempting suicide. *Public Health Reports* 78, 585–7.

—— —— (1968). A scale for assessing suicide risk of attempted suicide. *Journal of Clinical Psychology* **24**, 17–19.

Tuke, D.H. (1872). *Illustrations of the influence of the mind upon the body in health and disease*. J.& A. Churchill, London.

—— (1892). *A dictionary of psychological medicine*. J. and A. Churchill, London. (Reprinted by The Arno Press (1976).)

Tune, L.E., Folstein, M., Rabins, P., Jayaram, G., and McHugh, P. (1982). Familial manic-depressive illness and familial Parkinson's disease: a case report. *Johns Hopkins Medical Journal 151*, 65–70.

Turner, G. (1982). X-linked mental retardation. *Psychological Medicine* **12**, 471–3.

Turner, R.K. (1973). Conditioning treatment of nocturnal enuresis: present status. In Bladder control and enuresis. *Clinics in Developmental Medicine*, Nos. 48–49 (ed. I. Kolvin, R. McKeith, and S.R. Meadows). SIMP/Heinemann, London.

Twaddle, A. (1972). The concepts of the sick role and illness behaviour. In *Advances in psychosomatic medicine, 8. Psychological aspects of physical illness* (ed. Z.J. Lipowski). Karger, Basel.

Tylden, E. (1968). Hyperemesis and physiological vomiting. *Journal of Psychosomatic Research* **12**, 85–93.

Tyrell, D.A.J., Crown, T.J., Parry, R.P., Johnstone, E., and Ferrier, I.N. (1979). Possible virus in schizophrenia and some neurological disorders. *Lancet* **i**, 839–41.

Tyrer, P. (1976). Towards rational therapy with mono-amine oxidase inhibitors. *British Journal of Psychiatry* **128**, 354–60.

—— and Steinberg, D. (1975). Symptomatic treatment of agoraphobia and social phobias: a follow-up study. *British Journal of Psychiatry* **127**, 163–8.

—— and Tyrer, S. (1974). School refusal, truancy and neurotic illness. *Psychological Medicine* **4**, 416–21.

Udall, E.T. and Corbett, J.A. (1979). New hospital residential care for adults with mental retardation. In *Community care for the mentally disabled* (ed. J.K. Wing and R. Olsen). Oxford University Press.

Urwin, P. and Gibbons, J.L. (1979). Psychiatric diagnosis in self-poisoning patients. *Psychological Medicine* **9**, 501–8.

Van Krevelin, D.A. (1971). Early infantile autism and autistic psychopathy. *Journal of Autism and Child Schizophrenia* **1**, 82–6.

Van Loon, F.H.G. (1927). Amok and latah. *Journal of Abnormal and Social Psychology* **21**, 434–44.

Van Praag, H.M. (1982). Neurotransmitters and depression. Part B. catecholamines and depression. In *Handbook of psychiatry and endocrinology* (ed. P.J.V. Beumont and G.D. Burrows). Elsevier Biomedical, Amsterdam.

—— and Korf, J. (1971). Retarded depression and dopamine metabolism. *Psychopharmacologia* **19**, 199–203.

Van Putten, T. and May, P.R.A. (1978). 'Akinetic depression' in schizophrenia. *Archives of General Psychiatry* **35**, 1101–7.

Vaughn, C.E. and Leff, J.P. (1976). The influence of family and social factors as the course of psychiatric illness. *British Journal of Psychiatry* **129**, 125–37.

Vauhkonen, K. (1968). On the pathogenesis of morbid jealousy. *Acta Psychiatrica Scandinavica* Suppl. 202.

Veith, I. (1965). *Hysteria: the history of a disease*. University of Chicago Press.

Venables, P.M. (1977). The electrodermal physiology of schizophrenics and children at risk for schizophrenia. *Schizophrenia Bulletin* **3**, 28–48.

—— and Wing, J.K. (1962). Level of arousal and the subclassification of schizophrenia. *Archives of General Psychiatry* **7**, 114–19.

Victor, M. (1964). Observations on the amnesic syndrome in man and its anatomical basis. In *Brain function: RNA and brain function, memory and learning*, Vol. ii (ed. M.A.B. Brazier). University of California Press, Berkeley.

—— and Adams, R.D. (1953). The effect of alcohol on the nervous system. *Proceedings of the Association for Research in Nervous and Mental Diseases* **32**, 526–73.
—— —— and Collins, G.H. (1971). *The Wernicke–Korsakoff syndrome.* Blackwell, Oxford.

Virrkunnen, M. (1974). Alcohol as a factor precipitating aggression and conflict behaviour leading to homicide. *British Journal of Addiction* **69**, 149–54.

Vislie, H. (1956). Puerperal mental disorders. *Acta Psychiatrica et Neurologica Scandinavica* Suppl. 111.

Visotsky, H.M., Hamburg, D.A., Gross, M.E., and Lebovitz, B.Z. (1967). Coping behaviour under extreme stress. *Archives of General Psychiatry* **5**, 423–48.

Von Hartitzsch, B., Hoenich, N.A., Leigh, R.J., Wilkinson, R., Frost, T.H., Weddel, A., and Posen, G.A. (1972). Permanent neurological sequelae despite haemodialysis for lithium intoxication. *British Medical Journal* iv, 757–9.

Wadsworth, M.E.J., Butterfield, W.J.H., and Blaney, R. (1972). *Health and sickness, the choice of treatment.* Tavistock, London.

Wai, L., Burton, H., Richmond, J., and Lindsay, R.M. (1981). Home dialysis: influence of psychosocial factors on survival of home-dialysis patients. *Lancet* ii, 1155–6.

Wakeling, A. (1979). A general psychiatric approach to sexual deviation. In *Sexual deviation* (ed. I. Rosen) 2nd edn. Oxford University Press.

Walinder, J. (1967). *Transsexualism: a study of 43 cases.* Akademi-förlaget Göteborg.

—— (1968). Transsexualism – definition, prevalence and sex distribution. *Acta Psychiatrica et Neurologica Scandinavica* Suppl. 203, 255–8.

—— and Thuwe, I. (1977). A study of consanguinity between the parents of transsexuals. *British Journal of Psychiatry* **131**, 73–4.

Walker, N. (1965). *Crime and punishment in Britain.* Edinburgh University Press.

—— (1967). *Crime and insanity in England,* Vol. 1. *The historical perspective.* Edinburgh University Press.

—— and McCabe, S. (1973). *Crime and insanity in England,* Vol. 2. Edinburgh University Press.

Walker, S., Yesavage, J.A., and Tinklenberg, J.R. (1981). Acute phencylidine (PCP) intoxication: quantitative urine levels and clinical management. *American Journal of Psychiatry* **138**, 674–5.

Walker, V. and Beech, H.R. (1969). Mood state and the ritualistic behaviour of obsessional patients. *British Journal of Psychiatry* **115**, 1261–3.

Walters, A. (1961). Psychogenic regional pain alias hysterical pain. *Brain* **84**, 1–18.

Walton, D. (1961). Experimental psychology and the treatment of the ticquer. *Journal of Child Psychology* **2**, 148–55.

Walton, J.N. (1977). *Brain's diseases of the nervous system,* 8th edn. Oxford University Press.

Ward, C.H., Beck, A.T., Mendelson, M., Mock, J.E., and Erbaugh, J.K. (1962). The psychiatric nomenclature. *Archives of General Psychiatry* **7**, 198–205.

Warren, M.Q. (1969). The case for differential treatment of delinquents. *Annals of the American Academy of Political and Social Science* **381**, 47–59.

—— (1973). Correctional treatment in community settings. *Proceedings of the International Congress of Criminology,* Madrid.

Warren, W. (1965). A study of adolescent psychiatric inpatients and the outcome six or more years later: II. the follow-up study. *Journal of Child Psychology and Psychiatry* **6**, 141–60.

Warrington, E.K. and Weiskrantz, L. (1970). Amnesic syndrome – consolidation or retrieval? *Nature* **228**, 628–30.

Watanabe, S., Ishino, M., and Otsuki, S. (1975). Double blind comparison of lithium carbonate and imipramine in the treatment of depression. *Archives of General Psychiatry* **32**, 659–68.

Watson, B.U., Watson, C.S., and Fredd, R. (1982). Follow up studies of specific reading disability. Critical review of children and adolescents. *Journal of the American Academy of Child Psychiatry* **21**, 376–82.

Watson, J.B. and Rayner, R. (1920). Conditioned emotional reactions. *Journal of Experimental Psychology* **3**, 1–14.

Watson, J.M. (1982). Solvent abuse: presentation and clinical diagnosis *Human Toxicology* **1**, 249–56.

Watt, D.C. (1982). The search for genetic linkage in schizophrenia. *The British Journal of Psychiatry* **140**, 532–7.

Watts, F.N. and Bennett, D.H. (1983). *Theory and practice of psychiatric rehabilitation.* Wiley, Chichester.

Watzlawick, P., Bearn, J.H., and Jackson, D.D. (1968). *Pragmatics of human communication.* Faber, London.

Wechsler, H., Grosser, G.H., and Greenblatt, M. (1965). Research evaluating antidepressant medications on hospitalized mental patients: a survey of published reports during a five year period. *Journal of Nervous and Mental Disease* **141**, 231–9.

Weddell, R., Oddy, M., and Jenkins, D. (1980). Social adjustment after rehabilitation; a two year follow-up of patients with severe head injury. *Psychological Medicine* **10**, 257–63.

Weeks, D., Freeman, C.P.L., and Kendell, R.E. (1980). E.C.T.: III Enduring cognitive deficits. *British Journal of Psychiatry* **137**, 26–37.

Weeks, H.A. (1958). The Highfields project and its success. In *The sociology of punishment and correction* (ed. N. Johnston, L. Savitz, and M.W. Wolfgang). Wiley, New York.

Weinberger, D.R., Bigelow, L.B., Kleinman, J.E., Klein, S.T., Rosenblatt, J.E., and Wyatt, R.J. (1980). Cerebral ventricular enlargement in chronic schizophrenia. *Archives of General Psychiatry* **37**, 11–13.

—— Cannon-Spoor, E., Potkin, S.G., and Wyatt, R.J. (1980). Poor premorbid adjustment and CT scan abnormalities in chronic schizophrenia. *American Journal of Psychiatry* **137**, 1410–13.

—— —— —— (1981). Familial aspects of CT scan abnormalities in chronic schizophrenic patients. *Psychological Research* **4**, 65–71.

Weiner, H. (1977). *Psychobiology and human disease.* Elsevier, New York.

—— Thaper, M., Reiser, M.F., and Mirsky, I.A. (1957). Etiology of duodenal ulcer I: Relation of specific psychological characteristics to role of gastric secretion (serum pepsinogen). *Psychosomatic Medicine* **9**, 1–10.

Weinstein, E.A. and Kahn, R.L. (1955). *Denial of illness: symbolic and physiological aspects.* Thomas, Springfield, Ill.

Weinstein, M.R. (1980). Lithium treatment of women during pregnancy and in the post delivery period. In *Handbook of lithium therapy*, 2nd edn (ed. F.N. Johnson) pp. 421–9. MTP, Lancaster.

Weiss, E.M. and Berg, R.F. (1982). Child victims of sexual assault: impact of court procedures. *Journal of the American Academy of Child Psychiatry* **21**, 513–18.

Weissman, A.D. (1978). Coping with illness. In *Handbook of general hospital psychiatry* (ed. T.P. Hackett and N. Cassem). Mosby, St. Louis.

Weissman, M. and Slaby, A. (1973). Oral contraceptives and psychiatric disturbance: evidence from research. *British Journal of Psychiatry* **123**, 513–18.

—— (1974). The epidemiology of suicide attempts. 1960–1971. *Archives of General Psychiatry* **30**, 737–46.

—— and Klerman, G.L. (1978). Epidemiology of mental disorder: emerging trends in the U.S. *Archives of General Psychiatry* **35**, 705–12.

—— Pottenger, M., Kleber, H., Ruben, H.L., Williams, D., and Thompson, W.D. (1977). Symptom patterns in primary and secondary depression: a comparison of primary depressives, with depressed opiate addicts, alcoholics and schizophrenics. *Archives of General Psychiatry* **34**, 854–62.

—— Prusoff, B.A., DiMascio, A., Neu, C., Goklaney, M., and Klerman, G.L. (1979). The efficacy of drugs and psychotherapy in the treatment of acute depressive episodes. *American Journal of Psychiatry* **136**, 555–8.

Welch, C.A. (1981). Psychiatric medicine and the burn patient. In *Psychiatric medicine update: Massachusetts General Hospital reviews to physicians* (ed. T.C. Manschrek). Churchill Livingstone, Edinburgh.

Wells, C.E. (1978). Chronic brain disease: an overview. *American Journal of Psychiatry* **135**, 1–12.

Welner, J. and Strömgren, E. (1958). Clinical and genetic studies on benign schizophreniform psychoses based on a follow up. *Acta Psychiatrica Neurologica Scandinavica* **33**, 377–99.

Wender, P. (1971). *Minimal brain dysfunction in children.* Wiley, New York.

—— Rosenthal, D., Kety, S.S., Schulsinger, F., and Welner, J. (1974). Cross-fostering: a research strategy for clarifying the role of genetic and experimental factors in the aetiology of schizophrenia. *Archives of General Psychiatry* **30**, 121–8.

Wernicke, C. (1881). *Lehrbuch der Gehirnkrankheiten,* part 2, p. 229. Kassel, Berlin.

Werry, J.S. (1982). An overview of paediatric psychopharmacology. *Journal of the American Academy of Child Psychiatry* **21**, 3–9.

—— Minde, K., Guzman, A., Weiss, G., Dogan, K., and Hoy, E. (1972). Studies on the hyperactive child. VII: neurological status compared with neurotic and normal children. *American Journal of Orthopsychiatry* **42**, 441–50.

West, D. (1965). *Murder followed by suicide.* Heinemann, London.

—— (1974). Criminology, deviant behaviour and mental disorder. *Psychological Medicine* **4**, 1–3.

—— (1977). Delinquency. In *Child psychiatry: modern approaches* (ed. M. Rutter and L. Hersov). Blackwell, Oxford.

—— and Farrington, D.P. (1973). *Who becomes delinquent?* Heinemann Educational, London.

—— —— (1977). *The delinquent way of life.* Heinemann, London.

—— and Walk, A. (eds.) (1977). *Daniel McNaughton: his trial and aftermath.* Gaskell Books, Ashford, Kent.

Whalley, L.J., Carothers, A.D., Collyer, S., DeMey, R., and Frackiewicz, A. (1982). A study of familial factors in Alzheimer's disease. *British Journal of Psychiatry* **140**, 249–56.

Wheeler, E.O., White, P.D., Reed, E.W., and Cohen, M.E. (1950). Neurocirculatory asthenia (anxiety neurosis, effort syndrome, neurasthenia). A twenty year follow up of one hundred and seventy three patients. *Journal of the American Medical Association* **142**, 878–89.

Whitehorn, J.C. and Betz, B.J. (1954). A study of psychotherapeutic relationship between physicians and schizophrenic patients. *American Journal of Psychiatry* **111**, 321–31.

Whiteley, J., Stuart, J., and Gordon, J. (1979). *Group approaches in psychiatry.* Routledge and Kegan Paul, London.

Whiteley, S. (1975). The psychopath and his treatment. In *Contemporary psychiatry* (ed. T. Silverstone and R.B. Barraclough). *British Journal of Psychiatry* Special Publication No. 9.

Whitlock, F. (1961). The Ganser syndrome. *British Journal of Psychiatry* **113**, 19–29.

—— (1963). *Criminal responsibility.* Butterworth, London.

—— (1973). Suicide in England and Wales 1959–1963. Part 1. The country boroughs. *Psychological Medicine* **3**, 350–65.

—— (1973*b*). Suicide in England and Wales 1959–1963. Part 2, London. *Psychological Medicine* 3, 411–20.

—— (1976). *Psychological aspects of skin disease.* Saunders, London.

Whybrow, P.C. and Hurwitz, T. (1976). Psychological disturbances associated with endocrine disease and hormone therapy. In *Hormones, behaviour and psychopathology* (ed. E.J. Sachar). Raven Press, New York.

Wilkin, D. (1979). *Caring for the mentally handicapped child.* Croom Helm, London.

—— Evans, G., Hughes, B., and Jolley, D. (1982). The implications of managing confused and disabled people in non-specialist residential homes for the elderly. *Health Trends* 14, 98–100.

Wilkins, R.H. (1974). *The hidden alcoholic in general practice. A method of detection using a questionnaire.* Elek Science, London.

Wilkinson, D.G. (1981). Psychiatric aspects of diabetes. *British Journal of Psychiatry* 138, 1–9.

Williams, D. (1969). Neural factors related to habitual aggression: consideration of the differences between those habitual aggressive and others who have committed crimes of violence. *Brain* 92, 503–20.

Williams, R. and Davis, M. (1977). Alcohol liver injury. *Proceedings of the Royal Society of Medicine* 70, 33–6.

Williamson, J., Stokoe, I.H., Gray, S., Fisher, M., Smith, A., McGhee, A., and Stephenson, E. (1964). Old people at home: their unreported needs. *Lancet* i, 1117–20.

Willner, A.E. and Rabiner, C.J. (1979). Psychopathology and cognitive dysfunction five years after open heart surgery. *Comprehensive Psychiatry* 20, 409–18.

Wimmer, A. (1916). Psykogene sindssygdomsformer. [Psychogenic varieties of mental diseases.] In *St. Hans Hospital 1816–1916. Jubilee Publication,* pp. 85–216. Gad, Copenhagen.

Wilson, G.D. (1981). *Love and instinct.* Temple Smith, London.

Wilson, P. (1980). *Survey on drinking in England and Wales.* Office of population censuses and surveys. HMSO, London.

Wilson, S. (1978). The effect of treatment in a therapeutic community on intravenous drug abuse. *British Journal of Addiction* 73, 407–11.

—— and Mandelbrote, B. (1978). The relationship between duration of treatment in a therapeutic community for drug abusers and subsequent criminality. *British Journal of Psychiatry* 132, 487–91.

Wing, J.K. (1978). *Schizophrenia. Towards a new synthesis.* Academic Press, London.

—— (ed.) (1982). Long term community care: experience in a London Borough. *Psychological Medicine Monograph* Suppl. No. 2.

—— Bennett, D.H., and Denham, J. (1964). The industrial rehabilitation of long stay psychiatric patients. *Medical Research Council Memorandum. No. 42.* HMSO, London.

—— and Brown, G.W. (1970). *Institutionalism and schizophrenia.* Cambridge University Press, London.

—— Cooper, J.E., and Sartorius, N. (1974). *Measurement and classification of psychiatric symptoms.* Cambridge University Press.

—— and Fryers, T. (1976). *Psychiatric services in Camberwell and Salford.* MRC Social Psychiatry Unit, London.

—— and Hailey, A.M. (eds.) (1972). *Evaluating a community psychiatric service.* Oxford University Press, London.

—— and Olsen, R. (1979). *Community care for the mentally disabled.* Oxford University Press, London.

—— and Morris, B. (1981). *Handbook of rehabilitation practice.* Oxford University Press.

Wing, L. (1981). Management of early childhood autism. *British Journal of Hospital Medicine* 25, 53–9.

Winokur, G., Cardoret, R., Dorzab, J., and Baker, M. (1971). Depressive disease: a genetic study. *Archives of General Psychiatry* **24**, 135–44.
Witkin, H.A., Mednick, S.A., and Schulsinger, F. (1976). Criminality and XYY and XXY man. *Science* **193**, 547–8.
Witzig, J.S. (1968). The group treatment of male exhibitionists. *American Journal of Psychiatry* **125**, 179–85.
Wolberg, L.R. (1948). *Medical hypnosis.* 2 Vols. Grune and Stratton, New York.
—— (1977). *The techniques of psychotherapy.* 2 Vols. Grune and Stratton, New York.
Wolf, S. and Wolff, H.G. (1947). *Human gastric function.* Oxford University Press, New York.
Wolff, C. (1971). *Love between women.* Duckworth, London.
Wolff, H.G. (1962). A concept of disease in man. *Psychosomatic Medicine* **24**, 25–30.
—— and Curran, D. (1935). Nature of delirium and allied states. *Archives of Neurology and Psychiatry* **35**, 1175–215.
Wolff, S. (1961). Symptomatology and outcome of preschool children with behaviour disorders attending a child guidance clinic. *Journal of Child Psychology and Psychiatry* **2**, 269–76.
Wolkind, S.N. (1976). Psychogenic low back pain. *British Journal of Hospital Medicine* **15**, 17–24.
—— and Rutter, M.L. (1973). Children who have been 'in care': an epidemiological study. *Journal of Child Psychology and Psychiatry* **14**, 95–105.
—— and Zajicek, E. (1979). Psychosocial correlations of nausea and vomiting in pregnancy. *Journal of Psychosomatic Research* **22**, 1–5.
Wolpe, J. (1958). *Psychotherapy by reciprocal inhibition.* Stanford University Press.
Woodruff, R.A., Guze, S.B., Clayton, P.J., and Carr, D. (1973). Alcoholism and depression. *Archives of General Psychiatry* **28**, 97–100.
Woolley, D.W. and Shaw, E. (1954). A biochemical and pharmacological suggestion about certain mental disorders. *Proceedings of the National Academy of Sciences* **40**, 228–31.
Wootton, B. (1959). *Social science and social pathology,* Chapter 7, pp. 203–26. George Allen and Unwin, London.
World Health Organization (1978). *Report of the International Pilot Study of Schizophrenia,* Vol. 1. World Health Organization, Geneva.
—— (1978). *Mental disorders: glossary and guide to their classification in accordance with the ninth revision of the International Classification of Diseases.* World Health Organization, Geneva.
—— (1979). *Schizophrenia: an initial follow up.* Wiley, Chichester.
—— (1980). Changing patterns in mental health care. *Euro Reports and Studies 25.* WHO, Copenhagen.
—— (1981). *Current state of diagnosis and classification in the mental health field.* World Health Organization, Geneva.
Worrall, E.P., Moody, J.P., Peet, M., Dick, P., Smith, A., Chambers, C., Adams, M., and Naylor, G.J. (1979). Controlled studies of the antidepressant effects of lithium. *British Journal of Psychiatry* **135**, 255–62.
Wright, J., Perreault, R., and Mathieu, M. (1977). The treatment of sexual dysfunction: a review. *Archives of General Psychiatry* **34**, 881–90.
Wyant, G.M. and MacDonald, W.B. (1980). The role of atropine in electroconvulsive therapy. *Anaesthesia and Intensive Care* **8**, 445–50.
Wyke, T. (1980). Language and schizophrenia. *Psychological Medicine* **10**, 403–6.
—— (1982). Interhemispheric integration in man. *Psychological Medicine* **12**, 225–30.
Wynne, L.C. (1981). Current concepts about schizophrenics and family relationships. *The Journal of Nervous and Mental Disease* **169**, 82–9.
—— Ryckoff, I., Day, J., and Hirsch, S. (1958). Pseudomutuality in the family relations of schizophrenics. *Psychiatry* **21**, 205–20.

—— and Singer, M.T. (1963). Thought disorder and family relationships of schizophrenics: II A classification of forms of thinking. *Archives of General Psychiatry* **9**, 199–206.

Yalom, I. (1975). *The theory and practice of group psychotherapy,* 2nd edn. Basic Books, New York.

—— (1980). *Existential psychotherapy.* Basic Books, New York.

—— Green, R., and Fisk, N. (1973). Prenatal exposure to female hormones: effects on the psychosexual development of boys. *Archives of General Psychiatry* **28**, 554–61.

—— Hovts, P.S., Newell, G., and Rand, K.H. (1967). Preparation of patients for group therapy. *Archives of General Psychiatry* **17**, 416–27.

—— Linde, D., Moos, R.M., and Hamburg, D.A. (1968). 'Post partum blues' syndrome. A description and related variables. *Archives of General Psychiatry* **18**, 16–27.

Yap, P.M. (1951). Mental diseases peculiar to certain cultures: a survey of comparative psychiatry. *Journal of Mental Science* **97**, 313–27.

Yardley, K.M. (1976). Training in feminine skills in a male transsexual: a preoperative procedure. *British Journal of Medical Psychology* **49**, 329–39.

Yoss, R.E. (1970). The inheritance of diurnal sleepiness as measured by pupillography. *Proceedings of the Staff Meetings of the Mayo Clinic* **45**, 426–37.

Young, W., Goy, R., and Phoenix, C. (1964). Hormones and sexual behaviour. *Science* **143**, 212–18.

Yule, W. (1967). Predicting reading ages on Neale's analysis of reading ability. *British Journal of Educational Psychology* **37**, 252–5.

—— and Carr, J. (1980). *Behaviour modification for the mentally handicapped.* Croom Helm, London.

Zall, H., Therman, P.-O.G., and Myers, J.M. (1968). Lithium carbonate: a clinical study. *American Journal of Psychiatry* **125**, 549–55.

Zerssen, D. von (1976). Physique and personality. In *Human behaviour genetics* (ed. A.R. Kaplan) pp. 230–78. Thomas, Springfield, Ill.

Zitrin, C.M., Klein, D.F., and Woerner, M.G. (1978). Behaviour therapy, supportive psychotherapy, imipramine and phobias. *Archives of General Psychiatry* **35**, 307–16.

Author Index

835

Subject Index

857